BOLTON WANDERERS F.C.
The Official History
1877 ~ 2002
'Heroes, Heartbreakers & Headliners'

By Simon Marland

Published by:
Yore Publications
12 The Furrows, Harefield,
Middx. UB9 6AT.

© Simon Marland 2002
....

British Library Cataloguing-in-Publication Data.
A catalogue record for this book
is available from the British Library.

ISBN 1 874427 542

Printed and bound by
Bookcraft, Midsomer Norton, Bath.

Geoff Abey, Newton
Michael Ackers, Bolton
Sam Allardyce and family
Alf Ashworth, Harwood, Bolton
John S Aspery, Worsley
Alistair Aston, Droylsden, Manchester
Michael Austin, Mellor, Blackburn
The Austin Family, Warrington Whites
Keith Banks, Bolton
Jack Thompson, Worsley, Manchester
Andrew Barlow, Bury
Ian Barnes, Westhoughton, Bolton
Malcolm W Barrass
Steven Battersby
David Baxendale, Bolton
Roy Beardsworth, Heaton, Bolton
David Belfield, Walkden
Kenneth Bendelow, Little Lever
Salena, Michael Berry, Langwith
Dennis Birchall, Bolton, Lancs
Kevan Bird, Worsley
The Bisset Family, Turton, Bolton
David, Daniel, Jordan, Blinkhorn
Jarrod William Bolton, Bolton
Glen Booth, Farnworth
Tony Booth, Farnworth, Bolton
Steven Bothamley, Abram, Wigan
David Branwood
Florence Brandwood, Astley Bridge
Eric Brindle (Dad)
Bernard Broderick, Wimborne, Dorset
Andrew Broderick, Bridport
Daniel Bromilow, Harwood, Bolton
Eric Brooks, Breightmet, Bolton
Kath Brown, Little Lever
Vivian Brown, Horwich, Bolton
Phil Brown and family
Bunny and Karen
John Butler, Egerton, Bolton
Samuel Cannan, Hurst Green
Donald Carless, Bolton
Helen, Thomas, Robert, Bethan Carr, Bolton
David Casserly, Heaton, Bolton
Mark James Chadwick
Mr Desmond Christiani, Preston
Michael Clarkson, Lostock, Bolton
Wilson Clough, Westhoughton
Phil Collier, Westhoughton
Dave & Gill Cookson, Lostock Hall
Derek Cooper, Harwood, Bolton
John Coughlin, Heaton, Bolton
Alex Coward, 'Burden', Longridge
Andrew Cowsill, Horwich, Bolton
Graham Compton, Worsley
M J Crosbie, Peterbrough
Arthur Cross
David and Daniel Croughton
Geoffrey Culshaw, Sharples, Bolton
Colin & Daniel Cummings, Haslingden
Ian Currie and Family
Peter Daniels, Atherton
John Davidson, Leeds
Eddie Davies OBE, Isle of Man
Andrew Dean, Lostock, Bolton
Martin Dean, Lostock, Bolton

Gregory Dean, Lostock, Bolton
The Denham Family, Radcliffe
The Dodd Family
Tony Doyle, Lostock, Bolton
Allan Duckworth and Family
John Dutchman-Smith, Chorley
Lee Eastwood, Littlemoss
Sarah Eckersley, Bolton, Lancashire
David John Edwards, Bolton
Jack Enefer, Sowerby Bridge
Len Entwistle and family
Jack Enty, Morris Green
Robert Evan Fairclough, Bolton
Syd Farrimond, Leigh, Lancs
David Fearnley of Hindley
Harold Fellows, Garden City
The Fenton Brothers
Mark Fernside, Astley Bridge
Stephen Graham Fido, Worsley
Jane and Louise Flanagan
George David Fletcher
Paul Foley, Deane, Bolton
Steve Forkin, Llangollen, Denbighshire
Norman Fort, Bolton
Robert L.S. Francis, Harwood
Tom Fryer, Horwich
Carol Fryer, Horwich
Alan Gardiner, Wilmslow
Revd. Keith V Garner
Phil Gartside and Family
Martin Gibbons, Horwich, Bolton
Kevin Gibbons, Horwich, Bolton
Robin Gibbons, Horwich, Bolton
Phil & Linda Gill & family, Atherton
Peter Gilmore, Bolton
R&A Glover, Westhoughton
Wayne Glynn, Tyldesley White
Gregory Goldston, Bolton
Rory and Arran Gordon
Terence Martin Grant, Warrington
Michael Green, Horwich
Sue Green, Horwich, Bolton
Vincent Green, Atherton, Manchester
John Henry Greenhalgh, Leigh
Kyle Greenhalgh, Swinton, Manchester
Tim Greenhalgh
Lee Greenwood, Bolton
Nathan Gregory, Westhoughton
Colin Gregory, Wigston, Leicester
Ian & Alex Gregory, Hindley
Duncan and Scott Gregory
David Griffin, Astley Bridge, Bolton
Gary Halliwell, Heaton, Bolton
Gareth & Martin Hamer, Smithills
Chris Hamilton, High Wycombe
Mark Andrew Hampson, Kearsley
Michael Hardman, Swinton, Manchester
David Hardman, Clifton, Manchester
Roger Hart, Great Lever
David Hartley, Atherton
H Haythornthwaite, Queensgate, Bolton, BLI 4EB
Tony Heaney, Walton,Warrington
Jim Heathcote, Donisthorpe
Charles Heeley, Westhoughton, Bolton
Sue Hemmings, Preston, Lancs

Garry Herrity, Bolton
P.A. Hewitt, Heaton, Bolton
Stephen Robert Heyes, Westhoughton
Owen Heyworth, Bolton, Smithills
Norman William Heyworth, Bolton
Peter, Ian, Graeme Hill, Edingburgh
Michael Hobin, Boothstown, Manchester
Ronnie and Ruth Hobson
Joe & Louise Hodgkinson
Edwin & Mollie Hodgkiss, Ladybridge
George Hodgson, True Fan
Nicholas Jamie Holland, Gravesend
David Holland, Fleetwood
Graham Holliday
Graham Holliday for Trish
Martin Hooton, Nottingham
Christopher Hopkins, Whitby
Russell James Horton, Fleetwood
Callum Howarth, Bolton
Charlotte Amber Howarth, Harrogate
Barry Howarth, Aylesbury, Buckinghamshire
Phil Howcroft, Nottingham
Derek Hulme, Harwood, Bolton
Nick Hulme, Bolton
Glen Jackson, Bolton
Boyd Jackson, Egerton, Bolton
Philip John Jackson, Westhoughton
Alan Jackson, Bolton
Trevor James, Bolton
Michael Jeffries, Atherton
Harry Johnson, Swinton, M27 5LN
Stuart Johnston, Sale, Cheshire
Stephen Jolliffe from Bury
Glynn Jones, Bolton, Lancs
Stephen Jones, Harwood, Bolton
Paul Kateley, Whitefield
Alan Kay, Bolton
Gill Kay, Lostock, Bolton
Paul A Kaye, Brussels
David Kaye, Bolton
Andy & Martin Killas
Alex Kitchen, Bromley Cross
Jan Kozlowski and family
Simon G Leather, Bolton
Brian Lee of Ladybridge
Andrew Leech
Norman Lewis, Chorley
Stefan Lewis, Horwich
Keith Lewthwaite, Ladybridge, Bolton
Bob Lindsay, Bradshaw
Gareth Lindsay, Horwich
Joseph Lloyd Wisdom, Manchester
Wayne Lloyd, Manchester
Nat Lofthouse OBE, Bolton
Chris Lomax, Radcliffe
Milton Lomax, Fergus Ontario
Pauline Lord (Tatton), Horwich
Ian Makin, Daubhill, Bolton
Amanda Sarah Makinson, Bolton
Fiona Manning, Bromley Cross
Roderick Mark-Bell, Middleton
Clair Marland
Ally Marland
Dave Marsden, Cookridge, Leeds
Mr James Martell, Preston

Subscribers ~

Allan Martin of Hindley
Philip Massey, Lowton, Warrington
Alexis Massey, Lowton, Warrington
Bob Matthews began 1946
Des McBain and Family
James Edward McGann, Heaton
Daniel McKenna, Westhoughton
John McAtee, Bolton
Lauren McGrath, Newton le Wilows
Martin and Sam McMulkin
Rod Middleton, Bolton
Arthur Millington, Ladybridge, Bolton
Jack Minshull
James Miskell, Little Lever
Peter Miskell, Little Lever
Anthony Moore, Farnworth
Gareth Moores and family
Geoffrey Moorhouse, Hawes
Peter Morris, Great Lever
David Mort
Michael Moss, Changford, Devon
Ben and Dylan Moss, Stafford
Matthew Mullineaux, Farnworth, Bolton
Steve Newsham, Exile Sheffield
Steve Craig Nicholson, Cleveleys
Simon, Victoria, Robert Nightingale
Martin Nisbet, South Woodford
Margaret O'Brien, Horwich
Frank O'Connell, Bolton
Mo, The Wellington Great Harwood
Martin Parkinson, Hindley Green
David Parr, Oxted, Surrey
Trevor Peacock, Deane, Bolton
Adam Pearson, Ampthill, Beds
Brian Peers, Worsley
Roy Pennington, Bromley Cross
Paul Pennington, Bradshaw, Bolton
Matthew Phillips
J.M. Pickup & Family, Leigh, Lancs
Catherine and Andrew Pietralski
Kevin John Pilling, Preston
Denis Pomfret, Walkden
John Preston, Bolton
Harold Pye
Rob Rainford, Bolton
Lynda Wallace Rands, Sheffield
Les & May Rawsthorne, Bolton
Tom and Jack Reynolds, Lostock
Anthony Rigby, Thornton, Cleveleys
Eileen Rigby
Jonathon Roberts, Manchester
Graham Robinson, Bradshaw, Bolton
Bill Rose, Lutterworth, Leicestershire
Dave Rothwell, Harwood, Bolton
Dave Rothwell, Carlisle
Paul Rushton, Chiswick, London
Nigel & Susan Samuel, Heaton
Alex Sankey Newton-le-Willows
James Schofield, Bradshaw, Bolton
Robert Scholes, Bradshaw, Bolton
Vincent Settle, Turton
Gordon Seymour and Family
Stephen Shannon, Bolton
Terry Shaw, St Helens
Stanley Shaw

Dominic Shearer, Walkden
Grandad Bob Simm, Chorley
Chris Simm, Chorley
Garry Simm, Withnell Fold
Andy Simms, Guildford
Paul Simms (Simmy), Bolton
Richard Slater
Bernard & Malcolm Slater, London
Allan Slater, Bolton
The Slawson Family, Westhoughton
Stephen & Jen Smith, Lancaster
Ron Smith, Deane
Mark Stephan, Halliwell, Bolton
Dan Stephens, Crewe, Cheshire
Peter Sturgess, Bolton
Alan & Edith Sutton, Bolton
David Swanton, Heaton, Bolton
Brian Sweeney, Horwich, Bolton
Barrie Swift
Barry Taylor, Bradshaw
Rob Taylor, Blackrod, Bolton
Martin J Thompson, Tonbridge
Raymond Thornley, Horwich
Darren Thornley, Farnworth, Bolton
Martin Timothy, Radcliffe
Colin Timperley, Didsbury, Manchester
Brandon WFC Topp
Dennis Towler, Ivy Rd, Bolton
Darren Townsend, Westhoughton, Bolton
David Andrew Trimble, Bolton
Keith Turner, Leigh, Lancs
Tony Turner, Westhoughton
Michael Turner, Westhoughton
Craig Turner, Falmouth, Cornwall
Dave Unsworth, Warrington, Cheshire
Barry Walker, Bolton
Stephen Walmsley, Astley Bridge
Mark, Jane, Ross, Walsh
Bernard J Walsh, Adlington
John Walsh OBE - Mayor
Brett Warburton and Family
George Warburton and family
Ian Ward, Littlethorpe, Leicester
Steve Weir, Warrington
Chris White, Stoke, Staffs
Darren Lewis Jordan Whittaker, Bolton
Brandon, Jennifer & Lewis Whittaker
Andrew Wild, Baldivis, Australia
Steven Wilkinson, Leigh, Lancashire
Chris Williams, Poynton, Cheshire
Carole Wilson, Leigh
Dave Wolfnedale of Farnworth
David W Wolstencroft, Kearsley
Arnold Wood, Walkden
Peter Woodcock, Farnworth, Bolton
Tommy Woods, Great Lever
Martin Woof, Bolton, Lancashire
John Wroe

George Painter, Castle Cary
Dave Harby, Bakewell
David Elwyn Griffiths
John Treleven
David Windross, Selby
George Mason

Derek Latham
Michael Latham
P. Cogle, Aberdeen
Chas Sumner, Kelsall, Cheshire
Richard Wells
Allan Grieve, Tillicoultry
Derek Hyde
Richard Shore
David Keats, Thornton Heath
Richard Stocken, Cheshire
Mark Tyler, Billericay Town F.C.
J. Ringrose
L.A. Zammit
J.R. Orton
Raymond Shaw
Steve Phillipps
G.T. Allman
Graham Spackman
Paul Johnson, Birmingham City
Gordon Macey, Q.P.R. Historian
David Brealey, Chesterfield
David Jowett
C.N. Cresswell
Bob Lilliman
Jonny Stokkeland, Norway
John Holbrook, Southmead, Bristol
D.J. Bullock
A. & J. Waterman
Richard Whitehead
Keith & Kieron Coburn
John Rawnsley
A. Timlin
For Dick Pym
Willy Østby - Proud Potter
Sylvain Vernisse, France
Richard Owen, Portsmouth FC Historian
P.J. Newport
David W. Marsh
Phil Hollow
R. Brackley, Oundle, Peterborough
Geoffrey Wright
Thanks for Jimmy Rae
Graham E. Lunn, Tyldesley
Svein Borge Pettersen, Sandefjord
Christer Svensson, Ödeshög, Sweden
Terry Frost (Football Historian)
Chris Marsh, Chesterfield
Michael Grayson
Paul Snape - Stoke Potters
Gareth A. Evans
David J. Godfrey
S. Metcalfe
R.H. White.
Dave Woods, Bristol City Fan
Basil W. Godley
John Pietralski
Trond Isaksen, Norway
Steve Carr, West Bromwich
Mr. D.J. Brooker
Bert Tyldesley, MBE
Gordon Small, Penwortham
Roger Wash, Newmarket
David Yates, Leeds
Arran Matthews
Nicholas Matthews

FOREWORD

It gives me great pleasure to say a few words for this publication to celebrate the club's 125th anniversary.

It has been an honour for me to have been part of Bolton Wanderers for most of my life and to share not only life's ups and downs but also the club's ups and downs during that period.

Bolton Wanderers have a fantastic history. The magnificent team of the twenties that won the F.A. Cup on three occasions, the two F.A. Cup Finals in the fifties that I was fortunate enough to be involved in and now, the club making their mark in the elite of English football.

This book will bring back many memories for me as I am sure it will for everyone else who supports the club.

Nat Lofthouse OBE
President
Bolton Wanderers F.C.
October 2002.

Little could the men who founded Bolton Wanderers 125 years ago have realised what they were doing and the legacy that their actions would have on generations that came after them.

The history of the club is full of events that also reflect the growth of the game itself with Bolton Wanderers always at the forefront. In that respect it is perhaps therapeutic to be reminded of how we got to where we now are and the twists and turns in between.

The Trotters, (a local name for practical jokers in the nineteenth century) gave the town of Bolton an identity and indeed when the club does well so the town and its people seem to thrive. The club's motto, *Supera Moras*, (overcome all difficulties) has always prevailed, even in times of disappointment and despair and hopefully this history captures that along with the triumphs, failures, the great and good players and those that have helped shape 125 years of Bolton Wanderers.

Simon Marland
October 2002.

~ Contents ~

Bolton Wanderers ~ The Official History: 1877 ~ 2002
Heroes, Heartbreakers and Headliners......

.....Is the names and the faces of all the athletes and teams with whom we have shared our brightest expectations, fondest dreams and deepest disappointments. There is a wonder to Bolton Wanderers Football Club and this book invites you to join in on the goal line to look at the joys, sorrows, the failures and the spectacular triumphs of a century and a quarter of Bolton Wanderers, heroes, heartbreakers and headliners.

ACKNOWLEDGEMENTS

The Author wishes to thank the Bolton Evening News and Pete Phillips for permission to reproduce the bulk of the photographs used in this book. Every effort has been made to trace the ownership of other illustrative items, and apologies are given should copyright have inadvertently been broken.

Chapter 1 (1877 ~ 1888)
Pre-League

Like many other League clubs Bolton Wanderers had it's inception from the desire of scholars and teachers (in their case those of Christ Church Sunday School) to participate in outdoor recreation, but the beginnings of the game in Bolton go back even further. The game of Association football was introduced to Turton in 1870 by John Kay, who had learned his football skills at Harrow Public School. This was to be a significant move in the history of the game as Lancashire was to become a focal point for the formation of the sport we know today, the County itself being the centre of the commercial and industrial world in the 19th century.

In December 1871 the first general meeting of the Turton club was held and Kay's father, James, the squire of Turton, was elected as it's first president. John James Bentley was one of the club's first players and he went on to captain Turton, leading them to some notable performances in the F.A.Cup, including a couple of 'friendly' victories over Bolton Wanderers in 1880. Bentley was to become a great figure in the game, becoming secretary of the Wanderers and president of the Football League.

In July 1874, with the game flourishing in the area, Thomas Ogden, schoolmaster of Christ Church, called a meeting of teachers and other young men, and his idea to further the game in the area received plenty of support. Money was collected to buy a football and on the first Saturday of the month a practice match was arranged on a field known as Bob Wood's, which forms part of Heaton Cemetery, the game being postponed for a week because of heavy rain.

The Vicar of Christ Church, Rev.J.F.Wright, was elected president, Thomas Ogden assumed the captaincy, and Tom Rawsthorne was appointed secretary, with subscriptions set at one penny per week.

The club's first game was against Farnworth on a field called Smithfield, which was situated between Green Lane and Plodder Lane, and the game was played under rugby rules. It is not confirmed for how long the club played under rugby rules but they continued to play local clubs, although it is suggested that they played two halves, one under rugby rules and one under association rules.

Matches were played on the Recreation Ground or on a field opposite the Cross Guns Inn, known as Dick Cockle's field, with Chris Church School itself being used as headquarters.

Things went on smoothly until 1877 when a split arose with the Vicar, who objected to meetings being held in the school without his presence, and the fact that they had to wander to a neighbouring hostelry, the Gladstone Hotel, which in itself suggested the new name, "Bolton Wanderers". Thus on the 28th August 1877 the club, which has figured prominently in English football over the last 125 years, was formed. The headquarters were subsequently moved to the Britannia Hotel, at the corner of Deane Road, where they remained until becoming a limited liability company in 1895.

The rules of the club were quite strict. Members were fined if they did not turn up for meetings and players were treated likewise if they did not give notice of their inability to play, whilst swearing on the field of play would cost the offender two (old) pence. The club prospered, so much so that the gate receipts warranted an allowance to the players towards their expenses.

In 1878 Mr Peter Parkinson, manager of a mill in the town, became an honorary member and he was to be a main factor in bringing the club to the fore and obtaining its recognition throughout the country. He saw the advantages of having a successful team in the town as Bolton Wanderers were just one of a number of clubs within the locality. Bolton Hornets, Farnworth, Bolton Association, All Saints, St James', Eagley, Halliwell, Astley Bridge, Gilnow Rangers, Bolton Olympic, Emmanuel, Great Lever and of course, the most respected, Turton, were all competing for pride of place.

Turton F.C. instituted the Turton Challenge Cup in 1878, the first of its kind in Lancashire, Eagley being the inaugural winners. In the same year the Lancashire Football Association was formed with thirty members, of which only Bolton Wanderers and Blackburn Rovers made it to the Football League ten years later. The Lancashire F.A.Cup came into being in 1879 with Bolton being eliminated by Blackburn Rovers in that first competition. The Wanderers continued to improve and this was echoed when, in November 1880, full back Tom Naylor became the first player from the club to gain representative honours when he was selected for Lancashire against North Wales.

In 1881 the Wanderers made the short journey to make Pikes Lane their home with the sum of 150 being spent on pitch improvements. A basic wooden grandstand was erected and admission was set at sixpence (3p) and fourpence (2p) with season tickets priced at one guinea (£1-05).

At the annual meeting in 1881 Peter Parkinson was elected President of the club and he was instrumental in introducing Scottish players into Bolton. The first pair to arrive were W. Struthers and J. Devlin. The former being a young player who had already had a distinguished career as a member of Glasgow Rangers, for whom he once scored a goal against Queens Park while suffering from a dislocated shoulder, and was seen as the greatest centre forward of his day. Devlin, of Arbroath, was a full back who did not have a long stay in Bolton as he met with an accident at his work at Woods Foundry, which deprived him of the sight of one eye. Steele, Christie and Brogan all followed south and made their mark on the team. In the same year of 1881 the club resisted the suggestion by civic leaders that the name 'Wanderers' should be dropped in favour of simply 'Bolton'.

The Wanderers entered the F.A. Cup for the first time in 1881/82 and were knocked out at the second round stage by Blackburn Rovers. It was through English Cup-ties against Welsh club Druids that Wales also became a source of players for the Wanderers. The club obtained the services of Bob Roberts, Jacky Vaughan, Jack and Albert Powell, Dai Jones and Jimmy Trainer, who later became Preston's 'keeper in their double winning team.

In 1883 the club were threatened with expulsion from the Lancashire F.A. after the referee - Sam Ormerod, later to become secretary-manager at Manchester City - was booed off the field at Pikes lane and then assaulted at the railway station. Fortunately the Association decided to take no action.

Professionalism was not legalised but it was no secret that players were being paid. Goalkeeper Trainer was apparently earning 50 shillings (2-50) per week, whilst the other 'stars' were on anything between 30 shillings (1-50) and 2. They were also found 'jobs' although they hardly did any work and kept fit purely for the game.

The 'professional' player held all the cards as if a rival club offered better terms, then his current club were hardly in a position to make a complaint. A commission from the Football Association paid a visit to inspect the Wanderers books and complimented the

BOLTON WANDERERS v. GREAT LEVER.

The first match this season between these clubs was played on Saturday at Pike's lane. Both teams have been strengthened by the introduction of new players, and consequently great deal of interest was taken in the encounter. Though rain fell heavily during the whole of the game, about 2,000 persons were present. The Wanderers won the toss, and decided to play with the wind. The game had only been in progress a few minutes when the home team scored the first goal, the result of some clever dodging by Cox, who centred the ball nicely, and Fowler put it through. For some time the play was very even, and after some really good passing between Sharples, Fallen, and Lomax, the latter scored the first and only goal for Great Lever. The Wanderers now pressed their opponents, and from a corner well sent in Steel scored goal No. 2. From the kick-off P Howarth and Swithenby made a nice run, but the ball was returned by Young, and a series of attacks on the Great Lever stronghold ensued, A Jones defending grandly, but at length, from a good kick by Kennedy, Steel scored a third goal. Howarth and Swithenby again got the ball away for a few minutes, and made several good attempts to capture the Wanderers' goal, but Young and M'Kernan were always on the alert, and after a good run on the right by Cox, who centred well, the ball was shot in by Steel, and, slipping out of Higham's grasp, it went through. The second half was grandly contested, neither side having any perceptible advantage, but it was evident the heavy state of the ground told upon the diminutive Great Lever forwards, though Sharples, Howarth, and Swithenby put in some really good work, and made it rather warm for the Wanderers' backs and goalkeeper. E. Jones also made several good runs, and from a corner well put in by him the fifth goal was kicked; the game thus resulting in favour of the Wanderers by five goals to one. For the winners, Cox and E Jones were best amongst the forwards, though the former appeared to indulge in too much gallery play. All the backs and half-backs played well, M'Kernan being, perhaps, most prominent. A Jones played a grand game for Great Lever, keeping the ball out of the goal time after time. Scowcroft also played finely, looking after Cox extremely well. Sharples and Howarth were the best of the forwards. Teams:—

WANDERERS.—Wilson, goal; M'Kernan and Young, backs; eaves (captain) and Kennedy, half-backs; Cox, Fowler, T rth, Christie, Steel, and Jones, forwards.
LEVER.—Higham, goal; A Jones and Bradley, Hardman, and Scowcroft, half-backs; Sharples Howarth, Swithenby, Fallen, and Lomax, for

Messrs Parkinson ... ... Referee: Mr ...
... ... News.

30 September 1882

Secretary, Tom Rawsthorne, on the manner in which they were kept. The wily secretary of course did not inform the commission that he had sat up all night preparing a fresh set of books for their inspection!

In 1883/84 the Wanderers were involved in an F.A. Cup-tie that stirred the town for the first time. A draw had resulted at Trent Bridge and the replay aroused unheard of enthusiasm. Special preparations were made for the reception of the crowd, the grandstand being lengthened for the occasion, and Pikes Lane was a sight in terms of masses of people that was totally new. The dressing tents, refreshment tents, pay boxes and grandstand were all packed with people. No one knew for sure the actual attendance as many didn't pay, and the local farmers made a fortune by charging admission to their adjoining fields. Although the Wanderers took 468 in receipts, it was Notts who won through.

In 1884 the question of professionalism came to a head when Preston North End, Burnley and Great Lever were suspended by the Lancashire F.A. They called a crisis meeting at the Commercial Hotel in Bolton with Peter Parkinson suggesting that a British F.A. be formed and run independently from the Football Association. As a consequence the Wanderers were not involved in the 1884/85 F.A. Cup. The team had been drawn against Preston Zingari but both clubs were embroiled in the political issues and withdrew from the competition. Prestigious friendly games against the likes of Notts County and Aston Villa were also cancelled as Bolton's opponents attempted to avoid the issue by claiming amateur status.

The F.A. finally realised they had little option in the face of the British F.A. if they were to hold on to their grip on the game. The persistence of the Lancashire clubs ensured that at a meeting held by the F.A. in July 1885 ratified legal payments to players.

J. J. Bentley had been appointed secretary of the club in February 1885 and his knowledge of the game's finer points was to be of immense value in the coming months. The F.A. decreed that a professional player could only compete in the F.A. Cup if he had been born within a six miles radius of the club's H.Q., or ground, or had lived in that area for at least two years.

This was to have repercussions for the club. After defeating Eagley and Rawtenstall with weakened teams they were drawn to play Preston. Both clubs fielded ineligible players and both were disqualified from the competition. In the Wanderers case it was Jack Powell who had taken a job in Ruabon without telling the club.

The competition became farcical with clubs spying on their opponents' players. In 1887/88 Bolton met Everton in a long running saga. A goal from Bob Roberts appeared to have won the match for Bolton but Everton successfully appealed against the qualification of Bob Struthers, who proved ineligible by three days. The replayed game was drawn and a second replay also failed to produce a result, before Everton won the fourth game. Everton were then beaten by Preston, who in turn, went on to defeat Halliwell in the third round. Meanwhile Bolton protested that Everton had fielded two professionals who were registered as amateurs. The F.A. found the Toffees guilty and suspended the club for a month. Preston were brought back from the fourth round to face the Wanderers in the second, but North End showed no mercy by winning 9-1.

> **Bolton Wanderers v. Stoke.**—The return between these clubs was played on the Pike's-lane Ground, Bolton, yesterday afternoon. Stoke came short-handed, and after pressing the umpire into service they were left with ten men only, these including Cox and Wilson, of Walsall Town. Almost from start to finish the visitors were continually on the defence. Twenty-nine minutes passed away with a blank sheet, but Davenport having once found an opening, goals came pretty freely, five being scored before the interval. After the teams had crossed over, the Wanderers were busy peppering away at the Stoke citadel, six more goals being added, the last, just on "Time," from a foul close to the posts. The Wanderers thus ran into double figures, winning by eleven goals to nothing. Teams:—Wanderers: Trainer, goal; Powell and Hutchison, backs; Weir, Ramsey, and Roberts, half-backs; Brogan, Davenport, Struthers, Miller, and Parkinson, forwards. Stoke: Birch, goal; Cox and Munford, backs; Smith, Schutt, and Bettany, half-backs; Lawton, Edge, Wilson, and Cox, forwards. Referee: Mr W Fairhurst.

23 November 1885

7 December 1885

> **LANCASHIRE CUP.—Third Round.**
> **Bolton Wanderers v. Blackburn Olympic.**—These famous teams opposed each other at Bolton, before two thousand spectators. On paper the Olympic appeared to have the best chance, but were completely run away with. The Wanderers at once took up the attack, and Struthers scored the first goal. Yates made a good attempt at the other end, but the home team were again busy, and Parkinson notched the second from a long kick by Powell. Struthers added the third, and Hough the fourth. This brought about half-time. On changing ends, after some nice play by Costley and Bell, the latter scored the first goal for the Olympic. Struthers headed the Wanderers fifth, Parkinson the sixth from a corner, Struthers the seventh, Davenport the eighth, Struthers the ninth, Hough the tenth, and Struthers the eleventh. Yates added one for the Olympic just on "Time," leaving the Wanderers victorious by eleven to two. Teams.—Olympic: Walmsley, goal; Ward and Beverley, backs; Hunter, Jackson, and Towers, half-backs; Dewhurst, Bell, Costley, Yates, and Cottam, forwards. Wanderers: Bateson, goal; Powell and Parkinson, backs; Glaister, Steel, and Holden, half-backs; Davenport, Gregory, Hough, Parkinson, and Struthers, forwards. Referee: F. T. Norris.

In 1885/86 Bolton won the Lancashire Cup by defeating Blackburn, and also won the Bolton Charity Cup and the Derbyshire Charity Cup, but off the field politics took the headlines. Peter Parkinson resigned and, at the annual meeting, Billy Struthers was appointed secretary. He showed little inclination for the job and, in February 1887, he was replaced by Fitzroy Norris. Bentley's administrative skills were soon missed by the club and to compound the problems they were forced to release all their players at the season's end. Most of them joined Halliwell but many did return for the following season the main exceptions being Davie Weir and Jimmy Trainer. The loss of goalkeeper Trainer proved hard to swallow as he went on to have unrivalled success at Deepdale.

The Wanderers persuaded Bentley to return in October 1887 but, by now, they were in debt and the following year they organised a prize draw with a first prize of £100. The police objected and stationed officers at the secretary's house on the planned date of the draw. The club went ahead with the draw at a shop of one of the committee with the winner coming from the Manchester area. The main 'result' however was that the club were freed from debt.......

...........Then came the adoption of the league system that was to transform the game.................

Chapter 2 (1888 ~ 1899)
League Football... And The First Relegation

Season 1888/89

On April 17th 1888, at a meeting in Manchester, Bolton Wanderers became one of the twelve to form the Football League, the brain-child of a Mr William McGregor, a member of the Aston Villa club. Accrington, Aston Villa, Blackburn Rovers, Burnley, Derby County, Everton, Notts County, Preston North End, Stoke, West Bromwich Albion and Wolverhampton Wanderers were the other clubs chosen to constitute the League, which would end the non stimulating games of friendlies or ordinaries between clubs.

Bolton Wanderers commenced their league life on a sound financial footing, having paid off most of their debts thanks to a prize draw, held in March 1888. New dressing rooms were installed at Pikes Lane for the coming of the League, which were paid for by private benefactors, who were given five year season tickets in return. On September 8th 1888 the Football League got underway with all except Blackburn and Notts County playing their first game.

Harry Tyrer who scored two goals in the Trotters first ever League win. That came on 29th September 1888 when Everton were defeated 6-2 at Pikes Lane. Tyrer played 14 League games in that first season.

The Wanderers entertained Derby County with the kick-off advertised for 3.15pm. Unfortunately County arrived late and the game commenced half an hour after the scheduled start. Admission was 3d and 6d (2.5p) with the stands extra and season tickets could be bought from five shillings (25p) to a guinea (£1-05). A crowd of 5000 did not present a healthy appearance expected on the first day of the season but the supporters of the Wanderers were waiting for the club to revive its name after two poor seasons. So much so that the club were not one of the eighteen teams exempt from the qualifying rounds of the FA Cup and due to clashes with League games the reserves took part in the competition, getting through to the third qualifying round, before losing 4-0 at Lindfield Athletic in Belfast. Bolton's first international player Kenny Davenport, who was born and bred in Bolton, had the distinction of scoring the club's first League goal after only two minutes play. He scored again, and a minute later with a goal from James Brogan, who had been with the Wanderers since 1883, gave Bolton a three goal lead after only five minutes.

That was the end of the excitement for Bolton supporters as Derby came back to lead by a goal at half time, and end up as 6-3 winners. The Wanderers defence was labelled mediocre with goals conceded with an ease seldom witnessed.

A week later Burnley visited Pikes Lane and circumstances were again similar. The visitors arrived late, Bolton took a three goal lead but then went down 4-3, the winner coming in the 75th minute. Both sides had taken to the field in similar jerseys, the Wanderers having to change, and the same thing happened at Turf Moor the following month, in Burnley's first home game when they completed the double over Bolton.

After losing to the 'invincibles' of Preston at Deepdale 3-1, the Wanderers recorded their first League win by defeating Everton 6-2 at Pikes Lane, in their fourth game.

After a slow start the Wanderers produced some impressive results including a 5-1 win at West Brom who were the English FA Cup holders. The game was stopped three minutes from time after crowd disturbances which started when Seddons, who was making his Bolton debut, and Hendry were fighting. Both players were suspended for a month and Seddons didn't play for Bolton again.

On November 22nd 1888 it was decided to award points to decide the championship, two for a win and one for a draw, and the committees of clubs were also ordered to prevent disruption and improper demonstrations by spectators.

Although there were now 22 League games to be played, the club completed a total of 64 fixtures during the season. Glasgow Celtic were beaten 2-0 at Pikes Lane, on their first ever Lancashire appearance, another top Scottish club, Battlefield were also beaten, 5-0. A crowd of 7000 came to the Celtic game curious as to why such a club had become so popular in so short a time.

Sunderland also came to Pikes Lane and were thrashed 10-1, Jimmy Brogan scoring five times. Pikes Lane was certainly an uncomfortable place for visitors and for referees who were greeted with criticism and hooting.

Bolton climbed out of the bottom four of the League for the first time on March 5th 1889 with a 4-0 win at Notts County. This was the only occasion in the Wanderers first League season that both sides didn't score in a game. This victory was followed with a 7-3 home win over Notts County and a 3-2 win at Accrington, the winner coming three minutes into injury time, to place the Wanderers in a satisfactory place in the table. Only one of the final ten games was lost, a 6-2 reverse at Villa, and only double winners Preston North End, scored more away goals than Bolton. There were five ever presents during the season. Brogan, who was leading scorer, Davenport, Milne, Roberts, who weighed almost 16 stone (!) and Weir, who scored the Wanderers first League hat trick in a 4-1 win over Accrington just before Christmas. Another player worth mentioning was James Parkinson despite making only two League appearances. His first outing was at left back, in the second game of the season against Burnley, and his second as a goalkeeper in a 2-1 home defeat by West Brom; goalkeeping had not yet become a specialist job.

Season 1889/90

Six defeats in the opening seven games rooted Wanderers firmly at the foot of the Football League. The only victory during this spell came at fellow strugglers Stoke where Barbour scored the only goal of the game. A 3-0 home defeat at the hands of Notts County, which the visitors claimed as 4-0, was to have a significant effect at the end of the season.

New signings were made in an attempt to halt the slide. Rugby international John Sutcliffe, who was later to earn international recognition with the Wanderers, signed along with James McNee from Scottish crack side Renton. Bolton were later fined £5 by the Football League for fielding McNee, in a 6-2 home defeat by Preston in October 1889, having not served his proper qualification period.

Perhaps the most successful signing during the period was that of twenty year old James Cassidy from Glasgow Hibernians. Cassidy was to become a fixture in the Wanderers forward line and celebrated his first season for the club by becoming top scorer.

James Cassidy - five goals in the 13-0 demolition of Sheffield United in the F.A. Cup. He went on to score 101 first glass goals for the Wanderers.

A 3-2 win over Blackburn Rovers, at Pikes Lane, lifted the Wanderers off the foot of the table. Much credit for the victory went to goalkeeper James Parkinson who now saw his position under threat from Sutcliffe. As in the previous season, Parkinson also proved his worth away from the custodianship of the Wanderers goal, playing in the forward line and scoring in the opening day defeat by Accrington. During November the Wanderers took part in a floodlight game, defeating Sheffield United at Bramhall Lane, the crowd apparently astounded by the illumination, but it was to be over seventy years before the League accepted football under artificial light.

League form improved with the new signings settling in well. Derby County and West Brom were both hit for seven at Pikes Lane, with James Cassidy banging home four against County, his first for the club. John Sutcliffe made his debut against West Brom, but with an inch of snow on the ground it far from met the approval of the Throstles', and only 4000 braved the elements to see Sutcliffe keep a clean sheet.

On the 28th December 1889 the Wanderers defeated Burnley 6-3 on home soil in a scheduled League match. Both sides had protested to the referee over the hard ground, but he insisted that the game went ahead. The official reported the clubs disapproval of the conditions and the League ordered a replay. It was no coincidence that the best League form of the season came with the start of the season's FA cup rounds and the club's best ever victories in the competition.

Successes at both Notts County and Aston Villa sandwiched a first round FA Cup win over Belfast Distillery by 10-1.

Then in the second round the Wanderers were drawn to face Sheffield United at Bramhall Lane. The game was switched to Pikes Lane as Sheffield Wednesday were also at home, to Accrington, and it was expected that they would draw the crowds. The 1st February 1890 saw Bolton register their best ever victory in a major competition by seeing off United by 13-0. The Wanderers were urged by the crowd to make it twenty, although they saw James Cassidy score five goals, a feat that equalled Bob Struthers five against Bootle in 1882.

Cassidy followed this up a week later with a hat trick in a 5-0 home League win over Stoke, and then the Wanderers qualified for the semi-finals of the FA Cup with a 3-2 win at Preston, fighting back from a two goal deficit in only eight minutes.

After defeating high riding Wolves at the end of February the bubble burst. A 7-0 defeat was incurred at Burnley, the home side registering their first League win of the season, at the eighteenth attempt, and then defeat in the FA Cup by Sheffield Wednesday, in the semi-final at Perry Bar. The League season ended when Burnley visited Pikes Lane in the replayed game from December.

The Wanderers needed to win to stay out of the bottom four and to have to seek re-election. After leading 2-0, the game ended 2-2, and with Aston Villa beating Cup winners Blackburn, Bolton finished fourth from bottom on goal average the difference being one-hundredth, and in favour of Villa. At the League meeting Bolton stated the home defeat by Notts County had been by three goals and not four therefore placing them above Villa. The League settled the matter by stating that only Bolton and Burnley complied with the secretary's request for an official return of results. It was agreed that both Villa and Bolton should remain in the League without going to re-election, this being the closest the Wanderers have ever come to losing their League status. Sunderland were elected to the League in place of Stoke and the Wanderers became the first English club to defeat the newcomers on their own ground when, in an April friendly, James Brogan scored the only goal of the game.

Season 1890/91
Bolton were to get some indication of what was in store for them in the third season of League football when they were given three consecutive home games to kick off with. On the 6th September the Wanderers took the field in red and white quartered jersey's and duly defeated Notts County 4-2. Alec Barbour, who had become the Wanderers trainer, took his place at centre half due to injury problems and ended up playing fourteen games during the season. Derby County were then defeated 3-1, but this was followed by a crushing 5-0 defeat by Everton before Bolton's best League attendance to that date, of 12,000.

Fortunes fluctuated but home form took a turn for the worse after a 5-2 defeat by bottom club Sunderland at Pikes Lane. Harry Gardiner, transferred from Renton, made his debut in this game and perhaps spurred on the visitors as the Wanderers had pipped them for his signature. The Wanderers won their remaining six home League games of the season with a goal difference of 23-1.

Successive games at Pikes Lane produced a 6-0 win over Accrington, an identical result against Wolves, and a 7-1 win over West Bromwich. The heavy pitch certainly favoured Bolton and the defensive formation of Sutcliffe. Somerville and Jones ranked alongside the best in the country. There was disappointment in the FA Cup when Accrington won 5-1 at their Cricket Ground home venue.

A week earlier the sides had drawn 2-2 at the same venue in the Cup but both clubs agreed that the ground had been unfit before the kick off. Alec Barbour was sent off in the Cup defeat for *"wilfully kicking an opponent"*, and when it was discovered that the umpire was a former member of the Accrington club the Wanderers protested, but this was dismissed by the FA.

The latter stages of the season brought the Wanderers some success. On the 21st February, Everton, who were already champions, were defeated 6-0 at Pikes Lane in the Lancashire Cup quarter finals. Over 12,000 attended even though prices were raised to 1s-6d (7.5p). The Football Field stated that *"The Wanderers are a surprise packet one ought never to be amazed at anything they accomplish or for that matter fail to accomplish"*. Bolton then faced Lancashire rivals Blackburn Rovers three times in the space of a month.

Goals from Davenport and Turner won the Wanderers both points on their first visit to Rovers' new enclosure at Ewood Park; a fortnight later Rovers won the FA Cup, defeating Notts County in the final, at the Oval. Rovers visited Pikes Lane in the Wanderers final League game of the season and again a 2-0 scoreline went in favour of the Trotters, both goals coming in the final four minutes. The best crowd of the season, over 14000, saw Bolton finish in fine style to take fifth position in the League. The two sides faced each other again in the Lancashire Cup semi-final at Ardwick, with Bolton completing a hat trick of 2-0 wins over the FA Cup holders.

To complete a fine season the Wanderers won the County Cup by defeating Darwen 3-1 in the final at Anfield. Goal nets were used for the first time during the season, initially in one half of a friendly at Nottingham Forest in January 1891. They were invented by an engineer named Brodie who later helped design and build the first dual carriageway in the country in his home town of Liverpool. At the end of the season Bolton Wanderers were admitted to the Manchester Football Association, becoming the 46th member, and allowing them to compete in the Senior Cup competition.

In June 1891 the International Association decided that a penalty kick would be awarded if a player intentionally tripped or held a player, or handled the ball, within twelve yards from his own goal line. The penalty was to be taken at any point twelve yards from goal. It was also recommended that umpires should be abolished and replaced by linesmen.

Season 1891/92
The season kicked off on the 5th September with a visit to newcomers, Darwen, the League having been extended to fourteen clubs.

Pikes Lane - home of Bolton Wanderers until 1895.

The new twelve yard penalty line was well defined on the pitch, and the Wanderers got off to a good start with a 2-1 win. Then, three successive home games against Darwen, Sunderland and Preston all ended in victory and the club stood at the top of the League for the first time ever. Unfortunately this only lasted five days as a 2-0 reverse was suffered at Notts County, the match being part of the local Goose Fair celebrations.

The first penalty in a game involving the Wanderers came in the 4-3 home win over Sunderland. Auld converted the kick, awarded after Sutcliffe had kicked Hannah, the latter having to leave the field. The Wearsiders lost three of their first four games, yet then went on to take the League title by losing only twice in their next twenty two games.

Six straight wins in which only three goals were conceded put Bolton back on top of the table, and home games were each now attracting over 11,000 people. Twenty one years old David McFettridge, who signed in August from Cowlairs, faced his brother William in the 2-0 win over Burnley and the young Scot also scored the winner at Stoke in a game that was only eighty minutes long due to inclement weather.

Two November defeats against Lancashire rivals were to prove costly in the final analysis of the Wanderers attempts to secure the championship. A 4-0 loss at Blackburn, where the oldest member of the team, twenty seven years old James Brogan, fell ill, and a similar result at Preston, in which the first penalty goal was scored at Deepdale, were enough to handicap Bolton's chances. The Wanderers top spot was lost on New Years day, a position they were not to regain, and two months then passed without the club's involvement in a League game. During that time, Di Jones took and missed the club's first ever penalty in a 1-1 friendly draw at Everton, and Sheffield Wednesday and Blackburn Rovers ousted the Wanderers from the FA and Lancashire Cups respectively.

Any slim chances of success in the League went with a 4-1 Shrove Tuesday defeat at Sunderland, but only one defeat in the five League games gave Bolton third place. They wound up their programme with a 5-2 win at Everton thanks to a James Cassidy hat trick. It was Cassidy who also had the distinction of scoring Bolton's first penalty, converting in a 2-0 win over Notts County, at Pikes Lane.

Pikes Lane was honoured with what was advertised as the World's League Championship, between teams from the English and Scottish leagues. A 2-2 draw resulted, with Bolton's ever present centre half, Harry Gardiner, starring for the English eleven.

After defeat by Ardwick in the Manchester Cup final the Wanderers embarked on a Southern tour, defeating Leicester Fosse, drawing with Chatham, and losing to Royal Arsenal who recorded their first ever win over a Football League side. The Wanderers reserves also completed their first ever season of League competition, finishing fourth out of eight teams in the Lancashire Combination, which was won by Blackburn Rovers Reserves.

At the League AGM it was decided to again extend the First Division and form a Second consisting of twelve clubs. Eleven of these clubs came from the Football Alliance League therefore making that competition defunct. Test matches were also introduced to decide promotion and relegation.

Season 1892/93
Bolton opened the season by being the first visitors to Everton's new ground Goodison Park. The friendly resulted in a 4-2 win for the home side despite James Cassidy scoring the first goal, on the new enclosure, after only two minutes.

On the 13th September, at the Wanderers AGM, held at the public sale rooms on Bowkers Row, the issue of a new ground was raised. The Wanderers secretary, J.J. Bentley, stated that *"a ground was in view but Pikes Lane would still be available for two seasons before the builders take over."*

The opening game at Preston North End was lost by 2-1 then four consecutive home League matches all ended in Bolton victories, including a 5-0 win over Aston Villa, in which James Cassidy scored a hat trick. Three draws then followed with James Dickenson matching Cassidy's feat in a 4-4 draw with Stoke at Pikes Lane. Notice boards were erected around the ground requesting spectators to refrain from *"hooting"* or doing anything to annoy the referee.

After the promising start to the season, only one defeat in the first eleven games and fourth position in the League, things started to go wrong with only one win being chalked up in the next twelve games. That came in a 4-1 home win over Newton Heath, later to become Manchester United, in the first League meeting between the two clubs.

Christmas was spent away from home with a 1-1 draw at Aston Villa on Christmas Eve and the same score being repeated at Derby on Boxing Day. A crowd of only 2000 saw Derby win 3-0 at Pikes Lane on the 2nd January, the poor attendance being attributed to the good skating weather.

After two heavy defeats at Stoke and Burnley, along with an FA Cup exit at the hands of eventual winners, Wolves, the Wanderers found themselves in the bottom three. Davie Weir returned to the club from Ardwick, after heading their scoring charts in the Second, and he helped turn the tide with seven goals in the Wanderers last eight League games. Things improved with a 3-3 draw at runaway champions Sunderland, in which Weir scored twice and, indeed, the Wanderers were three goals to the good with only twenty five minutes remaining. Only one of the final eight games was lost, a 3-0 reverse in the final match at Everton. Six consecutive home wins, including a 2-1 victory over Sunderland before the best gate of the season of 13000, was enough to lift the Wanderers into a creditable final position of fifth.

During March a Lancashire Cup second round tie against Bury was abandoned after a spectator ran across

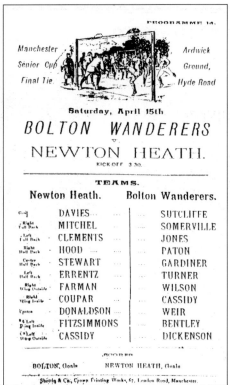

Programme from the Manchester Cup Final when Newton Heath ran out 2-1 winners at Hyde Road.

the pitch and kicked Wanderers' half back James Turner. The ground was overflowing and packed right up to the touchline with 16000 spectators, and despite the fact that Bolton were wining 3-1, the FA ordered a replay at Pikes Lane. Betting was given as the reasons for crowd disturbances but justice was done in the replay with Bolton wining 1-0.

The Wanderers qualified for both local cup finals but lost on each occasion, Newton Heath, who had finished bottom of the First Division, but had kept their place after the test matches, defeated the Wanderers 2-1 in the Manchester Cup Final at Ardwick. A week later Preston kept Bolton's trophy cabinet empty for the year with a 2-0 win in the Lancashire Cup Final at Blackburn.

Season 1893/94

Only 7000 spectators attended the opening day 4-1 win over Stoke at Pikes Lane. Preston being the only other club to attract less, and in an attempt to recoup some revenue the Wanderers increased prices for admission to the stand for the visit of North End at the end of the month, much to the protest of the patrons. Goals were hard to come by and after a 1-0 home defeat by League leaders Sheffield United, which meant only one goal had been scored in four games, the club were placed next to the bottom. A couple of victories at the end of October improved matters, when Cup winners Wolves were beaten 2-0 at Pikes Lane and a 3-1 win at bottom club Darwen gave the Wanderers their first away win for over twelve months.

On November 18th League leaders Aston Villa came to Bolton and won 1-0 before the lowest ever League gate in the town of 700. The game was not expected to take place and should have been abandoned with a storm of hail and wind lashing over the waterlogged pitch. The club took part in it's first ever Christmas Day League fixture, a tradition that was to continue for seventy years, drawing 1-1 with Sheffield Wednesday at Pikes Lane.

Although League form was poor it seemed the FA Cup could provide some silverware. The Wanderers had every reason to think it was their year, defeating Small Heath 4-3 in the first round, after being two down at half time, and ousting Newcastle in their own backyard after offering them a fee to switch the second round tie to Pikes Lane.

Special trains from fifteen Lancashire towns were to run to Bolton's third round game against Second Division leaders Liverpool at Pikes Lane. The ground was specially extended and 16000 saw the Wanderers cruise into the semis with a 3-0 win. Cup form extended to the League with a 3-2 win at champions elect Aston Villa, inflicting the Midlanders only home defeat of the season, a last minute winner from Cassidy sealing the points.

On the 10th March, two Handel Bentley goals secured Bolton's first ever FA Cup Final appearance, a 2-1 margin over Sheffield Wednesday at Fallowfield being recorded. Crowds increased with the Cup fever but results took a turn for the worse, as no one wanted to get injured before the final, and only one win in the last six League games saw the Wanderers keep out of the bottom three by the slender margin of one point.

The last League game before the FA Cup Final was lost 3-2 at Everton and five days later another trip was made to Goodison for the Cup Final. A poor crowd of 23000 saw the Wanderers freeze on the day and Notts County ran up a 4-0 lead before Cassidy grabbed a consolation goal, as County became the first Second Division side to win the FA Cup.

Only 2000 came to the next game, a 3-0 defeat by West Brom, and then Everton won the Lancashire Cup with a 2-1 win over the Wanderers in the final at Ardwick. Some pride was salvaged in the final League game of the season when runners up Sunderland, who had lost only twice since the turn of the year, were defeated 2-0 at Pikes Lane, with goals from Handel Bentley and Archie Hughes. These were the two of only eighteen scored at home, the lowest in the League, yet the club's defensive record of only fourteen conceded on home territory was only bettered by champions Villa. Incredibly the club actually lost money by reaching the FA Cup Final, a loss in revenue by not playing League games at the best time due to Cup commitments, and bonuses to player's for reaching the final, were blamed. At the end of the season only 36 players remained on the club's books whilst other First Division sides had over 70 registered players.

Season 1894/95
Total attendances on the first day of the season were up on the previous year with 9300 watching League football in comparison to 8200 twelve months earlier. The Wanderers kicked off their last season at Pikes Lanes with a 2-2 draw against Stoke, parading two new Scottish recruits, in William Andrews and Archie Freebairn.

The following week a visit to newly promoted Small Heath, later to become Birmingham City, saw the home side register their first win in the First Division, the Duke of York being in attendance.

Wanderers first win of the season came at Liverpool, goals from James Cassidy and the 'Kilmarnock Flyweight' Robert Tannahill, giving them a 2-1 result amid cheers from the Evertonian's present. Another scalp was taken in the form of Sunderland, named 'the team of all talents', by a 4-1 margin at Pikes Lane. It was the first of only four defeats during the season for Sunderland on their way to taking the League championship.

On the 5th October it was decided that Bolton Wanderers Football and Athletic should be incorporated under the company acts of 1862 and 1890, whereby the liability of each shareholder be limited to the amount of his shares. A capital of £4000 was to be raised and a plot of land at Burnden was to be leased in the sum of £130 per annum.

By the end of October the club had dropped into the bottom four but a run of ten games without a win came to an end when Wolves were beaten 6-1 at Pikes Lane. Christmas and New Year brought five points from three games including a 6-0 home win over Derby in which Charlie Henderson scored four times.

A 5-0 defeat at bottom club Stoke and a 2-1 reverse at high flying Aston Villa left the Wanderers in a precarious League position with almost two months to wait before their next encounter. This period was taken up with cup football. The third round of the FA Cup was reached, before defeat at Sunderland, after having conquered Arsenal and Bury. Everton defeated the Wanderers in the Lancashire Cup but interest was kept in the Manchester Cup which was won for the first time when Bury were beaten 3-2 in the Final at Hyde Road.

The Wanderers wound up League football at Pikes Lane in grand fashion. Cup Finalists, and eventual winners, Aston Villa were defeated 4-3, Nottingham Forest were thumped 4-1 on Good Friday before 12000, and the following day the other Cup Finalists, West Brom, were drubbed 5-0 before a crowd of 10000. Albion were handicapped as their keeper, James Reader, was sent off for pushing Willie Joyce. The Wanderers hammered home their advantage with Peter Turnbull, who had signed from Burnley a month earlier, grabbing a second half hat trick.

This result ensured Bolton's safety from the test matches and although the final game of the season was lost by 5-0 at Sheffield United, the club's home form of seven wins and one draw, in their last eight Pikes Lane appearances, pulled them through from an almost hopeless position. Along with the move to Burnden Park went the club's trainer/groundsman, Jack Nuttall, who moved into the house on the verge of the ground. The duties of both trainer and groundsman were proving to much for one man and not long after the move Bill Brierley was appointed Trainer.

Nuttall's son Henry, who was born in the house at Burnden, was to become a 1923 Cup winner with the club his father had served in the early days.

'Keeper James Sutcliffe, who missed only one League game during the campaign when he was dropped for insubordination, appeared for England in their 3-0 win over Scotland at Goodison Park, and also in the 9-0 win over Ireland.

Season 1895/96

Burnden Park was completed on August 10th and used for the first time a week later when the club's ninth annual athletic festival was held. A total of 35000 passed through the gates on the Saturday and bank Holiday Monday, the novelty of the new ground increasing the previous years attendance by 10000.

The Wanderers commenced the season with two away games losing 2-0 at Stoke and winning 3-0 at Bury in the first ever First Division game at Gigg Lane. Football was first played at Burnden on September 11th when the Wanderers took on Preston in a benefit for full back, Dave Jones, who had captained the club for the previous six years. A crowd of 3000 saw the winner come from the boot of Smith, for the visitors, late in the game.

David Jones - his benefit game was the first to be played at Burnden Park, he went on to play 255 League and Cup games for the club.

Three day's later 15000 attended the opening League game at Burnden. The four o'clock kick off was preceded by a cycle race. Everton were then beaten 3-1, the first goal coming from James Martin for the Wanderers, in the 25th minute. A 2-1 win at Small Heath put the Wanderers joint top of the League with Stoke. Robert Jack, who had signed from Alloa, was given his League debut in this game and so began an affinity that was to see the name become one of the most famous in the history of the club. Bury became the first and only side to win a League game at Burnden during the season but, five wins in the next six games kept the Wanderers in second position.

The first fatality at Burnden was recorded when, during a 3-1 win over Stoke, a spectator on the railway embankment, climbing for a better view, fell in front of an oncoming train. Stoke were to be the visitor's fifty one years later when the embankment witnessed one of the worst disasters at a football ground, when 33 people lost their lives.

Burnden Park caused plenty of headaches. The pitch was constantly waterlogged, six inches deep in places, the track around the pitch was breaking up due to the

elements and the overall drainage left a lot to be desired. Indeed the reserves had to switch a home game against Oswaldtwistle to Pikes Lane which was now a dreary place and half built on.

Erratic form again returned with only one win in the last eight games of 1895. A Boxing Day defeat at Derby produced record receipts for the home club and two days later a game with Preston at Burnden was abandoned at half time with no score when North End refused to come out owing to the state of the pitch.

New Year saw a change in fortunes with only one defeat in eleven League games. On New Year's day the Wanderers attracted 17000 for the visit of Derby with record receipts of £484. The Wanderers won 2-1 and three days later defeated Wolves 4-0, also on home soil. Unfortunately during this game, the club's centre forward and leading scorer, Willie Joyce, broke his leg whilst scoring the second goal, and his season finished there and then.

Interest in both the Lancashire and Manchester Cups ended in the first round, but by the end of February the quarter finals of the FA Cup had been reached. In successive weeks at Burnden, Small Heath were beaten 4-1 in a League game, Thomas Vail scoring on his debut after signing from Dundee, Bury were beaten 2-0 in the FA Cup quarter finals and League leaders and eventual champions Aston Villa were held to a 2-2 draw. An FA Cup Final appearance went by the board when bogey side Sheffield Wednesday won 3-1 in the semi-final replay at the Town Ground Nottingham.

The only League defeat since the turn of the year came in a 5-0 drubbing at Wolves, but even with this reverse only Derby, who finished in second place, had a better defensive away record than Bolton. The final League game of the season saw some consolation gained for the Cup defeat, with a win over Wednesday, who had won the Cup the week before, to take fourth position in the League.

Season 1896/97

During the summer the centre of the pitch at Burnden was raised to form a camber in an attempt to avoid the previous season's problem's and the season got off to a flying start when, after five games, the Wanderers found themselves heading the League. Sunderland were beaten at Burnden thanks to a David Jones free kick and a week later, the only other undefeated side, Preston, were thumped 3-1 despite them taking the lead after only 45 seconds.

The first reverse of the season came in the eighth game when a Chippendale goal gave Blackburn the points at Ewood. Recovery was swift and a week later Stoke fell to four goals without reply. The tenth game of the season saw the first change to the side, Bob Brown replacing Jimmy McGeachan who had fallen ill, and a 2-2 draw resulted at Bury.

New players were taken on in an attempt to keep hold of the leading position. Paddy Smith, a goalkeeper, was signed form Partick for £40 and centre forward, Tom Miller, was also found a position in the Bolton Theatre Orchestra as a cornet player.

After only two defeats in the first fifteen games, both by a goal to nil, the Christmas period produced four consecutive reversals. Motherwell were sent packing by 6-0 on Christmas Day and then two single goal defeats were incurred at Derby and Sheffield United.

Liverpool ended the Wanderers undefeated home record on New Year's Day when a crowd of 19000 paid record of receipts of £512. During January Burnden also hosted the mile championship of the world when James Craig won the race in a time of 4 minutes 30.25 seconds, in front of 3000 spectators.

Bolton were bundled out of the FA Cup in the second round at the hands of Derby County for whom Steve Bloomer notched a hat trick in a 4-1 win. The Cup defeat, coupled with the loss of League form, knocked the stuffing out of many players who were on a state bordering mutiny. Their complaints were long and loud with one player after another vowing to shake the soil of Burnden from their feet at the season's end. The players were badly managed with too many people in authority over them.

McGeachan was suspended for one month when he flatly refused to accompany the team to Sheffield. The storm which was brewing was reflected in results with only two victories in the final ten games, seven of which, were at home. The directorate claimed there was nothing wrong at the club and entertained the players for the purpose of a clear the air meeting.

Jim McGeachan - suspended for one month after refusing to travel.

McGeachan's suspension was lifted and he took part in a 2-1 home win over bottom club Burnley, although only 4000 were present.

Aston Villa took the Wanderers to task by completing a double within the space of five days. Robert Jack had given the Wanderers a two goal half time lead at Perry Bar before eventually going down 6-2, whilst the League champions and FA Cup winners elect won 2-1 at Burnden.

The final of the Manchester Cup was reached but there was little consolation there as Bury took the trophy by winning 3-1. After a brilliant start to the season the New Year had seen the team go to the dogs. Supporters were crying out for a manager to take over the running of team affairs instead of leaving it to a number of the directorate themselves who disagreed over selections. This was the first real crisis in the Wanderers League history and it was to have repercussions eventually resulting in the club's first ever relegation.

Season 1897/98
Early season fortunes were up and down with three wins and three defeats in the first six games. Bolton visited Everton on the opening day, a new covered stand, on the popular side of the ground was opened, and the home side won 2-1 despite Bob Thompson putting Bolton in front.

A centre forward was desperately required and James Cassidy was reinstated and he promptly scored the winner against Preston at Burnden. Early in October the League leaders Aston Villa were visited on their new ground at Villa Park. As in the previous season the Wanderers went in at half time two goals to the good, David Nicholl, who had signed from Arbroath, grabbing both goals. Villa hit back, and in the second period, went on to win the game 3-2.

On the 30th October, after a 1-0 win over Sunderland at Burnden, thanks to a Cassidy goal four minutes from time, the Wanderers were nicely placed in third position. Suddenly things began to look rosy after three consecutive November wins, including a 2-0 home win over Villa, who were in second place. Then came the crash. Ten League games without a win, scoring in only two, and only two points collected. The problems of the previous season were again becoming apparent. By the end of February a state of panic had set in. Without a League win since November, beaten in the Lancashire Cup, and ousted from the FA Cup by Southern League side Southampton.

A club record of five consecutive League games without a goal was recorded and a desperate remedy was required if the club were to avoid the test matches. The Wanderers had no game on the first Saturday in March and it seemed the rest did the team some good for Wolves were beaten 2-1 at Burnden the following week. A draw at Liverpool and a home win against Everton, before only 3000, saw the Wanderers climb away from danger. Victory over West Brom in April assured the Wanderers of safety, but the last three games of the season were all lost. The only consolation from these was a record gate at Burnden of 19350 for the visit of the new League champions Sheffield United who won 1-0.

Only eighteen goals had been scored at home, the worst in the division whilst only Preston scored less on their travels than the Wanderers. The total tally of 28 League goals for the season still remains the worst in the club's history, proving that the centre forward required at the start of the season still had to be found. Next season there would be no escape as automatic promotion and relegation was to be introduced.

During 1898, club secretary Frank Brettell, a founder member of Everton, left the club to join 'Spurs. Full back John Somerville took up the position continuing to play as required. In April a short Southern Tour was arranged. A 2-2 draw resulted at 'Spurs, one of their goals coming from former Wanderer Willie Joyce, and a 3-3 draw was played out with the Corinthians before a 30,000 crowd at Crystal Palace. The Wanderers had only expected a frivolous friendly at the Palace but the game had been billed as one of the Bank Holiday attractions within the great grounds.

Season 1898/99
Despite the waning interest in running and cycling, 10000 spectators attended the clubs 12th annual sports day on the 20th August, 5000 more than the practice match.

During the previous twelve months £3343 had been spent on players wages and the directorate decided this had to be reduced by £1200 in the ensuing year with another financial loss looming. This caused problems with the playing staff. Seven players left, including Welsh international David Jones, who joined Manchester City. Goalkeeper James Sutcliffe did not re-sign due to a disagreement over wages. He missed the first two League games before his situation was sorted out, an offer of £5 per week being accepted, whilst ex-Stockport keeper Joe Lee took over in his absence. The only changes at Burnden for the new season was a new coat of paint and an antiquated advertisement on the roof of the grandstand painted out.

7500 attended the first game, a 3-3 draw with West Brom, Tom Miller equalising for Bolton with the final kick of the game, after they had been three down at half time. Only two victories in the opening ten games placed the Wanderers in the bottom two. Wolves were beaten 2-1, thanks to a couple of Jocky Wright goals and the game at Stoke, which ended in a 3-2 win for Bolton, was held up for five minutes due to a downpour. The Wanderers lost 4-1 on their first ever League visit to Newcastle, who were at the foot of the table, and after a 1-0 home defeat by Bury on December 17th Bolton took the wooden spoon position.

Three representatives of the club were sent to Scotland with blank cheques and orders to return with a couple of first rate forwards and a full back with only well known men of repute to be bargained for. Unfortunately they returned with no new signings and everything seemed to be going against the club. On 2nd January the Wanderers were leading Aston Villa by 1-0 when the game was abandoned three minutes into the second half due to rain. The replayed match in April ended scoreless.

After another home defeat, this time by Blackburn Rovers, the *'Football Field'* stated: *"A team that can't win at home is doomed, the forwards have no sting and the defence lets them down."* The players responded by beating Sunderland 6-1 at Burnden in a continuous downpour before only 1500 spectators. This was however a flash in the pan as three consecutive League defeats followed as well as an exit from the FA Cup at the hands of Wolves.

During February, Hughie Morgan, an outside left, was signed form Sunderland for £250 and Tom Hynds, a centre half, was recruited from Celtic. Morgan finished the season as joint leading goalscorer with Albert Gilligan on six goals a piece, but four wins in the last eight games, including victories over Cup Finalists Derby and League runners up Liverpool, were not enough to save the Wanderers from relegation to the Second Division.

The clubs first ever relegation was a hard pill to swallow but there were some small crumbs of comfort. Hughie Morgan scored a last minute winner at Preston in the final game of the season to earn a 1-0 win and send the wooden spoon to Sheffield Wednesday who had a point less than the Wanderers.

Burnden Park also hosted a Cup semi final replay between Liverpool and Sheffield United that ended in a 4-4 draw and brought record receipts of £740.

Chapter 3 (1899 ~ 1914)
The Ups and Downs of Pre-War Football

Season 1899/1900

Only two major signings were made for Bolton's first ever campaign in the Second Division. William Halley rejoined the Wanderers from Bedminster and Lawrie Bell, a centre forward, came from Everton.

It was Bell who took the distinction of scoring the club's first Second Division goal in a 3-2 win over Loughborough. The game took place at Leicester, with Loughborough's ground being closed down due to crowd disturbances, in fact they were to win only one game all season and were not re-elected.

Lawrie Bell - leading scorer as the Trotters swept to promotion at the first attempt.

Bell scored twice on his home debut, a 2-1 win over Newton Heath, but the first reverse came a week later when Sheffield Wednesday won by the same score. Further players were taken on, for James Picken and Willie Brown came from the Kilmarnock Shawbank Club and local talent was not overlooked when Jimmy Hansen, from Little Hulton arrived. All three players were to play their part in a successful season. At the end of September the directorate offered the team £500 to win promotion and they didn't lose another League game that year. In fact the only reverses were a 4-0 friendly defeat at 'Spurs and a 3-2 Lancashire Cup knockout at Newton Heath

Burnden Park began to buzz when it was realised that the club had every chance to regain their First Division status and goals were scored in abundance. During October the South African touring side, known as the Kaffirs, were beaten 13-3, and even James Sutcliffe the Bolton goalkeeper got onto the scoresheet. The following month Burnden was awarded an Inter-League game against the Irish with Wanderers half back Jack Fitchett being selected for the English team. He was the only Second Division player in the side and the youngest at 19 years old, but a poor gate of only 5372 saw the English win 3-1.

It was during Christmas that Bolton really took their opponents to task with wins by 5-2 at Burton Swifts, 6-1 at Burnley and 7-0 against Loughborough at Burnden, all coming in the space of a week. The Wanderers then won their next three games before they faced the only side to have beaten them in a League game, Sheffield Wednesday. Bolton, who were top of the division, were a point in front of their Yorkshire visitors and a goal from Bob Jack after 65 minutes before a crowd of 12325 increased that advantage.

Wednesday took revenge by knocking Bolton out of the F.A. Cup at Owlerton and League form suffered with only one point being collected in three games. With nine games left to play the Wanderers had promotion still in their own hands. The challenge was taken on admirably with eight wins and only one defeat, which came in the seventh of this sequence, at New Brighton Tower on Easter Monday. During the nine games only three goals were conceded, and they all came in the defeat at New Brighton, giving Bolton a goal difference of 24 to 3. In fact the seven games played before conceding a goal is still a club record. Promotion was assured with a 3-0 home win over Gainsborough Trinity but there was disappointment in the crowd of only 4327.

Incredibly eleven penalties were awarded to the Wanderers during the season which were all missed! The season was wound up in style with a 5-0 win over Burton Swifts with Lawrie Bell scoring four times. This gave Bolton the runners up position, two points behind champions Sheffield Wednesday, and so the two clubs returned from whence they had departed twelve months earlier.

Club records of only four League defeats in a season and 25 goals conceded in a season were set, but off the field a high price was paid. Despite the success the poor gates contributed to the club increasing it's deficit. The £500 paid to the players for promotion was paid for by a local iron foundry owner and a bazaar and amateur athletics festival was arranged in an effort to raise money.

Season 1900/01

A maximum wage of £4 per week was fixed on the club's return to the First Division. The opening game on the 1st September saw Derby County win 1-0 at Burnden, before 10872, against a Bolton side made up of four Englishmen and seven Scotsmen. The Wanderers found themselves at the bottom of the League after the first three games had ended in defeat and the sum of £300 was offered to the players as an incentive to get into the top four.

The first point of the season was won in the next game, a 1-1 draw against Preston at Burnden. Half back Jack Fitchett was dropped from the Bolton side for this game due to his inattention to training, whilst the scorer of the Wanderers goal was William Tracey, a recent signing from Shrewsbury and a plasterer by trade.

Things continued to improve during October with a 5-0 Lancashire Cup win against Preston and the first League win of the season came against the leaders Aston Villa by a single goal at Burnden. Club Secretary John Somerville played his first League game of the season against Villa, replacing the injured William Halley at full back.

17810, the second best League gate at Burnden, saw the Wanderers inflict Newcastle's first defeat of the season by 3-2. In goal for Bolton was the famous amateur international W. H. Waller who hailed from Richmond. He had been guest of honour during the morning at the club's grand scenic bazaar, which took place between the 17th and 20th of October at the Albert Hall, in aid of club funds.

The record League gate at Burnden was broken for the visit of Manchester City on the 3rd November. 20,034 witnessed a dour goalless struggle against a City side who included former Wanderers captain Dai Jones. Burnley ousted the Wanderers from the Lancashire Cup and three successive away defeats plunged the club into the bottom three. Away form was a cause for concern as all were lost during December, including a 7-2 reverse at West Brom, on their new ground at The Hawthorns, despite Tracey giving Bolton the lead.

Fellow strugglers Stoke were beaten at Burnden thanks to a James McKie goal and for the visit of Everton three new local players were drafted in an attempt to halt the slide. Frank Bell, Robert Haslam and Bob Hodgkiss all made their League debuts. A crowd of 6,472 saw a 59th minute goal from Lawrie Bell settle the issue in Bolton's favour.

On Christmas Day the Wanderers went down 3-0 at Nottingham Forest with forward Jimmy Hanson in goal, Regular 'keeper James Sutclife had fractured a finger in the warm up and the players were now believing that luck was against them. They went into the game at Nottingham with 13 League points, travelled with 13 players, Sutcliffe stayed in room 13 at the Colwich Hall Hotel and just for good measure McAteer missed a penalty! The following day, again with Hanson in goal, a 3-0 result went in favour of Aston Villa in Birmingham.

1901 came in with Bolton next to bottom on the same points as Preston. Results did improve with a run of eight League games without defeat commencing on New Year's Day when Bolton came from two down to beat Nottingham Forest 4-2 at Burnden. Jimmy Hanson, now a reinstated forward, grabbed one of the goals.

Although enough points were taken to earn safety from relegation the F.A. Cup proved to be a disaster with Reading, who were in the Southern League, winning a second round tie at Burnden.

The following week only 2,017, the lowest gate of the season, turned up for a scoreless draw with Sheffield United.

During the season a total of 28 players were called upon for League duty, the highest of any First Division club. The twelve goals conceded at home during the campaign is the lowest ever by the club for a season in the top flight. On April 27th Burnden Park was privileged to stage the F.A. Cup final replay between Tottenham and Sheffield United. The previous Saturday a crowd of 114,815 had been at Crystal Palace to see a 2-2 draw fought out. An extra stand was erected on the cycle track so Burnden could accommodate as many as 47,000 spectators, but only 20,470 saw non-Leaguers Tottenham take the cup. The day became known as Pie Saturday as numerous pies remained unsold and rumour had it that Bolton Corporation bought these up for use as paving stones!

Season 1901/02
The club commenced the season practically out of debt thanks to the successful bazaar and increased takings at the gate. Once again there was an early struggle, for despite signing six new players, the club were positioned next to the bottom after four games. Centre half was proving to be a problem position with four different players taking the role in the first five games. Archie Freebairn, Sparrow Brown, Tom McAteer and Bob Taylor all tried their hand but it wasn't until December that the problem was solved with the arrival of Bill Bannister from Burnley. He had caught the eye of the Wanderers in a Lancashire Cup tie the previous month scoring the winner against his new club!

Fellow strugglers Manchester City recorded their first win of the season against Bolton at Hyde Road fielding three ex Wanderers in David Jones, Tom Hynds and Hugh Morgan. Wolves took a point from Burnden Park in a 2-2 draw thanks to a last minute penalty. The crowd rushed to the gate at the end of the game and the referee, Mr.Bye, needed police protection to the station.

In the next home game Newcastle were defeated with winger, Harold Williams, who had signed from Bury, netting twice on his home debut. He was barred from playing in the following game at Villa as he had not been registered with the Football League. The Wanderers were fined one guinea for this oversight.

During December there was a strange occurrence in that Bolton were refereed in three consecutive League games by the same official, a Mr Lewis. Two away defeats, at Everton and Blackburn, and a home win against Stoke were under Mr Lewis's charge. On New Years Day a visit from Manchester City attracted the best crowd of the season of 20,000 and provided an entertaining 3-3 draw. City were still at the foot of the League and scored more in this game than they had in the rest of their away games put together.

Four consecutive wins eased the pressure on the Wanderers and they climbed into seventh position after a 3-1 win over Sheffield Wednesday. Goalkeeper James Sutcliffe became the first Bolton player to be sent off at Burnden Park, when he was given his marching orders for bad language directed at the referee after he had allowed a goal that the custodian claimed did not cross the line. He was later suspended for fourteen days.

The other Sheffield side, United, knocked the Wanderers out of the F.A.Cup at Bramall Lane, the Yorkshire side going on to take the trophy. During this time Bolton were at loggerheads with Aston Villa over the signature of winger David Stokes from Brierley Hill. Villa claimed they had signed him on Birmingham and District League forms and that Bolton were poaching their player. The fact of the matter was that Stokes wanted to join Bolton and Villa only became interested in him when they heard of Bolton's interest.

James Sutcliffe - first Bolton player to be sent off at Burnden Park. The former international at both Football and Rugby Union played 364 League and Cup games for the club.

The League fined Bolton ten guineas and ordered Villa to give Stokes a free transfer. He made his League debut for his new club in a 2-1 win at Wolves, helping inflict their first home defeat of the season, his first goal coming, ironically, in a 2-2 draw with Villa at Burnden in March.

First Division safety was assured with six games remaining and all those ended in defeat with the exception of a 4-0 home win over Blackburn. More importantly Bolton's undefeated home record fell in the final game of the season when Everton won 3-1.

It was a disappointing end to the season that saw a top four place evaporate and 12th place had to be settled for. The season was wound up with a 4-2 home defeat by Preston, in a game organised to raise money for the Ibrox disaster fund.

Season 1902/03
The start of the 1902/03 season was met with new markings on the football pitch, the penalty area of a continuous twelve yard line being abandoned in favour of the markings as we know them today.

On the playing front the major change as far as the Wanderers were concerned was that of goalkeeper. The evergreen James Sutcliffe joined the flow of players south when he joined Millwall for a fee of £400. Five other Wanderers' players also went south, whilst Welsh rugby international, Dai Davies, was one of

eight new recruits and was Sutcliffe's replacement, having been playing under the League code for Swinton. Fred Thompson, another 'keeper, joined the club from Bury.

The season got off to a sad start with the death of former captain Dai Jones. The 35 years old Welshman fell on glass whilst playing for Manchester City and tetanus set in. He was well respected in Bolton and large numbers of people paid their last respects, as the funeral made it's way through Deane, to a player who had played 228 League games for the Wanderers. A benefit game for his family was played during September against City.

On the field the Wanderers made their worst start ever to a League season. The first six games all ended in defeat and, needless to say, the club was rooted at the foot of the table. The only respite was a Lancashire Cup win at Barrow.

John Lewis was appointed trainer at the beginning of October. He was awarded the position from over forty applications. The first point of the season came at the eighth attempt, a 1-1 draw with Liverpool at Burnden, but the Wanderers became something of a music hall joke as it was said, *"they're the most consistent team in the League- they never win!"*

Dai Davies - joined the club from Swinton R.F.L.C. He became the only man to have played in both the Rugby League Challenge Cup Final and F.A. Cup Final when he played for the Wanderers in the 1904 final. After 137 League and Cup appearances he returned to the Lions of Swinton.

And so it went on to sixteen games without a win and then, three heavy defeats during the Christmas period, with a goal difference of 3 for and 15 against this made relegation a virtual certainty with fifteen games still to play.

Then, on the 17th January, the first League win of the season was recorded at the 23rd attempt thanks to a 3-1 success at Notts County. "At last", was the cry, now some kind of normality could be returned to. The next two home games against Derby and Middlesbrough were won but Bristol City triumphed 5-0 in the first round of the F.A. Cup at Burnden to end any hopes of salvaging something from the season.

Sixteen points were taken from the last twelve games but the improvement came too late to save the club from relegation for the second time in its history. Thirty players were used during the season, most of whom were new to the rigours of First Division football, but it would have been difficult to believe that any club could go through its first twenty two League games without a win.

During his first two months in office, trainer John Lewis had eighteen injuries to deal with. Six players were carried from the field, James Picken and Jimmy Hanson broke their legs, David Stokes suffered from a long term injury and only once in the first half of the season did the same team appear consecutively.

Season 1903/04
The club was going all out once again for an immediate return to the top flight. Andrew Gardner, an outside left, was signed from Newcastle and Bill Yenson, a centre half, came from West Ham. Tom Barlow, who had been the leading goalscorer in 1901/02 returned to Burnden after twelve months at Southampton where he had helped them lift the Southern League championship. James Picken went in the other direction to the South Coast whilst William Bannister also went south to Arsenal.

The Wanderers were in good company in the Second Division with two other founder members, Burnley and Preston, also attempting to regain their place in the top tier. A 3-0 win over Burton United at Burnden was followed up with a 3-2 win at Burslem Port Vale and it seemed that another term similar to 1899/1900 was on the cards.

Five consecutive home games during the Christmas period in which only one point was dropped placed the Wanderers in third spot behind Arsenal and Preston.

Home form was fairly consistent but it was to be their interest in the FA Cup and poor away results that saw the Wanderers slip to seventh in the League.

Seven consecutive games, all away from home, which yielded only two draws, put the end to any hopes of promotion. Indeed in the last seven League games only two goals were scored, one of these being an own goal by a Bradford City defender that was to give Bolton their only League win in the last eleven games of the season. The players scoring ability seemed to have disappeared with the forwards that had netted eighteen goals in five games over Christmas and New Year missing the easiest of chances.

Whist League form was poor there was consolation in the FA Cup. Southern Leaguers, Reading, who had knocked the Wanderers out of the competition three seasons earlier, were accounted for after a replay. A tougher test awaited Bolton in the second round with the visit of Southern League champions Southampton to Burnden. The Saints were beaten 4-1 and the Wanderers were then drawn to face formidable opposition in First Division Sheffield United at Bramall Lane. Bolton were clear underdogs not only because of the divisional status but also because of their poor away form and United's impressive home record.

The sensation of the round was the headline as Bolton swept into the semi final with a 2-0 win. The disappointment of not returning to the First Division at the first attempt was now being forgotten as the club were now just two games away from getting their hands on the FA Cup.

A goal from Bob Taylor thirteen minutes from the end of the semi final against Derby at Molineux put Bolton into their second FA Cup Final. It was an all Lancashire affair with opponents Manchester City also chasing the First Division championship, and the Wanderers were virtually written off before a ball was kicked, but they remembered what happened in 1894 when they had lost out to Notts County. As it was the Cup once again eluded Bolton thanks to a disputed goal from Billy Meredith after 20 minutes. The Wanderers claimed the Welshman had been in an offside position when he received the ball before running clear to score.

THE ONLY AUTHORISED PROGRAMME.

TOPPING & SPINDLER, FLUSHING, HOLLAND.

The Oldest Established & Most Extensive Firm of Turf Commission Agents IN THE WORLD.

GREAT METROPOLITAN, CITY AND SUBURBAN, DERBY, CHESTER CUP, JUBILEE, etc.

"THE CONTINENTAL SPORTSMAN," containing latest market movements on above; also "YEAR BOOK and READY RECKONER," sent Free on receipt of Address.

All Letters to be addressed: TOPPING & SPINDLER, Flushing, Holland.

Postage, 2½d.   Post Cards, 1d.

CRYSTAL PALACE.

OFFICIAL PROGRAMME.

English Cup Tie

SATURDAY, APRIL 23, 1904.

MANCHESTER CITY v. BOLTON WANDERERS.

TEAMS.

MANCHESTER CITY.	BOLTON WANDERERS.
1 J. Hillman.	R. Taylor.
2 J. McMahon.	W. White.
3 Herbert Burgess.	W. Yenson.
4 Sam Frost.	S. Marsh.
5 T. Hynds.	D. Stokes.
6 G. B. Ashworth.	A. Freebairn.
7 W. Meredith.	B. Greenhalgh.
8 Geo. Livingstone.	Clifford.
9 W. Gillespie.	R. Struthers.
10 A. Turnbull.	W. Brown.
11 F. Booth.	D. Davies.

COLOURS. COLOURS.
Cambridge Blue Jerseys & White Knickers.   White Shirts and Blue Knickers.

Referee Mr. A. J. BARKER (Hanley).
Linesmen Mr. H. C. PLATT (London), and Mr. W. J. WILSON (Surrey).

KICK OFF AT 3.30. [P.T.O.

☞ **Frequent service of Trains after Match to all Parts** ☜

CRAMER PIANOS 25 GUINEAS. From

For HIRE, HIRE-PURCHASE SYSTEM, or for CASH.

126, OXFORD STREET, W.   46, MOORGATE STREET, E.C.

DR. DAVIS'S FAMOUS FEMALE PILLS

A BOON TO WOMANKIND. They are the best known Remedy for Depressions, Giddiness, Fulness and Swelling after Meals, Loss of Appetite, Hysteria, Palpitations of the Heart, Debility, Weakness, Irregularities, and all Female Ailments.

Price, 2s. 9d. and 4s. 6d.   May be had from Chemists and Patent Medicine Vendors everywhere Do not be persuaded to purchase a substitute. If not in stock ask them to obtain them, or to be had direct from the Proprietor,

DAVIS'S FAMOUS WHOOPING COUGH SPECIFIC.

Season 1904/05

Failure to return to the First Division prompted more comings and goings. William Brown went to Aston Villa for the highest fee received, Jocky Wright and Harry Gardiner went to Plymouth, Jimmy Hanson to Doncaster and Tom Barlow joined Millwall. Incomings were Tom Wilson from Queens Park Ranges, Archie Taylor from Dundee and George Eccles from West Ham, Albert Shepherd, later to become an English International, rejoined the Wanderers from Bolton St Lukes and was still only seventeen years old.

Burnden Park saw its last Annual Athletic Sports day, which still attracted over 10,000 spectators.

The League season opened with a visit to Bristol City's new ground at Ashton Gate. What was to be a rare victory on that ground was recorded with a last minute goal from Yenson securing a 4-3 result. Bolton hit the top of the Second Division after a 2-1 win at Bank Street, home of Manchester United, who had previously been un-defeated. The gates were closed with a crowd of 30,000 seeing both Bolton goals coming from Wattie White.

Six straight wins consolidated Bolton's position at the head of the table although both Liverpool and Manchester United were in hot pursuit. The first defeat of the season came in the seventh game, a 1-0 reverse at Chesterfield but the following week Doncaster were beaten 2-0 at Burnden to record the clubs 100th Second Division point.

Bradford City became the second club to defeat the Wanderers which prompted changes for the home game against third placed Gainsborough who were a point behind. Out went Bill Yenson and Bob Taylor and in came Albert Shepherd and Tom Wilson who both made their debuts. Gainsborough were promptly thrashed 5-1 and a run of eleven consecutive League wins then followed. Both Sam Marsh and Wattie White grabbed hat tricks in the 7-1 home win over Burton United and undefeated League leaders Liverpool were beaten 2-0 before a record Burnden gate of 27,824.

The struggle for promotion became a three cornered affair with Liverpool and Manchester United. The pendulum swung in United's favour early in January when they won 4-2 at Burnden still having only suffered a singe defeat inflicted by Bolton early in the season.

ENGLAND'S CENTRE FORWARD ALBERT SHEPHERD THE WONDERFUL GOAL SCORER.

Albert Shepherd - 26 League goals that earned him England International recognition.

Liverpool too continued to be consistent but it was during the Easter holiday that the momentous issue was resolved. The Anfielders won their last five games without conceding a goal; the only time during the season when they themselves failed to find the net was in defeat at Burnden, and they took the championship.

Both United and the Wanderers faced tough away games but there was a complete contrast in results. The Wanderers took maximum points, without conceding a goal, at Blackpool and West Brom, whilst United inexplicably lost their form and went down at Chesterfield and Liverpool without scoring a goal.

The struggle for promotion was terminated and fate decreed that United had to drag themselves through another season of weary existence in the Second Division. The season wound up with a visit to Barnsley and although the result was immaterial, a 2-1 Wanderers reverse ended a fine away record of six months without defeat.

In the FA Cup revenge for the previous season's defeat was gained over Manchester City when they were accounted for in the second round at Burnden. Eventual League champions and Cup finalists Newcastle United proved too good for the Wanderers in the next round with a 2-0 win, also at Burnden.

Season 1905/06

During the close season the cycling track at Burnden Park was removed thus making room for more spectators. Bolton Corporation renewed the lease of the ground for a further ten years, on the original terms, and the main stand on Manchester Road was erected at a cost of £3500. The new construction provided accommodation for 6000 spectators, 3420 of whom could be seated.

Having won promotion new talent was recruited in an attempt to strengthen the side. Edwin Jones from Tyldesley Albion, Charles Beckett from Atherton and Tom Wolstenholme from Blackpool were all recruited, but the most satisfying signing was that of Herbert Bavestock from Brierley Hill Alliance, a defender who was to give the Wanderers many years service. Archie Taylor left to join Bristol Rovers and James Picken went to Manchester United where he became their leading scorer after helping them return to the First Division.

The first half of the season was full of disappointment, for only two points were taken from the first five games and by the end of October thirteen points from a possible eighteen had slipped away. One problem that the Wanderers didn't have was scoring goals. The forward line of Stokes, Marsh, Shepherd, White and McEwan became the most feared in the First Division, so much so that Bolton were the League's leading goalscorers at the end of the season with a total of 81.

November saw a change in fortunes when three consecutive home games were won with fifteen goals being put into the opponents net and none conceded. Albert Shephed grabbed four goals in a 6-0 win over Nottingham Forest and a Sam Marsh hat trick was the highlight of a 5-0 win over Derby County.

Things looked much healthier by the turn of the year even though a 5-2 reverse was suffered at Sheffield United. The first nine League games of 1906 were all won although only two of these were away from Burnden. Albert Shepherd again found the net four times, in the 6-2 win over Sunderland, but there was disappointment when lowly Middlesbrough knocked the Wanderers out of the FA Cup by 3-0 at Ayresome Park.

The impressive run of League results came to an end in March and only three of the final nine games were won. One of these was a 3-2 win at Burnden over Liverpool who took the League championship twelve months after winning promotion with Bolton. Burnden's League record attendance was again increased when 37,322 attended a 3-1 defeat by Manchester City.

379,095 witnessed the 19 League games played at Burnden giving an average of over 19,000 per game. The side during 1905/06 was built around six players. David Stokes, Wattie White and John Boyd were ever-present whilst both Herbert Bavestock and Marshall McEwan only missed the opening game of the campaign. Keeper Dai Davies missed only three games, his understudy, Herbert Broomfield, keeping two clean sheets in his absence.

The seasons haul of 41 points was the clubs best in the First Division to that date and gave a final position of sixth. The Manchester Cup was won by defeating Bury 3-0 at Clayton although four attempts were required to defeat Manchester City in the first round. And so, after a successful term on the field the season finished as it had started with further ground improvements. Thirty-two terrace steps being laid on the slopes of the embankment.

Season 1906/07

The season opened full of optimism. There had been little change to the playing staff with no departures and six new local signings that raised the professional ranks to 31.

Goals from Shepherd and White earned Bolton a 2-1 win at Manchester United in September 1906.

Five wins and two draws in the opening seven games were enough to prove the club's optimism to the Bolton public. Maybe this would be the year that the League Championship would finally come to the town. Albert Shepherd, who had been capped by England the previous season, got off the mark with a hat trick in a 6-1 win over Sheffield United at Burnden. His striking partner, Walter White, also earned international recognition later in the season when he donned a Scottish shirt against England at Newcastle. White missed only two League games all season, both due to international appearances, but his fellow forwards were not so lucky.

It was remarkable that the Wanderers went through season 1906/07 without being able to field their five recognised forwards in the same game more than three times. Shepherd did well, netting 15 goals in 21 games to head the club's scoring charts, but the team suffered with too many changes.

After defeating Bury 3-2 at Burnden in the middle of November only one further win was recorded in the next eight games. This came at the previous year's champions, Liverpool, who were having a poor season this time around. New Year was celebrated with a return to form and two 3-0 home wins on successive days over Liverpool and Preston respectively. A home F.A. Cup victory over Brighton and a League win at Derby followed, but a home defeat by Manchester United brought things back to earth.

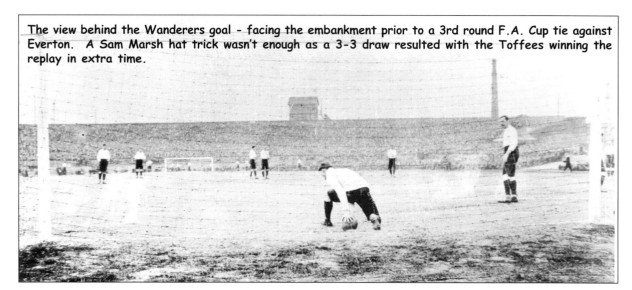

The view behind the Wanderers goal - facing the embankment prior to a 3rd round F.A. Cup tie against Everton. A Sam Marsh hat trick wasn't enough as a 3-3 draw resulted with the Toffees winning the replay in extra time.

This was the third home defeat of the season and, as Newcastle were to prove, League Championships are won by winning home games. The Tynesiders were to take the title thanks to collecting 37 points out of a possible 38 at St James Park whilst the Wanderers went down on two more occasions in the League at Burnden. Away form showed a different story where the Wanderers lost only seven times with only Bristol City, the runners up, having a better record on their travels.

Interest in the F.A. Cup ended when eventual runners up, Everton, won a third round tie at the second attempt although there was some satisfaction for the Wanderers followers before the season's end. Newly crowned Champions Newcastle United visited Burnden for their final game of the season, and Bolton managed to field their strongest forward line for only the second time during the season and ran out 4-2 winners. The Wanderers rounded off the season with an unchanged side winning 2-0 at Villa Park, their fourth win in succession, to once again finish in sixth spot, seven points behind the champions.

It was a case of what might have been once again for Bolton, but the cause wasn't helped by having to use thirteen different players in the forward line. Off the field things were rosy, for it had been the best season for the club financially with a profit of over £3,000 with the wage bill totalling the grand sum of £114 per week.

Season 1907/08

An air of expectancy again filled Burnden Park for the opening day of the season when the visitors were near neighbours Bury. The offside rule had been changed so that no player could be given offside when in his own half but this mattered little to Bury who went in 4-1 up at half time. Despite Albert Shepherd grabbing a hat trick, the Shakers eventually ran out 6-3 winners, their inside forward Billy Hibbert also netting three times.

Two further reverses, including one by 4-0 at home to Liverpool, were incurred before the first win of the

season was registered thanks to a Shepherd goal at Middlesbrough. The Burnden crowd didn't get to see a victory until the middle of October when a John Owen goal was enough to defeat Nottingham Forest. Sam Greenhalgh rejoined the Wanderers after 18 months with Aston Villa thus strengthening the half back line.

By the end of the year the Wanderers were placed in mid table with a total of 22 points from 23 games, but by the end of March had slumped to bottom having collected only a further three points from eight games. During this period the club also bowed out of the F.A. Cup in identical circumstances as the previous season, losing to Everton in a third round replay.

The critics returned to the fore, attacking the side as shapeless, the half back line was accused of being inept, and Edmundson, the goalkeeper, bewildered. Even leading scorer Albert Shepherd took some stick, being accused of selfishness, despite being one of the country's leading goalgetters.

Relegation looked a certainty after yet another home defeat, this time at the hands of Sunderland. There was however a change of fortune, not dissimilar to 1903, with five points being collected in the first three games of April. Newcastle United were thumped 4-0 at Burnden with Shepherd scoring his third hat trick of the season and, on Good Friday, over 27,000 saw the Wanderers defeat eventual League runners up Aston Villa 3-1.

The run came to an end when fellow strugglers Bristol City won 2-0 at Ashton Gate leaving the bottom of the League table on the evening of April 18th 1908 looking ominous.

		Pl.	W	D	L	F	A	Pts
17	Bolton	36	14	4	18	50	58	32
18	Bristol City	35	10	11	14	51	61	31
19	Notts Co	35	11	8	16	36	49	30
20	Birmingham	37	9	12	16	40	55	30

The Wanderers then faced League champions Manchester United at Burnden and forced a creditable draw whilst Notts County lost at Everton and Bristol City drew with Manchester City.

And so the scene was set for a relegation cliffhanger with Notts County visiting Burnden in the Wanderers final League match of the season. A draw would have ensured Bolton's First Division survival, but County took maximum points thanks to a fiftieth minute goal from Cantrell. Bristol City defeated Birmingham 4-0 in their final game and so the Wanderers last chance hinged on Chelsea avoiding defeat against Notts County at Stamford Bridge.

Unfortunately Notts County again tasted victory, winning 2-1 thanks to a dubious penalty, the Wanderers again falling into the Second Division, along with Birmingham.

Season 1908/09
John Somerville was given the title of Secretary-Manager as the professional staff increased to 35 in an attempt to regain First Division status at the first attempt. By the end of October the Wanderers were handily placed in the promotion race in 5th position, two points behind the leaders, Birmingham.

Unfortunately October had seen some indifferent results including three consecutive games without scoring a goal. This prompted further action with James Hogan, Willie Hughes, William Hunter and Bill Robinson signing for the club. During November, James McClarence went to Bradford, Albert Shepherd joined Newcastle United and both Bob Clifford and Wattie White signed for Everton.

By the last Saturday of 1908 the Wanderers were in 2nd spot, but then three games without any points, along with an F.A. Cup exit at West Brom, left them clinging on to third place behind both 'Spurs and the Baggies, who both had games in hand.

The pattern continued and the promotion race became a three horse race for the two places. There were four games remaining with only one point separating the sides when the Wanderers visited West Brom. Without the injured William Hunter, the Wanderers gave a debut to Joe Smith who was to write himself into the club's folklore, but unfortunately it wasn't a winning debut, Albion won 2-0 to become favourites for promotion.

The pendulum again swung with Albion dropping a point in their next game whilst both Bolton and 'Spurs won. And so promotion was to be decided at the death with each club having one game left to play. Strangely all three clubs had Derby County to face with Albion having a one point lead over both the Wanderers and Spurs.

Albion lost their final game at Derby 2-1 thus opening the door for their rivals. Two days later 'Spurs drew 1-1 at the Baseball Ground, and the following Friday evening, 30,000 cheered the Wanderers to a 1-0 win at Burnden over The Rams thanks to a Billy Hughes goal.

The championship had been won with an amazing run of consistency. Bolton's final twelve games of the season producing a record of ten wins, one draw and one defeat.

The following day the Manchester Senior Cup was also added to the Second Division trophy when Stockport's first team was defeated 3-0 at Hyde Road. The reserves were now captained by the experienced Sam Marsh and they had already defeated Manchester City's first team in an earlier round.

Returning to the First Division had cost the club over £3,000 in transfer fees and a wage bill of £6472 which was the highest of all the Lancashire clubs. The task that had been set eight months earlier had been successfully completed but there was once again cries to improve the playing staff to ensure their survival in the top grade. All these problems were put to one side whilst the Wanderers visited the continent and won all five games played in the Netherlands.

Season 1909/10
For the first time ever the Football League season almost failed to start on time with the Players Union at loggerheads with the F.A. over paying insurance to injured players. The dispute was settled in the nick of time but there was little to cheer about in Bolton.

The first four games, three of which were at Burnden, all ended in defeat. The first point of the season came at the fifth attempt when the Wanderers came from two down at half time to draw 2-2 at Sheffield United. This result was all the more admirable as they were down to ten men for most of the game, Robinson having been carried from the field injured.

Only four victories were recorded before the end of 1909 leaving the club at the foot of the table with ten points from nineteen games. On New Year's Day, Bolton were three up inside 35 minutes against Notts County at Burnden, only to go down 4-3 and to finish the game with nine men with both Greenhalgh and Owen getting injured. A Cup defeat by 4-1 at the hands of Second Division Stockport prompted some action.

On January 20th Will Settle, who had been a director of the club for 14 years, was appointed director/manager whilst trainer, Jack Lewis, severed his connections with the club. Two days later League leaders Sheffield United were beaten 1-0 at Burnden, Marshall McEwan scoring the all important goal in a side that showed four changes from the previous League game.

Two home defeats in as many days. Firstly (right) Sam Greenhalgh meets his Liverpool counterpart before going down 2-1 and then (above) Greenhalgh goes close in a 4-0 reverse against Newcastle United.

Unfortunately this wasn't the start of a revival, although during February six points were won from four consecutive home games, including a 5-2 win over fellow strugglers, Chelsea.

The Londoners were attempting to buy their way out of trouble and persuaded the Wanderers to part with Marshall McEwan. The finances of the club at the time were poor with the gate receipts some £3000 down on the previous season and rumours were spreading of a delay in paying players wages. Chelsea on the other hand, despite their poor League position, were commanding the best gates in the country.

Five games during March yielded only one point with the opposing net only being found in one of the games, that being a 4-2 reverse at Blackburn. With four games remaining Bolton found themselves six points behind 'Spurs who were in 18th place. The first two games were won but relegation was confirmed when 'Spurs came to Burnden and took both points in a 2-0 win.

The season wound up with a 1-0 defeat at Preston with the scene there being in stark contrast to the joyous celebrations witnessed twelve months earlier. Whilst injuries had once again plagued the side, the failure of the inside forwards to find the net hadn't helped the club's cause. Only five penalty conversions from a possible eleven awarded during the season had, on this occasion, proved that the players were not up to the rigours of First Division football.

The Reserves on the other hand had proved themselves admirably by finishing second in the Lancashire Combination, one point behind Everton, with Joe Smith, who was being groomed for greater things, scoring nine goals.

Season 1910/11

Once again the Wanderers were intent on making an attempt to return to the top flight at the first time of asking. Unfortunately money was short and the only major signings for the new season were Joe Hewitt, from Liverpool, and Fred Shinton from Leicester, both of whom were forwards. A 'raw' youngster from south Wales named Ted Vizard was also taken on to the payroll which had been drastically reduced from the previous season.

A poor opening was made, for after a home draw with Stockport, Leicester Fosse highlighted Bolton's weakness and ran up a 5-0 win. For the next game, against promotion favourites West Brom at Burnden, six changes were made. This had the desired effect with Bolton winning 3-1 thanks to a Billy Hughes hat trick.

During this game the Wanderers Bolton born captain, Sam Greenhalgh, was sent off for kicking an opponent and was subsequently suspended by the F.A. for fourteen days. The two games he missed whilst suspended were his only absences during the whole campaign.

The sweeping changes made for the game against West Brom were to strike the key note of success as the side went through the season without suffering a home reverse in the League. This wasn't, however, the case in the F.A. Cup as Chesterfield ousted the Wanderers from the competition on their home soil in the first round.

Ted Vizard made his League debut for the club in a 3-0 home win over Gainsborough, thus forming a partnership on the left wing with Joe Smith that was to serve the club for more than sixteen years. The Wanderers went to the top of the Second Division for the first time on November 26th after a 3-1 win at Lincoln City. On the last day of the year Leicester Fosse were beaten 6-2 at Burnden, the crowd of 9300 being the best of the season to date, Billy Hughes scoring his fourth hat trick of the year.

Two days later the attendance doubled for the visit of Barnsley who fell by 4-0, the faith of the local's in the club was returning. During January, Vizard made his Welsh international debut, whilst Fred Shinton, who had failed to establish himself as a regular, returned to Leicester. The race for promotion became a three horse race. The Wanderers, West Brom and Chelsea all holding the leadership at some stage during March.

It became obvious that the issue would not be settled until the final day of the season. On April 26th promotion rivals Chelsea were beaten 2-0 before a Burnden crowd of 40,000. This left both the Wanderers and West Brom level on 51 points with Chelsea two points adrift and all with one game left to play.

The Wanderers final game was at Birmingham where a win would give them the championship, a draw would be good enough for promotion, but a defeat could let in their rivals.

They lived dangerously, going down 2-1, West Brom defeating Huddersfield to take the championship and relief came when it was learned that Chelsea had lost at third from bottom Gainsborough, thus giving the Wanderers promotion as runners up.

The 'Football Field' summed up; *"the season has been one of the most critical periods through which the club has ever passed. Year by year, there have been times of stress and trouble in which great obstacles have had to be overcome. Up to now the club has survived all it's manifold disappointments and for the fourth time claims it's rightful place."*

Season 1911/12
Upon returning to the First Division the side was immediately rewarded with a proven goalscorer. A £1,000 fee was invested in the signing of Alf Bentley from Derby County. He had been their leading scorer in three of the previous four seasons scoring 102 goals in 151 games. Stan Gimblett from the Swansea and District League was also signed on professional forms and James Hogan returned to the club after a season coaching in Dordrecht.

A crowd of 25,344 saw the Wanderers lose their opening game 2-0 to Newcastle at Burnden. As far as the home spectators were concerned the only highlight was a fire in the stand that was quickly extinguished. On the same day the reserves entered new territory with their first ever game in the Central League, a 1-0 reverse at Liverpool being suffered.

Things improved on the League front and after seven games the club were in 4th place, one point behind the leaders – fellow promotion winners West Brom. The consistency position continued until mid December when after beating Spurs 1-0 at Burnden and climbing into 2nd place, the bubble burst and by the end of the year the club were found in mid table. During December the Lancashire Cup was won by defeating Burnley in the Final but injuries were beginning to take their toll.

The breaking point came when Hilton was out injured and Smith, Bentley, Marsh, Baverstock and Newton were all in hospital at one time,

Sam Marsh and David Stokes both played important parts in the Wanderers promotion.

to cap it all a number of other players caught flu. Two major signings were made when firstly Jimmy Fay, who was to gain Football League representative recognition, came from Oldham Athletic, and secondly Alec Donaldson, a future Scottish international, was signed from Ripley Athletic.

During this period Barnsley, the eventual winners, knocked the Wanderers out of the FA Cup at the third

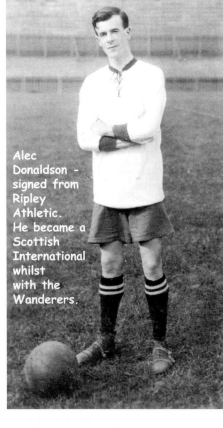

Alec Donaldson - signed from Ripley Athletic. He became a Scottish International whilst with the Wanderers.

round stage and the following week a 1-0 defeat was incurred at Everton. The next game, on March 2nd, saw West Brom visit Burnden. Once again internal problems came to the fore when they saw Greenhalgh refuse to play on the wing to help overcome selection problems. He was suspended for six weeks and his apologies to the Board were accepted. A 2-0 win over West Brom was however the start of six consecutive wins in which not one goal was conceded. Indeed in the club's final 10 games only two ended in defeat, both by a single goal at Middlesbrough and Spurs, and only five goals were conceded in the last 13.

The season wound up with a 1-1 draw versus Manchester United at Burnden, a game which saw Joe Edmondson take his benefit to the tune of £300 and leave the Wanderers in a healthy fourth place. The Bolton public had been treated to a season of scientific football – a clever thrilling game – not the crashing sort associated with the Second Division. They saw players in Wanderers colours produce a class of football that was normally associated with the likes of Aston Villa and Newcastle United.

At the season's end James Hogan returned to the continent to coach the Austrian National Team, whilst Sam Marsh, who had made his debut in the 23rd game and Bolton's first win of 1902/03, made the short trip to Bury.

Season 1912/13

Bolton prepared for the new season with a couple of signings from Oldham Athletic. Welsh international centre forward, Evan Jones and Farnworth born Walter Rowley, who was later to serve the club as coach and manager, came to Burnden along with Welsh Schoolboy International William Jennings from Barry. The Wanderers opened the season as usual – with a defeat – not having started with a win since 1904, on this occasion Newcastle winning 2-1 at Burnden.

Six victories in the next eight games however saw the Wanderers in 6th place but within the space of a week they were shocked when Manchester United won 3-0 in a Lancashire Cup tie and Blackburn Rovers hit six without reply at Ewood.

By the end of 1912 the club were still in 6th position and had parted with Tom Barber to Aston Villa after 107 League and Cup games with the club. Barber, who was born within 100 yards of Newcastle United, had been signed by John Somerville in 1908 and the profit from the fee of £1950 received went towards the erection of a cover on the Great Lever stand.

The first week of 1913 saw the Wanderers climb into second spot in the League with home wins over Sheffield United by 4-2 and Arsenal, 5-1. Attention turned to the FA Cup, but this was short-lived after Oldham ended Bolton's interest in the competition.

Six consecutive draws were enough to remain in third position by mid March. Of these the highlights were a 2-2 draw at Sheffield Wednesday, after being two down, and a 3-3 draw at Derby, after being 3-1 down, in which Edmondson saved a Barnes penalty and Greenhalgh hit the equaliser two minutes from time.

In an effort to reinforce the clubs championship ambitions Bob Glendenning was recruited from Cup winners Barnsley. One win in seven games however ended any hopes. The turning point came when Aston Villa won 3-2 at Burnden after the Wanderers had been 2-0 up

Bob Glendenning - recruited from Cup winners Barnsley. He became club captain and after retiring was a coach for the Dutch F.A.

thanks to goals from Smith and Hughes. Villa struck back with their first goal coming from Tom Barber, and their winner, in the final minute.

It was a poor finish to an otherwise profitable season for the club. This ended on the field with a seven game tour of Germany and Austria in which the Wanderers scored a 12-0 win against the German Association.

During the season the Great Lever stand was covered with an intention to join up the new roof with the old ones to make three sides of the ground completely covered. A profit of £4,000 was recorded after paying for the stand and manager Will Settle was engaged for a further 5 years.

Season 1913/14
A record fee of £1,300 was spent on bringing Barnsley centre forward George Lillycrop to Burnden Park. The new striker took the place vacated by Alf Bentley who returned to the Midlands with West Brom.

After the now customary opening League game defeat, 1-0 to Sheffield Wednesday at Burnden, the Wanderers clicked into gear with a 6-2 win over Oldham Athletic. George Lillycrop opened his account for Bolton in this game by scoring twice and the following week scored the only goal of the game at Manchester United.

Another departure from Burnden was that of Billy Hughes to Wolves, having failed to command a first team place in the 'new look' Bolton side. Hughes had scored 51 goals in 100 League appearances for the Wanderers and the club was later fined £25 by the League for misleading Hughes into believing he would receive a payment in lieu of a benefit which was against League rules.

During October and November three goals were scored in five consecutive games with only one point dropped in a 3-3 draw at Derby. The run came to an end in a 5-1 reverse at Bradford City where Oscar Fox scored four for the Yorkshiremen. A week later, on November 29th, Burnden's attendance record was broken when 53,747 saw the Wanderers defeat League leaders Blackburn Rovers thanks to a 60th minute Lillycrop goal.

Five games during December didn't produce a win. The rot started with a 3-2 defeat at Sunderland after being two up, and only two goals were scored in the next six hours of football. Despite the poor run Bolton were still in touch, being in 8th place, eight points behind leaders Blackburn but with three games in hand.

After a dark December, New Year started with a bang. 'Spurs were beaten 3-0 and second placed Manager United 6-1, both at Burnden. Joe Smith netted four times against United, his first hat trick in the League, with Edwin Jones and George Lillycrop scoring the others. Smith took his first benefit three weeks later against bottom of the League Preston, and although he took £500 from the game the result was a disappointment with North End winning 3-0.

FA Cup progress was also made with home wins over Port Vale and Swindon. A crowd of 50,558 saw the Wanderers beat the Wiltshire side 4-2, thanks to a Joe Smith hat trick, the visitors topping the Southern League at the time. Interest in the Cup ended in the 3rd round when Burnley won 3-0 at Burnden.

Another player who was to be a star of the 1920's made his debut at this time. James Seddon who had been signed from Hamilton Central, made his bow in a home draw with Middlesbrough, their goal coming from a dubious handball decision against the debutant.

The Wanderers kept up their title challenge and at the end of March were 3rd in the table, six points behind Blackburn. The crunch match came on 4th April when the Wanderers visited Blackburn but they were without Joe Smith and Alex Donaldson who were playing in the England v. Scotland International in Glasgow. Debuts were given to goalkeeper Eric Sidlow, Edmondson being injured, and to winger Alex Lockhart. Things seemed to be going well when the Wanderers were 2-1 up after 77 minutes but they eventually went down 3-2 and the club were now fighting for the runners-up spot. Only one win in the final five games saw the club slip into a final position of 6th but defeat at Ewood was akin to losing a Cup final.

Four goalkeepers were used during the season with neither John Baverstock nor James Tyldesley satisfying the management. John Edmondson took over until the Ewood Park engagement when young Eric Sidlow who was discovered around Christmas playing for Wharton Presbyterians, took over. He played in the final six games although he was only once on the winning side. Jack Feebury's free kicks and penalties became famous for their power with Lillycrop being the capture of the season, his 24 goals in 37 games supporting this claim.

Two old servants ended their Wanderers careers in Sam Greenhalgh, who took over the Cheetham Arms at Dunscar whilst playing for Chorley and Jack Slater who was transferred to South Liverpool.

Chapter 4 (1914 ~ 1940)
Three More F.A. Cup Finals

Season 1914/15

The Directors set out their objectives for the new season. To build up a strong enough squad so that every position was duplicated with a competent player and to remodel Burnden Park so that everyone who had paid could see in comfort and safety. Unfortunately these ambitions were to be interrupted by The Great War.

The season opened with a friendly, the proceeds of which went towards the war funds. The first two League games of the season were lost, despite scoring three times in each, and on 7th September 1914 the League Management Committee issued the following statement:- *"In view of requests from certain quarters to stop football the Management Committee have taken counsel with their clubs. The Committee are even more decidedly of the opinion that in the interests of the people of this Country football ought to continue."*

Goals came in abundance for the Wanderers and by the end of October only 2nd placed Sheffield Wednesday had scored more. Unfortunately Bolton had conceded more goals than any other club which placed them 15th. Attendances slumped, over 59000 spectators were lost in the first five games, peoples support now rested in the war effort.

Results continued to be inconsistent. After a 5-0 defeat at Burnley, Tottenham were beaten 4-2 at Burnden. Harold Hilton scoring the opening goal for Bolton after just 30 seconds in what was only his second League game since the end of 1911. Frank Roberts also scored his first League goal in this game the others coming from a couple of Joe Smith penalties.

On Boxing Day the Wanderers recorded their best ever away League victory with a 7-1 thumping of Aston Villa. Strangely both sides had travelled to Birmingham on the same train, Villa having won at Blackburn on Christmas Day. The return with Villa on New Year's Day ended in a draw but the Wanderers defeated League leaders Oldham 2-0 the following day to climb into 13th place.

Another League slump saw Bolton in the bottom four by mid March. One win in nine League games, including a 7-0 reverse at Sheffield Wednesday set the alarm bells ringing. There was, however, consolation in the FA Cup, Southern Leaguers Millwall were beaten after two replays, Burnley were defeated 2-1 after extra time, and a 4-2 win over Hull put the Wanderers into the semi finals. Sheffield United were the opponents and it was they who went on to win the trophy after defeating the Wanderers 2-1 at Ewood.

It was a miserable season against the two Sheffield clubs who also took maximum League points. Enough points were won in the final run-in, although not impressively, to keep their place in the First Division, although this became secondary when, on May 4th, it was announced that football was to be suspended. There were, however, second thoughts and regional tournaments, with unpaid players, were hastily organised.

Season 1915/16

The regional Leagues were commenced with all the games only being allowed to take place on a Saturday or on a public holiday, with no midweek games, so as not to interfere with the work of making munitions. The Wanderers had great difficulty in fielding teams and this was made harder when compulsory military service was introduced in 1916. The police kept watch at football games in an attempt to catch men shirking their responsibility to their country.

The quality of football was poor and gates collapsed. Prices were reduced at Burnden to 6d and this came into force for the visit of Everton in October. The visitors won 4-3 before a crowd of only 1483. People were also not attending football for moral reasons and this in turn put pressure on clubs, of which Bolton were no exception.

The club found themselves next to bottom of the Lancashire section after seven games without a win, which included a 7-0 home reverse at the hands of Southport Central. A typical problem occurred on November 27th when the Wanderers visited 2nd placed Stockport. Goalkeeper, Joe Lansdale, failed to turn up with leading scorer Tom Buchan taking over between the sticks.

Players who could get off from work, or released from their units, were keen to play for the club despite receiving no recompense but they were also keen to be at home with their families especially over Christmas. At the end of January table toppers Manchester City were defeated 4-2 at Burnden before the best crowd of the season, just 7000. It was the Wanderers of old with goals from Roberts, Lillycrop, an own goal from Fletcher and a Joe Smith penalty.

The first season in the Lancashire section was completed with a 4-2 home win over Stockport with Frank Roberts hitting his first hat trick for the club. 36 players were used, 17 of whom wore a Bolton shirt for the first time, the club ending in 12th position from the fourteen teams after 26 games.

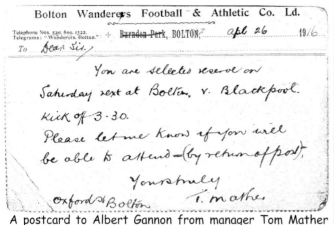

A postcard to Albert Gannon from manager Tom Mather advising that he was a reserve for the final game of the season against Blackpool. In the event Gannon actually played but the visitors won 2-1.

Tom Buchan - one of nine players who played twice on the same day. He played in every position except full back for the club in a career that saw him play 117 League and Cup games.

On the 4th March a new subsidiary competition of ten games began. Bolton lost the opening game 3-1 at Burnley whilst Joe Smith and Ted Vizard were guesting for Preston against Stockport. A week later Smith and Vizard were back in Bolton shirts against Preston North End winning 6-1 with Morris netting five.

The Wanderers did slightly better in this competition, finishing 4th from the six entrants. Interest in football didn't appear to be waning with the gates for the final two games at Burnden aggregating almost as big a figure as the first four games of the season.

In July the effect of the war struck home to the club when the first Wanderers professional fell whilst fighting in Picardy. Harold Greenhalgh, who was 23 years old, played his last game for the club on New Year's Day in a 3-1 defeat at Southport, having been ever-present up to his call up for duty.

Season 1916/17
The Wanderers continued to operate with a skeleton squad of players who were working in either local munitions or the local forces. Joe Smith was the team's inspiration during this season, being the country's leading goalscorer by December, until his call up for duty in his apt rank of bomber.

On 23rd September Stoke were beaten 9-2 at Burnden after they had previously been undefeated. Smith scored six goals, one from the penalty spot, the referee checking to see if his shot had broken the net! The crowd numbered 2116 plus a few hundred soldiers who were admitted free. A month later Smith scored four in a 6-0 win at Rochdale and on 9th December he netted his 20th goal of the season in a 5-1 home win over Manchester United.

Unfortunately 1917 didn't live up to expectations. Stoke gained revenge for their thrashing earlier in the season by handing Bolton a 7-0 defeat with four of their second half goals coming in as many minutes.

The first win of the year came on 10th March when Preston were beaten 2-1 at Deepdale. Ex-Wanderer Jimmy Fay guested for his old team as he was unable to get to Bury to play for his club Southport Central. On 6th April, Good Friday, the Wanderers played two games. In the morning they lost 2-0 at Stockport in the Lancashire Section Primary Competition and in the afternoon won 2-1 at Oldham in the Subsidiary Competition. Nine players took part in both games.

41 players were used in a total of 36 games as the season was rounded off in style with two home wins. Bury were beaten 6-0, Jimmy Fay grabbing four goals, champions Liverpool were also beaten 1-0.

Season 1917/18.
For the commencement of the 1917/18 season, the fixtures were arranged on a home and away basis so that clubs played each other on successive Saturday's and a 20% split of takings could be taken immediately to help the financial hardships. The people who seemed most interested in the opening of the new season were the men in Khaki although they had little to shout about as far as the Wanderers were concerned. The first four games all ended in defeat. Stoke winning 5-2 and 6-2 whilst Liverpool put nine into the Wanderers net without reply in the two games.

Changes were made in every department for the fifth game and the first win of the season ensued. Bury being the unlucky side who went down 4-1 at Burnden. November was a successful month for Bolton. An 8-0 win over Burnley was followed up with the double over Manchester United and a 3-2 win at Stockport.

Tom Buchan once again had to take over as an emergency 'keeper in this game, regular Bill Ellison missing his train. During January more of the old players returned home on leave. Nuttall, Rowley, Seddon, Davies, Smith and Vizard all took part in the 5-2 home success against Blackburn. A clean sweep over the Manchester clubs was completed in February when City were beaten 1-0 in both games but the chief source of satisfaction was the fact that the club had been able to carry on. Nothing had been added to their laurels and no tangible rewards gained, good victories were won and on the other hand there were bad defeats which were all part of the wartime regime.

Joe Smith ended the season by collecting a medal whilst guesting for Chelsea in the champion's game. The London Combination winners defeated Lancashire section champions Stoke 6-2 with Smith grabbing a hat trick.

Season 1918/19
Only one defeat in the opening 13 games saw a much settled team produce some entertaining football. The day that had been dreamt of for four years came on 16th November when peacetime football returned with the Wanderers defeating Southport Vulcan 3-2 at Burnden. Joe Thomas of the Guards had the honour of being the first Wanderer to return from the War to take his place in the team.

By the end of November rumour was rife that both Joe Smith and Ted Vizard would be in the colours of Chelsea, for whom they had been guesting, when League football returned to normal. This was immediately quashed by the Wanderers who declared they were on the lookout for players and in fact were later fined £25 by the League for an illegal approach to Bury centre forward Lythgoe. Centre forward was a problem position for the Wanderers and by the end of the year 12 different players had been tried.

As the season wore on the crowds started to return, 5271 saw Preston inflict Bolton's first home defeat of the season during January. A month later 10991 saw the return of Vizard, Hilton and Roberts to the forward line in a 3-2 win over Rochdale. On February 22nd, the directors placed the management of the team until the end of the season in the hands of Ted Vizard. 26,000 were at Burnden for his first home game in the position when Everton won 6-3. On the same day, the reserves returned to competitive football by entering the Liverpool section of the Lancashire Combination, taking over from Ashton Hospital.

The season was completed in style with seven wins and only one defeat in the final eight games. This left the club in 4th position of the Lancashire section and they were ousted out of the County Cup on goal average after six games.

The club also supplied players for the England v. Scotland International played at Goodison Park in April with Joe Smith and Alec Donaldson representing the whites and blues respectively.

Season 1919/20
For the recommencement of normal League football the Wanderers appointed, on 12th July, Mr Charles Foweraker as manager. He had been with the club since 1895 on the administration staff and was to serve the club through its most successful period. George Eccles was re-appointed as trainer whilst Joe Smith was handed the captaincy.

Bradford Park Avenue were the visitors to Burnden on the opening day and took a 2-1 win back to Yorkshire before a crowd of 17450. Both Joe Smith and Frank Roberts saw penalty shots saved by keeper Scattergood and Smith also missed one in the next game, a 1-1 home draw with Burnley. The first win of the season came at the fifth attempt, a 4-1 result at Manchester City, and the next four games were all won, including a return with City by 6-2.

Football was then faced with further problems due to railway strikes. Some of the less important games had to be postponed on account of the team being unable to get to their destinations. The Wanderers did get to their game at Derby, by means of private cars and two taxis, then went on to win 2-1. In goal for Derby was James Kidd who had been sold to County four days earlier by the Wanderers.

After a return win over Derby, Bolton were third in the table a point behind leaders West Brom, who were to be faced twice in eight days. Albion recorded a resounding 4-1 win on their home ground with their three second half goals coming in the space of eight minutes. Albion then completed the double with a 2-1 win at Burnden, their winner coming two minutes from time, although Bolton were without both Smith and Vizard, who were both on International duty.

On November 22nd Bolton took a point from a 3-3 draw at Everton and included in their side 39 year old David Stokes who remains as the oldest outfield player to have appeared for the club in the Football League. Stokes, who made his first Bolton appearance in season 1901/02 scored one of the goals to crown his comeback. Whilst there was enough consistency from results to keep the Wanderers in the top six of the League there was disappointment in the FA Cup. Chelsea won a first round tie by 1-0 at Burnden despite being down to ten men when McNeil was sent off for a foul on Donaldson.

Bolton's interest was not finished in the FA Cup however as the final between Aston Villa and Huddersfield was refereed by one of the many famous referees to come from the town J T Howcroft.

Jack Feebury - played the last of his
192 League and Cup games for the club.

Chelsea followed their Cup win by again winning at
Burnden by 2-1 in a League encounter but revenge was
gained a week later when the Wanderers won 3-2 in
London. Full back Jack Feebury played his final
Wanderers League game in the home defeat by
Chelsea. He was well known for his powerful shooting
and had scored four goals during the season, two from
free kicks and two from penalties, before his transfer to
Exeter with whom further transfer business was to take
place during the 1920's.

Season 1920/21
The rules were once again amended for the 1920/21
season with no offside to be awarded from throw-ins.
The Wanderers went into the transfer market and broke
their record by paying Luton Town £2,500 for full back
John Elvey. Goalkeeper Fred Hinton was also signed
from Southern Leaguers Swindon Town.

Only one defeat in the opening six games made Bolton
one of the favourites for the title. Manchester United
were beaten 3-2 at Old Trafford, and previous season's
champions West Brom, plus Aston Villa, were
overcome 3-0 and 5-0 respectively, both at Burnden.

The Wanderers continued to strengthen their side when
the Clubs transfer fee record was again broken in
signing Bolton born forward David Jack from
Plymouth Argyle. Attendances were on the up with the
first four home League games attracting an average of
38,380, 5000 more than any of the previous gates.

On Christmas Day Sunderland were beaten 6-2 at
Burnden with Joe Smith netting four to head the First
Division scoring chart with 22 goals. On New Year's
Day he hit another, the winner from the penalty spot
against Spurs at Burnden before 53,430 in what was
Walter Rowley's benefit.

England International Joe Smith fronts a
period postcard with the Wanderers
squad for season 1920/21.

The blue shirted Wanderers thus gained revenge for a
5-2 defeat at White Hart Lane a fortnight previously.
Bolton entered 1921, 2nd in the First Division and all
energies were able to concentrate on the League effort
after Preston won a first round Cup tie by 2-0. The
Wanderers gained revenge with a 2-1 League win at
Deepdale a month later thanks to a couple of Frank
Roberts goals, although an injury to Alec Donaldson, in
which he fractured a kneecap, quietened the
celebrations.

After a 2-2 draw at Bradford City the Wanderers then
visited the League leaders Burnley. The home side had
gone 26 games without defeat but found themselves a
goal down at the interval from Frank Roberts. The
leaders struck back in the second half and ran out 3-1
winners, following this up a week later with a 1-1 draw
at Burnden. These results virtually crushed Bolton's
championship aspirations but they battled on until the
end, losing only three of the last games. The first of
these defeats came by a single goal at Newcastle where
the team heard on the way to the game that the general
strike had been lifted.

On 30th April Joe Smith equalled the Football League record of 38 goals in a season held by Bert Freemans who established that number in 1908, scoring twice in a 3-2 win over Liverpool at Anfield. The win also put the team into the next round of the Lancashire Cup, however victory eventually went to Manchester City who defeated the Wanderers 2-1 in the final at Old Trafford.

During the season the Wanderers produced an income of £43,700 of which £672 was profit. The First Division leaders showing the most profit were Tottenham with a figure of £16,592 whilst only Derby County and Oldham Athletic showed losses on the season.

Season 1921/22

The close season of 1921 saw plenty of movement on the goalkeeping front. Joe Hughes went to Charlton and Frank Drabble to Southport, whilst Dick Pym was secured for the Wanderers from Exeter City. The fee for Pym was kept secret but was undoubtedly a record for a 'keeper at the time. Both clubs had been involved in weeks of negotiation for the 'keeper who had only missed three games in five seasons for City. For the first time the club were to run 3 teams during the season the 'A' team being set up to play competitive friendlies.

In the early games of the season late goals conceded cost the team dearly. In the opening game against Preston at Burnden, in which Pym made his debut, a last minute goal from North End produced a 2-2 draw. Bolton then led Bradford City 3-0 at Burnden after 49 minutes, Pym having saved a first half penalty from Bond, the Yorkshire side hit back to draw 3-3, Howson hitting the equaliser with two minutes remaining.

The 'Topsham Fisherman' - Dick Pym joined the Wanderers from Exeter City. He was to keep three clean sheets in Bolton's Wembley finals of the glorious twenties.

Cup holders Spurs were beaten twice in the space of a week and Huddersfield were beaten 3-1 at Burnden with the Wanderers including Bert Baverstock, in his 16th season with the club, in the side. After winning 2-1 at bottom club Cardiff on 8th October, the Welsh side turned the tables a week later to win by the same score at Burnden, the Wanderers then lost at home for the first time in the League since April 1920.

Three straight wins in November lifted the Wanderers into the top four and in a healthy position for the Christmas games. The double was accomplished over Manchester City, the only blemish being the sending off of Joe Smith, six minutes from the end of the 3-2 win in Manchester for a skirmish with Barnes. Smith was later acquitted from suspension by the FA.

The first defeat for two months came by a single goal reverse at Everton where Joe Smith shot a penalty tamely wide, and the Wanderers were without centre forward Frank Roberts for the first time in almost two seasons. Roberts returned to the side for the 5-1 win over Oldham on New Year's Day in which David Jack hit a hat trick. A Ted Vizard goal six minutes from time against Bury saw the Wanderers safely through to the second round of the FA Cup.

The last two Saturdays in January were a disaster for the Wanderers. Firstly Chelsea won 2-0 in a League game at Burnden, the homesters being without six regulars through flu, and Tom Buchan sent off after a challenge on South. Then came an FA Cup exit at the hands of Manchester City at Burnden by 3-1. City had been beaten 5-0 by the Wanderers six weeks earlier, and this defeat came despite holding a half time lead through Frank Roberts. There was some consolation in the fact that at the time the gate of 66442 was a record for Burnden and the 4th best ever receipts in English football at £5220. A week later only 7400 saw the Wanderers beat Sheffield United 3-1 to go into 2nd place in the League.

During March the Wanderers won 2-0 at League leaders Liverpool inflicting their first home defeat of the season. Such was the atmosphere that both teams had to be called into the middle by the referee for a cooling off period and a lecture to boot. The good win was thrown away seven days later when Liverpool won 3-1 at Burnden despite having McNabb sent off. Two successive away defeats at Sunderland, for whom Alec Donaldson starred, and Aston Villa, along with a 1-1 home draw with Sunderland once again put paid to any championship hopes.

The League season was rounded off with a 4-2 home win over Middlesbrough, but the Cupboard once again was not bare. The Lancashire Cup was won for the fourth time, against Bury at Gigg Lane, the Manchester Cup also being lifted with a win over Eccles United at Old Trafford. Full League elevens were fielded by the Wanderers for these competitions.

The Wanderers did plenty of experimenting during the season with no less than 11 debutants. Indeed an experiment which appeared to border on the ridiculous saw Fred Keetley move from forward to half back to full back where he found his true position. One exception was Tom Buchan who had long ceased to be marvelled at on his frequent change of position.

Season 1922/23

The Wanderers made a poor start to what was to become one of the most famous seasons ever, not just in the history of the club but to football in general. Bolton opened the season with a visit to Preston where they went down 3-1. Charles Flood, a forward signed from Hull City, scored the Wanderers goal only three minutes into his debut.

Burnden Park saw little change apart from the practice pitch behind the old stand, but only one win, by 3-1 against Oldham, saw the Wanderers languishing in 20th spot. Home form began to improve, and Burnden Park was awarded the English League game against the Irish League. David Jack scored twice for the English League and George Eccles was the victors trainer for the game.

During October Frank Roberts was suspended indefinitely by the club for taking the management of a licensed premises which was against club policy. The search for a new centre forward was on when Roberts signed for Manchester City, the striker scoring from the penalty spot a month later in City's 2-0 win.

For the return with City a week later the Wanderers had signed John Smith, a centre forward from Glasgow Rangers, and he soon began to repay some of this transfer fee with an 89th minute winner. The year ended with the Wanderers in a much healthier 10th position and they opened 1923 with a 4-2 home win over Nottingham Forest in which Joe Smith scored all four goals.

The first away win in the FA Cup since 1905 was recorded by the Wanderers with a 2-0 scoreline at Norwich and Leeds were accounted for by 3-1 at Burnden in the second round. In between these games League points were being accumulated with a 2-1 home win over Burnley and a 1-0 win at 'Spurs where on the way to the game the team had a passing glance of Wembley Stadium under construction.

The Wanderers qualified for the quarter finals of the FA Cup with a 1-0 replay win over Huddersfield Town at Burnden. Unfortunately Walter Rowley was sent off in the original game and received a six week suspension. Joe Smith missed his first game of the season in a 3-0 defeat at League leaders Liverpool but returned for the FA Cup tie at Charlton which was won thanks to a goal from David Jack.

Jack was again to be the Wanderers hero a fortnight later when his 46th minute goal won Bolton an FA Cup final appearance, by defeating Sheffield United at Old Trafford. The crowd of 72,000 was a record at the time even though ticket prices were excessive.

All eyes were focussed on the first Wembley Cup Final and only five further League points were won in nine games. Thirty players had been relied upon to carry the Wanderers through their League programmes with only Dick Pym ever-present.

On April 28th 1923 Bolton took the field with the then Second Division West Ham United for what came to be known as the White Horse Final. The greatest ever crowd at an FA Cup Final was present, estimated at 150,000 with hoards pushed back behind the touchline by a police white horse named Billy. When the game eventually got started goals from David Jack and John Smith brought the FA Cup back to Bolton for the first time.

Clubs were falling over themselves in an eagerness to entertain the Cup winners. A week later the Wanderers visited Chorley, where the home side displayed the Lancashire Combination Championship alongside the FA Cup, the Wanderers winning 8-0.

Joe Smith shoots at goal in the F.A. Cup semi final win over Sheffield United at Old Trafford.

The 1923
F.A.Cup Final

(Top) Photo call 1923 style. The Trotters line up for their Cup Final photo. (Middle left) Joe Smith greets former Wanderer George Kay before the Final with West Ham United. (Right) The crowds engulf Wembley prior to the Final. (Bottom) David Jack scores the first goal at Wembley.

A remembrance card sent to followers of West Ham after their final defeat.

A tour to Switzerland was undertaken where seven games were won and one drawn, but despite all the hullabaloo this was the end of an era at Burnden. Tom Buchan who had served the club throughout the First World War was given a free transfer for services rendered and he joined Tranmere where he teamed up with another old Bolton Wanderer, Harold Hilton.

Season 1923/24

The season opened full of promise with the club having won its first major trophy four months earlier, but the first two games marked the Wanderers as a team to be beaten. A 3-2 reverse at Cardiff was followed by a scoreless draw at Sheffield United where John Smith received his marching orders for kicking an opponent.

Dick Pym saved a Jack Evans penalty against Cardiff at Burnden to earn the Wanderers a 2-2 draw and the first League win of the season came in the fourth game when Sheffield United were beaten 4-2 at Burnden. John Smith netted a hat trick to gain some compensation for his sending off in the earlier match, whilst Harry Nuttall scored his first League goal for Bolton.

On the 8th September Bolton paid their first visit to Manchester City's new ground at Maine Road, drawing 1-1. John Smith had given Bolton a sixth minute lead but ex Wanderer Frank Roberts replied with City's equaliser. Only three defeats in the next 13 games kept Bolton with the leading group in the division although six of these games passed without them finding the net.

During November £1500 was spent on Rollo Jack, brother of David, from Plymouth Argyle for whom he had only played 15 league games. He made his debut on 22nd December in a 1-1 draw at Notts County, taking the place of his brother who had been injured a week earlier when County were trounced 7-1 at Burnden.

An undefeated seven games during December, in which only two points were dropped, saw the Wanderers in 2nd place at the turn of the year, just two points behind leaders Cardiff.

The impressive run continued into January when a David Jack equaliser in the 90th minute won a point in a 2-2 draw at Everton. Wanderers trainer George Eccles, the most superstitious man at the club, blamed the late reply on the fact that he hadn't worn his usual necktie until late in the game! A week later another late equaliser from Jack gave Bolton a 2-2 draw at Hull in the first round of the Cup, 40315 saw the replay at Burnden which was won 4-0.

The first defeat in 13 games came at the end of January when Aston Villa won 1-0 at Villa Park in a game that was attended by the Duke of York. Then came two successive defeats at the hands of Liverpool. Firstly the Anfielders won 4-1 at Burnden in the 2nd round of the FA Cup, the game being Joe Smith's and Ted Vizard's 29th consecutive FA Cup tie, they then registered a 3-1 League win on their own pitch.

Bolton got back to winning ways the following week by defeating Nottingham Forest at Burnden, but the crowd numbered only 12327. For the next home game it went down to 9886, the smallest of the season, a goalless draw with Burnley taking place during an arctic snap.

Joe Smith introduces the team to the Duke of York before a 1-0 reverse at Aston Villa in January 1924.

Things turned back into the Wanderers favour during March with four wins and one draw from their five outings which included a revenge victory over Liverpool by 4-1. David Jack also won his first England International Cap against Wales at Blackburn.

On March 29th the Wanderers won 2-0 at Preston thanks to a goal from each of the Jack brothers and, a week later, when Preston visited Burnden, the crowd were provided with a novelty in the shape of entertainment by way of the wireless, with the apparatus fixed at the Great Lever end of the new stand. The game ended in a scoreless draw. Three defeats in the final five games saw any title hopes vanish but 4th position was once again considered a successful nine months work. Only Blackburn and Liverpool had defeated the Wanderers by more than one goal and only champions Huddersfield had a better defensive record.

During May another tour to the Continent was undertaken and included a 9-0 win over Fortuna Leipzig plus 3-1 wins over both Ajax and Leeds United in Amsterdam.

Season 1924/25
Once again the club made a slow start to the League campaign not recording their first victory until the fifth game, by 1-0 over Notts County at Burnden.

The fixtures reverted to the pre-war system of playing each half of the season. The Wanderers engaged 34 professionals for the term, including paying £4,400 for Joe Cassidy, a centre forward from Glasgow Celtic. He scored his first goals for Bolton in a 3-3 draw with Bury at Burnden, but there was now plenty of competition for the forward places.

During October and November Bolton remained unbeaten. Arsenal were defeated 4-1 at Burnden in a game that saw Joe Cassidy, whose place had gone to John Smith, taking over the role of linesman, the official turning up late. A fortnight later it was Smith's turn to be ousted by Cassidy for the visit of League Champions Huddersfield. Cassidy scored the winning goal and Smith asked to go on the transfer list. He returned to the team for the next home game and scored a hat trick in 13 minutes as West Ham were beaten 5-0. The other two goals came from Cassidy.

Only a reverse at Sheffield United put a blot on Bolton's record to the end of 1924. On Boxing Day there were unprecedented scenes at Nottingham Forest when the home side were awarded a penalty. No Forest player wanted to take the kick and the game was held up for five minutes. Normal penalty taker Harold Martin had left the field injured and he returned to take the kick which he converted, to produce a 1-1 draw. Bolton entered the New Year in 3rd place and then took on and defeated Huddersfield by 3-0 before a 50412 Burnden crowd in the first round of the Cup.

On January 17th a 1-0 away win at Notts County put the Wanderers into 2nd place behind leaders West Brom. Four days later the Lancashire Cup was captured when Blackpool were beaten 2-1 at Burnden thanks to a last minute winner from Harry Nuttall. But any hopes of FA Cup glory again went at the 2nd round stage when, after a 1-1 draw in London, 'Spurs won 1-0, to become the only side to keep a clean sheet at Burnden during 1924/25.

Two successive away defeats, by 1-0 at Sunderland and Preston who were already doomed to relegation, saw the Wanderers slip to 5th place but home form remained impressive. Burnley were beaten 5-0, Manchester City 4-2 and Aston Villa 1-0. Joe Smith netted seven goals in these three games, grabbing a hat trick against City.

Whilst goals were flowing at Burnden the club had difficulty in finding the net on their travels. Apart from reverses at Spurs on the opening day and at Sheffield United, all the defeats came by a 1-0 margin. Despite only one reverse, at Leeds, in the final ten games the Wanderers had to settle for third place, three points behind champions Huddersfield Town.

The highlight of the season was undoubtedly the clubs sparkling home form. The last two matches of the season saw Blackburn defeated 6-0, David Jack scoring four times and Liverpool beaten 2-0 as the club recorded their 17th successive home League win.

During March the Wanderers took part in an experiment during a friendly against Manchester City. The Wanderers won 3-0 but there was no offside in operation 40 yards from goal. In the summer Walter Rowley was appointed Coach to the reserves in succession to Fred Scotchbrook who joined Southport as Manager.

Season 1925/26
For the start of the 1925/26 season the offside law was amended from requiring three opponents to only two between the attacker and the goal-line. In the opening game at home to Newcastle, in which the Wanderers fielded their Cup winning side of two years previous, there were only three offside decisions in the game that ended 2-2.

Eight League games were played in the opening three weeks, three of which were won, including a 5-0 win over Bury at Gigg Lane and a 5-2 reverse at Leicester. Joe Cassidy, who had failed to force his way into the League side during the opening weeks, left the club to join Cardiff City for £3,500. Successive wins over London clubs, 1-0 v. West Ham at Burnden and 3-2 over Arsenal at Highbury, in which Ted Vizard netted all three - the last in the 87th minute - lifted the club into 8th place.

For the next game against Blackburn at Burnden, John Smith was relegated to the reserves at his own request to recover his lost form; Jack Baggett came into the forward line and also scored in a 2-2 draw.

A run of three consecutive wins lifted the Wanderers into 5th place but at the end of November bottom club Cardiff came to Burnden and won 1-0. Home confidence was however soon restored when champions Huddersfield were thumped 6-1. Town were chasing their third title in a row and despite the final scoreline amazingly took the lead after only four minutes.

There was a mixed opening to 1926. John Smith hit a hat trick in a 5-3 home win over Birmingham on New Year's day and twenty four hours later the Wanderers went down 5-1 at Newcastle. The third round of the FA Cup paired the Wanderers with Accrington Stanley and the game was switched to Burnden in the interests of safety. Despite the switch it was a slender Wanderers win, David Jack scoring the only goal, although they were reduced to ten men when Ted Vizard was sent off for foul play.

A week later the best League gate of the season, 33738 excluding season tickets, saw the Wanderers inflict Bury's first defeat since 21st November, with a 3-2 win. A David Jack goal five minutes from time gave the Wanderers

(Above) Dick Pym punches clear in the F.A. Cup final win over Manchester City, and later.... (below) The Trotters celebrate the 1926 F.A. Cup win.

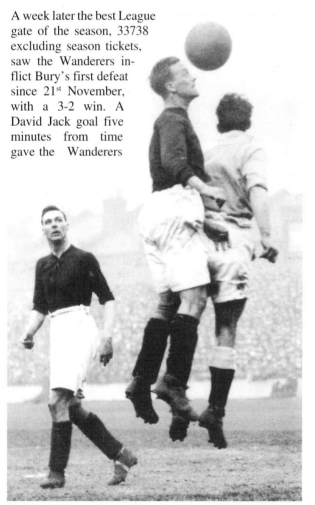

Jack Baggett go close with a header in the F.A. Cup semi final win over Swansea Town at White Hart Lane.

a 2-2 draw in the fourth round of the FA Cup at Bournemouth. The replay was won 6-2, and within an hour of the victory the Wanderers signed Charles Roberts from the south coast side in a dramatic piece of business. A 6-2 defeat was incurred at West Ham before a 3-0 win over South Shields in the 5th round of the FA Cup.

It took three attempts to defeat Nottingham Forest in the 6th round, Joe Smith scoring the only goal in the second replay at Old Trafford. Despite the importance of the Cup, League form remained consistent. Manchester United were beaten 3-1 at Burnden, in which Charles Roberts scored twice to register his first goals for the Wanderers. Unfortunately both John Smith and Alec Finney were long term injury victims, Smith missing his first Cup tie since joining the club, when the Wanderers defeated Swansea Town in the semi final. All the goals in the 3-0 win came in the first half, Jack Baggett and Joe Smith with a couple, sending the club to Wembley for the second time.

Two days after the semi final win the Wanderers faced Manchester City in a Cup final rehearsal. City were bottom of the League and the game ended a 1-1 draw. Ten League games were played in the final month of the season, three of which ended in defeat.

On April 24th, a 78th minute goal from David Jack won the FA Cup for Bolton before a crowd of 91447. It was expected to be the last Cup Final to be played at Wembley due to its impending sale but history has since proved otherwise.

Season 1926/27
For only the second time since the war the first game of the season was won, when Leeds were beaten 5-2, John Smith opening his account for the season with a hat trick. The fine start was hampered in the later games by injuries and it wasn't until the end of September that the first choice side could be selected again.

Progress was steadily maintained and Harry Nuttall took his benefit in the 4-0 win over Manchester United becoming the 6th captain in nine games. 39258, the best League gate, saw a 2-2 draw with Bury, and a 2-0 win over West Ham in the next home game saw Joe Smith net his 250th League goal.

At the end of November the Wanderers became the first team for seven weeks to prevent Dixie Dean scoring for Everton. The game at Goodison ended in a 1-1 draw, John Smith equalising an own goal from Jimmy Seddon. A week later Blackburn were beaten 5-1 at Burnden, a result that placed Wanderers 5th in the League, two points behind leaders Newcastle.

Inconsistent results saw 1927 come in without an improvement on that position and a hat trick from John Smith saw the Wanderers through to the 4th round of the FA Cup with a 3-1 win at Blackpool. For the visit to League leaders Newcastle, the Wanderers were without injured 'keeper Dick Pym, and they gave a debut to James Gill who hailed from Durham. A goal from McKay settled the game in favour of the Tynesiders.

Leeds United were accounted for in the 4th round of the FA Cup, after a replay, but the remainder of February virtually ended any hopes of a major trophy.

A 1-0 defeat at Cardiff was followed by the first home defeat of the season when Aston Villa won 2-0. Cardiff then visited Burnden in the 5th round of the FA Cup and won 2-0, before going on to win the trophy for the only time.

After the defeat by Villa the Wanderers were accused of putting more concern into winning the FA Cup than the League title and many supporters threatened to boycott the remaining League games. The Cup defeat heralded changes. Will Jennings asked for a transfer and Joe Smith was placed on the transfer list after 19 years of loyal service. His replacement was George Gibson, who signed from Hamilton Academicals, and he scored his first goal on March 26th in a 4-4 draw at West Ham. Coincidentally on the same day Joe Smith scored both goals for his new club Stockport County in their 2-1 win at Rotherham.

At the end of March the club went on a West Country tour winning 1-0 at Plymouth and losing 3-2 at Exeter. Two of the Exeter goals were scored by 21 years old Harold Blackmore and after the game he signed for the Wanderers in a £2150 deal. He made his debut on 2nd April scoring after only five minutes in a 3-2 home win over Sheffield Wednesday.

After a 6-1 reverse at Birmingham only one further defeat, by 6-2 at Sunderland, was incurred in the final seven games. George Gibson scored a hat trick in a 5-0 win over Everton and Willie Wright did likewise in a 4-0 win over runners up Huddersfield in the last League game of the season. The other goal in that game came from James Seddon his first League goal for six years, to enable the Wanderers to climb into 4th place.

The Lancashire Cup was again secured with a 1-0 win over Bury at Burnden, the winner coming from John Smith.

Season 1927/28
Bolton made a terrible start to the season, winning only once in the opening 10 games, this a 3-1 home victory over Blackburn on the second Saturday of the season. Loss of form and injuries to Harry Greenhalgh, Jimmy Seddon, John Smith, David Jack and Ted Vizard, all corner stones of the side, were heavily felt.

The Wanderers hit the bottom of the League, after a 2-1 defeat by Newcastle in the 9th game, for the first time since 1909/10. The following week a 1-0 reverse at Huddersfield was suffered, Dick Pym saving a 6th minute penalty from Kelly, only to be beaten by a 56th minute spot kick by Jackson. Two days later the tide appeared to turn when the Wanderers defeated Preston 6-3 at Deepdale in a 3rd round Lancashire Cup tie. Harold Blackmore netted four times George Gibson striking the other two. This form was transferred to the League when Liverpool were beaten at Burnden and Arsenal at Highbury both by 2-1. Burnley were then crushed 7-1 at Burnden with Harold Blackmore again netting four goals, including a first half hat trick, David Jack also claiming a hat trick of headed goals. Burnley were however handicapped when they lost goalkeeper Somerville with a broken collar bone and two other outfield players were subsequently tried between the posts. After the game the electric lights failed and the players had to bath by candlelight. The following week it was the Wanderers turn to lose their custodian when Dick Pym broke his wrist during a 4-2 defeat at Leicester.

By the end of November a much more satisfactory position of 15th had been reached although the Lancashire Cup had been lost when Bury won a semi final at Burnden. December saw steady progress with three victories and two defeats. Alec Finney netted his first goal for Bolton from a 50 yard free kick in a 3-1 home win over Aston Villa. David Jack grabbed his second hat trick of the season in a 4-3 reverse at Sheffield United on Christmas Eve. A special train with ten coaches was laid on from Bolton, but only 13 people made the journey!

Away results in the early part of the New Year were improved upon dramatically. Blackburn were beaten 6-1 at Ewood, Middlesbrough 5-2 at Ayresome and 'Spurs 2-1 at White Hart Lane. The FA Cup competition was however a short-lived affair. Luton Town were accounted for in the third round, but Stoke City, who were then in the Second Division, triumphed 4-2 in the Potteries at the next hurdle. Harry Nuttall missed a penalty during this game but Len Murphy scored his first goal for the Wanderers, after his transfer from Derby, Albert Picken having gone the other way in exchange.

A 3-2 home win over Birmingham put the Wanderers into 4th place in the League with an outside chance of championship success. League leaders Huddersfield Town were the next visitors to Burnden and won 1-0 before a season's best gate of 44082. This defeat put Bolton's form in reverse with only one win being recorded in the next six games. Changes in the forward line were made when John Smith was sold to Bury for £1590 whereupon he scored a hat trick on his debut. In his place came James McClelland from Middlesbrough for a fee of £6800, and he too scored on his debut, in a 2-2 draw at Burnley. The new signing netted eight goals in the final 10 games of the season.

The final game of the season attracted only 7958 to Burnden for a 1-1 draw with Sheffield United. There was controversy when United captain Billie Gillespie was sent off for butting Jimmy Seddon who was carried off injured. Seddon returned five minutes later only to be sent off as a joint offender in the incident. The receipts from the game of only £300 were the smallest in the League since the war.

Season 1928/29

Bolton kicked off 1928/29 with a visit from the previous season's champions Everton. The new stand on the Burnden side of the ground, costing £17712, was opened for the game with a crowd of 34637 attending. The Wanderers were without Jimmy Seddon, who was suspended for a month by the FA after his sending off in the final game of the previous term. Dixie Dean grabbed a hat trick as the visitors won 3-2, George Gibson scoring both the Wanderers goals.

Once again a poor start was encountered with only one win in nine games. Changes were made, for even Dick Pym was dropped, and half back Fred Kean arrived from Sheffield Wednesday for £5600. The first win of the season came coincidentally on Jimmy Seddon's return to action, with Derby being beaten 3-0 at Burnden, Murphy scoring one of the goals against his old club. This was a short-lived success however as Bury won 1-0 before 37181 and the Wanderers fell to the bottom of the table. This game proved to be David Jack's last in a Bolton shirt as a week later he was transferred to Arsenal for a fee of £10750, the first ten thousand pound player, the Londoners wanting his skills to replace those left by the retirement of Charles Buchan.

Three hat tricks in three successive games changed the Wanderers fortunes. Harold Blackmore did the trick in a 4-2 home win against Portsmouth, and a week later he repeated the dose in a 5-2 win at Aston Villa. George Gibson recorded his first Bolton hat trick in a 3-1 home win against Sheffield United.

The outside left position was strengthened when Billy Cook was signed for £5000 from Dundee and he made his debut in a 5-0 home win against Leicester City. The double was completed over Birmingham during Christmas including a Blackmore hat trick in a 6-2 home win on Boxing Day. Three days later however Dixie Dean notched his second hat trick of the season against Bolton scoring all his sides goals at Goodison.

David Jack returned to Bolton on 5th January and went away having scored both goals in Arsenal's 2-1 win. League form remained steady although points that appeared to be won were lost in the second half of games. League leaders Sheffield Wednesday drew 2-2 at Burnden after being two down and the Wanderers were 3-0 up at Portsmouth before having to settle for a 4-4 draw.

The FA Cup came around with the Wanderers in a mid table position. Oldham and Liverpool were defeated in the opening rounds and a rare goal from Jimmy Seddon helping the Wanderers to win 2-1 at Leicester in the 5th round. The Wanderers were then drawn to face the holders Blackburn at Ewood with over £500 worth of Wembley ticket applications having already been received at Burnden, such was the confidence of success.

62522 paid £4722, a then attendance and receipt record for the ground, with a 2-2 draw resulting. The replay attracted Burndens best mid-week crowd of 65295, a record not being established due to poor packing in of the crowd. Two Billy Butler goals gave the Wanderers a 2-1 win and a semi final match against Huddersfield at Anfield.

The Yorkshire side led at half time but the Wanderers struck back to win 3-1. Wembley approached, but League points and fit players were required, the team having slipped into 18th place. Home wins over Newcastle, without Seddon and Nuttall who were involved in international duty, and Aston Villa, assured League safety and so attentions were turned to the Cup Final.

Jimmy Seddon, Dick Pym and Fred Kean celebrate with the F.A. Cup after a 2-0 final success over Portsmouth.

On April 27th Bolton won the FA Cup for the third time, with two goals in the final 12 minutes against Portsmouth, with Billy Butler, and Harold Blackmore, who had scored in every round, finding the net. By now the Wanderers were a weary bunch of players. The season was wound up with a 6-1 reverse at Leicester, who gained revenge for their Cup defeat, another reverse in the Manchester Cup final at Manchester City, and a 4-0 loss against Cataluna in the opening of their 65000 seater Olympic Stadium in Barcelona.

Season 1929/30

The new paddock on the Burnden side of the ground was completed for the first game of the season on the 7th September, but unfortunately the visitors, Derby County, won 2-1. By then only one point had been taken from two away games, and that thanks to a last minute equaliser from Harold Blackmore in a 3-3 draw at Everton.

At the beginning of September, Rollo Jack was transferred to Clapton Orient but the London club had difficulty in settling the £1,000 fee due to financial problems. The Wanderers were having difficulties themselves being in bottom spot after five games.

The first win of the season came at the sixth attempt, Portsmouth being defeated 2-1 at Burnden, whilst the first away win of the term came a week later, when League leaders Arsenal were beaten 2-1 at Highbury, Harold Blackmore opening the scoring after just 40 seconds.

The Cup winning team was gradually being broken up, with Jim McClelland joining Second Division Preston North End and Dick Pym being dropped for the visit to Arsenal, his place going to Jimmy Gill. Another 'keeper in Robert Jones, was signed from Southport whilst £4150 was spent on bringing inside left Willie McKay to Burnden from Hamilton Academicals and £1750 on forward Jack Milsom from Rochdale.

The signings were initiated by another decline in results and attendances. A 5-2 reverse at Leicester included a hat trick by Lovatt who had dosed out the same medicine to the Wanderers the previous season. The following week only 8506 were at Burnden to see Grimsby win 3-2. Willie McKay made his debut in a 1-1 draw at Manchester United, where Dick Pym returned to the side, and Harold Blackmore scored his 50th First Division goal. The Wanderers went through December undefeated which culminated in a 5-0 home win over Everton, when Blackmore scored four times. Both Willie Cooke and Willie McKay also scored their first League goals for the club during the month that ended with the club in 7th position.

New Year's Day was celebrated with a 7-1 home win over Huddersfield, Blackmore netting another two, the scoring honours going to Billy Butler who grabbed a hat trick. Unfortunately this ended the club's consistent good run with only one draw and five defeats in the next six games. The FA Cup proved to be a disaster with a 1-0 defeat at Birmingham, played without regulars Finney and Blackmore.

The best crowd of the season, 42543, saw Manchester City win 2-1 at Burnden, the home supporters crying out for centre forward Jack Milsom who had scored 17 goals in 10 Central League games, to be given his opportunity.

This came when he was given his debut for the visit of Leeds who were defeated 4-2, Milsom obtaining a goal and Gibson a hat trick. After three games Blackmore was reinstated to the centre forward position where he scored twice in the first away win of 1930, 3-2 at Sheffield United, the first win there for 17 years.

During March the Club snapped up a youngster from Brierley Hill Alliance who was to become a household name in Bolton – his name – Ray Westwood. After two successive home wins that secured the club's First Division place there was a disappointing end to the season with three consecutive away defeats. At West Ham the Wanderers were two goals up in the first 12 minutes but eventually lost 5-3.

During the close season Jack Rimmer was signed from Southport and youngster Harry Goslin came from Nottingham club, Boots Athletic. 15th position in the First Division was an unwelcome position for the club considering their failure in the Cup competitions. It was however a transitionary period with comings and goings of younger players who were expected to immediately fill the boots of the 1920's 'old school', which was an almost impossible task considering the standard that had been set.

Season 1930/31
Bob Howarth was appointed captain for a season that opened with a 3-0 home win over Middlesbrough. Unfortunately the crowd of 13648 was the smallest opening day gate since the war. Only one point from the next four games left the club in the bottom four. A 7-2 defeat at Liverpool heralded the end of one era and the start of a new, for Dick Pym ended his Bolton League career, with Bob Jones taking over as number one custodian, whilst Harry Goslin made his debut.

The Wanderers remained in 20th position despite a 1-0 win at Chelsea. Harold Blackmore scored the all important goal but had Jackson to thank for missing a penalty for the home side. An improvement came during October to show some light on the horizon. Champions Sheffield Wednesday took the points at Hillsborough thanks to a disputed penalty, but Manchester City were beaten in the Lancashire Cup and Grimsby were defeated 4-2. There was a price to pay however with Jack Milsom fracturing a leg whilst scoring the winning goal over City.

There was another slump during November and centre forward Tommy Tait was purchased from Manchester City. He scored in each of his first two games but failed to satisfy the management and the position returned to Blackmore. George Taylor, a youngster from Ashton-under-Lyne was taken on as a professional during December in what was to be the start of a long and distinguished Wanderers career both on and off the field.

Due to the poor League position hopes were once again pinned on Cup success but that was short-lived. Carlisle were beaten in the 3rd round but Sunderland forced a draw in the next, thanks to an equaliser three minutes from time. Both sides were down to ten men Urwin and Nuttall having been sent off for fighting. The Wearsiders won the replay at Roker.

League form continued to deteriorate with further injuries taking their toll. Bob Haworth broke his leg in a 4-1 defeat at Grimsby and this ended his career as a Wanderer. George Gibson requested a transfer as he was finding it difficult to follow a public idol, namely Joe Smith. On 21st February George Taylor made his debut at Blackpool, who were also struggling to fight off relegation. Bolton fought back from 3-1 down to draw 3-3 with Blackmore netting the equaliser seven minutes from time.

Harold Blackmore - 27 League goals - including a run of scoring in seven consecutive games late in the season.

In March Ted Vizard, who had made his debut 20 years previously, and had not played a League game since October 1929, was reinstated. He took part in three games including a 6-2 win over Sheffield United, five of the goals coming in a 21 minute spell, with Blackmore hitting a hat trick. Vizard's place went to Ray Westwood as part of the club's policy to give youth a fling in its hour of need. Westwood, whose Uncle was David Stokes an old Bolton stalwart, had only taken part in 12 Central League games for the club.

The Wanderers re-corded four successive wins in the first eleven days of April to climb up to 12th place and safety. Westwood scored his first goal for the club in a 2-0 win at Cup Finalists Birmingham City, and Blackmore hit his 27th League goal of the season in a 4-1 home win over Leicester City. The final game of the season saw the Wanderers visit champions Arsenal where they were taught a lesson and went down 5-0. The term ended with the club looking to make economies, the first of which was the failure to offer terms to 34 years old Bob Haworth.

Too many positions required immediate attention for the club to become a great force. The two bright spots had been the discovery of Goslin and Westwood, both of whom had already become targets of other clubs. Tommy Tait's spell at the club was short lived and he left for Luton Town after scoring four goals in his nine games during the season.

Season 1931/32
Four debutants and eighteen new players were involved in the club's first four League games of the season. The immediate change after the opening day defeat by West Ham at Burnden highlighted the problems that the club now had. Out went Goslin, Seddon and Milsom and in came George Nicholson, signed from Washington Colliery, for his debut, Willie McKay and Harold Howarth.

A 2-2 draw at Liverpool was followed by a 7-1 defeat at Sheffield Wednesday in which Blackmore gave Bolton the lead after seven minutes. Jimmy Boyle, signed from the Bear Park club in Durham, was unfortunate enough to make his debut in this game. Other debutants in the early stages of the season were also non-League recruits in Tommy Walters from Merthyr Town and Tom Duckworth from local side Tonge, who were thrown in at the deep end in an attempt to find the formula that would turn the tide.

Home form kept the Wanderers in the top half of the table during the early weeks of the season, which included a 1-0 win over leaders West Brom. A couple of heavy away defeats at Sheffield United (0-4) and Derby County (1-5) - in which the home side's last four goals came in a 12 minute spell after Butler had given the Wanderers a half time lead - was followed by a home defeat by lowly Blackpool. This was a signal for the club to bring out the cheque book with £6500 going to Everton for Welsh international centre half Tom Griffiths.

A crowd of 33619, the best for two seasons, came to Burnden to see his debut against his old club. Dixie Dean opened the scoring for the visitors after 22 minutes but Jack Milsom struck twice in the 70th and 73rd minutes, in only his third game of the season, to see Bolton home. Christmas found the club in mid table and a double over Leicester City put the Wanderers in a confident mood for the FA Cup. Unfortunately this was unfounded as Preston won a third round replay at Burnden by 5-2.

Home crowds slumped with only 9694 seeing Sheffield Wednesday winning 4-2 at Burnden after the Wanderers had been leading 2-1 with 20 minutes remaining. Meanwhile, the reserves who were going well in the Central League were attracting crowds of 6500.

Tom Griffiths was appointed captain in place of George Gibson during February. Towards the end of the month a run of four successive home wins commenced. The drawing power of Arsenal was highlighted with a crowd of 20922 seeing a Jack Milsom goal defeat the Londoners. Only 11003 saw the next game at Burnden, a 5-1 win over Birmingham. The club's First Division security was assured with three games of the season remaining, a 3-0 win at Blackpool in which Milsom netted his second hat trick of the season, was enough to take the pressure off.

The League was wound up in style with an 8-1 demolition of Liverpool at Burnden. It was the second time during the season the Wanderers had defeated the Anfielders by that score, for they also won a 3rd round Lancashire Cup match during November. In that Cup tie Billy Butler hit four goals, and Milsom did likewise in the League encounter to take his overall record for the season to 51 goals in 43 games.

In the week prior to the final League game of the season £650 was paid to Liverpool for winger Dick Edmed. He made his debut for the Wanderers against his old club netting one of the goals in the process. The Lancashire Cup was secured on 14th May with a 3-2 win at Manchester City, all the Bolton goals coming from Scots McKay, Gibson and Cook.

Only 24 players of the 35 on the books at the end of the season were offered terms. Players however were not eager to put pen to paper with reduced terms being offered. Only the top players would receive £8 per week during the winter, whether playing or not, summer wages being cut to the bone. George Eccles the clubs trainer handed over the reins to Bob Young. Eccles who was now 60 decided to take over the reserves to cut down on travelling.

During June Jack Milsom gained undisputed posses-sion of the centre forward position when Harold Blackmore was sold to Middlesbrough for £4000 having scored 122 goals in 165 League and Cup games for the Wanderers.

Season 1932/33
Events of the previous season, with its disappointments and near disasters, had taught the club a sharp lesson but would it be heeded in the coming term?

The wage bill was cut to the bone and 28 professionals were engaged, the last being 18 year old George Eastham. Cup winners Newcastle United opened the season at Burnden with a 2-2 draw.

The Wanderers were without Milsom who had been injured in a practice game. His place went to Billy Wright who netted the second goal. Two heavy defeats at Wolves and Villa were offset by home wins over Wolves and Middlesbrough. Four goals in the last eight minutes of the first half against Boro' gave them a 3-1 lead, but the Wanderers hit back with three goals in 17 to win 4-3 and climb to 10th place.

Improved form continued with Ray Westwood hitting the only goal of the game, seven minutes from time, at Liverpool, and George Gibson scoring in only 21 seconds in the 5-0 win versus Leicester City. Jack Milsom went even better when he scored after 18 seconds in the 4-2 home win over Blackburn during a run which saw the Wanderers unchanged in nine games. An incredible 7-4 defeat at Sunderland was incurred, with the Wanderers finding themselves five down after half an hour. The Wanderers ended November with a 2-2 draw at champions Everton. Albert Geldard, later to star for the Wanderers after the war, scored on his home debut for the Goodison side.

Jack Milsom hit his first hat trick of the season when Wanderers inflicted Sheffield Wednesday's first defeat since August just before Christmas. Only one win in the next ten League fixtures put pressure back onto the club. Atherton full back Bob Smith made his debut in a 2-1 defeat at Middlesbrough where Harold Blackmore scored one of the home side's goals.

A week earlier the Wanderers had won 5-1 at Charlton in the third round of the FA Cup, and then accounted for Grimsby Town at the next stage. A defeat at bottom club Leicester City, their first Saturday win of the season, was hardly ideal preparation for a 5th round tie against Manchester City at Burnden. Despite Bolton taking the lead against City, the visitors ran out 4-2 winners but a record crowd of 69912 witnessed the game. Four days later another record was broken at Burnden when the lowest recorded crowd for a League game of 3101, which wasn't lowered further until 1983, saw Portsmouth defeated 4-1.

Wanderers supporters were accused of being disloyal by the media and as in previous years a Cup exit heralded changes. Tom Griffiths, who had been unable to settle in Bolton joined Middlesbrough for £6000, George Gibson was attracted by the bright lights of the capital and went to Chelsea for £5000. Both players final game for the club was against Portsmouth.

There were no new signings before the transfer deadline and after a 3-2 reverse at Blackburn the Wanderers were in 17th spot having played more games than any other club.

A 3-1 win at fellow strugglers Blackpool eased matters with George Eastham making his debut against his home town team.

George Eastham, made his Trotters debut against Blackpool, his home town club.

Unfortunately only one point was won from the next four games and only two points separated the bottom four clubs one of which was Bolton. The Wanderers crashed to the bottom of the table with a 2-0 defeat at Sheffield Wednesday, therefore requiring a win at home to Leeds in the last game of the season and other clubs to lose, to avoid relegation.

Leeds were crushed 5-0, Jack Milsom netting a first half hat trick, but all three struggling rivals also won leaving the Wanderers and Blackpool to face Second Division football thus ending a run of 22 years in the First Division.

The Lancashire Cup was also lost when the Wanderers went down 2-1 in the Final to Liverpool. Joe Smith now in the manager's seat at Reading came back to Burnden to snap up Billy Wright, Jack Boyle and his fellow 1923 Cup winner Billy Butler. Another Wanderers Cup winner cut his ties with the club, Ted Vizard leaving to manage Swindon Town, his charge of the 'A' team going to Jimmy Seddon.

Season 1933/34
Despite relegation a profit of £2173 was made on the season, and the club announced that an open cheque book was available to sign players, but there was a problem in tempting them to join a relegated club.

The opening game of the season was a 4-2 reverse at West Ham. Only two players remained from the 1923 Cup final sides - Alex Finney for the Wanderers, who were two down in eight minutes, and Willie Watson for West Ham who were grateful to see Willie McKay miss a penalty. For the first home game, Plymouth, who were managed by old Wanderer Bob Jack, made their first visit to the town.

Bolton won the game 2-0 but were brought back down to earth on Bank Holiday Monday when Grimsby won 4-0 at Burnden. Bolton then visited Manchester United, who had spent thousands on Scottish players, winning 5-1 with the Scottish selectors viewing Willie Cook and Willie McKay. After being two down at home to Brentford, the Wanderers eventually ran out 3-2 winners and went to the top of the Second Division after a 1-0 win over Oldham Athletic. £2400 was spent on bringing winger Kenny Cameron from Middlesbrough and he scored on his debut in a 1-1 draw at Preston. Further signings were those of Jim Winning from Canada and Jim Cochraine from South Africa, although neither got further than Central League matches.

Only one win in the next six games culminated in a 5-1 reverse at Bradford City where the Yorkshiremen scored three first half goals in a four minute spell. The following week League leaders Port Vale were defeated 3-0 at Burnden thanks to a Jack Milsom hat trick, his last goal being a penalty. Early December saw further activity in the transfer market with £3500 going to Notts County for the services of George.T.Taylor. He made his debut for the club in a 2-1 home win over Swansea but the next two games proved to be a disaster for the Wanderers and in the final analysis were to cost the club dear. Firstly a visit to bottom club Millwall ended in a 2-1 defeat with their winning goal coming in the final minute. A week later next to bottom side Lincoln City came to Burnden and won by the same score.

A slight improvement in form over Christmas lifted the club into second place. A 5-1 home win over West Ham United including four goals from Milsom, saw out the year in style. Unfortunately League form took a turn for the worse during the early part of 1934 as the club became involved in a good FA Cup run. Halifax and Brighton were accounted for in the first two hurdles, then 54912 saw First Division Liverpool beaten 3-0 at Anfield. Interest in the competition came to an end when Portsmouth won a sixth round tie at Burnden by the same score, before 52181.

The best League gate of the season was 27435 for the visit of Preston which ended in a 2-0 win for the visitors. G.T.Taylor missed a penalty during this game to become the third Wanderers player in successive games to miss from the spot, Harry Goslin against Burnley and Jack Milsom against Oldham, being the other culprits.

After the Cup defeat by Portsmouth the Wanderers played out their final dozen League games unbeaten. But five wins and seven draws were not enough to see the club return to the top flight after just one season's absence. A settled side contributed to the consistent run but the services of Willie McKay were lost during March, for after a number of transfer requests he joined Manchester United.

Preston North End and Grimsby Town were promoted with the Wanderers just one point behind in third spot leaving the club to ponder what might have been. There was some success at the end of the campaign however when the Lancashire Cup was lifted with a 4-2 win over Oldham Athletic at Maine Road.

Season 1934/35

Once again changes were made at Burnden during the close season, the most noticeable being the removal of four sided goal posts which were replaced by those of oval cross section. The pitch was also narrowed, so the Wanderers could adjust to the majority of 2nd Division grounds, although it would be extended for any games of importance such as Cup semi finals. The Great Lever corner of the new Burnden Stand was partitioned off for the exclusive use of youngsters which would accommodate 500 at 6d (2.5p) each.

The Burnden crowd must have enjoyed what they saw for the first seven games of the season were all won with only two goals being conceded. The first six victories equalled a feat set in 1899/1900 and created a new club record of 10 games, 12 from the previous season, without defeat. Jack Milsom had also started the season off with a wallop scoring in every game, a record shared by the legendary Ted Drake. The seventh consecutive win created a new club record for the start of the season, although Milsom failed to find the net. For the following game the club had to make the first change of the season to the side. Ken Cameron replaced Ray Westwood, who won his first international cap playing for England against Wales, the first such honour since Jimmy Seddon in 1929. The Wanderers went down 6-2 to Sheffield United at Bramall Lane thus ending a run of 19 League games without defeat, or 20 including the Lancashire Cup Final. The defeat didn't throw the Wanderers off the promotion rails as the following week the club recorded their best ever League win when a crowd of 15009 saw Barnsley thumped 8-0.

Two of Bolton's goals in the record 8-0 League win over Barnsley at Burnden in October 1934.

Barnsley, who were the previous season's Third Division North champions were three down in 39 minutes to a Westwood hat trick, his first for the club. Incredibly all the other five goals came in the final six minutes of the game and the Wanderers, understandably received a standing ovation.

Three defeats in the next four games allowed the chasing bunch to close the gap. One of these reverses was at Bradford where the home side's four goals were shared by ex-Wanderers Harold Blackmore and Jim McLelland. The leadership of the division was lost for the first time that season during December after a 4-1 defeat at West Ham. By the end of the year however Bolton were back on top, on goal average over the Hammers and their fellow Londoners Brentford. The New Year's Day encounter with Burnley was postponed due to the weather but was hastily arranged for the following day, with Bolton running out 7-0 winners, Milsom netting four.

The FA Cup campaign opened with a 2-0 win at Northampton Town when a ground attendance record at the time of 17962 was set. Alec Finney also took part in his 40th FA Cup tie for the club.

George Walton heads over the bar in the 2-1 reverse at Fulham in March 1935.

Jack Milsom:
31 League goals

Despite taking the lead, in the FA Cup semi final, through George Walton, a 1-1 draw resulted with West Brom at Leeds, and the midlanders won the replay 2-0 at Stoke before a then record attendance. Three successive League defeats saw the club slip down to 5th place and the crunch came in the final three games of the season. Second placed West Ham, who were three points in front of Bolton, were beaten 3-1 at Burnden, then Brentford, who were already champions, were defeated 2-0 before 46554. This left a point to be secured from the final game at Blackpool to make a return to Division One.

Plymouth were accounted for in the 4th round whilst League form remained steady with a three point lead at the top. 70347 were at Spurs for the 5th round FA Cup tie and despite going one down in the first minute Bolton fought back to draw the game. It took a second replay at Villa Park to decide the tie with Bolton winning 2-0, one of the goals coming from George Walton, who a week earlier had played his first senior game for two years.

The Wanderers won 2-1 at Everton, whose team included Dixie Dean, in the 6th round, the gates being closed an hour before the kick-off; but on the same day the leadership of the division was lost. The question was would the Cup campaign again interfere with the main goal of promotion, and this became more intensified when in the following mid-week game Hull won 2-1 at Burnden.

At Bloomfield Road, Ray Westwood grabbed his 30th goal of the season, in a 1-1 draw, which netted the club's 96th League goal of the season and set a club record. Westwood, along with Milsom who netted 31 goals, headed the division's goalgetters.

Season 1935/36
Burnden Park's capacity was increased to 70,000 for the start of the season thanks to the concreting of the Great Lever end and the disappearance of the remains of the cycle track. There was also a new top between the Burnden Terrace and Lever End. A season ticket for the new season back into the top flight cost £3 for men and £2-10s for women – no sex discrimination laws in those days! Record ticket sales of 3342 followed. Local brewery, Magee's, supplied clocks to be installed on the top of the stands which were to remain there for 40 years.

George Eastham, Fred Swift, George Nicholson, George Taylor, Jack Milsom, Bob Smith, Tom Clark and Willie Cook. Watch a tradesman work on the Burnden terrace.

The reserves were re-elected to the Central League after finishing next to bottom of the League the previous term.

After three games the Wanderers were at the foot of the table with one point. The first win came at the fifth attempt a 2-0 home win over Everton. During November, 42110 were attracted to Burnden for a 3-3 draw with Manchester City. This was the 12th League gate over 40000 since the war. The Wanderers found themselves 3-1 down but an equaliser from Westwood ten minutes from time won a point to lift the club into 8th place seven points behind leaders Sunderland. A visit to Roker Park the following month ended in disaster for Bolton when the defence went to pieces. Drawing 1-1 after 17 minutes the Wearsiders ran out 7-2 winners.

An early Cup exit at the hands of Blackburn, after a replay, along with a poor run of League results prompted the Wanderers to recruit. Full back John Tennant was signed from Liverpool for £2750 and debuts were given to Tom Clark, Cyril Woods and James Currier in an attempt to stop the slide. Goalkeeper Fred Swift, who was signed during the summer from Oldham Athletic, was given his debut in a 4-0 home win over Portsmouth on New Years Day.

No experienced players were signed before the transfer deadline and a young side took to the field against Stoke at Burnden. A debut was given to 18 years old winger Ton Woodward in a forward line that saw 25 years old Jack Rimmer the veteran, but Stoke ran out 2-1 winners. On March 21st the experienced Alec Finney and Harry Goslin were left out of the side for the visit to Manchester City.

George Goldsmith and George Nicholson, in his first game since February 1934, took over. Unfortunately the ploy failed and the Wanderers went down 7-0 thus equalling their worst ever League defeat. Neither Goldsmith nor Nicholson played in the first team again. Fred Swift, in the Wanderers goal, was opposed by his more illustrious brother Frank in goal for City.

The Wanderers got over the shock to take five points out of the following three games which virtually guaranteed survival. There was also successive home wins over the League champions and FA Cup winners. Champions Sunderland were beaten 2-1 with the Wanderers coming from behind after conceding a 2nd minute goal to Carter. The Wearsiders, despite losing remained seven points clear at the top. Arsenal were then defeated by the same score. Home lapses had led to a modest position although it was much better than had been feared during the early part of the New Year.

Willie Cook was placed on the transfer list after declining to accept terms at the end of April, and later left to join Blackpool. This left Alec Finney as the only member of the 1929 Cup winning team still in the club's employment.

Season 1936/37
Two new faces appeared in the opening day visit to Brentford which resulted in a 2-2 draw. Firstly, George Ainsley, a £2000 buy from Sunderland, was at outside left, and David Halford made his debut after arriving from Derby County. Unfortunately neither signing was successful, Ainsley's stay lasted only until December when he was sold to Leeds after just seven appearances, whilst Halford took to the field in only five games during the season.

GT Taylor commenced his seventh consecutive season without missing a game his sequence beginning on April 12th 1930 for Notts County at Southampton. Worrying times for the club were ahead with the team being far from consistent, thus a stable First Division place, which was needed from a financial angle, was not assured. The early season saw many drawbacks.

Bob Young, Harry Hubbick, Ray Westwood and Jack Hurst take time out to go through the Burnden mail.

Centre half Jack Atkinson fractured a shin bone in a home 0-0 draw with Preston and with only one win in the opening seven games the team were placed 20th in the table. One bright spot was the debut of Stan Hanson on September 19th in a 2-0 reverse at Huddersfield. Stan was to become another famous Wanderers custodian even serving the club when his playing days were over.

Another debutant was Ron Bower, an ex-South Liverpool full back, who first appeared in a 3-2 win at Wolves, but the same side was unable to play successive games due to injury. The jinx even struck GT Taylor when he ended a consecutive run of 290 first class games for Notts County and Bolton, missing the 3-1 home defeat by Derby County through a twisted knee. The first occasion that the side were unchanged was in the 12th game of the season, a 1-1 draw at Birmingham, where the Wanderers goal came from 18 year old Don Howe a Wakefield youth who had also recently received his League baptism.

Crowds during December went down to 13439 for the visit of Chelsea but doubled for the visit of League leaders Charlton Athletic, the Wanderers winning 2-1, Jack Milsom also missing a penalty in each half. Three consecutive home games during the Christmas period culminated in just a single point being collected with heavy defeats being handed out by Manchester United and Arsenal. A crowd of only 11801 saw the 4-0 reverse by fellow strugglers United whilst three days later, on New Year's Day, 42171 saw Arsenal win 5-0, Ted Drake netting four of their goals.

The management realised that the team had to be urgently strengthened. During January and February four new signings, three within the space of six days, joined the club. Alf Anderson, a left winger from Hibernian, Alec Carruthers, a right winger from Falkirk, John Calder, a centre forward from Morton and

the most expensive at £4000, and Harry Hubbick, a left back from Burnley, all came to Burnden whilst Jack Rimmer went in the opposite direction to Turf Moor after seven seasons with the Wanderers.

February was a dark month when a 3-0 defeat at Derby put Bolton into a relegation spot and an exit from the FA Cup was handed out when Manchester City won 5-0 at Burnden before 60979. The referee, whose unorthodox decisions had cost Bolton dearly, required a police escort from the field at the end of the game.

March opened with a scoreless home draw with Birmingham but the crowd of 21572 was exceptional considering the club's poor League position, along with the fact that nine home League defeats had already been suffered. The average crowd for the season at this time was almost 21000, excluding 3050 season ticket holders. The first League win of 1937 came on March 20th, when the FA Cup semi finalists West Brom were beaten 4-1, despite the fact that they had taken a 5th minute lead. This prompted the desired effect with only two of the final eight games ending in defeat. The highlights of this run-in were a 2-2 draw with eventual champions Manchester City at Maine Road, Don Howe hitting the Wanderers equaliser seven minutes from time, and a 1-0 win at Chelsea that was worth its weight in gold as the other struggling clubs slipped up to leave the club in a final position of 20th just two points clear of a relegation spot.

The season proved financially heavy to hold on to a First Division place with a loss of over £12,000 being the largest in the football League. To help offset this George Eastham was sold to Brentford for £4,500, after losing his place in the team during March.

Season 1937/38

George Eathsam made an early return to Burnden with his new club Brentford on the opening day of the season. The Wanderers made a good start winning 2-0 with Eastham's place going to Albert Grosvenor, an ex-England international who had joined Bolton from Sheffield Wednesday during the summer.

After four games the Wanderers sat on top of the League and despite a couple of defeats during September remained leaders after thrashing the previous season's Second Division champions Leicester City 6-1 at Burnden. Ray Westwood grabbed a couple of goals during this game, the first being his 100th League goal. A major change in the side took place when Alec Carruthers, who had signed the previous February from Falkirk, took the number seven shirt from GT Taylor. Taylor subsequently returned to the Midlands with Coventry City for a fee of £2250.

The spell at the top of the League came to an end with a 4-1 home defeat by Preston in a game that saw eight out of ten forwards on the field being Scottish. During this period the looming threat of war started to become more apparent with the club receiving a request from the government to appeal for home defence volunteers, but on the football front it was as you were.

Ray Westwood hit a hat trick in a 5-5 home draw with Chelsea, the Londoners then putting in a £12000 bid for the Wanderers star which was turned down, whilst a week later John Calder also did the trick in a 4-2 win at West Brom. December saw Charles Foweraker appointed Secretary-Manager for a further five years and Jack Milsom was placed on the transfer list at his own request after losing his centre forward spot to Calder.

A strange incident happened on New Year's Day when keeper Fred Swift received a £50 bribe to concede two goals at Brentford. He promptly handed it to his manager who advised the League but no action was taken, the game resulting in a 1-1 draw. An early exit from the Cup was sustained when Arsenal ran out 3-1 winners at Highbury all four goals coming in an eight minute spell just before half time.

A home defeat by Derby County during January was christened as Derby's benefit game. The original game commenced on Christmas Day but was abandoned after 37 minutes through fog with Bolton leading 2-0. The re-arranged match not only saw Derby take the points but also half of the gate receipts which under League rules they were entitled to.

Jack Milsom got his wish to leave the club during February when he made the short journey to Manchester City for a fee of £4000. His parting shot was to score the Wanderers goal in a 1-1 draw with Sunderland, the visitors equalising in the last minute.

February and March proved to be both experimental and transitional. Jack Roberts, from Swansea, made his debut as did ex Colwyn Bay winger Jimmy Jones. Half a dozen players normally on reserve duty took to the field in a 1-0 home win over Charlton. Milsom was quickly replaced when George Hunt joined the Wanderers for a £4000 fee from Arsenal and he scored six minutes into his debut, a 3-0 home win over West Brom on March 19th. Three defeats in the final nine games placed the club in a respectable seventh position. The final game of the season was a 5-0 defeat at

Arsenal, the Londoners winning the championship, thanks to this victory and Wolves' defeat at Sunderland.

There had been championship aspirations early in the season but even allowing for injuries the team had proved to be not quite good enough. There was some silverware won however with the Manchester Cup coming to Burnden after a 2-1 victory over Manchester United at Old Trafford. The team also won the West Lancashire Cup whilst the reserves finished runners-up in the Central League.

Season 1938/39
During the summer of 1938 there was again the usual crop of comings and goings from Burnden, with the wheeling and dealing by the management, in an attempt to bring the championship to Burnden. Goalkeeper Edward Goodall came from Hull City for a £3000 fee, ex-international and youngest ever League debutant Albert Geldard signed from Everton for £6500, and Lawrence Hamlett, a full back, came from non-League Congleton Town.

Departures were John Calder, who went to Barnsley and 'keeper Fred Swift who joined Birmingham League side Shrewsbury Town in an unusual arrangement. Swift had signed for Town without the Wanderers consent but they agreed to let the 'keeper remain there so long as Town gave Bolton first consideration on any of their players and that they kept Swifts registration for the Football League.

The Wanderers were without the influential Ray Westwood for the opening seven League games due to injury. He returned to the side in a 4-1 home win over Middlesbrough scoring twice and seeing his side handily placed in 5th position. On October 15th, League leaders Everton visited Burnden attracting the ground's Pre-war record League gate of 54,564. The Wanderers hero was Jack Roberts who hit a hat trick in a 4-2 victory, the game being won with a scintillating display in the final twenty minutes.

After only two defeats in the opening ten games of the season things suddenly turned sour with the following eleven games not producing a win. During this period the Wanderers twice came from behind to draw at Brentford, failed to defeat a ten man Grimsby side at Burnden, and Aston Villa, managed by ex Wanderer Jas Hogan came to Burnden and won 2-1. Full back Danny Winter also shot a penalty wide at Sunderland that would have earned the points. The club slipped to tenth in the League but the miserable run came to an end on New Year's Eve when Portsmouth were beaten 5-1 at Burnden.

The Cup was also to bring misery but plenty of drama. Having been drawn away to Middlesbrough in the third round Alf Anderson came in for his first senior game for four months. In the last minute of the first half Boro were awarded a penalty but Fenton shot against the bar and the ball rebounded to safety. The game thus ended scoreless, as did the replay at Burnden. It was Fenton however who had the final say, when in the second replay at Elland Road, he scored the only goal of the game two minutes from time.

Despite the Cup set back League form returned with three consecutive wins including revenge over Middlesbrough when the Wanderers won 2-1 at Ayresome Park. February and March saw George Hunt score in eight of the nine games, including one in a 2-1 win over bogey side Derby County at Burnden, to register Bolton's first win over them for ten years. There was however a poor finale to the season, for after a smart 3-1 win at Villa, only one goal was scored in the final four games, three of which were at home. The final game attracted only 7168, excluding ticket holders, despite the fact that neighbours Manchester United were the visitors.

Once again a season that had promised so much in the early stages had collapsed with the Wanderers finding themselves too much to do in the latter stages of the season to make up the lost ground.

Season 1939/40
The previous season had seen many professional footballers join the Territorial Army, or other National Service organisations, spending their leisure time preparing for what seemed to be the inevitable. Just three League games were completed before war was declared, the crowd of 12992 at Burnden against Cup holders Portsmouth, reflecting the tension.

On September 6th, the football League management committee met at Crewe and officially suspended League activities and contracts between players and clubs automatically terminated. The government had placed a ban on assemblies of crowds, but on September 14th it was announced that friendly matches could be arranged, even in areas barred by the Home Office under defence regulations, providing the local police gave their approval; therefore football only ceased for a matter of days.

Two clubs had signed up for army or service duty virtually en masse, one being the Wanderers and the other West Ham. Fifteen professionals from the club had enlisted in May 1939 and when war was declared all were immediately called up with the exception of Syd Jones and Charlie Hanks who were too

young. Stan Hanson, Danny Winter, George Catterall, Jimmy Thompson, Harry Goslin, Jack Hurst, Ernie Forrest, Jack Ithell, Albert Geldard, Tom Sinclair, Jack Roberts, Don Howe and Ray Westwood all joined the 53rd field regiment RA (Bolton Artillery). They spent much of the war together virtually as a team on many foreign fields. Of the 35 players on the staff in 1939, 32 eventually went into uniform, the other three either going into either coalmines or munitions.

The first game after the declaration of war was a friendly with Manchester United at Burnden. The game resulted in a 2-2 draw before a 4830 the side being chosen from members of staff in the Bolton Artillery. On October7[th], whilst the Wanderers were going down 6-1 at Preston, the 53rd Royal Artillery with the Wanderers stars defeated Ashington 5-1 in the North East. A few weeks later many guested for Newcastle as they defeated York 9-2, Don Howe scoring five and Ray Westwood grabbing three.

A North West regional tournament was organised and began on October 21st with a 1-1 draw at Burnley. Strangely the Wanderers played in claret and blue whilst the home side were in white. During November the reserves, who were competing in the Lancashire League, entertained Wigan Athletic at Burnden. The result a 3-3 draw whilst the visitors share of the gate amounted to 1d! At this time the club were taken to court by a season ticket holder who had claimed a refund due to not being able to see Football League games for which he had paid. The Wanderers won this test case allowing ticket holders into the regional tournament; if they had lost it would have cost many clubs up and down the country thousands of pounds they could ill afford.

On December 16th the Wanderers entertained the 53rd RA who were on leave, which was virtually a current Wanderers v. old Wanderers game. A crowd of 1509 saw an entertaining 3-3 draw but the footballing public of Bolton failed to be convinced that nothing short of the old League football and FA Cup would excite any interest. The club had a good run to win six of their final seven games, finishing in fourth position. The crowd of only 500 for the final home game with Accrington prompted the club to announce that they would not take part in any competition organised for the following season. A loss had been sustained on every home game and it was increasingly difficult to recruit a team.

Harry Goslin - ever present during 1938/39. The club captain lost his life in December 1943 whilst serving with the 53rd Field Regiment RA.

Chapter 5 (1940 ~ 1963)
War-time Struggles, Then First Division Prosperity

Season 1940/41

Despite the closure of the club, neither the players or the ground stood idle. Many of the players guested for other clubs whilst the playing area of Burnden Park was used by the Education Authority and the stands used by the Ministry of Supply to store food.

However, the Wanderers returned to action on Christmas Day 1940 with a friendly at Blackpool, who were also resuming after closure. League football returned to Bolton in the form of the Football League North's second competition of the season with a visit from Oldham. A crowd of 2038 saw the Wanderers win 2-1 in what was also the 1st leg of the 1st round of the Lancashire Cup. Guest players for Bolton included Butler of West Brom, Cunliffe of Everton, Eastwood of Manchester City, Martindale of Burnley and former Wanderer Eastham, now with Blackpool. Indeed the club were uncertain of the line up until almost the kick off.

On January 25th the Wanderers had to take to the field with only ten men against Manchester United. The aptly named Ron Bolton, a 19 year old 'keeper from Rotherham, had got lost on his way to the ground. Harry Goslin went into goal and United went one up inside a minute. Bolton (the player) eventually appeared after 12 minutes, going on to become man of the match with a magnificent exhibition.

A good start was made in the Football League War Cup. Bradford City were beaten 9-1 in the two-legged preliminary round, both games taking place at Burnden on City's request. Burnley were accounted for in the first round but Preston proved too strong for the Wanderers at the next hurdle, although the best gate since the start of the war, 7838, saw the first leg at Burnden.

During February after 21 years in the club's service, senior trainer Bob Young severed his connections with the Wanderers to become the licensee of the Shakespeare Hotel in Farnworth. His duties were taken over by George Eccles.

On March 22nd a surprise change was made in the Wanderers attack for the visit to Bury. Nathaniel Lofthouse, a former Folds Road and Bolton Town Team centre forward appeared for the first time, aged 15 years 207 days. Bolton won 5-1 with Lofthouse grabbing his side's fourth and fifth goals. Other amateurs were included in the side, Walter Grimsditch of Farnworth St Thomas's and Harry Cload of Halliwell were two, many of whom in normal circumstances would have been lucky to get a game in the 'A' team.

Whilst new blood was being introduced at Burnden the established stars were making a name for themselves elsewhere. Norwich City defeated a Dutch Army XI by 7-0, six of the goals coming from Wanderers by way of Don Howe, Tom Sinclair, and Jack Roberts, who hit a brace a piece.

Although only 10 games were won out of a total 27 played (including friendlies), since re-opening, the Wanderers could regard the return to football as amply justified. Junior talent was being explored pretty thoroughly at the loss of success on the field but many new professionals could be signed when normalities returned.

Season 1941/42

Once again the job of attempting to raise a team caused manager Foweraker numerous problems. He had to rely to a great extent on amateurs under military age or soldiers on leave.

BOLTON WANDERERS FOOTBALL & ATHLETIC CO. LTD.

WINNERS OF THE
FOOTBALL ASSOCIATION CUP 1923, 1926, 1929.

LANCASHIRE CUP 1885-6, 1890-I, 191I-2, 192I-2, 1924-5, 1926-7, 193I-2, 1933-4.
MANCHESTER CUP 1894-5, 1905-6, 1908-9, 1920-I, 192I-2.
RICHARDSON CUP 1929-9, 1930-I.
WEST LANCASHIRE CUP 1930-I.

TELEGRAMS:"WANDERERS, BOLTON"
TELEPHONE: BOLTON 800.

SECRETARY MANAGER.
C. E. FOWERAKER.

GROUND & REGISTERED OFFICE:
BURNDEN PARK,
BOLTON.

August 26th 1941.

Dear Mr Howarth,

C. Chadwick   Middlesbrough.

W. H. Johnson.   Charlton Athletic,

Will you kindly note that we have now obtained both these Clubs permission for the above players to assist us during the coming Season.

Yours faithfully,

C. E. Foweraker

F. Howarth Esq,
" Football League "
30 Winckley Square,
Preston.

2 7 AUG 1941

A letter from Charles Foweraker to the Football League before the first game of the season.
Both Chadwick and Johnson regularly guested for the Wanderers

~ 52 ~

Whilst stationed in this country the Wanderers players were guesting for other clubs. Geldard with Charlton, Currier with Manchester City, Hanson, Howe, Sinclair, Hurst, Roberts and Goslin all with Norwich City, the latter also turning out for Chelsea. During October Goslin won a couple of International places for England although these are not recognised as they would have been in peacetime. He played in a 2-0 win over Scotland at Wembley and a 2-1 win over Wales at Birmingham.

The Wanderers life was not made any easier by other League clubs unwilling to reciprocate in the loaning of guest players. Preston were asked permission for the loan of Wharton, a Bolton man, and Mansley for a game at Chester. Permission was refused despite the fact that North End did not require the services of the players themselves. Norwich City of all clubs - did they not have the services of a number of Bolton players - failed to reply to a request to play an RAF man stationed locally.

Other problems were those of guest players actually being given leave. For one game Johnson of Grimsby and Butler of Brentford were pencilled in but had to step down when they were ordered to change their RAF camps. A game scheduled to take place at Bradford City on March 25th had to be cancelled when only two players, Nat Lofthouse and Harry Hubbick, could be recruited with the release of guest players in the services unobtainable

Bolton got of to a reasonable start in the League with only one defeat in the opening six games. On the opening day at Bury a tremendous fight back saw the Wanderers draw 4-4 after being 3-1 down. A week later Bury visited Burnden and Lofthouse was left out of the team for the first time. George Hunt played at centre forward, to allow Harry Goslin, home on leave, his usual position. Goslin grabbed one of the goals in 2-1 win.

Five consecutive defeats left the Wanderers in a poor position, the last one of this spell being at Burnley where the team arrived in two trucks and a taxi after the coach had broken down. The first League competition ended on December 25th with the second commencing thereafter. This included the Football League War Cup qualifying competition played on a League basis to decide the 32 teams who would go into the knockout stages. Many of these games were cancelled through bad weather and so an average was calculated on 23 games. The Wanderers failed to qualify for the final stages of a competition that was eventually won by Wolves.

George Hunt, leading scorer with 20 goals, and Harry Hubbick were the backbone of the team throughout the season, missing only three games between them with a total of 62 players being called upon to play 33 games.

Season 1942/43
Results for the club were very poor with the opening eight games producing only one victory and seven defeats. The double was them completed over Burnley with the Wanderers having Preston winger Tom Finney as a guest at Turf Moor. This was the only occasion that the illustrious Finney guested for the club with both the Wanderers goals coming from Nat Lofthouse who a month earlier had signed professional forms. Another Preston player, Bill Shankly, who had promised to give the Wanderers the benefit of his services, was unfortunately transferred to Scotland with his unit. Whilst there he turned out for East Fife but wrote to manager Foweraker explaining his disappointment in his inability to become a wartime Wanderer. He stated that tears had almost come to his eyes when from the Northbound train he saw the deserted reaches of Burnden Park and thought of the scenes of the pre-war days.

Only three wins in the first League competition left the Wanderers placed 46th from 48 clubs with only Doncaster and Mansfield below them. There was a slight increase in the attendances with 8171 seeing the Boxing Day defeat by Manchester City. The second League competition of the season proved slightly more successful whilst the knockout stages of the War Cup weren't reached due to a poor goal average.

56 players were used throughout the season with only one ever-present, in Harry Hubbick who spent his time down the mines before turning out for the Wanderers. His team mates behind the lines were still involved in playing football despite the war activity. The Bolton boys faced some stiff competition on improvised pitches where, what was lacking in facilities was more than made up for by the partisan enthusiasm of their crowds.

In Egypt the Wanderers of the 53rd RA were out of practise when they went down 5-0 to an all star King Farouk XI in the desert heat. Their pride was soon regained with a 2-0 win over the Nile Sailing Club of Cairo. The National Sporting Club were also defeated 2-1 at the Farouk Stadium in Gezira. Eight of the Wanderers team took part; Hanson, Thompson, Catterall, Goslin, Hurst, Forrest, Woodward and Howe, the last two named although not in the 53rd RA were stationed in the RAF close by.

The Wanderers of the 53rd RA had built up a reputation and in the spring of 1943 were challenged by the self-styled champions of Persia and Iraq 'a team of hard bitten poles'. The game took place at Kifri in Iraq and the 53rd RA were captained by Harry Goslin before an excited crowd of sport-starved soldiers. It must have been some spectacle to see a team of sweaty long shirted gunners running around in the desert heat, but they took the honours with a 4-1 win.

Season 1943/44

There was little improvement on the playing side as far as the Wanderers were concerned. Failure to qualify for the League competitions were again the consequences of being unable to field settled teams. The most impressive win of the season came at the end of October, when goals from Lofthouse and Currier gave the Wanderers a 2-1 win at Blackpool, inflicting the seasiders first home defeat since Christmas Day 1941.

Attendances again increased with 10,969 attending the Christmas Day defeat by Manchester United and another three gates of over ten thousand seeing two games with Blackpool and one against Liverpool. The latter was the second leg of the Lancashire Cup final, the Wanderers having defeated Manchester United, Bury and Stockport County in previous rounds over two legs. Liverpool proved too strong however and they took the trophy with a 6-3 aggregate win. During the season the club at last received the services of Scottish international Bill Shankly although only for two games. He made his Wanderers debut in a 4-2 defeat by Bury at Burnden but the following week scored for his side in a 3-0 win at Oldham.

Football became secondary when the news of the death of the club's captain Harry Goslin reached the town. Lieutenant Goslin was wounded in action whilst with the 8th Army Central Mediterranean Forces and died on December 18th. Goslin was a popular captain and exemplary athlete and it was he who had inspired the Wanderers staff to join the Territorial Army in the summer of 1939. He had since led a bunch of them in France, Africa and Italy, and had escaped from the beaches of Dunkirk in 1940. His influence was a loss not only to the football club but to King and Country.

Harry Hubbick and Ted Goodall prepare to do a shift down the mine before returning to Burnden to play on Saturday afternoon.

Season 1944/45

The 1944/45 season saw a number of changes at Burnden Park. During August, secretary/manager Charles Foweraker retired, handing the reins over to his assistant, former player Walter Rowley. Unfortunately during November the club learned of another fatality when Walter Sidebottom lost his life after his ship was torpedoed in the English Channel.

The first League competition placed the club in 9th position, the team suffering only three defeats, and this was more than satisfactory considering previous seasons performances. The team began to have a more settled look about them with eight players making thirty or more appearances during the term. With one eye on the return to the normal League programme the club commenced recruiting, signing goalkeeper Bill Fielding on a permanent basis from Cardiff City, where he had been the first choice prior to the outbreak of war.

Bolton made a poor start to the qualifying competition of the League North Cup with three defeats in the first four games. Five wins in the final six games however gave the club a place in the knockout stages for the first time since the competition had been structured on a League basis. 27 goals were scored in ten cup qualifying games, Lofthouse grabbing 14 of them, including four in a 6-1 home win over Tranmere. Qualification for the knockout stages saw a return to Burnden of larger crowds and the making of a profit for the club. A new War record attendance of 14214 attended the Wanderers 0-0 draw with Accrington Stanley in the first round first leg with West Brom outside left, Stan Butler, guesting for the Wanderers. A week later Peel Park recorded a then record crowd of 11721 for the second leg, Bolton winning handsomely 4-0.

Walter Sidebottom - an able seaman who lost his life. He made his League debut in February 1939.

The second round looked a much tougher proposition when Blackpool were drawn as opponents. They could boast a squad of twelve players, nine of whom were internationals. This didn't deter the Wanderers and they shocked their rivals with a 4-1 win at Bloomfield Road, Lofthouse scoring all four, a penalty from Farrow seven minutes from time being their only reply. Bolton went through on aggregate despite losing the second leg 2-1. The War crowd record was again broken when Newcastle United visited Burnden for the first leg of the third round, Bolton enjoying a 3-0 win to take to St James' Park for the second leg.

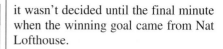

it wasn't decided until the final minute when the winning goal came from Nat Lofthouse.

The semi finals paired Bolton with Wolves, the games sandwiching VE Day. After a 2-2 draw at Molineux, Bolton won the second leg 2-1 with Willie Moir playing his first game at centre forward, in place of the injured Lofthouse, scoring one of the goals. Local neighbours Manchester United were the opponents for the final of the League North Cup. The first leg at Burnden was settled by a 50th minute goal from Lofthouse who bundled both the ball and 'keeper, Jack Crompton, into the net.

There were incredible scenes in the North East when Albert Stubbins scored three goals in eleven first half minutes to level the aggregate score. 38704 Geordies went into delight when Jackie Milburn put their side in front after 61 minutes but George Hunt levelled 15 minutes later. The game went into extra time and

The second leg took place at Maine Road, with Old Trafford being out of use due to bomb damage. A goal from Malcolm Barrass, his second of the game in the 90th minute earned Bolton a 2-2 draw and the Football League North War Cup, which was presented to captain Harry Hubbick.

(Above) The team show off the trophy through a crowded Town centre, (below) Harry Hubbick holds the trophy aloft.

On June 2nd the Wanderers visited Chelsea for the North v South Cup Winners Final. The proceeds went towards the King George Fund For Sailors, and despite coming from behind to win 2-1 the Bolton players received no medal but savings certificates instead!

The notes from the programme for the North Cup Final perhaps sum up best the feelings at the time. *"From this dark period we have emerged as a people and a nation, supreme in our steadfast courage and mighty deeds. Our football too, has passed through the valley of darkness. We have known the depths of despondency yet, we re-established ourselves with the advent of this programme in a better and brighter light."* The clubs best War season had been completed and augured well for normal resumption.

Season 1945/46

Football in general ran into a boom period after the hostilities and Bolton were no exception. But despite a successful season on the field, 1945/46 can only be remembered for the loss of 33 lives on March 9th 1946, when in an FA Cup 6th round second leg tie against Stoke City at Burnden, barriers collapsed causing not only death but injury to many. This particular incident is covered elsewhere in this book.

The League season opened with a 3-2 reverse at Everton, who included in their side Bolton born players Tommy Lawton and Norman Greenhalgh, along with ex-Wanderers youngster Stan Banham. Early season saw the club lose the services of Don Howe and Tom Sinclair when both were recalled for service abroad. Ray Westwood and Albert Geldard were still stationed in Italy the latter spending some time coaching.

After the opening day defeat seven games passed without loss until an unexpected reverse was incurred at bottom club Leeds who hit their winner two minutes from time to register their first win of the season. Revenge was swift however when a week later the Wanderers hit them for six without reply.

The first of the Wanderers professionals to be demobilised was George Taylor, during October 1945, he took up residence in his native Ashton-Under-Lyne, but played few games during the season after dislocating his shoulder against Manchester United. In the same month Mal Barrass was selected for England and Danny Winter for Wales in the victory international at West Brom.

George Hunt - a regular in the side during the War years in between his work in munitions.

Four consecutive defeats in November placed the Wanderers in a precarious position, but matters were improved when Hanson, Hurst, Westwood and Geldard were all demobbed. This allowed more normal preparations for League games for trainer Bob Young. After repeated requests, the club allowed Welsh international full back Danny Winter to join Chelsea, the side he had guested for during the War.

The return of the FA Cup stimulated a greater interest increasing crowds even further. The rounds were once again played over two legs to increase the clubs revenues which had been decimated during the War. The Wanderers entertained local rivals Blackburn Rovers in the third round, taking a single goal lead to Ewood for the second leg, thanks to a goal from Willie Moir four minutes from time on a glue pot pitch. Bolton took the second leg more comfortably by 3-1 before facing Liverpool in the next round.

They were sent packing with a 5-0 defeat, two Lofthouse goals being quickly followed up by an opportunist hat trick from Ray Westwood. The Wanderers lost the second leg 2-0 but the tie was academic. Westwood and Lofthouse were again the hero's in the fifth round when after a 1-0 win over Middlesbrough at Burnden the sides drew 1-1 at Ayresome, the crowd of 51612 paying record ground receipts at the time of £5708.

The game in the North East commenced a run of five consecutive away games for the club only one of which was lost. The last encounter of this sequence was the first leg of the 6th round of the FA Cup at Stoke City which resulted in favour of Bolton thanks to two Ray Westwood goals. The second leg ended scoreless to put the Wanderers into the semi-finals which was so overshadowed by events that victory couldn't be measured in terms of pleasure.

Unfortunately the Wanderers met their Waterloo in the semi final, when Charlton won 2-0 at Villa Park. League form however remained consistent and only one defeat, at home to Newcastle, in the final twelve League games was incurred.

A final position of third resulted, nine points behind champions Sheffield United, the best defensive record in the League with only 45 goals conceded, but with only 32 goals scored at home it gave the club a record that bettered only Chesterfield and Blackburn.

Season 1946/47

The Football League returned to normal with the fixtures originally scheduled for the 1939/40 season taking place. There were, however, a number of problems off the field that affected the club. Firstly the players union threatened to strike if the weekly wage was not increased and also a heavy financial burden was placed upon the club as a consequence of the disaster a few months earlier.

During August England drew 2-2 with Scotland at Maine Road in a game organised to raise money for the disaster fund. Towards the end of the season the Wanderers took part in a friendly at Hull where the home club donated £1,000 from the takings towards the fund. All in all this meant for the time being at least there would be no money to buy players.

The season opened with a 4-3 defeat at Chelsea which attracted the best crowd of the day 62850. After a mid-week win at Stoke, Portsmouth were the visitors to re-open League proceedings at Burnden.

A crowd of 33597, compared to 12992 in 1939, saw Willie Moir hit the winner two minutes from time after Lol Hamlett had earlier missed a penalty. Eight players remained in the side that had taken part in the last game before the War, five from the Wanderers and three from Pompey.

The first home defeat of the season came at the hands of Liverpool when their new signing, Albert Stubbins, a £12,500 buy from Newcastle, scored one of their goals. There was a swift recovery with a 4-0 win at Preston North End two days later, Stan Hanson saving a Bill Shankly penalty, but nine games without a win followed.

Goalkeeper Stan Hanson - ever present during 1946/47.

This run came to an end when Derby County were beaten 5-1 at Burnden, and November ended with a mid-table placing. Three of the top four teams in the First Division at this time were managed by former Wanderers players Joe Smith at Blackpool, David Jack at Middlesbrough and Ted Vizard at Wolves.

Towards the end of 1946 a number of injuries began to require changes in the side. Another reason for change was, in common with a number of other clubs, down to the fact that many players had lost their best footballing years because of the War. Goalkeeper Bill Fielding, who had just lost his place to Stan Hanson, went to Manchester United in exchange for winger Bill Wrigglesworth. Wrigglesworth had caught the eye of the Wanderers scoring one of United's goals in the final of the 1945 League North War Cup. After commencing the season in the right back berth, Dick Threlfall also left the club, to return to non-League football with Mossley.

The FA Cup provided little respite from a worsening League position. Third Division North side Stockport County were beaten 5-1 at Burnden in the third round and then the Wanderers entertained the Second Division leaders Manchester City. Bolton went two goals up inside nine minutes through Wrigglesworth and Lofthouse but City hit back in the second half with three goals in a thirteen minute spell. Mal Barrass equalised seven minutes from time to force a replay which City won 1-0.

The next home game, against Leeds United, attracted a crowd of only 4,280 which stood as a post-war low at Burnden until 1983. It was a dreadful end to the season with five consecutive defeats and a lone victory over already doomed Brentford, thanks to a Hamlett penalty goal, leaving the club in an unsavoury 18th position.

The Wanderers try out a new 'defensive formation' during training on Burnden Park.

Season 1947/48

The realities of League football struck home to the Wanderers when, after four games with only one goal scored, they found themselves rooted at the foot of the table.

New signings Walter Crook, a left back, from Blackburn and Harry McShane, an outside left, from Huddersfield made their Wanderers debuts in the opening defeat at home to Stoke.

The fifth game of the season brought the first victory, a 4-0 win over Portsmouth at Burnden, but this did not herald a revival with only two points being secured from the next seven games. After twelve games, in which twenty-three players had already been used, further changes in playing staff brought about the end of an era.

Ray Westwood, having been with the club for 18 years, played his final Wanderers League game in a defeat at Derby County. He signed for Chester on Boxing Day whilst another one of the clubs stalwarts of the war period, Harry Hubbick, was allowed to join Port Vale. Billy Wrigglesworth went to Southampton whilst in the opposite direction came John Bradley in exchange for £8,000.

The captaincy was handed to Walter Crook, Mat Gillies having been dropped, whilst Don Howe and Willie Moir were reinstated. The immediate effect was to record the second win of the season, when a Nat Lofthouse goal defeated third place Blackpool at Burnden, but the Wanderers were still firmly rooted at the foot of the table. Prospects hardly improved when five League games in December provided only a single win and four defeats and there was little relief in the arrival of the FA Cup, Tottenham winning a third round tie 2-0 after extra time at Burnden.

The turning point that was to eventually save the club from the threat of relegation came on January 24th when the Wanderers won 2-1 at Sunderland to register their first League win there for 36 years. The winning goal came four minutes from time when John Bradley hit only his second goal since signing for the club.

This prompted a run of ten wins, four of which were away from home, in thirteen games. By the end of March the Wanderers had climbed out of the bottom two and after defeating already doomed Grimsby Town by 2-0 at Burnden safety was assured. The highlight of this spell was undoubtedly a 2-0 victory over championship chasers Manchester United on Good Friday at Old Trafford before 72840. United eventually lost out on the title to Arsenal but they gained revenge over the Wanderers with a single goal win at Burnden on Easter Monday.

After fighting their way to safety the final three games failed to produce a goal in Bolton's favour but it did allow debuts to be given to local discoveries, Vince Dillon, John Smith and Tommy Banks. Tommy taking the place of his brother Ralph in the defeat at Wolves. Despite another disappointing season the term was completed by securing the Lancashire Cup when Southport were beaten 5-1 at Haig Avenue. Willie Moir hit a hat trick to help capture the Cup which didn't appear in the Wanderers trophy cabinet again until 1988.

Season 1948/49

A steady opening to the season increased confidence in the hope that the poor League form of the previous two years would not be repeated. The double over Aston Villa was completed during the first ten days of the new term with Willie Moir scoring all four goals in his side's 4-2 win at Villa Park. During this game Nat Lofthouse suffered an ankle injury and was unable to take his place again until Christmas. Both Moir and Barrass shared his centre forward duties with some success.

After learning of Lofthouse's indisposition the club spent £14,850 on inside right Jim Hernon of Leicester, he made his debut in a 1-0 win over Liverpool at Anfield, which placed the club in a mid-table position. Unfortunately the signing of Hernon proved to be unsuccessful and after nine appearances he lost his place until later in the season.

The previous season's champions Arsenal were beaten at Burnden, the winning goal coming from captain Don Howe, but then two heavy

Willie Moir - the First Divisions leading goalscorer in 1948/49.

defeats at Middles-brough, by 5-0 and at home to Newcastle by 5-1 prompted some team changes. Out went 'keeper Stan Hanson to be replaced by Reg Elvy, who had joined the club from Hal-ifax in March 1947, and he held the spot for the remainder of the season. Dan Murphy and Lol Ham-lett were brought back into the team and it was then the Wanderers turn to find the net regularly es-pecially at Burn-den.

Five goals against Manchester City and Preston, four in Sun-derland's net and six against Sheffield United all came in games at Burnden during November and December. Both Mal Barrass and Willie Moir each struck four goals in a game whilst Nat Loft-house celebrated his return from injury with two against Sunder-land. John Bradley also improved his poor scoring record with the club during this free scoring period, and his unselfish and highly discriminating football won him many admirers.

Field Marshall the Viscount Montgomery of Alamein is introduced to Jack Roberts prior to the Trotters 2-2 draw v. Newcastle United at Burnden in November 1949.

Tom Woodward signs for Middlesbrough in October 1949 watched by Walter Rowley and 'Boro Manager and ex-Wanderer David Jack.

Willie Moir is congratulated by Club Chairman Mr Duxbury on being selected for Scotland in April 1950. Walter Rowley looks on.

The club entered 1949 in 9th position in the League but the New Year proved to be disastrous. An early exit from the Cup at the hands of Aston Villa, after two re-plays, and scoring in only two of the first ten League games of the year ended any hopes of suc-cess.

The team was accused of giving tepid displays and lacking all the finer points and many of the best fundamen-tals of football. The management stated that *"an all out effort is required to recapture team balance, poise and accu-rate ball play that not only characterised early season displays but also won so many admir-ers."* A scent of relegation hovered over the club when Easter produced a single point, sur-prisingly from a 1-1 draw at championship chasers New-castle.

The final flurry of four points from the final three games was enough to lift the Wanderers into safety and a run of ten games with-out a win ended on the last day of the season when a Willie Moir goal was enough to beat Everton. Moir's 25 League goals gave him the distinction of becoming the First Di-vision's leading goalscorer.

Season 1949/50

The club again attempted to solve the problems in the full back position when £10,000 was spent on bringing Harry Kinsell from West Brom. Unfortunately he failed to live up to his early promise and after 17 appearances was dropped and later transferred to Reading. A 4-0 home win over Stoke opened the season but three consecutive defeats, including one at the re-opening of the repaired Old Trafford brought some swift action. Stan Hanson returned as custodian and produced a heroic performance on his home patch in a 1-1 draw at Liverpool. He caught the eye of the selectors and earned FA recognition by touring Canada at the end of the season along with Nat Lofthouse.

On October 13th Tom Woodward was sold to Middlesbrough for a £7,500 fee but wasn't away from Burnden long. Nine days later he returned to score for his new club against the Wanderers as the Teeside men won 2-1. November opened with the Wanderers in the bottom three and a visit from Field Marshall Viscount Montgomery of Alamein for the game with Newcastle United. The club, in the programme for the day, compared their current problems with ones that Montgomery had during the war and how success and ultimately goals could be achieved. To this end the club spent a record fee of £20,000 on signing winger Bobby Langton from Preston North End. He made his debut in a 3-0 home win over Manchester City which ended a run of eleven games without success.

There was a poor showing in the FA Cup, for after defeating Coventry City, the Wanderers went out to Leeds United on the snow and ice of Burnden in a fourth round replay.

Home results kept the Wanderers out of any real relegation threat during the second half of the season with only two defeats in nine games. Everton and Wolves were the successful sides at Burnden the latter winning 4-2 after the Wanderers had been two up. This game also produced the lowest Saturday gate of the season at Burnden of 13,380 (excluding season tickets) which was blamed on a live Cup Final broadcast. A defeat in the final game of the season, by 4-0 at Derby County, left the Wanderers without an away League victory for the first time in the club's history. But despite the poor League position both players and staff were recognised by their countries and Leagues.

Both Nat Lofthouse and Bobby Langton were selected for the Football League against the League of Ireland, whilst Lofthouse also appeared in an England B international against the Netherlands. Moir and Langton opposed one another at the Scotland v. England clash at Hampden, whilst at the season's end both Lofthouse and Hanson went on the FA tour of Canada. Trainer Bill Ridding went to Brazil with the England World Cup party as his country's chief trainer.

Season 1950/51

Despite a Nat Lofthouse hat trick the Wanderers went down 4-3 at Charlton Athletic on the opening day of the season. The main cause for concern in the early stages was the defensive problems with 19 goals being conceded in the opening five games including a 7-1 reverse at Wolves.

Full back Jack Roberts, who had started the season as captain, was allowed to join Swansea and his place went to John Ball who was recruited from Manchester United. Harry McShane went in the opposite direction to Old Trafford with United also adding £5,000 to the Burnden coffers. This was soon spent when left back George Kennedy was signed, ten days after the arrival of Ball, from Blackpool.

During September there was a dramatic improvement in results. The first away win in the League since November 1948 was recorded when Willie Moir scored the only goal of the game at Aston Villa. The defence was further strengthened when 20 years old Bryan Edwards was drafted into the team. The half back had joined the club as an unknown from a Leeds Junior club and had worked his passage through the 'A' and reserve sides.

On October 17th the directors received and accepted the resignation of Secretary-Manager Walter Rowley. It had been Rowley's 39th season at Burnden and it was ironic in the fact that the foundations had now been laid for the club to go on to greater things. Bill Ridding took over the appointment officially in February 1951 with the duties of chief coach going to George Taylor. His assistant was another ex-Wanderers player in George Hunt, who had retired to the coaching staff at Burnden after ending his playing days at Sheffield Wednesday in 1948.

November saw Nat Lofthouse recognised at full international level when he led England's forward line against Yugoslavia at Highbury. He fulfilled his promise scoring both goals in a 2-2 draw. Sharing the goalscoring duties in the first team with Lofthouse was Harry Webster who had also made his way through the clubs youth ranks and kept expensive signing Jim Hernon on the sidelines.

Seventh position at the turn of the year was a satisfying turnaround but problems in the defence were again looming. The successful partnership at full back of Ball and Kennedy was broken up when Kennedy tore his ligaments in a 2-1 win at Sunderland. He didn't play for the first team again and Banks, Howe and Murphy were all tried there with limited success. The loss of Kennedy was the club's second major injury of the season, Matt Gillies having his season written off with knee problems, his place going to the versatile Mal Barrass.

The FA Cup again brought hopes of success but these were dashed when Newcastle won a 4th round tie at St James' Park before 68659. There was some revenge for the Wanderers who again visited Newcastle in April and won a League encounter thanks to a Lofthouse goal.

Another Wanderer to win international recognition was Billy Hughes who had made his Northern Ireland debut in a game with Wales in Belfast, having won a regular first team place since McShane's departure.

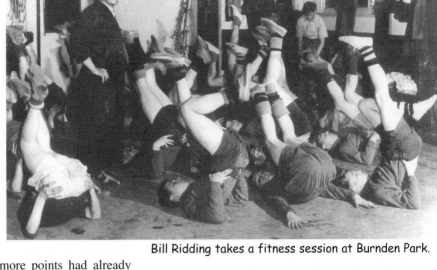

Bill Ridding takes a fitness session at Burnden Park.

With ten games remaining more points had already been accumulated than in any season since the resumption after the War, and if six defeats in those final games hadn't been incurred, there could have been a much higher finishing position than 8th. The last match of the season was a 4-0 defeat at Chelsea a result that kept the Londoners in the First Division on goal average.

Season 1951/52
The Wanderers sent their spending on full backs to nothing short of a small fortune when £10,000 was paid to bring George Higgins to Burnden Park from Blackburn Rovers. Higgins became the fifth big money full back signed by the club since the War and he replaced George Kennedy who had been lost the previous season through injury. The full back positions at last were settled with both Higgins and his partner John Ball missing only five games between them during the term.

Burnden's interior received modernisation during the close season with new baths and showers installed whilst in the stadium itself concrete trainers shelters were erected. A new club trainer was appointed in Bert Sproston allowing Bill Ridding more time on management duties. Sproston was a former England international full back who saw League services with Leeds, Tottenham and Manchester City.

Eleven points from the opening six games put the Wanderers on top of the League with a home victory over Manchester United attracting a post War record League crowd of 52239 along with another 3238 ticket holders. A settled team kept the momentum going with the only defeat during September coming at Spurs where the unfortunate Edwards put through his own goal.

The first significant change to the side came during October when Harry Webster was lost due to a cracked rib. In his place came Ray Parry, at 15 years 267 days old the club's youngest League player, although 111 days older than the youngest ever debutant, Albert Geldard then of Bradford. At the start of the season Parry had been in Bolton's fourth team and progressed swiftly through the ranks. Unfortunately, his debut was marred by the result, a 5-1 beating at Wolves.

There was a quick return to winning ways with a 2-1 success over Huddersfield a week later when the Wanderers were without both Mal Barrass and Nat Lofthouse who were on England Duty against Wales at Cardiff. During November and December the bubble appeared to have burst, with only three wins in eleven games, 1951 ending with the club in sixth position. A newcomer for the side was Doug Holden who had displaced Ron Codd on the left wing. Holden had originally signed for the club as a part time professional before completing his National Service.

Matt Gillies, unable to displace Mal Barrass in the centre half berth, left to join Leicester City, a club he later managed, for a £12,000 fee. That money was put towards a then Bolton record transfer of £27,000 spent on bringing England International Harold Hassall from Huddersfield Town, who made his debut in the first game of 1952, a 1-1 draw with Spurs at Burnden.

An early Cup exit at West Brom and successive home defeats by Burnley and Derby ended any faint championship hopes. Ambitions were now placed on a top four spot and the prize money that went with it. Despite winning four out of the five final games of the season the Wanderers missed out on 4th spot on goal average to Portsmouth but it was still the best post war year in terms of League performance.

For Nat Lofthouse the season was not yet over as he went with England on their European tour which kicked off with a 1-1 draw in Italy. The next game was against Austria in Vienna and this proved to be one of the classics with the home side laying claim to England's mantle of top European Country. With the game finely poised at 2-2 Tom Finney played the ball to Lofthouse in the middle of the field who then ran fully 50 yards with defenders in hot pursuit. The Wanderers centre forward shot and collided with the Austrian keeper unable to see the ball entering the net for what turned out to be his second goal of the game and the winner.

Ronnie Codd scores the Wanderers second goal in a 3-1 win at Chelsea in October 1951.

At the final whistle hundreds of British soldiers poured onto the pitch to cheer Lofthouse which earned him the tittle 'The Lion of Vienna'. Lofthouse grabbed another two goals in the final game of the tour, a 3-0 win over Switzerland.

Season 1952/53

After the previous season's dramatic improvement in League form, hopes were high that at last the championship could be coming to Burnden Park. Early season form pointed to the opposite scenario, and a relegation battle, when from the opening eight games only five points had been chalked up. One of the problems was a distinct lack of goals, only six being scored during this run.

A 5-0 home thrashing by Portsmouth appeared to spark something of a revival in the club's players although problems off the pitch remained. Both Bobby Langton and Harold Hassall were placed on the transfer list at their own request, the latter doing so on his wedding day, yet both were still at Burnden the following May. The tide turned with a 2-1 win at Middlesbrough, now managed by former Wanderers player and manager Walter Rowley, who had taken over from David Jack. Rowley at that time was, in fact, the only surviving life member of the Bolton Wanderers club, the honour being given to him upon his retirement from Burnden.

Only one defeat was suffered in the following eleven games, with Lofthouse regaining his goalscoring touch bagging six for the Football League against the League of Ireland at Wolverhampton. The improved run came to an end at Christmas with three consecutive defeats two of which were at home.

The Wanderers led a tremendous fight back in the 6-4 defeat by Arsenal on Christmas Day having been 6-2 down. Five minutes from time Bolton now on top and now only two in arrears, were awarded a penalty. Langton, who had been fouled, took the kick himself only to see Jack Kelsey save his effort, and that settled the issue.

The following game saw the introduction, at right back, of 21 year old Roy Hartle from Bromsgrove, in place of John Ball. The slump during Christmas didn't create any confidence for the Wanderers' patrons for a good Cup run, the team not having passed the fourth round since 1947. Fulham were accounted for in the third round, the game being played on a Wednesday afternoon, after fog had caused the postponement of Saturday's fixture. Second division Notts County provided stiff competition in the next round with the tie going to a second replay at Hillsborough before a Lofthouse goal settled the issue. Two away games in the fifth and sixth rounds at Luton Town and Gateshead respectively were each won by a single goal to put the Wanderers into the semi finals.

Average performances kept the clubs head above water in the League campaign with a 5-3 home win over Middlesbrough seeing the Wanderers field an all international forward line for the first time since the 1924/25 season: Hughes (Northern Ireland), Moir (Scotland), Lofthouse (England), Hassall (England) and Langton (England) were the five with only Hassall having failed to win a cap with Bolton, a fact which was rectified when he gained a further recognition in November 1953.

The FA Cup semi finals were remarkable in that all four clubs were captained by an international from the four home countries.

Bolton by Moir (Scotland), their opponents Everton by Farrell (Ireland), Blackpool by Johnson (England) and Tottenham by Burgess (Wales). 75,000 at Maine Road saw the all Lancashire semi final, the Wanderers stunning Everton and going into a four goal half time lead, the Toffeemen missing a penalty just before the break. It was Everton who produced the shock in the second half pulling three goals back but the Wanderers hung on to earn their first Wembley visit since 1929 where their opponents were to be Lancashire rivals Blackpool.

The 1953 final became legendary in the history of the FA Cup, as eventful as the 1929 final, and still today generally acknowledged to have been the most thrilling finish to any final in the annals of the FA Cup.

Cup finals are no place for sentiment and this was highlighted when John Ball regained his full back position a fortnight before the final at the expense of Roy Hartle who had played in every other Cup game.

Nat Lofthouse: Footballer of the Year 1953.

Ticket from the 1953 F.A. Cup 'Matthews' Final.
Eric Bell scores the Wanderers third, despite injury, in the final.

On the evening prior to the Cup Final Nat Lofthouse was awarded his footballer of the year trophy, having been leading scorer in the first division with 30 goals, eight of them coming in international matches.

He had also scored in every round of the FA Cup, a record he kept the following day, but after the Wanderers had led 3-1 with 20 minutes remaining, Blackpool hit back to take the trophy 4-3.

~ 63 ~

Season 1953/54

The Wanderers were without Nat Lofthouse for the opening six games of the season with the striker suffering a wrist injury in training. His replacement for the curtain-raiser was Ron Codd but he too got injured and Harry Webster, on leave from the RAF, took over with some success.

Only one defeat was suffered in the first seven games, this coming at Middlesbrough, where the Wanderers went two up in 29 minutes only to lose 3-2, with 'Boro gaining revenge for the same result inflicted on them a week earlier at Burnden. Harold Hassall came to the fore with a number of important goals netting five in his first six games. Three of these were penalties including an 89th minute winner at home to Sheffield Wednesday.

Hassall's penalty successes came to an end when he missed one in the 1-1 draw at Cardiff although he did score his team's goal. This match came in the middle of a run of three consecutive away games the other two being lost. At Preston, Willie Moir put the Wanderers in front in under half a minute but the game swung North End's way when Tommy Banks brought Tom Finney down to concede a penalty – North End eventually winning 3-1. Hassall missed this game, his place going to youngster Dennis Stevens from Dudley, who made his League debut.

Both Hassall and Lofthouse were selected for the Football League against the Irish League in Belfast which was won 5-0, all five goals going to the Wanderers pair – Lofthouse 3 Hassall 2. The pair were also selected for England against Wales but Hassall missed out on his first international, whilst a member of the Wanderers, due to injury. On the same day as the international the Wanderers entertained Manchester City. Webster replaced Lofthouse, whilst Terry Allcock made his League debut in place of Hassall, scoring twice in a 3-2 win.

November opened with a 6-1 home win over Portsmouth that saw the Wanderers climb into the top five. Hassall hitting a hat trick to celebrate his call up to the England squad for the game with Ireland at Goodison. On this occasion he was fit and scored twice in England's 3-1 win, Lofthouse making it a double by scoring the other goal. Injury hit Hassall at his most influential point in the Wanderers season, when during December he had to have a cartilage operation, his place in the side being shared between Parry and Stevens.

Towards the end of 1953 Ralph Banks left the club to join Aldershot, although he still trained at Burnden, and Bobby Langton was sold to Blackburn Rovers. Floodlight football was becoming more popular and the Wanderers were invited to Bury for a friendly under the Gigg Lane lights.

The result was a 2-2 draw but more interesting was the crowd of 20,622 which was attracted to the new conditions in which the game could be played.

The Wanderers opened the year seven points behind leaders Wolves and hopes were high that they could be caught and a good Cup run could be sustained. Bottom club Liverpool were beaten twice in the space of a week both in the League and Cup, and progress continued with a fourth round win at non-League Headington (later Oxford) United. A resounding 5-1 victory at fellow championship chasers Manchester United kept the Wanderers up with the pacemakers, the Busby Babes being humbled in the form of Burnden's own babes; 18 years old Ray Parry scoring twice as the Wanderers romped into a 4-0 half time lead.

Ticket from the Wanderers visit to Manchester United in January 1954. Bolton ran out 5-1 winners.

After climbing into third place by beating Cardiff 3-0 at Burnden the momentum was then lost with three consecutive League defeats. Harold Hassall returned after his operation but the muddy pitches didn't suit him whilst Johnny Wheeler missed the rest of the season with knee problems. His place went to another Wanderers debutant in Derek Hennin who had been secured from Prescot.

Cup progress was made at the expense of Portsmouth but an exit came in the sixth round when Sheffield Wednesday won a replay at Burnden. The Wanderers had ridden their luck in the first game at Hillsborough when with Wednesday winning 1-0, Willie Moir missed an 81st minute penalty, only to be awarded another a minute from time which he duly converted.

The chase for third place in the League was still on but it was eventually lost to Huddersfield Town when they defeated the Wanderers 2-1 in the final game of the season at Leeds Road – a result that pushed Bolton into fifth place.

Season 1954/55

The club squad was strengthened for the new season when Webster, Stevens and Edwards all finished their National Service whilst both Parry and Allcock, who were still in service, were stationed locally and would generally be available.

Three wins were secured from the first four games, the only defeat coming at Chelsea, where the *Sporting Life* said about Bolton's display: *"What a wonderful forward line Bolton have. Operating a combination of old and new styles which produce brilliant movements they threaten to sweep opponents out of the game. It was a treat to watch their display with the crossfield passing deadly. But underneath that brilliant football lies a shaky defence."*

Joint leaders of the League were played in consecutive weeks, drawing 1-1 with Manchester United at Burnden, both goals coming in the last six minutes, and then coming from behind to beat Wolves 2-1 at Molineux, to record the club's first post war win there.

Johnny Wheeler, back after his injury problem of the previous season, was recognised when he was selected for the Football League against the League of Ireland in Dublin. Injury however hit Doug Holden which allowed 16 year old Brian Birch in to make his debut against Aston Villa where the Wanderers came from 3-1 down to draw 3-3. After a 4-1 home win over Leicester, a game in which the woodwork was hit on no less than seven occasions, only one win was recorded in the following thirteen games, which sent the Wanderers hurtling down the League.

Five consecutive defeats around the Christmas period culminated in a 5-2 home reverse to Chelsea, but the game proved to be a disaster in more ways than one, for

Harold Hassall, playing at centre forward in place of the injured Lofthouse, tore his knee cap which, despite a comeback attempt, effectively ended his playing career.

FA Cup interest was short-lived, for after a third round win over Millwall, Birmingham City, thanks to a late winner and a Wheeler own goal, triumphed 2-1 at St Andrews in the next round. The first League win since November 20th was registered on February 5th, against most unlikely losers, League leaders Wolves. The result of 6-1 was particularly surprising to the footballing public. Ray Parry hitting his first League hat trick as the champions crumbled.

The League position was eased further with three consecutive home wins, but then the prophecies of the shaky defence came to light when the Wanderers netted twice in each of five games yet never earned both points. The second serious accident of the season occurred at Preston.

The Wanderers fought back from two down to draw 2-2 but this was overshadowed when Eric Bell suffered a broken leg. He had been selected by the FA for the close season tour to the West Indies and this was the last straw for the Wanderers in a most unfortunate season.

A point from a scoreless draw at Cup finalists Newcastle assured safety from relegation but the club's youngsters continued to make their mark by taking the Central League championship for the first time.

Season 1955/56

The club relied on home grown players to make the changes thought necessary to the side in the early part of the season. Lancashire cricketer Ken Grieves ousted Stan Hanson from the goalkeeping spot whilst Roy

Stan Hanson collects the ball during a 3-1 defeat at Arsenal on New Years Eve 1955. The Bolton defender is Tommy Banks.

Hartle made the right back position his own after replacing John Ball. Willie Moir lost his place after the opening two games and was subsequently sold to Stockport County. Ray Parry moved inside allowing Ralph Gubbins to become a regular in the number eleven shirt.

Inadequacies in defence were highlighted from time to time after three wins and two defeats in the opening games. The Wanderers led 3-0 with 13 minutes remaining at Portsmouth, only to surrender a point as the home side hit back. Harry Webster made his first appearance of the season in the absence of Lofthouse who was playing for England in Denmark. Webster scored one of the goals in a 2-1 win over Wolves but then suffered cartilage problems after being carried off in a floodlight game at Rhyl.

Nat Lofthouse continued to produce the goals, netting thirteen in the eight games prior to Christmas, which helped put the Wanderers in fifth position, three points behind leaders Manchester United, with two games in hand. Four consecutive defeats put a spanner in the works and FA Cup glory was all that could be hoped for. Huddersfield Town, who were at the foot of the First Division, visited Burnden in the third round with Nat Lofthouse captaining the club for the first time. The game was abandoned after 47 minutes due to fog with no goals having been recorded.

An end of an era was reached in this game when Stan Hanson made his last appearance for the club – the goalkeeping position being strong with the likes of Ken Grieves, Joe Dean, Eddie Hopkinson and Arthur Barnard all in reserve.

Huddersfield were beaten 3-0 when the game was replayed and confidence was high for the next round, after a 4-0 win over Portsmouth and a scoreless draw at Sunderland. Sheffield United were the visitors and they had problems as they were locked in a relegation battle, but they turned the tables to oust Bolton from the Cup.

The return to League football saw a debut given in goal to 16 years old Joe Dean, who, at the time was the youngest ever First Division keeper. He didn't finish the game having to leave the field for stitches. Nat Lofthouse took over between the sticks, as Wolves ran out 4-2 winners.

After two home wins in a week during March, against West Brom and Tottenham, the Wanderers climbed into third place although there was no realistic chance of the championship coming to Burnden, Manchester United having a twelve point lead. This was confirmed when the Wanderers went down 1-0 at Old Trafford and then, after drawing 0-0 at second placed Blackpool, the chase was on to equal the club's best finishing spot of third.

Once again the challenge in the final run-in faltered with Lancashire rivals, Blackpool and Burnley winning at Burnden over the Easter period. Two wins in the last four games were not enough and eighth place had to be settled for. A 5-2 defeat at Birmingham giving them revenge for the 6-0 defeat they had been given at Burnden, and relegated Huddersfield winning 3-1 at Leeds Road, to exact revenge for the Cup defeat.

Season 1956/57
The main talking point of the opening few weeks was the form of Nat Lofthouse. The Wanderers striker was in scintillating mood as he struck twelve goals in the opening nine games, failing to score in only one of these, a 3-0 reverse at Sunderland. He commenced with a hat trick in a 4-1 win over Blackpool at Burnden, a game which also gave Eddie Hopkinson his debut in goal, in what was to be the first of a record number of League appearances for the club.

John Ball returned to the side after a years absence, replacing the injured Tommy Banks, whilst John Higgins took the centre half berth from Mal Barrass. This prompted a move for the England international and Sheffield United paid £4,000 for his services at the end of September.

The flow of goals came to an abrupt end with the loss of an unbeaten home record, Wolves winning 3-0, and two visits to Birmingham, at City and Villa, ending scoreless. After this spell the net was found regularly for the remainder of the season, the team's problem lay in the number of goals conceded, only five clean sheets between the beginning of November and the end of the season.

Despite the loss of Lofthouse for a six game spell, due to a pulled muscle, his replacement Terry Allcock performed well, netting one of the goals in a 2-0 win over runaway League leaders Manchester United at Burnden. A prosperous Christmas was had with a double over Manchester City but a heavy defeat at Tottenham and a Cup defeat at home to Blackpool left the club once again chasing only a bonus place.

During February, Lofthouse the centre forward became Lofthouse the goalkeeper, curiously enough, again at Molineux. The Wanderers found themselves three goals down at the interval only to lose keeper Eddie Hopkinson after 65 minutes with a suspected broken finger. Lofthouse went into goal and despite being down to ten men the team produced a rally, only going down 3-2, and the stand-in keeper saving a penalty from Hooper.

In the same month Eric Bell returned to the side for his first League game for the club since April 1955. He stood in for Tommy Banks who had suffered a pulled muscle.

Home form remained consistent with only Preston winning at Burnden between the Cup exit and the end of the season. It was however a different story away from home with only one win in the same period, yet it was to say the least an unexpected win. The Wanderers visited Manchester United, who were League leaders, in what was the first game under the Old Trafford floodlights. The crowd of 61,100 were silenced as an own goal from Bill Foulkes and one from Ray Parry gave the Wanderers the double, and it is interesting to note that United only lost six games on their way to winning the championship.

The final six games of the season failed to produce a win, the team again sliding on the run in, but there was controversy brewing off the field when Nat Lofthouse became Licencee of the Castle Hotel, a move which was against club policy. During the 1920's Frank Roberts had been transferred for going against the club's wishes but on this occasion matters did not come to a head.

Season 1957/58

1957/58 heralded another new era at Burnden with the installation of floodlighting. They were officially opened on October 14th 1957 when the Wanderers entertained Heart of Midlothian before a crowd of 21,058 who witnessed a 1-1 draw. The cost of the lighting was put at £25,000 with the four pylons in each corner of the ground carrying 48 lights with an additional 170 lighting points provided in the stands, pay boxes, exit areas and car park. The lights which were switched on by club Chairman Harry Warburton, saw further renowned visitors when, during November, the Russian army side CDSA visited Burnden, the Wanderers winning 3-0 before a 34,139 crowd.

After a poor start in the League, including a 6-1 hammering at Wolves, which would later be revenged in the Cup, results steadily improved. Another Wanderer gained international recognition when Eddie Hopkinson won his first England cap against Wales at Cardiff. The 'keeper had a rapid rise to fame after only one full season in the seniors, which was the result of a number of outstanding displays. Ray Parry also impressed the selectors and he appeared for the England under 23 side.

The team again proved themselves not to be up to championship standard, a case of so near yet so far, when by the turn of the year they were in 9th position. The Cup had given the Wanderers a tough draw at third placed Preston but a second half goalrush, when the target was hit three times in 15 minutes, saw them through. It needed a replay to see off Third Division York City in the fourth round, and suddenly the Cup began to take precedence over the League.

Only one win in the first six games of 1958 was recorded, that being by 2-1 at Arsenal for the Wanderers first win there since 1929. A 7-2 defeat at Manchester United brought things back into prospective as they avenged a 4-0 defeat at Burnden from September. Stoke City were accounted for in the fifth round of the Cup but the draw was cruel handing out leaders Wolves to play at Burnden.

The sixth round tie became one of the most historic in Bolton's history, a titanic battle with neither side giving anything away, the home side being outplayed for long periods yet holding on to their 2-1 advantage in an epic struggle. Rarely had a defence seen as much luck as Eddie Hopkinson and his men kept Wolves down to a single goal, yet one of the stiffest obstacles any team could be asked to face on the Wembley trail had been overcome.

The semi final was contested with Second Division Blackburn Rovers before 74,000 at Maine Road. The Wanderers were without Nat Lofthouse but his stand in, Ralph Gubbins, became the hero as his goals in the 38th and 39th minutes saw Bolton through to Wembley with a 2-1 advantage. There was then a five week wait until the Final and although only one win was chalked up in the remaining eight League games there was never any real threat of relegation.

The backroom team in 1958. Bill Ridding, Bert Sproston, George Taylor and George Hunt.

For Roy Hartle the Final made up for the disappointment of missing the same in 1953, when he had been dropped after playing in all the rounds up to the big day. The Wanderers, a team that had cost nothing but signing on fees, took on a decimated Manchester United side that had a wave of sympathetic backing after the Munich Air disaster.

Nat Lofthouse hold the F.A. Cup aloft. Dennis Stevens stands alongside.

———————————

Nat Lofthouse became the Cup winner with both goals in a 2-0 win. The second of which, when he shoulder charged both United 'keeper Harry Gregg and the ball over the line, was still a talking point many years after the event.

Season 1958/59
Despite the Cup success, only 25922 were attracted to Burnden for the opening day win over Leeds United which was the second lowest attendance in the First Division. The fist six games saw an unchanged side produce some entertaining football to reach the top of the table. At Manchester City, the Wanderers fell two goals behind then fought back to take the lead only for City to make it 3-3 in the last minute. At Arsenal, who shared the leadership with the Wanderers, the Londoners hit six, a Ray Parry penalty being the only reply, but revenge was gained at Burnden a week later by a much closer margin of 2-1.

Injuries and international call-ups prompted a number of team changes with Fred Hill and Neville Bannister having a spell in place of the injured Brian Birch and Dennis Stevens. Left back Syd Farrimond made his debut in a scoreless draw at new League leaders Preston replacing Tommy Banks who was representing England against Ireland.

During October the Charity Shield was added to the Burnden trophy room with a 4-1 win over champions Wolves. Incredibly Lofthouse, who scored two goals,

had to have a stint in goal for the third occasion against Wolves when Joe Dean had to leave the field with a shoulder injury.

Lofthouse was also recalled to the England team for the first time in two seasons, scoring in the last minute of the game against the USSR to equal the English scoring record of 30 goals held by Tom Finney. Although Nat made one more appearance for his country, against Wales at Villa Park the following month, this was to be his last international goal.

Consecutive League defeats at Aston Villa, where Bolton born full back Stan Lynn hit their last minute winner, and at home to West Ham, dented the club's championship hopes.
However three consecutive wins reinstated Bolton as League leaders. Firstly, a 6-3 home win over Manchester United, in which many of the 33358 crowd were unable to see the traffic of goals due to fog, then a 2-1 win at second placed Wolves, despite falling behind, and finally a 2-1 home success over lowly Portsmouth did the trick.

There was a Christmas setback when Everton did the double, but the first hurdle in the defence of the FA Cup was completed with a 2-0 win at Scunthorpe United. The Wanderers were then handed a fourth round tie at Wolves and it seemed an exit was on the cards when Dennis Stevens had a recurrence of a groin strain early on and Derek Hennin put through his own goal. The tide turned in the second half and Ray Parry struck home a penalty before Nat Lofthouse hit the winner to send the favourites out of the competition for the

1958-59: Bolton's F.A. Cup hopes come to an end in a sixth round defeat at Nottingham Forest. Eddie Hopkinson, Tommy Banks, Graham Stanley and Roy Hartle can only watch Tommy Wilson score Forest's second.

second season in succession. Preston North End were faced in the next round, the clubs playing each other four times in the space of nine days, three of which were in the Cup. A Lofhouse goal in the second replay at Ewood Park settled the tie.

After a run of twelve consecutive FA Cup ties without defeat the Wanderers luck ran out at the thirteenth attempt when Nottingham Forest, the eventual winners, won a sixth round tie at the City Ground. The disappointment in the cup defeat was taken out on Chelsea in the next League game, the Londoners losing 6-0 at Burnden, Fred Hill hitting a hat trick.

The Wanderers now found themselves in fourth position, eight points behind leaders Wolves, with three games in hand. March however proved to be a lean month. The games in hand were swallowed up in defeats including one against relegation haunted Aston Villa at Burnden.

Despite a fighting finish which included only one defeat in the last six games, the Wanderers failed to equal their best ever position due to Arsenals better goal average. Eyes were cast back to the previous September and the six goal defeat at Highbury.

Season 1959/60

Problems hit the club before the start of the season with the loss of Nat Lofthouse who had been injured in a training incident. His centre forward position went to Ralph Gubbins, but he was dropped after two games and subsequently left to join Hull City. Fred Hill was also tried there, unsuccessfully, before Dennis Stevens settled into the role.

Only one win in the opening six games didn't augur well, more so considering the net was found in only two games, in the final analysis this was to cost the Wanderers dear. On the opening day Bolton romped into a two goal half time lead, only to lose 3-2, but things gradually improved during September when West Ham were beaten 5-1. One of the Wanderers goals came from Tommy Banks, his first for the club in over 200 appearances, whilst Ray Parry missed a penalty for the second game in succession.

Just when things started to look rosy an injury epidemic struck. Tommy Banks was hit by an ankle injury in a friendly at Hibernian, he then missed most of the season, Syd Farrimond acting as deputy. Bryan Edwards then broke a bone in training that put him out for the rest of the term. On a brighter note Ray Parry became the ninth Wanderer since the war to win an England cap when he played against Ireland at Wembley, and Nat Lofthouse made a comeback in the club's 'A' team scoring the winner against Blackburn Rovers.

Despite the injury setbacks results improved and during the Christmas period a double over Wolves was recorded. Bolton became the first club to win under the Molineux 'lights, and then the first win at Goodison for 39 years was recorded thanks to a Dennis Stevens goal. As the Wanderers prepared for their third round FA Cup tie with Bury at Gigg Lane, Nat Lofthouse announced his retirement from the game due to an ankle injury. It was premature as he attempted a comeback with a little success the following season.

The Cup tie attracted a record crowd at Bury of 35,000 and the Wanderers, who played in old gold shirts due to the clash, had to settle for a 1-1 draw. The replay proved to be tough and although Bury led with fifteen minutes remaining the Wanderers went through 4-2 after extra time. Interest in the Cup however, came to an end, when West Brom won 2-0 at the Hawthorns in the next round.

As if the club hadn't suffered enough with serious injuries, goalkeeper Eddie Hopkinson then fractured his shinbone in training, which ended his season prematurely. His replacement, Joe Dean, then dislocated his shoulder in a defeat at Sheffield Wednesday. Derek Hennin went into goal for the remainder of the game, the Wanderers also being handicapped following the sending off of John Higgins.

The Wanderers immediately went out and signed John Bollands from Sunderland he made his debut in a 2-1 home win over double-chasers Burnley, and kept his place for the remainder of the season. Fifth position in the League was reached before a halt in the form, when a 4-1 home defeat was inflicted by Newcastle.

The Wanderers are set to leave Burnden for the end of season tour to Germany, Belgium and Spain.

The following week, without the suspended Higgins, who was replaced by debutant and part time professional Dick Oxtoby, and the return of Graham Cunliffe, the Wanderers got back onto the rails with a 5-2 win at Birmingham.

The side now appeared to have a makeshift mixture of youth and experience, and a final run in of five wins and three defeats left the club in a final position of sixth, a mere seven points behind champions Burnley. It was a case of what might have been – what if the season had started with a more modest points return, but more importantly, what if the club hadn't lost four of its most influential players through serious injury.

Lofthouse's presence would surely not have left the Wanderers 'goals for' record better than only those of Nottingham Forrest and relegated Luton Town. Yet defensively only Tottenham had a better record.

Season 1960/61

The Wanderers commenced the season as they had the previous one with problems up front coupled with poor results. Nat Lofthouse, in his comeback attempt, was not yet fit whilst Dennis Stevens hadn't recovered from a cartilage operation. Ray Parry and Roy Hartle were used in the centre forward slot in the opening four games which produced only a point.

The cheque book was opened and £15,000 spent on bringing Irish International Bill McAdams from Manchester City to Burnden. He made his debut in the first win of the season scoring twice in a 4-1 defeat of Chelsea. This was swiftly followed by the first away victory at Blackpool, where a Fred Hill goal settled the issue in what was the first televised League game to be shown live.

Nat Lofthouse at this time was playing in the Central League side and had netted six goals in seven games, his goalscoring ability was urgently needed in the first team. He returned to the side for the first time since April 1959 for the visit of Manchester United. McAdams scored the Wanderers goal in a 1-1 draw but Roy Hartle, taking his third penalty in as many games, missed as he had done in a 4-3 defeat by Everton a fortnight earlier.

Pre-season 1960/61 and Bert Sproston prepares. From the left Billy McAdams, Ray Parry and Ralph Gubbins. Nat Lofthouse is in the background.

Lofthouse got back on the goal trail with the winner at Cardiff, a game in which Warwick Rimmer made his debut, and in his first League Cup tie Lofty hit a hat trick in a 6-2 win over Grimsby.

The Wanderers had a measured success in the inaugural season of the Football League Cup having already accounted for Hull City. Their visit to Darlington attracted a record crowd of 21,023 to Feethams, the Wanderers winning 2-1, but a fourth round home defeat by Rotherham ended any hopes of glory.

The club's youth policy was now beginning to show the promise of years of hard work with the debuts of Rimmer, Charlie Cooper and 16 years old Francis Lee. The youngster made his debut in a 3-1 win over Manchester City at Burnden, scoring one of the goals, his mentor Lofthouse also hitting the net. December commenced with the club in 21st position with fellow Lancashire clubs Blackpool, who had spent £25,000 on taking Ray Parry from Burnden, and Preston North End also struggling. On December 17th a further hammer blow hit the club when during a 2-2 draw with Birmingham at St Andrews, Lofhouse received a leg injury that finally ended his illustrious career.

A turning point in League fortunes came on the last day of the year, when, against West Ham at Burnden, the Wanderers found themselves trailing to the slick Londoners. Dennis Stevens, now leading the attack, netted a soft goal and the Wanderers went on to win 3-1. There followed only three defeats in the next twelve League games, not a brilliant run, but enough to keep the club away from the jaws of relegation. After defeating Hull City for the second time in the season's F.A. Cup competition Blackburn Rovers ended the Wanderers hopes with a 4-0 replay win. The club made another hefty signing during March when Brian Pilkington was secured from Burnley. The English international however, never reached the form that had distinguished him with the east Lancashire club. The same could not be said about the other signing, McAdams, for he had given the Wanderers value for money, netting 18 goals in his 27 games with only Dennis Stevens matching him in reaching double figures. Once again the problem was clear to see with only relegated Preston scoring less than the Wanderers.

Season 1961/62

Although only one point was secured from the opening three games, the goalscoring problem of the previous three years seemed to have been rectified. Hill, Stevens, and McAdams took the main responsibility and this helped pull the team together and enabled them to climb into the top half of the First Division.

Consecutive home wins over Sheffield Wednesday and Arsenal lifted the early season anxiety. Against the Gunners, McAdams came up against fellow Irishman Terry Neill, but the Wanderer took the honours by scoring twice to cancel out a Mel Charles goal. The team then lost McAdams through injury, and Doug Holden with appendicitis, and went on to record only one win in six games. As a result they slipped into the bottom three and suffered a League Cup exit at Sunderland.

It was no coincidence that a recovery only commenced when both McAdams and Holden returned, a Dennis Stevens goal was enough to beat Wolves and, a week later, a 3-0 win over Manchester United at Old Trafford lifted the pressure. The Wanderers made a second visit to Old Trafford to face United in the third round of the F.A. Cup but went out by 2-1 with the winner being a hotly disputed effort from David Herd who appeared to be yards offside.

Despite the improvement in the goals for column it was all change for the club's forward line when, in the space of three months, both McAdams and Stevens were replaced. McAdams was sold to Leeds United for £12,000 having scored 26 goals in 44 League appearances in just over a year. In came Ron McGarry from Workington for a £10,000 fee but his stay at Burnden was to be even shorter. A record fee of £35,000 was received by the Wanderers from Everton for the services of Dennis Stevens and his subsequent success at Goodison included a League championship medal.

Within two days of Steven's departure 19 years old Wyn Davies was recruited from Wrexham for a fee of £20,000 with the Wanderers reserve striker Ernie Phythian going to the Racecourse

Ground as part of the deal. Another, perhaps inconspicuous, signing during the early part of 1962 was that of goalkeeper Alex Smith from Accrington Stanley. He remained with the Wanderers for six years as understudy to Eddie Hopkinson and only managed 19 League games before his transfer to Halifax Town.

During the transition of the forward line results were not consistent. Both McGarry and Davies opened their goalscoring accounts for the club in a 4-2 home success over Chelsea and a final run-in, when nine points were taken from the final five games, placed the club in a respectable mid-table position.

Season 1962/63.

The 1962/63 season proved to be another difficult one for the Wanderers in terms of hanging on to their First Division status. The season, however, became most remembered not for the football, but more for the lack of it, when the game virtually closed down between the middle of December and the beginning of March due to the bad weather.

After the first eight weeks the Wanderers were to be found in the lower reaches of the table but there were some signs of hope. The England selectors had seen fit to give Freddie Hill recognition for an international against Ireland and the goalscoring of youngster Francis Lee made headline news.

Lee eventually won a fairly regular place in the team after the departure of Doug Holden to Preston. Other Burnden departures prior to Christmas were Jack Threlfall to Bury and Ron McGarry who was sold to Newcastle United at a profit. After a 1-0 home win over championship chasers Tottenham on December 8th, Peter Deakin hitting an 88th minute winner, the Wanderers didn't kick a ball in anger again until February 16th.

The atrocious weather took it's toll on hundreds of games and Bolton's mid season break came to an end thanks to Arsenal's undersoil heating at Highbury where George Armstrong scored a last minute winner for the Londoners.

Roy Hartle clears off his own goal line at West Ham in December 1961.
The Hammers ran out 1-0 winners.

Three days earlier the Wanderers had travelled to Ireland just to get some match practice. Their opponents in Cork were Manchester United who won the friendly by 4-2.

The third round F.A. Cup tie against Sheffield United at Bramall Lane was played at the thirteenth attempt but there was no joy for Bolton who went down 3-1. There was immediate revenge however, for United then visited Burnden, in Bolton's first home League game for three month's. A Freddie Hill hat trick secured the points as the Wanderers fielded their youngest ever forward line. Lee (18), Hill (23), Davies (20), Bromley (16) and Butler (18) were the forwards with Brian Bromley making his League debut after only six Central League appearances. Other youngsters were blooded before the season's end with John Hulme, Dave Lennard, Gordon Taylor and Albert Goulden all being thrown in against the threat of relegation.

£20,000 was spent on bringing forward Billy Russell to Burnden from Sheffield United and he scored on his debut in a 3-0 home win over West Ham United.

'Keeper Eddie Hopkinson and Roy Hartle combine to keep Arsenal out at Highbury in February 1963. This was Bolton's first League game for over two months due to the big freeze. The Gunners won 3-2.

Panic began to emerge when only one point was taken from five games at the end of April. The Wanderers defended like trojans at League Champions Everton but went down to a 72nd minute goal from Roy Vernon. Safety was assured however with two home victories in the space of three days. Cup Finalists Leicester City were defeated 2-0 and then Liverpool went down to a single goal which was scored by Brian Pilkington.

It was obvious that the club's youngsters were not yet ready for First Division football yet the club were not attracting large enough gates to buy players that would help the cause.

The season wound up with the first team winning the Manchester Senior Cup for the last time when they defeated Fourth Division promotion winners Oldham Athletic at Boundary Park.

The programme for the F.A.Cup match that was finally played - at the 13th attempt!

Chapter 6 (1963 ~ 1978)
Fifteen Years Away from The Top

Season 1963/64

The club continued to be dogged with a relegation fight, and 1963/64 was to prove decisive in ending their First Division status.

Of the team that opened the season only Roy Hartle proved to be consistent, missing just one game. Farrimond, Edwards, Lee and Pilkington all lost form and were dropped, whilst Stanley and Russell sustained injury, Rimmer and Hill required cartilage operations. Davies was the luckiest, he lasted until the early part of 1964 before his season finished after a hernia operation.

Ball work on Bromwich Street training ground. Left to right: Nat Lofthouse, Francis Lee, Freddie Hill, George Taylor, Brian Bromley and Gordon Taylor.

Even the replacements were in the wars with Butler also having a cartilage operation and Birch dislocating his shoulder.

In an early season game at Arsenal, Bolton held a half time lead of 3-1 before the Londoners struck back to equalise. Brian Pilkington then missed a penalty, Arsenal scored a last minute winner and Eddie Hopkinson received a kidney injury that was to keep him out of action until the end of October.

Only four victories in the opening 26 League and Cup games came against just two teams. A League double was recorded over Ipswich Town, who were at the bottom of the League, and a surprising double over Sheffield United at Bramhall Lane. Firstly the Wanderers won a second round League Cup tie, only to lose in the next round at Stoke, and then won 1-0 in a League game against a side who were at the top of the division and had only lost once in their previous fifteen games.

Money was spent in an attempt to rectify matters, £15,000 going to Sunderland in exchange for winger Jimmy Davison. There was some joy for the centre forward Wyn Davies when he was selected for Wales to became the club's first player for thirty years to win full Welsh honours.

Bolton found themselves in a desperate position just before Christmas when their nearest rivals Birmingham City won 2-0 at Burnden to open up a seven point gap.

Blushes were saved in the FA Cup when Francis Lee hit home a penalty at Southern League Bath City after they had taken a 78th minute lead. The replay at Burnden was a more comfortable affair but eventual finalists Preston ended Bolton's interest in a fourth round replay.

After 34 games had been played the Wanderers still found themselves in 21st place four points behind Birmingham City. It was then that a tremendous last ditch attempt to stave off relegation was put together when ten points from a possible twelve were won. This incredible turnaround was enough to lift the club out of the bottom two. A defeat at Tottenham was a set back, but with each club having one game left to play Bolton's future was at least in their own hands. Ipswich were relegated, and the last place rested between the Wanderers on 28 points and Birmingham on 27.

The Wanderers final game was at home to an average Wolves side, the match taking place on a Friday evening so as not to clash with the local Holcombe Brook races. Just when it really mattered Bolton slumped, going down 4-0, and Birmingham took the initiative the following day in defeating Sheffield United at St Andrews to assure their safety and to end Bolton's run of 29 years in the top flight.

Season 1964/65.

For the first season out of the top sphere since 1935 the Wanderers had to rely on a young team built around the experience of Hopkinson, Hartle and Edwards. The only new signing was that of Barry Fry who had been given a free transfer by Manchester United.

Only one point from the opening three games was hardly form to inspire a quick return, but things improved, especially on the goalscoring front.

Despite a heavy defeat by Blackburn Rovers in the League Cup, four consecutive League wins in which the Wanderers grabbed nineteen goals put them in touch with the leaders. The away form was something of a problem, whilst at Burnden nine consecutive League wins were reeled off with no less

Eddie Hopkinson saves from Liverpool's Hunt, in the F.A. Cup 5th round in February 1965.

leaders Newcastle and Northampton, but with three games in hand. Bolton at this stage looked to be a good bet. For, despite having to win games in hand, they still had to play Newcastle twice. It was unfortunate that the Wanderers then ran into what was their worst spell of the season.

than thirty goals hitting the opponents net. All this after losing the first home game of the season to Coventry City.

Francis Lee was again capturing the headlines when, in fourteen games between September 12th and November 28th, he failed to score in only two, grabbing sixteen goals altogether. Bolton made it four wins from four games during November with a 4-2 success at Manchester City after romping into a four goal half time lead. Unfortunately the goalscoring potential appeared to suffer a relapse when, after two Saturday postponements, it took an 86th minute Freddie Hill goal to defeat lowly Huddersfield Town at Burnden. This victory was followed by a couple of scoreless draws one of which was against promotion rivals Northampton Town.

The settled side which showed only one change from early season, Farrimond in for Lennard, came into 1965 in fourth place, nicely poised providing injuries could be avoided. Workington were defeated in the third round of the F.A. Cup and then the Wanderers won at Deepdale in the next round to gain revenge for the previous season's Cup defeat. 57,207 were at Burnden for a fifth round tie against Liverpool, an 86th minute Ian Callaghan goal separating the sides, and the visitors went on to take the trophy.

The Wanderers returned to the League under pressure. A surprising home defeat by Bury and a crushing 4-0 reverse at rivals Northampton Town were to cost the club dearly. During March Wyn Davies chipped a bone in his foot, and Francis Lee went to centre forward scoring in each of the three games that Davies missed, which were all won.

Further home points were dropped with draws against Swindon Town and Charlton Athletic, but the Wanderers remained in fourth spot, six points behind

The final eight games produced only two victories and only six goals were scored, four coming in one game, which finally left the Wanderers six points adrift of runners up Northampton. It was a hard pill to swallow knowing that anything like the form shown earlier in the season in the final run-in would have assured a quick return to the top flight.

Season 1965/66
Expectations for the new season were high with the Wanderers team having a more or less as you were look about it. Bids from both Newcastle and Sunderland for Wyn Davies had been turned down and Francis Lee's transfer request had been resolved. The only major change was at centre half where Irishman John Napier replaced Bryan Edwards who had retired.

A new innovation for this season was that of a substitute who could be brought on at any time for an injured player. The first appearance of a 'sub' in League football was at Burnden Park when Charlton Athletic's Keith Peacock came on as the Wanderers won 4-2. Gordon Taylor was Bolton's first substitute to appear. He made an appearance in the club's eleventh game of the season, a 3-2 home defeat by Southampton. Both Bolton goals came from local youngster Roy Greaves who had made his debut the previous week at Leyton.

The Wanderers were among the early pacesetters, topping the division after five games, but they then lost their way with only one point being won from a possible fourteen during September and October. Improvement had to come and it did in the shape of home wins over joint League leaders Coventry City and Manchester City.

Any real ambitions of promotion were finally erased with four consecutive losses either side of Christmas. The F.A. Cup brought some respite as First Division

West Brom were beaten 3-0 at Burnden Park. The bottom fell out of the Wanderers season when they went out of the Cup at Preston whom they had been drawn against for three consecutive seasons.

Now hovering in the relegation zone, emergency action had to be taken to prevent any further slide. A bid for Bury's Colin Bell was turned down but then a run of only one defeat in a

Wyn Davies heads toward goal during the Wanderers 2-1 home defeat to Birmingham City in September 1965.

nine game spell had the desired effect. Roy Hartle was left out of the side after eleven years in the line up and he appeared for the last time in a 3-1 home defeat by Preston. Warwick Rimmer took over the captaincy and moved to full back to allow another local debutant, Harry Beech, in at left back.

A 6-0 home win over lowly Middlesbrough late in the season was hardly compensation to the Wanderers followers for what had been a poor season. For once, injuries could not be blamed with only Davies being out for any length of time. John Napier, in his first full League season, was called up by Northern Ireland, thus forcing him to miss his first League game of the season in the final week of the term.

Season 1966/67.

The squad was strengthened for the third consecutive term in the Second Division with the acquisition of the charismatic John Byrom from Blackburn Rovers for a £25,000 fee. Byrom missed the start of the season through injury as he became only the third player on the then current staff to have been purchased. The others being Wyn Davies and Alex Smith.

A Wyn Davies header was enough to win Bolton the points in the first game against Charlton Athletic. In the opening home game against Rotherham United, the referee lost control of the game with players scything each other at will, which resulted in the sending off of Syd Farrimond for dissent, the game ending in a 2-2 draw.

The return at Rotherham a week later saw John Byrom make his Bolton debut as a Gordon Taylor goal in the last minute brought the points back over the Pennines. A League Cup defeat at Manchester City was perhaps only significant for the fact that it was to be Martin Dobson's only appearance in a Bolton shirt. He was later given a free transfer and further in his career played for Burnley and Everton as well as becoming an England international.

After only one defeat in eleven games, a 5-2 win at Cardiff put the Wanderers ahead of the pack. Unfortunately it was to be a watershed with the attacking trio

Despite the club's fall in League stature, Burnden Park still remained high on the F.A.'s list of venues. This was borne out when the ground was awarded an F.A. Cup semi final between Manchester United and Everton, which kept Bolton on the football map.

John Byrom waits to pounce as Arsenal's 'keeper Jim Furnell collects the ball during a goalless fourth round F.A. Cup tie at Burnden in February 1967.

of Byrom, Davies and Lee, who had won all three games in which they had played together, about to be broken up. Davies, who had netted twelve goals in as many games, was sold to Newcastle United for £80,000. His parting shot was to score in his final game, a 2-1 defeat at Bury a game that burst the Wanderers bubble. Home form kept the club in touch but it needed a dramatic improvement to move on from what looked like a mid-table finish by the turn of the year.

A Francis Lee penalty gave the Wanderers a third round F.A. Cup win over Crewe Alexandra but Arsenal ended any hopes of glory in a replay at Highbury thanks to three second half goals from John Radford. The heading power of Davies was being sorely missed and during March Bob Hatton was signed from Wolves for £35,000 in an attempt to plug the gap. Unfortunately the signing wasn't a success, for he netted only twice in ten games, both in a 3-1 home win over Bury.

It was once again home grown players who were relied upon. Both Ronnie Phillips and Arthur Marsh came through the ranks to make their mark. The final two fixtures of the season perhaps summed up Wanderers season. Firstly they knocked up their best win before Burnden's lowest gate of the term, thrashing Millwall 5-0. A week later the table's were turned as the Wanderers were turned over 6-1 at Carlisle United. They proved that they could beat the best in the division but were also capable of falling to the strugglers. This was borne in the final record, which showed an even distribution of wins, draws and losses.

Season 1967/68.
The new season kicked off in precisely the same way as the previous one had ended with erratic results. A heavy opening day defeat, at Birmingham by 4-0, was quickly followed by a resounding 6-1 thrashing of Hull City at Burnden. This provided great entertainment for home supporters but the Wanderers needed to plug the gaps in defence especially away from home.

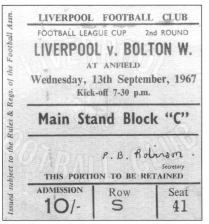

Steady progress was made with Francis Lee scoring in each of the opening seven games. The highlight was his goal against Liverpool at Anfield in the second round of the League Cup before a

Bolton won the replay 3-2.

crowd of 45,957 which, at the time, was a record for that ground in the competition. Peter Thompson hit Liverpool's equaliser ten minutes from time to bring a top First Division club to Burnden for the first time in the League Cup. The Wanderers caused a sensation when they won the replay 3-2 but this proved to be the last in a Bolton shirt for Lee.

After a number of transfer requests, Lee was allowed to join Manchester City for £60,000, the Wanderers, who had made plenty of noises about not wanting to sell their best players, could do little to dissuade Lee. Almost immediately, half back Gareth Williams was recruited from Cardiff City for a £50,000 fee and, a fortnight later £70,000 went to Wolves in exchange for Bolton born winger Terry Wharton.

The sale of Lee prompted the Wanderers to start the biggest spending spree in the club's history. In hindsight, although both players had some success, neither lived up to the fees paid in the long term. Interest in the League Cup ended in the third round with a 4-1 defeat at West Ham whilst League form was only adequate for another mid table position.

John Byrom improved his goal record for the club but an injury sustained at Portsmouth kept him out for two months and when he returned he couldn't recapture his earlier form. Dave Hatton was also absent for a long period after a shin-bone operation but when he returned he asked for a transfer and was later suspended for a fortnight by the club.

Nottingham Forest put the Wanderers out of the F.A. Cup competition at the third round stage with a 4-2 win on the City Ground. A return to League action brought rivals Blackburn Rovers to Burnden along with the best League gate of the season. Gareth Williams hit both Bolton goals in a 2-1 win, the referee, Mr Fussey, blowing for full time after only 85 minutes. His mistake was pointed out by a linesman and a further five minutes were played with Bolton holding on for victory.

Any outside chance of promotion disappeared during March with only one point from five games being secured and bottom club, Rotherham United, winning at Burnden. In the final fifteen games, only two of which were won, home gates plummeted to the six thousand mark. After suffering from such a long break out of the top League the club were now becoming isolated despite possessing a great tradition.

Season 1968/69.
Another difficult season was ahead for the club as a number of changes were made both on and off the field in an attempt to steady what had become a rocking ship. There was an early season change at the top when Nat Lofthouse took over as temporary manager from Bill

Chairman Harry Tyldesley congratulates Nat Lofthouse on his appointment as Manager in December 1968, with the players looking on

without anyone touching it. Eddie Hopkinson was booked for arguing the case and Gareth Williams received his marching orders.

The back room staff at the club was strengthened when Colin McDonald was recruited as Chief Scout and Jim Conway as assistant trainer. The latter coming from Portadown where he had been player-manager.

By the end of October the team were in mid table but changes were made for the visit to Crystal Palace. Both Williams and Gordon Taylor were dropped and in came Byrom, for his first appearance of the season, and 17 years old Paul Fletcher for his debut. The youngster netted his team's goal in a 2-1 defeat, but this game was to be the last appearance in a Bolton shirt for Brian Bromley. He joined Portsmouth for £25,000 to become the second departure with Bob Hatton having signed for Northampton Town.

Ridding who retired from management to concentrate on his work in physiotherapy. Another former player, Ted Rothwell, became Secretary.

The Burnden coffers were empty and so no new signings were made before the season commenced. The fixtures were, for the first time, worked out by computer and the Wanderers made a good start, taking eight points from the first six games, four of which were away from home.

19 year old John Ritson settled into the right back slot after he had made some steady performances towards the end of the previous season but there were no places for the experienced Warwick Rimmer and John Byrom in the early stages. The Wanderers crashed out of the League Cup for the second season in succession at West Ham United but it was a League defeat at Blackpool, in controversial circumstances, that turned the season into a downward spiral. The only goal of the game at Bloomfield Road was scored when, from an indirect free kick, the ball entered the net

After four months as caretaker manager Nat Lofthouse was officially appointed as team manager on December 18th having gone six games unbeaten since the reverse at Palace. His first game in full charge was a 2-1 home defeat by Cardiff City and it wasn't until March 15th that the next win in the League was recorded. There was little respite in the F.A. Cup, for, after defeating Northampton 2-1 thanks to an 83rd minute winner, Third Division Bristol Rovers then won by the same score at Burnden.

Injuries and suspensions began to take their toll and more teenagers were given their chance. Forward Garry Jones and full back Paul Hallows both made their bow but an attempt to sign experienced forward Frank Wignall from Derby County failed. There was success however in signing centre forward John Manning who joined for a £20,000 fee from Norwich City. He made his debut in a 3-2 home win over Fulham but the Burnden bogey struck again. Manning only managed one more game before a calf injury, his first injury of any sort for over three years, put him out for the rest of the season.

A run of four games in which nineteen goals were conceded all ended in heavy defeats, then a flu bug hit the club but the League refused to sanction any postponements. The last five games gave the Wanderers a chance to escape from the jaws of the Third Division with each one being against teams in and around the danger zone. Three home wins and two draws were enough to climb from danger but there could not be a continual Houdini act season after season.

Roy Greaves leaves the field after his hat-trick against Sheffield United at Burnden in August 1968.

Paul Fletcher in the thick of the action during a scoreless draw against Middlesbrough at Burnden in February 1969.

World Cup winner Roger Hunt comes out for his first home game for the club he supported as a boy. Watford ran out 2-1 winners in a F.A.Cup tie in January 1970.

Season 1969/70

A change in club colours was the most noticeable change for the supporters when the side appeared sporting an all white kit. On the playing front Irish international Charlie Hurley joined the club on a free transfer from Sunderland whilst Freddie Hill left the club to join Halifax Town.

Eddie Hopkinson began his fourteenth season as first choice goalkeeper and made his 500th League appearance in the opening day 4-1 win over Millwall at Burnden Park. John Byrom hit a hat trick against the Lions and repeated the feat four days later against Rochdale in a first round League Cup tie at Burnden. The visitors had held a 3-1 half time lead before the Wanderers hit back to win 6-3, but interest in the competition ended in the next round when Rotherham won through after a second replay at Millmoor. The club's disciplinary record was blemished when Roy Greaves was sent off in the League Cup replay at Rotherham. The club could ill afford any suspensions with both John Manning and Syd Farrimond out with long term injuries and the departure of another home grown player in Dave Hatton to Blackpool for £40,000.

The Wanderers slumped into the bottom four of the division and it was thanks to a tremendous last minute save by Eddie Hopkinson from Alan Woodward that a point was taken from a 0-0 home draw against Sheffield United on November 15th.

The game is now only significant for the fact that Hopkinson received a knock and it proved to be his last appearance for the club. He was later appointed assistant coach with Jim Conway being promoted to the position of Chief Coach.

Hopkinson's replacement was Alan Boswell who, three weeks earlier, had joined the club on a free transfer from Wolves. There was a continual search for players who would fit the bill with a bid for Blackburn's Eamon Rogers being turned down.

Bolton found themselves next to bottom of the Second Division at the end of November but there was still some will to win. After going three games without a goal, third placed Queens Park Rangers went ahead after just 45 seconds at Burnden, but the Wanderers hit back to win a thriller 6-4.

The club made a major coup during December when, for £32,000, Roger Hunt joined the Wanderers from Liverpool after initially turning down the offer. He made his debut in the first away win of the season, which came at Preston North End. Four League games had produced seven points and confidence was high for the visit of fellow Second Division strugglers Watford in the third round of the F.A. Cup. The attendance at Burnden jumped from 6,760, which had attended the previous League game, to 22,447.

The combination of Hunt's home debut and Cup football increasing interest. The result however was a let down with the Hornets, who were to reach the semi's, winning 2-1.

Despite the club's poor position, John Byrom hit his 16th goal of the season that earned a draw against League leaders Huddersfield Town, and Roger Hunt opened his account in a 2-1 home win over Middlesbrough that ended their run of seventeen games without defeat. A slump of four consecutive defeats followed and that put them back in trouble.

The Wanderers however surprised even their own followers with a 4-0 win at promotion chasing Queens Park Rangers during March. This proved to be a turning point to safety. Gareth Williams had been recalled to the side for his first game since November, in place of youngster Ian Seddon, and only one defeat was sustained in the final seven games with a clean sheet being kept in the last four.

Burnden Park was also honoured with the staging of the F.A. Cup semi final second replay between Leeds United and Manchester United.

Any lingering fears of relegation ended with Roger Hunt's 250th League goal that defeated Blackburn, whilst John Byrom struck his 25th of the season against Sheffield United. Youngsters Chris Duffey and Don McAllister were blooded in a more relaxed atmosphere in the final games but this was to be a lull before the storm.

Season 1970/71.
1970/71 season was to prove one of the most traumatic season's in the club's history both on and off the field, yet the first month gave little indication of what was to follow, which culminated in relegation to the Third Division for the first time.

After the opening five games, which had seen third position in the League reached, and a League Cup win over Blackburn, the tide turned. Leicester City ended all interest in the League Cup at Filbert Street, although the Wanderers didn't help themselves with Gordon Taylor failing to convert a penalty. Meanwhile the club's League form gradually got worse.

Jimmy McIlroy was appointed chief coach and aide to Nat Lofthouse and, on November 3rd, took over as team manager with Lofthouse taking over administrative duties. McIlroy's dilemma was whether to put out a young side and hope they could turn things around or rely on the more experienced members of the squad. His opening game in charge of the team ended in a 1-0 defeat by Norwich City and, a week later, the club fell into the bottom four after losing at Millwall.

Eighteen days after taking on the manager's job, McIlroy resigned and left the club, leaving Lofthouse again in charge of team affairs. He immediately brought back the old brigade, the only exception being Don McAllister, for the visit of Birmingham City. It produced the desired effect with Roger Hunt, who had been out in the wilderness for six weeks, hitting a hat trick as Bolton won 3-0 to record their sixth League win of the season.

Off the field, financial problems hung over the club. There had been a poor response to a share and loan notes issue and the Board of Directors had to give personal guarantees to keep the club afloat. Just before Christmas Gordon Taylor got his wish to leave the club when he joined Birmingham City for a fee of £18,000. Other players were offered in an attempt to raise money and both John Manning and John Byrom turned down moves.

The F.A. Cup proved to be a disaster with a 2-0 defeat at Third Division York City ending hopes of at least earning a pay day against a top club. The search for a team manager to assist Lofthouse continued and, on January 15th, after Wilf McGuiness had turned down the job, Jimmy Meadows, a Bolton born former England international, took over. The following day Bolton fielded their youngest ever side, which had been selected by Lofthouse, for the game against promotion chasing Sheffield United at Burnden. The average age was 20 years and included seven teenagers one of which, Paul Jones, was making his debut. John Tudor gave United the lead after only 95 seconds but the youngsters wouldn't lie down and they came back to win 2-1, which was to prove to be the last victory of the season.

At the end of January Terry Wharton was sold to Crystal Palace for £12,000 and the

Gordon Taylor puts Bolton ahead against Blackburn Rovers at Edwood Park in September 1970. The Wanderers went on to win 2-0 in what was the clubs only away success of the season.

following month the club's biggest asset, centre forward Paul Fletcher, joined Burnley for £60,000. There would be no money for replacements as this had to go on simply keeping the club alive. The scramble to avoid relegation became a four club race between the Wanderers, Blackburn Rovers, Bristol City and Charlton Athletic. Five consecutive defeats, including one at Birmingham where a young Trevor Francis scored all their four goals, left the Wanderers in a desperate position.

On April 6th Jimmy Meadows had had enough and he resigned leaving a bemused Lofthouse in charge once again. The final nail in the coffin came on April 17th when a further relegation, which had been brewing for a number of years, was finally confirmed after the team suffered a 4-1 defeat at Charlton Athletic. Despite what had happened, the best crowd of the season turned up at Burnden a month later for Eddie Hopkinson's testimonial, having attracted both Eusebio and Simoes from Benfica as star attractions.

On May 19th the managerial problems were finally sorted out when Jimmy Armfield was appointed manager. He had a monumental task before him to sort out players differences and get the club back on the rails in time for their first ever season in the Third Division.

Season 1971/72.

One of the first tasks to be performed by Jimmy Armfield was to revert the club's colours back to the traditional white shirts and navy blue shorts, for the first season outside the top two divisions. He then imported three capable campaigners from his old club, Blackpool. Grahame Rowe on a free transfer, and small fees for both Peter Nicholson and Henry Mowbray, brought some experience into the club. The close season dealings were finished when goalkeeper Charlie Wright arrived from Charlton on a free, Armfield fighting off hectic competition for his signature.

Charlie Hurley, Peter Clarke and John Manning all left the club, whilst early in the season £5,000 was accepted from local clubs Bury and Rochdale for Gareth Williams and Arthur Marsh respectively.

A confident start was made for, after two draws, a 2-1 win at Notts County gave the Wanderers their first League win since the previous January, and also ended the Meadow Lane club's 28 game unbeaten

home record. Two other club's who found themselves in a similar position to Bolton, Aston Villa and Blackburn Rovers, were both beaten to keep up their impressive Third Division opening. Meanwhile the team was initiating a League Cup run that would fill the club's coffers with the best Cup receipts for over ten years.

After something of a struggle to defeat Bradford City, a 2-0 win at First Division Huddersfield Town, in the second round, caused something of a stir. This was nothing compared to what happened in the next round when 42,039 at Burnden saw Manchester City thumped 3-0 thanks to a Garry Jones hat trick. City included in their side that evening former Wanderers players Francis Lee, Freddie Hill and Wyn Davies. The next round spelt elimination for, after a 1-1 draw at Chelsea, in which Bolton were unlucky not to win, the Londoners ran out 6-0 winners at Burnden.

Whilst prospering in the Cup, the League form declined with the major problem being a lack of goals. Roger Hunt lost his early season sparkle and was dropped, only to announce that he would retire at the end of the season. John Byrom was out for five weeks with injury which put more pressure on teenager Garry Jones who was unable to repeat the form that had toppled City. The Wanderers slumped to fifth from bottom and the enthusiasm of the Bolton public dropped to the extent that only 5,209 turned up for the visit of Brighton.

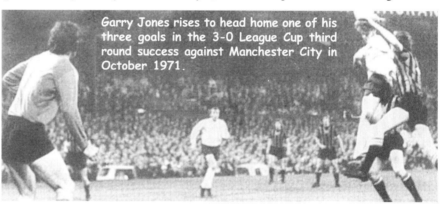

Garry Jones rises to head home one of his three goals in the 3-0 League Cup third round success against Manchester City in October 1971.

Roy Greaves waits to pounce in the snow during the 3-0 F.A. Cup first round win over Bangor City at Burnden the following month.

The club's disciplinary record also caught up with them. Too many bookings, along with suspensions for Warwick Rimmer and John Ritson, after being sent off, didn't help the team's consistency. Injuries also took their toll with the most serious being Paul Hallows who fractured his skull in the New Year's Day visit to York City.

The F.A. Cup provided another little earner. After defeating Bangor City in the first round the Wanderers faced Cheshire League champions Rossendale in a tie that was switched to Gigg Lane due to their opponents inadequate facilities. The minnows took a shock 16th minute lead, but a Roy Greaves hat trick put Bolton on the way to a 4-1 win, and, in the next round Torquay United were beaten at Burnden, before Chelsea again ended Cup ambitions with a 3-0 win at Stamford Bridge.

After defeating Torquay in the third round of the F.A. Cup the club was in a position where more Cup games than League games had been won. A Roger Hunt goal at Halifax ended a famine of ten League games without a win and then Plymouth were defeated at Burnden in which Stuart Lee, another Burnden youth product, made his debut. The youth team also had a measure of success in Cup football by reaching the quarter final of the F.A. Youth Cup. A crowd of 6,230, larger than for the previous first team game, saw them go down 1-0 to Arsenal at Burnden.

Attempts were made to strengthen the team, but Colin Dobson, Ray Treacy, Albert McCann and Peter Thompson all refused to step down into the Third Division. One player who did join the club was Ralph Wright who signed from Stockport County.

Only one defeat in the final eleven League games lifted the club into seventh spot but Armfield knew where the problems were. The defence had proved adequate, their record only being bettered by champions, Aston Villa and third placed Bournemouth, yet the goals for record had been poor.

Season 1972/73.
There was an early season bombshell when both full backs, Henry Mowbray and John Ritson, handed in transfer requests. Both were axed from the opening game which resulted in promotion favourites Bournemouth losing 3-0 at Burnden.

John Byrom leads out the team at Rochdale in October 1972. He scored one of the goals in a 2-2 draw.

Four wins and three defeats in the opening seven games eased the Wanderers into the top six, whilst there was to be no distraction in the League Cup after Sheffield Wednesday won a second round tie at Hillsborough, Roy Greaves missing a third minute penalty.

During September the Wanderers had to defend hard to earn draws at both Bristol Rovers and Hailfax Town whilst at home, opponents were difficult to break down. It needed a late penalty to break the deadlock against Tranmere whilst a twenty five yard winner in injury time from Alan Waldron was enough to defeat Chesterfield. Goalkeeper Charlie Wright missed his first game since joining the club during October owing to a rib injury. 18 Years old Barry Siddall came in to make his debut at League leaders Walsall. Bolton found themselves three down at half time but hit back to within one goal during the second period.

Gates at Burnden started to climb, going over 7,000 for the first time during the season against Scunthorpe, although receipts were some 40% down on the previous year. The top of the third division was reached for the first time after a 1-0 win at Chesterfield and the Wanderers remained there after a bizarre late winner against Rotherham at Burnden. The Yorkshire 'keeper, Jim McDonagh, later to star for the Wanderers, placed the ball for what he thought was a goal kick, the referee shouted play on and Garry Jones stepped up to put the ball into the empty net.

A good F.A. Cup run initially brought a few slip-ups in the League but by the end of January things started to look good with the club heading the division and into the fourth round of the F.A. Cup. Second Division Cardiff City were the visitors for a controversial and exciting tie. The Wanderers went 2-1 up in the 85th minute through a John Ritson goal and it appeared to be all over. Two minutes later Warwick Rimmer and Gil Reece were sent off and Cardiff hit an equaliser in the fifth minute of injury time.

The Wanderers eventually won through in a second replay at The Hawthorns before bowing out of the competition in the fifth round at home to Luton Town. A crowd of 39,556 attended the game, which ended a run of 26 games unbeaten at home, but a quick recovery was made with a home win over Walsall in the League.

Results continued to show promotion form until the delayed game with fellow promotion candidates Blackburn at Burnden. It was an intriguing game with the Wanderers, who had the best home record in the division, up against Rovers who had the best away record. As it was, a crowd of 33,010, the best in the League at Burnden since Division One days, witnessed a 78th minute winner from Derek Fazackerley to keep Rovers in the hunt.

There can be no doubt that the Wanderers missed their injured strike force of Garry Jones and John Byrom that night but they then unearthed another striker from the youth team for the visit to Swansea. 17 years old Neil Whatmore made his debut, scoring twice in a 3-2 win, all the Bolton goals coming in a five minute spell just before half time. After a 2-0 win at Shrewsbury the Wanderers held a five point lead at the top of the table and successive 3-0 home wins over Halifax, in which Stuart Lee grabbed a hat trick, and York, assured promotion.

The Third Division championship was presented to Warwick Rimmer after defeating already relegated Brentford at Burnden. The game turning out to be a curtain raiser to the celebrations. The club, which two years previous had been at its lowest ebb, had turned the tide. The youth policy, which had been the foundation stone of the promotion drive had succeeded without the need for big money signings along with some fast, entertaining and sometimes even spectacular football. Sixty one points was then a club record, whilst eighteen home wins and only nine goals conceded on home territory equalled previous club records.

Season 1973/74.

Rumours abounded that Jimmy Armfield would be moving from the manager's chair with both Everton and Sheffield United casting a roving eye. Other clubs were also keeping tabs on a number of the club's younger players which could potentially bring in half a million pounds but past mistakes of this nature were heeded. The only summer signings were those of Mike McBurney from Wrexham and the experienced Tony Dunne from Manchester United who both arrived on free transfers.

Three wins in the first four games placed Bolton joint top of the League which in reality was a false position. The honeymoon period ended with successive away defeats at Fulham and Carlisle. The third round of the League Cup was reached before losing in a replay at home to Millwall, whilst the squad was strengthened with the acquisition of forward Malcolm Darling from Rochdale for £16,000.

By the end of November things were starting to look bleak. After picking up only five points from a dozen games the club were now placed in the bottom three, this being the first season of three up and three down to settle promotion and relegation issues. Youngsters, Sam Allardyce and Peter Olinyk, were given their League debuts but Armfield made two significant moves to counter the worrying situation. Peter Thompson, the former England winger, was signed on loan from Liverpool and Neil Whatmore was reintroduced to first team football. No two players contributed more to the Wanderers climb away from danger.

Warwick Rimmer leads the team on a lap of honour with the Third Division Championship.

Thompson made his debut during the power strike at home to Sunderland when only 8,425, the lowest crowd of the season due to a midweek afternoon kick off, saw a Neil Whatmore goal defeat the Cup holders. Thompson's move was made permanent before the F.A. Cup began with the £18,000 fee being one of the best investments in a player ever made by the club.

Sixteen months earlier Thompson had been advised to give up the game through injury but he was to have an Indian Summer at Burnden in much the same way as Tony Dunne.

History was made on January 6th 1974 when the Wanderers entertained First Division Stoke City in the third round of the F.A. Cup on a Sunday. The club became one of the pioneers of Sunday football, the game attracting the best gate of the season, 39,138 witnessing a John Byrom hat trick which earned Bolton a 3-2 win.

A fortnight later the Wanderers attracted their best League gate of the season when 23,315 saw them come from behind to beat Bristol City again on a Sunday.

This win was followed by an exit from the Cup, but not before startling First Division Southampton. Trailing 3-1 to the Saints at The Dell, with only a few minutes remaining, the Wanderers stormed back to earn a replay. It took two goals in extra time from Southampton to end Bolton's interest in the replay, a mistake by 'keeper Barry Siddall, who had been selected as reserve for the England under 23 side, costing the game.

Only one defeat in nineteen League games put the club into the promotion frame but too many draws ended any real hopes. Despite this, promoted clubs Carlisle United and Luton Town were defeated at Burnden, whilst three points were taken in a week from the division's runaway champions Middlesbrough.

The last two games were something of a disappointment however. Relegated Preston becoming the first side to win a League game at Burnden since November, and an 86th minute Ken Knighton winner for Sheffield Wednesday at Hillsborough saving them from relegation. Consolidation had been earned however with 42 points from 42 games and 11th position being a satisfactory return to the higher level.

John Byrom completes his hat-trick in the 3-2 F.A. Cup win over Stoke City at Burnden in January 1974.

Season 1974/75.

After three seasons at the helm, Jimmy Armfield was finally tempted away from Burnden Park. It took some time, however for Armfield to put aside the club that gave him his first chance in management, but how many could have resisted the overtures of the League champions and European Cup contenders Leeds United? When he finally accepted the Yorkshire club's offer at the end of September Armfield had already created an obvious successor for the Burnden Board to consider.

Ian Greaves, manager of Huddersfield Town's Second Division championship winning side of 1970, linked up with Armfield in an assistant's capacity early in the season and his promotion to the manager's chair was rubber stamped within a matter of days.

The new boss brought in George Mulhall, former Halifax Town manager, and together the partnership brought Bolton steady improvement following an inconsistent start which threatened to deposit them among the sides battling against relegation.

Despite the arrival of experienced striker Hugh Curran, for £40,000 from Oxford United, results remained inconsistent. One week defeating high flying Aston Villa, then losing to lowly Sheffield Wednesday, both at Burnden. The situation was calmly dealt with. Youngsters Sam Allardyce, Peter Reid and Brian Smith all made their mark, but a run of four defeats just before Christmas left the Wanderers only three points clear of bottom club Sheffield Wednesday.

Paul Jones scores Bolton's second goal against Orient, October 1974, in Ian Greaves' first game in charge.

The following ten games produced only one defeat and included a 5-1 home win over Bristol Rovers, a pick up after an F.A. Cup defeat at West Brom, and a goalless draw at Aston Villa, four days after they had won the League Cup. Promotion had now become an outside possibility. Despite relative success to what had gone on in the early seventies the club still had a financial burden but this was eased when Don McAllister joined Tottenham for a fee of £80,000. His place in the team was taken by Sam Allardyce. Another player to part company was the experienced Warwick Rimmer. After fifteen years in League football he was given a free transfer and saw out his first class career with Crewe Alexandra.

Any promotion hopes ended when eventual champions Manchester United won 1-0 at Burnden before the best gate of the season. Only two wins in the final twelve games were recorded, both on away territory. One at West Brom avenged the earlier Cup exit, Peter Thompson scoring a rare goal to win the game, whilst the final outing of the season was a 2-1 win at Cardiff that sent the Welsh club into Division Three.

As in the previous season a point a game had been averaged and the team were now showing a neat blend of youth and experience that would send them on to greater things in the next few years.

Season 1975/76.
Despite the poor finish to the previous season the squad was not strengthened and things looked ominous after only one point was taken from the opening three games. The season then took off with a 2-1 win at York City which commenced a run of sixteen League games without defeat. The only reverse came in the League Cup when First Division Coventry City won a second round tie at Burnden.

The pattern of play had been switched to provide a patient build up, and a 5-0 home win over Charlton during October was to be the Wanderers best win of the season. After a 4-1 success against Portsmouth at Burnden at the beginning of November the club hit the top of the Second Division. The undefeated run which had seen the Wanderers climb from the bottom to the top of the table ended when West Brom won 2-1 at Burnden where Bryan Robson scored the winner. There was a quick return to

winning ways with successive wins in London over Chelsea and Fulham.

A defeat at Oldham Athletic on Boxing Day was the first on opponents territory since the first week of the season and the following day it was just like old times at Burnden when 42,680 saw the visit of League leaders Sunderland. The game was of the highest quality, the Roker side full of skill and character, had the Wanderers on the run for the first forty-five minutes. They should have had at least three goals to add to the messy affair that culminated in Tony Dunne firing a Tony Towers free kick into his own goal. No amount of defensive legislation in the world could have counteracted Sam Allardyce's brilliantly headed equaliser, and when John Byrom darted forward to nod in a second goal the contest was over; the Wanderers had proved they could beat the best.

The club went through January undefeated with F.A. Cup wins over Brentford and Huddersfield to boot and Ian Greaves collected the Second Division manager of the month award. A 1-0 win at Portsmouth on the first Saturday in February put Bolton back on top, but distraction was ahead in the form of a marathon 5th round Cup tie against League Cup finalists Newcastle United. Twice the Wanderers came from behind, to draw 3-3 at Burnden, and a goalless draw after extra time in the replay took a little more out of what was now becoming a drained team. The second replay at Leeds again attracted a crowd of over 40,000 but despite another exciting performance it was Newcastle who progressed through to the quarter-finals.

After a scrappy 1-0 home win over Hull City the following five games reaped only two points with home defeats at the hands of lowly Blackburn Rovers and Oxford United. 31 year old Willie Morgan, a former Scottish international winger, arrived on a free transfer from Burnley but he could do little to arrest the problem.

The Wanderers sudden stutter in their vociferous charge towards promotion continued even in victory. After failing to score in three successive games, two of which were at home, it needed two own goals to have the better of Chelsea at Burnden. Two goalless draws followed and the desperate search for goals and points had

Garry Jones finds the net during the 3-3 F.A. Cup 5th round draw at Burnden against Newcastle United.
The Magpies ran out winners in a second replay in February 1976.

reduced a once impressive side to mediocrity and near panic. A further disaster struck when already relegated York City won 2-1 at Burnden, Peter Nicholson scoring Bolton's goal two minutes from the end, to record their first goal from a Wanderer in 627 minutes of football. The club's fate still remained in its own hands as they were level on points, in third place, with West Brom, both having four games left to play.

A 4-1 success over Oldham raised confidence, but a 2-1 defeat at Sunderland, which won them the championship, left the Wanderers needing to win their final two games and hope that West Brom lost their final encounter at Oldham. Bolton went on to collect maximum points from their two games but, despite winning 4-0 at Charlton, it all meant nothing when the news came through that West Brom had won at Oldham to take the third promotion spot away from the Wanderers grasp.

Neil Whatmore (top) and Willie Morgan (below) score the goals that defeat Derby County at the Baseball Ground in the fifth round of the League Cup in December 1976.

Season 1976/77.

There was a danger that promotion could have been thought of as a divine right after going so close the previous term but early problems looked to have rocked the boat. Paul Jones asked for a transfer as he was looking for First Division football and John Byrom announced his retirement, although he had second thoughts and joined his former club Blackburn Rovers. The loss of Byrom caused something of a striker crisis with Hugh Curran out injured, 19 years old Steve Taylor grabbed his chance and became a regular goalscorer.

After losing on the opening day at Blackburn, five consecutive wins were recorded including a second round League Cup success at Bradford City. A fortnight travelling the length of the country didn't prove too successful. A League defeat at Chelsea was followed by a 2-2 draw at Fulham in the third round of the League Cup. A 1-1 draw at Plymouth, where both goals were scored by Argyle's Bolton born striker Paul Mariner, proved to be Barry Siddall's last game for the Wanderers. His transfer request was granted and he joined Sunderland in an £80,000 deal.

Jim McDonagh took over in goal, he had been signed from Rotherham United for a £15,000 fee after an initial loan period, and made his debut in a 1-0 defeat at Partick Thistle in the Anglo Scottish Cup. A disastrous 3-0 home defeat by Blackpool took place before a controversial League Cup replay with Fulham in which Mike Walsh made it 2-2 in the fifth minute of injury time. The referee blew for time three minutes later and was immediately surrounded by the Fulham players remonstrating at his time keeping. The outcome was that Bobby Moore was sent off and the Fulham players appeared to walk off in support. It need an ultimatum from the referee to get them to return for the extra time, which remained goalless, the Wanderers winning the second replay at St Andrews. Fulham were the visitors to Burnden in a League game which saw crowd segregation on the ground for the first time. Again the Wanderers ran out winners against Best, Marsh, Moore and Co by 2-1.

Results and the standard of football continued to be impressive with a run of twelve League and Cup games without defeat. The League Cup semi finals were reached for the first time after defeating First Division Derby County 2-1 at the Baseball Ground. The Wanderers had to fight their way back from conceding a Charlie George penalty and their battling qualities spilled over into the League when two goals in the last eight minutes gave them a point from a 3-3 draw at lowly Hereford United. League football took a back seat as the Wanderers played two Cup ties in a week. Firstly West Ham put any F.A. Cup hopes out of the players minds with a 2-1 third round win at Upton Park. The Wanderers then took on Everton at Goodison Park in the first leg of the League Cup semi final.

An 88th minute goal from Neil Whatmore gave Bolton a 1-1 draw and bookings for Wembley were already being made such was the confidence that the home leg would be a formality.

The club was hit with the news that Steve Taylor would be out of action for six weeks with cartilage problems. His replacement, Garry Jones, failed to keep up the scoring record that Taylor had set but even after returning to full fitness, Taylor struggled to regain his goal touch. Stage fright hit the Wanderers in the Cup second leg and it was Everton who made it to Wembley thanks to a goal from Bob Latchford. The crowd of 50,413 was the last over 50,000 to be seen at Burnden.

League form, as in previous years, then began to crumple. After taking a two goal lead at home to League leaders Chelsea, the Wanderers had to settle for a draw whilst clinging on to third place. A 1-0 defeat at promotion rivals Blackpool saw the debut of Ray Train who signed just before the transfer deadline for £35,000 from Sunderland.

One player that Bolton missed out on was Alan Hansen of Partick Thistle, the Scots club turning down a £75,000 offer.

The pressure again became too much with three defeats in four games. Relegation haunted Carlisle won 4-3 at Burnden and fellow challengers Nottingham Forest 3-1 at the City Ground. Eventually things began to settle with an unbeaten run of six games producing nine points.

The final third promotion place became a two horse race between the Wanderers and Nottingham Forest. Forest had completed their programme and Bolton required five points from three games to oust them. The first game produced what was required in the form of a 2-1 win over Cardiff.

But the dream was once again shattered when champions Wolves came to Burnden and won 1-0, leaving the final game, a 2-2 draw at Bristol Rovers, meaningless. The Wanderers had once again missed out by the slimmest of margins but they were looking to make it third time lucky the following term.

Season 1977/78.
After problems with crowd invasions Burnden Park greeted supporters for the new season with fences behind each of the goals. On the park, however, the Wanderers meant business. There was to be no slip up this time and they were quick off the mark, the first seven games producing six wins and a draw with only two goals conceded. Bolton went immediately to the top of the League and were in a class of their own in winning 2-0 at relegated Sunderland.

An inspired signing in the form of Frank Worthington was made, his debut, on loan from Leicester City, coming in a 1-1 draw with Stoke City in which he netted the Wanderers goal. His transfer was made permanent with £90,000 going to Leicester whilst £38,000 was recouped from the sale of Steve Taylor to Oldham Athletic, whose place in the team had been taken by Worthington. The strength of the squad was now greatly improved and this became obvious when a player of the calibre of Paul Jones was unable to get back into the team after injury. Even Peter Reid failed to return immediately after an F.A. ban for reaching twenty disciplinary points and he asked for a transfer. A fortnight later he had regained his place and he came off the list.

Burnden Park saw two crowds of over 30,000 in the space of four days. Firstly, for the visit of second placed Tottenham that was decided in Bolton's favour by an 89th minute Roy Greaves winner, to put them four points clear at the top. Then, for a fourth round League Cup defeat at the hands of Leeds United which brought Jimmy Armfield back to Bolton.

Christmas victories over Notts County and Blackpool kept the Wanderers marching along the promotion trail but New Year proved to be a disappointment with two defeats in three days. Millwall won 1-0 at The Den, a venue where the Wanderers never won, followed by a 2-1 home defeat by bottom club Burnley. This was enough to allow Tottenham to take over the leadership of the division.

It was ironic that the division's top two clubs should be drawn together in the third round of the F.A. Cup. A spectacular Glenn Hoddle goal in the 85th minute put Spurs 2-1 up at White Hart Lane and it seemed that a fierce and frantic Cup-tie had been settled. The celebrations were short-lived however as straight from the kick off Neil Whatmore hit home the equaliser. If either side feared that a Cup run would be an intrusion into any promotion ambitions they certainly didn't show it in the replay.

The Wanderers finally won a close encounter 2-1 with a superbly headed goal from substitute Garry Jones who converted John Ritson's cross fourteen minutes into extra time. This made it a personal triumph for both players who had seen little first team football during 1977 and Ritson had the additional glory of scoring the Wanderers first goal. The Cup win gave an immediate fillip to League form with a 5-1 win at Sheffield United, the first time that five goals had been scored away from home since March 1960, top spot also being regained from Spurs.

Mansfield Town were defeated in the fourth round of the F.A. Cup thanks to a Frank Worthington goal but Middlesbrough ended Bolton's interest in the next

The Wanderers show off the Second Division Championship trophy prior to Peter Thompson's testimonial in May 1978.

round at Ayresome Park. Now was the critical time, where, in the previous two years the club had slipped up. Only one defeat in the following eight games after the cup exit indicated the Wanderers had at last got it right and, just before the transfer deadline, a then club record fee of £120,000 was spent on signing Alan Gowling from Newcastle United.

Ray Train and Jim McDonagh show off their Second Division Championship medals.

But, on April 26th, three years of blood, sweat and tears came to fruition when a Frank Worthington goal won the Wanderers the two points needed to confirm promotion at Blackburn.

The fans used Ewood Park as the location for a late night party as the despair and disappointments of the previous two season's were washed away. Rarely could a single victory have released so much pent up emotion as Bolton returned to the top flight after fourteen long years. The final game proved to be an anti-climax with a 0-0 draw against Fulham at Burnden being enough to clinch the Second Division championship. At 4.45 the chant of 'champions' rolled around Burnden Park as the scene of players completing their lap of honour was in complete contrast to the previous season's final home game when promotion had slipped through their fingers.

Tottenham regained the leadership when they defeated the Wanderers 1-0 at White Hart Lane before 50,097, their winner coming from Bolton old boy Don McAllister, but two home wins recaptured top spot and, barring a complete collapse in the final three games, promotion would at last be confirmed.

True to form the Wanderers made their supporters sweat it out as they went down to a late goal at Cardiff City.

Chapter 7 (1978 ~ 1987)
A Gradual Slump.... To The Basement

Season 1978/79.

The face of Burnden Park changed for the club's first season back in the top flight with 4000 seats installed on the Great Lever End along with adjustable fencing on the Embankment to allow for easier segregation. The playing squad wasn't improved in the early weeks of the season, despite Peter Reid missing the opening two months after damaging his knee ligament in an Anglo Scottish Cup game against Sheffield United.

The team made an indifferent start. On the opening day Alan Gowling netted his first goal for the club to give the Wanderers a 32nd minute lead against Bristol City at Burnden. City hit back to win the game, but it was the Wanderers who twice came from behind to draw 2-2 at Southampton three days later to register their first point. The Wanderers were sunk 3-0 at League leaders Liverpool, where Jimmy Case struck a hat trick, and, after defeating Chelsea in the second round of the League Cup, Third Division Exeter City caused an upset by ending Bolton's interest in the competition at St James's Park.

Alan Gowling puts Bolton ahead at Chelsea in October 1978.

Home form improved but travelling proved to be unrewarding. At Chelsea, the Wanderers chalked up a 3-0 half time lead before the Londoners commenced a revival in the 76th minute before going on to win 4-3, their winner coming from an own goal by Sam Allardyce. £250,000, a then club record, was splashed out on bringing midfielder Neil McNab to Burnden from Tottenham whilst Ray Train left to join Watford in a £50,000 deal. Another departure from Burnden was that of George Mulhall who took over the reins at Bradford City, his replacement being former Middlesbrough manager Stan Anderson.

After taking only two points from eight games it appeared that a quick return to Division Two was on the cards. The first away win of the season heralded an improvement in results, a 3-1 success at Queens Park Rangers turning the tide, Frank Worthington netting twice, including one 'wonder' goal, to take over as the First Division's leading scorer.

December proved to be a productive month with only one defeat whilst the goalscoring twins of Worthington and Gowling kept up their act by demolishing Manchester United 3-0 at Burnden just before Christmas. The unluckiest player at Burnden during 1978 was undoubtedly Peter Reid. After recovering from his pre-season injury he again damaged ligaments in a collision with Everton 'keeper George Wood on New Years Day. The conditions were atrocious with heavy snow on the pitch and it came as no surprise when the game was abandoned at half time, but too late for Reid who missed the rest of the season.

Bad weather allowed only three games to go ahead during January and February. An F.A. Cup defeat at Bristol City was followed by a scoreless draw at Norwich City and a 2-1 home success over Chelsea where David Burke and Neil McNab scored their first goals for the club. A run of four consecutive away games produced only one point to keep the Wanderers in the relegation zone but then a run of seven games without defeat assured safety.

League Cup finalists Southampton were beaten 2-0 at Burnden thanks to two second half goals from Alan Gowling and, 48 hours later, F.A. Cup semi finalists Arsenal went down 4-2 with Gowling and Worthington hitting two apiece.

Gowling gave the Wanderers a surprise lead at League champions Nottingham Forest, who hadn't lost at home in the League for two years, their record remaining intact thanks only to a snatched equalizer from Trevor Francis in the dying minutes. Home wins over Queens Park Rangers and Everton were followed by a 2-1 success over Manchester United at Old Trafford, which made it eleven out of twelve points on the run.

For so long the Wanderers had been hawks at home and timid doves away, but once the job of preserving First Division status had been completed results waned with only a further three points being won.

The highlight during the final stages of the season was without doubt Frank Worthington's goal against Ipswich Town at Burnden that won him the goal of the season award. He also topped the division's scoring charts with 24 goals, whilst his partner Alan Gowling also finished in the top ten.

In preparation for the following season the Wanderers went behind the iron curtain to recruit new players and for £50,000 secured Polish international winger Tadeusz Nowak from Legia Warsaw.

Frank Worthington scores the winner at Manchester United in April 1979.

Season 1979/80.

The club's second season back in the top flight proved to be a disaster that had started with so much promise. Experienced campaigners were signed. Dave Clement, for £150,000 from Queens Park Rangers and Len Cantello for a then club record £350,000, from West Brom.

The first three League games produced a credible four points including a scoreless draw at Liverpool that had been earned with a dour defensive performance. The slump commenced when Third Division Southend United won the first leg of a second round League Cup tie at Burnden. The Wanderers then failed to win another League or Cup game during 1979, Southend completing the job in the second leg at Roots Hall, a scoreless draw resulting in which Neil Whatmore missed a penalty.

Hopes were raised for an improvement on the return of both Willie Morgan and Frank Worthington from their summer stints in the United States. Worthington, however, failed to find his previous form and left to join Second Division Birmingham City during October in a £150,000 deal. The club's big money buys failed to produce the form they had shown at their previous clubs and youngster's were given their chance. David Burke, Mike Graham, Mike Carter, Chris Thompson, Phil Wilson, Mick Bennett and David Hoggan were all products of the club's youth policy and all tasted First Division football.

The early part of 1980 saw hopes of a revival in fortunes when the Wanderers went to Second Division high flyers Sunderland and won a third round F.A.Cup tie. This game heralded the return of Peter Reid to the side after a twelve months absence through injury. A fourth round win over Halifax Town at Burnden earned the Wanderers a money-spinning tie at home to Arsenal, but it proved to be the end of the road for manager Ian Greaves. After the win over the Yorkshire side Greaves was sacked and Stan Anderson took over as caretaker boss. This game also proved to be the last in a Bolton shirt for Neil McNab who returned south with a £220,000 transfer to Brighton and Hove Albion.

After a 1-1 draw at Burnden, Arsenal ended Bolton's Cup hopes with a 3-0 win at Highbury. Stalwart Roy Greaves played his last game for the club in this game and joined Seattle Sounders in the North American League. Four days after the Cup defeat the Wanderers again visited Highbury, this time for a League encounter. Six players who had taken part in the Cup-tie were dropped and record signing Len Cantello was placed on the transfer list. The replacements put up a better showing, but still went down 2-0, to leave the Wanderers rooted at the foot of the table. The next match was another 2-0 defeat, this time at Manchester United, where Willie Morgan made his final Bolton appearance in a stadium where he had spent most of his illustrious career.

Len Cantello and Alan Gowling rush to congratulate Sam Allardyce after scoring against Leeds United at Burnden in September 1979. The game ended 1-1.

At the end of February Stan Anderson was appointed Manager with Tony Dunne taking over as coach. Both celebrated their initial game in charge as the Wanderers recorded their first League win for 24 games with a Neil Whatmore goal being enough to defeat Nottingham Forest at Burnden. This preceded the club's best run of the season with only two defeats in a seven game spell, although there was never any real chance of escaping the drop, and this was confirmed with five games remaining.

Peter Reid converts a penalty at Manchester City in a 2-2 draw in March 1980.

Within the space of eight days Burnden Park attracted its highest and lowest attendances of the season. 31,902 for the visit of Manchester United and only 8,995 seeing a 1-1 draw with Coventry City, this result being one of eleven home draws during the season which established a club record.

At the season's end more experienced players left the club. Sam Allardyce and Jim McDonagh departed, although both were later to return. The goalkeeping position had already been covered when, just before the transfer deadline, £70,000 was paid to Doncaster Rovers for Dennis Peacock.

Season 1980/81.
There was an international flavour to the club's pre-season games, for, after victories over Haarlem and Sparta Rotterdam in the Netherlands, Legia Warsaw paid a visit to Burnden and won 2-0.

The major signing prior to the new season was that of Brian Kidd who joined for a £150,000 fee from Everton. He made his League debut for the club in an opening day 2-1 defeat at Notts County and opened his goal account in the third game when he hit a hat trick in a 4-0 home win over Newcastle United.

Three days later he became the villain when he missed a penalty in a League Cup defeat by Crystal Palace as it became obvious that the Wanderers would struggle to win back their First Division place at the first attempt.

Other recruits were John Thomas, on a free transfer from Everton, and centre half Gerry McElhinney, who signed in a £25,000 deal from Distillery and was later to win international recognition for Northern Ireland whilst with the club.

Problems came to the fore when Swansea City came to Burnden and swept away the Wanderers with a 4-1 win. Big money signing Dave Clement and Polish import Tadeusz Nowak were dropped and didn't play for the club again. Goalkeeper Dennis Peacock was also dropped, which allowed Terry Poole to make his Bolton League debut three and a half years after signing for the Wanderers.

The club again went behind the iron curtain in search of players with £180,000 being spent on Dusan Nikolic from Red Star Belgrade. He made his debut in a 3-2 home defeat by Chelsea and in the following game he received an injury that was to keep him out for almost three months. The one consolation was that he had played his part in a 2-1 win at Shrewsbury Town that ended a run of 28 away League games without success.

Another plus was the return of Peter Reid, after sorting out his contractual difficulties, when moves to other clubs fell through. Brian Kidd recorded his second hat trick of the season in a 6-1 home win over Cambridge United. During December Mike Walsh ended a run of 126 consecutive League appearances when he was injured in a 3-1 win over Orient. His place went to Ian Brennan who had arrived from Burnley for £25,000.

Burnden attracted its two best gates of the season in the space of ten days. Unfortunately both games ended in defeat with Blackburn Rovers successful by 2-1 and Nottingham Forest, snatching a winner in extra time to win a third round F.A Cup replay, after a 3-3 draw at the City Ground.

The following months saw a pattern of winning at home and losing away but panic again set in when Shrewsbury won at Burnden during March. Changes were again drastic with home grown players David Burke and Mike Graham making their final appearances before being allowed to leave at the end of the season. In Burke's case he was to return for a happier spell in the early 1990's.

George Mulhall, former assistant to Ian Greaves in the promotion year of 1978, returned as coach and his influence had an immediate effect with a 2-1 win at fellow strugglers Preston North End. Results then picked up dramatically, only one defeat being sustained in the final eight games, but it wasn't until the penultimate match, a 2-2 Sunday morning draw at Orient, that the Wanderers were mathematically safe from relegation.

Manager Stan Anderson paid for a disastrous season with his job and George Mulhall took over as the club's financial problems began to take hold.

Season 1981/82.
An old face in the form of goalkeeper Jim McDonagh returned to Burnden in a deal that saw Mike Walsh go to Everton and £90,000 making it's way into the Wanderers coffers. Another departure was that of Neil Whatmore who joined his former team mate Frank Worthington at First Division Birmingham City in a deal worth £340,000 which made him the club's record sale.

It was a terrible start to the campaign with an early exit from the League Cup and the first four League games all ending in defeat. £120,000 of the cash received for Whatmore was spent on Tony Henry from Manchester City and Trevor Hebbard was taken on loan from Southampton. There was an immediate response with a 2-0 win at Derby County in which the Wanderers turned out in a new away kit of all green for the first time. It obviously suited Irishman Gerry McElhinney who scored his first goal for the club.

Three consecutive home games produced only one victory, John Thomas hitting the Wanderers 5000th League goal in a 2-1 defeat by Grimsby and £40,000 signing Jeff Chandler making his debut in a 3-0 reverse at the hands of Leicester City. November opened with the Wanderers recording their first win on a Saturday for eight months, by 2-0 over Watford at Burnden. But, a week later, a reverse by the same score was incurred at Shrewsbury, where Brian Kidd missed a penalty on what was to be his last appearance for the club.

Youngster Wayne Foster took over from Kidd but the majority of the goalscoring responsibility fell on the midfield with Tony Henry and Chris Thompson leading the way. The club's undersoil heating began to pay dividends during December and January with other teams idle. Five consecutive home games produced three wins and two draws.

Derby County were beaten in the third round of the F.A. Cup but the London jinx struck again when Crystal Palace won 1-0 at Selhurst Park at the next hurdle.

The experienced Mike Doyle was recruited from Stoke City in an attempt to bolster the defence but he had a nightmare start to his Bolton career. On his debut he conceded an own goal in a 1-1 draw at Oldham and, in his next game, was sent off at Newcastle. A disastrous League run culminated in a 7-1 defeat at Cup finalists Queens Park Rangers on their plastic pitch, a game which saw then record signing, Len Cantello, play his last game for the club.

The Wanderers then needed to win their final two games, both of which were at home, to stand any chance of survival and hope that Cardiff would slip up on the run in. It needed a goal in the final minute from Chris Thompson to give the Wanderers a 3-2 win in their penultimate game of the season against Derby County and to help keep hold of their hopes of safety.

The season ended with a visit from promotion chasing Sheffield Wednesday, but it was the Wanderers who showed the greater fighting spirit to win 3-1. One of the Wanderers goals in this game came from Alan Gowling who had reverted to his former role of striker having spent most of the season as a central defender. This proved to be his final game for the club but the issue of relegation wasn't settled until some weeks later when Cardiff finally ran out of games and slipped into Division Three.

Season 1982/83.
The close season saw another change in manager. After rumours that Pele was about to be interviewed for the job, the board invited former European Cup winner John McGovern to become the club's first player-manager. His first signing was the experienced Ian Moores from Orient. He was followed by Ray Deakin, from Port Vale, both players arriving on free transfers.

The first game of the season at Burnden also attracted what was to be the best gate of the season. Newcastle United, along with Kevin Keegan, were beaten 3-1 but five consecutive League defeats followed. The only respite during this spell was a 7-

Tony Henry scores against Watford in a 2-0 win at Burnden in November 1981.

3 aggregate Milk Cup win over Carlisle United. with Mike Doyle scoring the Wanderers 100th goal in the competition. First Division leaders Watford put the Wanderers out in the next round but not before extra time had been forced at Vicarage Road in the second leg, which saw John McGovern score what was to be his only goal for the club.

A run of eight League games without a win culminated in a humiliating 4-1 home defeat by Shrewsbury Town which attracted Bolton's lowest gate for 35 years. Six changes were made for the following game, a 0-0 draw at Derby, Steve Thompson making his debut.

Billy O'Rourke, Burnley's 'keeper is helpless to prevent Wanderers 'keeper Jim McDonagh scoring during a 3-0 win in January 1983.

Two consecutive home wins then lifted the Wanderers out of the bottom three. Mike Doyle scored his first League goal for the club in a 3-1 win against Leicester City whilst Peter Reid played his last game for the club in a 4-1 win over Charlton. Reid, after turning down a number of clubs in previous season's, joined Everton for a mere £60,000, some half a million pounds down on what could have been earned.

Six games without defeat over Christmas and early January improved the position but there was an early exit from the F.A. Cup when Arsenal won 2-1 at Highbury. The Wanderers goal came from Neil Whatmore, who had returned to the club on loan from Birmingham, whilst one of Bolton's goals in a 3-0 home win over Burnley came from goalkeeper Jim McDonagh from a long clearance.

The latter stages of the season were nothing short of disaster. Everything seemed rosy on March 12th when Tony Henry scored in what was his last appearance for Bolton before his £20,000 transfer to Oldham Athletic; such was the desperate need for cash to keep the club afloat.

In came Brian Borrows from Everton and Stuart Gray from Nottingham Forest, both on loan. Borrows later signed in a £6,000 deal to become one of the bargains of the season.

The final eleven games produced only a single victory, that by 2-0 over fellow strugglers Cambridge United, whilst only four goals were put into the opponents net in the same period. Youngsters Warren Joyce and Neil Redfearn, who had come through the youth ranks, were given their chance but little changed.

There was two encouraging results with scoreless draws at promotion chasing Leicester and Wolves, with Jim McDonagh saving a penalty at the former in his 400th League game. A home defeat by Chelsea, who were also in relegation trouble, left the Wanderers needing to win their last match to stay up. It became sudden death as the opponents were Charlton, at The Valley, who also needed victory to assure themselves of a Second Division place the following season.

The Wanderers supporters went wild when Ian Moores gave Bolton the lead early in the second half but this turned to disappointment as they slumped by 4-1, suffering relegation to the Third Division on the same ground, and by the same result, as they had done in 1971.

Season 1983/84.

The club began it's second stint in the Third Division without the services of some of the more experienced professionals who had left the club at the end of the previous season. Paul Jones, Jim McDonagh, Ian Moores, Mike Doyle and Steve Whitworth all departed leaving manager John McGovern with a young and inexperienced squad.

Jeff Chandler converts a penalty during the Wanderers 2-0 win over Wimbledon on the opening day of the 1983/84 season.

Arrivals during the summer were central defender Peter Valentine, a free transfer from Huddersfield Town, Eric Snookes, an experienced defender from Rochdale and forward Tony Caldwell, who was soon to hit the headlines, for a £2,000 fee from Horwich RMI.

Despite a 2-0 home win over Wimbledon on the opening day, which attracted the lowest League gate to Burnden at that time, and only 2,665 turned up for a first round first leg League Cup tie with Chester. Tony Caldwell registered his first goal for the club in this game as Bolton ran out 3-0 winners. Chester, however, won the second leg by the same score and went through on penalties after Bolton had missed four in succession.

In between these Cup ties, the Wanderers registered their best League win since 1934 when Walsall were thumped 8-1 at Burnden. Tony Caldwell grabbed five goals in this game to set a club record for the number of goals scored in a League match and, but for a last minute goal by Ally Robertson for Walsall, the record League win would have been equalled.

By early October the young Wanderers side were in sixth place and consistency was beginning to show when eleven games went without a team change. A 1-0 win at Wigan was recorded on Boxing Day before the home side's record League attendance and a day later League leaders Oxford United were beaten by an identical score at Burnden before the season's best League gate. Jeff Chandler scored the winner in each of these games.

Tony Caldwells five goals against Walsall in September 1983.

On New Years Eve, Sheffield United put five past the Wanderers without reply at Bramall Lane, Simon Farnworth saving a penalty for Bolton, then, Wimbledon, in their 300th League game won 4-0 at Plough Lane. In between, Sunderland ended the Wanderers F.A. Cup hopes with a 3-0 third round win at Burnden.

The pressure of slipping down the League was now beginning to take it's toll and Neil Redfearn was allowed to go out on loan to Lincoln City whom he was later to join on a permanent basis. John McGovern came back into the team for his first appearance in fourteen months. Unfortunately nothing changed as League leaders Walsall won 1-0 at Fellows Park with Tony Caldwell being sent off for fighting. The team appeared to get back onto the rails with the arrival of the experienced Graham Bell who came on a free transfer from Carlisle United. Neil Whatmore also returned to boost the fire power in a loan period from Oxford United.

Promotion remained a possibility during March but a 2-0 home defeat by Bradford City and a 2-2 draw at Burnley, in which a last minute goal was conceded, saw the club's fate take a change for the worse. The final nine games produced only two wins with the problem being a failure to score goals. Little could be done as the club could not find the money to secure Whatmore's return on a permanent basis and he returned to Oxford.

In the last home game of the season the team showed what they could achieve when Sheffield United, who were eventually promoted, were defeated 3-1 at Burnden.

Season 1984/85.
Money continued to be tight with the only new arrival at Burnden being Paul Lodge from Preston on a free transfer.

It wasn't until the sixth attempt that a League victory was posted, Tony Caldwell hitting a hat trick in a 7-2 thumping of Plymouth Argyle at Burnden, to lift the Wanderers off the bottom of division three.

There were some battling performances in the Milk Cup. Second Division Oldham were beaten 6-5 on aggregate in the first round, George Oghani scoring his first goals for the club, then Shrewsbury Town were ousted 4-3 on aggregate. At Gay Meadow, the Wanderers 'keeper, Simon Farnworth, saved a Ross MacLaren penalty to earn a 2-2 draw, and he repeated his penalty saving feats in the next two League games. Mark Came, who had been snapped up from Winsford United, made his first appearance in a Bolton shirt at Shrewsbury, coming on as a substitute for Jeff Chandler.

Jeff Chandler congratulates George Oghani on his hat-trick in a 4-0 Burnden win over Preston in October 1984.

Home form kept the Wanderers out of the bottom half of the League but away from home it was the worst start ever by the club. The poor travelling results included defeats at Notts County, by 6-1 in the third round of the Milk Cup, County being six up at half time with five goals being conceded in a five minute spell, and in the F.A. Cup at Hull, who won 2-1.

Once points started to slip away at Burnden the Wanderers started to drop down the League and by Christmas were in 18th place. Irish centre half Gerry McElhinney played his last game for the club in a 2-1 reverse at Bradford with Plymouth then paying £30,000 for his signature.

Manager John McGovern had lined up Peter Zelem from Chester as his replacement but he didn't get the chance to sign him as, after a goalless draw with Orient on New Years Day, he parted company with the club. Coach and former Wanderers 'keeper Charlie Wright took over as caretaker manager and the following four League games were all won, including a 2-1 success at Bristol Rovers that put the Wanderers first away points on the board for the season, Rovers having been previously unbeaten at home! It was inevitable that Wright would be appointed manager and his first game in full charge was a 2-0 defeat at Plymouth, where McElhinney made his home debut for the Devon side.

Nine games went by with only three goals being scored before the Wanderers put another win together. Tony Evans was taken on loan from Wolves and Ian Bailey, who had been with the club on loan two years previous, came on loan from Sheffield Wednesday. A 3-0 win at York City put the Wanderers back on the track with Jimmy Phillips scoring his first goal for the club. Only a single defeat came in the next seven games and that was a bizarre 4-3 reverse at Orient where the Wanderers had led 3-1 at half time after being a goal down. The London jinx was still in full force.

Promotion chasing Gillingham were stopped in their tracks when the Wanderers ran out 3-2 winners at The Priestfield Stadium, but the dose couldn't be repeated at another high flying club in Millwall, the Lions winning 5-2 after Bolton had led 2-1. The Wanderers gave a debut in this game to an unknown youngster, Paul Fitzpatrick, replacing the injured Brian Borrows whom, two months later joined First Division Coventry City for £80,000.

Interest in the Freight Rover Trophy ended in the Northern Semi Finals when Mansfield Town won at Burnden. The season ended with a win by 3-2 at Cambridge United where Roger Walker snatched a debut goal. This was, however, little comfort to add to the fact that the club had lost a record eighteen away League games and finished in it's lowest ever League position at the time.

Season 1985/86.
Burnden Park celebrated its 90th birthday by witnessing a 1-1 draw with Rotherham United in the opening game of the season. Tony Caldwell struck Bolton's goal which was the club's 250th in the Third Division. Experienced faces were added to the squad during the summer with Dave Sutton, David Cross, Asa Hartford, Derek Scott and the return of Sam Allardyce giving what appeared to be a steady base to build on.

Unfortunately League form proved to be erratic. Both Wolves and Plymouth were soundly beaten at Burnden but neighbours Bury gained an embarrassing 4-1 win.

A 2-0 defeat at Walsall was hardly surprising after the sending off of both George Oghani and David Cross in separate incidents whilst Nottingham Forest ended Milk Cup hopes with a 7-0 aggregate win.

Only one win in six League games during October sent the Wanderers into the relegation zone with a 1-0 defeat at League leaders Reading enabling them to equal a League record of eleven consecutive wins from the start of the season. £10,000 was spent on bringing forward Wayne Entwistle from Carlisle United but he struggled to find any form as things got worse both on and off the field. Only 2902 were at Burnden on bonfire night to see Darlington win 3-0 and this was followed by an early exit from the F.A. Cup at Wrexham in what was the Wanderers 300th game in the competition.

Action was taken in the form of a change of management, with Charlie Wright taking charge for the last time in a 2-0 defeat at Bristol City at the end of November, a game that saw Oghani sent off for a second time. Nat Lofthouse was put in temporary charge and he instilled some pride until the appointment of former Liverpool and England international full back Phil Neal on a player-manager basis. His first game was a 2-0 win over Doncaster Rovers at Burnden.

New Year found Bolton in 20th position, with Neal dropping himself in an attempt to view from the outside, as to what was going wrong. In the Freight Rover Trophy a 2-2 draw was earned at Stockport after being two down with three minutes remaining. A 1-0 win at Crewe put the Wanderers into the knockout stages of a competition that was to liven up the season.

A turning point in League form came at the end of February with the acquisition of goalkeeper Dave Felgate, and winger Stuart Ripley, both on loan. Felgate had come through the Wanderers youth ranks

whilst Ripley, who hadn't played a League game for his club Middlesbrough, set up a goal for Tony Caldwell after only 13 seconds of his debut and later scored himself in a 4-0 win over Newport County. A spirited revival then took place. League leaders Reading were beaten 2-0 at Burnden, only their third away defeat of the season, Tranmere were knocked out of the Freight Rover Trophy, and Cardiff were hit for five without reply with Phil Neal scoring his first goal for the club.

New signing Mark Gavin, a winger from Carlisle United, celebrated his debut by scoring in a 3-1 win at Wigan that ended their 33 home game unbeaten run. Although not mathematically safe from relegation attentions were turned towards the Freight Rover Trophy in the final weeks of the season. Darlington were beaten 3-0 at Feethams and then Wigan were accounted for in the two legged northern final to send the Wanderers to Wembley. All the frustrations of what had been another season of struggle were forgotten as the best crowd at Burnden since January 1983 saw the Wanderers, who had won 1-0 in the first leg, come from behind to win 2-1 on the night.

Other results assured Bolton's Third Division safety and the town came alive at the thought of a Wembley final, the club's first since the F.A. Cup success of 1958. There was sadness for on loan 'keeper Dave Felgate, whose loan period from Grimsby had expired, left Phil Neal with no other choice than to play out of favour Simon Farnworth in goal.

The opponents in the final were bogey side Bristol City who, a month earlier, had won 4-0 in a League game at Burnden. Although Tony Caldwell hit the bar early on in the game for the Wanderers it was Bristol who took the trophy with a 3-0 win.

Mark Gavin lets fly in the Freight Rover Trophy Final defeat by Bristol City.

Season 1986/87.

The Football League turned back the clock to introduce end of season play-off matches in a similar format to the old test matches that were part of the League in the 1890's.

Confidence at Burnden was high after the previous season's Wembley appearance but this proved to be a sense of false security. Goalkeeper Mike Salmon was signed from Stockport County but he struggled to be consistent whilst £25,000 was spent on forward Steve Elliott from Walsall. Despite his unselfish and workmanlike performances he couldn't live up to the scoring prowess that he had shown at his previous clubs.

It was a poor start to the season, Derek Scott suffering injury in the opening day home defeat by Swindon Town. Bury won a Littlewoods Cup tie by 2-1 on aggregate and then the Wanderers had both Steve Elliott and Mark Gavin sent off in a 2-1 defeat at Bournemouth. By the end of October the club was in the bottom four of the Third Division but November opened with the first success in London since 1978. A 2-1 victory at Brentford broke the bogey at the 32nd attempt to win in the capital. This was followed up with the first clean sheet away from home when a 0-0 draw resulted at League leaders Middlesbrough. Fellow strugglers Newport then highlighted the Wanderers failings by winning 1-0 at Burnden.

It needed a second replay to dispose of Halifax Town in the first round of the F.A. Cup, the Wanderers coming from behind to win away from home for the first time since April 1979. Tranmere were then accounted for in the second round, and Bolton then produced their best performance of the season in defeating League leaders Gillingham 3-0 at Burnden.

It looked as if the corner had been turned with nine League and Cup games without defeat, but all this changed after a 4-1 reverse at Bristol City where Steve Elliott had put Bolton in front with his 100th League goal. Eventual winners Coventry City put Bolton out of the F.A. Cup in the third round at Highfield Road and Chester City ended hopes of another trip to Wembley in the Freight Rover Trophy when they won 2-1 at Burnden, where Steve Thompson missed a last minute penalty.

A failure to score goals cost the Wanderers dearly with only seven going into the opponents net in the final seventeen League games, which left the team with no real chance of escaping from the bottom four. There was, however, a lifeline when the club finished in a play-off position. Aldershot proved to be too much of handful, winning 3-2 on aggregate, although it must be said that it was only in extra time, and after injury to goalkeeper Dave Felgate, that the Wanderers finally succumbed to relegation to Division Four for the first time in their history. Aldershot went on to win promotion after defeating Wolves in the play-off final.

The bright spots in the latter stages of the season were the discoveries of youngsters Nicky Brookman and Ian Stevens, although the club had failed to find a replacement at left back for Jimmy Phillips who had made a dream move to Glasgow Rangers. Dave Felgate eventually joined the club on a permanent basis during February whilst the other 'keepers, Mike Salmon and Simon Farnworth, joined Wrexham and Bury respectively.

The old regime went out with Hartford, Caldwell, Oghani and coach Colin Irwin all leaving Burnden whilst Phil Neal acted swiftly to bring in the new faces that would resurrect Bolton's flagging fortunes.

Steve Elliott scores the winner against Walsall at Burnden in March 1987.

Chapter 8 (1987 ~ 2002)
The Long Climb Up Again

Season 1987/88.

Phil Neal recruited five new faces for what was to be one of the most important seasons in the club's history. Old boy's, John Thomas (£30,000) and Jeff Chandler (£25,000), returned whilst the forward line was additionally strengthened by the arrival of Trevor Morgan, who had been a consistent goalscorer for his previous clubs, for a fee of £30,000. Gary Henshaw and Dean Crombie both came on a free from Grimsby Town whilst Mick Brown replaced Colin Irwin as first team coach. Outgoing was winger Mark Gavin who moved to Rochdale for £20,000.

Gary Henshaw opened the Wanderers account on his League debut for the club in a 1-1 home draw with Crewe Alexandra, but it was the long term loss of Jeff Chandler, injured in a Littlewoods Cup defeat by Wigan Athletic, that was the major concern. If there were thoughts of an easy passage out of the Fourth Division they were quickly dispelled with a 4-0 defeat at League new boys Scarborough. £30,000 was invested in Robbie Savage from Bradford City and he made his debut in a 2-0 home win over Halifax Town that lifted the Wanderers into second place in the table.

Robbie Savage grabs the goal that won promotion at Wrexham on the last day of the season.

Despite some poor performances, the results continued to be overall steady with only two defeats, both by the odd goal at Darlington and Burnley, being incurred during October and November. The defeat at Turf Moor was disappointing as a week earlier the Wanderers had won at the same venue in the first round of the F.A. Cup. John Thomas rounded off a run of scoring in six consecutive games by hitting two at Wrexham, which put the Wanderers into the third round of the F.A. Cup and, by the New Year, they were handily placed in fifth spot in the League.

January proved to be a bleak month with exits in the F.A. Cup at Barnsley, the Freight Rover Trophy at Bury but, more importantly, a 2-1 home defeat by fellow promotion challengers Torquay United. A 4-0 win at the end of the month over Peterborough United, at London Road, put the Wanderers back on the rails; Thomas grabbing a hat trick to become the first Wanderer since Francis Lee, back in February 1967, to hit three goals away from home in a League game.

A last minute goal at Crewe sent Bolton to defeat and, a week later, Wolves hit four without reply at Molineux, all their goals coming in the first half, to further increase the pressure. In hindsight the drubbing received there possibly instilled more spirit into the players, although Phil Neal continued to strengthen the squad for the run in. Winger Stuart Storer, who had arrived from Everton after an impressive loan period lost form, and Andy May came on loan from Huddersfield. Youngsters Paul Hughes, Ian Callaghan and Mark Winstanley all contributed towards what was to be an impressive final run in to the end of the season.

Neal had predicted the promotion issue would not be settled until the final day of the season and he was proved to be spot on, even after the Wanderers had lost just twice in the final thirteen games, both by 1-0 in South Wales, at Swansea and Cardiff. The last Saturday of the season arrived with most people expecting the Wanderers to end up in the play-offs. Wolves and Cardiff having already won promotion, the third spot was now between Torquay, Scunthorpe and the Wanderers.

Torquay, who for so long had looked favourites for the third automatic promotion spot had already blown one opportunity to secure promotion by losing at Burnley and they faced rivals Scunthorpe at Plainmoor needing just a point.

The Wanderers on the other hand had to win, and hope that Torquay lost, to snatch promotion. Although the Wanderers had already won at Wrexham in the F.A. Cup it was not going to be easy as the Welsh club had become one of the most improved sides in the League.

A goal from Robbie Savage, his third in as many games, settled the issue in Bolton's favour. After the tension of the second half, in which both John Thomas and Geoff Hunter had been sent off in separate incidents, it was party time when news came through that Scunthorpe had won 2-1 in Devon thus securing Bolton's climb out of the basement at the first attempt.

Season 1988/89.
A topsy-turvy season both on and off the field culminated with a club record unbeaten twenty game spell and success in the Sherpa Van Trophy final at Wembley. Strengthened in defence with the acquisition of full backs Phil Brown and Barry Cowdrill, the team made a steady start to the Third Division campaign. They climbed as high as third place after a 2-0 home success over Sheffield United on the opening day of October, only one defeat being suffered in the opening seven League games.

There was again a fleeting interest in the Littlewoods Cup in which an aggregate defeat by Chester was somewhat overshadowed when the Wanderers lost captain Mark Came with a broken leg. Despite playing some of their finest football of the season at Port Vale, the home side netted a winner in the seventh minute of injury time. From then on results were inconsistent.

Phil Brown and Steve Thompson with the Sherpa Van Trophy after the 4-1 success over Torquay United.

A 5-0 success over Chesterfield at Burnden was to be the best victory of the season but the same club proved to be a tough hurdle to overcome in the first round of the F.A. Cup. Bolton found themselves two down with 32 minutes remaining in a replay at Saltergate before striking three times to secure victory. Port Vale ended interest in the next round with a 2-1 win at Burnden.

Scoring goals became a problem with only one win in ten League games, which resulted in the club plummeting into the relegation zone. It was, however, in the Sherpa Van Trophy that some confidence was gained.

A last minute penalty secured success over Preston at Burnden and, despite defeat at Bury, the knockout stages were reached. Preston were again overcome, this time at Deepdale, whilst a spectacular long range goal from Mark Winstanley was the highlight of a 3-1 extra time win over Wrexham in February.

The same month saw the resignation of chairman Barry Chaytow after he had failed to gain enough support to oust Phil Neal from the manager's chair. The turnaround in results was nothing short of incredible, as, after a 1-0 defeat at Wolves in early March, defeat was a word that didn't exist in the Wanderers vocabulary for the remainder of the season. The character of the team was highlighted when the Wanderers fought back from three down at half time to earn a point at home to Notts County but it was success over both Crewe and Blackpool in the Sherpa Van Trophy that set the town buzzing with Wembley fever.

Defenders Winstanley and Brown got the goals in a 2-1 extra time win at Crewe and then, in the Northern Final, the Wanderers took a slender one goal lead thanks to a Julian Darby strike to Bloomfield Road for the second leg. The Seasiders levelled the scores but a Steve Thompson penalty in extra time earned a Wembley trip.

The Wanderers climbed into the top half of the League with consistency finally coming through. Brown, Darby, Felgate, Thompson and Winstanley missing only seven League games between them. Goalscoring form returned with fifteen goals coming in the final five games of the season and a 4-1 success against Torquay at Wembley after the Devon side had taken the lead.

Season 1989/90.
The Wanderers again kept their supporters on their toes until the final kick of the season, this time in an attempt to return to the Second Division for the first time since 1983. Early season form suggested that the Wanderers would be among the promotion contenders as the previous season's twenty game unbeaten run, which culminated in the Sherpa Van Trophy success, spilled over into 1989/90.

It was Rochdale who ended the club's undefeated run with a 2-1 win at Spotland in the Littlewood's Cup but Bolton bounced back in the second leg to win 6-3 on aggregate. A new club record of twenty League games without defeat was established after ending Bristol Rovers 100% record thanks to a David Reeves goal. Unfortunately, in the next game, defeat at Rotherham ended the run when a penalty miss by Steve Thompson allowed the home club to win by a single goal.

Tony Philliskirk turns away after scoring against Watford at Burnden in September 1989

After introducing both David Reeves (£80,000 from Sheffield Wednesday) and Tony Philliskirk (£50,000 from Preston), manager Phil Neal strengthened the squad further by paying £37,500 to Burnley for Paul Comstive. He quickly paid back some of that fee by scoring the goal at Watford that gave Bolton a 3-2 aggregate win over the Second Division club in the second round of the Littlewoods Cup.

Their reward in the third round was a visit to Swindon Town which proved to be a marathon tie. After twice leading the Wanderers found themselves 3-2 down with two minutes remaining. Substitute Mark Came struck an equaliser which set up two games at Burnden, both ending in draws after extra time, and produced the best gates since 1986. The tie was finally settled after seven and a half hours when Swindon scored in injury time at the County Ground in the third replay against a Wanderers line-up weakened through injury.

The Cup ties took their toll as in the same week Blackpool knocked the Wanderers out of the F.A. Cup and Birmingham City inflicted only the third League defeat of the season. By taking maximum points over Christmas and New Year, including success over promotion chasing rivals Bury and Tranmere, the Wanderers were handily placed in fifth spot. Once again the club put up a respectable performance in the Leyland DAF Cup but eventual winners Tranmere gained revenge for the League defeat by ending Bolton's interest in the semi finals.

Any hopes of automatic promotion soon disappeared and there was only one victory in the final eight League games of the season. That was a 1-0 home defeat of Bristol City, the goal coming from Scott Green who had been signed for a £50,000 fee from Derby County. A point from the final League game at Swansea confirmed the Wanderers participation in the play-offs but they went into those games a pale shadow of their form shown earlier in the season.

They came up against Notts County who had finished eighteen points in front of the Wanderers and the games went to form with County running out 3-1 winners on aggregate.

Season 1990/91.
For the second season in succession the Wanderers were to reach the end of season play-offs, only to miss out on returning to the Second Division once again.

The season began with optimism after securing the Lancashire Manx Cup trophy and the opening day saw a Stuart Storer goal secure victory at Shrewsbury Town. But this appeared to be false hope as there was only one more win in the following eight League games, the Wanderers coming from a two goal deficit to win 3-2 against Crewe Alexandra at Burnden.

The experienced Sammy Lee was recruited from Southampton, but he was involved in only five games before suffering a knee injury that left him out for the remainder of the season. Centre half Mark Seagraves made a £100,000 move from Manchester City and he made his debut in a Rumbelows Cup defeat against Coventry City.

By mid-October, Bolton were languishing next to the foot of the table, but the tide turned after a 2-2 draw at local rivals Bury. A club record 23 League games without defeat put the Wanderers into the promotion frame by the New Year. A first half goal from leading scorer Tony Philliskirk defeated Swansea City at Burnden to record the club's 1,000th home League victory.

The teams character was proved beyond doubt during November with some important victories in important games. The first was a 2-0 win at Chester, the club's 200th post war success in the League. Then, Reading were defeated 3-1 at Burnden, after they had held a half time advantage.

Finally, a Scott Green goal won the game at Grimsby Town to inflict their first home defeat of the season.

The run continued through the New Year, 1991 commencing with a 4-1 home success against Bournemouth which included two goals direct from corner kicks by Paul Comstive in the strong wind. Mark Patterson arrived from Bury in a £65,000 deal and he produced some workmanlike midfield performances before being struck down with a pelvic injury.

Manchester United ended F.A. Cup interest with a 79th minute Mark Hughes goal in the fourth round at Old Trafford, but the Wanderers had given them a scare. Mansfield Town ended the Wanderers unbeaten run with four second half goals without reply at Field Mill, but Bolton only failed to find the net in one more League game, that in a single goal defeat at Bournemouth where captain Phil Brown was missing through injury; this ended a 171 consecutive appearance run since he had joined the club.

The final weeks of the season had everything! Last minute goals to earn victory over Orient at Burnden, a point at Rotherham and then everything to play for in the final two games. The Wanderers came from behind to win at Swansea and misinformed reports came through that Grimsby had lost, thus securing third spot which would have left Bolton to win at home to Chester on the final day. Unfortunately Grimsby had in fact drawn and they went on to pip the Wanderers to promotion on goal difference.

Tony Kelly and Michael Brown were added to the squad from Shrewsbury Town, whilst the club's longest serving player, Steve Thompson, was an early season departure to Luton Town.

Early results were promising, just one defeat in the opening eight League games which came at Darlington where the Wanderers failed to recover from a three goal half time deficit. Nottingham Forest proved too strong for the Wanderers in the Rumbelows Cup with a 9-2 aggregate win in the second round. Three defeats in the next four games, culminating in a 3-0 home reverse to Fulham, set the alarm bells ringing as the club slipped to 14th in the League. But an undefeated run of seven games put them back into contention with David Reeves enjoying his best goalscoring spell since joining the Wanderers. Unfortunately he was injured in a home win over Hull City just before Christmas and he failed to find the net again.

Steady progress had been made in the F.A. Cup and, when a weakened Bolton side defeated Reading at Burnden to earn a fourth round home tie against Second Division Brighton, Cup tie fever took over to the detriment of the League.

The signing of Andy Walker, initially on loan from Celtic, proved to be a godsend. He scored within seconds of his introduction as substitute in a 2-2 draw at Exeter City and became a revelation with his goals helping to eventually keep the club away from relegation danger.

The play-offs saw the Wanderers reach Wembley after a 2-1 aggregate win over Bury but, in the final, an extra time goal from Chris Malkin condemned the Wanderers to another season in the Third Division and won promotion for Tranmere Rovers.

Goals from Walker and Philliskirk defeated Brighton to put Bolton into the fifth round of the F.A. Cup for the first time since 1980 and a home tie against Southampton who had won at Manchester United in the previous round. The Wanderers showed plenty of character by earning a replay after being two goals down with only eleven minutes left, and in doing so kept up their record of never having lost a game on a Sunday.

Tony Philliskirk scores the winner in the play off semi final second leg against Bury.

Season 1991/92.

After two disappointments in the play-offs in the previous two seasons, much was expected of the Wanderers in 1991/92.

In the replay at The Dell, Julian Darby appeared to have given Bolton a 2-1 win with an 89th minute strike, but then everything went wrong as Saints equalised in the third minute of injury time and won 3-2 in extra time. After the Cup exit there were still hopes of a play-off place as the club had games in hand over others.

A 4-0 win at Hartlepool, the club's best away win since February 1988, kept them in contention but injuries and a lack of form from a number of players began to take their toll. The final eleven games produced just one win, a 3-1 defeat of Stoke City at Burnden on the last day of the season, just eight points separating Bolton from relegated Bury.

Andy Walker and Nicky Spooner congratulate Julian Darby on his late goal in the fifth round of the F.A. Cup at Southampton.

Phil Neal ended his six and a half years in charge at Burnden and parted company along with coach Mick Brown.

Season 1992/93.

The Wanderers made 1992/93 a season to remember with a magnificent F.A. Cup run that saw them gain national prominence and put together a run that finished with promotion being won on the final day of the season, from what was now the Second Division, after the formation of the Premier League and consequent re-numbering of the divisions.

The goal of promotion that had slipped through the clubs hands in the recent past, despite setting many a new club record along the way, was finally secured under a new regime. Bruce Rioch took over as manager and appointed Colin Todd as his assistant, and they got the team playing some attractive football with the final goalscoring tally of 80 in the League being the best by the club since 1965.

By the middle of October things didn't look too good with the Wanderers lying seventh from the foot of the table and having gone out of the Coca-Cola Cup at the

Andy Walker rises to head home Wanderers second goal in the third round F.A. Cup success at Liverpool.

hands of Wimbledon, despite winning the second leg before just 1,987 at Selhurst Park. The turnaround, and perhaps the watershed in the club's fortunes since, began with a 2-2 draw at Chester City. Two down at half time, new signing John McGinlay headed his first goal for the club as Bolton hit back to go on a run of fifteen League and Cup games without defeat in which both McGinlay and Andy Walker became the scourge of opposing defences.

1993 opened brightly for the club who climbed to seventh place and also secured the services of winger David Lee from Southampton, after a loan spell, for a fee of £300,000 to become the second most expensive signing by the Wanderers. In the third round of the F.A. Cup, record receipts were paid to see the Wanderers draw 2-2 with Liverpool at Burnden, early goals from John McGinlay and Mark Seagraves being cancelled out in the second half. In the replay at Anfield, the Wanderers became front page news with a fully deserved 2-0 success thanks to goals from McGinlay and Walker. In the next round Wolves were accounted for at Molineux, but the dream came to an end at Derby County. In the Autoglass Trophy Huddersfield Town ended interest, at the northern quarter finals stage, at Leeds Road.

For weeks, automatic promotion looked to be just out of reach, with Stoke City and Port Vale having a cushion over the chasing clubs. Bolton made a fight of it by pushing Vale all the way with a magnificent run of consistency that saw fifteen wins and just one defeat in the final nineteen games of the season. There were times when they took it to the wire in the run in. It needed an 88th minute winner from Phil Brown to take the points at Bournemouth after stand-in centre forward Julian Darby had netted an early goal. Two goals in the last eleven minutes secured a 2-1 victory at Hull City, with the Wanderers down to ten men for most of the game after Alan Stubbs had been red carded for deliberate handball. The Wanderers finally overhauled Vale in the penultimate game of the season, ironically against Stoke City, thanks to a Julian Darby Goal. The final six games of the season had seen the team without leading scorer Andy Walker through injury but he had already equalled the club's post-war record of 33 goals in a season held by Nat Lofthouse.

On the final day, a crowd of 21,720, the clubs best League gate since April 1980, saw John McGinlay's penalty win promotion, send Preston North End into the Third Division, and create a new club record points total for a season of 90.

Season 1993/94.

For a second successive season the Wanderers gained national prominence from their exploits in the F.A. Cup. New arrivals for the return to the second tier of English football were Alan Thompson, from Newcastle United, Owen Coyle, from Airdrie and the return to the club of Jimmy Phillips from Middlesbrough.

Although the Wanderers were never in the running for promotion, conversely, relegation was never really an issue, although the club were propping up the table after three games and were briefly in 20th spot after a draw at West Brom in November. That draw came as part of a run of eleven undefeated League games, seven of which were drawn, and that after being two down at half time, Jason McAteer equalising six minutes from time.

John McGinlay's goals proved invaluable and, in the next two games, he struck the only goals to secure 1-0 wins at Middlesbrough and at home to Crystal Palace. In the new year the Scot hit hat tricks at Burnden against both Charlton Athletic and Middlesbrough, gained international recognition, and equalled the Wanderers record of 33 goals in a season.

Although the final game of the season saw little to play for, there was disappointment when Barnsley won 3-2 at Burnden to send the Wanderers to defeat for the first time on a Sunday, their nineteenth game to be played on the Sabbath.

In the Coca-Cola Cup there was a shock when Bury won 2-0 at Burnden, but the scoreline was reversed at Gigg Lane and the Wanderers won through on penalties, only to narrowly go down to Sheffield Wednesday in the second round.

The headlines came in the F.A. Cup although the team was nearly tripped up in the first round by non-League Gretna. The border side, who switched their home game to Burnden, twice led, and it need a penalty from John McGinlay and two Owen Coyle goals in the last eleven minutes to save any blushes.

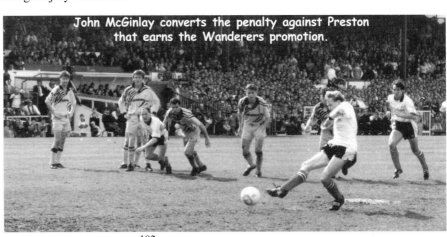

John McGinlay converts the penalty against Preston that earns the Wanderers promotion.

The second round saw a 3-1 success on a Saturday night for the Sky cameras at Lincoln City, and then a 1-1 draw resulted with Everton at Burnden.

In the replay the Wanderers came from two down, Everton fan Alan Stubbs equalising with seven minutes remaining and Owen Coyle hitting the winner in extra time. Coyle was again on target in the fourth round against Arsenal at Burnden. He equalised four minutes from time to make it 2-2 and earn a replay at Highbury. Ninety minutes failed to separate the sides but extra time strikes from Jason McAteer and Andy Walker made it another Cup night to remember for Bolton. An Alan Stubbs goal, eight minutes from time, defeated Aston Villa in the fifth round at Burnden but the quarter finals became an anti-climax when a fluke goal settled the game in Oldham Athletic's favour, again at Burnden.

If the F.A. Cup almost gave the Wanderers a Wembley trip they came even closer in the Anglo-Italian Cup when, after six games in the competition, they remained unbeaten. Victories in the qualifiers against Tranmere and Sunderland were followed by a 5-0 demolition of Ancona and a 3-3 draw against a Hagi inspired Brescia at Burnden. Away 1-1 draws at Pisa, where over 500 Wanderers supporters made up half the attendance, and at Ascoli were almost good enough to reach the final. Despite their run it was Notts County, who had a slightly better record, and they played in the final.

Season 1994/95.
Two Wembley appearances were just reward for some exciting football played by the club throughout the season which culminated in a seven goal play-off thriller and a return to the top flight after fifteen years absence.

The loss of Andy Walker, who returned to Celtic, was covered by the signings of strikers Mixu Paatelainen from Aberdeen and Fabien De Freitas from Vollendam, the latter setting a new record transfer fee paid for the club of £400,000. Another Dutchman, in Richard Sneekes, also joined the ranks. The Wanderers made their traditional slow start and were as low as 15th place during September. The Coca-Cola Cup proved to be a

John McGinlay celebrates after scoring in the F.A. Cup win at Arsenal in February 1994.

springboard to better results in the League and, after November had been reached, the team never fell out of the top six.

Defeat at Burnden in the opening home League fixture by Bristol City didn't augur well for the ground's centenary season but after that the Wanderers were unbeaten in 26 consecutive League and Cup games at Burnden. Included in that run were superb performances against Charlton Athletic and Wolves who were both beaten 5-1. Eventual champions Middlesbrough also fell at Burnden, a Mixu Paatelainen goal separating the sides.

Form away from Burnden told a different story with only five League victories, and eleven defeats being the highest suffered by any promotion winning Wanderers side. The final four away games of the season yielded only a single point and that fact was to deny the team any chance of automatic promotion, and they had to settle for a final finishing position of third.

In the play-offs the Wanderers appeared to gain a second wind. Wolves were beaten in the semi-final thanks to a memorable performance in the second leg at Burnden to overcome a 2-1 deficit from Molineux. That game saw Peter Shilton become the oldest player ever to wear a Bolton shirt at 45 years 239 days of age.

The Wanderers were full of confidence going into the final against Reading who had finished the season two points in front in second place. That confidence was severely tested when Reading stormed into a two goal lead inside twelve minutes and had the opportunity of making it three from the penalty spot just before half time. Keith Branagan's penalty save from Stuart Lovell proved to be a watershed as the second half saw Bolton get on top as Reading began to wilt. Goals from Coyle and De Freitas levelled the game and there was only going to be one winner in extra time with Bolton securing a 4-3 success.

In previous season's the Wanderers had made a name for themselves in the F.A. Cup, but during 1994/95 it was to be the Coca-Cola Cup that earned the club more national headlines.

Wanderers 'keeper Keith Branagan in front of a sea of sunlit faces during the Coca-Cola Cup final against Liverpool.

(Below) Play off celebrations with Mixu Paatelainen, Fabian deFreitas and Owen Coyle.

Premiership sides Ipswich Town, West Ham United and Norwich City were all accounted for with perhaps the hardest tie being the two-legged semi-final with Swindon Town. Trailing 2-1 from the first leg at the County Ground, Bolton again made things difficult by allowing Swindon to take the lead at Burnden, only to hit back with three late goals to reach the final for the first time.

Peter Shilton - the oldest player to wear a Wanderers shirt.

At Wembley Liverpool ran out 2-1 winners but the country saw how much progress Bolton Wanderers had made under the management team of Bruce Rioch and Colin Todd. Alan Thompson scored a spectacular goal but it was two efforts from Steve McManaman that took the Cup to Merseyside. Icelander Gudni Bergsson made his Wanderers debut in the final as a substitute and was to become a corner-stone of the Club's ups and down over the forthcoming seasons.

Season 1995/96.
The Wanderers went into their first Premiership season as favourites to return to the First Division. By Christmas the pundits looked to have got their forecast spot on but a spirited recovery at least gave the supporters something to shout about and took the issue to the penultimate game.

Bruce Rioch left to take over at Arsenal and a new joint management team of Colin Todd and Roy McFarland were put in charge. Pre-season additions to the squad were Gerry Taggart, Andy Todd and Chris Fairclough. The Wanderers had a baptism of fire in the first few weeks.

After losing 3-2 at Wimbledon on the opening day they then lost the opening game at Burnden by 3-1 to Newcastle United. They recovered to defeat Champions Blackburn Rovers four days later by 2-1 thanks to a goal from Alan Stubbs ten minutes from time.

Leading goalgetter John McGinlay missed the opening weeks through injury whilst all the talk in the press was about a transfer saga involving the departure of Jason McAteer and

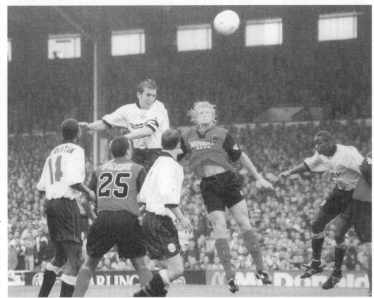

Alan Stubbs heads the winner against Blackburn Rovers at Burnden in August 1995.

against Manchester United at Burnden, that equalled the club's worst home defeat, hopes of avoiding the drop became a little more realistic. The Wanderers came from behind to defeat Sheffield Wednesday, a result that lifted the club off the bottom for the first time in four months and put them just three points from safety.

Unfortunately the final six games produced just one win and the clubs fate was sealed in a home

Alan Stubbs. As it was, Irish international McAteer joined Liverpool for a club record sale of £4.5 million, Stubbs remained in his role as team captain.

The Wanderers conceded a number of late goals that were to prove costly as time and again they matched sides blow for blow only to fail to convert chances that came their way. Goals conceded in the last five minutes denied the club points at home to Queens Park Rangers and Everton and at Nottingham Forest and Chelsea. Home victories over Blackburn and Arsenal, where McGinlay scored the winner, were the highlights of the first half of the season. The game against the Gunners saw the debut of Yugoslavian international Sasa Curcic, purchased for a club record £1.5 million and he added another dimension to the midfield.

Coca-Cola Cup interest ended when Norwich won a fourth round replay 3-2 on penalties after both sides had failed to find a goal in 210 minutes of open play. An F.A. Cup defeat by Leeds, in the fourth round, saw the club go out of both major competitions at home for the first time since the 1973/74 season.

In the first week of the new year, after a 4-2 defeat at Sheffield Wednesday, Colin Todd took sole charge with McFarland leaving the club and Ian Porterfield coming in as coach. They had some early success with a third round F.A. Cup win at Bradford and a home League victory against Wimbledon, but it wasn't until the middle of February that things began to pick up.

Four wins in six games began with a first away success of the season at Middlesbrough in which £1.2 million signing from Sheffield United, Nathan Blake, scored his first goal for the club. Despite a six goal reverse

defeat by Southampton which was the last top flight game on Burnden Park.

Season 1996/97.
Manager Colin Todd led the Wanderers to what could arguably be described as the club's most enthralling season in their 102 years at Burnden Park. The team set standards and broke records that had been set before the war but the so called experts didn't fancy the club's chances of a quick return to the top flight after the pre-season build up. Sasa Curcic left the club to join Aston Villa in a £4 million deal where he went on to make little impact, whilst Danes, Michael Johansen and Per Frandsen joined the club from F.C.Copenhagen. The latter performed so well he regained his international place.

During the season only four clubs could lay claim to a League win over the Wanderers. Southend by 5-2 in a rare off day at Roots Hall in September, plus Birmingham City, Reading and Ipswich Town who were the only victorious teams at Burnden. Indeed such was the margin of success that they could have afforded to lose all fourteen drawn games and still have secured the championship.

Highlights were a 7-0 defeat of Swindon at Burnden in March, that was just one short of equalling the club record League win, and completing the double over both Wolves and Manchester City who were pre-season favourites for promotion. The 2-1 success at Maine Road, with goals from Mixu Paatelainen and Scott Sellars, secured the championship just four days after a win over Queens Park Rangers at Burnden had confirmed promotion with five games remaining.

The Wanderers squad celebrate winning the First Division Championship after a 2-1 success at Manchester City in April 1997.

The team didn't take the run in easy and in the final games went all out for the double ton of 100 goals and 100 points. The 4-1 win over Charlton Athletic in the last ever game at Burnden Park was a tearful evening for many supporters.

The Londoners had held a half time lead but the Wanderers made the final 45 minutes on the ground something to remember, with John McGinlay netting the final

The goal that never was in the opener at the Reebok Stadium against Everton. Gerry Taggart's effort is clearly over the line but was missed by the officials.

Ball   Goal line

goal before the presentation of the championship trophy. The 28th League success of the season also set a new club record. The Scottish striker also netted in the final game, taking his tally to thirty for the season, in a 2-2 draw at Tranmere. Jamie Pollock scored the goal there that took the tally to 100 for the season but a last minute equaliser meant that another club record of 98 points for the season had to be settled for.

In Cup football the Wanderers shocked both Chelsea and Tottenham in the Coca-Cola Cup at Burnden. They came from behind to defeat Chelsea 2-1 whilst Spurs crumbled to a 6-1 defeat as a new club record victory in the competition was set with McGinlay claiming a hat trick. Wimbledon put paid to further progression in the quarter finals.

The season's F.A. Cup giantkillers Chesterfield ran out 3-2 winners in the fourth round at Burnden before going on to reach the semi's. In doing so they became the last visiting club to win at Burnden Park and had a Kevin Davies hat trick to thank for that fact.

Season 1997/98.
After making a record making return to the Premiership the squad was strengthened for the club's first season at the Reebok Stadium.

Neil Cox, for £1.2 million from Middlesbrough, Arnar Gunnlaugsson, for £100,000 from Akranes, and Robbie Elliott, for a club record £2.5 million from Newcastle all came during the close season.

Hopes were high of putting up a better show than the last time the club was in the Premiership and they opened up with three away games due to the Reebok Stadium not being ready until 1st September. A Nathan Blake goal secured a 1-0 win at Southampton for the Wanderers first opening day success in the top flight since 1958. A draw at Coventry and a defeat at Barnsley made up the trio by which time both Peter Beardsley and Mark Fish had been added to the ranks.

The opening game at the Reebok Stadium saw Everton as opponents. They had also been the first League visitors to Burnden back in 1895, and a TV audience of millions saw a scoreless draw that wasn't without incident. Gerry Taggart's second half header was clearly over the line but, unfortunately for the Wanderers, referee Steve Lodge didn't have the benefit of the TV replay. Of more concern to Bolton was the broken leg sustained by record signing Robbie Elliott that put a premature end to his season.

Another League success wasn't registered until the end of October when Chelsea were beaten 1-0 at the Reebok thanks to a Dean Holdsworth goal. He had been added to the Wanderers ranks for a new club record fee of £3.5 million whilst Mike Whitlow rejoined the club from Leicester City. John McGinlay ended his five year fairytale spell with the club when he joined Bradford City in November, but not before becoming the Wanderers record scorer in the League Cup. He notched his 14th in a 4-4 draw with Orient as Bolton ran out 7-5 aggregate winners. Middlesbrough put Bolton out of the competition at the fourth round stage.

Back to back home 1-0 wins against Wimbledon and Newcastle lifted Bolton up to 13th in the League but by January they were back in the bottom three and out of the F.A. Cup when Barnsley won 1-0 at Oakwell.

Evergreen Bob Taylor arrived from West Brom and his goal at Old Trafford secured a point after the pundits had forecast another defeat hot on the heels of a 5-1 home beating by Coventry. Home results kept the Wanderers in with an opportunity of escaping the drop but they remained in the bottom three until the last home game of the season. A 5-2 win over Crystal Palace at the Reebok Stadium lifted the club out of the relegation places and put Everton into trouble.

So, on the last day of the season, if Bolton could match Everton's result they would avoid relegation. The Wanderers had to visit Chelsea, who had the final of the European Cup Winners Cup the following mid-week, whilst Everton faced Coventry at Goodison.

At half time the Wanderers were drawing in London whilst Everton led Coventry by a single goal. A Coventry equaliser increased the tension but then, with just seventeen minutes remaining, a Vialli goal killed Bolton's hopes. Morris, almost regretfully, scored a second for Chelsea and the Wanderers went down on goal difference.

Season 1998/99.
The Wanderers set out their stall for a quick return to the Premier League and strengthened the squad during the summer with the signings of Claus Jensen from Lyngby, for £1.6 million and Jamaican World Cup star Ricardo Gardner for £1 million from Harbour View. Leaving the club was Northern Ireland international Gerry Taggart who joined Leicester City.

The early part of the season brought a glut of late goals. Arnar Gunnlaugsson struck late on to earn a point from a 2-2 draw at Crystal Palace on the opening day whilst Bradford City did likewise at Valley Parade in another 2-2 draw. Earlier in that game Gunnlaugsson had struck the Wanderers 6,000th League goal. Another 2-2 draw resulted against a ten man Sheffield United side at the Reebok Stadium where the Blades levelled in the 92nd minute. It was then the Wanderers turn to score late on with only ten men, Gudni Bergsson having been shown the red card which was followed by Ricardo Gardner's first goal for the club in a 3-2 win at West Brom.

By October the club was comfortably placed in the top four with a new club record unbeaten start to the season of eleven League games. The run came to an end when Watford struck an 87th minute winner at the Reebok to win 2-1. This prompted an inconsistent spell which included a 3-0 home defeat at the hands of League leaders Sunderland and a Worthington Cup exit at the hands of Wimbledon.

Nathan Blake made a £4 million move to Blackburn Rovers whilst the defence was bolstered with the loan signings of Jon Newsome, from Sheffield Wednesday and Paul Warhurst, from Crystal Palace. Back to back 1-0 away victories at Ipswich and Stockport, in which Bob Taylor netted the winners, put the team back on track.

An undefeated December, which included a home scoreless draw with Bradford City on Boxing Day before 24,625, the best gate of the season, saw the club finish the year in sixth spot. The first ever F.A. Cup tie at the Reebok Stadium put an end to an unbeaten nine game run when Wolves won a third round tie 2-1.

Paul Warhurst became a fully fledged Wanderer in a £1 million deal and he helped the Wanderers to a 3-0 home win against his old club before the TV cameras.

The Wanderers walk out at Wembley for the play off final against Watford.

February saw more comings and goings with Arnar Gunnlaugsson joining Leicester for £2 million, the clubs longest serving player Nicky Spooner joining Charleston Battery, and Bo Hansen a £1 million signing for the Wanderers from Brondby. Bottom club Crewe caused a major surprise when, in the Wanderers 2,000th League game, they ran out 3-1 winners. It was something that the team found difficult to recover from as they managed just one win in the next eight games.

The goalkeeping position was strengthened when Steve Banks joined for £50,000 from Blackpool and he made his debut in a 0-0 draw at Oxford. Automatic promotion hopes evaporated and a play-off place looked out of reach after nearest rivals Wolves had drawn 1-1 at The Reebok.

Fortunately they failed to win their game in hand which left Bolton needing to win the last game of the season, at Portsmouth, to claim a play-off place. Goals from Michael Johansen and Eidur Gudjohnsen secured a 2-0 victory.

Johansen scored the only goal of the first leg play-off semi final against Ipswich at the Reebok whilst the second leg was a game of twists and turns. Ipswich ran out 3-2 winners in the ninety minutes, the home side's third coming with just thirty seconds remaining. The game ended 4-3 after extra time with the tie going in the Wanderers favour on away goals. Watford proved one step too far for Bolton in the Final at Wembley as they ran out 2-0 winners to leave the Wanderers thinking what might have been.

Season 1999/2000.
This proved to be a season of change at the club, that lifted them from the bottom three in September to go on and reach three semi-finals that in the end were to prove heartbreaking.

The opening six League games of the season yielded a single victory. That came in a 2-1 success against Queens Park Rangers in what was the 50th first class game to be played at the Reebok. The best home gate of the season, 21,671 saw Manchester City win and then, in the next home game, the Wanderers came from a 3-1 half time deficit to draw 3-3 with Birmingham City.

Bolton had accounted for lower League opposition in the form of Darlington in the first round of the Worthington Cup but the second round game, against Gillingham at home, proved to be Colin Todd's last game in charge of the club. The Wanderers went through on a 6-1 aggregate before a Reebok crowd of just 3,673.

Phil Brown took over as caretaker and he started with a win thanks to a 90th minute winner from Neil Cox, against Nottingham Forest, to secure a 3-2 home success. This was followed up with a 4-0 win at Swindon, the Wanderers first 4-0 away win since 1992, all the goals coming in the first half. During October Phil Gartside took over as Chairman from Gordon Hargreaves. In his first game in the chair he saw the Wanderers win 2-1 at Premiership side Derby County in the third round of the Worthington Cup.

Former Wanderers favourite Sam Allardyce was appointed Manager and he had to settle for a 2-2 draw at home to Crewe in his first game when the visitors levelled with three minutes remaining. Results continued to improve. Whilst both Neil Cox and Andy Todd left the club, Gareth Farrelly was brought in, and he scored 82 seconds into his debut, on loan from Everton, in a 2-1 win at Sheffield United.

League results took a dip in December but the Wanderers reached the last four of the Worthington Cup by defeating Wimbledon 2-1 at The Reebok

Stadium with a spectacular goal from Eidur Gudjohnsen. Tranmere Rovers ended hopes of a trip to Wembley by winning in Bolton for the first time ever in the semi-final first leg. They then outplayed Bolton in the second leg to go through 4-0 on aggregate. The defeat at Prenton Park proved to be a turning point. Just one defeat in the next seven games saw the Wanderers climb the table and reach the semi-finals of the F.A. Cup for the first time since 1958, by defeating Charlton Athletic 1-0.

The Wanderers had the opportunities to defeat Aston Villa in the semi-final played at Wembley. After a scoreless two hours the Premiership side won through to the final by winning 4-1 on penalties with only Dean Holdsworth converting his kick.

Just three days after the disappointment of losing the semi-final Bolton went down 2-0 at promotion chasing Manchester City. The result left the Wanderers facing the last six League games in the knowledge that they couldn't afford to slip up in any more games if they were to pip Huddersfield Town for a play-off place.

Bolton came out on top in a seven goal thriller against Walsall at the Reebok and then took a point from a 4-4 draw at West Brom when Gudni Bergsson headed home a 90th minute equaliser. The result left Bolton seven points behind sixth placed Huddersfield. That gap was diminished when the Wanderers went to the McAlpine Stadium and won 3-0, one of the goals coming from Mike Whitlow, his first for the club.

Wins at Crewe and at home to Wolves took the fight to the last

Dean Holdsworth can't believe his miss against Aston Villa in the F.A. Cup semi final at Wembley.

Alan Johnston gets past Jamie Clapham in the play off semi final at Ipswich Town.

day of the League season. A Dean Holdsworth goal earned a 1-0 home win over Norwich and, when news came through that Huddersfield had lost at Fulham, the Reebok crowd began to party. The play-offs got off to the best possible start when Bolton went two up in the first leg at the Reebok only to be pegged back to 2-2. The season came to a disappointing and frustrating end at Portman Road. The Wanderers led three times and were 3-2 to the good in the final minute only for Ipswich to level and win 5-3 in extra time. By then the official had awarded Ipswich three dubious penalties, one of which was saved by Jussi Jaaskelainen, and showered the Wanderers with ten yellow cards and two red.

Season 2000/01.
The Wanderers added Anthony Barness, Simon Charlton, Ian Marshall and Michael Ricketts to the squad in an attempt to make it third time lucky at getting back into the Premiership. Major outgoings were Eidur Gudjohnsen, who joined Chelsea, and the Danes, Claus Jensen and Michael Johansen, who signed for Charlton and AB Copenhagen respectively.

A local Derby against Burnley finished 1-1 at the Reebok on the opening day with the Wanderers goal coming from a Per Frandsen penalty. It was to be the only one awarded to Bolton during the regular League season. Frandsen had returned to the club after spending less than a year with Blackburn Rovers. On loan striker Isaiah Rankin, from Bradford City, netted in a 2-0 win at West Brom and scored again in a 2-0 home win over Preston. Michael Ricketts scored his first goal for the club in that success as Bolton kept up with the early pacesetters.

Macclesfield Town put the Wanderers out of the Worthington Cup with a 3-1 win at the Moss Rose, going through 3-2 on aggregate. After the Cup exit the Wanderers put together three consecutive wins, two of which were away from home, and a point was earned at Blackburn. League leaders Fulham ended the run, wining 2-0 at the Reebok after taking a first minute lead.

October proved to be a difficult month with points being thrown away late in games. 2-0 up at Gillingham, only to draw 2-2, and three down at Stockport before making a great recovery to draw level only to lose the game in the last minute. It was a similar story at home when a 3-1 lead against Crystal Palace ended 3-3. But a 3-1 win over Queens Park Rangers at the Reebok on the last day of the month changed the fortunes.

The defence was strengthened with the arrival, on loan, of Colin Hendry from Coventry City and the move was made permanent in the New Year. He made his debut in a 1-0 win at Wimbledon where Dean Holdsworth netted against his former club. The Wanderers went into 2001 in second spot behind Fulham and made a great start to the year with a lunchtime 2-0 win at Preston. Gareth Farrelly and Michael Ricketts, who had now earned the title of super sub, grabbed the goals.

Jussi Jaaskelainen was lost for the remainder of the season when he injured his cruciate knee ligament in a 2-0 home win over Tranmere but the Wanderers kept picking up points even when the performances were not up to scratch. Blackburn Rovers were faced three times in quick succession. A 1-1 draw in a fifth round Cup tie at the Reebok was followed by a 4-1 home reverse in the League; the Wanderers were struggling to sustain their early season home form. In the Cup replay Rovers ran out 3-0 winners.

The Ewood side were now Bolton's main rivals for second spot with Fulham going well at the head of the table. Four consecutive home draws allowed the door to open to Blackburn's challenge, and in the final run in they held the initiative. A 1-0 win at Barnsley, their first at Oakwell for 92 years, and a 2-0 win at Wolves kept the pressure on Rovers but they secured the automatic promotion spot by winning at Preston.

Bolton faced West Brom in the play-offs and things weren't too rosy as the home side led 2-0 with ten minutes left. Gudni Bergsson then headed home and Per Frandsen converted a penalty to level matters. A 3-0 second leg success earned a final appearance against Preston at the Millennium Stadium.

Simon Charlton, Colin Hendry, Sam Allardyce and Dean Holdsworth celebrate after a 3-0 defeat of West Brom sent the Wanderers to Cardiff to face Preston.

Gareth Farrelly's first half goal settled any nerves and late goals from Michael Ricketts, his 24th of the season, and Ricardo Gardner secured a magnificent 3-0 win and a return to the Premiership.

Season 2001/02.

The Wanderers hit the headlines on the opening day of the Premiership season with a 5-0 success at Leicester City. It was the club's best ever opening day win and the first time five goals had been scored in the top flight since 1954. Michael Rickets continued where he had left off the previous season by scoring in the opening three games which were all won. Southampton burst the bubble with a 1-0 win at the Reebok Stadium but the Wanderers were still on top of the Premiership after a 1-1 draw against Arsenal at Highbury.

New faces in Henrik Pedersen, Rod Wallace, Bruno Ngotty and Jermaine Johnson all played a part in the opening weeks whilst Japanese striker Akinori Nishizawa scored in a 4-3 Worthington Cup win over Walsall. Back to back defeats at the Reebok Stadium by Sunderland and Newcastle United were tempered by a magnificent 2-1 win at Manchester United.

The home side had taken the lead, but the Wanderers triumphed and became the first side to win at Old Trafford, thanks to super goals from Kevin Nolan and Michael Ricketts.

Away form continued to be good and it was at home that points slipped away but a Monday evening visit to Tottenham, where the Wanderers were unlucky to go down 3-2, brought an end to away success in the Premiership until March. Another visit to Tottenham, in the fifth round of the Worthington Cup, saw the home side win 6-0 to equal the Bolton's worst ever defeat in the competition. It was to be a similar story in the F.A. Cup when yet another visit to Tottenham ended in a 4-0 defeat at the fourth round stage.

The Wanderers took the lead at Chelsea after only two minutes, only to go down 5-1, but the determination came through in the final home game of the year against Leicester City. Down to nine men for 67 minutes after the harsh dismissal of Dean Holdsworth and Paul Warhurst, the Wanderers hit back from 2-0 down to earn a point with a last minute goal from Per Frandsen.

Bolton slipped into the bottom three for the first time during the season after a 3-2 reverse at Newcastle but it was to be the arrival of French international Youri Djorkaeff, and Danish international Stig Tofting, along with the loan signing of

Michael Ricketts after his winner against Manchester United at Old Trafford.

World Cup winner Youri Djorkaeff arrived from Kaiserslautern.

Fredi Bobic that kept Bolton out of trouble. Djorkaeff made his debut in a scoreless draw at Southampton but came to the fore with the Wanderers' two goals in a 2-1 win at Charlton. This result came after a low point which saw Derby County win 3-1 at the Reebok Stadium to drag the club into the relegation melting pot.

A home win over Aston Villa, in which Fredi Bobic scored his first goal for the club, and England under 21 international midfielder Kevin Nolan took his season's League tally to eight, lifted the pressure. The proverbial six pointer came five games from the end of the season. Fellow relegation rivals Ipswich Town visited the Reebok Stadium and found themselves four down by the interval with Bobic grabbing Bolton's first top flight hat trick since Freddie Hill in 1962. Djorkaeff netted the other and although Ipswich pulled one back in the second half they were a broken team.

A point from a 1-1 home draw with Tottenham took the Wanderers to the mystical safety mark of 40 points and, a week later, that mark and Premiership status was confirmed when Ipswich lost at home to Manchester United. Two days later Arsenal won 2-0 at the Reebok Stadium on their way to the championship with a party atmosphere from both sets of supporters enveloping the stadium and watched by a record 27,351 crowd.

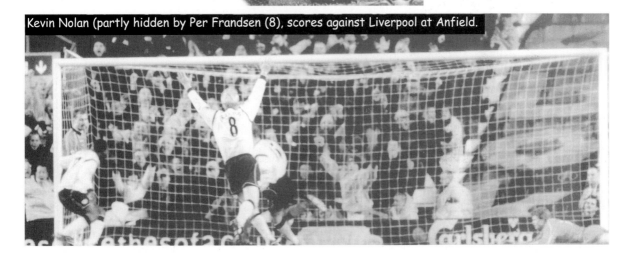

Kevin Nolan (partly hidden by Per Frandsen (8), scores against Liverpool at Anfield.

Places and People

The following sections deal with other aspects, which together build up to form a comprehensive 125 year history of Bolton Wanderers Football Club.

❋ ❋ ❋ ❋ ❋ ❋ ❋ ❋ ❋ ❋ ❋

The last decade or so has produced some big changes and not a few celebrations for Bolton Wanderers - the colour section that follows highlights some of those memorable moments.

❋ ❋ ❋ ❋ ❋ ❋ ❋ ❋ ❋ ❋ ❋

The move to the Reebok Stadium was a major transition in the history of the club, and so were the previous moves. The history of those Grounds is captured in words and pictures.

❋ ❋ ❋ ❋ ❋ ❋ ❋ ❋ ❋ ❋

In their heyday, Wanderers could boast of several household names in International football, and with the introduction of foreign players to this country, the list of such players continues to grow. The full record is included.

❋ ❋ ❋ ❋ ❋ ❋ ❋ ❋ ❋ ❋

The men that have steered the club to its glory days (and not so memorable occasions) are fully recorded.

❋ ❋ ❋ ❋ ❋ ❋ ❋ ❋ ❋ ❋

Every player, from the very early days of the F.A. Cup, through to the end of the 2001/02 season, to have made an appearance for the Wanderers is listed. A breakdown of appearances and goals scored in all major competitions, with the period spent at the club is also included.

❋ ❋ ❋ ❋ ❋ ❋ ❋ ❋ ❋ ❋

A major section is that of the statistical record of the club, where every known first team fixture (including friendly matches) is included in very detailed form. The statistics are supported by many named team/squad photographs that date back to 1881 right through to 2002.

1992-93

F.A.Cup third round replay.... Andy Walker heads the second goal in the shock 2-0 defeat of Liverpool

John McGinlay converts the penalty that secures victory over Preston at Burnden Park, and promotion to Division 1

Bruce Rioch leads the team out at Wembley for the Final of the Coca-Cola Cup, that Liverpool won 2-1

1994-95

Endsleigh **Play-off Winners 94/95 Season** Endsleigh

Promotion to the Premier League is won with a 4-3 extra time victory over Reading. The turning point was Keith Branagan's penalty save from Stuart Lovell.

The Decade

The end of an era at Burnden Park is celebrated with winning the First Division Championship.

John McGinlay scored the final goal at Burnden in the 4-1 win over Charlton...

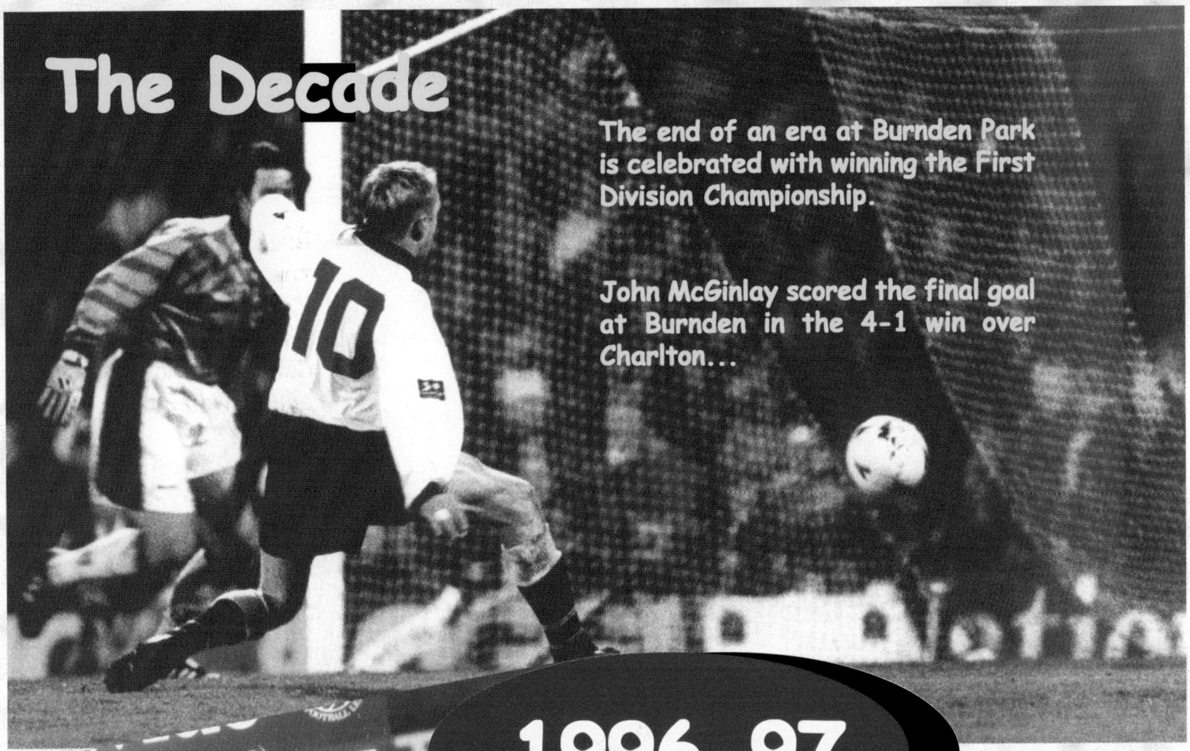

1996-97

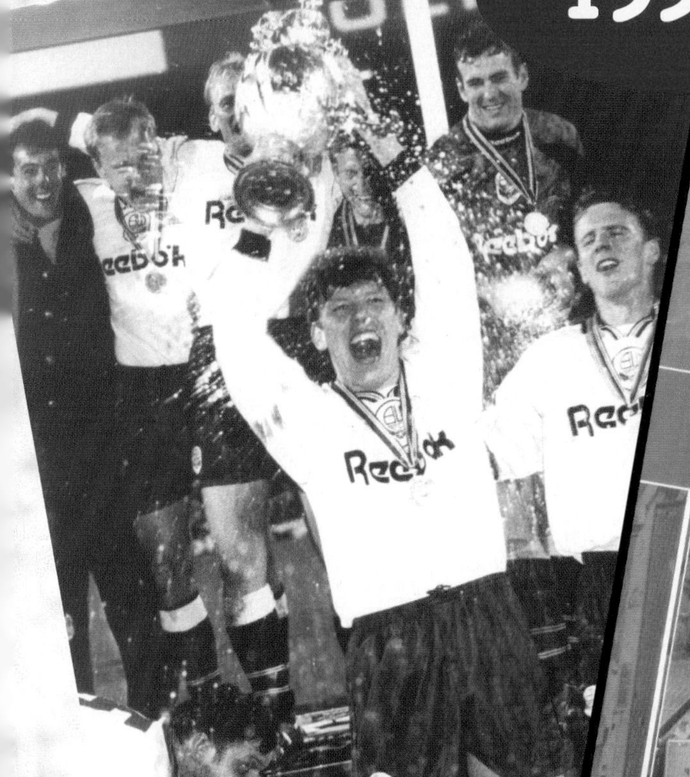
Reebok
ULATIONS

Alan Thompson shows off the Trophy with his team mates.

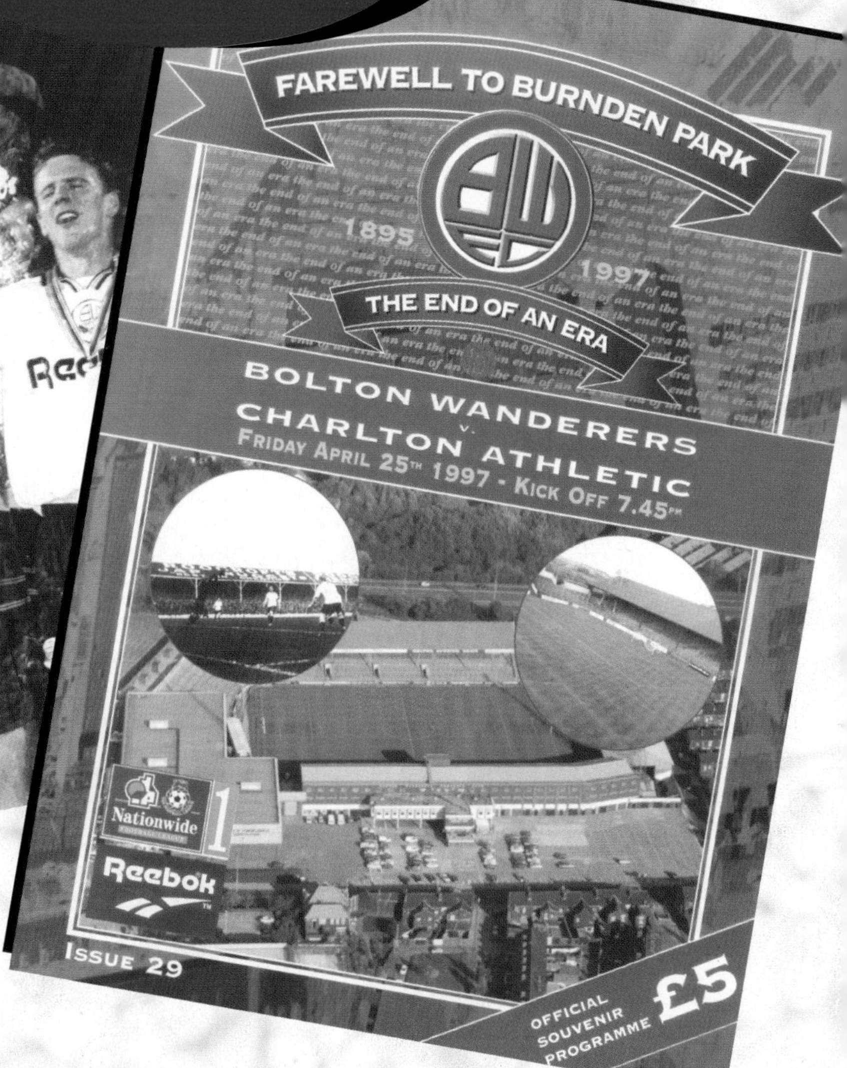
FAREWELL TO BURNDEN PARK
1895
1997
THE END OF AN ERA
BOLTON WANDERERS
v.
CHARLTON ATHLETIC
FRIDAY APRIL 25TH 1997 - KICK OFF 7.45PM
Nationwide
Reebok
ISSUE 29
OFFICIAL SOUVENIR PROGRAMME
£5

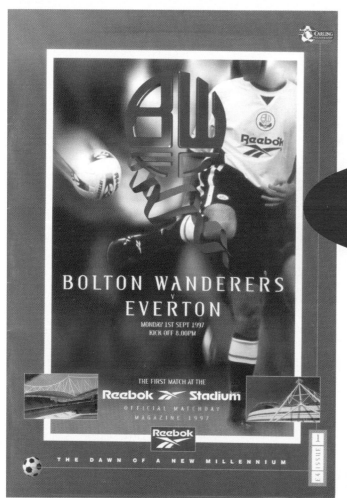

BOLTON WANDERERS
v
EVERTON

MONDAY 1ST SEPT 1997
KICK OFF 8.00PM

THE FIRST MATCH AT THE
Reebok ≫ Stadium

OFFICIAL MATCHDAY
MAGAZINE 1997

Reebok

T H E   D A W N   O F   A   N E W   M I L L E N N I U M

1997-98

The first match at the
Reebok Stadium.

Promotion to the Premier
League is celebrated after
a 3-0 play-off Final win
over Preston in Cardiff.

2000-01

The Grounds

Park Recreation Ground and Cockle's Field (to 1881)

Pikes Lane (1881 ~ 1895)

Situated in the Deane area of the Town, Pikes Lane was not a place for the faint hearted. A grandstand which held around 750 spectators, the remainder being sparse uncovered standing accommodation, was all that the Wanderers supporters of the day had to greet them. It was however a scenic spot to watch football. Houses on one side were flanked by the moors in the background along with a large oak tree that was situated some three yards from the touchline. The Wanderers paid £175 per year rent for Pikes Lane but it was obvious that the demands of an ambitious club could not be satisfied at the venue.

View of the Crowd watching a game at Pike's Lane

Indeed the owners of the land were looking to sell as building speculators were queuing up to buy the land.

In August 1893 the club made their first overtures to move away and won their final League game at the ground by 5-0 against F. A. Cup finalists West Brom in April 1895. The final months of the 1894/95 season at Pikes Lane were happy ones with seven victories and a draw in the final eight League games. Inconsistent away form had cost the Wanderers the chance of any major silverware but they did leave the old ground with the Manchester Cup secured.

Burnden Park (1895 ~ 1997)

'Burnden'- Scottish terminology for a brook or stream is a burn. 'Den' comes from an old English word dene or denu meaning valley. Thus in literal terms Burnden is a valley with a stream flowing through it. The particular stream was Burnden Brook which originally flowed from Rose Hill. Later culverted, it then ran underneath both Manchester Road and the ground itself.

In July 1894, four months after playing in their first F. A. Cup Final, the club agreed with the Gas Committee of the Bolton Corporation to pay a rent of £130 per year for a fourteen years period. The land, a five acre site on Manchester Road, which overlooked the River Croal, had previously been used as a tip whilst the Corporation had decided against extending the gasworks.

In October 1894 it was approved, at a general meeting, that a Limited Liability Company be formed and, on 15th January 1895, the company was incorporated and registered as the Bolton Wanderers Football and Athletic Company Limited under company registration number 43026. Preparation of the new ground was entrusted to a ground committee who employed a contractor from Scarborough to lay out the new stadium. Prior to work commencing, the site of Burnden Park was what could have been described at best a mess and a miserable place. One end being bound by a railway and the smell of dumped refuse and chemicals from nearby works did little to enhance the area.

In the early 1800's the Burnden area had been part of the countryside with several small bleaching crofts and works carrying on a thriving industry in the valley.

The Bolton to Manchester railway line was constructed in 1838 and, ten years later, a branch line to Bury cut the Burnden area into two thus robbing it of any charm that it did possess at the time. Added to this was the discovery of several rich coal seams which led to the establishing of a number of collieries which in turn brought about further industry and housing thus robbing the area of it's country image forever.

The Great Lever Colliery was situated on the site of the Greyhound Stadium at Raikes Lane with the pit yard fronting Manchester Road. The Rose Hill Colliery site was eventually covered by the car and coach park on the front of Burnden Park which in turn led to the odd cases of subsidence. In 1870 the car park was fronted by a collection of cottages whilst the playing pitch itself was occupied by a chemical works with numerous heaps of waste and slag covering the area.

The building of Burnden Park transformed the area with the club being able to boast one of the finest athletic enclosures in the country. The town itself had, for too long, been made to make do with inadequate facilities, yet in a short space of time one of the most desolate areas of Bolton was changed into a magnificent equipped enclosure.

The total area of the new site was almost six acres but an enormous amount of tipping had been necessary to level the area, thus making the ground well elevated. The turf was laid on a bed of cinders between 12" and 18" in depth with the area being 118 yards by 80 yards. The contractor advised that the drainage would be perfect but this was to prove a problem upon the onset of winter. The cycle track was 22ft in width and was banked up 6ft at the corners with one lap being the equivalent of a quarter of a mile.

Down each side of the ground stands were erected. The grandstand was on the Darcy Lever side of the ground and was 80 yards long with ten rows of seats capable of holding 1600 spectators. The central portion was reserved for 400 people and below the seating area was an enclosure which held 2500 standing spectators. Under the grandstand were two dressing rooms, each 22ft long, and a referee's retiring box. On the Manchester Road side an uncovered stand, some 120 yards long, ran the length of the ground. This was capable of holding 5000 standing spectators who paid 9d (4p) each for admission. The Great Lever End, the south side of the ground, had room for 2000 in a cramped area whilst the extensive Railway Embankment was terraced.

Ten turnstiles were in operation when Burnden Park opened, the nearest entrance being next to the terraced house, which was also taken over from the Corporation and was used as a groundsman's residence and secretary's office. This remained until it was demolished in 1946.

The ground was used for the first time on 17th August 1895 when the Wanderers held their ninth annual Athletic Festival. Admission was 6d (2.5p) and one shilling (5p) with extra payable to go into the stands. The somewhat incomplete entrances could not cope with the influx of people as there was immense local interest and the first chance of seeing the new ground. A crowd of 20,000 paid £453 on that historic day. A local cycle mile handicap at 2.30pm kicked off the proceedings whilst entertainment was provided in the shape of a high diver, a troupe of lady cyclists, a donkey riding a bicycle and a high stilt walker.

Two days later, a bank holiday Monday crowd of 15,000 attended the second day of the festival and, on 31st August, Bolton Harriers held their sixth annual sports day at Burnden Park. The ground was finally put to use for football on Wednesday 11th September 1895 when Preston North End were the visitors for a benefit game for Dai Jones. The crowd of 3,000 saw North End win with a solitary goal from David Smith.

Three days later the ground hosted it's first league game with Everton being the visitors. An hour before the 4pm kick off a crowd of 10,000 witnessed a cycle race and, by the kick off, this had risen to 15,000.

Billy Joyce kicked off the Wanderers League career at their new home and they played towards the Embankment. James Martin became the first player to score a League goal on the ground when he netted after 25 minutes as Bolton went on to win 3-1.

Within a month the ground saw it's first addition when a reporters box was erected on the Manchester Road side of the ground to save messengers having to dash about around the ground. In November 1895 the pitch failed its first test when it resembled a mini lake which was six inches deep in places. The cycle track also started to break up and emergency work was carried out but it meant that some of the club's reserve games took place at a derelict Pikes Lane.

A month later Preston North End refused to come out for the second half of a game due to the poor state of the pitch after torrential rain had caused waterlogging, leaving the referee no alternative but to abandon the match much to the displeasure of the 2,000 crowd. Although the pitch was a cause for concern the Lancashire F.A. still saw fit to award the Lancashire Cup Final between Blackburn and Bury in 1896 which

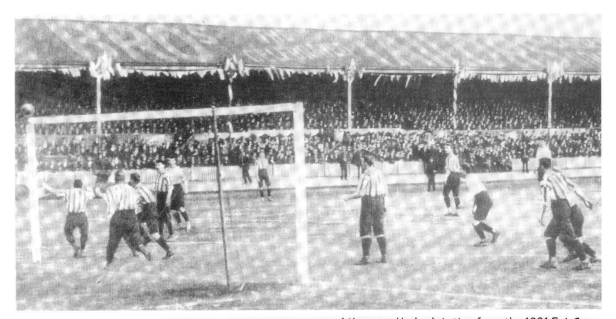

attracted 13,000 spectators. That close season was spent restoring the camber to the surface of the pitch, which had sunk in the bad weather, the centre being nine inches higher than the sides after restoration.

In January 1897 Burnden hosted the World Mile championship on the track. The winner of the £100 prize was a James Craig in a time of 4mins 30 secs. A month later a crowd of 9,007 witnessed the 400 yards championship of the

(Above and below) Action from the 1901 F.A.Cup Final at Burnden Park between Tottenham Hotspur and Sheffield United.

world. The following April the National Cyclists Union held their fifty miles championship on the cement track and even a brass band contest was held to make full use of the ground.

In 1899 Burnden Park was awarded its first F.A. Cup semi final, Liverpool and Sheffield United contesting a replay that ended 4-4, and later that year Burnden was the venue for a Football League representative game against the Irish League. Unfortunately only 5,372 attended, the Wanderers being in the Second Division at the time. In April 1901 the F.A. Cup Final replay was played on Burnden between Tottenham Hotspur and Sheffield United. The occasion became known as 'Pie Saturday' as a crowd of 50,000 was expected and only 20,470 actually turned up leaving many local caterers with mountains left over pies. The lack of cheap railway facilities was blamed on the poor attendance.

The last amateur athletic festival on the ground took place in August 1904 with less than 10,000 attending what was the 18th such event. A year later the cycle track was removed altogether to create more space for spectators and the lease on the ground was renewed with the Corporation for a further ten years.

The main stand on Manchester Road was erected at a cost of £3,500, providing seating for 3,420 and standing room for 3,000.

Further terraces were added to the Embankment in 1906 along with a terrace on the Great Lever End which was covered six years later. The Wanderers purchased the freehold of Burnden Park in July 1914 at a cost of £8,021 and 15 shillings (£8021. 75), this coming after patient shareholders had received a dividend of five per cent.

(Left) The Manchester Road Stand under construction in 1905.

(Below) The completed Stand. Note the bench seats that were placed on the old cycle track, and the pitch on a level rather than being raised.

In 1915 a wing stand was added to the main stand and, in 1928, the Burnden Stand replaced the old Darcy Lever Stand. The new structure seated 2,750 but it was built in controversial circumstances with proceeds of the sale of David Jack going towards the building cost of £17,712.

The largest 'official' crowd on Burnden came in February 1933 when 69,912 saw a fifth round F. A. Cup tie against Manchester City. Four days later only 3,101 attended a League game against Portsmouth to set up a record low that lasted until November 1985 when just 2,902 saw a Third Division game against Darlington. The largest League attendance at Burnden was recorded in September 1951 when 55,477 saw a Nat Lofthouse goal defeat Manchester United.

The government commandeered the ground during World War Two, the pitch being used by the Education Authorities and the stands by the Ministry of Supply. The Burnden Stand was still full of food supplies when Burnden Park saw it's darkest hour on the afternoon of the 9th March 1946.

An estimated 85,000 swarmed into Burnden Park, the official gate being 65,419, for the second leg of an F. A. Cup sixth round tie against Stoke City. Half an hour before kick off many people were in a crush outside the ground, attempting to gain entry to the Embankment from the Manchester Road terraces. Once inside the ground, it was impossible for spectators to move along the terrace to gain a position where they could feel comfortable, let alone see the pitch.

The forecourt of Burnden Park in the late 1940's

The turnstiles were eventually closed but people began climbing over the walls and there was an invasion over the railway line fence on the eastern side of the ground. The police, however, were reluctant to release more men from the Burnden Stand as they were guarding the stockpiles of food.

Inside the ground panic began to set in and a father and son, wanting to escape the crush, picked a padlock off an exit gate. They slipped out but the open gate allowed hundreds to rush in. A perimeter fence was ripped down on police instruction to relieve the crush but the keys could not be found to open the other exit doors. Ten minutes prior to kick off an estimated crowd of 1,000 climbed over the boy's entrance whilst the railway police were helpless to prevent 2,000 climbing onto a stationary train to view the game.

The pressure continued to mount despite passing people onto the track and, as the teams entered the field, two barriers near the north west corner flag collapsed. The crowd sunk and a number of people were smothered. Hundreds spilled onto the track as the game commenced but it was not until twelve minutes later that it became apparent that there had been fatalities and the game was held up. Many in the ground were unaware as to the extent of the disaster that was unfolding before their eyes. Thirty three bodies were found and laid out on the pitch whilst first aid was given to hundreds.

2 p.m. "An hour before the kick-off," said Gordon White, "Herald" photographer, "I took this picture of happy thousands singing and shouting in the spirit of cup-tie enthusiasm as they waited for admission to the ground."

3.15 p.m. "Referee Dutton stopped the match because spectators had encroached on the ground. Then it was found they had been crushed and trampled to death. Among the dead was the shoeless body of a woman."

2.45 p.m. "Crowds who had been shut out when the police closed the turnstiles, started climbing over the railway embankment. The great crush of people caused many to faint, and women were passed over the heads of spectators."

3.40 p.m. "Doreen Taylor, ATS girl, who helped to revive the injured, walked away," said White "But most of the crowd, unaware of the tragedy, yelled for the game to go on."

The turnstiles were not closed until some twenty minutes prior to kick off as the head checker could not be located. Inside the ground the police helped people out of the north west corner onto the track whilst instructions from outside failed to get through due to the density of the crowd.

After consultation, both the referee and the police decided to re-start the game. A few thousand were moved to other parts of the ground with the Burnden Stand being opened to accommodate some of them. Play resumed at 3.25pm, and continued without the traditional half time interval until 5pm, resulting in a goalless draw, the Wanderers going through to the semi final on a 2-0 aggregate.

A relief fund was set up which raised almost £40,000 whilst a shocked community came to terms with the loss of life. The Home Secretary, Mr Chuter Ede, ordered an enquiry by Mr Moelwyn Hughes KC, which lasted five days during March and April. The report made recommendations relating to the reception and control of crowds, not only at Burnden, but also at football grounds in general. The enquiry decided that the crowd had inflicted the disaster on itself. The club made alterations to the Embankment at a cost of £5,500 to enhance safety.

In October 1957 floodlit football came to Burnden Park. Heart of Midlothian were the visitors for the historic game with the four towers, some 160 feet in height, carrying 48 lamps of 1,500 watts each, being anchored with eight bolts 1¾" in diameter and 6 feet long. The lights were updated in 1975 whilst the whole towers and lamps were completely renewed in 1987.

Although the club slipped out of the top flight, Burnden was still honoured by the F. A. with selection for two F. A. Cup semi finals. In 1966, Everton defeated Manchester United and, in 1970, Leeds United also beat Manchester United in a second replay.

The front of Burnden Park changed significantly during the sixties with a supporters club built over the players entrance whilst in 1971 the

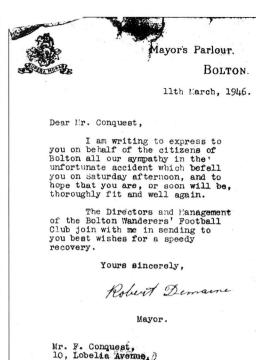

Mayor's Parlour,
BOLTON.
11th March, 1946.

Dear Mr. Conquest,

I am writing to express to you on behalf of the citizens of Bolton all our sympathy in the unfortunate accident which befell you on Saturday afternoon, and to hope that you are, or soon will be, thoroughly fit and well again.

The Directors and Management of the Bolton Wanderers' Football Club join with me in sending to you best wishes for a speedy recovery.

Yours sincerely,

Robert Demaine

Mayor.

Mr. F. Conquest,
10, Lobelia Avenue,
FARNWORTH.

Letter to the Author's Grandfather who was injured in the disaster

famous signal box behind the embankment was destroyed by fire. The clocks, which had been supplied by the brewers Magee's in 1935, were dismantled from the Burnden Stand in 1973 and, two years later, from the Manchester Road stand.

The last crowd of over fifty thousand came in February 1977 when 50,413 witnessed a League Cup semi final defeat by Everton and the following season segregation and fences were introduced. The Great Lever end was made all seater on the clubs return to the top flight in 1978 with 4,342 plastic seats being placed on the old terracing.

Despite the antiquated surroundings and off the field facilities the ground still managed to keep up with the times with the installation of sprinklers and undersoil heating. The greatest change to the inside of the ground came in 1986 when the then 16,000 capacity Embankment was cut in half to accommodate the Normid Superstore on the site of the 1946 disaster. Two years earlier the half time scoreboard had been pulled down after it had fallen into a state of disrepair.

During the late 1980's it wasn't football or Bolton Wanderers that attracted the biggest gates to the ground. With the Wanderers languishing in the lower reaches of the Football League it was Rugby League that attracted the crowds, the largest being 21,144 for the John Player Trophy final between Wigan and Warrington in January 1987. Other finals were also hosted whilst Swinton played some of their League fixtures on the ground.

The crowds returned to watch the Wanderers as they returned to the top flight in 1995 but the curtain finally fell on Burnden Park in April 1997. Charlton Athletic were the visitors for the final League game on the ground, the Wanderers running out 4-1 winners,

The signal box, overlooking the embankment, that caught fire in 1971.

John McGinlay netted the final goal, before the First Division championship trophy was presented. It was fitting that the old championship trophy, which the Wanderers have never won, should finally see the light of day in the stadium as it was about to take its final breath.

The ground was vacated, and after a fire in the main stand was finally pulled down. After a lengthy period in which the site was derelict Burnden Park is now home to a Big W superstore.

THE LAST MATCH
25 April 1997

NATIONWIDE LEAGUE DIVISION 1
FRI. 25TH APRIL K.O 7.45PM
WANDERERS
v
CHARLTON ATH.

A derelict ground - 1998

Reebok Stadium (1997 ~)

Work begins on the pitch - Early 1996.

Although it was in the mid 1980's that it was first muted that the club could relocate, it wasn't until the 90's that the Taylor report and the lack of space to rebuild Burnden forced the issue. From the fourteen sites that were looked at for a new facility it was a 200 acre site at Lostock that proved to be the most feasible and work got underway in November 1995 on the stadium.

At a cost of £35million the Reebok Stadium, with an initial capacity of 25,000, became the focal point of the Middlebrook development with a retail park, community facilities, indoor/outdoor tennis arena, athletics track, rail halt, hotel and housing all added to the area.

The sweeping curves of the upper tiers creates a bowl effect which means that no spectator is ever more that 90 metres from the centre of the field. The stand roofs are some 88 feet high whilst the floodlights, which have a maximum 1200 lux, are 182 feet high.

At the end of August 1997 over 10,000 spectators turned up for a 'dry run' to look around the inside of the stadium for the first time and watch a short game between the clubs youngsters. On the 1st September 1997 the first game took place when Everton were the visitors for a Premiership game, 102 years after they had been the first League visitors to Burnden Park.

Whilst the game itself was something of an anti climax, it became famous for the goal that never was from Gerry Taggart, the ball having crossed the line but missed by the 'unsighted' referee Steve Lodge. Alan Thompson scored the first goal in the stadium, converting a penalty in a 1-1 draw with Tottenham, Chris Armstrong netting their goal to have the distinction of scoring the first from open play.

In the five years since then the stadium has hosted international Rugby League games, with visits from both New Zealand and Australia, the World Club Championship won by St Helens and, in the summer of 2000, a rock concert over two evenings by Oasis.

The F.A also honoured the stadium by hosting four internationals in 2001 and 2002 at womens, under 17, under 20 and under 21 level, something that had never been seen at the club's other homes.

(Left) The steelwork goes up - October 1996...... (Above) February 1997, and the ground begins to take shape

April 1997

THE REEBOK STADIUM

~ Internationalists ~

Players capped whilst with Club (First number in brackets refers to number of appearances whilst with Bolton, followed by total number for Country as of final appearance whilst with Bolton) (comp. = competition, res. = result, gl = goals scored)

Country/Player)	Date	Opponents	Venue	comp.	res.	gl
FULL INTERNATIONALS						
ENGLAND						
T BANKS (6/6)	18.05.58	USSR	Moscow	FR	1-1	
	08.06.58	USSR (WC)	Gothenburg	WC	2-2	
	11.06.58	Brazil (WC)	Gothenburg	WC	0-0	
	15.06.58	Austria (WC)	Boras	WC	2-2	
	17.06.58	USSR(WC)	Gothenburg	WC	0-1	
	04.10.58	N Ireland	Belfast	HI	3-3	
W.BANNISTER (1/2)	22.03.02	Ireland	Belfast	HI	1-0	
M. BARRASS (3/3)	20.10.51	Wales	Cardiff	HI	1-1	
	14.11.51	N Ireland	Villa Park	HI	2-0	
	18.04.53	Scotland	Wembley	HI	2-2	
W. BUTLER (1/1)	12.04.24	Scotland	Wembley	HI	1-1	
J.K DAVENPORT (2/2)	14.03.1885	Wales	Blackburn	HI	1-1	
	15.03.1890	Ireland	Belfast	HI	9-1	2
G.R. EASTHAM (1/1)	18.05.35	Holland	Amsterdam	FR	1-0	
H.W. HASSALL (1/5)	11.11.53	N Ireland	Goodison	WCQ	3-1	2
F. HILL (2/2)	20.10.62	N Ireland	Belfast	HI	3-1	
	21.11.62	Wales	Wembley	HI	4-0	
A. D HOLDEN (5/5)	11.04.59	Scotland	Wembley	HI	1-0	
	06.05.59	Italy	Wembley	FR	2-2	
	13.05.59	Brazil	Rio	FR	0-2	
	17.05.59	Peru	Lima	FR	1-4	
	24.05.59	Mexico	Mexico C	FR	1-2	
E. HOPKINSON (14/14)	19.10.57	Wales	Cardiff	HI	4-0	
	06.11.57	N Ireland	Wembley	HI	2-3	
	27.11.57	France	Wembley	FR	4-0	
	19.04.58	Scotland	Glasgow	HI	4-0	
	07.05.58	Portugal	Wembley	FR	2-1	
	11.05.58	Yugoslavia	Belgrade	FR	0-5	
	11.04.59	Scotland	Wembley	HI	1-0	
	06.05.59	Italy	Wembley	FR	2-2	
	13.05.59	Brazil	Rio	FR	0-2	
	17.05.59	Peru	Lima	FR	1-4	
	24.05.59	Mexico	Mexico C	FR	1-2	
	28.05.59	USA	Los Angeles	FR	8-1	
	17.10.59	Wales	Cardiff	HI	1-1	
	28.10.59	Sweden	Wembley	FR	2-3	
D. JACK (4/4)	03.03.24	Wales	Blackburn	HI	1-2	
	12.04.24	Scotland	Wembley	HI	1-1	
	17.05.28	France	Paris	FR	5-1	1
	19.05.28	Belgium	Antwerp	FR	3-1	
F.W. KEAN (2/9)	09.05.29	France	Paris	FR	4-1	
	15.05.29	Spain	Madrid	FR	3-4	
R. LANGTON (2/11)	15.04.50	Scotland	Glasgow	HI	1-0	
	07.10.50	N Ireland	Belfast	HI	4-1	
N. LOFTHOUSE (33/33)	22.11.50	Yugoslavia	Highbury	FR	2-2	2
	20.10.51	Wales	Cardiff	HI	1-1	
	14.11.51	N Ireland	Villa Park	HI	2-0	2
	29.11.51	Austria	Wembley	FR	2-2	1
	05.04.52	Scotland	Glasgow	HI	2-1	
	18.05.52	Italy	Florence	FR	1-1	
	25.05.52	Austria	Vienna	FR	3-2	2
	28.05.52	Switzerland	Zurich	FR	3-0	2
	04.10.52	N Ireland	Belfast	HI	2-2	1
	12.11.52	Wales	Wembley	HI	5-2	2
	26.11.52	Belgium	Wembley	FR	5-0	2
	18.04.53	Scotland	Wembley	HI	2-2	
	17.05.53	Argentina	B Aires	FR	0-0	
	24.05.53	Chile	Santiago	FR	2-1	1
	31.05.53	Uruguay	Montevideo	FR	1-2	
	08.06.53	USA	New York	FR	6-3	2
	10.10.53	Wales	Cardiff	WCQ	4-1	2
	21.10.53	Rest Of Europe	Wembley	FR	4-4	
	11.11.53	N Ireland	Goodison	HI	3-1	1
	17.06.54	Belgium	Basle	WC	4-4	2
	26.06.54	Uruguay	Basle	WC	2-4	1
	02.10.54	N Ireland	Belfast	HI	2-0	
	02.04.55	Scotland	Wembley	HI	7-2	2
	18.05.55	France	Paris	FR	0-1	
	20.05.55	Spain	Madrid	FR	1-1	
	22.05.55	Portugal	Oporto	FR	1-3	
	02.10.55	Denmark	Copenhagen	FR	5-1	
Lofthouse (Cont.)	22.10.55	Wales	Cardiff	HI	1-1	
	30.11.55	Spain	Wembley	FR	4-1	
	14.04.56	Scotland	Glasgow	HI	1-1	
	20.05.56	Finland (Sub)	Helsinki	FR	5-1	2
	22.10.58	USSR	Wembley	FR	5-0	1
	26.11.58	Wales	Villa Park	HI	2-2	
H. NUTTALL (3/3)	22.10.27	Ireland	Belfast	HI	0-2	
	28.11.27	Wales	Turf Moor	HI	1-2	
	13.04.29	Scotland	Glasgow	HI	0-1	
R. A PARRY (2/2)	18.11.59	N Ireland	Wembley	HI	2-1	1
	19.04.60	Scotland	Glasgow	HI	1-1	
R. H PYM (3/3)	28.02.25	Wales	Swansea	HI	2-1	
	04.04.25	Scotland	Glasgow	HI	0-2	
	01.03.26	Wales	Selhurst	HI	1-3	
M. RICKETTS (1/1)	13.02.02	Holland	Amsterdam	FR	1-1	
J. SEDDON (6/6)	10.05.23	France	Paris	FR	4-1	
	21.05.23	Sweden	Stockholm	FR	4-2	
	24.05.23	Sweden	Stockholm	FR	3-1	
	01.11.23	Belgium	Antwerp	FR	2-2	
	12.02.27	Wales	Wrexham	HI	3-3	
	13.04.29	Scotland	Glasgow	HI	0-1	
A. SHEPHERD (1/1)	07.04.06	Scotland	Glasgow	HI	1-2	1
J. SMITH (5/5)	15.02.13	Ireland	Belfast	HI	1-2	
	16.03.14	Wales	Cardiff	HI	2-0	1
	04.04.14	Scotland	Glasgow	HI	1-3	
	25.10.19	Ireland	Belfast	HI	1-1	
	15.03.20	Wales	Arsenal	HI	1-2	
J.W SUTCLIFFE (4/4)	13.03.1893	Wales	Stoke	HI	6-0	
	09.03.1895	Ireland	Derby	HI	9-0	
	06.04.1895	Scotland	Goodison	HI	3-0	
	30.03.1901	Scotland	Crystal Pal.	HI	2-2	
J. A TURNER (1/1)	13.03.1893	Wales	Stoke	HI	6-0	
D. WEIR (2/2)	02.03.1889	Ireland	Everton	HI	6-1	1
	13.04.1889	Scotland	Kennington O.	HI	2-3	1
R. WESTWOOD (6/6)	29.09.34	Wales	Cardiff	HI	4-0	
	06.04.35	Scotland	Glasgow	HI	0-2	
	18.05.35	Holland	Amsterdam	FR	1-0	
	19.10.35	Ireland	Belfast	HI	3-1	
	04.12.35	Germany	Tottenham	FR	3-0	
	17.10.35	Wales	Cardiff	HI	1-2	
J.E. WHEELER (1/1)	02.10.54	N Ireland	Belfast	HI	2-0	
SCOTLAND						
W.L. COOK (3/3)	14.04.34	England	Wembley	HI	0-3	
	20.10.34	Ireland	Belfast	HI	1-2	
	21.11.34	Wales	Aberdeen	HI	3-2	
A. DONALDSON (6/6)	28.02.14	Wales	Glasgow	HI	0-0	
	14.03.14	Ireland	Belfast	HI	1-1	
	04.04.14	England	Glasgow	HI	3-1	
	13.03.20	Ireland	Glasgow	HI	3-0	
	10.04.20	England	Sheffield	HI	4-5	1
	04.03.22	Ireland	Glasgow	HI	2-1	
C.HENDRY (2/51)	24.03.01	Belgium	Glasgow	WCQ	2-2	
	28.03.01	San Marino	Glasgow	WCQ	4-0	2
A.JOHNSTON (2/9)	29.03.00	France(Sub)	Glasgow	FR	0-2	
	30.05.00	Ireland(Sub)	Dublin	FR	2-1	
J. MCGINLAY (14/14)	20.04.94	Austria	Vienna	FR	2-1	1
	27.05.94	Holland	Utrecht	FR	0-3	
	12.10.94	Faroe Islands	Glasgow	ECQ	5-1	1
	16.11.94	Russia	Glasgow	ECQ	1-1	
	18.12.94	Greece	Athens	ECQ	0-1	
	29.03.95	Russia	Moscow	ECQ	0-0	
	26.04.95	San Marino	Serravalle	ECQ	2-0	
	07.06.95	Faroe Islands	Toftir	ECQ	2-0	1
	11.10.95	Sweden	Stockholm	ECQ	0-2	
	09.10.96	Estonia (Aban.))	Tallinn	WCQ		
	10.11.96	Sweden	Ibrox	WCQ	1-0	1
	11.02.97	Estonia	Monaco	WCQ	0-0	
	29.03.97	Estonia (Sub)	Kilmarnock	WCQ	2-0	
	02.04.97	Austria (Sub)	Celtic Park	WCQ	2-0	
P.RITCHIE (2/6)	29.03.00	France	Glasgow	FR	0-2	
	26.04.00	Holland	Arnhem	FR	0-0	

Player	Date	Opponent		Venue	Comp	Score	G
W. MOIR (1/1)	15.04.50	England		Hampden	WCQ	0-1	1
W. WHITE (2/2)	06.04.07	England		Newcastle	HI	1-1	
	04.04.08	England		Glasgow	HI	1-1	

WALES

Player	Date	Opponent		Venue	Comp	Score	G
N. BLAKE (5/10)	24.01.96	Italy (Sub)		Terni	FR	0-3	
	20.08.97	Turkey		Istanbul	WCQ	4-6	1
	05.09.98	Italy		Liverpool	ECQ	0-2	
	10.10.98	Denmark		Copenhagen	ECQ	2-1	
	14.10.98	Belarus		Cardiff	ECQ	3-2	
D. DAVIES (3/3)	12.03.1904	Scotland		Dundee	HI	1-1	
	21.03.1904	Ireland		Bangor	HI	0-1	
	16.03.08	England	(Sub)	Wrexham	HI	1-7	
R. W DAVIES (16/16)	12.10.63	England		Cardiff	HI	0-4	
	03.10.64	Scotland		Cardiff	HI	3-2	1
	21.10.64	Denmark		Copenhagen	WCQ	0-1	
	18.11.64	England		Wembley	HI	1-2	
	09.12.64	Greece		Athens	WCQ	0-2	
	31.03.65	N Ireland		Belfast	FR	5-0	
	30.05.65	USSR		Moscow	WCQ	1-2	1
	02.10.65	England		Cardiff	HI	0-0	
	27.10.65	USSR		Cardiff	WCQ	2-1	
	24.11.65	Scotland		Hampden	HI	1-4	
	01.12.65	Denmark		Wrexham	WCQ	4-2	1
	30.03.66	N Ireland		Cardiff	HI	1-4	1
	14.05.66	Brazil		Rio	FR	1-3	
	18.05.66	Brazil		Belo Horionte	FR	0-1	
	22.05.66	Chile	(Sub)	Santiago	FR	0-2	
	22.10.66	Scotland		Cardiff	HI	1-1	
T. P GRIFFITHS (3/11)	26.10.32	Scotland		Edinburgh	HI	5-2	1
	16.11.32	England		Wrexham	HI	0-0	
	07.12.32	Ireland		Wrexham	HI	4-1	
W. JENNINGS (11/11)	28.02.14	Scotland		Glasgow	HI	0-0	
	16.03.14	England		Cardiff	HI	0-2	
	26.02.20	Scotland		Cardiff	HI	1-1	
	05.03.23	England		Cardiff	HI	2-2	
	14.04.23	Ireland		Wrexham	HI	0-3	
	16.02.24	Scotland		Cardiff	HI	2-0	
	03.03.24	England		Blackburn	HI	2-1	
	15.03.24	Ireland		Belfast	HI	1-0	
	30.10.26	Scotland		Glasgow	HI	0-3	
	09.04.27	Ireland		Cardiff	HI	2-2	
	27.10.28	Scotland		Glasgow	HI	2-4	
D. JONES (11/13)	23.02.89	England		Stoke	HI	1-4	
	15.04.89	Scotland		Wrexham	HI	0-0	
	27.04.89	Ireland		Belfast	HI	3-1	
	08.02.90	Ireland		Shrewsbury	HI	5-2	
	15.03.90	England		Wrexham	HI	1-3	
	21.03.91	Scotland		Wrexham	HI	3-4	
	27.02.92	Ireland		Bangor	HI	1-1	
	13.03.93	England		Stoke	HI	0-6	
	12.03.94	England		Wrexham	HI	1-5	
	18.03.95	England		London	HI	1-1	
	19.03.98	Scotland		Motherwell	HI	2-5	
E. JONES (1/7)	19.01.14	Ireland		Wrexham	HI	1-2	1
J. POWELL (1/10)	17.03.84	England		Wrexham	HI	0-4	
J. H. ROBERTS (1/1)	23.05.49	Belgium		Liege	FR	1-3	
R. ROBERTS (7/8)	21.03.87	Scotland		Wrexham	HI	0-2	
	04.02.88	England		Crewe	HI	1-5	
	10.03.88	Scotland		Edinburgh	HI	1-5	
	23.02.89	England		Stoke	HI	1-4	
	15.04.89	England		Wrexham	HI	0-0	
	22.03.90	Scotland		Glasgow	HI	0-5	
	27.02.92	Ireland		Bangor	HI	1-1	
J. TRAINER (1/1)	21.03.87	Scotland		Wrexham	HI	0-2	
J. VAUGHAN (1/11)	17.03.84	England		Wrexham	HI	0-4	
E. T VIZARD (22/22)	28.01.11	Ireland		Belfast	HI	2-1	
	06.03.11	Scotland		Cardiff	HI	2-2	
	13.03.11	England		London	HI	0-3	
	02.03.12	Scotland		Edinburgh	HI	0-1	
	11.03.12	England		Wrexham	HI	0-2	
	03.03.13	Scotland		Wrexham	HI	0-0	
	19.01.14	Ireland		Wrexham	HI	1-2	
	16.03.14	England		Cardiff	HI	0-2	
	15.03.20	England		London	HI	2-1	
	12.02.21	Scotland		Aberdeen	HI	1-2	
	16.03.21	England		Cardiff	HI	0-0	
	09.04.21	Ireland		Swansea	HI	2-1	
	04.02.22	Scotland		Wrexham	HI	2-1	
	13.03.22	England		Liverpool	HI	0-1	
	05.03.23	England		Cardiff	HI	2-2	

Player	Date	Opponent		Venue	Comp	Score	G
Vizard (Cont.)	14.04.23	Ireland		Wrexham	HI	0-3	
	16.02.24	Scotland		Cardiff	HI	2-0	
	03.03.24	England		Blackburn	HI	2-1	1
	15.03.24	Ireland		Belfast	HI	1-0	
	31.10.25	Scotland		Cardiff	HI	0-3	
	01.03.26	England		London	HI	3-1	
	30.10.26	Scotland		Glasgow	HI	0-3	

NORTHERN IRELAND

Player	Date	Opponent		Venue	Comp	Score	G
A. DAVISON (1/1)	24.4.96	Sweden		Belfast	FR	1-2	
W. HUGHES (1/1)	07.03.51	Wales		Belfast	HI	1-2	
W. MCADAMS (9/14)	08.10.60	England		Belfast	HI	2-5	2
	26.10.60	West Germany		Belfast	WCQ	3-4	3
	09.11.60	Scotland		Hampden	HI	2-5	
	12.04.61	Wales		Belfast	HI	1-5	
	25.04.61	Italy		Bologna	FR	2-3	1
	03.05.61	Greece		Athens	WCQ	1-2	
	10.05.61	West Germany		Berlin	WCQ	1-2	
	17.10.61	Greece		Belfast	WCQ	2-0	
	22.11.61	England		Wembley	HI	1-1	
G. MCELHINNEY (6/6)	16.11.83	West Germany		Hamburg	ECQ	1-0	
	13.12.83	Scotland		Belfast	HI	2-0	
	04.04.84	England		Wembley	HI	0-1	
	22.05.84	Wales		Swansea	HI	1-1	
	27.05.84	Finland		Pori	WCQ	0-1	
	12.09.84	Romania		Belfast	WCQ	3-2	
R. J NAPIER (1/1)	07.05.66	West Germany		Belfast	FR	0-2	
G. TAGGART (10/10 (10/46)	9.11.96	Germany		Nuremburg	WCQ	1-1	1
	14.12.96	Albania		Belfast	WCQ	2-0	
	22.1.97	Italy		Palermo	FR	0-2	
	11.2.97	Belgium		Belfast	FR	3-0	
	29.3.97	Portugal		Belfast	WCQ	0-0	
	2.4.97	Ukraine		Kiev	WCQ	1-2	
	30.4.97	Armenia		Erevan	WCQ	0-0	
	20.8.97	Germany		Belfast	WCQ	1-3	
	11.10.97	Portugal		Lisbon	WCQ	0-1	
	02.06.98	Spain		Santander	FR	1-4	1

EIRE

Player	Date	Opponent		Venue	Comp	Score	G
K. BRANAGAN (1/1)	11.2.97	Wales		Cardiff	FR	0-0	
O. COYLE (1/1)	20.04.94	Holland (Sub)		Tilburg	FR	1-0	
A.P. DUNNE (9/33)	05.05.74	Brazil (Sub)		Rio	FR	1-2	
	08.05.74	Uruguay		Montevideo	FR	0-2	
	12.05.74	Chile		Santiago	FR	2-1	
	20.11.74	Turkey		Izmir	ECQ	1-1	
	01.03.75	West Germany B		Dublin	FR	1-0	
	11.05.75	Switzerland		Dublin	ECQ	2-1	
	18.05.75	USSR		Kiev	ECQ	1-2	
	21.05.75	Switzerland		Berne	ECQ	0-1	
	29.10.75	Turkey		Dublin	ECQ	4-0	
G.FARRELLY (1/6)	06.06.00	USA		Boston	NIKECUP	1-1	
C. HURLEY (1/40)	08.06.69	Hungary		Dublin	WCQ	1-2	
A. KERNAGHAN (1/12)	12.10.94	Liechtenstein		Dublin	WCQ	4-0	
J. MCATEER (14/14)	23.03.94	Russia		Dublin	FR	0-0	
	20.04.94	Holland (Sub)		Tilburg	FR	1-0	
	24.05.94	Bolivia (Sub)		Dublin	FR	1-0	
	05.06.94	Czech Rep (Sub)		Dublin	FR	1-3	
	29.05.94	Germany		Hanover	FR	2-0	
	18.06.94	Italy (Sub)		New York	WC	1-0	
	24.06.94	Mexico (Sub)		Orlando	WC	1-2	
	28.06.94	Norway		New York	WC	0-0	
	04.07.94	Holland (Sub)		Orlando	WC	0-2	
	07.09.94	Latvia		Riga	ECQ	3-0	
	12.10.94	Liechtenstein		Dublin	ECQ	4-0	
	16.11.94	N Ireland		Belfast	ECQ	4-0	
	29.03.95	N Ireland (Sub)		Dublin	ECQ	1-1	
	03.06.95	Liechtenstein		Vaduz	ECQ	0-0	
J. MCDONAGH (9/13)	09.09.81	Holland		Rotterdam	WCQ	2-2	
	14.10.81	France		Dublin	WCQ	3-2	
	22.05.82	Chile		Santiago	FR	0-1	
	27.05.82	Brazil		Uderlandia	FR	0-7	
	22.09.82	Holland		Rotterdam	ECQ	1-2	
	13.10.82	Iceland		Dublin	ECQ	2-0	
	17.11.82	Spain		Dublin	ECQ	3-3	
	30.03.83	Malta		Valletta	ECQ	1-0	
	27.04.83	Spain		Zaragoza	ECQ	0-2	

DENMARK

Player	Date	Opponent		Venue	Comp	Score	G
P . FRANDSEN (18/22)	09.11.96	France		Copenhagen	FR	1-0	
	29.03.97	Croatia		Zagreb	WCQ	1-1	
	30.04.97	Slovakia (Sub)		Copenhagen	WCQ	4-0	
	08.06.97	Bosnia (Sub)		Copenhagen	WCQ	2-0	
	10.09.97	Cratia		Copenhagen	WCQ	3-1	
	26.03.98	Scotland (Sub)		Glasgow	FR	1-0	

Jason McAteer

Frandsen (Cont.)	22.04.98	Norway	Copenhagen	FR	0-2	
	28.04.98	Sweden	Malmo	FR	0-3	
	05.06.98	Cameroun (Sub)	Copenhagen	FR	1-2	
	12.06.98	Saudi Arabia (Sub)	Lens	WC	1-0	
	28.06.98	Nigeria (Sub)	Paris	WC	4-1	
	19.08.98	Czech Rep (Sub)	Prague	FR	0-1	
	10.10.98	Wales	Copenhagen	ECQ	1-2	
	14.10.98	Switzerland	Zurich	ECQ	1-1	
	10.06.99	Wales (Sub)	Liverpool	ECQ	2-0	
	16.08.00	Faroes (Sub)	Torshavn	FR	2-0	
	01.09.01	N. Ireland (Sub)	Copenhagen	WCQ	1-1	
	17.04.02	Israel (Sub)	Copenhagen	FR	3-1	

S. TOFTING (7/41)

	13.02.02	S. Arabia	Riyadh	FR	1-0	
	17.05.02	Cameroun	Copenhagen	FR	2-1	
	26.05.02	Tunisia	Wakayama	FR	2-1	
	01.06.02	Uruguay	Ulsan	WC	2-1	
	06.06.02	Senegal	Daegu	WC	1-1	
	11.06.02	France	Incheon	WC	2-0	
	15.06.02	England	Niigata	WC	0-3	

C. JENSEN (1/1)

| | 29.03.00 | Portugal(Sub) | Lisbon | FR | 1-2 | |

FINLAND
J. JAASKELAINEN (9/9)

	25.03.98	Malta	Valetta	FR	2-0	
	19.08.98	Slovakia (Sub)	Kosice	FR	0-0	
	10.02.99	Poland (Sub)	Valetta	FR	1-1	
	28.04.99	Slovenia (Sub)	Ljubljana	FR	1-1	
	16.08.00	Norway	Helsinki	FR	3-1	
	02.09.00	Albania	Helsinki	WCQ	2-1	
	15.11.00	Ireland	Dublin	FR	0-3	
	20.03.02	S. Korea	Cartagena	FR	0-2	
	22.05.02	Latvia (Sub)	Helsinki	FR	2-1	

M. PAATELAINEN (10/50) 17.08.94 Denmark

	17.08.94	Denmark	Copenhagen	FR	1-2	
	07.09.94	Scotland	Helsinki	ECQ	0-2	
	12.10.94	Greece	Salonika	ECQ	0-4	
	16.11.94	Faroes	Helsinki	ECQ	5-0	2
	14.12.94	San Marino	Helsinki	ECQ	4-1	4
	26.04.95	Faroes	Toftir	ECQ	4-0	1
	01.06.95	Denmark (Sub)	Helsinki	FR	0-1	
	11.06.95	Greece	Helsinki	ECQ	2-1	
	16.08.95	Russia	Helsinki	ECQ	0-6	
	02.04.97	Azerbaijan	Baku	WCQ	2-1	1

J. VIANDER (2/13)

| | 04.01.02 | Bahrain | Manama | FR | 2-0 | |
| | 10.01.02 | Macedonia | Manama | FR | 3-0 | |

FRANCE
Y. DJORKAEFF (6/81)

	27.03.02	Scotland (Sub)	Paris	FR	5-0	
	17.04.02	Russia	Paris	FR	0-0	
	18.05.02	Belgium	Paris	FR	1-2	
	26.05.02	South Korea	Suwon	FR	3-2	
	31.05.02	Senegal	Seoul	WC	0-1	
	11.06.02	Denmark (Sub)	Incheon	WC	0-2	

GREECE
K. KONSTANTINIDIS (2/33) 17.04.02 Czech Rep

| | 17.04.02 | Czech Rep | Athens | FR | 0-0 | |
| | 15.05.02 | Cyprus | Rhodes | FR | 3-1 | |

ICELAND
G.BERGSSON (18/77)

	22.04.95	Chile	Temuco	FR	1-1	
	01.06.95	Sweden	Solna	FR	1-1	
	11.06.95	Hungary	Reykjavic	ECQ	2-1	
	16.08.95	Switzerland	Reykjavic	ECQ	0-2	
	11.10.95	Turkey	Reykjavic	ECQ	0-0	
	11.11.95	Hungary	Budapest	ECQ	0-1	
	24.04.96	Estonia	Tallinn	WCQ	3-0	
	01.06.96	Macedonia	Reykjavic	WCQ	1-1	
	05.06.96	Cyprus	Reykjavic	FR	2-1	
	04.09.96	Czech Rep	Jablonec	FR	1-2	
	5.10.96	Lithuania	Vilnius	WCQ	0-2	
	09.10.96	Romania	Reykjavic	WCQ	0-4	
	29.04.97	Slovakia	Reykjavic	FR	1-3	
	07.06.97	Macedonia	Skopje	WCQ	0-1	
	11.06.97	Lithuania	Reykjavic	WCQ	0-0	
	20.07.97	Norway	Reykjavic	FR	0-1	
	20.08.97	Liechtenstein	Vaduz	WCQ	4-0	
	06.09.97	Ireland	Reykjavic	WCQ	2-4	

E. GUDJOHNSEN (3/4)

	04.09.99	Andorra (Sub)	Reykjavic	ECQ	3-0	1
	08.09.99	Ukraine (Sub)	Reykjavic	ECQ	0-1	
	09.10.99	France (Sub)	Paris	ECQ	2-3	

A. GUNNLAUGSSON (6/28)

	27.07.97	Faroe Islands	Reykjavic	FR	1-0	
	05.02.98	Slovenia	Cyprus	FR	2-3	
	09.02.98	Norway	Cyprus	FR	0-1	
	05.09.98	France	Reykjavic	ECQ	1-1	
	10.10.98	Armenia	Yerevan	ECQ	0-0	
	14.10.98	Russia	Reykjavic	ECQ	1-0	

B. KRISTINSSON (3/58)

	10.03.99	Luxembourg	Luxembourg	FR	2-1	
	27.03.99	Andorra	Andorra	ECQ	2-0	
	31.03.99	Ukraine	Kiev	ECQ	1-1	

JAMAICA
R. GARDNER (22/68)

	10.02.99	Costa Rica	Kingston	FR	1-1	
	28.03.99	Trinidad & Tobago	Port Of Spain	FR	0-2	
	31.03.99	Paraguay	Kingston	FR	3-0	
	07.06.99	Grenada	Port Of Spain	CC	2-1	
	10.06.99	Cuba	Port Of Spain	CC	0-2	
	08.09.99	USA	Port Of Spain	CC	2-2	2
	16.01.00	New Zealand	China	FR	2-1	
	08.02.00	Cayman Islands	USA	FR	3-0	
	12.02.00	Columbia	USA	GC	0-1	
	14.02.00	Honduras	USA	GC	0-2	
	15.11.00	El Salvador	San Salvador	WCQ	0-2	
	26.01.00	Bolivia	Miami	FR	3-0	
	28.01.00	Bulgaria	Kingston	FR	0-0	
	28.02.01	Trinidad & Tobago	Kingston	WCQ	1-0	
	25.03.01	Mexico	Mexico City	WCQ	0-4	
	25.04.01	Honduras	Kingston	WCQ	1-1	1
	10.06.01	Cuba	Kingston	WCQ	4-1	1
	16.06.01	USA	Kingston	WCQ	0-0	
	30.06.01	Trinidad & Tobago	Port Of Spain	WCQ	2-1	
	02.09.01	Mexico	Kingston	WCQ	1-2	
	05.09.01	Honduras	Tegucigalpa	WCQ	0-1	
	07.10.01	USA	Boston	WCQ	1-2	

J. JOHNSON (2/12)

| | 07.10.01 | USA (Sub) | Boston | WCQ | 1-2 | |
| | 16.05.02 | USA (Sub) | East Rutherford | FR | 0-5 | |

JAPAN
A. NISHIZAWA (2/26)

| | 07.10.01 | Nigeria | Southampton | FR | 0-2 | |
| | 07.11.01 | Italy (Sub) | Saitama | FR | 1-1 | |

SOUTH AFRICA
M. FISH (34/60)

	16.11.97	Germany	Dusseldorf	FR	0-3	
	07.12.97	Brazil	Johannesburg	FR	1-2	
	13.12.97	Czech Rep	Riyadh	PC	2-2	
	15.12.97	Uae	Riyadh	PC	0-1	
	17.12.97	Uruguay	Riyadh	PC	3-4	
	24.01.98	Namibia	Windhoek	COS	2-3	
	08.02.98	Angola	Bobo Dioulaso	ANC	0-0	
	11.02.98	Ivory Coast	Bobo Dioulaso	ANC	1-1	
	22.02.98	Morroco	Ouagoudougu	ANC	2-1	
	25.02.98	Congo	Ouagoudougu	ANC	2-1	
	28.02.98	Egypt	Ouagoudougu	ANCF	0-2	
	20.05.98	Zambia	Johannesburg	FR	1-1	
	25.05.98	Argentina	Buenos Aires	FR	0-2	
	06.06.98	Iceland	Balersbron	FR	1-1	
	12.06.98	France	Marseille	WC	0-3	
	18.06.98	Denmark	Toulouse	WC	1-1	
	24.06.98	Saudi Arabia	Bordeaux	WC	2-2	
	03.10.98	Angola	Johannesburg	ANC Q	1-0	
	16.12.98	Egypt	Johannesburg	FR	2-1	
	23.01.99	Mauritius	Port Louis	ANC Q	1-1	
	27.02.99	Gabon	Cape Town	ANC Q	4-1	
	10.04.99	Gabon	Libreville	ANC Q	0-1	
	28.04.99	Denmark	Copenhagen	FR	1-1	
	05.06.99	Mauritius	Durban	ANC Q	2-0	
	16.06.99	Zimbabwe	Johannesburg	FR	0-1	
	18.09.99	Saudi Arabia	Cape Town	AA	1-1	
	30.09.99	Saudi Arabia	Riyadh	AA	0-0	
	23.01.00	Gabon	Kumasi	ANC	3-1	
	27.01.00	Dr Congo	Kumasi	ANC	1-0	
	02.02.00	Algeria	Kumasi	ANC	1-1	
	06.02.00	Ghana	Kumasi	ANCQF	1-0	
	10.02.00	Nigeria	Accra	ANCSF	0-2	
	03.09.00	Congo	Pointe Noire	ANCQ	2-1	
	07.10.00	France	Johannesburg	FR	0-0	

Mark Fish

YUGOSLAVIA
S. CURCIC (3/10)

	27.03.96	Romania	Belgrade	FR	1-0	
	24.04.96	Faroe Islands	Belgrade	WCQ	3-1	
	23.05.96	Mexico	Japan	FR	0-0	
	26.05.96	Japan (Sub)	Japan	FR	0-1	

Under 23
ENGLAND
F. HILL (10/10)

	15.03.61	W. Germany	Tottenham	FR	4-1	
	09.11.61	Israel	Leeds	FR	7-1	2
	29.11.61	Holland	Rotterdam	FR	5-2	1
	28.02.62	Scotland	Aberdeen	FR	4-2	
	22.03.62	Turkey	Southampton	FR	4-1	2
	07.11.62	Belgium	Plymouth	FR	6-1	1
	28.11.62	Greece	Birmingham	FR	5-0	
	21.03.63	Yugoslavia	Manchester	FR	0-0	
	29.05.63	Yugoslavia	Belgrade	FR	4-2	
	02.06.63	Rumania	Bucharest	B FR	0-1	

E. HOPKINSON (6/6)

	19.05.57	Bulgaria	Sofia	FR	1-2	
	26.05.57	Rumania	Bucharest	B FR	1-0	
	30.05.57	Czechoslovakia	Bratislava	FR	2-0	
	25.09.57	Bulgaria	Chelsea	FR	6-2	
	15.01.58	Scotland	Everton	FR	3-1	
	18.03.59	France	Lyon	FR	1-1	

R. PARRY (4/4)

	16.10.57	Rumania	Wembley	FR	3-2
	18.03.59	France	Lyon	FR	1-1
	07.05.59	Italy	Milan	FR	3-0
	10.05.59	West Germany	Bochum	FR	2-2

D. STEVENS (2/2)

	26.05.57	Rumania	Bucharest	FR	1-0
	30.05.57	Czechoslovakia	Bratislava	FR	2-0

N. IRELAND
J. NAPIER (1/1)

	22.02.67	Wales	Belfast	FR	2-1

WALES
W. DAVIES (4/4)

	05.12.62	Scotland	Aberdeen	FR	0-2
	13.11.63	England	Bristol	FR	1-1
	30.11.64	Scotland	Wrexham	FR	6-0
	10.02.65	N Ireland	Cardiff	FR	2-2

M. EDWARDS (2/2)

	23.04.58	England	Wrexham	FR	1-2
	25.11.59	Scotland	Wrexham	FR	1-1

Under 21
DENMARK
C. JENSEN (8/19)

	18.08.98	Czech Rep	Prague	FR	1-0
	04.09.98	Belarus	Minsk	ECQ	2-0	1
	09.10.98	Wales	Odense	ECQ	2-2
	13.10.98	Switzerland	Basle	ECQ	0-2
	09.02.99	Croatia	Zagreb	FR	0-0
	04.06.99	Belarus	Odense	ECQ	3-0
	09.06.99	Wales	Wrexham	ECQ	2-1
	08.10.99	England	Bradford	FR	1-4

ENGLAND
P. REID(6/6)

	27.04.77	Scotland	Bramall Lane	FR	1-0
	26.05.77	Finland	Helsinki	ECQ	1-0
	01.06.77	Norway	Bergen	ECQ	2-1
	12.10.77	Finland	Hull	ECQ	8-1
	05.04.78	Italy	Rome	ECQ	0-0
	19.04.78	Yugoslavia	Novi Sad	ECQ	1-2

A. THOMPSON (2/2)

	07.06.95	Latvia	Burnley	ECQ	4-0
	02.09.95	Portugal	S M De Lamas	ECQ	0-2

NORTHERN IRELAND
W. BUCHANAN (1/1)

	12.02.02	Germany (Sub)	Belfast	FR	0-1

ICELAND
E. GUDJOHNSEN (1/1)

	09.10.98	Armenia	Yerevan	ECQ	1-3	1

B Internationals
ENGLAND
E. BELL (1/1)

	16.05.54	Yugoslavia	Lubljana	FR	1-2

N. LOFTHOUSE (1/1)

	22.02.50	Holland	Newcastle	FR	1-0

J. WHEELER (4/4)

	26.03.52	Holland	Amsterdam	FR	1-0
	22.05.52	France	Le Havre	FR	1-7
	23.03.55	West Germany	Hillsborough	FR	1-1
	29.02.56	Scotland	Dundee	FR	2-2

A. STUBBS (1/1)

	10.05.94	N Ireland	Hillsborough	FR	4-2

EIRE
K. BRANAGAN (1/1)

	13.12.94	England	Liverpool	FR	0-2

O. COYLE (1/1)

	13.12.94	England	Liverpool	FR	0-2

J. MCATEER (1/1)

	13.12.94	England	Liverpool	FR	0-2

SCOTLAND
J. MCGINLAY (1/1)

	15.04.96	Denmark	Aalborg	FR	0-2

FOOTBALL LEAGUE Under 21
S. TAYLOR (1/1)

	19.02.97	Italian League	Piacenza		1-1

Competition codes

WC	World Cup Finals	HI	Home International
WCQ	World Cup Finals qualifier	AA	Afro.Asian Cup
ECQ	European Champs. qualifier	PC	Presidents Cup
ANC	African Nations Cup	COS	Cosafa Castle Cup
ANCQ	African Nations Cup qualifier	CC	Copa Caribe Cup
FR	Friendly	GC	Gold Cup

ENGLAND YOUTH INTERNATIONALS

Aljofree H	1995
Holden D	1998
Bennett M	1980 1981
Jones D	1973
Birch B	1955
Lee F H	1961
Bromley B	1964/65
Nolan K	2000/01/02
Burke D	1979
Novaki Y	1977
Coghiel R	1984
Parry R	1952
Dean J	1957 1958
Phythian E	1959
Ellis R	1970
Redrobe E	1961
Farrimond S	1958
Robinson B	1961
Foster W	1982
Siddall B	1973
France K	1959
Smith B	1973 1974
Thompson C	1978

OTHER YOUTH INTERNATIONALS

Buchanan W	N Ireland
Power A	Ireland
Byrne M	Wales
Ross C	Ireland
Evans J	Scotland
Ryan C	Ireland
Macleod J	Scotland
Snorrason O	Iceland
Minchella M	Scotland

Nat Lofthouse

ENGLAND V YOUNG ENGLAND

Hill F	1961
Holden D	1959
Hopkinson E	1959

VICTORY AND WARTIME INTERNATIONALS

ENGLAND			WALES		
Barrass M	1946	(1)	Vizard T	1920	(1)
Goslin H	1940/41/42	(4)	Winter F	1945/46	(2)
Smith J	1919	(2)			

SCOTLAND

Donaldson A	1919	(1)

FOOTBALL LEAGUE REPRESENTATIVES

Ball J	1952/54	(2)	Hopkinson E	1958.1960	(2)
Banks T	1958	(1)	Jack DBN	1923.1928/29	(3)
Bannister W	1902	(1)	Langton R	12951/52	(3)
Barrass M	1952	(2)	Lofthouse N	1951/2/3/4/5/6/7	(14)
Bell. E	1954	(1)	Parry RA	1958.1960	(2)
Fay J	1912/13	(2)	Pym RH	1924/25	(2)
Fitchett J	1901/02	(2)	Shepherd A	1906	(1)
Gardiner H	1892	(1)	Stevens D	1958	(1)
Greenhalgh S	1904.1908.1910	(4)	Stokes D	1905.1907.1909	(4)
Hartle R	1959	(1)	Sutcliffe JW	1894.1896/97	(3)
Hassall H	1954/55	(2)	Westwood R	1935/6/7/8	(6)
Holden D	1959	(1)	Wheeler J	1955	(1)

John McGinlay
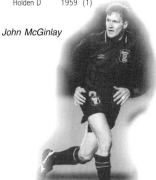

Eddie Hopkinson

The Managers

JOHN SOMERVILLE: 1908-1910.

Popular former player John Somerville was appointed the Wanderers first secretary-manager at the start of the 1908/09 season. He had joined the Wanderers in March 1890, from his native Ayr, and, as a player, helped the club to reach the 1894 F.A. Cup Final and to win promotion to Division One in 1899. As a right back he was a member of the clubs immaculate defensive line up of the 1890's and went on to play 293 first class games, the last being in April 1901.

His first season at the helm saw the Trotters win their first championship trophy. The Second Division title was secured and a return to the top flight after just one season's absence. Somerville had been allowed to spend over £3,000 in revamping the side for a quick return but the following season he found that the investments were not good enough to keep Bolton in the First Division.

In January 1910, the Wanderers found themselves bottom of Division One and knocked out of the F.A. Cup by Second Division Stockport County. Somerville was relieved of the manager's position but remained as secretary until the end of that fateful season.

He later became a Football League linesman and passed away in March 1917 aged 49.

WILL SETTLE: 1910-1915.

Will Settle's link with the club came from his father, Mr Miles Settle JP, who became a director of the club in 1895 in the year that Burnden Park was opened and the club became a limited company.

Both Will Settle and his father were involved in the control of Settle, Speakmen and Co, coal merchants. Will Settle took the place of his father on the board of directors in 1898 and became manager in January 1910.

There was little that could be done to arrest the club's free fall into Division Two in 1910 but the following season proved successful as Settle guided the club to promotion with the help of trainer George Eccles and assistant Peter Bullough. Investment in the team, in an attempt to remain in the First Division, was heavy with the likes of Fay, Donaldson, Gimblett, Bentley, Seddon, Lillycrop and Glendenning all secured under Settle's management. The discovery of left-wing pairing Ted Vizard and Joe Smith did save the club a considerable amount of money and they were to prove invaluable in the clubs improvement during the period.

Further secure financial management saw the club make a profit after selling Tom Barber to Aston Villa and, with the profits, pay for the roofing of the Great Lever End. Settle was awarded a five year contract and the club continued to prosper. In 1914 the club finished sixth in the First Division and the following year reached the F.A. Cup semi-finals only to lose out to Sheffield United. War time football intervened and this led to Settle ending his seventeen year association with the club after he was relieved of the day to day duties.

He left Bolton in 1918 and resided in Caernarfon where he passed away in September 1941 aged 73.

TOM MATHER: 1915-1919.

Chorley Born Tom Mather joined the club during Will Settle's stewardship and acted as secretary before being appointed manger-secretary in 1915. All the games played under Mather were during the First World War and, as such, proved to be a difficult time as the club did not know if they would be able to field a team from one week to the next. This experience was to stand Mather in good stead for his future roles at other clubs.

Further problems arose when he was called up by the Royal Navy and, during this period, his duties were carried out by his assistant, Charles Foweraker. In February 1919 the Bolton directors placed the management of the team in the hands of Ted Vizard. This was an interim measure to get the club through the remaining war time games with a return to normal League football being imminent.

After the War Mather left the club and took on the same role at Southend United. In October 1923 he was appointed manager at Stoke City, guiding them to the Second Division title in 1933. Two years later he joined Newcastle United and remained at St James's Park until 1939.

After the Second World War he managed Leicester City and Kilmarnock and after retirement settled in Stoke where he died in March 1957.

CHARLES FOWERAKER: 1919-1944.

Charles Foweraker served the Wanderers for 49 years having begun with the club as a checker in 1895. At that time he was employed by the Lancashire and Yorkshire Railway Company in the goods section and later became Tom Mather's assistant. In 1915, Foweraker was persuaded to become secretary, pro-tem, when Mather was called up. He ran the club during the First World War years and, in July 1919, was appointed secretary-manager.

It is debatable whether he knew the technical side of the game as well as some of his players as he had no experience of having played the game at a high level. He did however, have the skills and knowledge of man-management and, as time progressed had the assistance of the more experienced players such as Joe Smith and Ted Vizard.

Foweraker took charge at the beginning of what was to be the club's most successful period. Three F.A. Cup Final successes during the 1920's and serious contenders for the League championship lifted the club's profile. This and Foweraker's personality helped the club get many invites to play abroad and on one such trip he met King Alfonso of Spain.

Honours of the game fell to him more than to most officials. He was awarded the F.A's long service medal, awarded only to club secretaries with 21 or more years service. He also received the Lancashire F.A's equivalent and was also vice president of the latter body on which he served from 1922. After the success of the 1920's Foweraker had to deal with the transition of the following decade and the relegation in 1933. He made some astute signings and, two years later, the Trotters were back in the First Division.

In May 1938 he received a pleasant surprise prior to a game at Brighton and Hove organised for the benefit of the King. He received a handsome silver cigar case, a gift from the Bolton players inscribed, *To the Boss, with best wishes for good health, from the Lads.* The Bolton manager's fondness for cigars was well known but the esteem that he was held in by his own players also shone through.

With war looming in August 1939, he had two teams prepared for the visit to Chelsea in case of a sudden call on the players by the Territorial Army. In the circumstances he didn't need to call on the services of his 'second' team but, when war was declared, he became a manager without a team. He worked voluntarily for the club and spent many solitary days at Burnden with no electricity or water. He worked hard to get the club re-opened in January 1941 after the closure at the end of the 1939/40 season. Foweraker was keen to keep the club involved in whatever football was available as, in the long run, it would be to the club's advantage. He was helped in this by experienced campaigners such as George Hunt and Harry Hubbick, both were working locally in munitions and mining, and played regularly during the war years. He strongly believed in the development of players under military age and, from this belief, rose another Wanderers hero, Nat Lofthouse.

In August 1944, Foweraker retired through ill health and the most successful manager in the club's history left the game for good. He passed away at his home in Bolton in July 1950 aged 73.

WALTER ROWLEY: 1944-1950.

Walter Rowley was promoted from coach to secretary-manager on Charles Foweraker's retirement in August 1944.

It wasn't a difficult decision for the Wanderers directors to make as Rowley had been groomed and influenced all through his Bolton career by Foweraker.

As a player, Rowley started locally with Little Hulton, where he was born, before joining Oldham Athletic. He signed for the Wanderers in 1912 and became a regular after the First World War. He was 12th man for the 1923 F.A. Cup final and went on to play 191 first class games for the club before retiring through injury. He was appointed coach to the reserves and was first team coach at the outbreak of the Second World War.

His opening years in charge were promising with the Football League War Cup being won at the end of his first season. In his second, the club finished third in the Football League North and reached the F.A. Cup semi finals.

Unfortunately, after the resumption of League football, he found that despite having a number of good young players too many of the experienced players had seen their best go by them during the war. He had the unenviable task of ending the Bolton careers of the likes of Ray Westwood and George Hunt.

Rowley made steady progress despite some of the financial problems suffered due to the disaster in 1946. In October 1950 he resigned due to ill health and was awarded life membership of the club for services rendered in his 38 years with the club. He later returned to management with Middlesbrough and Shrewsbury Town.

BILL RIDDING: 1951-1968.

Bill Ridding's association with Bolton Wanderers began in 1946 after Walter Rowley appointed him as trainer.

Ridding was one of the last of the old school of secretary-managers. Born at Heswall, on the Wirral, he played with Tranmere Rovers and, after two brief spells with both Manchester clubs, a double cartilage injury forced his retirement from the game when only 22 years old. He rejoined Tranmere as 'A' team trainer, whilst also working as a tram conductor, and later qualified as a physiotherapist and chiropodist.

He became the club's trainer and manager after the death of Jimmy Morton. Walter Rowley appointed Ridding as trainer in 1946 and, on Rowley's resignation in October 1950, Ridding was put in temporary charge. In the same year the Football Association appointed him as trainer to the England team for the World Cup in Brazil.

Ridding was officially appointed secretary-manager of the club in February 1951 and also continued to act as trainer until the appointment of Bert Sproston. The Wanderers reached two F.A. Cup Finals under his charge but, on both occasions, the country's favour fell on their opponents. In 1953 it was Stan Matthews who had everyone's sympathy when he finally won a F.A. Cup winners medal at the Trotters expense. Blackpool ran out 4-3 winners, fighting back from a 3-1 deficit with twenty minutes remaining. In 1958 Ridding put together a team that had cost nothing apart from the signing-on costs of £110. They reached the final in which they faced a post Munich Manchester United side. On this occasion the Wanderers were successful thanks to two Nat Lofthouse goals.

The Wanderers continued to produce plenty of home grown players but Ridding found it difficult to hold on to them especially after the abolition of the maximum wage in 1961. After relegation from the First Division in 1964 the club's fortunes continued to decline and in 1968 Ridding relinquished the managers chair when second only to Matt Busby as the League's longest serving manager. He returned to physiotherapy and later joined Lancashire County Cricket Club.

He died in September 1981, aged 70.

NAT LOFTHOUSE: 1968-1970. 1971 & 1985.

The club's most successful goalscorer was appointed as temporary team manager after the departure of Bill Ridding in August 1968. His appointment as manager was confirmed the following December whilst another former player, Teddy Rothwell, became secretary.

Having been with the club since 1939, first as a player and then as a coach after his retirement through injury in 1960, Lofthouse was in a similar position to that which welcomed Walter Rowley after the war.

The club were in a difficult position financially, with very little to spend on players, responsibility was placed on the club's youngsters which was eventually to prove too much.

In 1969 Lofthouse managed to attract former World Cup winner Roger Hunt to the club he supported as a boy. In consecutive seasons relegation to the Third Division was a real possibility and only avoided late in the day.

Lofthouse made it known that he wanted to move away from team affairs and into a general manager's role and, in November 1970, Jimmy McIlroy took over. Unfortunately, after the short lived appointment of McIlroy, Lofthouse again took over as the club continued to struggle in the lower reaches of the Second Division. In January 1971 Lofthouse again stood aside when Jimmy Meadows was appointed. Lofthouse's last act was to select the club's youngest ever League side which defeated a strong Sheffield United line up at Burnden.

By April 1971 Meadows had also left the club leaving Lofthouse to again take charge as the club were relegated for the first ever time into the Third Division. Jimmy Armfield was appointed as manager and Lofthouse became chief scout until his departure from the club in 1972. Six years later he returned to Burnden Park when he became manager of the Burnden Executive Club.

In December 1985 he again tasted the manager's seat when he took over as an interim measure for one game whilst a successor to Charlie Wright was being recruited. He guided the team to a 2-1 win over Chesterfield and the following October capped almost a lifetime's service by becoming the club's president.

In 1994 he appeared in the New Year's honours list and was presented with an O.B.E in recognition for his services to the game.

JIMMY McILROY: 1970

Jimmy McIlroy was appointed chief coach and aide to manager Nat Lofthouse in August 1970. McIlroy had seen service as an inside forward with Burnley and Stoke City and appeared 55 times for Northern Ireland.

When his playing days ended he became manager at Oldham Athletic before moving to Stoke as chief coach. In 1969 he resigned his position at the Victoria Ground and was out of the game until joining the Wanderers.

McIlroy was officially appointed team manager on 4th November 1970, with assistance from coaches Jimmy Conway and Eddie Hopkinson. His first game in charge was a 1-0 home defeat by Norwich City which was followed by a 2-0 reverse at Millwall.

After just 18 days in charge, McIlroy parted company with the club after it became obvious that any offers received for the players would be accepted to relieve the financial pressure, and he felt he couldn't work within those constraints.

JIMMY MEADOWS: 1971.

Bolton born Jimmy Meadows took over as team manager on 15th January 1971 after leaving Blackpool where he had been chief coach. As a player he began with Bolton YMCA and progressed to League football with Southport. He joined Manchester City in 1951 and whilst at Maine Road became an England international, playing in a 7-2 win over Scotland at Wembley in April 1955.

His managerial career began at Stockport and he took them out of the Fourth Division in 1967 but he left Edgeley Park in 1969.

In an eleven week spell as Bolton manager the team didn't win once as the side that defeated Sheffield United the day after his appointment was selected by Nat Lofthouse. During this spell the club sold Terry Wharton and Paul Fletcher, attempted to sell John Byrom and John Manning and received transfer requests from John Ritson, Roy Greaves and John Hulme. Even with the recruitment of former Olympic athlete Joe Lancaster to bolster fitness, results continued to slump, and on 6th April Meadows resigned having seen his team go down 4-0 at Queens Park Rangers. His next managerial post took him to Southport where he won the Fourth Division championship in 1973. He later had another spell in charge at Stockport County.

He died in January 1994.

JIMMY ARMFIELD: 1971-1974.

The Wanderers handed Jimmy Armfield his first managerial position after ending his playing career at Blackpool. He played 568 League games for the Seasiders who were his only club and led England on 15 occasions. He was voted the finest right back in the world after his display in the 1962 World Cup finals and was also a member of the 1966 squad.

Armfield was appointed eighteen days after the Wanderers final League game and his immediate task was to restore confidence which he begun by bringing back the clubs traditional colours of white shirts and navy blue shorts. With little money to spend he returned to Bloomfield Road and brought in experienced players in Henry Mowbray, Peter Nicholson and Graeme Rowe and snapped up 'keeper Charlie Wright from Charlton Athletic.

In his first season in charge the club enjoyed a couple of good cup runs which included a memorable 3-0 win in the League Cup against Manchester City. He transformed the defence which produced the best goals against record by the club since 1925 but it wasn't enough to make a promotion chase.

In 1972/73 the Wanderers secured the Third Division championship and reached the fifth round of the F.A. Cup, whilst in the background a number of young players were starting to push through the ranks.

Armfield brought in the experience of Tony Dunne and Peter Thompson to add to some home grown talent and the team quickly acclimatised to Second Division football. After receiving a number of offers from top flight clubs he finally gave way to an offer from Leeds United in September 1974 and the following year took them to the final of the European Cup.

He left Elland Road in 1978 and turned to journalism and currently is a regular commentator/summariser on BBC radio.

IAN GREAVES: 1974-1980.

Ian Greaves was the obvious choice to take over from Armfield as he had been brought in as his assistant in August 1974.

As a player Greaves began his career with Buxton before joining Manchester United in May 1953. He played in the 1958 F.A. Cup final against the Wanderers and went on to make 67 League appearances as a full back before joining Lincoln City in December 1960. He ended his playing career with Oldham Athletic, his hometown club, in 1962 and turned to coaching.

He became Huddersfield Town manager in 1968 and two years later won the Second Division championship. He took them to a finishing place of 15th in the First Division but couldn't prevent them slipping into the Third Division by the time he left in 1974.

Armfield recommended that Greaves should take over at Bolton and he was appointed hours before a 2-0 win over Orient on 5th October 1974. He gave a number of youngsters a chance at first team level and, within his first ten weeks in charge, had used twenty players. The likes of Peter Reid, Brian Smith and Steve Taylor were blooded and at the end of his first season the Wanderers again finished mid-table to consolidate in the Division.

In 1975/76 he took the Wanderers to within a whisker of promotion to Division one only to miss out to West Brom. It was a similar story the following season when Nottingham Forest pipped the Wanderers in the run-in. In the same season he took the club to the League Cup semi-finals for the first time only to miss out to Everton. Greaves finally succeeded in taking the Wanderers into the top flight in 1978 when the championship was secured in front of both Tottenham and Southampton.

Unfortunately, after keeping the club in the top flight for one season, he was sacked in January 1980 with the club rooted at the foot of the table. His departure came just forty-eight hours after the club had reached the fifth round of the F.A. Cup.

Greaves had been given backing to the extent that he had broken the club's transfer record four times.

Unfortunately the arrival of the likes of Len Cantello and Dave Clement didn't work out despite the fact that they had performed well at their previous clubs. He returned to management with Oxford United and Wolverhampton Wanderers before becoming assistant at Hereford United. In January 1983 he took over at Mansfield Town and, in 1986, he led them to promotion from Division Four. A year later he tasted success as a manager at Wembley when Mansfield won the Freight Rover Trophy. He left Field Mill in 1988.

Greaves has continued to work in the game and in recent seasons has been scouting for Sunderland.

STAN ANDERSON: 1980-1981.

Stan Anderson joined the club in November 1978 as Ian Greaves' assistant after the departure of George Mulhall to Bradford City. Anderson took over as caretaker after Greaves left the club and, despite failing to win a game, he was appointed manager at the end of February 1980.

He tasted success in his first game in full charge when European Cup holders Nottingham Forest were beaten 1-0 at Burnden. This was only the Wanderers second League win of the season and, unfortunately, it didn't become a springboard to a miracle escape from relegation.

In his playing days, Anderson made over 500 League appearances as a wing half for Sunderland, Newcastle United and Middlesbrough and was capped twice by England. Between 1965 and 1970 he was in charge at Middlesbrough where he guided them out of the Third Division. He later had spells in charge at AEK Athens and as assistant at Queens Park Rangers. He spent four years in charge at Doncaster Rovers before joining the Wanderers.

After relegation from Division One the club continued to struggle in the lower division but results improved sufficiently to avoid relegation after the return of George Mulhall as his assistant in March 1981.

In May 1981 Anderson was relieved of his post despite having two years of his contract to run.

GEORGE MULHALL: 1981-1982.

George Mulhall began his second spell on the Wanderers management team in March 1981 as assistant to Stan Anderson. He had previously been assistant to Ian Greaves between 1974 and 1978 before leaving to take charge at Bradford City.

He became manager of the Wanderers in June 1981, and had to deal with a situation that had seen six players released on free transfers and six available for transfer due to the financial problems. He also had to recruit a backroom team.

As a player, Mulhall had been an outside left with Aberdeen and Sunderland, making 255 League appearances in which he scored 55 goals, for the Wearside club. He also made three Scottish international appearances. In October 1971 he joined Halifax Town as trainer-coach before being appointed manager in June 1972.

Season 1981/82 was again a struggle for the club with Mulhall claiming to be embarrassed at some of the team's performances. Wanderers, however, managed to keep their place in the Second Division by the narrowest of margins thanks to two home wins in the final week and Cardiff's failure to win their final game of the season.

The financial situation at the club got worse and Mulhall was forced to add Paul Jones to the nine players he had decided were to leave the club at the end of the season. In June 1982 he left the club as the Wanderers announced their intent to advertise for a player-manager.

Mulhall later scouted for Ipswich and between 1985 to 1987 was assistant manager to Frank Worthington at Tranmere. He has continued to work in the game as a scout latterly with Huddersfield and Halifax Town.

JOHN McGOVERN: 1982-1985.

CHARLIE WRIGHT: 1985.

The Wanderers appointed John McGovern as player-manager after he had been allowed to leave Nottingham Forest on a free transfer despite having over a year of his contract left to run.

Speculation prior to his appointment had included other player-manager possibilities including Mike Channon and John Wile, but the inclusion of Pele in the list at least put the club on the back page of the newspapers during the summer months.

Montrose born McGovern made 545 League appearances for Hartlepool, Derby County, Leeds United and Nottingham Forest with League championships and European Cup wins with Derby and Forest being part of a glittering career under Brian Clough.

It was expected that he would become part of the Wanderers midfield and pass his experience on to the younger players. Unfortunately he took over a squad that had just missed out on relegation and, with no money to recruit better players, had to make do with free transfers. His first season in charge ended in relegation to the Third Division and, as the financial situation got worse, he was left with a squad of young players.

McGovern got involved in raising money for the club, running in a fund-raising marathon and organising kit sponsorship schemes and supporters evenings.

The youngsters made a good start in Division three under McGovern but, with nothing available to build a team around them, they ran out of steam and finished in mid-table. The following season saw the team struggle at the wrong end of the division, and in January 1985 McGovern parted company with the Wanderers having played in only 16 League games in his two and a half years spell as player-manager.

He later went into business in Tenerife before returning to have spells at Chorley, Rotherham United, Hull City and Woking.

After a career that had seen him play 535 League games as a goalkeeper for Workington, Grimsby Town, Charlton Athletic and Bolton Wanderers, Charlie Wright turned to coaching.

He retired from League football following the winning of a Third Division championship medal with the Wanderers in 1973 after suffering with a back injury, and took charge of the youth team at Burnden.

The Glaswegian had an effervescent character that made him popular with the club's youth team players and he later became chief coach before leaving to become manager at York City in 1977. He had little success there and was sacked in March 1980, returning to Burnden the following year to take charge of the reserves and to work with the club's goalkeepers.

Wright became first team coach in November 1983, succeeding Walter Joyce, who switched to the reserves and after John McGovern's departure was put in temporary charge.

In three weeks, Wright steered the Wanderers to five consecutive wins, their best sequence of results in almost six years and, despite a number of applications from experienced managers, he was appointed Bolton manager on 7th February 1985, with Walter Joyce as his assistant. Unfortunately the results went backwards with only one win in the next ten games, and only a late improvement being enough to avoid relegation.

Wright signed a number of experienced players for the start of the 1985/86 season but they continued to struggle in the League and a first round F.A. Cup exit at Fourth Division Wrexham made matters worse.

In December 1985 Wright left the club along with Joyce by mutual consent after five consecutive defeats had seen Wright end his Wanderers managerial career in exactly the opposite way that he had started it.

PHIL NEAL: 1985-1992.

The Wanderers again went for inexperience at managerial level when Phil Neal was appointed on 18th December 1985.

Neal had played 635 League games for Northampton Town and Liverpool and had become one of the most decorated players in the game with fifty England caps to add to his League Championship and European Cup medals. He had turned down an offer to take over the reins at Second Division Grimsby two months earlier and upon his appointment at Burnden installed former Anfield team mate Colin Irwin as his assistant to make the Wanderers managerial set up one of the most inexperienced in the club's history.

In his first season in charge the club managed to hang on to their Third Division status and there was some consolation in the club's first visit to Wembley since 1958 when they won through to the Freight Rover Trophy final. Bristol City soured the day with a 3-0 win but there was a lack of improvement the following season when the Wanderers were relegated to the Fourth Division for the first time after a play-off defeat to Aldershot.

Neal announced his retirement from playing but was persuaded to change his mind by his new coach Mick Brown whose experience was to prove vital to the club. Within twelve months Neal and Brown had transformed the team with some new signings and won promotion at the first attempt. Things continued to improve and the team consolidated in the Third Division along with a Wembley success in the Sherpa Van Trophy against Torquay United in 1989.

Neal took the Wanderers to the Third Division play-offs in 1990 and 1991 only to miss out on a return to the Second Division on each occasion. In 1991/92 the team did well in the F.A. Cup, reaching the fifth round, but struggled in the League. Less than a week after the final game of the season Neal, who was the ninth longest serving manager in the Football League, left the club. He had brought stability and a measure of success to the club but the fact that the club was carrying one of their strongest squads for many a year the pressure of poor results and declining attendances brought about the inevitable.

Neal later had a spell as assistant at Peterborough, was in charge at Coventry and Manchester City, and was involved in the England set-up under Graham Taylor.

BRUCE RIOCH: 1992-1995.

The Wanderers wasted no time in appointing Bruce Rioch who had led Middlesbrough to promotion to the Second Division in 1987 and into the first a year later. Rioch appointed Colin Todd as his assistant.

As a midfield player he had won a First Division championship medal with Derby County in 1975 and also saw service with Luton Town, Aston Villa, Everton and Torquay United, a period that spanned 548 League games. He also represented Scotland on 24 occasions.

He cut his teeth as a manager at Plainmoor before joining Middlesbrough. He then had a spell with Millwall, taking them to the play-offs, before joining Bolton. After a slow start, in which the Wanderers were struggling at the wrong end of the table, there was a turn around with a fifteen game unbeaten spell. Two of his acquisitions, John McGinlay and Keith Branagan, who Rioch knew from Millwall, were to become the mainstays of the side for a number of years.

He led the Wanderers to promotion from the Second Division in 1993, and, in the same season the club enjoyed plenty of national coverage with a run to the fifth round of the F.A. Cup that included a win over Liverpool at Anfield in a third round replay. In 1993/94 he consolidated Bolton's position in the First Division and took the Wanderers to the sixth round of the F.A. Cup, their best effort in the competition since 1959.

Once again it was on two fronts that Rioch led the club to success in 1995. In the Coca-Cola Cup the Wanderers reached the final at Wembley for the first time, going down 2-1 to Liverpool, and then the play-off success over Reading won promotion into the Premier League and a return to the top flight for the first time since 1980.

In his three years at the helm he had brought a measure of success to the club that could only have been dreamt of on his appointment. He left the club to take over at Arsenal and in his only season at Highbury took them into Europe and started to transform their line-up with the acquisition of Dennis Bergkamp.

He later had a spell as assistant at Queens Park Rangers, and was in charge at Norwich City and Wigan Athletic.

ROY McFARLAND: 1995-96.

Roy McFarland was put in charge along with Colin Todd after the departure of Bruce Rioch.

As a player he had served Tranmere Rovers, Derby County and Bradford City and had been a team-mate of both Todd and Rioch at the Baseball Ground. Whilst with the Rams he won a Second Division championship medal in 1969 and a League championship medal in both 1972 and 1975 along with 28 full England caps.

He returned to Derby as a coach and then as manager but during his spell at Burnden Park the Wanderers managed to win only two Premier League games, one of those ironically coming against Rioch's Arsenal. After a 4-2 defeat at Sheffield Wednesday on New Year's day 1996, McFarland left the club by mutual consent.

He took charge at Cambridge United in November 1996, where he won promotion from the Third Division in 1998/99, and was later at the helm at Torquay United.

COLIN TODD: 1995-1999.

As a player, Colin Todd began his career at Sunderland before joining Derby County in February 1971, where he won League championship medals in both 1972 and 1975. He later played for Everton, Birmingham City, Nottingham Forest, Oxford United and ended his career with Luton Town in the 1984/85 season. He also represented England on 27 occasions.

He began coaching with Whitley Bay and held that position at Middlesbrough under Bruce Rioch when they won promotion from the Third Division in 1987 and from the Second a year later. As a manager he took 'Boro to the Second Division play-offs in 1991 and joined the Wanderers as coach to Rioch in 1992 after a spell at Bradford City

He was coach with the Wanderers during the promotion campaigns of 1993 and 1995, and after a spell in dual charge with Roy McFarland, took sole charge in January 1996. He could do little to prevent the Wanderers suffering relegation from the Premiership in 1996 during which time Ian Porterfield was the coach.

Todd appointed former Wanderer Phil Brown as his coach for the start of the 1996/97 season and Bolton won the First Division championship in record breaking style. Unfortunately the Premiership proved just too much in 1997/98 when Bolton were relegated on the final day on goal difference.

Todd took the Wanderers to the play-offs in 1999, only to lose in the final at the hands of Watford. The start of the following term saw them struggle at the wrong end of the table and in September 1999 he left the club to be replaced by caretaker Phil Brown.

Todd later took charge at Swindon Town and Derby County.

SAM ALLARDYCE: 1999-

Sam Allardyce was appointed manager of the Wanderers on his 45th birthday, the 19th October, and he began with a 2-2 draw at the Reebok Stadium on the same night. Phil Brown was appointed as his assistant.

As a player he played over four hundred League games which included two spells with the Wanderers. He came through the youth ranks at Burnden, turning professional in November 1971, and making his League debut in November 1973.

He was a regular member of the Wanderers side in the mid 1970's that twice narrowly missed out on promotion to the First Division before securing the Second Division championship in 1978.

The central defender played 214 first class games for Bolton before signing for Sunderland for a £150,000 fee in July 1980. He followed that with spells at Millwall, Tampa Bay Rowdies, Coventry City and Huddersfield Town before rejoining the Wanderers in 1985. He spent only one season back at Burnden, making seventeen first class appearances, before joining Preston where he helped them win promotion from Division four in 1987. His playing days came to an end at West Brom where he also served on the coaching staff.

Allardyce subsequently had spells as assistant manager at both Preston and Sunderland and had been in charge at Limerick, Blackpool, where he led them to the 1996 Second Division play-offs, and Notts County where he won the 1998 Third Division championship.

In his first season in charge at the Reebok Stadium the Wanderers reached the semi-finals of both the Worthington Cup and the F.A. Cup, the latter for the first time since winning the competition in 1958, and the First Division play-offs.

In 2000/01 he took the club back into the Premiership with a 3-0 success over Preston North End in the play-off final at Cardiff and then, with little money to spend in Premiership terms, moulded a team together that managed to hold their status the following year.

Sam Allardyce as a player.

Scoring against Sunderland at Burnden Park in December 1975.

Players - Appearances and Goals Summary

Player	Season(s)	League Apps	League Sub	League Goals	FA Cup Apps	FA Cup Sub	FA Cup Goals	League Cup Apps	League Cup Sub	League Cup Goals	FrtRov/A'glass Apps	FrtRov/A'glass Sub	FrtRov/A'glass Goals	Anglo Italian Apps	Anglo Italian Sub	Anglo Italian Goals	Total Apps	Total Sub	Total Goals
1 ABBOTT H	1904/05	1															1	0	0
2 ADAMSON HM	1909/10-10/11	15															15	0	0
3 AINSLEY GE	1936/37	7															7	0	0
4 ALEXANDER G	1895/96	2															2	0	0
5 ALJOFREE H	1997/98-99/00	6	8			2		4	2								10	12	0
6 ALLARDYCE S	*1973/74-85/86	194	4	21	14	1	2	18		1							226	5	24
7 ALLCOCK T	1953/54-57/58	31		9	1		2										32	0	11
8 ALLEN P	1986/87		1								2	1					2	1	1
9 ANDERSON A	1936/37-38/39	52		4	5		1										57	0	5
10 ANDREWS W	1894/95	12		3	1												13	0	3
11 ANTHONY A	1899/00	3															3	0	0
12 ASPINALL J	1946/47-49/50	14															14	0	0
13 ATHERTON J	Pre-League				5		3										5	0	3
14 ASTLEY H	1900/01-01/02	6															6	0	0
15 ATKINSON J	1905/06-06/07	3		1													3	0	1
16 ATKINSON JE	1932/33-47/48	240		4	23		1										263	0	5
17 ATKINSON P	1986/87	2	1														2	1	0
18 BAGGETT JW	1923/24-26/27	24		10	3		1										27	0	11
19 BAILEY D	1956/57	1															1	0	0
20 BAILEY IC	*1981/82-84/85	15									1	2					16	2	0
21 BALL J	1950/51-57/58	200		2	12												212	0	2
22 BANKS R	1946/47-52/53	104			14												118	0	0
23 BANKS S	1998/99-	23	1		5			7									35	1	0
24 BANKS T	1947/48-60/61	233		2	22												255	0	2
25 BANNISTER N	1955/56-60/61	26		4													26	0	4
26 BANNISTER W	1901/02-02/03	28		3	2												30	0	3
27 BARBER T	1908/09-12/13	102		14	5												107	0	14
28 BARBOUR A	1888/89-91/92	34		17	1												35	0	17
29 BARLOW TH	*1898/99-03/04	86		25	4												90	0	25
30 BARNARD A	1954/55-55/56	2															2	0	0
31 BARNES J	1898/99	9		1	2												11	0	1
32 BARNES P	*1987/88	4	1			1											4	2	0
33 BARNESS A	2000/01-	39	9		4			4									47	9	0
34 BARRASS MW	1946/47-56/57	329		25	28		2										357	0	27
35 BATES WE	1906/07	2															2	0	0
36 BATESON	Pre-League				1												1	0	0
37 BAVERSTOCK H	1905/06-21/22	366		4	22												388	0	4
38 BAVERSTOCK JJ	1913/14	2															2	0	0
39 BAXENDALE	Pre-League				1												1	0	0
40 BEARDS A	1950/51-53/54	14		2													14	0	2
41 BEARDSLEY P	1997/98-98/99	14	3	2		1		3									17	4	2
42 BECKETT C	1905/06	1															1	0	0
43 BEECH HW	1965/66-66/67	14	1					1									15	1	0
44 BELL E	1950/51-57/58	102		1	16		1										118	0	2
45 BELL F	1900/01-01/02	5															5	0	0
46 BELL G	1983/84-85/86	86	6	3	2			7		2	6	1					101	7	5
47 BELL L	1899/00-02/03	99		44	4		1										103	0	45
48 BENNETT M	1979/80-82/83	62	3	1	3			5									70	3	1
49 BENTLEY A	1910/11-12/13	51		15	4		1										55	0	16
50 BENTLEY H	1891/92-94/95	44		17	6		2										50	0	19
51 BERGSSON G	1994/95-	240	9	24	12		1	23	2	1							275	11	26
52 BERRY N	1981/82-84/85	25	7		1			4	2	1							30	9	1
53 BINGLEY W	1949/50-54/55	6															6	0	0
54 BIRCH B	1954/55-63/64	165		23	19		4	7		1							191	0	28
55 BLACKMORE HA	1926/27-31/32	153		111	12		11										165	0	122
56 BLAKE N	1995/96-1998/99	102	5	38	6		2	10	1	8							118	6	48
57 BOBIC F	2001/02	14	2	4													14	2	4
58 BOLLANDS JF	1959/60	13															13	0	0
59 BOLTON R	1898/99	2															2	0	0
60 BOOTH P	1984/85	1									1						2	0	0
61 BORROWS B	1982/83-84/85	95			4			7			4						110	0	0
62 BOSTON WJ	1923/24-28/29	37		2	2		1										39	0	3
63 BOSWELL AH	1969/70-70/71	51			2			3									56	0	0
64 BOURNE JT	1924/25	3															3	0	0

Player	Season(s)	League			FA Cup			League Cup			FrtRov/A'glass			Anglo Italian			Total		
		Apps	Sub	Goals	Apps	Sub	Goals	Apps	Sub	Goals	Apps	Sub	Goals	Apps	Sub	Goals	Apps	Sub	Goals
65 BOWER RW	1936/37	3															3	0	0
66 BOYD J	1902/03-08/09	189		7	19												208	0	7
67 BOYLE MJ	1931/32-32/33	13			1												14	0	0
68 BRACELIN J	1894/95	1															1	0	0
69 BRADLEY	Pre-League				1												1	0	0
70 BRADLEY J	1947/48-50/51	92		19	7		1										99	0	20
71 BRANAGAN K	1992/93-99/00	216			9			33			4			1			263	0	0
72 BRENNAN I	1980/81-81/82	16	1		2			1									19	1	0
73 BROGAN J	1888/89-91/92	74		26	12		6										86	0	32
74 BROMILOW G	1968/69	3	2														3	2	0
75 BROMLEY B	1962/63-68/69	165	1	25	10		1	8									183	1	26
76 BROOKMAN N	1986/87-89/90	47	10	10	5			1			7	1	2				60	11	12
77 BROOMFIELD H	1902/03-06/07	28															28	0	0
78 BROWN M	1991/92-92/93	27	6	3	3				1		2						32	7	3
79 BROWN P	1988/89-93/94	259	2	14	23		1	25		1	21		1	2			330	2	17
80 BROWN RN	1895/96-01/02	125		12	11		2										136	0	14
81 BROWN W	1899/00-03/04	106			8												114	0	0
82 BRYAN J	1929/30	1		1													1	0	1
83 BUCHAN TM	1914/15-22/23	116		14	1												117	0	14
84 BUCHANAN WB	2001/02-					1											0	1	0
85 BULLOUGH PA	1888/89-92/93	38		4	14		1										52	0	5
86 BURGESS AC	1946/47-47/48	5		3													5	0	3
87 BURKE DI	*1978/79-93/94	169	6	1	14	1	1	16	1		7						206	8	2
88 BURNETT W	1995/96-96/97		2														0	2	0
89 BURNISON J	1900/01-01/02	18															18	0	0
90 BUTLER DA	1962/63-67/68	62	3	11	2		1	2		1							66	3	13
91 BUTLER W	1921/22-32/33	407		65	42		9										449	0	74
92 BYROM J	1966/67-75/76	296	8	113	22	2	7	22	1	10							340	11	130
93 CALDER J	1936/37-37/38	27		11													27	0	11
94 CALDERBANK J	1900/01	3															3	0	0
95 CALDWELL A	1983/84-86/87	133	8	60	8		4	8	1	4	17		10				166	9	78
96 CALLAGHAN I	1987/88	1			1												2	0	0
97 CAME M	1984/85-92/93	192	7	7	16	2		15	4	2	23		2				246	13	11
98 CAMERON K	1933/34-34/35	24		3	3		1										27	0	4
99 CAMERON WS	1906/07-07/08	26		5	5		2										31	0	7
100 CAMPBELL A	2000/01	3	3														3	3	0
101 CANTELLO L	1979/80-81/82	89	1	3	3			4									96	1	3
102 CARR F	1997/98		5														0	5	0
103 CARR SR	1898/99	2															2	0	0
104 CARRUTHERS A	1936/37-37/38	26		4	1		1										27	0	5
105 CARTER M	1979/80-81/82	37	12	8	3			3	1								43	13	8
106 CARTMAN HR	1919/20-21/22	22															22	0	0
107 CASSIDY J	1889/90-97/98	194		84	25		17										219	0	101
108 CASSIDY J	1924/25	22		7													22	0	7
109 CHAMBERS F	1921/22-23/24	12			1												13	0	0
110 CHAMBERS WT	1934/35	2		1													2	0	1
111 CHANDLER JG	*1981/82-89/90	170	11	40	7		3	12	1	5	9	1					198	13	48
112 CHARLTON S	2000/01-	56	5		3	1		1									60	6	0
113 CHARNLEY J	1991/92	3															3	0	0
114 CHIRNSIDE JE	1891/92	1															1	0	0
115 CHORLTON HH	1897/98-00/01	9		2													9	0	2
116 CHRISTIE J	Pre-League				5												5	0	0
117 CHURCH HB	1930/31-34/35	41			1												42	0	0
118 CLARK TG	1935/36-36/37	21			2												23	0	0
119 CLARKE M	2000/01	11															11	0	0
120 CLARKE PA	1970/71	13															13	0	0
121 CLEMENT DT	1979/80-80/81	33			3			3									39	0	0
122 CLEMENTS AP	1977/78	1															1	0	0
123 CLIFFORD R	1903/04-08/09	152		5	15		1										167	0	6
124 CODD RW	1950/51-53/54	31		5													31	0	5
125 COLEMAN S	1994/95-97/98	34		5	2			4									40	0	5
126 COMSTIVE P	1989/90-91/92	45	8	3	3	1	1	6		1	3	1					57	10	5
127 CONNOR J	1934/35-38/39	29			7												36	0	0
128 COOK WL	1928/29-35/36	234		35	28		5										262	0	40
129 COOPER C	1960/61-68/69	79	4		5			2									86	4	0
130 COPE JW	1925/26-28/29	79			7												86	0	0

Player	Season(s)	League			FA Cup			League Cup			FrtRov/A'glass			Anglo Italian			Total		
		Apps	Sub	Goals	Apps	Sub	Goals	Apps	Sub	Goals	Apps	Sub	Goals	Apps	Sub	Goals	Apps	Sub	Goals
131 CORFIELD E	1949/50-51/52	6															6	0	0
132 COUPAR T	1888/89-89/90	5		1													5	0	1
133 COWDRILL B	1988/89-91/92	122	2	4	8			13		2	14	1					157	3	6
134 COX N	1997/98-99/00	80	3	7	1	1		9		1							90	4	8
135 COX W	Pre-League				5												5	0	0
136 COYLE OC	1993/94-95/96	37	20	13	8		5	5	3	1				5		4	55	23	23
137 CRAVEN R	1908/09	2															2	0	0
138 CREWE W	1922/23	4															4	0	0
139 CROMBIE D	1987/88-90/91	90	6	1	5		1	11	1		13		1				119	7	3
140 CROOK W	1947/48	28			1												29	0	0
141 CROSS D	1985/86	19	1	8				4		2							23	1	10
142 CUNLIFFE JG	1957/58-62/63	25			5			3									33	0	0
143 CUNNINGHAM T	1990/91	12		4													12	0	4
144 CURCIC S	1995/96-1996/97	28		4	2		2	3		1							33	0	7
145 CURRAN HP	1974/75-76/77	40	7	13	2			1									43	7	13
146 CURRIER J	1935/36-38/39	26		14													26	0	14
147 DARBY J	1985/86-93/94	263	12	36	19		3	25		8	25	1	5	1			333	13	52
148 DARLING M	1973/74	6	2														6	2	0
149 DAVENPORT JK	1888/89-92/93	56		25	21		11										77	0	36
150 DAVIES A	1919/20	8		1													8	0	1
151 DAVIES D	1902/03-09/10	123			14												137	0	0
152 DAVIES RH	1895/96-98/99	29			1												30	0	0
153 DAVIES RI	1924/25-25/26	3															3	0	0
154 DAVIES RW	1961/62-66/67	155		66	11		6	4		2							170	0	74
155 DAVIES WH	1898/99	21															21	0	0
156 DAVIN M	1930/31	3															3	0	0
157 DAVISON A	1993/94-96/97	35	2		8									4			47	2	0
158 DAVISON JH	1963/64	21		1	1												22	0	1
159 DAWSON T	Pre-League				1												1	0	0
160 DEFREITAS F	1994/95-1995/96	24	18	9	1			2	4								27	22	9
161 DEAKIN P	1957/58-63/64	63		13	7		2	3									73	0	15
162 DEAKIN RJ	1982/83-84/85	104	1	2	6			5			5						120	1	2
163 DEAN J	1955/56-59/60	17															17	0	0
164 DEMPSEY E	1906/07	7		1													7	0	1
165 DENTON R	1971/72	3	1														3	1	0
166 DEVLIN J	Pre-League				3												3	0	0
167 DIAWARA D	2001/02	4	5					2									6	5	0
168 DIBBLE A	1991/92	13									1						14	0	0
169 DICKENSON J	1892/93-93/94	42		11	5		2										47	0	13
170 DILLON V	1947/48-50/51	17		2													17	0	2
171 DJORKAEFF Y	2001/02-	12		4													12	0	4
172 DOBSON M	1966/67							1									1	0	0
173 DOCHERTY J	1894/95	2															2	0	0
174 DONALDSON A	1912/13-21/22	139		5	7		1										146	0	6
175 DOWNEY C	2000/01-		1														0	1	0
176 DOYLE M	1981/82-82/83	40		2				2		2							42	0	4
177 DRABBLE F	1919/20-20/21	29			1												30	0	0
178 DREYER J	1994/95	2	2														2	2	0
179 DUCKWORTH TC	1931/32-32/33	28			1												29	0	0
180 DUFFEY C	1969/70-71/72	8			2	1	1										10	1	1
181 DUNNE AP	1973/74-78/79	166	4		10			13									189	4	0
182 DYER F	1888/89	1															1	0	0
183 EASTHAM GR	1932/33-36/37	114		16	17		1										131	0	17
184 EATOCK T	1924/25-25/26	11		1													11	0	1
185 ECCLES GS	1904/05	6															6	0	0
186 EDISBURY W	1956/57-57/58	2															2	0	0
187 EDMED RA	1931/32-32/33	4		1	1												5	0	1
188 EDMONDS H	1909/10-10/11	10															10	0	0
189 EDMONDSON JH	1906/07-14/15	239			20												259	0	0
190 EDWARDS GB	1950/51-64/65	482		8	31		1	5									518	0	9
191 EDWARDS JG	1958/59	3															3	0	0
192 EDWARDS M	1956/57-60/61	14		1													14	0	1
193 EGERTON W	1911/12	2			1												3	0	0
194 ELLIOTT R	1997/98-00/01	76	17	5	5			4	1	2							85	18	7
195 ELLIOTT S	1986/87-88/89	59	3	11	6			4			4						73	3	11
196 ELVEY JR	1920/21-21/22	11															11	0	0

Player	Season(s)	League			FA Cup			League Cup			FrtRov/A'glass			Anglo Italian			Total		
		Apps	Sub	Goals	Apps	Sub	Goals	Apps	Sub	Goals	Apps	Sub	Goals	Apps	Sub	Goals	Apps	Sub	Goals
197 ELVY R	1947/48-49/50	31			3												34	0	0
198 ENTWISTLE W	1985/86	5	3		1						2						6	5	0
199 ESPARTERO M	2001/02		3														0	3	0
200 EVANS WP	1907/08	1															1	0	0
201 EVANS T	1984/85	4									1						5	0	0
202 FAIRCLOUGH C	1995/96-97/98	89	1	8	5			11									105	1	8
203 FALLON L	Pre-League				6		5										6	0	5
204 FARNWORTH S	1983/84-85/86	113			7			11			8						139	0	0
205 FARRELLY G	1999/00-	58	15	5	4	2		4									66	17	5
206 FARRIMOND S	1958/59-70/71	364	1	1	22			17									403	1	1
207 FAY J	1911/12-20/21	128		5	8												136	0	5
208 FEATHERSTONE F	1904/05	2		1													2	0	1
209 FEEBURY JH	1909/10-19/20	180		16	12												192	0	16
210 FELGATE D	*1985/86-92/93	245			17			14			24						300	0	0
211 FERGUSON G	1893/94-95/96	16		3	3												19	0	3
212 FINNEY A	1922/23-36/37	483		2	47												530	0	2
213 FISH M	1997/98-00/01	107	1	3	6			12	1	1							125	2	4
214 FISHER N	1990/91-94/95	17	7	1	1			4									22	7	1
215 FITCHETT J	1897/98-01/02	76		4	5												81	0	4
216 FITZPATRICK P	1984/85-85/86	13	1		1			3			1						18	1	0
217 FLECK R	1993/94	6	1	1										1			7	1	1
218 FLETCHER PJ	1968/69-70/71	33	3	5	2		1	3	1	1							38	4	7
219 FLITCROFT W	1888/89-89/90	8															8	0	0
220 FLOOD CW	1922/23	8		2													8	0	2
221 FORBES J	1924/25-25/26	3															3	0	0
222 FORREST E	1938/39-47/48	69		1	4												73	0	1
223 FOSTER J	1903/04	2															2	0	0
224 FOSTER WP	1981/82-84/85	92	13	13	6		3	3	2	1	2	2					103	17	17
225 FOWLER J	Pre-League				7												7	0	0
226 FRANDSEN P	*1996/97-	194	10	29	6	3		17	2	4							217	15	33
227 FREDGAARD C	2000/01	1	4														1	4	0
228 FREEBAIRN A	1894/95-06/07	286		9	29		1										315	0	10
229 FRY B	1964/65	3		1													3	0	1
230 FULLARTON J	1998/99	1															1	0	0
231 FULTON S	1993/94	4												2	1		6	1	0
232 GARDINER H	1890/91-93/94	80		5	4												84	0	5
233 GARDNER A	1903/04	8		1													8	0	1
234 GARDNER WR	1998/99-	107	20	15	6	3		11	2	2							124	25	17
235 GASKELL A	1905/06-09/10	105		2	5												110	0	2
236 GAVIN M	1985/86-86/87	50	1	3	5		1	1			8	1					64	1	5
237 GEE J	1907/08	6		1	1												7	0	1
238 GELDARD A	1938/39-46/47	29		1	10		1										39	0	2
239 GENT	Pre-League				1												1	0	0
240 GIALLANZA G	1997/98		3														0	3	0
241 GIBSON GB	1926/27-32/33	236		76	19		5										255	0	81
242 GILL JJ	1926/27-29/30	40			2												42	0	0
243 GILLAM SG	1888/89	2															2	0	0
244 GILLIES A	1895/96	6															6	0	0
245 GILLIES M	1946/47-51/52	145		1	9												154	0	1
246 GILLIGAN A	1893/94-99/00	99		17	8												107	0	17
247 GILLIGAN W	1898/99	3															3	0	0
248 GIMBLETT GS	1911/12-13/14	30			1												31	0	0
249 GIMBLETT WS	1919/20	2															2	0	0
250 GLAISTER	Pre-League				2												2	0	0
251 GLEAVES J	Pre-League				13		2										13	0	2
252 GLENDENNING R	1912/13-14/15	73			10												83	0	0
253 GOLDSMITH G	1934/35-35/36	19															19	0	0
254 GOODALL EI	1938/39	12															12	0	0
255 GOPE-FENEPEJ J	2000/01		2														0	2	0
256 GORRINGE FC	1930/31	1															1	0	0
257 GOSLIN HA	1930/31-38/39	303		23	31												334	0	23
258 GOUGH H	1927/28	4															4	0	0
259 GOULDEN AE	1962/63	1															1	0	0
260 GOWLING AE	1977/78-81/82	147	2	28	8		1	8		2							163	2	31
261 GRAHAM MA	1977/78-80/81	43	3		2			3									48	3	0
262 GRAY S	1982/83	10															10	0	0

Player	Season(s)	League			FA Cup			League Cup			FrtRov/A'glass			Anglo Italian			Total		
		Apps	Sub	Goals	Apps	Sub	Goals	Apps	Sub	Goals	Apps	Sub	Goals	Apps	Sub	Goals	Apps	Sub	Goals
263 GREAVES R	1965/66-79/80	487	8	66	39		10	41		9							567	8	85
264 GREEN S	1989/90-96/7	171	56	25	20	3	4	19	4	1	8			3	2	1	221	65	31
265 GREENHALGH	1888/89				3												3	0	0
266 GREENHALGH HW	1924/25-28/29	70			10												80	0	0
267 GREENHALGH S	*1902/03-13/14	259		19	19		1										278	0	20
268 GREGORY	Pre-League				2		1										2	0	1
269 GREGORY J	1897/98-98/99	6															6	0	0
270 GREGORY J	1989/90	2	6														2	6	0
271 GRIEVES KJ	1951/52-55/56	49			1												50	0	0
272 GRIFFIN P	1986/87										1						0	1	0
273 GRIFFITHS D	1908/09	4															4	0	0
274 GRIFFITHS J	1932/33-33/34	24			1												25	0	0
275 GRIFFITHS TP	1931/35-32/33	48		6	5		2										53	0	8
276 GRIME J	1902/03	3															3	0	0
277 GROSVENOR AT	1937/38-38/39	53		7	3												56	0	7
278 GRUNDY WA	1908/09	2															2	0	0
279 GUBBINS RG	1952/53-59/60	97		15	4		3										101	0	18
280 GUDJOHNSEN E	1998/99-99/00	52	7	19	4	1	4	8	1	4							64	9	27
281 GUEST A	1894/95	1															1	0	0
282 GUNN J	1895/96	6		5	2		2										8	0	7
283 GUNNLAUGSSON A	1997/98-1998/99	24	18	13	1	1		6	3	2							31	22	15
284 GUY G	1920/21	2		1													2	0	1
285 HALFORD D	1936/37-37/38	6		1	2		1										8	0	2
286 HALLEY W	1897/98-00/01	40			1												41	0	0
287 HALLIDAY JF	1901/02-02/03	27			3												30	0	0
288 HALLOWS PCR	1968/69-73/74	45	2		2			6									53	2	0
289 HAMILTON E	1895/96	1			2												3	0	0
290 HAMLETT TL	1946/47-48/49	72		9	13												85	0	9
291 HANSEN B	1998/99- 01/02	67	37	15	4	2	1	7	2	1							78	41	17
292 HANSON J	1898/99-03/04	64		9	3												67	0	9
293 HANSON S	1936/37-55/56	384			39												423	0	0
294 HARRISON CE	1888/89-89/90	24															24	0	0
295 HARTFORD A	1985/86-86/87	83		8	6			4		1	8		1				101	0	10
296 HARTLE LR	1952/53-65/66	446	1	11	39		1	13		1							498	1	13
297 HASLAM R	1900/01	1															1	0	0
298 HASSALL HW	1951/52-54/55	102		34	7												109	0	34
299 HATELEY CB	1913/14	1															1	0	0
300 HATTON DH	1961/62-69/70	231		8	14			14									259	0	8
301 HATTON RJ	1966/67-67/68	23	1	2													23	1	2
302 HAWORTH R	1921/22-30/31	322			35												357	0	0
303 HAY T	Pre-League				5												5	0	0
304 HAYDOCK J	1888/89-89/90	2			4												6	0	0
305 HEATON S	1903/04	4		1													4	0	1
306 HEBBERD TN	1981/82	6															6	0	0
307 HENDER P	1960/61							1									1	0	0
308 HENDERSON	Pre-League				1												1	0	0
309 HENDERSON C	1894/95	28		14	1												29	0	14
310 HENDRY C	2000/01-	28		3	1			4									33	0	3
311 HENNIN D	1953/54-60/61	164		8	17		1	2									183	0	9
312 HENRY T	1981/82-82/83	70		22	3			3		2							76	0	24
313 HENSHAW G	1987/88-90/91	49	21	4	4	1		8	1	1	4	2					65	25	5
314 HERBERT WE	1919/20-21/22	34		7	1												35	0	7
315 HERNON J	1948/49-50/51	43		2													43	0	2
316 HESLOP TW	1913/14-14/15	7															7	0	0
317 HEWITSON	Pre-League				2		3										2	0	3
318 HEWITT J	1910/11	11		3													11	0	3
319 HIGGINS G	1951/52-53/54	69			4												73	0	0
320 HIGGINS JO	1952/53-60/61	183			15			4									202	0	0
321 HILES A	1896/97	1															1	0	0
322 HILL F	1957/58-68/69	373	2	74	23		1	14		4							410	2	79
323 HILTON H	1909/10-19/20	62		23	3		1										65	0	24
324 HINTON F	1920/21-23/24	34			2												36	0	0
325 HODGKISS	1900/01	1															1	0	0
326 HODSON J	1919/20-21/22	22															22	0	0
327 HOGAN J	*1908/09-12/13	54		18	4		1										58	0	19
328 HOGGAN DM	1979/80-82/83	83	10	11	3	1	2	7		2							93	11	15

Player	Season(s)	League			FA Cup			League Cup			FrtRov/A'glass			Anglo Italian			Total		
		Apps	Sub	Goals	Apps	Sub	Goals	Apps	Sub	Goals	Apps	Sub	Goals	Apps	Sub	Goals	Apps	Sub	Goals
329 HOLDEN	Pre-League				5												5	0	0
330 HOLDEN AD	1951/52-62/63	419		40	40		3	4		1							463	0	44
331 HOLDEN D	1999/00-01/02	7	6	1	3	1		3									13	7	1
332 HOLDSWORTH D	1997/98-	97	57	42	5	2	3	11	4	4							113	63	49
333 HOLLOWAY D	1999/2000	3	1														3	1	0
334 HOPKINSON E	1956/57-69/70	519			38			21									578	0	0
335 HOUGH	Pre-League				2		1										2	0	1
336 HOULT R	1993/94	3	1											1			4	1	0
337 HOWARTH H	1929/30-33/34	59			2												61	0	0
338 HOWARTH JM	1919/20	1															1	0	0
339 HOWARTH N	1922/23-25/26	35		2	3												38	0	2
340 HOWARTH P	Pre-League				8		3										8	0	3
341 HOWARTH T	Pre-League				6		1										6	0	1
342 HOWCROFT H	1898/99	3			2												5	0	0
343 HOWE D	1936/37-51/52	266		35	20												286	0	35
344 HUBBICK H	1936/37-46/47	128			16												144	0	0
345 HUGHES A	1893/94	15		2	5		1										20	0	3
346 HUGHES J	1919/20-20/21	40			1												41	0	0
347 HUGHES JH	1933/34	9		3													9	0	3
348 HUGHES P	1987/88-90/91	12	1					1			2						15	1	0
349 HUGHES W	1908/09-12/13	100		51	2												102	0	51
350 HUGHES W	1948/49-52/53	47		2	2												49	0	2
351 HULME J	1962/63-71/72	186	2	7	9		1	18		1							213	2	9
352 HULME W	1919/20	3															3	0	0
353 HUNT GS	1937/38-46/47	45		24	6		2										51	0	26
354 HUNT N	2000/01-		1														0	1	0
355 HUNT R	1969/70-71/72	72	4	24	2	1	1	3	2								77	7	25
356 HUNTER WB	1908/09-11/12	53		15	2		1										55	0	16
357 HURLEY CJ	1969/70-70/71	41	1	3	1			3									45	1	3
358 HURST GJ	1934/35-46/47	60		2	13												73	0	2
359 HYNDS T	1898/99	8															8	0	0
360 JAASKELAINEN J	1998/99-	130	1		5			10									145	1	0
361 JACK DBN	1920/21-28/29	295		144	29		17										324	0	161
362 JACK R	1895/96-00/01	110		29	15												125	0	29
363 JACK RR	1923/24-28/29	29		9	2												31	0	9
364 JACKSON	Pre-League				3												3	0	0
365 JACKSON J	1947/48-49/50	11		1													11	0	1
366 JEFFREY M	1988/89-91/92	9	6		1			1	2		2	1					13	9	0
367 JEMSON N	1988/89	4	1														4	1	0
368 JARRETT RH	1890/91	5															5	0	0
369 JENNINGS W	1912/13-29/30	267		2	20												287	0	2
370 JENSEN C	1998/99-	90	1	8	6			12		2							108	1	10
371 JOHANSEN M	1996/97-99/00	117	25	17	7	1		16	4	4							140	30	21
372 JOHNSON J	2001/02-	4	6		1	1		2									7	7	0
373 JOHNSTON	1922/23	1															1	0	0
374 JOHNSTON A	1999/2000	19	2	4	2												21	2	4
375 JONES	Pre-League				2												2	0	0
376 JONES D	1888/89-97/98	228		4	27		4										255	0	8
377 JONES E	1912/13-14/15	90		24	9		4										99	0	28
378 JONES E	1933/34	1		1													1	0	1
379 JONES G	1909/10-11/12	22		6	1												23	0	6
380 JONES GE	1968/69-78/79	195	8	41	25	2	8	16	1	6							236	11	55
381 JONES J	1899/1900	2															2	0	0
382 JONES J	1919/20-21/22	70															70	0	0
383 JONES J	1937/38	6		1													6	0	1
384 JONES JLM	1922/23-25/26	12		3	3												15	0	3
385 JONES PB	1970/71-82/83	441	4	38	31		1	30		4							502	4	43
386 JONES R	1929/30-36/37	219			25												244	0	0
387 JOYCE W	1894/95-96/97	30		16	3		2										33	0	18
388 JOYCE WG	1982/83-87/88	182	4	17	11		1	14	1	1	9		2				216	5	21
389 KAPRIELIAN M	1999/00-00/01		1														0	1	0
390 KAY G	1910/11	3															3	0	0
391 KEAN FW	1928/29-30/31	80		1	9												89	0	1
392 KEELEY G	1988/89	20			1		1				2						23	0	1
393 KEETLEY JS	1921/22	1															1	0	0
394 KELLY A	1991/92-94/95	103	3	5	15	3		9		2	6		1	3			136	6	8

Player	Season(s)	League			FA Cup			League Cup			FrtRov/A'glass			Anglo Italian			Total		
		Apps	Sub	Goals	Apps	Sub	Goals	Apps	Sub	Goals	Apps	Sub	Goals	Apps	Sub	Goals	Apps	Sub	Goals
395 KENNEDY A	1991/92	1															1	0	0
396 KENNEDY J	Pre-League				10												10	0	0
397 KENNEDY GM	1950/51	17			1												18	0	0
398 KERNAGHAN A	1994/95	9	2														9	2	0
399 KIDD B	1980/81-81/82	40	3	14	2			4		2							46	3	16
400 KIDD J	1914/15	9															9	0	0
401 KING H	1905/06	1															1	0	0
402 KINSELL TH	1949/50	17															17	0	0
403 KIRKMAN G	1935/36	1															1	0	0
404 KONSTANTINIDIS K	2001/02	3															3	0	0
405 KNOWLES	1888/89				3		2										3	0	2
406 KNOWLES JH	1902/03	3		3													3	0	3
407 LANGLEY GR	1981/82	3	3		2												5	3	0
408 LANGTON R	1949/50-52/53	118		16	14		2										132	0	18
409 LAWRIE H	1905/06	3															3	0	0
410 LAWSON RR	1893/94-94/95	2		2													2	0	2
411 LEE D	1992/93-1996/97	125	31	17	13	2		19	1	2	4	1		3	1		164	35	20
412 LEE FH	1960/61-67/68	189		92	13		8	8		6							210	0	106
413 LEE FS	1971/72-74/75	77	8	20	11	1	3	3	1	4							91	10	27
414 LEE J	1897/98-98/99	6															6	0	0
415 LEE S	1990/91-91/92	4						1									5	0	0
416 LEES A	1947/48	2															2	0	0
417 LEIGH J	1903/04	2															2	0	0
418 LENNARD D	1962/63-68/69	114	5	3	6			1									121	5	3
419 LEVER A	1893/94	1															1	0	0
420 LILLYCROP GR	1913/14-14/15	52		31	3		1										55	0	32
421 LOCKHART A	1913/14	2															2	0	0
422 LOCKETT H	1909/10	16		4													16	0	4
423 LOCKHART G	1897/98-99/00	26			2												28	0	0
424 LODGE P	1984/85	4						1									5	0	0
425 LOFTHOUSE N	1946/47-60/61	452		255	49		27	2		3							503	0	285
426 LONG JP	1921/22	1															1	0	0
427 LONGWORTH B	1919/20-23/24	77			5												82	0	0
428 LOW J	1900/01	1															1	0	0
429 LOWE J	1921/22-22/23	5			1												6	0	0
430 LYDEN J	1894/95	3		1													3	0	1
431 LYDIATE J	1991/92-94/95	29	1		2			4			1						36	1	0
432 MANNING JJ	1968/69-70/71	27	2	7	1			2		1							30	2	8
433 MARSH A	1966/67-70/71	71	2		1			5									77	2	0
434 MARSH FK	1938/39	3															3	0	0
435 MARSH S	1902/03-11/12	185		72	16		9										201	0	81
436 MARSHALL I	2000/01-01/02	13	27	6	3			2									18	27	6
437 MARSHALL T	1898/99-02/03	4															4	0	0
438 MARTIN J	1894/95-95/96	7		1													7	0	1
439 MATHEWSON R	1950/51-52/53	3															3	0	0
440 MATTHEW H	1892/93	8															8	0	0
441 MATTHEWS N	1986/87	1															1	0	0
442 MATTHEWS VE	1922/23-24/25	3															3	0	0
443 MAXWELL A	1991/92	3															3	0	0
444 MAY A	1987/88	9	1	2													9	1	2
445 MCADAMS WJ	1960/61-61/62	44		26	3		1	5		2							52	0	29
446 MCAFFERTY W	1902/03	8															8	0	0
447 MCALLISTER D	1969/70-74/75	155	1	2	14			7									176	1	2
448 MCANESPIE S	1995/96-97/98	19	5					6									25	5	0
449 MCARTHUR W	1893/94	19		6													19	0	6
450 MCATEER J	1992/93-95/96	112	5	9	11		3	11		2	1	1		4		1	139	6	15
451 MCATEER T	1898/99-01/02	59		10	3												62	0	10
452 MCBURNEY ML	1973/74	1															1	0	0
453 MCCLARENCE JP	1907/08-08/09	15		6													15	0	6
454 MCCLELLAND J	1927/28-29/30	57		18	8		1										65	0	19
455 MCDONAGH JM	1976/77-82/83	242		1	13			19									274	0	1
456 MCDONALD N	1994/95-95/96	6															6	0	0
457 MCELHINNEY GR	1980/81-84/85	107	2	2	8			9			1						125	2	2
458 MCEWAN M	1904/05-09/10	152		13	12		2										164	0	15
459 MCFETTRIDGE D	1891/92-92/93	25		5	2												27	0	5
460 MCGARRY RJ	1961/62-62/63	27		7				1									28	0	7

Player	Season(s)	League			FA Cup			League Cup			FrtRov/A'glass			Anglo Italian			Total		
		Apps	Sub	Goals	Apps	Sub	Goals	Apps	Sub	Goals	Apps	Sub	Goals	Apps	Sub	Goals	Apps	Sub	Goals
461 MCGEACHAN J	1894/95-97/98	69		5	12												81	0	5
462 MCGINN J	1894/95	15		3													15	0	3
463 MCGINLAY J	1992/93-97/98	183	12	89	16	1	10	23	2	14	4		1	4		4	230	15	118
464 MCGOVERN JP	1982/83-83/84	16						4		1							20	0	1
465 MCGUINESS	1888/89	1		1													1	0	1
466 MCILWAINE M	1952/53	2															2	0	0
467 MCKAY D	1902/03	7			1												8	0	0
468 MCKAY P	1898/99	3															3	0	0
469 MCKAY W	1929/30-33/34	104		17	5												109	0	17
470 MCKERNON J	Pre-League				17												17	0	0
471 MCKIE J	1900/01-02/03	81		19	4		1										85	0	20
472 MCMAHON K	1971/72	4	2	1													4	2	1
473 MCNAB N	1978/79-79/80	33	2	4	2			2									37	2	4
474 MCNEE J	1889/90-92/93	87		23	9		2										96	0	25
475 MCREDDIE W	1895/96	2															2	0	0
476 MCSHANE H	1947/48-50/51	93		6	6		1										99	0	7
477 MCWHIRTER A	1889/90	4															4	0	0
478 MCWILLIAMS P	1902/03	1															1	0	0
479 MELLOR F	1920/21-21/22	2															2	0	0
480 MERCER	1888/89	1															1	0	0
481 MIDDLEBROUGH A	1946/47-47/48	5		1													5	0	1
482 MILLAR J	1894/95-95/96	9			1												10	0	0
483 MILLER J	1897/98	8			1												9	0	0
484 MILLER TA	1896/97-98/99	48		12	5		1										53	0	13
485 MILNE J	1888/89-89/90	39		9													39	0	9
486 MILSOM J	1929/30-37/38	235		142	20		11										255	0	153
487 MITCHELL J	1888/89	2															2	0	0
488 MOIR W	1946/47-55/56	325		118	33		16										358	0	134
489 MOORES	Pre-League				3												3	0	0
490 MOORES IR	1982/83	23	3	3				3	1	2							26	4	5
491 MOORES JC	1980/81		1														0	1	0
492 MORGAN H	1898/99-00/01	46		16	1												47	0	16
493 MORGAN T	1987/88-89/90	65	12	17	4			2		2	7		1				78	12	20
494 MORGAN W	1902/03	3															3	0	0
495 MORGAN W	1975/76-79/80	154	1	10	10			13	1	2							177	2	12
496 MORINI E	2000/01-01/02	1	1		1												2	1	0
497 MOSS AE	1920/21	1															1	0	0
498 MOWBRAY H	1971/72-72/73	31			3			6									40	0	0
499 MULLINEUX I	1986/87	1	1						1								1	2	0
500 MUNRO J	1890/91-92/93	50		20	2		1										52	0	21
501 MURPHY D	1946/47-50/51	66		1	10												76	0	1
502 MURPHY L	1927/28-28/29	33		7	1		1										34	0	8
503 NAPIER RJ	1964/65-66/67	69		2	3			2									74	0	2
504 NAPIER S	1905/06	4															4	0	0
505 NAYLOR T	Pre-League				3												3	0	0
506 NEAL P	1985/86-88/89	58	8	3	6	1		2	2		7	1					73	12	3
507 NELSON	Pre-League				1												1	0	0
508 NEILL TK	1952/53-56/57	40		2	2		1										42	0	3
509 NEWNES J	1922/23	7															7	0	0
510 NESOME J	1998/99	6															6	0	0
511 NEWTON S	1910/11-11/12	15															15	0	0
512 NEYLAND M	1901/02	2															2	0	0
513 NGOTTY B	2001/02-	24	2	1				2	1								26	3	1
514 NICHOLSON G	1931/32-35/36	67		1	4												71	0	1
515 NICHOLSON P	1971/72-81/82	303	15	12	23	3	2	26									352	18	14
516 NICOLL D	1895/96-01/02	61		11	4												65	0	11
517 NIKOLIC D	1980/81-81/82	22		2	2			1									25	0	2
518 NISHIZAWA A	2001/02							3		1							3	0	1
519 NOLAN K	1999/00-	61	11	9	4	2	2	1	1								66	14	11
520 NORRIS D	2000/01-				1			3	1								4	1	0
521 NOWAK T	1978/79-80/81	22	2	1				1	2								23	4	1
522 NUTTALL H	1921/22-31/32	294		6	32												326	0	6
523 OGHANI G	1983/84-86/87	86	13	27	2	4	1	9	2	3	13	1	7				110	20	38
524 OKANE J	1999/00-00/01	32	6	2	3	1	1	4									39	7	3
525 OLINYK P	1973/74-74/75	7	3														7	3	0
526 OLIVER D	1992/93	3						1									4	0	0

Player	Season(s)	League Apps	League Sub	League Goals	FA Cup Apps	FA Cup Sub	FA Cup Goals	League Cup Apps	League Cup Sub	League Cup Goals	FrtRov/A'glass Apps	FrtRov/A'glass Sub	FrtRov/A'glass Goals	Anglo Italian Apps	Anglo Italian Sub	Anglo Italian Goals	Total Apps	Total Sub	Total Goals
527 OSTICK C	1900/01-05/06	84			3												87	0	0
528 OWEN G	1888/89	7		3	1												8	0	3
529 OWEN JR	1906/07-10/11	90		19	8		1										98	0	20
530 OWEN R	Pre-League				3												3	0	0
531 OXTOBY R	1959/60	3						1									4	0	0
532 PAATELAINEN MM	1994/95-1996/97	61	11	16	1	1		8	1	2							70	13	18
533 PARKINSON DW	Pre-League				3												3	0	0
534 PARKINSON G	1992/93-93/94	1	2											4			5	2	0
535 PARKINSON J	1888/89-90/91	22		1	16												38	0	1
536 PARKINSON W	Pre-League				1												1	0	0
537 PARRY A	1929/30	5															5	0	0
538 PARRY RA	1951/52-60/61	270		68	28		11	1									299	0	79
539 PASSI F	1999/00-00/01	21	18		5	1		4									30	19	0
540 PATON A	1890/91-98/99	215		15	26												241	0	15
541 PATTERSON M	1990/91-95/96	158	11	11	17		1	16	4	2	5			4			200	15	14
542 PEACOCK D	1980/81-81/82	16			2			2									20	0	0
543 PEARSON J	1889/90	1			4												5	0	0
544 PEDERSEN H	2001/02-	5	6		2		1	1	1	1							8	7	2
545 PEYTON G	1991/92	1															1	0	0
546 PHILLIPS J	*1983/84-00/01	316	18	5	17			37	3	1	14			6		2	390	21	8
547 PHILLIPS RD	1966/67-74/75	135	10	17	13	1	1	12	4	1							160	15	19
548 PHILLISKIRK A	1989/90-92/93	144	2	54	10		7	18		12	8	2					180	2	75
549 PHYTHIAN ER	1959/60-61/62	10		3				1									11	0	3
550 PICKEN AH	1925/26-27/28	18		2													18	0	2
551 PICKEN JH	1899/00-02/03	101		22	5												106	0	22
552 PICKUP JH	1919/20	1															1	0	0
553 PIKE M	1989/90	5		1							1						6	0	1
554 PILKINGTON B	1960/61-63/64	82		11	1			3									86	0	11
555 PILLING V	1952/53-54/55	7															7	0	0
556 PLATT J	1983/84	10									1						11	0	0
557 POLLOCK J	1996/97-97/98	43	3	5	4		2	4	1	1							51	4	8
558 POTTER L	1999/2000								1								0	1	0
559 POOLE K	2001/02-	3															3		
560 POOLE T	1980/81	29						1									30	0	0
561 POWELL J	Pre-League				6												6	0	0
562 PULMAN J	1909/10	1															1	0	0
563 PYM RH	1921/22-30/31	301			35												336	0	0
564 RANKIN I	2000/01	9	7	2				2									11	7	2
565 REDFEARN ND	1982/83-83/84	35		1	4			2									41	0	1
566 REDFERN J	1969/70-72/73	19	5	2				3	1	1							22	6	3
567 REDROBE WE	1963/64-65/66	4		1													4	0	1
568 REEVES D	1989/90-92/93	113	24	29	8	5	5	14	1	1	7	1	7				142	31	42
569 REID P	1974/75-82/83	222	3	23	17		1	18	1	1							257	4	25
570 RICHARDSON L	2000/01-	5	8		1			3	1								9	9	0
571 RICKETTS M	2000/01-	51	28	33	3	3	3		4	3							54	35	39
572 RILEY BF	1956/57-58/59	8		1													8	0	1
573 RIMMER JW	1930/31-36/37	81		16	2												83	0	16
574 RIMMER WR	1960/61-74/75	462	7	17	30			29									521	7	17
575 RING M	1985/86	1	2														1	2	0
576 RIPLEY S	1985/86	5		1													5	0	1
577 RITCHIE P	1999/2000	15	1		3	1		1									19	2	0
578 RITSON JA	1967/68-77/78	321	3	9	30		4	24									375	3	13
579 ROBERTS CL	1925/26-26/27	6		2													6	0	2
580 ROBERTS D	1985/86										1						1	0	0
581 ROBERTS E	1921/22-22/23	5															5	0	0
582 ROBERTS F	1914/15-22/23	157		79	11		1										168	0	80
583 ROBERTS GM	1967/68-69/70	5															5	0	0
584 ROBERTS JH	1937/38-50/51	162		19	9												171	0	19
585 ROBERTS R	1888/89-91/92	71		3	14		2										85	0	5
586 ROBERTS WD	1926/27	5		4													5	0	4
587 ROBERTSON	Pre-League				3												3	0	0
588 ROBERTSON JN	1903/04-05/06	15															15	0	0
589 ROBINSON B	1888/89-90/91	38			3		1										41	0	1
590 ROBINSON WS	1908/09-10/11	31			1												32	0	0
591 ROLLINSON F	1907/08	1															1	0	0
592 ROSCOE A	1992/93-94/95	2	1								1			1			3	2	0

Player	Season(s)	League			FA Cup			League Cup			FrtRov/A'glass			Anglo Italian			Total		
		Apps	Sub	Goals	Apps	Sub	Goals	Apps	Sub	Goals	Apps	Sub	Goals	Apps	Sub	Goals	Apps	Sub	Goals
593 ROSE K	1989/90-91/92	10						6									16	0	0
594 ROTHWELL E	1937/38-48/49	48		2													48	0	2
595 ROUND JH	1925/26-29/30	56		1	3		1										59	0	2
596 ROWE GE	1971/72	4	2					2		1							6	2	1
597 ROWLEY WJ	1912/13-24/25	175		7	16												191	0	7
598 RUDGE SJ	1982/83-85/86	77	13	14	4	2	2	5			5						91	15	16
599 RUSHTON W	1889/90	2			5												7	0	0
600 RUSSELL W	1890/91-91/92	6															6	0	0
601 RUSSELL W	1962/63-64/65	22		2													22	0	2
602 RYDER G	1906/07-07/08	4															4	0	0
603 SALAKO J	1997/98		7														0	7	0
604 SALMON M	1986/87	26			4			2			4						36	0	0
605 SAUNDERS S	1983/84	3				1		1	1								4	2	0
606 SAVAGE R	1987/88-89/90	83	4	11	3			3		1	9		1				98	4	13
607 SCHOLES J	Pre-League				2		1										2	0	1
608 SCOTCHBROOK F	1896/97-99/00	5															5	0	0
609 SCOTT D	1985/86-87/88	121			8			4			14						147	0	0
610 SCOTT S	1896/97-97/98	19															19	0	0
611 SCOWCROFT J	1888/89	9		1	2												11	0	1
612 SEAGREAVES M	1990/91-94/95	155	5	7	17		1	8			6			4		1	190	5	9
613 SEDDON IW	1969/70-71/73	51	13	4	4	1		6	1								61	15	4
614 SEDDON J	1913/14-31/32	337		4	38		1										375	0	5
615 SELLARS S	1995/96-1998/99	106	6	15	5		1	8	1								119	7	16
616 SETTLE J	1894/95	13		4	2												15	0	4
617 SHAW J	1903/04-04/05	8															8	0	0
618 SHEPHERD A	1904/05-08/09	115		85	8		5										123	0	90
619 SHERIDAN J	1996/97-97/98	24	8	2	2			2									28	8	2
620 SHILTON P	1994/95	1	1														1	1	0
621 SHINTON F	1910/11	7		1													7	0	1
622 SHUTTLEWORTH T	1893/94-94/95	2															2	0	0
623 SIDDALL B	1972/73-76/77	137			11			10									158	0	0
624 SIDDONS	1888/89	1															1	0	0
625 SIDEBOTTOM W	1938/39	1															1	0	0
626 SIDLOW E	1913/14-14/15	19			1												20	0	0
627 SIMM J	1947/48	1															1	0	0
628 SIMMERS W	1888/89	2			2		2										4	0	2
629 SIMPSON H	1921/22-23/24	9		1													9	0	1
630 SINCLAIR TM	1938/39	10		5													10	0	5
631 SLATER J	1906/07-12/13	92			7												99	0	0
632 SLEIGHT G	1961/62	2						1									3	0	0
633 SMALL B	1995/96-97/98	11	1		3			1									15	1	0
634 SMITH A	1962/63-67/68	19						1									20	0	0
635 SMITH B	1974/75-78/79	43	6	3	2	1	1	5									50	7	4
636 SMITH CF	1921/22-22/23	7															7	0	0
637 SMITH DW	1895/96-96/97	3			1												4	0	0
638 SMITH GT	1900/01	1			1												2	0	0
639 SMITH H	1913/14	8		1													8	0	1
640 SMITH J	1908/09-26/27	449		254	43		23										492	0	277
641 SMITH J	2000/01-	1	1					1									2	1	0
642 SMITH JR	1922/23-27/28	147		72	27		15										174	0	87
643 SMITH R	1932/33-35/36	89			13												102	0	0
644 SMITH S	1974/75	3															3	0	0
645 SNEEKES R	1994/95-95/96	51	4	7	2		1	11	1	3							64	5	11
646 SNOOKES E	1983/84	6															6	0	0
647 SOMERVILLE J	1890/91-00/01	265		2	28												293	0	2
648 SOMMER J	2000/01				1												1	0	0
649 SOUTHALL N	2001/02-	10	8	1	2			4									16	8	1
650 SPENCE A	1894/95	4		2	1												5	0	2
651 SPOONER N	1991/92-1998/99	22	1	2	3			2				1					27	2	2
652 STANLEY G	1956/57-63/64	141		3	12		1	8									161	0	4
653 STANLEY J	1905/06-09/10	67			4												71	0	0
654 STATON L	1999/2000								1								0	1	0
655 STEEL R	Pre-League				14		8										14	0	8
656 STEEL W	Pre-League				8												8	0	0
657 STEVENS D	1953/54-61/62	273		90	30		9	7		2							310	0	101
658 STEVENS I	1986/87-90/91	26	22	7	4		2	1	2		3						34	24	9

Player	Season(s)	League			FA Cup			League Cup			FrtRov/A'glass			Anglo Italian			Total		
		Apps	Sub	Goals	Apps	Sub	Goals	Apps	Sub	Goals	Apps	Sub	Goals	Apps	Sub	Goals	Apps	Sub	Goals
659 STEVENSON J	1894/95	2															2	0	0
660 STOKES D	1901/02-19/20	387		43	33		3										420	0	46
661 STORER S	1987/88-92/93	100	28	12	7	3	2	9	2		11	5	1				127	38	15
662 STOTT W	1908/09-13/14	63			2												65	0	0
663 STRANG T	1902/03	3															3	0	0
664 STRONG G	1995/96-98/99	10	2	1				8	2								18	4	1
665 STRUTHERS R	1901/02-06/07	130			11												141	0	0
666 STRUTHERS WG	Pre-League				19		18										19	0	18
667 STUART W	1907/08-09/10	7		1													7	0	1
668 STUBBS A	1990/91-95/96	187	21	9	16	2	2	23		4	2	1		4			232	24	15
669 SUMMERBEE N	2000/01	9	3		3												12	3	0
670 SUTCLIFFE JW	1889/90-01/02	332			32												364	0	0
671 SUTTON D	1985/86-87/88	100		4	2			5			12						119	0	4
672 SWIFT F	1963/36-37/38	62			3												65	0	0
673 TAGGART G	1995/96-1997/98	68	1	4	4			8		1							80	1	5
674 TAIT T	1930/31	9		4	1												10	0	4
675 TANNAHILL R	1892/93-96/97	67		8	13		3										80	0	11
676 TATHAM W	1897/98	2															2	0	0
677 TAYLOR A	1904/05	3			3												6	0	0
678 TAYLOR C	2001/02-					1											0	1	0
679 TAYLOR G	1930/31-38/39	220		3	24												244	0	3
680 TAYLOR G	1962/63-70/71	253	5	41	14		2	14		3							281	5	46
681 TAYLOR GT	1933/34-37/38	150		27	20		2										170	0	29
682 TAYLOR R	1901/02-06/07	104		18	10		1										114	0	19
683 TAYLOR R	*1997/98-99/00	60	20	23	4	1	2	6	5	2							70	26	27
684 TAYLOR SJ	1974/75-77/78	34	6	16	1			9		4							44	6	20
685 TAYLOR SJ	1995/96-1998/99	2	10	1	1		1		4	1							3	14	3
686 TENNANT JW	1935/36-38/39	99		1	6												105	0	1
687 THIRKELL P	1922/23	14			1												15	0	0
688 THOMAS J	1912/13-14/15	30			6												36	0	0
689 THOMAS JW	*1980/81-88/89	89	6	37	2		3	5		2	6	2	2				102	8	44
690 THOMPSON A	1993/94-1997/98	146	14	34	6	2	2	24	1	5				4	1	1	180	18	42
691 THOMPSON CD	1979/80-82/83	66	7	18	3	1	1	3	1	1							72	9	20
692 THOMPSON F	1902/03	20			1												21	0	0
693 THOMPSON P	1973/74-77/78	111	6	2	10			5									126	6	2
694 THOMPSON SJ	1982/83-91/92	336	6	49	21		4	27		2	32		2				416	6	57
695 THOMSON W	1896/97-98/99	45		5	4		1										49	0	6
696 THORNBOROUGH EH	1925/26-29/30	69			11												80	0	0
697 THORP J	1906/07	2															2	0	0
698 THRELFALL J	1955/56-62/63	47		1	2												49	0	1
699 THRELFALL JR	1946/47	3			8												11	0	0
700 TIERNEY H	1907/08	1															1	0	0
701 TODD AJJ	1995/96-99/00	69	18	2	1			14	5	1							84	23	3
702 TOFTING S	2001/02-	6															6	0	0
703 TOONE PES	1914/15	3															3	0	0
704 TRACEY W	1900/01-02/03	56		11	3												59	0	11
705 TRAIN R	1976/77-78/79	49	2		3			3									55	2	0
706 TRAINER J	Pre-League				4												4	0	0
707 TURNBULL P	1894/95	4		5													4	0	5
708 TURNER JA	1888/89-93/94	96		8	12		4										108	0	12
709 TURNER R	1888/89				3												3	0	0
710 TYLDESLEY J	1911/12-13/14	10			2												12	0	0
711 TYRER H	1888/89	14		2													14	0	2
712 UNSWORTH W	Pre-League				5												5	0	0
713 VAIL T	1895/96	3		1	1												4	0	1
714 VALENTINE P	1983/84-84/85	66	2	1	4			4			5						79	2	1
715 VAUGHAN J	Pre-League				4		1										4	0	1
716 VIANDER J	2001/02				1												1	0	0
717 VIZARD ET	1910/11-30/31	467		64	45		6										512	0	70
718 WAGSTAFFE JT	1925/26-31/32	50		1	3												53	0	1
719 WALDRON A	1970/71-77/78	127	14	6	12	2	1	14	1	2							153	17	9
720 WALKER A	1991/92-93/94	61	6	44	9	3	8	3		1	5		2				78	9	55
721 WALKER R	1984/85-85/86	7	5	1				1				1					8	6	1
722 WALLACE R	2001/02	14	5	3	1			1	2	1							16	7	4
723 WALLACE W	1914/15	2		1													2	0	1
724 WALLER WH	1899/00-00/01	6															6	0	0

Player	Season(s)	League			FA Cup			League Cup			FrtRov/A'glass			Anglo Italian			Total		
		Apps	Sub	Goals	Apps	Sub	Goals	Apps	Sub	Goals	Apps	Sub	Goals	Apps	Sub	Goals	Apps	Sub	Goals
725 WALSH MT	1974/75-80/81	169	8	4	10	1		13		1							192	9	5
726 WALSH T	1920/21-23/24	22		4													22	0	4
727 WALTERS TC	1931/32	5		1													5	0	1
728 WALTON G	1932/33-36/37	26		1	2		2										28	0	3
729 WALTON M	1993/94	3															3	0	0
730 WARBURTON F	1903/04	1															1	0	0
731 WARD	Pre-League				3												3	0	0
732 WARD GJ	1995/96-1998/99	19	3		4			2									25	3	0
733 WARHURST P	1998/99-	78	10		3	1		3	3								84	14	0
734 WATSON AG	1919/20-21/22	35			1												36	0	0
735 WEAVER W	1906/07	4		1													4	0	1
736 WEBSTER H	1949/50-56/57	98		38	3												101	0	38
737 WEIR A	1912/13	2		2													2	0	2
738 WEIR D	1888/89-94/95	86		31	6		10										92	0	41
739 WESTWOOD RW	1930/31-47/48	301		127	32		17										333	0	144
740 WHARTON TJ	1967/68-70/71	101	1	28	2	1		5		2							108	2	30
741 WHATMORE N	*1972/73-83/84	279	15	107	21		7	22	1	7							322	16	121
742 WHEATCROFT P	2000/01-01/02					2			1								0	3	0
743 WHEELER JE	1950/51-55/56	189		18	16												205	0	18
744 WHITE W	1902/03-08/09	196		88	21		5										217	0	93
745 WHITESIDE E	1908/09-13/14	84			4												88	0	0
746 WHITESIDE J	1908/09-10/11	7		1													7	0	1
747 WHITLOW M	1997/98-	112	8	2	9			13	2								134	10	2
748 WHITTAKER S	1993/97-96/97	2	1						1								2	2	0
749 WHITTLE	1888/89				3		1										3	0	1
750 WHITWORTH S	1981/82-82/83	67			3			3									73	0	0
751 WILKINSON H	1909/10	1			1												2	0	0
752 WILKINSON RJ	1960/61-61/62	3															3	0	0
753 WILLCOCKS D	1892/93-93/94	32		8	4												36	0	8
754 WILLIAMS GC	1967/68-70/71	108	1	11	4		1	4									116	1	12
755 WILLIAMS H	1901/02-02/03	16		6	2		1										18	0	7
756 WILSON FW	1931/32-32/33	4		1													4	0	1
757 WILSON G	1914/15	26			7												33	0	0
758 WILSON J	1892/93-93/94	36		7	5		3										41	0	10
759 WILSON P	1979/80-80/81	35	4	4	2			1									38	4	4
760 WILSON T	1904/05-05/06	20		5	4												24	0	5
761 WILSON TR	Pre-League				8												8	0	0
762 WINSTANLEY M	1985/86-93/94	217	5	3	19			19	1		19		3	5			279	6	6
763 WINTER DT	1936/37-38/39	34			3												37	0	0
764 WINTERBURN A	1919/20	1															1	0	0
765 WOLSTENHOLME T	1905/06-06/07	9			1												10	0	0
766 WOODS C	1935/36				2		1										2	0	1
767 WOODS F	1889/90	5															5	0	0
768 WOODS S	1908/09-09/10	5		2													5	0	2
769 WOODWARD T	1935/36-49/50	152		18	17		1										169	0	19
770 WOOLFALL T	1900/01	21			2												23	0	0
771 WORTHINGTON W	1901/02	3		1													3	0	1
772 WORTHINGTON FS	1977/78-79/80	81	3	35	5		1	2	1	2							88	4	38
773 WIGGLESWORTH W	1946/47-47/48	13		1	2		1										15	0	2
774 WRIGHT CG	1971/72-72/73	88			13			8									109	0	0
775 WRIGHT J	1895/96-03/04	119		19	9		3										128	0	22
776 WRIGHT RL	1971/72-72/73	25	7	5				2									27	7	5
777 WRIGHT S	1920/21-21/22	10															10	0	0
778 WRIGHT T	2000/01	3	1														3	1	0
779 WRIGHT WB	1922/23-32/33	154		21	5		1										159	0	22
780 YATES W	1925/26-26/27	6															6	0	0
781 YENSON W	1925/26-26/27	28		8	6		2										34	0	10
782 YOUNG J	Pre-League				4												4	0	0
	Own Goals			100			12			4			1						117

* denotes more than one spell with the club

FA Cup figures do not include the game v Rawtenstall in 1885/86 No record of team available   League figures include play-offs

STATISTICAL SECTION
Notes

Generally this section is self-explantory, and is sub-divided into several sections:

1 (Pages 149-152) Details all known pre-Football League first team matches (1879 to 1888), but excluding F.A.Cup matches during this period. Cup or other competitive (not Friendly) matches are identified.

2 (Page 153) Details of all pre-Football League F.A.Cup matches (with complete line-ups, where known). See also below.

3 (Pages 154 - 314) Main Statistical Section. All Competitive matches (Football League and cup competitions) from 1888 to 2002 are included, with line-ups, plus all generally recognised first team friendly matches (no line-ups).

Key: First column shows the (League) match number or (Cup) round, e.g. Q = qualifying, 2r = 2nd round replay, 1/ 2r = 1st round second replay, SF = Semi-Final, etc.

Second column shows the date of the match

Third Column shows the opponents. Upper case (capitals) - Home game, lower case - Away game.

Fourth Column: Match result (Bolton score first)

Fifth Column: Goalscorers (OG indicates an 'own goal', eg indicates 'own' goal' and name of scorer) 'pen' indiates a goal scrored from a penalty.

Sixth Column: Provide the attendance. Official (these were not released for League matches until the 1925/26 season) and/or reasonably accurate (normally newspaper reports).

Players Grid: Shirt numbers worn are shown (or pre World War Two, adopting the normal numbering convention, e.g. 1 = goalkeeper, 4 = right half, 8 = inside left, etc. Substitutes replaced the same lettered player, e.g. A12 (player number 12) substituted A9 (player number 9). Since the use of squad numbering in the 1990's, and asterisk (*) indicates this player started the match, and a substitute ('S') replaced same lettered player, e.g. e.g. B* started the match and was replaced with substitute BS.

Other notes relating to additional players, different venues, etc. are self-explanatory.

1881 The earliest known team photograph
(Back) Parkinson, Howarth, Kennedy, Wilson, Devlin, Naylor, Steele
(Middle) Flower, Gleaves, Struthers, Christie   (Front) Scholes, Atherton

Pre-League Matches
1879 - 1888

(All friendly matches unless shown otherwise. Lancashire Cup matches, round numbers follow dates)

1879-80			
Dec 27	Turton	1-2	
Jan 3	Great Lever	6-0	
10	GREAT LEVER	0-0	
24	Eagley	4-2	
31	BOLTON OLYMPIC	3-2	
Feb 14	TURTON	1-4	
21	Accrington	2-1	
28	HALLIWELL	4-2	
Mar 6	BLACKBURN OLYMPIC	3-1	
27	Astley Bridge	4-4	
Apr 3	Bolton Olympic	3-5	
17	Blackburn Olympic	2-3	
24	Darwen (played at Bolton Rugby club)	3-3	

Lancashire Cup

1	ALL SAINTS	5-2	
2	Blackburn Rovers	0-4	

1880-81			
Oct 9	Blackburn Rovers	0-7	
16	Accrington	1-12	
23	EAGLEY	5-2	
Nov 6	Preston North End	7-2	
27	EARLSTOWN	8-1	
Dec 11	TURTON	1-1	
18	Eagley	1-4	
Jan 8	PRESTON NORTH END	4-0	
22	Northwich	2-1	
27	Accrington	1-8	
Feb 12	TURTON	3-2	
Mar 5	BLACKBURN OLYMPIC	2-1	
19	NORTHWICH	1-1	
26	MANCHESTER WANDERERS	10-0	
Apr 2	BLACKBURN ROVERS	3-5	
9	Blackburn Olympic	1-3	
15	Blackpool	3-3	
18	EDINBURGH HIBERNIANS	3-4	

Lancashire Cup

Oct 30	1	IRWELL SPINRGS	7-1
Nov 20	2	Great Harwood	2-0
Feb 5	3	Great Lever	3-2
27	4	BLACKBURN PARK ROAD	1-1
Mar 12	4r	Blackburn Park Road	1-6

1881-82			
Sep 10	GREAT LEVER	9-0	
17	ALL SAINTS (BOLTON & DISTRICT)	3-3	
24	Blackburn Park Road	3-0	
Oct 1	BLACKBURN ROVERS	2-2	
8	Bootle	7-1	
15	ASTLEY BRIDGE	8-1	
29	Edinburgh Hibernians	0-3	
Nov 26	Manchester Wanderers	11-0	
30	LIVERPOOL	13-1	
Dec 14	MACCLESFIELD	12-0	

17	VALE OF LEVEN	3-1	
24	NOTTS RANGERS	9-0	
31	3RD LANARK RV	4-1	
Jan 2	DUMBARTON	2-3	
14	GREAT LEVER	11-1	
21	BLACKBURN PARK ROAD	5-1	
28	EAGLEY	4-3	
Feb 4	MANCHESTER WANDERERS	15-0	
18	Darwen	2-2	
25	Turton	4-0	
Mar 4	Nottingham Forest	1-2	
11	DARWEN	2-2	
18	TURTON	3-2	
25	ACCRINGTON	2-3	

Bolton Charity Cup - Round 1

Apr 1	Turton (played at Eagley)	8-3	
8	VALE OF LEVEN	0-1	
10	EDINBURGH HIBERNIANS	1-3	
15	Astley Bridge	5-3	
17	BOOTLE	12-0	

Bolton Charity Cup - Semi-final

Apr 22	HALLIWELL	9-1	
26	OLYMPIC	4-0	

Bolton Charity Cup - Final

May 6	ASTLEY BRIDGE	3-3	

Devlin Benefit

May 10	DEVLINS TEAM	2-7	

Bolton Charity Cup - Final replay

May 20	Astley Bridge (played at Bolton Rugby club)	6-1	
27	WITTON	4-1	

Lancashire Cup

Nov 5	1	BLACKBURN PARK ROAD	10-4
Dec 10	2	Low Moor	13-0
Jan 7	3	LOWER DARWEN	9-0
Feb 11	4	Accrington	3-7

1882-83			
Sep 9	TURTON	3-1	
16	WEDNESBURY OLD ATHLETIC	1-3	
23	STAVELEY	4-1	
30	GREAT LEVER	5-1	
Oct 7	Druids	5-2	
14	DARWEN	1-1	
21	Accrington	3-3	
28	GLASGOW RANGERS	1-0	
Nov 6	SHEFFIELD WANDERERS	9-0	
11	NOTTINGHAM FOREST	9-0	
18	Darwen	2-3	
25	Eagley	7-1	
Dec 6	Co-operative Employees	8-0	
9	Great Lever (played at High Street)	1-1	
16	KILMARNOCK PORTLAND	9-0	
23	NORTHWICH VICTORIA	8-0	
26	Nottingham Forest	1-3	
30	HALLIWELL	14-2	
Jan 1	DUMBARTON	0-2	

13	PAISLEY ST. MIRREN	8-2
27	ACCRINGTON	4-8
Feb 10	Accrington	2-4
26	WEDNESBURY OLD ATHLETIC	6-0
Mar 3	Everton	8-1
5	WALSALL SWIFTS	2-1
10	CHURCH	7-0
21	OXFORD UNIVERSITY	2-2
24	DRUIDS	6-0
26	3RD LANARK RV	3-0
31	Paisley St. Mirren	4-3

Bolton Charity Cup - Round 1

Apr 7	Great Lever (played at Halliwell)	4-1
14	BLACKBURN ROVERS	6-3
21	Turton	4-1
24	EAGLEY	3-2

Bolton Charity Cup - Semi-final

Apr 28	TURTON	3-0
30	NORTH OF ENGLAND	4-2
May 5	EDINBURGH UNIVERSITY	2-1

Bolton Charity Cup - Final

May12	GILNOW RANGERS	3-0

Fowler Benefit

May15	BLACKBURN/DARWEN/BOLTON SELECT	2-1

Lancashire Cup

Nov 1	1	Egerton	6-2
15	2	BRADSHAW	9-2
Dec20	3	Rishton	2-2
Jan 20	3r	RISHTON	10-1
Feb 3	4	PEEL BANK ROVERS	7-0
17	5	DARWEN ST. JOHNS	5-1
Mar17	SF	Blackburn Rovers (played at Darwen)	1-4

1883-84

Aug25	Astley Bridge	4-3
Sep 1	OSWESTRY	8-0
8	STAVELEY	4-2
15	BIRMINGHAM ST. GEORGES	4-2
22	PADIHAM	6-1
29	Northwich Victoria	1-3
Oct 6	WALSALL SWIFTS	2-2
13	PRESTON NORTH END	1-1
20	Darwen	0-1
27	ACCRINGTON	5-1
Nov 3	Blackburn Rovers	0-0
12	STAVELEY	7-2
17	BOLTON ASSOCIATION	1-1
19	WEST BROMWICH ALBION	3-1
24	Turton	4-1
Dec13	Blackburn Park Road	3-2
15	LIVERPOOL RAMBLERS	11-1
22	Wednesbury Old Athletic	1-0
Jan 1	HEART OF MIDLOTHIAN	4-1
2	SHEFFIELD WEDNESDAY	4-1
5	HALLIWELL	2-1
12	DARWEN	4-0
17	Blackpool *	0-0

* (Abandoned after 15 mins, Tom Howarth - broken leg)

Feb 9	Accrington	0-1

Howarth Benefit

Feb23	BOLTON & DISTRICT	7-1
Mar 1	WALSALL TOWN	5-1
8	WEDNESBURY TOWN	10-0

10	BLACKBURN OLYMPIC	2-3
15	GLASGOW RANGERS	1-1
22	ACCRINGTON	7-0
29	WEDNESBURY OLD ATHLETIC	2-1
Apr 5	Walsall Swifts	2-1
7	Aston Villa	1-0
11	Halliwell	1-1
12	3RD LANARK RV	1-1
14	EDINBURGH HIBERNIANS	1-1
19	Preston North End	2-1
26	HALLIWELL	3-0
May 3	ASTON VILLA	2-1
10	GREAT LEVER	0-1
17	ASTLEY BRIDGE	2-0
24	WALSALL SWIFTS	5-0

Lancashire Cup

Sep29	1	DARWEN WANDERERS	1-2

1884/85

Sep 1	PADIHAM	3-4
6	BURNLEY	3-1
9	Padiham	2-4
13	STAVELEY	7-1
20	WALSALL TOWN	5-1
27	SHEFFIELD WEDNESDAY	2-1
Oct 4	Aston Villa	2-1
11	ASTLEY BRIDGE	7-3
18	Accrington	3-4
25	PADIHAM	7-0
27	Burnley	2-0
Nov 1	HALLIWELL	3-1
3	BURNLEY	3-1
8	CLITHEROE	6-1
10	Burslem Port Vale	6-1
15	Preston North End	1-4
22	ASTON VILLA	4-1
Dec 6	PRESTON NORTH END	2-2
13	BLACKBURN ROVERS	3-2
19	OLD CORINTHIANS	7-0
20	Blackburn Olympic	1-2
25	Burnley	2-3
27	WALSALL SWIFTS	2-0
Jan 1	PAISLEY ST. MIRREN	2-2
2	CAMBUSLANG	2-0
3	ST. BERNARDS	7-0
17	Halliwell	3-2
24	Sheffield Wednesday	6-2
Feb 2	BURNLEY	1-2
4	EVERTON	7-0
7	ASTLEY BRIDGE	4-0
14	ACCRINGTON	1-3
16	Burnley	2-3
17	DARWEN	3-0
21	DERBY COUNTY	4-1
28	BLACKBURN OLYMPIC	6-0
Mar 7	Stoke	3-0
9	Astley Bridge	7-2
14	NOTTS COUNTY	4-2
16	Wigan	9-1
21	ACCRINGTON	2-2
25	BOLTON ASSOCIATION	4-0
28	BURNLEY	4-0
Apr 3	KILMARNOCK	8-1

4	RENTON	2-1	
7	BATTLEFIELD	5-3	

Bolton Charity Cup - Semi-final

Apr 18	Astley Bridge (played at Halliwell)	3-1
20	WOLVERHAMPTON WANDERERS	3-1
25	West Bromwich Albion	1-0
27	Wolverhampton Wanderers	1-0
May 2	GREAT LEVER	2-1

Bolton Charity Cup Final

May 9	GREAT LEVER	5-1
16	Great Lever	1-1
18	Blackburn Rovers	4-1
23	ACCRINGTON	1-0
26	Everton	2-1
29	Arbroath	3-0
30	Old Boys (Dundee)	4-3
Jun 1	3rd Lanark RV	3-3

Lancashire Cup

Oct 4	1	HURST PARK ROAD	10-1
18	2	LOWERHOUSE	6-1
Nov 29	3	GREAT LEVER	5-2
Jan 10	4	LOW MOOR	3-0
31	5	DARWEN OLD WANDERERS	3-1
Apr 11	SF	Blackburn Rovers(played at Darwen) *	5-1

* (Bolton disqualified for fielding ineligable players)

1885-86

Aug 15	Padiham	1-1
22	Church	6-1
29	ASTON VILLA	7-2
Sep 3	TURTON	6-0
5	ASTLEY BRIDGE	7-0
12	WALSALL TOWN	5-0
19	BURNLEY	2-1
21	South Shore	3-0
26	NOTTS RANGERS	4-2
28	Stoke	4-2
Oct 3	PRESTON NORTH END	1-3
10	Wolverhampton Wanderers	2-0
17	Everton	4-1
19	BLACKBURN OLUMPIC	7-0
24	ACCRINGTON	2-0
31	Accrington	5-2
Nov 2	DERBY JUNCTION	11-0
2	Wigan	3-0
7	Corinthians (played at Kennington Oval)	2-0
14	Preston North End	0-5
21	Burnley	2-2
23	STOKE	11-0
25	EVERTON	10-0
28	Birmingham Excelsior	12-2
Dec 12	Aston Villa	3-4
19	Walsall Swifts	4-0
25	Great Lever *	2-1

* (Abandoned-fighting in crowd of 10,000 at Woodside)

26	Notts County	3-3
28	West Bromwich Albion	0-0
Jan 1	DERBY COUNTY	1-1
2	GREAT LEVER	7-1
4	BLACKBURN ROVERS	5-3
9	PADIHAM	0-1
9	Accrington	0-5
16	BIRMINGHAM ST. GEORGES	7-1

23	Nottingham Forest	7-0
25	Burslem Port Vale	4-0
30	DARWEN	3-4
Feb 6	WOLVERHAMPTON WANDERERS	5-0
8	BURNLEY	3-0
13	WITTON	4-0
20	Blackburn Rovers	3-1
27	HALLIWELL	7-1
Mar 6	Darwen	6-1
9	Staveley	6-0
13	DERBY COUNTY	7-0
15	Burnslem Port Vale	0-0
20	BLACKBURN ROVERS	5-2
22	Aston Villa	1-3
27	Grimsby Town	1-1
29	Burnley	2-3
Apr 3	NOTTS COUNTY	6-1
5	Stoke	1-0
7	Church	3-1
9	Glasgow Rangers	3-2
Apr 10	Heart of Midlothian(Opening of Tynecastle)	1-4
12	ACCRINGTON	4-0
23	EDINBURGH HIBERNIANS	6-2
24	BATTLEFIELD	2-1
26	HEART OF MIDLOTHIAN	2-2
27	Derby County	1-1

Bolton Charity Cup

May 1	Halliwell	4-1

Derby Charity Cup

8	Derby County	2-0

Lancashire Cup

Oct 13	1	Burnley Wanderers	0-0
21	1r	BURNLEY WANDERERS	7-0
Nov 13	2	South Shore	3-0
Dec 5	3	BLACKBURN OLYMPIC	11-2
19	4	Blackpool St. Johns	9-1
Feb 13	SF	Darwen	2-1
Apr 17	F	Blackburn Rovers (played at Preston)	1-0

1886-87

Jul 31	Crewe & Disrict	6-1
Aug 14	Everton	3-1
21	BURNLEY	5-1
23	Astley Bridge	7-0
27	Cowlairs	0-4
28	Edinburgh Hibernians	2-3
Sep 4	Preston North End	1-2
11	DRUIDS	7-1
18	WALSALL TOWN	5-2
25	WOLVERHAMPTON WANDERERS	9-0
27	Burslem Port Vale	0-3
Oct 2	Accrington	2-1
13	Burnley	4-3
16	Blackburn Rovers	2-6
23	WEST BROMWICH ALBION	1-0
28	Heart of Midlothian	2-2
Nov 1	Wigan	6-0
8	BLACKBURN ROVERS	5-4
20	PRESTON NORTH END	3-2
27	DERBY COUNTY	2-0
Dec 6	Stoke	1-1
18	BURNLEY	2-2
25	Preston North End	1-12

	28	West Bromwich Albion	3-1
Jan	1	GLASGOW RANGERS	3-2
	3	HEART OF MIDLOTHIAN	3-2
	4	COWLAIRS	3-1
	8	MITCHELL ST. GEORGES	6-1
	22	BLACKBURN OLYMPIC	6-0
	29	Burslem Port Vale	2-3
Feb	5	BLACKBURN ROVERS	2-2
	12	STOKE	4-0
	14	Blackburn Rovers	5-1
	26	ACCRINGTON	2-2
Mar	5	Burnley	0-6
	5	Derby County	0-3
Mar	12	Halliwell	3-2
	16	Middlesbrough	5-2
	19	PRESTON NORTH END	3-0
Apr	2	HALLIWELL	4-4
	4	Blackburn Olympic	2-1
	8	EDINBURGH HIBERNIANS	1-1
	9	3RD LANARK RV	2-1
	11	RENTON	3-3
	16	Mitchell St. Georges	2-0
	18	Bootle	1-0
	23	Bury	6-0
	25	Burnley	0-1
	30	Newton Heath	5-0

Bolton Charity Cup - Semi final

May	7	Halliwell	1-1
	14	DARWEN	3-2

Bolton Charity Cup - Semi-final replay

May	16	HALLIWELL	1-2
	21	Everton	0-5
	25	Crewe Alexandra	1-2
	28	West Bromwich Albion	0-2
	30	HALLIWELL	2-0

Charity Game

Jun	20	HALLIWELL	1-1

Lancashire Cup

Oct	9	1	WIGAN	14-0
Nov	6	2	Burnley	5-1
Dec	4	3	Rossendale	8-1
	14	4	Irwell Springs	4-1
Feb	19	SF	Padiham (played at Preston)	4-1
Mar	26	F	PRESTON NORTH END	0-3

1887-88

Aug	6	Accrington *	2-4

*(At Raikes Hall Gardens, Blackpool,: part of illuminations attractions)

	27	Earlstown (Engineers Strike Fund)	5-4
	29	Astley Bridge	3-0
Sep	3	LOCKWOOD BROS	0-1
	5	Wolverhampton Wanderers	1-1
	10	Hyde	8-2
	13	Bootle	2-3
	17	BURNLEY	1-4

	24	WEST BROMWICH ALBION	1-1
	26	Burslem Port Vale	4-1
	28	Newton Heath(Manchester Royal Jub.Exhib)	1-2
Oct	8	ACCRINGTON	1-1
	12	Northwich Victoria	1-1
	22	Derby County	0-3
Nov	5	Grimsby Town	0-2
	7	West Bromwich Albion	0-6
	26	HALLIWELL	4-3
Dec	3	WALSALL TOWN	6-1
	12	BURNLEY	4-3
	17	Halliwell	0-2
	24	WITTON	2-4
	26	Bootle	2-1
	27	Nottingham Forest	2-3
	31	KILMARNOCK	2-0
Jan	3	PAISLEY ABERCORN	0-2
	4	HEART OF MIDLOTHIAN	3-1
	7	Newton Heath	1-0
	14	Accrington	1-3
	21	HALLIWELL	3-4
	28	Lincoln City	3-4
Feb	4	BOOTLE	2-1
	11	Michell St. Georges	2-3
	14	Notts County	3-0
	18	BLACKBURN ROVERS	4-1
	25	Darwen	2-3
Mar	3	Preston North End	1-5
	5	Stoke	5-1
	10	DERBY COUNTY	5-5
	17	Halliwell	1-4
	24	Burnley	1-3
	30	MITCHELL ST GEORGES	3-4
	31	NOTTINGHAM FOREST	3-1
Apr	7	Blackburn Rovers	0-6
	14	PRESTON NORTH END	1-4
	17	FLETCHER STREET MEN	1-1
	21	DARWEN	3-3
	23	Newton Heath	3-3
	25	Middlesbrough	0-1
	28	ACCRINGTON	1-1

Bolton Charity Cup

	30	Astley Bridge (played at Halliwell)	4-2
May	2	Everton	0-4
	5	BURNLEY	4-1
	7	LANCASHIRE (Steel Benefit)	2-1
	12	ASTON VILLA	4-3
	19	HALLIWELL	3-1
	21	Blackburn Rovers	4-2
		(played at Eaton Hall Fete, Chester)	

Bolton Charity Cup - Final

Jun	9	FARNWORTH STANDARD	5-1

Lancashire Cup

Oct	1	1	BELLS TEMPERANCE	10-1
Nov	26	2	Burnley Union Star	0-5

Pre-League F.A.Cup Matches

1881/82

					Wilson TR	Devlin J	Naylor T	Gleaves J	Nelson	Howarth T	Dawson T	Struthers WG	Steel R	Atherton J	Robertson	Ward	Fowler J
1	Oct	22	EAGLEY	5-5 Atherton,Gleaves,Struthers,OG (2)	1	2	3	4	5	6	7	8	9	10	11		
1r	Nov	12	Eagley	1-0 Steel	1	2	3	4		6		8	9	10	11	5	7
2		19	Blackburn Rovers	2-6 Atherton, Struthers	1	2	3	4		6		8	9	10	11	5	7

1882/83

					Wilson TR	McKernon J	Young J	Kennedy J	Gleaves J	Cox W	Fowler J	Struthers WG	Christie J	Steel R	Jones E	Scholes J	Atherton J	Davenport JK
1	Nov	4	BOOTLE	6-1 Struthers (5), Steel	1	2	3	4	5	6	7	8	9	10	11			
2		30	LIVERPOOL RAMB.	3-0 Struthers (2), OG	1	2	3	4	5	6	7	8	9	10	11			
3	Jan	6	Druids	0-0	1	2	3	4	5	6	7	8	9	10		11		
3r		22	DRUIDS	1-1* Atherton	1	2	3	4	5	6	7	8	9	10			11	
3/2r		29	Druids+	0-1	1	2		4	5	6	7	8	9	10			11	3

* After extra time
\+ Played at Wrexham

1883/84

					Hay T	McKernon J	Powell J	Kennedy J	Gleaves J	Davenport JK	Fallon L	Struthers WG	Howarth T	Steel R	Scholes J	Vaughan J	Parkinson J
1	Nov	10	BOLTON OLYMPIC	9-0 Davenport,Struthers(3),Steel(2),Gleaves,Howarth,Scholes	1	2	3	4	5	6	7	8	9	10	11		
2	Dec	1	BOLTON ASSOC.	3-0 Steel(2), Struthers	1	2	3	4	5	6	7	8	9	10		11	
3		29	IRWELL SPRINGS	8-1 Davenport(2),Fallon(2),Steel(2),Struthers,OG	1	2	3	4	5	6	7	8	9	10		11	
4	Jan	19	Notts County	2-2* Davenport, Fallon	1	2	3	4	5	6	7	8		10		11	9
4r	Feb	2	NOTTS COUNTY	1-2 Vaughan	1	2	3	4	5	6	7	8		10		11	9

* After extra time

1884/85

Drawn against Preston Zingari, but both clubs withdrew due to professionalism argument with F.A.

1885/86

					Bateson	Holden	Gent	Parkinson J	Bullough P	Glaister	Fallon J	Gregory	Ward	Hough	Trainer J	Powell J	Steel R	Davenport JK	Parkinson W	Struthers WG
1	Oct	17	EAGLEY	6-0 Gregory,Fallon(2),Hough,Bullough,OG	1	2	3	4	5	6	7	8	9	10	11					
2	Nov	21	Rawtenstall*	3-3																
3	Dec	5	PRESTON N.E.#	2-3 Davenport, Struthers		5		3		4		7	11	10		1	2	6	8	9

* No record of team/goalscorers. Game played by reserves due to first team having a previous engagement. Rawtenstall disqualified for professionalism and for their pitch being too small.
# Both Bolton and Preston disqualified for professionalism.

1886/87

					Trainer J	Holden	McKernon J	Bullough P	Steel W	Roberts R	Parkinson J	Davenport JK	Struthers WG	Hewitson	Howarth P	Henderson
1	Oct	30	SOUTH SHORE	5-3 Hewitson,Struthers,Howarth,Davenport(2)	1	2	3	4	5	6	7	8	9	10	11	
2	Nov	13	Third Lanark	3-2 Hewitson(2), Struthers	1	2	3	6	5	4	8	7	10	9	11	
3	Dec	11	Darwen	3-4 Davenport, Howarth, Struthers	1	2	3	6	5	4	8	7	10		11	9

1887/88

					Unsworth W	Parkinson J	McKernon J	Roberts R	Steel W	Bullough P	Davenport JK	Brogan J	Owen G	Struthers WG	Howarth P	Owen R	Parkinson DW	Pearson	Baxendale
1	Oct	15	EVERTON *	1-0 Roberts	1	2	3	4	5	6	7	8	9	10	11				
1r		29	Everton	2-2 Brogan, Roberts	1	2	3	4	5	6	7	8			11	9	10		
1/2r	Nov	12	EVERTON	1-1 Brogan, Roberts	1	2	3	4	5	6	7	8			11	9	10		
1/3r		19	Everton+	1-2 Davenport	1	2	3	4	5	6	7	8			11	9	10		
2	Dec	10	Preston N.E.	1-9 Howarth	1	2		4	5	6	7	8		10	11			3	9

* Replay after protest by Everton that Bolton had fielded ineligible players.
\+ Everton disqualified for fielding ineligible players. Drawn against Preston Zingari in 1884-85 competition but both clubs withdrew due to professional argument with the F.A.

1883
(Back) Kennedy, Dobson, Bromley, McKernan, Steel, Parkinson
(Front) Howarth, Fallon, Struthers, Gleaves, Davenport, Scholes

1885-86 Season
(With the Bolton Charity Cup, The Lancashire Cup and the Derby Charity Cup)
(Back) Bentley, Weir, Hutchinson, Trainer, J.Parkinson(1), Roberts, J.Parkinson,(2), J.Parkinson(3)
(Front) Davenport, Brogan, Steele, Struthers, Hewitson, Hough

1888/89 5th in Division One

No	Date		Opponent	Score	Scorers	Barbour A	Brogan J	Bullough PA	Coupar T	Davenport JK	Dyer F	Flitcroft W	Gillam SG	Harrison CE	Jones D	McGuinness	Mercer	Milne J	Mitchell	Owen G	Parkinson J	Roberts R	Robinson B	Scowcroft J	Siddons	Simmers W	Turner IA	Tyrer	Weir D
1	Sep	8	DERBY COUNTY	3-6	Davenport 2, Brogan	10	11	6	9	7				1				8	3			4	2						5
2		15	BURNLEY	3-4	Brogan, Davenport, Coupar	8	7		9	5				1				10	2			3	6					11	4
3		22	Preston North End	1-3	Weir	9	7	4		8				1	3			10				6	2					11	5
4		29	EVERTON	6-2	Davenport 2, Tyrer 2, Milne 2	9	7			8				1	3			10				6	2			5		11	4
5	Oct	6	Burnley	1-4	Roberts	9	7			8				1	3			10				6	2			5		11	4
6		13	STOKE	2-1	Milne, (og)	9	7	4	8	5				1				10				3	2					11	6
7		20	ASTON VILLA	2-3	Weir, Barbour	9	7	4		8	3			1				10				6	2					11	5
8	Nov	3	Everton	1-2	Barbour	9	7	4		8			1					10				3	2	6				11	5
9		5	West Bromwich Albion	5-1	Barbour 2, Milne, Brogan, Weir	9	7			8				1				10				4	2	6	3			11	5
10		10	Wolverhampton Wan.	2-3	Brogan, McGuinness		7	4		8				1		9	3	10				6	2					11	5
11		17	WEST BROMWICH ALBION	1-2	Bullough		7	4		8				3				10			1	6	2	5				11	9
12		24	PRESTON NORTH END	2-5	Weir, Brogan		7			8	4	3	1					10				6	2	5				11	9
13	Dec	8	Blackburn Rovers	4-4	Scowcroft, Brogan 2, Milne		7			8	2			1	3			10		9		6		5				11	4
14		22	ACCRINGTON	4-1	Weir 3, Owen		7	4		8				1	3			10		11		6	2	5					9
15		26	Derby County	3-2	Brogan, Davenport, Milne		7	4		8				1	3			10		11		6	2	5					9
16		29	WOLVERHAMPTON W.	2-1	Weir, unknown		7	4		8				1	3			10				6	2	5				11	9
17	Jan	12	Aston Villa	2-6	Barbour 2	9	7			8				1	3			10		11		6	2	5					4
18		19	Stoke	2-2	Owen, Brogan		7	4		8	2			1	3			5		10		6						11	9
19		26	BLACKBURN ROVERS	3-2	Weir 2, Owen	9	7	4		8				1	3			5		10		6	2						11
20	Mar	5	Notts County	4-0	Brogan 2, Barbour, Davenport	9	7	4		8				1	3			5		10		6	2						11
21		9	NOTTS COUNTY	7-3	Turner, Brogan, Barbour 2, Davenport 3	9	7	4		8	2			1	3			5				6	3				11		10
22		23	Accrington	3-2	Brogan, Roberts, Davenport	9	7	4		8	2			1	3			5				6					11		10
					Apps	14	22	15	3	22	1	7	2	19	12	1	1	22	2	7	2	22	18	9	1	2	2	14	22
					Goals	9	13	1	1	11							1	6		3		2		1			1	2	10

Ave. Home Attendance: 5275

Two own goals

F.A. Cup

1	Oct	6	Hurst	0-0	
2		31	WEST MANCHESTER	9-0	J.Turner 3, Simmers 2, Knowles 2, Whittle, (og)
3	Nov	17	Linfield Athletic	0-4	

Round 2: Bolton and West Manchester met on October 27th, West Manchester winning 1-0. Game ordered to be replayed.

Reserve players appeared in all FA Cup matches. Versus Hurst: 1.Moores, 2.Haydock, 3.Jackson, 4.Greenhalgh, 5.Bullough, 6.Pearson, 7.Rushton, 8.Knowles, 9.R.Turner, 10.J.Turner, 11.Whittle

The same team was used in the other FA Cup-ties, except Simmers replaced Bullough

Lancashire Cup

Sep	29	Halliwell	1-8

Other Games

1	Sep	1	Newton Heath	0-1
2		2	Gorton Villa	2-0
3		17	Astley Bridge	1-0
4		24	Bootle	3-1
5	Oct	16	Port Vale	1-3
6		27	BOOTLE	4-0
7	Nov	28	Blackpool	4-2
8	Dec	1	Grimsby Town	0-3
9		15	SUNDERLAND	10-1
10		25	BATTLEFIELD	5-3
11		27	Nottingham Forest	4-1
12		31	PARTICK THISTLE	6-1
13	Jan	1	CAMBUSLANG	4-3
14		2	GLASGOW RANGERS	1-1
15		5	Sunderland Albion	3-1
16	Feb	2	NEWTON HEATH	3-1
17		9	Burnley	1-2
18		16	Sunderland	3-4
19		23	BURNLEY	2-1
20	Mar	2	Halliwell	3-1
21		16	GRIMSBY TOWN	5-3
22		25	Bootle	1-0
23		30	Lincoln	3-2
24	Apr	6	PRESTON NORTH END	5-1
25		8	Stoke	2-2
26		13	HALLIWELL	4-2
27		19	CELTIC	2-0
28		20	WOLVES	2-1
29		22	BATTLEFIELD	5-0
30		23	Rotherham	3-4
31		27	Heywood Central	1-4
32	May	1	Blackpool	4-2
33		4	Sunderland Albion	0-1
34		4	KEARSLEY *	4-0
35		6	Everton	0-1
36		8	BLACKBURN ROVERS	2-0
37		11	Hyde	2-3
38		18	Preston N.E.	2-2
39		20	Blackburn Rovers	1-1
40		23	Celtic	1-5
41		24	Glasgow Thistle	6-1
42		25	Dumfries Wanderers	3-8
43		30	Everton	2-2
44		30	Heywood Central +	3-2

* Bolton Charity Cup semi-final, + Bolton Charity Cup final

	FINAL TABLE	Pl.	Home				Away					F.	A.	Pts
			W	D	L	F	A	W	D	L	F	A	(Total)	
1	Preston North End	22	10	1	0	39	7	8	3	0	35	8	74	15	40
2	Aston Villa	22	10	0	1	44	16	2	5	4	17	27	61	43	29
3	Wolverhampton W.	22	8	2	1	30	14	4	2	5	20	23	50	37	28
4	Blackburn Rovers	22	7	4	0	44	23	3	2	6	22	23	66	45	26
5	BOLTON WANDERERS	22	6	0	5	35	30	4	2	5	28	29	63	59	22
6	West Bromwich Alb.	22	6	2	3	25	24	4	0	7	15	22	40	46	22
7	Accrington	22	5	3	3	26	17	1	5	5	22	31	48	48	20
8	Everton	22	8	0	3	24	17	1	2	8	11	29	35	46	20
9	Burnley	22	6	3	2	21	19	1	0	10	21	43	42	62	17
10	Derby County	22	5	1	5	22	20	2	1	8	19	41	41	61	16
11	Notts County	22	4	2	5	25	32	1	0	10	15	41	40	73	12
12	Stoke	22	3	4	4	15	18	1	0	10	11	33	26	51	12

1889/90   9th in Division One

#	Date	Opponent	Score	Scorers	Barbour A	Brogan J	Bullough PA	Cassidy J	Coupar T	Davenport JK	Flitcroft W	Harrison CE	Haydock J	Jones D	McNee J	McWhirter A	Milne J	Parkinson J	Pearson J	Roberts R	Robinson B	Rushton W	Scowcroft J	Sutcliffe W	Turner IA	Weir D	Woods F
1	Sep 14	ACCRINGTON	2-4	Weir, Parkinson		7	4			8		1		3			5	10		6	2					11	9
2	21	EVERTON	3-4	Brogan, Mlne, Barbour	9	7	4			8	2	1		3			5			6						11	10
3	28	Everton	0-3		9	7	4		11	8		1		3			5			6	2					10	
4	Oct 12	PRESTON N.E.	2-6	Bullough, Davenport	8	11	4			7		1		2	10	6	5				3						9
5	19	Stoke	1-0	Barbour	9	8	4			7		1		2	11	6	5				3					10	
6	26	NOTTS COUNTY*	0-4		9	8	4			7				2	11	6	5	1			3					10	
7	Nov 4	West Bromwich Albion	3-6	Davenport, Brogan, Weir		8		9		7				2	11		5	1	4	6	3					10	
8	9	BLACKBURN ROVERS	3-2	Davenport, Milne, Brogan		8	4	9		7				2	11		5	1		6	3					10	
9	16	ASTON VILLA	2-0	Davenport 2		8	4	9		7				2	11		5	1		6	3					10	
10	23	Preston North End	1-3	Weir		8	4	9		7				3	11		5	1		6	2					10	
11	30	DERBY COUNTY	7-1	Cassidy 4, Brogan, McNee, Davenport		8	4	9		7				2	11		5	1		6	3					10	
12	Dec 7	WEST BROMWICH ALBION	7-0	Weir 2, Brogan, Davenport 2, Bullough, Cassidy		8	4	9		7				2	11		5			6	3			1		10	
13	21	Blackburn Rovers	1-7	Cassidy		8	4	9		7				2	11		5	1		6	3					10	
14	26	Derby County	2-3	Brogan, Weir		8	4	9		7				2	11		5			6	3			1		10	
15	Jan 4	Accrington	1-3	Cassidy		7	4	9	8	5				3	11		1			6	2					10	
16	11	Notts County	5-3	Brogan, Weir 2, McNee, Cassidy		7	4	9		5				3	11		1			6		8				10	2
17	25	Aston Villa	2-1	Cassidy, Weir		8	4	9		7				3	11		1			6	2					10	5
18	Feb 8	STOKE	5-0	Cassidy 3, Weir, Brogan		8	4	9		5				3	11		1			6	2		7			10	
19	24	WOLVERHAMPTON W.	4-1	Weir, McNee 2, Turner	9	4				7			2	3	10		8	1							11	6	5
20	Mar 1	Burnley	0-7			8		9		7			2	3	11		5	1		6						10	4
21	15	Wolverhampton Wan.	1-5	Cassidy		8	4	9							11		7	1		6	2					10	5
22	17	BURNLEY	2-2	Milne, Jones		4		9		8				3	11		7	1		6	2					10	5
		Apps			5	21	20	15	2	21	1	5	2	21	19	4	17	16	1	17	19	2	2	6	21	5	
		Goals			2	8	2	13		8				1	4		3	1							1	11	

* Bolton claimed defeat was only by 3-0
Ave. Home Attendance: 5325

F.A. Cup

#	Date	Opponent	Score	Scorers	Brogan J	Bullough PA	Cassidy J	Davenport JK	Haydock J	Jones D	McNee J	Milne J	Roberts R	Robinson B	Scowcroft J	Weir D
1	Jan 18	BELFAST DISTILLERY	10-2	Weir 4, Cassidy 2, Davenport 2,2 'scrimmages'	8	4	9	5	2	3	11	1	6		7	10
2	Feb 1	SHEFFIELD WEDNESDAY	13-0	Cassidy 5, Weir 4, Brogan 3, Robinson	8	4	9	5		3	11	1	6	2	7	10
3	Feb 15	Preston North End	3-2	Weir 2, Brogan	8	4	9	5		3	11	1	6	2	7	10
SF	Mar 8	Sheffield Wednesday	1-2	McNee	8	4	9	5		3	11	1	6	2	7	10

SF at Perry Barr, Birmingham

Two scrimmaged-goals

Lancashire Cup

#	Date	Opponent	Score
1	Nov 2	ACCRINGTON	4-2
2	Dec 14	Darwen	2-4

Other Games

#	Date	Opponent	Score
1	Sep 2	Southport High Park	5-0
2	4	Blackpool	4-0
3	7	Newton Heath	1-1
4	9	Bootle	1-3
5	16	Chester	3-1
6	23	Port Vale	0-2
7	30	Birmingham St. Georges	1-3
8	Oct 5	SUNDERLAND	2-3
9	Nov 19	Sheffield United	2-0
10	Dec 25	BATTLEFIELD	9-1
11	28	BURNLEY	6-3
12	Jan 1	BIRMINGHAM ST. GEORGES	7-2
13	2	GLASGOW RANGERS	4-0
14	Feb 18	Rotherham	3-0
15	22	PRESTON NORTH END	2-4
16	Mar 22	Middlesbrough I.	2-1
17	29	Burnley	3-1
18	Apr 4	CELTIC	4-0
19	5	LONDON CALEDONIANS	2-0
20	7	Sunderland	1-0
21	8	Stockton	4-1
22	12	PRESTON NORTH END	2-1
23	19	Bootle	7-0
24	21	Rhos & District	5-0
25	24	EVERTON	0-0
26	26	Preston North End	0-5
27	28	Stoke	0-3
28	30	Middlesbrough	0-2
29	May 3	Southport Central	2-0
30	9	St. Bernards	2-1
31	10	Celtic	2-2
32	13	West Manchester	0-0
33	17	Newton Heath	1-1
34	19	Everton	0-1
35	24	Sunderland	0-1

	FINAL TABLE	Pl.	Home			Away			F.	A.	Pts
			W	D	L	F	A	W	D	L	F	A	(Total)
1	Preston North End	22	8	1	2	41	12	7	2	2	30	18	71	30	33
2	Everton	22	8	2	1	40	15	6	1	4	25	25	65	40	31
3	Blackburn Rovers	22	9	0	2	59	18	3	3	5	19	23	78	41	27
4	Wolverhampton W.	22	6	3	2	28	14	4	2	5	23	24	51	38	25
5	West Bromwich Alb.	22	8	1	2	37	20	3	2	6	10	30	47	50	25
6	Accrington	22	6	4	1	33	25	3	2	6	20	31	53	56	24
7	Derby County	22	6	2	3	32	13	1	9	11	42	43	55	21
8	Aston Villa	22	6	2	3	30	15	1	3	7	13	36	43	51	19
9	**BOLTON WANDERERS**	22	6	1	4	37	24	3	0	8	17	41	54	65	19
10	Notts County	22	4	3	4	20	19	2	2	7	23	32	43	51	17
11	Burnley	22	3	1	7	20	21	1	4	6	16	44	36	65	13
12	Stoke	22	2	3	6	18	20	1	1	9	9	49	27	69	10

1889-90 Season
(Back) Hargreaves, Hoyle, Robinson, Parkinson, Jones, Roberts, Bentley
(Middle) Davenport, Brogan, Cassidy, McNee, Weir   (Front) Milne, Bullough

1890/91 5th in Division One

#	Date	Opponent	Result	Scorers	Barbour A	Brogan J	Bullough PA	Cassidy J	Davenport JK	Gardiner H	Jarrett RH	Jones D	McNee J	Munro J	Parkinson J	Paton A	Roberts R	Robinson B	Russell W	Somerville J	Sutcliffe JW	Turner JA
1	Sep 6	NOTTS COUNTY	4-2	Roberts, Munro 2, Davenport	5	8		9	7			3	10	11	1	4	6			2		
2	13	DERBY COUNTY	3-1	Barbour, Davenport 2	5	8		9	7			3	10	11	1	4	6			2		
3	20	EVERTON	0-5		5	8		9	7			3	10	11	1	4	6			2		
4	27	Preston North End	0-1			8		9	5		7	3	10	11		4	6			2	1	
5	Oct 2	Notts County	1-3	Cassidy		8		9	5		7	3	10	11		4	6	2			1	
6	4	ASTON VILLA	4-0	McNee, Brogan, Turner, Bullough		8	4	9	7			3	10		1	5	6			2		11
7	11	Burnley	2-1	Barbour, McNee	9	8			7			3	10	11		4	6		5		1	2
8	18	Everton	0-2		9	8			5		7	3	10	11		4	6			2	1	
9	25	SUNDERLAND	2-5	Brogan 2		9			5	8	7	3	10	11		4	6			2	1	
10	Nov 3	West Bromwich Albion	4-2	Munro, McNee 2, Barbour	9	8	4				7	3	10	11		5				2	1	6
11	8	Wolverhampton Wan.	0-1		9	8				5	7	3	10	11		4				2	1	6
12	15	PRESTON NORTH END	1-0	Davenport	9	8			7			3	10	11		4	6			2	1	5
13	22	Aston Villa	0-5		7	8		9	5			3	10	11		4	6			2	1	
14	Dec 13	ACCRINGTON	6-0	Cassidy 2, Barbour 3, Munro	7	8		9	5			3	10	11		4	6			2	1	6
15	26	Derby County	1-1	McNee	7	8		9	5			3	10			4	6			2	1	11
16	29	WOLVERHAMPTON W.	6-0	Turner, mcNee 3, Gardiner, Cassidy	7	8		9		5		3	10			4	6			2	1	11
17	Jan 10	Accrington	1-2	Cassidy	7	8		9	5			3	10	11		4	6			2	1	
18	Feb 10	Sunderland	0-2		7	8		9	5			3	10	11		4	6			2	1	
19	Mar 7	Blackburn Rovers	2-0	Davenport, Turner		8		9	5			3	10	7		4	6			2	1	11
20	14	WEST BROMWICH ALBION	7-1	Turner, Munro 2, Cassidy 2, Brogan, McNee		8		9				3	10	7		4	6			2	1	11
21	21	BURNLEY	1-0	Cassidy		8		9					10	7		4	6		3	2	1	11
22	28	BLACKBURN ROVERS	2-0	Munro 2		8		9	5			3	10	7		4	6			2	1	11
				Apps	14	21	2	16	12	12	5	21	22	19	4	22	19	1	3	19	18	12
				Goals	6	4	1	8	5	1			9	8			1					4

Ave. Home Attendance: 7190

F.A. Cup

#	Date	Opponent	Result	Scorers	Barbour A	Brogan J	Cassidy J	Davenport JK	Jones D	McNee J	Munro J	Paton A	Somerville J	Sutcliffe JW	Turner JA
1	Jan 24	Accrington	1-5	Cassidy	7	8	10	5	3	11	9	4	2	1	6

Bolton met Accrington on January 17th - the game, which ended 2-2, was treated as a Friendly, due to an unfit ground.

Lancashire Cup

#	Date	Opponent	Result
1	Feb 7	Higher Walton	2-1
2	21	EVERTON	6-0
SF	Apr 11	Blackburn Rovers*	2-0
F	15	Darwen+	3-1

*Played at Ardwick.   + Played at Everton

Other Games

#	Date	Opponent	Result
1	Sep 1	Bootle	3-2
2	3	Southport High Park	2-1
3	8	Ardwick	5-1
4	22	Port Vale	6-1
5	Nov 1	Derby Co.	3-1
6	17	Sheffield United	1-2
7	27	Nottingham Forest	1-7
8	29	SHEFFIELD WEDNESDAY	3-0
9	Dec 3	Blackpool	1-2
10	6	Sheffield Wed.	6-3
11	25	HURLFORD	9-2
12	27	CHIRK	0-0
13	Jan 1	NOTTINGHAM FOREST	3-0
14	2	PAISLEY ST. MIRREN	1-1
15	3	BURNLEY	1-1
16	31	Everton	0-1
17	Feb 28	Everton	1-4
18	Mar 27	CELTIC	2-2
19	30	Linfield Athletic	1-0
20	31	Ulsterville R.	1-1
21	Apr 4	PRESTON NORTH END	2-0
22	6	Burnley	1-2
23	13	Stoke	0-1
24	15	Middlesbrough I	1-2
25	18	Celtic	0-2
26	27	INTERNATIONAL XI	1-2
27	29	HALLIWELL	4-0
28	30	Grimsby Town	0-0
29	May 2	BURY	2-0

FINAL TABLE

		Pl.	Home					Away					F.	A.	Pts
			W	D	L	F	A	W	D	L	F	A		(Total)	
1	Everton	22	9	0	2	39	12	5	1	5	24	17	63	29	29
2	Preston North End	22	7	3	1	30	5	5	0	6	14	18	44	23	27
3	Notts County	22	9	1	1	33	11	2	3	6	19	24	52	35	26
4	Wolverhampton W.	22	8	1	2	23	8	4	1	6	16	42	39	50	26
5	BOLTON WANDERERS	22	9	0	2	36	14	3	1	7	11	20	47	34	25
6	Blackburn Rovers	22	7	1	3	29	19	4	1	6	23	24	52	43	24
7	Sunderland	22	7	2	2	31	13	3	3	5	20	18	51	31	23
8	Burnley	22	7	1	3	33	24	2	2	7	19	39	52	63	21
9	Aston Villa	22	5	4	2	29	18	2	0	9	16	40	45	58	18
10	Accrington	22	5	1	5	19	19	1	3	7	9	31	28	50	16
11	Derby County	22	6	1	4	38	28	1	0	10	9	53	47	81	15
12	West Bromwich Alb.	22	3	1	7	17	26	2	1	8	17	31	34	57	12

1891/92 3rd in Division One

#	Mon	Date	Opponent	Score	Scorers	Barbour A	Bentley H	Brogan J	Cassidy J	Chirnside JE	Davenport	Gardiner H	Jones D	McFettridge D	McNee J	Munro J	Paton A	Roberts R	Russell W	Somerville J	Sutcliffe JW	Turner JA
1	Sep	5	Darwen	2-1	McNee, Cassidy			8	9			5	3	11	10	7	4			2	1	6
2		12	DARWEN	1-0	Brogan			8	9			5	3	11	10	7	4			2	1	6
3		19	SUNDERLAND	4-3	McNee, McFettridge, Cassidy 2			8	9			5	3	11	10	7	4			2	1	6
4		26	PRESTON NORTH END	3-0	McFettridge, Cassidy, McNee	8			9			5	3	11	10		4	6		2	1	7
5	Oct	1	Notts County	0-2					9			5	3	11	10	7	4			2	1	8
6		3	ACCRINGTON	3-4	McFettridge, Cassidy 2			8	9			5	3	11	10	7	4	6		2	1	
7		10	Aston Villa	2-1	Munro 2			8	9			5	3	11	10	7	4	6		2	1	
8		17	EVERTON	1-0	Cassidy			8	9			5	3	11	10	7	4	6		2	1	
9		24	BURNLEY	2-0	Munro, Cassidy			8	9			5	3	11	10	7	4			2	1	6
10		31	BLACKBURN ROVERS	4-2	McNee, Turner, Cassidy, Munro				9			5	3	11	10	7	4	6		2	1	8
11	Nov	2	West Bromwich Albion	2-0	Turner, Munro				9			5	3	11	10	7	4	6		2	1	8
12		7	Accrington	3-0	Munro 2, McNee			8	9			5	3	11	10	7	4			2	1	8
13		14	STOKE	1-1	Jones				9			5	3	11	10	7	4	6		2	1	8
14		21	Blackburn Rovers	0-4				8	9			5	3	11	10	7	4			2	1	6
15		28	Preston North End	0-4					9			5	3	11	10	7	4	6		2	1	8
16	Dec	5	WOLVERHAMPTON W.	3-0	Cassidy 2, Munro				9			5	3	11	10	7	4	6		2	1	8
17		12	Stoke	1-0	McFettridge				9			5	3	11	10	7	4	6		2	1	8
18		19	WEST BROMWICH ALB.	1-1	Munro				9			5	3	11	10	7	4			2	1	8
19		26	Derby County	2-3	Munro, McNee				9			5	3	11	10	7	4	6		2	1	8
20	Jan	1	DERBY COUNTY	3-1	Munro, Cassidy, McFettridge				9	7		5	3	11	10	8	4			2	1	6
21	Mar	1	Sunderland	1-4	Munro			8	9			5	3	11	10	7	4			2	1	6
22		5	Burnley	2-1	Cassidy, Bentley		11		9			5	3		10	7	4		6	2	1	8
23		26	NOTTS COUNTY	2-0	Cassidy, McNee		11		9			5	3		10	7	4		6	2	1	8
24	Apr	2	ASTON VILLA	1-2	Bentley		11		9			5	3		10	7	4		6	2	1	8
25		16	Wolverhampton Wan.	2-1	Bentley, Cassidy		11		9			5	3	6	10	7	4			2	1	8
26		18	Everton	5-2	Cassidy 3, Gardiner, Bentley		11		9			5	3	6	10	7	4			2	1	8
			Apps			1	5	10	26	1		26	26	23	26	25	26	13	3	26	26	23
			Goals				4	1	18			1	1	5	7	12						2

Ave. Home Attendance: 7625

F.A. Cup

#	Mon	Date	Opponent	Score	Scorers	Brogan J	Cassidy J	Davenport	Gardiner H	Jones D	McFettridge D	McNee J	Munro J	Paton A	Roberts R	Somerville J	Sutcliffe JW	Turner JA
1	Jan	16	Sheffield Wednesday	1-2	Munro	8	9	7		3	11	10		4	6	2	1	5
1r		23	Sheffield Wednesday	1-4	Jones	8			5	3	11	10	7	4	6	2	1	9

Replay ordered after protest over unfit ground

Lancashire Cup

#	Mon	Date	Opponent	Score
1	Feb	6	ROSSENDALE	4-1
2		20	Blackburn Rovers	2-3

Manchester Cup

#	Mon	Date	Opponent	Score	Note
1	Feb	13	Stockport Co.	2-1	
SF	Mar	12	Newton Heath	3-1	Played at Ardwick
F	Apr	23	Ardwick	1-4	Played at Newton Heath

Other Games

#	Mon	Date	Opponent	Score
1	Sep	3	Preston N.E.	2-4
2		7	Newton Heath	2-0
3		9	THE CANADIANS	1-1
4		21	Sheffield United	3-4
5	Oct	14	Accrington	1-1
6	Nov	12	Nottingham Forest	0-5
7	Dec	25	NEWTON HEATH	6-3
8	Jan	2	SHEFFIELD UNITED	3-3
9		4	KILMARNOCK	6-1
10		9	Ardwick	3-0
11		30	EVERTON	1-1
12	Feb	10	THE ALADDIN PANT. CO.	
13		13	Darwen	5-0
14		24	Lytham	1-1
15	Mar	19	Small Heath	0-7
16	Apr	7	Gorton Villa	2-1
17		9	PRESTON N.E.	3-1
18		15	NOTTINGHAM FOR.	1-0
19		25	Leicester	2-0
20		26	Arsenal	2-3
21		27	Chatham	1-1
22		28	Sheffield Wed.	1-1
23		30	Bury	2-5

FINAL TABLE

		Pl.	Home					Away					F.	A.	Pts
			W	D	L	F	A	W	D	L	F	A	(Total)		
1	Sunderland	26	13	0	0	55	11	8	0	5	38	25	93	36	42
2	Preston North End	26	12	0	1	42	8	6	1	6	19	23	61	31	37
3	**BOLTON WANDERERS**	26	9	2	2	29	14	8	0	5	22	23	51	37	36
4	Aston Villa	26	10	0	3	63	23	5	0	8	26	33	89	56	30
5	Everton	26	8	2	3	32	22	4	2	7	17	27	49	49	28
6	Wolverhampton W.	26	8	2	3	34	15	3	2	8	25	31	59	46	26
7	Burnley	26	9	1	3	34	14	2	3	8	15	31	49	45	26
8	Notts County	26	9	3	1	41	12	2	1	10	14	39	55	51	26
9	Blackburn Rovers	26	8	3	2	39	26	2	3	8	19	39	58	65	26
10	Derby County	26	6	3	4	28	18	4	1	8	18	34	46	52	24
11	Accrington	26	7	3	3	24	20	1	1	11	16	58	40	78	20
12	West Bromwich Alb.	26	6	3	4	37	24	0	3	10	14	34	51	58	18
13	Stoke	26	5	0	8	19	19	0	4	9	19	42	38	61	14
14	Darwen	26	4	1	8	31	43	0	2	11	7	69	38	112	11

1892/93   5th in Division One

#		Date	Opponent	Score	Scorers	Bentley H	Bullough PA	Cassidy J	Davenport JK	Dickenson J	Gardiner H	Jones D	McFettridge D	McNee J	Matthew H	Munro J	Paton A	Somerville J	Sutcliffe JW	Tannahill R	Turner JA	Weir D	Willocks D	Wilson J
1	Sep	3	Preston N.E.	1-2	Gardiner	10	9			11	5	3	6				7	4	2	1			8	
2		10	WEST BROM ALBION	3-1	Wilson, McNee, Dickenson		9			11	5	3		10			4	2	1		6		7	8
3		17	SHEFFIELD WEDNESDAY	1-0	Dickenson	7	9			11	5	3		10			4	2	1		6			8
4		24	ASTON VILLA	5-0	Cassidy 3, Willocks 2		9			11	5	3		10	6		4		1		2		8	7
5	Oct	1	WOLVERHAMPTON W.	3-1	Cassidy 2, Davenport		9	7	11	5	3		10	6		4		1		2		8		
6		6	Notts County	2-2	McNee, Cassidy		9			11	5	3		10	6		4		1		2		8	7
7		8	Accrington	1-1	Willocks		9			11	5	3		10			4	2	1		6		8	7
8		15	STOKE	4-4	Dickenson 3, Wilson		9			11	5	3		10			4	2	1		6		8	7
9		20	Nottingham Forest	0-2			9			11	5	3		10			4	2	1		6		8	7
10		22	Wolverhampton Wan.	2-1	Willocks 2		9			11		3		10	5		4	2	1		6		8	7
11		29	EVERTON	4-1	Willocks, Cassidy, Wilson, (og)		9			11		3		10	5		4	2	1		6		8	7
12	Nov	5	Sheffield Wednesday	2-4	Wilson, Dickenson		9			11		3		10	5		4	2	1		6		8	7
13		7	West Bromwich Albion	0-1			9			11		3		10	5		4	2	1		6		8	7
14		19	PRESTON NORTH END	2-4	Gardiner, Willocks		9			11	5	3		10			4	2	1		6		8	7
15		26	Blackburn Rovers	0-3		8	9			11	5	3			6		4	2	1		10			7
16	Dec	3	NEWTON HEATH	4-1	Bentley 2, Wilson, Cassidy	11	9				5	3		10			4	2	1		6		8	7
17		10	Newton Heath	0-1		11					5	3		10			4	2	1		6		8	7
18		24	Aston Villa	1-1	McNee		9			11	5	3		10			4	2	1		6		8	7
19		26	Derby County	1-1	Willocks		9			11	5	3		10			4	2	1		6		8	7
20	Jan	2	DERBY COUNTY	0-3		11	9				5	3				8	4	2	1		6			7
21		14	Stoke	0-6			9			11	5	3		10		7	4	2	1		6		8	
22	Feb	11	Burnley	0-3			8				5	3	6	10			4	2	1	7	11	9		
23		14	Sunderland	3-3	Weir 2, Dickenson	10	8			11	5	3					4	2	1		6	9		7
24		25	BURNLEY	1-0	(og)	10	8			11	5	3					4	2	1		6	9		7
25	Mar	4	ACCRINGTON	5-2	Weir 3, Bentley, Paton	10	8			11	5	3					4	2	1		6	9		7
26		18	BLACKBURN ROVERS	2-1	Dickenson, Weir	10	2	8		11	5	3					4		1		6	9		7
27		25	NOTTS COUNTY	4-1	Bentley 2, Cassidy, (og)	10		8		11	5	3					4	2	1		6	9		7
28		31	NOTTM. FOREST	3-1	Paton, Dickenson, Wilson	10				11	5	3				7	4	2	1		6		9	8
29	Apr	1	SUNDERLAND	2-1	Bentley, Weir	10				11		3				5	4	2	1		6	9	8	7
30		3	Everton	0-3		10				11		3				5	4	2	1		6	9	8	7

Ave. Home Attendance: 5790

	Bentley H	Bullough PA	Cassidy J	Davenport JK	Dickenson J	Gardiner H	Jones D	McFettridge D	McNee J	Matthew H	Munro J	Paton A	Somerville J	Sutcliffe JW	Tannahill R	Turner JA	Weir D	Willocks D	Wilson J
Apps	14	1	27	1	26	24	30	2	20	8	6	30	26	30	1	29	8	21	26
Goals	6		9	1	9	2			3			2					7	8	6

Three own goals

F.A. Cup

#		Date	Opponent	Score	Scorers	Cassidy J	Dickenson J	Gardiner H	Jones D	McNee J	Paton A	Somerville J	Sutcliffe JW	Turner JA	Willocks D	Wilson J
1	Jan	21	WOLVERHAMPTON W.	1-1*	Wilson	9	11	5	3	10	4	2	1	6	8	7
1r	Jan	28	Wolverhampton W.	1-2	McNee	9	11	5	3	10	4	2	1	6	8	7

* After extra time

Lancashire Cup

#		Date	Opponent	Score
1	Feb	18	ACCRINGTON	4-0
2	Mar	11	Bury*	3-1
2r		27	BURY	1-0
SF	Apr	8	ARDWICK	5-1
F		22	Preston N.E.+	0-2

* Game unfinished due to crowd invasion   + Played at Blackburn

Manchester Cup

#		Date	Opponent	Score
1	Feb	27	STOCKPORT COUNTY	4-1
SF	Mar	21	Heywood C.*	3-2
F	Apr	15	Newton Heath+	1-2

* Played at Bury   + Played at Ardwick

Other Games

#		Date	Opponent	Score
1	Sep	1	Everton	2-4
2		5	LANCASHIRE XI	3-5
3		6	Bury	1-0
4		19	DARWEN	2-5
5		21	Preston N.E.	3-2
6		27	Darwen	0-4
7	Nov	9	Blackpool	3-0
8		12	Ardwick	0-3
9		28	Sheffield Utd.	0-1
10	Dec	17	CREWE ALEXANDRA	9-1
11		31	THE CORINTHIANS	2-1
12	Jan	3	BURY	3-4
13		7	Newcastle United	1-3
14		23	Blackburn Rovers*	1-1
15	Feb	4	Small Heath	3-4
16		8	BOLTON WEDNESDAY	9-2
17	Apr	24	Liverpool	1-1
18		25	Heywood Central	2-1
19		29	SHEFFIELD UNITED	3-0

* Played at Swinton RLFC

	FINAL TABLE	Pl.	Home				Away					F.	A.	Pts
			W	D	L	F	A	W	D	L	F	A	(Total)	
1	Sunderland	30	13	2	0	58	17	9	2	4	42	19	100	36	48
2	Preston North End	30	11	2	2	34	10	6	1	8	23	29	57	39	37
3	Everton	30	9	3	3	44	17	7	1	7	30	34	74	51	36
4	Aston Villa	30	12	1	2	50	24	4	2	9	23	38	73	62	35
5	BOLTON WANDERERS	30	12	1	2	43	21	1	5	9	13	34	56	55	32
6	Burnley	30	10	2	3	37	15	3	2	10	14	29	51	44	30
7	Stoke	30	8	2	5	33	16	4	3	8	25	32	58	48	29
8	West Bromwich Alb.	30	9	2	4	35	17	3	3	9	23	52	58	69	29
9	Blackburn Rovers	30	5	8	2	29	24	3	5	7	18	32	47	56	29
10	Nottingham Forest	30	7	2	6	30	27	3	6	6	18	25	48	52	28
11	Wolverhampton W.	30	11	2	2	32	17	1	2	12	15	51	47	68	28
12	Sheffield Wed.	30	8	2	5	34	28	4	1	10	21	37	55	65	27
13	Derby County	30	5	6	4	30	28	4	3	8	22	36	52	64	27
14	Notts County	30	8	3	4	34	15	2	1	12	19	46	53	61	24
15	Accrington	30	5	5	5	29	34	1	6	8	28	47	57	81	23
16	Newton Heath	30	6	3	6	39	35	0	3	12	11	50	50	85	18

1893/94 13th in Division One

#	Date	Opponent	Score	Scorers	Bentley H	Cassidy J	Dickenson J	Ferguson G	Gardiner H	Gilligan A	Hughes A	Jones D	Lawson RR	Lever A	McArthur W	Paton A	Shuttleworth	Somerville J	Sutcliffe JW	Tannahill R	Turner JA	Weir D	Willcocks D	Wilson J
1	Sep 2	STOKE	4-1	Cassidy, Bentley(2), McArthur	11	8					10	3			9	4		2	1			6	5	7
2	9	Wolves	1-2	McArthur	11	8					10	3			9	4		2	1			6	5	7
3	16	BLACKBURN ROVERS	2-1	Cassidy, Hughes	11	8		5			10				9	4		2	1			6	5	7
4	23	Sheffield United	2-4	Cassidy, McArthur	10	8	11	5							9	4		2	1			6	5	7
5	30	PRESTON NORTH END	0-3		11	10				8		3			9	4		2	1			6	5	7
6	Oct 5	Nottingham Forest	0-1		10	8						3			9	4		2	1			6	5	7
7	7	DARWEN	1-0	Weir	10	8	11					3			9	4		2	1	7		6	5	
8	14	SHEFFIELD UNITED	0-1		10	8	11	5				3			9	4		2	1	7		6		
9	21	WOLVES	2-0	Cassidy, McArthur		8	11	5				3			9	4		2	1	7		6	10	
10	28	Darwen	3-1	Dickenson, Weir, Gardiner		8	11	5				3			9	4		2	1	7		6	10	
11	Nov 4	Preston North End	0-1			8	11	5				3			9	4		2	1	7		6	10	
12	6	West Bromwich Albion	2-5	Cassidy, McArthur		8	11	5				3			9	4		2	1	7		6	10	
13	18	ASTON VILLA	0-1			8	11	5			10	3			9	4		2	1	7		6		
14	Dec 2	Blackburn Rovers	1-0	McArthur	11			5	10			3			9	4		2	1	7		6		
15	9	NEWTON HEATH	2-0	Paton, Cassidy	11	8		5	10			3			9	4		2	1	7		6		
16	16	Sheffield Wed.	1-2	Cassidy	11	8		5	10			3			9	4	1	2		7		6		
17	25	SHEFFIELD WEDNESDAY	1-1	Cassidy	11	9		5	10			3				4		2	1	7		6	8	
18	26	Derby County	1-6	Tannahill		8	11	5	10			3			9			2	1	7		6	4	
19	30	Sunderland	1-2	Ferguson		8		5	10			3			9	4		2	1	7		6	11	
20	Jan 1	DERBY COUNTY	1-1	Ferguson		8	11	5	10			3				4		2	1	7		6	9	
21	6	BURNLEY	2-0	Ferguson, Weir	11	8		5	10			3				4		2	1	7		6	9	
22	13	Stoke	0-5		11	8		5	10			3				4		2	1	7		6	9	
23	Feb 3	Burnley	1-2	Tannahill	11	9		5	10			3				4		2	1	7		6	8	
24	Mar 3	Aston Villa	3-2	Bentley, Dickenson, Cassidy	10	9	11	5				3				4		2	1	7	6		8	
25	23	NOTTINGHAM FOREST	1-1	Cassidy	10	9	11	5			6	3				4		2	1	7			8	
26	24	Newton Heath	2-2	Cassidy, Tannahill	10	9	11	5				3				4		2	1	7	6		8	
27	26	Everton	2-3	Wilson, Bentley	10	9	11	5			6	3				4		2	1	7				8
28	Apr 7	WEST BROM ALBION	0-3		10	9	11				6	3	5	4				2	1	7			8	
29	16	EVERTON	0-1		11	9		6			10	3				4		2	1	7			5	8
30	23	SUNDERLAND	2-0	Bentley, Hughes	11	9					10	3				4		2	1	7	6		5	8
		Apps			21	29	16	13	18	1	15	28	1	1	19	21	1	25	29	23	24	24	11	10
		Goals			5	11	2	3	1		2				6	1				3		3		1

Ave. Home Attendance: 5350

F.A. Cup

#	Date	Opponent	Score	Scorers	Bentley H	Cassidy J	Dickenson J	Ferguson G	Gardiner H	Gilligan A	Hughes A	Jones D	Lawson RR	Lever A	McArthur W	Paton A	Shuttleworth	Somerville J	Sutcliffe JW	Tannahill R	Turner JA	Weir D	Willcocks D	Wilson J
1	Jan 27	Small Heath	4-3	Cassidy(2), Wilson(2)	11	9		5	10			3				4		2	1	7		6	8	
2	Feb 10	Newcastle United	2-1	Hughes, Turner	11	9		5				3				4		2	1	7	6		10	8
3	24	LIVERPOOL	3-0	Cassidy, Dickenson(2)	11	9	10	5				3				4		2	1	8	6		7	
SF	Mar 10	Sheffield Wednesday*	2-1	Bentley(2)	11	9	10	5				3				4		2	1	8	6		7	
F	31	Notts County+	1-4	Cassidy	11	9	10	6	5			3				4		2	1	8				7

* Played at Fallowfield, Manchester. + Played at Goodison Park, Liverpool

Lancashire Cup

#	Date	Opponent	Score
1	Jan 20	PRESTON NORTH END	4-1
2	Feb 17	Darwen	5-4
SF	Mar 17	Accrington*	1-0
F	Apr 14	Everton+	1-2

* Played at Everton. + Played at Ardwick

Manchester Cup

#	Date	Opponent	Score
1	Feb 3	NEATON HEATH	3-2
SF	Mar 3	Heywood C.*	1-2

* Played at Bury

Other Games

#	Date	Opponent	Score
1	Sep 4	Ardwick	5-0
2	6	Horwich	3-1
3	11	Everton	0-3
4	18	Farnworth S.	4-1
5	Nov 11	Southport Central	5-1
6	23	Southampton	5-0
7	24	Bournemouth	4-1
8	25	The Corinthians	1-2
9	Dec 20	PRESTON NORTH END	3-4
10	Apr 28	BLACKBURN ROVERS	0-4
11	30	Halliwell Rovers	4-0

FINAL TABLE

		Pl.	Home					Away					F.	A.	Pts
			W	D	L	F	A	W	D	L	F	A	(Total)		
1	Aston Villa	30	12	2	1	49	13	7	4	4	35	29	84	42	44
2	Sunderland	30	11	3	1	46	14	6	1	8	26	30	72	44	38
3	Derby County	30	9	2	4	47	32	7	2	6	26	30	73	62	36
4	Blackburn Rovers	30	13	0	2	48	15	3	2	10	21	38	69	53	34
5	Burnley	30	13	0	2	43	17	2	4	9	18	34	61	51	34
6	Everton	30	11	1	3	63	23	4	2	9	27	34	90	57	33
7	Nottingham Forest	30	10	2	3	38	16	4	2	9	19	32	57	48	32
8	West Bromwich Alb.	30	8	4	3	35	23	6	0	9	31	36	66	59	32
9	Wolverhampton W.	30	11	1	3	34	24	3	2	10	18	39	52	63	31
10	Sheffield United	30	8	3	4	26	22	5	2	8	21	39	47	61	31
11	Stoke	30	13	1	1	45	17	0	2	13	20	62	65	79	29
12	Sheffield Wed.	30	7	3	5	32	21	2	5	8	16	36	48	57	26
13	BOLTON WANDERERS	30	7	3	5	18	14	3	1	11	20	38	38	52	24
14	Preston North End	30	7	1	7	25	24	3	2	10	19	32	44	56	23
15	Darwen	30	6	4	5	25	28	1	1	13	12	55	37	83	19
16	Newton Heath	30	5	2	8	29	33	1	0	14	7	39	36	72	14

1893-94 Season
(Back) Bentley, McArthur, Cassidy,
Paton, Turner, Eastwood, Nuttall
(Middle) Gardiner, Sutcliffe, Somerville,
Weir, Bentley
(Front) Tannahill, Ferguson

1894/95 10th in Division One

#	Mon	Date	Opponent	Score	Scorers	Andrews W	Bentley H	Bracelin J	cassidy J	Docherty J	Ferguson G	Freebairn A	Guest A	Henderson C	Jones D	Joyce W	Lawson RR	Lyden J	McGeachan J	McGinn J	Martin J	Miller J	Paton A	Settle J	Shuttleworth T	Somerville J	Spence A	Stevenson J	Sutcliffe JW	Tannahill R	Turnbull P	Weir D
1	Sep	1	STOKE	2-2	Bentley, Jones	10	11		8			6		9	3								4			2		5	1	7		
2		8	Small Heath	0-2		10	11		8	5		6		9									4			2			1	7		3
3		13	Liverpool	2-1	Cassidy, Tannahill	8			11			6		9				5					4	10		2			1	7		3
4		15	PRESTON NORTH END	1-2	Settle	8			11			6		9				5					4	10		2			1	7		3
5		22	Sheffield Wednesday	1-2	Andrews	10	11		8			6		9	3								5	4		2			1	7		
6		29	SUNDERLAND	4-1	Paton, Henderson, Cassidy, Settle	8			11			6		9	3								5	4		2			1	7		
7	Oct	6	EVERTON	1-3	Henderson	8			11			6		9	3								4	10		2			1	7		5
8		13	Blackburn Rovers	1-2	Henderson	8			11			6		9	3								5	10		2		4	1	7		
9		20	BURNLEY	1-1	Andrews	10				5		6		9	3								4			2	8		1	7		11
10		27	Wolves	2-4	Lawson(2)			10	11		5	6		9	3		7				8		4			2			1			
11	Nov	3	BLACKBURN ROVERS	1-3	Paton	10						6	11	9	3					8		5	4			2			1	7		
12		5	West Bromwich Albion	1-2	Andrews	10						6		9	3					8		5	4			2			1	7		11
13		17	Sunderland	0-4					10			6		9	3					8		5	4			2			1	7		11
14		24	SMALL HEATH	1-2	Cassidy				11			6		9	3				8	5	10		4			2			1	7		2
15	Dec	1	Preston N.E.	2-2	Lyden, Henderson				11			6		9	3				8	5	10		4		1	2				7		
16		8	Everton	1-3	Henderson				11			6		9	3				8	5	10		4			2			1	7		
17		15	WOLVES	6-1	Henderson(3),Somerville,Settle,McGinn				11			6		9	3					5	10		4	8		2			1	7		
18		25	LIVERPOOL	1-0	Settle				11			6		9	3					5	10		4	8		2			1	7		
19		26	Derby County	2-2	Paton, McGinn				11			6		9	3					5	10		4	8		2			1	7		
20	Jan	1	DERBY COUNTY	6-0	Henderson(4), McGinn, Cassidy				11			6		9	3					5	10		4	8		2			1	7		
21		5	Burnley	0-1					11			6		9	3					5	10		4	8		2			1	7		
22		7	SHEFFIELD WED.	2-2	Paton(2)				11			6								5	10		4	9		2	8		1	7		3
23		12	Stoke	0-5					11			6			3					5	10		4	8		2			1	7		9
24		14	SHEFFIELD UTD	6-2	Cassidy(2),Spence(2),Paton,Tannahill				11			6		9	3						10	4	5			2	8		1	7		
25		26	Aston Villa	1-2	McGeachan					10		6		9	3					5			4	11		2	8		1			
26	Mar	16	Nottingham Forest	3-3	Cassidy(2), McGeachan	10			11			6		8	3	9				5		7	4			2			1			
27		23	ASTON VILLA	4-3	Bentley, Henderson(2), Turnbull		11		7			6		8	3	9				5			4			2			1		10	
28	Apr	12	NOTTINGHAM FOREST	4-1	Joyce(2), Cassidy, Turnbull				11			6		8	3	9				5			4			2			1	7	10	
29		13	WEST BROM ALBION	5-0	Joyce, Turnbull(3), Freebairn				11			6		8	3	9				5	7		4			2			1		10	
30		15	Sheffield United	0-5					11			6		8	3	9				5	7		4			2			1		10	
			Apps			12	4	1	26	2	2	29	1	28	26	5	1	3	16	15	3	8	30	13	1	29	4	2	29	25	4	11
			Goals			3	2		9			1		14	1	3	2	1	2	3			6	4		1	2			2	5	

Ave. Home Attendance: 7375

F.A. Cup

#	Mon	Date	Opponent	Score	Scorers	Andrews W	Bentley H	cassidy J	Docherty J	Freebairn A	Henderson C	Jones D	McGinn J	Miller J	Paton A	Settle J	Somerville J	Spence A	Sutcliffe JW	Tannahill R
1	Feb	2	ARSENAL	1-0	Jones			11		6		3	9	5	4	10	2	8	1	7
2		16	BURY	1-0	Cassidy		11	8	9	6		3	5		4	10	2		1	7
3	Mar	2	Sunderland	1-2	Cassidy	10		8	11	6	9	3	5		4		2		1	7

Lancashire Cup

#	Mon	Date	Opponent	Score
1	Jan	19	NEWTON HEATH	2-1
2	Feb	9	EVERTON	1-3

Manchester Cup

#		Mon	Date	Opponent	Score
1		Jan	26	Newton Heath	4-0
SF		Feb	23	Manchester City*	2-2
SFr		Mar	9	Manchester City+	2-1
F			30	Bury#	0-0
Fr		Apr	8	Bury +	3-2

* Played at Bury.   + Played at Hyde Road
# Played at Newton Heath

Other Games

#	Mon	Date	Opponent	Score
1	Sep	3	DARWEN	3-0
2		6	South Shore	4-2
3		18	Darwen	1-1
4		26	Manchester City	3-2
5	Oct	17	BOLTON WEDNESDAY	8-0
6		24	BOLTON WED. ROVERS	5-0
7	Nov	6	Millwall Athletic	1-5
8		7	New Brompton	4-1
9		8	Southampton	2-5
10		9	Bournemouth	5-0
11		10	The Corinthians	4-5
12	Jan	23	Blackpool	1-2
13	Mar	13	BOLTON WEDNESDAY	10-0
14	Apr	27	Chorley	0-2

Final Table

	FINAL TABLE	Pl.	Home					Away					F.	A.	Pts
			W	D	L	F	A	W	D	L	F	A		(Total)	
1	Sunderland	30	13	2	0	51	14	8	3	4	29	23	80	37	47
2	Everton	30	12	2	1	47	18	6	4	5	35	32	82	50	42
3	Aston Villa	30	12	2	1	51	12	5	3	7	31	31	82	43	39
4	Preston North End	30	9	3	3	32	14	6	2	7	30	32	62	46	35
5	Blackburn Rovers	30	9	5	1	40	15	2	5	8	19	34	59	49	32
6	Sheffield United	30	10	2	3	33	17	4	2	9	24	38	57	55	32
7	Nottingham Forest	30	10	1	4	33	22	3	4	8	17	34	50	56	31
8	Sheffield Wed.	30	10	2	3	36	19	2	2	11	14	36	50	55	28
9	Burnley	30	8	2	5	28	24	3	2	10	16	32	44	56	26
10	BOLTON WANDERERS	30	8	3	4	45	23	1	4	10	16	39	61	62	25
11	Wolverhampton W.	30	7	4	4	24	25	2	3	10	19	38	43	63	25
12	Small Heath	30	6	6	3	35	28	3	1	11	15	46	50	74	25
13	West Bromwich Alb.	30	9	2	4	38	21	1	2	12	13	45	51	66	24
14	Stoke	30	7	3	5	35	25	2	3	10	15	42	50	67	24
15	Derby County	30	4	5	6	23	23	3	4	8	22	45	45	68	23
16	Liverpool	30	6	4	5	38	28	1	4	10	13	42	51	70	22

1895/96 4th in Division One

#		Date	Opponent	Score	Scorers	Alexander G	Brown RN	Cassidy J	Davies RH	Ferguson G	Freebairn A	Gillies A	Gunn J	Hamilton E	Jack R	Jones D	Joyce W	Martin J	McGeachan J	McReddie W	Millar J	Nicoll D	Paton A	Smith DW	Somerville J	Sutcliffe JW	Tannahill R	Vail T	Wright J
1	Sep	2	Stoke	0-2			8	11			6					2	9		5		3		4			1	7		10
2		7	Bury	3-0	McGeachan, Brown, Paton		8	11			6					3	9		5				4		2	1	7		10
3		14	EVERTON	3-1	Martin, Cassidy, Joyce		8	11			6					3	9	7	5				4		2	1			10
4		21	BURNLEY	1-0	Gunn		7	11			6		9			3		8	5				4		2	1			10
5		28	Small Heath	2-1	Brown, Wright		8				6				11	3	9	7	5				4		2	1			10
6	Oct	5	BURY	2-4	Joyce 2		8				6				11	3	9	7	5				4		2	1			10
7		12	Burnley	2-1	Brown, Joyce		8	11			6					3	9		5				4		2	1	7		10
8		19	NOTTM. FOREST	2-1	Tannahill, Wright		8	11			6					3	9		5				4		2	1	7		10
9		26	STOKE	3-1	Joyce 2, Breown		8	7			6	11				3	9		5				4		2	1			10
10	Nov	2	Sheffield Wednesday	1-1	Joyce		8	7			6	11				3	9		5				4		2	1			10
11		4	West Bromwich Albion	3-2	McGeachan, Joyce 2		8	7			6	11				3	9		5				4		2	1			10
12		9	Preston North End	0-1			8	7			6	11				3	9		5				4		2	1			10
13		23	Sunderland	0-1			8	7			6	11				3	9		5				4		2	1			10
14		30	BLACKBURN ROVERS	1-1	Brown		8	7			6				11	3	9		5				4		2	1			10
15	Dec	7	Blackburn Rovers	2-3	Cassidy, Joyce		8	7			6				11	3	9		5				4		2	1			10
16		14	Aston Villa	0-2			8	7			6				11	3	9		5				4		2	1			10
17		21	SUNDERLAND	1-0	Joyce		8				6				11	3	9		5				4		2	1	7		10
18		26	Derby County	1-2	Jack		8				6				11	3	9		5				4		2	1	7		10
19		30	Sheffield United	0-1				8			6					3	9		5	11			4		2	1	7		10
20	Jan	1	DERBY COUNTY	2-1	Gunn 2			8			6		9		11	3			5				4		2	1	7		10
21		4	WOLVERHAMPTON W.	4-0	Tannahill, Joyce, Cassidy, Paton			8			6					3	9		5	11			4		2	1	7		10
22		11	Nottingham Forest	0-0				8			6	11				3	9		5				4		2	1	7		10
23	Feb	22	SMALL HEATH	4-1	Gunn 2, Paton, Vail						6		8		11	3			5				4		2	1	7	9	10
24	Mar	7	ASTON VILLA	2-2	Wright, Cassidy			8			6				11	3			5				4		2	1	7	9	10
25		14	PRESTON NORTH END	1-0	Jack						6		8	3	11				5				4		2	1	7	9	10
26	Apr	3	SHEFFIELD UNITED	4-1	Paton, Tannahill, Jack, Nicoll			8	3		6				11				5			9	4		2	1	7		10
27		4	WEST BROMWICH ALB.	2-1	Cassidy, Jack		7	8	3		6				11		9						4	5	2	1			10
28		6	Everton	1-1	Cassidy	1	5	8			6				11	3	9						4		2		7		10
29		11	Wolverhampton Wan.	0-5		1	7	8			6				11	3	9		5				4		2				10
30		25	SHEFFIELD WEDNESDAY	2-0	Jack, Cassidy		5	8			6				11	3	9						4		2	1	7		10
			Apps			2	22	22	2	1	30	6	6	1	15	27	20	4	27	2	1	5	30	1	29	28	16	3	30
			Goals				5	7					5		5		12	1	2			1	4				3	1	3

Ave. Home Attendance: 9535

F.A. Cup

#		Date	Opponent	Score	Scorers	Brown RN	Cassidy J	Freebairn A	Gunn J	Jack R	Jones D	Joyce W	McGeachan J	Paton A	Somerville J	Sutcliffe JW	Tannahill R	Vail T	Wright J
1	Feb	1	Crewe Alexandra	4-0	Brown, Gunn, Tannahill, Wright	8		6	9	11	3		5	4	2	1	7		10
2		15	Blackpool	2-0	Cassidy, Wright	8	9	6		11	3		5	4	2	1	7		10
3		29	BURY	2-0	Wright, Gunn		9	6	8	11	3		5	4	2	1	7		10
SF	Mar	21	Sheffield Wednesday	1-1	Tannahill	8	9	6		11	3		5	4	2	1	7		10
SFr		28	Sheffield Wednesday	1-3	Tannahill	8		6		11	3		5	4	2	1	7	9	10

SF at Goodison Park, Liverpool. SF replay at the Town Ground, Nottingham.

Lancashire Cup

1	Jan	19	BURNLEY	1-2

Manchester Cup

1	Jan	26	Manchester City	0-1

Other Games

1	Sep	11	PRESTON NORTH END	0-1
2		18	BOLTON WEDNESDAY	7-0
3		24	Bradford & District	7-2
4		26	Southport Central	1-2
5	Oct	23	BOLTON WED. ROVERS	13-2
6	Nov	11	BOLTON SHOP ASSIST.	9-1
7	Dec	25	LIVERPOOL	0-0
8	Feb	8	Celtic	1-4
9	Apr	16	Ayr	3-2
10		18	Clyde	3-0
11		20	Morton	1-0
12		21	St. Bernards	2-2
13		29	HALLIWELL ROVERS	5-0
14		30	Turton	0-0

FINAL TABLE

	Team	Pl.	Home W	D	L	F	A	Away W	D	L	F	A	F (Total)	A	Pts
1	Aston Villa	30	14	1	0	47	17	6	4	5	31	28	78	45	45
2	Derby County	30	12	2	1	42	13	5	5	26	22		68	35	41
3	Everton	30	10	4	1	40	17	6	3	6	26	26	66	43	39
4	**BOLTON WANDERERS**	30	12	2	1	34	14	4	3	8	15	23	49	37	37
5	Sunderland	30	10	5	0	36	14	5	2	8	16	27	52	41	37
6	Stoke	30	12	0	3	43	11	3	0	12	13	36	56	47	30
7	Sheffield Wed.	30	10	2	3	31	18	2	3	10	13	35	44	53	29
8	Blackburn Rovers	30	10	1	4	26	18	2	4	9	14	32	40	50	29
9	Preston North End	30	8	5	2	31	18	3	1	11	13	30	44	48	28
10	Burnley	30	8	5	2	33	11	2	2	11	15	33	48	44	27
11	Bury	30	7	1	7	32	24	5	2	8	18	30	50	54	27
12	Sheffield United	30	9	4	2	28	12	1	2	12	12	38	40	50	26
13	Nottingham Forest	30	11	1	3	34	16	0	2	13	8	41	42	57	25
14	Wolverhampton W.	30	10	0	5	43	18	0	1	14	18	47	61	65	21
15	Small Heath	30	7	2	6	22	24	1	2	12	17	55	39	79	20
16	West Bromwich Alb.	30	5	4	6	18	22	1	3	11	12	37	30	59	19

1895-96 season
(Back) McGeachan, Brierley, Somerville, Jones, Sutcliffe, Isherwood
(Middle) Paton, Martin, Joyce, Freebairn, Cassidy
(Front) Brown, Wright

1896/97 Season
(Back) Brettell (Sec.), Shutt, Sutcliffe, Scott, Gilligan, Jones (Capt.), Alexander
(Middle) Tannahill, Brown, McGeachan, Somerville, Brierley (Trainer), Thompson, Freebairn, Gunn, Paton
(Front) Caddidy, Nicholl, Joyce, Wright, Jack

1896/97 8th in Division One

						Brown RN	Cassidy J	Davies RH	Freebairn A	Gilligan A	Hiles A	Jack R	Jones D	Joyce W	McGeachan J	Miller TA	Nicoll D	Paton A	Scotchbrook F	Scott S	Smith DW	Somerville J	Sutcliffe JW	Tannahill R	Thomson W	Wright J
1	Sep	5	Sunderland	1-1	Jack				6	8		11	3		5		9	4				2	1		7	10
2		7	Liverpool	2-0	Nicoll, Jack				6	8		11	3		5		9	4				2	1		7	10
3		12	BLACKBURN ROVERS	0-0					6	8		11	3		5		9	4				2	1		7	10
4		19	Stoke	3-2	Thomson, Nicoll, Clare(og)				6	8		11	3		5		9	4				2	1		7	10
5		26	SUNDERLAND	1-0	Jones				6	8		11	3		5		9	4				2	1		7	10
6	Oct	3	PRESTON NORTH END	3-1	Wright, Jack, Gilligan				6	8		11	3		5		9	4				2	1		7	10
7		10	BURY	2-0	Paton, Nicoll				6	8		11	3		5		9	4				2	1		7	10
8		17	Blackburn Rovers	0-1					6	8		11	3		5		9	4				2	1		7	10
9		24	STOKE	4-0	Jack 2, Thomson, Gilligan				6	8		11	3		5		9	4				2	1		7	10
10		31	Bury	2-2	Jack, (og)	4			6	8		11	3				9	5				2	1		7	10
11	Nov	2	West Bromwich Albion	0-1					6	8		11	3		5		9	4				2	1		7	10
12		14	Everton	3-2	Thomson, Wright, Gilligan				6	8		11			5		9	4				2	1		7	10
13		21	Preston North End	3-2	Wright, Gilligan, Thomson				6	8		11	3		5		9	4				2	1		7	10
14	Dec	7	EVERTON	2-0	Jack, Gilligan				6	8		11	3		5		9	4				2	1		7	10
15		19	WEST BROMWICH ALB.	2-2	Nicoll, Gilligan				6	8		11	3		5		9	4				2	1		7	10
16		26	Derby County	0-1					6	8		11	3		5		9	4				2	1		7	10
17		29	Sheffield United	0-1					6	8		11	3		5	9	10	4				2	1		7	
18	Jan	1	LIVERPOOL	1-4	Jack				6			11	3		5	8	9	4		1	2				7	10
19		16	Nottingham Forest	0-2					6	8		11	3		5		9	4				2	1		7	10
20	Feb	6	Burnley	2-0	Cassidy, Jack		8		6			11	3	9	5		10	4				2	1		7	
21		27	Sheffield Wednesday	0-0		5	9		6			11				8	7	4	10	3		2	1			
22	Mar	6	DERBY COUNTY	1-3	Joyce	5	8		6					/		9	11	4		3		2	1			10
23		13	BURNLEY	2-1	Miller, Wright	4	8		6						5	9	11			3	1	2			7	10
24		20	NOTTM. FOREST	0-0			8		6			11			5	9		4		3		2	1		7	10
25		22	Aston Villa	2-6	Jack 2	5			6			11				9	10	4		3		2	1	7		8
26		27	ASTON VILLA	1-2	McGeachan		7	3	6			11		9	5		10	4		2			1			8
27	Apr	5	WOLVERHAMPTON W.	1-2	Nicoll		5		6	8		11					9	4		3		2	1	7		10
28		10	SHEFFIELD WEDNESDAY	2-1	Cassidy, Miller		8		6	10		11	3	9		7		4				2	5	1		
29		16	SHEFFIELD UNITED	0-2					6	8		11	3	9	5	7		4				2	1			10
30		20	Wolverhampton Wan.	0-4					6	8	1	11	3		5	7	9	4		2						10

Ave. Home Attendance: 8360

	Brown RN	Cassidy J	Davies RH	Freebairn A	Gilligan A	Hiles A	Jack R	Jones D	Joyce W	McGeachan J	Miller TA	Nicoll D	Paton A	Scotchbrook F	Scott S	Smith DW	Somerville J	Sutcliffe JW	Tannahill R	Thomson W	Wright J
Apps	4	9	1	30	22	1	28	22	5	24	10	27	29	1	10	2	28	27	2	22	26
Goals		2			6		11	1	1	1	2	5	1							4	4

Two own goals

F.A. Cup

						Brown RN	Cassidy J	Davies RH	Freebairn A	Gilligan A	Hiles A	Jack R	Jones D	Joyce W	McGeachan J	Miller TA	Nicoll D	Paton A	Scotchbrook F	Scott S	Smith DW	Somerville J	Sutcliffe JW	Tannahill R	Thomson W	Wright J
1	Jan	30	Grimsby Town	0-0					6	8		11	3		5	9	10	4				2	1		7	
1r	Feb	8	GRIMSBY TOWN*	3-3	Cassidy, Thompson, Jones		8		6			11	3	9	5		10	4		1	2				7	
1/2r		11	Grimsby Town+	3-2	Joyce 2, Jones		8		6			11	3	9	5		10	4				2	1		7	
2		13	Derby County	1-4	Brown	7	8		6	10		11	3	9	5			4				2	1			

* After extra time
+ Played at Bramall Lane, Sheffield

Lancashire Cup

1	Dec	5	NELSON	3-0
2	Jan	23	Liverpool	2-2
2r	Feb	15	LIVERPOOL	2-0
SF		20	Manchester City	1-2

Manchester Cup

1	Jan	16	FAIRFIELD	3-0
SF	Mar	17	Stalybridge Rovers*	1-1
SFr		29	Stalybridge Rovers*	4-3
F	Apr	3	Bury*	1-3

* Played at Hyde Road.

Other Games

1	Sep	1	Southport Central	1-0
2		3	Preston North End	0-3
3		9	BURY	4-0
4		16	DARWEN	0-1
5		22	Darwen	1-4
6		29	Oldham County	2-1
7	Dec	12	The Corinthians	1-4
8		15	Rochdale	1-3
9		25	MOTHERWELL	6-0
10	Jan	2	BURY	2-1
11		9	WEST BROM ALBION	2-2
12	Mar	31	Halliwell Rovers	2-1
13	Apr	12	EVERTON	8-0
14		28	West Manchester	1-2

FINAL TABLE		Pl.	Home					Away					F.	A.	Pts
			W	D	L	F	A	W	D	L	F	A			(Total)
1	Aston Villa	30	10	3	2	36	16	11	2	2	37	22	73	38	47
2	Sheffield United	30	6	4	5	22	16	7	6	2	20	13	42	29	36
3	Derby County	30	10	2	3	45	22	6	2	7	25	28	70	50	36
4	Preston North End	30	8	4	3	35	21	3	8	4	20	19	55	40	34
5	Liverpool	30	7	6	2	25	10	5	3	7	21	28	46	38	33
6	Sheffield Wed.	30	9	4	2	29	11	1	7	7	13	26	42	37	31
7	Everton	30	8	1	6	42	29	6	2	7	20	28	62	57	31
8	BOLTON WANDERERS	30	7	3	5	22	18	5	3	7	18	25	40	43	30
9	Bury	30	7	5	3	25	15	3	5	7	14	29	39	44	30
10	Wolverhampton W.	30	6	4	5	26	14	5	2	8	19	27	45	41	28
11	Nottingham Forest	30	8	3	4	30	16	1	5	9	14	33	44	49	26
12	West Bromwich Alb.	30	7	2	6	18	16	3	4	8	15	40	33	56	26
13	Stoke	30	8	3	4	30	18	3	0	12	18	41	48	59	25
14	Blackburn Rovers	30	8	1	6	27	25	3	2	10	8	37	35	62	25
15	Sunderland	30	4	6	5	21	21	3	3	9	13	26	34	47	23
16	Burnley	30	4	5	6	25	25	2	2	11	18	36	43	61	19

1897/98 11th in Division One

#	Mon	Date	Opponent	Score	Scorers	Brown RN	Cassidy J	Chorlton HH	Davies RH	Fitchett J	Freebairn A	Gilligan A	Gregory J	Halley W	Jack R	Jones D	Lee J	Lockhart G	McGeachan J	Miller J	Miller TA	Nicoll D	Paton A	Scotchbrook F	Scott S	Somerville J	Sutcliffe IW	Tatham W	Thomson W	Wright J
1	Sep	4	Everton	1-2	Thomson						6	8			11	3			5		7					2	1		9	10
2		11	Blackburn Rovers	3-1	Nicoll, Gilligan, Jack	5					6	8			11	3						9	4			2	1		7	10
3		18	NOTTS COUNTY	1-0	T. Miller	5					6	8			11	3					9		4			2	1		7	10
4		25	PRESTON NORTH END	1-0	Cassidy		9				6	8			11	3			5				4			2	1			10
5	Oct	2	Aston Villa	2-3	Jack, Wright		5				6	8			11	3					7	9	4			2	1			10
6		9	SHEFFIELD WEDNESDAY	0-3		5	11				6	8				3						9	4			2	1		7	10
7		16	Preston North End	0-0		5					6	8			11						9		4		3	2	1		7	10
8		23	NOTTM. FOREST	2-0	T. Miller, Jack	5	7				6	8			11						9		4		3	2	1			10
9		30	SUNDERLAND	1-0	Cassidy	5	7				6	8			11						9		4		3	2		1		10
10	Nov	1	West Bromwich Albion	0-2		5	7				6				11						9	8	4		3	2		1		10
11		6	Notts County	2-1	T. Miller, Jack	5	7				6	8			11						9		4		3	2	1			10
12		13	STOKE	2-1	Paton(pen), T. Miller	5	7				6	8			11						9		4		3	2	1			10
13		20	ASTON VILLA	2-0	Wright, Cassidy	5	7				6	8			11						9		4		3	2	1			10
14		27	Sheffield Wednesday	0-3		5	7				6	8			11						9		4		3	2	1			10
15	Dec	11	Bury	1-2	Cassidy		7				6	8			11	3				5	9		4			2	1			10
16		25	LIVERPOOL	0-2		5					6	8			11	3				10	9		4			2	1		7	
17		27	Derby County	0-1		5	7				6	11				3				9	8		4			2	1			10
18	Jan	1	DERBY COUNTY	3-3	T. Miller, Wright 2	5	7				6	11				3				9	8		4			2	1			10
19		3	BURY	0-0			5				6	11				3				9	8		4			2	1		7	10
20		8	Nottingham Forest	0-2			5				6	11				3				8		9			4	2	1		7	10
21		15	Stoke	0-2		5	7				6	11				3				9	8	10			4	2	1			
22	Feb	7	Sheffield United	0-4		5	7		3		6	9			11						8		4			2	1			10
23		22	Sunderland	0-2		5			4		6	8			11	3					9	7				2	1			10
24	Mar	12	WOLVERHAMPTON W.	2-1	Cassidy 2	5	10		3	4	6	8	11					1			9					2			7	
25		19	Liverpool	1-1	Gilligan	5	9	10	3	4	6	8	11													2			7	
26		26	EVERTON	1-0	Nicoll	5	9		3	4	6	8	11									10				2			7	
27	Apr	2	WEST BROMWICH ALB.	2-0	Fitchett, Nicoll	5	9		3	4	6	8	11									10				2			7	
28		8	SHEFFIELD UNITED	0-1		5	9		3	4	6	8	11									10				2			7	
29		9	Wolverhampton Wan.	0-2		5	9				6	8			11	1	3					10	4			2			7	
30		14	BLACKBURN ROVERS	1-2	Cassidy		7	10			6			3	11	2	1				5	9	4							8
			Apps			23	24	2	6	6	30	28	5	1	19	15	3	1	2	8	21	11	22	1	9	29	25	2	15	22
			Goals				7				1	2			4						5	3	1						1	4

Ave. Home Attendance: 8190

F.A. Cup

#	Mon	Date	Opponent	Score	Scorers	Brown RN	Cassidy J	Chorlton HH	Davies RH	Fitchett J	Freebairn A	Gilligan A	Gregory J	Halley W	Jack R	Jones D	Lee J	Lockhart G	McGeachan J	Miller J	Miller TA	Nicoll D	Paton A	Scotchbrook F	Scott S	Somerville J	Sutcliffe IW	Tatham W	Thomson W	Wright J
1	Jan	29	Luton Town	1-0	Cassidy	5	7		3		6	8			11						9		4			2	1			10
2	Feb	12	MANCHESTER CITY	1-0	T. Miller	5	7				6	8			11	3					9		4			2	1			10
3		26	SOUTHAMPTON	0-0		5	7			4	6	8			11	3					9					2	1			10
3r	Mar	2	Southampton	0-4		5					6	11				3				8	9		4			2	1		7	10

Lancashire Cup

#		Date	Opponent	Score
1	Dec	4	NELSON	3-3
1r		7	Nelson	1-0
2	Jan	22	Everton	2-1
SF	Feb	19	Newton Heath*	1-4

* Played at Hyde Road

Manchester Cup

#		Date	Opponent	Score
1	Feb	5	Stockport County	1-2

Other Games

#		Date	Opponent	Score
1	Sep	1	BURY	0-0
2		6	Bradfird	3-0
3		7	Stalybridge Rovers	2-0
4		20	Liverpool	1-3
5	Oct	11	LIVERPOOL	4-2
6	Jan	5	S.H. WOODS UNIVERSITY XI	4-0
7	Mar	23	Wigan County	2-1
8	Apr	11	The Corinthians	3-3
9		12	DUNDEE	0-0
10		23	HEART OF MIDLOTHIAN	0-0
11		25	Liverpool	1-1
12		26	St. Helens	1-2
13		30	Tottenham Hotspur	2-2

FINAL TABLE

		Pl.	Home W	D	L	F	A	Away W	D	L	F	A	F.	A. (Total)	Pts
1	Sheffield United	30	9	4	2	27	14	8	4	3	29	17	56	31	42
2	Sunderland	30	12	2	1	27	8	4	3	8	16	22	43	30	37
3	Wolverhampton W.	30	10	4	1	36	14	4	3	8	21	27	57	41	35
4	Everton	30	11	3	1	33	12	2	6	7	15	27	48	39	35
5	Sheffield Wed.	30	12	0	3	39	15	3	3	9	12	27	51	42	33
6	Aston Villa	30	12	1	2	47	21	2	4	9	14	30	61	51	33
7	West Bromwich Alb.	30	8	5	2	25	16	3	5	7	19	29	44	45	32
8	Nottingham Forest	30	7	5	3	30	19	4	4	7	17	30	47	49	31
9	Liverpool	30	7	4	4	27	16	4	2	9	21	29	48	45	28
10	Derby County	30	10	3	2	40	19	1	3	11	17	42	57	61	28
11	BOLTON WANDERERS	30	9	2	4	18	13	2	2	11	10	28	28	41	26
12	Preston North End	30	7	5	3	26	15	1	3	11	9	28	35	43	24
13	Notts County	30	4	6	5	23	23	4	2	9	13	23	36	46	24
14	Bury	30	8	3	4	25	19	0	5	10	14	32	39	51	24
15	Blackburn Rovers	30	4	7	4	20	22	3	3	9	19	32	39	54	24
16	Stoke	30	8	3	4	21	14	0	5	10	14	41	35	55	24

1897-98 Season
(Back) Bretell (Sec.), Lockhart, Brown, Sutcliffe, Chorlton, Freebairn, Brierley (Trainer)
(Front) Thomson, Barlow, Joyce, Paton, Jack
(n.b. only 10 players turned up for photo-call!)

1899
(Back) Brown, Lockhart, Fitchett, McAteer, Halley, Freebairn, Scotchbrook
(Front) Morgan, Gilligan, Picken, Barlow, Jack, Somerville

1898/99 17th in Division One (Relegated)

League Results

No	Date		Opponent	Score	Scorers
1	Sep	3	WEST BROM ALBION	3-0	Nicoll, Wright, Miller
2		10	Blackburn Rovers	1-4	Miller
3		17	SHEFFIELD WEDNESDAY	0-0	
4		24	Sunderland	0-0	
5	Oct	1	WOLVES	2-1	Wright(2)
6		8	Everton	0-1	
7		15	NOTTS COUNTY	0-1	
8		22	Stoke	3-2	Miller, Freebairn, Nicoll
9		29	Aston Villa	1-2	A.Gilligan
10	Nov	5	Burnley	0-2	
11		12	SHEFFIELD UNITED	3-0	A.Gilligan(2), Jack
12		19	Newcastle United	1-4	Miller
13		26	PRESTON NORTH END	2-2	A.Gilligan, Miller
14	Dec	3	Liverpool	0-2	
15		10	NOTTINGHAM FOREST	0-2	
16		17	BURY	0-1	
17		26	Derby County	1-1	Barlow
18		31	West Bromwich Albion	0-1	
19	Jan	3	BURNLEY	2-0	Brown, Jack
20		7	BLACKBURN ROVERS	0-2	
21		14	Sheffield Wednesday	0-2	
22		21	SUNDERLAND	6-1	A.Gilligan(2), Brown(2), Barlow, Barnes
23	Feb	18	STOKE	0-2	
24		25	EVERTON	2-4	Barlow(2)
25	Mar	11	Sheffield United	1-3	Morgan
26		18	NEWCASTLE UNITED	0-0	
27		31	DERBY COUNTY	2-1	Morgan, Barlow
28	Apr	1	Liverpool	2-1	McAteer, Morgan
29		3	Notts County	1-2	McAteer
30		4	Wolves	0-1	
31		8	Nottingham Forest	2-1	Morgan(2)
32		15	Bury	1-3	McAteer
33		17	ASTON VILLA	0-0	
34		29	Preston North End	1-0	Morgan

Ave. Home Attendance: 7075

Player Appearances / Goals

No	Barlow T	Barnes J	Bolton R	Brown RN	Carr SR	Chorlton HH	Davies RH	Davies WH	Fitchett J	Freebairn A	Gilligan A	Gilligan W	Gregory J	Hanson J	Howcroft H	Hynds T	Jack R	Lee J	Lockhart G	McAteer T	McKay P	Marshall T	Miller T	Morgan H	Nicoll D	Paton A	Somerville J	Sutcliffe JW	Thomson W	Wright J
1				5						4	6						11	1	3				8		9		2		7	10
2				5				2		4	6	7	11					1	3				8		9					10
3	11			5						4	6	8							3				7		9		2	1		10
4				5			7			4	6						11		3				8		9		2	1		10
5				5	7					4	6						11		3				8		9		2	1		10
6				5	7					4	6						11		3				8		9		2	1		10
7	10			5		11				4	6	7							3				8		9		2	1		
8				5						4	6					11			3				8		9		2	1	7	10
9				5						4	6					11			3				8		9		2	1	7	10
10				5						4	6					11		1	3				8		9		2		7	10
11				5				3		4	6						11						8		9		2	1	7	10
12				5				3		4	6						11						8		9		2	1	7	10
13				5				3		4	6						11						8		9		2	1	7	10
14				5				3		4	6						11						8		9		2	1	7	10
15			8	5		10	7	3		4	6						11								9		2	1		
16			8	5		10	7	3		4	6						11								9		2	1		
17	10	9		8			3	5		6	7						11										2	1		
18	10	7		9			3	5		6	8						11										2	1		
19		7		9			3	5		6	8						11					10					2	1		
20		7	8	9			3	5		6							11					10					2	1		
21	10	7		9						6	8				4		11			3	5						2	1		
22	10	7		9						5	8	6			4		11			3							2	1		
23	10	7		5						6	8				4		11			3				9			2	1		
24	10			5				4		6	8						11			3				9		7	2	1		
25	10			5				4		6	8					5	11			3				7		9		1		
26	10	11						4		6						8	5			3				7		9	1			
27	10			9				2	4	6	8					5	11				3			7				1		
28	10							2	4	6	8					5	11			9	3			7				1		
29	10							2	4	6	8					5	11			9	3			7				1		
30		10						2	4	6	8						11			3	5			7		9		1		
31	10							2	4	6	8					5	11			9	3			7				1		
32				10				2	4	6	8					5	11			9	3			7				1		
33	10							2	4	6	8					5	11				9			7			3	1		
34	10			9				2	4	6	8					5	11							7			3	1		
Apps	16	9	2	27	2	3	20	21	11	33	28	3	1	1	3	8	27	3	23	8	3	1	17	12	16	5	25	31	8	7
Goals	5	1		3						1	6						2			3			5	6	2					3

F.A. Cup

No	Date		Opponent	Score	Att	Barlow T	Barnes J	Brown RN	Freebairn A	Gilligan A	Hynds T	Jack R	McAteer T	Davies WH	Paton A	Somerville J	Sutcliffe JW
1	Jan	28	Wolves	0-0	12000	10	7	9	4	6	5	11	3	8		2	1
1r	Feb	1	WOLVES	0-1	5000	10	7		6	8	5	11	3	4	9	2	1

Lancashire Cup

	Date		Opponent	Score
1	Dec	5	BLACKPOOL	1-0
2	Feb	11	BURNLEY	3-2
SF	Mar	4	Blackburn Rovers	2-1
F		25	BURY	1-3

Manchester Cup

	Date		Opponent	Score
1	Feb	8	MANCHESTER CITY	3-9

Other Games

	Date		Opponent	Score
1	Sep	1	Wigan County	3-0
2		19	Liverpool	2-3
3		27	Stockport	6-1
4	Apr	26	BOLTON AMATEURS	5-1

Final Table

	FINAL TABLE	Pl.	Home W	D	L	F	A	Away W	D	L	F	A	F (Total)	A	Pts
1	Aston Villa	34	15	2	0	58	13	4	5	8	18	27	76	40	45
2	Liverpool	34	12	3	2	29	10	7	2	8	20	23	49	33	43
3	Burnley	34	11	5	1	32	15	4	4	9	13	32	45	47	39
4	Everton	34	10	2	5	25	13	5	6	6	23	28	48	41	38
5	Notts County	34	9	6	2	33	20	3	7	7	14	31	47	51	37
6	Blackburn Rovers	34	9	5	3	41	23	5	3	9	19	29	60	52	36
7	Sunderland	34	11	3	3	26	10	4	3	10	15	31	41	41	36
8	Wolverhampton W.	34	9	5	3	30	13	5	2	10	24	35	54	48	35
9	Derby County	34	11	5	1	46	19	1	6	10	16	38	62	57	35
10	Bury	34	9	5	3	31	18	5	2	10	17	31	48	49	35
11	Nottingham Forest	34	6	6	5	22	18	5	5	7	20	24	42	42	33
12	Stoke	34	10	4	3	29	17	3	3	11	18	35	47	52	33
13	Newcastle United	34	9	3	5	33	18	2	5	10	16	30	49	48	30
14	West Bromwich Alb.	34	11	1	5	28	9	1	5	11	14	48	42	57	30
15	Preston North End	34	10	4	3	29	14	0	5	12	15	33	44	47	29
16	Sheffield United	34	7	8	2	31	20	2	3	12	14	31	45	51	29
17	**BOLTON WANDERERS**	34	6	5	6	24	21	3	2	12	13	30	37	51	25
18	Sheffield Wed.	34	8	2	7	26	24	0	6	11	6	37	32	61	24

1899/1900 *2nd in Division Two (Promoted)*

#		Date	Opponent	Score	Scorers	Anthony A	Barlow T	Bell L	Brown RN	Brown W	Chorlton HH	Fitchett J	Freebairn A	Gilligan A	Halley W	Hanson J	Jack R	Jones J	Lockhart G	McAteer T	Morgan H	Picken JH	Scotchbrook F	Somerville J	Sutcliffe JW	Waller WH
1	Sep	2	Loughborough Town	3-2	Bell, McAteer, Jack		10	9	4			6	8	2			11			3	5	7			1	
2		9	NEWTON HEATH	2-1	Bell(2)		10	9	4			6		2			11			3	5	7		8	1	
3		16	Sheffield Wednesday	1-2	(og)		10	9	5			4	6	8	3						7	11		2	1	
4		23	LINCOLN CITY	4-0	Gilligan, Bell, Fitchett, Somerville		8	9	6			5	4	7	3	10			11					2	1	
5		30	Small Heath	0-0			10	9	5			4	6	11	3	7						8		2	1	
6	Oct	14	Grimsby Town	0-0			10	9	5			4	6	11	3			7				8		2	1	
7		21	WOOLWICH ARSENAL	1-0	Barlow		10	9	7			4	6	11	3					5	8			2	1	
8	Nov	4	LEICESTER FOSSE	2-2	Bell, Morgan		10	7	5			4	6	11	3					9	8			2	1	
9		11	Luton Town	2-0	Barlow(2)		10	9	4				6	7	3	11				5	8			2	1	
10		25	Walsall	2-2	Barlow, Picken		10	9	5			4	6	7	3						8	11		2	1	
11	Dec	2	MIDDLESBROUGH	3-0	Brown, Jack, Fitchett		10	9	5			4	6	7	3		11				8			2	1	
12		6	Chesterfield	3-3	Jack, Barlow, Picken		10		5				6	7	3	9	11					8	4	2	1	
13		16	Gainsborough Town	1-1	Barlow		8	9	4				6	10	3	11				5	7			2	1	
14		23	Burton Swifts	5-2	Bell(2), Morgan, Picken, Freebairn		10	9	5			4	6			8	11				7	3		2	1	
15		26	Barnsley	6-1	Picken, Freebairn, Hanson(3), Morgan			9	5	3		4	6			8	11				7	10		2	1	
16		30	LOUGHBOROUGH TOWN	7-0	Hanson(2), Morgan, Bell(3), McAteer			9		3		4	6			8	11			5	7	10		2	1	
17	Jan	1	NEW BRIGHTON TOWN	2-1	Bell(2)			9	5	3		4	6			8	11				7	10		2	1	
18		2	PORT VALE	5-0	McAteer(3), Jack(2)			9		3		4	6			8	11			5	7	10		2	1	
19		6	Newton Heath	2-1	Picken, Morgan							4	6	9	3	8	11			5	7	10		2	1	
20		13	SHEFFIELD WEDNESDAY	1-0	Jack			9	6			4			3	8	11			5	7	10		2	1	
21		20	Lincoln City	0-1				9	6	3		4				8	11			5	7	10		2	1	
22	Feb	3	SMALL HEATH	1-1	Fitchett			9		3		4	6		2	8	11			5	7	10			1	
23		17	GRIMSBY TOWN	1-2	Gilligan			9	4	3			6	11	2	8				5	7	10			1	
24		24	Woolwich Arsenal	1-0	Bell			8		3		4			2	7	11			5	10	9	6		1	
25	Mar	10	Leicester Fosse	0-0				9		3		4			2	8	11			5	7	10	6			1
26		17	LUTON TOWN	3-0	Jack, Morgan, (og)			9	5	3		4	6	8	2		11				7	10			1	
27		31	WALSALL	2-0	R.Brown, Bell			9	5	3		4	6	8	2		11				7	10			1	
28	Apr	7	Middlesbrough	3-0	Morgan, Hanson, Bell			9	5	3		4	6	11	2	8					7	10			1	
29		13	BARNSLEY	2-0	Bell, Morgan			9	5	3		4	6	11	2	8					7	10			1	
30		14	CHESTERFIELD	3-0	Picken, Gilligan, Morgan			9	5	3		4	6	11	2	8					7	10			1	
31		16	New Brighton Town	1-3	Picken			9	5	3		4	6	11	2	8					7	10			1	
32		21	GAINSBOROUGH TOWN	3-0	Chorlton(2), Bell	5		9	7	3	11	4	6		2	8						10			1	
33		23	Port Vale	2-0	Bell(2)	5		9	7	3	11		6		2	8				4		10			1	
34		28	BURTON SWIFTS	5-0	Bell(4), Morgan	5		9		3	11		6			8				4	7	10		2	1	
			Apps			3	14	32	27	18	3	27	29	20	27	22	19	2	2	17	30	25	3	20	33	1
			Goals				6	23	2		2	3	2	3		6	7			5	10	7		1		

Ave. Home Attendance: 4875

Two own goals

F.A. Cup

#		Date	Opponent	Score	Att.	Bell L	Brown RN	Brown W	Fitchett J	Halley W	Hanson J	Jack R	McAteer T	Morgan H	Picken JH	Sutcliffe JW
1	Jan	27	Sheffield Wednesday	0-1	12390	9	6	3	4	2	8	11	5	7	10	1

Lancashire Cup

#		Date	Opponent	Score
1	Dec	9	NEWTON HEATH	2-3

Manchester Cup

#		Date	Opponent	Score
1	Feb	19	ROCHDALE	3-0
SF	Mar	12	Manchester City	5-3
F	Apr	4	Bury*	0-2

* Played at Hyde Road

Other Games

#		Date	Opponent	Score
1	Sep	4	Burnley	0-0
2		5	Bury	2-2
3		18	BURY	3-2
4	Oct	7	New Brighton	0-1
5		28	THE KAFFIRS	13-3
6	Nov	18	Tottenham Hotspur	0-4
7	Apr	17	Hunslet	1-1

FINAL TABLE

		Pl.	Home W	D	L	F	A	Away W	D	L	F	A	F (Total)	A	Pts
1	Sheffield Wed.	34	17	0	0	61	7	8	4	5	23	15	84	22	54
2	BOLTON WANDERERS	34	14	2	1	47	7	8	6	3	32	18	79	25	52
3	Small Heath	34	15	1	1	58	12	5	5	7	20	26	78	38	46
4	Newton Heath	34	15	1	1	44	11	5	3	9	19	16	63	27	44
5	Leicester Fosse	34	11	5	1	34	8	6	4	7	30	36	64	43	43
6	Grimsby Town	34	10	3	4	46	24	7	3	7	21	22	67	46	40
7	Chesterfield Town	34	10	4	3	35	24	6	2	9	30	36	65	60	38
8	Woolwich Arsenal	34	13	1	3	47	12	3	3	11	14	31	61	43	36
9	Lincoln City	34	11	5	1	31	9	3	3	11	15	34	46	43	36
10	New Brighton T.	34	9	4	4	44	22	4	5	8	22	36	66	58	35
11	Burslem Port Vale	34	11	2	4	26	16	3	4	10	13	33	39	49	34
12	Walsall	34	10	5	2	35	18	2	3	12	15	37	50	55	32
13	Gainsborough Trinity	34	8	4	5	37	24	1	3	13	10	51	47	75	25
14	Middlesbrough	34	8	4	5	28	15	0	4	13	11	54	39	69	24
15	Burton Swifts	34	8	5	4	31	24	1	1	15	12	60	43	84	24
16	Barnsley	34	8	5	4	36	23	0	2	15	10	56	46	79	23
17	Luton Town	34	5	3	9	25	25	0	5	12	15	50	40	75	18
18	Loughborough	34	1	6	10	12	26	0	0	17	6	74	18	100	8

1900/01 10th in Division One

League Results

#	Date		Opponent	Score	Scorers
1	Sep	1	DERBY COUNTY	0-1	
2		8	Sheffield Wednesday	0-1	
3		15	Notts County	1-3	McAteer(pen)
4		22	PRESTON NORTH END	1-1	Tracey
5		29	Wolves	1-1	Tracey
6	Oct	6	ASTON VILLA	1-0	L.Bell
7		13	Liverpool	1-2	L.Bell
8		20	NEWCASTLE UNITED	3-2	Tracey(2), McKie
9		27	Sheffield United	2-0	L.Bell, McKie
10	Nov	3	MANCHESTER CITY	0-0	
11		10	Bury	0-3	
12		12	Stoke	1-2	Picken
13		24	Blackburn Rovers	0-2	
14	Dec	1	STOKE	1-0	McKie
15		8	West Bromwich Albion	2-7	Tracey, McKie
16		15	EVERTON	1-0	L.Bell
17		25	Nottingham Forest	0-3	
18		26	Aston Villa	0-3	
19		29	Derby County	2-4	Picken, L.Bell
20	Jan	1	NOTTINGHAM FOREST	4-2	R.Brown, Hanson, Freebairn, L.Bell
21		2	SUNDERLAND	0-0	
22		5	SHEFFIELD WEDNESDAY	1-1	Freebairn
23	Feb	16	LIVERPOOL	1-0	L.Bell
24	Mar	6	SHEFFIELD UNITED	0-0	
25		9	Manchester City	1-1	McKie
26		16	BURY	3-2	L.Bell, McKAteer, Picken
27		23	Preston North End	3-1	Picken(2), McKie
28		27	Newcastle United	0-3	
29		30	BLACKBURN ROVERS	1-0	Tracey
30	Apr	5	NOTTS COUNTY	0-0	
31		8	Sunderland	1-5	McKie
32		13	WEST BROM ALBION	3-2	Barlow, McKie, R.Brown
33		20	Everton	3-2	Barlow(2), Picken
34		29	WOLVES	1-0	Picken

Ave. Home Attendance: 10,175

Appearances

#	Astley H	barlow T	Bell F	Bell L	Brown RN	Brown W	Brunison J	Claderbank W	Chorlton HH	Fitchett J	Freebairn A	Halley W	Hanson J	Haslam R	Hodgkiss W	Jack R	Lowe J	McAteer T	McKie J	Morgan H	Ostick C	Picken JH	Smith GT	Somerville J	Sutcliffe JW	Tracey W	Waller WH	Woolfall T
1				9	5	3				4	6	2	8			11				7		10			1			
2				9		3		6		4		2	8					5		7		10			1	11		
3				9		3				4	6	2						5	8	7		10			1	11		
4		10				3			4		6	2						5	9	7		8			1	11		
5		10		7						4	6	2						5	9			8			1	11		3
6		10		7						4	6							5	9			8		2	1	11		3
7		10		7						4	6	2						5	9			8			1	11		3
8		10		7						4	6	2						5	9			8				11	1	3
9		10		7						4	6	2						5	9			8			1	11		3
10		10		7						4	6	2						5	9			8			1	11		3
11		10		7				4			6	2						5	9			8			1	11		3
12		10		7							6	2					4	5	9			8			1	11		3
13				7		2				4	6					10		5	9			8			1	11		3
14		10		7	4	2					6							5	9			8			1	11		3
15		10		7		2				4	6							5	9			8			1	11		3
16		10	4	7		2								5	6				9			8			1	11		3
17		10		7	4	2					6		1					5	9			8				11		3
18			4	7	5	2					6		1						9			10	8			11		3
19			4	7		2					6		10					5	9			8				11	1	3
20				7	4	2					6		8					5	9			10				11	1	3
21				7		2				4	6		8					5	9			10				11	1	3
22				7		2				4	6		8					5	9			10				11	1	3
23		10		7		3				4	6							5	9			8		2	1	11		
24		10		7		2				4	6							5	9			8			1	11		3
25		10		7		2				4	6							5	9			8			1	11		3
26		10		7						4	6							5	9			8		2	1	11		3
27		10		7						4	6							5	9		3	8		2	1	11		
28		10		7		6				2	4							5	9		3	8			1	11		
29		10		7			6				4							5	9		3	8		2	1	11		
30		10		7			6				4							5	9		3	8		2	1	11		
31				7	11		6				4		8					5	9		3	10		2	1			
32		10		7	11		6				4							5	9		3	8		2	1			
33		10		7	11		6			4	5								9		3	8		2	1			
34	8			7	11	2	6			5	4								9			10			1			3
Apps	1	23	3	33	10	19	6	3	1	22	29	12	10	1	1	2	1	29	32	4	7	34	1	9	26	29	5	21
Goals		3		8	2						2		1					2	8			7				6		

F.A. Cup

#	Date		Opponent	Score	Scorers	Att.	Bell L	Brown W	Fitchett J	Freebairn A	Hanson J	Jack R	McAteer T	McKie J	Ostick C	Picken JH	Somerville J	Sutcliffe JW	Tracey W	Woolfall T
1	Feb	9	DERBY COUNTY	1-0	L.Bell	13171	7	3	4	6	8		5	9		10	2	1	11	
2		23	READING	0-1		11592	8	2		6		4	5	9	7	10		1	11	3

Lancashire Cup

1	Oct	1	PRESTON NORTH END	5-0
2		22	Burnley	0-5

Manchester Cup

1	Mar	13	Manchester City	0-2

Other Games

1	Sep	12	MANCHESTER CITY	2-0
2		17	Burnley	1-3
3	Nov	17	Belfast Distillary	6-1
4	Jan	14	BURY	1-1
5	Mar	18	Blackpool	2-3
6	Apr	6	RANGERS	2-0
7		25	Shrewsbury Town	3-1

FINAL TABLE

	FINAL TABLE	Pl.	Home						Away					F.	A.	Pts
			W	D	L	F	A	W	D	L	F	A		(Total)		
1	Liverpool	34	12	2	3	36	13	7	5	5	23	22	59	35	45	
2	Sunderland	34	12	3	2	43	11	3	10	4	14	15	57	26	43	
3	Notts County	34	13	2	2	39	18	5	2	10	15	28	54	46	40	
4	Nottingham Forest	34	10	4	3	32	14	6	3	8	21	22	53	36	39	
5	Bury	34	11	3	3	31	10	5	4	8	22	27	53	37	39	
6	Newcastle United	34	10	5	2	27	13	4	5	8	15	24	42	37	38	
7	Everton	34	10	4	3	37	17	6	1	10	18	25	55	42	37	
8	Sheffield Wed.	34	13	2	2	38	16	0	8	9	14	26	52	42	36	
9	Blackburn Rovers	34	9	4	4	24	18	3	5	9	15	29	39	47	33	
10	BOLTON WANDERERS	34	10	5	2	21	12	3	2	12	18	43	39	55	33	
11	Manchester City	34	12	3	2	32	16	1	3	13	16	42	48	58	32	
12	Derby County	34	10	4	3	43	18	2	3	12	12	24	55	42	31	
13	Wolverhampton W.	34	6	10	1	21	15	3	3	11	18	40	39	55	31	
14	Sheffield United	34	8	4	5	22	23	4	3	10	13	29	35	52	31	
15	Aston Villa	34	8	5	4	32	18	2	5	10	13	33	45	51	30	
16	Stoke	34	8	3	6	23	15	3	2	12	23	42	46	57	27	
17	Preston North End	34	6	4	7	29	30	3	3	11	20	45	49	75	25	
18	West Bromwich Alb.	34	4	4	9	21	27	3	4	10	14	35	35	62	22	

1901/02 12th in Division One

#		Date	Opponent	Score	Scorers	Ashley H	Bannister W	Barlow TH	Bell F	Bell L	Brown RN	Brown W	Brunison J	Fitchett J	Freebairn A	Halliday JF	Hanson J	McAteer T	McKie J	Neyland M	Nicoll D	Ostick C	Picken J	Stokes D	Struthers R	Sutcliffe JW	Taylor R	Tracey W	Williams H	Woolfall T	Worthington W
1	Sep	7	Small Heath	0-2				10		7		2	6	4	5				9				8								
2		14	DERBY COUNTY	2-1	L.Bell, Picken			10		7	5	2	6	4					9			3	8		3	1			11		
3		21	Sheffield Wednesday	1-5	L.Bell	10				7		2		4	6		1	5	9			3	8						11		
4		28	NOTTS COUNTY	1-1	Tracey	10				7	5	2	6	4						9		3	8			1		5	11		
5	Oct	5	GRIMSBY TOWN	4-0	L.Bell(2), Picken(2)	10				7		2	6	4					9			3	8			1		5	11		
6		12	Manchester City	0-1		10				7		2	6	4					9			3	8			1		5	11		
7		19	WOLVES	2-2	L.Bell, Picken	10			4	7	5	2	6						9			3	8			1			11		
8		26	Liverpool	1-1	Barlow		10			7	5	2		4					9			3	8			1		6	11		
9	Nov	2	NEWCASTLE UNITED	3-1	Williams(2), L.Bell		10			7	5	2		4					9			3	8			1		6	11		
10		9	Aston Villa	0-1				11	4	7		2						5	10			3	8			1		6	8		
11		23	Nottingham Forest	1-4	Picken		10			7	5	2		4					9			3	8			1		6	11		
12		30	BURY	2-2	Barlow, Williams		10			7	5	2		4					9			3	8			1		6	11		
13	Dec	7	Blackburn Rovers	0-2				10	5	7	4	2				3	1		9				8					6	11		
14		14	STOKE	2-1	Barlow, Taylor			10	5	7		2			4				9			3	8			1		6			11
15		21	Everton	0-1				10	5	7		2			4				9		11	3	8			1		6			
16		28	SUNDERLAND	0-0				10	5	7		2			4				9		11	3	8			1		6			
17	Jan	1	MANCHESTER CITY	3-3	Bannister, L.Bell, Williams			10	5	7		2			4				9			3	8			1		6	11		
18		2	NOTTINGHAM FOREST	3-0	McKie, Picken, Williams			10	5	7					4	2			9			3	8			1		6	11		
19		4	SMALL HEATH	4-0	McKie(3), Williams			10	5	7					4	2			9			3	8			1		6	11		
20		11	Derby County	2-1	Barlow, L.Bell			10	5	7					4	2			9			3	8			1		6	11		
21		18	SHEFFIELD WEDNESDAY	3-1	Bannister(pen), L.Bell, Freebairn			10	5	7	6	2			4				9			3	8			1			11		
22	Feb	1	Grimsby Town	1-4	Picken			10	5	7		2			4				9			3	8			1		6	11		
23		15	Wolves	2-1	Barlow, Picken			10	5		6	2			4	3			9				8			1			11		
24		22	LIVERPOOL	1-0	McKie			10	5			2			4	3			9				8			1		6	11		
25	Mar	1	Newcastle United	1-4	Picken			10		7		2			4	3	1	5	9				8					6	11		
26		8	ASTON VILLA	2-2	McKie, Stokes			10			5	2			4	3	1		9	6			8						11		
27		28	SHEFFIELD UNITED	1-0	McKie			10	5		2	6			4	3			9				8			1			11		
28		29	Bury	2-2	Barlow(2)			10	5			6			4	2			9			3	8			1			11		
29		31	Notts County	1-2	Stokes			10	5			6			4	2			9			3	8			1			11		
30	Apr	5	BLACKBURN ROVERS	4-0	Barlow(2), McKie, Picken			10				6			4	2		5	9			3	8			1			11		
31		7	Sheffield United	0-2				10				6			4	2		5	9			3	8			1			11		
32		12	Stoke	0-4				10	5						4	2			9			3	8			1		6	11		
33		19	EVERTON	1-3	Barlow			10	5			8			4	2	1		9					3	6						11
34		26	Sunderland	1-2	Worthington				5			6			4	2	1		9					3	8						10
			Apps			5	18	28	2	22	12	24	12	10	23	16	6	5	33	2	2	27	32	12	3	28	19	15	15		3
			Goals				2	10				9			1				8				8	2				1	3	6		1

Ave. Home Attendance: 10,325

F.A. Cup

#		Date	Opponent	Score	Scorers	Att	Ashley H	Barlow TH	Bell L	Brown W	Fitchett J	Freebairn A	Halliday JF	McKie J	Picken J	Struthers R	Taylor R	Tracey W	Williams H	Woolfall T
1	Jan	25	Wolves	2-0	Williams, OG	15000	5	10	7	2		6	3	9	8		1	4	11	
2	Feb	8	Sheffield United	1-2	McKie	12000	5	10			4	6	2	9	8		1	7	11	3

Lancashire Cup

#		Date	Opponent	Score
1	Sep	30	BURY	2-1
2	Oct	21	BURNLEY	2-2
2r	Nov	4	Burnley	2-3

Manchester Cup

#		Date	Opponent	Score
1	Mar	3	BURY	2-0
SF	Apr	9	Newton Heath*	1-1
SFr		14	Newton Heath*	0-1

*Played at Hyde Road

Other Games

#		Date	Opponent	Score
1	Sep	2	Bradford	3-1
2		10	Bury	1-5
3	Mar	15	Bohemians	4-2
4	Apr	1	Brierley Hill	3-1
5		21	Barrow	3-1
6	May	3	PRESTON NORTH END	2-4

FINAL TABLE

		Pl.	Home					Away					F.	A.	Pts
			W	D	L	F	A	W	D	L	F	A		(Total)	
1	Sunderland	34	12	3	2	32	14	7	3	7	18	21	50	35	44
2	Everton	34	11	2	4	31	11	6	5	6	22	24	53	35	41
3	Newcastle United	34	11	3	3	41	14	6	3	8	7	20	48	34	37
4	Blackburn Rovers	34	12	2	3	36	16	3	4	10	16	32	52	48	36
5	Nottingham Forest	34	11	4	2	32	13	2	5	10	11	30	43	43	35
6	Derby County	34	11	5	1	26	10	2	4	11	13	31	39	41	35
7	Bury	34	11	5	1	31	9	2	3	12	13	29	44	38	34
8	Aston Villa	34	9	5	3	27	13	4	3	10	15	27	42	40	34
9	Sheffield Wed.	34	9	5	3	30	14	4	3	10	18	38	48	52	34
10	Sheffield United	34	10	5	2	38	13	3	2	12	15	35	53	48	33
11	Liverpool	34	8	3	6	28	16	2	9	6	14	22	42	38	32
12	BOLTON WANDERERS	34	10	6	1	38	17	2	2	13	13	39	51	56	32
13	Notts County	34	12	2	3	44	19	2	2	13	7	38	51	57	32
14	Wolverhampton W.	34	12	3	2	32	13	1	3	13	14	44	46	57	32
15	Grimsby Town	34	11	3	3	33	16	2	3	12	11	44	44	60	32
16	Stoke	34	10	4	3	31	12	1	5	11	14	43	45	55	31
17	Small Heath	34	8	5	4	31	14	3	3	11	16	31	47	45	30
18	Manchester City	34	10	3	4	28	17	1	3	13	14	41	42	58	28

1901-02 Season
(Back) Brown, Freebairn, Davies, Bannister, Thompson, Ostick, Halliday
(Middle) Stokes, Hanson, McKie, Taylor, Tracey
(Front) Brown, Picken

1903
(Back) Brown,Lewis,Freebairn,Clifford,Watson, Robertson, Broomfield, Greenhalgh,Davies,Yeuson,Struthers,Boyd
(Middle) Stokes, White, Marsh, Wright, Taylor   (Front) Hanson, Barlow

1902/03 18th in Division One (Relegated)

#	Date		Opponent	Score	Scorers	Bannister W	Bell L	Boyd J	Broomfield W	Brown W	Davies D	Freebairn A	Greenhalgh A	Grime J	Halliday JF	Hanson J	Knowles JH	McCafferty W	McKay D	McKie J	McWilliam P	Marsh S	Marshall T	Morgan W	Ostick C	Picken J	Stokes D	Strang T	Struthers R	Taylor R	Thompson F	Tracey W	White W	Williams H	Wright J
1	Sep	6	SHEFFIELD WEDNESDAY	0-2		5		6		2					3	8				9											1	11			
2		13	West Bromwich Albion	1-2	McKie	5				2		4	6		3	8				9						10	7				1	11			
3		20	NOTTS COUNTY	0-1						2		4	5							9					3	10	7			6	1	11	8		
4		27	Derby County	0-5						2		4	5							9					3	10	7			6	1	11	8		
5	Oct	4	Middlesbrough	3-4	Stokes, McKie, Tracey					2		4	5	3		10				9						8	7			6	1	11			
6		11	NEWCASTLE UNITED	0-2		5				2		4	6		3				10	9						8	7				1	11			
7		18	Wolves	1-3	Tracey	5		4		2			6		3	8			9							10	7				1	11			
8		25	LIVERPOOL	1-1	Bell	8	4			2			5		3	9										10	7			6	1			11	
9	Nov	1	EVERTON	1-3	Greenhalgh	8	4			2			5		3							9					7			6	1	11	11		
10		8	Grimsby Town	1-1	Stokes	5				2		4		1					11			9				8	7			3	6				10
11		15	Aston Villa	2-4	Bannister, Stokes	5				2		4		1				11				9				8	7			3	6				10
12		22	NOTTINGHAM FOREST	1-1	Hanson	5				2		4	6	1		8		11				9					7			3					10
13		29	Bury	0-3		5				2		4	6			8		11				9					7			3					10
14	Dec	6	BLACKBURN ROVERS	1-2	Knowles	9				2		4	5				8	11				9					7			3	6	1			10
15		13	Sunderland	1-3	Knowles	5						4	6	2			10	7				9					8			3	11	1			
16		20	STOKE	2-3	Knowles, Bell		8			2		4	5				10					9					7			3	6	1	11		
17		25	Liverpool	1-5	Freebairn	9			1	4		5										9							2	3	6	11	7		10
18		26	Sheffield United	1-7	Bell	9			1	4		5										9							2	3	6	11	7		10
19		27	Everton	1-3	McKie	8	4						6					5				9						10	2	3			7		11
20	Jan	2	GRIMSBY TOWN	0-1		9	4											5	6			9						10	2	3		1	7		
21		3	Sheffield Wednesday	0-3		7	6											5	4		3	9						10	2		1	8		
22		10	WEST BROM ALBION	0-1			6					4	5					7	10			9							2	3	11	1	8		
23		17	Notts County	3-1	Hanson, Marsh, Taylor		6					4	5					2	7			10		9						3	11	1	8		
24		24	DERBY COUNTY	2-0	Taylor, Marsh		6					4	5					2	7			10		9						3	11	1	8		
25		31	MIDDLESBROUGH	2-1	Marsh, Taylor		6					4	5					2	7			10		9						3	11	1	8		
26	Feb	14	WOLVES	4-1	Marsh(2), White, Bell	7	6	1		2		4	5									9								3		11	8		10
27		28	SHEFFIELD UNITED	1-0	Marsh	7	6	1		2		4	5									9								3		11	8		10
28	Mar	14	ASTON VILLA	0-1		7	6	1		2		4	5			11						9								3			8		10
29		21	Nottingham Forest	2-1	White, Marsh	7	6		1	2			5						7			9		4						3	11		8		10
30		28	BURY	1-0	Marsh		6		1	2			5									9	7	4						3	11		8		10
31	Apr	4	Blackburn Rovers	2-4	Taylor(2)		6		1	2			5									9	7	4						3	11		8		10
32		11	SUNDERLAND	2-0	White, Marsh		6		1	2		4	5									9	7							3	11		8		10
33		13	Newcastle United	0-2			6		1	2		4	5					7	10			9								3	11		8		
34		18	Stoke	0-2		7	6	1		2			5					4				9								3	11		8		10
	Apps					10	12	20	5	24	6	23	30	3	11	18	3	8	7	16	1	15	3	3	8	10	16	3	24	22	20	12	21	1	19
	Goals					1	4					1	1			2	3			3		9					3			5		2	3		

Ave. Home Attendance: 10,175

F.A. Cup

#	Date		Opponent	Score	Att	Bell L	Freebairn A	Greenhalgh A	McCafferty W	McKay D	Marsh S	Morgan W	Taylor R	Thompson F	Tracey W	White W
1	Feb	7	Bristol City	0-5	6000	6	4	5	2	7	10	9	3	11	1	8

Lancashire Cup

1	Sep	29	Barrow	4-2
2	Oct	20	BURY	2-2
2r		29	Bury	1-2

Manchester Cup

1	Feb	24	Stalybridge Rovers	0-1

Other Games

1	Sep	1	Barrow	2-1
2		9	Manchester City	1-3
3	Feb	21	Kidderminster	4-1
4	Mar	7	Third Lanark	2-0
5	Apr	10	THIRD LANARK	1-0
6		22	Northwich Vics.	7-0

FINAL TABLE

		Pl.	W	D	L	F	A	W	D	L	F	A	F.	A.	Pts (Total)
1	Sheffield Wed.	34	12	3	2	31	7	7	1	9	23	29	54	36	42
2	Aston Villa	34	11	3	3	43	18	8	0	9	18	22	61	40	41
3	Sunderland	34	10	5	2	27	11	6	4	7	24	25	51	36	41
4	Sheffield United	34	11	0	6	36	22	6	5	6	22	22	58	44	39
5	Liverpool	34	11	3	3	48	21	6	1	10	20	28	68	49	38
6	Stoke	34	11	2	4	29	11	4	5	8	17	27	46	38	37
7	West Bromwich Alb.	34	10	2	5	37	27	6	2	9	17	26	54	53	36
8	Bury	34	11	1	2	41	14	2	2	13	13	29	54	43	35
9	Derby County	34	13	2	2	34	11	3	1	13	16	36	50	47	35
10	Nottingham Forest	34	10	3	4	33	22	4	4	9	16	25	49	47	35
11	Wolverhampton W.	34	12	2	3	34	17	2	3	12	14	40	48	57	33
12	Everton	34	10	2	5	28	18	3	4	10	17	29	45	47	32
13	Middlesbrough	34	10	3	4	27	16	4	1	12	14	34	41	50	32
14	Newcastle United	34	12	1	4	31	11	2	3	12	10	40	41	51	32
15	Notts County	34	8	5	4	25	16	4	2	11	16	33	41	49	31
16	Blackburn Rovers	34	9	2	6	27	24	3	3	11	17	39	44	63	29
17	Grimsby Town	34	6	5	6	28	22	2	4	11	15	40	43	62	25
18	**BOLTON WANDERERS**	34	6	2	9	18	20	2	1	14	19	53	37	73	19

1903/04 7th in Division Two

#	Date		Opponent	Result	Scorers	Barlow T	Boyd J	Broomfield H	Brown W	Clifford R	Davies D	Foster J	Freebairn A	Gardner A	Greenhalgh S	Hanson J	Heaton S	Leigh J	Marsh S	Ostick C	Robertson JN	Shaw J	Stokes D	Struthers R	Taylor R	Warburton F	White W	Wright J	Yenson W
1	Sep	1	BURTON UNITED	3-0	White(2), Barlow	10	6		2		1		4	11	5				9	2			7	3			8		
2		7	Port Vale	3-2	Marsh, Freebairn, Gardner	10	6		2		1		4	11	5				9	2			7	3			8		
3		12	Burnley	0-0		10	6		2		1		4	11	5				9				7	3			8		
4		19	PRESTON NORTH END	0-2		10	6		2		1		4	11	5				9				7	3			8		
5		26	Grimsby Town	0-0			6		2		1		4	11	5				9				7	3			8		
6	Oct	3	LEICESTER FOSSE	3-1	Wright(2), Marsh		6		2		1		4	11	5				9				7	3	9		8	10	
7		10	Blackpool	4-1	Stokes(2), Marsh, White		6		2		1		4		5				9				7	3			8	10	
8		17	GAINSBOROUGH TOWN	5-0	Marsh(3), Wright(2)		6		2		1		4		5				9				7	3	11		8	10	
9		24	Burton United	1-2	Taylor		6		2		1		4		5				9				7	3	11		8	10	
10		31	BRISTOL CITY	1-1	White		6				1			11					9				7	3	11		8	10	
11	Nov	7	Manchester United	0-0		10	6		2						5				9	2			7	3	4		8	10	5
12		14	GLOSSOP NORTH END	0-1		10	6		2						5				9			7		11	3	4	8	10	
13		21	Bradford City	3-3	White, Taylor(2)		6		2		1		4		5				9			7		11	3	4	8		
14		28	WOOLWICH ARSENAL	2-1	Marsh, Heaton		6		2		1		4		5		9		10				7	3	11		8		
15	Dec	12	LINCOLN CITY	1-2	White		6		2		1		4	11	5		9		10				7	3	11		8		
16		19	Stockport City	2-3	Marsh, Stokes		6				1		4		5		9		10				7	3			8		
17		25	BARNSLEY	5-1	Marsh(3), Wright, Yenson		6				1				5	4			9	2		7		11	3		8	10	
18		26	CHESTERFIELD	4-0	Greenhalgh, Stokes, Taylor, Boyd		6				1				5	4			8	2			7	3	11		10		9
19	Jan	1	BLACKPOOL	3-0	Marsh, Stokes, Yenson		6				1				5		10		8	2			7	3	11		10		9
20		2	PORT VALE	5-0	Stokes,Yenson,Marsh,Greenhalgh,Taylor		6				1				5	4			8	2			7	3	11	4			9
21		9	BURNLEY	1-1	Yenson		6				1				5	4			8	2			7	3	11		10		9
22		16	Preston North End	1-3	White		6			4	1				5				8	2			7	3	11		10		9
23		23	GRIMSBY TOWN	4-0	Taylor, Marsh(2), Stokes		6			4	1				5				8	2			7	3	11		10		9
24		30	Leicester Fosse	2-2	Boyd, Marsh		6			4	1				5				8	2			7	3	11		10		9
25	Feb	13	Gainsborough Town	1-3	Taylor		6		2	4	1				5				8				7	3	11		10	8	9
26		27	Bristol City	0-2			6		2	4	1				5			7	8	2					11		10		9
27	Mar	12	Glossop North End	3-3	White, Stokes, Yenson			1	2	4		6			5								7	3	11		8	10	9
28		26	Woolwich Arsenal	0-3					2	4	1	6			5				8				7	3	11		10		
29	Apr	4	Barnsley	0-1					2	5	1	6	4						8				9	7	3	11	10		
30		9	Lincoln City	0-1					2	6	1		4		5		9		8				7	3	11		10		
31		11	BRADFORD CITY	1-0	(og)				2	6	1		4		5				8				7	3	11		10	8	9
32		13	Chesterfield	1-1	Taylor		6		2	5	1					4		7	8					3	11		10		9
33		16	Stockport City	0-1					2	4	1				5				8		6		7	3	11		10		9
34		25	MANCHESTER UNITED	0-0						4	1		6		5				8	2			7	3	11		10		9
			Apps			5	27	1	21	13	33	2	18	8	30	7	4	2	30	14	1	4	32	33	26	1	30	15	17
			Goals			1	2						1	1	2		1		16				8		8		8	5	5

Ave. Home Attendance: 7,975

One own goal

F.A. Cup

#	Date		Opponent	Result	Scorers	Att.	Boyd J	Brown W	Clifford R	Davies D	Foster J	Freebairn A	Greenhalgh S	Marsh S	Ostick C	Stokes D	Struthers R	Taylor R	White W	Yenson W
1	Feb	6	Reading	1-1	Marsh	10000	6			1		4	5	8	2	7	3	11	10	9
1r		10	READING	3-2	Freebairn, Marsh, Yenson	10082	6	2		1		4	5	8		7	3	11	10	9
2		20	SOUTHAMPTON	4-1	Marsh(2), White(2)	12000	6			1		4	5	8	2	7	3	11	10	9
3	Mar	5	Sheffield United	2-0	Marsh, Yenson	15000	6	2		1		4	5	8		7	3	11	10	9
SF		19	Derby County*	1-0	Taylor	25000	6	2		1		4	5	8		7	3	11	10	9
F	Apr	23	Manchester City+	0-1		61374		2	4	1	6		5	8		7	3	11	10	9

* Played at Molineux Grounds, Wolverhampton.   + Played at Crystal Palace, London.

Lancashire Cup

#	Date		Opponent	Result
1	Jan	19	St. Helens	1-1
1r		13	ST. HELENS	0-1

Manchester Cup

#	Date		Opponent	Result
SF	Mar	30	Bury*	1-1
SFr	Apr	26	Bury*	0-4

* Played at Clayton

Other Games

#	Date		Opponent	Result
1	Apr	1	THIRD LANARK	2-0
2		28	Bolton St. Lukes	2-1

FINAL TABLE

	Team	Pl.	Home W	D	L	F	A	Away W	D	L	F	A	F (Total)	A	Pts
1	Preston North End	34	13	4	0	38	10	7	6	4	24	14	62	24	50
2	Woolwich Arsenal	34	15	2	0	67	5	6	5	6	24	17	91	22	49
3	Manchester United	34	14	2	1	42	14	6	6	5	23	19	65	33	48
4	Bristol City	34	14	2	1	53	12	4	4	9	20	29	73	41	42
5	Burnley	34	12	2	3	31	20	3	7	7	19	35	50	55	39
6	Grimsby Town	34	12	5	0	39	12	2	3	12	11	37	50	49	36
7	**BOLTON WANDERERS**	34	10	3	4	38	11	2	7	8	21	30	59	41	34
8	Barnsley	34	10	5	2	25	12	1	5	11	13	45	38	57	32
9	Gainsborough Trinity	34	10	2	5	34	17	4	1	12	19	43	53	60	31
10	Bradford City	34	8	5	4	30	25	4	2	11	15	34	45	59	31
11	Chesterfield Town	34	8	5	4	22	12	3	3	11	15	33	37	45	30
12	Lincoln City	34	9	4	4	25	18	2	4	12	12	40	41	58	30
13	Burslem Port Vale	34	10	3	4	44	20	0	6	11	10	32	54	52	29
14	Burton United	34	8	6	3	33	16	3	1	13	12	45	45	61	29
15	Blackpool	34	8	2	7	25	27	3	3	11	15	40	40	67	27
16	Stockport County	34	7	7	3	28	23	1	4	12	12	49	40	72	27
17	Glossop	34	7	4	6	42	25	3	2	12	15	39	57	64	26
18	Leicester Fosse	34	5	8	4	26	21	1	2	14	16	61	42	82	22

1904/05 2nd in Division Two (promoted)

#			Opponent	Res	Scorers	Abbott H	Boyd J	Broomfield H	Clifford R	Davies D	Eccles GD	Featherstone F	Greenhalgh S	McEwan M	Marsh S	Ostick C	Shaw J	Shepherd A	Stokes D	Struthers R	Taylor A	Taylor R	White W	Wilson T	Yenson W
1	Sep	3	Bristol City	4-3	Marsh(2), Yenson, Clifford		6		4	1			5		8	2				7		3	11	10	9
2		10	BURNLEY	4-0	White, Marsh(2), Yenson		6		4	1			5		8	2				7		3	11	10	9
3		17	Manchester United	2-1	White(2)		6		4	1			5		8	2				7		3	11	10	9
4		24	GRIMSBY TOWN	4-1	R.Taylor, White(3,1pen)		6		4	1			5		8	2				7		3	11	10	9
5	Oct	1	Glossop North End	2-1	Stokes, White		6	1	4				5		8	2				7		3	11	10	9
6		8	BLACKPOOL	3-0	R.Taylor, Marsh Greenhalgh		6	1	4				5		8	2				7		3	11	10	9
7		15	Chesterfield	0-1			6	1	4				5		8	2			7			3	11	10	9
8		22	DONCASTER ROVERS	2-0	R.Taylor, Yenson	10	6	1	4				5		8	2				7		3	11		9
9		29	Bradford City	1-2	Marsh		4	1	6				5		8	2				7		3	11		9
10	Nov	5	GAINSBOROUGH TRIN.	5-1	White(2), Marsh(2), Greenhalgh		6		4	1			5		8	2		9		7		3	10	11	
11		12	LINCOLN CITY	4-1	Shepherd, Boyd, White, Wilson		6		4	1			5		8	2		9		7		3	10	11	
12		19	BURTON UNITED	7-1	Marsh(3), White(3), Shepherd		6		4	1			5		8	2		9		7		3	10	11	
13	Dec	3	LIVERPOOL	2-0	Marsh(2,1pen)		6		4	1			5		8	2		9		7		3	10	11	
14		10	Doncaster Rovers	4-0	White(3), Shepherd				4	1			5		8	2		9		7	6	3	10	11	
15		17	Port Vale	2-1	White(pen), Wilson		6		4	1	2		5		8			9		7		3	11	10	
16		24	WEST BROM ALBION	2-1	Marsh, Wilson		6		4	1	2		5		8			9		7		3	11	10	
17		26	Lincoln City	2-0	White, Marsh		6		4	1	2		5		8			9		7		3	11	10	
18		27	Leicester Fosse	4-2	Stokes, White(2), Marsh		6			1	2		5		8		4	9		7		3	11	10	
19		31	BRISTOL CITY	3-1	Shepherd(2), Marsh		6		4	1	2		5		8			9		7		3	11	10	
20	Jan	2	BARNSLEY	2-1	Shepherd(2)		6		4	1		7	5		8	2		9				3	11	10	
21		3	MANCHESTER UNITED	2-4	Shepherd, Marsh		6		4	1	2		5		8			9		7		3	11	10	
22		/	Burnley	1-0	R.Taylor		4		2	1					8			9		7	6	3	10	11	5
23		21	Grimsby Town	2-2	Marsh, Shepherd		6		4	1	2		5		8			9		7		3	10	11	
24		28	GLOSSOP NORTH END	4-0	Featherstone, Marsh, White, Boyd		6		4	1		9	5		8	2				7		3	10	11	
25	Feb	11	CHESTERFIELD	4-3	Marsh(2,1pen), Wilson, Shepherd		6		4	1			5		8	2		9		7		3	10	11	
26		25	BRADFORD CITY	2-0	Marsh(2), Yenson, Clifford		6		4	1			5	11	8			9		7	2	3	10		
27	Mar	18	Burton United	1-0	Stokes		6	1	4				5		8	2		9		7		3	10	11	
28		25	LEICESTER FOSSE	0-1			6	1	4				5		8	2		9		7		3	10	11	
29	Apr	1	Liverpool	1-1	Stokes		6	1	4				5		8	2		9		7		3	10	11	
30		12	Gainsborough Trinity	4-0	Shepherd(2), White, Marsh		6	1	4				5		8	2		9		7		3	10	11	
31		15	PORT VALE	3-1	White(2), Shepherd		6	1	4						8	2		9		7		3	10	11	5
32		21	Blackpool	2-0	Stokes, Shepherd		6	1	4				5		8	2		9		7		3	10	11	
33		22	West Bromwich Albion	1-0	Shepherd		6	1	4				5		8	2		9		7		3	10	11	
34		24	Barnsley	1-2	Marsh		6	1	4				5		8	2		9		7		3	10	11	
Apps						1	32	13	32	21	6	2	32	1	32	24	4	24	32	33	3	19	33	19	11
Goals							2		1			1	2		26			15	5			4	24	4	3

Ave. Home Attendance: 12,275

F.A. Cup

#			Opponent	Res	Scorers	Att	Boyd J	Clifford R	Davies D	Greenhalgh S	Marsh S	Ostick C	Shepherd A	Struthers R	Taylor A	Taylor R	White W	Wilson T
1	Feb	4	BRISTOL ROVERS	1-1	Marsh	10000	6	4	1	5	8	2	9	7		3	10	11
1r		8	Bristol Rovers	3-0	Stokes, Shepherd, OG	8000		4	1	5	8		9	7	2	3 6	10	11
2		18	Manchester City	2-1	Shepherd, White	37448	6	4	1	5	8		9	7	2	3	10	11
3	Mar	4	NEWCASTLE UNITED	0-2		20000	6	4	1	5	8		9	7	2	3	10	11

Lancashire Cup

1	Oct	10	MANCHESTER UNITED	4-2
2	Jan	9	BURY	5-1
SF	Mar	7	Everton	1-2

Manchester Cup

1	Jan	23	Bury	1-1
1r	Feb	6	BURY	1-2

Other Games

1	Sep	12	Wrexham	3-0
2	Mar	11	Corinthians	1-1
3	Apr	29	Bolton St. Lukes	8-2

Final Table

	FINAL TABLE	Pl.	Home W	D	L	F	A	Away W	D	L	F	A	F. (Total)	A.	Pts
1	Liverpool	34	14	3	0	60	12	13	1	3	33	13	93	25	58
2	BOLTON WANDERERS	34	15	0	2	53	16	12	2	3	34	16	87	32	56
3	Manchester United	34	16	0	1	60	10	8	5	4	21	20	81	30	53
4	Bristol City	34	12	3	2	40	12	7	1	9	26	33	66	45	42
5	Chesterfield Town	34	9	6	2	26	11	5	5	7	18	24	44	35	39
6	Gainsborough Trinity	34	11	4	2	32	15	3	4	10	29	43	61	58	36
7	Barnsley	34	11	4	2	29	13	3	1	13	9	43	38	56	33
8	Bradford City	34	8	5	4	31	20	4	3	10	14	29	45	49	32
9	Lincoln City	34	9	4	4	31	16	3	3	11	11	24	42	40	31
10	West Bromwich Alb.	34	8	2	7	28	20	5	2	10	28	28	56	48	30
11	Burnley	34	10	1	6	31	21	2	5	10	12	31	43	52	30
12	Glossop	34	7	5	5	23	14	3	5	9	14	32	37	46	30
13	Grimsby Town	34	9	3	5	22	14	2	5	10	11	32	33	46	30
14	Leicester Fosse	34	8	3	6	30	25	3	4	10	10	30	40	55	29
15	Blackpool	34	8	6	4	26	15	1	5	11	10	33	36	48	28
16	Burslem Port Vale	34	7	4	6	28	25	3	3	11	19	47	47	72	27
17	Burton United	34	7	2	8	20	29	1	2	14	10	55	30	84	20
18	Doncaster Rovers	34	3	2	12	12	32	0	0	17	11	49	23	81	8

1905/06 6th in Division One

League (Division One)

No		Date	Opponent	Score	Scorers
1	Sep	2	SHEFFIELD UNITED	1-2	Wilson
2		9	Notts County	3-3	Marsh, Greenhalgh, White
3		16	STOKE	1-2	Marsh
4		23	Wolves	0-2	
5		30	Woolwich Arsenal	0-0	
6	Oct	7	BLACKBURN ROVERS	1-0	Shepherd
7		14	Sunderland	3-3	Shepherd(2), McEwan
8		21	BIRMINGHAM	0-1	
9		28	Everton	1-3	White
10	Nov	4	DERBY COUNTY	5-0	Shepherd, Marsh(3), White
11		11	Sheffield Wednesday	2-1	McEwan, Stoke
12		18	NOTTINGHAM FOREST	6-0	Shepherd(4), Marsh, White
13		25	Manchester City	1-3	Shepherd
14	Dec	2	BURY	4-0	McEwan, Marsh, White(2)
15		9	Middlesbrough	4-4	White(2), Shepherd
16		16	PRESTON NORTH END	1-2	Shepherd
17		23	Newcastle United	1-2	Stokes
18		25	Liverpool	2-2	Shepherd(2)
19		26	Aston Villa	1-1	White
20		30	Sheffield Wednesday	2-5	Stokes, Shepherd
21	Jan	1	WOOLWICH ARSENAL	6-1	White(2), Marsh(2), Shepherd, McEwan
22		2	ASTON VILLA	4-1	White, Stokes, Marsh, Shepherd
23		20	Stoke	2-1	Marsh, White
24		27	WOLVES	3-2	Shepherd, White, (og)
25	Feb	3	NOTTS COUNTY	2-0	Shepherd(2)
26		17	SUNDERLAND	6-2	Clifford, Shepherd(4), White
27	Mar	3	EVERTON	3-2	White(2), McEwan
28		10	Derby County	1-0	McEwan
29		17	SHEFFIELD WEDNESDAY	1-0	Marsh
30		24	Nottingham Forest	0-4	
31		26	Birmingham	5-2	White(2), Atkinson, Stokes(2)
32		31	MANCHESTER CITY	1-3	White
33	Apr	2	Blackburn Rovers	1-4	White
34		7	Bury	1-2	White
35		14	MIDDLESBROUGH	2-1	White(2)
36		16	LIVERPOOL	3-2	Shepherd(2), McEwan
37		21	Preston North End	0-3	
38		28	NEWCASTLE UNITED	1-1	White

Ave. Home Attendance: 20,525

Appearances and Goals

	Atkinson J	Baverstone H	Beckett C	Boyd J	Broomfield H	Clifford R	Davies D	Freebairn A	Gaskell A	Greenhalgh S	King H	Lawrie H	McEwan M	Marsh S	Napier S	Ostick C	Robertson JN	Shepherd A	Stanley J	Stokes D	Struthers R	Taylor R	White W	Wilson T	Wolstenholme T
Apps	2	37	1	38	3	27	35	11	5	4	1	3	37	33	4	4	14	31	1	38	28	16	38	1	6
Goals	1					1		1					7	12				26		6			25	1	

One own goal

F.A. Cup

		Date	Opponent	Score	Att.
1	Jan	13	Middlesbrough	0-3	10000

Players: Baverstone 2, Boyd 6, Davies 1, Clifford(?) ..., McEwan 11, Marsh 8, Shepherd 9, Stokes 7, White 10, Wolstenholme 4

Lancashire Cup

		Date	Opponent	Score
1	Sep	19	BURNLEY	4-0
2	Oct	2	BLACKBURN ROVERS	5-2
SF		16	Bury	1-2

Manchester Cup

		Date	Opponent	Score
1	Jan	23	MANCHESTER CITY	1-1
1r		30	Manchester City	1-1
1/2r	Fri	12	Manchester City*	1-1
1/3r		19	Manchester City+	1-0
SF	Mar	9	STOCKPORT COUNTY	4-1
F		30	Bury*	2-0

* Played at Clayton.   + Played at Weaste

Other Games

		Date	Opponent	Score
1	Sep	11	Brierley Hill	4-1
2	Feb	24	West Ham	3-5
3	Mar	28	NORTHERN NOMADS	0-2
4	Apr	8	Pendlebury	0-1
5		20	CELTIC	1-3
6		22	Blackpool	1-1

FINAL TABLE

		Pl.	Home W	D	L	F	A	Away W	D	L	F	A	F. (Total)	A.	Pts
1	Liverpool	38	14	3	2	49	15	9	2	8	30	31	79	46	51
2	Preston North End	38	12	5	2	36	15	5	8	6	18	24	54	39	47
3	Sheffield Wed.	38	12	5	2	40	20	6	3	10	23	32	63	52	44
4	Newcastle United	38	12	4	3	49	23	6	3	10	25	25	74	48	43
5	Manchester City	38	11	2	6	46	23	8	3	8	27	31	73	54	43
6	BOLTON WANDERERS	38	13	1	5	51	22	4	6	9	30	45	81	67	41
7	Birmingham	38	14	2	3	49	20	3	5	11	16	39	65	59	41
8	Aston Villa	38	13	2	4	51	19	4	4	11	21	37	72	56	40
9	Blackburn Rovers	38	10	5	4	34	18	6	3	10	20	34	54	52	40
10	Stoke	38	12	5	2	41	15	4	2	13	13	40	54	55	39
11	Everton	38	12	1	6	44	30	3	6	10	26	36	70	66	37
12	Woolwich Arsenal	38	12	4	3	43	21	3	3	13	19	43	62	64	37
13	Sheffield United	38	10	4	5	33	23	5	2	12	24	39	57	62	36
14	Sunderland	38	13	2	4	40	21	2	3	14	21	49	61	70	35
15	Derby County	38	10	5	4	27	16	4	2	13	12	42	39	58	35
16	Notts County	38	8	9	2	34	21	3	3	13	21	50	55	71	34
17	Bury	38	8	5	6	30	26	3	5	11	27	48	57	74	32
18	Middlesbrough	38	10	4	5	41	23	0	7	12	15	48	56	71	31
19	Nottingham Forest	38	11	2	6	40	27	2	3	14	18	52	58	79	31
20	Wolverhampton W.	38	7	5	7	38	28	1	2	16	20	71	58	99	23

1905
Boyd, Stokes, Marsh, Baverstock, Greenhalgh, Davies, Shepherd, Struthers, Taylor, White, McEwan

1906
(Back) Lewis (Trainer), Settle, Bacerstock, Davies, Gaskill, Broomfield, Clifford, Boyd, Struthers, Tait, Somerville
(Middle) Ward, Dempsey, Cameron, Marsh, Shepherd, White, Hodgkinson, Hamer
(Front) Stokes, McEwen

1906/07 6th in Division One

#		Date	Opponent	Score	Scorers	Atkinson J	Bates WE	Baverstock H	Boyd J	Broomfield H	Cameron WS	Clifford R	Davies D	Dempsey E	Edmondsdon JH	Freebairn A	Gaskell A	McEwan M	Marsh S	Owen JR	Ryder G	Shepherd AS	Slater J	Stanley J	Stokes D	Struthers R	Taylor R	Thorp J	Weaver W	White W	Wolstenholme T
1	Sep	1	Notts County	0-0			2				8	5	1				4	11				9								10	
2		8	SHEFFIELD UNITED	6-1	White,McEwan,Shepherd(3),Cameron			2	6		8	5	1				4	11				9				7	3			10	
3		15	DERBY COUNTY	1-0	Boyd			2	6		8	5	1				4	11				9				7	3			10	
4		22	Manchester United	2-1	Shepherd, White			2	6		8	5	1				4	11				9				7	3			10	
5		29	STOKE	1-1	Shepherd			2	6		8	5	1				4	11				9				7	3			10	
6	Oct	6	Blackburn Rovers	3-2	White, Cameron, Clifford			2	6		9	5	1	8			4	11								7	3			10	
7		13	SUNDERLAND	1-0	White			2	6	1	9	5		8			4	11								7	3			10	
8		20	Birmingham	2-4	Shepherd(3)			2	6		8	5	1				4	11				9				7	3			10	
9		27	EVERTON	1-3	Shepherd			2	6			5	1	8			4	11				9				7	3			10	
10	Nov	3	Woolwich Arsenal	2-2	Clifford, Cameron			2	6	1	10	5					4	11				9	3			11				8	
11		10	SHEFFIELD WEDNESDAY	0-0				2	6	1	8	5					4	11				9		3	7					10	
12		17	Bury	3-2	Stokes, Marsh(3)			2	6		9	5	1				4	11	8					3	7					10	
13		24	MANCHESTER CITY	1-1	Shepherd			2	6			5	1				4	11	8			9		3	7					10	
14	Dec	1	Middlesbrough	0-0				2				5	1				4	11	8		9			3	7					10	6
15		8	Preston North End	1-3	Stokes, Marsh(3)			2				5	1				4	11	8					3	7		9			10	6
16		15	Newcastle United	0-4				2	6	1		5					4	11	8		9			3	7					10	
17		22	ASTON VILLA	1-2	Dempsey			2	6	1		5		8			4	11				9		3	7					10	
18		24	Stoke	0-3				2	6	1		5		8				11				9		3	7					10	4
19		26	Liverpool	2-0	Owen, Stokes			2	6			5	1				4	11	8	10				3	7					9	
20		29	NOTTS COUNTY	0-0				2	6			5	1				4	11	8	10				3	7					9	
21	Jan	1	LIVERPOOL	3-0	Stokes, Gaskell, Owen			2	6			5			1		4	11		8		9		3	7					10	
22		2	PRESTON NORTH END	3-0	Shepherd(2), White			2	6			5			1		4	11		8		9		3	7					10	
23		5	Sheffield United	1-2	White			2	6			5			1		4	11		8		9		3	7					10	
24		19	Derby County	1-0	Shepherd			2	6			5			1		4	11	8	10		9		3	7						
25		26	MANCHESTER UNITED	0-1		5		2	6					7	1		4	11		8		9		3						10	
26	Feb	9	BLACKBURN ROVERS	5-2	Clifford,Owen(2),White,Shepherd			2	6			5			1		4	11	8	7		9		3						10	
27		16	Sunderland	2-1	Shepherd, Weaver			2	6			5			1		4	11		8		9		3					7	10	
28	Mar	2	Everton	0-1				2	6		8	5			1		4	11				9	3		7					10	
29		9	BURY	1-0	White			2	6		9	5			1		4		8					3	7			11		10	
30		11	BIRMINGHAM	2-3	Owen, White			2	6		9				1	5	4		8					3	7			11		10	
31		16	Sheffield Wednesday	0-2				2	6		9	5			1		4	11		8				3	7					10	
32		27	WOOLWICH ARSENAL	3-0	White(2), Shepherd			2	6			5			1		4	11	8			9		3	7					10	
33		29	BRISTOL CITY	1-2	White			2	6			5			1		4	11	8			9		3	7					10	
34		30	Manchester City	1-1	Stokes			2				5			1		4	11	8			9		3	7		6			10	
35	Apr	2	Bristol City	2-1	Marsh, Boyd			2	6			5			1		4		8			9		3	7				11	10	
36		6	MIDDLESBROUGH	1-0	Marsh			2				5			1		4		8			9		3	7		6		11	10	
37		20	NEWCASTLE UNITED	4-2	Marsh(2), White, Gaskell			2	6			5			1		4	11	8			9		3	7					10	
38		27	Aston Villa	2-0	Shepherd, White			2	6			5			1		4	11	8			9		3	7					10	
Apps						1	2	38	34	6	14	36	14	7	18	1	37	35	15	19	2	21	2	27	33	9	2	2	4	36	3
Goals									2		3	3		1			2	1	6	5		16			5				1	14	

Ave. Home Attendance: 15,225

F.A. Cup

#		Date	Opponent	Score	Scorers	Att.	Baverstock H	Boyd J	Cameron WS	Clifford R	Edmondsdon JH	Gaskell A	McEwan M	Owen JR	Shepherd AS	Stanley J	Stokes D	White W
1	Jan	12	BRIGHTON & H.A.	3-1	Stokes, Clifford, Shepherd	19330	2	6		5	1	4	11	8	9	3	7	10
2	Feb	2	ASTON VILLA	2-0	Shepherd(2)	40367	2	6		5	1	4	11	8	9	3	7	10
3		23	Everton	0-0		52455	2	6		5	1	4	11	8	9	3	7	10
3r		27	EVERTON	0-3		54470	2	6	9	5	1	4	11	8		3	7	10

Lancashire Cup

#		Date	Opponent	Score
1	Oct	1	MANCHESTER CITY	4-3
2		16	DARWEN	3-0
SF	Nov	5	Blackburn Rovers*	0-2

* Played at Clayton

Manchester Cup

#		Date	Opponent	Score
1	Mar	18	Stockport County	0-0
1r	Apr	17	STOCKPORT COUNTY	1-2

Other Games

#		Date	Opponent	Score
1	Mar	21	Barnsley	1-1
2	Apr	13	Corinthians	0-0
3		15	Brighton & H.A.	2-2
4		25	Pendlebury	0-1

	FINAL TABLE	Pl.	Home			Away			F.	A.	Pts
			W	D	L	F A	W	D	L	F A	(Total)
1	Newcastle United	38	18	1	0	51 12	4	6	9	23 34	74 46 51
2	Bristol City	38	12	3	4	37 18	8	5	6	29 29	66 47 48
3	Everton	38	16	2	1	50 10	4	3	12	20 36	70 46 45
4	Sheffield United	38	13	4	2	36 17	4	7	8	21 38	57 55 45
5	Aston Villa	38	13	4	2	51 19	6	2	11	27 33	78 52 44
6	BOLTON WANDERERS	38	10	4	5	35 18	8	4	7	24 29	59 47 44
7	Woolwich Arsenal	38	15	1	3	38 15	5	3	11	28 44	66 59 44
8	Manchester United	38	10	6	3	33 15	7	2	10	20 41	53 56 42
9	Birmingham	38	13	5	1	41 17	2	3	14	11 35	52 52 38
10	Sunderland	38	10	4	5	42 31	4	5	10	23 35	65 66 37
11	Middlesbrough	38	11	2	6	33 21	4	4	11	23 42	56 63 36
12	Blackburn Rovers	38	10	3	6	40 25	4	4	11	16 34	56 59 35
13	Sheffield Wed.	38	8	5	6	33 26	4	6	9	16 34	49 60 35
14	Preston North End	38	13	4	2	35 19	1	3	15	9 38	44 57 35
15	Liverpool	38	9	2	8	45 32	4	5	10	19 33	64 65 33
16	Bury	38	9	4	6	30 23	4	2	13	28 45	58 68 32
17	Manchester City	38	7	7	5	29 25	3	5	11	24 52	53 77 32
18	Notts County	38	6	9	4	31 18	2	6	11	15 32	46 50 31
19	Derby County	38	8	6	5	29 19	1	3	15	12 40	41 59 27
20	Stoke	38	7	6	6	27 22	1	4	14	14 42	41 64 26

1907/08   19th in Division One (relegated)

#	Date	Opponent	Score	Scorers	Baverstock H	Boyd J	Cameron WS	Clifford R	Davies D	Edmondson JH	Evans WP	Gaskell A	Gee J	Greenhalgh S	McClarence JP	McEwan M	Marsh S	Owen JR	Rollinson F	Ryder G	Shepherd A	Slater J	Stanley J	Stokes D	Stuart W	Tierney H	White W
1	Sep 7	BURY	3-6	Shepherd(3)	2	6		5		1		4				11	8				9		3	7			10
2	14	Aston Villa	0-2		2	6		5		1		4				11	8			10	9		3	7			10
3	21	LIVERPOOL	0-4		2	6		5		1		4				11	8				9		3	7			10
4	28	Middlesbrough	1-0	Shepherd	2	6		5		1		4				11	8				9		3	7			10
5	Oct 5	SHEFFIELD UNITED	1-1	White		6		5		1		4				11		8			9	2	3	7			10
6	12	Chelsea	3-1	White(3)		6		5		1		4				11		8		10		2	3	7			9
7	19	NOTTINGHAM FOREST	1-0	Owen		6		5		1		4				11		8		10		2	3	7			9
8	26	Manchester United	1-2	Boyd		6		5		1		4				11		8			9	2	3	7			10
9	Nov 2	BLACKBURN ROVERS	3-1	Owen, Shepherd, White		6		5		1		4				11		8			9	2	3	7			10
10	9	Newcastle United	0-3			6		5		1		4				11		8			9	2	3	7			10
11	16	Birmingham	1-2	White	2		6	5		1		4				11		8			9		3	7			10
12	23	EVERTON	3-0	White(2), Shepherd	2	6		5		1		4				11		8			9		3	7			10
13	30	Sunderland	2-1	Shepherd(2)	2	6		5		1		4				11		8			9		3	7			10
14	Dec 7	WOOLWICH ARSENAL	3-1	Shepherd(3)	2	6		3		1			4	11	5	8					9			7			10
15	14	Sheffield Wednesday	2-5	White, Shepherd	2	6				1			4	11	5	8					9			7			10
16	21	BRISTOL CITY	1-2	Shepherd	2	6		5		1		4				11		8			9			7			10
17	25	Preston North East	0-2		2	6		5		1		4				11		8			9			7			10
18	26	Mancheser City	0-1		2	6				1		4	5			11		8			9		3	7			10
19	28	Notts County	1-0	Shepherd	2	6				1		4	5			11		8		10	9		3	7			
20	30	Sheffield United	0-1		2	6				1		4	5			11		8			9		3	7			
21	Jan 1	MANCHESTER CITY	2-0	Shepherd, Gee	2	6	8	5		1			4			11					9		3	7			10
22	2	PRESTON NORTH END	2-0	Owen, Cameron	2	6	8	5		1		4				11		9					3	7			
23	4	Bury	2-2	Cameron, Owen	2	6	8	5		1		4				11		9					3	7			10
24	18	Liverpool	0-1		2	6	8	5		1		4				11		9					3	7			10
25	25	MIDDLESBROUGH	1-1	Owen	2	6	8	5	1			4				11		9					3	7			10
26	Feb 8	CHELSEA	1-2	White	2		8	5	1			4		6		11		10					3	7			9
27	15	Nottingham Forest	0-1			6	8	2	1		10			8	4	11							3	7		5	
28	29	Blackburn Rovers	2-3	Shepherd, McEwan	2	6	8	5				4				11		10	1		9		3	7			
29	Mar 14	BIRMINGHAM	1-0	Marsh	2	6		5	1			4				11	8				9		3	7			10
30	21	Everton	1-2		2	6		5	1			4				11	8				9		3	7	10		
31	28	SUNDERLAND	2-3	White, McClarence	2	6		5	1			4			9	11	8						3	7			10
32	Apr 1	NEWCASTLE UNITED	4-0	White, Shepherd(3)		6		5	1			4			8	11					9	2	3	7			10
33	4	Woolwich Arsenal	1-1	Shepherd		6	8	5	1			4				11		10			9	2	3	7			
34	11	SHEFFIELD WEDNESDAY	2-1	Shepherd, Stokes		6		5	1			4			8	11					9	2	3	7			10
35	17	ASTON VILLA	3-1	Shepherd(2), McClarence		6		5	1			4			8	11					9	2	3	7			10
36	18	Bristol City	0-2			6		5	1			4			8	11					9	2	3	7			10
37	22	MANCHESTER UNITED	2-2	White, Shepherd		6		5	1			4			8	11					9	2	3	7			10
38	25	NOTTS COUNTY	0-1			6		5	1			4			8	11					9	2	3	7			10
		Apps			24	34	12	33	13	24	1	18	6	28	8	32	9	22	1	2	29	27	23	38	1	1	32
		Goals				1	2						1		2	1	1	5			25			1			13

Ave. Home Attendance: 14,450

F.A. Cup

#	Date	Opponent	Score	Scorers	Att	Baverstock H	Boyd J	Cameron WS	Clifford R	Davies D	Edmondson JH	Evans WP	Gaskell A	Gee J	Greenhalgh S	McClarence JP	McEwan M	Marsh S	Owen JR	Rollinson F	Ryder G	Shepherd A	Slater J	Stanley J	Stokes D	Stuart W	Tierney H	White W
1	Jan 11	WOKING	5-0	Cameron,Stoke,Owen,White,McEwan	8000	2	6	8	5		1		4				11		9					3	7			10
2	Feb 1	Notts County	1-1	McEwan	14000	2	6	8	5		1		4				11		9					3	7			10
2r	5	Notts County	2-1*	Cameron, White	17445	2	6	8	5		1		4				11		10					3	7			9
3	22	EVERTON	3-3	Marsh(3)	31113	2	6		5		1		4		10		11	8						3	7			9
3r	26	Everton	1-3*	Greenhalgh	32000	2	6	9	5		1		4				11	8						3	7			10

* After extra time

Lancashire Cup

#	Date	Opponent	Score
1	Sep 30	Blackburn Rovers	4-3
2	Oct 14	Manchester United	0-2

Manchester Cup

#	Date	Opponent	Score
1	Dec 2	STOCKPORT COUNTY	2-2
1r	Mar 2	Stockport County	1-4

Other Games

#	Date	Opponent	Score
1	Sep 18	Whitchurch	3-7
2	Apr 22	Eccles Borough	0-1

FINAL TABLE

		Pl.	Home					Away					F.	A.	Pts
			W	D	L	F	A	W	D	L	F	A	(Total)		
1	Manchester United	38	15	1	3	43	19	8	5	6	38	29	81	48	52
2	Aston Villa	38	9	6	4	47	24	8	3	8	30	35	77	59	43
3	Manchester City	38	12	5	2	36	19	4	6	9	26	35	62	54	43
4	Newcastle United	38	11	4	4	41	24	4	8	7	24	30	65	54	42
5	Sheffield Wed.	38	14	0	5	50	25	5	4	10	23	39	73	64	42
6	Middlesbrough	38	12	2	5	32	16	5	5	9	22	29	54	45	41
7	Bury	38	8	7	4	29	22	6	4	9	29	39	58	61	39
8	Liverpool	38	11	2	6	43	24	5	4	10	25	37	68	61	38
9	Nottingham Forest	38	11	6	2	42	21	2	5	12	17	41	59	62	37
10	Bristol City	38	8	7	4	29	21	4	5	10	29	40	58	61	36
11	Everton	38	11	4	4	34	24	4	2	13	24	40	58	64	36
12	Preston North End	38	9	7	3	33	18	3	5	11	14	35	47	53	36
13	Chelsea	38	8	3	8	30	35	6	5	8	23	27	53	62	36
14	Blackburn Rovers	38	10	7	2	35	23	2	5	12	16	40	51	63	36
14	Woolwich Arsenal	38	9	8	2	32	18	3	4	12	19	45	51	63	36
16	Sunderland	38	11	2	6	53	31	5	1	13	25	44	78	75	35
17	Sheffield United	38	8	6	5	27	22	4	5	10	25	36	52	58	35
18	Notts County	38	9	3	7	24	19	4	5	10	15	32	39	51	34
19	**BOLTON WANDERERS**	38	10	3	6	35	26	4	2	13	17	32	52	58	33
20	Birmingham	38	6	6	7	22	28	3	6	10	18	32	40	60	30

1907
(Back) Lewis (Trainer), Ward, Hodgkinson, Hamer, Tate, Settle, Somerville
(Middle) Edmonson, Stanley, Gaskell, Slater, Baverstock, Clifford, Davies, Boyd
(Front) Stokes, Greenhalgh, Marsh, Shepherd, Owen, White, McEwan

1909
(Back) Gaskell, Robinson, Baverstock, Edmondson, Slater, Barber
(Middle) Greenhalgh, Hogan, Hughes, Owen, McEwen
(Front) Stokes, Hunter

1908/09 1st in Division Two (promoted)

Manager: J.Somerville

#		Date	Opponent	Score	Scorers
1	Sep	2	Birmingham	0-2	
2		5	Barnsley	1-0	McClarence
3		12	GAINSBOROUGH TRIN	4-0	Baverstock, McClarence(2), White
4		14	HULL CITY	1-0	Stuart
5		15	WEST BROM ALBION	1-1	Owen
6		19	Tottenham Hotspur	1-2	Woods
7		26	GRIMSBY TOWN	2-0	Shepherd, McClarence
8	Oct	3	Hull City	0-2	
9		10	FULHAM	0-0	
10		17	Derby County	0-1	
11		24	BURNLEY	2-1	Wood, McEwan
12		31	Blackpool	2-1	Shepherd, Barber
13	Nov	7	BRADFORD	0-1	
14		14	Chesterfield	2-0	Hogan(2)
15		21	WOLVES	1-1	Shepherd
16		28	Glossop North End	2-0	Hogan(2)
17	Dec	5	OLDHAM ATHLETIC	3-0	Greenhalgh, Hughes, Hogan
18		12	Stockport County	0-1	
19		19	CLAPTON ORIENT	2-0	Hughes(2)
20		25	LEEDS CITY	2-0	Hogan, Hughes
21		26	Leeds City	2-1	Hughes, Stokes
22	Jan	1	BIRMINGHAM	2-1	Hughes, Hogan
23		2	BARNSLEY	3-0	Owen(2), Hughes
24		9	Gainsborough Trinity	1-2	Greenhalgh
25		23	TOTTENHAM HOTSPUR	0-1	
26		30	Grimsby Town	0-1	
27	Feb	13	Fulham	2-1	Hughes, Hogan
28		20	CHESTERFIELD	4-0	Hunter, Barber, Owen, Hughes
29		27	Burnley	2-1	Hughes, Hunter
30	Mar	6	BLACKPOOL	3-1	Owen(2), Hunter
31		13	Bradford	2-1	Greenhalgh, Hogan
32		27	Wolves	2-1	Hogan, Hughes
33	Apr	3	GLOSSOP NORTH END	2-0	Owen(2)
34		10	Oldham Athletic	1-1	Hogan
35		12	West Bromwich Albion	0-2	
36		17	STOCKPORT COUNTY	4-1	Hughes(2), Hunter(2)
37		24	Clapton Orient	2-0	Hughes(2)
38		30	DERBY COUNTY	1-0	Hughes

Ave. Home Attendance: 12,250

Appearances and Goals

Player	Apps	Goals
Barber T	20	2
Baverstock H	37	1
Boyd J	4	
Clifford R	11	
Craven R	2	
Edmondson JH	38	
Gaskell A	35	
Greenhalgh S	32	3
Griffiths D	4	
Grundy WA	2	
Hogan J	24	11
Hughes W	21	16
Hunter WB	14	5
McEwan M	21	1
McClarence JP	7	4
Marsh S	26	
Owen JR	10	8
Robinson WS	10	
Shepherd A	31	3
Slater J	1	
Smith J	8	
Stanley J	34	1
Stokes D	2	
Stott W	5	
Stuart W	6	1
White W	1	1
Whiteside E	1	
Whiteside J	1	
Woods S	4	2

F.A. Cup

	Jan	16	West Bromwich Albion	1-3	Hunter	19000
1						

Lancashire Cup

1	Oct	12	MANCHESTER UNITED	0-3

Manchester Cup

1	Jan	25	Glossop	3-1
SF	Mar	15	MANCHESTER CITY	1-0
F	Apr	29	Stockport County*	3-0

* Played at Hyde Road

Other Games

1	Nov	9	Blackburn Rovers	1-3
2	Apr	26	Woking	4-1
3	May	16	HBS Hague	4-1
4		20	Sporta Rotterdam	3-0
5		23	Swallows FC	6-0
6		30	A.F.S.	8-1
7	Jun	1	Dordrecht	10-1

FINAL TABLE

		Pl.	Home W	D	L	F	A	Away W	D	L	F	A	F. (Total)	A.	Pts
1	BOLTON WANDERERS	38	14	3	2	37	8	10	1	8	22	20	59	28	52
2	Tottenham Hotspur	38	12	5	2	42	12	8	6	5	25	20	67	32	51
3	West Bromwich Alb.	38	13	5	1	35	9	6	8	5	21	18	56	27	51
4	Hull City	38	14	2	3	44	15	5	4	10	19	24	63	39	44
5	Derby County	38	13	5	1	38	11	3	6	10	17	30	55	41	43
6	Oldham Athletic	38	14	4	1	39	9	3	2	14	16	34	55	43	40
7	Wolverhampton W.	38	10	6	3	32	12	4	5	10	24	36	56	48	39
8	Glossop	38	11	5	3	35	17	4	3	12	22	36	57	53	38
9	Gainsborough Trinity	38	12	3	4	30	20	3	5	11	19	50	49	70	38
10	Fulham	38	8	4	7	39	26	5	7	7	19	22	58	48	37
11	Birmingham	38	10	6	3	35	21	4	3	12	23	40	58	61	37
12	Leeds City	38	12	3	4	35	19	2	4	13	8	34	43	53	35
13	Grimsby Town	38	9	5	5	23	14	5	2	12	18	40	41	54	35
14	Burnley	38	8	4	7	33	28	5	3	11	18	30	51	58	33
15	Clapton Orient	38	7	7	5	25	19	5	2	12	12	30	37	49	33
16	Bradford Park Ave.	38	9	4	6	30	25	4	4	11	21	34	51	59	32
17	Barnsley	38	11	3	5	36	19	0	7	12	12	38	48	57	32
18	Stockport County	38	11	2	6	25	19	3	1	15	14	52	39	71	31
19	Chesterfield Town	38	10	3	6	30	28	1	5	13	7	39	37	67	30
20	Blackpool	38	9	6	4	30	22	0	5	14	16	46	46	68	29

1909/10 20th in Division One (relegated)

Manager: W.Settle

#				Score	Scorers
1	Sep	1	Newcastle United	0-1	
2		4	ASTON VILLA	1-2	Hughes
3		6	LIVERPOOL	1-2	Hogan
4		7	NEWCASTLE UNITED	0-4	
5		11	Sheffield United	2-2	Hughes, Hunter
6		18	WOOLWICH ARSENAL	3-0	Hunter, Hughes, Marsh
7		25	Middlesbrough	2-1	Hughes(2)
8	Oct	2	Chelsea	2-3	Hogan, Hunter
9		9	BLACKBURN ROVERS	1-2	Hunter
10		16	Nottingham Forest	0-2	
11		23	SUNDERLAND	2-1	Lockett, Hunter
12		30	Everton	1-3	Lockett
13	Nov	6	MANCHESTER UNITED	2-3	Hunter, Lockett
14		13	Bradford City	0-1	
15		27	Bristol City	0-1	
16	Dec	4	BURY	1-3	Hunter
17		11	Tottenham Hotspur	1-1	Baverstock(pen)
18		18	PRESTON NORTH END	3-1	Hughes, Baverstock(2pens)
19		25	Liverpool	0-3	
20	Jan	1	NOTTS COUNTY	3-4	Jones(2), Owen
21		3	SHEFFIELD WEDNESDAY	0-2	
22		8	Aston Villa	1-3	Hunter
23		22	SHEFFIELD UNITED	1-0	McEwan(pen)
24		29	Woolwich Arsenal	0-2	
25	Feb	5	MIDDLESBROUGH	1-1	Jones
26		12	CHELSEA	5-2	McEwan(2,1pen), Hunter(2), Lockett
27		19	BRADFORD CITY	1-1	Jones
28		26	NOTTINGHAM FOREST	2-1	Hughes, Barber
29	Mar	5	Sunderland	0-3	
30		12	EVERTON	0-1	
31		19	Manchester United	0-5	
32		26	Blackburn Rovers	2-4	Hughes(2)
33		28	Notts County	0-0	
34	Apr	2	Sheffield Wednesday	0-0	
35		9	BRISTOL CITY	4-2	Jones, Hughes(2), Stokes
36		16	Bury	2-1	Jones, Hughes
37		23	TOTTENHAM HOTSPUR	0-2	
38		30	Preston North End	0-1	

Ave. Home Attendance: 11,950

Apps: 13 15 34 1 4 33 22 10 23 4 14 31 28 17 16 26 21 19 1 19 16 6 8 24 1 1 7 2 1 1

Goals: 1 3 2 12 10 6 4 3 1 1 1 1

F.A. Cup

1	Jan	15	Stockport County	1-4	Hogan	8000

Lancashire Cup

1	Oct	11	OLDHAM ATHLETIC	1-2

Manchester Cup

1	Nov	27	NORTHERN NOMADS	1-2

	FINAL TABLE	Pl.	Home				Away					F.	A.	Pts
			W	D	L	F	A	W	D	L	F	A	(Total)	
1	Aston Villa	38	17	2	0	62	19	6	5	8	22	23	84	42	53
2	Liverpool	38	13	3	3	47	23	8	3	8	31	34	78	57	48
3	Blackburn Rovers	38	13	6	0	47	17	5	3	11	26	38	73	55	45
4	Newcastle United	38	11	3	5	33	22	8	4	7	37	34	70	56	45
5	Manchester United	38	14	2	3	41	20	5	9	5	28	41	69	61	45
6	Sheffield United	38	10	5	4	42	19	6	5	8	20	22	62	41	42
7	Bradford City	38	12	3	4	38	17	5	5	9	26	30	64	47	42
8	Sunderland	38	12	3	4	40	18	6	2	11	26	33	66	51	41
9	Notts County	38	10	5	4	41	26	5	5	9	26	33	67	59	40
10	Everton	38	8	6	5	30	28	8	2	9	21	28	51	56	40
11	Sheffield Wed.	38	11	4	4	38	28	4	5	10	22	35	60	63	39
12	Preston North End	38	14	2	3	36	13	1	3	15	16	45	52	58	35
13	Bury	38	8	3	8	35	30	4	6	9	27	36	62	66	33
14	Nottingham Forest	38	4	7	8	19	34	7	4	8	35	38	54	72	33
15	Tottenham Hotspur	38	10	6	3	35	23	1	4	14	18	46	53	69	32
16	Bristol City	38	9	5	5	28	18	3	3	13	17	42	45	60	32
17	Middlesbrough	38	8	4	7	34	36	3	5	11	22	37	56	73	31
18	Woolwich Arsenal	38	6	8	5	17	19	5	4	10	20	48	37	67	31
19	Chelsea	38	10	4	5	32	24	1	3	15	15	46	47	70	29
20	BOLTON WANDERERS	38	7	2	10	31	34	2	4	13	13	37	44	71	24

~ 181 ~

1910/11 2nd in Division Two (promoted)

Manager: W.Settle

Results & Scorers

No		Date	Opponent	Score	Scorers
1	Sep	1	STOCKPORT COUNTY	2-2	Greenhalgh, Hewitt
2		3	Leicester Fosse	0-5	
3		5	WEST BROM ALBION	3-1	Hughes(3)
4		10	HULL CITY	2-1	Hughes, Hewitt
5		17	Woles	0-3	
6		24	FULHAM	2-0	Hewitt, Hughes
7	Oct	1	Chelsea	0-3	
8		8	BRADFORD	1-0	Smith
9		15	Clapton Orient	0-0	
10		22	BURNLEY	1-1	Shinton
11		29	Blackpool	1-1	Hughes
12	Nov	5	GAINSBOROUGH TRINITY	3-0	Hilton, Smith(2)
13		12	Glossop north end	2-1	Greenhalgh, Vizard
14		19	LEEDS CITY	3-0	Vizard, Greenhalgh, Hilton
15		26	Lincoln City	3-1	Barber, Vizard, Stokes
16	Dec	3	HUDDERSFIELD TOWN	3-1	Hughes(3)
17		10	Huddersfield Town	1-1	Hughes
18		17	Derby County	2-2	Feebury, Vizard
19		24	BIRMINGHAM	5-1	Hilton, Stokes, Hughes(3,1pen)
20		26	West Bromwich Albion	0-2	
21		31	LEICESTER FOSSE	6-2	Hughes(3), Smith(2), Greenhalgh
22	Jan	2	BARNSLEY	4-0	Hughes(2), Smith, Barber
23		7	Hull City	1-1	Smith
24		21	WOLVES	4-1	Hilton(2), Stokes, Smith
25		28	Fulham	0-2	
26	Feb	11	Bradford	1-1	Smith
27		18	CLAPTON ORIENT	2-0	Hughes, Hilton
28		25	Stockport County	1-0	Hughes
29	Mar	4	BLACKPOOL	1-0	Smith
30		11	Gainsborough Trinity	0-1	
31		18	GLOSSOP NORTH END	4-0	J.Whiteside, Barber, Smith, Hilton
32		20	Burnley	3-1	Barber(2), Hilton
33		25	Leeds City	0-1	
34	Apr	1	LINCOLN CITY	3-1	Hilton, Hughes, Greenhalgh
35		17	Barnsley	0-0	
36		22	DERBY COUNTY	2-1	Hilton, Marsh
37		26	CHELSEA	2-0	Hilton(2)
38		29	Birmingham	1-2	Hilton

Ave. Home Attendance: 10,050

Appearances (shirt numbers)

No	Adamson HM	Barber T	Baverstock H	Edmonds H	Edmondson JH	Feebury JH	Greenhalgh S	Hewitt J	Hilton H	Hughes W	Hunter WB	Jones G	Kay G	Marsh S	Newton S	Owen JR	Robinson WS	Shinton F	Slater J	Smith J	Stokes D	Stott W	Vizard ET	Whiteside E	Whiteside J
1	6		1				3	5	10		11	8				4		9		7					
2	6		1				3	5	10		11	8					4	9		7					
3		2	1				4	8	10	9				5					3	11	7			6	
4		2	1				4	8	10	9				5					3	11	7			6	
5		2	1				4	8	10	9				5					3	11	7			6	
6		4	1					8	10	9						5			3	11	7	2		6	
7		2				1			10	9						4	5	8	3	11	7			6	
8		3	1				5	8		9	11					4				10	7	2		6	
9	4	3	1				5	8			11							9		10	7	2		6	
10	4	3	1				5	8			11							9		10	7	2		6	
11		3	1			6	5	8	10	9	11			4							7	2			
12		3	1			6	5		8	9				4						10	7	2	11		
13		3	1				4		8	9										10	7	2	11	6	
14		3	1				4		8	9										10	7	2	11	6	
15	10	3	1				4		8	9											7	2	11	6	
16		3	1				4		8	9										10	7	2	11	6	
17	10	3	1				4		8	9											7	2	11	6	
18	10	3	1			6	5		8	9				4							7	2	11		
19		3					4	5	8	9					1					10	7	2	11	6	
20		3	1				4	5	8	9										10	7	2	11	6	
21	6	3	1				4	5		9							8			10	7	2	11		
22	6	3	1				4	5		9							8			10	7	2	11		
23	6	3	1				4	5	8	9										10	7	2	11		
24	10	3	1				4	5	8	9										10	7	2		6	
25	10	3	1				4	5	8	9										10	7	2		6	
26		3	1				5		8	9				4						10	7	2	11	6	
27		3	1				5		8	9				4						10	7	2	11	6	
28		3	1				5		8	9				4						10	7	2	11	6	
29		3	1				5		8	9				4						10	7	2	11	6	
30		3	1				5		8	9				4						10	7	2	11	6	
31	9	3	1				5		8					4						10		2	11	6	7
32	9	3	1				5		8					4						10		2	11	6	7
33	9	3	1				5		8		11			4						10		2		6	7
34	10	3	1				5		8	9				4						11		2		6	7
35		3	1				5		8	9				4						10	7	2	11	6	
36	9		1		3		5		8					4						10	7	2	11	6	
37	9	3	1				5		8					4						10	7	2	11	6	
38	9		1		3		5		8					4						10	7	2	11	6	
Apps	2	17	36	6	31	19	36	11	30	28	7	2	3	16	1	4	2	7	5	32	34	32	23	30	4
Goals		5				1	5	3	13	21				1				1		11	3		4		1

F.A. Cup

No		Date	Opponent	Score	Att	Adamson HM	Barber T	Baverstock H	Edmondson JH	Greenhalgh S	Hilton H	Hughes W	Marsh S	Smith J	Stokes D	Stott W	Vizard ET
1	Jan	14	CHESTERFIELD	0-2	6193		6	1	3	5	8	9	4	10	7	2	11

Lancashire Cup

No		Date	Opponent	Score
1	Oct	10	BURY	3-2
2		24	BLACKBURN ROVERS	0-4

Manchester Cup

No		Date	Opponent	Score
1	Oct	3	Stockport County	0-3

Other Games

No		Date	Opponent	Score
1	Jan	3	Rest of Lancs	0-0

FINAL TABLE

		Pl.	Home W	D	L	F	A	Away W	D	L	F	A	F. (Total)	A.	Pts
1	West Bromwich Alb.	38	14	2	3	40	18	8	7	4	27	23	67	41	53
2	BOLTON WANDERERS	38	17	2	0	53	12	4	7	8	16	28	69	40	51
3	Chelsea	38	17	2	0	48	7	3	7	9	23	28	71	35	49
4	Clapton Orient	38	14	4	1	28	7	5	3	11	16	28	44	35	45
5	Hull City	38	8	10	1	38	21	6	6	7	17	18	55	39	44
6	Derby County	38	11	5	3	48	24	6	3	10	25	28	73	52	42
7	Blackpool	38	10	5	4	29	15	6	5	8	20	23	49	38	42
8	Burnley	38	9	9	1	31	18	4	6	9	14	27	45	45	41
9	Wolverhampton W.	38	10	5	4	26	16	5	3	11	25	36	51	52	38
10	Fulham	38	12	3	4	35	15	3	4	12	17	33	52	48	37
11	Leeds City	38	11	4	4	35	18	4	3	12	23	38	58	56	37
12	Bradford Park Ave.	38	12	4	3	44	18	2	5	12	9	37	53	55	37
13	Huddersfield Town	38	10	4	5	35	21	3	4	12	22	37	57	58	34
14	Glossop	38	11	4	4	36	21	2	4	13	12	41	48	62	34
15	Leicester Fosse	38	12	3	4	37	19	2	2	15	15	43	52	62	33
16	Birmingham	38	10	4	5	23	18	2	4	13	19	46	42	64	32
17	Stockport County	38	10	4	5	27	26	1	4	14	20	53	47	79	30
18	Gainsborough Trinity	38	9	5	5	26	16	0	6	13	11	39	37	55	29
19	Barnsley	38	5	7	7	36	26	2	7	10	16	36	52	62	28
20	Lincoln City	38	5	7	7	16	23	2	3	14	12	49	28	72	24

~ 182 ~

1911-12
(top to bottom left to right)
Edmondson, Eccles, Tyldesley,
Baverstock, Stott, Newton, Feebury,
Slater, Greenhalgh, Marsh,
Whiteside, Barber, Gimblett, Fay,
Dodds, Hilton, Hogan, Bentley,
Stokes, Egerton, Hunter, Hughes,
Smith, Vizard, Hobson, Jones,
Griffiths, Pritchard

1910-11 Season
(Back) Stott, Kay, Slater, Adamson
(2nd Row)Eccles (Trainer), Tate (Dir.), Baverstock, Gaskell, Greenhalgh, Feebury, Edmundson, Edmunds,
Settle (Manager), Sankey (Ass.Manager)
(3rd Row)Stokes,Hilton,Shinton,Hewitt,Hughes, Whiteside, Hunter   (Front)Owen,Whiteside,Smith,Barber,Vizzard

1911/12 4th in Division One

Manager: W.Settle

#		Date	Opponent	Res	Scorers	Barber T	Baverstock H	Bentley A	Edmondson JH	Egerton W	Fay J	Feebury JH	Gimblett GS	Greenhalgh S	Hilton H	Hogan J	Hughes W	Hunter WB	Jones G	Marsh S	Newton S	Slater J	Smith J	stokes D	Stott W	Tyldesley J	Vizard ET	Whiteside E
1	Sep	2	NEWCASTLE UNITED	0-2		4	3	9	1					5	8								10	7	2		11	6
2		4	LIVERPOOL	2-1	Bentley, Hilton	4	3	9	1					5	8								10	7	2		11	6
3		9	Sheffield United	5-0	Hilton, Bentley(2), Smith(2)	4	2	9	1					5	8							3	10	7			11	6
4		16	OLDHAM ATHLETIC	2-1	Hilton, Greenhalgh	4	2	9						5	8						1	3	10	7			11	6
5		23	Preston North End	2-1	Greenhalgh, Bentley	4	2	9						5	8			11			1	3	10	7				6
6		30	Bradford City	0-1		6	2	9			4			5	8			11			1	3	10	7				
7	Oct	7	WOOLWICH ARSENAL	2-2	Hilton, Barber	4	2	9						5	8			11			1	3	10	7				6
8		14	Manchester City	1-3	Smith	6		9			4			5	8						1	3	10	7	2		11	
9		21	EVERTON	1-2	Smith	6	2	9	1		5	3			8				7	4			10				11	
10		28	West Bromwich Albion	0-0		6	2	9			5	3			8					4	1		10	7			11	
11	Nov	4	SUNDERLAND	3-0	Vizard, Bentley, Smith	6	2	9			5	3			8					4	1		10	7			11	
12		11	Blackburn Rovers	0-2		6	2	9			5	3			8					4	1		10	7	2		11	
13		18	SHEFFIELD WEDNESDAY	4-2	Smith(2), Hilton, Stokes	6	2	9			5	3			8					4	1		10	7			11	
14		25	Bury	3-1	Smith(2), Hilton	6	2	9			5	3			8					4	1		10	7			11	
15	Dec	2	MIDDLESBROUGH	1-0	Smith	4	2	9			5	3			8						1		10	7			11	6
16		9	Notts County	2-3	Smith(2)	4	2	9			5	3			8						1		10	7			11	6
17		16	TOTTENHAM HOTSPUR	1-0	Barber	10	2	9			5	3	4		8						1			7			11	6
18		23	Manchester United	0-2		8		9			5	3	4								1	2	10	7			11	6
19		25	Liverpool	0-1		4		9	1		5	3					8					2	10	7			11	6
20		30	Newcastle United	2-5	Smith, Bentley	4		9	1	8	5	3											10	7	2		11	6
21	Jan	1	ASTON VILLA	3-0	Smith, Fay, Vizard	6		9	1		5	3	4				8						10	7	2		11	
22		6	SHEFFIELD UNITED	0-3		6		9	1		5	3	4				8						10	7	2		11	
23		20	Oldham Athletic	1-3	Smith	4	2	9		8	5	3											10	7		1	11	6
24		27	PRESTON NORTH END	3-0	Feebury(2pens), Barber	10	2	9			5	3	4				8						11	7		1		6
25	Feb	10	Woolwich Arsenal	0-3		4	2	9			5	3				8							10	7		1	11	6
26		14	BRADFORD CITY	2-0	Smith, Hogan	4	2	9	1		5	3				8							10	7			11	6
27		17	MANCHESTER CITY	2-1	Bentley, Stokes	4	2	9	1			3		5		8							10	7			11	6
28		28	Everton	0-1		10	6		1		5	3	8			9				4				7			11	2
29	Mar	2	WEST BROM ALBION	2-0	Smith, Stokes	6			1		5	3	4			8	9						10	7	2		11	
30		9	Sunderland	1-0	Smith	6			1		5	3	4			8	9						10	7			11	
31		16	BLACKBURN ROVERS	2-0	Fay, Barber	6			1		5	3	4			8	9						10	7	2		11	
32		23	Sheffield Wednesday	1-0	Smith	6			1		5	3	4			8	9						10	7	2		11	
33		30	BURY	1-0	Smith	6			1		5	3	4			8	9						10	7	2		11	
34	Apr	5	Aston Villa	1-0	Hogan	6	2		1		5	3	4			8	9						10	7			11	
35		6	Middlesbrough	0-1		6			1		5	3	4			8	9						10	7	2		11	
36		13	NOTTS COUNTY	3-0	Hogan(2), Smith	6	3		1		5		4			8	9						10	7	2		11	
37		20	Tottenham Hotspur	0-1		6	3		1				4			8	9				5		10	7	2		11	
38		27	MANCHESTER UNITED	1-1	Smith	6	3		1				4	5		8	9						10	7	2		11	
			Apps			38	26	27	21	2	29	26	13	13	16	13	13	4	3	7	14	8	37	37	16	3	33	19
			Goals			4		7			2	2		2	6	4							22	3			2	

Ave. Home Attendance: 18,450

F.A. Cup

		Date	Opponent	Res	Scorer	Att	Barber T	Baverstock H	Bentley A	Edmondson JH	Egerton W	Fay J	Feebury JH	Hogan J	Smith J	stokes D	Tyldesley J	Vizard ET	Whiteside E
1	Jan	13	ARSENAL	1-0	Smith	24854	4	2	9		8	5	3		10	7	1	11	6
2	Feb	3	BLACKPOOL	1-0	Bentley	18651	4	2	9			5	3	8	10	7	1	11	6
3		24	BARNSLEY	1-2	Smith	34598	4	2	9	1		5	3	8	10	7		11	6

Lancashire Cup

		Date	Opponent	Res
1	Oct	10	Nelson	4-2
2		23	BARROW	1-0
SF	Nov	20	MANCHESTER UNITED	2-1
F	Dec	13	Burnley	4-1

Manchester Cup

		Date	Opponent	Res
1	Oct	16	GLOSSOP	3-1
SF	Feb	12	Manchester United*	0-4

* Played at Hyde Road

Other Games

		Date	Opponent	Res
1	Apr	9	Blackpool	1-1
2		10	Brierley Hill	6-5

	FINAL TABLE	Pl.	Home W	D	L	F	A	Away W	D	L	F	A	F (Total)	A	Pts
1	Blackburn Rovers	38	13	6	0	35	10	7	3	9	25	33	60	43	49
2	Everton	38	13	5	1	29	12	7	1	11	17	30	46	42	46
3	Newcastle United	38	10	4	5	37	25	8	4	7	27	25	64	50	44
4	BOLTON WANDERERS	38	14	2	3	35	15	6	1	12	19	28	54	43	43
5	Sheffield Wed.	38	11	3	5	44	17	5	6	8	25	32	69	49	41
6	Aston Villa	38	12	2	5	48	22	5	5	9	28	41	76	63	41
7	Middlesbrough	38	11	6	2	35	17	5	2	12	21	28	56	45	40
8	Sunderland	38	10	6	3	37	14	4	5	10	21	37	58	51	39
9	West Bromwich Alb.	38	10	6	3	23	15	5	3	11	20	32	43	47	39
10	Woolwich Arsenal	38	12	3	4	38	19	3	5	11	17	40	55	59	38
11	Bradford City	38	12	3	4	31	15	3	5	11	15	35	46	50	38
12	Tottenham Hotspur	38	10	4	5	35	20	4	5	10	18	33	53	53	37
13	Manchester United	38	9	5	5	29	19	4	6	9	16	41	45	60	37
14	Sheffield United	38	10	4	5	47	29	3	6	10	16	27	63	56	36
15	Manchester City	38	10	5	4	39	20	3	4	12	17	38	56	58	35
16	Notts County	38	9	4	6	26	20	5	3	11	20	43	46	63	35
17	Liverpool	38	8	4	7	27	23	4	6	9	22	32	49	55	34
18	Oldham Athletic	38	10	4	5	32	19	2	7	10	14	35	46	54	34
19	Preston North End	38	8	4	7	26	25	5	3	11	14	32	40	57	33
20	Bury	38	6	5	8	23	25	0	4	15	9	34	32	59	21

1912/13 8th in Division One

Manager: W.Settle

Match results

#	Date	Opponent	Score	Scorers
1	Sep 2	NEWCASTLE UNITED	1-2	Vizard
2	7	CHELSEA	1-0	Jones
3	11	Newcastle United	1-2	Jones
4	14	Woolwich Arsenal	2-1	Smith, Jones
5	21	BRADFORD CITY	2-0	Hogan, Vizard
6	28	Manchester City	0-2	
7	Oct 5	WEST BROM ALBION	2-1	Smith, Vizard
8	12	Everton	3-2	Jones, Barber, Donaldson
9	19	SHEFFIELD WEDNESDAY	3-0	Smith, Barber, Worrall(og)
10	26	Blackburn Rovers	0-6	
11	Nov 2	DERBY COUNTY	1-1	Jones
12	9	Tottenham Hotspur	1-0	Smith
13	16	MIDDLESBROUGH	3-2	Smith, Bentley(2)
14	23	Notts County	0-1	
15	30	MANCHESTER UNITED	2-1	Smith Bentley
16	Dec 7	Aston Villa	1-1	Smith
17	14	LIVERPOOL	1-1	Smith
18	21	Sunderland	1-2	Greenhalgh
19	26	Sheffield United	2-0	Bentley, Donaldson
20	28	Chelsea	3-2	Smith, Greenhalgh, Hughes
21	Jan 1	SHEFFIELD UNITED	4-2	Jones, Smith(2), Bentley
22	4	WOOLWICH ARSENAL	5-1	Donaldson,Jones,Bentley,Smith,Feebury(pen)
23	18	Bradford City	1-4	Bentley
24	25	MANCHESTR CITY	2-2	Smith, Bentley
25	Feb 8	West Bromwich Albion	2-2	Weir(2)
26	15	EVERTON	0-0	
27	24	Sheffield Wednesday	2-2	Smith, Feebury
28	Mar 1	BLACKBURN ROVERS	1-1	Smith
29	8	Derby County	3-3	Feebury(pen), Smith, Greenhalgh
30	15	TOTTENHAM HOTSPUR	2-0	Feebury, Smith
31	21	OLDHAM ATHLETIC	3-0	Feebury(pen), Smith(2)
32	22	Middlesbrough	0-4	
33	25	Oldham Athletic	3-2	Jones(2), Smith
34	29	NOTTS COUNTY	0-0	
35	Apr 5	Manchester United	1-2	Smith
36	12	ASTON VILLA	2-3	Smith, Hughes
37	19	Liverpool	0-5	
38	26	SUNDERLAND	1-3	Jones

Ave. Home Attendance: 20,920

Player appearances

Columns: Barber T, Baverstock H, Bentley A, Donaldson A, Edmondson JH, Fay J, Feebury JH, Gimblett GS, Glendenning R, Greenhalgh S, Hilton H, Hogan J, Hughes W, Jennings W, Jones E, Rowley WI, Slater J, Smith J, Stokes D, Stott W, Thomas J, Tyldesley J, Vizard ET, Weir A

#	Bar	Bav	Ben	Don	Edm	Fay	Fee	Gim	Gle	Gre	Hil	Hog	Hug	Jen	Jon	Row	Sla	Smi	Stk	Stt	Tho	Tyl	Viz	Wei
1	6	2			1	5	3			4		8			9			10	7				11	
2	6	2	8	7	1	5	3			4					9			10					11	
3	6	2	8	7	1	5	3			4					9			10					11	
4	6	2	8	7	1	5	3			4					9			10					11	
5	6	2	8	7	1	5	3			4		10			9								11	
6	6	2	8	7	1	5	3			4		10			9								11	
7		2	8	7	1	5	3			4					9			10				6	11	
8	8	2		7	1	5	3			4					9			10				6	11	
9	8	2		7	1	5	3			4					9			10				6	11	
10	8	2		7		5	3			4					9			10				1	11	
11	8	2		7				4		5				3	9			10				1	11	
12	4		9	7	1		2			5				3	8			10					11	
13			9	7	1	5	2			4				3	8			10					11	
14			9	7	1	5	2			4				3	8								11	
15			8		1	5	2			4					9						11		10	
16			9	7	1		2	4		5					8		3	10	7				11	
17			9	7	1		2	4		5					8		3	10					11	
18	8		9	7	1		3	4		5							3	10	2				11	
19			9	7	1		2	4		5				3	8			10						
20				7	1		3	4		5			9		8			10	2		6		11	
21			9	7	1		3	4		5					8			10	2				11	
22			9	7			3	4		5					8			10	2		6	1	11	
23			9				3	4		5					8			10	7	2	6	1	11	
24			9		1	5	3	4							8			10	7	2			11	
25		2	9		1		3	4							8	5		7					11	10
26		2	9		1		3	4							8	5		7					11	10
27		2			1		3	4					9		8	5		10	7				11	
28		2			1		3		4		8				8	5		10	7				11	
29		2			1		3		4	5			9		8			10	7				11	
30		2			1		3		4	5			9		8			10	7				11	
31		2	9	7	1				4	5					8			10		11				
32		2	9	7	1				4	5					8			10		11	2			
33		3		7	1				4				9		8	5		10		11	2			
34		2	9	7			3		4						8	5		10		11		1		
35		2	9				3		4						8	5		10	7			1	11	
36		2		7	1		3		4				9		8	5		10			6			
37		2		7	1		3	6	4	5			9		8			10		11				
38		2		7	1		3		4	5					8			10		11				
Apps	12	25	24	27	32	14	35	15	9	30	1	3	7	5	37	9	3	33	18	8	7	6	31	2
Goals	2		8	3			5			3		1	2		10			22					3	2

One own goal

F.A. Cup

#	Date	Opponent	Score	Att	Bar	Bav	Ben	Don	Edm	Fay	Fee	Gim	Gle	Gre	Hil	Hog	Hug	Jen	Jon	Row	Sla	Smi	Stk	Stt	Tho	Tyl	Viz	Wei
1	Jan 11	Oldham Athletic	0-2	23300			9		1		3	4		5					8			10	7	2			11	

Lancashire Cup

#	Date	Opponent	Score
1	Oct 7	SOUTHPORT CENTRAL	2-1
2	23	MANCHESTER UNITED	0-3

Manchester Cup

#	Date	Opponent	Score
1	Feb 10	HURST	3-1
SF	Mar 12	ROCHDALE	1-1
SFr	Apr 1	Rochdale	1-1
F	21	Manchester United*	1-4

* Played at Hyde Road

Other Games

#	Date	Opponent	Score
1	May 1	Duisberg Spieldaerein	5-1
2	4	Victoria Berliner	1-2
3	11	Weiner	3-0
4	12	Vienna ASC	3-0
5	15	Sports Club Rapid	3-3
6	16	Austria Vienna	2-2
7	18	German Association	12-0

FINAL TABLE

		Pl.	Home W	D	L	F	A	Away W	D	L	F	A	F. (Total)	A.	Pts
1	Sunderland	38	14	2	3	47	17	11	2	6	39	26	86	43	54
2	Aston Villa	38	13	4	2	57	21	6	8	5	29	31	86	52	50
3	Sheffield Wed.	38	12	4	3	44	23	9	3	7	31	32	75	55	49
4	Manchester United	38	13	3	3	41	14	6	5	8	28	29	69	43	46
5	Blackburn Rovers	38	10	5	4	54	21	6	8	5	25	22	79	43	45
6	Manchester City	38	12	3	4	34	15	6	5	8	19	22	53	37	44
7	Derby County	38	10	2	7	40	29	7	6	6	29	37	69	66	42
8	BOLTON WANDERERS	38	10	6	3	36	20	6	4	9	26	43	62	63	42
9	Oldham Athletic	38	11	7	1	33	12	3	7	9	17	43	50	55	42
10	West Bromwich Alb.	38	8	7	4	30	20	5	9	5	27	30	57	50	38
11	Everton	38	8	2	9	28	31	7	5	7	20	23	48	54	37
12	Liverpool	38	12	2	5	40	24	4	3	12	21	47	61	71	37
13	Bradford City	38	10	5	4	33	22	2	6	11	17	38	50	60	35
14	Newcastle United	38	8	5	6	30	23	5	3	11	17	24	47	47	34
15	Sheffield United	38	10	5	4	36	24	4	1	14	20	46	56	70	34
16	Middlesbrough	38	6	9	4	29	22	5	1	13	26	47	55	69	32
17	Tottenham Hotspur	38	9	3	7	28	25	3	3	13	17	47	45	72	30
18	Chelsea	38	7	2	10	29	40	4	4	11	22	33	51	73	28
19	Notts County	38	6	4	9	19	20	1	5	13	9	36	28	56	23
20	Woolwich Arsenal	38	1	8	10	11	31	2	4	13	15	43	26	74	18

1912-13 Season
(Back) Donaldson, Stott, Baverstock, Edmondson, Tyldesley, Feebury, Greenhalgh, Thomas
(Middle) Eccles, Gimblett, Rowley, Egerton, Fay, Barber, Whiteside, Dr Burnham, Sankey
(Front) Hogan, Stokes, Hilton, Jones, Smith, Vizard, Hughes, Bentley, Jennings

1913-14 Season
(Back) Gimblett, Jennings, J.Baverstock, Tyledsley, Edmondson, Thomas, Greenhalgh, Feebury
(Middle) Eccles (Trainer), Cartwright, Cooke, Slater, Glendenning, Fay, Rowley, Bullogh,
Whiteside, H.Baverstock, Hughes, Sanley (Ass,Trainer)
(Front) Stott, Donaldson, Hilton, Weir, Jones, Lillycrop, Smith, Vizard, Westwood, Stokes

1913/14 6th in Division One

Manager: W.Settle

#		Date	Opponent	Score	Scorers	Baverstock H	Baverstock JI	Donaldson A	Edmondson JH	Fay J	Feebury JH	Gimblett GS	Glendenning R	Greenhalgh S	Hateley CB	Heslop TW	Jennings W	Jones E	Lillycrop GR	Lockhard A	Rowley WI	Seddon J	Sidlow E	Smith H	Smith J	Stokes D	Stott W	Thomas J	Tyldesley J	Vizard ET	Whiteside E
1	Sep	1	SHEFFIELD WEDNESDAY	0-1		2		7	1		3		4	5				8	9						10					11	6
2		6	OLDHAM ATHLETIC	6-2	Lillycrop(2),J.Smith,Feebury,Jones,Vizard	2		7	1		3		4					8	9		5				10			6		11	
3		13	Manchester United	1-0	Lillycrop	2		7	1		3	4						8	9		5				10			6		11	
4		20	BURNLEY	0-0		2		7	1		3	4						8	9		5				10			6		11	
5		27	Preston North End	1-1	Lillycrop	2		7	1	5	3		4					8	9						10			6		11	
6	Oct	4	NEWCASTLE UNITED	3-1	Lillycrop, Vizard, J.Smith	2		7	1	5	3		4					8	9						10			6		11	
7		11	Liverpool	1-2	Vizard	2		7	1	5	3		4					8	9						10			6		11	
8		18	ASTON VILLA	3-0	Rowley, Fay, Donaldson	2		7	1	9	3		4					8			5				10			6		11	
9		25	Middlesbrough	3-2	Lillycrop, J.Smith(2)	2		7			3		4					8	9		5				10			6	1	11	
10	Nov	1	SHEFFIELD UNITED	3-1	Lillycrop(2), J.Smith	2		7	1	5	3		4					8	9						10			6		11	
11		8	Derby County	3-3	Jones(2), J.Smith	2		7	1	5	3		4					8	9						10			6		11	
12		15	MANCHESTER CITY	3-0	J.Smith, Jones(2)	2		7	1	5	3		4					8	9						10			6		11	
13		22	Bradford City	1-5	Lillycrop	2		7	1	5	3		4					8	9						10			6		11	
14		29	BLACKBURN ROVERS	1-0	Lillycrop	2		7	1	5	3		4					8	9		6				10					11	
15	Dec	6	Sunderland	2-3	Feebury, Lillycrop	2	1	7		5	3		4				6	8	9						10					11	
16		13	EVERTON	0-0		2		7	1	5	3		4				6	8	9						10					11	
17		20	West Bromwich Albion	1-1	Lillycrop	2		7	1	5	3		4				6	8	9						10					11	
18		27	Oldham Athletic	0-2		2		7	1	5	3		4				6	8	9						10					11	
19		29	Sheffield Wednesday	1-1	Lillycrop	2	1	7		5	3		4				6	8	9						10					11	
20	Jan	1	TOTTENHAM HOTSPUR	3-0	Lillycrop(2), Fay	2		7	1	5	3		4				6	8	9						10					11	
21		3	MANCHESTER UNITED	6-1	J.Smith(4), Lillycrop, Jones			7	1	5	3		4				6	8	9						10		6			11	
22		17	Burnley	2-2	J.Smith, Donaldson			7	1	5	3		4				6	8	9						10					11	
23		24	PRESTON NORTH END	0-3		2		7	1	5	3		4				6	8	9						10					11	
24	Feb	7	Newcastle United	3-4	Lillycrop, Feebury(2,1pen)			7	1	5	3		4				6	8	9						10		6			11	
25		11	CHELSEA	1-1	Lillycrop	2		7	1	6	3		4			10		8	9		5									11	
26		14	LIVERPOOL	2-1	Lillycrop(2)	2		7	1		3		4			10		8	9		5									11	6
27		25	Aston Villa	0-1		2		7	1	5	3		4				6	8	9						10					11	
28		28	MIDDLESBROUGH	1-1	Jones	2			1		3		4				6	8	9	5					10		7			11	
29	Mar	7	WEST BROM ALBION	1-0	Jones	2		7	1		3		4					8	9	5					10			6		11	
30		14	DERBY COUNTY	3-1	Vizard(2), Stokes	2			1		3		4			6			9		5			8	10	7				11	
31		21	Manchester City	1-0	Lillycrop	2		7	1		3		4		11	6			9		5			8	10						
32		28	BRADFORD CITY	3-0	J.Smith(3)	2		7	1		3		4			6			9		5			8	10					11	
33	Apr	4	Blackburn Rovers	2-3	Lillycrop(2)	2				5	3		4			6		8	9				1		10	7				11	
34		6	Sheffield United	0-2		2				5	3		4					8	9				1			7	6			11	
35		10	Tottenham Hotspur	0-3		2		7		5	3		4					8	9				1		10		6			11	
36		11	SUNDERLAND	2-1	J.Smith(2)	2		7		5	3		4					8	9				1		10	6				11	
37		13	Chelsea	1-2	H.Smith	2				5	3		4						9				1	8	10	7	6			11	
38		18	Everton	1-1	Lillycrop	2		7		5	3		4					8	9				1		10	6				11	
			Apps			31	2	33	29	27	37	2	36	1	1	6	10	32	37	2	24	1	6	8	35	7	4	13	1	31	2
			Goals					2		2	4							8	24		1			1	17	1				5	

Ave. Home Attendance: 24,950

F.A. Cup

#		Date	Opponent	Score	Scorers	Att.											
1	Jan	10	PORT VALE	3-0	Smith, Donaldson, Lillycrop	18975	2	7	1	5	3	4	8	9	6	10	11
2		31	SWINDON TOWN	4-2	Smith(3),Jones	50558	2	7	1	5	3	4	8	9	6	10	11
3	Feb	21	Burnley	0-3		32734	2	7	1	5	3	4	8	9	6	10	11

Lancashire Cup

2	Oct	6	PRESTON NORTH END	3-1
3		20	Rochdale	2-3

Manchester Cup

1	Feb	10	Hurst	0-2

	FINAL TABLE	Pl.	Home				Away					F.	A.	Pts
			W	D	L	F	A	W	D	L	F	A	(Total)	
1	Blackburn Rovers	38	14	4	1	51	15	6	7	6	27	27	78	42	51
2	Aston Villa	38	11	3	5	36	21	8	3	8	29	29	65	50	44
3	Middlesbrough	38	14	2	3	55	20	5	3	11	22	40	77	60	43
4	Oldham Athletic	38	11	5	3	34	16	6	4	9	21	29	55	45	43
5	West Bromwich Alb.	38	11	7	1	30	16	4	6	9	16	26	46	42	43
6	BOLTON WANDERERS	38	13	4	2	41	14	3	6	10	24	38	65	52	42
7	Sunderland	38	11	3	5	32	17	6	3	10	31	35	63	52	40
8	Chelsea	38	12	3	4	28	18	4	4	11	18	37	46	55	39
9	Bradford City	38	8	6	5	23	17	4	8	7	17	23	40	40	38
10	Sheffield United	38	11	4	4	36	19	5	1	13	27	41	63	60	37
11	Newcastle United	38	9	6	4	27	18	4	5	10	12	30	39	48	37
12	Burnley	38	10	4	5	43	20	2	8	9	18	33	61	53	36
13	Manchester City	38	9	3	7	28	23	5	5	9	23	30	51	53	36
14	Manchester United	38	8	4	7	27	23	7	2	10	25	39	52	62	36
15	Everton	38	8	7	4	32	18	4	4	11	14	37	46	55	35
16	Liverpool	38	8	4	7	27	25	6	3	10	19	37	46	62	35
17	Tottenham Hotspur	38	9	6	4	30	19	3	4	12	20	43	50	62	34
18	Sheffield Wed.	38	8	4	7	34	34	5	4	10	19	36	53	70	34
19	Preston North End	38	9	4	6	39	31	3	2	14	13	38	52	69	30
20	Derby County	38	6	5	8	34	32	2	6	11	21	39	55	71	27

1914/15 17th in Division One

Manager: W.Settle

#		Date	Opponent	Score	Scorers	Baverstock H	Buckan TM	Donaldson A	Edmondson JH	Fay J	Feebury JH	Glendenning R	Heslop TW	Hilton H	Jennings W	Jones E	Kidd J	Lillycrop G	Roberts F	Rowley WJ	Seddon J	Sidlow E	Smith J	Stokes D	Thomas J	Toone P	Vizard ET	Wallace W	Wilson G
1	Sep	2	Liverpool	3-4	Jones(2), Smith	2		7	1	5	3	4			6	8		9					10				11		
2		5	Oldham Athletic	3-5	Vizard, Smith, Fay	2		7	1	5	3	4			6	8		9					10				11		
3		7	BLACKBURN ROVERS	3-2	Lillycrop(2), Smith	2		7		5		4			3	8		9		6			10			1	11		
4		12	MANCHESTER UNITED	3-0	Lillycrop(2), Smith	2				5		4			3	8		9		6			10	7		1	11		
5		19	MANCHESTER CITY	2-3	Vizard, Smith	2				5		4			3	8		9		6			10	7		1	11		
6		26	Blackburn Rovers	2-2	Vizard, Lillycrop	2				5		4			3	8		9				1	10	7	6		11		
7	Oct	3	NOTTS COUNTY	1-2	Lillycrop	2				5		4			3	8		9		6		1	10	7			11		
8		7	Bradford Park Avenue	2-1	Smith(2)	2		7		6		4			3			9	8		5	1	10				11		
9		10	Sunderland	3-4	Smith(2), Vizard	2		7		6		4			3			9	8		5	1	10				11		
10		17	SHEFFIELD WEDNESDAY	0-3		2		7	1	4	3				6			9	8		5		10				11		
11		24	West Bromwich Albion	0-3		2				1	5	3			6	8		9		4			10	7			11		
12		31	EVERTON	0-0		2	9			1	6		4					8	5				10	7			11		3
13	Nov	7	Chelsea	1-2	Lillycrop	2				1	6		4					9	8	5			10	7			11		3
14		14	BRADFORD CITY	3-5	Stokes, Smith (2,1pen)	2				1	6		4					9	8	5			10	7			11		3
15		21	Burnley	0-5		2	10			1	5		4			9			8				10	7			11		3
16		28	TOTTENHAM HOTSPUR	4-2	Hilton, Roberts, Smith(2 pens)			7					4	8					9	5			1	10		6		11		2
17	Dec	5	Newcastle United	2-1	Wallace, Roberts								4	8					9	5			1	10		6		11	7	2
18		12	MIDDLESBROUGH	4-0	Hilton, Stokes, Rowley, Smith								4	8					9	5			1	10	7	6		11		2
19		19	Sheffield United	1-3	Hilton								4	8					9	5			1	10	7	6		11		2
20		25	LIVERPOOL	0-1									4	8					9	5			1	10		6		11	7	2
21		26	Aston Villa	7-1	Smith(4,1pen), Roberts(2), Hilton								4	8					9	5			1	10	7	6		11		2
22	Jan	1	ASTON VILLA	2-2	Stokes, Smith								4	8	6				9	5			1	10	7			11		2
23		2	OLDHAM ATHLETIC	2-0	Roberts, Smith (pen)	2							4	8	6				9	5			1	10	7			11		2
24		16	Manchester United	1-4	Smith	2							4	8		6			9	5			1	10	7			11		3
25		23	Manchester City	1-2	Smith			7	1			3	4		8	6			9	5				10				11		2
26	Feb	27	WEST BROM ALBION	1-1	Smith(pen)			7	1	4	3					8		9		5				10		6		11		2
27	Mar	1	Sheffield Wednesday	0-7				7	1	4	3					8		9		5				10		6		11		2
28		10	SUNDERLAND	1-1	Jones	2			1							8			9	5				10	7	6		11		3
29		13	BURNLEY	3-1	Jones(2), Smith	2			1						6	8			9	5	4			10	7			11		3
30		17	Notts County	0-0		2									6	8	1		9	5	4			10	7			11		3
31		20	Bradford City	2-4	Roberts, Jones							3			6	8	1		9	5	4			10	7			11		3
32		22	Everton	3-5	Roberts, Buchan, Smith	2	8			4					6		1		9	5				10	7			11		3
33	Apr	2	BRADFORD PARK AVE	3-2	Roberts(2), Smith	2		7				4			6	8	1		9	5				10				11		3
34		3	Tottenham Hotspur	2-4	Smith(2,1pen)	2		7				4			6	8	1		9	5				10				11		3
35		10	NEWCASTLE UNITED	0-0		2		7		4					6	8	1		9	5				10				11		3
36		14	CHELSEA	3-1	Roberts, Smith, Vizard	2		7		4					6	8	1		9	5				10				11		3
37		17	Middlesbrough	0-0		2		7				5	4		6	8	1		9					10	7			11		3
38		26	SHEFFIELD UNITED	0-1		2		7				5	4		6	8	1		9					10				11		3

Ave. Home Attendance: 13,625

	Apps	27	3	15	13	22	16	28	1	10	24	21	9	15	28	29	6	13	38	21	10	3	38	2	26
	Goals		1					1		4	6			7	10	1			29	3			5	1	

F.A. Cup

#		Date	Opponent	Score	Scorers	Att	Baverstock H		Donaldson A		Fay J	Feebury JH		Heslop TW	Hilton H	Jennings W		Kidd J		Roberts F	Rowley WJ			Smith J	Stokes D	Thomas J		Vizard ET		Wilson G
1	Jan	9	NOTTS COUNTY	2-1	Smith, Hilton	17871	2							4	8					9	5			1	10	7	6		11		3
2		30	MILLWALL	0-0*		22418						1		3	4	8	6			9	5				10	7			11		2
2r	Feb	6	Millwall	2-2*	Vizard, Smith(pen)	24801						1		3	4			8		9	5				10	7	6		11		2
2/2r		13	MILLWALL	4-1	Jones(2), Vizard(2)	20962						1		3	4		8			9	5				10	7	6		11		2
3		20	BURNLEY	2-1*	Smith(2)	42932						1		3	4		8			9	5				10	7	6		11		2
4	Mar	6	HULL CITY	4-2	Vizard, Jones, Smith(2pens)	24379	2					1			4		8			9	5				10	7	6		11		2
SF		27	SHEFFIELD UNITED +	1-2	Smith	22404						1			4	3	8			9	5				10	7	6		11		2

* after extra time   + At Ewood Park, Blackburn

Lancashire Cup

2	Oct	5	Preston North End	0-1

Manchester Cup

1	Feb	10	BURY	2-2
1r	Mar	2	Bury	3-2
2		15	Stockport	0-3

FINAL TABLE	Pl	Home					Away					F. A	Pts
		W	D	L	F	A	W	D	L	F	A	(Total)	
1 Everton	38	8	5	6	44	29	11	3	5	32	18	76 47	46
2 Oldham Athletic	38	11	5	3	46	25	6	6	7	24	31	70 56	45
3 Blackburn Rovers	38	11	4	4	51	27	7	3	9	32	34	83 61	43
4 Burnley	38	12	1	6	38	18	6	6	7	23	29	61 47	43
5 Manchester City	38	9	7	3	29	15	6	6	7	20	24	49 39	43
6 Sheffield United	38	11	5	3	28	13	4	8	7	21	28	49 41	43
7 Sheffield Wed.	38	10	7	2	43	23	5	8	6	18	31	61 54	43
8 Sunderland	38	11	3	5	46	30	7	2	10	35	42	81 72	41
9 Bradford Park Ave.	38	11	4	4	40	20	6	3	10	29	45	69 65	41
10 West Bromwich Alb.	38	11	5	3	31	9	4	5	10	18	34	49 43	40
11 Bradford City	38	11	5	3	41	19	4	5	10	20	50	55 49	40
12 Middlesbrough	38	10	6	3	42	24	3	6	10	20	50	62 74	38
13 Liverpool	38	11	5	3	45	34	3	4	12	20	41	65 75	37
14 Aston Villa	38	10	5	4	39	32	3	6	10	23	40	62 72	37
15 Newcastle United	38	8	4	7	29	20	3	6	10	17	28	46 48	32
16 Notts County	38	8	7	4	28	18	1	6	12	13	39	41 57	31
17 BOLTON WANDERERS	38	8	5	6	35	27	3	3	13	33	57	68 84	30
18 Manchester United	38	6	7	6	27	17	3	5	11	19	43	46 62	30
19 Chelsea	38	8	6	5	32	25	0	7	12	19	40	51 65	29
20 Tottenham Hotspur	38	7	7	5	30	29	1	5	13	27	61	57 90	28

1914-15 Season
(Back) Wilson, Rowley, Thomas, Beaverstock, Sidlow, Toone, Edmonston, Feebery, Wallace
(Middle) Eccles, ?, Heslop, Roberts, Gimblets, Fay, Hilton, Jennings, Hodkinns, Seddon, ?
(Front) Thomas, Glendenning, Stokes, Donaldson, Jones, Lillycrop, Smith, Vizard, Burton

1915/16   12th in Lancs section Principal Comp., 4th in Subsidiary Competition

Manager: T.Mather

#	Date		Opponent	Score	Scorers
1	Sep	4	LIVERPOOL	1-1	T.Buchan
2		11	Bury	2-4	Foulkes, Roberts
3		18	MANCHESTER UNITED	3-5	T.Buchan(2), Foulkes
4		25	Blackpool	1-2	Mather
5	Oct	2	SOUTHPORT CENTRAL	0-7	
6		9	Oldham Athletic	2-6	J.Buchan, J.Smith
7		16	EVERTON	3-4	T.Buchan(pen), Mather
8		23	Rochdale	4-2	J.Smith(pen), Roberts(2), Hampson
9		30	Manchester City	2-1	Jennings(2)
10	Nov	6	STOKE	2-1	T.Buchan, J.Smith(pen)
11		13	Burnley	0-3	
12		20	PRESTON NORTH END	1-0	J.Smith
13		27	Stockport County	2-4	J.Smith(2)
14	Dec	4	Liverpool	3-3	T.Buchan, Roberts, J.Smith
15		11	BURY	1-2	J.Smith
16		18	Manchester United	0-1	
17		25	BLACKPOOL	0-2	
18	Jan	1	Southport Central	1-3	Hulme
19		8	OLDHAM ATHLETIC	1-6	J.Smith
20		15	Everton	1-2	J.Smith
21		2	ROCHDALE	3-0	Roberts(2), Lillycrop
22		29	MANCHESTER CITY	4-2	J.Smith2*(1pen), Roberts, Lillycrop
23	Feb	5	Stoke	1-1	J.Smith
24		12	BURNLEY	3-0	Roberts, J.Smith, Lillycrop
25		19	Preston North End	3-1	J.Smith, Roberts, Lillycrop
26	Mar	4	Burnley	1-3	H.Smith
27		11	PRESTON NORTH END	1-6	J.Smith
28		18	SOUTHPORT CENTRAL	2-0	Lillycrop, Vizard
29		25	Blackpool	1-3	T.Buchan
30	Apr	1	Bury	4-3	J.Smith(3,1pen), Roberts
31		8	BURNLEY	2-0	J.Smith, Vizard
32		15	Preston North End	1-1	Vizard
33		21	Bury	2-4	Roberts, Vizard
34		22	Southport Central	1-0	J.Smith
35		24	STOCKPORT COUNTY	4-2	Roberts(3), J.Smith
36		29	BLACKPOOL	1-2	Waller

* In some records Smith's first goal is credited as an own-goal

Player appearances (shirt numbers)

Columns: Baverstock R, Buchan TM, Devitt T, Donaldson A, Entwistle W, Foulkes R, Gannon A, Glendenning R, Greenhalgh H, Guy G, Hallows C, Hampson J, Heslop T, Hilton H, Hodgkiss J, Hulme W, Hurst G, Jennings W, Kay T, Lansdale J, Lillycrop G, Mather W, Roberts F, Rowley W, Shipperbottom, Smith H, Smith J, Vizard ET, Waller W, Wilson G

#	Bav	Buc	Dev	Don	Ent	Fou	Gan	Gle	Gre	Guy	Hal	Ham	Hes	Hil	Hod	Hul	Hur	Jen	Kay	Lan	Lil	Mat	Rob	Row	Shi	SmH	SmJ	Viz	Wal	Wil
1		8	10		6			4	2	11										1						5	3		7	
2		4			6	8			2	11										1				9			3		7	
3		9			6	8		4	2	11										1						5	3		7	
4		9	10		6			4	2	11												1		8		5	3		7	
5			10		6		8		2	11												1		8		5	3		7	
6		8						4	2	11						6		1								5	3	10		
7		9						4	2	11	7						5	3		1	8							10		
8		8						6	2	11							4	3		1			9	5				10		
9		8						6	2	11							4	3	10	1			9	5						
10		8						6	2				7				4	3	11	1			9	5				10		
11		8						6	2			11	7				4	3		1			9	5				10		
12		8							2			11	7				4	3		1			9	5	6			10		
13		1							2			11	7				4	3			8		9	5	6			10		
14		8							2			11		7			4	3		1			9	5				10		
15		8	7						2								4	3		1			9	5	6			10	11	
16		8	7					4	2							6		3		1			9	5				10	11	
17		8	7					4			11	8				6		3		1						5		10		2
18		8						4			7	5				6		3		1			9					10	11	2
19		8										7		4				3		1			9	5	6			10	11	2
20	2	5						4						7	1	6	3				8		9				11	10		
21	2	6						4						7	1		3				8		9		5		11	10		
22	2	6						4						7	1		3				8		9		5		11	10		
23	2	6						4						7	1		3				8		9		5		11	10		
24	2	6						4						7	1		3				8		9		5		11	10		
25	2	6						4						7	1		3				8		9		5		11	10		
26	2	6						4				11		7	1		3				8		9		5	10				
27	2	6						4				7		8	1		3						9		5		11	10		
28	2	6						4						7	1		3				8		9		5		11	10		
29		6						4	2						1		3				8		9		5		11	10	7	
30	2	6						4							1		3				8		9		5		11	10	7	
31		6						4							1		3				8		9		5		11	10	7	
32		6						4							1		3				8		9		5		11	10	7	
33		6						4						7	1		3				8		9		5		11	10		
34		6						4						7	1		3				8		9		5		11	10		
35		6						4				11		7	1		3				8		9		5			10		
36	2	6						4				11			1		3				8		9		5			10	7	
Apps	15	35	3	3	10	3	2	16	18	12	4	13	6	11	16	22	28	3	5	14	10	3	29	31	13	9	27	17	6	3
Goals		8				2						1				1		2			5	2	14			1	22	4	1	

Additional Players: J Buchan 6/7(1 goal), FH Garrett 35/2, A Hatfield 14/6, T Hesmondhalgh 1/9, H Hothersall 2/5 5/4, W Lovett 2&3/10, JR Sloan 6/9

Note
Matches 26-34 & 36 were in the Lancashire Section Subsidiary Tournament.

FINAL LEAGUE TABLE

		P	W	D	L	F	A	Pts
1	Manchester City	26	16	3	7	61	35	35
2	Burnley	26	14	5	7	71	43	33
3	Blackpool	26	14	3	9	54	41	31
4	Everton	25	15	0	10	59	42	30
5	Stockport County	26	13	3	10	47	43	29
6	Liverpool	26	11	7	8	48	42	29
7	Oldham Athletic	25	13	3	9	52	44	29
8	Stoke	26	10	7	9	43	46	27
9	Southport Central	26	9	6	11	41	41	24
10	Bury	26	10	3	13	46	52	23
11	Manchester United	26	7	8	11	41	51	22
12	BOLTON WANDERERS	26	9	3	14	48	65	21
13	Rochdale	26	7	5	14	34	56	19
14	Preston North End	26	4	2	20	23	67	10

Oldham .v. Everton not played

FINAL LEAGUE TABLE Subsidiary Tournament - North. Div.

		Pl	W	D	L	F	A	Pts
1	Burnley	10	8	0	2	29	12	16
2	Blackpool	10	8	0	2	24	13	16
3	Preston North End	10	4	2	4	22	19	10
4	BOLTON WANDERERS	10	4	1	5	16	22	9
5	Bury	10	3	0	7	17	26	6
6	Southport Central	10	1	1	8	12	28	3

1916/17

Manager: T.Mather

#		Date	Opponent	Score	Scorers
1	Sep	2	Liverpool	1-3	Geddes
2		9	STOCKPORT COUNTY	1-1	Buchan
3		16	Bury	0-2	
4		23	STOKE	9-2	Sharp(2), Smith(6,1pen), Vizard
5		30	Southport Central	0-3	
6	Oct	7	BLACKBURN ROVERS	0-0	
7		14	Manchester City	0-1	
8		21	EVERTON	1-3	Smith
9		28	Rochdale	6-0	Buchan(2), Smith(4,1pen)
10	Nov	4	BLACKPOOL	4-1	Smith, Sharp, Vizard(2)
11		11	PORT VALE	3-2	Smith, Buchan(2)
12		18	Oldham Athletic	1-2	Sharp
13		25	PRESTON NORTH END	6-2	Smith(4), Buchan, Vizard
14	Dec	2	Burnley	2-2	Smith, Jones
15		9	MANCHESTER UNITED	5-1	Jones, Buchan(2), Smith(2)
16		30	BURY	2-3	Nuttall(2)
17	Jan	1	Oldham Athletic	0-3	
18		6	Stoke	0-7	
19		13	SOUTHPORT CENTRAL	0-0	
20		20	Blackburn Rovers	1-5	Pickup
21		27	MANCHESTER CITY	2-2	Heslop, Buchan
22	Feb	3	Everton	0-1	
23		10	ROCHDALE	1-3	Appleton
24		17	Blackpool	3-5	Brookes, Jones, Winterburn
25		24	Port Vale	0-2	
26	Mar	3	OLDHAM ATHLETIC	2-2	Gimblett, Sharp
27		10	Preston North End	2-1	Geddes, Pickup
28		17	BURNLEY	3-1	Jones(2), Keenan
29		24	Manchester United	3-6	Jones, Geddes(2)
30		31	ROCHDALE	0-1	
31	Apr	6	Stockport County	0-2	
32		6	Oldham Athletic	2-1	Hulme, Cavanagh (og)
33		7	Bury	3-2	Geddes(2), Davies
34		14	Rochdale	1-5	Stanley
35		21	BURY	6-0	Fay(4), Davies, Geddes
36		28	LIVERPOOL	1-0	Geddes

Appearances / Goals

	Appleton L	Brooks J	Buchan TM	Clayton P	Davies W	Fay J	Geddes R	Gimblett GS	Hallows C	Hamer J	Haslam G	Heslop TW	Hilton J	Hodgkiss J	Hodson J	Hulme W	Hurst G	Johnson F	Jones A	Keenan H	Livesey F	Nuttall J	Nuttall W	Pickup JH	Sharp S	Shufflebottom F	Smith J	Stanley G	Vizard ET	Winterburn A
Apps	2	6	35	15	6	3	15	14	2	2	4	18	3	33	4	12	30	3	15	26	3	31	3	36	11	2	16	6	16	10
Goals	1	1	9		2	4	8	1				1				1			6	1			2	2	5		20	1	4	1

One own goal

Additional Players: H Bradbury 18/10, J Farnworth 4&5/2, J Garside 18/11, R Glendenning 19/9, R Hayes 29/11, WJ Holgate 23/11, H Johnson 2/8, J Lane 21/10, F McMillan 19&20/11, H Smith 30/3, J Wray 7&8/9

Note:
Matches 17, 30 & 32-35 were in the Lancashire Section Subsidiary Tournament.

Other Games

#	Date		Opponent	Score
1	Dec	25	PRESTON GARRISON RFA	2-4
2	May	12	Atherton	1-5

FINAL LEAGUE TABLE

		Pl	W	D	L	F	A	Pts
1	Liverpool	30	19	8	3	62	26	46
2	Stockport County	30	18	7	5	61	31	43
3	Stoke	30	16	7	7	64	36	39
4	Manchester City	30	14	9	7	49	29	37
5	Everton	30	15	7	8	62	41	37
6	Burnley	30	15	4	11	73	56	34
7	Manchester United	30	13	6	11	48	54	32
8	Rochdale	30	12	5	13	47	54	29
9	Southport Central	30	10	8	12	40	43	28
10	BOLTON WANDERERS	30	9	6	15	59	65	24
11	Blackburn Rovers	30	10	4	16	52	66	24
12	Preston North End	30	8	7	15	47	65	23
13	Bury	30	7	8	15	40	63	22
14	Oldham Athletic	30	8	6	16	36	65	22
15	Port Vale	30	7	7	16	50	60	21
16	Blackpool	30	6	7	17	44	80	19

FINAL LEAGUE TABLE Subsidiary Tournament

		Pl	W	D	L	F	A	Pts
1	Rochdale	6	5	1	0	15	6	11
2	Everton	6	4	1	1	16	5	9
3	Burnley	6	4	1	1	14	9	9
4	Manchester United	6	4	0	2	15	9	8
5	Stockport County	6	2	3	1	6	10	7
6	Stoke	6	3	0	3	11	6	6
7	Preston North End	6	2	2	2	8	7	6
8	BOLTON WANDERERS	6	3	0	3	12	12	6
9	Liverpool	6	2	1	3	13	10	5
10	Oldham Athletic	6	2	1	3	9	8	5
11	Blackpool	6	2	1	3	10	12	5
12	Port Vale	6	2	1	3	9	12	5
13	Manchester City	6	2	1	3	3	11	5
14	Blackburn Rovers	6	2	0	4	11	15	4
15	Southport Central	6	1	1	4	5	15	3
16	Bury	6	1	0	5	6	16	2

1917/18 7th in Lancs Section Principal Comp., 6th in Subsidiary Competition

			Manager: T.Mather			Barrett H	Buchan TM	Clayton P	Cousins W	Davies A	Davies W	Ellison W	Fay J	Geddes R	Heathcote J	Hilton H	Hodgkiss JH	Hodson J	Hurst G	Kelly P	Longworth B	Mather W	Nuttall J	Pasquill E	Pickup JH	Pilkington F	Rowley W	Rutter M	Seddon J	Smith J	Thomas J	Vizard ET	Wilson J	Winterburn A	Young A
1	Sep	1	STOKE	2-5	Pilkington, Geddes			6			8			7					3			4	2			9		10					5	11	
2		8	Stoke	2-6	Kelly, Geddes			4			10			9				3		8			2		7			6					5	11	
3		15	LIVERPOOL	0-3			6	4			10	1	5	9						8			3		7									11	
4		22	Liverpool	0-6			9	4			10	1		7				3		8			2	6									5	11	
5		29	BURY	4-1	W.Davies, Hilton(2), Winterburn		7	5	4		10	1				8			3	9			2					6						11	
6	Oct	6	Bury	1-1	W.Davies		7	5	4		10	1						3	2	9				8				6						11	
7		13	SOUTHPORT CENTRAL	1-1	Winterburn		8	5	4		10	1						3					2	7		9		6						11	
8		20	Southport Central	2-6	W.Davies, Buchan		4	5	2		10	1		9	7	8							3					6						11	
9		27	Burnley	1-2	Heathcote		4	6	2		10	1		8	7				3				5									9		11	
10	Nov	3	BURNLEY	8-0	Heathcote,Clayton(2),Rutter,Geddes,Winterburn(2,1p),unknown(og)		4	6			10	1		9	7				3				2					8			5			11	
11		10	Manchester United	3-1	Geddes(2), Winterburn		4				10	1		9	7			3	2				5		8			6						11	
12		17	MANCHESTER UNITED	4-2	W.Davies,Heathcote,Geddes,unknown(og)		4				10	1		9	8			3	2				5		7			6						11	
13		24	Stockport County	3-2	Winterburn, W.Davies, Pickup		1	6	4		10			9	8				3				2		7			5						11	
14	Dec	1	STOCKPORT COUNTY	1-3	W.Davies		5	4			10	1		9	8				3				2		7			6						11	
15		8	Oldham Athletic	3-6	Rutter, W.Davies, Heathcote		4	6			10	1			8			3	2				2		7			9						11	
16		15	OLDHAM ATHLETIC	3-5	Geddes, Heathcote, unknown (og)		4		2		10	1		9	8			3					2		7			6						11	
17		22	PORT VALE	0-2			9			5	10				8			3	4				2		7			6						11	
18		25	Bury	2-2	Buchan, Geddes		11					1		9	8				3				2		7			6							5
19		29	Port Vale	2-1	Smith, Geddes		4				8	1		9				3					2		7			6	5	10				11	
20	Jan	1	BURY	4-0	Smith(2), Buchan, Geddes		8							9				3					2		7		5	6	4	10		11			
21		5	BLACKBURN ROVERS	5-2	Smith, Buchan(3), Pickup		9			6		1			8			3					2		7		4		5	10		11			
22		12	Blackburn Rovers	3-1	Winterburn(2), Heathcote	9	4			5	10	1			8				3				2		7			6						11	
23		19	Preston North End	0-2			4			5	10	1	9		8			3					2		7			6						11	
24		26	PRETON NORTH END	4-0	Heathcote(2), Barrett, Winterburn	9	4			5	10	1			8			3					2		7			6						11	
25	Feb	2	Blackpool	5-0	W.Davies(2),Pickup,Heathcote,A.Davies	9	4			5	10	1			8			3					2		7			6						11	
26		9	BLACKPOOL	1-1	Geddes		4			5	10	1		9	8			3					2		7			6						11	
27		16	MANCHESTER CITY	1-0	Heathcote		4				10	1		9	8			3					2		7			6						11	
28		23	Manchester City	1-0	W.Davies	9	4				10	1	5		8				3				2		7			6						11	
29	Mar	2	ROCHDALE	1-1	Winterburn	9	4				10	1			8			3					2		7			6						11	
30		9	Rochdale	2-5	Winterburn, Hurst		4				10	1			8			3	5	9			2		7			6						11	
31		16	EVERTON	2-3	Winterburn, Pickup		5				10				8		1		3	9			2		7			4						11	
32		23	Everton	3-2	Heathcote(2), Pickup		4						5	9	8		1	3		10			2		7			6						11	
33		30	OLDHAM ATHLETIC	2-0	Winterburn, Geddes		4			5				9	8		1	3			7	10	2					6						11	
34	Apr	6	Oldham Athletic	1-2	Heathcote		4			5					8		1	3		10	7	9	2					6						11	
35		13	ROCHDALE	2-1	J.Nuttall, Winterburn		4			5				9	10		1	3					2		7			6						11	
36		22	Rochdale	0-4			4			5					7		1	3	8				2	10				6						11	
					Apps	5	34	13	7	12	28	25	4	20	27	2	6	24	17	9	2	3	35	4	25	2	2	32	3	3	1	3	3	33	1
					Goals	1	6	2		1	10			12	13	2		1		1			1		5	1		2		4				14	

Three own goals

Additional Players: L Abrams31/6, AM Baverstock 3/2, A Clunie 35/8, W Glover 17/1, H Greenhalgh36/9, J Hilton 2/1, W Hulme 29/5, T Kay 20/1, J Livesey 18/10, W Makin 1/1, W Nuttall 18/4

Note
Matches 18, 20 & 33-36 were in the Lancashire Section Subsidiary Compeition

Other Games

1	Mar	29	R.F.A. [Home game]	4-0
2	Apr	27	Blackpool	5-2

FINAL LEAGUE TABLE

		Pl	W	D	L	F	A	Pts
1	Stoke	30	22	4	4	109	27	48
2	Liverpool	30	21	6	3	101	26	48
3	Everton	30	19	6	5	92	36	44
4	Rochdale	30	15	9	6	78	47	39
5	Manchester City	30	15	8	7	57	28	38
6	Stockport County	30	17	3	10	59	32	37
7	BOLTON WANDERERS	30	13	4	13	68	70	30
8	Manchester United	30	11	8	11	45	49	30
9	Oldham Athletic	30	11	6	13	50	59	28
10	Preston North End	30	12	3	15	38	53	27
11	Port Vale	30	9	8	13	47	58	26
12	Blackpool	30	9	6	15	38	67	24
13	Southport Central	30	8	6	16	33	69	22
14	Bury	30	8	5	17	46	64	21
15	Burnley	30	4	5	21	29	100	13
16	Blackburn Rovers	30	2	1	27	22	127	5

FINAL LEAGUE TABLE Subsidiary Tournament

		Pl	W	D	L	F	A	Pts
1	Liverpool	6	5	0	1	24	7	10
2	Everton	6	5	0	1	19	7	10
3	Manchester City	6	4	1	1	11	4	9
4	Preston North End	6	4	1	1	10	8	9
5	Blackpool	6	4	0	2	18	9	8
6	BOLTON WANDERERS	6	3	1	2	11	9	7
7	Oldham Athletic	6	3	1	2	9	9	7
8	Manchester United	6	3	1	2	6	7	7
9	Stoke	6	2	2	2	10	5	6
10	Rochdale	6	3	0	3	13	8	6
11	Burnley	6	2	1	3	10	11	5
12	Bury	6	1	2	3	8	15	4
13	Stockport County	6	2	0	4	6	13	4
14	Port Vale	6	1	0	5	4	15	2
15	Blackburn Rovers	6	1	0	5	3	13	2
16	Southport Central	6	0	0	6	1	23	0

1918/19 4th in Lancs Section Principal Comp., 2nd in Subsidiary Competition

Manager: T. Mather until 21 February then E.Vizard

#		Date	Opponent	Score	Scorers	Ashurst R	Buchan TM	Colbourn J	Cooper E	Davies A	Davies W	Donaldson A	Ellison W	Feebury J	Geddes R	Heathcote J	Hilton H	Hodgkiss JH	Hodson J	Hulme W	Hurst G	Jennings W	Kelly P	Lawrence J	Morris R	Nuttall J	Pickup JH	Roberts F	Rowley W	rutter M	Seddon J	Smith J	Vizard ET	Winterburn A	Woods J
1	Sep	7	Blackpool	4-1	W.Davies, Rutter, Ashurst(2)	9	4			5	10					8		1	3							2	7			6				11	
2		14	BLACKPOOL	2-1	Lythgoe(2)		4			5	10					8		1	3							2	7			6				11	
3		21	Stockport County	2-2	Buchan, Winterburn	9	4			5	10					8		1	3							2	7			6				11	
4		28	STOCKPORT COUNTY	3-1	Heathcote(2), Winterburn	9	4			5	10					8		1	3							2	7			6				11	
5	Oct	5	Bury	5-1	Cooper,Heathcote,Winterburn(2),A.Davies		4		9	5	10					8		1	3							2	7			6				11	
6		12	BURY	3-1	W.Davies, Buchan(2)		4			5	10					8		1	3							2	7			6				11	
7		19	Liverpool	1-6	Heathcote		4			5	10					8		1	3							2	7			6				11	
8		26	LIVERPOOL	2-2	Heathcote(pen), Geddes		4			5	10				9	8		1	3				2				7			6					
9	Nov	2	BURNLEY	2-1	Heathcote(pen), Buchan		4			5	10	1			9	8			3				2				7			6					
10		9	Burnley	4-0	Pickup,Heathcote,W.Davies,Winterburn		4	9		5	10	1				8			3							2	7			6				11	
11		16	SOUTHPORT VULCAN	3-2	W.Davies, Heathcote(2)		4			5	10					8		1	3							2	7			6				11	
12		23	Southport Vulcan	0-0			4	9		5	10					8		1	2	3							7			6				11	
13		30	MANCHESTER UNITED	3-1	W.Davies(2), Jennings		4				10					8		1	3	2		9					7							11	
14	Dec	7	Manchester United	0-1			4	9		5	10					8		1	3	2							7							11	
15		14	STOKE	1-1	Lord		4			5								1	3							7	2							11	
16		21	Stoke	1-7	Roberts		4			5	10					8		1	3				2				7	9		6				11	
17		25	Bury	0-1						5	10					8		1	3				2				7	9	4	6				11	
18		28	Port Vale	1-3	Roberts					5	10							1	3				2				8	7	9	6				11	
19	Jan	1	BURY	2-1	Roberts, Heathcote											8		1	3				2				7	9		6		10		11	
20		11	Blackburn Rovers	3-2	Winterburn(2), Morris													1	3				2	10	8		7	9		6	5			11	
21		18	BLACKBURN ROVERS	3-0	Seddon(2), P.Hilton		44											1	3				2	10	9		7			6	5			11	
22		25	PRESTON NORTH END	2-4	Morris, Buchan		4									8		1	3				2	10	9		7			6	5			11	
23	Feb	1	Preston North End	0-0			4												1	8	2		2	10		3	7	9		6	5			11	
24		8	ROCHDALE	3-2	A.Davies, H.Hilton, Roberts		4			5							8	1					2			3	7	9		6			11		
25		15	Rochdale	2-2	Vizard, Roberts		4			5							8	1	3							2	7	9		6			11	10	
26		22	Everton	1-4	Vizard		4			5							8		3							2	7	9		6			11	10	1
27	Mar	1	EVERTON	3-6	Roberts(2), Rowley		4										8		3				2				7	9	5	6			11	10	1
28		8	Oldham Athletic	1-3	Roberts			10	5								8	1	3	2							7	9	4	6				11	
29		15	OLDHAM ATHLETIC	2-1	Smith, Roberts					5			7		2		8	1	3								9		4	6		10		11	
30		22	Manchester City	2-1	Roberts(2)					5					2		8	1	3								7	9	4	6		10	11		
31		29	MANCHESTER CITY	3-1	Roberts, Smith, Vizard					5			7		2		8	1	3			6					9	4				10	11		
32	Apr	5	Oldham Athletic	1-4	Buchan	8				5			7		2			1	3			6					9	4	10				11		
33		12	OLDHAM ATHLETIC	3-1	Roberts(3)	8				5			7		2				3			6					9	4				10	11		1
34		18	PORT VALE	2-1	Roberts, Vizard	8				5					2				3	10							7	9	4	6			11		
35		19	Rochdale	2-1	Roberts(pen), Feebury	8				5				2					3								7	9	4	6			11	10	1
36		26	ROCHDALE	2-1	Rutter, Roberts(pen)					5				2					3			6					7	9	4	10			11		
			Apps			3	27	3	2	29	17	4	2	8	2	19	8	28	32	2	18	5	5	3	3	16	31	19	11	34	4	5	11	27	5
			Goals			2	6		1	2	6			1	1	10	1					1			2		1	18	1	2	2	2	2	4	7

Additional Players: J Bleakley 18/4, E Boardman 7/9, P Clayton 19&20/4, J Fay 19/5, W Fitton 6/9, P Hilton 21/8 (1 goal),
J Hughes 36/1, B Longworth 36/8, J Lord 15/10 (1 goal), J Lythgoe 2/9 (2 goals), J Spiby 15/9, J Thomas 11/4

Other Games

#		Date	Opponent	Score
1	Apr	21	Derby County	1-5
2	May	8	Oldham Athletic	3-3
3		10	OLDHAM ATHLETIC	6-2

Note:
Matches 5,6,32,33,35 and 36 were in the Lancashire Section Subsidiary Compeition and Lancashire Cup.

FINAL LEAGUE TABLE

	Pl	W	D	L	F	A	Pts
Everton	30	27	2	1	108	26	56
Stoke	30	20	3	7	84	36	43
Liverpool	30	19	4	7	82	33	42
BOLTON WANDERERS	30	15	6	9	58	58	36
Manchester City	30	15	3	12	57	36	33
Southport Vulcan	30	15	3	12	49	53	33
Preston North End	30	12	6	12	41	51	30
Stockport County	30	11	7	12	48	52	29
Manchester United	30	11	5	14	51	50	27
Rochdale	30	11	5	14	56	61	27
Blackpool	30	10	5	15	45	61	25
Port Vale	30	10	4	16	39	77	24
Burnley	30	10	3	17	54	76	23
Bury	30	7	6	17	27	58	20
Oldham Athletic	30	7	4	19	39	62	18
Blackburn Rovers	30	5	4	21	35	83	14

Subsidiary Tournament Section B (Lancashire Senior Cup)

	Pl	W	D	L	F	A	Pts
Oldham Athletic	6	5	0	1	17	4	10
BOLTON WANDERERS	6	5	0	1	16	9	10
Rochdale	6	1	0	5	5	13	2
Bury	6	1	0	5	4	16	2

1919/20   6th in Division One

Manager C.E. Foweraker

#	Date		Opponent	Score	Scorers	Baverstock H	Buchan TM	Cartman HR	Davies A	Donaldson A	Drabble F	Fay J	Feebury JH	Gimblett WS	Herbert WE	Hodson J	Howarth JM	Hughes HJ	Hulme W	Jennings W	Jones J	Pickup JH	Roberts F	Rowley WJ	Seddon J	Smith J	Stokes J	Vizard ET	Watson AG
1	Aug	30	BRADFORD	1-2	Roberts		8			7								1	4	6			9	2	5	10		11	2
2	Sep	1	BURNLEY	1-1	Roberts		8			7		1							4	6			9	2	5	10		11	2
3		6	Bradford	0-2			9			7		1			3					6			8	4	5	10		11	2
4		10	Burnley	1-2	Smith		8			7		1			3					6			9		5	10		11	2
5		13	Manchester City	4-1	Rowley, Smith(2), Roberts		8		5	7	1		3							6			9	4		10		11	2
6		17	Middlesbrough	3-1	Smith(3)		8		5	7	1		3							6			9	4		10		11	2
7		20	MANCHESTER CITY	6-2	Roberts(2), Feebury, Smith(2), Davies		8		5	7	1		3							6			9	4		10		11	2
8		27	Derby County	2-1	Smith, Feebury		8		5	7	1		3							6			9	4		10		11	2
9	Oct	4	DERBY COUNTY	3-0	Roberts, Smith, Feebury(pen)		8			7	1		5	3						6			9	4		10		11	2
10		11	West Bromwich Albion	1-4	Feebury(pen)		8						5	3						1	6		7	9	4	10		11	2
11		18	WEST BROM ALBION	1-2	Roberts		10			7			8	3			1			6			9	4	5				2
12		25	Sunderland	0-2			10			7	1		8	3						6			9	4	5				2
13	Nov	1	SUNDERLAND	1-0	Rowley		8			7	1			3						6			9	4	5	10		11	2
14		8	Arsenal	2-2	Vizard, Buchan		10			7			5	3			1			6			9	4				11	2
15		15	ARSENAL	2-2	Jennings, Buchan		10			7	1		8	3						6			9	4	5			11	2
16		22	Everton *	3-3	Buchan, Stokes, Herbert	2	10				1		5	3	8					6			9	4			7	11	
17		29	EVERTON *	0-2		2	10				1		5	3	4	8				6			9				7	11	
18	Dec	6	Bradford City	1-0	Roberts	2	10	11			1		5	3	8					6			9		4		7		
19		13	BRADFORD CITY	1-1	Buchan	2	10				1		5	3	8					6			9		4		7	11	
20		20	Blackburn Rovers	2-2	Roberts, Herbert	2	10				1		5	3	8					6			9		4		7	11	
21		25	PRESTON NORTH END	4-1	Buchan(3), Herbert	2	10			7	1		5	3	8					6			9		4			11	
22		26	Preston North End	1-1	Broadhurst (og)	2	10				1		5	3	8					6			9		4		7	11	
23		27	BLACKBURN ROVERS	2-1	Roberts, Buchan	2	10			7			5	3	4	8					6		9					11	
24	Jan	1	SHEFFIELD WEDNESDAY	2-0	Roberts(2)		10			7			5	3	8					6			9		4			11	2
25		3	NOTTS COUNTY	1-0	Roberts		10	5		7				3	8					6			9		4		7	11	2
26		17	Notts County	2-2	Seddon, Vizard		6			7	1		5	3	8								9		4	10		11	2
27		24	LIVERPOOL *	0-3			8			7	1		5	3	9					6					4	10		11	2
28	Feb	4	Liverpool *	0-2		2	10			7	1		5	3	8					6			9		4			11	
29		7	CHELSEA	1-2	Vizard	2	8			7			3					1		6			9	4	5	10		11	
30		14	Chelsea	3-2	Roberts, Smith(2)	2	6			7	1			3						9			8	4		10		11	
31		21	NEWCASTLE UNITED	0-3		2	6			7	1	5		3						9			8	4		10		11	
32		28	Newcastle United	1-0	Roberts	2	8		5	7				3		1				6			9	4		10			
33	May	13	ASTON VILLA	2-1	Roberts(2pens)		8		5					3		1				6			9	4		10	7	11	2
34		20	Oldham Athletic	0-2		2	8		5	7				3		1							9	6	4	10		11	
35		27	OLDHAM ATHLETIC	1-0	Smith		6					5			8	1						3	9	4		10	7	11	2
36	Apr	3	Manchester United	1-1	Roberts		6			7		5			8	1						3	9	4		10		11	2
37		5	Sheffield Wednesday	2-0	Roberts, Smith		6			7		5			8	1						3	9	4		10		11	2
38		7	Aston Villa	6-3	Smith(2), Roberts(3,1pen), Vizard		6					5			8	1						3	9	4		10	7	11	2
39		10	MANCHESTER UNITED	3-5	Herbert, Smith, Roberts		6					5			8	1						3	9	4		10	7	11	2
40		17	Sheffield United	2-3	Roberts, Smith	2	4			7					8							6	3	9	5	10		11	
41		24	SHEFFIELD UNITED	1-0	Roberts	2	4			7	1				8							6	3	9	5	10		11	
42	May	1	MIDDLESBROUGH	2-1	Roberts, Herbert	2	4	11		7	1				8							6	3	9	5	10		11	
			Apps			17	42	2	8	30	28	25	25	2	21	7	1	13	3	34	8	1	40	26	24	27	11	39	25
			Goals				8		1				4		5					1			26	2	1	18	1	4	

Ave, Home Attendance: 22,910

Additional Players: H Hilton 14/8, B Longworth 4/4, A Winterburn 11/11

One own goal

F.A. Cup

| 1 | Jan | 10 | CHELSEA | 0-1 | | 35398 | | | | | | | | 7 | 1 | 5 | 3 | | | 8 | | | | 6 | | 9 | | 4 | 10 | | 11 | 2 |

Lancashire Cup

* League games counted as qualifiers for knockout.
Failed to qualify

Manchester Cup

| 1 | Mar | 24 | STALYBRIDGE CELTIC | 3-2 |
| SF | Apr | 12 | Manchester United | 2-5 |

Other Games

| 1 | Apr | 2 | ARSENAL | 4-2 |
| 2 | | 28 | DUBLIN BOHEMIANS | 2-4 |

FINAL TABLE

		Pl.		Home					Away				F.	A.	Pts
			W	D	L	F	A	W	D	L	F	A			(Total)
1	West Bromwich Alb.	42	17	1	3	65	21	11	3	7	39	26	104	47	60
2	Burnley	42	13	5	3	43	27	8	4	9	22	32	65	59	51
3	Chelsea	42	15	3	3	33	10	7	2	12	23	41	56	51	49
4	Liverpool	42	12	5	4	35	18	7	5	9	24	26	59	44	48
5	Sunderland	42	17	2	2	45	16	5	2	14	27	43	72	59	48
6	**BOLTON WANDERERS**	42	11	3	7	35	29	8	6	7	37	36	72	65	47
7	Manchester City	42	14	5	2	52	27	4	4	13	19	35	71	62	45
8	Newcastle United	42	11	5	5	31	13	6	4	11	13	26	44	39	43
9	Aston Villa	42	11	3	7	49	36	7	3	11	26	37	75	73	42
10	Arsenal	42	11	5	5	32	21	4	7	10	24	37	56	58	42
11	Bradford Park Ave.	42	8	6	7	31	26	7	6	8	29	37	60	63	42
12	Manchester United	42	6	8	7	20	17	7	6	8	34	33	54	50	40
13	Middlesbrough	42	10	5	6	35	23	5	5	11	26	42	61	65	40
14	Sheffield United	42	14	5	2	43	20	2	3	16	16	49	59	69	40
15	Bradford City	42	10	6	5	36	25	4	5	12	18	38	54	63	39
16	Everton	42	8	6	7	42	29	4	8	9	27	39	69	68	38
17	Oldham Athletic	42	12	4	5	33	19	3	4	14	16	33	49	52	38
18	Derby County	42	12	5	4	36	18	1	7	13	11	39	47	57	38
19	Preston North End	42	9	6	6	35	27	5	4	12	22	46	57	73	38
20	Blackburn Rovers	42	11	4	6	48	30	2	7	12	16	47	64	77	37
21	Notts County	42	9	8	4	39	25	3	4	14	17	49	56	74	36
22	Sheffield Wed.	42	6	4	11	14	23	1	5	15	14	41	28	64	23

~ 193 ~

1919-20 Season
(Back) Rowley, Eccles (Trainer), Watson, Hughes, Feebery, Fay, Davies, Jennings
(Front) Pickup, Buchan, Roberts, Smith (Capt.), Vizard

1920-21 Season
(Back) Eccles, Elvey, Jones, Hinton, Seddon, Jennings
(Front) Rowley, Donaldson, Herbert, Roberts, Smith, Buchan

1920/21   3rd in Division One

Manager: C.E. Foweraker

No	Date		Opponent	Score	Scorers	Baverstock H	Buchan TM	Cartman HR	Donaldson AP	Drabble F	Elvey JR	Fay JA	Guy G	Herbert WE	Hinton WFW	Hodson J	Hughes J	Jack DBN	Jennings W	Jones J	Longworth B	Mellor F	Moss AE	Roberts F	Rowley WJ	Seddon J	Smith J	Vizard ET	Walsh T	Watson AG	Wright S
1	Aug	28	Manchester United	3-2	Roberts(2), Guy		11	7			2		8		1					6	3			9	4	5	10				
2	Sep	1	Chelsea	0-1			11	7			2		8		1					6	3			9	4	5	10				
3		4	MANCHESTER UNITED	1-1	Smith		11	7			2			8	1					6	3			9	4	5	10				
4		6	CHELSEA	3-1	Roberts(2), Smith	2	11	7						8	1					6	3			9	4		10				5
5		11	WEST BROMWICH ALB.	3-0	Smith(2), Roberts	2	11	7						8	1					6	3			9	4		10				5
6		15	ASTON VILLA	5-0	Roberts(2), Buchan, Smith(2)	2	11	7						8	1					6	3			9	4		10				5
7		18	West Bromwich Albion	1-2	Herbert	2	11		7					8	1					6	3			9	4		10				5
8		25	MANCHESTER CITY	3-0	Smith(2), Roberts	2	11		7					8	1					6	3			9	4	5	10				
9	Oct	2	Manchester City	1-3	Smith	2	11		7					8	1					6	3			9	4	5	10				
10		9	Arsenal	0-0		2			7					8	1					6	3			9	4		10	11			5
11		16	ARSENAL	1-1	Smith	2	4		7					8	1					6	3			9	5		10	11			
12		23	Middlesbrough	1-4	Smith	2			7					8	1					6	3			9	4	5	10	11			
13		30	MIDDLESBROUGH	6-2	Buchan, Smith(3), Roberts(2)	2	8		7			5			1					6	3			9	4		10	11			
14	Nov	6	Derby County	0-0		2	8		7			5			1					6	3			9	4		10	11			
15		13	DERBY COUNTY	1-0	Seddon		10		7			5					1			6	3			9		4		11		8	2
16		20	Blackburn Rovers	2-2	Smith, Roberts	2	8		7								1			6	3			9	4	5	10	11			
17		27	BLACKBURN ROVERS	2-1	Roberts(2)	2	8		7			5					1			6	3			9		4	10	11			
18	Dec	4	Huddersfield Town	0-0		2	8		7			5					1			6	3			9		4	10	11			
19		11	HUDDERSFIELD TOWN	3-1	Smith, Herbert, Roberts	2	4	11	7			5		8			1				3			9		6	10				
20		18	Tottenham Hotspur	2-5	Smith, Rowley	2	11		7			5		8			1				3			9	4	6	10				
21		25	SUNDERLAND	6-2	Smith(4), Seddon, Roberts	2	8		7			5					1		3	4				9		6	10	11			
22		27	Sunderland	0-0		2	8		7			5					1		3	4				9		6	10	11			
23	Jan	1	TOTTENHAM HOTSPUR	1-0	Smith	2	6		7			5					1		3	8				9	4		10	11			
24		15	Oldham Athletic	0-0			6		7								1	8	3	4				9		5	10	11		2	
25		22	OLDHAM ATHLETIC	1-1	Smith		6		7								1	8	3	4				9		5	10	11		2	
26	Feb	5	BRADFORD CITY	1-1	Smith	2	6		7								1	8	3					9	4		10	11			5
27		12	Preston North End	2-1	Roberts(2)	2	6	11	7								1	9	3	4				8		5	10				
28		16	Bradford City	2-2	Roberts, Smith	2	6									7	1	9	3	4				8		5	10	11			
29		26	Burnley	1-3	Roberts	2	6									7	1	9	3	4				8		5	10	11			
30	Mar	5	BURNLEY	1-1	Smith	2	6					5				7	1	9	3	4				8			10	11			
31		12	Sheffield United	2-2	Roberts(2)		6									7	1	9	3	4				8		5	10	11		2	
32		19	SHEFFIELD UNITED	2-2	Smith, Vizard	2	6									7	1	9	3	4				8		5	10	11			
33		25	EVERTON *	4-2	Jack, Roberts, Smith(2)	2	6									7	1	9	3	4				8		5	10	11			
34		26	BRADFORD PARK AVE.	2-0	Jack(2)	2	6			7							1	9	3	4				8		5	10	11			
35		28	Everton *	3-2	Vizard, Smith, Roberts	2	6		7								1	8	3	4				9		5	10	11			
36	Apr	2	Bradford Park Avenue	1-2	Smith	2	6		7								1	8	3	4				9		5	10	11			
37		4	PRESTON NORTH END	3-0	Roberts, Smith, Walsh		6										1	8	3	4				9		5	10	11	7	2	
38		9	NEWCASTLE UNITED	3-1	Smith(3)	2	6		7								1	8	3	4	11		9		5	10				
39		16	Newcastle United	0-1			6		7								1	9	3	4	11	2	8		5	10				
40		23	LIVERPOOL *	1-0	Smith	2	6		7								1	8	3	4			9		5	10	11			
41		30	Liverpool *	3-2	Smith(2), Jack	2	6		7								1	8	3	4			9		5	10	11			
42	May	7	Aston Villa	0-2		2	6		7								1	8	3	4			9		5	10	11			
			Apps			33	40	6	27	1	3	11	2	12	14	10	29	8	27	33	20	2	1	42	16	32	41	29	12	5	6
			Goals				2						1	2				4						24	1	2	38	2	1		

Ave. Home Attendance: 34,320

F.A. Cup

No	Date		Opponent	Score	Att.	Baverstock H	Buchan TM	Donaldson AP	Fay JA	Hughes J	Jack DBN	Jennings W	Roberts F	Rowley WJ	Smith J	Vizard ET
1	Jan	8	Preston North End	0-2	27000	2	6	7	5	1	8	3	9	4	10	11

Lancashire Cup

* League games counted as qualifiers for knockout.

	Date		Opponent	Score
SF	May	9	BURY	4-1
F		14	Manchester City *	1-2

* Played at Old Trafford

Manchester Cup

No	Date		Opponent	Score
1	Mar	14	NEW MOSS COLLIERY	4-1
2	Apr	11	Stalybridge Celtic	2-2
2r		19	STALYBRIDGE CELTIC	6-0
SF	May	2	MOSSLEY	8-0
F		11	MANCHESTER UNITED	2-0

Other Games

No	Date		Opponent	Score
1	Oct	11	Bournemouth	5-0
2	Jan	3	CARDIFF CITY	4-2
3	Feb	19	Sunderland	3-2
4	Apr	20	Broughton & District	2-1
5		27	INTERNATIONAL XI	4-0

FINAL TABLE

		Pl.	Home					Away					F.	A.	Pts
			W	D	L	F	A	W	D	L	F	A		(Total)	
1	Burnley	42	17	3	1	56	16	6	10	5	23	20	79	36	59
2	Manchester City	42	19	2	0	50	13	5	4	12	20	37	70	50	54
3	BOLTON WANDERERS	42	15	6	0	53	17	4	8	9	24	36	77	53	52
4	Liverpool	42	11	7	3	41	17	7	8	6	22	18	63	35	51
5	Newcastle United	42	14	3	4	43	18	6	7	8	23	27	66	45	50
6	Tottenham Hotspur	42	15	2	4	46	16	4	7	10	24	32	70	48	47
7	Everton	42	9	8	4	40	26	8	5	8	26	29	66	55	47
8	Middlesbrough	42	10	6	5	29	21	7	6	8	24	32	53	53	46
9	Arsenal	42	9	8	4	31	25	6	6	9	28	38	59	63	44
10	Aston Villa	42	11	4	6	39	21	7	3	11	24	49	63	70	43
11	Blackburn Rovers	42	7	9	5	36	27	6	6	9	21	32	57	59	41
12	Sunderland	42	11	4	6	34	19	3	9	9	23	41	57	60	41
13	Manchester United	42	9	4	8	34	26	6	6	9	30	42	64	68	40
14	West Bromwich Alb.	42	8	6	7	31	23	5	7	9	23	35	54	58	39
15	Bradford City	42	7	9	5	38	28	5	6	10	23	35	61	63	39
16	Preston North End	42	10	4	7	38	25	5	5	11	23	40	61	65	39
17	Huddersfield Town	42	11	4	6	26	16	4	5	12	16	33	42	49	39
18	Chelsea	42	9	7	5	35	24	4	6	11	13	34	48	58	39
19	Oldham Athletic	42	6	9	6	23	26	3	6	12	26	60	49	86	33
20	Sheffield United	42	5	11	5	22	19	1	7	13	20	49	42	68	30
21	Derby County	42	3	12	6	21	23	2	4	15	11	35	32	58	26
22	Bradford Park Ave.	42	6	5	10	29	35	2	3	16	14	41	43	76	24

~ 195 ~

1921/22 6th in Division One

Manager: C.E. Foweraker

No		Date	Opponent	Score	Scorers	Baverstock H	Buchan TM	Butler W	Cartman HR	Chambers F	Donaldson A	Elvey JR	Haworth R	Hinton F	Hodson J	Jack DBN	Jennings W	Jones J	Longworth B	Lowe J	Mellor F	Nuttall H	Pym RH	Roberts E	Roberts F	Rowley WJ	Seddon J	Simpson H	Smith CF	Smith J	Vizard ET	Watson AG	Wright S
1	Aug	27	PRESTON NORTH END	2-2	J Smith(2,1pen)						2				3	8	6		4				1				5			10	11		
2		29	Tottenham Hotspur	2-1	J Smith(pen), Vizard		6		7		2				3	8			4				1		9		5			10	11		
3	Sep	3	Preston North End	1-3	Jack		6		7		2				3	8			4				1		9					10	11		5
4		5	TOTTENHAM HOTSPUR	1-0	Vizard						2					8	6	3	4			7	1		9		5			10	11		
5		10	BRADFORD CITY	3-3	Jack(2), Roberts						2					8	6	3	4			7	1		9		5			10	11		
6		17	Bradford City	3-4	Jack(2), J Smith				7							8	6	3	4				1		9		5			10	11	2	
7		24	HUDDERSFIELD T	3-1	Jack, J Smith, Roberts						2			1		8	6	3	4						9		5			10	11		
8	Oct	1	Huddersfield Town	0-3		2	7							1		8	6	3	4	11					9		5			10			
9		8	Cardiff City	2-1	Buchan, Jack		10		11					1		8	6	3				7			9	4	5					2	
10		15	CARDIFF CITY	1-2	Roberts		10		7					1		8	6	3							9	4	5				11	2	
11		22	Birmingham	1-1	Roberts				7					1		8	6	3							9		5			10	11	2	4
12		29	BIRMINGHAM	1-2	Roberts				7					1		8	6	3							9		5			10	11	2	4
13	Nov	5	West Bromwich Albion	1-0	Jack		6		7				2	1	3	8			4						9		5			10	11		
14		12	WEST BROMWICH ALB.	2-0	Vizard, Roberts		6		7				2	1		8		3	4						9		5			10	11		
15		19	ARSENAL	1-0	Jack		6		7				2	1		8		3	4						9		5			10	11		
16	Dec	3	Manchester City	3-2	Jack, Roberts(2)		6						2	1		8		3	4					7	9	5				10	11		
17		10	MANCHESTER CITY	5-0	Roberts(2), Jack(2), J Smith		6						2	1		8		3	4					7	9	5				10	11		
18		12	Arsenal	1-1	Jack		6						2	1		8		3	4					7	9	5				10	11		
19		17	Blackburn Rovers	2-1	Roberts, Jack							7	2	1		8	6	3	4						9					10	11		5
20		24	BLACKBURN ROVERS	1-1	Jack							7	2	1		8	6	3	4						9		5			10	11		
21		26	Oldham Athletic	0-0					7				2	1		8	6	3	4						9		5			10	11		
22		31	Everton	0-1								7	2	1		8	6	3	9							4	5			10	11		
23	Jan	2	OLDHAM ATHLETIC	5-1	Roberts, Jack(3), J Smith (pen)				7				2	1		8	6	3	4						9		5			10	11		
24		14	EVERTON	1-0	Jack		6						2	1		8		3	4					7	9	5				10	11		
25		18	Chelsea	3-0	Buchan, Jack(2,1pen)		8		7				2				6	3	4				1		9		5			10	11		
26		21	CHELSEA	0-2			10	8		7			2	1			6	3	4	11					9		5						
27	Feb	4	SHEFFIELD UNITED	3-1	Roberts(2), Jack	11			7				2			8	6	3	4						9		5		10				
28		11	Sheffield United	0-1					7				2			8	6	3	4						9		5			10	11		
29		18	BURNLEY	0-1					7				2			8	6	3	4						9				5	10	11		
30		25	Burnley	0-2			6			2	7					3	8		4						9				5	10	11		
31	Mar	4	NEWCASTLE UNITED	3-2	Roberts, J Smith (pen), Bradley (og)		6	8	3				2						4			7	1		9		5			10	11		
32		11	Newcastle United	1-2	J Smith			7	3				2			8			4					6	9	5				10	11		
33		18	Liverpool	2-0	Jack, J Smith (pen)			7	3				2			8			4					6	9					10	11		
34		25	LIVERPOOL	1-3	J Smith			7	3				2			8			4					6	9				5	10	11		
35	Apr	1	Manchester United	1-0	J Smith	11	7						2			8		3	4					6	9	5		10				
36		8	MANCHESTER UNITED	1-0	Jack		7						2			8			4					6	9	5	11	10				
37		14	Sunderland	2-6	Roberts, J Smith (pen)		7						2			8		3	4					6	9	5			10	11		
38		15	Aston Villa	1-2	Roberts		6	7					2			8			4			3	1		9	5			10	11		
39		17	SUNDERLAND	1-1	J Smith		6	7			2	3				8			4				1		9	5			10	11		
40		22	ASTON VILLA	1-0	Roberts		6	7			2	3				8			4				1		9		5		10	11		
41		29	Middlesbrough	2-4	Jack, J Smith		6	7					2			8			4			3	1		9		5		10	11		
42	May	6	MIDDLESBROUGH	4-2	Jack, J Smith, Rowley, Butler		9						2			8		3	4	7			1			5		11	10			
					Apps	1	22	13	13	5	8	8	29	19	5	39	20	29	38	4	1	10	23	4	39	13	27	2	3	39	35	5	4
					Goals		2	1								24									18	1				18	3		

Ave. Home Attendance: 24,800

One own goal

Additional Players: WE Herbert 1/7, JS Keetley 36/1, JP Long 7/7, T Walsh 41/9

F.A. Cup

		Date	Opponent	Score	Scorer	Att.			Haworth R	Hinton F		Jack DBN	Jennings W	Jones J	Longworth B			Pym?	Roberts F		Seddon J			Smith J	Vizard ET
1	Jan	7	BURY	1-0	Vizard	42831		7	2	1		8	6	3	4				9		5			10	11
2		28	MANCHESTER CITY	1-3	Roberts	66442		7	2	1		8	6	3	4				9		5			10	11

Lancashire Cup

Q	Apr	26	EVERTON	6-0
Q	May	3	LIVERPOOL	3-1
SF		8	Manchester City *	0-0
SFr		13	Manchester City +	1-0
F		17	Bury	3-1

* Played at Old Trafford   + Played at Bury

Manchester Cup

1	Feb	28	ROCHDALE	2-1
2	Mar	28	STALYBRIDGE CELTIC	2-0
SF	May	1	Stockport County	4-4
SFr		10	STOCKPORT COUNTY	6-0
F		20	Eccles United *	3-1

* Played at Old Trafford

Other Games

1	Aug	30	Witton Albion	2-2
2	Oct	10	Swansea	2-0
3		19	NORTHERN NOMADS	3-0
4		26	BOLTON WED. LEAGUE	6-0

	FINAL TABLE	Pl	Home					Away					F.	A.	Pts
			W	D	L	F	A	W	D	L	F	A		(Total)	
1	Liverpool	42	15	4	2	43	15	7	9	5	20	21	63	36	57
2	Tottenham Hotspur	42	15	3	3	43	17	6	6	9	22	22	65	39	51
3	Burnley	42	16	3	2	49	18	6	2	13	23	36	72	54	49
4	Cardiff City	42	13	2	6	40	26	6	8	7	21	27	61	53	48
5	Aston Villa	42	16	3	2	50	19	6	0	15	24	36	74	55	47
6	BOLTON WANDERERS	42	12	4	5	40	24	8	3	10	28	35	68	59	47
7	Newcastle United	42	11	5	5	36	19	7	5	9	23	26	59	45	46
8	Middlesbrough	42	12	6	3	46	19	4	8	9	33	50	79	69	46
9	Chelsea	42	9	6	6	17	16	8	6	7	23	27	40	43	46
10	Manchester City	42	13	7	1	44	21	5	2	14	21	49	65	70	45
11	Sheffield United	42	11	3	7	32	17	4	7	10	27	37	59	54	40
12	Sunderland	42	13	4	4	46	23	3	4	14	14	39	60	62	40
13	West Bromwich Alb.	42	8	6	7	26	23	7	4	10	25	40	51	63	40
14	Huddersfield Town	42	12	3	6	33	14	3	6	12	20	40	53	54	39
15	Blackburn Rovers	42	8	6	7	35	31	6	6	9	19	26	54	57	38
16	Preston North End	42	12	7	2	33	20	1	5	15	9	45	42	65	38
17	Arsenal	42	10	6	5	27	19	5	1	15	20	37	47	56	37
18	Birmingham	42	9	2	10	25	29	6	5	10	23	31	48	60	37
19	Oldham Athletic	42	8	7	6	21	15	5	4	12	17	35	38	50	37
20	Everton	42	10	7	4	42	22	2	5	14	15	33	57	55	36
21	Bradford City	42	8	5	8	28	30	3	5	13	20	42	48	72	32
22	Manchester United	42	7	7	7	25	26	1	5	15	16	47	41	73	28

1921-22 Season
(Back) Wright, Broome, Hinton, John Jones, Nuttall
(Middle) Corbett, Walsh, Hodsosn, Eivey, Seddon, Jennings, Pym, Kidd
(Front) Longworth, Buchan, Jack, Roberts, Smith, Vizard, Jim Jones, Cartman, Mills

1922-23 Season
(Back) Haworth, Finney, Seddon, Pym, Jennings, Greenhalgh
(Front) Butler, Jack, J.R.Smith, J.Smith, Vizard

1922-23 13th in Division One

Manager : C.E. Foweraker

Match Results

#	Date		Opponent	Score	Scorers
1	Aug	26	Preston North End	1-3	Flood
2	Sep	2	PRESTON NORTH END	1-1	F Roberts
3		4	OLDHAM ATHLETIC	3-1	Flood, J Smith (pen), Rowley
4		9	SUNDERLAND	1-1	Vizard
5		11	Oldham Athletic	1-3	J Smith
6		16	Sunderland	1-5	J Smith
7		23	BIRMINGHAM	3-0	Vizard, J Smith(2)
8		30	Birmingham	0-2	
9	Oct	5	Nottingham Forest	1-1	J Smith
10		7	HUDDERSFIELD T	1-0	Jack
11		14	Huddersfield Town	2-0	J Smith, Jack
12		21	Aston Villa	0-2	
13		28	ASTON VILLA	3-0	Butler, Walsh, Buchan
14	Nov	4	STOKE	1-1	J Smith
15		11	Stoke	0-2	
16		18	Manchester City	0-2	
17		25	MANCHESTER CITY	2-1	Jack, JR Smith
18	Dec	2	West Bromwich Albion	1-1	J Smith
19		9	WEST BROMWICH ALB.	3-0	Jack(3)
20		16	Blackburn Rovers	0-1	
21		23	BLACKBURN ROVERS	3-0	J Smith(2), Jack
22		25	ARSENAL	4-1	JR Smith, Butler, J Smith, Jack
23		26	Arsenal	0-5	
24		30	CARDIFF CITY	0-0	
25	Jan	2	NOTTM. FOREST	4-2	J Smith(4)
26		6	Cardiff City	0-1	
27		20	SHEFFIELD UNITED	1-1	JR Smith
28		27	Sheffield United	2-2	Walsh, Jack
29	Feb	10	BURNLEY	2-1	J Smith, Jack
30		17	Tottenham Hotspur	1-0	Jones
31	Mar	3	Liverpool *	0-3	
32		12	Burnley	1-2	Jennings
33		17	NEWCASTLE UNITED	1-0	Walsh
34		30	EVERTON *	0-2	
35		31	MIDDLESBROUGH	1-1	JR Smith
36	Apr	2	Everton	1-1	Jones
37		7	Middlesbrough	2-1	Jack, JR Smith
38		11	TOTTENHAM HOTSPUR	0-2	
39		14	CHELSEA	1-1	JR Smith
40		16	Newcastle United	0-1	
41		18	LIVERPOOL	1-1	JR Smith
42		21	Chelsea	0-3	

Ave. Home Attendance: 21,250

Appearances / Goals

	Buchan TM	Butler W	Chambers F	Crewe W	Finney A	Flood CW	Haworth R	Howarth N	Jack DBN	Jennings W	Johnston JB	Jones JLM	Longworth B	Lowe J	Matthews VE	Newnes J	Nuttall H	Pym RH	Roberts EF	Roberts F	Rowley WJ	Seddon J	Simpson H	Smith CF	Smith J	Smith JR	Thirkell P	Vizard ET	Walsh T	Wright WB
Apps	9	30	2	4	26	8	30	2	41	32	1	9	5	1	2	7	20	42	1	8	33	16	5	4	37	22	14	38	7	6
Goals	1	2				2			11	1		2								1	1				17	7		2	3	

F.A. Cup

#	Date		Opponent	Score	Scorers	Att.
1	Jan	13	Norwich City	2-0	J Smith, JR Smith	15286
2	Feb	3	LEEDS UNITED	3-1	Jack(2), J Smith	43341
3		24	Huddersfield Town	1-1	Jack	39442
3r		28	HUDDERSFIELD TOWN	1-0	Jack	61609
4	Mar	10	Charlton Athletic	1-0	Jack	41033
SF		24	Sheffield United	1-0	Jack	72000
F	Apr	28	West Ham United	2-0	Jack, JR Smith	126047

SF at Old Trafford, Manchester. Final at Wembley Stadium.

Lancashire Cup

* League games counted as cup tie qualifying rounds.

Q	Mar	3	Liverpool	0-3
Q		30	EVERTON	0-2

Manchester Cup

1	Feb	7	MOSSLEY	6-0
2	Apr	10	Stockport County	0-2

Other Games

1	Sep	25	Plymouth Argyle	0-3
2		27	Exeter City	2-0
3	May	5	Chorley	8-0
4		20	Servette Geneva	2-2
5		21	Young Boys Berne	2-0
6		23	Norastern Basle	2-1
7		26	La Chaux de Fond	5-0
8		27	Zurich XI	5-1
9		30	Young Boys Berne	2-1
10	Jun	2	Mullhouse	6-0
11		3	Alsace XI	3-0

Final Table

		Pl.	Home W	Home D	Home L	Home F	Home A	Away W	Away D	Away L	Away F	Away A	F. (Total)	A. (Total)	Pts
1	Liverpool	42	17	3	1	50	13	9	5	7	20	18	70	31	60
2	Sunderland	42	15	5	1	50	25	7	5	9	22	29	72	54	54
3	Huddersfield Town	42	14	2	5	35	15	7	9	5	25	17	60	32	53
4	Newcastle United	42	13	6	2	31	11	5	6	10	14	26	45	37	48
5	Everton	42	14	4	3	41	20	6	3	12	22	39	63	59	47
6	Aston Villa	42	15	3	3	42	11	3	7	11	22	40	64	51	46
7	West Bromwich Alb.	42	12	7	2	38	10	5	4	12	20	39	58	49	45
8	Manchester City	42	14	6	1	38	16	3	5	13	12	33	50	49	45
9	Cardiff City	42	15	2	4	51	18	3	5	13	22	41	73	59	43
10	Sheffield United	42	11	7	3	41	20	5	3	13	27	44	68	64	42
11	Arsenal	42	13	4	4	38	16	3	6	12	23	46	61	62	42
12	Tottenham Hotspur	42	11	3	7	34	22	6	4	11	16	28	50	50	41
13	**BOLTON WANDERERS**	42	11	8	2	36	17	3	4	14	14	41	50	58	40
14	Blackburn Rovers	42	12	7	2	32	19	2	5	14	15	43	47	62	40
15	Burnley	42	12	3	6	39	24	4	3	14	19	35	58	59	38
16	Preston North End	42	12	3	6	41	26	1	8	12	19	38	60	64	37
17	Birmingham	42	10	4	7	25	19	3	7	11	16	38	41	57	37
18	Middlesbrough	42	11	4	6	41	25	2	6	13	16	38	57	63	36
19	Chelsea	42	5	13	3	29	20	4	5	12	16	33	45	53	36
20	Nottingham Forest	42	12	2	7	25	23	1	6	14	16	47	41	70	34
21	Stoke	42	7	9	5	28	19	3	1	17	19	48	47	67	30
22	Oldham Athletic	42	9	6	6	21	20	1	4	16	14	45	35	65	30

1923/24 4th in Division One

Manager: C.E. Foweraker

#	Date		Opponent	Score	Scorers	Baggett WJ	Boston HJ	Butler W	Chambers F	Finney A	Haworth R	Hinton WFW	Howarth N	Jack DBN	Jack RR	Jennings W	Jones JLM	Longworth B	Nuttall H	Pym RH	Rowley WJ	Seddon J	Simpson H	Smith J	Smith JR	Vizard ET	Walsh T	Wright WB
1	Aug	25	Cardiff City	2-3	D Jack(2)			7		3	2			8		6			4	1		5		10	9	11		
2		27	Sheffield United	0-0				7		3	2			8		6			4	1		5		10	9	11		
3	Sep	1	CARDIFF CITY	2-2	J Smith(2)			7		3	2		6	8					4	1		5		10	9	11		
4		3	SHEFFIELD UNITED	4-2	JR Smith(3), Nuttall			7		3	2		6	8					4	1	5			10	9	11		
5		8	Manchester City	1-1	JR Smith			7		3	2			8		6			4	1		5		10	9	11		
6		10	Birmingham	3-0	JR Smith(2), D Jack			7		3	2			8		6			4	1		5		10	9	11		
7		12	Newcastle United	0-1				7		3	2			8		6			4	1		5		10	9	11		
8		15	MANCHESTER CITY	0-0				7		3	2			8		6			4	1		5		10		11	9	
9		22	Tottenham Hotspur	0-0				7		3	2			8		6			4	1		5		10	9	11		
10		29	TOTTENHAM HOTSPUR	3-1	JR Smith, D Jack(2)			7		3	2	1		8		6			4			5		10	9	11		
11	Oct	6	Sunderland	2-2	JR Smith(2)			7		3	2			8		6			4	1		5		10	9	11		
12		13	SUNDERLAND	1-0	Nuttall			7		3	2			8		6			4	1		5		10	9	11		
13		20	ARSENAL	1-2	JR Smith	8		7	2	3						6			4	1		5		10	9	11		
14		27	Arsenal	0-0				7		3				8		6			4	1	2	5		10	9	11		
15	Nov	3	Chelsea	0-0				7		3	2			8		6			4	1		5		10		11	9	
16		10	CHELSEA	4-0	J Smith, D Jack(3)			7		3	2			8		6			4	1	5			10	9	11		
17		17	HUDDERSFIELD T	3-1	J Smith, JR Smith, D Jack			7		3	2			8		6			4	1	5			10	9	11		
18		24	Huddersfield Town	0-1				7		3	2			8		6			4	1		5		10	9	11		
19	Dec	1	WEST HAM UNITED	1-1	Bishop (og)			7		3	2			8		6			4	1		5		10	9	11		
20		8	West Ham United	1-0	D Jack			7		3	2		6	8					4	1		5		10	9	11		
21		15	NOTTS COUNTY	7-1	J Smith(2), D Jack(2), JR Smith, Butler			7		3	2		6	8					4	1		5		10	9	11		
22		22	Notts County	1-1	J Smith			7		3	2			8		6		4		1		5		10	9	11		
23		25	WEST BROMWICH ALB.	2-0	J Smith, JR Smith			7		3	2			8		6		4		1	5			10	9	11		
24		26	West Bromwich Albion	5-0	D Jack(3), J Smith, JR Smith			7		3	2			8		6		4		1	5			10	9	11		
25		29	EVERTON	2-0	Vizard, D Jack			7		3	2			8		6		4		1	5			10	9	11		
26	Jan	1	BIRMINGHAM	1-1	J Smith			7		3	2			8		6		4		1	5			10	9	11		
27		5	Everton	2-2	J Smith, D Jack			7		3	2			8		6		4		1	5			10	9	11		
28		19	ASTON VILLA	1-0	JR Smith			7		3	2			8		6		4		1	5			10	9	11		
29		26	Aston Villa	0-1				7		3	2			8		6		4		1	5			10	9	11		
30	Feb	9	Liverpool	1-3	J Smith			7		3	2			8		6		4		1	5			10	9	11		
31		16	NOTTM. FOREST	4-0	D Jack(2), Howarth, JR Smith			7		3	2		6	8				4		1		5	11	10	9			
32		23	Nottingham Forest	0-1				7		3	2			8		6		4		1		5		10	9	11		
33	Mar	1	BURNLEY	0-0				7		3	2			8		6		4		1		5		10	9	11		
34		12	Liverpool	4-1	J Smith(2), JR Smith, D Jack			7		3	2			8		6			4	1	5			10	9	11		
35		15	Middlesbrough	2-1	Simpson, R Jack			7		3	2		6	8	9				4	1		5	11	10				
36		22	MIDDLESBROUGH	2-0	D Jack			7		3	2		6	8	9				4	1		5		10		11		
37		29	Preston North End	2-0	D Jack, R Jack		7			3	2			8	9	6			4	1		5				11		10
38	Apr	1	Burnley	0-1			7			3	2			8	9	6			4	1		5				11		10
39		5	PRESTON NORTH END	0-0			7			3	2			8	9	6			4	1		5				11		10
40		12	Blackburn Rovers	1-3	J Smith	8	7			3	2		6		9				4	1		5		10		11		
41		18	NEWCASTLE UNITED	0-1			7			3	2			8		6			4	1		5		10		11		9
42		19	BLACKBURN ROVERS	3-0	Jones, J Smith, D Jack		7			3	2			8		6	9		4	1		5		10		11		
			Apps			2	6	36	5	42	36	1	8	39	7	34	1	12	30	41	14	29	2	39	32	40	2	4
			Goals					2					1	24	2		1		2				1	16	17	1		

Ave. Home Attendance: 20,480

One own goal

F.A. Cup

#	Date		Opponent	Score	Scorers	Att	Butler W	Finney A	Haworth R	Jack DBN	Jack RR	Jennings W	Nuttall H	Pym RH	Seddon J	Smith J	Smith JR	Vizard ET
1	Jan	12	Hull City	2-2	JR Smith, D Jack	28000		3	2	8	7	6	4	1	5	10	9	11
1r		16	HULL CITY	4-0	JR Smith(2), D Jack(2)	40315	7	3	2	8		6	4	1	5	10	9	11
2	Feb	2	LIVERPOOL	1-4	JR Smith	51596	7	3	2	8		6	4	1	5	10	9	11

Lancashire Cup

#	Date		Opponent	Score
1	Sep	24	Burnley	0-2

Manchester Cup

#	Date		Opponent	Score
1	Feb	20	ECCLES UNITED	8-2
2	Mar	26	STALYBRIDGE CELTIC	2-1
SF	Apr	30	Manchester United	0-4

Other Games

#	Date		Opponent	Score
1	Oct	9	Celtic	1-1
2		31	Bournemouth	0-0
3	Mar	6	Nuneaton Borough	3-2
4		8	Corinthians	0-0
5	Apr	21	CELTIC	0-0
6		23	Llandudno	3-1
7		26	Hearts	1-1
8		29	Atherton	2-1
9	May	4	Gutmus	3-1
10		7	Fortuna	9-0
11		11	Sparta Praque	3-1
12		13	Nurnberg	4-0
13		15	Munich	3-1
14		18	Union Club	4-0
15		19	Aberdeen *	3-1
16		21	Ajax	3-1
17		25	Leeds United +	3-1
18		29	Sparta Rotterdam	5-1

* Played in Leipzig   + Played in Amsterdam

FINAL TABLE

		Pl.	Home W	D	L	F	A	Away W	D	L	F	A	F.	A.	Pts (Total)
1	Huddersfield Town	42	15	5	1	35	9	8	6	7	25	24	60	33	57
2	Cardiff City	42	14	5	2	35	13	8	8	5	26	21	61	34	57
3	Sunderland	42	12	7	2	38	20	10	2	9	33	34	71	54	53
4	BOLTON WANDERERS	42	13	6	2	45	13	5	8	8	23	21	68	34	50
5	Sheffield United	42	12	5	4	39	16	7	7	7	30	33	69	49	50
6	Aston Villa	42	10	10	1	33	11	8	3	10	19	26	52	37	49
7	Everton	42	13	7	1	43	18	5	6	10	19	35	62	53	49
8	Blackburn Rovers	42	14	5	2	40	13	6	12	14	37	54	54	50	45
9	Newcastle United	42	13	5	3	40	21	4	5	12	20	33	60	54	44
10	Notts County	42	9	7	5	21	15	5	7	9	23	34	44	49	42
11	Manchester City	42	11	7	3	34	24	4	5	12	20	47	54	71	42
12	Liverpool	42	11	5	5	35	20	4	6	11	14	28	49	48	41
13	West Ham United	42	10	6	5	26	17	3	9	14	26	40	43	41
14	Birmingham	42	10	4	7	25	19	3	9	9	16	30	41	49	39
15	Tottenham Hotspur	42	9	6	6	30	22	3	8	10	20	34	50	56	38
16	West Bromwich Alb.	42	10	6	5	43	30	2	8	11	8	32	51	62	38
17	Burnley	42	10	5	6	39	27	2	7	12	16	33	55	60	36
18	Preston North End	42	8	4	9	34	27	4	6	11	18	40	52	67	34
19	Arsenal	42	8	5	8	25	24	4	4	13	15	39	40	63	33
20	Nottingham Forest	42	7	5	9	19	15	3	3	15	23	49	42	64	32
21	Chelsea	42	7	9	5	23	21	2	5	14	8	32	31	53	32
22	Middlesbrough	42	6	4	11	23	23	1	4	16	14	37	37	60	22

1924/25 3rd in Division One

Manager: C.E. Foweraker

#	Date	Opponent	Score	Scorers	Boston HJ	Bourne JT	Butler W	Cassidy J	Davies RI	Eatock T	Finney A	Forbes J	Greenhalgh HW	Haworth R	Howarth N	Jack DBN	Jack RR	Jennings W	Matthews VE	Nuttall H	Pym RH	Rowley WI	Seddon J	Smith J	Smith JR	Vizard ET	Wright WB	Chambers J
1	Aug 30	Tottenham Hotspur	0-3				7	9			3			2		8		6		4	1		5	10		11		
2	Sep 1	WEST BROMWICH ALB.	1-1	D Jack			7	9			3			2		8		6	5	4	1			10		11		
3	6	BURY	3-3	Cassidy(2), J Smith			7	9			3			2		8		6		4	1		5	10		11		
4	8	Birmingham	0-1				7	9			3			2		8		6		4	1		5	10		11		
5	13	NOTTS COUNTY	1-0	J Smith(pen)			7	10			3					8				4	1	2	5	6	9	11		
6	20	Everton	2-2	JR Smith, D Jack			7	10			3					8				4	1	2	5	6	9	11		
7	27	SUNDERLAND	1-2	D Jack			7	10			3					8				4	1	2	5	6	9	11		
8	Oct 4	Cardiff City	2-1	J Smith, D Jack	7			9			3					8		6		4	1	2	5	10		11		
9	11	PRESTON NORTH END	6-1	Vizard, D Jack(2), J Smith(2), Cassidy	7			9			3					8		6		4	1	2	5	10		11		
10	18	Burnley	0-0				7	9			3			2		8		6		4	1		5	10		11		
11	25	Manchester City	2-2	J Smith(2,1 pen)			7				3			2		8		6		4	1		5	10	9	11		
12	Nov 1	ARSENAL	4-1	JR Smith, D Jack(2)			7				3		11	2		8		6		4	1		5	10	9			
13	8	Aston Villa	2-2	JR Smith, J Smith			7				3		11	2		8		6		4	1		5	10	9			
14	15	HUDDERSFIELD T	1-0	Cassidy(2), J Smith			7	9			3			2		8		6		4	1		5	10		11		
15	22	Blackburn Rovers	2-0	J Smith, Eatock			7	9		11	3			2		8		6		4	1		5	10				
16	29	WEST HAM UNITED	5-0	JR Smith(3), Cassidy(2)			7	10		11	3			2		8		6		4	1		5		9			
17	Dec 6	Sheffield United	0-2				7	10		11	3			2		8		6		4	1		5		9			
18	13	NEWCASTLE UNITED	3-2	JR Smith(2), D Jack			7	10		11	3			2		8		6		4	1		5		9			
19	20	Liverpool	0-0				7		10	11	3			2	6	8				4	1		5		9			
20	25	NOTTM. FOREST	1-0	JR Smith			7			11	3			2	6	8				4	1		5		9		10	
21	26	Nottingham Forest	1-1	Wright			7			11	3			2	6	8				4	1		5		9		10	
22	27	TOTTENHAM HOTSPUR	3-0	D Jack, J Smith(pen), JR Smith			7			11	3			2	6	8				4	1		5	10	9			
23	Jan 1	BIRMINGHAM	3-0	J Smith(2), D Jack			7				3			2	6	8				4	1		5	10	9	11		
24	3	Bury	0-1				7				3			2	6	8				4	1		5	10	9	11		
25	17	Notts County	1-0	D Jack			7	9			3			2	6	8				4	1		5	10		11		
26	24	EVERTON	1-0	D Jack			7				3	9		2	6	8				4	1		5	10		11		
27	Feb 7	CARDIFF CITY	3-0	Vizard(2), D Jack			7	9			3		5	2	6	8				4	1			10		11		
28	11	Sunderland	0-1				7	9			3			2	6	8				4	1		5	10			11	
29	14	Preston North End	0-1				7	9			3			2	6	8				4	1		5	10		11		
30	21	BURNLEY	5-0	J Smith(2), Cassidy, D Jack(2)	7			9			3			2	6	8				4	1		5	10		11		
31	28	MANCHESTER CITY	4-2	J Smith(3), D Jack	7			9			3			2	6	8				4	1		5	10		11		
32	Mar 7	Arsenal	0-1		7			9			3			2	6	8				4	1		5	10		11		
33	14	ASTON VILLA	4-0	J Smith(2), D Jack(2)		1	7				3			2	6	9	8			4			5	10		11		
34	21	Huddersfield Town	0-0			1	7				3			2	6	9	8			4			5	10		11		
35	Apr 4	West Ham United	1-1	Vizard		1	7				3			2		9	8	6		4			5	10		11		
36	10	LEEDS UNITED	1-0	JR Smith			7				3			2		8		6		4	1		5	10	9	11		
37	11	SHEFFIELD UNITED	3-1	D Jack, J Smith(2,1 pen)			7				3			2		8		6		4	1		5	10	9	11		
38	14	Leeds United	1-2	J Smith(pen)			7				3			2		8		6		4	1		5	10	9	11		
39	18	Newcastle United	1-0	D Jack	7						3			2		8		6		4	1		5	10	9	11		
40	22	Blackburn Rovers	6-0	D Jack(4), JR Smith, J Smith	7						3			2		8		6		4	1		5	10	9	11		
41	25	LIVERPOOL	2-0	D Jack, J Smith(pen)	7						3			2		8		6		4	1		5	10	9	11		
42	May 2	West Bromwich Albion	0-0		7						3			2		8		6		4	1		5	10	9	11		
		Apps			9	3	33	22	2	10	31	1	13	35	16	42	3	23	1	41	39	11	35	36	21	31	4	
		Goals						7	1							26								24	13	4	1	

Ave. Home Attendance: 22,770

F.A. Cup

#	Date	Opponent	Score	Scorers	Att.	Butler W	Finney A	Haworth R	Howarth N	Jack DBN	Nuttall H	Pym RH	Seddon J	Smith J	Smith JR	Vizard ET	Chambers J
1	Jan 10	HUDDERSFIELD TOWN	3-0	D Jack, J Smith(pen), Vizard	50412	7	3		6	8	4	1	5	10	9	11	2
2	31	Tottenham Hotspur	1-1	J Smith	52631	7	3	2	6	8	4	1	5	10	9	11	
2r	Feb 4	TOTTENHAM HOTSPUR	0-1		51774	7	3	2	6	8	4	1	5	10	9	11	

Lancashire Cup

#		Date	Opponent	Score
1	Oct	15	STOCKPORT COUNTY	4-0
2	Nov	5	SOUTHPORT CENTRAL	3-1
SF	Dec	10	Everton *	4-1
F	Jan	21	BLACKPOOL	2-1

* Played at Old Trafford

Manchester Cup

#	Date	Opponent	Score
1	Feb 25	MOSSLEY	4-0
2	Mar 24	Bury	1-3

Other Games

#	Date	Opponent	Score
1	Sep 24	Colwyn Bay	5-1
2	Mar 28	MANCHESTER CITY	3-0
3	May 8	Hakoah	2-1
4	10	MTK Budapest	1-1
5	14	Austrian/Budapest Select	4-2
6	17	Budapest League XI	1-3
7	21	City of Prague	0-2

FINAL TABLE

		Pl.	Home W	D	L	F	A	Away W	D	L	F	A	F. (Total)	A.	Pts
1	Huddersfield Town	42	10	8	3	31	10	11	8	2	38	18	69	28	58
2	West Bromwich Alb.	42	13	6	2	40	17	10	4	7	18	17	58	34	56
3	BOLTON WANDERERS	42	18	2	1	61	13	4	9	8	15	21	76	34	55
4	Liverpool	42	13	5	3	43	20	7	5	9	20	35	63	55	50
5	Bury	42	13	4	4	35	20	4	11	6	19	31	54	51	49
6	Newcastle United	42	11	6	4	43	18	5	10	6	18	24	61	42	48
7	Sunderland	42	13	6	2	39	14	6	4	11	25	37	64	51	48
8	Birmingham	42	10	8	3	27	17	7	4	10	22	36	49	53	46
9	Notts County	42	11	6	4	29	12	5	7	9	13	19	42	31	45
10	Manchester City	42	11	7	3	44	29	6	2	13	32	39	76	68	43
11	Cardiff City	42	11	5	5	35	19	5	6	10	21	32	56	51	43
12	Tottenham Hotspur	42	9	8	4	32	16	6	4	11	20	27	52	43	42
13	West Ham United	42	12	7	2	37	12	3	5	13	25	48	62	60	42
14	Sheffield United	42	10	6	5	34	25	3	8	10	21	38	55	63	39
15	Aston Villa	42	10	7	4	34	25	3	6	12	24	46	58	71	39
16	Blackburn Rovers	42	7	6	8	31	26	4	7	10	22	40	53	66	35
17	Everton	42	11	4	6	25	20	1	7	13	15	40	40	60	35
18	Leeds United	42	9	8	4	29	17	2	4	15	17	42	46	59	34
19	Burnley	42	7	8	6	28	31	4	4	13	18	44	46	75	34
20	Arsenal	42	12	3	6	33	17	2	2	17	13	41	46	58	33
21	Preston North End	42	8	2	11	29	35	2	4	15	8	39	37	74	26
22	Nottingham Forest	42	5	6	10	17	23	1	6	14	12	42	29	65	24

1923-24 Season
Seddon, Pym, Rowley, Finney, Jennings, Jack, Vizard, Nuttall, J.R.Smith, Haworth, Butler, J.Smith

1925-26 Season
(Back) Haworth, Nuttall, Pym, Jennings, Greenhalgh
(Front) Butler, Jack, J.R.Smith, Vizard, Seddon

1925/26 8th in Division One

Manager: C.E. Foweraker

#	Date		Opponent	Score	Scorers	Att.
1	Aug	29	NEWCASTLE UNITED	2-2	J Smith, D Jack	30998
2		31	Leeds United	1-2	Vizard	24188
3	Sep	5	Bury	5-0	JR Smith(2), J Smith(2,1pen), D Jack	23093
4		7	LEEDS UNITED	1-0	J Smith	23343
5		9	Burnley	1-1	Butler	14295
6		12	Notts County	0-3		18587
7		16	BURNLEY	4-2	D Jack, JR Smith, J Smith(2)	16647
8		19	ASTON VILLA	1-3	Vizard	16982
9		26	Leicester City	2-5	JR Smith, D Jack	23820
10	Oct	3	WEST HAM UNITED	1-0	D Jack	20923
11		10	Arsenal	3-2	Vizard(3)	41076
12		17	BLACKBURN ROVERS	2-2	J Smith(pen), Baggett	19648
13		24	Sunderland	1-2	J Smith(pen)	23516
14		31	WEST BROMWICH ALB.	2-2	Howarth, D Jack	17063
15	Nov	7	Birmingham	1-0	Baggett	22134
16		14	MANCHESTER CITY	5-1	D Jack(2), Vizard, Smith J, Baggett	22326
17		21	Tottenham Hotspur	3-2	Baggett, D Jack, Vizard	26792
18		28	CARDIFF CITY	0-1		21520
19	Dec	5	Sheffield United	0-2		20014
20		12	HUDDERSFIELD T	6-1	Butler, J Smith(2), D Jack, JR Smith(2)	25823
21		19	Everton	1-2	Butler	26400
22		25	Manchester United	1-2	D Jack	38503
23	Jan	1	BIRMINGHAM	5-3	D Jack, Vizard, JR Smith(3)	22240
24		2	Newcastle United	1-5	Vizard	34136
25		16	BURY	3-2	Baggett, Vizard, JR Smith	36654
26		23	NOTTS COUNTY	2-1	JR Smith(2)	15507
27	Feb	6	LEICESTER CITY	2-2	J Smith(2pens)	17939
28		13	West Ham United	0-6		24062
29		27	Blackburn Rovers	0-3		21348
30	Mar	13	West Bromwich Albion	3-0	Baggett(2), R Jack	15833
31		17	MANCHESTER UNITED	3-1	Roberts(2), Baggett	10794
32		29	Manchester City	1-1	Vizard	21720
33	Apr	2	LIVERPOOL	0-1		30298
34		3	TOTTENHAM HOTSPUR	1-1	Vizard	21364
35		5	Liverpool	2-2	Boston, R Jack	21398
36		7	SUNDERLAND	3-2	D Jack(2), R Jack	12076
37		10	Cardiff City	1-0	R Jack	13787
38		12	Huddersfield Town	0-3		20829
39		17	SHEFFIELD UNITED	2-1	Butler, J Smith(pen)	13133
40		26	Aston Villa	2-2	Butler, Vizard	13093
41		28	ARSENAL	1-1	J Smith	22198
42	May	1	EVERTON	0-2		11883

Player columns: Baggett WJ, Boston HJ, Butler W, Cope JW, Davies RI, Eatock T, Finney A, Forbes J, Greenhalgh HW, Haworth R, Howarth N, Jack DBN, Jack RR, Jennings W, Jones JLM, Nuttall H, Picken AH, Pym RH, Roberts CL, Round JH, Seddon J, Smith J, Smith JR, Thornborough EH, Vizard ET, Wagstaffe JT, Yates W

Apps: 19 10 32 19 1 1 5 2 17 39 9 37 7 29 2 22 3 39 4 10 29 36 22 23 38 4 3

Goals: 8 1 5 — — — — — — 1 14 4 — — — — — — 2 — — 15 12 — 13

F.A. Cup

#	Date		Opponent	Score	Scorers	Att.
3	Jan	9	Accrington Stanley	1-0	D Jack	32875
4		30	Bournemouth	2-2	JR Smith, D Jack	12000
4r	Feb	3	BOURNEMOUTH	6-2	Boston, J Smith(2), D Jack, JR Smith(2)	24798
5		20	South Shields	3-0	J Smith(pen), D Jack, JR Smith	48166
6	Mar	6	Nottingham Forest	2-2	Butler(2)	26216
6r		10	NOTTINGHAM FOREST*	0-0		29752
6/2r		15	Nottingham Forest ~	1-0	J Smith (p), D Jack, JR Smith	30952
SF		27	Swansea Town+	3-0	Baggett, J smith 2 (1p)	25476
F	Apr	24	Manchester City#	1-0	D Jack	91447

~ Played at Old Trafford. +Played at White Hart Lane.
# Played at Wembley Stadium. * after extra time

Lancashire Cup

1	Nov	3	Nelson	6-0
2		30	Oldham Athletic	0-3

Manchester Cup

1	Feb	10	ECCLES UNITED	9-0
2	Mar	22	Stockport County	1-2

	FINAL TABLE	Pl.	Home					Away					F.	A.	Pts
			W	D	L	F	A	W	D	L	F	A	(Total)		
1	Huddersfield Town	42	14	6	1	50	17	9	5	7	42	43	92	60	57
2	Arsenal	42	16	2	3	57	19	6	6	9	30	44	87	63	52
3	Sunderland	42	17	2	2	67	30	4	4	13	29	50	96	80	48
4	Bury	42	12	4	5	55	34	8	3	10	30	43	85	77	47
5	Sheffield United	42	15	3	3	72	29	4	5	12	30	53	102	82	46
6	Aston Villa	42	12	7	2	56	25	4	5	12	30	51	86	76	44
7	Liverpool	42	9	8	4	43	27	5	8	8	27	36	70	63	44
8	BOLTON WANDERERS	42	11	6	4	46	31	6	4	11	29	45	75	76	44
9	Manchester United	42	12	6	3	40	26	7	2	12	26	47	66	73	44
10	Newcastle United	42	13	3	5	59	33	3	7	11	25	42	84	75	42
11	Everton	42	9	9	3	42	26	3	9	9	30	44	72	70	42
12	Blackburn Rovers	42	11	6	4	59	33	4	5	12	32	47	91	80	41
13	West Bromwich Alb.	42	13	5	3	59	29	3	3	15	20	49	79	78	40
14	Birmingham	42	11	2	5	35	25	2	6	13	31	56	66	81	40
15	Tottenham Hotspur	42	11	4	6	45	36	4	5	12	21	43	66	79	39
16	Cardiff City	42	8	5	8	30	25	8	2	11	31	51	61	76	39
17	Leicester City	42	11	3	7	42	32	3	7	11	28	48	70	80	38
18	West Ham United	42	14	2	5	45	27	1	5	15	18	49	63	76	37
19	Leeds United	42	11	5	5	38	28	3	3	15	26	48	64	76	36
20	Burnley	42	7	7	7	43	35	6	3	12	42	73	85	108	36
21	Manchester City	42	8	7	6	48	42	4	4	13	41	58	89	100	35
22	Notts County	42	11	4	6	37	26	2	3	16	17	48	54	74	33

1926/27   4th in Division One

Manager: C.E. Foweraker

The player-appearance grid column headers (left to right) are:
Baggett WJ · Blackmore HA · Boston HJ · Butler W · Cope JW · Finney A · Gibson GB · Gill JJ · Greenhalgh HW · Haworth R · Jack DBN · Jack RR · Jennings W · Nuttall H · Picken AH · Pym RH · Roberts CL · Roberts WD · Round JW · Seddon J · Smith J · Smith JR · Thornborough EH · Vizard ET · Wagstaffe JT · Wright WB · Yates W

#		Date	Opponent	Res	Scorers	Att
1	Aug	28	Leeds United	5-2	J Smith(pen), D Jack, JR Smith(3)	23699
2	Sep	1	Arsenal	1-2	Butler	23002
3		4	NEWCASTLE UNITED	2-1	D Jack, JR Smith	25049
4		6	ARSENAL	2-2	JR Smith, D Jack	19717
5		11	Burnley	3-4	Baggett(2), D Jack	23730
6		18	CARDIFF CITY	2-0	Vizard, D Jack	18737
7		25	Aston Villa	4-3	Vizard, Jakeman(og), D Jack, JR Smith	20696
8	Oct	2	BIRMINGHAM	1-0	D Jack(pen)	20006
9		9	MANCHESTER UNITED	4-0	JR Smith, Wright(2), Butler	17869
10		16	West Bromwich Albion	1-1	Wright	16622
11		23	BURY	2-2	Butler, Wright	39258
12		30	Tottenham Hotspur	0-1		29999
13	Nov	6	WEST HAM UNITED	2-0	D Jack, J Smith	13934
14		13	Sheffield Wednesday	1-2	J Smith	21033
15		20	LEICESTER CITY	2-0	Butler, D Jack	15255
16		27	Everton	1-1	JR Smith	28091
17	Dec	4	BLACKBURN ROVERS	5-1	D Jack, Butler, J Smith, Vizard(2)	25614
18		11	Huddersfield Town	0-1		24667
19		18	SUNDERLAND	2-2	J Smith(2)	24232
20		25	DERBY COUNTY	3-1	Butler(3,1pen)	31533
21		27	Derby County	0-2		30557
22		28	Liverpool	2-3	J Smith, R Jack	14802
23	Jan	1	LIVERPOOL	2-1	JR Smith(2)	34513
24		15	Leeds United	3-0	Vizard, D Jack, JR Smith	19149
25		22	Newcastle United	0-1		57431
26	Feb	5	Cardiff City	0-1		12721
27		12	ASTON VILLA	0-2		17745
28		26	Manchester United	0-0		29618
29	Mar	5	WEST BROM ALBION	1-1	Vizard	12954
30		9	BURNLEY	3-1	D Jack, W Roberts(2)	13331
31		12	Bury	0-2		30532
32		19	TOTTENHAM HOTSPUR	2-2	W Roberts(2)	17762
33		26	West Ham United	4-4	Vizard, D Jack(2), Gibson	17752
34	Apr	2	SHEFFIELD WEDNESDAY	3-2	Blackmore, Marsden (og), Butler	16195
35		4	Birmingham	1-6	Gibson	6321
36		9	Leicester City	1-0	Blackmore	20768
37		15	SHEFFIELD UNITED	4-1	Gibson(2), Butler, D Jack	23149
38		16	EVERTON	5-0	JR Smith, Gibson(3), Vizard	26381
39		18	Sheffield United	1-1	Blackmore	12893
40		19	Sunderland	2-6	Gibson, JR Smith	14316
41		23	Blackburn Rovers	3-0	Vizard, D Jack, Gibson	14816
42		30	HUDDERSFIELD TOWN	4-0	Wright(3), Seddon	21229

Appearances (Apps) and Goals by player:

Player	Apps	Goals
Baggett WJ	3	2
Blackmore HA	5	3
Boston HJ	3	
Butler W	39	10
Cope JW	26	
Finney A	33	
Gibson GB	14	9
Gill JJ	2	
Greenhalgh HW	34	
Haworth R	14	
Jack DBN	38	16
Jack RR	5	1
Jennings W	10	
Nuttall H	35	
Picken AH	6	
Pym RH	37	
Roberts CL	2	
Roberts WD	5	4
Round JW	5	
Seddon J	35	1
Smith J	12	7
Smith JR	32	13
Thornborough EH	15	
Vizard ET	29	9
Wagstaffe JT	3	
Wright WB	17	7
Yates W	3	

Two own goals

F.A. Cup

#		Date	Opponent	Res	Scorers	Att
3	Jan	8	Blackpool	3-1	JR Smith(3)	16297
4		29	Leeds United	0-0		42694
4r	Feb	2	LEEDS UNITED	3-0	Wright, D Jack, JR Smith	46686
5		19	CARDIFF CITY	0-2		49465

Lancashire Cup

		Date	Opponent	Res
2	Oct	6	Everton	2-1
3	Nov	2	Burnley	3-0
SF		29	Manchester City	6-1
F	May	14	BURY	1-0

Manchester Cup

		Date	Opponent	Res
1	Mar	16	Crewe Alexandra	1-5

Other Games

		Date	Opponent	Res
1	Mar	28	Plymouth Argyle	1-0
2		30	Exeter City	2-3
3	May	5	INTERNATIONAL XI	4-7

FINAL TABLE

		Pl.	Home W	D	L	F	A	Away W	D	L	F	A	F. (Total)	A.	Pts
1	Newcastle United	42	19	1	1	64	20	6	5	10	32	38	96	58	56
2	Huddersfield Town	42	13	6	2	41	19	4	11	6	31	41	76	60	51
3	Sunderland	42	15	3	3	70	28	4	11	28	42		98	70	49
4	BOLTON WANDERERS	42	15	5	1	54	19	4	5	12	30	43	84	62	48
5	Burnley	42	15	4	2	55	30	4	5	12	36	50	91	80	47
6	West Ham United	42	9	6	6	50	36	10	2	9	36	34	86	70	46
7	Leicester City	42	13	4	4	58	33	4	8	9	27	37	85	70	46
8	Sheffield United	42	12	6	3	46	33	5	4	12	28	53	74	86	44
9	Liverpool	42	13	4	4	47	27	5	3	13	22	34	69	61	43
10	Aston Villa	42	11	4	6	51	34	7	3	11	30	49	81	83	43
11	Arsenal	42	12	5	4	47	30	5	4	12	30	56	77	86	43
12	Derby County	42	14	4	3	60	28	3	3	15	26	45	86	73	41
13	Tottenham Hotspur	42	11	4	6	48	33	5	5	11	28	45	76	78	41
14	Cardiff City	42	12	3	6	31	17	4	6	11	24	48	55	65	41
15	Manchester United	42	9	8	4	29	19	4	6	11	23	45	52	64	40
16	Sheffield Wed.	42	15	3	3	49	29	0	6	15	26	63	75	92	39
17	Birmingham	42	13	3	5	36	17	4	1	16	28	56	64	73	38
18	Blackburn Rovers	42	9	5	7	40	40	6	3	12	37	56	77	96	38
19	Bury	42	8	5	8	43	38	4	7	10	25	39	68	77	36
20	Everton	42	10	6	5	35	30	2	4	15	29	60	64	90	34
21	Leeds United	42	9	7	5	43	31	2	1	18	26	57	69	88	30
22	West Bromwich Alb.	42	10	4	7	47	33	1	4	16	18	53	65	86	30

1926-27 Season
(Back) Cope, Greenhalgh, Pym, Seddon, Nuttall
(Front) Butler, Jack, J.R.Smith, Baggett, Vizard, Finney   (inset) Joe Smith

1928-29 Season
(Back) Kean, Haworth, Pym, Finney, Nuttall
(Front) Butler, McCelland, Seddon, Blackmore, Gibson, Cook

1927/28 7th in Division One

Manager: C.E. Foweraker

No	Date	Opponent	Score	Scorers	Att	Blackmore HA	Boston HJ	Butler W	Cope JW	Finney A	Gibson GB	Gill JJ	Gough H	Greenhalgh HW	Haworth R	Jack DBN	Jack RR	Jennins W	McClelland J	Murphy L	Nuttall H	Picken AH	Pym RH	Round JH	Seddon J	Smith JR	Thornborough EH	Vizard ET	Wagstaffe JT	Wright WB
1	Aug 27	Cardiff City	1-2	Smith	24107			7		3	10			2							4		1		5	9	6	11		
2	Sep 3	BLACKBURN ROVERS	3-1	Smith(2), Picken	25711			7		3	10			2							4	11	1		5	9	6			
3	5	EVERTON	1-1	R.Jack	18734			7		3	10			2							4	11	1		5	9	6			
4	10	Bury	0-1		24593			7		3	10			2							4	11	1		5	9	6			8
5	14	Everton	2-2	Butler, Picken	22726			7	4	3	10			2								11	1		5	9	6			8
6	17	Sheffield Wednesday	0-3		19111			7	4	3	10			2							6	11	1		5	9				8
7	24	MIDDLESBROUGH	0-0		21720		7	8			10			2					6		4	11	1		5	9			3	
8	Oct 1	Birmingham	1-1	D Jack	15988	9		7		3	10			2		8					4	11	1		5	6				
9	8	NEWCASTLE UNITED	1-2	D Jack	30676	9		7		3	10			2		8					4	11	1		5	6				
10	15	Huddersfield Town	0-1		19818	9		7		3	10				2	8					4		1	5			6	11		
11	22	LIVERPOOL	2-1	Vizard, Blackmore	12024	9		7	4	3	10				2	8							1	5			6	11		
12	29	Arsenal	2-1	Gibson, Vizard	35787	9		7	4	3	10				2	8					6		1	5				11		
13	Nov 5	BURNLEY	7-1	Blackmore(4,1pen), D Jack(3)	14340	9		7	4	3	10				2	8					6		1	5				11		
14	12	Leicester City	2-4	Wright, Blackmore	21249	9		7	4	3					2	8					6		1	5				11		10
15	19	PORTSMOUTH	3-1	D Jack, Wright, Blackmore	14302	9		7	4	3		1			2	8					6			5				11		10
16	26	Sunderland	1-1	D Jack	20406			7	4	3	10	1			2	8					6			5				11		10
17	Dec 10	West Ham United	0-2		18926			7	4	3	10	1			2	8					6			5				11		10
18	17	ASTON VILLA	3-1	Finney, Smith, Vizard	14852			7	4	3	10	1			2	8					6			5		9		11		
19	24	Sheffield United	3-4	D Jack(3)	10503			7	4	3	10	1			2	8					6			5		9		11		
20	26	TOTTENHAM HOTSPUR	4-1	D Jack(2), Nuttall, Gibson	25229	9		7	4		10	1			2	8		3			6			5				11		
21	31	CARDIFF CITY	2-1	D Jack, Blackmore	15748	9		7	4		10	1			2	8		3			6			5				11		
22	Jan 2	DERBY COUNTY	1-3	Gibson	23569	9		7	4		10	1			2	8		3			6			5			2	11		
23	7	Blackburn Rovers	6-1	D Jack(2), Gibson(2), Smith(2)	14660			7	4		10	1			2	8		3			6	11		5		9				
24	21	Bury	2-1	D Jack, Smith	23487			7	4		10	1			2	8		3		9				5		6				
25	Feb 4	Middlesbrough	5-2	D Jack(2), Smith, Butler, Murphy	21109			7	4		10	1			2	8		3		11	6			5		9				
26	6	Tottenham Hotspur	2-1	Smith(2)	18183			7	4		10	1			2	8		3		11				5		9				
27	11	BIRMINGHAM	3-2	D Jack(2), Gibson	11747			7	4		10	1			2	8		3		11	6			5		9				
28	18	Newcastle United	2-2	D Jack, Murphy	28932			7		3	10	1			2	8				11	4			5		9				
29	25	HUDDERSFIELD TOWN	0-1		44082			7		3	10	1			2	8				11	4			5		9				
30	29	SHEFFIELD WEDNESDAY	2-0	D Jack(2)	9786			7		3	10	1			2	8	9			11	4			5						
31	Mar 3	Liverpool	2-4	D Jack, Gibson	37115			7	4	3	10	1			2	8	9			11	6			5						
32	10	ARSENAL	1-1	R Jack	15546		7	8	4		10				2		9	3		11	6		1	5						
33	17	Burnley	2-2	Butler, McClelland	15865			7	4	3	10	1			2				9	11	6			5						
34	24	LEICESTER CITY	3-3	McClelland(2), Butler	18142			7	4		10				2		9	3			2			5				11		6
35	31	Portsmouth	0-1		21846			7			10				2		9	3	9		4		1	5						6
36	Apr 6	MANCHESTER UNITED	3-2	McClelland, Vizard, Round	23795			7		3	10				2				9		4		1	5				11		6
37	7	SUNDERLAND	1-2	McClelland(pen)	18064			7	4		10				2		9	3						5				11		6
38	9	Manchester United	1-2	McClelland	28590	9	11	7	4	3	10				2				9				1	5			6			
39	14	Derby County	0-1		12378		7		4	3	10				2		9				6		1	5				11		
40	21	WEST HAM UNITED	4-0	McClelland, Murphy, Butler, Nuttall	8520			7	4		10				2		9	3	9	11	6		1	5						
41	28	Aston Villa	2-2	Gibson, Boston	22895		7		4	3	10				2		9			11	6		1	5						
42	Mar 5	SHEFFIELD UNITED	1-1	McClelland	7958		7			3	10				2		9		9		4		1	5			6			

| | | | | Apps | | 12 | 6 | 39 | 28 | 33 | 38 | 17 | 4 | 3 | 28 | 33 | 6 | 18 | 10 | 14 | 36 | 9 | 21 | 21 | 21 | 18 | 21 | 18 | 1 | 16 |
| | | | | Goals | | 8 | 1 | 5 | | 1 | 8 | | | | | 24 | 2 | | 8 | 3 | 2 | 2 | | 1 | | 10 | | 4 | | 2 |

F.A. Cup

Rd	Date	Opponent	Score	Scorers	Att	Butler W	Cope JW	Finney A	Gibson GB	Gill JJ	Haworth R	Jack DBN	Jennins W	McClelland J	Round JH	Smith JR	Thornborough EH	Wright WB
3	Jan 14	LUTON TOWN	2-1	Butler, Smith	20266	7	4		10	1	2	8	3		5	9	6	11
4	28	Stoke City	2-4	Round, Murphy	25000	7	4	3	10	1	2	8		11 6	5	9		

Lancashire Cup

Rd	Date	Opponent	Score
2	Sep 27	Burnley	3-1
3	Oct 17	Preston North End	6-3
SF	Nov 30	BURY	0-2

Manchester Cup

Rd	Date	Opponent	Score
3	Mar 21	WIGAN BOROUGH	1-4

Other Games

No	Date	Opponent	Score
1	Aug 29	Barry	3-1
2	Apr 25	HAMILTON ACC.	4-0
3	30	Atherton	4-1
4	May 21	Helsingborg	3-1
5	25	Gothenburg	2-2
6	28	Elfsborg	4-0
7	30	Stockholm	2-3
8	Jun 1	Stockholm XI	3-1
9	3	Oslo	3-1

FINAL TABLE

		Pl.	Home W	D	L	F	A	Away W	D	L	F	A	F (Total)	A	Pts
1	Everton	42	11	8	2	60	28	9	5	7	42	38	102	66	53
2	Huddersfield Town	42	15	1	5	57	31	7	6	8	34	37	91	68	51
3	Leicester City	42	14	5	2	66	25	4	7	10	30	47	96	72	48
4	Derby County	42	12	4	5	59	30	5	6	10	37	53	96	83	44
5	Bury	42	13	1	7	53	35	7	3	11	27	45	80	80	44
6	Cardiff City	42	12	7	2	44	27	5	3	13	26	53	70	80	44
7	BOLTON WANDERERS	42	12	5	4	47	26	6	1	14	34	40	81	66	43
8	Aston Villa	42	13	3	5	52	30	4	6	11	26	43	78	73	43
9	Newcastle United	42	9	7	5	49	41	6	6	9	30	40	79	81	43
10	Arsenal	42	10	6	5	49	33	3	9	9	33	53	82	86	41
11	Birmingham	42	10	7	4	36	25	3	8	10	34	50	70	75	41
12	Blackburn Rovers	42	13	5	3	41	22	3	4	14	25	56	66	78	41
13	Sheffield United	42	12	4	5	56	42	3	6	12	23	44	79	86	40
14	Sheffield Wed.	42	9	6	6	45	29	4	7	10	36	49	81	78	39
15	Sunderland	42	9	5	7	37	29	6	4	11	37	47	74	76	39
16	Liverpool	42	10	6	5	54	36	3	7	11	30	51	84	87	39
17	West Ham United	42	9	7	5	48	34	5	4	12	33	54	81	88	39
18	Manchester United	42	12	6	3	51	27	4	1	16	21	53	72	80	39
19	Burnley	42	12	5	4	43	29	4	2	15	27	67	82	98	39
20	Portsmouth	42	13	4	4	40	23	3	3	15	26	67	66	90	39
21	Tottenham Hotspur	42	12	3	6	47	34	3	5	13	27	52	74	86	38
22	Middlesbrough	42	7	9	5	46	35	4	6	11	35	53	81	88	37

League — Division One

#	Date		Opponent	Score	Scorers	Att.
1	Aug	25	EVERTON	2-3	Gibson(2)	34637
2		27	Huddersfield Town	1-4	Murphy	15710
3	Sep	1	Arsenal	0-2		35124
4		3	HUDDERSFIELD TOWN	1-1	D Jack	15532
5		8	BLACKBURN ROVERS	0-3		15633
6		15	Sunderland	0-4		29617
7		22	DERBY COUNTY	3-0	Murphy, Blackmore(2)	20406
8		29	Sheffield Wednesday	0-0		25098
9	Oct	6	BURY	0-1		37181
10		13	PORTSMOUTH	4-2	Butler, Blackmore(3)	16101
11		20	Aston Villa	5-3	Butler, Gibson, Blackmore(3)	29827
12		27	SHEFFIELD UNITED	3-1	Gibson(3)	18802
13	Nov	3	Manchester United	1-1	Murphy	21185
14		10	LEEDS UNITED	4-1	McClelland, Gibson, Blackmore(2)	16308
15		17	Liverpool	0-3		27904
16		24	WEST HAM UNITED	4-1	Murphy, Kean, Blackmore(2)	12371
17	Dec	1	Newcastle United	1-4	McClelland	31420
18		8	BURNLEY	0-1		17222
19		15	Cardiff City	1-1	Vizard	11286
20		22	LEICESTER CITY	5-0	Butler, McClelland, Gibson, Blackmore(2)	16030
21		25	Birmingham	2-0	Blackmore, McClelland	31358
22		26	BIRMINGHAM	6-2	Butler, Blackmore(3), Gibson(2)	22117
23		29	Everton	0-3		34443
24	Jan	1	CARDIFF CITY	1-0	Blackmore	33651
25		5	ARSENAL	1-2	Gibson	17597
26		19	Blackburn Rovers	3-1	McClelland, Blackmore, Gibson	22037
27	Feb	2	Derby County	1-2	Wright	9319
28		9	SHEFFIELD WEDNESDAY	2-2	Blackmore(2)	22387
29		20	SUNDERLAND	2-2	McClelland, Blackmore	11315
30		23	Portsmouth	4-4	Gibson(2), Blackmore, Butler	15068
31	Mar	9	Sheffield United	1-1	Blackmore	23927
32		16	MANCHESTER UNITED	1-1	Wright	17354
33		29	Manchester City	1-5	Butler	45838
34		30	LIVERPOOL	0-0		20460
35	Apr	1	MANCHESTER CITY	1-1	Gibson	21955
36		6	West Ham United	0-3		20973
37		13	NEWCASTLE UNITED	1-0	Blackmore	10463
38		17	ASTON VILLA	3-1	McClelland, Gibson, Vizard	10271
39		20	Burnley	1-3	Blackmore	14584
40		29	Leeds United	2-2	Blackmore(2)	12877
41	May	1	Bury	4-3	McClelland(2), Gibson, Vizard	9419
42		4	Leicester City	1-6	Blackmore	19912

Appearances (by shirt number)

#	Blackmore HA	Boston HJ	Butler W	Cook WL	Cope JW	Finney A	Gibson GB	Gill JJ	Greenhalgh HW	Haworth R	Jack DBN	Jack RR	Jennings W	Kean RW	McClelland J	Murphy L	Nuttall H	Pym RH	Round JH	Seddon J	Thornborough EH	Vizard ET	Wagstaffe JT	Wright WB
1			7		4	3	10			2	8				9	11	6	1		5				
2			7		4		10			2	8		3		9	11		1		5				6
3			7			3	10	1		2	8		5		9		4					11		6
4			7			3	10			2	8				9	11	4	1		5				6
5			7				10		3	2	8				9	11	4	1		5				6
6			7				10		3	2	8			5	9	11	4	1						6
7	9		7			3	10			2				4	8	11	6	1		5				
8	9		7			3	10			2				4	8	11	6	1		5				
9	9		7			3	10			2				4	8	11	6	1		5				
10	9		7			3	10			2				4	8	11	6	1		5				
11	9		7			3	10			2				4	8	11	6	1		5				
12	9		7			3	10			2				4	8	11	6	1		5				
13	9		7			3	10			2				4	8	11	6	1		5				
14	9	7				3	10			2				4	8	11	6	1		5				
15	9	7			4	3	10			2					8	11	6	1		5				
16	9		7			3	10			2				4	8	11	6	1		5				
17	9		7			3				2				4	8	11	6	1		5				10
18	9		7			3	10			2				4	8	11	6	1		5				
19	9		7			3	10			2				4	8		6	1		5		11		
20	9		7	11		3	10			2				4	8		6	1		5				
21	9		7	11		3	10			2				4	8		6	1		5				
22	9		7	11		3	10			2				4	8		6	1		5				
23	9		7	11	4	3	10			2					8		6	1		5				
24	9		7	11		3	10			2				4	8		6	1		5				
25	9		7	11		3	10			2				4	8			1	5		6			
26	9		7	11		3	10			2				4	8			1	5		6			
27			7	11			10	1	3	2				4	8				5		6			9
28	9		7	11		3	10			2				5	8		6	1			4			
29	9		7	11			10			2				4	8		6	1		5			3	
30	9		7	11			10			2			3	4	8		6	1	5					
31	9		7	11		3	10	1		2				4	8				5		6			
32	9		7	11		3	10			2				4				1	5		6			8
33	9		7	11		3	10			2				4	8		6	1		5				
34	9		7	11			10			2			3	4	8		6	1	5					
35	9		7	11			10			2			3	4	8		6	1	5					
36	9		7			3	10	1		2				4	8	11	6			5				
37	9		7		4	3	10	1		2					8				5		6	11		
38	9		7			3	10	1		2					8				5		6	11		
39	9		7					1		2			3	4	8				5		6	11		10
40	9		7			3	10	1		2				4	8				5		6	11		
41	9		7			3	10	1		2				4	8				5		6	11		
42	9		7		4	3	10	1		2									5		6	11		8
Apps	35	3	38	16	6	32	40	10	3	40	7		9	32	39	19	31	32	13	26	14	7	1	8
Goals	30		6				17				1			1	9	4						3		2

F.A. Cup

#	Date		Opponent	Score	Scorers	Att.
3	Jan	12	OLDHAM ATHLETIC	2-0	Gibson, Blackmore	34499
4		26	Liverpool	0-0		55055
4r		30	LIVERPOOL	5-2*	Butler, McClelland, Gibson, Blackmore(2)	41808
5	Feb	16	Leicester City	2-1	Seddon, Blackmore	30591
6	Mar	2	Blackburn Rovers	1-1	Blackmore	62522
6r		6	BLACKBURN ROVERS	2-1	Butler(2)	65295
SF		23	Huddersfield Town+	3-1	Butler, Gibson, Blackmore	39000
F	Apr	27	Portsmouth#	2-0	Butler, Blackmore	92576

In each F.A. Cup tie the side was: Pym 1, Haworth 2, Finney 3, Kean 4, Seddon 5, Nuttall 6, Butler 7, McClelland 8, Blackmore 9, Gibson 10, Cook 11.

* After extra-time. + Played at Anfield, Liverpool. # Played at Wembley Stadium.

Lancashire Cup

#	Date		Opponent	Score
2	Sep	19	Manchester City	1-1
2r	Oct	17	MANCHESTER CITY	3-1
3	Nov	7	Liverpool	2-2
3r		21	LIVERPOOL	7-2
SF	Dec	12	MANCHESTER UNITED	2-2
SFr	Apr	3	MANCHESTER UNITED	0-1

Manchester Cup

#	Date		Opponent	Score
3	Mar	11	MANCHESTER UNITED	4-1
SF	Apr	10	MANCHESTER NORTH END	1-0
F	May	11	Manchester City	0-2

Other Games

#	Date		Opponent	Score
1	May	2	Hinckley	2-1
2		20	Cataluna	0-4

Final Table

		Pl.	Home W	D	L	F	A	Away W	D	L	F	A	F. (Total)	A.	Pts
1	Sheffield Wed.	42	18	3	0	55	16	3	7	11	31	46	86	62	52
2	Leicester City	42	16	5	0	67	22	5	4	12	29	45	96	67	51
3	Aston Villa	42	16	2	3	62	30	7	2	12	36	51	98	81	50
4	Sunderland	42	16	2	3	67	30	4	5	12	26	45	93	75	47
5	Liverpool	42	11	4	6	53	28	6	8	7	37	36	90	64	46
6	Derby County	42	12	5	4	56	24	6	5	10	30	47	86	71	46
7	Blackburn Rovers	42	11	6	4	42	26	6	5	10	30	37	72	63	45
8	Manchester City	42	12	3	6	63	40	6	6	9	32	46	95	86	45
9	Arsenal	42	11	6	4	43	25	5	7	9	34	47	77	72	45
10	Newcastle United	42	15	2	4	48	29	4	4	13	22	43	70	72	44
11	Sheffield United	42	12	5	4	57	30	3	6	12	29	55	86	85	41
12	Manchester United	42	8	8	5	32	23	6	5	10	34	53	66	76	41
13	Leeds United	42	11	5	5	42	28	5	4	12	29	55	71	83	41
14	BOLTON WANDERERS	42	10	6	5	44	25	4	6	11	29	55	73	80	40
15	Birmingham	42	8	7	6	37	32	7	3	11	31	45	68	77	40
16	Huddersfield Town	42	9	6	6	45	23	5	5	11	25	38	70	61	39
17	West Ham United	42	11	6	4	55	31	3	3	14	31	65	86	96	39
18	Everton	42	11	2	8	38	31	6	2	13	25	44	63	75	38
19	Burnley	42	12	5	4	55	32	3	3	15	26	71	81	103	38
20	Portsmouth	42	13	2	6	43	26	2	4	15	13	54	56	80	36
21	Bury	42	9	5	7	38	35	3	2	16	24	64	62	99	31
22	Cardiff City	42	7	7	7	34	26	1	6	14	9	33	43	59	29

1929/30 15th in Division One

Manager: C.E. Foweraker

#		Date	Opponent	Score	Scorers	Att	Blackmore HA	Bryan J	butler W	Cook WL	Finney A	Gibson GB	Gill JJ	Haworth R	Howarth H	Jennings W	Jones R	Kean FW	McClelland J	McKay W	Milsom J	Nuttall H	Parry AS	Pym RH	Round JH	Seddon J	Thornborough EH	Vizard ET	Wagstaffe JT	Wright WB
1	Aug	31	Everton	3-3	Butler, Blackmore(2)	40808	9		7	11	3	10		2				4	8			6			1	5				
2	Sep	2	Sheffield Wednesday	0-1		26480	9		7	11	3	10		2				4	8						1	5	6			
3		7	DERBY COUNTY	1-2	Blackmore	20918	9			11	3	10		2				4	7						1	5	6			8
4		14	Manchester City	0-2		36972	9			11	3	10		2				4	7			6			1	5				8
5		18	MIDDLESBROUGH	2-2	McClelland, Bryan	13795	9	7		11	3	10		2				4	8			6			1	5				
6		21	PORTSMOUTH	2-1	Blackmore(2)	13491	9		7	11	3	10		2				4	8			6			1	5				
7		25	SHEFFIELD WEDNESDAY	1-3	Gibson	11136	9			7	3	10		2					8			6			1	5	4	11		
8		28	Arsenal	2-1	Blackmore, Wright	42723	9				3	10	1	2				4	7			6				5		11		8
9	Oct	5	ASTON VILLA	3-0	Blackmore, Wright(2)	19187	9			7	3	10	1	2				4				6				5		11		8
10		12	Leeds United	1-2	Wright	29749	9			7	3	10	1	2				4				6				5		11		8
11		19	BLACKBURN ROVERS	2-1	Blackmore, Rankin(og)	25756	9		7	11	3	10	1	2				4				6				5				8
12		26	Newcastle United	3-2	Blackmore,(2), Gibson	28636	9		7	11	3	10	1	2				4				6				5				8
13	Nov	2	SHEFFIELD UNITED	2-1	Butler, Gibson	15066	9		7	11	3	10	1	2			6	4								5				8
14		9	Liverpool	0-3		29071	9		7	11	3	10	1	2				4				6				5				8
15		16	BIRMINGHAM	0-0		15922	9		7	11	3	10	1	2				4				6				5				8
16		23	Leicester City	2-5	Butler, Blackmore	15330	9		7	11	3	10	1	2				5				6					4			8
17		30	GRIMSBY TOWN	2-3	Gibson, Wright	8506	9		7	11	3	10	1	2				4				6				5				8
18	Dec	7	Manchester United	1-1	Blackmore	5656	9		7	11	3	10		2				4		8		6		1		5				
19		14	WEST HAM UNITED	4-1	Nuttall, Cook(3)	11421	9		7	11	3	10		2				4		8		6		1		5				
20		21	Huddersfield Town	2-0	Blackmore, McKay	12625	9		7	11	3	10		2				4		8		6		1		5				
21		25	BURNLEY	1-1	Gibson	21533	9		7	11	3	10		2				4		8		6		1		5				
22		26	Burnley	2-2	McKay, Blackmore	27515	9		7	11	3	10		2				4		8		6		1		5				
23		28	EVERTON	5-0	Blackmore(4), Gibson	15928	9		7	11	3	10		2				4		8		6		1		5				
24	Jan	1	HUDDERSFIELD TOWN	7-1	Butler(3),Blackmore(2),Gibson,Cook	27355	9		7	11	3	10		2				4		8		6		1		5				
25		4	Derby County	1-2	Blackmore	16508	9		7	11		10		2				4		8				1		5			3	6
26		18	MANCHESTER CITY	1-2	Blackmore	42543	9		7	11	3	10		2				4		8		6		1		5				
27	Feb	1	ARSENAL	0-0		27336	9		7	11	3	10		2				4		8		6		1		5				
28		5	Portsmouth	0-3		13155	9		7	11	3	10		2				4		8		6		1		5				
29		8	Aston Villa	0-2		26235	9		7	11	3	10	1	2				4		8		6				5				
30		15	LEEDS UNITED	4-2	Gibson(3), Milsom	18104			7	11	3	10		2				4		8	9	6	5	1						
31		22	Blackburn Rovers	1-3	Gibson	19362			7	11	3	10		2				4		8	9		5	1			6			
32	Mar	1	MANCHESTER UNITED	4-1	Butler, Blackmore(2), Cook	17714	9		7	11		10		2				4		8				1		5			3	6
33		8	Sheffield United	3-2	Blackmore(2), Cook	21032	9		7	11		10		2				4		8				1		5			3	6
34		15	LIVERPOOL	0-2		14330	9		7	11		10		2				4		8				1		5			3	6
35		22	Birmingham	1-3	Gibson	18262	9		7	11	3	10		2				4		8			5	1						6
36		29	LEICESTER CITY	1-0	Wright	13644	9		7	11	3	10		2	6			4					5	1						8
37	Apr	5	Grimsby Town	1-1	Milsom	12081			7	11	3	10		2	4		6				9			1		5				8
38		9	NEWCASTLE UNITED	1-1	Milsom	6990			7	11	3	10		2	4		6				9			1		5				8
39		18	SUNDERLAND	3-0	McKay, Blackmore(2)	16333	9		7	11	3	10		2				4		8		6		1		5				
40		19	West Ham United	3-5	McKay, Blackmore, Gibson	12837	9		7	11	3	10		2				4		8			6	1		5				
41		21	Sunderland	1-4	McKay	28072	9		7	11	3	10		2				4		8				1		5				6
42	May	3	Middlesbrough	1-3	Blackmore	9816	9		7	11	3	10		2			6	4		8				1		5				
			Apps				38	1	35	41	38	42	11	42	4	1	7	39	8	22	4	27	5	24	7	32	5	4	4	21
			Goals				30	1	7	6		13								1	5	3	1							6

One own goal

F.A. Cup

#		Date	Opponent	Score	Att	butler W	Cook WL	Gibson GB	Haworth R	Kean FW	McKay W	Nuttall H	Pym RH	Seddon J	Wagstaffe JT	Wright WB
3	Jan	11	Birmingham	0-1	36011	7	11	10	2	4	8	6	1	5	3	9

Lancashire Cup

#		Date	Opponent	Score
1	Sep	9	Blackburn Rovers	2-1
2	Oct	30	Manchester United	1-6

Manchester Cup

#		Date	Opponent	Score
1	Feb	12	Wigan Borough	0-1

Other Games

#		Date	Opponent	Score
1	May	12	Macclesfield	4-0

FINAL TABLE

| | | Pl. | Home | | | | | Away | | | | | F | A | Pts |
			W	D	L	F	A	W	D	L	F	A	(Total)		
1	Sheffield Wed.	42	15	4	2	56	20	11	4	6	49	37	105	57	60
2	Derby County	42	16	4	1	61	32	5	4	12	29	50	90	82	50
3	Manchester City	42	12	5	4	51	33	7	4	10	40	48	91	81	47
4	Aston Villa	42	13	1	7	54	33	8	4	9	38	50	92	83	47
5	Leeds United	42	15	2	4	52	22	5	4	12	27	41	79	63	46
6	Blackburn Rovers	42	15	2	4	65	36	4	5	12	34	57	99	93	45
7	West Ham United	42	14	2	5	51	26	5	3	13	35	53	86	79	43
8	Leicester City	42	12	5	4	57	42	5	4	12	29	48	86	90	43
9	Sunderland	42	13	3	5	50	35	5	4	12	26	45	76	80	43
10	Huddersfield Town	42	9	7	5	32	21	8	2	11	31	48	63	69	43
11	Birmingham	42	13	3	5	40	21	3	6	12	27	41	67	62	41
12	Liverpool	42	11	5	5	33	29	5	4	12	30	50	63	79	41
13	Portsmouth	42	10	6	5	43	25	5	4	12	23	37	66	62	40
14	Arsenal	42	10	2	9	49	26	4	9	8	29	40	78	66	39
15	BOLTON WANDERERS	42	11	5	5	46	24	4	4	13	28	50	74	74	39
16	Middlesbrough	42	11	3	7	48	31	5	3	13	34	53	82	84	38
17	Manchester United	42	11	4	6	39	34	4	4	13	28	54	67	88	38
18	Grimsby Town	42	8	6	7	39	39	7	1	13	34	50	73	89	37
19	Newcastle United	42	13	4	4	52	32	2	3	16	19	60	71	92	37
20	Sheffield United	42	12	2	7	59	39	4	4	13	32	57	91	96	36
21	Burnley	42	11	5	5	53	34	3	3	15	26	63	79	97	36
22	Everton	42	6	7	8	48	46	6	4	11	32	46	80	92	35

1929-30 Season
(Back) Haworth, Kean, Gill, Finney, Nuttall, Blackmore
(Front) Butler, Wright, Seddon, Gibson, Cook

1930-31 Season
(Back) Haworth, Wagstaffe, Seddon, Jones, Finney, Wright
(Front) Butler, McKay, Blackmore, Taylor, Rimmer

1930/31 14th in Division One

Manager: C.E. Foweraker

#	Date	Opponent	Score	Scorers	Att	Blackmore HA	Butler W	Church HB	Cook WL	Davin M	Finney A	Gibson GB	Gorringe FC	Goslin HA	Haworth R	Haworth H	Jones R	Kean FW	McKay W	Milsom J	Nuttall H	Pym RH	Rimmer JW	Seddon J	Tait T	Taylor G	Vizard ET	Wagstaffe JT	Westwood RW	Wright WB
1	Aug 30	MIDDLESBROUGH	3-0	McKay, Cook, Blackmore	13648	9	7		11		3	10			2			4	8		6	1		5						
2	Sep 1	ARSENAL	1-4	Cook	20684	9	7		11		3	10			2	5		4	8		6	1								
3	6	Huddersfield Town	2-3	McKay, Gibson	15018	9	7		11		3	10			2	5	1	4	8		6									
4	10	Liverpool	2-7	Milsom, Gibson	20808		7		11		3	10		4	2				8	9	6	1		5						
5	13	ASTON VILLA	1-1	Blackmore	17207	9	7		11	8	3			4	2		1		10					5						6
6	20	Chelsea	1-0	Blackmore	48349	9	7		11	8	3			4	2		1		10					5						6
7	27	NEWCASTLE UNITED	0-3		17988	9	7		11	8	3			4	2		1	5	10											6
8	Oct 4	Sheffield Wednesday	0-1		21310	9	7		11		3	8		4	2		1		10					5						6
9	11	GRIMSBY TOWN	4-2	Cook, Nuttall, Blackmore(2)	14979	9	7		11		3	10		4	2		1		8		6			5						
10	18	BLACKPOOL	1-0	Butler	26651	9	7		11		3	10		4	2		1		8		6			5						
11	25	Blackburn Rovers	2-2	Blackmore, Cook	18649	9	7		11		3	10		4	2		1		8		6			5						
12	Nov 1	DERBY COUNTY	1-2	Goslin	15571	9	7		11		3	10		4	2		1		8					5						6
13	8	Sheffield United	0-2		19649	9	7		11			8		4	2	5	1		10									3		6
14	15	SUNDERLAND	2-2	Gibson, Cook	10835	9	7		11			8		4	2	5	1		10									3		6
15	22	Manchester City	0-3		23481	9	7		11		3	8		4	2		1		9					5						10
16	29	BIRMINGHAM	2-0	Tait, Blackmore	15361	10	7				3	8			2		1	4						5	9					6
17	Dec 6	Leeds United	1-3	Tait	7595	10		7			3	8	11		2		1	4						5	9					6
18	13	PORTSMOUTH	3-1	Cook(2), Butler	13345	8	7		11		3	10			2		1	4			5				9					6
19	20	Leicester City	1-2	Blackmore	12660	8	7		11		3	10			2		1	4			5				9					6
20	25	MANCHESTER UNITED	3-1	Blackmore(2), Gibson	22262	9	7		11		3	10		4	2		1		8		6			5						
21	26	Manchester United	1-1	Blackmore	12741	9	7		11		3	10		4	2		1		8		6									10
22	27	Middlesbrough	0-3		16084	8	7		11						2	5	1	4	10						9			3		6
23	Jan 3	HUDDERSFIELD T	1-0	McKay	15665	9	7		11		3	10		4	2		1		8		6			5						
24	14	LIVERPOOL	2-0	Gibson, Blackmore	10361	9	7		11		3	10		4	2		1		8					5						6
25	17	Aston Villa	1-3	Blackmore	21950	9	7		11		3	10		4	2		1		8					5						6
26	31	Newcastle United	0-4		9159	9	7				3	10		4	2		1		8		6			5						11
27	Feb 4	CHELSEA	1-1	Blackmore	9678	9	7				3	10		4	2		1		8		5		11							6
28	7	SHEFFIELD WEDNESDAY	2-2	Tait, Blackmore	19594	10	7				3	8		4	2		1						11	5	9					
29	17	Grimsby Town	1-4	Tait	5741	10	7				3			4	2		1		8				11	5	9					
30	21	Blackpool	3-3	Butler(2), Blackmore	16695	9	7				3					4	1		8				11	5		10			2	6
31	28	BLACKBURN ROVERS	1-1	Blackmore	9462	9	7		11		3	10			2	4	1		8					5						6
32	Mar 7	Derby County	1-4		8843	9	7				3	8			2		1							5		10	11			6
33	14	SHEFFIELD UNITED	6-2	Butler, Blackmore(3), Gibson(2)	13113	10	7	1			3	8		4										5	9		11	2		
34	21	Sunderland	1-3	Blackmore	17143	9	7	1			3	10		5				4							8		11	2		
35	28	MANCHESTER CITY	1-1	Blackmore	17398	9	7				3	10		4			1		8					5				2	11	6
36	Apr 3	West Ham United	4-1	Milson(2), Gibson, Blackmore	19116	9	7				3	10		4		5	1			8								2	11	6
37	4	Birmingham	2-0	Gibson, Westwood	18083	9	7				3	10		4		5	1			8								2	11	6
38	6	WEST HAM UNITED	4-2	Gibson, Blackmore, Butler, Cadwell (og)	20229	9	7				3	10		4		5	1			8								2	11	6
39	11	LEEDS UNITED	2-0	Butler, Blackmore	15438	9	7				3	10		4		5	1			8								2	11	6
40	18	Portsmouth	0-1		12519	9	7				3	10		4		5	1			8								2	11	6
41	25	LEICESTER CITY	4-1	Blackmore, Gibson(2), Butler	8962	9	8				3	10		4		5	1						7					2	11	6
42	May 2	Arsenal	0-5		35406	9	7				3	10		4		5	1							8				2	11	6
			Apps			40	41	2	26	3	39	35	1	33	29	15	37	9	28	6	20	3	6	21	9	2	3	14	8	32
			Goals			27	8		7			12	1						3	3	1				4					1

One own goal

F.A. Cup

#	Date	Opponent	Score	Scorers	Att	Blackmore HA	Butler W	Cook WL	Finney A	Gibson GB	Goslin HA	Haworth R	Jones R	McKay W	Nuttall H	Seddon J	Tait T
3	Jan 10	CARLISLE UNITED	1-0	Blackmore	23029	9	7	11	3	10	4	2	1	8	6	5	
4	24	SUNDERLAND	1-1	Blackmore	36602	9	7	11	3	10	4	2	1	8	6	5	
4r	28	Sunderland	1-3	Blackmore	46000	9	7	11	3	10	4	2	1		6	5	8

Lancashire Cup

2	Oct 8	MANCHESTER CITY	2-1
3	Nov 3	Blackburn Rovers	1-2

Manchester Cup

3	Feb 25	BURY	0-0
3r	Mar 25	Bury *	1-2

* after extra time

Other Games

1	Apr 6	Brierley Hill Alliance	6-2
2	27	PAST PLAYERS	2-1

FINAL TABLE		Pl.	Home					Away					F.	A.	Pts
			W	D	L	F	A	W	D	L	F	A	(Total)		
1	Arsenal	42	14	5	2	67	27	14	5	2	60	32	127	59	66
2	Aston Villa	42	17	3	1	86	34	8	6	7	42	44	128	78	59
3	Sheffield Wed.	42	14	3	4	65	32	8	5	8	37	43	102	75	52
4	Portsmouth	42	11	7	3	46	26	7	6	8	38	41	84	67	49
5	Huddersfield Town	42	10	8	3	45	27	8	4	9	36	38	81	65	48
6	Derby County	42	12	6	3	56	31	6	4	11	38	48	94	79	46
7	Middlesbrough	42	13	5	3	57	28	6	3	12	41	62	98	90	46
8	Manchester City	42	13	2	6	41	29	5	8	8	34	41	75	70	46
9	Liverpool	42	11	6	4	48	28	4	6	11	38	57	86	85	42
10	Blackburn Rovers	42	14	3	4	54	28	3	5	13	29	56	83	84	42
11	Sunderland	42	12	4	5	61	38	4	5	12	28	47	89	85	41
12	Chelsea	42	13	4	4	42	19	2	6	13	22	48	64	67	40
13	Grimsby Town	42	13	2	6	55	31	4	3	14	27	56	82	87	39
14	BOLTON WANDERERS	42	12	6	3	45	26	3	3	15	23	55	68	81	39
15	Sheffield United	42	10	7	4	49	31	4	3	14	29	53	78	84	38
16	Leicester City	42	12	4	5	50	38	4	2	15	30	57	80	95	38
17	Newcastle United	42	9	2	10	41	45	6	4	11	37	42	78	87	36
18	West Ham United	42	11	3	7	56	44	3	5	13	23	50	79	94	36
19	Birmingham	42	11	3	7	37	28	2	7	12	18	42	55	70	36
20	Blackpool	42	8	7	6	41	44	3	3	15	30	81	71	125	32
21	Leeds United	42	10	3	8	49	31	2	4	15	19	50	68	81	31
22	Manchester United	42	6	6	9	30	37	1	2	18	23	78	53	115	22

~ 209 ~

1931/32 — 17th in Division One

League — Division One

#	Date		Opponent	Score	Scorers	Att.
1	Aug	29	WEST HAM UNITED	0-1		15740
2	Sep	2	Liverpool	2-2	Gibson, Westwood	20090
3		5	Sheffield Wednesday	1-7	Blackmore	14544
4		9	GRIMSBY TOWN	5-3	Westwood(2), Blackmore(2), Gibson	9700
5		12	PORTSMOUTH	4-0	Blackmore, Butler(2), Walters	12258
6		15	Grimsby Town	0-2		10857
7		19	MIDDLESBROUGH	4-2	Blackmore(3), Wagstaffe	14180
8		26	Huddersfield Town	0-2		12901
9	Oct	3	NEWCASTLE UNITED	2-1	Blackmore, Davidson (og)	13833
10		10	Aston Villa	1-2	Gibson	39673
11		17	Arsenal	1-1	Blackmore	42141
12		24	WEST BROMWICH ALB.	1-0	Westwood	19695
13		31	Birmingham	2-2	Gibson, Butler	16163
14	Nov	7	SUNDERLAND	3-1	Blackmore(2), Butler	14928
15		14	Sheffield United	0-4		15057
16		21	BLACKBURN ROVERS	3-1	Imrie (og), Butler(2)	18164
17		28	Derby County	1-5	Butler	9786
18	Dec	5	BLACKPOOL	1-2	Cook	14294
19		12	Manchester City	1-2	Westwood	20283
20		19	EVERTON	2-1	Milsom(2)	33619
21		25	LEICESTER CITY	1-0	Blackmore	32544
22		26	Leicester City	3-1	Taylor(2), Milsom	24675
23	Jan	1	CHELSEA	1-0	Milsom	28232
24		2	West Ham United	1-3	Gibson	15997
25		16	SHEFFIELD WEDNESDAY	2-4	Gibson, Blackmore	9694
26		30	Middlesbrough	1-3	Gibson	10502
27	Feb	6	HUDDERSFIELD T	1-2	Griffiths	11876
28		17	Newcastle United	1-3	Butler	22618
29		20	ASTON VILLA	2-1	Milsom(2)	12682
30	Mar	2	ARSENAL	1-0	Milsom	20922
31		5	West Bromwich Albion	0-3		16050
32		9	Portsmouth	2-3	Wright, Cook	7974
33		12	BIRMINGHAM	5-1	Cook(2), Gibson(2), Milsom	11003
34		19	Sunderland	0-3		21765
35		25	Chelsea	0-3		38515
36		26	SHEFFIELD UNITED	3-1	Milsom(3)	13737
37	Apr	2	Blackburn Rovers	1-3	Binns (og)	12100
38		9	DERBY COUNTY	1-2	Milsom	7722
39		16	Blackpool	3-0	Milsom(3)	16890
40		23	MANCHESTER CITY	1-1	Wright	8680
41		30	Everton	0-1		28546
42	May	7	LIVERPOOL	8-1	Milsom(4), Edmed, Westwood(2), Wilson	9209

Appearances / Goals

	Blackmore HA	Boyle MJ	Butler W	Cook WL	Duckworth TC	Edmed RA	Finney A	Gibson GB	Goslin HA	Griffiths TP	Howarth H	Jones R	McKay W	Milsom J	Nicholson G	Nuttall H	Rimmer JW	Seddon J	Taylor G	Wagstaffe JT	Walters TC	Westwood RW	Wilson FW	Wright WB
Apps	23	4	36	34	18	1	38	40	10	23	7	42	13	22	30	22	2	3	9	23	5	21	3	33
Goals	13		8	4		1		9		1				19					2		1	7	1	2

Three own goals

F.A. Cup

	Date		Opponent	Score	Scorers	Att.
3	Jan	9	Preston North End	0-0		29057
3r		13	PRESTON NORTH END	2-5	Blackmore, Gibson	32862

Lancashire Cup

	Date		Opponent	Score
2	Oct	7	Accrington Stanley	0-0
2r		19	ACCRINGTON STANLEY	4-1
3	Nov	4	Liverpool	1-1
3r		11	LIVERPOOL	8-1
SF	Apr	20	Blackpool	1-1
SFr	May	4	BLACKPOOL	5-1
F		14	Manchester City	3-2

Manchester Cup

	Date		Opponent	Score
3	Mar	16	OLDHAM ATHLETIC	1-2

FINAL TABLE

		Pl.	W	Home D	L	F	A	W	Away D	L	F	A	F.	A.	Pts (Total)
1	Everton	42	18	0	3	84	30	8	4	9	32	34	116	64	56
2	Arsenal	42	14	5	2	52	16	8	5	8	38	32	90	48	54
3	Sheffield Wed.	42	14	4	3	60	28	8	2	11	36	54	96	82	50
4	Huddersfield Town	42	11	8	2	47	21	8	2	11	33	42	80	63	48
5	Aston Villa	42	15	1	5	64	28	4	7	10	40	44	104	72	46
6	West Bromwich Alb.	42	12	4	5	46	21	8	2	11	31	34	77	55	46
7	Sheffield United	42	13	3	5	47	32	7	3	11	33	43	80	75	46
8	Portsmouth	42	14	2	5	37	21	5	5	11	25	41	62	62	45
9	Birmingham	42	13	5	3	48	22	5	3	13	30	45	78	67	44
10	Liverpool	42	13	4	4	56	38	6	2	13	25	55	81	93	44
11	Newcastle United	42	13	5	3	52	31	5	1	15	28	56	80	87	42
12	Chelsea	42	12	4	5	43	27	4	4	13	26	46	69	73	40
13	Sunderland	42	11	4	6	42	29	4	6	11	25	44	67	73	40
14	Manchester City	42	10	5	6	49	30	3	7	11	34	43	83	73	38
15	Derby County	42	13	5	3	51	25	1	5	15	20	50	71	75	38
16	Blackburn Rovers	42	12	3	6	57	41	4	3	14	32	54	89	95	38
17	**BOLTON WANDERERS**	42	15	1	5	51	25	2	3	16	21	55	72	80	38
18	Middlesbrough	42	12	3	6	41	29	3	5	13	23	60	64	89	38
19	Leicester City	42	11	3	7	46	39	4	4	13	28	55	74	94	37
20	Blackpool	42	9	4	8	42	40	3	5	13	23	62	65	102	33
21	Grimsby Town	42	11	4	6	39	28	2	2	17	28	70	67	98	32
22	West Ham United	42	9	5	7	35	37	3	2	16	27	70	62	107	31

~ 210 ~

1932/33 21st in Division One (relegated)

Manager: C.E. Foweraker

#		Date	Opponent	Score	Scorers	Att	Atkinson JE	Boyle MJ	Butler W	Church HB	Cook WL	Duckworth TC	Eastham GR	Edmed RA	Finney A	Gibson GB	Goslin HA	Griffiths J	Griffiths TP	Howarth H	Jones R	McKay W	Milsom J	Nicholson G	Rimmer JW	Smith R	Walton G	Westwood RW	Wilson FW	Wright WB
1	Aug	27	NEWCASTLE UNITED	2-2	Butler, Wright	16245			7		11	2			3	8			5	6	1	4						10		9
2		29	Wolverhampton Wan.	1-4	Butler	28197			7		11	2			3	8			5	6	1	4						10		9
3	Sep	3	Aston Villa	1-6	Griffiths	31296			7		11	2			3	8			5	6	1	4	9					10		
4		5	WOLVERHAMPTON W.	2-0	Cook, Butler	11353			7		11				3	8	2		5		1	4	9					10		6
5		10	MIDDLESBROUGH	4-3	Milsom, McKay, Gibson, Butler	12035			7		11				3	8	2		5		1	4	9					10		6
6		17	Arsenal	2-3	Milson, Westwood	42395			7		11				3	8	2		5	6	1	4	9					10		
7		24	Liverpool	1-0	Westwood	26019			7		11				3	8	2		5	6	1	4	9					10		
8	Oct	1	LEICESTER CITY	5-0	Gibson, Westwood(2), Milsom, Cook	12342			7		11				3	8	2		5	6	1	4	9					10		
9		8	Portsmouth	1-2	Westwood	17397			7		11				3	8	2		5	6	1	4	9					10		
10		15	CHELSEA	2-3	Milsom(2)	15021			7		11				3	8	2		5	6	1	4	9					10		
11		22	MANCHESTER CITY	2-1	Griffiths, Milsom	14468			7		11				3	8	2		5	6	1	4	9					10		
12		29	Sunderland	4-7	Gibson(2), Butler(2)	10182			7		11				3	8	2		5	6	1	4	9					10		
13	Nov	5	BLACKBURN ROVERS	4-2	Milsom, Butler(2), Griffiths	20225			7		11				3	8	2		5	6	1	4	9					10		
14		12	Derby County	1-4	Milsom	14922			7		11				3	8	2		5	6	1	4	9					10		
15		19	BLACKPOOL	1-0	Milsom	14468			7		11				3	8	2		5	6	1	4	9					10		
16		26	Everton	2-2	Griffiths, Goslin	27529			7						3	8	4	2	5		1		6	9	11			10		
17	Dec	3	BIRMINGHAM	2-2	Goslin, Gibson	8970			7						3	8	4	2	5		1		6	9	11			10		
18		10	West Bromwich Albion	0-4		12778				7					3	8	4	2		5	1			9	11			10		6
19		17	SHEFFIELD WEDNESDAY	3-0	Milsom(3)	11409			7						3		4	2	5		1		9	8	11			10		6
20		24	Leeds United	3-4	Westwood(2), Nicholson	15804			7						3		4	2	5		1		9	8	11			10		6
21		26	HUDDERSFIELD T	2-1	Butler, Milsom	23967			7						3		4	2	5		1		9	8	11			10		6
22		27	Huddersfield Town	1-2	Griffiths	19797			7	10					3		4	2	5		1		9	8	11					6
23		31	Newcastle United	1-3	Milsom	18101		2	7						3	10	4		5		1		9	8	11					6
24	Jan	2	SHEFFIELD UNITED	3-3	Goslin, McKay, Gibson	15360		2	7						3	10	4		5		1	9		8	11					6
25		7	ASTON VILLA	0-1		17624			7		11				3	10	4		5		1	9		8						6
26		21	Middlesbrough	1-2	Milsom	9256			7		11					10	8	2	5		1	4	9			3				6
27	Feb	1	ARSENAL	0-4		13401		2	7		11				3	8	4		5		1		6	9				10		
28		4	LIVERPOOL	3-3	Milsom, Cook, Westwood	11314		2	7	1	11				3	8	4		5				9	6				10		
29		11	Leicester City	0-2		14178		2		1			7		3	8	4		5	6				9	11			10		
30		22	PORTSMOUTH	4-1	Gibson, Westwood, Milsom(2)	3101				1		2	7		3	8	4		5	6			9		11			10		
31		25	Chelsea	1-1	Gibson	12590				1		2	7		3	8	4		5	6			9		11			10		
32	Mar	8	Manchester City	1-2	Milsom	19144				1		2	7		3		4		5	6			9		11			10	8	
33		11	SUNDERLAND	0-0		10353			7	1					3		4			5	6		9		11		8	10		
34		18	Blackburn Rovers	2-3	Rimmer(2)	10423				1	7	2			3		4			5	6		9		11		8	10		
35		25	DERBY COUNTY	1-1	Milsom	9585				1	7	2			3		4			5	6		9		11			10		8
36	Apr	1	Blackpool	3-1	McKay, Rimmer(2)	15849		2		1	7			8	3		4				5	9		6	11			10		
37		8	EVERTON	2-4	Milsom, Rimmer	12112		2		1	7			8	3		4				5	9		6	11			10		
38		15	Birmingham	1-2	Butler	13541			7	1		2		8	3		4				5	9		6	11			10		
39		17	Sheffield United	2-3	Milsom, McKay	9410	2		7	1	8				3		5					4	9	6	11			10		
40		22	WEST BROMWICH ALB.	2-2	Goslin, Westwood	11647	5	2	7	1					3	8						4	9	6	11			10		
41		29	Sheffield Wednesday	0-2		4810	5		7	1					3	8						4	9	6	11	2		10		
42	May	6	LEEDS UNITED	5-0	Milsom(3), Westwood(2)	10048			7	1					3					6		4	9	8	11	2		10		
						Apps	3	9	35	15	26	10	3	3	41	27	26	21	25	30	27	22	39	21	23	3	2	37	1	13
						Goals			10		3					8	4		5			4	25	1	5			12		1

F.A. Cup

#		Date	Opponent	Score	Scorers	Att	Atkinson JE	Boyle MJ	Butler W	Church HB	Cook WL	Duckworth TC	Eastham GR	Edmed RA	Finney A	Gibson GB	Goslin HA	Griffiths J	Griffiths TP	Howarth H	Jones R	McKay W	Milsom J	Nicholson G	Rimmer JW	Smith R	Walton G	Westwood RW	Wilson FW	Wright WB
3	Jan	14	Charlton Athletic	5-1	T.Griffiths, Gibson, Cook(2), Milsom	17402			7		11				3	10	8	2	5	6	1		9	4						
4		28	GRIMSBY TOWN	2-1	T.Griffiths, Butler	25866		2	7		11				3	10	8		5		1	4	9							6
5	Feb	18	MANCHESTER CITY	2-4	Westwood, Milsom	69912			8	1		2	7		3	10	4		5	6			9					11		

Lancashire Cup

1	Sep	18	Southport	2-1
2	Oct	18	Oldham Athletic	1-0
SF	Mar	4	PRESTON NORTH END	4-2
F	May	13	Liverpool	1-2

Manchester Cup

1	Mar	8	BURY	2-3	Aw.

Other Games

1	Apr	24	Accrington Stanley	4-0

FINAL TABLE

	FINAL TABLE	Pl.	Home W	D	L	F	A	Away W	D	L	F	A	F. (Total)	A.	Pts
1	Arsenal	42	14	3	4	70	27	11	5	5	48	34	118	61	58
2	Aston Villa	42	16	2	3	60	29	7	6	8	32	38	92	67	54
3	Sheffield Wed.	42	15	5	1	46	20	6	4	11	34	48	80	68	51
4	West Bromwich Alb.	42	16	1	4	50	23	4	8	9	33	47	83	70	49
5	Newcastle United	42	15	2	4	44	24	7	3	11	27	39	71	63	49
6	Huddersfield Town	42	11	6	4	32	17	7	5	9	34	36	66	53	47
7	Derby County	42	11	8	2	49	25	4	6	11	27	44	76	69	44
8	Leeds United	42	10	6	5	39	24	5	8	8	20	38	59	62	44
9	Portsmouth	42	14	3	4	39	22	4	4	13	35	54	74	76	43
10	Sheffield United	42	14	3	4	50	30	3	6	12	24	50	74	80	43
11	Everton	42	13	6	2	54	24	3	3	15	27	50	81	74	41
12	Sunderland	42	8	7	6	33	31	7	3	11	30	49	63	80	40
13	Birmingham	42	13	3	5	40	23	1	8	12	17	34	57	57	39
14	Liverpool	42	10	6	5	53	33	4	5	12	26	51	79	84	39
15	Blackburn Rovers	42	11	6	4	48	41	3	4	14	28	61	76	102	38
16	Manchester City	42	12	3	6	47	30	4	2	15	21	41	68	71	37
17	Middlesbrough	42	8	5	8	35	33	6	4	11	28	40	63	73	37
18	Chelsea	42	9	4	8	38	29	5	3	13	25	44	63	73	35
19	Leicester City	42	9	9	3	43	25	2	4	15	32	64	75	89	35
20	Wolverhampton W.	42	10	4	7	56	48	3	5	13	24	48	80	96	35
21	BOLTON WANDERERS	42	10	7	4	49	33	2	2	17	29	59	78	92	33
22	Blackpool	42	11	2	8	44	35	3	3	15	25	50	69	85	33

1932-33 Season
(Back) McKay, Duckworth, Jones, Smith, Finney, Howarth
(Front) Butler, Gibson, Milsom, Griffiths, Westwood, Cook

1933-34 Season
(Back) Goslin, Atkinson, Smith, Jones, Finney, G.Taylor
(Front) G.T.Taylor, Eastham, Milsom, Westwood, Cook

1933/34 3rd in Division Two

Manager: C.E. Foweraker

#		Date	Opponent	Score	Scorers	Att	Atkinson JE	Cameron K	Church HB	Cook WL	Eastham GR	Finney A	Goslin HA	Griffiths J	Howarth H	Hughes JH	Jones E	Jones R	McKay W	Milson J	Nicholson G	Rimmer JW	Smith R	Taylor G	Taylor GT	Westwood RW
1	Aug	26	West Ham United	2-4	Hughes, McKay	24825	5		1	11		3		2	6	7			8	9	4					10
2		29	Grimsby Town	3-2	Westwood(2), Milsom	9961	5		1	11		3				7			8	9	4		2	6		10
3	Sep	2	PLYMOUTH ARGYLE	2-0	Hughes, Westwood	11388	5		1	11		3				7			8	9	4		2	6		10
4		4	GRIMSBY TOWN	0-4		9370	5		1	11		3				7			8	9	4		2	6		10
5		9	Manchester United	5-1	Milsom(2), Hughes, McKay, Cook	21779	5			11		3				7		1	8	9	4		2	6		10
6		16	BURY	2-0	McKay, Westwood	18982	5			11		3				7		1	8	9	4		2	6		10
7		23	BRENTFORD	3-2	Westwood, Milsom(2)	9894	5		1	11		3	4						8	9	7		2	6		10
8		30	Burnley	3-1	Westwood(2), McKay	12672	5		1	7		3							8	9	4	11	2	6		10
9	Oct	7	OLDHAM ATHLETIC	1-0	Atkinson	14206	5		1	11		3				7			8	9	4		2	6		10
10		14	Preston North End	1-1	Cameron	20054	5	7	1	11		3	4						8	9			2	6		10
11		21	Hull City	0-1		16167	5	7	1	11		3	4						8	9			2	6		10
12		28	FULHAM	3-1	Cook, Milsom, Westwood	14190	5	7	1	11		3	4						8	9			2	6		10
13	Nov	4	Southampton	0-1		15084	5		1	11	8	3	4						7	9			2	6		10
14		11	BLACKPOOL	1-2	McKay	19947	5	9	1	11	8	3							7		4		2	6		10
15		18	Bradford City	1-5	Westwood	10223	5	8	1	11		3				7				9	4		2	6		10
16		25	PORT VALE	3-0	Milsom(3)	14925	5	8	1	7		3	4						6	9		11	2			10
17	Dec	2	Notts County	2-1	Rimmer, Milsom	11279	5	8	1	7		3	4						6	9		11	2			10
18		9	SWANSEA TOWN	2-1	Rimmer, Westwood	12595	5	8	1			3	4						6	9		11	2		7	10
19		16	Millwall	1-2	Rimmer	10181	5	8	1			3	4						6	9		11	2		7	10
20		23	LINCOLN CITY	1-2	Milsom	9174		8	1				4	2	5					9		11	3	6	7	10
21		25	Bradford Park Avenue	4-1	Cameron, Milsom, Westwood(2)	17527	5	8	1			3	4							9		11	2	6	7	10
22		30	WEST HAM UNITED	5-1	Milsom(4), Westwood	9551	5	8	1			3	4							9		11	2	6	7	10
23	Jan	1	BRADFORD PARK AVE.	0-1		19433	5	8	1			3	4						10	9		11	2	6	7	
24		2	Bury	1-1	Westwood	17969		8	1			3			5					9	4	11	2	6	7	10
25		6	Plymouth Argyle	0-3		18348		8	1			3	4							9		11	2	6	7	10
26		20	MANCHESTER UNITED	3-1	Westwood, GT Taylor, Goslin	11887		8		11		3	5					1		9	4		2	6	7	10
27	Feb	3	Brentford	1-3	Westwood	16037		8					5	2				1		9	4	11	3	6	7	10
28		10	BURNLEY	4-1	GT Taylor, Milsom(2), Westwood	13214	5			11	8	3	4					1		9			2	6	7	10
29		20	Oldham Athletic	3-1	Eastham(2), GT Taylor	7604	5			11	8	3	4					1		9			2	6	7	10
30		24	PRESTON NORTH END	0-2		27435				11	8	3	5					1		9	4		2	6	7	10
31	Mar	7	HULL CITY	3-3	Rimmer, GT Taylor, Milsom	5175	5	10			8	3	4					1		9		11	2	6	7	
32		10	Fulham	2-0	Eastham, Milsom	18636	5	10		11	8	3	4					1		9			2	6	7	
33		17	SOUTHAMPTON	2-0	Milsom(2)	11029	5				8	3	4					1		9		11	2	6	7	10
34		24	Blackpool	1-1	GT Taylor	17464	5			11	8	3	4					1		9			2	6	7	10
35		30	NOTTM. FOREST	1-1	GT Taylor	16526	5	10		11	8	3	4					1		9			2	6	7	
36		31	BRADFORD CITY	3-0	Goslin, Eastham, Westwood	15270	5			11	8	3	4					1		9			2	6	7	10
37	Apr	2	Nottingham Forest	2-2	GT Taylor, Westwood	13444				11	8	3	4		5			1		9			2	6	7	10
38		7	Port Vale	0-0		9923				11	8	3	4					1		9			2	6	7	10
39		14	NOTTS COUNTY	1-0	Eastham	11652	5	10			8	3	4					1		9		11	2	6	7	
40		21	Swansea Town	0-0		10569	5			11	8	3	4					1		9			2	6	7	10
41		28	MILLWALL	5-0	GT Taylor(2), Milsom, Westwood(2)	13268	5			11	8	3	4					1		9			2	6	7	10
42	May	5	Lincoln City	2-2	E Jones, Finney	6412	5			11	8	3	4				7	1					2	6	9	10
					Apps		36	21	23	30	17	40	32	3	3	9	1	19	19	38	15	16	41	37	25	37
					Goals		1	2		2	5	1	2			3	1		5	23		4			9	21

F.A. Cup

#		Date	Opponent	Score	Scorers	Att	Atkinson JE	Cameron K	Church HB	Cook WL	Eastham GR	Finney A	Goslin HA	Jones R	Milson J	Nicholson G	Smith R	Taylor G	Taylor GT	Westwood RW
3	Jan	13	HALIFAX TOWN	3-1	Cook(2), Westwood	24885		8		11		3	5	1	9	4	2	6	7	10
4		27	Brighton & Hove Albion	1-1	Westwood	25535		8		11		3	5	1	9	4	2	6	7	10
4r		31	BRIGHTON & HOVE ALB.	6-1	Milsom(3), Westwood, G.T.Taylor, Came[ron]	24047		8		11		3	5	1	9	4	2	6	7	10
5	Feb	17	Liverpool	3-0	G.T.Taylor, Milsom, Westwood	54912	5			11	8	3	4	1	9		2	6	7	10
6	Mar	3	PORTSMOUTH	0-3		52181	5			11	8	3	4	1	9		2	6	7	10

Lancashire Cup

		Date	Opponent	Score
1	Sep	18	BURNLEY	3-0
2	Oct	4	ACCRINGTON STANLEY	5-2
SF	Nov	15	MANCHESTER CITY	3-2
F	May	12	Oldham Athletic*	4-2

* Played at Maine Road

Manchester Cup

		Date	Opponent	Score
SF	Apr	25	Manchester United	0-4

FINAL TABLE

		Pl.	Home					Away					F.	A.	Pts
			W	D	L	F	A	W	D	L	F	A	(Total)		
1	Grimsby Town	42	15	3	3	62	28	12	2	7	41	31	103	59	59
2	Preston North End	42	15	3	3	47	20	8	3	10	24	32	71	52	52
3	**BOLTON WANDERERS**	42	14	2	5	45	22	7	7	7	34	33	79	55	51
4	Brentford	42	15	2	4	52	24	6	5	9	33	36	85	60	51
5	Bradford Park Ave.	42	16	2	3	63	27	7	1	13	23	40	86	67	49
6	Bradford City	42	14	4	3	46	25	6	2	13	27	42	73	67	46
7	West Ham United	42	13	5	3	51	28	4	9		27	42	78	70	45
8	Port Vale	42	14	4	3	39	14	5	3	13	21	41	60	55	45
9	Oldham Athletic	42	12	5	4	48	28	5	5	11	24	32	72	60	44
10	Plymouth Argyle	42	12	7	2	43	20	3	6	12	26	50	69	70	43
11	Blackpool	42	10	8	3	39	27	5	5	11	23	37	62	64	43
12	Bury	42	12	4	5	43	31	5	5	11	27	42	70	73	43
13	Burnley	42	14	2	5	40	29	4	4	13	20	43	60	72	42
14	Southampton	42	15	2	4	40	21	0	6	15	14	37	54	58	38
15	Hull City	42	11	6	4	33	20	2	8	11	19	48	52	68	38
16	Fulham	42	13	3	5	29	17	2	4	15	19	50	48	67	37
17	Nottingham Forest	42	11	4	6	50	27	2	5	14	23	47	73	74	35
18	Notts County	42	9	7	5	32	22	3	4	14	21	40	53	62	35
19	Swansea Town	42	10	9	2	36	19	0	6	15	15	41	51	60	35
20	Manchester United	42	9	3	9	29	33	5	3	13	30	52	59	85	34
21	Millwall	42	8	8	5	21	17	3	3	15	18	51	39	68	33
22	Lincoln City	42	7	7	7	31	23	2	1	18	13	52	44	75	26

1934/35   2nd in Division Two (promoted)

Manager: C.E. Foweraker

No	Date	Opponent	Score	Scorers	Att	Atkinson JE	Chameron K	Chambers WT	Church HB	Connor J	Cook WL	Eastham GR	Finney A	Goldsmith G	Goslin HA	Hurst J	Jones R	Milson J	Rimmer JW	Smith R	Taylor G	Taylor GT	Walton G	Westwood RW
1	Aug 25	Oldham Athletic	4-1	Westwood, Milsom(2), Cook	12842	5					11	8	3		4		1	9		2	6	7		10
2	Sep 1	BURY	2-0	Milsom, Atkinson	18186	5					11	8	3		4		1	9		2	6	7		10
3	3	MANCHESTER UNITED	3-1	Milsom, Atkinson, Vose(og)	16238	5					11	8	3		4		1	9		2	6	7		10
4	8	SOUTHAMPTON	4-0	Milsom(2), Westwood(2)	15383	5					11	8	3		4		1	9		2	6	7		10
5	12	Manchester United	3-0	Milsom, Westwood, Eastham	24760	5					11	8	3		4		1	9		2	6	7		10
6	15	Notts County	2-0	Milsom(2)	13783	5					11	8	3		4		1	9		2	6	7		10
7	22	BRADFORD CITY	3-0	Eastham, Cook, Westwood	14181	5					11	8	3		4		1	9		2	6	7		10
8	29	Sheffield United	2-6	Cameron, Milsom	12788	5	10				11	8	3		4		1	9		2	6	7		
9	Oct 6	BARNSLEY	8-0	Westwood(4), GT Taylor 2, Shotton(og), Milsom	15009	5					11	8	3		4		1	9		2	6	7		10
10	13	Port Vale	3-1	Westwood, Milsom(2)	16839	5					11	8	3		4		1	9		2	6	7		10
11	20	Hull City	2-0	Rimmer, Milsom	12758							8	3		4	5	1	9	11	2	6	7		10
12	27	NOTTM. FOREST	2-3	Milsom, Westwood	21298	5						8	3		4		1	9	11	2	6	7		10
13	Nov 3	Brentford	0-1		22322	5					11	8	3		4		1	9		2	6	7		10
14	10	FULHAM	4-0	Hindson(og), Cook, Westwood, Chambers	19612	5		9			11	8	3		4					2	6	7		10
15	17	Bradford Park Avenue	0-4		12627	5		9			11	8	3		4		1			2	6	7		10
16	24	PLYMOUTH ARGYLE	3-2	Westwood(2), Milsom	18210	5					11	8	3		4		1	9		2	6	7		10
17	Dec 1	Norwich City	3-2	Rimmer, GT Taylor, Westwood	20556	5						8	3		4		1	9	11	2	6	7		10
18	8	NEWCASTLE UNITED	1-0	GT Taylor	22170	5						8	3		4		1	9	11	2	6	7		10
19	15	West Ham United	1-4	Atkinsom	27489	5						8	3		4		1	9	11	2	6	7		10
20	22	BLACKPOOL	4-2	Milson(2), Westwood	22255	5					11	8	3		4		1	9		2	6	7		10
21	25	Burnley	1-2	Milsom	26518	5					11	8	3		4		1	9		2	6	7		10
22	29	OLDHAM ATHLETIC	2-0	Eastham, Westwood	16859	5						8	3		4		1	9	11	2	6	7		10
23	Jan 2	BURNLEY	7-0	Milsom(4), Westwood, Goslin, Eastham	19354	5						8	3		4		1	9	11	2	6	7		10
24	5	Bury	1-2	Eastham	31032	5						8	3		4		1	9	11	2	6	7		10
25	19	Southampton	2-1	Milsom, Westwood	16525	5			1		11	8	3		4			9		2	6	7		10
26	30	NOTTS COUNTY	5-1	Westwood, Rimmer, Milsom(3), GT Taylor	8220	5						8	3		4		1	9	11	2	6	7		10
27	Feb 2	Bradford City	1-1	Rimmer	9023	5						8	3		4		1	9	11	2	6	7		10
28	9	SHEFFIELD UNITED	1-1	Goslin	23976	5	10					8	3		4		1	9	11	2	6	7		
29	23	PORT VALE	2-0	GT Taylor, Milsom	18897	5	10			3	11				4	6	1	9		2		7	8	
30	Mar 6	HULL CITY	1-2	Westwood	13715	5					11	8	3		4		1	9		2	6	7		10
31	9	Nottingham Forest	1-0	Westwood	16269	5					11	8	3		4		1	9		2	6	7		10
32	23	Fulham	1-2	Walton	21747	5					11		3		4		1	9		2	6	7	8	10
33	30	BRADFORD PARK AVE.	1-2	GT Taylor	19357	5					11		3		4		1	9		2	6	7	8	10
34	Apr 6	Plymouth Argyle	0-1		16238	5						10	3		4		1	9	11	2	6	7	8	
35	10	Barnsley	1-1	Eastham	13171	5						8	3		4		1	9	11	2	6	7		10
36	13	NORWICH CITY	4-0	Westwood, Milsom(2), Cook	16218	5					11		3		4		1	9		2	6	7	8	10
37	19	SWANSEA TOWN	1-0	Cook	26583	5					11		3		4		1	9		2	6	7	8	10
38	20	Newcastle United	3-1	Westwood(2), Milsom	28277	5					11		3		4		1	9		2	6	7	8	10
39	22	Swansea Town	1-2	Cook	19693						11		3		4	5	1	9		2	6	7	8	10
40	27	WEST HAM UNITED	3-1	Walton, Westwood(2)	34909	5					11			3	4		1	9		2	6	7	8	10
41	May 1	BRENTFORD	2-0	Milsom, GT Taylor	46554	5					11			3	4		1	9		2	6	7	8	10
42	4	Blackpool	1-1	Westwood	25550	5					11			3	4		1	9		2	6	7	8	10
				Apps		40	3	2	1	1	29	33	38	3	42	3	41	40	13	42	41	42	10	38
				Goals		2	1	1			6	6			2			31	4			8	1	30

Three own goals

F.A. Cup

Rd	Date	Opponent	Score	Scorers	Att	Atkinson JE	Chameron K	Chambers WT	Church HB	Connor J	Cook WL	Eastham GR	Finney A	Goldsmith G	Goslin HA	Hurst J	Jones R	Milson J	Rimmer JW	Smith R	Taylor G	Taylor GT	Walton G	Westwood RW
3	Jan 12	Northampton Town	2-0	Milsom, Cook	17962	5					11	8	3		4		1	9		2	6	7		10
4	26	Plymouth Argyle	4-1	Milsom(2), Westwood, OG	41403	5						8	3		4		1	9	11	2	6	7		10
5	Feb 16	Tottenham Hotspur	1-1	Atkinson	70347	5					11	8	3		4		1	9		2	6	7		10
5r	20	TOTTENHAM HOTSPUR*	1-1	Westwood	47453	5				3		8			4		1	9	11	2	6	7		10
5/2r	25	Tottenham Hotspur+	2-0	Westwood, Walton	22692	5				3	11	8			4		1			2	6	7	9	10
6	Mar 2	Everton	2-1	Eastham, Milsom	67696	5					11	8	3		4		1	9		2	6	7		10
SF	16	West Bromwich Albion#	1-1	Walton	49605	5					11	8	3		4		1			2	6	7	9	10
SFr	20	West Bromwich Albion"	0-2		49110	5					11	8	3		4		1	9		2	6	7		10

* After extra time. + Played at Villa Park, Birmingham. # Played at Elland Road, Leeds. " Played at the Victoria Gound, Stoke.

Lancashire Cup

1	Sep 10	Preston North End	1-5

Manchester Cup

1	Mar 13	OLDHAM ATHLETIC	1-0
SF	Apr 24	Bury	2-2
SFr	Feb 29	BURY	0-3

FINAL TABLE

		Pl.	Home W	D	L	F	A	Away W	D	L	F	A	F (Total)	A	Pts
1	Brentford	42	19	2	0	59	14	7	7	7	34	34	93	48	61
2	BOLTON WANDERERS	42	17	1	3	63	15	9	3	9	33	33	96	48	56
3	West Ham United	42	18	1	2	46	17	8	3	10	34	46	80	63	56
4	Blackpool	42	16	4	1	46	18	5	7	9	33	39	79	57	53
5	Manchester United	42	16	2	3	50	21	7	2	12	26	34	76	55	50
6	Newcastle United	42	14	2	5	55	25	8	2	11	34	43	89	68	48
7	Fulham	42	15	3	3	62	26	2	9	10	14	30	76	56	46
8	Plymouth Argyle	42	13	3	5	48	26	6	5	10	27	38	75	64	46
9	Nottingham Forest	42	12	5	4	46	23	5	3	13	30	47	76	70	42
10	Bury	42	14	1	6	38	26	5	3	13	24	47	62	73	42
11	Sheffield United	42	11	4	6	51	30	5	5	11	28	40	79	70	41
12	Burnley	42	11	2	8	43	32	5	7	9	20	41	63	73	41
13	Hull City	42	9	6	6	32	26	7	2	12	31	48	63	74	40
14	Norwich City	42	11	6	4	51	23	5	1	15	20	38	71	61	39
15	Bradford Park Ave.	42	7	8	6	32	28	4	8	9	23	35	55	63	38
16	Barnsley	42	8	10	3	32	22	5	2	14	28	61	60	83	38
17	Swansea Town	42	13	5	3	41	22	1	3	17	15	45	56	67	36
18	Port Vale	42	10	7	4	42	28	1	5	15	13	46	55	74	34
19	Southampton	42	9	8	4	28	19	2	4	15	18	56	46	75	34
20	Bradford City	42	10	7	4	34	20	1	1	18	16	48	50	68	32
21	Oldham Athletic	42	10	3	8	44	40	0	3	18	12	55	56	95	26
22	Notts County	42	8	3	10	29	33	1	4	16	17	64	46	97	25

1934-35 Season
(Back) Goslin, Atkinson, Smith, Jones, Finney, G.Taylor
(Front) G.T.Taylor, Eastham, Milsom, Westwood, Cook

1935-36 Season
(Back) Goslin, Tennant, Atkinson, Swift, Finney, G.Taylor
(Front) G.T.Taylor, Walton, Milsom, Westwood, Rimmer

1935/36 13th in Division One

Manager: C.E. Foweraker

#	Date	Opponent	Score	Scorers	Att	Atkinson JE	Clark TG	Cook WL	Connor J	Currier J	Eastham GR	Finney A	Goldsmith G	Goslin HA	Hurst GJ	Jones RH	Kirkman G	Milsom J	Nicholson G	Rimmer JW	Smith R	Swift FV	Taylor G	Taylor GT	Tennant JW	Walton G	Westwood RW	Woodward T
1	Aug 31	BRENTFORD	0-2		31949	5		11			8	3		4		1		9			2		6	7			10	
2	Sep 2	SHEFFIELD WEDNESDAY	1-1	Eastham	21655	5		11			8	3		4		1					2		6	7		9	10	
3	Sep 7	Derby County	0-4		25716	5		11			8	3		4		1		9			2		6	7			10	
4	Sep 9	Sheffield Wednesday	2-2	Westwood, Goslin	12912	5		11				3	2	4		1		9					6	7		8	10	
5	Sep 14	EVERTON	2-0	Milsom, Cook	28391	5		11				3	2	4		1		9					6	7		8	10	
6	Sep 21	Grimsby Town	1-3	GT Taylor	12768	5		11				3	2	4		1		9					6	7		8	10	
7	Sep 28	Huddersfield Town	0-0		22564	5		11			10	3	2	4		1		9					6	7		8		
8	Oct 5	MIDDLESBROUGH	3-1	Milson, GT Taylor, Eastham	29910	5		11			8	3	2	4		1		9					6	7			10	
9	Oct 12	Aston Villa	2-1	Milsom(2)	36297	5		11			8	3	2	4		1		9					6	7			10	
10	Oct 19	LIVERPOOL	0-0		19322	5		11			10	3	2	4		1		9					6	7		8		
11	Oct 26	Chelsea	2-1	Milsom	36080	5		11			8	3	2	4		1		9					6	7			10	
12	Nov 2	BLACKBURN ROVERS	3-1	Milsom, Cook, Westwood	28981	5		11			8	3	2	4		1		9					6	7			10	
13	Nov 9	Stoke City	2-1	Westwood(2)	21771	5		11			8	3	2	4		1		9					6	7			10	
14	Nov 16	MANCHESTER CITY	3-3	Westwood(2), Milsom	42110	5		11			8	3	2	4		1		9					6	7			10	
15	Nov 23	Leeds United	2-5	Cook(2)	22973	5		11			8	3	2	4		1		9					6	7			10	
16	Nov 30	BIRMINGHAM	2-0	Cook, Milsom	21684	5		11			8	3	2	4		1		9					6	7			10	
17	Dec 7	Sunderland	2-7	Eastham, Westwood	27375	5		11			8	3	2	4		1		9					6	7			10	
18	Dec 14	WEST BROMWICH ALB.	3-1	Westwood, Milsom, Cook	21736	5		11			8	3	2	4		1		9					6	7			10	
19	Dec 25	WOLVERHAMPTON W.	0-3		30438	5		11	3		8	2		4		1		9					6	7			10	
20	Dec 26	Wolverhampton Wan.	3-3	Westwood, Milsom(2)	35672	5		11	3		8	2		4		1		9					6	7			10	
21	Dec 28	Brentford	0-4		27156			11			8	3		2	5	1	4	9					6	7			10	
22	Jan 1	PORTSMOUTH	4-0	Milsom(2), Westwood(2)	28300		4	11			8	3		2	5			9				1	6	7			10	
23	Jan 4	DERBY COUNTY	0-2		31392	5	4	11			8			2				9				1	6	7	3		10	
24	Jan 22	Everton	3-3	GT Taylor(3)	14562	5		11			8	3		4				9				1	6	7	2		10	
25	Jan 29	GRIMSBY TOWN	4-0	GT Taylor, Westwood, Cook, Carrier	10068	5		11		9	8	3		4								1	6	7	2		10	
26	Feb 1	HUDDERSFIELD T	1-2	Eastham	30852	5	6	11		9	8	3		4								1		7	2		10	
27	Feb 8	Middlesbrough	0-0		18377	5		11		9	8	3		4								1	6	7	2		10	
28	Feb 15	ASTON VILLA	4-3	Westwood, Currier(2), Rimmer	30834	5				9	8	3		4	6					11		1		7	2		10	
29	Feb 22	Liverpool	1-1	Currier	24543	5				9	8	3		4	6					11		1		7	2		10	
30	Feb 29	STOKE CITY	1 2	Goslin	14906	5				9	8	3		4						11		1		6	2		10	7
31	Mar 7	Birmingham	0-0		20170	5		7			8	3		4				9		11		1		6	2		10	
32	Mar 14	CHELSEA	2-3	Milsom, O'Hare(og)	18925	5		7			8	3		4				9		11		1		6	2		10	
33	Mar 21	Manchester City	0-7		40779	5		7			8		2					9	4	11		1		6	3		10	
34	Mar 28	LEEDS UNITED	3-0	Milsom, Westwood, Eastham	21289	5					11	3		4				9				1	6	7	2	8	10	
35	Apr 1	Arsenal	1-1	Milsom	10485	5					11	3		4				9				1	6	7	2	8	10	
36	Apr 4	Blackburn Rovers	3-0	Milsom(2), Westwood	13779	5						3		4				9		11		1	6	7	2	8	10	
37	Apr 10	PRESTON NORTH END	1-1	Milsom	35992	5						3		4				9		11		1	6	7	2	8	10	
38	Apr 11	SUNDERLAND	2-1	Milsom, Atkinson	32306	5						3		4				9		11		1	6	7	2	8	10	
39	Apr 13	Preston North End	0-1		25996	5		7			8	3		4				9		11		1	6		2		10	
40	Apr 18	West Bromwich Albion	2-2	Currier, Westwood	27468	5				9		3		4						11		1	6	7	2	8	10	
41	Apr 29	ARSENAL	2-1	GT Taylor, Goslin	29479	5						3		4				9		11		1	6	7	2	8	10	
42	May 2	Portsmouth	1-2	Hurst	13314						8	3		4	5			9		11		1	6	7	2		10	
		Apps				39	3	31	2	7	34	40	16	41	5	21	1	34	1	13	3	21	34	42	20	13	40	1
		Goals				1		7		5	5			3	1			20		1				7			16	

One own goal

F.A. Cup

Rd	Date	Opponent	Score	Scorers	Att	Atkinson	Clark	Cook	Eastham	Finney	Goslin	Swift	Taylor G	Taylor GT	Westwood	Woodward
3	Jan 11	Blackburn Rovers	1-1	Woods	41000	5	4	11	8	3	2	1	6	7	10	9
3r	Jan 14	BLACKBURN ROVERS	0-1		40800	5	4	11	8	3	2	1	6	7	10	9

Lancashire Cup

Rd	Date	Opponent	Score
1	Sep 2	Rossendale	1-1
1r	Oct 8	Rossendale	0-1

Manchester Cup

Rd	Date	Opponent	Score
SF	Mar 18	Manchester United	0-3

Other Games

	Date	Opponent	Score
1	May 9	Grimsby Town	0-1

	FINAL TABLE	Pl.	Home W	D	L	F	A	Away W	D	L	F	A	F (Total)	A	Pts
1	Sunderland	42	17	2	2	71	33	8	4	9	38	41	109	74	56
2	Derby County	42	13	5	3	43	23	5	7	9	18	29	61	52	48
3	Huddersfield Town	42	12	7	2	32	15	6	5	10	27	41	59	56	48
4	Stoke City	42	13	3	5	35	24	7	4	10	22	33	57	57	47
5	Brentford	42	11	5	5	48	25	6	7	8	33	35	81	60	46
6	Arsenal	42	9	9	3	44	22	6	6	9	34	26	78	48	45
7	Preston North End	42	15	3	3	44	18	3	5	13	23	46	67	64	44
8	Chelsea	42	11	7	3	39	27	4	6	11	26	45	65	72	43
9	Manchester City	42	13	2	6	44	17	4	6	11	24	43	68	60	42
10	Portsmouth	42	14	4	3	39	22	3	4	14	15	45	54	67	42
11	Leeds United	42	11	5	5	41	23	4	6	11	25	41	66	64	41
12	Birmingham	42	10	6	5	38	31	5	5	11	23	32	61	63	41
13	BOLTON WANDERERS	42	11	4	6	41	27	3	9	9	26	49	67	76	41
14	Middlesbrough	42	12	6	3	56	23	3	4	14	28	47	84	70	40
15	Wolverhampton W.	42	13	7	1	59	28	2	3	16	18	48	77	76	40
16	Everton	42	12	5	4	61	31	1	8	12	28	58	89	89	39
17	Grimsby Town	42	13	4	4	44	20	4	1	16	21	53	65	73	39
18	West Bromwich Alb.	42	12	3	6	54	31	4	3	14	35	57	89	88	38
19	Liverpool	42	11	4	6	43	23	2	8	11	17	41	60	64	38
20	Sheffield Wed.	42	9	8	4	35	23	4	4	13	28	54	63	77	38
21	Aston Villa	42	7	8	4	47	56	6	3	12	34	54	81	110	35
22	Blackburn Rovers	42	10	6	5	32	24	2	3	16	23	72	55	96	33

1936/37 *20th in Division One*

Manager: C.E. Foweraker

No	Mon	Date	Opponent	Score	Scorers	Att	Ainsley GE	Anderson AJ	Atkinson JE	Bower RWC	Calder J	Carruthers AN	Clark TC	Connor J	Currier J	Eastham GR	Finney A	Goslin HA	Halford D	Hanson S	Howe D	Hubbick H	Hurst J	Jones RH	Milson J	Rimmer IW	Swift F	Taylor G	Taylor GT	Tennant IW	Walton G	Westwood RW	Winter DT
1	Aug	29	Brentford	2-2	Currier(2)	27524	8		5						9		3	4	11									6	7	2		10	
2		31	Preston North End	2-1	Goslin, GT Taylor	23449	8		5						9		3	4	11				6	1					7	2		10	
3	Sep	5	GRIMSBY TOWN	1-2	Betwood (og)	21207	8		5						9		3	4	11					1				6	7	2		10	
4		7	PRESTON NORTH END	0-0		17622	8		5					3	9			4	11				6	1					7	2		10	
5		12	EVERTON	1-2	Westwood	18029	8						6	3	9	10		4			5			1					7	2		11	
6		19	Huddersfield Town	0-2		15992	8							3		10		4			5			1	9			6	7	2		11	
7		26	SUNDERLAND	1-1	Milsom	28453							6	3		8		4			5			1	9	11			7	2		10	
8	Oct	3	Wolverhampton Wan.	3-2	Westwood(2), Rimmer	28100		2					6	3		8		4			5			1	9	11			7			10	
9		10	DERBY COUNTY	1-3	Milsom	27893		2					4		9	8	3				5			1	9	11		6	7			10	
10		17	Liverpool	0-0		21701							4	3		10					5			1	9			6	7	2	8		
11		24	LEEDS UNITED	2-1	Milsom, Hurst	20411							4	3		8	11				5			1	9			6	7	2		10	
12		31	Birmingham	1-1	Howe	23288							4	3		8	11				5			1	9			6	7	2		10	
13	Nov	7	MIDDLESBROUGH	1-3	Howe	18264	8						4	3		10	11				5			1	9			6	7	2			
14		14	West Bromwich Albion	2-0	Milsom, Rimmer	20125							4	3		8		5			10			1	9	11		6	7	2			
15		21	MANCHESTER CITY	0-2		32003							4	3		8		5			10			1	9	11		6	7	2			
16		28	Portsmouth	1-1	Milsom	18259							4	3		8		5			11			1	9			6	7	2		10	
17	Dec	5	CHELSEA	2-1	Milsom(2)	13439							4	3		8		5			11			1	9			6	7	2		10	
18		12	Stoke City	2-1	Milsom(2)	8469							4	3		8		5			11			1	9			6	7	2		10	
19		19	CHARLTON ATHLETIC	2-1	Milsom, Westwood	25202							4	3		8		5			11			1	9			6	7	2		10	
20		25	Manchester United	0-1		47658							4	3		8		5			11			1	9			6	7	2		10	
21		26	BRENTFORD	2-2	Milsom, Westwood	36962							4	3				5			8			1	9	11		6	7	2		10	
22		26	MANCHESTER UNITED	0-4		11801							4	3				5			8			1	9	11		6	7	2		10	
23	Jan	1	ARSENAL	0-5		42171										8	3	5			11		4	1	9			6	7	2		10	
24		2	Grimsby Town	1-3	Howe	9719								3		10		4			5		8	1	9	11		6	7	2			
25		9	Everton	2-3	GT Taylor, Halford	24422		5								10	2	4	11		8			1	9			6	7			3	
26		23	HUDDERSFIELD T	2-2	Milsom, Goslin(pen)	15746	11	5	2					3		8		4						1	9			6	7			10	
27	Feb	6	WOLVERHAMPTON W.	1-2	Anderson	19576	11	5					6	3		8		4						1	9				7	2		10	
28		10	Sunderland	0-3		10975	7	5						3		8		4					11	1	9			6				10	2
29		13	Derby County	0-3		23046	11	5						3		8		2			7	4	6	1	9						10	
30		24	LIVERPOOL	0-1		15960	11				9	7				8		4			5	3					1	6		2			
31		27	Leeds United	2-2	Howe, Calder	15090	11				9			3		8		4			5					7	1	6		2			
32	Mar	6	BIRMINGHAM	0-0		21572	11				9			3		10		4			8					7	1	6		2			
33		13	Middlesbrough	0-2		20025					9			3		10		4			8					7	1	6		2		11	
34		20	WEST BROMWICH ALB.	4-1	Goslin(pen), Westwood, Calder(2)	20268	11	5			9							4			8	3				7	1	6		2		10	
35		26	SHEFFIELD WEDNESDAY	1-0	Milsom	26780	11	5			9							4			10	3			8		1	6	7	2			
36		27	Manchester City	2-2	Calder, Howe	51714	11	5			9							4			10	3	6		8		1		7	2			
37		29	Sheffield Wednesday	0-2		30859	11	5			9							4				3	6		8		1		7	2		10	
38	Apr	3	PORTSMOUTH	1-0	Howe	22552		5			9						11	4			10	3			8		1	6	7	2			
39		10	Chelsea	1-0	GT Taylor	23271	11	5			9							4			10	3			8		1	6	7	2			
40		17	STOKE CITY	0-0		16962	11	5			9							4			10	3			8		1	6	7	2			
41		24	Charlton Athletic	0-1		23684		5			9						11	4				3			8		1	6	7	2		10	
42	May	1	Arsenal	0-0		22875		5			9						11	4				3			8		1	6	7	2		10	
				Apps			7	13	17	3	13	1	18	21	6	27	7	37	5	4	30	13	24	25	35	9	13	31	35	37	1	29	1
				Goals				1			4				2			3	1		6		1		13	2			3			6	

One own goal

F.A. Cup

Rnd	Mon	Date	Opponent	Score	Scorers	Att	Ainsley	Atkinson	Connor	Eastham	Goslin	Halford	Howe	Hubbick	Hurst	Jones	Milson	Rimmer	Swift	Taylor G	Taylor GT	Tennant	Westwood
3	Jan	16	West Ham United	0-0		42300		5	3	8	4	11				9			1	6	7	2	10
3r		20	WEST HAM UNITED	1-0	Halford	21539		5	3	8	4	11				1	9			6	7	2	10
4		30	NORWICH CITY	1-1	Westwood	24791	11	5	3	8	4					1	9			6	7	2	10
4r	Feb	4	Norwich City*	2-1	Anderson, Milsom	30108	11	5	3	8	4				6	1	9				7	2	10
5		20	MANCHESTER CITY	0-5		60979	11	5	3	8	4					1	9			6	7	2	10

* After extra time

Lancashire Cup

Rnd	Mon	Date	Opponent	Score
1	Sep	28	Preston North End	2-2
1r	Oct	28	PRESTON NORTH END	2-1
2	Nov	16	Barrow	5-2
SF	May	3	BLACKBURN ROVERS	0-1

Manchester Cup

Rnd	Mon	Date	Opponent	Score
SF	Apr	14	Manchester United	0-1

	FINAL TABLE	Pl.		Home					Away					F.	A.	Pts
			W	D	L	F	A	W	D	L	F	A		(Total)		
1	Manchester City	42	15	5	1	56	22	7	8	6	51	39	107	61		57
2	Charlton Athletic	42	15	5	1	37	13	6	7	8	21	36	58	49		54
3	Arsenal	42	10	10	1	43	20	8	6	7	37	29	80	49		52
4	Derby County	42	13	3	5	58	39	8	4	9	38	51	96	90		49
5	Wolverhampton W.	42	16	2	3	63	24	5	3	13	21	43	84	67		47
6	Brentford	42	14	5	2	58	32	4	5	12	24	46	82	78		46
7	Middlesbrough	42	14	6	1	49	22	5	2	14	25	49	74	71		46
8	Sunderland	42	17	2	2	59	24	2	4	15	30	63	89	87		44
9	Portsmouth	42	13	3	5	41	29	4	7	10	21	37	62	66		44
10	Stoke City	42	12	6	3	52	27	3	6	12	20	30	72	57		42
11	Birmingham	42	9	7	5	36	24	4	9	8	28	36	64	60		41
12	Grimsby Town	42	13	3	5	60	32	4	4	13	26	49	86	81		41
13	Chelsea	42	11	6	4	36	21	3	7	11	16	34	52	55		41
14	Preston North End	42	10	6	5	35	28	4	7	10	21	39	56	67		41
15	Huddersfield Town	42	12	5	4	39	21	0	10	11	23	43	62	64		39
16	West Bromwich Alb.	42	13	3	5	45	32	3	3	15	32	66	77	98		38
17	Everton	42	12	7	2	56	23	2	2	17	25	55	81	78		37
18	Liverpool	42	9	8	4	38	26	3	3	15	24	58	62	84		35
19	Leeds United	42	14	3	4	44	20	1	1	19	16	60	60	80		34
20	BOLTON WANDERERS	42	6	6	9	22	33	4	8	9	21	33	43	66		34
21	Manchester United	42	8	9	4	29	26	2	3	16	26	52	55	78		32
22	Sheffield Wed.	42	8	5	8	32	29	1	7	13	21	40	53	69		30

1937
(Back) Winter, Roberts, Clark, Swift, Hanson, Catterall, Brown, Rothwell, Baum, J.Jones, Woodward
(Middle) Young(Trainer), David, Davies, Halford, Connor, Goslin, Hurst, Atkinson, Sinclair, Ithell, Eccles(Trainer)
(Front) Hubbick, G.T Taylor, Grosvenor, Calder, Howe, Milsom, Westwood, Anderson, G.Taylor, Currier, Carruthers

1938
(Back) Goslin, Atkinson, Hanson, Hubbick, tennant, Taylor
(Front) Woodward, Grosvenor, Calder, Howe, Anderson

1937/38 7th in Division One

Manager: C.E. Foweraker

No	Date		Opponent	Score	Scorers	Att	Anderson AJ	Atkinson JE	Calder J	Carruthers AN	Connor J	Currier J	Goslin HA	Grosvenor AT	Halford D	Hanson S	Howe D	Hubbick H	Hunt GS	Hurst GJ	Jones J	Milsom J	Roberts JH	Rothwell E	Swift FV	Taylor G	Taylor GT	Tennant JW	Westwood RW	Winter DT	Woodward T
1	Aug	28	BRENTFORD	2-0	Milsom, Westwood	31572	11	5					4	8				3				9			1	6	7	2	10		
2		30	Blackpool	2-2	Westwood, Milsom	24929	11	5					4	8				3				9			1	6	7	2	10		
3	Sep	4	Grimsby Town	1-0	G Taylor	10642	11	5					4	8				3				9			1	6	7	2	10		
4		6	BLACKPOOL	3-0	Grosvenor(2), Westwood	23606	11	5					4	8				3				9			1	6	7	2	10		
5		11	Huddersfield Town	0-1		20758	11	5					4	8				3				9			1	6	7	2	10		
6		15	ARSENAL	1-0	Westwood	39750	11	5					4	8				3				9			1	6	7	2	10		
7		18	EVERTON	1-2	Westwood	35691	11	5		7			4	8				3				9			1	6		2	10		
8		25	Wolverhampton Wan.	1-1	Carruthers	36995	11	5		7			4	8				3				9			1	6		2	10		
9	Oct	2	LEICESTER CITY	6-1	Goslin(2), Milsom, Carruthers, Westwood(2)	26498	11	5		7			4	8				3				9			1	6		2	10		
10		9	Sunderland	1-3	Tennant	29932	11	5		7			4	8				3				9			1	6		2	10		
11		16	PRESTON NORTH END	1-4	Westwood	37911	11	5	9	7			4	8				3							1	6				10	2
12		23	Charlton Athletic	1-1	Goslin	24000	11	5		7	3		4	8						6		9			1					10	2
13		30	CHELSEA	5-5	Westwood(3), Calder, Grosvenor	22293	11	5	9	7	3		4	8						6					1			2	10		
14	Nov	6	West Bromwich Albion	4-2	Calder(3), Westwood	20485	11	5	9	7			4	8				3		6					1			2	10		
15		13	STOKE CITY	1-0	Westwood	29870	11	5	9	7			4	8				3							1	6		2	10		
16		20	Leeds United	1-1	Westwood	23687	11	5	9	7			4	8				3							1	6		2	10		
17		27	BIRMINGHAM	1-1	Goslin	21999	11	5		7			4	8				3				9			1	6		2	10		
18	Dec	4	Portsmouth	1-1	Westwood	14508	11	5		7			4	8				3				9			1	6		2	10		
19		11	LIVERPOOL	0-0		15073	11	5		7			4	8				3				9			1	6		2	10		
20		18	Middlesbrough	2-1	Hardwick(og), Milsom	21407	11	5		7			4	8				3				9			1	6		2	10		
21		27	Derby County	2-4	Westwood, Currier	31679	11	5		7		9	4	8				3							1	6		2	10		
22	Jan	1	Brentford	1-1	Carruthers	23210	11	5	9	7			4	8				3							1	6		2	10		
23		15	GRIMSBY TOWN	3-1	Westwood(3)	14342	11	5	9	7			4	8				3							1	6		2	10		
24		22	DERBY COUNTY	0-2		26351	11	5	9	7			4	8				3							1	6		2	10		
25		26	HUDDERSFIELD T	2-0	Calder(2)	9722	11	5	9	7			4	8			10	3		6					1			2			
26		29	Everton	1-4	Calder	25848	11	5	9	7			4	8				3							1	6		2	10		
27	Feb	5	WOLVERHAMPTON W.	1-2	Grosvenor	38101	11	5	9	7			4	8				3							1	6		2	10		
28		12	Leicester City	1-1	Howe	15069	11	5	9				4			1	8	3					7			6		2	10		
29		19	SUNDERLAND	1-1	Milsom	23943	11	5		7			4			1	10	3				9		8		6		2			
30		26	Preston North End	2-2	Anderson(2)	29335	11	5	9				4	8		1	10	3								6		2			7
31	Mar	5	CHARLTON ATHLETIC	1-0	Howe	23051	11				3	9	4	8		1	10		2			5				6					7
32		12	Chelsea	0-0		38171	11	5					4	8		1	9	3						7		6		2	10		
33		19	WEST BROMWICH ALB.	3-0	Hunt, Westwood(2)	23098	11	5					4	8		1		3	9					7		6		2	10		
34		26	Stoke City	2-3	Jones, Currier	19431		5		7		9	4	8		1	10	3			11					6		2			
35	Apr	2	LEEDS UNITED	0-0		18492		5		7		9	4	8		1	10	3			11					6		2			
36		9	Birmingham	0-2		19889		5					4	8		1	10	3			11	9		7		6		2			
37		15	Manchester City	2-1	Westwood, Carruthers	53328	11	5		7			4	8		1		3				9				6		2	10		
38		16	PORTSMOUTH	1-1	Goslin(pen)	21854		5		7			4	8		1		3	9	6	11							2	10		
39		18	MANCHESTER CITY	2-1	Currier, Grosvenor	29872		5				9	4	8	11	1	10	3								6		2			7
40		23	Liverpool	1-2	Currier	26370						9	4	8		1	11	3	5		10					6		2			7
41		30	MIDDLESBROUGH	3-1	Woodward, Howe, Westwood	12164						9	4	8		1	11	3	5							6		2	10		7
42	May	7	Arsenal	0-5		40500						9	4	8		1	11	3	5							6		2	10		7
			Apps				34	37	14	25	3	7	40	41	1	14	14	40	5	9	6	17	1	3	28	37	6	38	33	3	6
			Goals				2		7	4		4	5	5			3			1		1				1		1	23		1

One own goal

F.A. Cup

| 3 | Jan | 8 | Arsenal | 1-3 | Carruthers | 64244 | 11 | 5 | | 7 | | | 4 | 8 | | | | 3 | | | | 9 | | | 1 | 6 | | 2 | 10 | | |

Lancashire Cup

1	Mar	30	NEW BRIGHTON	5-1
2	Apr	27	Southport	1-1
2r	May	9	Southport	1-3

Manchester Cup

SF	Mar	23	Manchester City	1-1
SFr	May	2	MANCHESTER CITY	1-0
F		14	Manchester United	2-1

Other Games

1	Sep	8	Morton	0-2
2	Apr	27	Flint Town	2-1
3	May	4	Brighton	5-1

	FINAL TABLE	Pl.	W	D	L	F	A	W	D	L	F	A	F.	A.	Pts
				Home					Away				(Total)		
1	Arsenal	42	15	4	2	52	16	6	6	9	25	28	77	44	52
2	Wolverhampton W.	42	11	8	2	47	21	9	3	9	25	28	72	49	51
3	Preston North End	42	9	9	3	34	21	7	8	6	30	23	64	44	49
4	Charlton Athletic	42	14	5	2	43	14	2	9	10	22	37	65	51	46
5	Middlesbrough	42	12	4	5	40	26	7	4	10	32	39	72	65	46
6	Brentford	42	10	6	5	44	27	8	3	10	25	32	69	59	45
7	BOLTON WANDERERS	42	11	6	4	38	22	4	9	8	26	38	64	60	45
8	Sunderland	42	12	6	3	32	18	2	10	9	23	39	55	57	44
9	Leeds United	42	11	6	4	38	26	3	9	9	26	43	64	69	43
10	Chelsea	42	11	6	4	40	22	3	7	11	25	43	65	65	41
11	Liverpool	42	9	5	7	40	30	6	6	9	25	41	65	71	41
12	Blackpool	42	10	5	6	33	26	6	3	12	28	40	61	66	40
13	Derby County	42	10	5	6	42	36	5	5	11	24	51	66	87	40
14	Everton	42	11	5	5	54	34	5	2	14	25	41	79	75	39
15	Huddersfield Town	42	11	3	7	29	24	6	2	13	26	44	55	68	39
16	Leicester City	42	9	6	6	31	26	5	5	11	23	49	54	75	39
17	Stoke City	42	10	7	4	42	21	3	5	13	16	38	58	59	38
18	Birmingham	42	7	11	3	34	28	3	7	11	24	34	58	62	38
19	Portsmouth	42	11	6	4	41	22	2	6	13	21	46	62	68	38
20	Grimsby Town	42	11	5	5	29	23	2	7	12	22	45	51	68	38
21	Manchester City	42	12	2	7	49	33	2	6	13	31	44	80	77	36
22	West Bromwich Alb.	42	10	5	6	46	36	4	3	14	28	55	74	91	36

1938/39   8th in Division One

Manager: C.E. Foweraker

No	Date		Opponent	Score	Scorers	Att	Anderson AJ	Atkinson JE	Connor J	Currier J	Forrest E	Geldard A	Goodall EI	Goslin HA	Grosvenor AT	Hanson S	Howe D	Hubbick H	Hunt GS	Hurst GJ	Marsh FK	Roberts JH	Rothwell E	Sidebottom W	Sinclair TMcK	Taylor G	Tennant JW	Westwood RW	Winter DT	Woodward T
1	Aug	27	CHARLTON ATHLETIC	2-1	Hunt, Anderson	21809	11	5				7	1	4	8		10	3	9								6	2			
2		31	Manchester United	2-2	Hunt(2)	37950	11	5				7	1	4	8		10	3	9							6	2			
3	Sep	3	Portsmouth	1-2	Grosvenor	28452	11	5					1	4	8		10	3	9							6	2			7
4		5	CHELSEA	0-2		19616	11	5			6		1	4	8		10	3	9								2			7
5		10	Leeds United	2-1	Woodward, Hunt	20381		5					1	4			10	3	9			8	11			6			2	7
6		17	LIVERPOOL	3-1	Roberts, Hunt(2)	22409		5						4		1	10	3	9			8	11			6			2	7
7		24	Leicester City	0-0		18263		5		9				4		1	10	3				8	11			6			2	7
8	Oct	1	MIDDLESBROUGH	4-1	Westwood(2), Roberts, Rothwell	28505		5		9				4		1		3				8	11			6		10	2	7
9		8	Birmingham	2-0	Westwood, Hunt	21855		5						4		1		3	9			8	11			6		10	2	7
10		15	EVERTON	4-2	Roberts(3), Woodward	54564		5						4		1		3	9			8	11			6		10	2	7
11		22	Huddersfield Town	1-2	Roberts	18027		5						4		1		3	9			8	11			6		10	2	7
12		29	ARSENAL	1-1	Woodward	46611		5				7	1	4				3	9			8				6		10	2	11
13	Nov	5	Brentford	2-2	Westwood, Hunt	24594		5					1	4			6	3	9			8	11					10	2	7
14		12	BLACKPOOL	0-1		35782		5					1	4			6	3	9			8	11					10	2	7
15		19	Derby County	0-3		26062		5					1	4			10	3	9			8	11			6			2	7
16		26	GRIMSBY TOWN	1-1	Currier	16229		5		9			1	4			10	3			6	8	11						2	7
17	Dec	3	Sunderland	2-2	Howe, Hunt	17815		5					1	4	8		10	3	9				11			6			2	7
18		10	ASTON VILLA	1-2	Currier	22552		5		9		7	1	4	8		10	3								6			2	11
19		17	Wolverhampton Wan.	1-1	Howe	19316		5						4		1	10	3	9			8	11			6			2	7
20		24	Charlton Athletic	1-2	Howe	6590		5						4		1	10	3	9			8	11			6			2	7
21		27	Preston North End	2-2	Roberts, Howe	38240		5						4	8	1	10	3	9			6	11						2	7
22		31	PORTSMOUTH	5-1	Hunt(2), Goslin(pen), Grosvenor, R	15679		5						4	8	1	10	3	9			6	11						2	7
23	Jan	2	STOKE CITY	1-3	Roberts	24767		5	3	9				4	8	1	10	2				6	11							7
24		14	LEEDS UNITED	2-2	Goslin(2,1pen)	14893		5	3			7		4		1	10		9				11		8	6			2	
25		25	Liverpool	2-1	Hunt, Sinclair	17705		5				7		4		1	10	3	9				11		8	6			2	
26		28	LEICESTER CITY	4-0	Hunt, Howe(2), Sinclair	18621		5				7		4		1	10	3	9				11		8	6			2	
27	Feb	4	Middlesbrough	2-1	Sinclair(2)	16416	11	5				7		4		1	10	3	9						8	6			2	
28		18	Everton	1-2	Geldard	38961		5				7		4		1	10	3	9						8	6			2	
29		22	BIRMINGHAM	3-0	Hunt(2), Howe	11696		5				7		2		1	10	3	9			4	11		8	6				
30		25	HUDDERSFIELD T	3-2	Howe, Hunt(2)	19332		5				7		2	8	1	10	3	9			4		11		6				
31	Mar	4	Arsenal	1-3	Hunt	29814		5				7		4		1	8	3	9				11			6		10	2	
32		11	BRENTFORD	1-1	Hunt	15161		5				7		4		1	8	3	9				11			6		10	2	
33		18	Blackpool	0-0		18896		5				7		4		1	10	3	9				11			6		8	2	
34		25	DERBY COUNTY	2-1	Westwood, Hunt	20543		5				7		4		1	10	3	9				11			6		8	2	
35	Apr	1	Grimsby Town	1-1	Hunt	8558		5				7		4		1	8	3	9				11			6		10	2	
36		8	Sunderland	2-1	Westwood, Hunt	22692		5				7		4		1	8	3	9				11					10	2	
37		10	Stoke City	1-4	Hunt	29042		5						4		1	8	3	9				11			6		10	2	7
38		15	Aston Villa	3-1	Currier, Sinclair, Cobley(og)	23160				9	6			2		1	4	3		5			11		8					7
39		22	WOLVERHAMPTON W.	0-0		23976					6			2		1	4	3	9	5			11		8					7
40		26	PRESTON NORTH END	0-2		15353					6	7		2		1	4	3	9	5			11		8					
41		29	MANCHESTER UNITED	0-0		10314					6	7		4		1	10	3	9	5			11		8				2	
42	May	6	Chelsea	1-1	Howe	18232		5				7		4		1	8	3	9				11			6			2	

		Anderson AJ	Atkinson JE	Connor J	Currier J	Forrest E	Geldard A	Goodall EI	Goslin HA	Grosvenor AT	Hanson S	Howe D	Hubbick H	Hunt GS	Hurst GJ	Marsh FK	Roberts JH	Rothwell E	Sidebottom W	Sinclair TMcK	Taylor G	Tennant JW	Westwood RW	Winter DT	Woodward T
Apps		5	38	2	6	5	20	12	42	12	30	36	41	37	16	3	17	24	1	10	29	4	18	30	24
Goals		1			4		1		3	2		9		23			8	1		5			6		3

One own goal

F.A. Cup

Rd	Date		Opponent	Score	Att	Anderson AJ	Atkinson JE	Goslin HA	Grosvenor AT	Hanson S	Howe D	Hubbick H	Hunt GS	Hurst GJ	Roberts JH	Rothwell E	Taylor G	Winter DT	Woodward T
3	Jan	7	Middlesbrough	0-0	32790	11		4	8	1	6	3	9	5	10			2	7
3r		11	MIDDLESBROUGH*	0-0	16981		5	4		1	10	3	9	6	8	11		2	7
3/2r		16	Middlesbrough +	0-1	25577		5	4	8	1	10	3	9	6		11		2	

* After extra time   + played at Elland Road, Leeds

Lancashire Cup

1	Oct	5	Blackpool	1-0
2		25	Bury	2-1
SF	Feb	11	MANCHESTER CITY	4-0
F	May	10	Preston North End	1-1

No replay due to War - Trophy shared

Manchester Cup

1	Mar	14	Bury	0-5

Other Games

1	Aug	20	BURY	1-2
2	Sep	19	Coalville	6-1
3	Apr	12	Flint Town	2-3
4	May	14	Norwegian XI	4-0
5		16	Fredrikstad	2-1
6		18	Skien	5-1
7		21	Drammen	2-0
8		23	Stavanger	4-0

	FINAL TABLE	Pl.	Home					Away					F.	A.	Pts
			W	D	L	F	A	W	D	L	F	A	(Total)		
1	Everton	42	17	3	1	60	18	10	2	9	28	34	88	52	59
2	Wolverhampton W.	42	14	6	1	55	12	8	5	8	33	27	88	39	55
3	Charlton Athletic	42	16	3	2	49	24	6	3	12	26	35	75	59	50
4	Middlesbrough	42	13	6	2	64	27	7	3	11	29	47	93	74	49
5	Arsenal	42	14	3	4	34	14	5	6	10	21	27	55	41	47
6	Derby County	42	12	6	3	39	22	7	5	9	27	33	66	55	46
7	Stoke City	42	13	6	2	50	25	6	4	11	21	43	71	68	46
8	BOLTON WANDERERS	42	10	6	5	39	25	5	9	7	28	33	67	58	45
9	Preston North End	42	13	7	1	44	19	3	5	13	19	40	63	59	44
10	Grimsby Town	42	11	6	4	38	26	5	5	11	23	43	61	69	43
11	Liverpool	42	12	6	3	40	24	2	8	11	22	39	62	63	42
12	Aston Villa	42	11	3	7	44	25	5	6	10	27	35	71	60	41
13	Leeds United	42	11	5	5	40	27	5	4	12	19	40	59	67	41
14	Manchester United	42	7	9	5	30	20	4	7	10	27	45	57	65	38
15	Blackpool	42	9	8	4	37	26	6	3	12	19	42	56	68	38
16	Sunderland	42	7	7	7	30	29	6	5	10	24	38	54	67	38
17	Portsmouth	42	10	7	4	25	15	2	6	13	22	55	47	70	37
18	Brentford	42	11	2	8	30	27	3	6	12	23	47	53	74	36
19	Huddersfield Town	42	11	4	6	38	18	1	7	13	20	46	58	64	35
20	Chelsea	42	10	5	6	43	29	4	4	15	21	51	64	80	33
21	Birmingham	42	10	5	6	40	27	2	3	16	22	57	62	84	32
22	Leicester City	42	7	6	8	35	35	2	5	14	13	47	48	82	29

1939

The 53rd .RA. Regiment Team that drew 3-3 with the Wanderers at Burden on 16th December, 1939.
All the players were on the Wanderers Books having signed up 'en masse'.

(Back) Winter, Goslin, Ithell, Hanson, Catterall, Hurst   (Front) Geldard, Sinclair, Howe, Roberts, Thompson

1940
(Back) Goslin, Hanson, Catterall, Ithell, Hurst
(Front) Geldard (part hidden), Howe, Westwood, Roberts, Sinclair

Manager: C.E. Foweraker

#	Date	Opponent	Score	Scorers	Att.	Atkinson JE	Burgess AC	Butler S	Chadwick C	Connor J	Cunliffe JN	Eastwood E	Forrest E	Geldard A	Goodall EI	Goslin HA	Graham RE	Grosvenor A	Hanks CW	Hanson S	Howe D	Hubbick H	Hunt GS	Hurst J	Jones WEA	Richardson N	Rothwell E	Sidebottom W	Taylor G	Walton G	Westwood RW	Whalley H	Winter D	Woodward T
1	Aug 26	Chelsea	2-3	Howe, Westwood	33902								7		4					1	8	3	9	5			11				10	2		
2	28	Stoke City	2-1	Hunt, Rothwell	13151								7		4					1	8	3	9	5			11				10	2		
3	Sep 2	PORTSMOUTH	2-1	Hubbick, Howe	12992								7		4					1	8	3	9	5			11				10	2		

The above games were played in Division One before the League closed down.

4th in North West Division of War Regional League

#	Date	Opponent	Score	Scorers	Att.	Atkinson JE	Burgess AC	Butler S	Chadwick C	Connor J	Cunliffe JN	Eastwood E	Forrest E	Geldard A	Goodall EI	Goslin HA	Graham RE	Grosvenor A	Hanks CW	Hanson S	Howe D	Hubbick H	Hunt GS	Hurst J	Jones WEA	Richardson N	Rothwell E	Sidebottom W	Taylor G	Walton G	Westwood RW	Whalley H	Winter D	Woodward T
1	Oct 21	Burnley	1-1	Hubbick(pen)	3000	5	8	7		6		2				1						3	9				11				10	4		
2	28	CARLISLE UNITED	4-1	Hunt(2), Rothwell, Butler	2000	5	8	7		6		2				1						3	9				11				10	4		
3	Nov 11	Oldham Athletic	2-2	Rothwell, Butler	8254			7		6	8	2				1						3	9			4	11				10	5		
4	18	ROCHDALE	4-0	Hunt(2), Cunliffe(2)	2113			7		6	8	2				1						3	9			4	11				10	5		
5	25	Blackburn Rovers	1-3	Walton	1221					6	8	2				1						3	9			4				11	10	5		7
6	Dec 2	BLACKPOOL	3-1	Howe(2), Cunliffe	2777		8									1					10	3	9	5	7		11	6				4	2	
7	23	SOUTHPORT	2-1	Connor(pen), Cunliffe	1033	5			11		8	2				1						3	9	6	7							4		
8	Jan 6	Accrington	1-1	Hunt	3000	5		7	11		8	2				1						3	9								10	6		
9	13	OLDHAM ATHLETIC	3-0	Hunt, Connor(pen), Burgess	1000	5	10			6	8	2				1						3	9	7			11					4		
10	20	Bury	1-4	Connor(pen)	3045	5	10			6	8	2				1						3	9	7			11					4		
11	Feb 24	Carlisle United	3-2	Connor(pen), Burgess(2)	2000	5		7	11		8	2				1						3	9								10	6		
12	Mar 16	Rochdale	2-2	Woodward, Burgess	3000	5	10			6	8	2				1						3	9				11					4		7
13	22	Barrow	2-4	Hunt, Burgess	3000	5	10			3	8	2	6		1								9	7			11					4		
14	23	BLACKBURN ROVERS	2-0	Rothwell, Sidebottom	3490	5	9				8	2		4					1			3					11	10				6		7
15	30	Blackpool	1-3	Burgess	6000	5	10			6	8	2				1						3	9				11					4		
16	Apr 6	BARROW	2-0	Hunt(2)	2000	5	10			6	8	2				1						3	9	7			11					4		
17	10	BURNLEY	5-1	Hunt(3), Cunliffe, Chadwick	700	5			11	6	8	2				1						3	9				10					4		7
18	13	PRESTON NORTH END	1-0	Sidebottom	2000	5			10	6	8	2				1						3	9				11					4		7
19	May 4	Preston North End	3-1	Chadwick(2), Sidebottom	2000	5			11	6	8	2				1			4			3	9	7			10							
20	11	BURY	0-1		950	5				6	8	2				1			4			3	9	7	11		10							
21	13	Southport	8-1	Sidebottom(4), A Jones(2), Hunt, Chadwick	1500	5			11	6	8	2				1			4			3	9	7			10							
22	18	ACCRINGTON	4-1	Hunt(2,1pen), Sidebottom(2)	500	5			11		8	2				1			4			3	9	7			10					6		

	Atkinson JE	Burgess AC	Butler S	Chadwick C	Connor J	Cunliffe JN	Eastwood E	Forrest E	Geldard A	Goodall EI	Goslin HA	Graham RE	Grosvenor A	Hanks CW	Hanson S	Howe D	Hubbick H	Hunt GS	Hurst J	Jones WEA	Richardson N	Rothwell E	Sidebottom W	Taylor G	Walton G	Westwood RW	Whalley H	Winter D	Woodward T
Apps	18	11	4	5	19	20	21	1	20	1				4	1	2	1	21	21	2	10	3	5	22	3	1	19	1	6
Goals		6	2	4	4	5										2	1	15	2			3	9	1					1

War League Cup

#	Date	Opponent	Score	Scorers	Att.	Atkinson JE	Connor J	Cunliffe JN	Eastwood E	Geldard A	Hanks CW	Hubbick H	Hunt GS	Rothwell E	Westwood RW	Woodward T
1/1	Apr 20	Blackburn Rovers	1-5	Hunt	7451	5	6	10	2	1	8	3	9	4	11	7
1/2	27	BLACKBURN ROVERS	1-3	Hanks	1500	5	6	2		1	8 11	3	9	7 4	10	

Lancashire Cup

#	Date	Opponent	Score
1	Nov 4	LIVERPOOL	1-3

Manchester Cup

No Competition held

Other Games

#	Date	Opponent	Score
1	Aug 19	BURY	2-1
2	Sep 16	MANCHESTER UNITED	2-2
3	23	Liverpool	0-3
4	30	Blackpool	0-2
5	Oct 7	Preston North End	1-6
6	14	MANCHESTER CITY	2-2
7	Dec 16	53rd FIELD REG. R.A.	3-3
8	25	STOKE CITY	3-0
9	26	Stoke City	5-1
10	Jan 1	PRESTON NORTH END	3-1
11	Feb 17	Blackpool	1-2
12	Mar 2	Oldham Athletic	2-4
13	9	Sheffield Wednesday	3-3
14	25	Liverpool	1-0

FINAL TABLE

	P	W	D	L	F	A	Pts.
Bury	22	16	4	2	64	30	34
Preston North End	22	15	5	2	63	27	32
Blackpool	22	13	3	6	75	36	32
BOLTON WANDS.	22	13	5	4	55	30	30
Oldham Athletic	22	11	9	2	55	61	24
Burnley	22	9	8	5	48	43	23
Barrow	22	8	10	4	54	57	20
Blackburn Rovers	22	7	11	4	37	40	18
Rochdale	22	5	12	5	38	58	15
Southport	22	5	13	4	34	62	14
Carlisle United	22	4	14	4	38	68	12
Accrington Stan.	22	2	14	6	31	78	10

~ FINAL TABLES 1940/41 - 1944/45 SEASONS ~

1940/41 Season

North League

	P	W	L	D	F	A	G/Ave
Preston N.E.	29	18	4	7	81	37	2.189
Chesterfield	35	20	9	6	76	40	1.900
Manchester City	35	18	7	10	104	55	1.890
Barnsley	30	18	8	4	86	49	1.775
Everton	34	19	8	7	85	51	1.666
Blackpool *	20	13	4	3	56	34	1.646
Halifax Town	30	10	7	13	64	51	1.254
Manchester Utd.	35	14	13	8	80	65	1.249
Lincoln City	27	13	7	7	65	53	1.226
Newcastle United	23	12	11	0	49	41	1.195
Huddersfield Town	33	11	16	6	69	58	1.189
Middlesbrough	27	16	10	1	84	71	1.183
New Brighton	26	15	10	1	97	82	1.182
Burnley	35	17	11	7	62	53	1.169
Leeds United	30	13	9	8	62	54	1.148
Liverpool	37	15	16	6	91	82	1.102
Wrexham	29	15	9	5	78	71	1.098
Chester	35	14	15	6	94	89	1.056
Doncaster Rovers	32	15	10	7	77	74	1.040
Oldham Athletic	37	17	16	4	78	77	1.012
Grimsby Town	27	12	13	2	60	63	.952
Bradford PA	31	9	15	7	64	74	.864
Rotherham Utd.	29	12	12	5	48	57	.842
Blackburn Rovers	32	9	13	10	49	60	.816
Bury	38	10	19	9	80	100	.800
BOLTON WANDS.*	16	6	8	2	31	40	.775
Tranmere Rovers	25	9	11	5	67	90	.744
Sheffield Utd.	25	6	13	6	44	60	.733
Bradford City	29	8	18	3	72	99	.727
Rochdale	32	12	15	5	64	92	.695
Southport	28	7	19	2	61	88	.693
York City	25	7	14	4	49	71	.690
Hull City	23	8	12	3	44	67	.656
Sheffield Wed.	30	9	15	6	50	78	.641
Stockport County	29	9	15	5	54	93	.580
Crewe Alex.	24	2	19	3	32	84	.380

* Competed in second part of season only.
(Final positions determined on goal average)

1941/42 Season

North League 1st Championship

	P	W	L	D	F	A	Pts
Rotherham United	18	6	10	2	33	47	14
New Birghton	18	4	8	6	39	75	14
Tranmere Rovers	18	5	10	3	35	60	13
York City	18	4	10	4	41	55	12
Mansfield T.	18	6	12	0	29	50	12
BOLTON WANDS.	18	3	10	5	35	48	11
Southport	18	5	12	1	33	61	11
Bury	18	3	12	3	37	59	9
Wrexham	18	2	11	5	40	69	9
Stockport County	18	2	14	2	34	73	6

Bottom 10 clubs only shown (of 38 total)

2nd Championship

	P	W	L	D	F	A	Pts
BOLTON WANDS.	15	5	6	4	26 33 14		

Only those clubs playing 18 matches or more qualified for the Championship, of which there were 22 (varied between 18 and 23 matches), Bolton Wanderers were one of 29 who played less than the min. (varied between 8 and 17).

League Cup Qualifying Competition

	P	W	L	D	F	A	Pts	Ave.
York City	10	2	3	5	22	27	9	.900
Chesterfield	10	4	5	1	15	20	9	.900
Wrexham	9	3	4	2	22	23	8	.888
BOLTON WANDS.	9	3	4	2	16	17	8	.888
Leeds United	10	4	6	0	22	15	8	.800
Newcastle United	10	2	4	4	15	23	8	.800
New Brighton	10	4	6	0	18	38	8	.800
Bournemouth & B.	8	2	4	2	11	21	6	.750
Swansea Town	8	1	3	4	9	21	6	.750
Halifax Town	9	2	5	2	11	20	6	.666
Rochdale	9	3	6	0	13	29	6	.666
Gateshead	10	2	6	2	15	30	6	.600
Luton Town	10	2	6	2	12	30	6	.600
Tranmere Rovers	10	2	6	2	16	42	6	.600
Doncaster Rovers	8	2	6	0	10	27	4	.500
Stockport County	10	1	6	3	12	38	5	.500
Mansfield Town	7	1	5	1	10	19	3	.428
Walsall	10	2	8	0	9	29	4	.400
Sheffield Wed.	8	1	6	1	8	25	3	.375

Only top 32 qualified. Bottom 19 clubs did not qualify, those only shown above. Final positions based on average points from games played

1942/43 Season

North League 1st Championship

	P	W	L	D	F	A	Pts
Tranmere Rovers	18	5	10	3	36	63	13
Wolverhampton W.	18	5	11	2	28	41	12
Crewe Alexandra	18	5	11	2	43	64	12
Middlesbrough	18	4	10	4	30	50	12
Rochdale	18	5	11	2	34	57	12
Wrexham	18	5	12	1	43	67	11
Leeds United	18	3	11	4	28	45	10
Oldham Athletic	18	4	12	2	29	54	10
Bradford City	18	4	12	2	30	63	10
BOLTON WANDS.	18	3	12	3	31	52	9
Doncaster Rovers	17	3	11	3	23	41	9
Mansfield Town	18	2	12	4	25	65	8

Bottom 12 only shown (of 48 total)

2nd Championship

	P	W	L	D	F	A	Pts
BOLTON WANDS.	17	7	8	2	34	42	16
Tranmere Rovers	20	6	10	4	37	48	16
Halifax Town	18	7	9	2	30	39	16
Chester	20	6	11	3	40	49	15
Northampton Town	17	6	9	2	30	37	14
Wolverhampton W.	17	5	8	4	38	45	14
Swansea Town	18	4	8	6	36	52	14
Grimsby Town	13	4	4	5	30	27	13
Bury	16	5	8	3	44	42	13
Doncaster Rovers	17	5	9	3	27	41	13
Rotherham United	18	4	9	5	28	43	13
Gateshead	13	6	7	0	29	36	12
Stockport County	19	4	11	4	37	76	12
Southport	18	4	11	3	38	58	11
Leeds United	16	5	10	1	32	50	11
Oldham Athletic	18	4	11	3	28	47	11
Middlesbrough	18	5	13	0	31	69	10
Lincoln City	10	4	5	1	23	18	9
Burnley	14	3	8	3	17	31	9
Walsall	16	3	11	2	22	35	8
Cardiff City	17	2	12	3	22	47	7
Mansfield Town	10	1	8	1	12	41	3

Bottom 22 clubs shown only (of 54 total)

League North Cup Qualifying Competition

	P	W	L	D	F	A	Pts
Grimsby Town	10	3	3	4	22	20	10
BOLTON WANDS.	10	4	4	2	20	24	10
Gateshead	10	5	5	0	25	30	10
Lincoln City	10	4	5	1	23	18	9
Sunderland	10	3	4	3	31	26	9
Northampton Town	10	4	5	1	19	19	9
Birmingham	10	3	6	1	15	17	7
Wrexham	10	2	5	3	16	23	7
Stockport County	10	3	6	1	22	46	7
Walsall	10	2	6	2	13	18	6

Only top 28 qualified. Bottom 26 did not qualify, top 10 non-qualifiers only shown.

1943/44 Season

North League 1st Championship

	P	W	L	D	F	A	Pts
York City	18	7	9	2	35	40	16
Halifax Town	18	6	8	4	27	36	16
Southport	18	7	9	2	33	51	16
Stoke City	18	6	9	3	40	35	15
Chesterfield	18	7	10	1	29	31	15
Oldham Athletic	18	7	10	1	30	44	15
Stockport County	18	5	8	5	24	43	15
Coventry City	18	4	8	6	25	23	14
Newcastle United	18	5	9	4	32	37	14
Sheffield Wed.	18	5	9	4	29	34	14
Middlesbrough	18	4	8	6	35	52	14
Wolverhampton W.	18	5	10	3	30	42	13
Bury	18	6	11	1	31	44	13
Barnsley	18	5	11	2	32	42	12
Bradford City	18	4	11	3	27	47	11
Wrexham	18	5	12	1	43	63	11
Notts County	18	4	11	3	26	53	11
BOLTON WANDS.	18	5	13	0	24	46	10
Tranmere Rovers	18	4	13	1	39	71	9
Crewe Alexandra	18	4	13	1	29	62	9

Bottom 20 clubs only shown (of 50 total)

North League 2nd Championship

	P	W	L	D	F	A	Pts
West Bromwich A.	21	5	7	9	46	48	19
BOLTON WANDS.	21	8	10	3	42	49	19
Leeds United	18	8	7	3	34	40	19
Northampton Town	19	9	10	0	37	39	18
Burnley	18	6	6	6	39	42	28
Bristol City	20	6	9	5	38	42	17
York City	20	7	11	2	37	40	16
Middlesbrough	21	6	11	4	41	51	16
Swansea Town	20	7	11	2	42	67	16
Grimsby Town	15	6	6	3	23	28	15
Bury	20	6	11	3	38	55	15
Oldham Athletic	18	5	9	4	28	36	14
Sunderland	19	6	11	2	44	58	14
Chestefield	19	5	10	4	31	41	14
Mansfield Town	14	6	7	1	23	25	13
Wolverhampton W.	20	3	11	6	28	56	12
Walsall	17	3	8	6	17	35	12
Tranmere Rovers	20	6	14	0	29	62	12

Bottom 18 clubs only shown (of 50 total)

North Cup Qualifying Competition

	P	W	L	D	F	A	Pts
Stockport County	10	5	5	0	23	28	10
Nottingham Forest	9	3	3	3	8	7	9
Chester	10	4	5	1	31	31	9
Mansfield Town	10	4	5	1	12	19	9
Huddersfield Town	10	3	5	2	16	19	8
West Bromwich A.	10	2	4	4	24	29	8
Doncaster Rovers	9	3	4	2	14	24	8
Middlesbrough	10	2	5	3	14	20	7
BOLTON WANDS.	10	3	6	1	15	27	7
Walsall	10	2	5	3	11	22	7

Only top 32 qualified. Bottom 24 did not qualify, top 10 non-qualifers only shown.

1944/45 Season

North League 1st Championship

	P	W	L	D	F	A	Pts
Huddersfield Town	18	14	1	3	50	22	31
Derby County	18	14	3	1	54	19	29
Sunderland	18	12	2	4	52	25	28
Aston Villa	18	12	3	3	54	19	27
Everton	18	12	4	2	58	25	26
Wrexham	18	11	4	3	40	18	25
Doncaster Rovers	18	12	6	0	48	27	24
Bradford PA	18	10	4	4	45	31	24
BOLTON WANDS.	18	9	3	6	34	22	24
Manchester City	18	9	5	4	53	31	22
Stoke City	18	9	5	4	37	25	22
Birmingham	18	8	4	6	30	21	22
Barnsley	18	10	6	2	42	32	22
Rotherham United	18	9	5	4	31	25	22
West Bromwich A	18	9	5	4	36	30	22

Top 15 clubs only shown.

2nd Championship

	P	W	L	D	F	A	Pts
Derby	26	19	4	3	78	28	41
Everton	27	17	7	3	79	43	37
Liverpool	24	16	5	3	67	26	35
Burnley	26	15	8	3	56	36	33
Newcastle United	23	15	7	1	71	38	31
Aston Villa	25	14	9	2	70	45	30
Chesterfield	24	10	5	9	40	24	29
Wolvershampton W.	2411	6	7	45	31	29	
Manchester United	22	13	6	3	47	33	29
Darlington	24	13	8	3	61	45	29
Bristol City	22	13	7	2	55	33	28
Blackburn Rovers	24	13	9	2	62	51	28
Huddersfield T.	27	12	11	4	52	49	28
Wrexham	22	10	5	7	55	36	27
BOLTON WANDS.	23	11	7	5	52	35	27
Blackpool	24	12	9	3	58	42	27
Stoke City	23	12	9	2	67	42	26
Lovell's Ath.	19	12	5	2	44	27	26

Top 18 clubs only shown.

League North Cup Qualifying Competition

	P	W	L	D	F	A	Pts
Derby County	10	7	0	3	38	9	17
Aston Villa	10	8	1	1	31	13	17
Bristol City	10	8	2	0	27	10	16
Everton	10	8	2	0	39	15	16
Burnley	10	7	2	1	25	10	15
Cardiff City	10	7	2	1	26	11	15
Doncaster Rovers	10	7	2	1	30	13	15
Liverpool	10	7	2	1	34	15	15
Stoke City	10	6	2	2	35	14	14
Lovell's Athletic	10	7	3	0	24	15	14
Barnsley	10	7	3	0	18	14	14
Wrexham	10	5	1	4	30	17	14
BOLTON WANDS.	10	6	3	1	27	15	13
Bradford P.A.	10	6	3	1	23	19	13
Manchester City	10	6	3	1	23	19	13

Only top 32 qualified. Bottom 28 did not qualify. top 15 clubs only shown.

Note: During the War-time seasons, leagues were formed on a general countrywide regional basis. Fixtures were then played against others on a more local basis, i.e. each club did not play every other on a 'home' and 'away' format within their league (e.g. Bolton never played the likes of Middlesbrough or Bristol City). Consequently the final league tables were on a composite basis. In addition, some matches were 'double-headers' for other competitions - as indicated on the detailed statistics pages

N.B. In the tables shown here the order of match records are as follows:P (played) W (Won) L (lost) D (Drawn)

1940/41   26th in Football Lge North, decided on goal average of all Members (36)

Manager: C.E. Foweraker

#		Date	Opponent	Score	Scorers	Att	Atkinson JE	Banks R	Berry J	Bolton R	Butler S	Chadwick C	Cload H	Cooper JE	Connor J	Cunliffe JN	Eastham GR	Eastwood E	Finan RJ	Goodall EI	Goslin HA	Grosling G	Grainger R	Grimsditch SW	Heslop N	Howe D	Hubbick H	Hunt GS	Hurst J	Johnson WH	Knight J	Lofthouse N	Martindale L	Morrison ER	Pearson TU	Rothwell E	Sidebottom W	Winter DT
1	Jan	4	OLDHAM ATHLETIC	2-1	Eastham, Butler	2038		2			11				6	7	8	5		1							3							4				9	
2		11	Oldham Athletic*	5-3	Hunt(4,1pen), Eastham	2800		2		1	11				6	8	7										3	9							4				9	
3		18	MANCHESTER UNITED	3-2	Chadwick, Goslin, Howe	2146	5				7				6		8			1	4					10	3	9											11	2
4		25	Manchester United	1-4	Cunliffe	2649	5			1	7				6	8		2		4							3	9										10	11	
5	Mar	15	Bury	1-4	Hunt	2437	5	2		1	11				6				7						4		3	9		10								8	
6		22	BURY	5-1	Lofthouse(2),Cload,Connor,Johnson	1587	5	2					11		6				7							1	3	4		10		9						8	
7		29	Southport	1-2	Sidebottom	1800	5						11		6											1	3	4				9						8	
8	Apr	12	Burnley	2-2	Lofthouse(2)	3729	5	2	7				11		6											1	8	3	4			9						10	
9		14	BURNLEY	0-2		1500	5	2	7						6							8		1	11		3	4				9						10	
10		19	Rochdale	3-1	Sidebottom, Lofthouse(2)	800	5	2					11		6										1		3	7	4			9						10	8
11		26	BLACKBURN ROVERS	2-0	Sidebottom, Lofthouse	1441	5	2					11		6										1		3	8				9						10	
12	May	10	Chester	0-8		1500	5	2					7	11	10	6											3	8				9							2
13		17	MANCHESTER CITY	1-1	Lofthouse	1500	5	4							6									7			3			10		9		1	11				
14		24	Manchester City	4-6	Chadwick, Howe(2), Johnson	1500	5	2					7		6					4						10	3			8		9		1	11				
15		31	OLDHAM ATHLETIC	3-1	Grainger, Lofthouse(2)	1000		2					8		5								7				3	4				9		1	11				
16	Jun	7	Oldham Athletic	2-3	Knight, Lofthouse	1000	4	2																			3	8			10	9							
			Additional players: H Barker 7/10, A Burgess 15/10, D Clancy 13/4, JW Gallon 13/8,				Apps	13	13	2	3	3	5	6	1	14	3	3	2	2	2	3	1	2	7	3	2	16	13	2	5	1	11	2	3	3	2	11	2
			S Hanson 12/1, W Houghton 7/7, EC Leyland 16/6,				Goals					1	2	1			1	1	2				1		1				3		5		2	1	11				3	

D Mann 7/2, W O'Neill 7/6, E Platt 16/11, RI Pryde 16/5, A Richardson 11/4, R Ryder 16/7, JD Smith 11/7, G Taylor 1/10,

Notes: * After extra time. Full time Oldham 2 Bolton 1 - League result. Extra time played to settle Lancashire Cup tie. Matches 1-4 also counted as Lancashire Cup games.

Football League War Cup

#		Date	Opponent	Score	Scorers	Att	Atkinson JE	Banks R	Bolton R	Butler S	Chadwick C	Cload H	Cooper JE	Connor J	Cunliffe JN	Eastham GR	Eastwood E	Finan RJ	Goslin HA	Grainger R	Hubbick H	Hunt GS	Johnson WH	Rothwell E	Sidebottom W	Winter DT
P	Feb	1	BRADFORD CITY	6-0	Hunt(3),Chadwick,Sidebottom,Butler	3210	5	2	1	11	7			6				4	8		3	9				10
P		8	Bradford City*	3-1	Cunliffe(2), Finan(pen)	1567	5	2	1	11	7			6	10			4	8		3	9				
1/1		15	BURNLEY	3-1	Hunt(2), Finan(pen)	3820	5	2	1	11	7			6				4	8		3	9				
1/2		22	Burnley	2-2	Hunt, Chadwick	2400	5	2	1	11	7			6				4	8		3	9	10			11
2/1	Mar	1	PRESTON NORTH END	1-4	Hunt	7838	5	2	1	11	7			6	8			4			3	9				10
2/2		8	Preston North End	0-2		9000	5	2	1	11						8			7		3	9				10

* Played at Burnden Park, Bolton at Bradford City's request.   Additional player: SJ Pugh 2/2 /4

Other Games

#		Date	Opponent	Score
1	Dec	25	Blackpool	1-3
2		28	Halifax Town	1-4
3	Apr	5	RAF XI	3-3
4	Jun	2	RAF KIRKHAM	3-3
5		6	RAF*	1-2

* Played at Blackpool

1941/42   34th in Football Lge - Northern Sect (1st Comp), failed to qualify for 2nd.

Manager: C.E. Foweraker

#		Date	Opponent	Score	Scorers	Att	Atkinson JE	Banks R	Brown W	Brown W	Burgess AC	Chadwick C	Cload H	Connor J	Eastham GR	Foster R	Gallon JW	Goslin HA	Grimsbitch SW	Hanks CW	Haslam AD	Hubbick H	Hunt GS	Jackson J	Johnson JW	Johnson WH	Knight J	Lofthouse N	Mawdsley LAC	McCormick JM	Morris J	Myers J	Rothwell E	Russell DW	Smith JD	Swinburne TA	Wright H
1	Aug	30	Bury	4-4	Lofthouse,Chadwick,WH Johnson,Bacuzzi(og)	2730		2				7	11	6								3	4			10		8					1				
2	Sep	6	BURY	2-1	Jones, Goslin	2646	5	2				11		6			4					3	9			10	7	8									
3		13	HALIFAX TOWN	1-1	Hunt	1869	5	2					11	6								3	4			10	7	8	9								
4		20	Halifax Town	0-2		4000	5	2					11	6								3	4				7	8	9								
5		27	BLACKBURN ROVERS	2-2	Myers, Hunt	1986	5	2			10		11	6								3	4					8				9		1			
6	Oct	4	Blackburn Rovers	3-3	Chadwick, Hunt(2)	2500	5	2	4				11	6	1							3	10				7	8	9								
7		11	BLACKPOOL	2-6	Hunt(2)	5203	5	2					11	6							10	3	9				4	7	8					1			
8		18	Blackpool	1-2	Hunt	3000	5	2					11	6							10	3	9				4	7	8					1			
9		25	OLDHAM ATHLETIC	3-5	Rothwell, Hunt(2)	1600	5	2					11								8	3	9				7			6		10	1			
10	Nov	1	Oldham Athletic	0-2		2000	5		4	10				6								3	9				7	8				11				
11		8	Burnley	1-2	Chadwick(pen)	3000		2					7	6								3	8	9		10				4						
12		15	BURNLEY	3-1	Wright, Hunt(2)	2000	5	2							8							3	9					10		4							11
13		22	ROCHDALE	3-3	Knight, Lofthouse, G Eastham	2684	5	2	4					6	8				1			3					10	9									11
14		29	Rochdale	0-1		1500		2						5						7		3					10			6							11
15	Dec	6	Preston North End	2-4	Wright, Chadwick	1500	5					7		6	10				1			3	8	9						4							11
16		13	PRESTON NORTH END	2-6	Knight, Chadwick(pen)	2000		2	4	10		7		5								3	9					8								1	11
17		20	Southport	2-3	Wright(2)	2700	5	2				7				4						3	9			10		8		6					1	11
18		25	SOUTHPORT	4-0	Burgess, Hunt(2), Myers	4086	5	2			10			6		5						3	9				4	8				7			1		
19		27	Manchester United	1-3	Hunt	5000	5				10			6		4						3	9					8	7						1		
20	Jan	3	MANCHESTER UNITED	2-2	Chadwick(2)	2500		2	10		11			5								3	4		6	7	8				9					
21		10	CHESTER	1-0	Knight	2673		2	10					5								3	4	9				8				7					
22		17	Chester	1-3	Speak	1000		2						5								3	9		10	6		8									
23	Feb	14	Stoke City	1-3	Franklin(og)	3224		2						5								3	9		8	6						4					
24		28	YORK CITY	4-3	Knight(2), Hunt(pen), JW Johnson	2109		2					11	5	8							3	4		7	6		10									
25	Mar	14	BRADFORD CITY	4-0	Lofthouse, Hunt, Knight, Morris	2624	5						11							2	3	8				6		10	9	7						
26		21	STOKE CITY	1-1	Morris	4371	5						11						4	1	2	3	8				6		10	9	7						
27		28	York City	1-2	Hunt	3700										7	11	2		2	3	8		6			10									
28	Apr	4	Halifax Town	2-2	Morris, Lofthouse	2000							7				11		2	3	8				6	10	9	8							
29		6	SHEFFIELD WEDNESDAY	3-3	Knight, Hunt(pen), Lofthouse	2000												2	3	8				6	10	9										
30		11	Blackpool	1-7	Hunt	4000	6						11						2	3	9				7		8					4				
31		18	BLACKPOOL	2-1	Knight, Hunt(pen), Lofthouse	3760							11				10		2	3	9			7		8		5				4				
32		25	Bury	0-2		1222							11				7	1	2	3	8			4		10	9	5								
33	May	2	BURY	2-1	Lofthouse, Gallon	2900							11				10	1	2	3	9			6		8						7	4			

			Addit.players:EC Beardsman 27/5,LM Boulter 23/10,J Breedon 25/1,G Catterall 14/3			Apps	18	22	4	6	3	20	3	21	5	5	5	6	11	4	8	32	31	4	6	19	9	30	12	3	7	4	5	3	5	4	6
			RM Cross 27/4 & 28/5, H Eastham 12,13/7, E Eastwood 29/4, E Forrest 9/4,			Goals			1	7			1	1	1						20			1	1	8	6			3	2	1				4
			S Hanson 14/1, D Howe 16/6, J Hurst 11/5 & 12/6, W Mangham 10/2																								Two own goals									

R Marsh 18,19/11, L Martindale 22/4 & 30/5, W McEwan 27/8, ER Morrison 3,4/1, RR Newton 29/1, E Platt 11/11, JJ Robinson 27/1, W Schofield 11,12/1,

J Shields 24/9, J Shore 31,32/6, J Shuttleworth 29/5 K Speak 21/6 & 22/11(1), AW Steen 22,23/7, E Walker 29/11, H Whalley 25/4, GK Whitehead 21,31/1, DT Winter 19/2, J Wright 5/7.

Notes: Matches 1-18 inclusive were Football League - Northern Section (1st Comp.) comprising 38 clubs.

Matches 19-33 inclusive were Football League - Northern Section (2nd Comp.), Bolton failed to qualify for a Championship placing having played less than 18 games.

Matches 19-27 inclusive were Football League War Cup, Qualifying Comp., early stages of which were played on 'mini-league' basis. Matches 30 & 31 also counted as Lancashire Cup games.

1942/43   46th in Football Lge - Northern Sect (1st Comp), 33rd in (2nd Comp)

Manager: C.E. Foweraker

#		Date	Opponent	Score	Scorers	Att	Atkinson JE	Chadwick C	Charlesworth S	Colclough W	Connor JE	Crozier J	Gee H	Gillies MM	Gorman WE	Gunner R	Harker J	Hopkins RW	Hubbick H	Hughes GE	Hunt GS	John WR	Johnson IW	Johnson WH	Knight J	Lofthouse N	Longman FH	Maudsley RC	Murphy D	Parker LT	Power GF	Rothwell E	Russell DW	Tate N	Taylor G	Watson I	Wharton JE	Wright H
1	Aug	29	Bury	3-4	Hunt(pen), Gee(2)	2485		10					7				4		3		8			6		9											11	
2	Sep	5	BURY	2-3	Harker, Chadwick	1185		10					7				9		3		8							6				4					11	
3		12	SOUTHPORT	1-3	Hunt	1885		11					7						3		9							5				4					10	
4		19	Southport	2-6	Lofthouse, Hunt	2000		11					7						3	4				6		9				5	8						10	
5		26	Manchester City	0-2		4000				5	1			2					3			8	6	9				4									10	11
6	Oct	3	MANCHESTER CITY	2-1	Hunt, Chadwick	3736		11			1			2					3	4		7	6	9						5	8						10	
7		10	Blackpool	0-2		4000		11			1			2					3	4		7	6	9						5	8						10	
8		17	BLACKPOOL	0-2		4982								5	2				3	8	1	6	10	9											11	4	7	
9		24	BURNLEY	7-4	W.Johnson, Lofthouse, Rothwell, Chadwick(3), Hunt	2664		7						5	4				3	8	1			6		9									10		11	
10		31	Burnley	2-1	Lofthouse(2)	3000	4	11						5	2				3	8	1	6				9											10	
11	Nov	7	BLACKBURN ROVERS	3-3	Lofthouse(2), Hunt	3748		11							2			7	3	8	10	6				9				5								
12		14	Blackburn Rovers	2-4	Lofthouse(2)	2000		11						5	2			10	3			6				9				8								
13		21	Oldham Athletic	1-3	Chadwick(pen)	2000		11						5	2				3	8	1	7	6			9							4				10	
14		28	OLDHAM ATHLETIC	1-1	Lofthouse	2990		7						5	2				3	4		8	6			9											11	
15	Dec	5	ROCHDALE	4-4	Chadwick, Watson, Hughes, Wharton	873		11						5	2				3	8	10					9									4	7		
16		12	Rochdale	1-3	Tate	1000		11						5	2				3		10					9				1				8	4	7		
17		19	MANCHESTER UNITED	0-2		1578		11						5	2				3		10		4			9				1				8	7			
18		25	Manchester United	0-4		6000		7		6				5	2			10	3							9				1						8	11	
19		26	MANCHESTER CITY	2-4	Hunt, Chadwick	8171	8		11					5	2				3							9	10			1							6	7
20	Jan	2	Manchester City	0-2		3000		10							2	4			3							9	6			1					5		7	11
21		9	Oldham Athletic	3-3	Wharton, Lofthouse, Gillies	1000	5	11						4	2				3		10					9				1							7	
22		16	OLDHAM ATHLETIC	5-0	Hunt(4,2pens), Chadwick	2374	5	11						4	2				3		10							8	9	1		6						
23		23	BURNLEY	4-1	Hunt(2), Colclough, Wharton	3863	5	11		8					2				3		9							10		1		6					7	
24		30	Burnley	1-0	Colclough	2000	5	11		8				4	2				3		10								9	1		6					7	
25	Feb	6	BLACKBURN ROVERS	3-1	Hunt(3,1pen)	4501	5	10						4	2				3		9									1		6					7	11
26		13	Blackburn Rovers	1-7	Chadwick	3000	5	8						4	2				3		9									1		6			10		7	11
27		20	BLACKPOOL	1-1	Chadwick	9000	5	10							2				3		9							8		1		6			4		7	11
28		27	Blackpool	0-5		5000	5								2				3										9	1		6		8	4	10	7	11
29	Mar	6	BURNLEY	4-1	Lofthouse(3), Chadwick	2900		7						5	2	4			3		8					10				1								11
30		13	Burnley	1-4	Chadwick	2000		7						5	2	4			3	10	8					9				1								11
31	Apr	3	Blackburn Rovers	3-1	W.Johnson, Lofthouse, Wright	2800		7	5					4	2				3	8				9		10				1					6			11
32		10	BLACKBURN ROVERS	0-1		2971		7						5	2				3	4						10		9	1						6			11
33		17	CHESTER	3-1	Chadwick(2), Gillies	2000		7	5					4					3		9					8					1				6	10		11
34		24	LIVERPOOL	3-6	W.Johnson, Knight, Hunt	7566	5							4	2				3		8			10	7	9					1				6			11
35	May	1	Liverpool	0-4		10000	5	10							2				3		4			6	7	9					1							11
			Apps				10	31	3	2	3		4	23	28	3	2	3	35	5	31	5	6	25	4	25	4	8	7	16	4	3	3	3	9	6	26	13
			Goals					15		2			2	2			1			1	17			3	1	14						1		1		1	3	1

Additional players: R Banks 9,23/2, EC Beardshaw 1/2, R Bolton 11/1, J Bray 4/1, S Briddon 33,34/2, AC Burgess 3/8, RM Cross 2/5 & 3/6,
J Crossley 35/8, JK Davies 3/1, T Finney 10/7, JW Gallon 14/10 &20/8, A Geldard 5/7, S Grimsditch 2/1, J Hall 14,15/1, AD Haslam 4/2
WJ Ithell 18,19/4, L Lievesley 2,3/2, R Marsh 11/4, JM McCormick 12/4, T Middleton 25,28/8, W Moir 35/7, RG Savage 1/1, H Stephan 32/8, FW West 1/5.

Notes:
Matches 1-18 inclusive were Football League - Northern Section (1st Comp.) comprising 48 clubs.
Matches 19-35 inclusive were Football League - Northern Section (2nd Comp.), comprising 54 clubs.
Matches 19-28 inclusive were Football League War Cup, Qualifying Comp., Bolton failed to qualify for the knock-out stages.
Matches 31, 32, 34 & 35 also counted as Lancashire Cup games, semi-final games against Liverpool.

Other Games

1	Mar	27	RAF	7-3
2	Apr	26	RAF paras	5-2

Manager: C.E. Foweraker

#	Date	Opponent	Score	Scorers	Att	Anderson J	Berry J	Chadwick C	Connor J	Currier J	Foxton JD	Gillies MM	Gorman WC	Hall HHC	Hamlett TL	Hubbick H	Johnson WH	Knight J	Lancaster JN	Liddle J	Lofthouse N	Marshall D	McClelland C	Middlebrough A	Murphy D	Rigby E	Rimmer J	Rothwell E	Shankly W	Smith K	Speak K	Taylor G	Whaley H	Winter DT	Woodburn J	Woodburn T	Wright H
1	Aug 28	Burnley	0-4		1700			7		9			2			3	10								5							6			4	8	11
2	Sep 4	BURNLEY	0-2		2945			7		9		5	2			3	8		1						6								10		4		
3	11	BLACKBURN ROVERS	1-4	Currier	2661			7		9			2			3	4		1						6								10				11
4	18	Blackburn Rovers	1-3	Wright	3000	4				8			2	1		3						9			5							6				10	11
5	25	MANCHESTER CITY	4-1	Chadwick(p),Woodward,Currier,Lofthouse	2756	4		7		8			2	1		3						9			5							6				10	11
6	Oct 2	Manchester City	0-4		3000			7		8			2	1		3	4								5		11					6				10	
7	9	SOUTHPORT	3-1	Currier, R.Smith, Woodward	2771			7		9			2	1		3	4													5		6				10	11
8	16	Southport	0-2		3000			7	5	9			2	1		3	4	8														6				10	11
9	23	BLACKPOOL	1-2	Woodward	10243		11			9			2	1		3	4	8										5				7	6			10	
10	30	Blackpool	2-1	Lofthouse, Currier	7000					8			2	1		3	4				9	10				5						6					11
11	Nov 6	Bury	3-2	Chadwick, Lofthouse(2)	5000			7		8			2	1		3	4				9	10				5											11
12	13	BURY	2-4	Woodward, Marshall	4546		11	7		9			2	1		3	6						10			5			4								
13	20	OLDHAM ATHLETIC	3-0	Lofthouse(2), Shankly	3644			7					2	1		3	8				9	10				5			4			6					11
14	27	Oldham Athletic	2-4	Lofthouse, Hurst(og)	2000			7		8	4		2	1		3	10				9					6	5										11
15	Dec 4	Huddersfield Town	0-2		3091		10			8	4		2	1		3					9						5					7					
16	11	HUDDERSFIELD TOWN	0-4		4125		10	7		4			2	1		3	6							9	5											8	11
17	18	Manchester United	1-3	Gorman	4800			7		8			4	1		3									9	5						6				10	11
18	25	MANCHESTER UNITED	1-3	Woodward	10696			7		8			2			3								9	5	1										10	
19	27	Rochdale	0-5		3000			7		8			2	1		3	4				9					6	5									10	11
20	Jan 1	ROCHDALE	2-2	Lofthouse, Currier	6766		10			8			2	1		3	4				9					5										7	
21	8	BURNLEY	2-1	Lofthouse, Woodward	5423					5			4	1		3	8				9				10							11	6	2		7	
22	15	Burnley	1-5	Currier	3000					8			2			3	10				9				5	1						11	6			7	
23	22	Blackpool	0-6		8000		11						2	1	4	3					9	10										6				7	
24	29	BLACKPOOL	1-2	Knight	10254		11		5	9				1	2	3	4	8					10									6				7	
25	Feb 5	Blackburn Rovers	0-2		3000								2	1	5	3	4	8			9	10					11					6				7	
26	12	BLACKBURN ROVERS	4-1	Middlebrough(2), Johnson, Currier	6208					8				1	5	3	4					10		9	6									2		7	11
27	19	SOUTHPORT	5-1	Currier(4), Middlebrough	4888		10			8			2	1	5	3	4							9								6				7	
28	26	Southport	0-2		2000		10			8			2	1		3	4							9	5							6				7	
29	Mar 4	BURY	6-1	Johnson,Lofthouse(2),Currier,Berry,Hamlett(p)	2750		10			8			2	1	5	3	4				9											6				7	
30	11	Bury	2-5	Wright, Taylor	2126		10			8			2	1		3	4				9							5				6				7	11
31	18	Wrexham	3-3	Hamlett(pen), Currier, Lofthouse	5000		10			8			2	1	5	3					9						6							4			7	
32	25	WREXHAM	1-1	Jones(og)	5335		10			8			2			5	3	4	1	9														6		7	11
33	Apr 1	MANCHESTER UNITED	3-0	Middlebrough(2), Currier	5791		10			8			4	1	5	3	6							9										2		7	11
34	8	Manchester United	2-3	Currier(2)	13044					8			2		5	3	4		1	9		10										6				7	11
35	10	BURY	3-2	Rothwell, McClelland(2)	7021					8	4		2		5	3	6				9		10					1	11							7	
36	15	Bury*	1-1	Woodward	4187					9			2		5	3	4						10					1				6				7	
37	22	STOCKPORT COUNTY	4-2	Hamlett(pen), Carter, Lofthouse(2)	5003					8			2	1	5	3	4				9	10										6				7	
38	29	Stockport County	2-1	Lofthouse, Woodward	3500					8			2	1	5	3	10				9	11										6	4			7	
39	May 6	Liverpool	1-3	Currier	16591					8			2	1	5	3	10				9	11										6	4			7	
40	13	LIVERPOOL	2-3	Lofthouse, Hughes(og)	10254					8			2	1	5	3	10				9	11										6	4			7	
		Apps				2	10	19	2	35	3	3	34	30	17	39	33	4	2	2	24	8	6	6	24	6	3	2	2	2	3	27	4	3	2	35	23
		Goals					1	2		17			1		3	2	1				15	1	2	5				1	1			1	1				8	2

Three own goals

Additional players: DF Carter 37/11(1), SW Grimsditch 1/1, FH Harrison 22/4, H Higham 17/2, AL Hughes 36/11, JG Owens 23/5, R MacFarlane 18/11, R Marsh 18/4, JR Smith 36/1, RAG Smith 7/8(1), A Sullivan 15/11, A Watson 36/8, F Windsor 4/7.

Notes:
* After extra time. Full time Bury 1 Bolton 0 - League result. Extra time played to settle Lancashire Cup tie.
Matches 1-18 inclusive were Football League - Northern Section (1st Comp.) comprising 50 clubs.
Matches 19-39 inclusive were Football League - Northern Section (2nd Comp.), comprising 50 clubs.
Matches 19-28 inclusive were Football League War Cup, Qualifying Comp., Bolton failed to qualify for the knock-out stages.
Matches 33 - 40 also counted as Lancashire Cup games, 2 legged final against Liverpool (second leg not counted a League game, figures not included in appearance or goals total)

1944/45 9th in Football Lge - Northern Sect (1st Comp), 15th in (2nd Comp)

Manager: W. Rowley

#	Date	Opponent	Score	Scorers	Att	Barrass WM	Berry J	Butler S	Connor J	Dailey H	Fielding W	Foxton JD	Gillies MM	Hall HHC	Hamlett TL	Hanson AJ	Hubbick H	Hunt GS	Johnson WH	Jones S	Koffman SJ	Knight J	Lofthouse N	McClelland C	McCormick JM	Middlebrough A	Milne JL	Moir W	Murphy D	Rigby E	Rothwell E	Taylor G	Threlfall JR	Topping H	Whalley H	Winter DT	Woodward T
1	Aug 26	HALIFAX TOWN	0-0		6504	10								1	5	11	3	9	4									7				6				2	8
2	Sep 2	Halifax Town	0-2		4000									1	2	11	3	8	4				9	10						5		6					7
3		9 Blackpool	2-1	Hanson, Johnson	8000	10						5		1	2	11	3	8	4				9									6					7
4		16 BLACKPOOL	1-0	Hamlett(pen)	10148	10					1				2	11	3	8	4				9		5							6					7
5		23 BLACKBURN ROVERS	0-0		7057	10					1				2	11	3	8	4				9									6				5	7
6		30 Blackburn Rovers	1-2	Barrass	5000	10					1	4		5			3	9	8								11		6							2	7
7	Oct 7	Rochdale	2-2	Barrass, Middlebrough	4100	10						5		1	2		3	11	4							9			6								7
8		14 ROCHDALE	0-0		4752	10	8					5		1	2		3	8	4				11	6		9											7
9		21 Burnley	3-6	Hunt(2), Middlebrough	4500	10						4		1	5		3	8					11	6		9							2				7
10		28 BURNLEY	4-0	Middlebrough,Woodward,Barrass,McClelland	3458	10			5					1	2		3	8						11		9			6			4					7
11	Nov 4	ACCRINGTON STANLEY	3-3	Barrass(2), Hunt	4301	10			5		1				2		3	8					11			9			6			4					7
12		11 Accrington Stanley	3-2	Barrass, Hunt, Middlebrough	3500	10					1				5		3	8	4				11			9			6					2			7
13		18 Preston North End	3-2	Hunt, Barrass(2)	4000	10					1				5		3	8	4				9					7	6				2				11
14		25 PRESTON NORTH END	0-0		6950	10					1				5		3	8	4				9			11		9	6					2			7
15	Dec 2	SOUTHPORT	3-1	Middlebrough, McClelland, Barrass	3621	10					1				5		3	8						11		9			6			4	2				7
16		9 Southport	2-0	Barrass(2)	3000	10					1				5		3	8					9	11					6			4	2				7
17		16 Oldham Athletic	5-0	Lofthouse(2),Barrass,Rothwell,Hamlett(p)	3000	10					1				5		3	8					9						6		11	4	2				7
18		23 OLDHAM ATHLETIC	2-1	Lofthouse, Woodward	9271	10			8		1				5		3	4					9						6		11		2				7
19		26 STOCKPORT COUNTY	2-0	Lofthouse, Barrass	2934	10					1				5		3	8					9						6		11	4	2				7
20		30 Stockport County	0-2		3000	10					1				5		3	8					9						6		11	4	2				7
21	Jan 6	Everton	1-2	Lofthouse	18123	10					1		5		2		3	8					9	11					6			4					7
22		13 EVERTON	1-3	Lofthouse	14204	10					1				5		3	8			11		9						6			4		2			7
23		27 Southport	4-3	Hunt, Barrass, Murphy, Lofthouse	1800	10					1				5		3	8					9	11					6			4		2			7
24	Feb 3	Tranmere Rovers	4-1	Lofthouse(3), Hunt	2500	10					1				5		3	8					9	11					6			4		2			7
25		10 TRANMERE ROVERS	6-1	Lofthouse(4), Barrass(2)	6273	10		11			1				5		3	8					9						6			4		2			7
26		17 LIVERPOOL	2-1	Woodward, Moir	11494	10			5		1				2		3	8					9					7	6			4					11
27		24 Liverpool	1-1	Barrass	20966	10					1				5		3	8			11		9						6			4				2	7
28	Mar 3	Crewe Alexandra	1-4	Lofthouse	5059				5		1				2		3	8					9	10			11		6			4					7
29		10 SOUTHPORT	6-1	Lofthouse(3),Woodward,Murphy,Hamlett	8745	10		11			1				5		3	8					9						6			4		2			7
30		17 BURY	3-3	Hunt, Lofthouse, Barrass	10503	10					1				5		3	8					9				11		6			4					7
31		24 ACCRINGTON STANLEY	0-0		14214	10		11			1				5		3	8					9						6		4						7
32		31 Accrington Stanley	4-0	Lofthouse(2), Murphy, Woodward	11721	10		11			1				5		3	8					9						6			4	2				7
33	Apr 2	Bury	0-1		9314	5					1	4			2		3			11		8	9	10					6				2				7
34		7 Blackpool	4-1	Lofthouse(4)	20000	10					1				5		3	8					9					11	6			4	2				7
35		14 BLACKPOOL	1-2	Loftjouse	13613	10		11			1				5		3	8					9						6			4					7
36		21 NEWCASTLE UNITED	3-0	Barrass, Lofthouse(2)	25924	10		11			1				5		3	8					9						6			4	2				7
37		28 Newcastle United*	2-4	Hunt, Lofthouse	38704	10		11			1				5		3	8					9						6			4					7
38	May 5	Wolves	2-2	Barrass, Butler	29861	10		11			1				5		3	8					9						6			4	2				7
39		12 WOLVES	2-1	Moir, Hunt	29683	10		11			1				5		3	8										9	6			4	2				7
40		19 MANCHESTER UNITED	1-0	Lofthouse	40785	10		11			1				5		3	8					9						6			4	2				7
41		26 Manchester United	2-2	Barrass(2)	57395	10		11			1				5		3	8					9						6			4	2				7
42	Jun 2	Chelsea	2-1	Hunt, Hamlett(pen)	45000	10					1				5		3	8					9					11	6			4	2				7
		Apps				40	1	9	6	1	34	5	2	8	42	5	42	41	11	1	2	1	31	16	2	9	3	6	33	1	4	30	14	12	2	6	42
		Goals				22		1							4	1		11	1				30	2		5		2	3		1						5

Notes:
* After extra time.
Matches 1-18 inclusive were Football League - Northern Section (1st Comp.) comprising 54 clubs.
Matches 19-41 inclusive were Football League - Northern Section (2nd Comp.), comprising 54 clubs.
Matches 19-27 & 29 inclusive were Football League War Cup (North), Qualifying Comp., Bolton finished 13th out of 32 qualifiers.
Matches 30-41 also counted towards Football League War Cup (North), matches 40 & 41 being the final.
Matches 30 & 33 also counted as Lancashire Cup 1st round games.
Match 42 was the Football League War Cup, North v South Final.

1945/46 3rd in Football League North

Manager: W. Rowley

No	Date	Opponent	Score	Scorers	Att	Aspinall J	Atkinson JE	Barrass MW	Fielding W	Forrest E	Geldard A	Hamlett TL	Hanson S	Hanks C	Dowe D	Hubbick H	Hunt GS	Hurst J	Lofthouse N	Moir W	Murphy D	Neal C	Roberts JH	Rothwell E	Sinclair TM	Sullivan A	Taylor G	Threlfall JR	Tomlinson F	Westwood RW	Woodward T
1	Aug 25	Everton	2-3	Lofthouse, Barrass,	24898			10	1			5				11	3	8	9		6						4	2			7
2	29	Liverpool	2-2	Howe, Lofthouse	17437			10	1			5				11	3	8	9		6						4	2			7
3	Sep 1	EVERTON	3-1	Lofthouse, Woodward, Howe	16683			10	1			5				11	3	8	9		6						4	2			7
4	8	BURNLEY	2-0	Lofhouse, Hamlett(pen)	16652			10	1			5				4	3	8	9	7	6		11					2			7
5	12	Blackpool	1-1	Lofthouse	15207			5	1							4	3		9	7	6		10		8			2	11		
6	15	Burnley	2-2	Lofthouse, Sullivan	9212			10	1			5				4	3		9	7	6				8	11		2			
7	22	PRESTON NORTH END	0-0		17983			10	1			5				4	3	9	11		6				8			2			7
8	29	Preston North End	2-1	Hunt, Moir	14000			10	1			5				4	3	8	9	11	6							2			7
9	Oct 6	Leeds United	1-2	Hunt	11836			10	1			5				4	3	8	9	11	6							2			7
10	13	LEEDS UNITED	6-0	Howe, Lofthouse(2), Moir(2), Hunt	17770				1			5				10	3	8	9	11	6						4	2			7
11	20	MANCHESTER UNITED	1-1	Woodward	23829				1			5				10	3	8	9	11	6						4	2			7
12	27	Manchester United	1-2	Lofthouse	27472			10				5				3	8	4	9	11	6	1						2			7
13	Nov 3	Sunderland	0-1		13381				1			5				3	8	4	9	7	6		10					2	11		
14	10	SUNDERLAND	1-2	Barrass	18336			10	1			5				3	8	4	9	11	6							2			7
15	17	SHEFFIELD UNITED	1-4	Hunt	19391			10	1			5				3	8	4	9	11	6							2			7
16	24	Sheffield United	3-2	Hunt, Hamlett([pen), Lofthouse	19832			10				5	1	7		3	8	4	9		6		11					2			
17	Dec 1	Middlesbrough	0-1		16666			10				5	1	11		3	8	4	9	7	6							2			
18	8	MIDDLESBROUGH	2-1	Geldard, Westwood	16812						7	5	1			3	8	4	9	11	6							2		10	
19	15	STOKE CITY	2-2	Westwood, Hamlett	251000						7	5	1			3	8	4	9		6							2		10	11
20	22	Stoke City	1-4	Barrass	12974			11			7	5	1			3	8		9		6						4	2		10	
21	25	Grimsby Town	2-0	Geldard, Moir	10075						7	5	1			3	8	4	9	10	6							2			11
22	29	BLACKPOOL	1-1	Lofthouse	28775						7	5	1			3	8	4	9	10	6							2			11
23	Jan 1	GRIMSBY TOWN	0-0		20953						7	5	1	9		3	8	4		10	6							2			11
24	12	BURY	1-0	Moir	25064		5				7	2	1		11	3	8	4		9	6										10
25	19	Bury	2-0	Howe(2)	14451			10			7	5	1		8	3		4	9	11	6							2			
26	Feb 2	BLACKBURN ROVERS	1-2	Lofthouse	14169		5				7	4	1			3	8		9	10	6							2			11
27	16	Bradford	5-0	Lofthouse(3), Howe, Hamlett(pen)	20358						7	5	1		8	3		4	9		6							2		10	11
28	20	Blackburn Rovers	1-0	Barrass	4400			10			7	5	1		8	3		4	9		6			11				2			
29	23	Manchester City	0-1		25000							5	1		8	3		4	9		6				7			2		10	11
30	Mar 13	BRADFORD	0-0		5162						7	5	1		8	3		4	9	10	6							2			11
31	16	Newcastle United	4-3	Lofthouse, Moir(2), Westwood	30000		5				7	2	1		8	3		4	9	11	6									10	
32	27	MANCHESTER CITY	3-1	Lofthouse, Barrass, Hamlett(pen)	17500			10			7	5	1			4	3		9	8	6							2			11
33	30	SHEFFIELD WEDNESDAY	2-1	Barrass, Moir	20531			10			7	5	1			4	3	9		8	6							2			11
34	Apr 1	Sheffield Wednesday	0-0		13500	2		10	11	7			1			4	3	8	5	9		6									
35	6	HUDDERSFIELD TOWN	2-1	Lofthouse(2)	15000		5	10			7		1			4	3			9	8	6						2			11
36	10	NEWCASTLE UNITED	0-1		9386		5	11					1			4	3			9	8							2		10	7
37	13	Huddersfield Town	1-1	Lofthouse	11996		5	8		6	7	2	1			4	3			9	11										10
38	19	Chesterfield	2-1	Hamlett(pen), Woodward	25000		5			6	7	2	1			4	3			9	8									10	11
39	20	BARNSLEY	2-0	Hunt, Moir	10000			10		6		5	1		8	3	9	4		11								2			7
40	22	CHESTERFIELD	1-0	Hamlett(pen)	24000			11		6		2	1		4	3	9	5		8										10	7
41	27	Barnsley	3-0	Barrass(2), Hunt	12000			11		6		2	1		4	3	9	5		7			8							10	
42	29	LIVERPOOL	1-0	Roberts	18000			11		6		2	1		4	3	9	5		7			8							10	
		Apps				1	7	28	14	8	19	38	27	2	29	42	29	23	34	32	35	1	6	2	3	1	6	34	2	13	26
		Goals						8			2	7				6	7		20	9			1				1			3	3

F.A. Cup

Rnd	Date	Opponent	Score	Scorers	Att	Atkinson JE	Geldard A	Hamlett TL	Hanson S	Dowe D	Hubbick H	Hunt GS	Hurst J	Lofthouse N	Moir W	Murphy D	Rothwell E	Threlfall JR	Westwood RW	Woodward T
3/1 Jan	5	BLACKBURN ROVERS	1-0	Moir	26307		7	5	1		3	8	4	9	6			2	10	11
3/2	9	Blackburn Rovers	3-1	Westwood(2), Hunt	20000	5	7	2	1		3	8	4	9	6			2	10	11
4/1	26	LIVERPOOL	5-0	Lofthouse(2), Westwood(3)	39682		7	5	1	8	3		4	9		6		2	10	11
4/2	30	Liverpool	0-2		35000	5	7	4	1	8	3			9		6		2	10	11
5/1 Feb	9	MIDDLESBROUGH	1-0	Westwood	43453		7	5	1	8	3		4	9		6		2	10	11
5/2	13	Middlesbrough	1-1	Hunt	51612		7	5	1	8	3	9	4		11	6		2	10	
6/1 Mar	2	Stoke City	2-0	Westwood(2)	50735			5	1	8	3		4	9	11	6		2	10	7
6/2	9	STOKE CITY	0-0		65419		7	5	1	8	3		4	9		6		2	10	11
SF	23	Charlton Atheltic*	0-2		69500		7	5	1	8	3		4	9		6		2	10	11

* Played at Villa Park, Birmingham

Lancashire Cup

Rnd	Date	Opponent	Score
1/1 Sep	3	ACCRINGTON	2-0
1/2	25	Accrington	0-1
2 Mar	6	Liverpool	1-3

FINAL TABLE

	P	W	D	L	F	A	Pts
Sheffield United	42	27	6	9	112	62	60
Everton	42	23	9	10	88	54	55
BOLTON WANDERERS	42	20	11	11	67	45	51
Manchester United	42	19	11	12	98	62	49
Sheffield Wednesday	42	20	8	14	67	60	48
Newcastle United	42	21	5	16	106	70	47
Chesterfield	42	17	12	13	68	49	46
Barnsley	42	17	11	14	76	68	45
Blackpool	42	18	9	15	94	92	45
Manchester City	42	20	4	18	78	75	44
Liverpool	42	17	9	16	80	70	43
Middlesbrough	42	17	9	16	75	87	43
Stoke City	42	18	6	18	88	79	42
Bradford PA	42	17	6	19	71	84	40
Huddersfield Town	42	17	4	21	90	89	38
Burnley	42	13	10	19	63	84	36
GRIMSBY TOWN	42	13	9	20	61	89	35
Sunderland	42	15	5	22	55	83	35
Preston North End	42	14	6	22	70	77	34
Bury	42	12	10	20	60	85	34
Blackburn Rovers	42	11	7	24	60	111	29
Leeds United	42	9	7	26	66	118	25

1946
(Back) Ridding, Connor, Gillies, Hurst, Hanson, Atkinson, Aspinall
(Front) Howe, Roberts, Moir, Hubbick, Hunt, Westwood, Forrest, Rothwell

1947
(Back) Ridding (Trainer), Forrest, Robert, Hanson, Atkinson, Banks, Howe, Murphy
(Front) Woodward, Rothwell, Lofthouse, Taylor (Coach), Bradley, Moir, Hamblett

1946/47 18th in Division One

Manager: W.Rowley

No	Date		Opponent	Score	Scorers	Att	Aspinall J	Atkinson JE	Banks R	Barrass MW	Burgess AC	Forrest E	Geldard A	Gillies MM	Hamlett TL	Hanson S	Howe D	Hubbick H	Hunt GS	Hurst J	Lofthouse N	Middlebrough A	Moir W	Murphy D	Roberts JH	Rothwell E	Threlfall JR	Westwood RW	Woodward T	Wrigglesworth W
1	Aug	31	Chelsea	3-4	Lofthouse(2), Forrest	62850						6			5	1	4	3			9		8			11	2	10	7	
2	Sep	2	Stoke City	2-1	Woodward, Westwood	22559						6			5	1	4	3			9		8			11	2	10	7	
3		7	PORTSMOUTH	1-0	Moir	33597						6			5	1	4	3			9		8			11	2	10	7	
4		11	STOKE CITY	3-2	Roberts, Barrass(2)	26366		5		10		6			2	1	4	3			9		11		8				7	
5		14	LIVERPOOL	1-3	Woodward	35861		5		10		6			2	1	4	3	8		9		11						7	
6		16	Preston North End	4-0	Lofthouse(2), Westwood, Roberts	32536		5		10		6			2	1	4	3			9				8			11	7	
7		21	Leeds United	0-4		25739		5		10		6			2	1	4	3			9				8			11	7	
8		28	GRIMSBY TOWN	1-2	Hamlett(pen)	30547		5		10		6			2	1	4	3			9				8			11	7	
9	Oct	5	Charlton Athletic	0-2		33859	3	5				6		11	2	1	4		8		9							10	7	
10		12	MIDDLESBROUGH	1-1	Lofthouse	32000	3	5				6		11	2	1	4		8		9							10	7	
11		19	Everton	1-2	Roberts	45104		5	3			6			2	1	4				9				8	11		10	7	
12		26	BLACKPOOL	1-1	Westwood	35896		5				6	7		2	1	4	3			9		8			11		10		
13	Nov	2	Brentford	0-1		23782		5				6	7		2	1	4	3			9		11		8			10		
14		9	BLACKBURN ROVERS	0-0		31727		5				6	7	4	2	1	8	3			9							10	11	
15		16	Aston Villa	1-1	Lofthouse	40399		5				6		4	2	1	8	3			9		11					10	7	
16		23	DERBY COUNTY	5-1	Woodward, Moir(2), Lofthouse(2)	28127		5				6		4	2	1		3			9		10		8				11	
17		30	Arsenal	2-2	Woodward, Roberts	42522		5				6		4	2	1		3			9		10		8				11	
18	Dec	7	HUDDERSFIELD T	4-0	Moir, Lofthouse, Roberts, Gillies	21975		5				6		4	2	1		3			9		10		8				11	
19		14	Wolverhampton Wan.	0-5		37775		5				6		4	2	1		3			9		10		8				11	
20		21	SUNDERLAND	0-1		19757		5				6			2	1	4	3			9		10		8				11	
21		25	MANCHESTER UNITED	2-2	Woodward, Lofthouse	30511		5				6		4	2	1		3			9		10		8				11	
22		26	Manchester United	0-1		57446		5				6		4	2	1		3			9		10		8				11	
23		28	CHELSEA	1-1	Hamlett(pen)	36048				10		6		4	2	1		3		5	9				8				11	
24	Jan	1	PRESTON NORTH END	1-2	Lofthouse	47040				10		6		4	2	1		3		5	9				8				11	
25		4	Portsmouth	0-2		25221		5				6		4	2	1	8	3			9		11					10	7	
26		18	Liverpool	3-0	Lofthouse, Moir, Barrass	49820		2		10		6		4	5	1		3			9		8						7	11
27	Feb	1	Grimsby Town	2-2	Lofthouse, Hamlett(pen)	11467						6		4	5	1	10	3			9		8		2				7	11
28		3	LEEDS UNITED	2-0	Woodward, Hamlett	4280				10		6			5	1	4	3			9		8		2				7	11
29		15	Middlesbrough	1-3	Hamlett(pen)	31437						6	7	4	5	1	10	3			9		8		2					11
30		19	CHARLTON ATHLETIC	0-1		16489						6	7	4	5	1		3			9		8		2			10		11
31		22	EVERTON	0-2		21080						6		4	5	1		3			9		8		2			10	7	11
32	Mar	1	Blackpool	1-0	Woodward	20356						6		4	5	1	10	3			9		8		2				7	
33		15	Blackburn Rovers	1-2	Moir	31262						6		4	5	1	10	3			9		8		2				7	
34		22	ASTON VILLA	2-1	Lofthouse, Moir	26417						6		4	5	1		3			9		8		2			10	7	11
35		29	Derby County	3-1	Lofthouse, Westwood, Hamlett(pen)	18767						6		4	5	1		3			9		8		2			10	7	11
36	Apr	4	SHEFFIELD UNITED	3-2	Hamlett(pen), Roberts, Lofthouse	34109						6		4	5	1		3			9		8		2			10	7	11
37		5	ARSENAL	1-3	Wrigglesworth	34398		5				6		4	2	1	8				9				3			10	7	11
38		7	Sheffield United	2-4	Lofthouse, Muir	29170						6		4	5	1		3			9		8		2			10	7	11
39		12	Huddersfield Town	0-1		21639		5				6		4	2	1					9		8		3			10	7	11
40		19	WOLVERHAMPTON W.	0-3		34419		5				6	7	4	2	1					9		8		3			10		11
41		26	Sunderland	1-3	Lofthouse	19359		5				6	7	4	2	1					9		8		3			10		11
42	May	10	BRENTFORD	1-0	Hamlett(pen)	19887		5			8	6		4	2	1					9	7			3			10		11
			Apps				2	25	2	8	1	41	9	27	42	42	23	34	3	3	40	1	31	1	32	11	3	29	40	12
			Goals							3		1		1	8						18		8		6			4	7	1

F.A. Cup

No	Date		Opponent	Score	Scorers	Att	Atkinson JE	Barrass MW	Forrest E	Geldard A	Gillies MM	Hamlett TL	Hanson S	Howe D	Hubbick H	Lofthouse N	Moir W	Roberts JH	Woodward T	Wrigglesworth W
3	Jan	11	STOCKPORT COUNTY	5-1	Lofthouse(2),Geldard,Barrass,Woodward	30024	2	10	6	7	4	5	1		3	9	8			11
4		25	MANCHESTER CITY	3-3	Lofthouse,Barrass,Wrigglesworth	41286	2	10	6		4	5	1		3	9	8		7	11
4r		29	Manchester City	0-1		39355			6		4	5	1	10	3	9	8	2	7	11

Lancashire Cup

1/1	Oct	16	Manchester City	1-0
1/2		30	MANCHESTER CITY	2-3
1r	Nov	27	Manchester City	2-1
2/1	Dec	4	Chester	2-1
2/2		11	CHESTER	3-0
SF/1	May	7	BURY	3-1
SF/2		14	Bury	0-3

Other Games

1	May	3	Hull City	1-0
2		17	Carlisle United	1-4

FINAL TABLE

		Pl.	Home W	D	L	F	A	Away W	D	L	F	A	F. (Total)	A.	Pts
1	Liverpool	42	13	3	5	42	24	12	4	5	42	28	84	52	57
2	Manchester United	42	17	3	1	61	19	5	9	7	34	35	95	54	56
3	Wolverhampton W.	42	15	1	5	66	31	10	5	6	32	25	98	56	56
4	Stoke City	42	14	5	2	52	21	10	2	9	38	32	90	53	55
5	Blackpool	42	14	1	6	38	32	8	5	8	33	38	71	70	50
6	Sheffield United	42	12	4	5	51	32	9	3	9	38	43	89	75	49
7	Preston North End	42	10	7	4	45	27	8	4	9	31	47	76	74	47
8	Aston Villa	42	9	6	6	39	24	9	3	9	28	29	67	53	45
9	Sunderland	42	11	3	7	33	27	7	5	9	32	39	65	66	44
10	Everton	42	13	5	3	40	24	4	4	13	22	43	62	67	43
11	Middlesbrough	42	11	3	7	46	32	6	5	10	27	36	73	68	43
12	Portsmouth	42	11	3	7	42	27	5	6	10	24	33	66	60	41
13	Arsenal	42	9	5	7	43	33	7	4	10	29	37	72	70	41
14	Derby County	42	13	2	6	44	28	5	3	13	29	51	73	79	41
15	Chelsea	42	9	3	9	33	39	7	4	10	36	45	69	84	39
16	Grimsby Town	42	9	6	6	37	35	4	6	11	24	47	61	82	38
17	Blackburn Rovers	42	6	5	10	23	27	8	3	10	22	26	45	53	36
18	**BOLTON WANDERERS**	42	8	5	8	30	28	5	3	13	27	41	57	69	34
19	Charlton Athletic	42	6	6	9	34	32	5	6	10	23	39	57	71	33
20	Huddersfield Town	42	11	4	6	34	24	2	3	16	19	55	53	79	33
21	Brentford	42	5	5	11	19	35	4	2	15	26	53	45	88	25
22	Leeds United	42	6	5	10	30	30	0	1	20	15	60	45	90	18

1947/48 17th in Division One

Manager: W.Rowley

#		Date	Opponent	Score	Scorers	Att	Aspinall J	Atkinson JE	Banks R	Banks T	Barrass MW	Bradley J	Burgess AC	Crook W	Dillon V	Elvy R	Forrest E	Gillies MM	Hamlett TL	Hanson S	Howe D	Jackson J	Lees A	Lofthouse N	McShane H	Middlebrough A	Moir W	Murphy D	Roberts JH	Rothwell E	Simm J	Westwood RW	Woodward T	Wrigglesworth W
1	Aug	23	STOKE CITY	0-1		31189							3				4	5	1					9	11		8	6	2				10	7	
2		25	Preston North End	0-1		33901							3				4	5	1					9	11		8	6	2				10	7	
3		30	Burnley	0-2		35835					10		3				6	4	5	1	8			9	11			2					7		
4	Sep	1	PRESTON NORTH END	1-2	Woodward	31867							3				4		1	8	5	9					6	2				10	7	11
5		6	PORTSMOUTH	4-0	Burgess, Middlebrough, Flewin (og)	26597							8	3			4	5		1					11	9		6	2				10	7	
6		10	Arsenal	0-2		46969							8	3			4	5		1					11	9		6	2				10	7	
7		13	Chelsea	1-1	Howe	41242							3			9	4	5	1	8					11			6	2				10	7	
8		20	Liverpool	0-0		43920							3				4	5	1	8				9	11			6	2				10	7	
9		27	MIDDLESBROUGH	1-3	Woodward	30641							3				4	5	1	8					11	9		6	2				10	7	
10	Oct	4	Charlton Athletic	1-2	Rothwell	31284							3				4	5		1				9	11			6	2	8			10	7	
11		11	HUDDERSFIELD T	1-5	Lofthouse	27590							3				6	4	5	1				9	11			2	8				10	7	
12		18	Derby County	1-2	Lofthouse	24134	5	2			10			3			4		1					9			6		8				11	7	
13		25	BLACKPOOL	1-0	Lofthouse	45037	5	2			10		3				4		1	6				9			11		8					7	
14	Nov	1	Blackburn Rovers	0-4		31721	5	2			10		3				4		1	6				9			11		8					7	
15		8	SUNDERLAND	3-1	Moir, Hamlett (pen)	26729		3			10						4		5	1	6			9			11		2	8				7	
16		15	Aston Villa	1-3	Bradley	43531		3			10						4		5	1	6			9			11		2	8				7	
17		22	MANCHESTER CITY	2-1	Lofthouse	28883		2		8	10		3				4		5	1	6			9			11							7	
18		29	Grimsby Town	2-0	Lofthouse	11901				8	10		3				4		5	1	6			9			11		2					7	
19	Dec	6	WOLVERHAMPTON W.	3-2	Lofthouse, Moir	28438				8	10		3				4		5	1	6			9			11		2					7	
20		13	Everton	0-2		33458				8	10		3				4		5	1	6			9			11		2					7	
21		20	Stoke City	0-2		23469				8	10		3		1	4			5		6			9			11		2					7	
22		25	Sheffield United	1-2	Lofthouse	36670					10	8	3				4		5	1	6			9			11		2					7	
23		27	SHEFFIELD UNITED	2-3	Barrass	29262				8	10		3				4		5	1	6			9			11		2					7	
24	Jan	1	ARSENAL	0-1		30028	5			8	10		3				4			1	6			9			11		2					7	
25		3	BURNLEY	1-1	Barrass	43442	5			8	10		3				4			1	6			9	11				2					7	
26		17	Portsmouth	0-2		25347					10		3				4	5	1	6				8		9	11		2					7	
27		24	Sunderland	2-1	Lofthouse,Bradley	24326				8	10		3					5		1	4			9			11	6	2					7	
28		31	CHELSEA	2-1	Lofthouse Moir	24232				8	10		3					5		1	4			9			11	6	2					7	
29	Feb	7	LIVERPOOL	3-0	Howe(pen), Barrass, Lofthouse	22895				8	10		3					5		1	4			9			11	6	2					7	
30		14	Middlesbrough	1-4	Howe (pen)	24234				8	10		3					5		1	4			9			11	6	2					7	
31		21	CHARLTON ATHLETIC	1-0	Lofthouse	16792	6		3	8	10							5		1	4			9			11		2					7	
32		28	Huddersfield Town	2-1	Moir, Barrass	14273			3	8	10							5		1	4						11	6	2		9			7	
33	Mar	20	BLACKBURN ROVERS	1-0	Woodward	34520			3	8	10						6	5		1	4			9			11		2					7	
34		26	Manchester United	2-0	Woodward, Barrass	72840			3	8	10							5		1	4			9			11	6	2					7	
35		29	MANCHESTER UNITED	0-1		46322			3	8	10							5		1	4			9	11		7	6	2						
36	Apr	3	ASTON VILLA	1-0	Burgess	26403			3	8		10						5		1	4			9			11	6	2					7	
37		5	Blackpool	1-1		25050	6		3	8								5		1	4	10		9			11		2					7	
38		10	Manchester City	2-0	Lofthouse	36409	6		3	8								5		1	4	10		9			11		2					7	
39		17	GRIMSBY TOWN	2-0	Lofthouse	23378	6		3	8	10							5		1	4			9			11		2					7	
40		21	DERBY COUNTY	0-3	Lofthouse, Bradley	25938	6			8	10					9		5	2	1	4						11		3					7	
41		24	Wolverhampton Wan.	0-1		25751			3		10					9	6		2	1	4	8	5				11					7			
42	May	1	EVERTON	0-0		17391			3		10					9	6	5		1	4	8					11		2					7	

	Aspinall J	Atkinson JE	Banks R	Banks T	Barrass MW	Bradley J	Burgess AC	Crook W	Dillon V	Elvy R	Forrest E	Gillies MM	Hamlett TL	Hanson S	Howe D	Jackson J	Lees A	Lofthouse N	McShane H	Middlebrough A	Moir W	Murphy D	Roberts JH	Rothwell E	Simm J	Westwood RW	Woodward T	Wrigglesworth W
Apps	5	5	16	1	23	28	4	28	3	1	23	25	21	41	33	6	2	34	12	4	31	18	37	8	1	11	40	1
Goals					6	3	3					1	3		18			1	5			4						

One own goal

F.A. Cup

| 3 | Jan | 10 | TOTTENHAM HOTSPUR* | 0-2 | | 37075 | 5 | | | 8 | 10 | | 3 | | | | 4 | | | 1 | 6 | | | 9 | | | 11 | | 2 | | | | | 7 | |

* After Extra time

Lancashire Cup

1	Oct	7	Everton	4-3
2	Nov	4	Bury	3-2
SF	Apr	28	BLACKBURN ROVERS	1-0
F	May	8	Southport	5-1

Manchester Cup

SF	Mar	13	Oldham Athletic	2-1
F	May	5	MANCHESTER UNITED *	1-3

* After extra time

Other Games

1	Mar	6	MOTHERWELL	3-4

	FINAL TABLE	Pl.		Home					Away					F.	A.	Pts
			W	D	L	F	A	W	D	L	F	A			(Total)	
1	Arsenal	42	15	3	3	56	15	8	10	3	25	17	81	32	59
2	Manchester United	42	11	7	3	50	27	8	7	6	31	21	81	48	52
3	Burnley	42	12	5	4	31	12	8	7	6	25	31	56	43	52
4	Derby County	42	11	6	4	38	24	8	6	7	39	33	77	57	50
5	Wolverhampton W.	42	12	4	5	45	29	7	5	9	38	41	83	70	47
6	Aston Villa	42	13	5	3	42	22	6	4	11	23	35	65	57	47
7	Preston North End	42	13	4	4	43	35	7	3	11	24	33	67	68	47
8	Portsmouth	42	13	5	3	44	17	6	2	13	24	33	68	50	45
9	Blackpool	42	13	4	4	37	14	4	6	11	20	27	57	41	44
10	Manchester City	42	13	3	5	37	22	2	9	10	15	25	52	47	42
11	Liverpool	42	9	4	8	39	23	7	2	12	26	38	65	61	42
12	Sheffield United	42	13	4	4	44	24	3	6	12	21	46	65	70	42
13	Charlton Athletic	42	8	4	9	33	29	9	2	10	24	37	57	66	40
14	Everton	42	10	2	9	30	26	7	4	10	22	40	52	66	40
15	Stoke City	42	9	5	7	29	23	5	5	11	12	32	41	55	38
16	Middlesbrough	42	8	7	6	37	27	6	2	13	34	46	71	73	37
17	**BOLTON WANDERERS**	42	11	2	8	29	25	5	3	13	17	33	46	58	37
18	Chelsea	42	11	6	4	38	27	3	3	15	15	44	53	71	37
19	Huddersfield Town	42	7	6	8	25	24	5	6	10	26	36	51	60	36
20	Sunderland	42	11	4	6	33	18	2	6	13	23	49	56	67	36
21	Blackburn Rovers	42	8	5	8	35	30	3	5	13	19	42	54	72	32
22	Grimsby Town	42	5	5	11	20	35	3	1	17	25	76	45	111	22

1948/49   14th in Division One

Manager: W.Rowley

No	Date	Opponent	Score	Scorers	Att	Aspinall J	Banks R	Banks T	Barrass MW	Bradley J	Dillon V	Elvy R	Gillies MM	Hamlett TL	Hanson S	Hernon J	Howe D	Hughes W	Jackson J	Lofthouse N	McShane H	Moir W	Murphy D	Roberts JH	Rothwell E	Woodward T
1	Aug 21	Sunderland	0-2		47854		3			10			5		1		4		8	9		11	6	2		7
2	25	ASTON VILLA	3-0	Bradley, Dillon(2)	24774		3			10	8		5		1		4			9		11	6	2		7
3	28	WOLVERHAMPTON W.	0-5		35878	4	3			10	8		5		1					9		11	6	2		7
4	30	Aston Villa	4-2	Moss(4,1pen)	26890		3		6	10			5		1		4			9		11	8	2		7
5	Sep 4	Chelsea	2-2	Howe(pen), McShane	42971		3		6	10	9		5		1		4				11	8		2		7
6	6	HUDDERSFIELD T	1-2	Jackson	25332		3		6	10			5		1		4		9		11	8		2		7
7	11	Liverpool	1-0	McShane	56561	6	3			10			5		1	8	4				11	9		2		7
8	15	Huddersfield Town	2-0	Moir(2)	16046		3		6	10			5		1	8	4				11	9		2		7
9	18	BLACKPOOL	2-2	Moir, Hernon	46779		3		6	10			5		1	8	4				11	9		2		7
10	25	Derby County	0-1		33972		3		6	10			5		1	8	4				11	9		2		7
11	Oct 2	ARSENAL	1-0	Howe	45228		3		6	10			5		1	8	4				11	9		2		7
12	9	BIRMINGHAM CITY	0-0		45494		3		6	10			5		1		4				11	9		2		7
13	16	Middlesbrough	0-5		28628		3		6	10			5		1	8	4					9		2	11	7
14	23	NEWCASTLE UNITED	1-5	Moir	39071			3	6	10			5		1	8	4					9		2	11	7
15	30	Portsmouth	0-0		29760		3			10			5	2	1	8	4				11	9	6			7
16	Nov 6	MANCHESTER CITY	5-1	Moir, Barrass(4,1pen)	40089		3		9	10		1	5	2			4				11	8	6			7
17	13	Charlton Athletic	4-1	Barrass, Moir(2), Woodward	37047		3		9	10		1	5	2			4				11	8	6			7
18	20	STOKE CITY	2-1	Moir, Barrass	37249		3		9	10		1	5				4				11	8	6	2		7
19	27	Burnley	0-3		37291		3		9	10		1	5	2			4				11	8	6			7
20	Dec 4	PRESTON NORTH END	5-3	Bradley(2), Moir(2), Barrass	40140		3		9	10		1	5				4				11	8	6	2		7
21	11	Everton	0-1		40407		3		9	10		1	5				4				11	8	6	2		7
22	18	SUNDERLAND	4-1	Moir, Lofthouse(2), Bradley	24309		3		6	10		1	5				4			9	11	8		2		7
23	25	Sheffield United	1-1	Bradley	39676		3		6	10		1	5				4			9	11	8		2		7
24	27	SHEFFIELD UNITED	6-1	Moir(4), Lofthouse(2)	42630		3		6	10		1	5				4			9	11	8		2		7
25	Jan 1	Wolverhampton Wan.	0-2		27110		3		6	10		1	5				4			9	11	8		2		7
26	22	LIVERPOOL	0-3		35668		3		9	10		1	5				4				11	8	6	2		7
27	Feb 12	Blackpool	0-1		23210		3		6	10		1	5			8	4				11	9		2		7
28	19	DERBY COUNTY	4-0	Woodward, Moir, Lofthouse, Bradley	37948		3		6	10		1	5				4			9	11	8		2		7
29	26	Arsenal	0-5		50263		3			10		1	5				4			9	11	8	6	2		7
30	Mar 5	Birmingham City	0-0		20730					6		1	5	3		10	4	7		9	11	8		2		
31	12	MIDDLESBROUGH	4-1	Moir(3,1pen), Lofthouse	28783					4		1	5	3		10		7		9	11	8	6	2		
32	19	Stoke City	0-4		24350					6		1	5	3		10	4	7		9	11	8		2		
33	26	BURNLEY	0-1		26593		3			6		1	5			10	4	7		9	11	8		2		
34	Apr 2	Manchester City	0-1		27241		3		6	10		1	5				4			9	11	8		2		7
35	9	CHARLTON ATHLETIC	2-2	Bradley(2)	20371	5	3		6	10	9	1					4				11	8		2		7
36	15	MANCHESTER UNITED	0-1		47157	5	3		6	10		1					4			9	11	8		2		7
37	16	Newcastle United	1-1	Moir	39999	5	3		6	10		1					4			9	11	8		2		7
38	18	Manchester United	0-3		50504	5	3		6	10		1					4			9	11	8		2		7
39	23	PORTSMOUTH	1-2	Roberts	31063		3					1	5			10	4			9	11	8	6	2		7
40	30	Preston North End	1-1	Lofthouse	33495		3					1	5			10	4			9	11	8	6	2		7
41	May 4	CHELSEA	1-1	Roberts	19084		3					1	5			10	4			9	11	8	6	2		7
42	7	EVERTON	1-0	Moir	22725		3					1	5			10	4			9	11	8	6	2		7
		Apps				6	38	1	37	36	8	27	33	9	15	17	40	3	3	22	36	42	17	36	2	34
		Goals							7	8	2					1	2		1	7	2	25		2		2

F.A. Cup

No	Date	Opponent	Score	Scorers	Att	Aspinall J	Banks R	Banks T	Barrass MW	Bradley J	Dillon V	Elvy R	Gillies MM	Hamlett TL	Hanson S	Hernon J	Howe D	Hughes W	Jackson J	Lofthouse N	McShane H	Moir W	Murphy D	Roberts JH	Rothwell E	Woodward T
3	Jan 8	Aston Villa*	1-1	Bradley	53459		3		6	10		1	5				4			9	11	8		2		7
3r	15	ASTON VILLA*	0-0		38706		3		6	10		1	5				4			9	11	8		2		7
3/2r	17	Aston Villa*	1-2	Lofthouse	49709		3			10		1	5	2			4			9	11	8	6			7

* After extra time

Lancashire Cup

1	Oct	27	ACCRINGTON STANLEY	3-1
2	Nov	24	MANCHESTER UNITED	2-4

Manchester Cup

1	Apr	25	MANCHESTER UNITED	1-0
SF	May	9	Manchester City	0-0
SFr		14	MANCHESTER CITY	0-2

Other Games

1	Feb	5	Middlesbrough	1-1
2	Apr	6	Chester*	3-2
3	May	9	Norwich City	2-0

* Game abandoned after 70 mins due to bad light.

FINAL TABLE

		Pl	Home					Away					F.	A.	Pts
			W	D	L	F	A	W	D	L	F	A	(Total)		
1	Portsmouth	42	18	3	0	52	12	7	5	9	32	30	84	42	58
2	Manchester United	42	11	7	3	40	20	10	4	7	37	24	77	44	53
3	Derby County	42	17	2	2	48	22	5	7	9	26	33	74	55	53
4	Newcastle United	42	12	5	4	35	29	8	7	6	35	27	70	56	52
5	Arsenal	42	13	5	3	51	18	5	8	8	23	26	74	44	49
6	Wolverhampton W.	42	13	5	3	48	19	4	7	10	31	47	79	66	46
7	Manchester City	42	10	8	3	28	21	5	7	9	19	30	47	51	45
8	Sunderland	42	8	10	3	27	19	5	7	9	22	39	49	58	43
9	Charlton Athletic	42	10	5	6	38	31	5	7	9	25	36	63	67	42
10	Aston Villa	42	10	6	5	40	36	6	4	11	20	40	60	76	42
11	Stoke City	42	14	3	4	43	24	2	6	13	23	44	66	68	41
12	Liverpool	42	5	10	6	25	18	8	4	9	28	25	53	43	40
13	Chelsea	42	10	6	5	43	27	2	8	11	26	41	69	68	38
14	BOLTON WANDERERS	42	10	4	7	43	32	4	6	11	16	36	59	68	38
15	Burnley	42	10	6	5	27	19	2	8	11	16	31	43	50	38
16	Blackpool	42	8	8	5	24	25	3	8	10	30	42	54	67	38
17	Birmingham City	42	9	7	5	19	10	2	8	11	17	28	36	38	37
18	Everton	42	12	5	4	33	25	1	6	14	8	38	41	63	37
19	Middlesbrough	42	10	6	5	37	23	1	6	14	9	34	46	57	34
20	Huddersfield Town	42	6	7	8	19	24	6	3	12	21	45	40	69	34
21	Preston North End	42	8	6	7	36	36	3	5	13	26	39	62	75	33
22	Sheffield United	42	8	9	4	32	25	3	2	16	25	53	57	78	33

1948-49 Season
(Back) Ridding (Trainer), Howe, Roberts, Hanson, Banks, Barrass, Murphy
(Front) Woodward, Moir, Lofthouse, Rowley (Manager), Bradley, McShane, Gillies

1949-50 Season
(Back) Ridding (Trainer), Howe, Roberts, Kinsell, Elvy, Barrass, Gillies, Hernon
(Front) Woodward, Moir, Lofthouse, Bradley, McShane

1949/50   16th in Division One

Manager: W.Rowley

No	Date		Opponent	Result	Scorers	Att	Aspinall J	Banks R	Banks T	Barrass MW	Bingley W	Bradley J	Corfield E	Dillon V	Elvy R	Gillies MM	Hanson S	Hernon J	Howe D	Hughes W	Jackson J	Kinsell TH	Langton R	Lofthouse N	McShane H	Moir W	Murphy D	Roberts JH	Webster H	Woodward T
1	Aug	20	STOKE CITY	4-0	Bradley(2), Lofthouse, Moir	32222				6		10			1	5			4			3		9	11	8		2		7
2		24	Manchester United	0-3		42515				6		10			1	5			4			3		9	11	8		2		7
3		27	Burnley	1-2	Woodward	31581				6		10			1	5			4			3		9	11	8		2		7
4		31	MANCHESTER UNITED	1-2	McShane	39226				6						5	1	10	4			3		9	11	8		2		7
5	Sep	3	SUNDERLAND	2-1	Howe(pen), Moir	32092				6		10				5	1	7	4			3		9	11	8		2		
6		5	DERBY COUNTY	0-0		29558				6		10				5	1	8	4		9	3			11	7		2		
7		10	Liverpool	1-1	Bradley	44212		2				10				5	1	8	4	7	9	3			11		6			
8		17	ARSENAL	2-2	Roberts(pen), Barrass	33867		3		9		10				5	1	8	4					7	11		6	2		
9		24	Portsmouth	1-1	Lofthouse	35188						10				5	1	8	4			3		9	11		6	2		7
10	Oct	1	Birmingham City	0-0		33142						10				5	1	8	4			3		9	11		6	2		7
11		8	HUDDERSFIELD T	1-2	Lofthouse	31048						10				5	1	8	4			3		9	11	8	6	2		7
12		15	Everton	0-0		38421		2								5	1	10	4	7		3		9	11	8	6			
13		22	MIDDLESBROUGH	1-2	Murphy	30095		2		9						5	1	10	4	7		3			11	8	6			
14		29	Blackpool	0-2		23233			3			10		8		5	1		4					9	11	7	6	2		
15	Nov	5	NEWCASTLE UNITED	2-2	Howe, Lofthouse	31728			3	4						5	1	10	8					9	11	7	6	2		
16		12	Fulham	0-3		30197			3	4						5	1	10	8					9	11	7	6	2		
17		19	MANCHESTER CITY	3-0	Roberts(pen), Lofthouse(2)	35376				4		10				5	1		8			3	11	9	7		6	2		
18		26	Charlton Athletic	0-0		19755				4		10				5	1		8			3	11	9	7		6	2		
19	Dec	3	ASTON VILLA	1-1	Barrass	22861				4		10				5	1		8			3	11	9	7		6	2		
20		10	Wolverhampton Wan.	1-1	Bradley	30768				4		10				5	1					3	11	9	7	8	6	2		
21		17	Stoke City	2-3	Moir, Bradley	17031				4		10	9			5	1					3	11		7	8	6	2		
22		24	BURNLEY	0-1		34461		3		4		10	9			5	1						11		7	8	6	2		
23		26	WEST BROMWICH ALB.	3-0	Moir(2), Bradley	38764		3		4		10				5	1	6					11	9	7	8		2		
24		27	West Bromwich Albion	1-2	Bradley	41746		3		4		10				5	1						11	9	7	8	6	2		
25		31	Sunderland	0-2		38135		3		9		10				5	1	4					11	7		8	6	2		
26	Jan	14	LIVERPOOL	3-2	Howe, Bradley, McShane	41507		3		4		10				5	1	6					11	9	7	8		2		
27		21	Arsenal	1-1	Moir	47493		3		4		10				5	1	6					11	9	7	8		2		
28	Feb	4	PORTSMOUTH	1-0	Lofthouse	32441	5	3		4		10					1	6					11	9	7	8		2		
29		18	BIRMINGHAM CITY	1-0	Roberts(pen)	30383		3		4		10				5	1	6					11	9	7	8		2		
30		25	Huddersfield Town	0-2		12352		3		4		10	8	9		5	1	6					11		7			2		
31	Mar	8	EVERTON	1-2	Lofthouse	14807		2		4	3	10	8			5	1	6					11	9	7					
32		11	Manchester City	1-2		43764		2		4						5	1	10	6				11	9		8		3	7	
33		18	CHARLTON ATHLETIC	3-0	Howe(pen), Moir, Langton	24895		3		4						5	1	10	6				11	9	7	8		2		
34		25	Newcastle United	1-3	Moir	33752		3		4						5	1	10	6	7				9	11	8		2		
35	Apr	1	FULHAM	2-1	Moir, Lofthouse	23658		3		4						5	1	10	6				11	9	7	8		2		
36		7	Chelsea	1-1	McShane	52985		3		4						5	1	10	6				11	9	7	8		2		
37		8	Middlesbrough	0-2		21674		3		4						5	1	10	6				11	9	7	8	3	2		
38		10	CHELSEA	1-0	Hernon	24441		3		4			8			5	1	6					11	9	7			2		
39		15	BLACKPOOL	0-0		25800		3		4					9	5	1		6	7			11					2	8	
40		22	Aston Villa	0-3		29820				4	3					5	1	10	6	7				9	11	8		2		
41		29	WOLVERHAMPTON W.	2-4	Howe(pen), McShane	16336				4						5	1	10	3				11	9	7	8	6	2		
42	May	6	Derby County	0-4		14622		3		4						5	1	10	6				11	9	7	8		2		
			Apps				1	22	3	36	2	27	2	5	3	41	39	22	38	6	2	17	23	35	40	31	21	37	2	7
			Goals							2		8					1	5					1	10	4	9	1	3		1

F.A. Cup

	Date		Opponent	Result	Scorers	Att	Banks R	Barrass MW	Bradley J	Gillies MM	Hanson S	Hernon J	Langton R	Lofthouse N	McShane H	Moir W	Roberts JH
3	Jan	7	Coventry City	2-1	Lofthouse, Langton	29090	3	4	10	5	1	6	11	9	7	8	2
4		28	Leeds United	1-1	Lofthouse	51000	3	4	10	5	1	6	11	9	7	8	2
4r	Feb	1	LEEDS UNITED*	2-3	Lofthouse, McShane	29440	3	4	10	5	1	6	11	9	7	8	2

* After extra time

Lancashire Cup

1	Oct	18	ACCRINGTON STANLEY	4-1
1	Feb	8	ROCHDALE	0-1

Manchester Cup

SF	Apr	19	MANCHESTER CITY *	0-1

* After extra time

Other Games

1	Feb	11	ST MIRREN	4-2
2	May	12	Drumcondra	2-1
3		14	Sligo Rovers	4-2
4		16	Derry City	3-1

FINAL TABLE		Pl.	Home					Away					F.	A.	Pts
			W	D	L	F	A	W	D	L	F	A	(Total)		
1	Portsmouth	42	12	7	2	44	15	10	2	9	30	23	74	38	53
2	Wolverhampton W.	42	11	8	2	47	21	9	5	7	29	28	76	49	53
3	Sunderland	42	14	6	1	50	23	7	4	10	33	39	83	62	52
4	Manchester United	42	11	5	5	42	20	7	9	5	27	24	69	44	50
5	Newcastle United	42	14	4	3	49	23	5	8	8	28	32	77	55	50
6	Arsenal	42	12	4	5	48	24	7	7	7	31	31	79	55	49
7	Blackpool	42	10	8	3	29	14	7	7	7	17	21	46	35	49
8	Liverpool	42	10	7	4	37	23	7	7	7	27	31	64	54	48
9	Middlesbrough	42	14	2	5	37	18	6	5	10	22	30	59	48	47
10	Burnley	42	9	7	5	23	17	7	6	8	17	23	40	40	45
11	Derby County	42	11	5	5	46	26	6	5	10	23	35	69	61	44
12	Aston Villa	42	10	7	4	31	19	5	5	11	30	42	61	61	42
13	Chelsea	42	7	7	7	31	30	5	9	7	27	35	58	65	40
14	West Bromwich Alb.	42	9	7	5	28	16	5	5	11	19	37	47	53	40
15	Huddersfield Town	42	11	4	6	34	22	3	5	13	18	51	52	73	37
16	**BOLTON WANDERERS**	42	10	5	6	34	22	0	9	12	11	37	45	59	34
17	Fulham	42	8	6	7	24	19	2	8	11	17	35	41	54	34
18	Everton	42	6	8	7	24	20	4	6	11	18	46	42	66	34
19	Stoke City	42	10	4	7	27	28	1	8	12	18	47	45	75	34
20	Charlton Athletic	42	7	5	9	33	35	1	14	20	30	53	65	32
21	Manchester City	42	7	8	6	27	24	1	5	15	9	44	36	68	29
22	Birmingham City	42	6	8	7	19	24	1	6	14	12	43	31	67	28

1950 - 51 Season
(Back) Ridding (Manager), Moir, Barrass, Hanson, Gillies, Howe, Ball
(Front) R.Banks, McShane, Lofthouse, Duxbury (Chair.), T.Banks, Hernon, Langton
(insets) Hughes, Webster

1951
The Players and Officials at Lucerne during the end of season tour.

1950/51   8th in Division One

Manager: W.Rowley until 17/10/50, W.Ridding from 7/2/51

No	Date	Opponent	Res	Scorers	Att	Ball J	Banks R	Banks T	Barrass MW	Beards A	Bell E	Bradley J	Codd RW	Corfield E	Dillon V	Edwards GB	Gillies MM	Hanson S	Hernon J	Howe D	Hughes W	Kennedy GM	Langton R	Lofthouse N	McShane H	Matthewson R	Moir W	Murphy D	Roberts JH	Webster H	Wheeler JE
1	Aug 19	Charlton Athletic	3-4	Lofthouse(3)	30487	3			4			10					5	1		6			11	9	7		8		2		
2	23	TOTTENHAM HOTSPUR	1-4	Langton	21745	3			4		10						5	1		6			11	9	7		8		2		
3	26	MANCHESTER UNITED	1-0	Lofthouse	40759		2	3	4								5	1	10	6			11	9	7		8				
4	28	Tottenham Hotspur	2-4	Moir(2)	44246		2	3	4								5	1	10	6			11	9	7		8				
5	Sep 2	Wolves	1-7	Moir	46764		2	3	4								5	1	10	6			11	9	7		8				
6	4	CHELSEA	1-0	Hughes	25457	3			4							9	5	1		2	7		11				8	6		10	
7	9	SUNDERLAND	1-2	Webster	30745	3			4								5	1		2	7		11	9			8	6		10	
8	16	Aston Villa	1-0	Moir	32817	2	3										5	1		4	7		11	9			8	6		10	
9	23	DERBY COUNTY	3-0	Howe(pen), Lofthouse, Webster	36745	2										6	5	1		4	7	3	11	9			8			10	
10	30	Liverpool	3-3	Moir, Lofthouse, Webster	44534	2										6	5	1		4	7	3	11	9			8			10	
11	Oct 7	PORTSMOUTH	4-0	Lofthouse(2), Webster(2)	36995	2				6	11						5	1		4	7	3		9			8			10	
12	14	Everton	1-1	Moir	53421	2				6							5	1		4	7	3	11	9			8			10	
13	21	NEWCASTLE UNITED	0-2		49213	2										6		1		4	7	3	11	9		5	8			10	
14	28	Huddersfield Town	4-0	Howe(pen),Moir,Lofthouse,Webster	30989	2										6	5	1		4	7	3	11	9			8			10	
15	Nov 4	STOKE CITY	1-1	Webster	34244	2				6							5	1		4	7	3	11	9			8			10	
16	11	West Bromwich Albion	1-0	Kennedy(og)	28816	2			5							6		1		4	7	3	11	9			8			10	
17	18	MIDDLESBROUGH	0-2		37296	2			5							6		1		4	7	3	11	9			8			10	
18	25	Sheffield Wednesday	4-3	Lofthouse(2), Webster(2)	37053	2			5							6		1		4	7	3	11	9			8			10	
19	Dec 2	ARSENAL	3-0	Moir, Langton(2)	43484	2			5				9			6		1		4	7	3	11				8			10	
20	9	Burnley	0-2		31124	2			5							6		1		4	7	3	11	9			8			10	
21	16	CHARLTON ATHLETIC	3-0	Moir, Webster(2)	19207	2			5							6		1		4	7	3	11	9			8			10	
22	23	Manchester United	3-2	Lofthouse(2), Webster	37235	2			5							6		1		4	7	3	11	9			8			10	
23	25	Fulham	1-0	Lofthouse	21712	2			5							6		1		4	7	3	11	9			8			10	
24	26	FULHAM	0-1		43116	2			5				9			6		1		4	7	3	11				8			10	
25	Jan 13	Sunderland	2-1	Moir, Webster	47197	2			5							6		1		4	7	3	11	9			8			10	
26	20	ASTON VILLA	1-0	Moss(og)	29233	2	3		5							6		1		4	7		11	9			8			10	
27	Feb 3	Derby County	2-2	Lofthouse, Webster	19879	2	3		5							6		1	11	4	7			9			8			10	
28	10	BURNLEY	1-1	Howe(pen)	35540	2	3		5							6		1		4	7		11	9			8			10	
29	17	LIVERPOOL	2-1	Howe, Lofthouse	34807	2			5							6		1		4	7		11	9				3		10	8
30	24	Portsmouth	1-2	Lofthouse	27222	2			5							6		1		4	7		11	9			8	3		10	
31	Mar 3	EVERTON	2-0	Codd, Langton	36752	2			5				9			6		1		3	7		11				8			10	4
32	17	HUDDERSFIELD TOWN	4-0	Lofthouse,Langton(p),Webster,Wheeler	29796	2			5							6		1		3	7		11	9			8			10	4
33	23	Blackpool	0-2		33627	2			5				7			6		1		3			11	9			8			10	4
34	24	Stoke City	1-2	Lofthouse	20682	2			5				7			6		1		3			11	9			8			10	4
35	26	BLACKPOOL	1-2	Langton	42265	2			5							6		1		4	7		11	9			10	3			8
36	31	WEST BROMWICH ALBION	0-2		21860	2			5							6		1		4	7		11	9			10	3			8
37	Apr 7	Middlesbrough	1-1	Moir	24423	2			5							6		1		4	7		11	9			10	3			8
38	14	SHEFFIELD WEDNESDAY	0-1		19956	2			5							6		1		4	7		11	9			10	3			8
39	18	Newcastle United	1-0	Lofthouse	39099	2			5				7			6		1		3			11	9			8			10	4
40	21	Arsenal	1-1	Lofthouse	42050	2			5				7			6		1		3			11	9			8			10	4
41	28	WOLVES	2-1	Moir, Codd	26775	2			5				7	8		6		1		3			11	9			10				4
42	May 5	Chelsea	0-4		38928	2			5				7	8		6		1		3			11	9			10				4
		Apps				35	11	3	38	1	1	1	9	2	1	30	14	42	4	42	31	17	40	38	5	1	41	9	2	31	13
		Goals											2							4	1		6	21			12			15	1

Two own goals

F.A. Cup

No	Date	Opponent	Res	Scorers	Att	Ball J	Banks R	Banks T	Barrass MW	Edwards GB	Hanson S	Howe D	Hughes W	Kennedy GM	Langton R	Lofthouse N	Moir W	Webster H
3	Jan 6	YORK CITY	2-0	Lofthouse, Langton	26652	2			5	6	1	4	7	3	11	9	8	10
4	27	Newcastle United	2-3	Moir(2)	68659	2	3		5	6	1	4	7		11	9	8	10

Lancashire Cup

1	Oct 25	MANCHESTER UNITED	2-3

Manchester Cup

1	Mar 4	MANCHESTER UNITED	2-0
SF	23	OLDHAM ATHLETIC	1-2

Other Games

1	May 7	Norwich City	2-3
2	9	DUNDEE	2-1
3	14	Lucerne	3-0
4	16	Zurich XI	0-1
5	17	Berne	1-1
6	22	Basle	0-1
7	25	Schaafhausen	2-0

FINAL TABLE

		Pl.	Home					Away					F.	A.	Pts
			W	D	L	F	A	W	D	L	F	A	(Total)		
1	Tottenham Hotspur	42	17	2	2	54	21	8	8	5	28	23	82	44	60
2	Manchester United	42	14	4	3	42	16	10	4	7	32	24	74	40	56
3	Blackpool	42	12	6	3	43	19	8	4	9	36	34	79	53	50
4	Newcastle United	42	10	6	5	36	22	8	7	6	26	31	62	53	49
5	Arsenal	42	11	5	5	47	28	8	4	9	26	28	73	56	47
6	Middlesbrough	42	12	7	2	51	25	6	4	11	25	40	76	65	47
7	Portsmouth	42	8	10	3	39	30	8	5	8	32	38	71	68	47
8	BOLTON WANDERERS	42	11	2	8	31	20	8	5	8	33	41	64	61	45
9	Liverpool	42	11	5	5	28	25	5	6	10	25	34	53	59	43
10	Burnley	42	9	7	5	27	16	5	7	9	21	27	48	43	42
11	Derby County	42	10	5	6	53	33	6	3	12	28	42	81	75	40
12	Sunderland	42	8	9	4	30	21	4	7	10	33	52	63	73	40
13	Stoke City	42	10	5	6	28	19	3	9	9	22	40	50	59	40
14	Wolverhampton W.	42	9	3	9	44	30	6	5	10	30	31	74	61	38
15	Aston Villa	42	9	6	6	39	29	3	7	11	27	39	66	68	37
16	West Bromwich Alb.	42	7	4	10	30	27	6	7	8	23	34	53	61	37
17	Charlton Athletic	42	9	4	8	35	31	5	5	11	28	49	63	80	37
18	Fulham	42	8	5	8	35	37	5	6	10	17	31	52	68	37
19	Huddersfield Town	42	8	4	9	40	40	7	2	12	24	52	64	92	36
20	Chelsea	42	9	4	8	31	25	3	4	14	22	40	53	65	32
21	Sheffield Wed.	42	9	6	6	43	32	3	2	16	21	51	64	83	32
22	Everton	42	7	5	9	26	35	5	3	13	22	51	48	86	32

1951/52 5th in Division One

Manager: W.Ridding

#	Date	Opponents	Result / Scorers	Att	Ball J	Banks R	Barrass MW	Bell E	Codd R	Corfield E	Edwards GB	Gillies MM	Grieves KJ	Hanson S	Hassall HW	Higgins G	Holden AD	Howe D	Hughes W	Langton R	Lofthouse N	Moir W	Parry RA	Webster H	Wheeler JE
1	Aug 18	ASTON VILLA	5-2 Moir,Lofthouse,Webster(2),Langton(p)	30253	2		5				6			1		3			7	11	9	8		10	4
2	22	NEWCASTLE UNITED	0-0	39942	2		5		9		6			1		3			7	11		8		10	4
3	25	Stoke City	2-1 Lofthouse, Webster	22442	2		5				6			1		3			7	11	9	8		10	4
4	29	Newcastle United	1-0 Moir	49587	2		5		7		6			1		3				11	9	8		10	4
5	Sep 1	MANCHESTER UNITED	1-0 Lofthouse	55477	2		5		7		6			1		3				11	9	8		10	4
6	3	MIDDLESBROUGH	3-1 Moir, Webster, Codd	33811	2		5		7		6			1		3				11	9	8		10	4
7	8	Tottenham Hotspur	1-2 Langton(pen)	61838	2		5		7		6			1		3				11	9	8		10	4
8	15	PRESTON NORTH END	1-1 Webster	46523	2		5		7		6			1		3				11	9	8		10	4
9	22	Burnley	3-1 Wheeler, Moir, Webster	37196	2		5		7		6			1		3				11	9	8		10	4
10	29	CHARLTON ATHLETIC	2-1 Moir, Webster	37719	2		5		7		6			1		3				11	9	8		10	4
11	Oct 6	SUNDERLAND	1-1 Lofthouse	43887	2		5		7		6			1		3				11	9	8		10	4
12	13	Wolves	1-5	38413	2		5		7		6			1		3				11	9	8		10	4
13	20	HUDDERSFIELD TOWN	2-1 Langton(pen), Codd	33670					9	7	6	5		1		3				11		8		10	4
14	27	Chelsea	3-1 Lofthouse(2), Codd	45287	2		5		7		6			1		3		10		11	9	8			4
15	Nov 3	PORTSMOUTH	0-3	26299	2		5		7		6			1		3				11	9	8		10	4
16	10	Liverpool	1-1 Wheeler	49537	2		5		7		6			1		3	11				9	8		10	4
17	17	BLACKPOOL	1-0 Garrett(og)	38990	2				7		6	5		1		3				11	9	8		10	4
18	24	Arsenal	2-4 Moir, Webster	50790	2				7		6	5		1		3				11	9	8		10	4
19	Dec 1	MANCHESTER CITY	2-1 Lofthouse, Howe	43405	2		5				6			1		3	7	10		11	9	8			4
20	8	Derby County	2-5 Lofthouse, Howe	23838	2		5				6			1		3	7	10		11	9	8			4
21	15	Aston Villa	1-1 Howe	28907	2		5				6			1		3	7	10		11	9	8			4
22	22	STOKE CITY	1-1 Moir	19235	2		5				6			1		3	7	10		11	9	8			4
23	25	WEST BROMWICH ALBION	3-2 Moir (2,1pen), Lofthouse	32562	2		5				6			1		3	7	10		11	9	8			4
24	26	West Bromwich Albion	2-3 Moir, Lofthouse	37698	2						6	5		1		3	7			11	9	8		10	4
25	29	Manchester United	0-1	55073	2						6	5		1		3	7	10		11	9	8			4
26	Jan 5	TOTTENHAM HOTSPUR	1-1 Langton(pen)	46354	2	3	5				6			1	10		7			11	9	8			4
27	19	Preston North End	2-2 Lofthouse, Langton	38646		2	5	4			6			1	10	3	7			11	9			8	
28	26	BURNLEY	1-4 Hassall	38149	2		5				6			1	10	3	7			11	9	8			4
29	Feb 2	DERBY COUNTY	1-2 Holden	26596	2		5	4					7	1	10	3	11	6			9				8
30	9	Charlton Athletic	0-1	23480	2		5	4					7	1	10	3	11	6			9				8
31	16	Sunderland	2-0 Moir, Holden	43397	2		5				6			1	10		7	3		11	9	8			4
32	Mar 1	WOLVES	2-2 Moir, Lofthouse	33294	2		5				6			1	10	3	7			11	9	8			4
33	8	Huddersfield Town	2-0 Moir, Lofthouse	24045	2		5				6			1	10	3	7			11	9	8			4
34	15	CHELSEA	3-0 Lofthouse, Holden, Hassall	31448	2		5				6			1	10	3	7			11	9	8			4
35	22	Portsmouth	0-3	31135	2		5				6			1	10	3	7			11	9	8			4
36	29	LIVERPOOL	1-1 Wheeler	17459		2	5				6			1	10	3	7			11	9	8			4
37	Apr 5	Blackpool	0-1	17374		2	5				6			1	10	3	7			11		8	9		4
38	11	Fulham	2-1 Wheeler, Moir	38304	2		5			11	6			1	10	3	7					8	9		4
39	12	ARSENAL	2-1 Moir, Lofthouse	47940	2		5				6			1		3	7			11	9	8			4
40	14	FULHAM	2-1 Lofthouse, Holden	29461	2		5			11	6			1		3	7				9	8			4
41	19	Manchester City	3-0 Moir, Lofthouse, Hassall	28388	2		5				6			1	10	3	7				9	8		11	4
42	23	Middlesbrough	0-2	23591	2		5				6			1	10	3	7				9	8		11	4
		Apps			39	4	37	5	18	2	40	5	2	40	17	40	25	10	3	35	38	39	2	21	40
		Goals							3						3		4	3		5	18	16		8	4

One own goal

F.A. Cup

	Date	Opponents	Result	Att	Ball J	Banks R	Barrass MW	Bell E	Codd R	Corfield E	Edwards GB	Gillies MM	Grieves KJ	Hanson S	Hassall HW	Higgins G	Holden AD	Howe D	Hughes W	Langton R	Lofthouse N	Moir W	Parry RA	Webster H	Wheeler JE
3	Jan 12	West Bromwich Albion	0-4	37900	2	3	5				6			1			7			11	9	8		10	4

Lancashire Cup

1	Oct 24	MANCHESTER UNITED	1-0
2	Feb 20	Burnley	1-2

Manchester Cup

SF	Mar 12	Manchester United	0-0
SFr	26	MANCHESTER UNITED	1-0
F		Bury	1-2

Other Games

1	Feb 23	Nottingham Forest	3-3
2	Mar 5	Dutch XI	2-2
3	Apr 26	Hibernian	2-2

FINAL TABLE

		Pl.	Home					Away					F.	A.	Pts
			W	D	L	F	A	W	D	L	F	A	(Total)		
1	Manchester United	42	15	3	3	55	21	8	8	5	40	31	95	52	57
2	Tottenham Hotspur	42	16	1	4	45	20	6	8	7	31	31	76	51	53
3	Arsenal	42	13	7	1	54	30	8	4	9	26	31	80	61	53
4	Portsmouth	42	13	3	5	42	25	7	5	9	26	33	68	58	48
5	BOLTON WANDERERS	42	11	7	3	35	26	8	3	10	30	35	65	61	48
6	Aston Villa	42	13	3	5	49	28	6	6	9	30	42	79	70	47
7	Preston North End	42	10	5	6	39	22	7	7	7	35	32	74	54	46
8	Newcastle United	42	12	4	5	62	28	6	5	10	36	45	98	73	45
9	Blackpool	42	12	5	4	40	27	6	4	11	24	37	64	64	45
10	Charlton Athletic	42	12	5	4	41	24	5	5	11	27	39	68	63	44
11	Liverpool	42	6	11	4	31	25	6	8	7	26	36	57	61	43
12	Sunderland	42	8	6	7	41	28	7	6	8	29	33	70	61	42
13	West Bromwich Alb.	42	8	9	4	38	29	6	4	11	36	48	74	77	41
14	Burnley	42	9	6	6	32	19	4	6	11	24	44	56	63	40
15	Manchester City	42	7	5	9	29	28	6	8	7	29	33	58	61	39
16	Wolverhampton W.	42	8	6	7	40	33	4	8	9	33	40	73	73	38
17	Derby County	42	10	4	7	43	37	5	3	12	21	43	63	80	37
18	Middlesbrough	42	12	4	5	37	25	3	2	16	27	63	64	88	36
19	Chelsea	42	10	3	8	31	29	4	5	12	21	43	52	72	36
20	Stoke City	42	8	6	7	34	32	4	1	16	15	56	49	88	31
21	Huddersfield Town	42	9	3	9	32	35	1	5	15	17	47	49	82	28
22	Fulham	42	5	7	9	38	31	3	4	14	20	46	58	77	27

1951-52 Season
(Back) Wheeler, Edwards, Ball, Hanson, Higgins, Barrass
(Front) Hughes, Moir, Lofthouse, Webster, Langton

1953-54 Season
(Back) Taylor (Coach), Ball, Wheeler, Hanson, Barrass, Bell, Higgins, Ridding (Manager)
(Front) Holden, Moir, Lofthouse, Hassall, Langton, Sproston (Trainer)

1952/53 14th in Division One

Manager: W.Ridding

#		Date	Opponent	Result	Scorers	Att.	Ball J	Banks R	Banks T	Barrass MW	Beards A	Bell E	Codd RW	Edwards GB	Gubbins RG	Hanson S	Hartle LR	Hassall HW	Higgins G	Higgins JO	Holden AD	Hughes W	Langton R	Lofthouse N	Matthewson R	McIlwaine M	Moir W	Neill TK	Parry RA	Pilling V	Webster H	Wheeler JE
1	Aug	23	DERBY COUNTY	2-0	Holden, Langton	35551	2			5				6		1		10	3		7		11	9			8					4
2		25	Wolves	1-3	Moir	32449	2			5				6		1		10	3		7		11	9			8					4
3		30	Blackpool	0-3		31317	2			5				6		1		11	3		7			9			8				10	4
4	Sep	1	WOLVES	2-1	Moir, Hassall	28057	2			5				6		1		10	3		7			9			8				11	4
5		6	CHELSEA	1-1	Lofthouse	29877	2			5				6		1		10	3		7			9			8				11	4
6		10	Charlton Athletic	0-2		14900	2	11		5				6		1		10	3		7			9			8					4
7		13	Manchester United	0-1		42370	2			5	8			6		1			3		7			9			10		11			4
8		20	PORTSMOUTH	0-5		29590	2			5	8			6		1			3		7			9			11		10			4
9		27	Middlesbrough	2-1	Moir, Hassall	26679	2			5	11					1		10	3		7			9			8	6				4
10	Oct	4	Aston Villa	1-1	Beards	32242	2			5	11		9			1		10	3		7						8	6				4
11		11	LIVERPOOL	2-2	Lofthouse(2)	38450	2			5	11					1		10	3		7			9			8	6				4
12		18	Manchester City	2-1	Lofthouse, Langton	42369	2			5						1		10	3		7		11	9			8	6				4
13		25	STOKE CITY	2-1	Moir(2)	28295	2			5						1		10	3		7		11	9			8	6				4
14	Nov	1	Preston North End	2-2	Hassall, Langton(pen)	37848	2			5						1		10	3		7		11	9			8	6				4
15		8	BURNLEY	1-2		37603	2			5						1		10	3		7		11	9			8	6				4
16		15	Tottenham Hotspur	1-1	Lofthouse	31442	2			5	11					1		10	3		7			9			8	6				4
17		22	SHEFFIELD WEDNESDAY	1-1	Moir	34435	2			5	11					1		10	3		7			9			8	6				4
18	Dec	6	NEWCASTLE UNITED	4-2	Moir, Lofthouse, Hassall(2)	28577	2			5	11					1		10	3		7			9			8	6				4
19		13	West Bromwich Albion	1-0	Beards	16148	2			5	11					1		10	3		7			9			8	6				4
20		20	Derby County	3-4	Moir, Lofthouse, Hassall	12884	2			5	11					1		10	3		7			9			8	6				4
21		25	ARSENAL	4-6	Moir(2), Lofthouse(2)	45432	2			5						1			3		7		11	9			8	6			10	4
22	Jan	1	CHARLTON ATHLETIC	1-2	Holden	32614				5	11		6			1	2		3		7				5						10	4
23		3	BLACKPOOL	4-0	Wheel(3), Moir	36572				4	11					1	2		3		7			9			8	6	10			9
24		17	Chelsea	0-1		36572				5		6				1	2		3		7		11	9			8		10			4
25		24	MANCHESTER UNITED	2-1	Moir(2)	46818				5		6				1	2	10	3		7		11	9			8					4
26	Feb	7	Portsmouth	1-3	Parry	25240	2		3							1	2	10			7			9			8	6	11			4
27		18	MIDDLESBROUGH	5-3	Lofthouse(3), Hassall, Hughes	15041				5		6				1	2	10	3			7	11	9			8					4
28		21	ASTON VILLA	0-0		24446				5		6				1	2	10	3			7		9			8		11			4
29	Mar	4	Liverpool	0-0		24999		3		5		6	7			1	2	10						9					8	11		4
30		7	MANCHESTER CITY	1-0	Lofthouse	39585		3		5		6				1	2	10						9			8			11	7	4
31		11	Cardiff City	0-1		31099		3		5		6				1	2	10					11	9				4	8		7	
32		14	Stoke City	2-1	Lofthouse, Webster	28070				5		6				1	2		3				11	9				4	10	7		8
33		25	PRESTON NORTH END	0-2		22173		3		5		6				1	2				7		11					8	4			9
34		28	Burnley	1-0	Moir	20392		3				6				1	2		10	5	7		11				8	9				4
35	Apr	3	SUNDERLAND	5-0	Lofthouse(3), Langton, Neill	34862		3		5		6				1	2		10		7		11	9			8	4				
36		4	TOTTENHAM HOTSPUR	2-3	Moir(2)	40185		3		5		6				1	2		10		7		11	9			8	4				
37		6	Sunderland	0-2		32227		3		5			6			1	2		10				11	9				4	8	7		
38		11	Sheffield Wednesday	1-1	Lofthouse	39893		3		5			6			1	2		10		7			9	4	8		11				
39		15	Arsenal	1-4	Moir	35381	2	3					6			1				5	7		11			8	9	4	10		
40		18	CARDIFF CITY	0-1		18037	2	3					6			1		10				7				5	9	4	8	11	
41		22	WEST BROMWICH ALBION	0-1		17189	2	3		5			6			1		10			7		11	9			8					4
42		25	Newcastle United	3-2	Lofthouse(3)	34824	2	3		5					10	1					7		11	9			8					4
			Apps				26	11	4	38	10	15	2	14	1	42	17	33	28	2	33	4	20	36	2	2	37	23	15	6	7	34
			Goals								2							7			2	1	4	22			17	1	1		1	3

F.A. Cup

#		Date	Opponent	Result	Scorers	Att.	Ball J	Banks R	Banks T	Barrass MW	Beards A	Bell E	Codd RW	Edwards GB	Gubbins RG	Hanson S	Hartle LR	Hassall HW	Higgins G	Higgins JO	Holden AD	Hughes W	Langton R	Lofthouse N	Matthewson R	McIlwaine M	Moir W	Neill TK	Parry RA	Pilling V	Webster H	Wheeler JE
3	Jan	14	FULHAM	3-1	Holden, Moir, Lofthouse	32235				5		6				1	2		3		7		11	9			8		10			4
4		31	NOTTS COUNTY	1-1	Lofthouse	40048		3		5		6				1	2	10			7		11	9			8					4
4r	Feb	5	Notts County*	2-2	Moir(2)	33668		3		5		6				1	2	10			7		11	9			8					4
4/2r		9	Notts County+	1-0	Lofthouse	23171		3		5		6				1	2	10			7		11	9			8					4
5		16	Luton Town	1-0	Lofthouse	23735				5		6				1	2	10	3		7		11	9			8					4
6		28	Gateshead	1-0	Lofthouse	17692				5		6				1	2	10	3		7		11	9			8					4
SF	Mar	21	Everton#	4-3	Moir, Lofthouse(2), Holden	75000				5		6				1		10			7		11	9			8					4
F	May	2	Blackpool'	3-4	Moir, Bell, Lofthouse	100000	2		3	5		6				1		10			7		11	9			8					4

* After extra time. + Played at Hillsborough, Sheffield. # Played at Maine Road, Manchester. ' Played at Wembley Stadium.

Lancashire Cup

#		Date	Opponent	Result
1	Oct	1	BURY	2-2
1r		14	Bury	3-1
2	Feb	24	Preston North End	0-1

Manchester Cup

#		Date	Opponent	Result
1	Apr	15	BURY	2-1
SF		22	Manchester United	1-0
F	May	4	Oldham Athletic	1-3

Other Games

#		Date	Opponent	Result
1	May	9	Germany B	2-1
2		14	Germany A	0-2
3		16	German Select	1-1
4		20	Germany B	3-3
5		24	Select XI	3-2
6		31	Dutch XI	6-1

Final Table

	FINAL TABLE	Pl.	Home W	Home D	Home L	Home F	Home A	Away W	Away D	Away L	Away F	Away A	F. (Total)	A. (Total)	Pts
1	Arsenal	42	15	3	3	60	30	6	9	6	37	34	97	64	54
2	Preston North End	42	15	3	3	46	25	6	9	6	39	35	85	60	54
3	Wolverhampton W.	42	13	5	3	54	27	6	8	7	32	36	86	63	51
4	West Bromwich Alb.	42	13	3	5	35	19	8	5	8	31	41	66	60	50
5	Charlton Athletic	42	12	6	3	47	22	7	3	11	30	41	77	63	49
6	Burnley	42	11	6	4	36	20	7	6	8	31	32	67	52	48
7	Blackpool	42	13	5	3	45	22	6	4	11	26	48	71	70	47
8	Manchester United	42	11	5	5	35	30	7	5	9	34	42	69	72	46
9	Sunderland	42	11	9	1	42	27	4	4	13	26	55	68	82	43
10	Tottenham Hotspur	42	11	6	4	55	37	4	5	12	23	32	78	69	41
11	Aston Villa	42	9	7	5	36	23	5	6	10	27	38	63	61	41
12	Cardiff City	42	7	8	6	32	17	7	4	10	22	29	54	46	40
13	Middlesbrough	42	12	5	4	46	27	2	6	13	24	50	70	77	39
14	**BOLTON WANDERERS**	42	9	4	8	39	35	6	5	10	22	34	61	69	39
15	Portsmouth	42	10	6	5	44	34	4	13	30	49	74	83	38	
16	Newcastle United	42	9	5	7	34	33	5	4	12	25	37	59	70	37
17	Liverpool	42	10	6	5	36	28	4	2	15	25	54	61	82	36
18	Sheffield Wed.	42	8	6	7	35	32	4	5	12	27	40	62	72	35
19	Chelsea	42	10	4	7	35	24	2	7	12	21	42	56	66	35
20	Manchester City	42	12	2	7	45	28	2	5	14	27	59	72	87	35
21	Stoke City	42	10	4	7	35	26	2	6	13	18	40	53	66	34
22	Derby County	42	9	6	6	41	29	2	4	15	18	45	59	74	32

~ 239 ~

1953/54   5th in Division One

Manager: W.Ridding

No	Date	Opponent	Score	Scorers	Att	Allcock T	Ball J	Banks T	Barrass MW	Beards A	Bell E	Codd RW	Edwards GB	Grieves KJ	Hanson S	Hassall HW	Hennin D	Higgins G	Higgins JO	Holden AD	Lofthouse N	Moir W	Neill TK	Parry RA	Stevens D	Webster H	Wheeler JE
1	Aug 22	West Bromwich Albion	1-1	Moir	28975		2		5		6	9			1	10			3	7		8		11			4
2	26	MIDDLESBROUGH	3-2	Hassall(2,1pen), Webster	29502		2	3	5		6				1	10				7		8		11		9	4
3	29	LIVERPOOL	2-0	Moir, Webster	27258		2	3	5		6				1	10				7		8		11		9	4
4	Sep 2	Middlesbrough	2-3	Wheeler, Hassall	25458		2	3	5		6				1	10				7		8		11		9	4
5	5	Newcastle United	3-2	Hassall(pen), Webster(2)	61321		2	3	5		6				1	10				7		8		11		9	4
6	9	SHEFFIELD WEDNESDAY	2-1	Moir, Hassall(pen)	31143		2	3	5		6				1	10				7		8		11		9	4
7	12	MANCHESTER UNITED	0-0		48591		2	3	5		6				1	10				7	9	8		11			4
8	16	Sheffield Wednesday	1-2	Hassall	26025		2	3	5		6				1	10				7	9	8		11			4
9	19	Cardiff City	1-1	Hassall	35788		2	3	5		6				1	10				7	9	8		11			4
10	26	Preston North End	1-3	Moir	39553		2	3	5		6				1					7	9	8		11	10		4
11	Oct 3	TOTTENHAM HOTSPUR	2-0	Hassall, Lofthouse	39842		2	3	5		6				1	10				7	9	8		11			4
12	10	MANCHESTER CITY	3-2	Moir, Allcock(2)	34443	8	2	3	5		6				1					7		10		11		9	4
13	17	Sunderland	2-1	Wheeler, Lofthouse	45358	8	2	3	5		6				1					7	9	10		11			4
14	24	WOLVES	1-1	Moir	40027		2	3	5		6				1	10				7	9	8		11			4
15	31	Aston Villa	2-2	Moir, Lofthouse	25325		2	3	5		6				1	10				7	9	8		11			4
16	Nov 7	PORTSMOUTH	6-1	Holden, Lofthouse(2), Hassall(3,1p)	22441		2	3	5		6				1	10				7	9	8	4	11			
17	14	Arsenal	3-4	Moir, Hassall(pen), Wheeler	52319		2	3	5		6				1	10				7		8	4	11			9
18	21	CHELSEA	2-2	Wheeler, Lofthouse	30635		2	3	5		6				1	10				7	9	8		11			4
19	28	Blackpool	0-0		29464		2	3	5		6				1	10				7	9	8		11			4
20	Dec 5	HUDDERSFIELD TOWN	0-0		36077		2	3			6				1	10		5		7	9	8		11			4
21	12	Sheffield United	0-3		27769	8	2	3	5		6				1					7	9	10	4	11			
22	19	WEST BROMWICH ALBION	2-1	Wheeler, Lofthouse	32246		2	3	5		6				1	10				7	9	8		11			4
23	25	Charlton Athletic	0-1		19226		2	3	5		6				1	10				7	9	8		11			4
24	26	CHARLTON ATHLETIC	3-1	Wheeler, Moir, Lofthouse	36065		2	3	5		6				1	10				7	9	8		11			4
25	Jan 1	SHEFFIELD UNITED	2-1	Lofthouse, Caldwell(og)	37484		2	3	5		6				1					7	9	8		11	10		4
26	2	Liverpool	2-1	Moir, Stevens	44383		2	3	5		6				1					7		8	4	11	10		9
27	16	NEWCASTLE UNITED	2-2	Moir, Lofthouse	29476		2	3	5		6				1					7	9	8		11	10		4
28	23	Manchester United	5-1	Moir, Parry(2), Lofthouse(2)	48505		2	3	5		6				1					7	9	8		11	10		4
29	Feb 6	CARDIFF CITY	3-0	Moir, Stevens, Lofthouse	30777		2	3	5		6				1					7	9	8		11	10		4
30	13	PRESTON NORTH END	0-2		44639		2	3	5		6	9			1	10				7		8		11			4
31	27	Manchester City	0-3		39340		2	3		5	6				1					7	9	8	4	11	10		
32	Mar 3	Tottenham Hotspur	2-3	Moir, Lofthouse	16720		2	3		5	6				1	10	4			7	9	8		11			
33	6	SUNDERLAND	3-1	Moir, Parry, Stevens	26379		2	3		5	6				1		4			7	9	8		11	10		
34	20	ASTON VILLA	3-0	Hassall(2), Stevens	26292		2		5		6		3		1	10	4			7	9			11	8		
35	24	Wolves	1-1	Lofthouse	19617		2	3	5		6				1	10	4			7	9	8		11			
36	27	Portsmouth	2-3	Moir, Parry	22784		2	3	5		6				1	10	4			7	9	8		11			
37	Apr 3	ARSENAL	3-1	Moir, Hassall(pen), Lofthouse	30525		2	3	5		6				1	10	4			7	9	8		11			
38	10	Chelsea	0-2		49433		2	3	5		6				1	10	4			7	9	8		11			
39	16	BURNLEY	0-0		34394		2	3	5		6				1	10	4			7	9	8		11			
40	17	BLACKPOOL	3-2	Moir, Hassall, Lofthouse	40291		2	3	5		6				1	10	4			7	9	8		11			
41	19	Burnley	1-1	Parry	25857		2	3	5		6				1	8	4			7	9			11	10		
42	24	Huddersfield Town	1-2	Parry	25635		2	3	5		6				1	8	4			7	9			11	10		
				Apps		3	42	40	38	3	40	2	2	2	40	28	11	1	4	42	32	39	6	41	12	6	28
				Goals		2										16					17	18		6	4	4	6

One own goal

F.A. Cup

Rd	Date	Opponent	Score	Scorers	Att	Ball J	Banks T	Barrass MW	Bell E	Hanson S	Hennin D	Holden AD	Lofthouse N	Moir W	Parry RA	Stevens D	Wheeler JE
3	Jan 9	LIVERPOOL	1-0	Moir	45340	2	3	5	6	1		7	9	8	11	10	4
4	30	Headington United	4-2	Moir, Parry, Lofthouse, Stevens	16600	2	3	5	6	1		7	9	8	11	10	4
5	Feb 20	PORTSMOUTH	0-0		53883	2	3	5	6	1		7	9	8	11	10	4
5r	24	Portsmouth	2-1	Moir(2)	45806	2	3	5	6	1		7	9	8	11	10	4
6	Mar 13	Sheffield Wednesday	1-1	Moir	65000	2	3	5	6	1	4	7	9	8	11	10	
6r	17	SHEFFIELD WEDNESDAY	0-2		52568	2	3	5	6	1	4	7	9	8	11	10	

Lancashire Cup

| 1 | Oct 20 | Preston North End | 0-3 |

Manchester Cup

| SF | Mar 31 | OLDHAM ATHLETIC | 1-0 |
| F | Apr 26 | Manchester United | 1-0 |

Other Games

1	Oct 13	Bury	2-2
2	May 5	Dutch XI	0-2
3		9	Bangu de Rio	3-0
4		12	Liege XI	2-1
5		16	Borussia/Rheydt XI	1-0

FINAL TABLE

		Pl.	Home					Away					F.	A.	Pts
			W	D	L	F	A	W	D	L	F	A	(Total)		
1	Wolverhampton W.	42	16	1	4	61	25	9	6	6	35	31	96	56	57
2	West Bromwich Alb.	42	13	5	3	51	24	9	4	8	35	39	86	63	53
3	Huddersfield Town	42	13	6	2	45	24	7	5	9	33	37	78	61	51
4	Manchester United	42	11	6	4	41	27	7	6	8	32	31	73	58	48
5	BOLTON WANDERERS	42	14	6	1	45	20	4	6	11	30	40	75	60	48
6	Blackpool	42	13	6	2	43	19	6	4	11	37	50	80	69	48
7	Burnley	42	16	2	3	51	23	5	2	14	27	44	78	67	46
8	Chelsea	42	12	3	6	45	26	4	9	8	29	42	74	68	44
9	Charlton Athletic	42	14	4	3	51	26	5	2	14	24	51	75	77	44
10	Cardiff City	42	12	4	5	32	27	6	4	11	19	44	51	71	44
11	Preston North End	42	12	2	7	43	24	7	3	11	44	34	87	58	43
12	Arsenal	42	8	8	5	42	37	7	5	9	33	36	75	73	43
13	Aston Villa	42	12	5	4	50	28	4	4	13	20	40	70	68	41
14	Portsmouth	42	13	5	3	53	31	1	6	14	28	58	81	89	39
15	Newcastle United	42	9	2	10	43	40	5	8	8	29	37	72	77	38
16	Tottenham Hotspur	42	11	3	7	38	33	5	2	14	27	43	65	76	38
17	Manchester City	42	10	4	7	35	31	4	5	12	27	46	62	77	37
18	Sunderland	42	11	4	6	50	37	3	4	14	31	52	81	89	36
19	Sheffield Wed.	42	12	4	5	43	30	3	2	16	27	61	70	91	36
20	Sheffield United	42	9	5	7	43	38	4	6	13	26	52	69	90	33
21	Middlesbrough	42	6	6	9	29	35	4	4	13	31	56	60	91	30
22	Liverpool	42	7	8	6	49	38	2	2	17	19	59	68	97	28

1954/55   18th in Division One

Manager: W.Ridding

#	Date		Opponent	Score	Scorers	Att	Allcock T	Ball J	Banks T	Barnard A	Barrass MW	Bell E	Bingley W	Birch B	Edwards GB	Grieves KJ	Gubbins RG	Hanson S	Hassall HW	Hennin D	Higgins JO	Holden AD	Lofthouse N	Moir W	Neill TK	Parry RA	Pilling V	Stevens D	Webster H	Wheeler JE
1	Aug	21	CHARLTON ATHLETIC	3-2	Lofthouse, Hassall, Webster	34526		2	3		5				6			1	10				7	9	8				11	4
2		23	Blackpool	3-2	Lofthouse, Webster(2)	33915		2	3		5				6			1	10				7	9	8				11	4
3		28	Chelsea	2-3	Moir, Parry	52756		2	3		5				6			1	10				7	9	8	11				4
4	Sep	1	BLACKPOOL	3-0	Lofthouse, Hassall, Edwards	47013		2	3		5				6			1	10				7	9	8	11				4
5		4	Huddersfield Town	0-2		28726		2	3		5				6			1	10				7	9	8	11				4
6		6	PORTSMOUTH	3-1	Lofthouse(2), Hassall	26629		2	3		5				6			1	10				7	9	8				11	4
7		11	MANCHESTER UNITED	1-1	Lofthouse	50708		2	3		5				6			1	10				7	9	8				11	4
8		15	Portsmouth	0-1		24113		2	3		5				6			1	10				7	9	8				11	4
9		18	Wolves	2-1	Hassall, Parry	40899		2	3		5	4			6			1	10				7		8	11				9
10		25	ASTON VILLA	3-3	Wheeler, Moir, Lofthouse	28335		2	3		5	6		7				1	10					9	8	11				4
11	Oct	2	Sunderland	1-1	Hassall	50486		2	3		5	4		7	6			1	10						8	11		9		
12		9	LEICESTER CITY	4-1	Moir(2), Lofthouse, Hassall	34358		2	3		5				6			1	10				7	9	8	11				4
13		16	Burnley	0-2		30016		2	3		5				6			1	10				7	9	8	11				4
14		23	MANCHESTER CITY	2-2	Wheeler, Lofthouse	29841		2	3		5	6						1	10				7	9	8	11				4
15		30	Cardiff City	2-2	Parry, Hassall	31698		2	3		5	6						1	10				7	9	8	11				4
16	Nov	6	ARSENAL	2-2	Moir, Parry	31223		2	3		5	6						1	10				7	9	8	11				4
17		13	West Bromwich Albion	0-0		34961		2	3		5	4			6			1	10				7	9	8	11				4
18		20	NEWCASTLE UNITED	2-1	Hassall(pen), Webster	25936		2	3		5	4			6			1	10				7		8	11			9	
19		27	Everton	0-0		43681		2	3		5	4			6			1	10				7		8	11	9			
20	Dec	11	Sheffield United	0-2		22947		2	3		5				6			1	10	4			7	9	8	11				
21		18	Charlton Athletic	0-2		16491		2			5		3		6			1	11	4			7		8			10	9	
22		25	TOTTENHAM HOTSPUR	1-2	Stevens	25978		2			5		3		6			1	11	4			7		8			10		9
23		27	Tottenham Hotspur	0-2		41063		2			5		3		6		11	1	9				7			10		8		4
24	Jan	1	CHELSEA	2-5	Barrass(2)	30998		2			10		3		6			1	9	8	5					11	7			4
25		22	Manchester United	1-1	Stevens	41719		2			5	6			3			1					7	9	8	11		10		4
26	Feb	5	WOLVES	6-1	Moir, Webster, Bell, Parry(3)	37427		2			5	6			3			1					11	9	7	10			8	4
27		12	Aston Villa	0-3		21447		2			5	6			3	1		1					11	9	7	10			8	4
28	Mar	2	SUNDERLAND	3-0	Moir, Lofthouse, Webster	17190		2			5	6			3			1					11	9	7			10	8	4
29		5	SHEFFIELD UNITED	1-0	Lofthouse	26837		2			5	6			3			1					11	9	7			10	8	4
30		9	PRESTON NORTH END	2-1	Lofthouse, Webster	19250		2			5	6			3			1					11	9	7			10	8	4
31		16	Manchester City	2-4	Lofthouse, Barrass(pen)	27742		2			5	6			3			1					11	9	7			10	8	4
32		19	CARDIFF CITY	0-0		25321		2			5	6			3			1					11	9	7	6	10		8	
33		26	Arsenal	0-3		32852		2			5	6			3			1					7	9	8	11			10	4
34	Apr	2	WEST BROMWICH ALBION	2-4	Parry, Allcock	17715	8	2			5	6			3			1					7			11		10	9	4
35		8	SHEFFIELD WEDNESDAY	2-2	Moir, Barrass	22909		2			5	6			3	1	11						7	9	8	10				4
36		9	Preston North End	2-2	Parry, Wheeler	25213		2			5	6			3	1	11						7	9		10				4
37		11	Sheffield Wednesday	2-3	Lofthouse(2)	16569		2			5				3	1	11						7	9		10				4
38		16	EVERTON	2-0	Stevens, Barrass(pen)	26722		2	3		5				6	1	11			4			7	9		6		10		8
39		23	Newcastle United	0-0		48194		2	3						6	1	11			4	5		7	9				10		8
40		27	HUDDERSFIELD TOWN	1-0	Holden	16184		2	3		5				6	1	11			4			7					10	8	9
41		30	BURNLEY	0-1		20671		2	3						5	1	11			4			7			6		10	9	8
42	May	4	Leicester City	0-4		12223		2	3	1	5				6		11			4			7	9				10		8

	Allcock T	Ball J	Banks T	Barnard A	Barrass MW	Bell E	Bingley W	Birch B	Edwards GB	Grieves KJ	Gubbins RG	Hanson S	Hassall HW	Hennin D	Higgins JO	Holden AD	Lofthouse N	Moir W	Neill TK	Parry RA	Pilling V	Stevens D	Webster H	Wheeler JE
Apps	1	42	25	1	40	21	4	2	38	8	9	33	24	9	2	39	31	32	3	28	1	14	21	34
Goals	1				5	1			1				8			1	15	8		9		3	7	3

F.A. Cup

#	Date		Opponent	Score	Scorers	Att	Ball J	Barrass MW	Bell E	Edwards GB	Hanson S	Lofthouse N	Moir W	Neill TK	Parry RA	Stevens D	Wheeler JE
3	Jan	8	MILLWALL	3-1	Moir(2,1pen), Parry	33597	2	5	6	3	1	7	9	8	11	10	4
4		29	Birmingham City	1-2	Moir	56800	2	5	6	3	1	7	9	8	11	10	4

Lancashire Cup

1	Nov	23	Bury	1-0
2	Mar	16	PRESTON NORTH END	2-2
2r	May	1	Preston North End	0-1

Manchester Cup

1	Oct	26	Bury	1-1
1r	Nov	10	BURY	3-4

Other Games

1	Aug	7	Edinburgh Select	2-3
2	Oct	5	Bury	3-2
3	Apr	19	Tranmere Rovers	2-2
4	May	7	Rot-Weiss Essen	1-3
5		11	Schalke 04	2-2
6		15	Athletic Bilbao	1-2
7		19	Royal Antwerp	1-2

FINAL TABLE

		Pl.	Home					Away					F.	A.	Pts
			W	D	L	F	A	W	D	L	F	A	(Total)		
1	Chelsea	42	11	5	5	43	29	9	7	5	38	28	81	57	52
2	Wolverhampton W.	42	13	5	3	58	30	6	5	10	31	40	89	70	48
3	Portsmouth	42	13	5	3	44	21	5	7	9	30	41	74	62	48
4	Sunderland	42	8	11	2	39	27	7	7	7	25	27	64	54	48
5	Manchester United	42	12	4	5	44	30	8	3	10	40	44	84	74	47
6	Aston Villa	42	11	3	7	38	31	9	4	8	34	42	72	73	47
7	Manchester City	42	11	5	5	45	36	7	5	9	31	33	76	69	46
8	Newcastle United	42	12	5	4	53	27	5	4	12	36	50	89	77	43
9	Arsenal	42	12	3	6	44	25	5	6	10	25	38	69	63	43
10	Burnley	42	11	3	7	29	19	6	6	9	22	29	51	48	43
11	Everton	42	9	6	6	32	24	7	4	10	30	44	62	68	42
12	Huddersfield Town	42	10	4	7	28	23	4	9	8	35	45	63	68	41
13	Sheffield United	42	10	3	8	41	34	7	4	10	29	52	70	86	41
14	Preston North End	42	8	5	8	47	33	8	3	10	36	31	83	64	40
15	Charlton Athletic	42	8	6	7	43	34	7	4	10	33	41	76	75	40
16	Tottenham Hotspur	42	9	4	8	42	35	7	4	10	30	38	72	73	40
17	West Bromwich Alb.	42	11	5	5	44	33	5	3	13	32	63	76	96	40
18	BOLTON WANDERERS	42	11	6	4	45	29	2	7	12	17	40	62	69	39
19	Blackpool	42	8	6	7	33	26	6	4	11	27	38	60	64	38
20	Cardiff City	42	9	4	8	41	38	4	7	10	21	38	62	76	37
21	Leicester City	42	9	6	6	43	32	3	5	13	31	54	74	86	35
22	Sheffield Wed.	42	7	7	7	42	38	1	3	17	21	62	63	100	26

1954-55 Season
(Back) Wheeler, Barrass, Hanson, Edwards, Ball, Banks
(Front) Moir, Lofthouse, Hassall, Parry, Holden

1955-56 Season
(Back) Ridding (Manager), Higgins, Ball, Wheeler, Grieves, Barrass, Hanson, Hennin, Edwards, Banks
(Front) Webster, Holden, Moir, Lofthouse, Stevens, Gubbins, Sproston (Trainer)

1955/56   8th in Division One

Manager: W.Ridding

#	Date	Opponent	Score	Scorers	Att	Allcock T	Ball J	Banks T	Bannister N	Barnard A	Barrass MW	Birch B	Dean J	Edwards GB	Grieves KJ	Gubbins RG	Hanson S	Hartle LR	Hennin D	Holden AD	Higgins JO	Lofthouse N	Moir W	Neill TK	Parry RA	Stevens D	Threlfall J	Webster H	Wheeler JE
1	Aug 20	Chelsea	2-0	Stevens, Holden	44454		2	3			5			6	1					7		9	8		11	10			4
2	27	CHARLTON ATHLETIC	1-3	Lofthouse	25989		2	3			5			6	1					7		9	8		11	10			4
3	31	Cardiff City	0-1		26973	8		3			5			6	1	11		2		7		9				10			4
4	Sep 3	ARSENAL	4-1	Lofthouse(3), Parry	26324			3			5			6	1	11		2		7		9			10	8			4
5	7	CARDIFF CITY	4-0	Lofthouse, Stevens, Parry(2)	25012			3			5			6	1	11		2		7		9			10	8			4
6	10	Portsmouth	3-3	Lofthouse(2), Stevens	30904			3			5			6	1	11		2		7		9			10	8			4
7	17	SUNDERLAND	0-3		33178			3			5			6	1	11		2		7		9			10	8			4
8	24	Aston Villa	2-0	Lofthouse(2)	28418			3			5	11		6	1			2		7		9			10	8			4
9	Oct 1	WOLVES	2-1	Stevens, Webster	34134			3			5			6	1	11		2		7					10	8		9	4
10	8	Tottenham Hotspur	3-0	Lofthouse, Gubbins(2)	35237			3			5			6	1	11		2		7		9			10	8			4
11	15	EVERTON	1-1	Stevens	32999			3			5			6	1	11		2		7		9			10	8			4
12	22	Burnley	0-2		23839			3			5			6	1	11		2		7					10	8		9	4
13	29	LUTON TOWN	4-0	Lofthouse(2), Holden(2)	26794			3			5			6	1	11		2		7		9			10	8			4
14	Nov 5	West Bromwich Albion	0-2		23651			3			5			6	1	11		2		7		9			10	8			4
15	12	MANCHESTER UNITED	3-1	Lofthouse(2), Parry	41829			3			5			6	1	11		2		7		9			10	8			4
16	19	Sheffield United	3-1	Lofthouse(2), Holden	21002			3			5			6	1	11		2		7		9			10	8			4
17	26	PRESTON NORTH END	0-0		32630			3			5			6	1	11		2		7		9			10	8			4
18	Dec 3	Newcastle United	0-3		36856			3			5			6	1	11		2		7		9			10	8			4
19	10	BIRMINGHAM CITY	6-0	Lofthouse(4), Wheeler, Stevens	15793			3			5			6	1	11		2		7		9			10	8			4
20	17	CHELSEA	4-0	Lofthouse(3), Gubbins	24129			3			5			6	1	11		2		7		9			10	8			4
21	24	Charlton Athletic	1-3	Parry	18746			3						6	1	11		2		7		9			10	8			4
22	26	MANCHESTER CITY	1-3	Hartle	43947			3						6	1	11		2		7	5	9			10	8			4
23	27	Manchester City	0-2		38407			3						6	1	11		2		7	5	9			10	8			4
24	31	Arsenal	1-3	Lofthouse	43757			3						6		11	1	2		7	5	9			10	8			4
25	Jan 2	HUDDERSFIELD TOWN	2-2	Lofthouse, Parry(pen)	39524			3						6		11	1	2		7	5	9			10	8			4
26	14	PORTSMOUTH	4-0	Gubbins, Parry, Lofthouse, Edwards	24093			3						6	1	11		2		7	5	9		4	10	8			
27	21	Sunderland	0-0		38871			3			5			6	1	11		2		7		9		4	10	8			
28	Feb 11	Wolves	2-4	Lofthouse, Stevens	24919			3			5		1	6		11		2		7		9			10	8			4
29	18	ASTON VILLA	1-0	Lofthouse	19737			3			5	11		6	1			2		7		9			10	8			4
30	25	Everton	0-1		47293			3	11		5			6	1			2		7		9			10	8			4
31	Mar 3	SHEFFIELD UNITED	2-1	Lofthouse, Stevens	20521			3			5	11		6	1			2		7		9			10	8			4
32	10	Luton Town	0-0		20432			3			5	11		6	1			2		7		9			10	8			4
33	17	WEST BROMWICH ALBION	4-0	Lofthouse(2), Stevens(2)	23603			3			5	11		6	1	10		2		7		9				8			4
34	21	TOTTENHAM HOTSPUR	3-2	Barrass(2,1pen), Edwards	10942			3			5	11		6	1	10		2		7		9				8			4
35	24	Manchester United	0-1		46346			3			5	11		6	1	10		2		7		9				8			4
36	30	Blackpool	0-0		34764			3			5	11		6	1			2	4	7					10	8			9
37	31	BURNLEY	0-1		29488	8		3				11		6	1	10		2		7	5			9					4
38	Apr 2	BLACKPOOL	1-3	Allcock	39208	8								6	1	11		2	4	7	5			10			3		9
39	7	Preston North End	1-0	Gubbins	18834	9						11		6	1	10		2		7	5					8	3		4
40	14	NEWCASTLE UNITED	3-2	Stevens, Neill, Gubbins	17378	9							1	6		11		2		7	5			10		8	3		4
41	21	Birmingham City	2-5	Stevens(2)	29640			3	7		5			6	1	11		2				9			10	8			4
42	28	Huddersfield Town	1-3	Lofthouse	18877			3		1	5	7		6		11		2				9			10	8			4
					Apps	5	2	39	2	1	32	11	2	42	37	34	2	40	2	40	10	36	2	6	33	39	3	2	40
					Goals	1					2			2		6		1		4		32		1	7	13		1	1

F.A. Cup

#	Date	Opponent	Score	Scorers	Att	Allcock T	Ball J	Banks T	Bannister N	Barnard A	Barrass MW	Birch B	Dean J	Edwards GB	Grieves KJ	Gubbins RG	Hanson S	Hartle LR	Hennin D	Holden AD	Higgins JO	Lofthouse N	Moir W	Neill TK	Parry RA	Stevens D	Threlfall J	Webster H	Wheeler JE
3	Jan 11	HUDDERSFIELD TOWN	3-0	Lofthouse, Stevens, Neill	20862			3						6		11	1	2		7		9		6	10	8			4
4	28	SHEFFIELD UNITED	1-2	Hartle	47105			3			5			6	1	11		2		7		9		4	10	8			4

Lancashire Cup

#	Date	Opponent	Score
1	Oct 24	Rochdale	1-1
1r	Nov 2	Rochdale	0-1

Manchester Cup

#	Date	Opponent	Score
1	Apr 30	MANCHESTER CITY	5-0

Competition abandoned

Other Games

#	Date	Opponent	Score
1	Oct 11	Bury	2-2
2	31	Rhyl	3-1
3	Nov 28	Accrington	1-3
4	Apr 18	International XI	2-3
5	May 10	Larvik Turn	3-3
6	12	Lyn Oslo	6-1
7	15	Brann Bergen	4-0
8	18	Stavanger	5-0

FINAL TABLE

		Pl.	Home W	D	L	F	A	Away W	D	L	F	A	F. (Total)	A.	Pts
1	Manchester United	42	18	3	0	51	20	7	7	7	32	31	83	51	60
2	Blackpool	42	13	4	4	56	27	7	5	9	30	35	86	62	49
3	Wolverhampton W.	42	15	2	4	51	27	5	7	9	38	38	89	65	49
4	Manchester City	42	11	5	5	40	27	7	5	9	42	42	82	69	46
5	Arsenal	42	13	4	4	38	22	5	6	10	22	39	60	61	46
6	Birmingham City	42	12	4	5	51	26	6	5	10	24	31	75	57	45
7	Burnley	42	11	3	7	37	20	7	5	9	27	34	64	54	44
8	BOLTON WANDERERS	42	13	3	5	50	24	5	4	12	21	34	71	58	43
9	Sunderland	42	10	8	3	44	36	7	1	13	36	59	80	95	43
10	Luton Town	42	12	4	5	44	27	5	4	12	22	37	66	64	42
11	Newcastle United	42	12	4	5	49	24	5	3	13	36	46	85	70	41
12	Portsmouth	42	9	8	4	46	38	7	1	13	32	47	78	85	41
13	West Bromwich Alb.	42	13	3	5	37	25	5	2	14	21	45	58	70	41
14	Charlton Athletic	42	13	2	6	47	26	4	4	13	28	55	75	81	40
15	Everton	42	11	5	5	37	29	4	5	12	18	40	55	69	40
16	Chelsea	42	10	4	7	32	26	4	7	10	32	51	64	77	39
17	Cardiff City	42	11	4	6	36	32	4	5	12	19	37	55	69	39
18	Tottenham Hotspur	42	9	4	8	37	33	6	3	12	24	38	61	71	37
19	Preston North End	42	6	5	10	32	36	8	3	13	41	36	73	72	36
20	Aston Villa	42	9	6	6	32	29	2	7	12	20	40	52	69	35
21	Huddersfield Town	42	9	4	8	32	30	5	3	13	22	53	54	83	35
22	Sheffield United	42	8	6	7	31	35	4	3	14	32	42	63	77	33

1956/57 9th in Division One

Manager: W.Ridding

#	Date		Opponent	Result	Scorers	Att	Allcock T	Bailey D	Ball J	Banks T	Barrass MW	Bell E	Birch B	Edisbury W	Edwards GB	Edwards M	Gubbins RG	Hartle LR	Hennin D	Higgins JO	Holden AD	Hopkinson E	Lofthouse N	Neill TK	Parry RA	Riley BF	Stanley G	Stevens D	Threlfall J	Webster H
1	Aug	18	BLACKPOOL	4-1	Lofthouse(3), Stevens	33310				3	5				6		11	2	4		7	1	9		10			8		
2		22	Sunderland	0-3		33307				3	5				6		11	2	4		7	1	9		10			8		
3		25	Everton	2-2	Lofthouse(2)	40816				3					6		11	2	4	5	7	1	9		10			8		
4	Sep	1	TOTTENHAM HOTSPUR	1-0	Lofthouse	30889				3					6		11	2	4	5	7	1	9		10			8		
5		5	SUNDERLAND	2-1	Lofthouse(2)	33786				3					6		11	2	4	5	7	1	9		10			8		
6		8	Leeds United	2-3	Lofthouse, Holden	40010				3					6		11	2	4	5	7	1	9		10			8		
7		12	CHARLTON ATHLETIC	2-0	Lofthouse, Holden	19846			3						6		11	2	4	5	7	1	9		10			8		
8		15	CARDIFF CITY	2-0	Lofthouse, Parry	28738			3						6		11	2	4	5	7	1	9		10			8		
9		20	Charlton Athletic	1-2	Lofthouse	13649			3						6		11	2	4	5	7	1	9		10			8		
10		22	WOLVES	0-3		35720			3						6		11	2	4	5	7	1	9		10			8		
11		29	Aston Villa	0-0		34402	8			3					6			2	4	5	7	1	9	10	11					
12	Oct	6	Birmingham City	0-0		29614	8			3					6			2	4	5	7	1	9	10	11					
13		13	WEST BROMWICH ALBION	1-1	Stevens	24969	8			3					6			2	4	5	7	1	9		11			10		
14		20	Preston North End	2-2	Lofthouse, Stevens	26994	8	11		3					6			2	4	5	7	1	9					10		
15		27	CHELSEA	2-2	Stevens, Gubbins	21299	9			3			7		6		10	2	4	5	11	1						8		
16	Nov	3	Sheffield Wednesday	2-1	Gubbins, Allcock	23968	9			3					6		11	2	4	5	7	1			10			8		
17		10	MANCHESTER UNITED	2-0	Allcock, Holden	39922	9			3					6		11	2	4	5	7	1			10			8		
18		17	Arsenal	0-3		33377	9			3					6		11	2	4	5	7	1			10			8		
19		24	BURNLEY	3-0	Stevens, Parry, Gubbins	26062	9			3					6		11	2	4	5	7	1			10			8		
20	Dec	1	Portsmouth	1-1	Stevens	19021	9			3					6		11	2	4	5	7	1						8		10
21		8	NEWCASTLE UNITED	3-1	Lofthouse(2), Webster	25131				3					6		11	2	4	5	7	1	9					8		10
22		15	Blackpool	2-4	Stevens, Lofthouse	17556				3					6		11	2	4	5	7	1	9		10			8		
23		25	Manchester City	3-1	Stevens, Lofthouse(2)	19731									6		11	2	4	5	7	1	9		10			8	3	
24		26	MANCHESTER CITY	1-0	Stevens	20856	10								6		11	2	4	5	7	1	9					8	3	
25		29	Tottenham Hotspur	0-4		42030	10								6		11	2	4	5	7	1	9					8	3	
26	Jan	12	LEEDS UNITED	5-3	Holden, Gubbins, Lofthouse(2), Dunn(og)	25705									6		11	2	4	5	7	1	9					8	3	10
27		19	Cardiff City	0-2		12810									6		11	2	4	5	7	1	9					8	3	10
28	Feb	2	Wolves	2-3	Stevens, Webster	30520									6			2	4	5	7	1	9		11			8	3	10
29		9	ASTON VILLA	0-0		21012									6			2	4	5	7	1	9		11			8	3	10
30		20	BIRMINGHAM CITY	3-1	Lofthouse, Parry, Warhurst(og)	11284						6			3		11	2	4	5	7	1	9		10			8		
31		23	Chelsea	2-2	Hennin, Lofthouse	13647						6			3		11	2	4	5	7	1	9		10			8		
32	Mar	2	PRESTON NORTH END	2-3	Stevens, Lofthouse	37090						6			5		11	2	4		7	1	9		10			8	3	
33		9	Newcastle United	0-4		34073			3			6			5		10	2	4		7	1	9		11			8		
34		16	SHEFFIELD WEDNESDAY	3-2	Lofthouse, Ball, Hennin*	18424			3			6			5		10	2	4		7	1	9			11		8		
35		25	Manchester United	2-0	Parry, Foulkes(og)	61100			3			6			5		11	2	4		7	1	9		10			8		
36		30	ARSENAL	2-1	Stevens, Lofthouse	23897			3			6			5		11	2	4		7	1	9		10			8		
37	Apr	6	Burnley	0-1		23250			3			6			5		11	2	4		7	1	9		10			8		
38		13	PORTSMOUTH	1-1	Parry	16969						6		3	5		11	2	4		7	1	9		10			8		
39		19	LUTON TOWN	2-2	Lofthouse((2))	18666					3	6	7		5			2	4		11	1	9		10			8		
40		20	West Bromwich Albion	2-3	Stevens, Birch	18351						6	7		5			2			11	1	9		10		4	8	3	
41		22	Luton Town	0-1		13396			2	3		6	7		5						11	1	9				4	8		10
42		27	Everton	1-1	Lofthouse	16016	10			3		6	7		5	6		2				1	9				4	8		10

* Some records credit Lofthouse with two goals, the goal in question coming from a shot by Hennin that was caught by the goalkeeper to barge both player and ball over the line.

| Apps | | | | | | | 13 | 1 | 10 | 21 | 2 | 12 | 5 | 1 | 42 | 1 | 32 | 41 | 39 | 29 | 42 | 42 | 36 | 2 | 31 | 1 | 3 | 39 | 9 | 8 |
| Goals | | | | | | | 2 | | 1 | | | | | | 1 | | 4 | | 2 | | 4 | | 28 | | 5 | | | 13 | | 2 |

Three own goals

F.A. Cup

| 3 | Jan | 5 | BLACKPOOL | 2-3 | Hennin(pen), Gubbins | 42515 | | | | | | | | | 6 | | 11 | 2 | 4 | 5 | 7 | 1 | 9 | | | | | 8 | 3 | 10 |

Lancashire Cup

1	Mar	12	Bury	2-5

Manchester Cup

SF	Apr	29	OLDHAM ATHLETIC	2-4

Other Games

1	Oct	2	Bury	2-2
2	Jan	26	LIVERPOOL	5-3
3	Feb	16	Hearts	6-3
4	Mar	10	La Gantoise	1-1
5	Apr	23	ALL STARS XI*	3-0
6		29	Tranmere Rovers	2-0

* Harold Hassall testimonial

FINAL TABLE

Pos	Team	Pl.	Home W	D	L	F	A	Away W	D	L	F	A	F (Total)	A	Pts
1	Manchester United	42	14	4	3	55	25	14	4	3	48	29	103	54	64
2	Tottenham Hotspur	42	15	4	2	70	24	7	8	6	34	32	104	56	56
3	Preston North End	42	15	4	2	50	19	8	6	7	34	37	84	56	56
4	Blackpool	42	14	3	4	55	26	8	6	7	38	39	93	65	53
5	Arsenal	42	12	5	4	45	21	9	3	9	40	48	85	69	50
6	Wolverhampton W.	42	17	2	2	70	29	3	6	12	24	41	94	70	48
7	Burnley	42	14	5	2	41	21	5	12	15	29	56	56	50	46
8	Leeds United	42	10	8	3	42	18	5	6	10	30	45	72	63	44
9	BOLTON WANDERERS	42	13	6	2	42	23	3	6	12	23	42	65	65	44
10	Aston Villa	42	10	8	3	45	25	4	7	10	20	30	65	55	43
11	West Bromwich Alb.	42	8	8	5	31	25	6	6	9	28	36	59	61	42
12	Chelsea	42	7	8	6	43	36	6	5	10	30	37	73	73	39
12	Birmingham City	42	12	5	4	52	25	3	4	14	17	44	69	69	39
14	Sheffield Wed.	42	14	3	4	55	29	2	3	16	27	59	82	88	38
15	Everton	42	10	5	6	34	28	4	5	12	27	51	61	79	38
16	Luton Town	42	10	4	7	32	26	4	5	12	26	50	58	76	37
17	Newcastle United	42	10	5	6	43	31	4	3	14	24	56	67	87	36
18	Manchester City	42	10	2	9	48	42	3	7	11	30	46	78	88	35
19	Portsmouth	42	8	6	7	37	35	2	7	12	25	57	62	92	33
20	Sunderland	42	9	5	7	40	30	3	3	15	27	58	67	88	32
21	Cardiff City	42	7	6	8	35	34	3	3	15	18	54	53	88	29
22	Charlton Athletic	42	7	3	11	31	44	2	1	18	31	76	62	120	22

1956-57 Season

(Back) Taylor (Coach), Bell, Ball, Banks, Hopkinson, Hennin, Edwards, Higgins, Webster, Sproston (Trainer)
(Front) Ridding (Manager), Allcock, Holden, Stevens, Lofthouse, Parry, Gubbins, Hartle

1957-58 Season

(Back) Hennin, Hartle, Higgins, Hopkinson, Banks, Edwards
(Front) Birch, Stevens, Gubbins, Parry, Holden

1957/58 15th in Division One

Manager: W.Ridding

#		Date	Opponent	Score	Scorers	Att	Allcock T	Ball J	Banks T	Bell E	Birch B	Cunliffe JG	Deakin P	Dean J	Edwards GB	Edwards M	Edisbury W	Gubbins RG	Hartle LR	Hennin D	Higgins JO	Hill F	Holden AD	Hopkinson E	Lofthouse N	Parry RA	Riley BF	Stanley G	Stevens D
1	Aug	24	Luton Town	0-1		17591			3	4					6			11	2		5		7	1	9	10			8
2		28	Wolves	1-6	Lofthouse	30790			3	4					6			11	2		5		7	1	9	10			8
3		31	BLACKPOOL	3-0	Stevens, Allcock(2)	31491	9		3		7				6				2	4	5		11	1		10			8
4	Sep	4	WOLVES	1-1	Stevens	25845	9			6	7				3				2	4	5		11	1		10			8
5		7	Leicester City	3-2	Holden, Stevens, Lofthouse	30033		2		6					3					4	5		11	1	7	10			8
6		11	SUNDERLAND	2-2	Parry, Allcock	17647	9	2		6					3					4	5		11	1	7	10			8
7		14	MANCHESTER UNITED	4-0	Stevens,Lofthouse,Parry(p),Birch	48003		2		6	7				3					4	5		11	1	9	10			8
8		18	Sunderland	2-1	Lofthouse, Parry	30021	8			6	7				3				2	4	5		11	1	9	10			
9		21	Leeds United	1-2	Parry(pen)	18379	8			6	7				3				2	4	5		11	1	9	10			
10		28	PORTSMOUTH	1-0	Stevens	13184					7				3	6			2	4	5		11	1	9	10			8
11	Oct	5	ARSENAL	0-1		20212	9				7				3	6		8	2	4	5		11	1		10			
12		12	West Bromwich Albion	2-2	Sanders(og), Stevens	31370			3		7				6				2	4	5		11	1	9	10			8
13		19	TOTTENHAM HOTSPUR	3-2	Lofthouse(2), Parry	20381			3				1		6				2	4	5		7		9	10	11		8
14		26	Birmingham City	1-5	Parry*	26225			3						6				2	4	5		7	1	9	10	11		8
15	Nov	2	SHEFFIELD WEDNESDAY	5-4	Holden,Lofthouse(2),Parry,Birch	18072			3		7				6				2	4	5		11	1	9	10			8
16		9	Manchester City	1-2	Birch	34147					7		1		3				2	4	5		11		9	10			8
17		16	NOTTINGHAM FOREST	2-0	Holden, Lofthouse	24562					7				3				2	4	5		11	1	9	10			8
18		23	Preston North End	0-3		28036					7				3				2	4	5		11	1	9	10			8
19		30	CHELSEA	3-3	Stevens(2), Parry	18815					7				3				2	4	5		11	1	9	10			8
20	Dec	7	Newcastle United	2-1	Lofthouse, Parry	29886					7				6		3		2	4	5		1		9	10			8
21		14	BURNLEY	2-1	Stevens, Parry	20197			3		7				6				2	4	5		1	1	9	10			8
22		21	LUTON TOWN	1-2	Hennin	16754			3		7				6				2	4	5		11	1	9	10			8
23		25	Everton	1-1	Birch	29584			3		7				6				2	4	5		11	1	9	10			8
24		26	EVERTON	1-5	Lofthouse	23462			3		7				6				2		5		11	1	9	10		4	8
25		28	Blackpool	3-2	Lofthouse, Parry, Armfield(og)	19858			3		7								2	4	5		8	1	9	10	11	6	
26	Jan	11	LEICESTER CITY	2-3	Stevens, Parry	17884			3						6			7	2	4	5		11	1	9	10			8
27		18	Manchester United	2-7	Stevens, Lofthouse	41360			3		7				6				2	4	5			1	9	10	11		8
28	Feb	1	LEEDS UNITED	0-2		18558	9		3		7				6			11	2		5			1				4	8
29		8	Portsmouth	2-2	Parry, Hennin	21950			3		7				6			11	2	4	5			1		10			8
30		18	Arsenal	2-1	Lofthouse, Gubbins	28425			3						6			11	2	4	5		7	1	9	10			8
31		22	WEST BROMWICH ALBION	2-2	Stevens, Gubbins	19132	9		3		7				6			11	2	4	5		1			10			8
32	Mar	8	BIRMINGHAM CITY	1-0	Lofthouse	18309			3		7				6				2		5		11	1	9	10		4	8
33		12	Tottenham Hotspur	1-4	Parry	22978			3		7			1	6				2		5		11			10			8
34		15	Sheffield Wednesday	0-1		24085			3		7			1	6			9	2	4	5		11			10			8
35		29	Nottingham Forest	0-0		24060			3		7			1	6			9	2	4	5		11			10			8
36	Apr	4	ASTON VILLA	4-0	Stevens, Hennin(3,1pen)	19026			3		7			1	6			10	2	9	5		11					4	8
37		5	MANCHESTER CITY	0-2		27733			3		7			1	6			10	2	9	5		11					4	8
38		8	Aston Villa	0-4		32745			3		7		10	1	6			9	2		5		11					4	8
39		12	Chelsea	2-2	Gubbins, Ball(pen)	27994		3			7		10	1	6			9	2		5		11	1				4	8
40		19	NEWCASTLE UNITED	1-1	Lofthouse	19284			3		7			1	6			11	2		5	8			9	10		4	
41		21	PRESTON NORTH END	0-4		24067			3		7			1	6				2	4	5		11	1	9	10		4	8
42		26	Burnley	1-3	Lofthouse	17419			3		7				6				2	4	5		11	1	9	10			8

* Some records show scorer as Stevens who deflected Parry's shot after only 25 seconds of the game.

	Allcock T	Ball J	Banks T	Bell E	Birch B	Cunliffe JG	Deakin P	Dean J	Edwards GB	Edwards M	Edisbury W	Gubbins RG	Hartle LR	Hennin D	Higgins JO	Hill F	Holden AD	Hopkinson E	Lofthouse N	Parry RA	Riley BF	Stanley G	Stevens D
Apps	9	4	28	8	34	4	2	9	41	2	1	15	39	32	42	1	37	33	31	38	4	11	37
Goals	3	1			4							3		5			3		17	14			13

F.A. Cup

Two own goals

#		Date	Opponent	Score	Scorers	Att	Allcock T	Ball J	Banks T	Bell E	Birch B	Cunliffe JG	Deakin P	Dean J	Edwards GB	Edwards M	Edisbury W	Gubbins RG	Hartle LR	Hennin D	Higgins JO	Hill F	Holden AD	Hopkinson E	Lofthouse N	Parry RA	Riley BF	Stanley G	Stevens D
3	Jan	4	Preston North End	3-0	Stevens, Parry(2)	32641			3		7				6				2	4	5		11	1	9	10			8
4		25	York City	0-0		23460			3		7	6							2		5		11	1	9	10		4	8
4r		29	YORK CITY	3-0	Birch, Allcock(2)	35194	9		3		7	6							2		5		11	1		10		4	8
5	Feb	15	STOKE CITY	3-1	Lofthouse, Stevens, Parry	56667			3		7				6				2	4	5		11	1	9	10			8
6	Mar	1	WOLVES	2-1	Stevens, Parry	56306			3		7				6				2	4	5		11	1	9	10			8
SF		22	Blackburn Rovers*	2-1	Gubbins(2)	74800			3		7				6			9	2	4	5		11	1		10			8
F	May	3	Manchester United+	2-0	Lofthouse(2)	100000			3		7				6				2	4	5		11	1	9	10			8

* Played at Maine Road, Manchester.   + Played at We.......

Lancashire Cup

1	Nov	6	Manchester United	1-3

Manchester Cup

SF	Mar	18	Manchester City	0-1

Other Games

1	Oct	14	HEARTS	1-1
2	Nov	4	CDSA MOSCOW	3-1
3		28	Feyenoord	0-3
4	Dec	9	BLACKBURN ROVERS	4-1
5	May	8	Fortuna Geleen	0-2
6		10	Dusseldorf/Rotwess Essen Select	3-2
7		13	F.C. Sochaux	0-2
8		15	Olympique Lyonnais	3-2
9		21	Flamengo de Rio	1-1
10		23	Racing Club Paris	1-2

FINAL TABLE

		Pl.	Home W	D	L	F	A	Away W	D	L	F	A	F. (Total)	A. (Total)	Pts
1	Wolverhampton W.	42	17	3	1	60	21	11	5	5	43	26	103	47	64
2	Preston North End	42	18	2	1	63	14	8	5	8	37	37	100	51	59
3	Tottenham Hotspur	42	13	4	4	58	33	8	5	8	35	44	93	77	51
4	West Bromwich Alb.	42	14	4	3	59	29	4	10	7	33	41	92	70	50
5	Manchester City	42	14	4	3	58	33	8	1	12	46	67	104	100	49
6	Burnley	42	16	2	3	52	21	5	3	13	28	53	80	74	44
7	Blackpool	42	11	2	8	47	35	8	4	9	33	32	80	67	44
8	Luton Town	42	13	5	3	45	22	6	3	12	24	41	69	63	44
9	Manchester United	42	10	4	7	45	31	6	7	8	40	44	85	75	43
10	Nottingham Forest	42	10	4	7	41	27	6	6	9	28	36	69	63	42
11	Chelsea	42	10	5	6	47	34	5	7	9	36	45	83	79	42
12	Arsenal	42	10	4	7	48	39	6	3	12	25	64	73	85	39
13	Birmingham City	42	8	6	7	43	37	6	5	10	33	52	76	89	39
14	Aston Villa	42	12	4	5	46	26	4	3	14	27	60	73	86	39
15	BOLTON WANDERERS	42	9	5	7	38	35	5	5	11	27	52	65	87	38
16	Everton	42	5	9	7	34	35	8	2	11	31	40	65	75	37
17	Leeds United	42	10	6	5	33	23	4	3	14	18	40	51	63	37
18	Leicester City	42	11	4	6	59	41	3	1	17	32	71	91	112	33
19	Newcastle United	42	6	4	11	38	42	6	4	11	35	39	73	81	32
20	Portsmouth	42	10	4	7	45	34	2	2	17	28	54	73	88	32
21	Sunderland	42	7	7	7	32	33	3	5	13	22	64	54	97	32
22	Sheffield Wed.	42	12	2	7	45	40	0	5	16	24	52	69	92	31

1958/59 4th in Division One

Manager: W.Ridding

#		Date	Opponent	Score	Scorers	Att	Banks T	Bannister N	Birch B	Deakin P	Dean J	Edwards GB	Edwards JG	Edwards M	Farrimond S	Gubbins RG	Hartle LR	Hennin D	Higgins JO	Hill F	Holden AD	Hopkinson E	Lofthouse N	Parry RA	Riley BF	Stanley G	Stevens D
1	Aug	23	LEEDS UNITED	4-0	Birch, Parry, Lofthouse(2)	25922	3		7			6					2	4	5		11	1	9	10			8
2		27	Manchester City	3-3	Birch, Parry(pen), Lofthouse	40844	3		7			6					2	4	5		11	1	9	10			8
3		30	West Bromwich Albion	1-1	G.B.Edwards	37244	3		7			6					2	4	5		11	1	9	10			8
4	Sep	3	MANCHESTER CITY	4-1	Birch, Stevens, Lofthouse, Parry	39727	3		7			6					2	4	5		11	1	9	10			8
5		6	BIRMINGHAM CITY	2-0	G.B.Edwards, Lofthouse	24707	3		7			6					2	4	5		11	1	9	10			8
6		9	Arsenal	1-6	Parry(pen)	45276	3		7			6					2	4	5		11	1	9	10			8
7		13	Luton Town	0-0		19699	3		7			6				9	2		5		11	1		10		4	8
8		17	ARSENAL	2-1	Birch, Lofthouse	42200	3		7			6					2		5		11	1	9	10		4	8
9		20	NOTTINGHAM FOREST	3-2	Stevens, Lofthouse(2)	28486	3		7			6					2		5		11	1	9	10		4	8
10		27	BURNLEY	1-2	Lofthouse	32359	3		7			6					2		5		11	1	9	10			8
11	Oct	4	Preston North End	0-0		28769		7				6		3			2	4	5	8	11	1	9	10			
12		11	Chelsea	1-0	Lofthouse	49229		7				3		6			2	4	5	10	11	1	9				8
13		18	BLACKPOOL	4-0	Stevens, Holden, Hill(2,1pen)	37045		7				3		6			2	4	5	10	11	1	9				8
14		25	Aston Villa	1-2	Stevens	28740		7				3		6			2	4	5	10	11	1		9			8
15	Nov	1	WEST HAM UNITED	0-2		31067		7				3		6			2	4	5	10	11	1					8
16		8	Tottenham Hotspur	1-1	Lofthouse	39820	3		7			6					2	4	5	10	11	1	9				8
17		15	MANCHESTER UNITED	6-3	G.B.Edwards,Stevens(2),Parry(p),Gubbins	33358	3		7			6				9	2	4	5		11	1		10			8
18		22	Wolves	2-1	Stevens, Lofthouse	33489	3		7			6					2	4	5		11	1	9	10			8
19		29	PORTSMOUTH	2-1	Stevens, Lofthouse	20624	3		7			6					2	4	5		11	1	9	10			8
20	Dec	6	Blackburn Rovers	1-1	Stevens	38027	3		7			6						4	5		11	1	9	10		4	8
21		13	NEWCASTLE UNITED	1-1	Stevens	23020	3		7			6					2	4	5		11	1	9	10			8
22		20	Leeds United	4-3	G.B.Edwards,Lofthouse(2),Gibson(og)	28534	3		7			6					2	4	5		11	1	9	10			8
23		26	Everton	0-1		61692	3		7			6					2	4	5	8	11	1	9	10			
24		27	EVERTON	0-3		37263	3		7			6					2	4	5	8	11	1	9	10			
25	Jan	3	WEST BROMWICH ALBION	2-1	Lofthouse(2)	27847	3		7			6					2	8	5	8	11	1	9	10		4	
26		31	LUTON TOWN	4-2	Lofthouse(3), Holden	27787	3		7			6					2	4	5		11	1	9	10			
27	Feb	7	Nottingham Forest	0-3		29703	3		7			6					2	9	5	8	11	1		10		4	
28		21	PRESTON NORTH END	2-1	Birch, Hill	16472	3		7			6				9	2	4	5	8		1		10		6	8
29	Mar	4	CHELSEA	6-0	Lofthouse(2), Parry, Hill(3,1pen)	24258	3		7			6					2	4	5	8	11	1	9	10			
30		7	Blackpool	0-4		21072	3		7			6					2	4	5	8	11	1	9				8
31		18	ASTON VILLA	1-3	Lofthouse	21808	3		7	1		6					2	4	5	10	11						8
32		21	West Ham United	3-4	Stevens, Parry, Hill	27722	3					6					2	4	5	10	7	1	9	11			8
33		27	LEICESTER CITY	3-3	Ogilvie(og), Stevens, Lofthouse	21212	3	7				6					2	4			11	1	9	10			8
34		28	TOTTENHAM HOTSPUR	4-1	Parry(2), Stevens, Baker(og)	21384	3	7				6	5				2	4			11	1	9	10			8
35		30	Leicester City	0-0		20329	3	7				6	5				2	4			11	1	9	10			
36	Apr	4	Manchester United	0-3		61528	3	7				6	5				2	4			11	1	9	10			
37		8	Birmingham City	3-1	Birch, Riley, Lofthouse	24608	3		7		1	5					2	4					9	10	11	6	8
38		11	WOLVES	2-2	Lofthouse, Parry(pen)	26019	3		7		1	5					2	4	5	8			9	10	11		
39		14	Burnley	1-0	Lofthouse	23664	3		7			6					2	4	5			1	9	10			
40		18	Portsmouth	1-0	Lofthouse	14161	3		7		1	6					2	4	5	10			9		11		
41		22	Newcastle United	0-2		17451	3			7		6					2	4	5			1	9	10	11		
42		25	BLACKBURN ROVERS	3-1	Lofthouse, Parry(2,1pen)	18268	3					6				11	2	4	5	7		1	9	10			
			Apps				37	11	28	1	3	41	3	4	1	4	41	38	38	18	37	39	37	37	3	9	32
			Goals						6			4				2				7	2		29	12	1		13

Three own goals

F.A. Cup

#		Date	Opponent	Score	Scorers	Att	Banks T	Bannister N	Birch B	Deakin P	Dean J	Edwards GB	Edwards JG	Edwards M	Farrimond S	Gubbins RG	Hartle LR	Hennin D	Higgins JO	Hill F	Holden AD	Hopkinson E	Lofthouse N	Parry RA	Riley BF	Stanley G	Stevens D
3	Jan	10	Scunthorpe United	2-0	Lofthouse(2)	23708	3		7			6					2	8	5		11	1	9	10		4	
4		24	Wolves	2-1	Lofthouse, Parry(pen)	55921	3		7			6					2	4	5		11	1	9	10			8
5	Feb	14	PRESTON NORTH END	2-2	Birch, Parry	58692	3		7			6					2	4	5		11	1	9	10			8
5r		18	Preston North End*	1-1	Holden	36866	3		7			6					2	4	5		11	1	9	10			8
5/2r		23	Preston North End+	1-0	Lofthouse	51090	3		7			6					2	4			11	1	9	10		6	8
6		28	Nottingham Forest	1-2	Birch	45000	3		7			6					2	4			11	1	9	10		6	8

* After extra time.   + Played at Ewood Park, Blackburn.

Lancashire Cup

1	Oct	27	BURY	3-2
2	Feb	11	Liverpool	0-3

Manchester Cup (Did not enter)

Other Games - South African Tour

1	May	16	Southern Transvaal	2-1
2		20	Eastern Transvaal	1-2
3		23	Natal	0-1
4		27	Border F.A.	6-1
5		30	Western Province	3-0
6	Jun	1	Northern Transvaal	2-1
7		6	South Africa	1-0
8		8	South Africa	2-1
9		17	Southern Rhodesia	5-0
10		21	Northern Rhodesia	5-3

	FINAL TABLE	Pl.	Home					Away					F.	A.	Pts
			W	D	L	F	A	W	D	L	F	A	(Total)		
1	Wolverhampton W.	42	15	3	3	68	19	13	2	6	42	30	110	49	61
2	Manchester United	42	14	4	3	58	27	10	3	8	45	39	103	66	55
3	Arsenal	42	14	3	4	53	29	7	5	9	35	39	88	68	50
4	BOLTON WANDERERS	42	14	3	4	56	30	6	7	8	23	36	79	66	50
5	West Bromwich Alb.	42	8	5	6	41	33	10	6	5	47	35	88	68	49
6	West Ham United	42	15	3	3	59	29	6	3	12	26	41	85	70	48
7	Burnley	42	11	4	6	41	29	8	6	7	40	41	81	70	48
8	Blackpool	42	12	5	4	39	13	6	4	11	27	36	66	49	47
9	Birmingham City	42	14	1	6	54	35	6	5	10	30	33	84	68	46
10	Blackburn Rovers	42	12	3	6	48	28	5	7	9	28	42	76	70	44
11	Newcastle United	42	11	3	7	40	29	6	4	11	40	51	80	80	41
12	Preston North End	42	9	3	9	40	39	8	4	9	30	38	70	77	41
13	Nottingham Forest	42	9	4	8	37	32	8	2	11	34	42	71	74	40
14	Chelsea	42	13	2	6	52	37	5	2	14	25	61	77	98	40
15	Leeds United	42	8	7	6	28	27	7	2	12	29	47	57	74	39
16	Everton	42	11	3	7	39	38	6	1	14	32	49	71	87	38
17	Luton Town	42	11	6	4	50	26	1	7	13	18	45	68	71	37
18	Tottenham Hotspur	42	10	3	8	56	42	3	7	11	29	53	85	95	36
19	Leicester City	42	7	6	8	34	36	4	4	13	33	62	67	98	32
20	Manchester City	42	8	7	6	40	32	3	2	16	24	63	64	95	31
21	Aston Villa	42	8	5	8	31	33	3	3	15	27	54	58	87	30
22	Portsmouth	42	5	4	12	38	47	1	5	15	26	65	64	112	21

1959/60 6th in Division One

Manager: W.Ridding

#		Date	Opponent	Score	Scorers	Att.	Banks T	Bannister B	Birch B	Bollands JF	Cunliffe JG	Deakin P	Dean J	Edwards GB	Edwards M	Farrimond S	Gubbins RG	Hartle LR	Hennin D	Higgins JO	Hill F	Holden AD	Hopkinson E	Oxtoby R	Parry RA	Phythian ER	Stanley G	Stevens D
1	Aug	22	Blackpool	2-3	Hill, Parry(pen)	29216	3							6			9	2	4	5	10	7	1		11			8
2		26	BLACKBURN ROVERS	0-3		42324	3							6			9	2	4	5	10	7	1		11			8
3		29	EVERTON	2-1	Stevens, Parry	26792	3	7						6				2		5	9	11	1		10		4	8
4		31	Blackburn Rovers	0-1		39039	3	7						6				2		5	9	11	1		10		4	8
5	Sep	5	Luton Town	0-0		15604	3	7						6				2		5	8	11	1		10		4	9
6		9	ARSENAL	0-1		32571	3	7						6				2		5	8	11	1		10		4	9
7		12	WEST HAM UNITED	5-1	Banks, Stevens, Hill, Bannister(2)	24240	3	7						6				2		5	8	11	1		10		4	9
8		15	Arsenal	1-2	McCullough(og)	38634	3	7						6				2		5	8	11	1		10		4	9
9		19	FULHAM	3-2	Stevens, Hill, Lampe(og)	24751	3	7						6				2		5	8	11	1		10		4	9
10		26	Nottingham Forest	0-2		28930	3	7						6				2	4	5	8	11	1		10			9
11	Oct	3	SHEFFIELD WEDNESDAY	1-0	Parry	23990	3	7						6				2	4	5	8	11	1		10			9
12		10	Chelsea	2-0	Parry, Hill	28707	3	7						6	9			2	4	5	8	11	1		10			
13		17	WEST BROMWICH ALBION	0-0		22581	3	7					1	6				2	4	5	8	11			10			9
14		24	Newcastle United	2-0	Parry(2)	34679			7					6		3		2	9	5	8	11	1		10		4	
15		31	LEEDS UNITED	1-1	Hennin	20183			7					6		3		2	9	5	8	11	1		10		4	
16	Nov	7	Tottenham Hotspur	2-0	Stevens, Parry	41909			7					6		3		2		5	8	11	1		10		4	9
17		14	MANCHESTER UNITED	1-1	Stevens	37892			7					6		3		2		5	8	11	1		10		4	9
18		21	Preston North End	0-1		28723			7						6	3		2		5	8	11	1		10		4	9
19		28	LEICESTER CITY	3-1	Stevens, Hartle(pen), Parry	19834			7						6	3		2		5	8	11	1		10		4	9
20	Dec	5	Burnley	0-4		26510			7						6	3		2		5	8	11	1		10		6	9
21		12	BIRMINGHAM CITY	4-1	Holden, Stevens, Parry(2)	16074			7							3		2	4	5	8	11	1		10		6	9
22		19	BLACKPOOL	0-3		17308			7							3		2	4	5	8	11	1		10		6	9
23		26	WOLVES	2-1	Hartle(pen), Stevens	36039			7							3		2	4	5	8	11	1		10		6	9
24		28	Wolves	1-0	Birch	28424			7							3		2	4	5	8	11	1		10		6	9
25	Jan	2	Everton	1-0	Stevens	37513			7							3		2	4	5	8	11	1		10		6	9
26		23	West Ham United	2-1	Stevens, Parry	21155			7							3		2	4	5	8	11	1		10		6	9
27	Feb	6	Fulham	1-1	Birch	24743			9			8				3		2	4	5		11	1				6	10
28		13	NOTTINGHAM FOREST	1-1	Stanley	16218			9			8	1			3		2	4	5		11					6	10
29		24	Sheffield Wednesday	0-1		34464			7				1			3		2	4	5	8	11				9	6	10
30		27	BURNLEY	2-1	Hartle, Birch	28772			7	1		8				3		2	4	5	10	11					6	9
31	Mar	5	West Bromwich Albion	1-1	Holden	23707			7	1		8				3		2	4	5	10	11					6	9
32		9	LUTON TOWN	2-2	Hill, Birch	14791			7	1						3		2	4	5	8	11					6	9
33		12	NEWCASTLE UNITED	1-4	Stevens	24648	6		7	1						3		2		5	8	11			10		4	9
34		19	Birmingham City	5-2	Stevens, Hill(2), Bannister, Hartle(p)	24183	3	7		1	6							2			8	11		5	10		4	9
35		26	TOTTENHAM HOTSPUR	2-1	Holden, Parry	31106	3		7	1	6							2			8	11		5	10		4	9
36	Apr	2	Manchester United	0-2		45482	3		7	1	6							2			8	11		5	10		4	9
37		9	PRESTON NORTH END	2-1	Hartle(pen), Stevens	30816	3		7	1	6	10						2		5	8	11					4	9
38		15	Manchester City	0-1		50053	3		7	1	6							2		5	8	11					4	9
39		16	Leeds United	0-1		19272			7	1	6					3		2		5	8	11			10		4	9
40		18	MANCHESTER CITY	3-1	Holden, Stevens, Birch	35591			7	1	6	10				3		2		5	8	11					4	9
41		23	CHELSEA	2-0	Hill, Birch	19432			7	1	6	10				3		2		5	8	11					4	9
42		30	Leicester City	2-1	Deakin(2)	19527	3		7	1	6	10						2		5	8	11					4	9
			Apps				20	12	30	13	9	8	3	17	4	23	2	35	27	39	40	42	26	3	33	1	36	39
			Goals				1	3	6			2						5	1		8	4			12		1	14

Two own goals

F.A. Cup

3	Jan	9	Bury	1-1	Parry	35000		7				3	2	4	5	8	11	1	10	6	9
3r		13	BURY*	4-2	Stevens, Parry(2), Birch	43616		7				3	2	4	5	8	11	1	10	6	9
4		30	West Bromwich Albion	0-2		36207		7				3	2	4	5	8	11	1	10	6	9

* After extra time

Lancashire Cup

1	Dec	9	PRESTON NORTH END	2-5

Manchester Cup (Did not enter)

Other Games

1	Oct	19	Hibernian	2-5
2	May	17	Royal Beerschot	1-1
3		20	Borussia Dortmund	1-0
4		22	VFB Stuttgart	3-2
5		26	Seville	1-2
6		29	Borussia Dortmund*	2-3

* Played in Seville

	FINAL TABLE	Pl.		Home					Away					F.	A.	Pts
			W	D	L	F	A	W	D	L	F	A	(Total)			
1	Burnley	42	15	2	4	52	28	9	5	7	33	33	85	61	55	
2	Wolverhampton W.	42	15	3	3	63	28	9	3	9	43	39	106	67	54	
3	Tottenham Hotspur	42	10	6	5	43	24	11	5	5	43	26	86	50	53	
4	West Bromwich Alb.	42	12	4	5	48	25	7	7	7	35	32	83	57	49	
5	Sheffield Wed.	42	12	7	2	48	20	7	4	10	32	39	80	59	49	
6	BOLTON WANDERERS	42	12	5	4	37	27	8	3	10	22	24	59	51	48	
7	Manchester United	42	13	4	4	53	30	6	4	11	49	50	102	80	45	
8	Newcastle United	42	10	5	6	42	32	8	3	10	40	46	82	78	44	
9	Preston North End	42	10	6	5	43	34	6	6	9	36	42	79	76	44	
10	Fulham	42	12	4	5	42	28	5	6	10	31	52	73	80	44	
11	Blackpool	42	9	6	6	32	32	6	4	11	27	39	59	71	40	
12	Leicester City	42	8	6	7	38	32	5	7	9	28	43	66	75	39	
13	Arsenal	42	9	5	7	39	38	6	4	11	29	42	68	80	39	
14	West Ham United	42	12	3	6	47	33	4	3	14	28	58	75	91	38	
15	Everton	42	13	3	5	50	20	0	8	13	23	58	73	78	37	
16	Manchester City	42	11	2	8	47	34	6	1	14	31	50	78	84	37	
17	Blackburn Rovers	42	12	3	6	38	29	4	2	15	22	41	60	70	37	
18	Chelsea	42	7	5	9	44	50	7	4	10	32	41	76	91	37	
19	Birmingham City	42	9	5	7	37	36	4	5	12	26	44	63	80	36	
20	Nottingham Forest	42	8	6	7	30	28	5	3	13	20	46	50	74	35	
21	Leeds United	42	7	5	9	37	46	5	5	11	28	46	65	92	34	
22	Luton Town	42	6	5	10	25	29	3	7	11	25	44	50	73	30	

1959-60 Season
(Back) Hennin, Higgins, Hopkinson, Hartle, Stanley, Farrimond
(Front) Birch, Parry, Stevens, Hill, Holden

1960-61 Season
(Back) Hennin, Banks, Edwards, Farrimond, Hopkinson, Bollands, Hill, Higgins, Hartle
(Front) Lofthouse, Deakin, Stanley, Stevens, Holden, Birch, Parry

1960/61   18th in Division One

Manager: W.Ridding

#		Date	Opponent	Score	Scorers	Att	Ban	Bn	Bir	Coo	Cun	Dea	EdG	EdM	Far	Har	Hen	Hnn	Hig	Hil	Hol	Hop	Lee	Lof	McA	Par	Phy	Pil	Rim	Sta	Ste	Wil
1	Aug	20	BIRMINGHAM CITY	2-2	Birch, Parry	20543	3		7							2				5	8	1			11	9				4		
2		24	WOLVES	0-2		20132	3		7			8	6			2				5	10	1			11	9				4		
3		27	West Ham United	1-2	Deakin	24283	3		7			8	6			2				5	10	1			11	9				4		
4		31	Wolves	1-3	Banks	37313	3		7				6		9	2		2		5	8	1			11	10				4		
5	Sep	3	CHELSEA	4-1	G.B.Edwards, Holden, McAdams(2)	21609	3		7				6			2				5	8	1		9	10					4		
6		7	TOTTENHAM HOTSPUR	1-2	McAdams	41565	3		7				6			2				5	8	1		9	10					4		
7		10	Blackpool	1-0	Hill	17166			7				6			3	2			5	8	1		9	10					4		
8		14	Tottenham Hotspur	1-3	McAdams	43559			7				5			3	2	4			8	1		9	10					6		
9		17	EVERTON	3-4	McAdams, Parry, Hill	30405			7				5			3	2	4			8	1		9	10					6		
10		24	Blackburn Rovers	1-3	Hartle(pen)	29236			7				6			3	2			5	8	1		9	10					4		
11	Oct	1	MANCHESTER UNITED	1-1	McAdams	39197							6	3	2					5	10	7	1		9	8	11				4		
12		8	WEST BROMWICH ALBION	0-1		18672			7					3	2	4	5				11	1		9		10				6	8	
13		15	Cardiff City	1-0	Lofthouse	22672								3	2				5	11	7	1		9	8				4	6	10	
14		22	FULHAM	0-3		19816			11					3	2				5	10	7	1		9					6	8	
15		29	Sheffield Wednesday	0-2		25708				3		10			2		4		5	11	7	1		9					6	8	
16	Nov	5	MANCHESTER CITY	3-1	Stanley, Lofthouse, Lee	34005				3	6				2				5		11	1	7	8	9				4	10	
17		12	Nottingham Forest	2-2	Lofthouse, Iley(og)	18812				3	6				2				5		11	1	7	8	9				4	10	
18		19	BURNLEY	3-5	McAdams(2), Lee	23830				3	6				2				5	8	11	1	7	9					4	10	
19	Dec	3	NEWCASTLE UNITED	2-1	M.Edwards, Stevens	12921				3	6		5	10	2						11	1	7						4	8	
20		10	Arsenal	1-5	McAdams	30598				3	6		5	10	2						11	1	7						4	8	
21		17	Birmingham City	2-2	Stevens(2)	19051	3		11						2				5	10		1	7	9					6	4	8	
22		24	LEICESTER CITY	2-0	Deakin, Stevens	11534	3		7			10	5		2						11	1		9					6	4	8	
23		26	Leicester City	0-2		23806	3		7			10	5		2						11	1		9					6	4	8	
24		31	WEST HAM UNITED	3-1	Birch, McAdams, Stevens	15931			7		6	10	5	3	2						11	1		9					4	8	
25	Jan	14	Chelsea	1-1	McAdams	20641			7		6		5	3	2					10	11	1		9					4	8	
26		21	BLACKPOOL	3-1	McAdams, Stanley(pen), Stevens	15909			7		6		5	3	2					10	11	1		9					4	8	
27	Feb	4	Everton	2-1	McAdams(2,1pen)	35654	2		7			10	5	3							11	1		9					6	4	8	
28		11	BLACKBURN ROVERS	0-0		16183	2		7			10	5	3							11	1		9					6	4	8	
29		18	Manchester United	1-3	McAdams	38146			7			10	5	3	2						11	1		9					6	4	8	
30		25	West Bromwich Albion	2-3	Stevens, Bannister	15171	7						5	3	2					10	11	1		9					6	4	8	
31	Mar	4	CARDIFF CITY	3-0	Holden, Stevens(2)	21815						10	5	3	2						7	1				9	11	6	4	8	
32		11	Fulham	2-2	Holden, Phythian	18794						10	5	3	2						7	1				9	11	6	4	8	
33		18	SHEFFIELD WEDNESDAY	0-1		19418							5	3	2					10	7	1				9	11	6	4	8	
34		25	Manchester City	0-0		21816				8			5	3	2					10	7	1					11	6	4	9	
35	Apr	1	ARSENAL	1-1	Neill(og)	18618				8			5	3	2					10	7	1					11	6	4	8	
36		3	ASTON VILLA	3-0	McAdams(3)	21721							5	3	2					10	7	1			9		11	6	4	8	
37		4	Aston Villa	0-4		15732							5	3	2					10	7	1					11	6	4	8	
38		8	Burnley	0-2		22998							5	3	2					10	7	1			9		11	6	4	8	
39		15	NOTTINGHAM FOREST	3-1	Hartle, Birch, Hill	18601			8				5	3	2					10	7	1					11	6	4	9	
40		18	Preston North End	0-0		17786			8				5	3	2					10	7	1					11	6	4	9	
41		22	Newcastle United	1-4	Pilkington	18820			8				5	3	2					10	7	1					11	6	4	9	
42		29	PRESTON NORTH END	1-1	Stevens	12637			8				5	3	2					10	7	1					11	4	9	6
			Apps				11	1	27	6	8	12	33	3	27	40		6	17	31	39	42	6	6	27	12	3	12	20	41	31	1
			Goals				1	1	3			2	1	1					3	3			2	3	18	2	1	1			2	10

Two own goals

F.A. Cup

#		Date	Opponent	Score	Scorers	Att	Ban	Bir	Cun	EdG	EdM	Far	Hig	Hil	Hol	Hop	McA	Sta	Ste
3	Jan	7	Hull City	1-0	Stevens	18771		7	6	10	5	3	2		11	1	9	4	8
4		28	BLACKBURN ROVERS	3-3	Stanley(pen), McAdams, Stevens	29804		7	6	5	3	2		10	11	1	9	4	8
4r	Feb	1	Blackburn Rovers	0-4		31000	3	7	6	5		2		10	11	1	9	4	8

League Cup

#		Date	Opponent	Score	Scorers	Att	Bir	Coo	Cun	Dea	EdG	Far	Hig	Hil	Hol	Hop	Lee	Lof	McA	Par	Sta	Ste	Rim
1	Oct	10	Hull City	0-0		11890	7					3	2	5	11	1		9	10		4	6	8
1r		19	HULL CITY	5-1	Birch, Hill(2), McAdams(2)	10781	11					3	2	4	5	10	7	1	9		6	8	
2		26	GRIMSBY TOWN	6-2	Hill, Stevens, Lofthouse(3), Keeble(og)	7992		3		10	5	2	4	11	7	1	9				6	8	
3	Nov	14	Darlington	2-1	Hartle, Holden	21023		3	6			2	5	11	7	1	8	9			4	10	
4	Dec	20	ROTHERHAM UNITED	0-2		6594	7			10		3	2	11	5	1		9			6	4	8

Lancashire Cup

| 1 | Dec | 7 | Manchester United | 1-3 |

Manchester Cup

| F | Nov | 13 | Manchester United | 1-0 |

Final planned for April 1961: postponed due to waterlogged pitch. Played Nov 1961

Other Games

1	Aug	14	Le Havre	1-1
2	Mar	15	LE HAVRE	4-0
3	May	6	Karlsruher	2-1
4		11	Saarbrucken	0-1
5		13	Mestalla	0-1
6		14	Espanyol	0-2

	FINAL TABLE	Pl.	Home					Away					F. A.		Pts
			W	D	L	F	A	W	D	L	F	A	(Total)		
1	Tottenham Hotspur	42	15	3	3	65	28	16	1	4	50	27	115	55	66
2	Sheffield Wed.	42	15	4	2	45	17	8	5	8	33	30	78	47	58
3	Wolverhampton W.	42	17	2	2	61	32	8	5	8	42	43	103	75	57
4	Burnley	42	11	4	6	58	40	11	3	7	44	37	102	77	51
5	Everton	42	13	4	4	47	23	9	2	10	40	46	87	69	50
6	Leicester City	42	12	4	5	54	31	6	5	10	33	39	87	70	45
7	Manchester United	42	14	5	2	58	20	4	4	13	30	56	88	76	45
8	Blackburn Rovers	42	12	3	6	48	34	3	10	8	29	42	77	76	43
9	Aston Villa	42	13	3	5	48	28	4	6	11	30	49	78	77	43
10	West Bromwich Alb.	42	10	8	3	43	32	8	2	11	24	39	67	71	41
11	Arsenal	42	12	3	6	44	35	3	8	10	33	50	77	85	41
12	Chelsea	42	10	5	6	61	48	5	2	14	37	52	98	100	37
13	Manchester City	42	10	5	6	41	30	3	6	12	38	60	79	90	37
14	Nottingham Forest	42	8	7	6	34	33	6	2	13	28	45	62	78	37
15	Cardiff City	42	11	5	5	34	26	2	6	13	26	59	60	85	37
16	West Ham United	42	12	4	5	53	31	1	6	14	24	57	77	88	36
17	Fulham	42	5	8	8	39	39	6	0	15	33	56	72	95	36
18	BOLTON WANDERERS	42	9	5	7	38	29	3	6	12	20	44	58	73	35
19	Birmingham City	42	10	4	7	35	31	4	2	15	27	53	62	84	34
20	Blackpool	42	9	3	9	44	34	3	6	12	24	39	68	73	33
21	Newcastle United	42	7	7	7	51	49	4	3	14	35	60	86	109	32
22	Preston North End	42	7	6	8	28	25	3	4	14	15	46	43	71	30

1961/62　11th in Division One

Manager: W.Ridding

#		Date	Opponent	Result	Scorers	Att	Birch B	Cunliffe JG	Deakin P	Davies RW	Edwards GB	Farrimond S	Hartle LR	Hatton DH	Hill F	Holden AD	Hopkinson E	Lee FH	McAdams WJ	McGarry RJ	Phythian ER	Pilkington B	Rimmer WR	Sleight G	Stanley G	Stevens D	Threlfall J	Wilkinson RJ
1	Aug	19	IPSWICH TOWN	0-0		16708					5	3	2		10	7	1		9			11	4			8		6
2		23	Sheffield Wednesday	2-4	Holden, McAdams	35460					5	3	2		10	7	1		9			11	4			8		6
3		26	Burnley	1-3	Threlfall	24167					5	3	2		10	7	1		9			11	6			8	2	
4		30	SHEFFIELD WEDNESDAY	4-3	Holden, McAdams, Hill(2)	19559					5	3	2		10	7	1		9			11	6			4	8	
5	Sep	2	ARSENAL	2-1	McAdams(2)	18414					5	3	2		10	7	1		9			11	6			4	8	
6		6	Fulham	2-2	Hill(2)	12639					5	3	2		10	7	1		9			11	6			4	8	
7		9	Cardiff City	2-1	Holden, McAdams	22076					5	3	2		10	7	1		9			11	6			4	8	
8		16	Manchester City	1-2	Stevens	27275	7	6			5	3	2		10		1						9		4	11	8	
9		20	FULHAM	2-3	Stevens, Phythian	16748	7	6			5	3	2		10		1				9				4	11	8	
10		23	WEST BROMWICH ALBION	3-2	Hill, Pilkington, Phythian	14155	7				5	3	2		10		1				9	11	6			8	
11		30	Birmingham City	1-2	Stevens	17214					5	3	2		10		1				9	11	6			8	
12	Oct	9	TOTTENHAM HOTSPUR	1-2	Hill	24726					5	3	2		10		1	7	9			11	6			8	
13		14	Blackpool	1-2	McAdams	22062					5	3	2		10		1	7	9			11	6			8	
14		21	WOLVES	1-0	Stevens	14755	11				5	3	2		10	7	1		9				6			8	4	
15		28	Manchester United	3-0	McAdams, Hill, Pilkington	31442					5	3	2		10	7	1		9			11	6			8	4	
16	Nov	4	SHEFFIELD UNITED	2-0	Hartle, Coldwell(og)	12563					5	3	2		10	7	1		9			11	6			8	4	
17		11	Chelsea	0-1		12404				10	5	3	2			7	1		9			11	6			8	4	
18		18	ASTON VILLA	1-1	McAdams	13198					5	3	2		10	7	1		9			11	6			8	4	
19		25	Nottingham Forest	1-0	Hill	23914					5	3	2		10	7	1		9			11	6			8	4	
20	Dec	2	BLACKBURN ROVERS	1-1	Holden	12855					5	3	2		10	7	1		9			11	6			8	4	
21		9	West Ham United	0-1		19492					5	3	2		10	7	1		9			11	6			8	4	
22		16	Ipswich Town	1-2	Holden	16587					5	3	2		10	7	1				9	11	6			8	4	
23		26	Everton	0-1		45462	11				5	3	2		10	7	1				9		6			8	4	
24	Jan	13	Arsenal	2-1	Holden, Stevens	33451			8		5	3	2		10	7	1					11	6			9	4	
25		20	CARDIFF CITY	1-1	Stevens	11231			8		5	3	2		10	7	1					11	6			9	4	
26	Feb	3	MANCHESTER CITY	0-2		18454					5	3	2		10	7	1					11	6			9	4	
27		10	West Bromwich Albion	2-6	Hartle, Hill	20226	7				5	3	2		8		1					11	6			9	4	
28		17	BIRMINGHAM CITY	3-2	Stevens, Hill, Hennessey(og)	13308	7				5	3	2		8		1			10		11	6			9	4	
29		24	Tottenham Hotspur	2-2	Hill(2)	36470	7				5	3	2		8		1			10		11	6			9	4	
30	Mar	3	BLACKPOOL	0-0		14831					5	3	2		8	7	1			10		11	6			9	4	
31		10	Wolves	1-5	Holden	18882				9	5	3	2		8	7	1			10		11	6				4	
32		17	MANCHESTER UNITED	1-0	Pilkington	34366				9	5	3	2		8	7	1			10		11	6		4			
33		24	Sheffield United	1-3	Pilkington	18324				9	5	3	2		8	7	1			10		11	6		4			
34		31	CHELSEA	4-2	Holden,McGarry,Davies,Harris(og)	15495				9	5	3	2		8	7	1			10		11	6				4	
35	Apr	4	EVERTON	1-1	Rimmer	20428				9	5	3	2		8	7	1			10		11	6				4	
36		7	Aston Villa	0-3		23571	7			9	5	3	2		8		1			10		11	6				4	
37		11	BURNLEY	0-0		26615				9	5	3	2		8	7	1			10		11	6				4	
38		14	NOTTINGHAM FOREST	6-1	Rimmer,Holden,Hill,Birch,Davies,McGarry	12891	7			9	5	3	2		8	11	1			10			6				4	
39		21	Blackburn Rovers	3-2	Holden, Hill, McGarry(pen)	15459	7			9	5	3	2		8	11	1			10			6				4	
40		23	LEICESTER CITY	1-0	Davies	19264	7			9	5	3	2		8	11	1			10			6				4	
41		24	Leicester City	1-1	McGarry	14093				9	5	3	2	4	8	7	1			10		11	6				4	
42		28	WEST HAM UNITED	1-0	Holden	17333				9	5	3	2	4	8	7	1			10		11	6				4	
			Apps				12	2	3	12	42	42	41	2	41	32	42	5	17	15	6	35	42	2	11	30	26	2
			Goals				1			3			2		14	11			8	4	2	4	2			7	1	

Three Own Goals

F.A. Cup

							Birch B	Cunliffe JG	Deakin P	Davies RW	Edwards GB	Farrimond S	Hartle LR	Hatton DH	Hill F	Holden AD	Hopkinson E	Lee FH	McAdams WJ	McGarry RJ	Phythian ER	Pilkington B	Rimmer WR	Sleight G	Stanley G	Stevens D	Threlfall J	Wilkinson RJ
3	Jan	6	Manchester United	1-2	Stevens	42202			8		5	3	2		10	7	1					11	6			9	4	

League Cup

							Birch B	Cunliffe JG			Edwards GB	Farrimond S	Hartle LR	Hatton DH	Hill F	Holden AD	Hopkinson E		McAdams WJ			Pilkington B	Rimmer WR		Stanley G	Stevens D		
1	Sep	13	SUNDERLAND	1-1	Stevens	13125	7				5	3	2		10		1		9			11	6		4	8		
1r		25	Sunderland	0-1		19557	7	6			5	3	2	4	10		1				9				11	8		

Lancashire Cup

2	Oct	23	Manchester City	4-3
SF	Feb	14	Blackburn Rovers	1-4

Manchester Cup (Did not enter)

Other Games

1	Nov	22	SAARBRUCKEN	4-1
2	Jan	23	Barnsley	0-2
3		27	Hibernian	0-2
4	May	2	AEK Athens	1-4
5		4	Loval	2-1
6		6	Panathanaikos	1-1
7		7	Olympiakos	2-1
8		9	Racing Club Paris	0-1

FINAL TABLE

		Pl.	Home W	D	L	F	A	Away W	D	L	F	A	F. (Total)	A.	Pts
1	Ipswich Town	42	17	2	2	58	28	7	6	8	35	39	93	67	56
2	Burnley	42	14	4	3	57	26	7	7	7	44	41	101	67	53
3	Tottenham Hotspur	42	14	4	3	59	34	7	6	8	29	35	88	69	52
4	Everton	42	17	2	2	64	21	3	9	9	24	33	88	54	51
5	Sheffield United	42	13	5	3	37	23	6	4	11	24	46	61	69	47
6	Sheffield Wed.	42	14	4	3	47	23	6	2	13	25	35	72	58	46
7	Aston Villa	42	13	5	3	45	20	5	3	13	20	36	65	56	44
8	West Ham United	42	11	6	4	49	37	6	4	11	27	45	76	82	44
9	West Bromwich Alb.	42	10	7	4	50	23	5	6	10	33	44	83	67	43
10	Arsenal	42	9	6	6	39	31	7	5	9	32	41	71	72	43
11	BOLTON WANDERERS	42	11	7	3	35	22	5	3	13	27	44	62	66	42
12	Manchester City	42	11	3	7	46	38	6	4	11	32	43	78	81	41
13	Blackpool	42	10	4	7	41	30	5	7	9	29	45	70	75	41
14	Leicester City	42	12	2	7	38	27	5	4	12	34	44	72	71	40
15	Manchester United	42	10	3	8	44	31	5	6	10	28	44	72	75	39
16	Blackburn Rovers	42	10	6	5	33	22	4	5	12	17	36	50	58	39
17	Birmingham City	42	9	6	6	37	35	5	4	12	28	46	65	81	38
18	Wolverhampton W.	42	8	7	6	38	34	5	3	13	35	52	73	86	36
19	Nottingham Forest	42	12	4	5	39	23	1	6	14	24	56	63	79	36
20	Fulham	42	8	3	10	38	34	5	4	12	28	40	66	74	33
21	Cardiff City	42	6	9	6	30	33	3	5	13	20	48	50	81	32
22	Chelsea	42	7	7	7	34	29	2	3	16	29	65	63	94	28

1961-62 Season
(Back) Stanley, Farrimond, McAdams, Hill, Birch
(Middle) Hartle, Dean, Hopkinson, Cunliffe, Wilkinson, Holden
(Front) Deakin, Stevens, Edwards, Pilkington, Rimmer

1962-63 Season
(Back) Hatton, Smith, Hopkinson, Hartle
(Middle) Threlfall, Holden, Edwards, Rimmer, Farrimond
(Front) Deakin, McGarry, Davies, Hill, Pilkington

1962/63 18th in Division One

Manager: W.Ridding

No	Date	Opponent	Score	Scorers	Att	Birch B	Bromley B	Butler DA	Cooper C	Cunliffe JG	Davies RW	Deakin P	Edwards GB	Farrimond S	Goulden AE	Hartle LR	Hatton DH	Hill F	Holden AD	Hopkinson E	Hulme J	Lee FH	Lennard D	McGarry RJ	Oxtoby R	Pilkington B	Rimmer WR	Russell W	Smith A	Stanley G	Taylor G	Threlfall J
1	Aug 18	Sheffield Wednesday	1-1	Davies	28036						9	10	5	3		2		8	7	1						11	6					4
2	22	BURNLEY	2-2	Rimmer, Davies	28897						9	10	5	3		2		8	7	1						11	6					4
3	25	FULHAM	1-0	Hill	16666						9	10	5	3		2		8	7	1						11	6					4
4	28	Burnley	1-2	Pilkington	27529						9	10	5	3		2		8	7	1						11	6					4
5	Sep 1	Leicester City	1-4	Norman(og)	19113						9		5	3		2		8	7	1		10				11	6					4
6	5	MANCHESTER UNITED	3-0	Pilkington(pen), Hill, Davies	45097						9		5	3		2		8	7	1		10				11	6					4
7	8	IPSWICH TOWN	1-3	Holden	17790						9		5	3		2		8	7	1		10				11	6					4
8	12	Manchester United	0-3		37951				3							2	6	8	7	1						11						4
9	15	EVERTON	0-2		27404	11				6	9	10	5	3			4	8		1			7							2		
10	22	West Bromwich Albion	4-5	Lee(3,2pens), Davies	18209	7				6	9		5	3		2			10	11	1	8						4				
11	29	ARSENAL	3-0	Lee(2,1pen), McGarry	16634						9		5	3		2	4	8	11	1		7		10			6					
12	Oct 6	Liverpool	0-1		41115						9		5	3		2	4	8	11	1		7		10			6					
13	13	WOLVES	3-0	Pilkington, Lee(2)	27838						9		5	3		2		8		1		7		10		11	6				4	
14	20	Sheffield United	1-4	Davies	19862						9	8	5	3		2				1		7		10		11	6					4
15	27	NOTTINGHAM FOREST	1-0	Lee	13614						9			3		2		8		1		7	5	10		11	6					4
16	Nov 3	West Ham United	2-1	McGarry(2)	19885						9		5	3		2		8		1		7		10		11	6				4	
17	10	MANCHESTER CITY	3-1	Lee(2,1pen), Davies	21700						9		5	3		2		8		1		7		10		11	6				4	
18	17	Blackpool	1-3	Lee	12930						9		5	3		2		8		1		7		10		11	6				4	
19	24	BLACKBURN ROVERS	0-0		26868						9		5	3		2		8		1		7		10		11	6				4	
20	Dec 1	Aston Villa	0-5		37075			11			9	10	5	3		2		8		1		7					6				4	
21	8	TOTTENHAM HOTSPUR	1-0	Deakin	20737			11			9	10	5	3		2		8		1		7					6				4	
22	Feb 16	Arsenal	2-3	Hill, Baker	25203			11			9	10	5	3		2		8		1		7					6				4	
23	Mar 9	SHEFFIELD UNITED	3-2	Hill	12925		10	11			9		5	3		2		8		1		7					6				4	
24	16	Nottingham Forest	0-1		16294		10	11			9		5	3		2		8		1		7					6				4	
25	20	Wolves	0-4		17648		10	11			9		5	3		2				1		7					6				4	8
26	23	WEST HAM UNITED	3-0	Russell, Butler, Lee	19177			11			9		5	3		2		10		1		7					6	8			4	
27	25	WEST BROMWICH ALBION	1-2	Davies	14997			11			9		5	3		2		10		1		7					6	8			4	
28	29	Blackburn Rovers	0-5		11533			11			9		5	3		2		10		1		7					6	8			4	
29	Apr 3	Birmingham City	2-2	Hill, Birch	13200	7		11			9		5	3		2		10									6	8	1		4	
30	6	BLACKPOOL	3-0	Hartle, Rimmer, Birch	14584	7		11			9		5	3		2		10		1							6	8			4	
31	12	Leyton Orient	1-0	Butler(2)	15389	7		11			9		5	3		2		10		1							6	8			4	
32	13	Manchester City	1-2	Deakin	18551			11			9	8	5		3	2		10				7					6		1		4	
33	15	LEYTON ORIENT	0-1		16752	11					9		5			2	3	10				7					6	8	1		4	
34	20	ASTON VILLA	7-1	Davies(2), Deakin, Butler	13411	7		11			9	10	5			2	3										6	8	1		4	
35	24	BIRMINGHAM CITY	0-0		12949	7		11			9	10	5			2	3										6	8	1		4	
36	27	Tottenham Hotspur	1-4	Deakin	40965	7						8	5			2	3	10		1						11	6	9			4	
37	May 1	Fulham	1-0	Deakin	10896	7					9	8	5			2	3	10		1						11	6				4	
38	4	Everton	0-1		52047	7						8	5			2	3	10		1						11	6	9			4	
39	6	SHEFFIELD WEDNESDAY	0-4		12905	7					9	5				2	3	10		1						11	6				4	
40	11	LEICESTER CITY	2-0	Deakin, Russell	10734						9	10	5			2	3	7		1						11	6	8			4	
41	13	LIVERPOOL	1-0	Pilkington	15837						9	10	5			2	3	7		1						11	6	8			4	
42	17	Ipswich Town	1-4	Davies	19088						9	10	5			2	3	8		1						11	6				4	
		Apps				11	3	16	1	2	40	19	41	30	1	41	14	38	11	39	1	23	7	12		22	40	14	3	1	23	9
		Goals				2		4			10	6				1		7	1			12		3		4	2	2				

One own goal

F.A. Cup

No	Date	Opponent	Score	Scorers	Att	Butler DA	Davies RW	Deakin P	Edwards GB	Farrimond S	Hartle LR	Hill F	Hopkinson E	Lee FH	Rimmer WR	Taylor G
3	Mar 6	Sheffield United	1-3	Lee	27184	11	9	10	5	3	2	8	1	7	6	4

League Cup

No	Date	Opponent	Score	Att	Birch B	Cunliffe JG	Farrimond S	Hartle LR	Hatton DH	Hill F	Hopkinson E	Lennard D	Pilkington B	Rimmer WR	Russell W
2	Sep 26	Norwich City	0-4	19258	7	6	3	2	4	8	1	9	10	5	11

Lancashire Cup

No	Date	Opponent	Score
1	Nov 14	BURY	4-0

Competition abandoned

Manchester Cup

	Date	Opponent	Score
F	May 20	Oldham Athletic	3-1

Other Games

No	Date	Opponent	Score
1	Aug 11	Middlesbrough	2-0
2	Dec 3	RFC LIEGE	3-2
3	Feb 13	Manchester United*	2-4

*Played in Cork

	FINAL TABLE	Pl.	Home					Away					F.	A.	Pts
			W	D	L	F	A	W	D	L	F	A		(Total)	
1	Everton	42	14	7	0	48	17	11	4	6	36	25	84	42	61
2	Tottenham Hotspur	42	14	6	1	72	28	9	3	9	39	34	111	62	55
3	Burnley	42	14	4	3	41	17	8	6	7	37	40	78	57	54
4	Leicester City	42	14	6	1	53	23	6	6	9	26	30	79	53	52
5	Wolverhampton W.	42	11	4	6	51	25	9	4	8	42	40	93	65	50
6	Sheffield Wed.	42	10	5	6	38	26	9	5	7	39	37	77	63	48
7	Arsenal	42	11	4	6	44	33	7	6	8	42	44	86	77	46
8	Liverpool	42	13	5	3	45	22	4	7	10	26	37	71	59	44
9	Nottingham Forest	42	12	4	5	39	28	5	6	10	28	41	67	69	44
10	Sheffield United	42	11	7	3	33	20	5	5	11	25	40	58	60	44
11	Blackburn Rovers	42	11	4	6	55	34	4	8	9	24	37	79	71	42
12	West Ham United	42	8	6	7	39	34	6	6	9	34	35	73	69	40
13	Blackpool	42	8	7	6	34	27	5	7	9	24	37	58	64	40
14	West Bromwich Alb.	42	11	1	9	40	37	5	6	10	31	42	71	79	39
15	Aston Villa	42	12	2	7	38	23	3	6	12	24	45	62	68	38
16	Fulham	42	8	6	7	28	30	6	4	11	22	41	50	71	38
17	Ipswich Town	42	8	8	3	34	39	7	1	13	25	39	59	78	35
18	BOLTON WANDERERS	42	13	3	5	35	18	2	2	17	20	57	55	75	35
19	Manchester United	42	6	6	9	36	38	6	4	11	31	43	67	81	34
20	Birmingham City	42	6	8	7	40	40	4	5	12	23	50	63	90	33
21	Manchester City	42	7	5	9	30	45	3	6	12	28	57	58	102	31
22	Leyton Orient	42	4	5	12	22	37	2	4	15	15	44	37	81	21

1963/64   21st in Division One (relegated)

Manager: W.Ridding

#	Date	Opponent	Res	Scorers	Att	Birch B	Bromley B	Butler DA	Cooper C	Davies RW	Davison JH	Deakin P	Edwards GB	Farrimond S	Hartle LR	Hatton DH	Hill F	Hopkinson E	Hulme J	Lee FH	Lennard D	Pilkington B	Redrobe WE	Rimmer WR	Russell W	Smith A	Stanley G	Taylor G
1	Aug 24	Birmingham City	1-2	Davies	24817					9			5	3	2		10	1		7	6	11				8	4	
2	31	WEST BROMWICH ALBION	1-2	Hill	14398					9			5	3	2		10	1		7	6	11				8	4	
3	Sep 4	EVERTON	1-3	Rimmer	34093	7				9	8	5		3	2		10	1			6	11					4	
4	7	Arsenal	3-4	Bromley, Davies(2)	26016		8	7		9				3	2		10	1	5		6	11					4	
5	11	Everton	0-2		28301		8	7		9				2	3	10			5		6	11				1	4	
6	14	LEICESTER CITY	0-0		12753		8	7		9				2	3	10			5		6	11				1	4	
7	18	IPSWICH TOWN	6-0	Pilkington, Davies(2), Lennard(2), Taylor	12917			7		9				2	3	10			5		6	11				1	4	8
8	21	Nottingham Forest	1-3	Taylor	23712			7		9				2	3	10			5		6	11				1	4	8
9	28	Fulham	1-3	Lee	17345	7	11			9				2	3				5	8	6					1	4	10
10	Oct 1	Ipswich Town	3-1	Butler, Taylor(2)	11363	7	11			9				2	3				5	8	6					1	4	10
11	5	MANCHESTER UNITED	0-1		36183	7	11			9				2	3				5	8	6					1	4	10
12	9	Blackburn Rovers	0-3		18675			7		9				2	3				5	8	6	11				1	4	10
13	12	STOKE CITY	3-4	Lee(2,1pen), Butler	17560		8	7						2	3				5	9	6	11				1	4	10
14	19	Wolves	2-2	Butler, Pilkington	19420			7		9		10		2	3				5	8	6	11				1	4	
15	26	BLACKPOOL	1-1	Rimmer	14359	7	11			9		10		2	3			1	5	8	6						4	
16	Nov 2	Aston Villa	0-3		18847		8	11				10		3	2	4		1	5	7	6			9				
17	9	LIVERPOOL	1-2	Hatton	24049		11			9	7	10		3	2	4		1	5	8	6							
18	16	Sheffield United	1-0	Deakin	21518	8				9	7	10		3	2	4		1	5	11	6							
19	23	WEST HAM UNITED	1-1	Lee(pen)	11041	8				9	7	10		3	2	4		1	5	11	6							
20	30	Chelsea	0-4		19969	10						7		3	2	4	11	1	5	8	6			9				
21	Dec 7	TOTTENHAM HOTSPUR	1-3	Davies	18394					9	7	10	5	3	2		8	1			6	11					4	
22	14	BIRMINGHAM CITY	0-2		9663					9	7		5	3	2		10	1			6	11				8	4	
23	21	West Bromwich Albion	1-1	Deakin	10705					9	7	10		3	2	4	11		5	8	6					1		
24	26	Sheffield Wednesday	0-3		30532					9	7	10		3	2	4	11	1	5	8	6							
25	28	SHEFFIELD WEDNESDAY	3-0	Lee, Davies, Deakin	12376					9	7	10	5	3	2	4	11	1		8	6							
26	Jan 11	ARSENAL	1-1	Lee	14830					9	7	10	5	3	2	4	11	1		8	6							
27	18	Leicester City	0-1		15902					9	7	10	5	3	2		11	1		8	6				4			
28	Feb 1	NOTTINGHAM FOREST	2-3	Lee(2,1pen)	10770	10				9	7		6	3	2	4		1	5	8								11
29	8	FULHAM	2-1	Robson(og), Taylor	9615							7	5	3	2	4	10	1		8	6			9				11
30	19	Manchester United	0-5		33426							7	5	3	2	4	10	1		8	6			9				11
31	22	Stoke City	1-0	Lee	20419							7	5	3	2	4	10	1		8	6			9				11
32	29	BLACKBURN ROVERS	0-5		18343				2			7	5	3		4	10	1		8	6			9				11
33	May 7	Blackpool	0-2		12242				4			8	5	3	2	9	10	1		7	6							11
34	20	Liverpool	0-2		38583							7	5	3	2	9	10	1		8	6				4			11
35	28	ASTON VILLA	1-1	Davison	8348						7		5	3	2	9	10	1		8	6				4			11
36	30	BURNLEY	2-1	Hatton, Lee	14112		8					7	5	3	2	4	10	1		9	6							11
37	31	Burnley	1-1	Hatton	12554		8					7	5	3	2	4	10	1		9	6							11
38	Apr 4	West Ham United	3-2	Taylor, Lee, Bromley	19398		8					7	5	3	2		10	1		9	6				4			11
39	8	SHEFFIELD UNITED	3-0	Hill, Lee, Bromley	16905		8					7	5	3	2		10	1		9	6				4			11
40	11	CHELSEA	1-0	Bromley	18868		8					7	5	3	2		10	1		9	6				4			11
41	18	Tottenham Hotspur	0-1		32507		8					7	5	3	2		10	1		9	6				4			11
42	24	WOLVES	0-4		27808		8					7	5	3	2		10	1		9	6				4			11
				Apps		5	18	14	2	23	21	18	23	31	41	29	29	31	20	34	37	13	2	24	5	11	7	24
				Goals			4	3		7	1	3				3	2			12	2	2		2				6

One own goal

F.A. Cup

#	Date	Opponent	Res	Scorers	Att	Davies RW	Davison JH	Deakin P	Edwards GB	Farrimond S	Hartle LR	Hatton DH	Hill F	Hopkinson E	Lee FH	Lennard D	Russell W	Taylor G
3	Jan 4	Bath City	1-1	Lee(pen)	12779	9	7	10	5	3	2	4	11	1	8	6		
3r	8	BATH CITY	3-0	Taylor, Lee(pen), Davies	26983	9		10	5	3	2	4	11	1	8	6		7
4	25	PRESTON NORTH END	2-2	Deakin(2)	39234	9		10	5	3		2	8	1	7	6	4	11
4r	27	Preston North End	1-2	Edwards	38290	9		10	5	3		2	8	1	7	6	4	11

League Cup

#	Date	Opponent	Res	Scorers	Att	Birch B	Bromley B	Davies RW	Deakin P	Edwards GB	Farrimond S	Hartle LR	Hatton DH	Hopkinson E	Hulme J	Lee FH	Lennard D	Pilkington B	Smith A	Stanley G	Taylor G
2	Sep 25	Sheffield United	2-1	Lee(2)	10000			9			2	3	11		5	8	6	7	1	4	10
3	Oct 29	Stoke City	0-3		11825	7	11	9	10	6	2	3		1	5					4	8

Lancashire Cup

#	Date	Opponent	Res
3	Oct 30	BLACKBURN ROVERS	1-1
3r	Nov 13	Blackburn Rovers	0-3

Manchester Cup (Did not enter)

Other Games

#	Date	Opponent	Res
1	Aug 17	Sunderland	4-3

FINAL TABLE

		Pl.	Home W	D	L	F	A	Away W	D	L	F	A	F. (Total)	A.	Pts
1	Liverpool	42	16	0	5	60	18	10	5	6	32	27	92	45	57
2	Manchester United	42	15	3	3	54	19	8	4	9	36	43	90	62	53
3	Everton	42	14	4	3	53	26	7	6	8	31	38	84	64	52
4	Tottenham Hotspur	42	13	3	5	54	31	9	4	8	43	50	97	81	51
5	Chelsea	42	12	5	4	36	24	8	7	6	36	32	72	56	50
6	Sheffield Wed.	42	15	3	3	50	24	4	8	9	34	43	84	67	49
7	Blackburn Rovers	42	10	4	7	44	28	8	6	7	45	37	89	65	46
8	Arsenal	42	10	4	7	56	37	7	4	10	34	45	90	82	45
9	Burnley	42	14	3	4	46	23	3	7	11	25	41	71	64	44
10	West Bromwich Alb.	42	9	6	6	43	35	7	5	9	27	26	70	61	43
11	Leicester City	42	9	4	8	33	27	7	7	7	28	31	61	58	43
12	Sheffield United	42	10	6	5	35	22	6	5	10	26	42	61	64	43
13	Nottingham Forest	42	9	5	7	34	24	7	4	10	30	44	64	68	41
14	West Ham United	42	8	7	6	45	38	6	5	10	24	36	69	74	40
15	Fulham	42	11	8	2	45	23	2	5	14	13	42	58	65	39
16	Wolverhampton W.	42	6	9	6	36	34	6	9	3	44	46	70	80	39
17	Stoke City	42	9	6	6	49	33	5	4	12	28	45	77	78	38
18	Blackpool	42	8	6	7	26	29	5	3	13	26	44	52	73	35
19	Aston Villa	42	8	6	7	35	29	3	6	12	27	42	62	71	34
20	Birmingham City	42	7	7	7	33	32	4	0	17	21	60	54	92	29
21	BOLTON WANDERERS	42	6	5	10	30	35	4	3	14	18	45	48	80	28
22	Ipswich Town	42	9	3	9	38	45	0	4	17	18	76	56	121	25

~ 254 ~

1963-64 Season
(Back) Threlfall, Hartle, Hatton, Stanley, Hopkinson, Edwards, Rimmer, Farrimond, Butler
(Front) Lennard, Lee, Hill, Davies, Deakin, Russell, Pilkington

1964-65 Season
(Back) Edwards, Hulme, Davies, Smith, Hopkinson, Hartle, Farrimond, Hill
(Front) Rimmer, Taylor, Hatton, Lee, Bromley, Lennard, Fry

1964/65   3rd in Division Two

Manager: W. Ridding

No	Date	Opponent	Score	Scorers	Att	Bromley B	Butler DA	Cooper C	Davies RW	Edwards GB	Farrimond S	Fry B	Hartle LR	Hatton DH	Hill F	Hopkinson E	Hulme J	Lee FH	Lennard D	Napier RJ	Redrobe WE	Rimmer WR	Russell W	Smith A	Taylor G
1	Aug 22	Huddersfield Town	1-1	Davies	12657	10			9	5			2	3	8			7				4			11
2	26	Southampton	2-3	Lee, Davies	17240	10			9	5			2	3	8	1		7	6			4			11
3	29	COVENTRY CITY	1-3	Davies	15969	10			9	5			2	3	8	1		7	6			4			11
4	Sep 2	SOUTHAMPTON	3-0	Davies(3)	10943	10			9	5		7	2	3	8	1			6			4			11
5	5	Cardiff City	3-1	Charter(og), Hill, Fry	13501	10			9	5	3	7	2	6	8	1		7				4			11
6	7	Middlesbrough	2-5	Hill, Bromley	22670	10			9	5	3		2		8	1		7	6			4			11
7	12	PRESTON NORTH END	5-1	Lee, Hill(2), Davies(2)	18186	10			9	5	3		2	6	8	1		7				4			11
8	16	MIDDLESBROUGH	4-2	Lee(2,pen), Hill, Bromley	13912	10			9	5	3		2	6	8	1		7				4			11
9	19	Ipswich Town	4-1	Lee(2), Thrower(og), Elsworthy(og)	12558	10			9	5	3		2	6	8	1		7				4			11
10	26	PLYMOUTH ARGYLE	6-1	Hill(2), Davies(2), Bromley, Taylor	13670	10			9	5	3		2	6	8	1		7				4			11
11	28	Leyton Orient	1-3	Lee	11385	10			9	5	3		2	6	8	1		7				4			11
12	Oct 2	Bury	1-2	Lee(pen)	23321	10			9		3		2	6	8	1	5	7				4			11
13	10	CRYSTAL PALACE	3-0	Lee, Hill, Davies	13671	10			9		3		2	6	8	1	5	7				4			11
14	17	Norwich City	2-3	Lee, Butler(og)	18065	10			9		3		2	6	8	1	5	7				4			11
15	24	ROTHERHAM UNITED	2-0	Lee(pen), Taylor	14173	10			9	5	3		2	6	8	1		7				4			11
16	31	Swansea Town	0-2		10651	10			9	5	3		2	6	8	1		7				4			11
17	Nov 7	DERBY COUNTY	3-1	Lee, Davies, Bromley	12903	10			9	5	3		2	6	8	1		7				4			11
18	14	Swindon Town	3-1	Lee(2), Davies	14445	10			9	5	3		2	6	8	1		7				4			11
19	21	PORTSMOUTH	3-2	Lee, Hill, Davies	13181	10			9	5	3		2	6	8	1		7				4			11
20	28	Manchester City	4-2	Lee(2,pen), Davies(2)	21895	10			9	5	3		2	6	8	1		7				4			11
21	Dec 15	HUDDERSFIELD TOWN	1-0	Hill	11782	10			9	5	3		2	6	8	1		7				4			11
22	19	Coventry City	0-0		23387	10			9	5	3		2	6	8	1		7				4			11
23	26	NORTHAMPTON TOWN	0-0		24487	10		2	9	5	3			6	8	1		7				4			11
24	Jan 16	Preston North End	2-2	Hill, Davies	19187	10	7		9	5	3		2	6	8	1						4			11
25	23	IPSWICH TOWN	0-0		13557	10	7		9	5	3		2	6	8	1						4			11
26	Feb 6	Plymouth Argyle	3-1	Lee, Bromley, Taylor	14553	10			9	5	3		2	6	8	1		7				4			11
27	13	BURY	0-1		16726	10			9	5	3		2	6	8	1		7				4			11
28	27	NORWICH CITY	5-2	Lee, Hill, Davies(2), Taylor	14130	10			9	5	3		2	6	8	1		7				4			11
29	Mar 2	Northampton Town	0-4		15515	10			9	5	3		2	6	8	1		7				4			11
30	6	Charlton Athletic	3-1	Lee(pen), Bromley, Butler	8634	10	7			5	3		2	6	8	1		9				4			11
31	13	SWANSEA TOWN	2-1	Lee, Hill	14027	10	7			5	3		2	6	8	1		9				4			11
32	20	Derby County	3-2	Lee, Hill, Taylor	16178	10	7			5	3		2	6	8	1		9				4			11
33	26	SWINDON TOWN	1-1	Lee(pen)	20731	10			9	5	3		2	6	8	1		7				4			11
34	29	CHARLTON ATHLETIC	1-1	Rimmer	19563	10			9	5	3		2	6	8	1		7				4			11
35	Apr 3	Portsmouth	0-3		11214	10			9	5	3		2	6	8	1		7				4			11
36	7	Crystal Palace	0-2		14022	10			9	5	3		2	6	8	1		7				4			11
37	10	MANCHESTER CITY	4-0	Hill, Davies(2), Bromley	14546	10			9		3		2	6	8	1	5	7				4			11
38	16	Newcastle United	0-2		59960	10			9	5	3		2	6	8	1		7				4			11
39	17	Rotherham United	0-0		7685		7			5	3		2	6	8	1		9				4	10		11
40	19	NEWCASTLE UNITED	1-1	Butler	15979		7			5	3		2	6	8	1		9				4	10		11
41	24	LEYTON ORIENT	0-0		9016		7				3		2	6	8			9		5		4	10	1	11
42	28	CARDIFF CITY	1-0	Hatton	6498		7				3		2	6	8				6	5		4		1	11
	Apps					38	9	1	34	36	38	3	41	41	41	40	4	38	6	2	1	42	3	2	42
	Goals					7	2		21		1		1		15			23			1		1		5

Four own goals

F.A. Cup

No	Date	Opponent	Score	Scorers	Att	Bromley B	Butler DA	Davies RW	Edwards GB	Farrimond S	Hartle LR	Hatton DH	Hill F	Hopkinson E	Lee FH	Rimmer WR	Taylor G
3	Jan 9	WORKINGTON TOWN	4-1	Hill, Butler, Davies(2)	14743	10	7	9	5	3	2	6	8	1		4	11
4	30	Preston North End	2-1	Lee(pen), Davies	33553	10		9	5	3	2	6	8	1	7	4	11
5	Feb 20	LIVERPOOL	0-1		57207	10		9	5	3	2	6	8	1	7	4	11

League Cup

No	Date	Opponent	Score	Scorers	Att	Bromley B	Davies RW	Edwards GB	Farrimond S	Hartle LR	Hatton DH	Hill F	Hopkinson E	Lee FH	Rimmer WR	Taylor G
2	Sep 23	BLACKBURN ROVERS	1-5	Davies	17335	10	9	5	3	2	6	8	1	7	4	11

Lancashire Cup

No	Date	Opponent	Score
1	Nov 3	BLACKPOOL	1-1
1r	13	Blackpool	1-1
1/2r	Jan 17	Blackpool	2-2
1/3r	19	BLACKPOOL	1-2

Manchester Cup (Did not enter)

Other Games

No	Date	Opponent	Score
1	Aug 10	Blackburn Rovers	1-4
2	13	BLACKBURN ROVERS	3-2

FINAL TABLE	Pl.	Home					Away					F. A. (Total)		Pts
		W	D	L	F	A	W	D	L	F	A			
1 Newcastle United	42	16	4	1	50	16	8	5	8	31	29	81	45	57
2 Northampton Town	42	14	7	0	37	16	6	9	6	29	34	66	50	56
3 BOLTON WANDERERS	42	13	6	2	46	17	7	4	10	34	41	80	58	50
4 Southampton	42	12	6	3	49	25	5	8	8	34	38	83	63	48
5 Ipswich Town	42	11	7	3	48	30	4	10	7	26	37	74	67	47
6 Norwich City	42	15	4	2	47	21	5	3	13	14	46	61	67	47
7 Crystal Palace	42	11	6	4	37	24	5	7	9	18	27	55	51	45
8 Huddersfield Town	42	12	4	5	28	15	5	6	10	25	36	53	51	44
9 Derby County	42	11	5	5	48	35	5	6	10	36	44	84	79	43
10 Coventry City	42	10	5	6	41	29	7	4	10	31	41	72	70	43
11 Manchester City	42	12	3	6	40	24	4	6	11	23	38	63	62	41
12 Preston North End	42	11	8	2	46	29	3	5	13	30	52	76	81	41
13 Cardiff City	42	10	7	4	43	25	3	7	11	21	32	64	57	40
14 Rotherham United	42	10	7	4	39	25	4	5	12	31	44	70	69	40
15 Plymouth Argyle	42	10	7	4	36	28	6	1	14	27	51	63	79	40
16 Bury	42	9	4	8	36	30	5	6	10	24	36	60	66	38
17 Middlesbrough	42	8	5	8	40	31	5	4	12	30	45	70	76	35
18 Charlton Athletic	42	8	5	8	35	34	5	4	12	29	44	64	78	35
19 Leyton Orient	42	10	4	7	36	34	2	7	12	14	38	50	72	35
20 Portsmouth	42	11	4	6	36	22	1	6	14	20	55	56	77	34
21 Swindon Town	42	9	3	6	43	30	2	2	17	20	51	63	81	33
22 Swansea Town	42	9	7	5	40	29	2	3	16	22	54	62	84	32

1965/66 9th in Division Two

Manager: W.Ridding

#	Date		Opponent	Score	Scorers	Att	Beech HW	Bromley B	Butler DA	Cooper C	Davies RW	Farrimond S	Greaves R	Hartle LR	Hatton DH	Hill F	Hopkinson E	Hulme J	Lee FH	Lennard D	Napier RJ	Redrobe WE	Rimmer WR	Taylor G
1	Aug	21	CHARLTON ATHLETIC	4-2	Rimmer, Lee(2,1pen), Bonds(og)	12744	10				9	3		2	6	8	1		7		5		4	11
2		25	Crystal Palace	1-1	Bromley	20784	10				9	3		2	6	8	1		7		5		4	11
3		28	Plymouth Argyle	3-1	Davies(2), Taylor	16444	10				9	3		2	6	8	1		7		5		4	11
4	Sep	1	CRYSTAL PALACE	3-0	Lee(pen), Davies, Taylor	15617	10				9	3		2	6	8	1		7		5		4	11
5		4	PORTSMOUTH	2-0	Lee, Hill	12107	10	7				3		2	6	8	1		9		5		4	11
6		7	Huddersfield Town	0-1		24532	10	7		2		3			6	8	1		9		5		4	11
7		15	HUDDERSFIELD TOWN	1-1	Butler	16614	10	7				3		2	6	8	1		9		5		4	11
8		18	Ipswich Town	0-2		12775	10	7				3		2	6	8	1		9		5		4	11
9		25	BIRMINGHAM CITY	1-2	Hill	12117	10				9	3		2	6	8	1		7		5		4	11
10	Oct	2	Leyton Orient	0-1		7774	10					3	8	2	6	11	1		7	6	5		4	
11		9	SOUTHAMPTON	2-3	Greaves(2)	12511	10	7				3	9	2	6	11	1		8		5*		4	12
12		16	Derby County	0-2		11418	10				9	3	8	2	6	11	1		7		5		4	
13		23	CARDIFF CITY	2-1	Davies, Taylor	11088					9	3	8	2	6	10	1		7		5		4	11
14		30	Carlisle United	1-1	Hill	11114	10				9	3		2	6	8	1		7		5		4	11
15	Nov	6	COVENTRY CITY	4-2	Davies(2), Bromley, Butler	13499	10	7			9	3		2	6	8	1				5		4	11
16		13	Bristol City	2-2	Davies, Opp own-goal	19912	10	7			9	3		2	6	8	1				5		4	11
17		16	Bury	1-1	Hill	12686	10	7			9	3		2	6	8	1				5		4	11
18		20	MANCHESTER CITY	1-0	Hatton	22927	10	7			9	3		2	6		1		8		5		4	11
19		27	Rotherham United	1-2	Redrobe	9785	10	7				3		2	6		1		8		5	9	4	11
20	Dec	4	WOLVES	2-1	Hill, Davies	12276		7			9	3		2	6	10	1		8		5		4	11
21		11	Norwich City	0-3		14363		7		12	9	3		2	6	10*	1		8		5		4	11
22		18	DERBY COUNTY	0-1		8578		7			9	3	10	2	6		1		8		5		4	11
23	Jan	1	Southampton	1-5	Lee	18807	10				9	3		2	6	8	1		7		5		4	11
24		8	BRISTOL CITY	1-2	Lee(pen)	10405	8				9	3		2	6	10	1		7		5		4	11
25		29	Charlton Athletic	1-0	Bromley	10227	8				9			2	3	10	1		7	6	5		4	11
26	Feb	5	PLYMOUTH ARGYLE	0-1		10705	8				9*		12	2	3	10	1		7	6	5		4	11
27		19	Portsmouth	0-1		11995	6	8	7		9	3		12	2*	10	1				5		4	11
28		26	BURY	2-1	Lee, Hill	12528		8			9	3		2		10	1		7	6	5		4	11
29	Mar	5	Cardiff City	1-1	Davies	8951		8			9	3		2		10	1		7	6	5		4	11
30		12	IPSWICH TOWN	3-1	Lee, Hill, Davies	9180		8	11		9	3		2		10	1		7	6	5		4	11
31		16	PRESTON NORTH END	1-3	Davies	13961		8	11		9	3		2		10	1		7	6	5		4	11
32		19	Birmingham City	1-0	Lee	13770	4	8		3	9					10	1		7	6	5		2	11
33		26	LEYTON ORIENT	2-0	Rimmer, Lee(pen)	8713	4	8		3	9					10	1		7	6	5		2	11
34	Apr	2	Coventry City	2-2	Lee, Taylor	19461	4	8		3	9					10	1		7	6	5		2	11
35		11	MIDDLESBROUGH	6-0	Lee, Hill, Davies, Bromley, Taylor(2)	11948	4	8		3	9					10	1		7	6	5		2	11
36		12	Middlesbrough	1-1	Greaves(2)	11384	4		7	3	9		8			10	1			6	5		2	11
37		16	Manchester City	1-4	Taylor	29459	4		12	3	9*		8		11	10	1			6	5		2	7
38		19	Preston North End	1-0	Hatton	11231	4		11	3			8		9	10	1			6	5		2	7
39		25	ROTHERHAM UNITED	1-3	Davies	10622	4		7*		9	3	12		8	10	1			6	5		2	11
40		30	Wolves	1-3	Taylor	15770	4				9	3	8			10	1	5	7	6			2	11
41	May	4	CARLISLE UNITED	4-0	Hatton(2), Lee, Taylor	6536	6			2	9	3	12		8	10*	1	5	7				4	11
42		7	NORWICH CITY	1-1	Rimmer	7420	6		12	2	9	3	10		8		1	5*	7				4	11
			Apps				12	31	19	10	34	33	9	29	33	38	42	3	34	16	39	1	42	37
			Subs						2	1			3											1
			Goals					4	2		13		3		4	8			13			1	3	9

Two own goals

F.A. Cup

#	Date		Opponent	Score	Scorers	Att	Beech HW	Bromley B	Butler DA	Cooper C	Davies RW	Farrimond S	Greaves R	Hartle LR	Hatton DH	Hill F	Hopkinson E	Hulme J	Lee FH	Lennard D	Napier RJ	Redrobe WE	Rimmer WR	Taylor G
3	Jan	22	WEST BROMWICH ALBION	3-0	Lee(2), Bromley	24425	8				9	3		2	6	10	1		7		5		4	11
4	Feb	12	PRESTON NORTH END	1-1	Davies	35680	8				9	3		2	6	10	1		7		5		4	11
4r		14	Preston North End	2-3	Lee, Davies	31131	8				9	3		2	6	10	1		7		5		4	11

League Cup

#	Date		Opponent	Score	Scorers	Att	Beech HW	Bromley B	Butler DA	Cooper C	Davies RW	Farrimond S	Greaves R	Hartle LR	Hatton DH	Hill F	Hopkinson E	Hulme J	Lee FH	Lennard D	Napier RJ	Redrobe WE	Rimmer WR	Taylor G
2	Sep	22	ALDERSHOT	3-0	Lee(2), Davies	8329	10				9	3		2	6	8	1		7		5		4	11
3	Oct	13	Grimsby Town	2-4	Butler, Greaves	8824	10	7				3	9	2	6		1		8		5		4	11

Lancashire Cup

#	Date		Opponent	Score
1	Jan	14	Bury	0-0
1r	Mar	21	BURY	1-2

Other Games

#	Date		Opponent	Score
1	Aug	14	Crewe Alexandra	1-0

	FINAL TABLE	Pl.	Home					Away					F.	A.	Pts
			W	D	L	F	A	W	D	L	F	A	(Total)		
1	Manchester City	42	14	7	0	40	14	8	8	5	36	30	76	44	59
2	Southampton	42	13	4	4	51	25	9	6	6	34	31	85	56	54
3	Coventry City	42	14	5	2	54	31	6	8	7	19	22	73	53	53
4	Huddersfield Town	42	12	7	2	35	12	7	6	8	27	24	62	36	51
5	Bristol City	42	9	10	2	27	15	8	7	6	36	33	63	48	51
6	Wolverhampton W.	42	15	4	2	52	18	5	6	10	35	43	87	61	50
7	Rotherham United	42	12	6	3	48	29	4	8	9	27	45	75	74	46
8	Derby County	42	13	2	6	48	31	3	9	9	23	37	71	68	43
9	BOLTON WANDERERS	42	12	2	7	43	25	4	7	10	19	34	62	59	41
10	Birmingham City	42	10	6	5	41	29	6	3	12	29	46	70	75	41
11	Crystal Palace	42	11	7	3	29	16	3	6	12	18	36	47	52	41
12	Portsmouth	42	13	4	4	47	26	3	4	14	27	52	74	78	40
13	Norwich City	42	8	7	6	33	27	4	8	9	19	25	52	52	39
14	Carlisle United	42	16	2	3	43	19	1	3	17	17	44	60	63	39
15	Ipswich Town	42	12	6	3	38	23	3	3	15	20	43	58	66	39
16	Charlton Athletic	42	10	6	5	39	29	2	8	11	22	41	61	70	38
17	Preston North End	42	7	7	10	34	27	4	5	12	25	47	62	70	37
18	Plymouth Argyle	42	7	8	6	37	26	5	5	11	17	37	54	63	37
19	Bury	42	12	5	4	45	25	2	2	17	17	51	62	76	35
20	Cardiff City	42	10	3	8	37	35	2	7	12	34	56	71	91	34
21	Middlesbrough	42	8	8	5	36	28	2	5	14	22	58	58	86	33
22	Leyton Orient	42	3	9	9	19	36	2	4	15	19	44	38	80	23

1965-66 Season
(Back) Farrimond, Rimmer, Napier, Hatton, Hopkinson, Cooper, Edwards, Hartle
(Front) Butler, Russell, Taylor, Hill, Bromley, Lee, Davies

1966-67 Season
(Back) Lennard, Hill, Davies, Napier, Cooper, D.Hatton, Hulme, Farrimond, Byrom
(Front) Butler, Bromley, Smith, Rimmer, Hopkinson, Lee, Beech, Taylor

1966/67 9th in Division Two

Manager: W.Ridding

League — Division Two

#	Date		Opponent	Score	Scorers	Att
1	Aug	20	Charlton Athletic	1-0	Davies	10429
2		24	ROTHERHAM UNITED	2-2	Davies, Hill	14389
3		27	DERBY COUNTY	3-1	Napier, Lee(pen), Bromley	11656
4		30	Rotherham United	1-0	Taylor	11943
5	Sep	3	Crystal Palace	2-3	Rimmer, Greaves	16578
6		7	CARLISLE UNITED	3-0	Davies(3)	15282
7		10	HUDDERSFIELD TOWN	1-0	Lee	17600
8		17	Cardiff City	5-2	Lee(2,1p), Davies(2), Murray(og)	7594
9		24	WOLVES	0-0		21149
10	Oct	1	Ipswich Town	2-2	Lee, Davies	16019
11		8	PRESTON NORTH END	4-2	Davies(3), Cranston(og)	20239
12		14	Bury	1-2	Davies	21545
13		22	COVENTRY CITY	1-1	Byrom	14561
14		29	Norwich City	0-1		12593
15	Nov	5	BIRMINGHAM CITY	3-1	Rimmer, Lee, Byrom	10030
16		12	Portsmouth	1-2	Lee	12665
17		19	HULL CITY	2-1	Lee(2,1pen)	14950
18		26	Plymouth Argyle	0-2		13635
19	Dec	3	NORTHAMPTON TOWN	1-2	Byrom	10352
20		10	Millwall	0-2		13222
21		17	CHARLTON ATHLETIC	2-1	Lee(pen), Bromley	7911
22		26	Bristol City	1-1	Lee	16725
23		31	Derby County	2-2	Bromley, Byrom	14619
24	Jan	14	Huddersfield Town	1-2	Byrom	18176
25		21	CARDIFF CITY	3-1	Rimmer, Lee, Byrom	9071
26	Feb	4	Wolves	2-5	Bromley(2)	24015
27		11	IPSWICH TOWN	1-1	Taylor	12565
28		25	Preston North End	3-1	Lee(3,1pen)	16067
29	Mar	4	NORWICH CITY	1-1	Farrimond	12483
30		11	CRYSTAL PALACE	0-0		9784
31		18	Coventry City	1-1	Phillips	28674
32		25	BURY	3-1	Lee, R.Hatton(2)	20320
33		27	BLACKBURN ROVERS	0-1		21740
34	Apr	1	Birmingham City	2-2	Lee, Isherwood(og)	18187
35		8	PORTSMOUTH	0-1		11281
36		15	Hull City	1-1	Lee	16480
37		19	BRISTOL CITY	0-0		8647
38		22	PLYMOUTH ARGYLE	1-2	Phillips	7427
39		25	Blackburn Rovers	0-0		12403
40		29	Northampton Town	1-2	Lee	9387
41	May	6	MILLWALL	5-0	Napier, Lee(2), Bromley, Lennard	6502
42		13	Carlisle United	1-6	Lee	8493

Appearances (shirt numbers)

#	Beech HW	Bromley B	Butler DA	Byrom J	Cooper C	Davies RW	Dobson M	Farrimond S	Greaves R	Hatton DH	Hatton RJ	Hill F	Hopkinson E	Hulme J	Lee FH	Lennard D	Marsh A	Napier RJ	Phillips RD	Rimmer WR	Smith A	Taylor G
1		8			2	9		3		6		10	1		7			5		4		11
2		8			2	9		3		6		10	1		7			5		4		11
3	12	8*			2	9		3		6		1	1		7			5		4		11
4				8	2	9		3	7	6		10	1					5		4		11
5			7	8	2	9		3	10	6			1		7			5		4		11
6		8			2	9		3		6		10	1		7			5		4		11
7		8			2	9		3		6		10	1		7			5		4		11
8		8			2	9		3		6		10	1		7			5		4		11
9		8			2	9		3		6		10	1		7			5		4		11
10		8			2	9		3		6		10	1		7			5		4		11
11		8			2	9		3		6		10	1		7			5		4		11
12		8			2	9		3	12	6		10*	1		7			5		4		11
13	6	8		9	3			2					1		7	10		5		4		11
14	6	8		9	3			2					1		7	10		5		4		11
15		8		9	3			2		6			1		7	10		5		4		11
16		8		9	3			2		6		10	1		7			5		4		11
17		8		9	3			2		6		10	1		7			5		4		11
18		8		9	3			2		6		10	1		7	11		5		4		
19		8		9	3			2		6		10	1		7			5		4		11
20		8		9	3			2		6			1		7	10		5		4		11
21		8	7	10	3					6			1		9	6		5		4		11
22			7	8	3					6			1	12	9	10		5*		4		11
23		7		8	3			2		6			1		9	10		5		4		11
24		7	12	8	3			2		6			1		9	10*		5		4		11
25		7		8	3			2		6		10	1	5	9				11	4		
26		7		8	3			2		6			1	5	9	10			11	4		
27		10		8	3			2					1	5	9				11	4		7
28		7		8				2			10		1	5	9	6	3		11	4		
29		7		8				2			10		1	5	9	6	3		11	4		
30		10						3	2	7			1	5	9	6			11	4		
31		10						3	2	9	11		1	5	8	6			7	4		
32		10						3	2	9	7		1	5	8	6			11	4		
33		10						3	2	9	7		1	5	8	6			11	4	1	
34		10						3	2	9	7		1	5	8	6			11	4		
35		10						3	2	9	7		1	5	8	6			11	4		
36		10	8*					3	2	9			1	5	7	6			12	4		11
37		10	11					3	2	9			1	5	8	6				4		7
38		10	8					3	2				1	5	9	6			11	4		7
39		7						2			8*		1	5	9	10	3	6		12		11
40		8						3*		4	9		1	5	7	10	2	6		12		11
41		8								4	9		1	5	7	10	3	6		2		11
42		8								4	9		1	5	7	10	3	6		2		11
Apps	2	27	3	25	27	12		37	2	40	10	25	41	18	40	25	6	28	11	40	1	32
Subs	1		1						1					1								
Goals		6		6		12		1	1		2	1			22	1		2	2	3		2

Three own goals

F.A. Cup

Rd	Date		Opponent	Score	Scorers	Att
3	Jan	28	CREWE ALEXANDRA	1-0	Lee(pen)	23730
4	Feb	18	ARSENAL	0-0		31870
4r		22	Arsenal	0-3		47050

Rd	Bromley B	Butler DA	Cooper C	Farrimond S	Greaves R	Hatton DH	Hill F	Hopkinson E	Hulme J	Lee FH	Lennard D	Phillips RD	Rimmer WR	Taylor G
3	7		3	2		6	10	1	5	9		11	4	
4	10	12	3	2	6*	8		1	5	9		11	4	7
4r	10		3	2		8		1	5	9	6	11	4	7

League Cup

Rd	Date		Opponent	Score	Scorers	Att
2	Sep	14	Manchester City	1-3	Lee	9006

Rd	Beech HW	Bromley B	Davies RW	Farrimond S	Hatton DH	Hill F	Hopkinson E	Lee FH	Napier RJ	Rimmer WR	Taylor G
2	4	8	9	3	6	10	1	7	5	2	11

Lancashire Cup

#	Date		Opponent	Score
1	Oct	11	Morecambe	0-2

Other Games

#	Date		Opponent	Score
1	Aug	15	Manchester City	0-0

FINAL TABLE

		Pl.	Home W	D	L	F	A	Away W	D	L	F	A	F (Total)	A	Pts
1	Coventry City	42	17	3	1	46	16	6	10	5	28	27	74	43	59
2	Wolverhampton W.	42	15	4	2	53	20	10	4	7	35	28	88	48	58
3	Carlisle United	42	15	3	3	42	16	8	3	10	29	38	71	54	52
4	Blackburn Rovers	42	13	6	2	33	11	6	7	8	23	35	56	46	51
5	Ipswich Town	42	11	8	2	45	25	6	8	7	25	29	70	54	50
6	Huddersfield Town	42	14	4	3	36	17	6	9		22	29	58	46	49
7	Crystal Palace	42	14	4	3	42	23	5	6	10	19	32	61	55	48
8	Millwall	42	14	5	2	33	17	4	4	13	16	41	49	58	45
9	BOLTON WANDERERS	42	10	7	4	36	19	4	7	10	28	39	64	58	42
10	Birmingham City	42	11	5	5	42	23	5	3	13	28	43	70	66	40
11	Norwich City	42	10	7	4	31	21	3	7	11	18	34	49	55	40
12	Hull City	42	11	5	5	46	25	5	2	14	31	47	77	72	39
13	Preston North End	42	14	3	4	44	23	2	4	15	21	44	65	67	39
14	Portsmouth	42	7	5	9	34	37	6	8	7	25	33	59	70	39
15	Bristol City	42	10	8	3	38	22	2	6	13	18	40	56	62	38
16	Plymouth Argyle	42	12	4	5	42	21	2	5	14	17	37	59	58	37
17	Derby County	42	8	5	8	42	30	4	6	11	28	40	68	72	36
18	Rotherham United	42	10	5	6	39	28	3	5	13	22	42	61	70	36
19	Charlton Athletic	42	11	4	6	34	16	2	5	14	15	37	49	53	35
20	Cardiff City	42	9	5	7	43	28	3	2	16	18	59	61	87	33
21	Northampton Town	42	8	6	7	28	33	0		17	19	51	47	84	30
22	Bury	42	9	3	9	31	30	2	3	16	18	53	49	83	28

Manager: W.Ridding

No	Date	Opponent	Score	Scorers	Att	Bromley B	Butler D	Byrom J	Cooper C	Farrimond S	Greaves R	Hatton DH	Hatton RJ	Hill F	Hopkinson E	Hulme J	Lee FH	Lennard D	Marsh A	Phillips RD	Rimmer WR	Ritson JA	Roberts GM	Smith A	Taylor G	Wharton TJ	Williams GC
1	Aug 19	Birmingham City	0-4		23537	8				3	4	5	9	10	1		7	6	2						11		
2	23	HULL CITY	6-1	Lee(2), Taylor(2), Byrom(2)	9653			8		3	4	5	9	10	1		7	6	2						11		
3	26	CARDIFF CITY	1-1	Lee	10654			8		3	4	5	9	10	1		7	6	2						11		
4	30	Hull City	2-1	Lee, Byrom	15776			8		3	4	5	9	10			7	6	2					1	11		
5	Sep 2	HUDDERSFIELD TOWN	3-1	Lee(2), Byrom	11544			8	12	3	4	5	9*	10			7	6	2					1	11		
6	6	MILLWALL	1-1	Lee	11360	8		9		3	4	5		10	1		7	6	2						11		
7	9	Ipswich Town	1-1	Lee	14903	8		9		3	4	2		10	1	5	7	6							11		
8	16	CARLISLE UNITED	2-3	Greaves, Bromley	12809	8		9		3	4	6	12	10	1	5	7		2*						11		
9	23	Blackburn Rovers	1-2	Byrom	19933	8		10		3	4		9*		1	5	7	6	12						11		
10	30	BLACKPOOL	1-2	Phillips	16695	8	7	9		3	4	2		10	1	5		6		11							
11	Oct 7	Queens Park Ranger	0-1		16848	10		9		3	4	2*		10	1	5		6		12	7				11		
12	14	NORWICH CITY	2-0	Bromley, Byrom	8503	7		9		3	8	2		10	1	5		6							11		4
13	21	Rotherham United	2-2	Greaves, Byrom	7229			9		3	8	2		10	1	5		6			7				11		4
14	28	DERBY COUNTY	5-3	Greaves, Byrom(2), Williams(2)	12631	7		9		3	8	2		10	1	5		6							11		4
15	Nov 4	Preston North End	1-1	Taylor	19796			9		3	8	2		10	1	5		6							11	7	4
16	18	Portsmouth	0-3		21437	8		9*	2	3	6			10	1	5				12					11	7	4
17	22	CHARLTON ATHLETIC	2-0	Williams, Wharton	12043	8			2	3	9			10	1	5					6	12			11	7	4*
18	25	ASTON VILLA	2-3	Hill, Deakin(og)	13064	8			2	3	9			10	1	5					6				11	7	4
19	Dec 2	Cyrstal Palace	3-0	Taylor, Wharton(2)	15780	8			2	3	9			10	1	5					6				11	7	4
20	9	PLYMOUTH ARGYLE	1-2	Taylor	9505	8			2	3	9			10	1	5					6				11	7	4
21	16	BIRMINGHAM CITY	1-1	Greaves	10468				2	3	9	6		8	1	5					10				11	7	4
22	23	Cardiff City	3-1	Taylor, Greaves, Carver(og)	11082				2	3	9	6		8	1	5					10				11	7	4
23	26	MIDDLESBROUGH	2-0	Rimmer, Wharton	16067				2	3	9	6		8	1	5					10				11	7	4
24	30	Middlesbrough	2-1	Rimmer, Horner(og)	29217				2	3	9	6		8	1	5					10				11	7	4
25	Jan 6	Huddersfield Town	1-1	Hill	14147				2	3	9	6		8	1	5					10				11	7	4
26	20	Carlisle United	0-3		11065				2	3	9			8	1	5				12	10	6			11	7	4
27	Feb 3	BLACKBURN ROVERS	2-1	Williams(2)	17334			9	2	3	12	6		8	1	5					10				11	7*	4
28	10	Blackpool	1-1	Taylor(pen)	19183			9	2	3	7	6		8	1	5					10				11	7*	4
29	16	Millwall	1-1		12457			9	2	3	7	6		8	1	5					10				11		4
30	24	QUEENS PARK RANGERS	1-1	Hulme	14956	12		8	2	3	9	6		7	1	5*					10				11		4
31	Mar 2	Norwich City	1 3	Taylor	14694			9	2	3	5		7	8	1						10	6			11		4
32	9	Ipswich Town	1-2	Greaves	8695				2	3	9	6		8	1	5					10	7			11		4
33	16	ROTHERHAM UNITED	0-2		8682	8			2	3	5		9	10	1						11*	6	12		7		
34	23	Derby County	1-2	Greaves	16054	8			2	3	9	6			1	5					10	7			11		
35	30	PRESTON NORTH END	0-0		14664			9	2	3	7	6			1	5					10	8			11		
36	Apr 2	Bristol City	1-1	Greaves	11047	8			2	3	9	6			1	5					10	7			11		
37	6	Charlton Athletic	0-2		10571	8			2	3	9	6			1	5					10	2			11	7	4
38	13	PORTSMOUTH	1-2	Smith(og)	7833	10				3	9	6		8	1	5						2			11	7	4
39	17	BRISTOL CITY	1-0	Greaves	7289	10				3	9	6		8	1	5						2			11	7	4
40	20	Aston Villa	1-1	Taylor	16860	10				3	9	6		8	1	5						2			11	7	4
41	27	CRYSTAL PALACE	2-2	Greaves, Hulme	6768	10				3	9	6		8	1	5						2			11	7	4
42	May 4	Plymouth Argyle	2-1	Hill, Wharton(pen)	5371	10					9	6		8	1	5						2	3		11	7	4

					Apps	21	1	23	22	41	36	35	13	36	40	34	9	15	8	3	24	7	1	2	41	19	31
					Subs	1		1	1		1		1			1		1	2	1		2					
					Goals	2		9			10			3		2	8			1	2				9	5	5

Four own goals

F.A. Cup

Rd	Date	Opponent	Score	Scorers	Att	Bromley B	Byrom J	Cooper C	Farrimond S	Greaves R	Hill F	Hopkinson E	Hulme J	Rimmer WR	Taylor G	Williams GC
3	Jan 27	Nottingham Forest	2-4	Taylor, Hulme	37229	7	9	2	3	10	8	1	5	6	11	4

League Cup

Rd	Date	Opponent	Score	Scorers	Att	Bromley B	Byrom J	Farrimond S	Greaves R	Hatton DH	Hill F	Hopkinson E	Hulme J	Lee FH	Lennard D	Marsh A	Rimmer WR	Taylor G	Williams GC
2	Sep 13	Liverpool	1-1	Lee	45957	8	9	3	4	6	10	1	5	7		2		11	
2r	27	LIVERPOOL	3-2	Hill, Taylor(2)	30669	8	9	3	4	2	10	1	5	7	6			11	
3	Oct 11	West Ham United	1-4	Byrom	20450	8	9	3	6	2	10	1	5				7	11	4

Lancashire Cup

Rd	Date	Opponent	Score
2	Nov 20	Barrow	1-4

Other Games

#	Date	Opponent	Score
1	Aug 12	Tranmere Rovers	1-3

FINAL TABLE

		Pl.	Home W	D	L	F	A	Away W	D	L	F	A	F. (Total)	A.	Pts
1	Ipswich Town	42	12	7	2	45	20	10	8	3	34	24	79	44	59
2	Queen's Park Rgs.	42	18	2	1	45	9	7	6	8	22	27	67	36	58
3	Blackpool	42	12	6	3	33	16	12	4	5	38	27	71	43	58
4	Birmingham City	42	12	6	3	54	21	7	8	6	29	30	83	51	52
5	Portsmouth	42	13	6	2	43	18	5	7	9	25	37	68	55	49
6	Middlesbrough	42	10	7	4	39	19	7	5	9	21	35	60	54	46
7	Millwall	42	9	10	2	35	16	5	7	9	27	34	62	50	45
8	Blackburn Rovers	42	13	5	3	34	16	3	6	12	22	33	56	49	43
9	Norwich City	42	12	5	4	40	30	4	7	10	20	35	60	65	43
10	Carlisle United	42	9	9	3	38	22	4	4	12	20	30	58	52	41
11	Crystal Palace	42	11	4	6	34	19	3	7	11	22	37	56	56	39
12	BOLTON WANDERERS	42	8	6	7	37	28	5	7	9	23	35	60	63	39
13	Cardiff City	42	9	6	6	35	29	4	6	11	25	37	60	66	38
14	Huddersfield Town	42	10	6	5	29	23	3	6	12	17	38	46	61	38
15	Charlton Athletic	42	10	6	5	43	25	2	7	12	20	43	63	68	37
16	Aston Villa	42	10	3	8	35	30	5	4	12	19	34	54	64	37
17	Hull City	42	6	8	7	25	23	6	5	10	33	50	58	73	37
18	Derby County	42	8	5	8	40	35	5	5	11	31	43	71	78	36
19	Bristol City	42	7	7	7	26	25	6	3	12	22	37	48	62	36
20	Preston North End	42	8	7	6	29	24	4	4	13	14	41	43	65	35
21	Rotherham United	42	7	4	10	22	32	3	7	11	20	44	42	76	31

1967-68 Season
(Back) Hulme, Marsh, Farrimond, Cooper, Byrom
(Middle) Napier, Hill, Smith, Hopkinson, Lennard, D.Hatton
(Front) Lee, R.Hatton, Bromley, Taylor, Phillips

1968-69 Season
(Back) Jones, Hulme, Farrimond, Hill, Cooper, Hopkinson
(Middle) D.Hatton, R.Hatton, Rimmer, Byrom, Williams
(Front) Taylor, Wharton, Ritson, Bromley, Phillips, Lennard, Greaves

1968/69 17th in Division Two

Manager: N. Lofthouse

Player columns (left to right): Bromilow G, Bromley B, Byrom J, Cooper C, Farrimond S, Fletcher PJ, Greaves R, Hallows PCR, Hatton DH, Hill F, Hopkinson E, Hulme J, Jones GE, Lennard D, Manning JJ, Marsh A, Phillips RD, Rimmer WR, Ritson JA, Roberts GM, Taylor G, Wharton TJ, Williams GC

#		Date	Opponent	Result	Scorers	Att.	BrmlwG	BrmlyB	ByrmJ	CoopC	FarrS	FletPJ	GrvsR	HalPCR	HatDH	HillF	HopE	HulmJ	JonGE	LenD	ManJJ	MarA	PhilRD	RimWR	RitJA	RobGM	TayG	WhaTJ	WilGC
1	Aug	10	Oxford United	1-1	Williams	11427		10			3		9		6	8	1	5							2		11	7	4
2		17	BURY	2-0	Greaves, Bromley	16627		10			3		9		6	8	1	5							2		11	7	4
3		20	Bristol City	2-2	Wharton(2)	17353		10			3		9		6	8	1	5							2		11	7	4
4		24	Fulham	2-0	Hulme, Hill	12830		10			3		9		6	8	1	5							2		11	7	4
5		26	Millwall	1-3	Wharton	15655		10			3		9		6	8	1	5							2		11	7	4
6		31	SHEFFIELD UNITED	4-2	Greaves(3), Wharton(pen)	14636		10			3		9		6	8	1	5							2		11	7	4
7	Sep	7	Blackpool	0-1		22688		10			3		9		6	8	1	5							2		11	7	4
8		14	BLACKBURN ROVERS	1-1	Bromley	16097		10			3		9		6	8	1	5							2		11	7	4
9		18	ASTON VILLA	4-1	Greaves(2), Hill, Hulme	14513		10			3		9		6	8	1	5						12	2		11	7	4*
10		21	Hull City	0-1		13487		10			3		9		6	8	1	5		12				4	2		11*	7	
11		28	DERBY COUNTY	1-2	Wharton	15202		10			3		9		6	8	1	5					11		2			7	4
12	Oct	5	Carlisle United	1-1	Hill	8846		10			3		9*		6	8	1	5		12				4	2		11	7	
13		9	MILLWALL	0-4		12715		10			3		9		6*	8	1	5		12				4	2		11	7	
14		12	CHARLTON ATHLETIC	3-0	Greaves, Hill, Curtis(og)	9060	12	8*			3		9			10	1	5		6		2	4					7	
15		19	Cardiff City	2-0	Wharton, Taylor	12026		10			3		9		6	8	1	5							2		11	7	4
16		26	HUDDERSFIELD TOWN	2-3	Wharton(pen), Hill	12431		10			3		9		6	8	1	5							2		11	7	4
17	Nov	2	Crystal Palace	1-2	Fletcher	13027		10*	8		3	9	4		6	11	1	5		12					2			7	
18		16	Middlesbrough	0-0		18458			8		3		9		6	11	1	5					10		2			7	4
19		23	BIRMINGHAM CITY	0-0		7175	8*		9		3				6	11	1	5					10	12	2			7	4
20		30	Preston North End	4-1	Byrom(2), Rimmer, Williams	15252			9		3				6	11	1	5					10	4	2			7	8
21	Dec	4	NORWICH CITY	1-1	Byrom	9842			9		3				6	11	1	5					10	4	2			7	8
22		7	PORTSMOUTH	1-0	Taylor	7805			9		3				6	8	1	5					10	4	2		11	7	
23		14	Charlton Athletic	2-2	Williams, Fletcher	9270					3	9			6	11	1	5					10	4	2			7	8
24		21	CARDIFF CITY	1-2	Wharton	8895			9		3	12			6	11	1	5					10	4	2			7	8*
25		26	CARLISLE UNITED	0-1		13922			8		3	9			6	10	1	5							2		11	7	4
26	Jan	11	CRYSTAL PALACE	2-2	Greaves(2)	9082					3	9	8		6	10	1	5							2		11	7	4
27		18	Norwich City	0-2		11997						9	8		6	10	1	5							2	3	11	7	4
28	Feb	1	MIDDLESBROUGH	0-0		7658			8		3		9		6	10	1					5			2		11	7	4
29		22	Portsmouth	2-2	Wharton, Taylor	16500			8		3		9		6	10	1					5		12	2		11*	7	4
30	Mar	1	OXFORD UNITED	1-1	Byrom	6707			8		3		9		6	10	1			12		5*			2		11	7	4
31		4	Huddersfield Town	0-3		8614			8		3		9		6	10	1					5	7	2			11		4
32		7	Bury	1-2	Williams	11755			9	12	3			8	6*	10	1					5	7		2		11		4
33		15	FULHAM	3-2	Conway(og), Rimmer, Taylor	8323			9		3			8		10	1					5	7	6	2		11		4
34		22	Sheffield United	2-5	Hill, Phillips	12467	12				3			8		10	1		5*		9	6	7	2			11		4
35		25	Birmingham City	0-5		20454	6				3			8		10	1				9	5	7	2			11		4
36		29	BLACKPOOL	1-4	Taylor(pen)	9264			10	2	3	12	9			8	1					5	7	6*			11		4
37	Apr	5	Derby County	1-5	Greaves	30684			9	2	3		10			8	1					5	7	6			11		4
38		7	BRISTOL CITY	1-0	Byrom	8172			9	2	3					8	1					5	10	6			11	7	4
39		8	Aston Villa	1-1	Hulme	25442			9	2	3					8	1	5					10	6			11	7	4
40		12	HULL CITY	1-0	Phillips	5106			9	2	3					8	1		5*			12	10	6			11	7	4
41		16	PRESTON NORTH END	0-0		8028			9	2	3		10			8	1					5		6			11	7	4
42		19	Blackburn Rovers	3-2	Greaves, Wharton, Bryom	8178			9	2	3		10			8	1	12				5		6			11	7	4*
			Apps				3	17	21	10	38	9	32	3	31	35	42	32	2	8	2	15	13	19	29	1	29	35	36
			Subs				2			2		1						2		1	4					3				
			Goals					2	6			2	11		6			3					2	2			5	10	4

Two own goals

F.A. Cup

#		Date	Opponent	Result	Scorers	Att.	FarrS	FletPJ	GrvsR	ByrmJ	HatDH	HillF	HopE	HulmJ	MarA	PhilRD	WhaTJ	RitJA	TayG	WilGC
3	Jan	4	NORTHAMPTON TOWN	2-1	Fletcher, Greaves	12632	3	9	8		6	10	1	5				2	11	4
4		25	BRISTOL ROVERS	1-2	Williams	16707	3		8	9*	6	11	1	5	10		12	2	7	4

League Cup

#		Date	Opponent	Result	Scorers	Att.	BrmlyB	FarrS	GrvsR	HatDH	HillF	HopE	HulmJ	RitJA	TayG	WhaTJ	WilGC
2	Sep	4	West Ham United	2-7	Wharton(pen), Taylor	24737	10	3	9	6	8	1	5	2	11	7	4

Lancashire Cup

2	Oct	15	BURY	4-1
3	Dec	11	MANCHESTER CITY	1-2

Other Games

1	Jul	31	Twente Enschede	1-1
2	Aug	3	VFR Neuss	1-0
3	Nov	12	BREMHERHAVEN	4-2
4	Apr	27	Bremherhaven	1-1
5		30	Hvidovre	2-0
6	May	2	Holbaek	2-0
7		5	South Jutland Alliance	4-0
8		8	Freja Randers	4-3

FINAL TABLE

		Pl.	W	D	L	F	A	W	D	L	F	A	F	A	Pts
				Home					Away				(Total)		
1	Derby County	42	16	4	1	43	16	10	7	4	22	16	65	32	63
2	Crystal Palace	42	14	4	3	45	24	8	8	5	25	23	70	47	56
3	Charlton Athletic	42	11	8	2	39	21	7	8	6	22	31	61	52	50
4	Middlesbrough	42	13	7	1	36	13	6	4	11	22	36	58	49	49
5	Cardiff City	42	13	3	5	38	19	7	4	10	29	35	67	54	47
6	Huddersfield Town	42	13	6	2	37	14	4	6	11	16	32	53	46	46
7	Birmingham City	42	13	3	5	52	24	5	5	11	21	35	73	59	44
8	Blackpool	42	9	8	4	33	20	5	7	9	18	21	51	41	43
9	Sheffield United	42	14	4	3	41	15	2	7	12	20	35	61	50	43
10	Millwall	42	10	6	5	33	23	7	4	10	24	26	57	49	43
11	Hull City	42	10	7	4	38	20	3	9	9	21	32	59	52	42
12	Carlisle United	42	10	5	6	25	17	6	5	10	21	32	46	49	42
13	Norwich City	42	7	5	9	24	25	8	4	9	29	31	53	56	40
14	Preston North End	42	8	8	5	23	19	4	7	10	15	25	38	44	39
15	Portsmouth	42	11	5	5	39	22	1	9	11	19	36	58	58	38
16	Bristol City	42	9	9	3	30	15	2	7	12	16	38	46	53	38
17	BOLTON WANDERERS	42	8	7	6	29	26	4	7	10	26	41	55	67	38
18	Aston Villa	42	10	8	3	22	11	2	6	13	15	37	37	48	38
19	Blackburn Rovers	42	9	6	6	30	24	4	5	12	22	39	52	63	37
20	Oxford United	42	8	8	5	21	16	4	4	13	13	32	34	55	33
21	Bury	42	8	4	9	35	33	3	4	14	16	47	51	80	30
22	Fulham	42	6	7	8	20	28	1	4	16	20	53	40	81	25

1969/70 16th in Division Two

Manager: N. Lofthouse

Player columns (in order): Boswell AH, Byrom J, Duffey CP, Farrimond S, Fletcher PJ, Greaves R, Hallows PCR, Hatton DH, Hopkinson E, Hulme J, Hunt R, Hurley C, McAllister D, Manning JJ, Marsh A, Phillips RD, Redfern J, Rimmer WR, Ritson JA, Roberts GM, Seddon IW, Taylor G, Wharton TJ, Williams GC

League (Division Two)

#	Date	Opponent	Result	Scorers	Att.
1	Aug 9	MILLWALL	4-1	Byrom(3), Greaves	10402
2	16	Watford	0-0		15975
3	20	Leicester City	2-2	Wharton(pen), Phillips	27673
4	23	PRESTON NORTH END	2-0	Phillips, Wharton(pen)	15009
5	26	Carlisle United	1-2	Wharton	11682
6	30	Cardiff City	1-2	Wharton	21048
7	Sep 6	BIRMINGHAM CITY	2-0	Taylor, Byrom	11303
8	13	Hull City	2-4	Greaves, Byrom	10646
9	17	ASTON VILLA	2-1	Byrom, Greaves	11700
10	20	PORTSMOUTH	0-1		10579
11	27	Huddersfield Town	0-1		12326
12	Oct 4	SWINDON TOWN	0-1		9372
13	8	WATFORD	2-3	Hulme, Seddon	7443
14	11	Middlesbrough	0-4		14020
15	18	OXFORD UNITED	1-1	Byrom	7030
16	25	Blackpool	1-1	Manning	17179
17	Nov 1	BRISTOL CITY	3-1	Byrom, Wharton, Rooks(og)	6757
18	8	Blackburn Rovers	1-3	Wharton	13175
19	12	LEICESTER CITY	2-3	Taylor, Wharton(pen)	7219
20	15	SHEFFIELD UNITED	0-0		7992
21	19	Aston Villa	0-3		22951
22	22	Norwich City	0-1		10809
23	29	QUEENS PARK RANGERS	6-4	Manning(2), Byrom(2), Taylor, Wharton	7253
24	Dec 6	Charlton Athletic	1-1	Byrom	7644
25	13	HULL CITY	2-1	Byrom(2)	7059
26	26	Preston North End	3-1	Manning, Byrom, Hurley	23934
27	Jan 10	Portsmouth	1-1	Byrom	10464
28	17	HUDDERSFIELD TOWN	1-1	Byrom	14272
29	31	Swindon Town	2-3	Wharton, Manning	18564
30	Feb 11	MIDDLESBROUGH	2-1	Hunt, Hurley	9928
31	14	Millwall	0-2		9881
32	21	BLACKPOOL	0-2		14431
33	24	Birmingham City	0-2		19489
34	28	Oxford United	1-3	Byrom	9627
35	Mar 14	Queens Park Rangers	4-0	Hunt(2), Greaves, Byrom	13596
36	18	CARDIFF CITY	0-1		10434
37	21	CHARLTON ATHLETIC	1-1	Hunt	8367
38	27	Bristol City	2-2	Hulme, Byrom	17298
39	28	Sheffield United	1-0	Byrom	18539
40	30	BLACKBURN ROVERS	1-0	Hunt	18032
41	Apr 4	CARLISLE UNITED	0-0		9120
42	9	NORWICH CITY	0-0		7164

Appearances / Goals summary

	Boswell AH	Byrom J	Duffey CP	Farrimond S	Fletcher PJ	Greaves R	Hallows PCR	Hatton DH	Hopkinson E	Hulme J	Hunt R	Hurley C	McAllister D	Manning JJ	Marsh A	Phillips RD	Redfern J	Rimmer WR	Ritson JA	Roberts GM	Seddon IW	Taylor G	Wharton TJ	Williams GC
Apps	22	40	2	5	4	37	26	6	20	15	17	28	1	14	37	13	1	36	39	3	13	28	38	17
Subs				1	1								1								2	3		1
Goals		20				4				1	5	3		5		2					1	3	9	

One own goal

F.A. Cup

#	Date	Opponent	Result	Scorers	Att.
3	Jan 3	WATFORD	1-2	Greaves	22447

League Cup

#	Date	Opponent	Result	Scorers	Att.
1	Aug 13	ROCHDALE	6-3	Byrom(3), Wharton(p), Greaves(2)	10097
2	Sep 3	ROTHERHAM UNITED	0-0		11043
2r	9	Rotherham United*	3-3	Hulme, Byrom(2)	7924
2/2r	11	Rotherham United	0-1		9018

* After extra-time

Lancashire Cup

#	Date	Opponent	Result
2	Oct 21	MANCHESTER UNITED	1-2

Other Games

#	Date	Opponent	Result
1	July 26	Walsall	0-1
2	30	BURNLEY	1-1
3	Aug 2	Ayr United	2-1
4	Nov 24	VFR NEUSS	3-0
5	Jan 24	Halifax Town	2-0
6	Feb 6	Tranmere Rovers	1-1
7	Apr 14	South Liverpool	1-1

FINAL TABLE

		Pl	Home W	D	L	F	A	Away W	D	L	F	A	F (Total)	A	Pts
1	Huddersfield Town	42	14	5	2	36	10	10	6	5	32	27	68	37	60
2	Blackpool	42	10	9	2	25	16	10	4	7	31	29	56	45	53
3	Leicester City	42	12	6	3	37	22	7	7	7	27	28	64	50	51
4	Middlesbrough	42	15	4	2	36	14	5	6	10	19	31	55	45	50
5	Swindon Town	42	13	7	1	35	17	4	9	8	22	30	57	47	50
6	Sheffield United	42	16	2	3	50	10	6	3	12	23	28	73	38	49
7	Cardiff City	42	12	7	2	38	14	6	6	9	23	27	61	41	49
8	Blackburn Rovers	42	15	2	4	42	19	5	5	11	12	31	54	50	47
9	Queen's Park Rgs.	42	13	5	3	47	24	4	6	11	19	33	66	57	45
10	Millwall	42	14	4	3	38	18	1	10	10	18	38	56	56	44
11	Norwich City	42	13	5	3	37	14	3	6	12	12	32	49	46	43
12	Carlisle United	42	10	6	5	39	28	4	7	10	19	28	58	56	41
13	Hull City	42	11	6	4	43	28	4	5	12	29	42	72	70	41
14	Bristol City	42	11	7	3	37	13	2	6	13	17	37	54	50	39
15	Oxford United	42	9	9	3	23	13	3	6	12	12	29	35	42	39
16	BOLTON WANDERERS	42	9	6	6	31	23	3	6	12	23	38	54	61	36
17	Portsmouth	42	8	4	9	39	35	5	5	11	27	45	66	80	35
18	Birmingham City	42	9	7	5	33	22	2	4	15	18	56	51	78	33
19	Watford	42	6	8	7	26	21	3	5	13	18	36	44	57	31
20	Charlton Athletic	42	7	8	6	23	20	1	9	12	12	48	35	76	31
21	Aston Villa	42	7	8	6	23	21	1	5	15	13	41	36	62	29
22	Preston North End	42	7	6	8	31	28	1	6	14	12	35	43	63	28

1969-70 Season
(Back) Hulme, Seddon, Williams, Marsh, Hopkinson, Clarke, Manning, Hurley, Hatton, Taylor, Greaves
(Front) Ritson, Rimmer, Roberts, Phillips, Fletcher, Wharton, Byrom, Jones, Hallows

1970-71 Season
(Back) Farrimond, Boswell, Clarke, Redfern, Duffey, Hallows, Ritson, Waldron, Fletcher, Wharton
(2nd Row) Hopkinson (Ass.Trainer) Manning, P.Jones, Marsh, Lucas, G.Jones, Hulme,
Seddon, McAllister, Bourne, Conway (Coach)
(3rd Row) Phillips, Taylor, Greaves, Hunt, Lofthouse (Manager), Hurley, Williams, Rimmer, Byrom
(Front) Welsh, McGill, Graham, Lee, Olinyk. Sproston (Trainer)

1970/71 22nd in Division Two (relegated)

Manager: *

#		Date	Opponent	Score	Scorers	Att	Boswell AH	Byrom J	Clarke PA	Duffey CP	Farrimond S	Fletcher PJ	Greaves R	Hallows PCR	Hulme J	Hunt R	Hurley CJ	Jones GE	Jones PB	McAllister D	Manning JJ	Marsh A	Phillips RD	Redfern J	Rimmer WR	Ritson IA	Seddon IW	Taylor G	Waldron A	Wharton TJ	Williams GC
1	Aug	15	LUTON TOWN	4-2	Wharton(3,2pens), Greaves	11664		8	1		3		10		5	9									6	2		11		7	4
2		19	SHEFFIELD WEDNESDAY	2-1	Ritson, Hunt	13462		8	1		3		10		5	9									6	2		11		7	4
3		22	Portsmouth	0-4		15743		8	1		3		10		5	9		12							6	2*		11		7	4
4		29	QUEENS PARK RANGERS	2-2	Williams, Wharton(pen)	11242	1	8			3		10		2	5		9							6			11		7	4
5	Sep	2	Sheffield Wednesday	1-1	Hunt	12420	1	8			3		10		2	5		9							6			11		7	4
6		5	Hull City	0-1		16290	1	8*			3		9	7	2	5		10					12		6		4	11			
7		12	CARDIFF CITY	0-2		11086	1				3		9	10	2			8		7			5		6			11			4
8		19	Blackburn Rovers	2-0	Taylor, Byron	10421	1	10			3		9	7	2			8							6			11			4
9		26	OXFORD UNITED	0-2		9095	1	10*			3		9	7	2			8					12		6			11			4
10		30	ORIENT	0-1		7165	1				3		9		2	5		10		7*			11		6		8	12	4		
11	Oct	3	Sunderland	1-4	Fletcher	15972	1				3		9		2	5		10					11		6		8	7	4		
12		10	CHARLTON ATHLETIC	4-0	Fletcher, Byrom(2), Taylor	7937	1	8			3	7			6			5			9		10			2		11			4
13		17	Luton Town	0-2		19055	1	8			3	7			6			5			9		10			2		11			4
14		20	Sheffield United	2-2	Hulme, Phillips	18216	1	8			3		9		6			5					11		10	2		7			4
15		24	BRISTOL CITY	1-0	Williams	7749	1	8			3		9		6			5					11		10	2		7			4
16		31	Leicester City	0-1		24623	1	8			3		9		6			5					11		10	2		7			4
17	Nov	7	NORWICH CITY	0-1		7201	1				3		12		10			6		5	7		9*		11	8	2				
18		14	Millwall	0-2		6410	1				3		8		10			5		7*	9		11		6	2			12		
19		21	BIRMINGHAM CITY	3-0	Hunt(3)	7432	1						10		6	8	5			3	9					2		11		7	4
20		28	Watford	1-1	Manning	12020	1						10		6	8	5			3	9					2		11		7	4
21	Dec	5	SWINDON TOWN	0-3		7826	1						10		6	8	5			3	9					2		11		7	4
22		12	Middlesbrough	0-1		12873	1						10		6	8*	5			3	9		12			2		11		7	4
23		19	PORTSMOUTH	1-1	Manning	5813	1	8					10		5			7		3	9		11		6	2*				12	
24		26	Carlisle United	0-1		11132	1	8					9	10	2			5		7	3		11		6						
25	Jan	9	Orient	1-3	Redfern	6580	1	8					9	10*		5		7		3			11	12	6	2	8				
26		16	SHEFFIELD UNITED	2-1	Seddon, Fletcher	10146	1						9		5			10	6	3			11	7		2	8		4		
27		30	WATFORD	0-1		10239	1						9		6	5*		10		3			11	7	12	2	8		4		
28	Feb	6	Swindon Town	1-3	Hunt	15325	1						9		6	8	5	10		3*			11			2	7		12		4
29		13	MIDDLESBROUGH	0-3		9877	1						9		6	8	5	10	4	3			11		12	2	7*				4
30		20	Birmingham City	0-4		25600	1						9			8	5	10		3		12	11*		6	2	7				4
31		27	LEICESTER CITY	0-3		8663		8	1				7		6	12				3	9*		11		5	2	10		4		
32	Mar	6	Bristol City	1-1	Waldron	10550		8	1				6		7	9				3			11		5	2	10		4		
33		13	MILLWALL	1-1	G.Jones	6308		8	1				6		9	12		7		3				11*	5	2	10		4		
34		20	Norwich City	1-2	G.Jones(pen)	9051		8	1				6		9			7		3			11		5	2	10		4		
35		27	HULL CITY	0-0		8759		8	1				6		9	12		7		3			11		5	2	10		4*		
36	Apr	3	Queens Park Rangers	0-4		8613		8	1				6		9	4		7		3			11		5	2	10				
37		7	Cardiff City	0-1		21282			1				4		5	8		9		3		6	11		7	10*	2	12			
38		10	CARLISLE UNITED	0-3		8038			1				4		5	8		9		3		6	11		7	2	10*		12		
39		12	SUNDERLAND	1-3	Hunt	5937			1				4		2	5		8		9		3	6	11*	7		12	10			
40		17	Charlton Athletic	1-4	Greaves	10295			1	11			8		5	9				3		6			7	2	10		4		
41		24	BLACKBURN ROVERS	1-1	Goodwin(og)	7195		12	1	11*			8		5	9				3		6			7	2	10		4		
42	May	1	Oxford United	1-1	Hunt	7357		9	1				8		5	10	11*	6		3			12		7	2			4		

						Apps	29	22	13	2	18	20	34	11	37	22	13	22	4	24	11	5	20	13	27	32	17	19	14	9	24
						Subs		1			1	1		1		2	1	1				1	4	2	1		2	1	3	1	
						Goals		3				3	2		1	8		2			2		1	1		1	1	2	1	4	2

One own goal

*N.Lofthouse until 2/11/70; J.McIlroy 3-20/11/70;
N.Lofthouse until 14/1/71; J.Meadows 15/1 until 6/4/71;
N.Lofthouse until 5/71

F.A. Cup

		Date	Opponent	Score		Att	Boswell AH	Byrom J	Greaves R	Hulme J	Hunt R	Jones GE	McAllister D	Manning JJ	Phillips RD	Redfern J	Rimmer WR	Ritson IA	Seddon IW	Taylor G	Williams GC
3	Jan	2	York City	0-2		10113	1	8	9		10	5	3	7*	11		6	2	12		4

League Cup

		Date	Opponent	Score	Scorers	Att															
2	Sep	9	BLACKBURN ROVERS	1-0	Fletcher	12000	1		3 9	10 2	8	7			5		6			11	4
3	Oct	7	LEICESTER CITY	1-1	Manning	8623	1 12	3 10		6	5	9			11	8* 2			7		4
3r		12	Leicester City	0-1		18068	1 8	3 7*		6 12 5		9			10		2			11	4

Lancashire Cup

		Date	Opponent	Score
2	Oct	19	Manchester City	1-2

Other Games

		Date	Opponent	Score
1	Aug	2	SPVGG. Bayreuth	0-0
2		4	Celle	2-0
3		5	VFL Osnabruck	2-1
4		8	Newcastle United	0-3
5	Jan	23	Grimsby Town	0-2
6	Mar	1	FREJA RANDERS	2-1

FINAL TABLE

		Pl.	Home W	D	L	F	A	Away W	D	L	F	A	F. (Total)	A.	Pts
1	Leicester City	42	12	7	2	30	14	11	6	4	27	16	57	30	59
2	Sheffield United	42	14	6	1	49	18	7	8	6	24	21	73	39	56
3	Cardiff City	42	12	7	2	39	16	8	6	7	25	25	64	41	53
4	Carlisle United	42	16	3	2	39	13	4	10	7	26	30	65	43	53
5	Hull City	42	11	5	5	31	16	8	5	8	23	25	54	41	51
6	Luton Town	42	12	7	2	40	18	6	6	9	22	25	62	43	49
7	Middlesbrough	42	13	6	2	37	16	4	8	9	23	27	60	43	48
8	Millwall	42	13	5	3	36	12	6	4	11	23	30	59	42	47
9	Birmingham City	42	12	7	2	30	12	5	5	11	28	36	58	48	46
10	Norwich City	42	11	8	2	34	20	4	6	11	20	32	54	52	44
11	Queen's Park Rgs.	42	11	5	5	39	22	5	6	10	19	31	58	53	43
12	Swindon Town	42	12	7	2	38	14	3	5	13	23	37	61	51	42
13	Sunderland	42	11	6	4	34	21	4	6	11	18	33	52	54	42
14	Oxford United	42	8	8	5	23	23	6	6	9	18	25	41	48	42
15	Sheffield Wed.	42	10	7	4	32	27	2	5	14	19	42	51	69	36
16	Portsmouth	42	9	4	8	32	28	1	10	10	14	33	46	61	34
17	Orient	42	5	11	5	16	15	4	5	12	13	36	29	51	34
18	Watford	42	6	6	9	18	22	4	6	11	20	38	38	60	33
19	Bristol City	42	9	6	6	30	28	1	5	15	16	36	46	64	31
20	Charlton Athletic	42	7	6	8	28	28	1	8	12	13	35	41	65	30
21	Blackburn Rovers	42	5	8	8	20	28	1	7	13	17	41	37	69	27
22	BOLTON WANDERERS	42	6	5	10	22	31	1	5	15	13	43	35	74	24

1971/72 7th in Division Three

Manager: J.Armfield

#		Date	Opponent	Score	Scorers	Att.	Byrom J	Denton R	Duffey CP	Greaves R	Hallows PCR	Hulme J	Hunt R	Jones GE	Jones PB	Lee FS	McAllister D	McMahon K	Mowbray H	Nicholson P	Phillips RD	Redfern J	Rimmer WR	Ritson JA	Rowe GE	Seddon IW	Waldron A	Wright CG	Wright RL
1	Aug	14	Oldham Athletic	2-2	Byrom(2)	14372	10			9		5	8*	11						3	4		12	6	2	7			1	
2		21	BOURNEMOUTH	0-0		8962	8			9		5	10	11						3	4		7	6	2				1	
3		28	Notts County	2-1	Hunt(2)	15658	11		3	10		5	8	9	7						4			6	2				1	
4	Sep	4	ASTON VILLA	2-0	Hunt, Byrom	11470	11		3	10		5	8	9	7*						4			6	2		12		1	
5		11	Blackburn Rovers	3-0	Hunt, Byrom(2)	13938	11			10		5	8	9	7					3	4			6	2				1	
6		18	YORK CITY	0-1		12192	11			10		5	8	9	7*					3	4			6	2		12		1	
7		24	Tranmere Rovers	0-0		6988	11			10		5	8	9	7					3	4		12	6	2				1	
8		29	HALIFAX TOWN	1-1	Greaves	9304	11			10		5	8	9	7*					3	4			6	2	12			1	
9	Oct	2	MANSFIELD TOWN	2-0	Greaves, G.Jones	8751	11			10		5		9						3			6	2	7	8	4*	1	
10		9	Port Vale	1-1	Nicholson	6394	11			10		5	12	9						3	7		6	2		8	4*	1	
11		12	Plymouth Argyle	0-2		13336	11			10		5	8	9	7*					3	4		6	2		12		1	
12		16	OLDHAM ATHLETIC	2-1	Ritson(pen), Greaves	13302	11			10		5		9						3	7	12	6	2		8	4*	1	
13		23	SWANSEA CITY	0-0		11242	11*			10		5		9						3	7		6	2	12	8	4	1	
14		30	Bristol Rovers	0-2		11532				10*		5		9	12					3	7		6	2	11	8	4	1	
15	Nov	6	WREXHAM	0-2		8953				10		5	12	9						3	7	4*	6	2	11	8		1	
16		13	Chesterfield	1-2	Hunt	9423		12		9		5*	8	11						3			7	6	2	10	4	1	
17		26	Shrewsbury Town	0-1		6605			11	8				9	5					3	7		6	2		10	4	1	
18	Dec	4	BRIGHTON & HOVE ALBION	1-1	Greaves	5209	7		11	10				9	5					3			6	2		8	4	1	
19		18	Aston Villa	2-3	Seddon, Waldron	27767			11	8	2			9	5			12		3	7		6			10	4*	1	
20		27	BARNSLEY	0-0		6973	7		3	11	10	2	6*	9	5						12					8	4	1	
21	Jan	1	York City	0-0		4467	11			9	2*	6	10		5	12	3				7					8	4	1	
22		8	NOTTS COUNTY	1-2	Byrom	8096	11			9		6	8	7	5					3	2					10	4	1	
23		22	Halifax Town	1-0	Hunt	3919	11			9		6	8	7	5					3				2		10	4	1	
24		29	PLYMOUTH ARGYLE	2-1	Greaves, Seddon	5856				9		6	8	11	5	7	2			3						10	4	1	
25	Feb	12	Swansea City	2-3	Greaves, Byrom	4962	10			9		6	7	11	5		2			3	4					8		1	
26		19	BRISTOL ROVERS	0-0		5819	10			9			8	11	5		2			3	7		6				4	1	
27		26	Wrexham	2-1	Hunt(2)	3851	10			9			8		5		2			3	7		6				4	1	11
28	Mar	4	CHESTERFIELD	1-0	R.Wright	5607	10			9			8		5		2			3	7		6	2			4	1	11
29		11	PORT VALE	3-0	Nicholson, Hunt, McMahon	5956	10			9			8		5		2	12	3	7			6*				4	1	11
30		15	BRADFORD CITY	0-0		7818	10			9			8	12	5		2	7	3	6							4	1	11*
31		18	Bournemouth	2-1	Hunt(2)	15123	12			9			8	10	5		2	7*	3	4			6					1	11
32		22	WALSALL	0-1		6786				9			8	11	5		2	7	3*	4			6				12	1	10
33		25	BLACKBURN ROVERS	1-0	G.Jones	11026	7			9			8	11	5		3			2	10		6				4	1	
34		27	Mansfield Town	0-1		5398	7						8	11	5		3*	9		2	10		6				4	1	12
35	Apr	1	Barnsley	0-1		3925	7*			9			8	11	5				12	3	10		6	2			4	1	
36		3	TRANMERE ROVERS	1-0	Byrom	6216	7			9			8	11	5					3	4	10	6	2				1	
37		8	Walsall	1-1	Byrom	4735	7			9			8	11	5					3	4	10	6	2				1	
38		12	ROCHDALE	2-1	Byrom, P.Jones	5773	7			9			8	11	5					3	4	10	6	2				1	
39		15	SHREWSBURY TOWN	2-0	Greaves(pen), Phillips	5447	7			9			8	11	5		3				4	10	6	2				1	
40		19	TORQUAY UNITED	2-0	Byrom, G.Jones	5193	9						8*	11	5		3				4	10	6	2		7	1	12
41		22	Brighton & Hove Albion	1-1	G.Jones(pen)	25074	10						8	9	5		3			4*	11		6	2		7	1	12
42		24	Rochdale	2-2	G.Jones, Phillips	4826	10						8	9	5		3			4*	11		6	2		7	1	12
43		29	ROTHERHAM UNITED	2-2	Phillips(2)	5345	9						8	11	5		3			4	10		6	2			1	7
44	May	2	Rotherham United	0-2		3945	9							11	5		3			4	10		6	2		7	1	8
45		5	Torquay United	1-1	McAllister	2081	9							11	5		3			4			6	2		10	7	1	8
46		10	Bradford City	3-0	McAllister, Lee, R.Wright	2468								11	5	9	3			4	7		6	2		10		1	8
			Apps				37	3	4	38	3	22	33	41	37	2	21	4	30	40	13	2	39	32	4	18	27	46	10
			Subs				1	1					2	1	1	1	2			1	1	2				2	3	1	
			Goals				11			7			11	5	1	1	2	1			2	4			1			2	2

F.A. Cup

#		Date	Opponent	Score	Scorers	Att.	Byrom J	Greaves R	Hulme J	Hunt R	Jones GE	Jones PB	McAllister D	Mowbray H	Nicholson P	Phillips RD	Rimmer WR	Ritson JA	Seddon IW	Waldron A	Wright CG	Wright RL
1	Nov	20	BANGOR C	3-0	Ritson(pen), Nicholson, Duffy	6252		11 8			9	5			3	7	6	2	10	4	1	
2	Dec	11	Rossendale United	4-1	Greaves(3), Byrom	12100	7	11 10			9	5			3		6	2	8	4	1	
3	Jan	15	TORQUAY UNITED	2-1	Hunt, Greaves	7551	11	12 9		6	8	7* 5	3					2	10	4	1	
4	Feb	5	Chelsea	0-3		38066	8	9		6	12	11 5	2		3	7			10	4*	1	

League Cup

#		Date	Opponent	Score	Scorers	Att.	Byrom J	Greaves R	Hallows PCR	Hulme J	Hunt R	Jones GE	Jones PB	Lee FS	Nicholson P	Phillips RD	Redfern J	Rimmer WR	Ritson JA	Rowe GE	Seddon IW	Waldron A	Wright CG	Wright RL
1	Aug	18	Bradford City	1-1	Byrom	5742	8	9		5	12	11			3	4		7	6	2	10*		1	
1r		25	BRADFORD CITY	2-1	Redfern, Phillips	8256	10	9	3	5	8					4	11	7	6	2			1	
2	Sep	7	Huddersfield Town	2-0	Greaves(2)	10131	11	9		5	8*	10	7		3	4		6	2		12		1	
3	Oct	5	MANCHESTER CITY	3-0	G.Jones(3,1pen)	42039	11	10		5		9			3	7		6	2		8	4	1	
4		27	Chelsea	1-1	Rowe	27679		10		5		9			3	7		6	2	11	8	4	1	
4r	Nov	8	CHELSEA	0-6		29805		10		5	11	9			3	4*		7	6	2		4	1	

Lancashire Cup

#		Date	Opponent	Score
1	Nov	12	Chorley	0-2

Other Games

#		Date	Opponent	Score
1	Jul	31	BURNLEY	1-0
2	Aug	7	CHELSEA	2-0
3	Nov	29	HVIDOVRE	4-0

FINAL TABLE

		Pl.	Home W	D	L	F	A	Away W	D	L	F	A	F.	A.	Pts (Total)
1	Aston Villa	46	20	1	2	45	10	12	5	6	40	22	85	32	70
2	Brighton & Hove A.	46	15	5	3	39	18	12	6	5	43	29	82	47	65
3	Bournemouth	46	16	6	1	43	13	7	10	6	30	24	73	37	62
4	Notts County	46	16	3	4	42	19	9	9	5	32	25	74	44	62
5	Rotherham United	46	12	8	3	46	25	8	7	8	23	27	69	52	55
6	Bristol Rovers	46	17	2	4	54	26	4	10	9	21	30	75	56	54
7	BOLTON WANDERERS	46	11	8	4	25	13	6	8	9	26	28	51	41	50
8	Plymouth Argyle	46	13	6	4	43	26	7	4	12	31	38	74	64	50
9	Walsall	46	12	8	3	38	16	3	10	10	24	41	62	57	48
10	Blackburn Rovers	46	14	4	5	39	22	5	5	13	15	35	54	57	47
11	Oldham Athletic	46	11	4	8	37	35	6	7	10	22	28	59	63	45
12	Shrewsbury Town	46	13	5	5	50	29	4	5	12	23	44	73	65	44
13	Chesterfield	46	10	5	8	25	23	8	3	12	32	34	57	57	44
14	Swansea City	46	10	6	7	27	21	7	4	12	19	38	46	59	44
15	Port Vale	46	10	10	3	27	21	3	5	15	16	38	43	59	41
16	Wrexham	46	10	5	8	33	26	6	3	14	26	37	59	63	40
17	Halifax Town	46	11	6	6	31	22	2	6	15	17	39	48	61	38
18	Rochdale	46	11	7	5	35	26	1	6	16	22	57	57	83	37
19	York City	46	8	8	7	32	22	4	4	15	25	44	57	66	36
20	Tranmere Rovers	46	9	7	7	34	30	1	9	13	16	41	50	71	36
21	Mansfield Town	46	6	6	6	29	26	3	8	12	32	37	41	63	36
22	Barnsley	46	6	10	7	23	30	3	8	12	9	34	32	64	36
23	Torquay United	46	8	9	6	31	21	2	6	15	10	38	41	59	32
24	Bradford City	46	6	6	8	27	32	5	2	16	18	45	45	77	32

1971-72 Season
(Back) Ritson, P.Jones, Rowe, Marsh, Mowbray, Hallows
(Middle) Nicholson, McAllister, Wright, Greaves, Boswell, Byrom, Williams, Rimmer
(Front) Waldron, Redfern, Seddon, Armfield, Hulme, G.Jones, Phillips

1973 (Third Division Champions)
Armfield, Waldron, Ritson, G.Jones, Byrom, R.Wright, Nicholson, C.Wright, P.Jones,
McAllister, Greaves, Seddon, Rimmer, Lee, Phillips, Conway

1972/73   1st in Division Three (promoted)

Manager: J.Armfield

No		Date	Opponent	Score	Scorers	Att
1	Aug	12	BOURNEMOUTH	3-0	Byrom(2), Machin(og)	7133
2		19	Notts County	0-1		11129
3		26	OLDHAM ATHLETIC	2-1	R.Wright, Phillips	7019
4		28	Brentford	1-2	Byrom	11800
5	Sep	2	Blackburn Rovers	3-0	Byrom, R.Wright, Phillips	9546
6		9	PLYMOUTH ARGYLE	2-0	Byrom, G.Jones(pen)	5515
7		16	Grimsby Town	0-2		8678
8		19	Bristol Rovers	1-1	G.Jones(pen)	9572
9		23	TRANMERE ROVERS	2-0	G.Jones(pen), R.Wright	6139
10		27	CHESTERFIELD	1-0	Waldron	6532
11		30	Halifax Town	1-1	P.Jones	4664
12	Oct	7	Walsall	2-3	P.Jones, Greaves	7631
13		11	SWANSEA CITY	3-0	Byrom(2), G.Jones	6112
14		14	SCUNTHORPE UNITED	0-0		7175
15		21	Rochdale	2-2	Byrom, Nicholson	7165
16		28	SOUTHEND UNITED	1-1	Phillips	7342
17		30	Wrexham	3-1	G.Jones, Phillips, Lee	5547
18	Nov	4	Chesterfield	1-0	Lee	6576
19		11	BRISTOL ROVERS	2-0	Byrom, Lee	8419
20		25	ROTHERHAM UNITED	2-1	Byrom, G.Jones	7980
21	Dec	2	Watford	1-2	Byrom	7349
22		16	Charlton Athletic	3-2	P.Jones, Byrom, G.Jones	6489
23		23	PORT VALE	2-0	Byrom, G.Jones	12354
24		26	Tranmere Rovers	1-1	G.Jones	14356
25		30	NOTTS COUNTY	2-2	Byrom, Lee	17515
26	Jan	6	Oldham Athletic	0-2		19745
27		27	Plymouth Argyle	0-1		8592
28		30	WREXHAM	1-0	P.Jones	16732
29	Feb	10	GRIMSBY TOWN	2-0	G.Jones, Waldron	16588
30		17	Bournemouth	0-2		18384
31		20	CHARLTON ATHLETIC	3-0	Nicholson, P.Jones, Phillips	18146
32	Mar	3	WALSALL	3-1	P.Jones, Byrom, G.Jones	14924
33		5	York City	1-0	Lee	9038
34		10	Scunthorpe United	1-1	Lee	4424
35		17	ROCHDALE	2-1	Byrom, G.Jones	17870
36		21	SHREWSBURY TOWN	2-0	Lee, Redfern	18193
37		24	Southend United	1-1	P.Jones	8046
38		28	BLACKBURN ROVERS	0-1		33010
39		31	Rotherham United	0-1		6506
40	Apr	4	Swansea City	3-2	Byrom, Whatmore(2)	3096
41		7	WATFORD	1-1	Lee(pen)	17462
42		13	Shrewsbury Town	2-0	Byrom, G.Jones	6574
43		16	HALIFAX TOWN	3-0	Lee(3)	20062
44		21	YORK CITY	3-0	Nicholson, Lee(2)	19999
45		23	Port Vale	2-2	Nicholson, Byrom	14168
46		28	BRENTFORD	2-0	Nicholson, Byrom	21646

Appearances (by match number)

Players: Byrom J, Greaves R, Hallows PCR, Jones GE, Jones PB, Lee FS, McAllister D, Mowbray H, Nicholson P, Phillips RD, Redfern J, Rimmer WR, Ritson JA, Seddon IW, Siddall B, Waldron A, Whatmore N, Wright CG, Wright RL

No	By	Gr	Ha	JGE	JPB	Lee	McA	Mo	Ni	Ph	Re	Ri	Rit	Se	Si	Wal	Wha	WCG	WRL
1	7	9		8	5		3			2	11		6				12	1	10
2	7	9		8	5		3	3*		4	11		6				12	1	10
3	7	9		8	5		3			2	11		6				4	1	10
4	7	9		8	5		3			2	11		6				4	1	10
5	7	9		8	5		3			2	11		6				4	1	10
6	7	9		8	5		3			2	11		6	12			4	1	10*
7	7	9		8	5	12	3			2	11		6	12			4	1	10*
8	7	9		8	5		3			2	11		6	2			4	1	10
9	7	9		8	5		3			11			6	2			4	1	10
10	7	9		8	5		3				11		6	2			4	1	10
11	7	9		8	5		3				11		6	2			4*	1	12
12	7	12		8	5		3			10	11		6*	2	1		4	1	10
13	7	9		8	5		3			9	11			2			4	1	10*
14	7	9		8	5	12	3			6	11			2			4	1	10*
15	7	9		8*	5	10	3			6	11			2			4	1	12
16	7	9		8	5	12	3			6	11			2			4*	1	10
17	7	9		8	5	10	3			6	11		4	2				1	
18	7	9		8	5	10	3			6	11		4	2				1	
19	7	9		8	5	10	3			6*	11		4	2	12			1	
20	7	9		8	5	10	3*			6	11		4	2	12			1	
21	7	9		8	5	10				6	11		4	2	3			1	
22	7	9		8	5	10					11		4	2		6		1	
23	7	9		8	5	10	3				11		4	2		6		1	
24	7	9		8	5	10	3				11		4	2		6		1	
25	7	9		8	5	10	3			12	11		4	2		6*		1	
26	7*	9		8	5	10	3				11		4	2	12	6		1	
27	12	9		8	5	10	3			7	11*		4	2		6		1	
28	7	9		8	5	10	3				11		4	2		6		1	
29	7*	9		8	5	10	3			2	11		4			6		1	
30		9	2	8	5	10	3			7	11		4		12	6		1	
31		9*		8	5	10*	3			7	11		4	2	12	6		1	
32	7	9		8	5	10	3			7	11	6	4	2				1	
33	7	9		8	5	10	3			6	11		4	2				1	
34	7	9		8	5	10	3			7	11		4	2			12	1	
35	6	9		8	5	10*	3			12	11		4	2			6	1	
36	7	9		8*	5	10	3			8	11	7	4	2			6	1	
37		9			5	10	3			8	11	7*	4	2	12		6	1	
38		9			5	10	3			7	11		4	2	8		6*	1	12
39		9			5	10	3			6	11	12	4	2	7			1	8*
40		9			5	10	3			6	11		4	2			8	1	
41	7	9			5	10	3			6	11		4	2			12	1	
42	7	9		8*	5	10	3			6	11		4	2		1		1	
43	7	9		8	5	10	3			6	11		4	2		1		1	
44	7	9		8	5	10	3			6	11		4	2			12	1	
45	8	9		8*	5	10	3			6	11		4	2		1	7		
46	8	9		8	5	10	3			6	11		4	2			7		
Apps	39	45	1	39	46	31	45		1	36	45	3	42	37	3	4	31	1	42
Subs	1	1	1					3		2		1			1	6	4		1
Goals	20	1		14	7	12			5	5	1					2	2		3

One own goal.

F.A. Cup

No		Date	Opponent	Score	Scorers	Att	By	Gr	JGE	JPB	Lee	McA	Ph	Re	Rit	Se	Wal	WCG	WRL
1	Nov	18	CHESTER	1-1	Byrom	9620	7	9	8	5	10	3	6	11	4	2		1	
1r		22	Chester	1-0	G.Jones	7611	7	9	8	5	10	3	6	11	4	2		1	
2	Dec	9	SHREWSBURY TOWN	3-0	Phillips, Lee, Ritson	8403	7	9	8	5*	10	3	12	11	4	2	6	1	
3	Jan	13	Charlton Athletic	1-1	Lee	10688		9	8	5	10	3	7	11	4	2	6	1	
3r		17	CHARLTON ATHLETIC	4-0	Nicholson, Greaves(2), G.Jones	21195		9	8	5	10	3	7	11	4	2	6	1	
4	Feb	3	CARDIFF CITY	2-2	G.Jones, Ritson	24729		9	8	5	10	3		11	4	2	6	1	
4r		7	Cardiff City	1-1	G.Jones	14849		9	8	5	10	3	6	11	4	2*	12	1	
4/2r		12	Cardiff City*	1-0	Lee	6609		9	2	8	5	10	3	7	11	4	6	1	
5		24	LUTON TOWN	0-1		39556		9	8	5	10	3	7	11	4	2	6	1	

* Played at The Hawthorns, West Bromwich, score after extra time.

League Cup

No		Date	Opponent	Score	Scorers	Att	By	Gr	JGE	JPB	Lee	McA	Ph	Re	Rim	Rit	Wal	WCG	WRL
1	Aug	16	OLDHAM ATHLETIC	3-0	Byrom, G.Jones(2)	7947	7	9	8	5		3	2	11	12	6	4*	1	10
2	Sep	6	Sheffield Wednesday	0-2		15903	7	9	8	5	12	3	2	11*		6	4	1	10

Lancashire Cup

No		Date	Opponent	Score
1	Oct	25	CHORLEY	0-1

Other Games

No		Date	Opponent	Score
1	Jul	29	PRESTON NORTH END	2-0
2	Aug	2	BOHEMIANS PRAGUE	1-1
3		5	Raith Rovers	1-2
4	May	2	BURNLEY*	3-1

* Rimmer testimonial

FINAL TABLE

		Pl.	Home W	D	L	F	A	Away W	D	L	F	A	F	A	Pts
1	BOLTON WANDERERS	46	18	4	1	44	9	7	7	9	29	30	73	39	61
2	Notts County	46	17	4	2	40	12	6	7	10	27	35	67	47	57
3	Blackburn Rovers	46	12	8	3	34	16	8	7	8	23	31	57	47	55
4	Oldham Athletic	46	12	7	4	40	18	7	9	7	32	36	72	54	54
5	Bristol Rovers	46	17	4	2	55	20	3	9	11	22	36	77	56	53
6	Port Vale	46	15	6	2	41	21	6	5	12	15	48	56	69	53
7	Bournemouth	46	14	6	3	44	16	3	10	10	22	28	66	44	50
8	Plymouth Argyle	46	14	3	6	43	26	6	7	10	31	40	74	66	50
9	Grimsby Town	46	16	2	5	45	18	4	6	13	22	43	67	61	48
10	Tranmere Rovers	46	12	8	3	38	17	3	8	12	18	35	56	52	46
11	Charlton Athletic	46	12	7	4	46	24	5	4	14	23	43	69	67	45
12	Wrexham	46	11	9	3	39	23	3	8	12	16	31	55	54	45
13	Rochdale	46	8	8	7	22	26	6	9	8	26	28	48	54	45
14	Southend United	46	13	6	4	40	14	4	4	15	21	40	61	54	44
15	Shrewsbury Town	46	10	10	3	31	21	5	4	14	15	33	46	54	44
16	Chesterfield	46	13	4	6	37	22	4	5	14	20	39	57	61	43
17	Walsall	46	14	3	6	37	26	4	4	15	19	40	56	66	43
18	York City	46	8	10	5	24	14	5	5	13	18	32	42	46	41
19	Watford	46	11	8	4	32	23	1	9	13	11	25	43	48	41
20	Halifax Town	46	9	8	6	29	23	4	7	12	14	30	43	53	41
21	Rotherham United	46	12	4	7	34	27	3	15	17	38	51	65	41	
22	Brentford	46	12	5	6	33	18	3	2	18	18	51	51	69	37
23	Swansea City	46	11	9	3	37	29	3	4	16	14	44	51	73	37
24	Scunthorpe United	46	8	7	8	18	25	2	3	18	15	47	33	72	30

~ 268 ~

Manager: J. Armfield

						Allardyce S	Byrom J	Darling M	Dunne AP	Greaves R	Hallows PCR	Jones GE	Jones PB	Lee FS	McAllister D	McBurney ML	Nicholson P	Olinyk P	Phillips RD	Rimmer WR	Ritson JA	Siddall B	Thompson P	Waldron A	Whatmore N
1	Aug	25	Bristol City	0-1		13288		7		3	9		8	5	10	2		6*		11	4		1		12	
2	Sep	1	HULL CITY	1-0	Greaves	12708		7			9		8*	5	10	3		12		11	4	2	1		6	
3		8	Portsmouth	2-0	Byrom(2)	13367		7			9			5	10	3		8		11	4	2	1		6	
4		11	ORIENT	1-1	Byrom	16761		7			9			5	10	3		8		11	4	2	1		6	
5		15	CRYSTAL PALACE	2-0	Lee, Byrom	18392		7			9			5	10	3		8		11	4	2	1		6	
6		22	Fulham	0-1		9556		7			9			5	10	3		8*		11	4	2	1		6	12
7		29	NOTTINGHAM FOREST	1-0	Byrom	15101		7	8		9			5	10	3				11	4	2	1		6	
8	Oct	6	Carlisle United	0-1		8365		7	8		9			5	10*	3		12		11	4	2	1		6	
9		13	ASTON VILLA	1-2	Whatmore	19206			7		9			5	10	3		8		11	4	2	1		6*	12
10		20	MILLWALL	0-1		13022					9		7	5	10	3		8*	12	11	4	2	1			9
11		22	Orient	0-3		11702			7	12	9		10	5		3			6	11*	4	2	1			8
12		27	West Bromwich Albion	0-0		15604		12	7		9		10*	5		3		11			4	2	1		6	8
13	Nov	3	OXFORD UNITED	2-1	Shuker(og), Byrom	12709		7			9		8	5		3		11			4	2	1		6	10*
14		10	Luton Town	1-2	Whatmore	9628			7		9		8	5	12	3		11			4	2	1		6	10*
15		13	Sunderland	0-3		26454			12		9		8	5*	11	3		7	10		4	2	1		6	
16		17	NOTTS COUNTY	1-3	Greaves	11850	5				9				7*	3	8	11	10		4	2	1		6	12
17		24	Cardiff City	0-1		9606		8			9			5	12	3		10*		11	4	2	1		6	7
18	Dec	5	SUNDERLAND	1-0	Whatmore	8425		7			9			5	8	3					4	2	1	11	6	10
19		8	Preston North End	1-2	Byrom	14715		7			9			5	8	3					4	2	1	11	6	10
20		15	SWINDON TOWN	2-0	Byrom, Whatmore	8846		7			9			5		3		8			4	2	1	11	6	10
21		22	Nottingham Forest	2-3	Byrom, G.Jones	9498		7			9		8	5		3		4				2	1	11	6	10
22		26	BLACKPOOL	1-1	Suddaby(og)	18150		7		3	9		8	5							4	2	1	11	6	10
23		29	PORTSMOUTH	4-0	G.Jones(p),Byrom,Whatmore(2)	13684		7			9		8	5		3*		12			4	2	1	11	6	10
24	Jan	1	Hull City	0-0		12210		7			9		8	5		3			11	4	2	1		6	10
25		12	Crystal Palace	0-0		15804	6	7			9	2	8	5		3					4	1	11			10
26		20	BRISTOL CITY	2-1	Merrick(og), Greaves	23315	6	7			9		8*	5		3		4	12		2	1	11			10
27	Feb	3	Swindon Town	2-2	Whatmore(2)	8835	4	7		3	9		8	5				6	12		2	1	11*			10
28		16	SHEFFIELD WEDNESDAY	4-2	Ritson, Byrom(2), G.Jones	13405		7		3	9		8	5		4		6			2	1	11			10
29		23	CARLISLE UNITED	2-0	Byrom, G.Jones(pen)	16675		7		3	9		8	5		4		6			2	1	11			10
30		27	Aston Villa	1-1	Byrom	18952		7		3	9		8	5		4		6			2	1	11			10
31	Mar	2	Blackpool	2-0	G.Jones, Ritson	18575		7		3	9		8	5		4		6			2	1	11			10
32		9	WEST BROMWICH ALBION	1-1	Byrom	17760		7		3	9		8	5		4		6			2	1	11			10
33		16	Millwall	1-2	Byrom	6419		7		3	9		8	5		4		6*			2	1	11	12		10
34		23	LUTON TOWN	1-0	Greaves	15616		7			9		8	5		4		3			2	1	11		6	10
35		30	Oxford United	2-0	Whatmore, Byrom	6223		7			9		8	5		4		3			2	1	11		6	10
36	Apr	2	FULHAM	0-0		18636		7*		12	9		8	5		4		3			2	1	11		6	10
37		6	CARDIFF CITY	1-1	Waldron	14857					9		8	5	7	4		3			2	1	11		6	10
38		9	Middlesbrough	0-0		27143					9		8	5		4		3	7		2	1	11		6	10
39		13	Notts County	0-0		8349	5		12		9		8*			4		3	7		2	1	11		6	10
40		15	MIDDLESBROUGH	2-1	Byrom, G.Jones	22246	5	9					8			4		3	7		2	1	11		6	10
41		20	PRESTON NORTH END	0-2		17273	5	7			9		8			4		3*		12	2	1	11		6	10
42		27	Sheffield Wednesday	0-1		23264		7		3	9		8	5		4					2	1	11		6	10
			Apps			7	32	6	10	41	1	30	38	15	38	1	33	6	13	23	41	42	24	30	31	
			Subs				1	2	2					2			3	3	1					2	3	
			Goals				18			4		6		1							2				1	9	

Three own goals

F.A. Cup

3	Jan	6	STOKE CITY	3-2	Byrom(3)	39138		7			9		8	5	12			3		4*	2	1	11	6	10
4		26	Southampton	3-3	Byrom(2), G.Jones(pen)	20265	12	7		3	9		8	5				6		4*	2	1	11		10	
4r		30	SOUTHAMPTON *	0-2		21788		7		3	9		8	5				6		12	4*	2	1	11		10	

* After extra time

League Cup

1	Aug	28	PRESTON NORTH END	1-1	Byrom	17101		7		3	9		8	5	10	2				11	4		1		6	
1r	Sep	3	Preston North End	2-0*	Lee(2)	18571		7			9			5	10	3		8		11	4	2	1		6	
2	Oct	10	Rochdale	4-0	Lee(2), P.Jones, Waldron	7241		7*			9			5	10	3		8		11	4	2	1		6	12
3		31	Millwall	1-1	P.Jones	9281		7			9		8	5		3		11			4	2	1		6	10
3r	Nov	6	MILLWALL	1-2	Greaves	13501	5	7*			9		8			3		11		12	4	2	1		6	10

Lancashire Cup

1	Oct	23	ROCHDALE	4-0
2	Feb	12	BLACKPOOL	1-0
SF	Mar	19	MANCHESTER CITY	2-3

Other Games

1	Aug	1	Helmond	3-0
2		4	Mulheim	0-2
3		5	Dordrecht	1-2
4		11	HUDDERSFIELD	0-1
5		17	BLACKBURN ROVERS	2-0

	FINAL TABLE	Pl.	Home						Away						F.	A.	Pts
			W	D	L	F	A	W	D	L	F	A		(Total)			
1	Middlesbrough	42	16	4	1	40	8	11	7	3	37	22	77	30	65
2	Luton Town	42	12	5	4	42	25	7	7	7	22	26	64	51	50
3	Carlisle United	42	13	5	3	40	17	7	4	10	21	31	61	48	49
4	Orient	42	9	8	4	28	17	6	10	5	27	25	55	42	48
5	Blackpool	42	11	5	5	35	17	6	8	7	22	23	57	40	47
6	Sunderland	42	11	6	4	32	15	8	3	10	26	29	58	44	47
7	Nottingham Forest	42	12	6	3	40	19	3	9	9	17	24	57	43	45
8	West Bromwich Alb.	42	8	9	4	28	24	6	7	8	20	21	48	45	44
9	Hull City	42	9	9	3	25	15	4	8	9	21	32	46	47	43
10	Notts County	42	8	6	7	30	35	7	7	7	25	25	55	60	43
11	BOLTON WANDERERS	42	12	5	4	30	17	3	7	11	14	23	44	40	42
12	Millwall	42	10	6	5	28	16	4	8	9	23	35	51	51	42
13	Fulham	42	11	4	6	26	20	5	6	10	13	23	39	43	42
14	Aston Villa	42	8	9	4	33	21	5	6	10	15	24	48	45	41
15	Portsmouth	42	9	8	4	26	16	4	12	19	46	45	62	40	
16	Bristol City	42	9	5	7	25	20	5	5	11	22	34	47	54	38
17	Cardiff City	42	8	7	6	27	20	2	9	10	22	42	49	62	36
18	Oxford United	42	8	8	5	27	21	2	8	11	8	25	35	46	36
19	Sheffield Wed.	42	9	6	6	33	24	3	5	13	18	39	51	63	35
20	Crystal Palace	42	6	7	8	24	24	5	5	11	19	32	43	56	34
21	Preston North End	42	7	8	6	24	23	2	6	13	16	39	40	62	31
22	Swindon Town	42	6	7	8	22	27	1	4	16	14	45	36	72	25

1974/75 10th in Division Two

Manager: J.Armfield until 30/9/74; I.Greaves from 5/10/74

League

#		Date	Opponent	Score	Scorers	Att.
1	Aug	17	PORTSMOUTH	3-0	P.Jones(2), Byrom	12776
2		24	Blackpool	1-2	Whatmore	15513
3		31	ASTON VILLA	1-0	P.Jones	12976
4	Sep	7	Bristol City	1-2	Ritson	9263
5		14	SHEFFIELD WEDNESDAY	0-1		14597
6		21	Sunderland	0-0		28453
7		25	Manchester United	0-3		47084
8		28	NOTTS COUNTY	1-1	Whatmore	10045
9	Oct	5	ORIENT	2-0	Greaves, P.Jones	9769
10		12	Hull City	0-2		7353
11		19	CARDIFF CITY	2-1	Curran(2)	9439
12		22	BLACKPOOL	0-0		12574
13		26	York City	3-1	Lee, Curran, Allardyce	8804
14	Nov	2	NOTTINGHAM FOREST	2-0	Curran, Smith	12395
15		9	Millwall	1-1	Curran	7136
16		12	OLDHAM ATHLETIC	1-1	Curran	14667
17		16	SOUTHAMPTON	3-2	Lee, Byrom(2)	14348
18		23	Norwich City	0-2		18649
19		30	Bristol Rovers	0-1		9369
20	Dec	7	WEST BROMWICH ALBION	0-1		12315
21		14	Portsmouth			7612
22		21	OXFORD UNITED	3-1	Greaves, Curran, Nicholson	9588
23		26	Sheffield Wednesday	2-0	Lee, Curran	17153
24		28	FULHAM	0-0		14703
25	Jan	18	BRISTOL ROVERS	5-1	Byrom(2), Lee(2), Curran	11432
26	Feb	1	MILLWALL	2-0	Lee, Byrom	12920
27		4	Oldham Athletic	0-1		16303
28		8	Nottingham Forest	3-2	Byrom(2), Curran	11922
29		15	NORWICH CITY	0-0		15506
30		22	Southampton	1-0	Curran	18339
31	Mar	5	Aston Villa	0-0		39322
32		8	MANCHESTER UNITED	0-1		37759
33		15	Notts County	1-1	Byrom	8196
34		22	BRISTOL CITY	0-2		11066
35		28	Fulham	1-2	Byrom	9453
36		29	Oxford United	1-2	Whatmore	6742
37		31	SUNDERLAND	0-2		18220
38	Apr	5	YORK CITY	1-1	P.Jones(pen)	7876
39		8	West Bromwich Albion	1-0	Thompson	7937
40		12	Orient	0-0		5478
41		19	HULL CITY	1-1	Allardyce	8208
42		26	Cardiff City	2-1	Nicholson, Allardyce	6396

Appearances (shirt numbers)

#	Allardyce S	Byrom J	Curran HP	Dunne AP	Greaves R	Jones EG	Jones PB	Lee FS	McAllister D	Nicholson P	Olinyk P	Phillips RD	Reid P	Rimmer WR	Ritson JA	Siddall B	Smith B	Smith S	Taylor S	Thompson P	Waldron A	Walsh M	Whatmore N
1		7		3			5	9	6	4					2	1				11			10
2		7		3	9		5	12	6	4					2	1				11		8*	10
3		7		3	9	8	5		6	4					2	1				11			10
4		7		3	9	8*	5		6	4					2	1			12	11			10
5		7	8	3	9		5		6	4		10			2	1				11			
6			8	3	9		5		6	4		10			2	1				11			7
7		7	8	3	9		5		6	4		10			2	1				11			
8		10	8	3	9		5		6	4					2	1				11			7
9		7	8*	3	9		5		6	4		12			2	1				11			10
10		7	8	3*	9		5		6	2			4	12		1				11			
11		7	8		9		5	10	6	3			4		2	1				11			
12			8		9		5	10	6	3	7		4		2	1				11			
13	12		8	3*	9		5	10	6	4					2	1		7		11			
14			8	3	9		5	10	6	4					2	1		7		11			
15			8	3	9		5	10	6	4			12		2	1		7*		11			
16			8	3	10		5	9	6	4			12		2	1		7*		11			
17		7	8	3	10		5	9	6	4					2	1			8	11			
18	6	7	8	3	10		5	9		2			4			1				11			
19	6	7*	9	3	8		5	10		2			4			1			12	11			
20	6		8		10		5	9		3			4	6	2	1	12		7*	11			
21			8	3	10	12	5*	9		4				6	2	1	7			11			
22			8		10*			9		3		7	6		2	1		4		11			12
23		7	8				5	9	6	3			10		2	1		4		11			
24		7	8				5	9	6	3			10		2	1		4		11			
25		7	8	3			5	9	6	4			10		2	1				11			
26		7	8	3			5	9	6	4			10		2	1				11			
27		7	8	3			5	9	6	4			10		2*	1				11			12
28		7	8	3*	4		5	9	6	2			10			1				11	12		
29	6	7	8	3	4		5	9					10		2	1				11			
30	6	7	8	3	4		5	9			12		10*		2	1				11			
31	6	7	8	3	4		5	9					10		2	1				11			
32	6	7	8	3	4		5	9				12	10*		2	1				11			
33	6	7	8	3	4		5	9					10		2	1				11			
34	6	7	8*	3	4		5	9					10		2	1				11			12
35	6	7		3			5			4			10		2	1			8	11			9
36	6	7	8	3	12		5*			4			10		2	1				11			9
37	6		8*	3	7		5			4	12		10		2	1				11			9
38	6		8*	3			5	12		4			10		2	1				11			9
39	6		12	3*			5	8		4			10		2	1				11	7		9
40	6				7		5	8		4			10		2	1				11	3		9
41	6		12		8		5	9		4*			10		2	1			7	11		3	
42	6		12	3	8		5	9		4			10		2	1				11		7*	
Apps	17	28	32	34	29	5	42	29	26	36	1	4	24	2	38	42	6	3	3	41	2	4	14
Subs	1		3			1		1			2	1	2		3		1		2		1		3
Goals	3	10	11		2		5	6		2					1			1		1			3

F.A. Cup

Rd		Date	Opponent	Score	Att.	Curran HP	Greaves R	Jones EG	Jones PB	Lee FS	McAllister D	Nicholson P	Reid P	Ritson JA	Siddall B	Thompson P	Allardyce S
3	Jan	4	WEST BROMWICH ALBION	0-0	17305	8	10	7	5	9	6	3	4	2	1	11	
3r		8	West Bromwich Albion	0-4	21210	8	10	7	5	9	6*	3	4	2	1	11	12

League Cup

Rd		Date	Opponent	Score	Scorers	Att.	Byrom J	Dunne AP	Greaves R	Jones EG	Jones PB	McAllister D	Nicholson P	Phillips RD	Reid P	Ritson JA	Siddall B	Thompson P	Whatmore N
2	Sep	11	NORWICH CITY	0-0		11205	7	3	9	8	5	6	4	12		2	1	11	10*
2r		17	Norwich City	1-3	P.Jones	14417	7	3	9		5		4	10	6	2	1	11	8

Other Games

#		Date	Opponent	Score
1	Jul	28	Erkenschwick	1-2
2		30	Gutersloh	1-1
3	Aug	1	Haltern	4-0
4		3	Nac Breda	1-1
5		7	PLYMOUTH ARGYLE	1-1
6		10	BLACKBURN ROVERS	2-2
7	Jan	24	BLACKBURN ROVERS	3-1

FINAL TABLE

		Pl.	Home					Away					F.	A.	Pts
			W	D	L	F	A	W	D	L	F	A		(Total)	
1	Manchester United	42	17	3	1	45	12	9	6	6	21	18	66	30	61
2	Aston Villa	42	16	4	1	47	6	9	4	8	32	26	79	32	58
3	Norwich City	42	14	3	4	34	17	6	10	5	24	20	58	37	53
4	Sunderland	42	14	6	1	41	8	5	7	9	24	27	65	35	51
5	Bristol City	42	14	5	2	31	10	7	3	11	16	23	47	33	50
6	West Bromwich Alb.	42	13	4	4	33	15	5	5	11	21	27	54	42	45
7	Blackpool	42	12	6	3	31	17	2	11	8	7	16	38	33	45
8	Hull City	42	12	8	1	25	10	3	6	12	15	43	40	53	44
9	Fulham	42	9	8	4	29	17	4	8	9	23	22	44	39	42
10	BOLTON WANDERERS	42	9	7	5	27	16	6	5	10	18	25	45	41	42
11	Oxford United	42	14	3	4	30	19	1	9	11	11	32	41	51	42
12	Orient	42	8	9	4	17	16	3	11	7	11	23	28	39	42
13	Southampton	42	10	6	5	29	20	5	5	11	24	34	53	54	41
14	Notts County	42	7	11	3	34	26	5	5	11	15	33	49	59	40
15	York City	42	9	9	5	28	18	5	3	13	23	37	51	55	38
16	Nottingham Forest	42	7	7	7	24	23	5	7	9	19	32	43	55	38
17	Portsmouth	42	9	7	5	28	20	3	6	12	14	32	42	52	37
18	Oldham Athletic	42	10	7	4	28	16	0	8	13	12	32	40	48	35
19	Bristol Rovers	42	10	4	7	25	23	2	7	12	17	41	42	64	35
20	Millwall	42	8	9	4	31	19	2	3	16	13	37	44	56	32
21	Cardiff City	42	7	8	6	24	21	2	6	13	12	41	36	62	32
22	Sheffield Wed.	42	3	7	11	17	29	2	4	15	12	35	29	64	21

1974-75 Season
(Back) Taylor, Ritson, Nicholson, Greaves, Dunne, Olinyk
(Middle) P.Jones, Byrom, Allardyce, Siddall, Holbrook, McBurney, G.Jones, McAllister
(Front) Waldron, Whatmore, Rimmer, Armfield, Phillips, Darling, Thompson, Lee

1975-76 Season
(Back) Waldron, Whatmore, Siddall, G.Jones, Greaves
(Middle) Walsh, P.Jones, Byrom, Allardyce, Nicholson, Curran   (Front) Lee, Thompson, Ritson, Reid, Dunne

1975/76 4th in Division Two

Manager: I.Greaves

#	Date	Opponent	Score	Scorers	Att	Allardyce S	Byrom J	Curran HP	Dunne AP	Greaves R	Jones GE	Jones PB	Morgan W	Nicholson P	Reid P	Ritson JA	Siddall B	Smith B	Taylor SJ	Thompson P	Waldron A	Walsh MT	Whatmore N
1	Aug 16	Bristol City	0-1		10510		7	8	3	4	9	5			10	2	1			11		6	
2	20	Oxford United	0-2		5277		7	8	3	4	9*	5		12	10	2	1			11		6	
3	23	FULHAM	2-2	G.Jones, Byrom	8786	6	7	8	3	4	9	5			10	2	1			11			
4	30	York City	2-1	P.Jones, G.Jones	5640	6	7	8	3	4	9	5			10	2	1			11			
5	Sep 6	SOUTHAMPTON	3-0	Curran, G.Jones, Byrom	9188	6	7	8	3	4	9	5			10	2	1			11			
6	13	Luton Town	2-0	P.Futcher(og), Curran	11217	6	7	8		4	9	5		3	10	2	1			11			
7	20	ORIENT	1-1	Greaves	10218	6	7	8*		4	9	5			10	2	1			11		12	
8	23	Bristol Rovers	2-2	P.Jones, Greaves	7992	6	7		3	4	9	5			10	2	1			11			8
9	27	Nottingham Forest	2-1	Whatmore, P.Jones(pen)	10775	6	7		3	4	9	5		2	10		1			11			8
10	Oct 4	CHARLTON ATHLETIC	5-0	Whatmore(2), Ritson, Byrom(2)	9895	6	7*		3	4	9	5			10	2	1			11		12	8
11	11	Plymouth Argyle	3-2	Whatmore(2), Reid	14595	6	7		3	4	9*	5		2	10		1			11		12	8
12	18	NOTTS COUNTY	2-1	Allardyce, Whatmore	16080	6			3	4	9	5			10	2	1			11		7	8
13	25	Hull City	2-2	Byrom, G.Jones	7369	6	7		3	4	9	5			10	2	1			11			8
14	Nov 1	BLACKPOOL	1-0	Ritson	17274	6	7		3	4	9	5			10	2	1			11			8
15	4	PORTSMOUTH	4-1	P.Jones, G.Jones(2), Whatmore	18538	6	7		3	4	9	5			10	2	1			11			8
16	8	Blackburn Rovers	1-1	G.Jones	24480	6	7		3	4	9	5			10	2	1			11			8
17	15	CARLISLE UNITED	0-0		14556	6	7*	12	3	4	9	5			10	2	1			11			8
18	22	Notts County	1-1	G.Jones	12964	6			3	4	9	5		7	10	2	1			11			8
19	29	WEST BROMWICH ALBION	1-2	Greaves	18710	6		9*	3	4		5			10	2	1		12	11		7	
20	Dec 6	Chelsea	1-0	Greaves	20896	6			3	4	9	5			10	2	1			11		7	
21	13	Fulham	2-1	Whatmore, G.Jones	8720	6			3	4	9	5			10	2	1	12		11*		7	8
22	20	BRISTOL CITY	1-0	Whatmore	18505	6	12		3	4	9	5			10	2	1			11*		7	8
23	26	Oldham Athletic	1-2	Whatmore	24537	6	12		3	4	9	5			10	2	1	11				7*	8
24	27	SUNDERLAND	2-1	Allardyce, Byrom	42680	6	7		3	4	9	5			10	2	1			11			8
25	Jan 17	Southampton	0-0		20363	6	7		3	4	9	5			10	2	1			11			8
26	27	LUTON TOWN	3-0	G.Jones, Byrom, Allardyce	21358	6	7*		3	4	9	5		12	10	2	1			11			
27	Feb 7	Portsmouth	1-0	Went(og)	8958	6	7		3	4	9	5			10	2	1			11			
28	21	Carlisle United	2-3	Reid, Allardyce	12809	6	7		3	4	9			5	10	2	1			11			
29	28	HULL CITY	1-0	Thompson	21781	6	7*		3	4	9	5			10	2	1			11		12	8
30	Mar 2	OXFORD UNITED	0-1		22340	6			3	4	9	5		2	10		1	7	12	11			8*
31	6	Blackpool	1-1	G.Jones	18548	6			3	4	9	5			10	2*	1	7	12	11			8
32	13	PLYMOUTH ARGYLE	0-0		21147	6	7		3	4	9	5	12		10		1			11		3	8*
33	20	West Bromwich Albion	0-2		25319	6			3	4	9	5	7	2	10		1			11			8*
34	23	BLACKBURN ROVERS	0-1		24780	6			3	4		5	7	2	10		1	9	12	11			8*
35	27	CHELSEA	2-1	Hay(og), G.Wilkins(og)	20817	6	9		3	4		5	7	2	10		1			11			8
36	Apr 3	NOTTINGHAM FOREST	0-0		21464	6	9			4	12	5	7	2	10		1			11*	3		8
37	10	Orient	0-0		6294	6	11		3*	4	9	5	7	12	10	2	1						8
38	13	YORK CITY	1-2	Nicholson	19048	6	11			4	9	5	7	3	10	2	1						8
39	17	OLDHAM ATHLETIC	4-0	Greaves(2), P.Jones(2pens)	22455	6	12			4	9*	5	7	3	10		1			11		2	8
40	19	Sunderland	1-2	Allardyce	51943	6	12			4	9*	5	7	3	10		1			11		2	8
41	24	Charlton Athletic	4-0	Whatmore, Greaves, Byrom(2)	14415	6	9			4		5	7	3	10	2	1			11			8
42	28	BRISTOL ROVERS	3-1	Nicholson, Byrom(2)	12815	6	9			4		5	7	3	10	2	1			11			8
				Apps		40	29	8	35	42	36	41	10	15	42	32	42	5		38	6	6	35
				Subs			4	1			1			1				1	3			2	3
				Goals		5	11	2		7	11	6		2	2	2				1			11

Four own goals

F.A. Cup

#	Date	Opponent	Score	Scorers	Att	Allardyce S	Byrom J	Dunne AP	Greaves R	Jones GE	Jones PB	Nicholson P	Reid P	Ritson JA	Siddall B	Smith B	Thompson P	Walsh MT	Whatmore N
3	Jan 3	Brentford	0-0		12450	6	7	3	4	9	5		10	2	1		11		8
3r	6	BRENTFORD	2-0	Whatmore(2)	18538	6	7	3	4	9	5		10	2	1	12	11*		8
4	24	Huddersfield Town	1-0	Reid	27824	6	7	3	4	9	5		10	2	1		11		8
5	Feb 14	NEWCASTLE UNITED	3-3	G.Jones, P.Jones, Allardyce	46584	6	7	3	4	9	5		10	2	1		11		8
5r	18	Newcastle United*	0-0		50381	6	7	3	4	9	5		10	2	1		11		8
5/2r	23	Newcastle United+	1-2	G.Jones	42280	6	7	3	4	9		5	10	2*	1		11	12	8

* After extra time + Played at Elland Road, Leeds

League Cup

#	Date	Opponent	Score	Scorers	Att	Allardyce S	Byrom J	Curran HP	Dunne AP	Greaves R	Jones GE	Jones PB	Reid P	Ritson JA	Siddall B	Thompson P
2	Sep 10	Coventry City	1-3	Byrom	12743	6	7	8	3	4	9	5	10	2	1	11

Other Games

#	Date	Opponent	Score
1	July 19	Westphalia Herne	2-0
2	23	Homburg	3-2
3	27	NAC Breda	0-4
4	Aug 2	CHESTERFIELD	2-1
5	5	Rotherham United	2-0
6	9	Wolves	1-1
7	May 3	ALL STAR XI*	1-2

* Greaves' testimonial

FINAL TABLE

		Pl	Home					Away					F	A	Pts
			W	D	L	F	A	W	D	L	F	A	(Total)		
1	Sunderland	42	19	2	0	48	10	5	6	10	19	26	67	36	56
2	Bristol City	42	11	7	3	34	14	8	8	5	25	21	59	35	53
3	West Bromwich Alb.	42	10	9	2	29	12	10	4	7	21	21	50	33	53
4	BOLTON WANDERERS	42	12	5	4	36	14	8	7	6	28	24	64	38	52
5	Notts County	42	11	6	4	33	13	8	5	8	27	28	60	41	49
6	Southampton	42	18	2	1	49	16	3	5	13	17	34	66	50	49
7	Luton Town	42	13	6	2	38	15	6	4	11	23	36	61	51	48
8	Nottingham Forest	42	13	1	7	34	18	4	11	6	21	22	55	40	46
9	Charlton Athletic	42	11	5	5	40	34	4	7	10	21	38	61	72	42
10	Blackpool	42	9	9	3	26	22	5	5	11	14	27	40	49	42
11	Chelsea	42	7	9	5	25	20	5	7	9	28	34	53	54	40
12	Fulham	42	9	8	4	27	14	4	6	11	18	33	45	47	40
13	Orient	42	10	6	5	21	12	3	8	10	16	27	37	39	40
14	Hull City	42	9	5	7	29	23	5	6	10	16	26	45	49	39
15	Blackburn Rovers	42	8	6	7	27	22	4	8	9	18	28	45	50	38
16	Plymouth Argyle	42	13	4	4	36	20	0	8	13	12	34	48	54	38
17	Oldham Athletic	42	11	8	2	37	24	2	4	15	20	44	57	68	38
18	Bristol Rovers	42	7	5	9	20	15	4	7	10	18	35	38	50	38
19	Carlisle United	42	9	8	4	29	22	3	5	13	16	37	45	59	37
20	Oxford United	42	7	7	7	23	25	4	4	13	16	34	39	59	33
21	York City	42	8	3	10	28	34	2	5	14	11	37	39	71	28
22	Portsmouth	42	4	6	11	15	23	5	1	15	17	38	32	61	25

1976/77 4th in Division Two

Manager: I.Greaves

No	Date	Opponent	Score	Scorers	Att	Allardyce S	Carter M	Curran HP	Dunne AP	Greaves R	Jones GE	Jones PB	McDonagh JM	Morgan W	Nicholson P	Reid P	Ritson JA	Siddall B	Smith B	Taylor SJ	Thompson P	Train R	Waldron A	Walsh MT	Whatmore N
1	Aug 21	Blackburn Rovers	1-3	Reid	14368	6			3	4	8	5				7	10	2	1	12	11				9*
2	Aug 24	ORIENT	2-0	P.Jones(pen), Taylor	11600	6			3*	4	8	5				7	10	2	1	11	9			12	
3	Aug 28	MILLWALL	3-1	Taylor(2), Smith	13628	6			3	4	8*	5				7	10	2	1	11	9				12
4	Sep 4	Notts County	1-0	P.Jones	9266	6			3	4		5				7	10	2	1	11*	9	12			8
5	Sep 11	HULL CITY	5-1	Whatmore, P.Jones(2), Taylor(2)	12495	6			3	4		5				7	10	2	1	9	11				8
6	Sep 18	Chelsea	1-2	Taylor	24835	6			3	4		5				7	10	2	1	9	11				8
7	Sep 25	Plymouth Argyle	1-1	Mariner(og)	12564	6			3	4		5				7	10	2	1	9	11				8
8	Oct 2	BLACKPOOL	0-3		18680	6			3	4		5	1	7	2	10				12	9	11*			8
9	Oct 9	Cardiff City	2-3	P.Jones(pen), Taylor	11007	6				4		5	1	7	2	10				11	9		12	3	8*
10	Oct 16	BRISTOL ROVERS	1-0	P.Jones(pen)	12771	6			3	4		5	1	7	2	10				9	11				8
11	Oct 23	Oldham Athletic	2-2	Greaves, Taylor	15811	6			3	4		5	1	7	2	10				9	11				8
12	Oct 30	FULHAM	2-1	Whatmore, Allardyce	24228	6			3	4		5	1	7	2	10				9	11				8
13	Nov 6	Carlisle United	1-0	P.Jones	8811	6			3*	4		5	1	7	2	10				11	9			12	8
14	Nov 9	BURNLEY	2-1	Taylor, Reid	20681	6	12			4		5	1	7	2	10				11	9			3	8*
15	Nov 20	Southampton	3-1	Whatmore, Taylor(2)	17611	6			3	4		5	1	7	2	10				11	9				8
16	Nov 27	CHARLTON ATHLETIC	1-0	Allardyce	17842	6			3	4		5	1	7	2	10				11	9				8
17	Dec 15	Hereford United	3-3	Whatmore, Allardyce, Greaves	5025	6			3	4		5	1	7	2	10				11	9				8
18	Dec 18	Wolves	0-1		18444	6			3	4		5	1	7	2	10				11	9				8
19	Dec 21	LUTON TOWN	2-1	Whatmore, Greaves	17475	6			3	4		5	1	7	2	10				11*	9	12			8
20	Dec 27	NOTTINGHAM FOREST	1-1	Whatmore	31313	6	12		3	4*		5	1	7	2	10				11	9				8
21	Dec 28	Sheffield United	3-2	Whatmore(2), Taylor	25503	6			3			5	1	7*	2	10				11	9	12	4		8
22	Jan 3	Fulham	2-0	Whatmore, Reid	12594	6			3	4		5	1	7	2	10				11	9				8
23	Jan 22	BLACKBURN ROVERS	3-1	Whatmore(2), Reid	28525	6			3	4		5	1	7	2	10				9			11		8
24	Feb 5	Millwall	0-3		10461	6	12		3*		9	5	1	7	2	10							11		8
25	Feb 12	NOTTS COUNTY	4-0	Richards(og), P.Jones, Whatmore, Morgan	21171	6			3	4*	9	5	1	7	2	10						12	11		8
26	Feb 19	Hull City	2-2	Reid, Whatmore	9913	6			3	4	9	5	1	7	2	10							11		8
27	Feb 26	CHELSEA	2-2	Whatmore, G.Jones	31600	6			3	4	9	5	1	7	2	10							11		8
28	Mar 5	PLYMOUTH ARGYLE	3-0	Whatmore(2), P.Jones(pen)	18496	6			3*	4	9	5	1	7	2	10							11	12	8
29	Mar 12	Blackpool	0-1		23659	6			3	4	9	5	1	7	2	10								11*	8
30	Mar 15	Orient	2-2	Greaves, G.Jones	5413	6				4	9	5	1	7	2	10					12			3	8
31	Mar 22	CARLISLE UNITED	3-4	Allardyce, Whatmore(2)	18471	6				4	9*	5	1	7	2	10					12		11	3	8
32	Apr 2	OLDHAM ATHLETIC	3-0	Taylor, Allardyce, Whatmore	18130	6			3	4	12	5	1	7	2*	10				9			11		8
33	Apr 6	Nottingham Forest	1-3	P.Jones	24580	6			3	4	12	5	1	7		10		2		9*			11		8
34	Apr 9	SHEFFIELD UNITED	1-2	Taylor	19576	6			3	4	12	5	1	7*	2	10				9			11		8
35	Apr 12	Burnley	0-0		20342	6			3*	4	12	5	1	7	2	10				9			11		8
36	Apr 16	SOUTHAMPTON	3-0	Whatmore(2), P.Jones	20095					4		5	1	7	3	10		2		9			11	6	8
37	Apr 22	Charlton Athletic	1-1	Whatmore	10517	6				4		5	1	7	3	10		2		9			11		8
38	Apr 30	HEREFORD UNITED	3-1	Hughes(og), Allardyce, Taylor	18874	6				4		5	1	7	3	10		2		9			11		8
39	May 7	Luton Town	1-1	Reid	11164	6				4		5	1	7	3	10		2					11		8
40	May 10	CARDIFF CITY	2-1	Whatmore, G.Jones	22060	6				4	9	5	1	7	3	10		2					11		8
41	May 14	WOLVES	0-1		35603	6				4	9	5	1	7	3	10		2					11		8
42	May 17	Bristol Rovers	2-2	Whatmore(2)	6991	6				4	9*	5	1	7	3	10		2			12		11		8
		Apps				41			31	41	14	42	35	41	34	42	15	7	14	30	6	13	11	5	40
		Subs					3		4											2	1	5	1	3	1
		Goals				6				4	3	11		1		5			1	16					25

Three own goals

F.A. Cup

No	Date	Opponent	Score	Scorers	Att	Allardyce S	Carter M	Curran HP	Dunne AP	Greaves R	Jones GE	Jones PB	McDonagh JM	Morgan W	Nicholson P	Reid P	Ritson JA	Siddall B	Smith B	Taylor SJ	Thompson P	Train R	Waldron A	Walsh MT	Whatmore N
3	Jan 8	West Ham United	1-2	Waldron	24147				3	4		5*	1	7	2	10				11	9		12	6	8

League Cup

Rd	Date	Opponent	Score	Scorers	Att	Allardyce S	Carter M	Curran HP	Dunne AP	Greaves R	Jones GE	Jones PB	McDonagh JM	Morgan W	Nicholson P	Reid P	Ritson JA	Siddall B	Smith B	Taylor SJ	Thompson P	Train R	Waldron A	Walsh MT	Whatmore N
2	Sep 1	Bradford City	2-1	Whatmore(2)	7479	6				4		5				7	10	2	1	11	9			3	8
3	Sep 22	Fulham	2-2	Greaves, Reid	14961	6			3	4		5				7	10	2	1	9	11				8
3r	Oct 5	FULHAM*	2-2	Taylor, Walsh	15010	6				4		5	1	7	2	10				11	9			3	8
3/2r	Oct 18	Fulham+	2-1	P.Jones, Whatmore	9315	6				4		5	1	7	2	10				9	11			3	8
4	Oct 26	Swansea City	1-1	Taylor	14000	6			3	4		5	1		2	10				9	11	7			8
4r	Nov 2	SWANSEA CITY	5-1	Morgan, Greaves, Taylor(2), Whatmore	14955	6	12		3	4		5	1	7	2	10				9				11*	8
5	Dec 1	Derby County	2-1	Whatmore, Morgan	26734	6			3	4		5	1	7	2	10				11	9				8
SF1	Jan 18	Everton	1-1	Whatmore	54032				3	4		5	1	7	2	10				11*	9		12	6	8
SF2	Feb 15	EVERTON	0-1		50413	6			3	4	9	5	1	7	2	10							11		8

+ At St. Andrews.   * After extra time

Other Games

No	Date	Opponent	Score
1	July 24	Paderborn	1-0
2	July 25	Rotweiss Ludenschied	1-1
3	July 27	VFB Rhine	2-1
4	July 31	Westphalia Herne	0-1
5	Jan 28	Huddersfield Town	2-2

Anglo Scottish Cup

No	Date	Opponent	Score
1	Aug 7	BLACKPOOL	0-0
2	Aug 10	BLACKBURN ROVERS	2-0
3	Aug 14	Burnley	0-1
4	Sep 14	PARTICK THISTLE	0-0
5	Sep 29	Partick Thistle	0-1

FINAL TABLE

		Pl.	Home W	D	L	F	A	Away W	D	L	F	A	F. (Total)	A.	Pts
1	Wolverhampton W.	42	15	3	3	48	21	7	10	4	36	24	84	45	57
2	Chelsea	42	15	6	0	51	22	6	7	8	22	31	73	53	55
3	Nottingham Forest	42	14	3	4	53	22	7	7	7	24	21	77	43	52
4	BOLTON WANDERERS	42	15	2	4	46	21	5	9	7	29	33	75	54	51
5	Blackpool	42	11	7	3	29	17	6	10	5	29	25	58	42	51
6	Luton Town	42	13	5	3	39	17	8	1	12	28	31	67	48	48
7	Charlton Athletic	42	14	5	2	52	27	2	11	8	19	31	71	58	48
8	Notts County	42	11	5	5	29	20	8	5	8	36	40	65	60	48
9	Southampton	42	12	6	3	40	24	5	4	12	32	43	72	67	44
10	Millwall	42	9	6	6	31	22	6	7	8	26	31	57	53	43
11	Sheffield United	42	9	8	4	32	25	5	4	12	22	38	54	63	40
12	Blackburn Rovers	42	12	4	5	31	18	3	5	13	11	36	42	54	39
13	Oldham Athletic	42	11	6	4	37	23	3	4	14	15	41	52	64	38
14	Hull City	42	9	8	4	31	17	1	9	11	14	36	45	53	37
15	Bristol Rovers	42	9	8	4	32	27	4	4	13	21	41	53	68	37
16	Burnley	42	8	9	4	27	20	3	5	13	19	44	46	64	36
17	Fulham	42	8	9	4	27	25	2	6	13	15	36	54	61	35
18	Cardiff City	42	7	6	8	30	30	5	4	12	26	37	56	67	34
19	Orient	42	4	8	9	18	23	5	8	8	19	32	37	55	34
20	Carlisle United	42	7	5	9	31	33	4	5	12	18	42	49	75	32
21	Plymouth Argyle	42	5	9	7	27	25	3	7	11	19	40	46	65	32
22	Hereford United	42	6	9	6	28	30	2	6	13	29	48	57	78	31

1976-77 Season
(Back) Reid, G.Jones, Greaves, Walsh, Smith
(Middle) Byrom, Allardyce, Siddall, Slack, Nicholson, Whatmore
(Front) Curran, Taylor, Ritson, Morgan, Dunne   (insets) P.Jones, Thompson

1977-78 season
(Back) Morgan, Nicholson, Carter, G.Jones, Walsh, Graham, McDonagh, Poole, Allardyce, Gowling, Worthington
(Front) Thompson, Reid, Smith, Greaves, Burke, Dunne, Train

1977/78 1st in Division Two - Promoted

Manager: I.Greaves

#	Date		Opponent	Score	Scorers	Att	Allardyce S	Clements AP	Dunne AP	Gowling AE	Greaves R	Graham MA	Jones GE	Jones PB	McDonagh JM	Morgan W	Nicholson P	Reid P	Ritson JA	Taylor SJ	Thompson CD	Thompson P	Train R	Waldron A	Walsh MT	Whatmore N	Worthington FS
1	Aug	20	Burnley	1-0	Greaves	14716	6	2	3		4				1	7		10								9	5	8
2		23	MILLWALL	2-1	Allardyce, Whatmore	14874	6		3		4				1	7		10				2	11	9		5	8
3		27	SHEFFIELD UNITED	2-1	Reid, Whatmore	16840	6		3		4				1	7		10			11	2		9		5	8
4	Sep	3	Hull City	0-0		10106	6		3					11	1	7		10				2		9	4	5	8
5		10	OLDHAM ATHLETIC	1-0	Whatmore	16033	6		3					11	1	7		10				2		9	4	5	8
6		17	Sunderland	2-0	Whatmore, Reid	30342	6				4			11	1	7	3	10				2		9		5	8
7		24	Crystal Palace	1-2	Whatmore	23604	6		3		4			11	1	7	2	10						9		5	8
8	Oct	1	STOKE CITY	1-1	Worthington	20799	6		3		4				1	7	2	10						9		5	8	11
9		4	BLACKBURN ROVERS	4-2	Reid, Allardyce, Greaves(2)	18240	6		3		4				1	7	2	10						9		5	8	11
10		8	Brighton & Hove Albion	2-1	Reid, Greaves(pen)	27430	6		3		4				1	7	2	10						9		5	8	11
11		15	MANSFIELD TOWN	2-0	Worthington(2)	18937	6		3		4				1	7	2	10*						9	12	5	8	11
12		22	Southampton	2-2	Worthington, Morgan	27296	6		3		4				1	7	2	10						9		5	8	11
13		29	LUTON TOWN	2-1	Morgan, Worthington	20113	6		3		4				1	7	2	10						9		5	8	11
14	Nov	5	Orient	1-1	Greaves(pen)	7547	6		3		4			12	1	7*	2							9	10	5	8	11
15		12	CHARLTON ATHLETIC	2-1	Whatmore, Wood(og)	15977	6		3		4			12	1	7	2							9	10	5	8	11
16		19	Bristol Rovers	1-0	Waldron	7870	6		3		4				5	1	7	2							10	9	8	11
17		26	TOTTENHAM HOTSPUR	1-0	Greaves	32266	6		3		4				5	1	7	2							10	9	8	11
18	Dec	3	Fulham	0-2		8162	6		3		4				5	1	7	2	10							9	8	11
19		10	CARDIFF CITY	6-3	P.Jones(2),Reid,Whatmore,Walsh,Morgan	16090	6		3*		4				5	1	7	2	10					12			9	8	11
20		17	Charlton Athletic	1-2	Whatmore	12800	6		3		4				5	1	7	2	10							9	8	11
21		26	NOTTS COUNTY	2-0	Allardyce, Whatmore	22647	6		3		4				5	1	7	2	10						9		8	11
22		27	Blackpool	2-0	Worthington, Whatmore	25789	6		3*		4				5	1	7	2	10					9		12	8	11
23		31	Millwall	0-1		6720	6				4				1	7	2	10	3					9		5	8	11
24	Jan	2	BURNLEY	1-2	Whatmore	26334	6				4				1	7	2	10	3					9		5	8	11
25		14	Sheffield United	5-1	Reid,Worthington,Nicholson,Greaves(pen),Whatmore	22603	6				4				1	7	3	10	2					9		5	8	11
26		21	HULL CITY	1-0	Whatmore	18256	6				4				1	7	3	10	2					9		5	8	11
27	Feb	18	Oldham Athletic	2-2	Reid, Whatmore	20810	6				4		5		1	7		10	2					9		3	8	11
28		25	Stoke City	0-0		19280	6				4		5		1	7	12	10	2					9*		3	8	11
29	Mar	4	BRIGHTON & HOVE ALBION	1-1	Reid	21405	6				4		9		5	1	7	10	2							3	8	11
30		7	SUNDERLAND	2-0	Whatmore, Morgan	20972	6				4		9		5*	1	7	12	10	2						3	8	11
31		11	Mansfield Town	1-0	Ritson	12329			3*	9	4	12			5	1	7		10	2						6	8	11
32		18	SOUTHAMPTON	0-0		23770	6			9	4				5	1	7		10	2						3	8	11
33		21	Luton Town	1-2	P.Jones	8306	6		2	12	4				5	1	7		10					9		3	8	11*
34		25	BLACKPOOL	2-1	Reid, P.Jones	20506	6		3	11	4				2	1	7		10					9*			8	12
35		27	Notts County	1-1	Whatmore	15718	6		3	9	4				2	1	7		10							5	8	11
36	Apr	1	ORIENT	2-0	Allardyce, Whatmore	17957	6		3	9*	4				2	1	7		10				12			5	8	11
37		8	Tottenham Hotspur	0-1		50097	6		3		4				2	1	7		10					9		5	8	11
38		15	BRISTOL ROVERS	3-0	Whatmore, Worthington(2)	20393	6		3		4				2	1	7		10					9		5	8	11
39		18	CRYSTAL PALACE	2-0	Whatmore, Worthington	23980	6		3		4					1	7		10	2				9		5	8	11
40		22	Cardiff City	0-1		12566	6		3		4					1	7		10	2				9		5	8	11
41		26	Blackburn Rovers	1-0	Worthington	27835	6		3	12	4					1	7*		10	2				9		5	8	11
42		29	FULHAM	0-0		34110	6		3	7	4					1			10	2				9		5	8	11
					Apps		41	1	32	6	40		6		19	42	41	21	38	19	1		2	31	6	40	42	34
					Subs					2		1		2			2						1	1	1	1		1
					Goals		4				7				4		4	1	9	1					1	1	19	11

One own goal

F.A. Cup

#	Date		Opponent	Score	Scorers	Att	AS		DAP		GR	GMA		JPB	McD	MW	NP	RP	RJA	TSJ			TR	WA	WMT	WN	WFS
3	Jan	7	Tottenham Hotspur	2-2	Greaves(pen), Whatmore	43731	6				4				5*	1	7	12	10	2				9		3	8	11
3r		10	TOTTENHAM HOTSPUR*	2-1	Ritson, G.Jones	31314	6				4*	12				1	7	3	10	2				9		5	8	11
4	Feb	6	MANSFIELD TOWN	1-0	Worthington	23830	6				4					1	7	3	10	2				9		5	8	11
5		27	Middlesbrough	0-2		36662	6				4	12	5			1	7	3	10*	2						9	8	11

* After extra time

League Cup

#	Date		Opponent	Score	Scorers	Att	AS		DAP		GR			JPB	McD	MW	NP	RP	RJA	TSJ			TR	WA	WMT	WN	WFS
2	Aug	31	LINCOLN CITY	1-0	Waldron	11467	6		3					12	1	7		10	2	11*				9	4	5	8
3	Oct	25	PETERBOROUGH UNITED	3-1	Greaves,Allardyce,Whatmore(pen)	14990	6		3		4				1	7	2	10					11	9		5	8
4	Nov	30	LEEDS UNITED	1-3	G.Jones	33766	6		3		4			11	5	1		2	10				7			9	8

Other Games

#	Date		Opponent	Score
1	July	23	Bayreuth	1-5
2		26	VFB Stuttgart	1-3
3		28	Atlas Delmenhorst	2-1
4	Aug	1	SV Troisdorf	2-3
5	May	12	Liverpool/Everton XI *	5-5

* Thompson Testimonial

FINAL TABLE

		Pl.	Home					Away					F.	A.	Pts
			W	D	L	F	A	W	D	L	F	A	(Total)		
1	BOLTON WANDERERS	42	16	4	1	39	14	8	6	7	24	19	63	33	58
2	Southampton	42	15	4	2	44	16	7	9	5	26	23	70	39	57
3	Tottenham Hotspur	42	13	7	1	50	19	7	9	5	33	30	83	49	56
4	Brighton & Hove A.	42	15	5	1	43	21	7	7	7	20	17	63	38	56
5	Blackburn Rovers	42	12	4	5	33	16	4	9	8	23	44	56	60	45
6	Sunderland	42	11	6	4	36	17	3	10	8	31	42	67	59	44
7	Stoke City	42	13	5	3	38	16	3	5	13	15	33	53	49	42
8	Oldham Athletic	42	9	10	2	32	20	4	6	11	22	38	54	58	42
9	Crystal Palace	42	9	7	5	31	20	4	8	9	19	27	50	47	41
10	Fulham	42	9	8	4	32	19	5	5	11	17	30	49	49	41
11	Burnley	42	11	6	4	35	20	4	4	13	21	44	56	64	40
12	Sheffield United	42	13	4	4	38	22	3	4	14	24	51	62	73	40
13	Luton Town	42	11	4	6	35	20	3	6	12	19	32	54	52	38
14	Orient	42	8	11	2	30	20	2	7	12	13	29	43	49	38
15	Notts County	42	10	9	2	36	22	1	7	13	18	40	54	62	38
16	Millwall	42	8	8	5	23	20	4	6	11	26	37	49	57	38
17	Charlton Athletic	42	11	6	4	38	27	2	6	13	17	41	55	68	38
18	Bristol Rovers	42	10	7	4	40	26	3	5	13	21	51	61	77	38
19	Cardiff City	42	12	6	3	32	23	1	6	14	19	48	51	71	38
20	Blackpool	42	7	8	6	35	25	5	5	11	24	35	59	60	37
21	Mansfield Town	42	6	6	9	30	34	4	5	12	19	35	49	69	31

1978/79 17th in Division One

Manager: I Greaves

#		Date	Opponent	Score	Scorers	Att	Allardyce S	Burke DI	Dunne AP	Gowling AE	Graham MA	Greaves R	Jones GE	Jones PB	McDonagh JM	McNab N	Morgan W	Nicholson P	Nowak T	Poole T	Reid P	Smith B	Thompson CD	Train R	Walsh MT	Whatmore N	Worthington FS
1	Aug	19	BRISTOL CITY	1-2	Gowling	21355	6*		12	9		4		5	1									11	3	8	10
2		22	Southampton	2-2	Worthington(2)	21059	6		3	9		4		12	1		7	2*						11	5	8	10
3		26	West Bromwich Albion	0-4		23237	6		3	9		4	12	2*	1		7							11	5	8	10
4	Sep	2	BIRMINGHAM CITY	2-2	Worthington(2,1pen)	20234	6	3		9	2	4			1		7							11	5	8	10
5		9	DERBY COUNTY	2-1	Gowling(2)	20331		6	3	9		4			1		7	2				12		11*	5	8	10
6		16	Arsenal	0-1		31024		3		9		4	6		1		7	2				11			5	8	10
7		23	NORWICH CITY	3-2	Whatmore, Worthington(2)	19901	12	3		9		4	6		1		7	2				11			5*	8	10
8		30	Liverpool	0-3		47099		3		9		4	6		1		7	2				11			5	8	10
9	Oct	7	LEEDS UNITED	3-1	Worthington, Morgan, Smith	27751	6	3	12	9*		4	2		1		7				8	11			5		10
10		14	Chelsea	3-4	Gowling(2), Worthington(pen)	19879	6	3		9*		4	2		1		7				8	11			5	12	10
11		21	MANCHESTER CITY	2-2	Gowling, Worthington	32249	6	3		9		4			1		7	2			8	11			5		10
12		28	Tottenham Hotspur	0-2		37337	6	3		9		4			1		7	2			8	11			5		10
13	Nov	4	COVENTRY CITY	0-0		22379			3	9		4	6		1	11	7	2			8				5		10
14		11	Bristol City	1-4	Walsh	18168			3*	9		4			1	11	7	2			8	6			5	12	10
15		18	WEST BROMWICH ALBION	0-1		22278		3		9		4		5	1	11	7	2			8				6		10
16		21	Birmingham City	0-3		21643		3		9		4		5	1	11	7	2			8*				6	12	10
17		25	NOTTINGHAM FOREST	0-1		25692	6			9		4		5	1	11	7	2			8				3		10
18	Dec	2	Queens Park Rangers	3-1	Gowling, Worthington(2)	11635			3	9		4		5	1	11	7	2			8				6		10
19		9	WOLVES	3-1	Greaves, Gowling, Worthington(pen)	21006			3	9		4		5	1	11	7	2			8				6		10
20		16	Ipswich Town	0-3		16953			3	9		4		5	1	11	7	2			8				6		10
21		22	MANCHESTER UNITED	3-0	Worthington(2), Gowling	32390			3	9		4		5	1	11	7	2			8				6		10
22		26	Middlesbrough	1-1	Worthington	20125			3	9		4		5	1	11	7	2			8				6		10
23	Feb	3	Norwich City	0-0		15589		8	3			4		5	1	11	7	2							6	9	10
24		24	CHELSEA	2-1	Burke, McNab	19457		8	3			4		5	1	11	7	2							6		10
25	Mar	3	Manchester City	1-2	Worthington	41127		8*	3	9		4		5	1	11	7	2							6	12	10
26		7	Aston Villa	0-3		28053		8*	3	9		4		5	1	11	7	2							6	12	10
27		17	Coventry City	2-2	Worthington, McNab	15231	8	12	3*	9		4		5	1	11	7	2							6		10
28		21	Derby County	0-3		15227	8		3	9		4		5*	1	11	7	2							6	12	10
29		24	SOUTHAMPTON	2-0	Gowling(2)	19879			3	9		4		5	1		7	2				11			6	8	10
30		27	ARSENAL	4-2	Worthington(2pens), Gowling(2)	20704			3	9		4		5	1		7	2				11			6	8	10
31		31	Nottingham Forest	1-1	Gowling	29015			3	9		4		5	1		7	2				11			6	8	10
32	Apr	3	EVERTON	3-1	Morgan, Whatmore, P.Jones	27263			3	9		4		5	1		7	2				11			6	8	10
33		7	QUEENS PARK RANGERS	2-1	Worthington, Gowling	21119			3	9		4		5	1	12	7	2*				11			6	8	10
34		11	Manchester United	2-1	Worthington(2)	49617			3	9	2	4		5	1		7					11			6	8	10
35		14	MIDDLESBROUGH	0-0		22621	12		3*	9	2	4		5	1		7					11			6	8	10
36		16	Everton	0-1		31214	6			9	2	4		5	1		7					11			3	8	10
37		21	IPSWICH TOWN	2-3	Worthington, Allardyce	20073	6			9				5*	1	4	7	2	12			11			6	8	10
38		25	Leeds United	1-5	McNab	20218	5	3			2	4			1	11	7							9	6	8	10
39		28	Wolves	1-1	Whatmore	18125	5	3			11	4			1	9	7	2							6	8	10
40	May	1	LIVERPOOL	1-4	Souness(og)	35200	5	3			11	4			1	9	7	2							6	8	10
41		5	ASTON VILLA	0-0		17394	5	3			11	4			1	9	7	2							6	8	10
42		8	TOTTENHAM HOTSPUR	1-3	Worthington	17879	5	3*			11	4			1	9	7	2					12		6	8	10
			Apps				18	19	24	36	9	41		31	42	22	41	34	1		14	18		5	42	23	42
			Subs				2	1	2				1	1					1			2				6	
			Goals				1	1		15		1		1		3	2					1			1	3	24

One own goal

F.A. Cup

3	Jan	9	Bristol City	1-3	Smith	17392			3	9		4		5	1	11	7	2			8				6		10

League Cup

2	Aug	29	CHELSEA	2-1	Worthington(2,1pen)	10449	6	3		9	2	4			1		7							11	5	8	10
3	Oct	4	Exeter City	1-2	Gowling	9151	6	3		9	2*	4			1		7			1			12	11	5	8	10

Other Games

1	July	28	Bradford City	2-2
2	Aug	1	Doncaster Rovers	1-1
3	Nov	6	BLACKBURN ROVERS*	3-4

* Byrom testimonial

FINAL TABLE

		Pl.	Home						Away						F.	A.	Pts
			W	D	L	F	A	W	D	L	F	A		Total		
1	Liverpool	42	19	2	0	51	4	11	6	4	34	12		85	16	68
2	Nottingham Forest	42	11	10	0	34	10	10	8	3	27	16		61	26	60
3	West Bromwich Alb.	42	13	5	3	38	15	11	6	4	34	20		72	35	59
4	Everton	42	12	7	2	32	17	5	10	6	20	23		52	40	51
5	Leeds United	42	11	4	6	41	25	7	10	4	29	27		70	52	50
6	Ipswich Town	42	11	4	6	34	21	9	5	7	29	28		63	49	49
7	Arsenal	42	11	8	2	37	18	6	6	9	24	23		61	48	48
8	Aston Villa	42	8	9	4	37	26	7	7	7	22	23		59	49	46
9	Manchester United	42	9	7	5	29	25	6	8	7	31	38		60	63	45
10	Coventry City	42	11	7	3	41	29	3	9	9	17	39		58	68	44
11	Tottenham Hotspur	42	7	8	6	19	25	6	7	8	29	36		48	61	41
12	Middlesbrough	42	10	5	6	33	21	5	5	11	24	29		57	50	40
13	Bristol City	42	11	6	4	34	19	4	4	13	13	32		47	51	40
14	Southampton	42	9	10	2	35	20	3	6	12	12	33		47	53	40
15	Manchester City	42	9	5	7	34	28	4	8	9	24	28		58	56	39
16	Norwich City	42	7	10	4	29	19	0	13	8	22	38		51	57	37
17	BOLTON WANDERERS	42	10	5	6	36	28	2	6	13	18	47		54	75	35
18	Wolverhampton W.	42	10	4	7	26	26	3	4	14	18	42		44	68	34
19	Derby County	42	8	5	8	25	25	2	6	13	19	46		44	71	31
20	Queen's Park Rgs.	42	4	9	8	24	33	2	4	15	21	40		45	73	25
21	Birmingham City	42	5	9	7	24	25	1	1	19	13	39		37	64	22
22	Chelsea	42	3	5	13	23	42	2	5	14	21	50		44	92	20

1978-79 Season
(Back) Nicholson, Gowling, Walsh, Jones
(Middle) I.Greaves, Poole, Allardyce, McDonagh, Worthington, Mulhall, Headridge
(Front) Train, Whatmore, R.Greaves, Reid, Ritson, Dunne

1979-80 Season
(Back) Jones, Nowak, Cantello, Walsh, Allardyce, McNab
(Middle) Anderson, Nicholson, McDonagh, Gowling, Poole, Graham, Headridge, I.Greaves
(Front) Burke, Smith, R.Greaves, Whatmore, Reid, Clement

1979/80 22nd in Division One (relegated)

Manager: I.Greaves until 26/01/80, then S.Anderson from 02/80

#	Date	Opponent	Score	Scorers	Att	Allarduce S	Bennett M	Burke DI	Cantello L	Carter M	Clement DT	Gowling AE	Graham MA	Greaves R	Hoggan DM	Jones PB	McDonagh JM	McNab N	Morgan W	Nicholson P	Nowak T	Reid P	Thompson CD	Walsh MT	Whatmore N	Wilson P	Worthington FS
1	Aug 18	ASTON VILLA	1-1	Whatmore	19795				10		2	9		4		5	1	11		3		7		6	8		
2	21	Liverpool	0-0		45900			7	10		2	9		4		5	1	11		3				6	8		
3	25	SOUTHAMPTON	2-1	McNab, Whatmore	17417				10		2	9		4		5	1	11		3		7		6	8		
4	Sep 1	Brighton & Hove Albion	1-3	Walsh	20171			3	10		2	9		4		5	1	11			12			6	8*		7*
5	8	WEST BROMWICH ALBION	0-0		17033			11	10		2	9		4		5	1		7	3				6	8		12
6	15	Coventry City	1-3	Morgan	15555			11	10		2	9		4		5	1		7	3*			12	6			12
7	22	LEEDS UNITED	1-1	Allardyce	21724	5		3	10*		2	8		4			1	11	7					6	11		9
8	29	Norwich City	1-2	Whatmore	16500	5		3	8		2	9		4			1	11	7					6	11		10
9	Oct 6	Derby County	0-4		16810	5		3	12		2	9*		4			1	11	7					6	8		10
10	9	LIVERPOOL	1-1	Whatmore	25571	4		3			2	9				5	1		7		10		11	6*	8		12
11	13	ARSENAL	0-0		17032	4		3			2					5	1		7		10		11	6	8		9
12	20	Nottingham Forest	2-5	Thompson, Morgan(pen)	24564	4		3			2*	9				5	1	12	7		10		11	6	8		
13	27	CRYSTAL PALACE	1-1	Gowling	15132	4		3	10			9				5	1		7		2		11	6	8		
14	Nov 3	Aston Villa	1-3	Whatmore	24744	4*		3	10			9	12			5	1		7		2		11	6	8		
15	10	Tottenham Hotspur	0-2		33155			3			2	9		4		5	1	10	7				11	6	8		
16	17	MANCHESTER CITY	0-1		25515			3	10		2	9		4		5	1	11	7					6	8		
17	24	Stoke City	0-1		15435			12	10		2*	9		4		5	1	11	7	3				6	8		
18	Dec 1	BRISTOL CITY	1-1	Greaves	12074			3	10	12		9*				5	1	11	7		2			6	8		
19	8	Wolves	1-3	Whatmore	20169		2	11	10			9		4		5	1		7					6	8		
20	15	IPSWICH TOWN	0-1		10929			3	10	12		9				5	1		7*		2		11	6	8		
21	21	Middlesbrough	1-3	Morgan(pen)	11813	5		3	10*	12		9	2	4			1		7				11	6	8		
22	26	EVERTON	1-1	Carter	18220	5		3	10	12	2	9		4			1	11	7					6	8*		
23	29	Southampton	0-2		21605	5		12	10	8	2	9		4			1			3		7	11*	6			
24	Jan 12	BRIGHTON & HOVE ALBION	0-2		13963	5			10	12	2	9*		4			1		7	3				6	11		
25	Feb 9	Leeds United	2-2	Whatmore, Greaves	16428	5		12	10	9*	2			4			1		7	3			11	6	8		
26	23	Arsenal	0-2		24383			3			2	9		4		5	1		7	11				6	8	10	
27	27	Manchester United	0-2		47546			3			2	9		4		5	1		7	11				6	8	10	
28	Mar 1	NOTTINGHAM FOREST	1-0	Whatmore	16164			3*		12	2	9		4		5	1		7	11				6	8	10	
29	8	Crystal Palace	1-3	Jones	18728			3			2*	9	12	4		5	1		7	11				6	8	10	
30	11	NORWICH CITY	1-0	Whatmore	10442			3		12	2	9		4*		5	1		7	11				6	8	10	
31	15	Derby County	1-2	Reid	13236			3		12	2	9*		4		5	1		7	11				6	8	10	
32	18	West Bromwich Albion	4-4	Carter(2), Reid, Whatmore	11721			3			2	9		4		5	1		7	11				6	8	10	
33	22	TOTTENHAM HOTSPUR	2-1	Carter, Whatmore	14734			3			2	9		4		5	1		7	11				6	8	10	
34	29	Manchester City	2-2	Whatmore, Reid(pen)	33500		12	3			2	9		4		5*	1		7	11				6	8	10	
35	Apr 5	Everton	1-3	Whatmore	28030		12	3*			2	9		4		5	1		7	11				6	8	10	
36	7	MANCHESTER UNITED	1-3	Whatmore	31902			3		4	2		9			5	1		7	11				6	8	10	
37	8	MIDDLESBROUGH	2-2	Nowak, Whatmore	10613			3		4*	2		9			5	1		7	11			12	6	8	10	
38	12	Bristol City	1-2	Allardyce	13584	12		3			2		9	4		5	1		7	11				6	8*	10	
39	15	COVENTRY CITY	1-1	Wilson	8995			3			2		9	4		5	1		7	11				6	8	10	
40	19	STOKE CITY	2-1	Carter, Whatmore	11304	5		3			2		9	4			1		7	11				6	8	10	
41	26	Ipswich Town	0-1		21447			3			2		9	4		5	1		7	11				6	8	10	
42	May 3	WOLVES	0-0		11710	5	11	3			2		9	4					7		12			6	8	10	
		Apps				16	6	24	30	14	29	24	8	20	2	32	42	11	21	30	19	17	13	42	40	17	5
		Subs				1	2	3	1	8			1	1	1			1		1		1		1	2	1	2
		Goals				2				5	1			2			1		3		1	3	1	1	16	1	

F.A. Cup

Rd	Date	Opponent	Score	Scorers	Att	Allarduce S	Burke DI	Cantello L	Carter M	Clement DT	Gowling AE	Greaves R	McDonagh JM	McNab N	Morgan W	Nicholson P	Nowak T	Reid P	Thompson CD	Walsh MT	Whatmore N	Wilson P
3	Jan 5	Sunderland	1-0	Whatmore	24464	5		10		2	9	4	1		7	3				6	8	
4	26	HALIFAX TOWN	2-0	Greaves, Whatmore	21085	5	3		9			4	1	10	7		2		11	6	8	
5	Feb 16	ARSENAL	1-1	Allardyce	23530	5	12	10	9*	2		4	1		7	3			11	6	8	
5r	19	Arsenal	0-3		40140	5*		10	9	2		4	1		7	3			11	12	8	

League Cup

Rd	Date	Opponent	Score	Scorers	Att	Burke DI	Cantello L	Clement DT	Gowling AE	Greaves R	Jones PB	McDonagh JM	McNab N	Morgan W	Nicholson P	Nowak T	Reid P	Walsh MT	Whatmore N	Worthington FS
2/1	Aug 28	SOUTHEND UNITED	1-2	Gowling	7861		10	2	9	4	5	1	11		12	3	7*	6	8	
2/2	Sep 3	Southend United	0-0		9140	3	10	2	9	4	5	1	11	7				6	8*	12

Other Games

#	Date	Opponent	Score
1	Aug 13	AJAX AMSTERDAM	1-3
2	Sep 11	Malawi*	3-1

*Played at Chorley

FINAL TABLE

	Team	Pl.	Home W	D	L	F	A	Away W	D	L	F	A	F (Total)	A (Total)	Pts
1	Liverpool	42	15	6	0	46	8	10	4	7	35	22	81	30	60
2	Manchester United	42	17	3	1	43	8	7	7	7	22	27	65	35	58
3	Ipswich Town	42	14	4	3	43	13	8	5	8	25	26	68	39	53
4	Arsenal	42	8	10	3	24	12	10	6	5	28	24	52	36	52
5	Nottingham Forest	42	16	4	1	44	11	4	4	13	19	32	63	43	48
6	Wolverhampton W.	42	9	6	6	29	20	10	3	8	29	27	58	47	47
7	Aston Villa	42	11	5	5	29	22	5	9	7	22	28	51	50	46
8	Southampton	42	14	2	5	53	24	4	7	10	12	29	65	53	45
9	Middlesbrough	42	11	7	3	31	14	5	5	11	19	30	50	44	44
10	West Bromwich Alb.	42	9	8	4	37	23	2	11	8	17	27	54	50	41
11	Leeds United	42	10	7	4	30	17	3	7	11	16	33	46	50	40
12	Norwich City	42	10	8	3	38	30	3	6	12	20	36	58	66	40
13	Crystal Palace	42	9	9	3	26	13	3	7	11	15	37	41	50	40
14	Tottenham Hotspur	42	11	5	5	30	22	4	5	12	22	40	52	62	40
15	Coventry City	42	12	2	7	34	24	4	5	12	22	42	56	66	39
16	Brighton & Hove A.	42	8	8	5	25	20	3	7	11	22	37	47	57	37
17	Manchester City	42	8	8	5	28	25	4	5	12	15	41	43	66	37
18	Stoke City	42	9	4	8	27	26	4	6	11	17	32	44	58	36
19	Everton	42	7	7	7	28	25	2	10	9	15	26	43	51	35
20	Bristol City	42	6	6	9	22	30	3	7	11	15	36	37	66	31
21	Derby County	42	9	4	8	36	29	2	4	15	11	38	47	67	30
22	BOLTON WANDERERS	42	5	11	5	19	21	0	4	17	19	52	38	73	25

1980/81   18th in Division Two

Manager: S.Anderson

Player columns (left→right): Bennett M · Brennan I · Burke DI · Cantello L · Carter M · Clement D · Gowling AE · Graham MA · Hoggan DA · Jones PB · Kidd B · McElhinney GR · Moores JC · Nicholson P · Nikolic D · Nowak T · Peacock D · Poole T · Reid P · Thomas JW · Thompson CD · Walsh MT · Whatmore N · Wilson P

#	Date	Opponent	Res	Scorers	Att	Bennett	Brennan	Burke	Cantello	Carter	Clement	Gowling	Graham	Hoggan	Jones	Kidd	McElhinney	Moores	Nicholson	Nikolic	Nowak	Peacock	Poole	Reid	Thomas	Thompson	Walsh	Whatmore	Wilson
1	Aug 16	Notts County	1-2	Whatmore	7459			3	11	9		7	2		5	10						1					6	8	4
2	19	SHEFFIELD WEDNESDAY	0-0		15926			3	11	9		7	2		5	10						1					6	8	4
3	23	NEWCASTLE UNITED	4-0	Kidd(3), Whatmore	11835			3	11	9		7	2		5	10						1					6	8	4
4	30	Derby County	0-1		17378			3	4	9	2	7		11	5	10						1					6	8	
5	Sep 6	BRISTOL ROVERS	2-0	Griffiths(og), Gowling(pen)	8712			3	4	9	2	7		11		10	5					1					6*	8	12
6	13	Cardiff City	1-1	Walsh	6649			3	4		2	9		11	5*	10					7	1					6	8	12
7	20	SWANSEA CITY	1-4	Whatmore	9419			3	4		2	9		11	5	10					7	1					6	8	
8	27	Oldham Athletic	1-1	Cantello	10174			3	4	9	2			11	5	10						1				7	6	8	
9	Oct 4	CHELSEA	2-3	Thompson, Gowling	11888			3	4*	9	2	12			5	10			11			1				7	6	8	
10	7	Shrewsbury Town	2-1	Carter, Kidd	5077			3	4	8		9	12		5	10			2	11*		1					6		7
11	11	Queens Park Rangers	1-3	Kidd	8641			3	4	11		9			5	10			2			1					6	8	7
12	18	BRISTOL CITY	1-1	Gowling	8988			11	4	8		9	2		5	10	3					1				7	6		
13	21	PRESTON NORTH END	2-1	Carter, Whatmore	10713			3	4	9		11	2		5	10				7		1					6	8	
14	25	West Ham United	1-2	Kidd	25277			3	4	9		11	2		5	10				7			1				6	8	
15	Nov 1	CAMBRIDGE UNITED	6-1	Kidd(3),Whatmore,Hoggan,Cantello	8016			3	4	9*		11	2	12	5	10				7			1				6	8	
16	8	Watford	1-3	Hoggan	11296			3	4			11	2	9	5	10				7			1				6	8	
17	15	Sheffield Wednesday	0-2		16262			3	4			11	2	9	5*	10				7			1				6	8	12
18	22	GRIMSBY TOWN	1-1	Hoggan	9031			3		9		4	2	11	5	10*		12		7			1				6	8	
19	25	NOTTS COUNTY	3-0	Wilson(2), Kidd	7344							11	2	9	5	10	3			7			1				6	8	4
20	29	Luton Town	2-2	Whatmore(2)	8300							11	2	9	5	10	3		7				1				6	8	4
21	Dec 6	ORIENT	3-1	Whatmore, Kidd(2)	8228							11	2	9	5	10	3		7				1			12	6*	8	4
22	13	Bristol City	1-3	Gowling(pen)	7384		6					11	2	9	5	10	3		7*				1			12		8	4
23	19	QUEENS PARK RANGERS	1-2	Gowling	6315			3				11	2	9	5	10	3		7				1			12		8*	4
24	26	Wrexham	1-0	Whatmore	7635	6						11	2	9		10	3			7	5		1					8	4
25	27	BLACKBURN ROVERS	1-2	Hoggan	18184	6*	5			12		11	2	9		10	3			7			1				8		4
26	Jan 10	Grimsby Town	0-1		9320	11	6					5	2	9		10	3		12	7*			1					8	4
27	24	DERBY COUNTY	3-1	Gowling(2), Thomas	9937		6					11*	2	9	5	10	3			7			1		12			8	
28	31	Newcastle United	1-2	Bennett	19108	11	6						2	9	5	10	3			7			1					8	4
29	Feb 7	CARDIFF CITY	4-2	Thomas(2), Wilson, Nikolic	8115	10	6						2	9	5		3			7			1		11			8	4
30	14	Bristol Rovers	1-2	Gowling	5368	4*	6					11	2	9	5		3			7			1		10			8	12
31	24	OLDHAM ATHLETIC	2-0	Whatmore, Thomas	9641		6	4				11	2	9	5		3			7			1		10			8	
32	28	Swansea City	0-3		9468		6					11	2	9*	5		3			7			1		10	12		8	
33	Mar 7	Chelsea	0-2		12948		6		4			11	2*	12	10		3			7			1	9				8	
34	14	SHREWSBURY TOWN	0-2		7900			3*	4			11	2	12		10	6			7			1	9				8	
35	24	Preston North End	2-1	Reid, Gowling	8505				6			11	2		5	10	12			7*			1	4	9			8	
36	28	WEST HAM UNITED	1-1	Whatmore	13271				6			11	2		5	10				7			1	4	9			8	
37	Apr 4	Cambridge United	3-2	Reid, Nikolic, Whatmore	4512				6			11	2		5	10				7			1	4	9			8	
38	11	WATFORD	2-1	Thomas, Whatmore	8461							11	2		5	10	12			7			1	4	9			8	6*
39	18	Blackburn Rovers	0-0		16357				6			11	2		5	10				7			1	4	9			8	
40	20	WREXHAM	1-1	Kidd(pen)	6194		3		6			11	2		5	10*	12			7			1	4	9			8	
41	26	Orient	2-2	Gowling, Whatmore	3824		12		6			11	2		5	10				7*			1	4	9			8	
42	May 2	LUTON TOWN	0-3		7268		3		4	12		11			5					7			1	10*	9		6	8	

	Bennett	Brennan	Burke	Cantello	Carter	Clement	Gowling	Graham	Hoggan	Jones	Kidd	McElhinney	Moores	Nicholson	Nikolic	Nowak	Peacock	Poole	Reid	Thomas	Thompson	Walsh	Whatmore	Wilson
Apps	6	12	22	25	12	4	41	26	29	35	30	17		18	21	2	13	29	18	15	3	30	36	18
Subs		1			2			1	4			3		1	1					2	3			4
Goals	1			2	2		10		4		13				2				2	5	1	1	14	3

One own goal

F.A. Cup

	Date	Opponent	Res	Scorers	Att	Brennan	Gowling	Graham	Hoggan	Jones	Kidd	McElhinney	Nicholson	Nikolic	Poole	Whatmore	Wilson
3	Jan 3	Nottingham Forest	3-3	Hoggan(2), Whatmore	22520	3	11	2	9	5*	10	6	12	7	1	8	4
3r	6	NOTTINGHAM FOREST*	0-1		22799	6	11	2	9		10	3	5	7	1	8	4

* After extra time

League Cup

	Date	Opponent	Res	Scorers	Att	Burke	Cantello	Carter	Clement	Gowling	Graham	Hoggan	Jones	Kidd	Thompson	Peacock	Walsh	Whatmore	Wilson
2/1	Aug 26	CRYSTAL PALACE	0-3		9913	3		9		7	2	11	5	10	12	1	6	8	4*
2/2	Sep 2	Crystal Palace	1-2	Kidd	14764	3	4	9	2	7		11	5*	10	12	1	6	8	

Other Games

	Date	Opponent	Res
1	Aug 1	Darlington	0-0
2	5	Harlem	1-0
3	7	Sparta Rotterdam	2-1
4	9	LEGIA WARSAW	0-2
5	Nov 4	HARLEM	5-0
6	Mar 17	SPARTA ROTTERDAM	2-1
7	May 4	Rotherham United*	0-2

* Breckin Testimonial

FINAL TABLE

		Pl.	Home W	D	L	F	A	Away W	D	L	F	A	F.(Total)	A.	Pts
1	West Ham United	42	19	1	1	53	12	9	9	3	26	17	79	29	66
2	Notts County	42	10	8	3	26	15	8	9	4	23	23	49	38	53
3	Swansea City	42	12	5	4	39	19	6	9	6	25	25	64	44	50
4	Blackburn Rovers	42	12	8	1	28	7	4	10	7	14	22	42	29	50
5	Luton Town	42	10	6	5	35	23	8	6	7	26	23	61	46	48
6	Derby County	42	9	8	4	34	26	6	7	8	23	26	57	52	45
7	Grimsby Town	42	10	8	3	21	10	5	7	9	23	32	44	42	45
8	Queen's Park Rgs.	42	11	7	3	36	12	4	6	11	20	34	56	46	43
9	Watford	42	13	5	3	34	18	3	6	12	16	27	50	45	43
10	Sheffield Wed.	42	14	4	3	38	14	3	4	14	15	37	53	51	42
11	Newcastle United	42	11	7	3	22	13	3	7	11	8	32	30	45	42
12	Chelsea	42	8	6	7	27	15	6	6	9	19	26	46	41	40
13	Cambridge United	42	13	1	7	36	23	4	5	12	17	42	53	65	40
14	Shrewsbury Town	42	9	7	5	33	22	2	10	9	13	25	46	47	39
15	Oldham Athletic	42	7	9	5	19	16	5	6	10	20	32	39	48	39
16	Wrexham	42	5	8	8	22	24	7	6	8	21	21	43	45	38
17	Orient	42	9	8	4	34	20	4	4	13	18	36	52	56	38
18	BOLTON WANDERERS	42	10	5	6	40	27	4	5	12	21	39	61	66	38
19	Cardiff City	42	7	7	7	23	24	5	5	11	21	36	44	60	36
20	Preston North End	42	8	7	6	28	26	3	7	11	13	36	41	62	36
21	Bristol City	42	6	10	5	19	15	1	6	14	10	36	29	51	30
22	Bristol Rovers	42	4	9	8	21	24	1	4	16	13	41	34	65	23

~ 279 ~

1980-81 Season
(Back) Moores, Bennett, Langley, Carter, Graham, Hoggan
(2nd Row) Nicholson, Nowak, Jones, Poole, Walsh, Peacock, Thompson, Felgate, Kidd
(3rd Row) Keighley, Thomas, Heaney, McGlynn, Reid, Cantello, Gowling, Burke, Wilson
(Front) Berry, Taylor, Foster, Atherton, Conway, Kay

1981-82 Season
(Back) Jenkins, Rudge, Saunders, S.Thompson, Walsh, Mulligan, Fitzharris, Kay,
Taylor, Foster, Gratton, Lee, Atherton
(Middle) Wright, Nightingale, Conway, Berry, C.Thompson, Nicholson, Peacock, Farnworth,
McDonagh, McElhinney, Jones, Brennan, Hoggan, Joyce
(Front) Nikolic, Bennett, Carter, Gowling, Mulhall, Cantello, Whatmore, Reid, Thomas

1981/82 19th in Division Two

Manager: G.Mulhall

Player columns (left to right): Bailey IC, Bennett M, Berry M, Brannan I, Cantello L, Carter M, Chandler JG, Doyle M, Foster WP, Gowling AE, Hebberd TN, Henry A, Hoggan DM, Jones PB, Kidd B, Langley GR, McDonagh JM, McElhinney GR, Nicholson P, Nikolic D, Peacock D, Reid P, Thomas JW, Thompson CD, Whitworth S

#	Date	Opponent	Score	Scorers	Att.	Appearances (by player column)
1	Aug 29	Chelsea	0-2		16606	Brannan 3, Cantello 10, Gowling 6, Jones 9, Kidd 5, McDonagh 1, McElhinney 4, Nicholson 2, Thomas 11, Thompson 7, Whitworth 8
2	Sep 5	LUTON TOWN	1-2	Gowling	6911	Bennett 3, Cantello 10, Gowling 6, Jones 9, Kidd 5, Langley 8, McDonagh 1, McElhinney 4, Nicholson 2, Thomas 11, Thompson 7
3	12	Barnsley	0-3		13844	Bennett 3, Cantello 10*, Gowling 6, Jones 9, Kidd 5, Langley 8, McDonagh 1, McElhinney 4, Nicholson 2, Nikolic 7, Thomas 11, Thompson 12
4	19	OLDHAM ATHLETIC	0-2		7222	Bennett 3, Brannan 4, Cantello 10*, Carter 11, Gowling 6, Hebberd 2, Jones 9, Kidd 5, Langley 8, McDonagh 1, McElhinney 12, Thompson 7
5	23	Derby County	2-0	Thompson, McElhinney	12066	Bennett 3, Cantello 10, Gowling 6, Henry 11, Hoggan 4, Jones 9, Kidd 8, McDonagh 1, McElhinney 5, Nicholson 2, Thompson 7
6	26	Rotherham United	0-2		6998	Bennett 3, Cantello 10, Doyle 8, Gowling 6, Henry 11, Hoggan 4, Jones 9, McDonagh 1, McElhinney 5, Nicholson 2, Peacock 1, Thompson 7
7	29	NEWCASTLE UNITED	1-0	Thompson	6429	Bennett 3, Cantello 10, Doyle 8, Gowling 6, Henry 11, Hoggan 4, Jones 9, McDonagh 1, McElhinney 5, Nicholson 2, Peacock 1, Thompson 7
8	Oct 3	GRIMSBY TOWN	1-2	Thomas	7217	Bennett 3, Cantello 10, Doyle 8, Gowling 6, Henry 11, Hoggan 4, Jones 9*, McDonagh 1, McElhinney 5, Nicholson 2, Peacock 1, Thomas 12, Thompson 7
9	10	LEICESTER CITY	0-3		7361	Bennett 3, Cantello 10, Foster 7, Gowling 6, Henry 11, Hoggan 2, Jones 8, McDonagh 1, McElhinney 5*, Thompson 12, Whitworth 9
10	17	Cardiff City	1-2	Cantello	3879	Bennett 2, Brannan 3, Cantello 10, Foster 7, Gowling 6, Henry 11, Hoggan 4, Jones 5, Kidd 8, McDonagh 1, Whitworth 9
11	24	CAMBRIDGE UNITED	3-4	Henry(2), Kidd	5751	Bennett 11, Brannan 3*, Carter 12, Foster 7, Gowling 6, Henry 4, Hoggan 10, Jones 5, Kidd 8, McDonagh 1, Reid 9, Whitworth 2
12	31	Norwich City	0-0		12991	Bennett 3, Foster 7, Gowling 6, Henry 4, Jones 9, Kidd 5, Langley 8, McDonagh 1, Thompson 11, Whitworth 2
13	Nov 7	WATFORD	2-0	Henry, Thompson	7066	Bennett 3, Cantello 10, Foster 7, Gowling 6, Henry 4, Jones 9, Kidd 5, Langley 8, McDonagh 1, Thompson 11, Whitworth 2
14	14	Shrewsbury Town	0-2		4062	Bennett 3, Cantello 10, Carter 12, Foster 7, Gowling 6, Henry 4, Jones 9, Kidd 5, Langley 8*, McDonagh 1, Thompson 11, Whitworth 2
15	21	ORIENT	1-0	Carter	5737	Bailey 3, Cantello 10, Carter 9, Chandler 7, Doyle 12, Henry 4, Hoggan 11, Jones 5, McDonagh 1, McElhinney 6, Thompson 8*
16	24	Luton Town	0-2		8889	Bailey 3, Cantello 10, Carter 9, Chandler 7, Doyle 12, Henry 4, Hoggan 11, Jones 5, McDonagh 1, McElhinney 6, Thompson 8*
17	28	Crystal Palace	0-1		8839	Bailey 3, Cantello 10, Chandler 9, Doyle 8, Foster 7*, Gowling 6, Henry 4, Hoggan 11, Jones 5, McDonagh 1, Thompson 12
18	Dec 5	QUEENS PARK RANGERS	1-0	Hoggan	6076	Bailey 3, Cantello 10, Chandler 9, Doyle 8, Foster 7, Gowling 6, Henry 4, Hoggan 11, Jones 5, McDonagh 1, Whitworth 2
19	19	CHARLTON ATHLETIC	2-0	Henry, Chandler	5085	Bailey 3, Cantello 10, Chandler 7, Foster 8, Henry 9, Jones 5, McDonagh 1, McElhinney 6, Thompson 11, Whitworth 2
20	28	BLACKBURN ROVERS	2-2	Thompson, Henry	16577	Bennett 3, Cantello 10*, Doyle 8, Foster 7, Gowling 9, Henry 4, Jones 5, McDonagh 1, McElhinney 6, Thompson 11, Whitworth 2
21	Jan 16	CHELSEA	2-2	Foster, Henry	7278	Bennett 3, Foster 7, Gowling 9, Henry 4, Jones 5, Kidd 10, McDonagh 1, McElhinney 6, Thompson 11, Whitworth 2
22	30	Oldham Athletic	1-1	Thompson	9271	Bennett 3, Cantello 10, Carter 12, Doyle 8, Foster 7*, Gowling 6, Henry 9, Hoggan 4, Jones 5, McDonagh 1, Thompson 11, Whitworth 2
23	Feb 3	Newcastle United	0-2		14761	Bennett 3, Cantello 10, Carter 12, Doyle 8, Foster 9, Gowling 6, Henry 4, Hoggan 7, Jones 5, McDonagh 1, Thompson 11*
24	6	Barnsley	2-1	Henry, Thompson	11680	Bennett 3, Doyle 8, Foster 9, Gowling 6, Henry 4, Hoggan 10, Jones 5, McDonagh 1, Thompson 11, Whitworth 2
25	16	Sheffield Wednesday	1-0	Foster	16555	Bennett 3, Cantello 10*, Doyle 8, Foster 9, Gowling 6, Henry 4, Hoggan 12, Jones 5, McDonagh 1, Thompson 11, Whitworth 2
26	20	ROTHERHAM UNITED	0-1		9466	Bennett 3, Cantello 10, Doyle 8, Foster 9, Gowling 6, Henry 4, Hoggan 11, Jones 5, McDonagh 1, McElhinney 6, Whitworth 2
27	27	Leicester City	0-1		10678	Bennett 3, Cantello 10, Chandler 9, Doyle 8, Foster 7, Gowling 6, Henry 4, Jones 5, McDonagh 1, Thompson 11, Whitworth 2
28	Mar 2	Grimsby Town	1-1	Henry	6525	Cantello 10, Doyle 8, Foster 7, Gowling 6, Henry 9, Hoggan 4, Jones 5, McDonagh 1, McElhinney 3, Thompson 11, Whitworth 2
29	6	CARDIFF CITY	1-0	Jones(pen)	6269	Bennett 3, Cantello 10, Doyle 8, Foster 7, Gowling 6, Henry 9, Hoggan 4, Jones 5, McDonagh 1, Thompson 11, Whitworth 2
30	9	Wrexham	1-2	Thompson	3220	Bennett 3, Cantello 10*, Doyle 8, Foster 7, Gowling 6, Henry 9, Hoggan 4, Jones 5, McDonagh 1, Nicholson 12, Thompson 11, Whitworth 2
31	13	Cambridge United	1-2	Henry	3430	Bailey 10, Bennett 8, Foster 7, Gowling 6*, Henry 9, Hoggan 4, Jones 5, Langley 12, McDonagh 1, McElhinney 3, Thompson 11, Whitworth 2
32	20	NORWICH CITY	0-1		6199	Bennett 3, Foster 7, Gowling 9, Henry 4, Hoggan 10, Jones 5, Kidd 11, McDonagh 1, McElhinney 6, Whitworth 2
33	27	Watford	0-3		12937	Bennett 3, Berry 12, Foster 7, Gowling 9, Henry 4, Hoggan 10, Jones 5, Kidd 11*, McDonagh 1, McElhinney 6, Whitworth 2
34	Apr 3	SHREWSBURY TOWN	1-1	Thompson	5833	Bennett 3, Doyle 8, Foster 7, Gowling 9, Henry 4*, Jones 5, Langley 12, McDonagh 1, McElhinney 6, Reid 10, Thompson 11, Whitworth 2
35	10	WREXHAM	2-0	Henry(pen), Reid	6221	Bennett 3, Doyle 8, Foster 7, Gowling 9, Hebberd 6, Henry 4, Hoggan 12, Jones 5, McDonagh 1, Reid 10, Thompson 11*
36	12	Blackburn Rovers	2-0	Thompson(2)	11912	Bennett 3, Doyle 8, Foster 7, Gowling 9, Hebberd 6, Henry 4, Jones 5, McDonagh 1, Reid 10, Thompson 11, Whitworth 2
37	17	Orient	0-3		2851	Bennett 3, Berry 2, Doyle 8, Foster 7, Gowling 9*, Henry 4, Hoggan 12, Jones 5, McDonagh 1, Reid 10, Thompson 11
38	24	CRYSTAL PALACE	0-0		6280	Bennett 3, Doyle 8*, Foster 7, Gowling 9, Hebberd 6, Henry 4, Jones 5, McDonagh 1, Nicholson 12, Reid 10, Thompson 11, Whitworth 2
39	28	Charlton Athletic	0-1		3379	Bennett 3, Chandler 12, Doyle 8, Foster 7, Gowling 9, Hebberd 6, Henry 4, Jones 5, McDonagh 1, McElhinney 2*, Reid 10, Thompson 11
40	May 1	Queens Park Rangers	1-7	Henry(pen)	10002	Bennett 3, Doyle 8, Foster 9, Gowling 7, Hebberd 6, Henry 4, Jones 5, McDonagh 1, Reid 10, Thompson 11, Whitworth 2
41	4	DERBY COUNTY	3-2	Thompson(2), Henry	5226	Bennett 3, Foster 7, Gowling 6, Hebberd 9, Henry 4, Hoggan 8, Jones 5, McDonagh 1, Reid 10, Thompson 11, Whitworth 2
42	8	SHEFFIELD WEDNESDAY	3-1	Chandler, Gowling, Henry	13656	Bennett 3, Foster 7, Gowling 6, Hebberd 9, Henry 4, Hoggan 8, Jones 5, McDonagh 1, Reid 10, Thompson 11, Whitworth 2

Apps: Bailey 5, Bennett 35, Berry 2, Brannan 4, Cantello 34, Carter 11, Chandler 32, Doyle 10, Foster 20, Gowling 40, Hebberd 6, Henry 39, Hoggan 25, Jones 41, Kidd 10, Langley 3, McDonagh 39, McElhinney 18, Nicholson 6, Nikolic 1, Peacock 3, Reid 12, Thomas 3, Thompson 34, Whitworth 29

Subs: Bennett 1, Carter 2, Chandler 1, Foster 3, Hoggan 4, McElhinney 3, Nicholson 1, Nikolic 2, Thompson 2, Whitworth 2

Goals: Cantello 1, Carter 1, Chandler 2, Foster 2, Gowling 2, Henry 13, Hoggan 1, Jones 1, Kidd 1, McElhinney 1, Reid 1, Thomas 1, Thompson 12

F.A. Cup

Rd	Date	Opponent	Score	Scorers	Att.	Appearances
3	Jan 2	DERBY COUNTY	3-1	Gowling, Foster, Thompson	9534	Bennett 3, Foster 7, Gowling 8, Henry 9, Hoggan 4, Jones 5, Kidd 10, McDonagh 1, McElhinney 6, Thompson 11, Whitworth 2
4	23	Crystal Palace	0-1		9719	Bennett 3, Foster 7, Gowling 8, Henry 9, Hoggan 4, Hoggan 12, Jones 5, Kidd 10*, McDonagh 1, McElhinney 6, Thompson 11, Whitworth 2

League Cup

Rd	Date	Opponent	Score	Scorers	Att.	Appearances
1/1	Sep 1	OLDHAM ATHLETIC	2-1	Kidd, Thomas	5156	Bennett 3, Cantello 10, Gowling 6, Jones 9, Kidd 5, Langley 8, McDonagh 1, McElhinney 4, Nicholson 2, Thomas 11, Thompson 7
1/2	15	Oldham Athletic *	2-4	Thompson, Berry	4779	Bennett 3, Berry 12, Brannan 4, Cantello 11, Gowling 6, Jones 9, Kidd 5, Langley 8, McDonagh 1, McElhinney 2, Nicholson 7*, Thompson 10

* After extra time

Other Games

#	Date	Opponent	Score
1	Aug 10	Hartlepool United	3-2
2	24	BIRMINGHAM CITY	1-1
3	Feb 11	Nigerian XI	1-4
4	May 11	Wigan Athletic*	0-1

* Brown testimonial

FINAL TABLE

		Pl.	Home W	D	L	F	A	Away W	D	L	F	A	F	A	Pts (Total)
1	Luton Town	42	16	3	2	48	19	9	10	2	38	27	86	46	88
2	Watford	42	13	6	2	46	16	10	5	6	30	26	76	42	80
3	Norwich City	42	14	3	4	41	19	8	2	11	23	31	64	50	71
4	Sheffield Wed.	42	10	8	3	31	23	10	2	9	24	28	55	51	70
5	Queen's Park Rgs.	42	15	4	2	40	9	6	2	13	25	34	65	43	69
6	Barnsley	42	13	4	4	33	14	6	6	9	26	27	59	41	67
7	Rotherham United	42	13	5	3	42	19	7	2	12	24	35	66	54	67
8	Leicester City	42	12	5	4	31	19	6	7	8	25	29	56	48	66
9	Newcastle United	42	14	4	3	30	14	4	4	13	22	36	52	50	62
10	Blackburn Rovers	42	11	4	6	26	15	5	7	9	21	28	47	43	59
11	Oldham Athletic	42	9	9	3	28	23	6	5	10	22	28	50	51	59
12	Chelsea	42	10	5	6	37	30	5	7	9	23	30	60	60	57
13	Charlton Athletic	42	11	5	5	33	22	2	7	12	17	43	50	65	51
14	Cambridge United	42	11	4	6	31	19	2	5	14	17	34	48	53	48
15	Crystal Palace	42	9	2	10	25	26	4	7	10	9	19	34	45	48
16	Derby County	42	9	8	4	32	23	3	4	14	21	45	53	68	48
17	Grimsby Town	42	8	8	5	29	30	6	5	10	24	35	53	65	46
18	Shrewsbury Town	42	10	6	5	26	19	1	7	13	11	38	37	57	46
19	BOLTON WANDERERS	42	10	4	7	28	24	3	3	15	11	37	39	61	46
20	Cardiff City	42	9	2	10	28	32	3	6	12	17	29	45	61	44
21	Wrexham	42	9	4	8	22	24	3	7	12	18	34	40	56	44
22	Orient	42	6	8	7	23	24	4	1	16	13	37	36	61	39

1982/83 22nd in Division Two (relegated)

Manager: J.McGovern

Player columns (left → right): Bennett M · Berry M · Borrows B · Chandler IG · Deakin RI · Doyle M · Foster WP · Gray S · Henry A · Hoggan DM · Jones PB · Joyce WG · McDonagh JM · McElhinney GR · McGovern JP · Moores IR · Redfearn ND · Reid P · Rudge SJ · Thompson CD · Thompson SJ · Whatmore N · Whitworth S

#		Date	Opponent	Result	Scorers	Att	Ben	Ber	Bor	Cha	Dea	Doy	Fos	Gra	Hen	Hog	Jon	Joy	McDo	McEl	McGo	Moo	Red	Rei	Rud	ThC	ThS	Wha	Whi
1	Aug	28	Burnley	0-0		10527	3	12		7		6			8	11	5		1		4	9		10*					2
2	Sep	4	NEWCASTLE UNITED	3-1	Henry(2,1pen), Reid	17738	3			7		6			8	11	5		1		4	9		10					2
3		7	Sheffield Wednesday	1-3	Henry	17307	3			7		6			8	11	5		1		4	9		10					2
4		11	Fulham	0-4		5688	3	11		7					8	12	5		1	6*	4	9		10					2
5		18	WOLVES	0-1		9264	3	11		7		6			8		5		1		4*	9		10		12			2
6		25	Grimsby Town	0-1		7583	3			7					8		5		1		4	9		10		11			2
7		28	Oldham Athletic	2-3	Henry, Moores	5605	3			7					8		5		1	6	4	9		10		11			2
8	Oct	2	CRYSTAL PALACE	1-0	Hoggan	5804				7	3				8	11	5		1	6	4			10	9				2
9		9	ROTHERHAM UNITED	2-2	C.Thompson, Moores	6577				7	3		12		8		5		1	6	4	10			9	11			2*
10		16	Middlesbrough	0-1		5529	2			7	3				8		5		1	6	4	9		10		11			2
11		23	Barnsley	0-2		7339				7	3				8	11	5		1	6	4	9		10					2
12		30	Queens Park Rangers	0-1		9363	3	2					7		10		5		1	6	4	9			8	11			2
13	Nov	6	SHREWSBURY TOWN	1-4	Henry(pen)	4879	3	2		12			7		10		5		1	6	4	9			8*	11			2
14		13	Derby County	0-0		10999	12			7	3	6*	9		4		5		1					10	8		11		2
15		20	Blackburn Rovers	1-1	Chandler	7428				7	3	6	9	8	4		5		1					10			11		2
16		27	LEICESTER CITY	3-1	Foster, Doyle, C.Thompson	5060				7	3	6	9		4		5		1					10	8	11			2
17	Dec	4	Cambridge United	0-0		2622	3			7		6	9		4	10	5		1						8			11	2
18		11	CHARLTON ATHLETIC	4-1	Whatmore(2), Chandler, Foster	5645				7	3	6	9		4	10	5		1						8			11	2
19		18	Chelsea	1-2	Henry	6903		2		7	3	6	9		4	10	5		1						8			11	
20		27	CARLISLE UNITED	1-0	Jones	8171				7	3	6	9		4	10	5		1						8			11	2
21		28	Leeds United	1-1	Whatmore	16180				7	3	6	9		4	10	5		1						8			11	2
22	Jan	1	BLACKBURN ROVERS	1-0	Henry	11481				7	3	6*	9		4	10	5		1			12			8			11	2
23		3	Newcastle United	2-2	Foster, C.Thompson	23533	3			7		6	9		4	10	5		1						8			11	2
24		15	BURNLEY	3-0	Henry, Hoggan, McDonagh	8894				7	3	6	9		4	10	5		1						8			11	2
25		22	Oldham Athletic	3-2	C.Thompson, Chandler, Foster	8510				7	3	6	9		4	10	5*		1			12			8			11	2
26	Feb	5	FULHAM	0-1		6748				7	3	6	9		4	10	5		1						8			11	2
27		19	Rotherham United	1-1	Chandler	5646	3			7		6	9			10	5		1				4				11		2
28		22	Crystal Palace	0-3		4456	11			7		6	9*	8			5		1				4	10		12			2
29		26	MIDDLESBROUGH	3-1	Deakin, Hoggan(2)	5598				7	3	6	9		11	10	5		1				4		8				2
30	Mar	5	Barnsley	1-3	Rudge	10403				7	3	6	9*		11	10	5		1			12	4		8				2
31		12	QUEENS PARK RANGERS	3-2	Doyle, Henry, Rudge	6373				7	3	6			4	11	5		1				9	10	8				2
32		19	Shrewsbury Town	0-1		4163				7	3	6				10	5		1				4		9		11		2
33		26	DERBY COUNTY	0-2		7041			3	7		6		11		10	5		1				4		9	8			2
34	Apr	2	LEEDS UNITED	1-2	Rudge	10784	5		3	7		6		10		11			1				4		9	8			2
35		5	Carlisle United	0-5		5615	5		10	7*	3	6	9	11				12	1				4			8			2
36		9	SHEFFIELD WEDNESDAY	0-2		6408			7		3	6		8*	11		5	12	1				9	4				2
37		16	Wolves	0-0		12723			7		3	6			11		5		1				9	4	8				2
38		23	CAMBRIDGE UNITED	2-0	Hoggan(2)	4636			10	7		6			11		5	12	1	5*			9						2
39		30	Leicester City	0-0		13959			11			6					5	7	1	5			9		8				2
40	May	1	GRIMSBY TOWN	0-0		5866			11*	12		6			4		5	7	1	5			9		8				2
41		7	CHELSEA	0-1		8687			11*	12		6					5	7	1	5			9		8				2
42		14	Charlton Athletic	1-4	Moores	8720			11	12		6			4		5	7*	1	5		9				8			2

	Ben	Ber	Bor	Cha	Dea	Doy	Fos	Gra	Hen	Hog	Jon	Joy	McDo	McEl	McGo	Moo	Red	Rei	Rud	ThC	ThS	Wha	Whi
Apps	15	8	9	35	30	30	21	10	31	27	33	5	42	16	14	23	10	15	21	16	3	10	38
Subs	1	1		2			3			1		3				3				2			
Goals				4	1	2	4		9	6	1		1			3		1	3	4		3	

F.A. Cup

Rd		Date	Opponent	Result	Scorers	Att	Ben	Cha	Doy	Fos	Hen	Hog	Jon	McDo	Rud	Wha	Whi
3	Jan	8	Arsenal	1-2	Whatmore	22576	3	7	6	9	4	10	5	1	8	11	2

League Cup

Rd		Date	Opponent	Result	Scorers	Att	Ben	Ber	Cha	Dea	Doy	Fos	Hen	Hog	Jon	McDo	McEl	McGo	Moo	Rei	Rud	ThC	ThS	Whi
1/1	Aug	31	Carlisle United	3-3	Doyle, Hoggan, Moores	4313	3	12	7		6		8	11	5*	1		4	9	10				2
1/2	Sep	14	CARLISLE UNITED	4-0	Henry(2,1pen), Doyle, Moores	4039	3	11	7		6		8		5	1		4	9	10				2
2/1	Oct	5	WATFORD	1-2	Hoggan	5664			7	3			8	11	5	1	6	4	12	10*	9			2
2/2		26	Watford*	1-2	McGovern	11520	3	2				7		11	5	1	6	4	9	8*		10	12	2

* after extra time

Lancashire Cup

1	Aug	14	Preston North End	2-3
2		17	BLACKBURN ROVERS	0-1
3		21	Blackpool	2-2

Other Games

1	Aug	6	Fleetwood	6-1
2		9	Morecambe	2-0
3		24	Manchester United*	2-2
4	Oct	19	1978 XI+	4-0
5	Jan	28	SUNDERLAND	0-1

* Headridge testimonial
+ Nicholson testimonial (home match)

FINAL TABLE

		Pl.	Home W	D	L	F	A	Away W	D	L	F	A	F (Total)	A	Pts
1	Queen's Park Rgs.	42	16	3	2	51	16	10	4	7	26	20	77	36	85
2	Wolverhampton W.	42	14	5	2	42	16	6	10	5	26	28	68	44	75
3	Leicester City	42	11	4	6	36	15	9	6	6	36	29	72	44	70
4	Fulham	42	13	3	5	36	20	7	4	10	28	27	64	47	69
5	Newcastle United	42	13	6	2	43	21	5	7	9	32	32	75	53	67
6	Sheffield Wed.	42	9	8	4	33	23	7	7	7	27	24	60	47	63
7	Oldham Athletic	42	8	10	3	38	24	6	9	6	26	23	64	47	61
8	Leeds United	42	7	11	3	28	22	6	10	5	23	24	51	46	60
9	Shrewsbury Town	42	8	9	4	20	15	7	5	9	28	33	48	48	59
10	Barnsley	42	9	8	4	37	28	5	7	9	20	27	57	55	57
11	Blackburn Rovers	42	11	7	3	38	21	4	5	12	20	37	58	58	57
12	Cambridge United	42	11	7	3	26	17	2	5	14	16	43	42	60	51
13	Derby County	42	7	10	4	27	24	3	9	9	22	34	49	58	49
14	Carlisle United	42	10	6	5	44	28	2	6	13	24	42	68	70	48
15	Crystal Palace	42	11	7	3	31	17	1	5	15	12	35	43	52	48
16	Middlesbrough	42	8	7	6	27	29	3	8	10	19	38	46	67	48
17	Charlton Athletic	42	11	3	7	40	31	2	6	13	23	55	63	86	48
18	Chelsea	42	8	8	5	31	22	3	6	12	20	39	51	61	47
19	Grimsby Town	42	9	7	5	32	26	3	4	14	13	44	45	70	47
20	Rotherham United	42	6	7	8	22	29	4	8	9	23	39	45	68	45
21	Burnley	42	10	4	7	38	24	2	4	15	18	42	56	66	44
22	BOLTON WANDERERS	42	10	2	9	30	26	1	9	11	12	35	42	61	44

1982-83 Season
(Back) McElhinney, Jones, McDonagh, Farnworth, Moores, Whitworth
(Middle) Wright, Bennett, Berry, Thompson, Doyle, Allatt, Henry, Joyce
(Front) Hoggan, Foster, McGovern, Chandler, Reid, Deakin

1983-84 Season
(Back) Borrows, Berry, Platt, Farnworth, McElhinney, Valentine
(Middle) Joyce, Redfearn, Thompson, Caldwell, Snookes, Foster
(Front) Wright, Chandler, Saunders, McGovern, Deakin, Rudge, Nightingale

1983/84 10th in Division Three

Manager: J.McGovern

#	Date	Opponent	Score	Scorers	Att	Bell G	Berry N	Borrows B	Caldwell A	Chandler IG	Deakin RJ	Farnworth S	Foster WP	Joyce WG	McElhinney GR	McGovern JP	Oghani G	Phillips JN	Platt JR	Redfearn NE	Rudge SJ	Saunders S	Snookes E	Thompson SJ	Valentine P	Whatmore N
1	Aug 27	WIMBLEDON	2-0	Rudge, Chandler(pen)	3992			2	10	8	3	1		4	5					11	9	7			6	
2	Sep 3	Bradford City	2-0	Caldwell, Rudge	3324			2	10	8	3	1		4	5					11	9	7			6	
3	6	Gillingham	0-2		3087		12	2	10	8	3	1		4	5					11	9	7*			6	
4	10	WALSALL	8-1	Caldwell(5),Deakin,Rudge,Valentine	4375			2	10	8	3	1		4	5					11	9			7	6	
5	16	Sunthorpe United	0-1		4406			2	10	8	3	1		4	5					11	9			7	6	
6	24	ROTHERHAM UNITED	2-0	Caldwell, Redfearn	5592			2	10	8	3	1		4	5					11	9			7	6	
7	27	BURNLEY	0-0		9709			2	10	8	3	1		4	5					11	9			7	6	
8	Oct 1	Bristol Rovers	1-2	Rudge	5651		12	2	10	8	3	1		4*	5					11	9			7	6	
9	8	Exeter City	2-2	Caldwell(2)	3478			2	10	8	3	1		4	5					11	9			7	6	
10	15	NEWPORT COUNTY	2-3	Caldwell, Chandler	4928			2	10	8	3	1		4	5					11	9			7	6	
11	18	HULL CITY	0-0		6397			2	10	8	3	1		4	5					11	9			7	6	
12	22	Port Vale	2-1	Caldwell, Caldwell	4269			2	10	8*	3	1		4	5					11	9			7	6	
13	29	SOUTHEND UNITED	2-0	Caldwell(2)	5366			2	10	8	3	1	12	4	5					11	9*			7	6	
14	Nov 2	Lincoln City	0-0		3988			2	10	8	3	1	12	4	5					11	9			7	6	
15	5	ORIENT	3-2	McElhinney, Foster, Joyce	5859			2	10	8	3	1	9	4	5					11				7	6	
16	12	Plymouth Argyle	0-2		6424		12	2	10	8	3	1	9*	4	5					11				7	6	
17	26	Bournemouth	2-2	Chandler, Thompson	3941			2	10	8	3	1	9	4	5					11				7	6	
18	Dec 3	BRENTFORD	1-0	Chandler	5416			2	10	8	3	1	9	4	5					11				7	6	
19	17	PRESTON NORTH END	2-2	Foster, Chandler	6245		5	2		8	3	1	9	4						11	10			7	6	
20	26	Wigan Athletic	1-0	Chandler	10045		5	2		8	3	1	9	4						11	10			7	6	
21	27	OXFORD UNITED	1-0	Chandler	11059		6	2		8	3	1	9	4	5					11	10			7		
22	31	Sheffield United	0-5		14252			2		8	3	1	9	4	5					11	10			7	6	
23	Jan 2	MILLWALL	2-0	Rudge, Joyce	7054		2			8	3	1	9	4	5					11	10			7	6	
24	14	Wimbledon	0-4		2955		2			8	6	1	9*	4	5		12			11	10	3		7		
25	21	SCUNTHORPE UNITED	0-0		5379			2	12	8	3	1		4	5					11	10*			7	6	
26	28	Walsall	0-1		7812		2	7	10	8		1	9	4	5	11						3			6	
27	Feb 4	BRISTOL ROVERS	3-0	Caldwell(2), Chandler(pen)	5399	11		2	10	8		1	9	4	5							3		7	6	
28	6	Southend United	1-0	Caldwell	1594	11		2	10	8		1	9	4	5							3		7	6	
29	11	Rotherham United	1-1	Rudge	5043	11		2		8		1*	9	4	5			10			12	3		7	6	
30	14	LINCOLN CITY	0-2		5450	11		2		8			9	4	5			12	1		10	3		7*	6	
31	25	PORT VALE	2-0	Caldwell(2)	5818	11		2	10	8	3		9	4	5				1					7	6	
32	Mar 3	Hull City	1-1	Chandler	6869	11		2		8	3		9	4	5				1		10			7	6	
33	6	Orient	1-2	Chandler	2449	11	12	2		8	3		9	4	5				1		10*			7	6	
34	17	EXETER CITY	1-0	Foster	5161	11		2		8	3		9	4	5				1		12			7*	6	10
35	24	Newport County	3-2	Whatmore, Thompson, Joyce	2436	11		2		8	3		9	4	5						12			7	6	10*
36	27	BRADFORD CITY	0-2		5994	11		2		8	3		9	4	5						12			7	6	10*
37	31	Burnley	2-2	Thompson, Whatmore	8359	11		2	9*	8	3	1	12	4	5									7	6	10
38	Apr 7	GILLINGHAM	0-1		4815	11		2	9	8	3*	1		4	5	12								7	6	10
39	14	Brentford	0-3		3831	11		2	10	8	3	1		4	5									7	6	9
40	16	PLYMOUTH ARGYLE	2-1	Chandler(pen), Bell	3266	11		2	10	8	3	1		4	5									7	6	9
41	20	Oxford United	0-5		9788	11	12	2	10	8	3	1	9	4*	5									7	6	
42	21	WIGAN ATHLETIC	0-1		6142	11		2	10	8	3		9	4	5						12			7*	6	
43	28	BOURNEMOUTH	0-1		3045	11		2	10	8	3		9		5				1				4	7	6	
44	May 5	Millwall	0-3		2346	11	5	2	10	8	3		7	4					1		9				6	
45	7	SHEFFIELD UNITED	3-1	Chandler(2), Caldwell	9036	11	6	2	10	8	3		7	4					1		9					
46	12	Preston North End	1-2	Rudge	5077	11	6	2	10	8	3			4	5				1		9			7		
		Apps				20	9	44	32	46	41	36	27	45	43	2	1		10	25	27	3	6	40	42	7
		Subs					5		1				3				2	1				5				
		Goals				1			19	14	1		3	3	1					1	7			3	1	2

F.A. Cup

#	Date	Opponent	Score	Scorers	Att	Bell G	Berry N	Borrows B	Caldwell A	Chandler IG	Deakin RJ	Farnworth S	Foster WP	Joyce WG	McElhinney GR	Redfearn NE	Rudge SJ	Saunders S	Thompson SJ	Valentine P
1	Nov 19	Tranmere Rovers	2-2	Joyce, Chandler(pen)	5497			2	10	8	3	1		4	5	11	9		7	6
1r	22	TRANMERE ROVERS*	4-1	Chandler(2,1pen), Rudge, Caldwell	6305			2	10*	8	3	1		4	5	11	9	12	7	6
2	Dec 10	MANSFIELD TOWN	2-0	Foster, Rudge	6934			2	10*	8	3	1	9	4	5	11	12		7	6
3	Jan 7	SUNDERLAND	0-3		14018			2		8	3	1	9	4	5	11	10		7	6

* After extra time

League Cup

#	Date	Opponent	Score	Scorers	Att	Borrows B	Caldwell A	Chandler IG	Deakin RJ	Farnworth S	Foster WP	Joyce WG	McElhinney GR	Redfearn NE	Rudge SJ	Saunders S	Thompson SJ	Valentine P	Whatmore N
1/1	Aug 30	CHESTER CITY	3-0	Joyce, Caldwell(2)	2665	2	10	8*	3	1	12	4	5	11	9	7			
1/2	Sep 14	Chester City*	0-3		1502	2		8	3	1	10	4	5	11	9	12	7	6*	

* After extra time (lost 2-0 on penalties)

Associate Members Cup

#	Date	Opponent	Score	Scorers	Att	Bell G	Borrows B	Caldwell A	Chandler IG	Deakin RJ	Foster WP	Joyce WG	McElhinney GR	Platt JR	Thompson SJ	Valentine P
1	Feb 21	Burnley	1-2	Caldwell	3355	11	2	10	8	3	9	4	5	1	7	6

Lancashire Cup

#	Date	Opponent	Score
1	Aug 13	Rochdale	3-3
2	16	Wigan Athletic	0-0
3	20	BURY	2-3

Other Games

#	Date	Opponent	Score
1	Aug 2	Sligo Rovers	2-1
2	4	Finn Harps	2-1
3	6	Carrick Rangers	6-0
4	8	Glentoran	0-0
5	Mar 9	Hamilton Accademicals	1-3

FINAL TABLE

		Pl.	Home W	D	L	F	A	Away W	D	L	F	A	F (Total)	A (Total)	Pts
1	Oxford United	46	17	5	1	58	22	11	6	6	33	28	91	50	95
2	Wimbledon	46	15	5	3	58	35	11	4	8	39	41	97	76	87
3	Sheffield United	46	14	7	2	56	18	10	4	9	30	35	86	53	83
4	Hull City	46	16	5	2	42	11	7	9	7	29	27	71	38	83
5	Bristol Rovers	46	16	5	2	47	21	6	8	9	21	33	68	54	79
6	Walsall	46	14	4	5	44	22	8	5	10	24	39	68	61	75
7	Bradford City	46	14	9	0	50	20	6	2	15	24	45	74	65	71
8	Gillingham	46	13	4	6	50	29	7	6	10	24	40	74	69	70
9	Millwall	46	11	6	6	42	18	9	6	8	29	29	71	65	67
10	BOLTON WANDERERS	46	13	4	6	36	17	5	6	12	20	43	56	60	64
11	Orient	46	13	5	5	40	27	5	4	14	31	54	71	81	63
12	Burnley	46	12	5	6	52	25	4	9	10	24	36	76	61	62
13	Newport County	46	11	9	3	35	27	5	5	13	23	48	58	75	62
14	Lincoln City	46	11	4	8	42	29	6	6	11	17	33	59	62	61
15	Wigan Athletic	46	11	5	7	26	18	5	8	10	20	38	46	56	61
16	Preston North End	46	12	5	6	42	27	3	6	14	24	39	66	66	56
17	Bournemouth	46	11	5	7	38	27	5	2	16	24	46	63	73	55
18	Rotherham United	46	10	5	8	29	17	5	4	14	28	47	57	64	54
19	Plymouth Argyle	46	11	9	4	38	17	2	4	17	18	45	56	62	51
20	Brentford	46	8	9	6	41	30	4	7	13	28	49	69	79	49
21	Scunthorpe United	46	9	9	5	40	31	0	10	13	14	54	54	73	46
22	Southend United	46	9	9	5	34	24	1	5	16	21	52	55	76	44
23	Port Vale	46	9	6	8	33	29	1	6	16	18	54	51	83	43
24	Exeter City	46	6	4	13	27	39	2	7	14	23	45	50	84	33

League Tables: 1984/85 - 1989/90

1984/85 Third Division

	FINAL TABLE	Pl.	Home W	D	L	F	A	Away W	D	L	F	A	F. (Total)	A.	Pts
1	Bradford City	46	15	6	2	44	23	13	4	6	33	22	77	45	94
2	Millwall	46	18	5	0	44	12	8	7	8	29	30	73	42	90
3	Hull City	46	16	4	3	46	20	9	8	6	32	29	78	49	87
4	Gillingham	46	15	5	3	54	29	10	3	10	26	33	80	62	83
5	Bristol City	46	17	2	4	46	19	7	7	9	28	28	74	47	81
6	Bristol Rovers	46	15	6	2	37	13	6	6	11	29	35	66	48	75
7	Derby County	46	14	7	2	40	20	5	6	12	25	34	65	54	70
8	York City	46	13	5	5	42	22	7	4	12	28	35	70	57	69
9	Reading	46	8	7	8	31	29	11	5	7	37	33	68	62	69
10	Bournemouth	46	16	3	4	42	16	3	8	12	15	30	57	46	68
11	Walsall	46	9	7	7	33	22	9	6	8	25	30	58	52	67
12	Rotherham United	46	11	6	6	36	24	7	5	11	19	31	55	55	65
13	Brentford	46	13	5	5	42	27	3	9	11	20	37	62	64	62
14	Doncaster Rovers	46	11	5	7	42	33	6	3	14	30	41	72	74	59
15	Plymouth Argyle	46	11	7	5	33	23	4	7	12	29	42	62	65	59
16	Wigan Athletic	46	12	6	5	36	22	3	8	12	24	42	60	64	59
17	BOLTON WANDS.	46	12	5	6	38	22	4	1	18	31	53	69	75	54
18	Newport County	46	9	6	8	30	30	4	7	12	25	37	55	67	52
19	Lincoln City	46	8	11	4	32	20	3	7	13	18	31	50	51	51
20	Swansea City	46	7	5	11	31	39	5	6	12	22	41	53	80	47
21	Burnley	46	6	8	9	30	24	5	5	13	30	49	60	73	46
22	Orient	46	7	7	9	30	36	4	6	13	21	40	51	76	46
23	Preston North End	46	9	5	9	33	41	4	2	17	18	59	51	100	46
24	Cambridge United	46	2	3	18	17	48	2	6	15	20	47	37	95	21

1985/86 Third Division

	FINAL TABLE	Pl.	Home W	D	L	F	A	Away W	D	L	F	A	F. (Total)	A.	Pts
1	Reading	46	16	3	4	39	22	13	4	6	28	29	67	51	94
2	Plymouth Argyle	46	17	3	3	56	20	9	6	8	32	33	88	53	87
3	Derby County	46	13	7	3	45	20	10	8	5	35	21	80	41	84
4	Wigan Athletic	46	17	4	2	54	17	6	10	7	28	31	82	48	83
5	Gillingham	46	14	5	4	48	17	8	8	7	33	37	81	54	79
6	Walsall	46	15	7	1	59	23	7	2	14	31	41	90	64	75
7	York City	46	16	4	3	49	17	4	7	12	28	41	77	58	71
8	Notts County	46	12	6	5	42	26	7	8	8	29	34	71	60	71
9	Bristol City	46	14	5	4	43	19	4	9	10	26	41	69	60	68
10	Brentford	46	8	8	7	29	29	10	4	9	29	32	58	61	66
11	Doncaster Rovers	46	7	10	6	20	21	9	6	8	25	31	45	52	64
12	Blackpool	46	11	6	6	38	19	6	6	11	28	36	66	55	63
13	Darlington	46	10	7	6	39	33	5	6	12	22	45	61	78	58
14	Rotherham United	46	13	5	5	44	18	2	7	14	17	41	61	59	57
15	Bournemouth	46	9	6	8	41	31	6	3	14	24	41	65	72	54
16	Bristol Rovers	46	9	8	6	27	21	5	4	14	24	54	51	75	54
17	Chesterfield	46	10	6	7	41	30	3	8	12	20	34	61	64	53
18	BOLTON WANDS	46	10	4	9	35	30	5	4	14	19	38	54	68	53
19	Newport County	46	7	8	8	35	33	4	10	9	17	32	52	65	51
20	Bury	46	11	7	5	46	26	1	6	16	17	41	63	67	49
21	Lincoln City	46	7	9	7	33	34	3	7	13	22	43	55	77	46
22	Cardiff City	46	7	5	11	22	29	5	4	14	31	54	53	83	45
23	Wolverhampton W.	46	6	6	11	29	47	5	4	14	28	51	57	98	43
24	Swansea City	46	9	6	8	27	27	2	4	17	16	60	43	87	43

1986/87 Third Division

	FINAL TABLE	Pl.	Home W	D	L	F	A	Away W	D	L	F	A	F. (Total)	A.	Pts
1	Reading	46	16	3	4	39	22	13	4	6	28	29	67	51	94
2	Plymouth Argyle	46	17	3	3	56	20	9	6	8	32	33	88	53	87
3	Derby County	46	13	7	3	45	20	10	8	5	35	21	80	41	84
4	Wigan Athletic	46	17	4	2	54	17	6	10	7	28	31	82	48	83
5	Gillingham	46	14	5	4	48	17	8	8	7	33	37	81	54	79
6	Walsall	46	15	7	1	59	23	7	2	14	31	41	90	64	75
7	York City	46	16	4	3	49	17	4	7	12	28	41	77	58	71
8	Notts County	46	12	6	5	42	26	7	8	8	29	34	71	60	71
9	Bristol City	46	14	5	4	43	19	4	9	10	26	41	69	60	68
10	Brentford	46	8	8	7	29	29	10	4	9	29	32	58	61	66
11	Doncaster Rovers	46	7	10	6	20	21	9	6	8	25	31	45	52	64
12	Blackpool	46	11	6	6	38	19	6	6	11	28	36	66	55	63
13	Darlington	46	10	7	6	39	33	5	6	12	22	45	61	78	58
14	Rotherham United	46	13	5	5	44	18	2	7	14	17	41	61	59	57
15	Bournemouth	46	9	6	8	41	31	6	3	14	24	41	65	72	54
16	Bristol Rovers	46	9	8	6	27	21	5	4	14	24	54	51	75	54
17	Chesterfield	46	10	6	7	41	30	3	8	12	20	34	61	64	53
18	BOLTON WANDS	46	10	4	9	35	30	5	4	14	19	38	54	68	53
19	Newport County	46	7	8	8	35	33	4	10	9	17	32	52	65	51
20	Bury	46	11	7	5	46	26	1	6	16	17	41	63	67	49
21	Lincoln City	46	7	9	7	33	34	3	7	13	22	43	55	77	46
22	Cardiff City	46	7	5	11	22	29	5	4	14	31	54	53	83	45
23	Wolverhampton W.	46	6	6	11	29	47	5	4	14	28	51	57	98	43
24	Swansea City	46	9	6	8	27	27	2	4	17	16	60	43	87	43

1987/88 Fourth Division

	FINAL TABLE	Pl.	Home W	D	L	F	A	Away W	D	L	F	A	F. (Total)	A.	Pts
1	Wolverhampton W.	46	15	3	5	47	19	12	6	5	35	24	82	43	90
2	Cardiff City	46	15	6	2	39	14	9	7	7	27	27	66	41	85
3	BOLTON WANDS.	46	15	6	2	42	12	7	6	10	24	30	66	42	78
4	Scunthorpe United	46	14	5	4	42	20	6	12	5	34	31	76	51	77
5	Torquay United	46	10	7	6	34	16	11	7	5	32	25	66	41	77
6	Swansea City	46	9	7	7	35	28	11	3	9	27	28	62	56	70
7	Peterborough Utd.	46	10	5	8	28	26	10	5	8	24	27	52	53	70
8	Leyton Orient	46	13	4	6	55	27	6	8	9	30	36	85	63	69
9	Colchester United	46	10	5	8	23	22	9	5	9	24	29	47	51	67
10	Burnley	46	12	5	6	31	22	8	2	13	26	40	57	62	67
11	Wrexham	46	13	3	7	46	26	7	3	13	23	32	69	58	66
12	Scarborough	46	12	8	3	38	19	5	6	12	18	29	56	48	65
13	Darlington	46	13	6	4	39	25	5	5	13	32	44	71	69	65
14	Tranmere Rovers	46	14	2	7	43	20	5	7	11	18	33	61	53	64
15	Cambridge United	46	10	6	7	32	24	6	7	10	18	28	50	52	61
16	Hartlepool United	46	9	7	7	25	25	6	7	10	25	32	50	57	59
17	Crewe Alexandra	46	7	11	5	25	19	6	8	9	32	34	57	53	58
18	Halifax Town	46	11	7	5	37	25	3	7	13	17	34	54	59	55
19	Hereford United	46	8	7	8	25	27	6	5	12	16	32	41	59	54
20	Stockport County	46	7	7	9	26	26	5	8	10	18	32	44	58	51
21	Rochdale	46	5	9	9	28	34	6	6	11	19	42	47	76	48
22	Exeter City	46	8	6	9	33	29	3	7	13	20	39	53	68	46
23	Carlisle United	46	9	5	9	38	33	3	3	17	19	53	57	86	44
24	Newport County	46	4	5	14	19	36	2	2	19	16	69	35	105	25

1988/89 Third Division

	FINAL TABLE	Pl.	Home W	D	L	F	A	Away W	D	L	F	A	F. (Total)	A.	Pts
1	Wolverhampton W.	46	18	4	1	61	19	8	10	5	35	30	96	49	92
2	Sheffield United	46	16	3	4	57	21	9	6	8	36	33	93	54	84
3	Port Vale	46	15	3	5	46	21	9	9	5	32	27	78	48	84
4	Fulham	46	12	7	4	42	28	10	2	11	27	39	69	67	75
5	Bristol Rovers	46	9	11	3	34	21	10	6	7	33	30	67	51	74
6	Preston North End	46	14	7	2	56	31	5	8	10	23	29	79	60	72
7	Brentford	46	14	5	4	36	21	4	9	10	30	40	66	61	68
8	Chester City	46	12	6	5	38	18	7	5	11	26	43	64	61	68
9	Notts County	46	11	7	5	37	22	7	6	10	27	32	64	54	67
10	BOLTON WANDS.	46	12	8	3	42	23	4	8	11	16	31	58	54	64
11	Bristol City	46	10	3	10	32	25	8	6	9	21	30	53	55	63
12	Swansea City	46	11	8	4	33	22	4	8	11	18	31	51	53	61
13	Bury	46	11	7	5	27	22	5	6	12	28	45	55	67	61
14	Huddersfield Town	46	10	8	5	35	25	7	1	15	28	48	63	73	60
15	Mansfield Town	46	10	8	5	32	22	4	9	10	16	30	48	52	59
16	Cardiff City	46	10	9	4	30	16	4	6	13	14	40	44	56	57
17	Wigan Athletic	46	9	5	9	28	22	5	9	9	27	31	55	53	56
18	Reading	46	10	6	7	37	29	5	5	13	31	43	68	72	56
19	Blackpool	46	10	6	7	36	29	4	7	12	20	30	56	59	55
20	Northampton Town	46	11	2	10	41	34	5	4	14	25	42	66	76	54
21	Southend United	46	10	9	4	33	26	3	6	14	23	49	56	75	54
22	Chesterfield	46	9	5	9	35	35	5	2	16	16	51	51	86	49
23	Gillingham	46	7	3	13	25	32	5	1	17	22	49	47	81	40
24	Aldershot	46	7	6	10	29	29	1	7	15	19	49	48	78	37

1989/90 Third Division

	FINAL TABLE	Pl.	Home W	D	L	F	A	Away W	D	L	F	A	F. (Total)	A.	Pts
1	Bristol Rovers	46	15	8	0	43	14	11	7	5	28	21	71	35	93
2	Bristol City	46	15	5	3	40	16	12	5	6	36	24	76	40	91
3	Notts County	46	17	4	2	40	18	8	8	7	33	35	73	53	87
4	Tranmere Rovers	46	15	5	3	54	22	8	6	9	32	27	86	49	80
5	Bury	46	11	7	5	35	19	10	4	9	35	30	70	49	74
6	BOLTON WANDS.	46	12	7	4	32	19	6	8	9	27	29	59	48	69
7	Birmingham City	46	10	7	6	33	19	8	5	10	27	40	60	59	66
8	Huddersfield Town	46	11	5	7	30	23	6	9	8	31	39	61	62	65
9	Rotherham United	46	12	6	5	48	28	5	7	11	23	34	71	62	64
10	Reading	46	10	9	4	33	21	5	10	8	24	32	57	53	64
11	Shrewsbury Town	46	10	9	4	38	24	6	6	11	21	30	59	54	63
12	Crewe Alexandra	46	10	8	5	32	24	5	9	9	24	29	56	53	62
13	Brentford	46	11	4	8	41	31	7	3	13	25	35	66	66	61
14	Leyton Orient	46	9	6	8	28	24	7	4	12	24	32	52	56	58
15	Mansfield Town	46	13	2	8	34	25	3	5	15	16	40	50	65	55
16	Chester City	46	11	7	5	30	23	2	8	13	13	32	43	55	54
17	Swansea City	46	10	6	7	25	27	4	6	13	20	36	45	63	54
18	Wigan Athletic	46	10	6	7	29	22	3	8	12	19	42	48	64	53
19	Preston North End	46	10	7	6	42	30	4	3	16	23	49	65	79	52
20	Fulham	46	8	8	7	33	27	4	7	12	22	39	55	66	51
21	Cardiff City	46	6	9	8	30	35	6	5	12	21	35	51	70	50
22	Northampton Town	46	7	7	9	27	31	4	7	12	24	37	51	68	47
23	Blackpool	46	8	6	9	29	33	2	10	11	20	40	49	73	46
24	Walsall	46	6	8	9	23	30	3	6	14	17	42	40	72	41

1984/85 17th in Division Three

Manager: J.McGovern until 7/1/85, C.Wright from 8/2/85

No	Mth	Day	Opponent	Score	Scorers	Att	Bailey IC	Bell G	Berry N	Borrows B	Booth P	Caldwell A	Came M	Chandler JG	Deakin RJ	Evans A	Farnworth S	Fitzpatrick P	Foster WP	Joyce WG	Lodge P	McElhinney GR	Oghani G	Phillips JN	Rudge SJ	Thompson SJ	Valentine P	Walker R
1	Aug	25	BRISTOL ROVERS	0-1		4469		11	5	2		10		8	6		1			4			9	3		7		
2	Sep	1	Derby County	2-3	Caldwell, Chandler(pen)	11478		11	6	2		10		8			1			4	7	5	9	3				
3		8	HULL CITY	0-0		5403		11		2		10		8	3		1			4	7	5	9				6	
4		15	Rotherham United	1-3	Oghani	3926		11		2		10		8	3		1			4	7*	5	9		12		6	
5		18	Swansea City	1-2	Oghani	3636				2					3		1		10	4		5	9	11	8	7	6	
6		22	PLYMOUTH ARGYLE	7-2	Caldwell(3),Oghani,Joyce,Chandler(2,1p)	3876		11		2		10		8			1			4			9	3		7	6	
7		29	Doncaster Rovers	0-2		4850		11		2		10	12	8			1			4			9	3		7*	6	
8	Oct	2	WALSALL	3-1	Oghani, Thompson, Caldwell	4445		11		2		10		8			1			4			9	3		7	6	
9		6	Reading	1-3	Chandler	3253		11		2		10		8			1			4			9	3		7	6	
10		13	BOURNEMOUTH	2-1	Foster, Chandler(pen)	4651		11	5	2				8			1		10	4			9	3		7	6	
11		20	PRESTON NORTH END	4-0	Chandler, Oghani(3)	5691		11	5	2				8			1		10	4			9	3		7	6	
12		23	Bristol City	2-3	Foster, Oghani	7715		11	5	2				8			1		10	4			9	3		7	6	
13		27	Burnley	2-3	Oghani(2)	6460		11	5	2				8			1		10	4			9	3		7	6	
14	Nov	3	LINCOLN CITY	1-0	Thompson	4019		11		2			5	8*	6		1		10	4		12	9	3		7		
15		6	YORK CITY	2-1	Rudge, Oghani(pen)	4672		11		2			5		6		1		10	4			9	3	8	7		
16		10	Newport County	2-3	Foster, Thompson	2073		11*		2			5		6		1		10	4			9	3	8	7	12	
17		24	GILLINGHAM	1-2	Chandler	4381		11		2			5	8	6		1		10	4			9*	3	12	7		
18	Dec	1	Brentford	1-2	Joyce	3668		11		2				6	8	7	1		10	4		5	9	3				
19		15	MILLWALL	2-0	Caldwell(2)	4544		11		2		10		6	8	7	1			4		5						
20		22	CAMBRIDGE UNITED	0-0		4310		11		2		10		6	8	7	1		9	4*		5	12	3				
21		26	Wigan Athletic	0-1		8871		11		2		10		6	8	3	1		9*	4		5	12			7		
22		29	Bradford City	1-2	Caldwell	6255		11*		2		10		6	8	3	1			4		5	9		12	7		
23	Jan	1	ORIENT	0-0		4710				2		10		6	8		1			4			9	3	11	7	5	
24		12	DERBY COUNTY	3-0	Caldwell, Chandler(2,1pen)	6491		11		2		10	5	8	6		1			4			9	3		7		
25		26	ROTHERHAM UNITED	2-0	Caldwell(2)	5059		11		2		10	5	8	6		1			4			9	3		7		
26		29	Bristol Rovers	2-1	Caldwell, Chandler(pen)	3982		11		2		10	5	8	6		1			4			9	3		7		
27	Feb	2	DONCASTER ROVERS	3-1	Came, Caldwell, Chandler(pen)	5810		11		2		10	5	8	6		1			4			9	3*		7	12	
28		9	Plymouth Argyle	0-2		4978		11		2		10*	5	8	3		1		9	4					12	7	6	
29		16	SWANSEA CITY	0-0		5448		11		2	7*	10	5	8	6		1		12	4			9	3				
30		23	Lincoln City	0-2		2448		11		2		10	5	8	6		1			4	7		9	3				
31	Mar	2	BURNLEY	1-3	Joyce	6468		11*		2		10	5	8	6	9	1			4			12	3		7		
32		5	BRISTOL CITY	1-4	Joyce	3774		11		2		10	5	8	6	9	1			4				3		7		
33		9	Preston North End	0-1		5478		11		2		10		8	6	9*	1		12	4				3		7	5	
34		16	Bournemouth	0-4		2715	3	11		2				6		9*	1		10	4			12		8	7	5	
35		19	Walsall	0-1		4941	3	11		2		10	12				1		9	4				6	8*	7	5	
36		23	READING	1-2	Caldwell	3627	3	11*		2		10	12				1		9	4				6	8	7	5	
37		29	York City	3-0	Jones(og), Phillips, Foster	4363	11			2			12		6		1		9	4			10	3	8	7	5*	
38	Apr	2	Hull City	2-2	Oghani, Joyce	7863	3			2				8	6		1		9	4			10	5	11	7		
39		6	WIGAN ATHLETIC	1-0	Chandler(pen)	6067	3			2		12		8	6		1		9	4			10*	5	11	7		
40		9	Orient	3-4	Chandler(2), Rudge	2197	3			2		12		8	6		1		9	4			10*	5	11	7		
41		13	NEWPORT COUNTY	3-1	Caldwell(2), Chandler	4011				2*		10		8	6		1		9	4			12	3	11	7	5	
42		20	Gillingham	3-2	Caldwell, Chandler, Oghani	5132				2*		10		8	6		1		12	4			9	3	11	7	5	
43		27	BRENTFORD	1-1	Thompson	4230		4				10		8	6		1		12	2*			9	3	11	7	5	
44	May	4	Millwall	2-5	Oghani(2)	7202	3	4					5	8			1	2	10				9		11	7		
45		6	BRADFORD CITY	0-2		7712	3						5	8	6*		1	2	10	4			9	12	11	7		
46		11	Cambridge United	3-2	Walker, Oghani, Caldwell	1694	3					10*	5	8			1	2		4			9	12	11		6	7
			Apps				10	36	6	42	1	29	22	39	33	4	46	3	24	45	4	13	37	37	16	34	24	1
			Subs									2	1	2	1				4		1	4	3	4			2	
			Goals									18	1	16					4	5			16	1	2	4		1

One own goal

F.A. Cup

No	Mth	Day	Opponent	Score	Scorers	Att	Bell G	Borrows B	Came M	Deakin RJ	Farnworth S	Foster WP	Joyce WG	Oghani G	Phillips JN	Rudge SJ	Thompson SJ
1	Nov	17	Hull City	1-2	Foster	6424	11	2	5	6	1	10	4	9	3	8	7

League Cup

No	Mth	Day	Opponent	Score	Scorers	Att	Bell G	Berry N	Borrows B	Caldwell A	Came M	Chandler JG	Deakin RJ	Farnworth S	Foster WP	Joyce WG	Lodge P	McElhinney GR	Oghani G	Phillips JN	Thompson SJ	Valentine P
1/1	Aug	28	OLDHAM ATHLETIC	2-1	Caldwell, Chandler(pen)	3286	11	5	2	10		8	6	1		4			9	3	7	
1/2	Sep	4	Oldham Athletic	4-4*	Oghani(2), Bell, Chandler	4111	11	6	2	10		8	3	1		4	7	5	9			
2/1		25	Shrewsbury Town	2-2	Chandler, Oghani	3720	11		2	10	12	8*		1		4		5	9	3	7	6
2/2	Oct	9	SHREWSBURY TOWN	2-1	Thompson, Chandler	5445	11		2	10*		8		1	12	4		5	9	3	7	6
3		30	Notts County	1-6	Foster	4547	11		2			6	8	1	10	4		5	9	3	7	

* After extra time

Freight Rover Trophy

No	Mth	Day	Opponent	Score	Scorers	Att	Bailey IC	Bell G	Borrows B	Caldwell A	Came M	Chandler JG	Deakin RJ	Evans A	Farnworth S	Fitzpatrick P	Foster WP	Joyce WG	Oghani G	Phillips JN	Rudge SJ	Thompson SJ	Valentine P	Walker R
1/1	Jan	22	CREWE ALEXANDRA	3-2	Joyce(2), Caldwell	2345		11	2	10*	5	8	6		1		12	4	9	3		7		
1/2	Feb	5	Crewe Alexandra	0-0		3303		11	2	10	5	8		3	1		12	4	9*			7	6	
2	Mar	12	Rochdale	1-0	Caldwell	2650	12	11	2	10			6	9	1		8	4		3*		7	5	
3	Apr	16	DARLINGTON	2-1	Oghani(2)	3769	A12			A2	B10	8	6		1			4	9	3	11	7	5	B14
SF	May	8	MANSFIELD TOWN	1-2	Caldwell	6706	3			10	5	8	6		1	2		4	9		11	7		

Lancashire Cup

No	Mth	Day	Opponent	Score
1	Aug	11	Preston N.E.	1-1
2		14	BLACKBURN ROVERS	1-1
3		18	Bury	4-3

Other Games

No	Mth	Day	Opponent	Score
1	Aug	1	Glenavon	2-3
2		3	Portadown	4-2
3		4	Linfield	2-1
4		6	Moyola Park	8-0
5		8	Bangor	2-0
6	Oct	17	Winsford United	6-3
7	Nov	19	Hyde United	3-3
8	Dec	8	Rochdale	3-2

1984-85 Season
(Back) Valentine, Phillips, Came, McElhinney, Berry, Booth, Oghani
(Middle) Joyce, Borrows, Thompson, Caldwell, Farnworth, Platt, Deakin, Lodge, Joyce, Nightingale
(Front) Foster, Wright, Chandler, Rudge, Saunders, McGovern, Bell

1985-86 Season
(Back) Thompson, Farnworth, Scott
(Middle) Nightingale, Phillips, Came, Sutton, Allardyce, Entwistle, Irwin, Carroll
(Front) Bell, Hartford, Oghani, Neal, Caldwell, Gavin, Joyce

1985/86   18th in Division Three

Manager: C.Wright until 6/12/85; N.Lofthouse (caretaker) 6-17/12/85; P.Neal from 18/12/85

#	Date	Opponent	Score	Scorers	Att	Allardyce S	Bell G	Caldwell A	Came M	Cross D	Darby J	Entwistle W	Farnworth S	Felgate DW	Fitzpatrick P	Gavin MW	Hartford RA	Joyce WG	Neil P	Oghani G	Phillips JN	Ring MP	Ripley SE	Roberts	Rudge SJ	Scott DE	Sutton D	Thompson SJ	Walker R	Winstanley M
1	Aug 17	ROTHERHAM UNITED	1-1	Caldwell	5129		11	8	6	9			1				10	2			3					4*	5	7	12	
2	24	Doncaster Rovers	1-1	Cross	3414	6	11	8*		9			1				10	4		12	3					2	5	7		
3	26	BURY	1-4	Cross	8772	6	11*	8		9			1				10	4		12	3					2	5	7		
4	31	Gillingham	1-2	Cross	2773	6	11	8		9			1				10	2		12					4	3	5	7*		
5	Sep 7	WOLVES	4-1	Thompson(2,1pen), Cross(2)	4986	6		8*	5	9			1		2		10	4		11	3							7	12	
6	14	Walsall	0-2		5432	6		8	5	9			1		2		10	4		11	3							7		
7	17	LINCOLN CITY	1-1	Thompson	3928		11	8	5	9			1		2		10				3					4		7		
8	21	Newport County	1-0	Oghani	2212	6	7		5	9			1		2		10			11					8	3	4			
9	28	PLYMOUTH ARGYLE	3-1	Joyce, Caldwell, Rudge	4270	6		8	5				1		2		10	7							9*	3	4		11	
10	Oct 1	York City	0-3		4680	6	12	8	5				1		2		10	7		11					9*	3	4			
11	5	Reading	0-1		8000	6	12	8	5	9			1				10	4		11	3					2*		7		
12	12	BRENTFORD	1-2	Joyce	4106	6	11		5	9			1		2		10	4		8	3							7*	12	
13	19	SWANSEA CITY	1-1	Thompson(pen)	3558		7	8*	5	9			1				10	2		11	3				6		4	12		
14	22	Bristol Rovers	1-2	Caldwell	4308		11	8	5	9*			1			12	10	2			3				6		4	7		
15	26	Cardiff City	1-0	Bell	2502	6	11	8				9	1				10	2			3				5		4	7		
16	Nov 2	BOURNEMOUTH	1-0	Thompson	3800	6	11	8		12		9*	1				10	2			3				5		4	7		
17	5	DARLINGTON	0-3		2902	6	11	8			8	9	1				10	2			3				5		4*	7		
18	9	Notts County	0-1		4497		7	8	5			9	1				10	2		11	3				6		4			
19	23	DERBY COUNTY	0-1		5887		11	12	5				1		7*		10	4		8	3				9	2	6			12
20	30	Bristol City	0-2		6253		11*	8	5				1		7		10	2		9					4	3	6			
21	Dec 14	CHESTERFIELD	2-1	Thompson, Hartford	3621		11	8	5	9			1				10	4								2	6	7		
22	21	DONCASTER ROVERS	2-0	Cross(2)	5456		11	8	5	9*			1				10	4	3						12	2	6	7		
23	26	Blackpool	1-1	Cross	9473		11	7	4	9			1				10	6	3							2	5	8		
24	Jan 1	WIGAN ATHLETIC	1-2	Thompson(pen)	9252		11*	7		9			1				10	6	3	12					4		5	8		
25	11	GILLINGHAM	0-1		5232		11	7		9			1				10	6	4	12	3					2	5	8*		
26	18	Rotherham United	0-1		3821		11		5	9			1				10		4	8	3				7	2	6			
27	25	WALSALL	3-1	Caldwell, Bell, Oghani	4088		11	9	5				1				10			8	3				7	2	6		4	
28	Feb 1	Wolves	2-0	Rudge, Oghani	3110			9	5				1			11	10			8	3				7	2	6		4	
29	4	BRISTOL ROVERS	0-2		3672			9	5			12	1				10	11		8	3*				7	2	6		4	
30	8	Swansea City	1-3	Hartford	4242			9	5			12	1				10		3	8					7	2	6		4*	
31	22	NEWPORT COUNTY	4-0	Caldwell(2), Oghani, Ripley	4063		11	9	5				1				10	6		8	3		7			2	4			
32	25	Bury	1-2	Caldwell(pen)	6006		11	9	5					1			10	6	7	8	3					2	4			
33	Mar 4	YORK CITY	1-1	Hartford	3589			9	5					1			10	6	7	8	3		11			2	4			
34	8	READING	2-0	Caldwell(pen), Joyce	4903		12	9	5					1			10	6	7	8	3		11*			2	4			
35	14	Brentford	1-1	Sutton	3284		11	9	5					1			10		7	8	3		6			2	4			
36	18	Bournemouth	1-2	Oghani	2063		11	9*				12		1			10		7	8	3		6			2	4			5
37	22	CARDIFF CITY	5-0	Joyce, Came, Neil, Oghani, Caldwell	4114		11	9	5					1			10	6*	7	8	3				12	2	4			
38	25	Lincoln City	1-1	Neil	2329			9	5					1			10	6	7	8	3					2	4			11
39	29	Wigan Athletic	3-1	Hartford, Gavin, Caldwell	8009		12	9						1		11	10	7		8	3					2*	4	6		5
40	31	BLACKPOOL	1-3	Thompson	7878			9			2			1		11	10	7		8*	3	12					4	6		5
41	Apr 12	Notts County	1-0	Phillips	4688			9*	5					1		11	10	7		8	3	12				2	4	6		
42	19	Derby County	1-2	Hartford	12232				5					1		11	10	7		8	3		9			2	4	6		
43	22	Plymouth Argyle	1-4	Sutton	12183		12	9*	5					1		11	10	7		8	3					2	4	6		
44	24	Darlington	1-0	Oghani	1870			9	5					1		11	10	7		8	3					2	4	6		
45	26	BRISTOL CITY	0-4		4493		6		5		7	9	1			11	10			8	3					2	4			
46	May 3	Chesterfield	0-3		3183				5					1		11*	10	7		8	3					2	4	6		
		Apps				14	30	38	35	19	2	5	31	15	10	8	46	31	20	31	33	1	5		13	43	32	35	6	3
		Subs					6	2	1			3				1				5			2			2				5
		Goals					2	10	1	8						1	5	4	2	7	1		1		2		2	8		

F.A. Cup

#	Date	Opponent	Score	Scorers	Att	Bell G	Came M	Entwistle W	Farnworth S	Fitzpatrick P	Hartford RA	Joyce WG	Oghani G	Phillips JN	Rudge SJ	Scott DE	Thompson SJ
1	Nov 16	Wrexham	1-3	Thompson	2738	11	5	9*	1	2	10	4	8	3	12	6	7

League Cup

#	Date	Opponent	Score	Scorers	Att	Allardyce S	Bell G	Caldwell A	Came M	Cross D	Farnworth S	Fitzpatrick P	Hartford RA	Joyce WG	Neil P	Oghani G	Phillips JN	Ring MP	Rudge SJ	Scott DE	Sutton D	Thompson SJ	Walker R
1/1	Aug 20	STOCKPORT COUNTY	4-1	Hartford, Cross(2), Bell	3311		11	8	6*	9	1		10	4		12	3			2	5	7	
1/2	Sep 3	Stockport County*	1-1	Caldwell	2573	6	12	8		9	1	2	10	4*		8	3					7	11
2/1	25	Nottingham Forest	0-4		10530	6	7		5	9	1	2	10		12	11			8*	3	4		
2/2	Oct 8	NOTTINGHAM FOREST	0-3		4010	6		8	5	9	1	2	10	4		11	3					7	

* Played at Burnden Park, Stockport's ground under repair.

Freight Rover Trophy

#	Date	Opponent	Score	Scorers	Att	Bell G	Caldwell A	Came M	Entwistle W	Farnworth S	Felgate DW	Gavin MW	Hartford RA	Joyce WG	Neil P	Oghani G	Phillips JN	Roberts	Rudge SJ	Scott DE	Sutton D	Thompson SJ	Walker R
Q	Jan 20	Stockport County	2-2	Came, Caldwell	1874	11	9	5	12	1			10		4	8	3		7*	2	6		
1	28	CREWE ALEXANDRA	1-0	Oghani	2428		9	5	12	1			10			8	3	11*	7	2	6		4
Q/F	Mar 11	TRANMERE ROVERS	2-1	Caldwell, Oghani	3865	11	9	5			1		10	6	7	8	3			2	4		
SF	May 1	Darlington	3-0	Oghani, Caldwell, Hartford	3771		9	5			1	11	10	7		8	3			2	4	6	
F/1	6	Wigan Athletic	1-0	Caldwell	6975		9	5			1	11	10	7		8	3			2	4	6	
F/2	9	WIGAN ATHLETIC	2-1	Oghani, Caldwell	12120		9	5			1	11	10	7		8	3			2	4	6	
F	24	Bristol City*	0-3		54502	12	9	5			1	11	10	7		8	3			2	4	6*	

* Played at Wembley Stadium.

Lancashire Cup

#	Date	Opponent	Score
1	Aug 3	ROCHDALE	2-0
2	6	BURY	1-0
3	10	Burnley	0-4

Other Games

#	Date	Opponent	Score
1	Jul 24	Chorley	0-0
2	25	Macclesfield Town	2-1
3	27	Workington	0-0
4	30	Southport	5-2

1986/87 21st in Division Three (relegated after play offs)

Manager: P.Neal

No		Date	Opponent	Score	Scorers	Att	Allan P	Atkinson P	Brookman N	Caldwell A	Came M	Darby J	Elliott SB	Farnworth S	Felgate DW	Gavin MW	Griffin P	Hartford RA	Joyce WG	Matthews N	Mullineux I	Neal P	Oghani G	Phillips JN	Salmon MB	Scott DE	Stevens I	Sutton D	Thompson SI	Winstanley M
1	Aug	23	SWINDON TOWN	1-2	Oghani	5684						4	9			7		10	12			2*	11	3	1	5			8	6	
2		30	Bristol Rovers	0-1		4092				7	5	12	9						4			2	11	10*	1			8	6	3
3	Sep	6	DARLINGTON	4-3	Elliott, Thompson, Oghani, Joyce	3952					5		9			7			4			2	11	10	1			8	6	3
4		13	Bournemouth	1-2	Caldwell	3031				10	5	12	9			7			4			2		11	1			8	6	3*
5		16	Fulham	2-4	Elliott, Thompson	2434				10	5	12	9			7			4			2*	11	3	1			8	6	
6		20	PORT VALE	3-0	Caldwell, Elliott, Joyce	4872				10	5	6	9			7*			4	12		2	11		1			8		3
7		26	Wigan Athletic	1-2	Joyce	4986				10	5	6	9			7			4			2	12	11*	1			8		3
8		30	CHESTERFIELD	1-2	Caldwell	3931				9	5	6						10	4		7*	2	11	12*	1			8		3
9	Oct	4	NOTTS COUNTY	1-1	Oghani	4248				9	5	6						10	4			2	7	11	1		3	8		12
10		11	Walsall	3-3	Thompson(pen), Caldwell, Elliott	4677				9*	5	6	7			12		10	4			2		11	1			8*		
11		18	Rotherham United	0-1		3430				9	5	6	7			4		10					12	11	1	2		3	8	
12		21	BLACKPOOL	1-0	Thompson	6534				9	5*	6				11		10	4				7	3	1	2	5	8		
13		25	CHESTER CITY	1-1	Elliott	4607						6	9			11*		10	4				7	3	1	2	5	8		
14	Nov	1	Brentford	2-1	Gavin, Thompson	3522					12	6	9			11		10	4				7	3	1	2	5*	8		
15		4	Middlesbrough	0-0		10096				12		6	9			11		10	4				7	3	1	2				
16		8	NEWPORT COUNTY	0-1		4530					5	6	9			11		10	4				7*	3	1	2				
17		22	Mansfield Town	2-2	Caldwell, Joyce	3096				12	5	6*	9			11		10	4			12		3	1	2				
18		29	YORK CITY	3-2	Hartford, Caldwell(2)	4528				7	5		9			11		10	4			2	9	3	1			6		
19	Dec	13	GILLINGHAM	3-0	Caldwell(2), Gavin	4867				7	5					11		10	4			2		3	1			6		
20		20	Bristol City	1-4	Elliott	8028				7	5		9			11		10	4			2		3	1			6		
21		26	BURY	2-3	Thompson, Oghani	10135				7	5		9			11		10	4			2	9	3	1			6		
22		27	Doncaster Rovers	0-3		3301				7	5					11		10	4			12	9	3	1			6	8*	
23	Jan	3	Mansfield Town	0-1		5058				7	5	2				11		10	4			2	9	3	1			6		
24		17	BRISTOL ROVERS	2-2	Sutton, Caldwell	4087				7	9							11						3	1	2		5	8	6
25		31	BOURNEMOUTH	0-1		4219				7	6	10						11					9	3	1	2		5	8	
26	Feb	3	Carlisle United	0-0		2535				7	6	10						11						3	1	2		5	8	
27		7	FULHAM	3-2	Joyce, Thompson, Caldwell	4128				7	6	10	9		1			11				5		3		2			8	
28		14	Port Vale	1-1	Elliott	3628		10		7	6	10	9		1			11						3		2			8	
29		18	Darlington	1-0	Elliott	1464				7	6	5	9		1			11	10			4		3		2		5	8	
30		28	Chesterfield	0-0		3202		7			6		9		1			11	10			4		3		2		5	8	
31	Mar	3	BRENTFORD	0-2		3563		12			6		9		1			11	10	4*			7	3		2		5	8	
32		7	Chester City	0-0		2764				7	6		9		1				10	4				3		2		5	8	
33		14	ROTHERHAM UNITED	0-0		3748				7	6	11	9		1			11	10*	4				3		2		5	8	
34		17	Blackpool	1-1	Sutton	14717				7	6	12	9		1			11	10	4				3		2		5		
35		21	WALSALL	1-0	Elliott	4308				7	6	8	9		1			11	10	4		2*				3		5	12	
36		24	Swindon Town	0-2		8110				7	6	8	9		1			11	10	4				2				5	12	3
37		28	Notts County	0-0		4776					6	8	9*		1			11	10	7*		4				2	12	5	8	3
38	Apr	4	Newport County	1-2	Stevens	1193				12	6		9		1			11	10	4*				2			7	5	8	
39		7	WIGAN ATHLETIC	1-2	Hartford(pen)	5321					6	3	9		1			11	10	4		2					7	5	8	3
40		11	MIDDLESBROUGH	0-1		5858				7*	6		9		1			11	10	4		2				3	12	5	8	
41		18	CARLISLE UNITED	2-0	Neal, Stevens	4241			8*		6		9		1			11	10	4		2				3	7	5	12	
42		20	Bury	0-0		4969			8		6		9		1			11	10	4		2				3*	7	5	12	
43		25	BRISTOL CITY	0-0		4414			8	7	6		9		1			11*	10	4		2				3	12	5		
44	May	2	York City	1-2	Hartford	4079			11	7	6		9		1				10	4		2				3	8*	5	12	
45		4	DONCASTER ROVERS	0-1		4838	12			7*	6		9		1			11	10	4		2				3			8	5
46		9	Gillingham	0-1		5561					7	6	9		1			11	10	4		2				3			8	5
			Apps					2	4	32	42	24	38		20	40		35	43	1	1	26	17	33	26	36	5	30	39	12
			Subs				1	1		3	1	4				1				1		1	2	2	1			3		5	1
			Goals							11			9			2		3	5			1	4				2	2	7	

Play Offs

No		Date	Opponent	Score	Scorers	Att	Caldwell A	Came M	Elliott SB	Felgate DW	Hartford RA	Joyce WG	Neal P	Phillips JN	Scott DE	Stevens I	Sutton D	Thompson SI
SF1		14	Aldershot	0-1		4164	7	6	9	1	11	10	4	2	3		5	8
SF2		17	ALDERSHOT	2-2*	Caldwell(2,1pen)	7445	7	6	9	1	11	10	4*	2	3	12	5	8

* After extra time

F.A. Cup

No		Date	Opponent	Score	Scorers	Att	Came M	Darby J	Elliott SB	Farnworth S	Felgate DW	Hartford RA	Joyce WG	Neal P	Oghani G	Phillips JN	Scott DE	Sutton D	Thompson SI
1	Nov	15	Halifax Town	1-1	Oghani	3370	7	5	6	9	1	11	10	4	12	3	2		8*
1r		18	HALIFAX TOWN	1-1	Caldwell	4652	7*	5	6	9		11	10	4	2	12	3	1	8
1/2r		24	Halifax Town	3-1	Thompson, Caldwell, Gavin	3338	7	5		9*		11	10	4	2	12	3	1	6	8
2	Dec	6	TRANMERE ROVERS	2-0	Caldwell, Thompson	6193	7	5	9			11	10	4	2		3	1	6	8
3	Jan	10	Coventry City	0-3		12044	7	9	2			11	10*	4	12	3	1	6	5	8

League Cup

No		Date	Opponent	Score	Scorers	Att	Caldwell A	Came M	Darby J	Elliott SB	Gavin MW	Joyce WG	Neal P	Oghani G	Phillips JN	Salmon MB	Sutton D	Thompson SI	Winstanley M
1/1	Aug	26	Bury	1-2	Ross(og)	3217			4	9	7		10	2	11	3	1	8	6	5
1/2	Sep	2	BURY	0-0		4330	10	5	A7	9		4	B14	2	A12	11	1	8	6	B3

Freight Rover Trophy

No		Date	Opponent	Score	Scorers	Att	Allan P	Caldwell A	Came M	Darby J	Elliott SB	Hartford RA	Joyce WG	Neal P	Oghani G	Phillips JN	Salmon MB	Scott DE	Sutton D	Thompson SI	Winstanley M
Q	Dec	2	BLACKPOOL	1-0	Gavin	3395		7	5	2	9*	11	10	4	12	3	1		6	8	
Q		16	Burnley	2-0	Oghani, Darby	1464	4	7*		10		11	12		9	3	1	2	5	8	6
1	Jan	27	BURNLEY	2-1	Allen, Caldwell	3698	4	7	6	10		11			9	3	1	2	5	8	
Q/F	Feb	10	CHESTER CITY	1-2	Came	3900		7	6	10	9	11		4	5	3	1	2		8	

Lancashire Cup

No		Date	Opponent	Score
1	Aug	9	PRESTON NORTH END	0-0
2		12	Burnley	3-2
3		16	WIGAN ATHLETIC	3-4

Other Games

No		Date	Opponent	Score
1	Jul	30	Morecambe	2-0
2	Aug	2	Fleetwood	2-1
3		4	Workington	3-0
4	Feb	20	Scarborough	3-0

1986-87 Season
(Back) Came, Salmon, Mailey, Farnsworth, Phillips
(Middle) Carroll, Thompson, Winstanley, Oghani, Elliott, Sutton, Joyce, Clark, Irwin, Nightingale
(Front) Allen, Darby, Gavin, Neal, Scott, Caldwell, Hartford

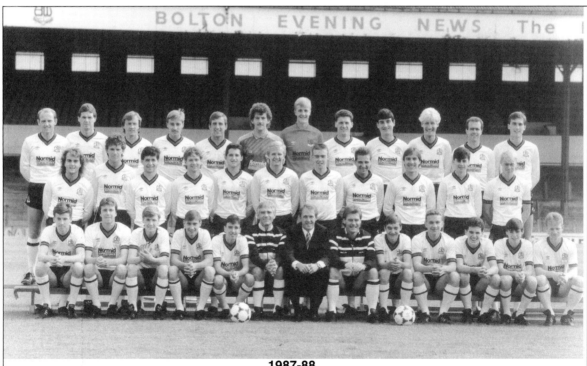

1987-88
(Back) Whatmore, Elliott, Thomas, Darby, Thompson, Felgate, Price, Came, Morgan, Sutton, Crombie, Winstanley
(Middle) Bell, Stevens, Callaghan, Chandler, Banks, Hughes, Brookman, Joyce, Scott, Henshaw, Booth
(Front) Jackson, Still, Halligan, Roberts, Gaskell, Nightingale, Neal, Carroll, Fisher, Raven, Spooner, Jeffrey, O'Brien

1987/88 3rd in Division Four (promoted)

Manager: P. Neal

#		Date	Opponent	Score	Scorers	Att	Barnes P	Brookman N	Callaghan I	Came M	Chandler JG	Crombie D	Darby J	Elliott SB	Felgate DW	Henshaw G	Hughes P	Joyce WG	May AM	Morgan T	Neal P	Savage RJ	Scott DE	Stevens I	Storer SJ	Sutton D	Thomas JW	Thompson SJ	Winstanley M
1	Aug	15	CREWE ALEXANDRA	1-1	Henshaw	4792		A14		6	11	3	A2			1	7		8		9						5	10	4
2		22	CARDIFF CITY	1-0	Chandler	4530				5	11	3	2			1	7		8		9						6	10	4
3		29	Scarborough	0-4		4462		11		5		3				1	7		8		9		2				6	10	A4
4		31	PETERBOROUGH UNITED	2-0	Thomas(pen), Thompson	3746		11		5		3		A12		1	7		8		9		2				6	10	4
5	Sep	5	Hereford United	3-0	Thomas(2), Morgan	2541		11		5		3				1	7		8		9		2				6	10	4
6		12	HALIFAX TOWN	2-0	Henshaw, Shaw(og)	4445				5		3				1	7		8		9	11	2				6	10	4
7		15	Scunthorpe United	1-1	Morgan	2501				5		3				1	7		8		9	11	2				6	10	4
8		19	Torquay United	1-2	Savage	2247		B14		5		3	2	A12		1	7		8		9	11					6	A10	B4
9		26	HARTLEPOOL UNITED	1-2	Came	4398		4		5		3	B2	A12		1	7		8	A9	B14	11					6	10	
10	Oct	3	WOLVES	1-0	Thomas(pen)	3833				5		3				1	7		8		9	11	2				6	10	4
11		10	Darlington	0-1		1763	11			5		3			10	B7	8				A9	4	2				6	A12	B14
12		17	CARLISLE UNITED	5-0	Brookman(2),Darby,Elliott,Wright(og)	4184	B11	7		5		3	B14	10	1							4	2	A12		6	A9	8	
13		20	EXETER CITY	1-0	Came	4165		7		5			A3	11	10	1						4	2	A12		6	9	8	
14		24	Rochdale	2-2	Thomas(2,1pen)	4294		7		5			A3	11	10	1						4	2	A12		6	9	8	
15		31	SWANSEA CITY	1-1	Thompson	4607		7		5			A3	11	10	1			A12			4	2			6	9	8	
16	Nov	3	Newport County	1-0	Elliott	1566		7		5		3		11	10	1						4	2			6	9	8	
17		7	LEYTON ORIENT	1-0	Thomas	5189		7		5		3		11	10	1				A14		4	2			6	9	8	A6
18		21	Burnley	1-2	Thomas	7489		7		5		6	11	10	1	A3				A14		4	2				9	8	
19		28	CAMBRIDGE UNITED	2-2	Thomas(2,1pen)	4294		7		5		3	11	10	1					A14	A6	4	2				9	8	
20	Dec	11	Colchester United	0-3		1743		B7	A8	5			11	10	1					A12		B14	3	4	2		6	9	
21		15	Tranmere Rovers	0-2		3064				5			11	10	1	7				A14		4	A2			6	9	8	3
22		19	WREXHAM	2-0	Thompson, Morgan	3701		4		5			11	A10	1	7				A14		3	2			6	9	8	
23		26	Hartlepool United	0-0		4102				5			11		1	4						10	3	2	7	6	9	8	
24		28	STOCKPORT COUNTY	2-1	Storer, Morgan	6607				5			11		1	4	2			A10		3		A12	7	6	9	8	
25	Jan	1	SCARBOROUGH	3-1	Came, Thomas, Thompson	6295				5			11		1	4				10		3	2	A12	7	6	A9	8	
26		12	Halifax Town	0-0		2663				5			11		1	4				10	3		2	9	7	6		8	
27		16	TORQUAY UNITED	1-2	Came	5993		A12		5			11		1	A4	2			10		6	3	9	7			8	
28		30	Peterborough United	4-0	Thomas(3,2pens), Brookman	3412		11		5			11		1	A14	2			10		4	3		7	6	9	A8	
29	Feb	6	HEREFORD UNITED	1-0	Savage	4559		11		5					1		2			10		4	3		7	6	9	8	
30		12	Stockport County	2-1	Brookman, Morgan	4814		11		5					1		2			10		4	3		7	6	9	8	
31		20	Crewe Alexandra	1-2	Morgan	4340		11					5		1	A14	2			10		4	3		A7	6	9	8	
32		27	Wolves	0-4		12430		A11							1	A12	2			10		4	3	B14	B7	6	9	8	
33	Mar	1	TRANMERE ROVERS	2-0	Thompson, Thomas	3979				5					1	7	2			10		4	3			6	9	8	
34		5	Carlisle United	2-0	Thomas(pen), Brookman	2760		5		5			11		1	7	2			10		4	3			6	9	8	
35		11	DARLINGTON	1-1	Brookman	4948		5					11		1	A7	2			10		4	3		A12	6	9	8	
36		18	Swansea City	0-1		3990		4					11		1	A12				A10		3	2		7	6	9	8	
37		26	ROCHDALE	0-0		4173		4		5			11		1	B14			A12	A10		3	2		B7	6	9	8	
38	Apr	2	Leyton Orient	2-1	Darby, May	4537				5		3	11	10	1			7				4	2			6	9	8	
39		4	BURNLEY	2-1	May, Thompson	9921				5		3	11	10	1			7				4	2			6	9	8	
40		9	Exeter City	1-1	Thomas	1962				5		3	11	10	1		2	7				4				6	9	8	
41		15	Cardiff City	0-1		6703				5		A3	11		1	A12		7	10			4	2		B14	B6	9	8	
42		19	SCUNTHORPE UNITED	0-0		6669				5			11	10	1	B4		7		3			2		B14		9	8	6
43		23	NEWPORT COUNTY	6-0	Thomas(3,1p),Morgan,Winstanley,Thompson	4357				5		3	B11		1	B14		A7	10			4	2	A12			9	8	6
44		29	Cambridge United	2-2	Thomas, Savage	2063				5					1			7	10	3		4	2				9	8	6
45	May	2	COLCHESTER UNITED	4-0	Thomas, Savage, Came, Chandler	5540				5	A14		11		1			7	10	3		4	2			A9	8	6	
46		7	Wrexham	1-0	Savage	5977				5			11		1			7	10	3		4	2			9	8	6	

	Barnes P	Brookman N	Callaghan I	Came M	Chandler JG	Crombie D	Darby J	Elliott SB	Felgate DW	Henshaw G	Hughes P	Joyce WG	May AM	Morgan T	Neal P	Savage RJ	Scott DE	Stevens I	Storer SJ	Sutton D	Thomas JW	Thompson SJ	Winstanley M
Apps	2	23	1	43	2	24	34	16	46	23	11	11	9	31	7	39	40	2	12	36	43	43	8
Subs		3			1		1	3			8			1	7	1			7	3		1	1
Goals		6		5	2		2	2		2			2	7					1		22	7	1

Two Own Goals

F.A. Cup

#		Date	Opponent	Score	Scorers	Att	Brookman N	Came M	Chandler JG	Crombie D	Darby J	Elliott SB	Felgate DW	Henshaw G	Savage RJ	Scott DE	Stevens I	Storer SJ	Sutton D	Thomas JW	Thompson SJ
1	Nov	14	Burnley	1-0	Thomas(pen)	10788	7	5	6		11	10	1	3	4	2				9	8
2	Dec	5	Wrexham	2-1	Thomas(2)	4703	7	8	5	3	11	10	1		6	4	2			9	
3	Jan	9	Barnsley	1-3	Stevens	9667		5			11		1	4	10	3	2	9	7	6	8

League Cup

#		Date	Opponent	Score	Scorers	Att	Came M	Chandler JG	Crombie D	Darby J	Henshaw G	Hughes P	May AM	Morgan T	Savage RJ	Thomas JW	Thompson SJ	Winstanley M
1/1	Aug	18	Wigan Athletic	3-2	Morgan(2), Chandler	4115	6	11	3	2	1	7	8	9		5	10	4
1/2		25	WIGAN ATHLETIC	1-3	Thomas	5847	5	A11	3		1	7	8	9	A14	6	10	4

Sherpa Van Trophy

#		Date	Opponent	Score	Scorers	Att	Brookman N	Came M	Crombie D	Darby J	Felgate DW	Henshaw G	Hughes P	Joyce WG	Morgan T	Savage RJ	Scott DE	Stevens I	Storer SJ	Sutton D	Thomas JW	Thompson SJ	Winstanley M
Q	Oct	13	PRESTON NORTH END	0-0		3375	11	5	3	7	10	1				4	2			6	9	8	
Q	Nov	24	Stockport County	3-1	Thomas(2), Bookman	2123	7	5	3	11	10	1				4	2			6	9	8	
1	Jan	19	Bury	0-1		3796	B12	B5		11	1		2		10	4	3	9	A7	6	A14	8	

Lancashire Cup

#		Date	Opponent	Score
1	Aug	1	BLACKBURN ROVERS	1-2
2		4	Blackpool	0-0
3		7	BURNLEY	1-1

Other Games

#		Date	Opponent	Score
1	Jul	29	Port Vale	3-2

1988/89 10th in Division Three

Manager: P.Neal

#	Date		Opponent	Score	Scorers	Att	Barnes P	Brookman N	Brown P	Came M	Chandler J	Cowdrill B	Crombie D	Darby J	Elliott S	Felgate D	Henshaw G	Jeffrey M	Jemson N	Keeley G	Morgan T	Neal P	Savage R	Stevens I	Storer S	Thomas J	Thompson S	Winstanley M
1	Aug	27	Southend United	0-2		4075		7	2	5	3			4	10	1	A12						11	A9			8	6
2	Sep	3	CARDIFF CITY	4-0	Thomas, Henshaw, Darby(2)	4831		4	2	5	3			11	10	1	7									9	8	6
3		10	Reading	1-1	Thomas	4660			2		3		7	11		1	4			5	10					9	8	6
4		17	BRISTOL ROVERS	1-1	Brown	4821			2		3		A12	11	B10	1	4			5	B14				A7	9	A9	6
5		20	FULHAM	3-2	Savage, Thompson, Morgan	4289			2		3			11		1	7			5	10		4	A12		A9	8	6
6		24	Aldershot	3-0	Stevens(2), Brookman	2127	A12		2		3			11		1	7			5	9		A4	10			8	6
7	Oct	1	SHEFFIELD UNITED	2-0	Thompson(2,1pen)	9345			2				3	11		1	7			5	9		4	10			8	6
8		4	Swansea City	0-1		3283	A12		2				3	11		1	A7			5	9		4	10			8	6
9		8	BLACKPOOL	2-2	Morgan, Thompson(pen)	7106			2				3	11		1	7			5	9		4	A10		A12	8	6
10		15	Port Vale	1-2	Brookman	7985		8	2				3	11		1	7			5	9		4			10		6
11		22	WOLVES	1-2	Morgan	8174		5	2			B3		11		1	7				9	B14	4	A12		A10	8	6
12		25	Wigan Athletic	1-1	Brookman	4438		11	2			3	5			1	7				9		4				8	6
13		29	CHESTERFIELD	5-0	Brown(2), Morgan(2), Stevens	4783		7	2			3	A12	11		1				5	9		B4	10	B14		8	A6
14	Nov	5	Bristol City	1-1	Morgan	8808		5	2			3	7	11		1					9		A4	10	A12		8	6
15		8	Huddersfield Town	1-0	Morgan	7802		5	2			3	7	11		1					9		A10	A12			8	6
16		12	Bury	2-4	Brown, Thompson	7897		5	2			3	7	11		1					9	B14	A4	A12			8	B6
17		26	NORTHAMPTON TOWN	2-1	Stevens, Brookman	4446		4	2			3	5	11		1	A12				9			10	A7		8	6
18	Dec	3	Brentford	0-3		4600		4	2		A14	3	5	11		1					A9		A12	10	B7		8	6
19		17	CHESTER CITY	0-1		4318		10	2				3	11		1	A7						4	A12			8	6
20		26	Preston North End	1-3	Savage	12124		A12	2				3	11		1	A7						4				8	6
21		31	Notts County	0-2		5096			2		7	3		11		1			10	5	9		A4	A12			8	6
22	Jan	2	MANSFIELD TOWN	0-0		4936			2		A12	3		11		1			B10	5	9		A4	B14	7		8	6
23		6	GILLINGHAM	2-1	Stevens, Thompson(pen)	4178			2		11	3	4			1			A12	5	9			A10	7		8	6
24		14	Cardiff City	0-1		4212			2		A14	3	4	11		1	A12		B10	5	9				A7		8	6
25		21	READING	1-1	Henshaw	5172	A12	4	2		A11	3				1	7				9					10		6
26		28	Bristol Rovers	0-2		5311	11	4	2			3	B14			1	B7			5	A9		8	A12		10		6
27	Feb	4	Sheffield United	0-4		11162	A11	7	2			3		4		1				5	9	A12	8			10		6
28		11	SWANSEA CITY	1-0	Savage	4178		7	2			3		11		1				5	9		4			10		6
29		18	Blackpool	0-2		5552		A7	2			3		11		1				5	9		4	A12		10	8	6
30	Mar	4	Wolves	0-1		13521		7	2			3	5	11		1		B14	B10			A12	A4			9	8	6
31		11	BRISTOL CITY	2-0	Darby(2)	4423		A4	2		7	3	5	11		1				10				A12		9	8	6
32		14	Chesterfield	1-1	Thompson	2877			2		A12	3	5	11		1				A10			4	7	9		8	6
33		18	SOUTHEND UNITED	0-0		3505		B14	2		A12	3	5	11		1				10			B4	A7	9		8	6
34		25	Mansfield Town	1-1	Savage	3256			2		7	3	5	11		1				A10		A12	4		9		8	6
35		27	PRESTON NORTH END	1-0	Thompson	10281			2		7	3	5	11		1				10		A12	B4	B14	A9		8	6
36	Apr	1	Chester City	0-0		3225			2		11	B3	5			1	7	A10				A12	B14			9	8	6
37		4	Gillingham	1-0	Thomas	3096			2		7		5			1						3	4	10		9	8	6
38		8	NOTTS COUNTY	3-3	Thomas, Thompson, Morgan	4521	11		2		7		6	5		1					A12	B3	4	A10	B14	9	8	
39		15	Fulham	1-1	Morgan	4950			2		A7	3	5	11		1					10	6	4	A12		9	8	
40		22	ALDERSHOT	1-0	Savage	4407			2		A7	3	5	11		1		B14			B10		4			9	8	6
41		25	PORT VALE	1-1	Chandler	5296			2		7	3	5	11		1					10		4			9	8	6
42		29	Bury	0-0		4393			2		A7	3	5	11		1		B14			10		4	A12	B9	8		6
43	May	1	HUDDERSFIELD TOWN	3-1	Chandler, Morgan, Thomas	5511			2		7	3	5	11		1					10		4			9	8	6
44		6	Brentford	4-2	Thomas(2), Darby, Savage	4627			2		A7	3	5	11		1					10		4	A12		9	8	6
45		9	WIGAN ATHLETIC	1-1	Storer	6166			2			3	5	11		1					A10		4	A12	7	9	8	6
46		13	Northampton Town	3-2	Thomas(2), Storer	3655			2			3	A5	11		1	A12				10		4		7	9	8	6
					Apps		2	20	46	2	16	38	28	44	3	46	16	7	4	20	34	3	37	15	10	28	43	44
					Subs		1	5			4		3							5	2	1	5	5	1	6	13	1
					Goals			4	4		2			5			2				10		6	5	2	9	9	

F.A. Cup

#	Date		Opponent	Score	Scorers	Att	Barnes P	Brookman N	Brown P	Chandler J	Cowdrill B	Crombie D	Darby J	Felgate D	Henshaw G	Keeley G	Morgan T	Savage R	Stevens I	Storer S	Thompson S	Winstanley M
1	Nov	19	CHESTERFIELD	0-0		4840		4	2		3	5	11	1	A12		9	A14	A10	7	8	B6
1r		28	Chesterfield	3-2	Stevens, Storer, Darby	4168		4	2		3	5	11	1			9	A7	10	A12	8	6
2	Dec	10	PORT VALE	1-2	Keeley	7499	A12	7	2		3		11	1		5	9	A4	10		8	6

League Cup

#	Date		Opponent	Score	Scorers	Att	Brookman N	Brown P	Came M	Chandler J	Crombie D	Darby J	Elliott S	Felgate D	Henshaw G	Stevens I	Thomas J	Thompson S	Winstanley M
1/1	Aug	30	CHESTER CITY	1-0	Darby	3535		2	5	3		11	10	1	7	4		9	8	6
1/2	Sep	7	Chester City	1-3	Cowdrill	3784	4	2	A5	3	A12	11	B10	1	7	B14		9	8	6

Sherpa Van Trophy

#	Date		Opponent	Score	Scorers	Att	Barnes P	Brookman N	Brown P	Chandler J	Cowdrill B	Crombie D	Darby J	Felgate D	Henshaw G	Jeffrey M	Keeley G	Morgan T	Neal P	Savage R	Stevens I	Storer S	Thomas J	Thompson S	Winstanley M
Q	Dec	6	PRESTON NORTH END	1-0	Thompson(pen)	2695		4	2		3	5	11	1	7	A14				10	A9			8	6
Q		20	Bury	0-1		2023	A7		2		3		11	1	A12		5	B9	B14	4	10			8	6
1	Jan	17	Preston North End	1-0	Darby	5569		10	2	11	3	4		1	7		5	9						8	6
2	Feb	21	WREXHAM +	3-1	Winstanley(2), Savage	3833			2		3	5	11	1			10	9		4		A7	A12	8	6
S/F	Mar	21	Crewe Alexandra +	2-1	Winstanley, Brown	5875			2	A14	3	5	11	1			10			4		A7	9	8	6
F/1	Apr	11	BLACKPOOL	1-0	Darby	10345			2	7	3	5	11	1					10	A4	A12		9	8	6
F/2		18	Blackpool +	1-1	Thompson(pen)	9027			2	7	3	5	11	1					10	4			9	8	6
F	May	28	Torquay United*	4-1	Darby, Morrison(og), Crombie, Morgan	46513			2	A7	3	5	11	1					10	4	A12		9	8	6

* Played at Wembley Stadium   + After extra time

Lancashire Cup

#	Date		Opponent	Score
1	Aug	6	BURY	1-0
2		11	Wigan Athletic	1-0
3		13	ROCHDALE*	1-1
F		16	PRESTON NORTH END	1-0

* won 5-4 on pens

1988-89 Season
(Back) Callaghan, Henshaw, Hughes, Felgate, Darby, Stevens, O'Brien
(Middle) Neal, Carroll, Brookman, G.Brown, Storer, Morgan, McKearney, Savage, Chandler, M.Brown, Stock
(Front) Thomas, Elliott, P.Brown, Came, Winstanley, Crombie, Cowdrill, Thompson

1989-90 Season
(Back) Crombie, Came, Felgate, Rose, Gray, Winstanley, Cowdrill
(Middle) Carroll, G.Brown, P.Brown, Darby, Reeves, Philliskirk, Thompson, Storer, Henshaw, Jeffrey, Simpson
(Front) Stevens, Fisher, Hughes, Brookman, M.Brown, Neal, Roberts, Chandler, Savage, Spooner

1989/90 6th in Division Three

Manager: P.Neal

#		Date	Opponent	Score	Scorers	Att
1	Aug	19	Cardiff City	2-0	Philliskirk, Darby	4376
2		26	FULHAM	0-0		5524
3	Sep	2	Huddersfield Town	1-1	Crombie	7872
4		9	BRISTOL ROVERS	1-0	Reeves	5913
5		16	Rotherham United	0-1		6846
6		23	LEYTON ORIENT	2-1	Cowdrill, Philliskirk	5951
7		26	Notts County	1-2	Philliskirk	5392
8		30	MANSFIELD TOWN	1-1	Winstanley	5797
9	Oct	7	WIGAN ATHLETIC	3-2	Philliskirk(pen), Darby(2)	6462
10		14	Crewe Alexandra	2-2	Reeves(2)	4284
11		17	Brentford	2-1	Reeves(2)	4537
12		21	CHESTER CITY	1-0	Philliskirk	6496
13		28	Preston North End	4-1	Philliskirk,Thompson,Darby,Kelly(og)	9135
14		31	WALSALL	1-1	Darby	7363
15	Nov	4	SWANSEA CITY	0-0		6618
16		11	Bristol City	1-1	Brown	11994
17		25	Birmingham City	0-1		8081
18	Dec	2	NORTHAMPTON TOWN	0-3		5501
19		16	Shrewsbury Town	3-3	Thompson(2), Philliskirk	3443
20		26	BLACKPOOL	2-0	Darby, Cowdrill	9944
21		30	BURY	3-1	Reeves(2), Storer	10628
22	Jan	6	Tranmere Rovers	3-1	Dowdrill, Darby, Storer	8273
23		13	Fulham	2-2	Pike, Storer	4523
24		20	CARDIFF CITY	3-1	Philliskirk(2,1pen), Comstive	7017
25		28	Bristol Rovers	1-1	Philliskirk	7722
26	Feb	10	ROTHERHAM UNITED	0-2		7728
27		17	Northampton Town	2-0	Darby, Thompson	3432
28		24	BIRMINGHAM CITY	3-1	Reeves(2), Thompson	7681
29	Mar	3	Reading	0-2		4461
30		6	Mansfield Town	1-0	Darby	3334
31		10	NOTTS COUNTY	3-0	Darby, Philliskirk, Reeves	8420
32		16	Wigan Athletic	0-2		6850
33		20	CREWE ALEXANDRA	0-0		7241
34		24	BRENTFORD	0-1		6156
35		27	Leyton Orient	0-0		3296
36		31	Chester City	0-2		2738
37	Apr	3	READING	3-0	Philliskirk(2), Thompson	4679
38		7	PRESTON NORTH END	2-1	Philliskirk(2)	8266
39		10	Walsall	1-2	Philliskirk(pen)	3376
40		14	TRANMERE ROVERS	1-1	Storer	9070
41		16	Blackpool	1-2	Philliskirk	6435
42		21	SHREWSBURY TOWN	0-1		5665
43		24	Bury	0-2		6551
44		26	BRISTOL CITY	1-0	Green	11098
45	May	1	HUDDERSFIELD TOWN	2-2	Green, Philliskirk(pen)	8550
46		5	Swansea City	0-0		5623

Apps: 46 15 30 43 36 46 40 4 2 9 1 1 45 5 41 6 7 3 38 45 43
Subs: 2 4 1 1 2 1 5 5 1 3 3 1
Goals: 1 1 3 1 10 2 18 1 10 4 6 1

One own goal

Play-Offs

#		Date	Opponent	Score	Scorers	Att
1	May	13	NOTTS COUNTY	1-1	Philliskirk(pen)	15105
2		16	Notts County	0-2		15200

F.A. Cup

#		Date	Opponent	Score	Scorers	Att
1	Nov	18	Blackpool	1-2	Crombie	7309

League Cup

#		Date	Opponent	Score	Scorers	Att
1/1	Aug	22	Rochdale	1-2	Thompson(pen)	3464
1/2		29	ROCHDALE	5-1	Philliskirk,Reeves,Savage,Cowdrill,Darby	4637
2/1	Sep	19	WATFORD	2-1	Philliskirk(2)	6856
2/2	Oct	3	Watford	1-1	Comstive	8452
3		24	Swindon Town	3-3	Henshaw, Philliskirk, Came	8318
3r	Nov	7	SWINDON TOWN*	1-1	Brown	11533
3/2r		14	SWINDON TOWN*	1-1	Philliskirk(pen)	14126
3/3r		21	Swindon Town*	1-2	Came	11238

* After extra time

Leyland Daf Cup

#		Date	Opponent	Score	Scorers	Att
Q	Nov	29	CREWE ALEXANDRA	2-0	Darby, Brookman	3868
Q	Dec	5	Wigan Athletic	0-1		2306
1	Jan	9	LINCOLN CITY	2-1	Reeves(2)	4420
Q/F		31	ROTHERHAM UNITED	1-0	Storer	6838
S/F	Feb	20	Tranmere Rovers	1-2	Philliskirk	9315

Lancashire Cup

#		Date	Opponent	Score
1	Aug	5	Burnley	2-2
2		8	Wigan Athletic	0-1
3		12	BLACKBURN ROVERS	3-1

Isle of Man Tournament

#		Date	Opponent	Score
1	Jul	23	Motherwell	0-1
2		25	Dundalk	1-0
3		28	Swansea City	1-2
4	Aug	10	MANCHESTER CITY*	0-2

* Lofthouse testimonial

League Tables: 1990/91 - 1995/96

1990/91 Third Division

#	FINAL TABLE	Pl.	Home W	D	L	F	A	Away W	D	L	F	A	F. (Total)	A.	Pts
1	Cambridge United	46	14	5	4	42	22	11	6	6	33	23	75	45	86
2	Southend United	46	13	6	4	34	23	13	1	9	33	28	67	51	85
3	Grimsby Town	46	16	3	4	42	13	8	8	7	24	21	66	34	83
4	BOLTON WANDS.	46	14	5	4	33	18	10	6	7	31	32	64	50	83
5	Tranmere Rovers	46	13	5	5	38	21	10	4	9	26	25	64	46	78
6	Brentford	46	12	4	7	30	22	9	9	5	29	25	59	47	76
7	Bury	46	13	6	4	39	26	7	7	9	28	30	67	56	73
8	Bradford City	46	13	3	7	36	22	7	7	9	26	32	62	54	70
9	Bournemouth	46	14	3	6	37	20	5	7	11	21	38	58	58	70
10	Wigan Athletic	46	14	3	6	40	20	6	6	11	31	34	71	54	69
11	Huddersfield Town	46	13	3	7	37	23	5	10	8	20	28	57	51	67
12	Birmingham City	46	8	9	6	21	21	8	8	7	24	28	45	49	65
13	Leyton Orient	46	15	2	6	35	19	3	8	12	20	39	55	58	64
14	Stoke City	46	9	7	7	36	29	7	5	11	19	30	55	59	60
15	Reading	46	11	5	7	34	28	6	3	14	19	38	53	66	59
16	Exeter City	46	12	6	5	35	16	4	3	16	23	36	58	52	57
17	Preston North End	46	11	5	7	33	29	4	6	13	21	38	54	67	56
18	Shrewsbury Town	46	8	7	8	29	22	6	3	14	32	46	61	68	52
19	Chester City	46	10	3	10	27	27	4	6	13	19	31	46	58	51
20	Swansea City	46	8	6	9	31	33	5	3	15	18	39	49	72	48
21	Fulham	46	8	8	7	27	22	2	8	13	14	34	41	56	46
22	Crewe Alexandra	46	6	9	8	35	35	5	2	16	27	45	62	80	44
23	Rotherham United	46	5	10	8	31	38	5	2	16	19	49	50	87	42
24	Mansfield Town	46	5	8	10	23	27	3	6	14	19	36	42	63	38

1991/92 Third Division

#	FINAL TABLE	Pl.	Home W	D	L	F	A	Away W	D	L	F	A	F. (Total)	A.	Pts
1	Brentford	46	17	2	4	55	29	8	5	10	26	26	81	55	82
2	Birmingham City	46	15	6	2	42	22	8	6	9	27	30	69	52	81
3	Huddersfield Town	46	15	4	4	36	15	7	8	8	23	23	59	38	78
4	Stoke City	46	14	5	4	45	24	7	9	7	24	25	69	49	77
5	Stockport County	46	15	5	3	47	19	7	5	11	28	32	75	51	76
6	Peterborough Utd.	46	13	7	3	38	20	7	7	9	27	38	65	58	74
7	West Bromwich Alb.	46	12	6	5	45	25	7	8	8	19	24	64	49	71
8	Bournemouth	46	13	4	6	33	18	7	7	9	19	30	52	48	71
9	Fulham	46	11	7	5	29	16	8	6	9	28	37	57	53	70
10	Leyton Orient	46	12	7	4	36	18	6	4	13	26	34	62	52	65
11	Hartlepool United	46	12	5	6	30	21	6	6	11	27	36	57	57	65
12	Reading	46	9	8	6	33	27	7	5	11	26	35	59	62	61
13	BOLTON WAND.	46	10	9	4	26	19	4	8	11	31	37	57	56	59
14	Hull City	46	9	4	10	28	23	7	7	9	26	31	54	54	59
15	Wigan Athletic	46	11	6	6	33	21	4	8	11	25	43	58	64	59
16	Bradford City	46	8	10	5	36	30	5	9	9	26	31	62	61	58
17	Preston North End	46	12	7	4	42	32	3	5	15	19	40	61	72	57
18	Chester City	46	10	6	7	34	29	4	8	11	22	30	56	59	56
19	Swansea City	46	10	9	4	35	24	4	5	14	20	41	55	65	56
20	Exeter City	46	11	7	5	34	25	3	4	16	23	55	57	80	53
21	Bury	46	8	7	8	31	31	5	5	13	24	43	55	74	51
22	Shrewsbury Town	46	7	7	9	30	31	5	4	14	23	37	53	68	47
23	Torquay United	46	13	7	3	29	19	0	5	18	13	49	42	68	47
24	Darlington	46	5	5	13	31	39	5	2	16	25	51	56	90	37

1992/93 Second Division (Formerly Third Division)

#	FINAL TABLE	Pl.	Home W	D	L	F	A	Away W	D	L	F	A	F. (Total)	A.	Pts
1	Stoke City	46	17	5	2	41	13	10	8	5	32	21	73	34	93
2	BOLTON WANDS.	46	18	2	3	48	14	9	7	7	32	27	80	41	90
3	Port Vale	46	14	7	2	44	17	12	4	7	35	27	79	44	89
4	West Bromwich Alb.	46	17	3	3	56	22	8	7	8	32	32	88	54	85
5	Swansea City	46	12	7	4	38	17	8	6	9	27	30	65	47	73
6	Stockport County	46	11	11	1	47	18	8	4	11	34	39	81	57	72
7	Leyton Orient	46	16	4	3	49	20	5	5	13	20	33	69	53	72
8	Reading	46	14	4	5	44	20	4	11	8	22	31	66	51	69
9	Brighton & Hove A.	46	13	4	6	36	24	7	5	11	27	35	63	59	69
10	Bradford City	46	12	5	6	36	24	6	9	8	33	43	69	67	68
11	Rotherham United	46	9	7	7	30	27	8	7	8	30	33	60	60	65
12	Fulham	46	9	9	5	28	22	7	8	8	29	38	57	60	65
13	Burnley	46	11	8	4	38	21	4	8	11	19	38	57	59	61
14	Plymouth Argyle	46	11	6	6	38	28	5	6	12	21	36	59	64	60
15	Huddersfield Town	46	10	6	7	30	22	7	3	13	24	39	54	61	60
16	Hartlepool United	46	8	6	9	19	23	6	6	11	23	37	42	60	54
17	Bournemouth	46	7	10	6	28	24	5	7	11	17	28	45	52	53
18	Blackpool	46	9	9	5	40	30	3	6	14	23	45	63	75	51
19	Exeter City	46	5	8	10	26	30	4	9	8	28	39	54	69	50
20	Hull City	46	9	5	9	28	26	4	6	13	18	43	46	69	50
21	Preston North End	46	8	5	10	41	47	5	3	15	24	47	65	94	47
22	Mansfield Town	46	7	8	8	34	34	4	3	16	18	46	52	80	44
23	Wigan Athletic	46	6	6	11	26	34	4	5	14	17	38	43	72	41
24	Chester City	46	6	2	15	30	47	2	3	18	19	55	49	102	29

1993/94 First Division

#	FINAL TABLE	Pl.	Home W	D	L	F	A	Away W	D	L	F	A	F. (Total)	A.	Pts
1	Crystal Palace	46	16	4	3	39	18	11	5	7	34	28	73	46	90
2	Nottingham Forest	46	12	9	2	38	22	11	5	7	36	27	74	49	83
3	Millwall	46	14	8	1	36	17	9	9	5	22	32	58	49	74
4	Leicester City	46	11	9	3	45	30	8	7	8	27	29	72	59	73
5	Tranmere Rovers	46	15	3	5	48	23	6	6	11	21	30	69	53	72
6	Derby County	46	15	3	5	44	25	8	5	10	29	43	73	68	71
7	Notts County	46	16	3	4	43	26	4	5	14	22	43	65	69	68
8	Wolverhampton W.	46	10	10	3	34	19	7	7	9	26	28	60	47	68
9	Middlesbrough	46	12	6	5	40	19	6	7	10	26	35	66	54	67
10	Stoke City	46	14	4	5	35	19	4	9	10	22	40	57	59	67
11	Charlton Athletic	46	14	3	6	39	22	5	5	13	22	36	61	58	65
12	Sunderland	46	14	2	7	35	22	5	6	12	19	35	54	57	65
13	Bristol City	46	11	7	5	27	18	5	9	9	20	32	47	50	64
14	BOLTON WANDS.	46	10	8	5	40	31	5	6	12	23	33	63	64	59
15	Southend United	46	10	5	8	34	28	7	3	13	29	39	63	67	59
16	Grimsby Town	46	7	14	2	26	16	6	6	11	26	31	52	47	59
17	Portsmouth	46	10	6	7	29	22	5	7	11	23	36	52	58	58
18	Barnsley	46	9	3	11	25	26	7	4	12	30	41	55	67	55
19	Watford	46	10	5	8	39	35	5	4	14	27	45	66	80	54
20	Luton Town	46	12	4	7	38	25	2	7	14	18	35	56	60	53
21	West Bromwich Alb.	46	9	7	7	38	31	4	5	14	22	38	60	69	51
22	Birmingham City	46	9	7	7	28	29	4	5	14	24	40	52	69	51
23	Oxford United	46	10	5	8	33	33	3	5	15	21	42	54	75	49
24	Peterborough Utd.	46	6	9	8	31	30	2	4	17	17	46	48	76	37

1994/95 First Division

#	FINAL TABLE	Pl.	Home W	D	L	F	A	Away W	D	L	F	A	F. (Total)	A.	Pts
1	Middlesbrough	46	15	4	4	41	19	8	9	6	26	21	67	40	82
2	Reading	46	12	7	4	34	21	11	3	9	24	23	58	44	79
3	BOLTON WANDS.	46	16	6	1	43	13	5	8	10	24	32	67	45	77
4	Wolverhampton W.	46	15	5	3	39	18	6	9	8	38	43	77	61	76
5	Tranmere Rovers	46	17	4	2	51	23	5	6	12	16	35	67	58	76
6	Barnsley	46	15	6	2	42	19	5	6	12	21	33	63	52	72
7	Watford	46	14	6	3	33	17	5	7	11	19	29	52	46	70
8	Sheffield United	46	12	9	2	41	21	5	8	10	33	34	74	55	68
9	Derby County	46	12	6	5	44	23	6	6	11	22	28	66	51	66
10	Grimsby Town	46	12	7	4	36	19	5	7	11	26	37	62	56	65
11	Stoke City	46	10	7	6	31	21	6	8	9	19	32	50	53	63
12	Millwall	46	11	8	4	36	22	5	6	12	24	38	60	60	62
13	Southend United	46	13	2	8	33	25	5	6	12	21	48	54	73	62
14	Oldham Athletic	46	12	7	4	34	21	4	6	13	26	39	60	60	61
15	Charlton Athletic	46	11	6	6	33	25	5	5	13	25	41	58	66	59
16	Luton Town	46	8	6	9	35	30	7	7	9	26	34	61	64	58
17	Port Vale	46	11	5	7	30	24	4	8	11	28	40	58	64	58
18	Portsmouth	46	9	8	6	31	28	6	5	12	22	35	53	63	58
19	West Bromwich Alb.	46	13	3	7	33	24	3	7	13	18	33	51	57	58
20	Sunderland	46	5	12	6	22	22	7	6	10	19	23	41	45	54
21	Swindon Town	46	9	6	8	28	27	3	6	14	26	46	54	73	48
22	Burnley	46	8	7	8	36	33	3	6	14	13	41	49	74	46
23	Bristol City	46	8	7	8	26	28	3	5	15	19	35	45	63	45
24	Notts County	46	7	8	8	26	28	2	5	16	19	38	45	66	40

1995/96 Premier League

#	FINAL TABLE	Pl.	Home W	D	L	F	A	Away W	D	L	F	A	F. (Total)	A.	Pts
1	Manchester United	38	15	4	0	36	9	10	3	6	37	26	73	35	82
2	Newcastle United	38	17	1	1	38	9	7	5	7	28	28	66	37	78
3	Liverpool	38	14	4	1	46	13	6	7	6	24	21	70	34	71
4	Aston Villa	38	11	5	3	32	15	7	4	8	20	20	52	35	63
5	Arsenal	38	10	7	2	30	16	7	5	7	19	16	49	32	63
6	Everton	38	10	5	4	35	19	7	5	7	29	25	64	44	61
7	Blackburn Rovers	38	14	2	3	44	19	4	5	10	17	28	61	47	61
8	Tottenham Hotspur	38	9	5	5	26	19	7	8	4	24	19	50	38	61
9	Nottingham Forest	38	11	6	2	29	17	4	7	8	21	37	50	54	58
10	West Ham United	38	9	5	5	25	21	4	9	6	18	31	43	52	51
11	Chelsea	38	7	7	5	30	22	5	7	7	16	22	46	44	50
12	Middlesbrough	38	8	3	8	27	27	3	7	9	8	23	35	50	43
13	Leeds United	38	8	3	8	21	21	4	4	11	19	36	40	57	43
14	Wimbledon	38	8	6	5	27	33	5	5	9	28	37	55	70	41
15	Sheffield Wed.	38	7	5	7	30	31	3	5	11	18	30	48	61	40
16	Coventry City	38	6	7	6	21	23	2	7	10	21	37	42	60	38
17	Southampton	38	7	7	5	21	18	2	4	13	13	34	34	52	38
18	Manchester City	38	7	7	5	21	19	2	4	13	12	39	33	58	38
19	Queen's Park Rgs.	38	6	5	8	25	26	3	1	15	13	31	38	57	33
20	BOLTON WANDS.	38	5	4	10	16	31	3	1	15	23	40	39	71	29

1990/91 4th in Division Three

Manager: P. Neal

#	Date		Opponent	Score	Scorers	Att	Brown P	Burke D	Came M	Comstive P	Cowdrill B	Crombie D	Cunningham T	Darby J	Felgate D	Green S	Henshaw G	Lee S	Patterson M	Philliskirk T	Reeves D	Seagraves M	Stevens I	Storer S	Stubbs A	Thompson S	Winstanley M
1	Aug	25	Shrewsbury Town	1-0	Storer	4608	2	3	5		A4			11	1	4				10	9			A12		8	6
2	Sep	1	BRADFORD CITY	0-1		7031	2	3	B5		A4			11	1	4				10	9			A12	B14	8	6
3		8	Huddersfield Town	0-4		5419	2	3		A14				11	1	4				10	9			7	5	8	6
4		15	CREWE ALEXANDRA	3-2	Philliskirk, Green, Darby	4933	2	3	A5					11	1	4				10	9			7	A12	8	6
5		19	PRESTON NORTH END	1-2	Darby	5844	2	3						11	1	4				10	9			7	5	8	
6		22	Brentford	2-4	Green, Reeves	5077	2	3		A11		6			1	4	7			10	9			A12	5	8	
7		28	Wigan Athletic	1-2	Philliskirk(pen)	4366	2	A3						11	1	4	A12			10	9	5		7		8	6
8	Oct	2	MANSFIELD TOWN	1-1	Reeves	3631	2	3						11	1	4				10	9	5		7		8	6
9		6	STOKE CITY	0-1		8521	2	A3			A12			11	1	4		7		10	B9	5	B14			8	6
10		13	Bury	2-2	Thompson, Philliskirk(pen)	5634	2				3			11	1	4		7		10	A12			A9	5	8	6
11		20	Leyton Orient	1-0	Storer	4121	2				3			11	1	4		7		10	9			5		8	6
12		23	ROTHERHAM UNITED	0-0		4692	2				3			11	1	4			A7	B10	9			B12	5	8	6
13		27	SWANSEA CITY	1-0	Philliskirk	4158	2				3			11	1	B4	B14			10	A9	A12		7	5	8	6
14	Nov	3	Chester City	2-0	Green, Reeves	2553	2				3			11	1	4				10	9	5		7		8	6
15		10	READING	3-1	Thompson(2,1pen), Reeves	4648	2				3			11	1	4	A12			10	9	5		7		8	6
16		24	Grimsby Town	1-0	Green, Reeves	6240	2							11	1	10					A9	5	A12	7		8	6
17	Dec	1	TRANMERE ROVERS	2-1	Green, Philliskirk	6941	2			4				11	1	8				10	9	5		7			6
18		15	Fulham	1-0	Philliskirk	3466	2			4				11	1	4				10	9	5		7		8	6
19		22	CAMBRIDGE UNITED	2-2	Storer, Thompson	5800	2			4				11	1					10	9	5		7		8	6
20		26	Southend United	1-1	Green	7539	2		5		A4			11	1	A12				10	9			7		8	6
21		29	Birmingham City	3-1	Philliskirk, Darby, Reeves	7318	2		5		4			B11	1	A12				10	9			A7	B14	8	6
22	Jan	1	BOURNEMOUTH	4-1	Darby,Comstive(2),Philliskirk(pen)	7639	2		5	4				11	1					10	9			7		8	6
23		12	Bradford City	1-1	Philliskirk	8764	2		5	A4				11	1				A14	10	9			7		8	6
24		19	SHREWSBURY TOWN	1-0	Thompson	6164	2							A11		A12			4	10	9	5		7		8	6
25	Feb	2	Preston North End	2-1	Philliskirk(2,1pen)	9844	2							11	1	7			4	10	9	5				8	6
26		5	BRENTFORD	1-0	Evans(og)	6731	2							11	1	7			4	10	9	5				8	6
27		9	HUDDERSFIELD TOWN	1-1	Philliskirk	7947	2				A14			11	1	A7			4	10	9	5				8	6
28		13	EXETER CITY	1-0	Reeves	5532	2							11	1	7			4	10	9	5				8	6
29		16	GRIMSBY TOWN	0-0		10318	2				B14			A11	1	B7			4	10	9	5			A12	8	6
30		23	Reading	1-0	Cowdrill	5997	2				3			11	1	7			4	10	9	5				8	6
31	Mar	1	Tranmere Rovers	1-1	Patterson	10076	2				3			11	1	7			4	10	9	5				8	6
32		9	FULHAM	3-0	Philliskirk(2,1pen), Patterson	7316	2				3			11	1	7			4	10	9	5				8	6
33		12	Mansfield Town	0-4		3611	2				B14			11	1	7			B4	A10	9	5			A12	8	6
34		16	WIGAN ATHLETIC	2-1	Reeves, Darby	7812	2							11	1	7			4		9	5		10	A12	8	A6
35		19	BURY	1-3	Green	9006	2	B14			A12		B3	11	1	A7			4		9	5		10	6	8	
36		23	Stoke City	2-2	Darby, Storer	13869	2	3						11	1	A12			A4	10	9	5		7		8	
37		26	Exeter City	1-2	Reeves	4009	2	3		4				11	1	A12				10	9	5		A7		8	
38		30	SOUTHEND UNITED	1-0	Darby	10666	2	3					9	11	1	7			A4	10		5			B14	8	6
39	Apr	2	Cambridge United	1-2	Philliskirk	7763	2	3		B4			A9	11	1	7				10		A12	5		B14	8	6
40		7	BIRMINGHAM CITY	3-1	Philliskirk, Darby, Cunningham	11280	2				3		A9	11	1	7			4	10	A12	5				8	6
41		13	Bournemouth	0-1		7156	2			4	B14		A9	11	1	B7				10	A12	5		2		8	6
42		16	Crewe Alexandra	3-1	Philliskirk(2,1pen), Reeves	4419	2				3		A9	11	1	B14			B4	10	A12	5		7		8	6
43		20	LEYTON ORIENT	1-0	Reeves	7926	2				3		9	11	1	B14			B4	10	A12	5		A7		8	6
44		27	Rotherham United	2-2	Cunningham(2)	8045	2				3		9	11	1				A4	10	A12	5		7		8	6
45	May	4	Swansea City	2-1	Darby, Storer	4713	2				A4		3	11	1					10	A12	5		7		8	6
46		11	CHESTER CITY	1-0	Cunningham	12826	2				A4		3	11	1				A14	10		5		7		8	6
			Apps				45	13	8	12	35	2	9	45	46	33	1	4	18	43	36	32	1	30	16	45	32
			Subs					1		6	1						8	3		1		8		4	5	7	
			Goals							2	1		4	9		6				2	19	10			5		5	

One own goal

Play Offs

	Date		Opponent	Score	Scorers	Att	Brown P	Comstive P	Cowdrill B	Cunningham T	Darby J	Felgate D	Green S	Philliskirk T	Reeves D	Seagraves M	Storer S	Stubbs A	Thompson S	Winstanley M
1/1	May	19	Bury	1-1	Philliskirk(pen)	8000	2	4	3	9	11	1	A14	10		5	7	A6	8	
1/2		22	BURY	1-0	Philliskirk	19198	2	4	3	9	11	1		10		5	7	6	8	
F	Jun	1	Tranmere Rovers*	0-1		30217	2	4	3	A9	11	1	B14	10	A12	5	7	6	8	

* After extra time

F.A. Cup

#	Date		Opponent	Score	Scorers	Att	Brown P	Came M	Comstive P	Cowdrill B	Darby J	Felgate D	Green S	Henshaw G	Philliskirk T	Reeves D	Seagraves M	Storer S	Thompson S	Winstanley M
1	Nov	17	Witton Albion	2-1	Darby, Comstive	3790	2		A12	3	11	1	10	A4		9	5	7	8	6
2	Dec	11	Chesterfield	4-3	Reeves,Philliskirk,Thompson,Storer	4836	2	5		3	11	1	4		10	9		7	8	6
3	Jan	5	BARROW	1-0	Philliskirk	11475	2	5	4	3	11	1			10	9		7	8	6
4		26	Manchester United	0-1		43293	2		4	3	11	1	A12		10	9	5	A7	8	6

League Cup

	Date		Opponent	Score	Scorers	Att	Brown P	Burke D	Came M	Cowdrill B	Darby J	Felgate D	Green S	Henshaw G	Philliskirk T	Reeves D	Seagraves M	Storer S	Stubbs A	Thompson S	Winstanley M
1/1	Aug	29	Huddersfield Town	3-0	Darby(2), Philliskirk(pen)	4444	2	3	5	4	11	1	7		10	9				8	6
1/2	Sep	4	HUDDERSFIELD TOWN	2-1	Stubbs, Darby	3101	2	3	A14		11	1	4		A10	9		7	5	8	6
2/1		26	Coventry City	2-4	Philliskirk(2)	6193	2	3			11	1	4		10	9	6	7		8	
2/2	Oct	9	COVENTRY CITY	2-3	Philliskirk(2,1pen)	5222	2			3	11	1	4	7	10	9	A12	5	8	6	

Leyland Daf Cup

	Date		Opponent	Score	Scorers	Att	Brown P	Came M	Comstive P	Cowdrill B	Darby J	Felgate D	Green S	Philliskirk T	Reeves D	Seagraves M	Storer S	Thompson S	Winstanley M
Q	Nov	6	TRANMERE ROVERS	1-0	Reeves	3178	2			3	11	1	4	10	9	5	7	8	6
Q	Dec	18	Blackpool	0-3		2579	2	5	A12	3	11	1	4	10	9		7	8	6

Lancashire Cup

#		Date	Opponent	Score
1	Aug	11	Wigan Athletic	0-0
2		14	BLACKPOOL	2-0
3		18	BURNLEY	3-0
F		21	PRESTON NORTH END	2-1

Other Games

#		Date	Opponent	Score
1	Jul	31	Lancaster City	5-1
2	Aug	7	Lincoln United	3-0
3	Oct	15	MANCHESTER CITY*	2-1

* Hill testimonial

1990-91 (Lancashire Cup Final)
(Back) Came, Brown, Green, Cowdrill, Reeves, Philliskirk, Felgate
(Front) Burke, Storer, Winstanley, Darby, Thompson

1991-92 Season
(Back) Cowdrill, Comstive, Winstanley, Stubbs, Darby, Roscoe
(2nd Row) Seagraves, Philliskirk, Rose, Felgate, Cunningham, Reeves, Came
(3rd Row) Crombie, Spooner, Jeffrey, Brown, Storer, Green, Thompson, Burke, Simpson
(Front) Oliver, Patterson, Carroll, Neal, Brown, Fisher, Lee

1991/92 13th in Division Three

Manager: P. Neal

#	Date		Opponent	Result	Scorers	Att.	Brown M	Brown P	Burke D	Came M	Charnley C	Comstive P	Cowdrill B	Darby J	Dibble A	Felgate D	Fisher N	Green S	Jeffrey M	Kelly T	Kennedy A	Lydiate J	Maxwell A	Patterson M	Peyton G	Philliskirk T	Reeves D	Rose K	Seagraves M	Spooner N	Storer S	Stubbs A	Thompson S	Walker A	Winstanley M
1	Aug	17	HUDDERSFIELD TOWN	1-1	Philliskirk	7606	A12	2					3	11	1		A7			4						10	9		5			6	8		
2		24	Swansea City	1-1	Reeves	3578		2	3					11						4						10	9	1	5		7	6	8		
3		31	LEYTON ORIENT	1-0	Reeves	5058	7	2	3					11						4				8		10	9	1	A5			A12			6
4	Sep	3	Darlington	2-3	Philliskirk, Reeves	3385	7	2	A3					11						4		A14		8		10	9	1	5						6
5		7	WEST BROMWICH ALBION	3-0	Philliskirk(2), M.Brown	7980	7	2	3					11	1					4				8		10	9		5						6
6		14	Bournemouth	2-1	Reeves, P.Brown	5690	A7	2	3					11	1		A14			4				8		10	9		5						6
7		17	Bradford City	4-4	Darby(2), Patterson(pen), Reeves	5669	7	2	3					11	1					4				8		10	9		A5			A14			6
8		21	WIGAN ATHLETIC	1-1	Darby	6923	A7	2	3	5				11	1		B14			B4				8		10	9					A12	6		
9		28	Brentford	2-3	Reeves, Darby	5658		2	3	5				11			7			A4				8		10	9	1				A12	6		
10	Oct	5	TORQUAY UNITED	1-0	Green	5092		2	3	5				11	1			10		4				8					7			6			
11		12	Stoke City	0-2		12420	7	2	A3	5				11	1			B10		4				8			9		A14			B12	6		
12		19	FULHAM	0-3		5152	7	2	A3					11	1			A12		4				8		10	9		5			6			
13		26	Chester City	1-0	Darby	1867	B7	2	3					11	1			A14		4		9		A8		10	B12		5						6
14	Nov	2	READING	1-1	Philliskirk(pen)	3632	7	2	3					11	1					4				A8		10	9		5						6
15		5	Stockport County	2-2	Philliskirk(2,1pen)	5036	7	2	3					11	1			A12		4				A8		10	9		5						6
16		9	Bury	1-1	M.Brown	5886	7	2	3					11	1					4				8		10	9		5						6
17		23	PRESTON NORTH END	1-0	Reeves	7033	7	2	3					11	1					8						10	9		5						6
18		30	Shrewsbury Town	3-1	Philliskirk(pen), Kelly, Reeves	3937	7	2	3					11	1					8						10	9		5			A12			A6
19	Dec	14	HULL CITY	1-0	Philliskirk(pen)	5273		2	3	6				11	1		1			4						10	A9		5			A14			
20		26	Leyton Orient	1-2	Green	4896	A7	2	3	6				11	1			9		4				8		10			5			A14			
21		28	Huddersfield Town	0-1		11884		2	3	6				11	1			9		4				8		10			5			A7	A12		
22	Jan	1	DARLINGTON	2-0	Fisher, Philliskirk	5841	A2		3	6				11	1		B14	9		4				8		10			5			B7	A12		
23		11	Exeter City	2-2	Philliskirk, Walker	3336			3	6				11	1		7	A9	A4	4				8		10			5			2		A12	
24		18	HARTLEPOOL UNITED	2-2	Walker, Derby	6129			3	6				11	1		7			7				8		10			5			2		9	
25	Feb	1	Fulham	1-1	Walker	3804	B14		3	6				11	1		A7			4				B8		10	A12		5	2				9	
26		8	CHESTER CITY	0-0		6609			3	6				11	1		B14	A7		4				B8		10	A12		5	2				9	
27		11	SHREWSBURY TOWN	1-0	Walker	2576	A14		3	6				11	1			A7		4				B10			B12		5	2				9	
28		22	EXETER CITY	1-2	Walker	5631		B12	3	6				11				A14		A4				8	1	10	7		5	B2				9	
29		29	Peterborough United	0-1		6270				6						1	A8	7		4							10	A12	5			11		9	3
30	Mar	3	Hartlepool United	4-0	Kelly, Walker(2), M.Brown	2244	7	2		6						1				4				8			10		5			11		9	3
31		10	STOCKPORT COUNTY	0-0		7635	7	2		6				A14		1				A4				B11			10	B12	5			8		9	3
32		14	Reading	0-1		3515	7	2		6				4		1	B14							11			10	A12	5			8		9	A3
33		17	BIRMINGHAM CITY	1-1	P.Brown	7329	B12	2	3					5		1		B4						11			10	7		A14		A8		9	6
34		21	BURY	2-1	Walker(2)	7619		2	3					A12		1		4						11			A10	7	5			8		9	6
35		24	PETERBOROUGH UNITED	2-1	Walker, Charlery(og)	5421		2	3					4		1		7						11				10	5			8		9	6
36		28	Preston North End	1-2	Philliskirk	7327		2	3		8			4		1		A7						11			10	A12	5					9	6
37		31	BOURNEMOUTH	0-2		4955	7	2	B3		A8			4		1		B14						11			A12	10	5					9	6
38	Apr	4	West Bromwich Albion	2-2	Walker, Stubbs	10287	B7		3		A8			4		1		B14						11			10		5	2		A12		9	6
39		7	SWANSEA CITY	0-0		3535	A7		3					4		1		A12						11			10		5	2		8		9	6
40		11	BRADFORD CITY	1-1	Walker	4892	7		3					4				11					1				10	12	5	2		8		9	6
41		14	Birmingham City	1-2	Walker	14440		B14	B3					4				11					1	11			A10	A12	5	2		8		9	6
42		18	Wigan Athletic	1-1	Spooner	3357		7	A3					11				A14		4			1				10	A12	5	2		8		9	6
43		20	BRENTFORD	1-2	Walker	4382		3						11				1	7	A4							10	A12	5	2		8		9	6
44		25	Torquay United	0-2		2178		3						11				1	7	A4							10	A12	5	2		8		9	6
45		29	Hull City	0-2		3997		3						4				1	A7	A12							10	8	5	2		8		9	
46	May	2	STOKE CITY	3-1	Patterson, Seagreaves, Walker	10000		3						4				7			6			11				10	5	2		8		9	
			Apps				23	35	37	18	3		1	42	13	25	4	26	1	31	1	1	3	36	1	42	24	4	39	14	4	26	2	23	27
			Subs				4	2						2			3	11	1					1		1	1		1	1		5	6		1	
			Goals				3	2						6			1	2		2				2		12	8		1	1		1		15	

F.A. Cup

One own goal

#	Date		Opponent	Result	Scorers	Att.	Brown M	Brown P	Burke D	Came M	Darby J	Dibble A	Fisher N	Green S	Kelly T	Kennedy A	Patterson M	Peyton G	Philliskirk T	Reeves D	Rose K	Seagraves M	Spooner N	Storer S	Stubbs A	Walker A	Winstanley M
1	Nov	17	Emley*	3-0	Reeves(2), Philliskirk	9035	A7	2	3		11	1	B8		4				10	9		5			A14 B12		6
2	Dec	7	BRADFORD CITY	3-1	Burke, Reeves, Philliskirk(pen)	7129	7	2	3	A14	11	1	8		4				10	9		5			A6		
3	Jan	4	READING	2-0	Philliskirk	7301			3	6		1	11	7	4	9	8		10			5			2		
4		25	BRIGHTON	2-1	Walker, Philliskirk(pen)	12636			3	6	11	1	A7		4		8		10	A12		5			2	9	
5	Feb	16	SOUTHAMPTON	2-2	Walker, Green	20136	B7		3	6	11	1	B14		4		A8		10	A12		5	2			9	
5r		26	Southampton+	2-3	Walker, Darby	18009			3	6	11	1	A7		4		B8		10	A12		5	2		B14	9	

* Played at Leeds Road   + After extra time

League Cup

#	Date		Opponent	Result	Scorers	Att.	Brown P	Burke D	Charnley C	Comstive P	Cowdrill B	Darby J	Dibble A	Fisher N	Kelly T	Patterson M	Philliskirk T	Reeves D	Rose K	Seagraves M	Spooner N	Storer S	Stubbs A	Walker A	Winstanley M
1/1	Aug	20	YORK CITY	2-2	Philliskirk, Darby	3017	2	A12		A8	3	11			4		10	9	1	5		7	6		
1/2		27	York City	2-1	Darby, Patterson	2757	2	3				11		A8	4	A12	10	9	1	5		B7	6		B14
2/1	Sep	25	Nottingham Forest	0-4		19936	2	3	5			11		A7	4	8	B10	9	1			A12	6		
2/2	Oct	8	NOTTINGHAM FOREST	2-5	Darby, Kelly	5469	2	3	5			11		10	4	8		9	1			7	6		

Autoglass Trophy

#	Date		Opponent	Result	Scorers	Att.	Brown M	Brown P	Burke D	Came M	Comstive P	Darby J	Felgate D	Fisher N	Kelly T	Patterson M	Philliskirk T	Reeves D	Seagraves M	Spooner N	Stubbs A	Walker A	Winstanley M
Q	Nov	17	Preston North End	1-2	Reeves	2709	7	2	3	5	A14	11	1			A8		9			10		6
Q	Dec	10	ROCHDALE	4-1	Reeves(3), Philliskirk	1507	7	2	3	6		11	1			8	10	9	5				
1	Jan	14	Crewe Alexandra	0-2		2155			3	6		11	1			B8	10		5	B14 A12	2	9	

Lancashire Cup

#	Date		Opponent	Result
1	Aug	5	ROCHDALE	0-1
2		7	Blackpool	2-1
3		10	WIGAN ATHLETIC	0-1

Other Games

#	Date		Opponent	Result
1	Jul	28	Sunderland*	2-2
2		29	Shelbourne*	0-0
3	Aug	2	Isle of Man*	6-0
4	Jan	7	Leek Town	0-0

* Isle of Man Tournament

1992/93 2nd in Division Two (promoted)

Manager: B. Rioch

League

#	Month	Date	Opponent	Score	Scorers	Att	Branagan K	Brown M	Brown P	Burke D	Came M	Darby J	Fisher N	Green S	Kelly T	Lee D	Lydiate J	McAteer J	McGinlay J	Oliver D	Parkinson G	Patterson M	Philliskirk T	Reeves D	Roscoe A	Seagraves M	Spooner N	Storer S	Stubbs A	Walker A	Winstanley M
1	Aug	15	HUDDERSFIELD TOWN	2-0	Walker, Darby	7897	1	A7	2	3		4		B14								11		B10	A12				8	9	6
2		22	Brighton	1-2	Walker	6205	1	A12	2	3		4		A7								11		10					8	9	6
3		29	Reading	2-1	Seagraves, Walker	4877	1		2	3		4		7	A14							A11		10					8	9	6
4	Sep	1	BLACKPOOL	3-0	Philliskirk, Walker, Green	7291	1		2	3		4		7	11									10					8	9	6
5		5	Stoke City	0-0		14252	1	A14	2	3		4		7	11								A10						8	9	6
6		12	Rotherham United	1-2	P.Brown	5227	1		2	3	B14	4		7	11								A10	A12		B5			8	9	6
7		15	WEST BROMWICH ALBION	0-2		8531	1	9	2	3	A3	5	4	7	11											A14	10		8		6
8		19	BOURNEMOUTH	1-1	Philliskirk, Walker, Green	4623	1	9	2	3	5	A4		7	11								A12	B14	B10				8		6
9		26	Plymouth Argyle	1-2	Darby	6829	1		2	3	A5	A12	B14	7	B4							11	10						8	9	6
10	Oct	3	Leyton Orient	0-1		3946	1			2				4	8	7		9		3		11	10						8		6
11		10	HARTLEPOOL UNITED	1-2	Green	5097	1							4	A8	7		5	A14	3		11	9					2	10		6
12		17	Chester City	2-2	Reeves, McGinlay	3394	1							A8	7	4		5	9	3		11		A12				2	10		6
13		24	HULL CITY	2-0	McGinlay, Paterson	4136	1							7	4			5	9			11						2	8		6
14		31	Preston North End	2-2	Green, Stubbs	7013	1	A4		3				7				5	B9			11	10			A12	2		8	B14	6
15	Nov	3	Exeter City	3-1	Spooner, Walker(2)	2431	1			3				7			4					11	10			5	2		8	9	6
16		7	PORT VALE	1-1	McGinlay	7349	1			3				7			4		A14			11	10			5	A2		8	9	6
17		21	Fulham	4-1	Walker(2), Stubbs, Lee	4049	1		2	3				7			4		A14			11	10			5			B8	9	6
18		28	BURNLEY	4-0	Lee, Walker(2,1pen), P.Brown	11438	1		2	3				A7	8	4		A14	10			11		A10		5				9	6
19	Dec	19	BRADFORD CITY	5-0	Seagraves,McGinlay(2),Lee,Walker	6887	1		2	3				7	8	4			10			11				5				9	6
20		26	WIGAN ATHLETIC	2-1	Walker(2)	11493	1		2	3				A7	8	4			10			11				5				9	6
21		28	Swansea City	2-1	P.,Brown, McGinlay	7220	1		2	3				7	8	4			10			11				5				9	6
22	Jan	9	West Bromwich Albion	1-3	Walker(pen)	14581	1		2	3				A7	8	4		A12	10			11				5			B14	9	6
23		16	PLYMOUTH ARGYLE	3-1	Walker, Seagraves, Morrison(og)	8256	1		2	3				A7	8	4			10			11				5			A14	9	6
24		27	Reading	2-1	Walker, Lee	4640	1		2	3				7	8	4			10			11				5				9	6
25		30	BRIGHTON	0-1		8929	1		2	3				A7	8	4			10			11		A12		5			6	9	
26	Feb	6	Huddersfield Town	1-1	Walker	8858	1		2	3		7		8	B4							11		A10		5			B14	9	
27		9	Stockport County	0-2		7363	1		2	3				B7					10			11		9		5			B14	A12	A6
28		20	Blackpool	1-1	McGinlay(pen)	8054	1		2	3				A14	4		5	8	10			11		9				A7	6		
29		27	Hartlepool United	2-0	McGinlay, Green	2756	1		2	3				7	4		5	8	10			11							6	9	
30	Mar	6	LEYTON ORIENT	1-0	Walker	7763	1		2	3				7	4			8	10			11				5			6	9	
31		9	MANSFIELD TOWN	2-1	Walker(2)	6557	1		2	3			B12	A7	A14	4			8			B10				5			6	9	
32		13	Port Vale	0-0		11055	1		2	3			10	A14	7	A4			8			11				5			6	9	
33		20	EXETER CITY	4-1	McGinlay(2), Walker, Kelly	6819	1		2	3				7	4				8	10		11				5			6	9	
34		23	Burnley	1-0	McGinlay	15085	1		2	3				7	4				8	10		11				5			6	9	
35		27	FULHAM	1-0	Walker	8402	1		2	3				A14	7	A4			8	10		11				5			6	9	
36		30	ROTHERHAM UNITED	2-0	Walker(2,1pen)	7985	1		2	3		11			7	4			8	10						5			6	9	
37	Apr	3	Mansfield Town	1-1	Seagraves	5366	1		2	3			A11	A12	7	4			8	10						5			6	9	
38		6	STOCKPORT COUNTY	2-1	Walker, McGinlay	13773			2	3				A11	7	4			8	10	A14					5			6	9	
39		10	Wigan Athletic	2-0	Kelly, Walker	5408	1		2	3				11	7	4			8	10						5			6	9	
40		12	SWANSEA CITY	3-1	Green(2), Lee	10854	1		2	3				11	7	4			8	B10	B14					5			6	A9	A12
41		17	Bradford City	1-2	McGinlay	9813	1		2	3				11	7	4			8	10						5			6		9
42		24	CHESTER CITY	5-0	P.Brown,Seagraves,Patterson,McGinlay,Winstanley	8514	1		2	3		A14		A9	7	4			8	10		B11				5			6		B12
43		27	Bournemouth	2-1	Darby, P.Brown	4434	1		2	3		A9		A12	7	4			8	10		11				5			6		
44		30	Hull City	2-1	Windass(og), McGinlay	8785	1		2	3		9			7	4			8	10		11				5			6		
45	May	4	STOKE CITY	1-0	Darby	19238	1		2	3		A9		A12	7	4			8	10		11				5			6		
46		8	PRESTON NORTH END	1-0	McGinlay(pen)	21720	1		2	3		A9		A12	7	4			8	10		11				5			6		
			Apps				46	4	40	43	3	18	3	33	33	32	6	19	31	3		35	9	10		36	6	1	37	31	27
			Subs					2			1	3	1	8	3			2	3		2	2	1	4		1		2	5	1	2
			Goals						5			4		6	2	5			16			2	2	1		5	1		2	26	1

Two own goals

F.A. Cup

#	Month	Date	Opponent	Score	Scorers	Att	Branagan K	Brown P	Burke D	Darby J	Green S	Kelly T	Lee D	McAteer J	McGinlay J	Patterson M	Reeves D	Seagraves M	Spooner N	Stubbs A	Walker A	Winstanley M
1	Nov	14	SUTTON COLDFIELD TOWN	2-1	Reeves, Walker	5345	1		A3		7	A12		4		11	10	5	2	8	9	6
2	Dec	5	ROCHDALE	4-0	McAteer, McGinlay(2), Walker	6876	1	2	3		7	8		4	10	A11	A12	5			9	6
3	Jan	3	LIVERPOOL	2-2	McGinlay, Seagraves	21502	1	2	3		7	8	4		10	11		5			9	6
3r		13	Liverpool	2-0	McGinlay, Walker	34790	1	2	3		7	8	4		10	11		5			9	6
4		24	Wolves	2-0	Green, McGinlay	19120	1	2	3		7	8	4		10	11	A12	5			A9	6
5	Feb	13	Derby County	1-3	Walker	20289	1	2	3			4	5	8	10	11				7	6	9

League Cup

#	Month	Date	Opponent	Score	Scorers	Att	Branagan K	Brown M	Brown P	Burke D	Came M	Darby J	Green S	Kelly T	McAteer J	Patterson M	Philliskirk T	Reeves D	Seagraves M	Spooner N	Stubbs A	Walker A	Winstanley M
1/1	Aug	18	PORT VALE	2-1	Stubbs, Green	3282	1		2	3		4	7			11	10	A12	5		8	A9	6
1/2		25	Port Vale	1-1	Walker	4870	1	A12	2	3		4	7			11	A10		5		8	9	6
2/1	Sep	22	WIMBLEDON	1-3	Stubbs	5049	1		2	3	5		7	4		11	10				8	9	6
2/2	Oct	6	Wimbledon	1-0	Philliskirk	1987	1				4	8	7		5	11	9			2	10		6

Autoglass Trophy

#	Month	Date	Opponent	Score	Scorers	Att	Branagan K	Brown M	Brown P	Burke D	Darby J	Green S	Kelly T	Lee D	McAteer J	McGinlay J	Oliver D	Patterson M	Reeves D	Seagraves M	Stubbs A	Walker A	Winstanley M
Q	Dec	1	Rochdale	0-0		1348	1		2	3		A7	8	4		10		11	A14	5		9	6
Q		8	BURY	1-1	McGinlay	3278	1		A2	3		7			8	5	4	10	11		A14	9	6
1	Jan	19	Darlington *	4-3	Walker(2), Lee, Kelly	1265	1		2	3		A7	8	4		10		11	B12	5	A14	B9	6
2	Feb	2	Huddersfield	0-3		2996	1		2	3	A12		A8	4		B14	10	11		5	7	6	9

* After extra time

Lancashire Cup

#	Month	Date	Opponent	Score
1	Jul	27	BURY	0-0
2	Aug	1	ROCHDALE	0-0

Other Games

#	Month	Date	Opponent	Score
1	Jul	22	Atherton LR	4-0
2		25	Barnsley	2-0
3	Nov	17	MANCHESTER CITY*	4-2

1992-93 Season
(Back) Lydiate, Seagraves, Winstanley, Came, Stubbs, Darby, Spooner
(2nd Row) Roscoe, McAteer, Reeves, Philliskirk, Storer, Smith, Lewin
(3rd Row) Simpson, Oliver, Burke, Branagan, Clarke, Felgate, Green, M.Brown, Crombie
(Front) Carroll, Patterson, Fisher, Rioch, P.Brown, Todd, Walker, Kelly

1993-94 Season
(Back) Lydiate, Mason, Brown, Stubbs, Phillips, Parkinson,
(2nd Row) Fisher, Oliver, Patterson, Branagan, Clarke, Davison, Winstanley, Seagraves, Burke
(3rd Row) Carroll, Whittaker, Thompson, McAteer, Coyle, Roscoe, Walker, Lee, Simpson
(Front) Green, McGinlay, Darby, Rioch, Todd, Fulton, Kelly, Spooner

1993/94   14th in Division One

Manager: B.Rioch

#	Date		Opponent	Score	Scorers	Att	Branagan K	Brown P	Burke D	Coyle O	Darby J	Davison A	Fisher N	Fleck R	Fulton S	Green S	Hoult R	Kelly T	Lee D	Lydiate J	McAteer J	McGinlay J	Parkinson G	Patterson M	Phillips J	Roscoe A	Seagraves M	Spooner N	Stubbs A	Thompson A	Walker A	Walton M	Whittaker S	Winstanley M
1	Aug	14	Grimsby Town	0-0		8593	1	2	5	9						A12		4	7		8	A10			3					11				6
2		21	STOKE CITY	1-1	Coyle	11328	1	2	5	A9								4	7		8	10		A12	3					6	11			
3		28	Charlton Athletic	0-3		7573	1	2	5	9								A4	7		8	10		11	3					6	A14			
4		31	OXFORD UNITED	1-0	McGinlay	8230	1	2	5	B9	B14							4	7		8	10		A11	3					6	A12			
5	Sep	11	Luton Town	2-0	McGinlay(2)	7189	1	2		9	5							4	7		A8	10		B11	3		B14			6	A12			
6		18	LEICESTER CITY	1-2	McGinlay(pen)	12049	1	2		9	5							4	7		8	10		A11	3					6	A12			
7		26	NOTTINGHAM FOREST	4-3	Lee(2), Thompson, Patterson	10578	1	2		A9	B5					A12		4	7		8			11	3		B14			6	10			
8	Oct	2	Bristol City	0-2		7704	1	2			A14					B12		A4	7		8	10		11	3		5			6	B9			
9		9	Tranmere Rovers	1-2	Brown	10128	1	2								A12		4	7		8	10		11	3		5			6	A9			
10		16	MILLWALL	4-0	McGinlay(2), McAteer, Lee	9386		2				1				A12		4	7		8	10		11	3		5				A9			6
11		19	Birmingham City	1-2	Thompson	12071		2				1						4	7		8	10		11	3		5			6	9			6
12		23	Watford	3-4	McAteer, Lee, Thompson	7492		2				1						4	7		8	10		11	3		5			6	9			6
13		30	DERBY COUNTY	0-2		11464	A1	2			B12	A16						4	7		8	10		11	3		5			6	B9			6
14	Nov	2	PETERBOROUGH UNITED	1-1	McGinlay	7058		2			1					9		4	7		8	10		11	3		5			6				6
15		6	West Bromwich Albion	2-2	Green, McAteer	15709		2			B12	1				9		A16	A4	B7	8	10		11	3		5			6				6
16		21	Middlesbrough	1-0	McGinlay	6828		2		9						1		4		A12	7	A10			3		5			8	11			6
17		24	CRYSTAL PALACE	1-0	McGinlay	7486		2		9						1		4			7	10			3		5			8	11			6
18		27	Barnsley	1-1	Coyle	6755		2		9						1		4			7	10			3		5			8	11			6
19	Dec	7	WEST BROMWICH ALBION	1-1	Coyle	9277	A2			9						1		4	A12		7	A10			3		5							6
20		11	Oxford United	2-0	Kelly, Thompson	5559		2		9						1		4	A12		7	A10			3		5			8	B11			6
21		18	GRIMSBY TOWN	1-1	Coyle	9431		2		9				A12	B14	1		4	B10		7				3	A5				8	11			6
22		27	SUNDERLAND	0-0		18496		2	3	A9		1		10				5			7	4					A12			6				6
23		28	Portsmouth	0-0		14276			3			1		10		9		4			7		2	11			5		8					6
24	Jan	1	NOTTS COUNTY	4-2	Fleck, Green, Thompson, Devlin(og)	11041		2	A3	B9		1		10		5			7		4			11	A12				8	B14				6
25		3	Wolves	0-1		24053		2				1		10	A9			4			7			11	3		5		8	A14				6
26		12	Southend United	2-0	Stubbs, McGinlay	4969		2	3			1		9	6				7		4	10		11					8					6
27		15	Millwall	0-1		9772		2	3			1		A9	A14			4	7		5	10		11					8					6
28		23	TRANMERE ROVERS	2-1	McGinlay(2)	11550		2		A9		1						4	7		5	10		11	3				8	A14				6
29	Feb	5	WATFORD	3-1	Coyle, Watson(og), McGinlay(pen)	10150		2	A14	9		1						4	7		5	10		B11	3				8		B12			A6
30		12	Derby County	0-2		16698		2		9		1						4	A7		5	10		11	3		6		8		A12			
31		22	Stoke City	0-2		14257			8	B9		1						4	B10		2	5	10	11	3		6			A7	A12			
32		26	Crystal Palace	1-1	Coyle	17245			3	9		1						4	7	5	8	10		11	3		6							
33	Mar	5	CHARLTON ATHLETIC	3-2	McGinlay(3,1pen)	13027		2		9		1						4	7		8	10		11	3		5		6					
34		19	Nottingham Forest	2-3	Brown, Green	23846		2		9		1				A12		A4	7		8	B10		11	3		5		6					B14
35		26	BRISTOL CITY	2-2	Lee, Coyle	10221		2		9		1				A12		4	A7		8			11	3		5		6		B10			B14
36		29	WOLVES	1-3	McGinlay	12405		2		9		1						A14			8	10		11	3		5		A4	7				6
37	Apr	2	Sunderland	0-2		18574		2		B9		1						A4	7		8	10		11	3		5				A14	B12		6
38		4	PORTSMOUTH	1-1	McGinlay	9560		2						7	A14				6		8	10			3	11	5		4		A9			
39		9	Notts County	1-2	McGinlay	7270		2						7	9				A14	6	8	10			3	A11	5		4			1		
40		12	SOUTHEND UNITED	0-2		7140		2										4	7		8	10		11	3		5		6		9	1		
41		16	Peterborough United	3-2	Walker(2), Welsh(og)	6616		2		A12			B14					B4	7		8	10		11	3		5		6		A9	1		
42		23	MIDDLESBROUGH	4-1	McGinlay(3), Green	9220		2		A12		1				4			7		8	10		11	3		5		6		A9			
43		30	BIRMINGHAM CITY	1-1	Walker	13602		2		A12		1				4			7		8	10		11	3		5		6		A9			5
44	May	3	Leicester City	1-1	McGinlay	18145		2			1					A4			7	8	A12	10		11	3				6		9			5
45		5	LUTON TOWN	2-1	McGinlay, Thompson	7102					1					4			7		8	10			3			5	2	6	11		9	
46		8	BARNSLEY	2-3	Seagraves, McGinlay	11661		2			1				A14	B4			7		8	10			3		B12	5		6	A11		9	
				Apps			10	42	11	25	3	30		6	4	11	3	35	35	5	45	39	1	34	41	2	32	1	41	19	7	3	2	19
				Subs					1	5	2	1	2	1		11	1		6		1			1	1	1	3				8	4			2
				Goals				2		7				1		4		1	5		3	25		1			1			1	6	3			

Three own goals

F.A.Cup

#	Date		Opponent	Score	Scorers	Att	Brown P	Burke D	Coyle O	Darby J	Davison A	Green S	Hoult R	Kelly T	Lee D	Lydiate J	McAteer J	McGinlay J	Patterson M	Phillips J	Seagraves M	Stubbs A	Thompson A	Walker A	Winstanley M
1	Nov	13	Gretna*	3-2	McGinlay, Coyle(2)	6447	2		9	1				A8			A12	7		4	10		3	5	11	6
2	Dec	4	Lincoln City	3-1	Thompson, Brown, Coyle	6250	2		9	1							4	7	10	3	5		8	11	6
3	Jan	8	EVERTON	1-1	Patterson	21072	2	3		1		5			7		4	10	11				8	9	6
3r		19	Everton+	3-2	McGinlay, Stubbs, Coyle	34652	2		9	1		A5		A12	7		4	10	11	3			8		6
4		31	ARSENAL	2-2	McAteer, Coyle	18891	2		9	1							4	7	5	10		A11	3	8	A14	6
4r	Feb	9	Arsenal +	3-1	McGinlay, McAteer, Walker	33863	2		9	1							4	7	5	10	A11	3		6	8	A12	6
5		20	ASTON VILLA	1-0	Stubbs	18817	2		9	1							4	7	5	10	11	3		6	8	6
6	Mar	12	OLDHAM ATHLETIC		20321	2		9	1						4	7	8	10	A11	3		5	6	A12	6

* Played at Burnden Park   + After extra time

League Cup

#	Date		Opponent	Score	Scorers	Att	Branagan K	Brown P	Burke D	Coyle O	Darby J	Kelly T	Lee D	McAteer J	McGinlay J	Patterson M	Phillips J	Seagraves M	Thompson A	Walker A	Winstanley M
1/1	Aug	17	BURY	0-2		6455	1	2	5	9		4	7	8	10		3		6	11	
1/2		24	Bury*	2-0	Coyle, McGinlay	4528	1	2	5	9		4	7	8	10	A11	3		6	A12	
2/1	Sep	21	SHEFFIELD WEDNESDAY	1-1	Kelly(pen)	11590	1	2		A9	5	4	7	8		11	3		6	10	A12
2/2	Oct	6	Sheffield Wednesday	1-1		16194	1	2		A12		A4	7	8	10	11	3	5	6	9	

* won 3-0 on penalties (After extra time)

Anglo Italian Tournament

#	Date		Opponent	Score	Scorers	Att	Branagan K	Brown P	Coyle O	Darby J	Davison A	Fisher N	Fleck R	Fulton S	Green S	Hoult R	Kelly T	Lee D	McAteer J	McGinlay J	Parkinson G	Patterson M	Phillips J	Roscoe A	Seagraves M	Spooner N	Stubbs A	Thompson A	Walker A	Winstanley M
1	Sep	7	Tranmere Rovers	2-1	McGinlay, Coyle	2786			9	5	1		8	4				7				10	2		11	3				6
2		14	SUNDERLAND	2-0	Coyle(2)	3460			9		1		8	7								2	11	3	4	5			10	6
3	Oct	12	ANCONA	5-0	McGinlay(2), Thompson, McAteer, Ph	3448	1	2							A12		4	7	A8	10		11	3		5			6	9	6
4	Nov	9	BRESCIA	3-3	Coyle, McGinlay, Green	3021			9	1			B17	4			A7		8	10		2	B11	3				5	A15	6
5		14	Pisa	1-1	Phillips	1000		2	A9	1				4			A12		7	10			3		5		8	11	6
6	Dec	22	Ascoli	1-1	Seagraves	1000			A9			10		A17	1	4		7		2		3	5		8	11	6

Lancashire Cup

#	Date		Opponent	Score
1	Jul	23	Rochdale	4-3
2		27	Burnley	1-0
3		30	BLACKPOOL	1-3

Other Games

#	Date		Opponent	Score
1	Jul	21	Atherton LR	2-0
2	Aug	7	Chorley	2-1

1994/95 3rd in Division One (promoted via play-offs)

Manager: B. Rioch

#		Date	Opponent	Score	Scorers	Att	Bergsson G	Branagan K	Coleman S	Coyle O	Davison A	Dreyer J	Fisher N	de Freitas F	Green S	Kelly T	Kernaghan A	Lee D	Lydiate J	McAteer J	McDonald N	McGinlay J	Paatelainen M	Patterson M	Phillips J	Seagraves M	Shilton P	Sneekes R	Spooner N	Stubbs A	Thompson A	Whittaker S
1	Aug	13	Grimsby Town	3-3	Paatelainen(2), McGinlay(pen)	8393		1		A14				7			5	4		2		A10	9	8	3			B12			6	B11
2		20	BRISTOL CITY	0-2		12127		1		B14							5	7		4	A2	B10	9	8	3			11			6	A12
3		27	Middlesbrough	0-1		19570		1					7	10			5			2	A4	A12	9	11	3					8	6	
4		30	MILLWALL	1-0	Patterson	9519		1					7	A10			5			2	4	A12	9	11	3					8	6	
5	Sep	3	STOKE CITY	4-0	McGinlay(p),McAteer(2),Paatelainen	11515		1					7			11	5			2	4	10	9		3					8	6	
6		10	Sheffield United	1-3	McGinlay	14116		1		B12			7			11	5			2	4	B10	9		A3					8	6	A14
7		13	Luton Town	3-0	McGinlay(2), Sneekes	5764		1					7			11	5			2	4	10	9		3					8	6	
8		17	PORTSMOUTH	1-1		11284		1					7			A11	5	A12		2	4	10	9		3					8	6	
9		24	Southend United	1-2	Sneekes	4507		1					7	B12			A14	11	2	4		10	B9		3					8	A6	5
10	Oct	1	DERBY COUNTY	1-0	McGinlay	12015		1					7				6	11	2	4		10	9		3					8		5
11		8	Burnley	2-2	McGinlay, Coleman	16687		1	7					B12	A14		B11		2	4		10	9		3					8	6	A5
12		16	OLDHAM ATHLETIC	2-2	Paatelainen, Lee	11106		1	7						6		A12	11	2	4		B10	9		3					A8		5
13		22	Port Vale	1-1	Green	10003		1	7					A6	B14	A12	2		11	4		B10	9		3					8		5
14		29	WATFORD	3-0	Paatelainen, McGinlay(2,1pen)	10483		1	7						6			11	2			10	9	4	3					8		5
15	Nov	1	SWINDON TOWN	3-0	Coleman, Thompson, DeFreitas	10046		1	7					B12				B10	6	A11	2	A14	9	4	3					8		5
16		5	Charlton Athletic	2-1	Sneekes(2)	9793		1	7					B12				B10	6	A11	2	A14	9	4	3					8		5
17		19	NOTTS COUNTY	2-0	DeFreitas, Paatelainen	11698		1	7					B12				B10	6	11	2		9	4	3					A8	A14	5
18		23	Wolves	1-3	Paatelainen	25903		1	7					A12				A10	6	11	2		9	4	3					B8	B14	5
19		26	Barnsley	0-3		8507		1	7					A12				6	B14	B2	11	10	9		3					8	4	A5
20	Dec	6	PORT VALE	1-0	Patterson	10324		1	5								2			7	4	10	9	11	3					8	6	
21		10	Bristol City	1-0	Patterson	6144		1	5	A12							2			7	4	10	9	11	3					A8	6	
22		17	GRIMSBY TOWN	3-3	Coyle(2), Lee	10522		1	5	10							2			7	4		9	A11	3					8	6	BA12
23		26	Sunderland	1-1	Paatelainen	18758		1	5	10							2			7	4		9		3					8	6	11
24		27	TRANMERE ROVERS	1-0	Thompson	16782		1	5	A12							2			7	4	A10	9	8	3						6	11
25		31	West Bromwich Albion	0-1		18184		1	5								2			7	4	10	9	A12	3					8	6	11
26	Jan	2	READING	1-0	Coleman	14705		1	5	11							2			7	4	B10	B12	9	3					A8	6	A14
27		14	Watford	0-0		9113		1	5								2			7	4	10	9		3					8	6	11
28		21	CHARLTON ATHLETIC	5-1	McGinlay(2),McAteer,Coyle,Paatelainen	10516		1	5	A12B							2			7	B14	A10	9		3					8	6	11
29	Feb	4	WOLVES	5-1	Sneekes,Coleman,Phillips,Coyle,Thompson	16964		1	5	10							2			7	4		9		3					8	6	11
30		7	Notts County	1-1	Coyle	7553		1	5	B10	A16								B12	A7	4		9		3					8	6	11
31		18	BARNSLEY	2-1	Thompson, Sneekes	12463		1	5								2			7	4		9		3					8	6	11
32		26	Derby County	1-2	McAteer	11003	A5	1			1			B12			2			7	4	B10	9	A14	3					8	6	11
33	Mar	4	SOUTHEND UNITED	3-0	Thompson, Lee, McAteer	10766		1		9							2			7	4	10	9	A8	3	5					6	11
34		11	MIDDLESBROUGH	1-0	Paatelainen	18370		1									2			A12		10	9	A8	3	5				/	6	11
35		19	Millwall	1-0	McGinlay	6103		1												4	8	10	9		3	5		7			6	11
36		22	SHEFFIELD UNITED	1-1	Stubbs	16756		1									7			4		10	9		3	5		8			6	11
37		25	Portsmouth	1-1	Paatelainen	7765		1		10										A12	4	A8	9		3	5		7			6	11
38	Apr	5	Swindon Town	1-0	Thompson	8100	2	1									A12			7		A10	9	8	3	5					6	11
39		8	WEST BROMWICH ALBION	1-0	Thompson(pen)	16207	2	1						B14	A12		A7			4		B10	9	8	3	5					6	11
40		11	LUTON TOWN	0-0		13619	2	1						A10	7					4		A14	9		3	5					6	11
41		14	Tranmere Rovers	0-1		15595	2	1									7					10	A9	A12	3	5					6	11
42		17	SUNDERLAND	1-0	McGinlay	15030	2	1					B14		A12		B7			4		10	9	11	3	5		A8			6	
43		21	Reading	1-2	Lee	13223		1		9	2						7			4		10		8	3	5					6	11
44		29	Oldham Athletic	1-3	McGinlay	11901	2	1									7			4		10	9	8	3	5					6	11
45	May	3	Stoke City	1-1	McGinlay	15557	2				1			B14			A7			4		10	9	8	3	B5	A16				6	11
46		7	BURNLEY	1-1	Paatelainen	16853	5				1						7			4		10	9	8	3						6	11
			Apps				8	43	22	8	3	1	10	7	26	4	9	35	17	41	4	34	43	23	46	13		37	1	37	34	
			Subs							11	1	1	1	6	5		2	4	1	2		3	1	3		1		1		2	3	1
			Goals						4	5				2	1			4		5		16	12	3	1			6		1	7	

Play Offs

		Date	Opponent	Score	Scorers	Att	Bergsson G	Branagan K	Coleman S	Coyle O	Davison A	Dreyer J	Fisher N	de Freitas F	Green S	Kelly T	Kernaghan A	Lee D	Lydiate J	McAteer J	McDonald N	McGinlay J	Paatelainen M	Patterson M	Phillips J	Seagraves M	Shilton P	Sneekes R	Spooner N	Stubbs A	Thompson A	Whittaker S
SF1	May	14	Wolves	1-2	McAteer	26153	5			A14			8				2			4	7	A10	9		3	1					6	11
SF2		17	WOLVES*	2-0	McGinlay	20041	5	1		8				B14		A12	2			A7	4	10	9		3					B6		11
F		29	Reading*	4-3	DeFreitas(2), Coyle, Paatelainen	64107	5	1		8					A12	2				4	A7	10	9		3						6	11

* After extra time

F.A. Cup

		Date	Opponent	Score	Scorers	Att	Bergsson G	Branagan K	Coleman S	Coyle O	Davison A	Dreyer J	Fisher N	de Freitas F	Green S	Kelly T	Kernaghan A	Lee D	Lydiate J	McAteer J	McDonald N	McGinlay J	Paatelainen M	Patterson M	Phillips J	Seagraves M	Shilton P	Sneekes R	Spooner N	Stubbs A	Thompson A	Whittaker S
3	Jan	7	Portsmouth	1-3	Sneekes	9721		1	5	9							2			A12		4			10	A7		B11	3		8	6

League Cup

		Date	Opponent	Score	Scorers	Att	Bergsson G	Branagan K	Coleman S	Coyle O	Davison A	Dreyer J	Fisher N	de Freitas F	Green S	Kelly T	Kernaghan A	Lee D	Lydiate J	McAteer J	McDonald N	McGinlay J	Paatelainen M	Patterson M	Phillips J	Seagraves M	Shilton P	Sneekes R	Spooner N	Stubbs A	Thompson A	Whittaker S
2/1	Sep	21	Ipswich Town	3-0	McAteer, McGinlay, Thompson	7787		1		B14			7	A12			11		2	4		B10	A9		3					8	6	5
2/2	Oct	5	IPSWICH TOWN	1-0	Sneekes	8212		1					7	A14			11		2	B4		10	A9		3					8	6	5
3		25	Sheffield United	2-1	Paatelainen, Scott(og)	6939		1	7					A12	6		A11	2				10	9		3					8	6	5
4	Nov	30	West Ham United	3-1	McGinlay(2,1pen), Lee	18190		1	5						2		A7			4		10	9	A14	3					8	6	11
5	Jan	12	NORWICH CITY	1-0	Lee	17029		1	5						2		7			4		10	9		3					8	6	11
SF1	Feb	12	Swindon Town	1-2	Stubbs	15341		1	5	A10					2		7			4		A12	9		3					8	6	11
SF2	Mar	8	SWINDON TOWN	3-1	McAteer, Paatelainen, McGinlay	19851		1		A9					2		B7			4		10	A12	8	3	5		B14			6	11
F	Apr	2	Liverpool	1-2	Thompson	75595	A14	1							A2		7			4		10	9		3	5				8	6	11

Other Games

1	Jul	22	Atherton LR	1-0	
2		26	LIVERPOOL	4-1	
3		30	Dunfermline	0-0	won 5-4 on penalties
4	Aug	1	Ross County	7-0	
5		3	Caledonian Thistle	2-0	
6		6	St Johnstone	3-1	

1994-95 Season
(Back) Paatelainen, Bergsson, Davison, Seagraves, Branagan, Stubbs, McDonald
(Middle) Sneekes, Defreitas, McAteer, Phillips, Coyle, Green
(Front) Thompson, Lee, McGinlay, Fisher, Patterson

1995-96 Season
(Back) Sneekes, Phillips, Green, Fairclough, Coleman, McDonald, Todd, Spooner
(Middle)Simpson,McAteer,Defreitas,Bergsson, Branagan, Taggart, Davison,Thompson,Patterson,Carroll,McNeill
(Front) Lee, Coyle, Stubbs, Todd, McFarland, Paatelainen, McGinlay, Whittaker

1995/96   20th in Premiership (relegated)

Manager: C.Todd/R.McFarland until 2.1.96. C.Todd from 2.1.96

#		Date	Opponent	Score	Scorers	Att	Bergsson G (5)	Blake N (20)	Branagan K (1)	Burnett W (26)	Coleman S (17)	Coyle O (20)	Curcic S (4)	Davison A (13)	Fairclough C (21)	Defreitas F (14)	Green S (2)	Lee D (7)	McAnespie S (24)	McAteer J (4)	McGinlay J (10)	Paatelainen M (9)	Patterson M (15)	Phillips J (3)	Sellars S (12)	Small B (15)	Sneekes R (8)	Strong G (29)	Stubbs A (6)	Taggart G (22)	Taylor S (25)	Thompson A (11)	Todd A (23)	Ward G (16)	Whittaker S (19)
1	Aug	19	Wimbledon	2-3	Thompson, Defreitas	9317	A*		*			BS				*	*			AS			B*	*						*			A*			
2		22	NEWCASTLE UNITED	1-3	Bergsson	20243	*		*			*			B*	*	*		BS		*			*	*				AS		*		A*			
3		26	BLACKBURN ROVERS	2-1	Defreitas, Stubbs	20253	*		*			A*			*	*	*		AS		*			*	*				*		*		*			
4		30	Aston Villa	0-1		31770	*		*						*	*	B*	BS		*	A*		*	*				AS		*		*			
5	Sep	9	MIDDLESBROUGH	1-1	McGinlay	18376	*		*			AS			*	*	*				A*		*	*				*		*	*		*			
6		16	Manchester United	0-3		32812	*		*						*	*	*	*			B*		AS	*				*	BS	A*	*					
7		23	Liverpool	2-5	Todd, Patterson(pen)	40104	*		*			AS			*	*	*	*			A*		*	*				*			B*	BS				
8		30	QUEENS PARK RANGERS	0-1		17362	*		*						*	*	*				*		*	*				*	*		*					
9		14	EVERTON	1-1	Paatelainen	20427	*		*						AS	BS	*		A*	B*	*		*	*				*	*		*					
10		21	Nottingham Forest	2-3	Sneekes, Defreitas	25426	*		*						*	AS	BS		A*	*	B*		*	*				*	*		*					
11		31	ARSENAL	1-0	McGinlay	18682	*		*			A*			*	BS	*	*	*	*	AS		*	*				*			B*					
12	Nov	4	Manchester City	0-1		28397	*		*			B*			*	BS	CS	*	*	*	A*	AS	C*	*				*			*					
13		18	WEST HAM UNITED	0-3		19047	*		*			*			*	AS	A*	B*	*	*			*	*							*	BS				
14		22	Chelsea	2-3	Curcic, Green	17496	*		*			*			*	*	*		*				*	*					*		*	*				
15		25	Southampton	0-1		14404	*		*			*			*	*	*		*				*	*					*		*	*				
16	Dec	2	NOTTINGHAM FOREST	1-1	Defreitas	17342	*		*			*			*	*	*		*					*					*		*	*				
17		9	LIVERPOOL	0-1		21042	*		*			*			*	*	*		*		AS	*	*						*		A*				
18		16	Queens Park Rangers	1-2	Sellars	11456	*		*			*			*	*	*		*			*	*						*		A*				
19		23	Tottenham Hotspur	2-2	Green, Bergsson	30702	*	*	*			*			*	BS	*		B*			*	*		AS				*		A*				
20		27	LEEDS UNITED	0-2		18414	*	*	*	AS		*			*	BS	*		*		B*	*	A*						*						
21		30	COVENTRY CITY	1-2	McGinlay	16678	*	*				*			*	*	*		*			*	*		*				*		*				
22	Jan	1	Sheffield Wednesday	2-4	Curcic, Taggart	24872	*					*			*	BS	*		B*			*	*		*	AS	*	*		A*				
23		13	WIMBLEDON	1-0	McGinlay(pen)	16216	*	A*	*			*			*	*		AS	*	*	*	*	*		*				*					
24		20	Newcastle United	1-2	Bergsson	36543	*	B*	*			A*			C*	*			*	AS	*	*		*					*			BS		
25	Feb	3	Blackburn Rovers	1-3	Green	30419	*	AS	*			*			B*	*	BS		A*	*	*	*		*				*			*			
26		10	ASTON VILLA	0-2		18099	A*	*	*			*			*	*				BS			*	B*	*				*	AS				
27		17	Middlesbrough	4-1	Blake, Coleman, Defreitas, Lee	29354	*	*	*		*	*		*	*	*	*						*	*					*					
28		25	MANCHESTER UNITED	0-6		21381	*	*	*		*	*		*	*	*	*	A*	AS				*	*					*					
29	Mar	2	Leeds United	1-0	Bergsson	30106	*	A*	*		*		*			*	AS	*			*		*	*					*					
30		16	Coventry City	2-0	Stubbs(2)	17226	*	A*	*		*		*			*	AS	*			*		*	*					*					
31		20	TOTTENHAM HOTSPUR	2-3	Stubbs, Sellars	17829	*	A*			*		*			CS	C*				AS	B*	*	*				*		BS				
32		23	SHEFFIELD WEDNESDAY	2-1	Sellars, Curcic	18368	*				*		*	*	*	*					*	*	*				*		*				
33		30	MANCHESTER CITY	1-1	McGinlay	21050	*	CS			*		B*	A*	AS		*	BS	*	*				C*		*				
34	Apr	6	Everton	0-3		37974	*	BS			*		*		AS	A*		*	B*	*		*				*				
35		8	CHELSEA	2-1	McGinlay, Curcic	18021	*	A*			*		*		*		*	*		*			AS	*				*		
36		13	West Ham United	0-1		23086	*	A*			*		*		AS		*	*		*				*				*		
37		27	SOUTHAMPTON	0-1		18795	*				*		*	A*	B*	AS	*	BS	*	*				*		*		*		
38	May	5	Arsenal	1-2	Todd	38104	*	BS	*		B*	B*				*		*	*				*	*				AS	*	

						Apps	34	14	31		12	2	28	2	33	17	26	9	7	4	29	12	12	37	22	1	14		24	11		23	9	5	
						Subs		4		1		3						10	5	9	2		3	3	4			3	1	1		1	3	3	
						Goals	4	1			1		4			5	3	1			6	1	1		3		1		4	1		1	2		

F.A. Cup

		Date	Opponent	Score	Scorers	Att																												
3	Jan	6	Bradford City	3-0	McGinlay, Curcic(2)	10265	*	*				*			*		*				*			*	*		*		*	*				
4	Feb	14	LEEDS UNITED	0-1		16694	B*	*				*			*	*	*	A*			AS	BS		*				*	*	*				

League Cup

		Date	Opponent	Score	Scorers	Att																												
1/1	Sep	19	BRENTFORD	1-0	Sneekes	5243	*		*			AS			*	A*	*	*			*		B*	*				*			*	BS		
1/2	Oct	3	Brentford	3-2	Patterson, McGinlay, Thompson	4861	*		*						*		AS	*	*		*		*	*		B*		*		A*	BS		
3		25	LEICESTER CITY	0-0		9166	*		*						*	BS		AS	*		*	B*	A*	*		*		*		*			
3r	Nov	8	Leicester City	3-2	McGinlay, Sneekes, Curcic	14884	*		*					*		BS	*	*		*	AS	*		*	A*		B*			
4		29	Norwich City	0-0		13820	*		*			*			*	*		*			*		*	*		*		*	*		
4r	Dec	20	NORWICH CITY*	0-0		8736	*		*			*			*	*		*			*	A*	*		*		*		AS	

* After extra time, lost 2-3 on penalties

Other Games

#		Date	Opponent	Score
1	Jul	28	Atherton LR	1-0
2		31	Queens Park	3-0
3	Aug	2	Dundee	2-2
4		5	Dunfermline	2-3
5		8	ABERDEEN	3-1
6		12	Kilmarnock	2-1

League Tables: 1996/97 - 2000/02

1996/97 First Division

	FINAL TABLE	Pl.	Home W	Home D	Home L	Home F	Home A	Away W	Away D	Away L	Away F	Away A	F. (Total)	A. (Total)	Pts
1	BOLTON WANDS.	46	18	4	1	60	20	10	10	3	40	33	100	53	98
2	Barnsley	46	14	4	5	43	19	8	10	5	33	36	76	55	80
3	Wolverhampton W.	46	10	5	8	31	24	12	5	6	37	27	68	51	76
4	Ipswich Town	46	13	7	3	44	23	7	7	9	24	27	68	50	74
5	Sheffield Utd.	46	13	5	5	46	23	7	8	8	29	29	75	52	73
6	Crystal Palace	46	10	7	6	39	22	9	7	7	39	26	78	48	71
7	Portsmouth	46	12	4	7	32	24	8	4	11	27	29	59	53	68
8	Port Vale	46	9	9	5	36	28	8	7	8	22	27	58	55	67
9	Queens Park Rgs.	46	10	5	8	33	25	8	7	8	31	35	64	60	66
10	Birmingham City	46	11	7	5	30	18	6	8	9	22	30	52	48	66
11	Tranmere Rovers	46	10	9	4	42	27	7	5	11	21	29	63	56	65
12	Stoke City	46	15	3	5	34	22	3	7	13	17	35	51	57	64
13	Norwich City	46	9	10	4	28	18	8	2	13	35	50	63	68	63
14	Manchester City	46	12	4	7	34	25	5	6	12	25	35	59	60	61
15	Charlton Athletic	46	11	8	4	36	28	5	3	15	16	38	52	66	59
16	West Bromwich Alb.	46	7	7	9	37	33	7	8	8	31	39	68	72	57
17	Oxford United	46	14	3	6	44	26	2	6	15	20	42	64	68	57
18	Reading	46	13	7	3	37	24	2	5	16	21	43	58	67	57
19	Swindon Town	46	11	6	6	36	27	4	3	16	16	44	52	71	54
20	Huddersfield Town	46	10	7	6	28	20	3	8	12	20	41	48	61	54
21	Bradford City	46	10	5	8	29	32	2	7	14	18	40	47	72	48
22	Grimsby Town	46	7	7	9	31	34	4	6	13	29	47	60	81	46
23	Oldham Athletic	46	6	8	9	30	30	4	5	14	21	36	51	66	43
24	Southend United	46	7	9	7	32	32	1	6	16	10	54	42	86	39

1997/98 Premier League

	FINAL TABLE	Pl.	Home W	Home D	Home L	Home F	Home A	Away W	Away D	Away L	Away F	Away A	F. (Total)	A. (Total)	Pts
1	Arsenal	38	15	2	2	43	10	8	7	4	25	23	68	33	78
2	Manchester United	38	13	4	2	42	9	10	4	5	31	17	73	26	77
3	Liverpool	38	13	2	4	42	16	5	9	5	26	26	68	42	65
4	Chelsea	38	13	2	4	37	14	7	1	11	34	29	71	43	63
5	Leeds United	38	9	5	5	31	21	8	3	8	26	25	57	46	59
6	Blackburn Rovers	38	11	4	4	40	26	5	6	8	17	26	57	52	58
7	Aston Villa	38	9	3	7	26	24	8	3	8	23	24	49	48	57
8	West Ham United	38	13	4	2	40	18	3	4	12	16	39	56	57	56
9	Derby County	38	12	3	4	33	18	4	4	11	19	31	52	49	55
10	Leicester City	38	6	10	3	21	15	7	4	8	30	26	51	41	53
11	Coventry City	38	8	9	2	26	17	4	7	8	20	27	46	44	52
12	Southampton	38	10	1	8	28	23	4	5	10	22	32	50	55	48
13	Newcastle United	38	8	5	6	22	20	3	6	10	13	24	35	44	44
14	Tottenham Hotspur	38	7	8	4	23	22	4	3	12	21	34	44	56	44
15	Wimbledon	38	5	6	8	18	25	5	8	6	16	21	34	46	44
16	Sheffield Wednesday	38	9	5	5	30	26	3	3	13	22	41	52	67	44
17	Everton	38	7	5	7	25	27	2	8	9	16	29	41	56	40
18	BOLTON WANDS.	38	7	8	4	25	22	2	5	12	16	39	41	61	40
19	Barnsley	38	7	4	8	25	35	3	1	15	12	47	37	82	35
20	Crystal Palace	38	2	5	12	15	39	6	4	9	22	32	37	71	33

1998/99 First Division

	FINAL TABLE	Pl.	Home W	Home D	Home L	Home F	Home A	Away W	Away D	Away L	Away F	Away A	F. (Total)	A. (Total)	Pts
1	Sunderland	46	19	3	1	50	10	12	9	2	41	18	91	28	105
2	Bradford City	46	15	4	4	48	20	11	5	7	34	27	82	47	87
3	Ipswich Town	46	16	1	6	37	15	10	7	6	32	17	69	32	86
4	Birmingham City	46	12	7	4	32	15	11	5	7	34	22	66	37	81
5	Watford	46	12	8	3	30	19	9	6	8	35	37	65	56	77
6	BOLTON WANDS.	46	13	6	4	44	25	7	10	6	34	34	78	59	76
7	Wolverhampton W.	46	11	10	2	37	19	8	6	9	27	24	64	43	73
8	Sheffield United	46	12	6	5	42	29	6	7	10	29	37	71	66	67
9	Norwich City	46	7	12	4	34	28	8	5	10	28	33	62	61	62
10	Huddersfield Town	46	11	9	3	38	23	4	7	12	24	48	62	71	61
11	Grimsby Town	46	11	6	6	25	18	6	4	13	15	34	40	52	61
12	West Bromwich Alb.	46	12	4	7	43	33	4	7	12	26	43	69	76	59
13	Barnsley	46	7	9	7	35	30	7	8	8	24	26	59	56	59
14	Crystal Palace	46	11	10	2	43	26	3	6	14	15	45	58	71	58
15	Tranmere Rovers	46	8	7	8	37	30	4	13	6	26	31	63	61	56
16	Stockport County	46	7	9	7	24	21	5	8	10	25	39	49	60	53
17	Swindon Town	46	7	8	8	40	44	6	3	14	19	37	59	81	50
18	Crewe Alexandra	46	7	6	10	27	35	5	6	12	27	43	54	78	48
19	Portsmouth	46	10	5	8	34	26	1	9	13	23	47	57	73	47
20	Queen's Park Rangers	46	9	7	7	34	22	3	4	16	18	39	52	61	47
21	Port Vale	46	10	3	10	22	28	3	5	15	23	47	45	75	47
22	Bury	46	9	7	7	24	27	1	10	12	11	33	35	60	47
23	Oxford United	46	7	8	8	31	30	3	6	14	17	41	48	71	44
24	Bristol City	46	7	8	8	35	36	2	7	14	22	44	57	80	42

1999/2000 First Division

	FINAL TABLE	Pl.	Home W	Home D	Home L	Home F	Home A	Away W	Away D	Away L	Away F	Away A	F. (Total)	A. (Total)	Pts
1	Charlton Athletic	46	15	3	5	37	18	12	7	4	42	27	79	45	91
2	Manchester City	46	17	2	4	48	17	9	9	5	30	23	78	40	89
3	Ipswich Town	46	16	3	4	39	17	9	9	5	32	25	71	42	87
4	Barnsley	46	15	4	4	48	24	9	6	8	40	43	88	67	82
5	Birmingham City	46	15	5	3	37	16	7	6	10	28	28	65	44	77
6	BOLTON WANDS.	46	14	5	4	43	26	7	8	8	26	24	69	50	76
7	Wolverhampton W.	46	15	5	3	45	20	6	6	11	19	28	64	48	74
8	Huddersfield Town	46	14	5	4	43	21	7	6	10	19	28	62	49	74
9	Fulham	46	13	7	3	33	13	4	9	10	16	28	49	41	67
10	Queen's Park Rangers	46	9	12	2	30	20	7	6	10	32	33	62	53	66
11	Blackburn Rovers	46	10	9	4	33	20	5	8	10	22	31	55	51	62
12	Norwich City	46	11	6	6	26	22	3	9	11	19	28	45	50	57
13	Tranmere Rovers	46	10	8	5	35	27	5	4	14	22	41	57	68	57
14	Nottingham Forest	46	9	10	4	29	18	5	4	14	24	37	53	55	56
15	Crystal Palace	46	7	11	5	33	26	6	4	13	24	41	57	67	54
16	Sheffield United	46	10	8	5	38	24	3	7	13	21	47	59	71	54
17	Stockport County	46	8	8	7	33	31	5	7	11	22	36	55	67	54
18	Portsmouth	46	9	6	8	36	27	4	6	13	19	39	55	66	51
19	Crewe Alexandra	46	9	5	9	27	31	5	4	14	19	36	46	67	51
20	Grimsby Town	46	10	8	5	27	25	3	4	16	14	42	41	67	51
21	West Bromwich Alb.	46	6	11	6	25	26	4	8	11	18	34	43	60	49
22	Walsall	46	7	6	10	26	34	4	7	12	26	43	52	77	46
23	Port Vale	46	6	6	11	27	30	1	9	13	21	39	48	69	36
24	Swindon Town	46	5	6	12	23	37	3	6	14	15	40	38	77	36

2000/01 First Division

	FINAL TABLE	Pl.	Home W	Home D	Home L	Home F	Home A	Away W	Away D	Away L	Away F	Away A	F. (Total)	A. (Total)	Pts
1	Fulham	46	16	5	2	49	14	14	6	3	41	18	90	32	101
2	Blackburn Rovers	46	15	5	3	43	20	11	8	4	33	19	76	39	91
3	BOLTON WANDS.	46	10	10	3	40	28	14	5	4	36	17	76	45	87
4	Preston North End	46	12	6	5	32	18	11	3	9	32	34	64	52	78
5	Birmingham City	46	14	3	6	34	22	9	6	8	25	26	59	48	78
6	West Bromwich Alb.	46	13	5	5	37	23	8	6	9	23	29	60	52	74
7	Burnley	46	14	5	4	30	17	7	4	12	20	37	50	54	72
8	Wimbledon	46	7	11	5	33	26	10	7	6	38	24	71	50	69
9	Watford	46	11	6	6	46	29	9	3	11	30	38	76	67	69
10	Sheffield United	46	14	4	5	34	18	5	7	11	18	31	52	49	68
11	Nottingham Forest	46	11	3	9	28	24	9	5	9	27	29	55	53	68
12	Wolverhampton W.	46	7	9	7	25	20	7	4	12	20	28	45	48	55
13	Gillingham	46	9	6	8	32	28	4	10	9	29	38	61	66	55
14	Crewe Alexandra	46	12	5	6	30	24	3	5	15	17	38	47	62	55
15	Norwich City	46	10	7	6	25	18	4	5	14	21	40	46	58	54
16	Barnsley	46	11	3	9	32	26	4	6	13	17	36	49	62	54
17	Sheffield Wed.	46	9	4	10	34	38	6	4	13	18	33	52	71	53
18	Grimsby Town	46	10	4	9	26	27	4	6	13	17	35	43	62	52
19	Stockport County	46	6	11	6	29	26	5	7	11	29	39	58	65	51
20	Portsmouth	46	9	8	6	31	25	1	11	11	16	34	47	59	49
21	Crystal Palace	46	6	6	11	28	34	6	7	10	29	36	57	70	49
22	Huddersfield Town	46	7	6	10	29	26	4	9	10	19	31	48	57	48
23	Queen's Park Rangers	46	6	9	8	24	28	1	10	12	21	47	45	75	40
24	Tranmere Rovers	46	8	7	8	30	33	1	4	18	16	44	46	77	38

2001/02 Premier League

	FINAL TABLE	Pl.	Home W	Home D	Home L	Home F	Home A	Away W	Away D	Away L	Away F	Away A	F. (Total)	A. (Total)	Pts
1	Arsenal	38	12	4	3	42	25	14	5	0	37	11	79	36	87
2	Liverpool	38	12	5	2	33	14	12	3	4	34	16	67	30	80
3	Manchester United	38	11	2	6	40	17	13	3	3	47	28	87	45	77
4	Newcastle United	38	12	3	4	40	23	9	5	5	34	29	74	52	71
5	Leeds United	38	9	6	4	31	21	9	6	4	22	16	53	37	66
6	Chelsea	38	11	4	4	43	21	6	9	4	23	17	66	38	64
7	West Ham United	38	12	4	3	32	14	3	4	12	16	43	48	57	53
8	Aston Villa	38	8	7	4	22	17	4	7	8	24	30	46	47	50
9	Tottenham Hotspur	38	10	4	5	32	24	4	4	11	17	29	49	53	50
10	Blackburn Rovers	38	8	6	5	33	20	4	4	11	22	31	55	51	46
11	Southampton	38	7	5	7	23	22	5	4	10	23	32	46	54	45
12	Middlesbrough	38	7	5	7	23	26	5	4	10	12	21	35	47	45
13	Fulham	38	7	7	5	21	16	3	7	9	15	28	36	44	44
14	Charlton Athletic	38	5	6	8	23	30	5	8	6	15	19	38	49	44
15	Everton	38	8	4	7	26	23	3	6	10	19	34	45	57	43
16	BOLTON WANDS.	38	5	7	7	20	31	4	6	9	24	31	44	62	40
17	Sunderland	38	7	7	5	18	16	3	3	13	11	35	29	51	40
18	Ipswich Town	38	6	4	9	20	24	3	5	11	21	40	41	64	36
19	Derby County	38	5	4	10	20	26	3	2	14	13	37	33	63	30
20	Leicester City	38	3	7	9	15	34	2	6	11	15	30	30	64	28

1996/97 1st in Division One (promoted)

Manager: C.Todd

#	Mon	Date	Opponent	Score	Scorers	Att	Bergsson G	Blake N	Branagan K	Burnett W	Coleman S	Fairclough C	Frandsen P	Green S	Johansen M	Lee D	McAnespie S	McGinlay J	Paatelainen M	Phillips J	Pollock J	Sellars S	Sheridan J	Small B	Taggart G	Taylor S	Thompson A	Todd A	Ward G
1	Aug	17	Port Vale	1-1	Thompson	10057		9	1			6	4	2	7	A14		10		3		A8			5		11		
2		20	MANCHESTER CITY	1-0	Frandsen	18257		9	1			6	4	2	7	A14		10		3		A8			5		11		
3		24	NORWICH CITY	3-1	Blake(2), Johansen	13507		9	1	A13		6	4	A2	7	8		10		3					5		11		
4	Sep	1	Queen's Park Rangers	2-1	McGinlay, Thompson	11225		9	1			6	4		A7	8	2	10		3		A14			5		11		
5		7	Southend United	2-5	Blake, McGinlay	4475	B14	9	1			6	4		A7	C8	B2	10		3					5	C12	11	A13	
6		10	GRIMSBY TOWN	6-1	Johansen(2), Blake, Lee, Fairclough, Taylor	12448	A14	9	1			6	B4		7	C8	A2	10		3					5	C12	11	B13	
7		14	PORTSMOUTH	2-0	Blake, Fairclough	14248	B14	9	1			6	4		C7	A8	B2	10		3					5	A12	11	C13	
8		21	Bradford City	4-2	Thompson, Blake(2), Frandsen	12034	2	9	1			6	4		C7	C8		B10		3					5	B12	11	A13	
9		28	STOKE CITY	1-1	Blake	16195	2	9	1			6	4		B7	A14		C10		3		A8			5	C12	11	B13	
10	Oct	2	Wolves	2-1	McGinlay(2)	26540	5	9	1			6	4		7		2	10		3		8					11		
11		12	OLDHAM ATHLETIC	3-1	Johansen, McGinlay(2)	14813	2	B9	1			6	4		C7	C14		10		3		8			5	B12	A11	A13	
12		15	TRANMERE ROVERS	1-0	Sellars	14136	2	9	1			6	4		7			10		3		8			5		11		
13		19	Charlton Athletic	3-3	McGinlay(2), Blake	11091	2	9	1			6	4		7	A14		10		3		A8			5		11		
14		25	Barnsley	2-2	McGinlay, Thompson	9413	2	9	1			6	4		7			10		3		8			5		11		
15		29	READING	2-1	Sellars, McGinlay	12677	A2		1			6	4		B7	B12		10		3		8			5	9	11	A13	
16	Nov	2	HUDDERSFIELD TOWN	2-0	Thompson, McGinlay	15865		A9	1			6	4		7			10		3		8			5	A12	11	2	
17		13	Birmingham City	1-3	Sheridan	17033		9				6	A4		7	A14		10		3		8	11		5			2	1
18		16	CRYSTAL PALACE	2-2	Sheridan, McGinlay(pen)	16892	4	9	1			6		A13	7			10		3		A8	11		5			2	
19		19	Oxford United	0-0		7517	4	9	1			6			A7	A14		10		3		8	11		5			2	
20		22	Sheffield United	1-1	Blake	17069	2	9	1			6				7		10		3		8	11		5	4			
21		30	BARNSLEY	2-2	Blake, Thompson	16852	2	9	1			6			A14	B13		7		B3		8	A11		5	4	B13		
22	Dec	8	West Bromwich Albion	2-2	Frandsen, Fairclough	13082	2	9	1			6	4		A14	A7		10		3					5		11		
23		14	IPSWICH TOWN	1-2	Bergsson	13314	5		1			6	4	2	7	A12		10		3	A11	8				9			
24		22	Swindon Town	2-2	Green, McGinlay	8948	2	9				6	4	A14	A7			10		3		8	11		5				1
25		26	Grimsby Town	2-1	Taggart, Blake	8185	2	9				6	4		7			A10	A12	3		8	11		5				1
26		28	SOUTHEND UNITED	3-1	Sellars(2), McGinlay(pen)	16357	2	9				6	C4		A7			A14	B12	3	B11	8			5			C13	1
27	Jan	1	BRADFORD CITY	2-1	Lee, Sellars	16192	A2	9				6	4		B7	B14		10		3	11	8			5			A13	1
28		11	Portsmouth	3-0	Blake(2), Johansen	10467		9				6		A14	10	7				3	4	8	11		5			A2	1
29		18	WOI VFS	3-0	McGinlay, Curle(og), Blake	18980	2	9				6	A12		7			A10		3	4	8	11		5				1
30		29	Stoke City	2-1	Pollock, McGinlay	15645	2	9				6	7					10		3	4	8	11		5				1
31	Feb	1	BIRMINGHAM CITY	2-1	Pollock, McGinlay(pen)	16737	2	9				6	7		A13			10		3	4	A8			5		11		1
32		8	Reading	2-3	Thompson, McGinlay	10739	2					6	A7					10	B13	B3	4	8	11		5	A14	11		1
33		15	SHEFFIELD UNITED	2-2	Paatelainen, Fairclough	17922	2		1			6	7		A14			10	9	A4	4	8			5	9			
34		22	Huddersfield Town	2-1	Fairclough, Taggart	10661	2		A9	1		6	7		11			10	A13	3	4	8			5		11		
35	Mar	2	WEST BROMWICH ALBION	1-0	Blake	13258	2	9	1			6	7		A14	A11		10		3	4	8			5				
36		4	Crystal Palace	1-1	Fairclough	16035	2	9	1			6	C7		A14				B10	B13	3	4	A8	C12	5		11		
37		8	SWINDON TOWN	7-0	Thompson, Frandsen, Pollock, Bergsson(2), McGinlay, Blake	13981	2	9	1			6	A7		B14			10	C13	3	4	B8	A12		5		C11		
38		15	Ipswich Town	1-0	McGinlay	16187	A2	9	1			6	7					10		3	4	8	A12		5		11		
39		18	PORT VALE	4-2	Frandsen, Glover(og), Fairclough, Blake	14150		A9	1			6	7		4		2	10	A13	3		8			5		11		
40		22	Norwich City	1-0	Sellars	17585		9	1			6	7				2	10		3	4	8			5		11		
41	Apr	5	QUEENS PARK RANGERS	2-1	Fairclough, McGinlay	19198		C9	1			6	B7		A12		2	10	C13		A4	8	B14	3	5		11		
42		9	Manchester City	2-1	Paatelainen, Sellars	28026		9	1			6	7				2	A10	A13	3	4	8			5		11		
43		12	OXFORD UNITED	4-0	Thompson(2), Sellars, Blake	15994		9	1			6	C7	B13	A12		2		B10	A3	4	8	C14		5		A11		
44		19	Oldham Athletic	0-0		10702		9	1			6	C7				2		B10	A3	4	8	C14	A12	5	B13	11		
45		25	CHARLTON ATHLETIC	4-1	Thompson, Taggart, McGinlay(2,1pen)	22030	B2	C9	1			6	7		A4			B12	C10	C13	3	8	A14		5		11		
46	May	4	Tranmere Rovers	2-2	McGinlay, Pollock	14309	2	B9	C1			A6	7			B13		10			3	4	8	A14	5		11		C12

						Apps	30	42	36			46	40	7	24	13	11	43	3	36	18	40	12	10	43	2	34	6	10
						Subs	3			1			1	5	9	12	2		7		2	2	8	1		9		9	1
						Goals	3	19				8	5	1	5	2		24	2		4	8	2		3	1	11		

Two own goals

F.A. Cup

#	Mon	Date	Opponent	Score	Scorers	Att	Bergsson G	Blake N	Coleman S	Fairclough C	Frandsen P	Green S	Johansen M	Lee D	Pollock J	Sellars S	Sheridan J	Phillips J	Taggart G	Taylor S	Thompson A	Ward G
3	Jan	21	Luton Town	1-1	Pollock	7414	2	9	5	6	A12	A10	7		4	8	11	3				1
3r		25	LUTON TOWN	6-2	McGinlay, Blake(2), Thompson, Pollock, Green	9713	2	9		6	7	C14/B13			4	B8	A11	3	5	A12		1
4	Feb	5	CHESTERFIELD	2-3	Taylor, Green	10852		9		6	7	2	8	A12	4			3	5	A10	11	1

League Cup

#	Mon	Date	Opponent	Score	Scorers	Att	Bergsson G	Blake N	Branagan K	Fairclough C	Frandsen P	Green S	Johansen M	Lee D	McAnespie S	McGinlay J	Paatelainen M	Phillips J	Sellars S	Sheridan J	Taggart G	Taylor S	Thompson A	Todd A	Ward G
1/1	Sep	18	Bristol City	0-0		6351		9	1	6	4		7	a8	2	10		3			5		11	A13	
1/2		24	BRISTOL CITY	3-1	McGinlay, Blake, Thompson	6367	2	c9	1	6	4		a7	b8		10		3	A14		5	B12	11	C13	
3	Oct	22	CHELSEA	2-1	McGinlay, Blake	16867	2	9	1	6	4		7			A10		3	8		5	A12	11		
4	Nov	27	TOTTENHAM HOTSPUR	6-1	McGinlay(3,1p), Taggart, Blake, Taylor	18621	2	9	1	6		c14	7			A10		3	8	B11	5	A12	C4	B13	
5	Jan	8	WIMBLEDON	0-2		16968		9		6	4	a13	7			A10	B14	3	8	B11	5			2	1

Other Games

#	Mon	Date	Opponent	Score
1	Jul	19	Atherton LR	5-0
2		24	Queen of the South	3-1
3		27	Hull City	0-1
4		31	Wrexham	1-1
5	Aug	3	York City	2-0
6		6	Rotherham United	1-0
7		10	Carlisle United	0-1

1996-97 Season
(Back) McAnespie, Blake, Fairclough, Phillips, Paatelainen, Frandsen, Johansen, Branagan
(Front) Sellars, Sheridan, Taggart, Bergsson, McGinlay, Thompson

1997-98 Season
(Back) Spooner, Sheridan, Frandsen, Todd, Cox, Branagan, Glennon, Ward, Blake, Taylor, Coleman, Thompson
(Middle) Simpson, McAnespie, McGinlay, Fairclough, Taggart, Aljofree, Fish, Strong,
Whitehead, Doherty, Potter, Beardsley, Sellars, Dyson
(Front) Carroll, Johansen, Gunnlaugsson, Bergsson, Todd, Pollock, Holdsworth, Phillips, Brown

1997/98 18th in Premiership (relegated)

Manager: C.Todd

#		Date	Opponent	Score	Scorers	Att	Aljofree H (28)	Beardsley P (13)	Bergsson G (12)	Blake N (9)	Branagan K (1)	Carr F (32)	Cox N (2)	Elliott R (3)	Fairclough C (6)	Fish M (21)	Frandsen P (4)	Giallanza G (34)	Gunnlaugsson A (30)	Holdsworth D (23)	Johansen M (14)	McAnespie S (24)	McGinlay J (10)	Phillips J (18)	Pollock J (7)	Salako J (10)	Sellars S (8)	Sheridan J (15)	Strong G (26)	Taggart G (5)	Taylor R (33)	Taylor S (25)	Thompson A (11)	Todd A (17)	Ward G (16)	Whitlow M (22)
1	Aug	9	Southampton	1-0	Blake	15206		*	*	*	*		*				*						*		*		*			*			*			
2		23	Coventry City	2-2	Blake(2)	16633	BS	*	*	*	*		A*	*			*							B*	AS		*			*			*			
3		27	Barnsley	1-2	Beardsley	18236	*	*	*	*					B*		*				AS			BS	*	A*	*			*			*			
4	Sep	1	EVERTON	0-0		23131	C*	*	*	*			A*				B*				BS	AS	CS	*	*		*			*			*			
5		13	Arsenal	1-4	Thompson	38138	B*	*	*	*							*			BS				*	*		*			*			*	AS		
6		20	MANCHESTER UNITED	0-0		25000	AS	*	*	*					*	*							*	*		A*	*			*			*			*
7		23	TOTTENHAM HOTSPUR	1-1	Thompson(pen)	23433	*	*	*	*					*	*								*	*		*			*			*			*
8		27	Crystal Palace	2-2	Beardsley, Johansen	17134	*	*	*	*					*						AS			*	A*		*			*			*	*	*
9	Oct	4	ASTON VILLA	0-1		24196	*	*		*						*			AS	*			A*		*		*			*			*	*	*
10		18	West Ham United	0-3		24865	B*	*		*						*			*	AS	BS		A*		*		*			*			A*		*
11		26	CHELSEA	1-0	Holdsworth	24080	A*	*	*						*	*								*	AS		*			*			*			
12	Nov	1	LIVERPOOL	1-1	Blake	25000	A*	*	*	*	BS				*	B*	*		AS	*				*	*					*			*			*
13		8	Sheffield Wednesday	0-5		25027		*	*	*	BS				*	B*			*	*			A*	*						*			*	AS		*
14		22	Leicester City	0-0		20464		*	*	*					*	*			AS	*	A*			*						*			*	*		
15		29	WIMBLEDON	1-0	Blake	22703		*	*	*					*	*			AS	*				*	*					*			A*	*		
16	Dec	1	NEWCASTLE UNITED	1-0	Blake	24494		*	*	*					*	*								*	*					*			A*	*		
17		6	Blackburn Rovers	1-3	Frandsen	25503		*	*	B*					*	*			AS	A*				*	*					*			*	*	BS	*
18		14	DERBY COUNTY	3-3	Thompson(pen), Blake, Pollock	23027	B*	*	*						*				BS		AS			*	*	A*				*			*	*	*	
19		20	Leeds United	0-2		31163	*	*	*		AS				*						A*			*	*					*			*	*	*	
20		26	BARNSLEY	1-1	Bergsson	25000	*	*	*		CS				*	B*			AS		A*			*	*				BSC	*			*	*	*	
21		28	Everton	2-3	Bergsson, Sellars	37149	A*	*	*		BS	*		*	C*	*			ASB		CS			*	*					*			*	*	*	
22	Jan	10	SOUTHAMPTON	0-0		23333		*	*	*	BS	*			*				AS					*	B*	A*				*			*	*		
23		17	Newcastle United	1-2	Blake	36767		*	*	*		*			*	*			AS					*	*					A*			*	*		
24		31	COVENTRY CITY	1-5	Sellars	25000	BS	*	*	*			*	*	*					AS				*	B*	*	*			A*			*	*		
25	Feb	7	Manchester United	1-1	Taylor	55156		*	*	*			*		*					AS					*		*			A*	*		*			
26		21	WEST HAM UNITED	1-1	Blake	25000		*	*	*				*	A*	*			AS	*	*				*					*			*	*		
27	Mar	1	Tottenham Hotspur	0-1		29032		*	*	*				*	B*	*			AS	*	BS			*	A*					*			*	*		
28		7	Liverpool	1-2	Thompson	44532		*	*	*				*	*	*	*		*						*					*			*	*		
29		14	SHEFFIELD WEDNESDAY	3-2	Frandsen, Blake, Thompson(pen)	24847		*	*	*				*	*				*					*			*			*			*	*		
30		28	LEICESTER CITY	2-0	Thompson(2)	25000		*		*				*	*				A*	BS				*		ASB	*			*		*	*	*		
31		31	ARSENAL	0-1		25000		*	*	*				*	*				*	BS				B*	AS		*			*			*	A*		
32	Apr	4	Wimbledon	0-0		11356		*	*	*				*	*		B*		A*					*			BS			*		AS	*	*		
33		11	BLACKBURN ROVERS	2-1	Holdsworth, Taylor	25000	*		*	*			*	*	*		A*								*					*		AS	*	*		
34		13	Derby County	0-4		29126	*	CS	*	A*			B*	C*	*										BS		*			*			*	*	*	AS
35		18	LEEDS UNITED	2-3	Thompson, Fish	25000		*	*	*				*	*	BS							A*		AS	B*	*			*			*	*	*	
36		25	Aston Villa	3-1	Cox, Taylor, Blake	38392		*	*	*				BS	B*	A*	CS					AS			*					*	*	C*	*			
37	May	2	CRYSTAL PALACE	5-2	Blake,Fish,Phillips,Thompson,Holdsworth	24449		*	B*	*				*		*			AS	CS				*			BS			C*	*	A*	*			
38		10	Chelsea	0-2		34845		B*	*	*				*	*	*	AS			BS				*			CS			C*	*	A*	*			

	Aljofree	Beardsley	Bergsson	Blake	Branagan	Carr	Cox	Elliott	Fairclough	Fish	Frandsen	Giallanza	Gunnlaugsson	Holdsworth	Johansen	McAnespie	McGinlay	Phillips	Pollock	Salako	Sellars	Sheridan	Strong	Taggart	Taylor R	Taylor S	Thompson	Todd	Ward	Whitlow
Apps	2	14	34	35	34		20	4	10	22	38		2	17	4	1	4	21	25		22	12		14	10	1	33	23	4	13
Subs	3	1			5	1		1				3	13	3	12	1	3	1	7			1	2						2	2
Goals		2	2	12			1			2	2		3	1				1	1		2				3		9			

F.A. Cup

		Date	Opponent	Score		Att	Aljofree	Beardsley	Bergsson	Blake	Branagan	Carr	Cox	Elliott	Fairclough	Fish	Frandsen	Giallanza	Gunnlaugsson	Holdsworth	Johansen	McAnespie	McGinlay	Phillips	Pollock	Salako	Sellars	Sheridan	Strong	Taggart	Taylor R	Taylor S	Thompson	Todd	Ward	Whitlow
3	Jan	3	Barnsley	0-1		15042	BS	*	*				AS		*	*		*						B*	*								*	*	*	A*

League Cup

		Date	Opponent	Score	Scorers	Att	Aljofree	Beardsley	Bergsson	Blake	Branagan	Carr	Cox	Elliott	Fairclough	Fish	Frandsen	Giallanza	Gunnlaugsson	Holdsworth	Johansen	McAnespie	McGinlay	Phillips	Pollock	Salako	Sellars	Sheridan	Strong	Taggart	Taylor R	Taylor S	Thompson	Todd	Ward	Whitlow
1/1	Sep	16	Leyton Orient	3-1	Todd, Frandsen, McGinlay	4128		B*	*	*						*				AS	*		*	BS	*	A*	*						*	*		
1/2		30	LEYTON ORIENT	4-4	Blake(2), McGinlay(pen),Gunnaugs	6444	*		B*						*				ASC	A*	*	BS	*	*			CS						*	*	*	*
3	Oct	14	WIMBLEDON*	2-0	Pollock, McAllister(og)	9875	*	*		*					*				ASC			A*	*		*			*					*	*		*
4	Nov	18	Middlesbrough*	1-2	Thompson	22801	*	*	*	*					*	*			BS	AS				A*	B*								*	*		*

* After extra time

Other Games

#		Date	Opponent	Score
1	Jul	16	Crewe Alexandra	1-2
2		19	Notts County	4-3
3		22	Colchester United	1-1
4		25	Norwich	1-0
5		29	Bury	2-1
6	Aug	2	Port Vale	2-1
7	Oct	9	Rochdale	0-2

1998/99 6th in Division One

Manager: C.Todd

Player columns (left to right): Aljofree H, Banks S, Bergsson G, Blake N, Branagan K, Cox N, Elliott R, Fish M, Frandsen P, Fullarton J, Gardner R, Gudjohnsen E, Gunnlaugsson A, Hansen B, Holdsworth D, Jaaskelainen J, Jensen C, Johansen M, Nwesome J, Phillips J, Sellars S, Strong G, Taylor R, Taylor S, Todd A, Warhurst P, Whitlow M

#			Opponent	Score	Scorers	Att
1	Aug	8	Crystal Palace	2-2	Holdsworth, Gunnlaugsson	19029
2		15	GRIMSBY TOWN	2-0	Blake, Holdsworth	16584
3		23	Bradford City	2-2	Gunnlaugsson, Blake	13163
4		29	SHEFFIELD UNITED	2-2	Strong, Blake	18263
5	Sep	8	West Bromwich Albion	3-2	Gunnlaugsson, Blake, Gardner	15789
6		12	BIRMINGHAM CITY	3-1	Taylor(2), Frandsen	19637
7		19	Crewe Alexandra	4-4	Gunnlaugsson(2),Taylor,Frandsen	5744
8		26	HUDDERSFIELD TOWN	3-0	Frandsen, Blake, Gunnlaugsson	20971
9		29	SWINDON TOWN	2-1	Blake, Gunnlaugsson	16497
10	Oct	3	Barnsley	2-2	Gunnlaugsson, Johnsen	17382
11		17	OXFORD UNITED	1-1	Frandsen, Blake, Gunnlaugsson	17064
12		20	WATFORD	1-2	Gunnlaugsson	15921
13		23	Bristol City	1-2	Gunnlaugsson	12026
14	Nov	1	SUNDERLAND	0-3		21676
15		4	PORT VALE	3-1	Taylor, Frandsen, Gunnlaugsson	14324
16		7	Queens Park Rangers	0-2		11814
17		14	TRANMERE ROVERS	2-2	Johnsen, Holdsworth	16564
18		21	Ipswich Town	1-0	Taylor	17225
19		24	Stockport County	1-0	Taylor	8520
20		28	BURY	4-0	Gunnlaugsson(2)	21028
21	Dec	5	Wolves	1-1	Taylor	22537
22		12	Tranmere Rovers	1-1	Taylor	6959
23		19	PORTSMOUTH	3-1	Taylor, Frandsen, Holdsworth	15981
24		26	BRADFORD CITY	0-0		24625
25		28	Port Vale	2-0	Sellars, Holdsworth	8201
26	Jan	10	CRYSTAL PALACE	3-0	Taylor, Johansen, Jensen	15410
27		16	Sheffield United	2-1	Holdsworth(2)	15787
28		30	NORWICH CITY	2-0	Holdsworth, Cox	18766
29	Feb	6	Grimsby Town	1-0	Holdsworth	8674
30		13	WEST BROMWICH ALBION	2-1	Taylor, Cox	20657
31		21	Birmingham City	0-0		26051
32		27	CREWE ALEXANDRA	1-3	Holdsworth	19437
33	Mar	2	Huddersfield Town	2-3	Holdsworth, Johansen	13867
34		6	Swindon Town	3-3	Fish, Jensen, Gudjohnsen	8392
35		9	BARNSLEY	3-3	Sellars,Holdsworth(pen),Gudjohnse	16537
36		13	QUEENS PARK RANGERS	2-1	Taylor(2)	17919
37		20	Sunderland	1-3	Frandsen	41505
38	Apr	3	Oxford United	0-0		7547
39		5	STOCKPORT COUNTY	1-2	Taylor	18587
40		10	Watford	0-2		13001
41		13	BRISTOL CITY	1-0	Gudjohnsen	14459
42		17	IPSWICH TOWN	2-0	Taylor, Gudjohnsen	19894
43		20	Norwich City	2-2	Cox, Frandsen	11137
44		23	Bury	1-2	Cox, Frandsen	7680
45		30	WOLVES	1-1	Gardner	20208
46	May	9	Portsmouth	2-0	Johansen, Gudjohnsen	16015

Totals:

- Apps: Aljofree 1, Banks 9, Bergsson 15, Blake 11, Branagan 3, Cox 42, Elliott 14, Fish 36, Frandsen 44, Fullarton 1, Gardner 19, Gudjohnsen 8, Gunnlaugsson 22, Hansen 1, Holdsworth 22, Jaaskelainen 34, Jensen 44, Johansen 40, Nwesome 6, Phillips 14, Sellars 22, Strong 4, Taylor R 32, Todd 18, Warhurst 17, Whitlow 27
- Subs: Aljofree 3, Bergsson 2, Blake 1, Cox 2, Fish 8, Gudjohnsen 10, Gunnlaugsson 6, Hansen 5, Holdsworth 7, Johansen 10, Phillips 3, Sellars 1, Strong 3, Taylor R 1, Todd 6, Warhurst 2, Whitlow 1
- Goals: Bergsson 6, Blake 4, Fish 1, Frandsen 8, Gardner 2, Gudjohnsen 5, Gunnlaugsson 13, Holdsworth 12, Jensen 2, Johansen 7, Sellars 2, Strong 1, Taylor R 15

Play-offs

			Opponent	Score	Scorers	Att
SF1	May	16	IPSWICH TOWN	1-0	Johansen	18295
SF2		19	Ipswich Town*	3-4	Taylor(2), Frandsen	21755
F		31	Watford	0-2		70343

* After extra time, won on away goals, score at full time 2-3

F.A. Cup

			Opponent	Score	Scorers	Att
3	Jan	2	WOLVES	1-2	Sellars	18269

League Cup

			Opponent	Score	Scorers	Att
1/1	Aug	11	HARTLEPOOL UNITED	1-0	Taylor	6429
1/2		25	Hartlepool United	3-0	Blake(3)	3185
2/1	Sep	15	HULL CITY	3-1	Phillips, Gunnlaugsson, Frandsen	7544
2/2		22	Hull City	3-2	Jensen, Johansen, Gardner	4226
3	Oct	27	Norwich City*	1-1	Elliott	14189
4	Nov	10	WIMBLEDON	1-2	Jensen	7868

* After extra time, won 3-1 on penalties

Other Games

1	Jul	18	Galway	5-0
2		21	Waterford	2-3
3		24	Sligo Rovers	3-0
4		25	St. Patricks Athletic	1-0
5	Aug	1	Blackpool	1-2
6		4	CELTIC	1-1	Jimmy Phillips Testimonial
7	Oct	13	Leigh RMI	2-0

1998-99 Season
(Back) Aljofree, Phillips, Holdsworth, Frandsen, Branagan, Jaaskelainen, Ward, Strong, Cox, Whitlow
(Middle) Fish, Todd, Elliott, Jensen, Taylor, Spooner, Gunnlaugsson, Taylor, Beardsley
(Front) Johansen, Blake, Brown, Todd, Bergsson, Sellars

1999-2000 Season
(Back) Frandsen, Bergsson, Branagan, Jaaskelainen, Banks, Strong, Phillips
(Middle) Todd, Elliott, Hansen, Gudjohnsen, Cox, Warhurst, Whitlow, Taylor, Jensen
(Front) Holdsworth, Johansen, Carroll, Brown, Todd, Simpson, Page, Crombie, Gardner, Aljofree

1999/2000 6th in Division One

Manager: C.Todd to 22.09.99. S.Allardyce from 19.10.99

		Opponent	Score	Scorers	Att	19 Aljofree H	20 Banks S	4 Bergsson G	1 Branagan K	2 Cox N	15 Elliott R	23 Farrelly G	17 Fish M	18 Frandsen P	11 Gardner R	12 Gudjohnsen E	14 Hansen B	41 Holden D	10 Holdsworth D	30 Holloway D	22 Jaaskelainen J	8 Jensen C	7 Johansen M	32 Johnston A	36 Nolan K	24 Okane J	25 Passi F	16 Phillips J	31 Ritchie P	21 Strong G	9 Taylor R	6 Todd A	5 Warhurst P	3 Whittlow M
1	Aug 7	Tranmere Rovers	0-0		7674	AS			*	*						*	A*		*				*						BS			B*	*
2	14	QUEENS PARK RANGERS	2-1	Holdsworth(pen), Gudjohnsen	13019	AS			*	*					*	*			*				*						BS			B*	*
3	21	Ipswich Town	0-1		17696				*	*					*	*			*				*						*		*	*	*
4	28	MANCHESTER CITY	0-1		21671	AS			*	*	*				*	*	B*	BS				A*	*						*		*	*	*
5	Sep 5	BIRMINGHAM CITY	3-3	Frandsen(2), Holdsworth(pen)	11668			AS	*	*	*					BS			*				*					CS		A*	B*	C*	
6	11	Charlton Athletic	1-2	Johansen	19028			C*	*	*	*				*	BS	B*		A*				*						AS	*	CS	*
7	18	BARNSLEY	2-2	Tuttle(og), Gardner	14621			*	*	*	*				*	*			AS				*						A*	*		*	
8	25	NOTTINGHAM FOREST	3-2	Gardner, Holdsworth(pen), Cox	14978			*	*	*	*			*		*		AS	A*				*					*				*	
9	Oct 2	Swindon Town	4-0	Cox, Holdsworth, Gardner, Elliott	6711			*	*	*	*				*	B*			A*			AS	*					*	BS			*	
10	9	Wolves	0-1		18665	BS		*	*	*	C*			*		*		AS					B*					*	A*			*	CS
11	16	HUDDERSFIELD TOWN	1-0	Gardner	16603			*	A*	*	B*			*		*			C*		AS	*	*					*	CS	BS		*	
12	19	CREWE ALEXANDRA	2-2	Gudjohnsen, Holdsworth	12676			*		*				*		A*			*			*	*					*	*		*	AS	
13	24	Norwich City	1-2	Gardner	12468			*		*		A*		*	*	BS			*		*	B*					C*			AS	*	AS	CS
14	27	Nottingham Forest	1-1	Gudjohnsen	15572			*		*				*	A*				*		*	*	*						AS	*	*	*	
15	30	SWINDON TOWN	2-0	Taylor, Hansen	12486			*		*				*	B*	AS		A*		*	*	*						BS		*	*	
16	Nov 6	CRYSTAL PALACE	2-0	Gudjohnsen, Jensen	12744	CS		*				*		*		AS		A*		*	*	C*							BS	B*	*	
17	14	Sheffield United	2-1	Farrelly, Hansen	10013	AS		*				*		*		B*			*		*	A*							BS		*	*	
18	20	GRIMSBY TOWN	2-0	Hansen(2)	12415	*		*				*		*		*			*		*	*							*		*	*	
19	23	Fulham	1-1	Gudjohnsen	9642	*		*				*		*		C*	BS		*		*	A*		AS			B*		CS		*	*	
20	27	Portsmouth	0-0		10431			*				*		*		B*	A*	BS	*		*	A*		*					AS		*	*	
21	Dec 4	TRANMERE ROVERS	2-3	Gudjohnsen, Taylor	13534	*				AS		*		*		*	B*		*		*	A*							C*		*	*	
22	7	Blackburn Rovers	1-3	Elliott	21046					B*		*		*		*	*		AS	BS	*	A*			CS		*	C*		*	*	
23	18	STOCKPORT COUNTY	0-1		13285			*				*		*		*	*		AS	BS	*	B*							A*		*	*	
24	28	WEST BROMWICH ALBION	1-1	Jensen	16269			*				*		*		AS	*		BS		*			AS					B*		A*	*	
25	Jan 3	Walsall	0-2		6873			*				C*		*		AS			BS		*	*	A*	CS					B*		*	*	
26	15	Queens Park Rangers	1-0	Jensen	11396	*	*	*							A*			B*	AS		*	*		*	*		*		BS			*	
27	22	IPSWICH TOWN	1-1	Holdsworth(pen), Gudjohnsen	13266	*	*	*				AS			BS	*		*			B*	*		A*	*	*			B*		*	*	
28	Feb 5	BLACKBURN ROVERS	3-1	Bergsson, Johansen, Gudjohnsen	17687			*				*			A*	*		*	BS		*	*	C*	CS					B*		A*	*	
29	8	Port Vale	1-0	Gudjohnsen	5092			*				*	AS			*		*	BS		*	*		CS					CS		*	*	
30	12	Birmingham City	1-2	Johnston	18426			*				*	C*			*	BS		A*		*	*	B*		AS		*		CS		*	*	
31	22	PORTSMOUTH	3-0	Taylor, Jensen, Elliott	12672			*				*		B*	AS	*			CS		*	*	A*			BS			C*		*	*	
32	26	Barnsley	1-1	Holdsworth(pen)	14604			*				*		A*		*	BS	*	*		C*	AS			CS			B*			*	*
33	Mar 4	CHARLTON ATHLETIC	0-2		13788			*				*			AS	*			*		*	B*	BS		C*			A*			*	*
34	7	Crystal Palace	0-0		15236			*				*			*			*			B*	A*	CS	BS	AS			C*			*	*
35	11	FULHAM	3-1	Holdsworth(2,1pen), Gudjohnsen	12761			*				*			*			A*			*	*	AS					*			*	*
36	14	Stockport County	0-0		6412			*				*			*			A*			*	*						*		AS	*	*
37	18	Grimsby Town	1-0	Bergsson	5289			B*				AS				C*	BS	CS			*	*		*	A*				*		*	*	
38	21	SHEFFIELD UNITED	2-0	Johnston, Okane	11891			*				*				*		BSC	CS		*	*	B*		AS			*	*			A*	
39	25	PORT VALE	2-1	Gudjohnsen, Johnston	12292			*				*				*	BS		B*		*	*	A*	AS	*			*	*		*	
40	Apr 5	Manchester City	0-2		32927							*				*	BS		B*		*	*	C*	CS	A*	AS			*			*	*
41	8	WALSALL	4-3	Johansen(pen), Hansen(2), Phillips	11777			*			A*		B*			*	C*		CS		*	*	*			AS			*		BS	*	*
42	15	West Bromwich Albion	4-4	Hansen, Gudjohnsen, Bergsson(2)	12802			*			A*		*			*			BS		*	*	B*			AS			*		A*	*	*
43	22	Huddersfield Town	3-0	Hansen(2), Whittlow	16404			*				CS	B*			*	C*				*	*	*		AS	BS			*		A*	*	*
44	29	Crewe Alexandra	3-1	Gudjohnsen,Holdsworth(pen),Jensen	8015			*				CS	*			C*	B*		BS		*	*	*		AS	A*			*		*	*	*
45	May 3	WOLVES	2-1	Jensen, Gudjohnsen	18871			*				AS	*			*	B*		BS		*	*	C*			CS			*		*	*	*
46	7	NORWICH CITY	1-0	Holdsworth	17987			*				BS	*			C*	A*		AS		*		B*			CS			*		*	*	*

Additional players: M.Kaprielian 33/CS

	Apps	3	2	37	11	15	22	8	3	17	26	40	15	6	22	3	33	41	44	17		7	7	15	13	6	15	10	15	35
	Subs	5		1			5	3			3	1	15	6	13	1	1	1	2	4	4	8	8	1		12	4	2	4	2
	Goals			4		2	3	1		2	5	13	9		11				4	2		3	1		1		3			1

One own goal

Play-offs

SF1	May 14	IPSWICH TOWN	2-2	Holdsworth, Gudjohnsen	18814			*				CS		*		B*	BS		*			*	C*	*						AS	A*		*	*
SF2	16	Ipswich Town+	3-5	Holdsworth(2), Johnston	21543			*				*		*		CS			C*			*	B*	*						AS	BS		A*	*

+ After extra time

FA Cup

3	Dec 21	CARDIFF CITY	1-0	Gudjohnsen	5734	AS	*	*						*		*		*			*	*	*					*			A*		*	
4	Jan 8	Grimsby Town	2-0	Gudjohnsen, Hansen	4270	CS	*							*		C*	A*	B*	BS		*	*		*	*	*		*		AS		*		
5	29	Cambridge United	3-1	Taylor(2), Gudjohnsen	7523			*			*	CS			AS	BS		*	B*		*	*	*					A*		C*		*		
6	Feb 19	CHARLTON ATHLETIC	1-0	Gudjohnsen	20131			*				*			BS	*			*		*	*	C*	B*		CS		AS	A*			*		
SF	Apr 2	ASTON VILLA+	0-0		62000			B*				*		*		*			AS*	*	*		BS			*		AS			*			

+ After extra time, lost 1-4 on penalties

League Cup

1/1	Aug 10	Darlington	1-1	Frandsen	5361	BS			*	*				B*	*	*	A*		AS			*	*						*		*		
1/2	24	DARLINGTON	5-3	Gudjohnsen,Gardner,Taylor,Frandsen,Johansen(p)	4991	*			*	*				*	*	*			*				*						*	*			
2/1	Sep 14	Gillingham	4-1	Cox, Gudjohnsen(2), Bergsson	4996			*	B*	*	*				*	*			*				*				AS		*	*		BS	A*
2/2	21	GILLINGHAM	2-0	Hansen, Holdsworth	3673	C*	*	*	A*				AS	B*		*			*				*				*		*	*		*	
3	Oct 13	Derby County	2-1	Fish, Johansen	20242			*	*	*	*		*			*			*			*	*						*			*	
4	Nov 30	SHEFFIELD WEDNESDAY	1-0	Elliott	12543	*		A*		AS			*			*	B*	CS		*	*	*		C*				BS			*		
5	Dec 14	WIMBLEDON	2-1	Gudjohnsen, Johansen(pen)	9463	CS		*					*		C*	B*	BS	*		*	*	*					AS	A*			*		
SF1	Jan 12	TRANMERE ROVERS	0-1		13303		*	*						*	*	A*		AS		*	B*			*	*				BS			*	
SF2	26	Tranmere Rovers	0-3		15834		*	*			*			*	*	C*			*	BS			A*	*				CS		AS	B*

Additional Players: I.Potter 2/2,CS; I.Staton 2/2,BS

Other Games

1	Jul 17	Stoke City	1-2
2	21	Blackpool	1-1
3	24	Cambridge United	1-0
4	28	Wrexham	1-0
5	Aug 1	PRESTON NORTH END+	2-1

+ Abandoned

2000/01 3rd in Division One (promoted via play-offs)

Manager: S.Allardyce

Player columns (left to right): Banks S, Barness A, Bergsson G, Campbell A, Charlton S, Clarke M, Elliott R, Farrelly G, Fish M, Frandsen P, Fregaard C, Gardner R, Gope-Fenepej J, Hansen B, Hendry C, Holdsworth D, Jaaskelainen J, Marshall I, Morini E, Nolan K, O'Kane J, Passi F, Rankin I, Richardson I, Ricketts M, Smith J, Summerbee N, Warhurst P, Whitlow M, Wright T

#		Date	Opponent	Score	Scorers	Att
1	Aug	12	BURNLEY	1-1	Frandsen(pen)	20622
2		19	West Bromwich Albion	2-0	Rankin, Farrelly	17316
3		26	PRESTON NORTH END	2-0	Rankin, Ricketts	19954
4		28	Tranmere Rovers	1-0	Whitlow	9350
5	Sep	9	Huddersfield Town	3-2	Holdsworth, Richetts(2)	12248
6		12	Grimsby Town	1-0	Ricketts	3732
7		16	PORTSMOUTH	2-0	Holdsworth, Richetts	14113
8		23	Blackburn Rovers	1-1	Hansen	23660
9		30	FULHAM	0-2		19924
10	Oct	6	Gillingham	2-2	Hansen, O'Kane	9311
11		14	WOLVES	2-1	Holdsworth, Bergsson	15585
12		17	NOTTINGHAM FOREST	0-0		13017
13		21	Stockport County	3-4	Marshall(2), Richetts	8266
14		24	Watford	0-1		11799
15		28	CRYSTAL PALACE	3-3	Bergsson, Ricketts, Frandsen	12872
16		31	QUEENS PARK RANGERS	3-1	Bergsson, Elliott, Ricketts	10180
17	Nov	4	Birmingham City	1-1	Ricketts	20043
18		11	BARNSLEY	2-0	Ricketts, Gardner	13406
19		18	Norwich City	2-0	Ricketts, Bergsson	15224
20		25	Sheffield United	0-1		14962
21	Dec	3	WATFORD	2-1	Gardner, Marshall	13904
22		9	CREWE ALEXANDRA	4-1	Frandsen,Marshall,Bergsson,Nolan	12836
23		16	Wimbledon	1-0	Holdsworth	6076
24		23	Burnley	2-0	Ricketts(2)	19552
25		26	SHEFFIELD WEDNESDAY	2-0	Holdsworth, Hendry	21316
26		30	WEST BROMWICH ALBION	0-1		18986
27	Jan	1	Preston North End	2-0	Farrelly, Richetts	15863
28		13	TRANMERE ROVERS	2-0	Hansen, Hill(og)	15493
29		20	Sheffield Wednesday	3-0	Gardner, Ricketts, Marshall	17638
30	Feb	3	Queens Park Rangers	1-1	Frandsen	10283
31		10	HUDDERSFIELD TOWN	2-2	Bergsson, Frandswen	14866
32		13	Portsmouth	2-1	Ricketts, Frandsen	11337
33		20	GRIMSBY TOWN	2-2	Bergsson, Hansen	24249
34		23	BLACKBURN ROVERS	1-4	Richetts	20017
35	Mar	4	Fulham	1-1	Frandsen	16468
36		10	GILLINGHAM	3-3	Frandsen,Patterson(og),Holdsworth	13161
37		17	Nottingham Forest	2-0	Holdsworth, Farrelly	22162
38		31	WIMBLEDON	2-2	Elliott, Hendry	14562
39	Apr	3	STOCKPORT COUNTY	1-1	Hendry	12492
40		13	BIRMINGHAM CITY	2-2	Bergsson, Holdsworth	15025
41		16	Crystal Palace	2-0	Marshall, Kolinko(og)	16268
42		18	Crewe Alexandra	1-2	Holdsworth	8054
43		21	NORWICH CITY	1-0	Holdsworth	17967
44		28	Barnsley	1-0	Ricketts	13979
45	May	1	Wolves	2-0	Holdsworth, Ricketts	16242
46		6	SHEFFIELD UNITED	1-1	Holden	14836

Additional Players: C.Downey 46/AS, D.Holden 46/*(1 gl), N.Hunt 46/CS

League appearances (columns: Banks S, Barness A, Bergsson G, Campbell A, Charlton S, Clarke M, Elliott R, Farrelly G, Fish M, Frandsen P, Fregaard C, Gardner R, Gope-Fenepej J, Hansen B, Hendry C, Holdsworth D, Jaaskelainen J, Marshall I, Morini E, Nolan K, O'Kane J, Passi F, Rankin I, Richardson I, Ricketts M, Smith J, Summerbee N, Warhurst P, Whitlow M, Wright T):

	Banks S	Barness A	Bergsson G	Campbell A	Charlton S	Clarke M	Elliott R	Farrelly G	Fish M	Frandsen P	Fregaard C	Gardner R	Gope-Fenepej J	Hansen B	Hendry C	Holdsworth D	Jaaskelainen J	Marshall I	Morini E	Nolan K	O'Kane J	Passi F	Rankin I	Richardson I	Ricketts M	Smith J	Summerbee N	Warhurst P	Whitlow M	Wright T
Apps	8	17	44	3	18	8	31	36	13	35	1	27		38	22	22	27	13	1	25	25	14	9	5	24	1	9	19	7	3
Subs	1	3		3	4		2	5	1	4	4	5	2	3		9		23	1	6	2	9	7	7	15		3	1	1	1
Goals			8				2	3		7		3		5	3	11		6		1	1			2	19				1	

Three own goals

Play-offs

		Date	Opponent	Score	Scorers	Att
SF1	May	13	West Bromwich Albion	2-2	Bergsson, Frandsen(pen)	18167
SF2		17	WEST BROMWICH ALBION	3-0	Bergsson, Gardner, Ricketts	23515
F		28	Preston North End	3-0	Farrelly, Ricketts, Gardner	54328

FA Cup

		Date	Opponent	Score	Scorers	Att
3	Jan	6	YEOVIL TOWN	2-1	O'Kane, Ricketts	11161
4		28	SCUNTHORPE UNITED	5-1	Holdsworth(3), Nolan(2)	11737
5	Feb	17	BLACKBURN ROVERS	1-1	Ricketts	22048
5r	Mar	7	Blackburn Rovers	0-3		20318

Additional players: J.Sommer 5/*, P.Wheatcroft 4&5/CS

League Cup

		Date	Opponent	Score	Scorers	Att
1/1	Aug	22	MACCLESFIELD	1-0	Holdsworth	4957
1/2	Sep	6	Macclesfield	1-3	Ricketts	2235

Additional players: D.Norris 1/1,* & 1/2,*; P.Wheatcroft 1/2,CS

Other Games

		Date	Opponent	Score
1	Jul	12	Brondby	1-2
2		15	Lyngby	0-6
3		17	Odense	1-6
4		25	Indiana Blast *	2-0
5		30	USA U23 *	0-1
6	Aug	5	Bury	2-1
7		7	Chester	0-0

* In Indianapolis

League appearance marks (columns 1–30 = Banks S, Barness A, Bergsson G, Campbell A, Charlton S, Clarke M, Elliott R, Farrelly G, Fish M, Frandsen P, Fregaard C, Gardner R, Gope-Fenepej J, Hansen B, Hendry C, Holdsworth D, Jaaskelainen J, Marshall I, Morini E, Nolan K, O'Kane J, Passi F, Rankin I, Richardson I, Ricketts M, Smith J, Summerbee N, Warhurst P, Whitlow M, Wright T):

#	1	2	3	4	5	6	7	8	9	10	11	12	13	14	15	16	17	18	19	20	21	22	23	24	25	26	27	28	29	30
1		*	*					*	*	*				A*				*		AS			B*	*	*	BS				
2		*	*		A*			*	*	*				*	BS		*	CS			C*		B*	AS						
3		*	*					*	*	*				C*	A*		AS					B*	CS	BS				*		
4		*	*					*	*	*				C*	AS		*	A*				BS	CS	B*				*		
5		*	*					*		*				C*	B*		BS			*	*	A*	CS	AS				*		
6		*	*							*				C*	B*		*	CS		*	*	AS	BS					*		
7		*	*					*	B*	*				*	C*		BS	CS		*	A*		AS							
8		*	*					*	*	*				*	A*		AS	BS		B*	CS		C*							
9		B*	*		BS			*	*	*				C*	A*		AS			*	CS		*							
10	*		*		*		BS	C*	*					*	*			B*		CS	A*		AS							
11			C*		*		CS		AS	*				*	A*		*	*		*	B*		BS							
12					*		B*	*	*	*	AS			*	*		BS	*		A*	*									
13	BS		*		*		*	C*	*		AS	A*		*	*		CS	B*					*							
14	*	*			*		B*	AS	*	*			C*	*			*		BS	CS		A*								
15	C*	*		A*			*	AS	*	*				*			B*			CS		BS								
16		*					*	*	*	*				*			*			AS	*	BS								
17		*					*	*	B*	*				A*			*			*	AS			BS						
18		*					*	*	*					B*	AS		*	BS		*	A*			*						
19	*	*					*		AS	C*	CS			*			A*	BS		BS	*			*						
20		*					*	*	BS	A*				AS			*	B*		*	*			*						
21		*					*	*	BS	B*				*	AS		*	*	*	A*				*						
22		*					A*	CS	C*	AS				B*	*		BS	*		BS				*						
23		*					*	A*	*	BS				B*	B*		AS			AS				*						
24		*					*	BS	B*	A*				*	*	*	AS			AS				*						
25		*	BS				*	C*	*	A*				AS	*	CS	B*			B*				*						
26		*	BS				*	C*	*	AS	CS			B*			A*			A*				*						
27		*					*	C*	B*	BS	A*	AS		CS				*		CS				*						
28	AS	*					*	C*	*	A*	BS			B*				*		B*		CS		*						
29	AS	*					*	C*		BS				B*		CS	*	A*						*						
30	*	*			B*		BS	*	CS	*				A*	C*							AS								AS
31	*	*			*		BS	C*	*	AS	B*	CS						*		*	A*									
32	BS	*			*		*	*	ASC	*	B*	CS					A*													
33	*				*	*	AS	BS	*	B*	A*																			
34	*	BS			*		A*	*	A*	C*	B*	CS					AS													
35	*	*	A*		C*		B*	BS			*						AS	CS	*											
36	AS	*	*		*	B*	BS	*	*	CS							A*													
37	B*	*	CS		*		C*	A*		*	BS	AS																		
38	A*	*	*	BS	*	AS	C*	CS		*	B*																			
39	B*	*	*	AS	BS	*	*	CS		*	C* A*																			
40	BS	*	*		A*	AS	*	CS	C*		B*																			
41	*	*	*	BS	*		A*	B*			AS																			
42	*	CS	*	*	BS	C*	*	AS	A*		*			B*																
43	*	*	*	*	AS	*	A*		BS		B*																			
44	*	*	*	B*	BS	C*	AS				CS	A*																		
45	*	*	*	AS	*		A*	BS		B*		*																		
46	*				C*		* A*	BS	B*		*																			

2000-01 Season
(Back) Crombie, Richardson, Gardner, Elliott, Frandsen, Whitlow, Holdsworth, Barness, Wheatcroft
(Middle) Page, Warhurst, Holden, Bergsson, Glennon, Jaaskelainen, Banks, Fish, Nolan, Ricketts, Leather
(Front) Kaprielian, Passi, Charlton, O'Kane, Allardyce, Brown, Farrelly, Phillips, Hansen, Norris

2002
(Back) Ngotty, Jaaskelainen, Bergsson, Nolan, Farrelly, Bobic
(Front) Charlton, Djorkaeff, Barness, Frandsen, Wallace

2001/02 16th in the Premiership

Manager: S.Allardyce

#		Date	Opponent	Result	Scorers	Att	Bank S	Barnes A	Bergsson G	Bobic F	Charlton S	Diawara D	Djorkaeff Y	Espartero M	Farrelly G	Frandsen P	Gardner R	Hansen B	Hendry C	Holdsworth D	Jaaskelainen J	Johnson J	Konstantinidos K	Marshall I	Ngotty G	Nolan K	Pedersen H	Poole K	Ricketts M	Smith J	Southall N	Tofting S	Wallace R	Warhurst P	Whitlow M
1	Aug	18	Leicester City	5-0	Nolan(2), Ricketts, Frandsen(2)	19987		*	*							*	A*	*							CS		*			BS					B*	*
2		21	MIDDLESBROUGH	1-0	Ricketts	20747		*	*		*					*	*	*		BS	*				CS		C*			B*		AS			A*	*
3		27	LIVERPOOL	2-1	Ricketts, Holdsworth	27205		*	*		*	CS			BS	B*	*	*		AS	*						C*			A*					*	*
4	Sep	8	Leeds United	0-0		40153		*	*		*				*	*		A*		BS	*						*	*		B*					*	*
5		15	SOUTHAMPTON	0-1		24378		*	*		*				A*	CS	*			BS	*						C*	*		B*	AS				*	*
6		19	Blackburn Rovers	1-1	Wallace	25949		*	*		*					*	A*			AS	*				CS		C*	*		B*				BS	*	*
7		22	Arsenal	1-1	Ricketts	38014		*	*		*	BS				*				A*	*	*					*	C*		AS				CS	B*	*
8		29	SUNDERLAND	0-2		24520		*	*		*				AS	*	CS			*	*	C*					AS			BS				B*	*	*
9	Oct	13	NEWCASTLE UNITED	0-4		25631	A*		*		C*	CS				*	*			*	*	*			AS		*			BS	B*				*	*
10		20	Manchester United	2-1	Nolan, Ricketts	67559	BS	*	*							*	*	B*			*	AS					*			*					A*	*
11		27	Aston Villa	2-3	Ricketts(2)	33599	*	CS	*		*	*			B*	*	*	A*		BS					C*		*			*				AS			
12	Nov	3	EVERTON	2-2	Frandsen, Ricketts	27343			*		A*	AS			BS	*	*			CS					*	*		*	*					C*	B*	*
13		18	Ipswich Town	2-1	Bergsson, Ricketts	22335			*		*				AS	*	*			BS	*				*	*			*					B*	A*	*
14		24	FULHAM	0-0		23848			*		*				BS	B*	A*			AS	*				*	*			*					*	*	*
15	Dec	3	Tottenham Hotspur	2-3	Ricketts, Wallace	32971			*		*				B*	*	C*	BS		AS	*	CS			*	*			A*					*		*
16		8	Derby County	0-1		25712	*	*	*		*				AS	A*	*			BS	*	CS			*			*						B*	C*	*
17		15	CHARLTON ATHLETIC	0-0		20834			*		*					*	*			AS	*				*	*			*					A*	*	*
18		23	Chelsea	1-5	Nolan	34063			*		*				AS	A*	*	CS	*	VS		B*			*	*			*						C*	*
19		26	LEEDS UNITED	0-3		27060	C*		*	*					A*	*	*			*	*	BS			*	AS				CS				B*		*
20		29	LEICESTER CITY	2-2	Nolan, Ricketts	23037	A*			*	AS				B*	*		C*	*	*					*	*	CS			*	BS			*			
21	Jan	1	Liverpool	1-1	Nolan	43710			*	*					AS	*		A*	B*	*					*	*	BS			*	*			*		
22		12	CHELSEA	2-2	Ricketts, Nolan	23891	CS	*	AS	*	*				*	B*	BS				*				C*	*	A*			*	*					
23		19	Middlesbrough	1-1	Hansen	26104	AS	*	C*	B*					*	A*	*	BS			*				*	*	CS			*	*					
24		30	MANCHESTER UNITED	0-4		27350	*	*	C*	AS					*		*	B*		CS	*	BS			*					*	A*					*
25	Feb	2	Newcastle United	2-3	Gardner, Southall	52094	*	*	B*	*					*		*	CS		BS	*				A*	AS			C*	*						
26		9	WEST HAM UNITED	1-0	Gardner	24342		*	C*	*						*	*	CS		BS	*				*	*			B*	AS	*		A*			*
27		23	Southampton	0-0		31380		*	C*	A*		B*	CS			*	*	AS			*				*	*			*		*	BS				
28	Mar	2	BLACKBURN ROVERS	1-1	Wallace	27203	BS	*	A*		*					*				CS	*				*	*			AS	B*	C*					
29		5	Sunderland	0-1		43011	AS	*			*	CS				*				BS	*				*	S			B*	*	*	*	C*	A*		
30		16	DERBY COUNTY	1-3	Gardner	25893		A*	CS	*	*				BS	*					*				*				*	AS	C*	*	*	B*		
31		23	Charlton Athletic	2-1	Djorkaeff(2)	26358	*		B*	*					C*	*			A*	*				*	*			BS	AS				*			
32		30	ASTON VILLA	3-2	Delaney(og), Bobic, Nolan	24600		*	*		B*				A*	*			*			*		*	*			BS							*	AS
33	Apr	1	Everton	1-3	Ngotty	39784		B*	*		C*				AS	*			A*			*		*	*			BS				CS	*	*	
34		6	IPSWICH TOWN	4-1	Bobic(3), Djorkaeff	25817	*	C*	*		*				AS	B*			CS	*				*	*			BS				*	A*	*	
35		20	TOTTENHAM HOTSPUR	1-1	Holdsworth	25817		*	A*	*		*			*				AS	*				*	*			BS	*		B*		*		
36		23	Fulham	0-3		18107	*	*	B*	*		*	AS		*				CS	*				*	*			BS	A*		C*				
37		29	ARSENAL	0-2		27351	*	*	A*	*			*		*	*				*	BS				*	*			AS			B*			
38	May	11	West Ham United	1-2	Djorkaeff	35546	*	*	*	*			*		*	*			AS	*	C*				BS			A*	CS	B*				

Additional players: L.Richardson 4/AS

	Bank S	Barnes A	Bergsson G	Bobic F	Charlton S	Diawara D	Djorkaeff Y	Espartero M	Farrelly G	Frandsen P	Gardner R	Hansen B	Hendry C	Holdsworth D	Jaaskelainen J	Johnson J	Konstantinidos K	Marshall I	Ngotty G	Nolan K	Pedersen H	Poole K	Ricketts M	Smith J	Southall N	Tofting S	Wallace R	Warhurst P	Whitlow M
Apps	1	19	30	14	35	4	12		11	25	29	10	3	9	34	4	3		24	34	5	3	26		10	6	14	25	28
Subs	6		2	1	5		3	7	4	2	7		22		6		2	2	1	6			11	1	8		5		1
Goals		1	4			4				3	3	1		2					1	8			12		1		3		

One own goal

F.A. Cup

		Date	Opponent	Result	Scorers	Att	Bank S	Barnes A	Bergsson G	Bobic F	Charlton S	Diawara D	Djorkaeff Y	Espartero M	Farrelly G	Frandsen P	Gardner R	Hansen B	Hendry C	Holdsworth D	Jaaskelainen J	Johnson J	Konstantinidos K	Marshall I	Ngotty G	Nolan K	Pedersen H	Poole K	Ricketts M	Smith J	Southall N	Tofting S	Wallace R	Warhurst P	Whitlow M
3	Jan	16	Stockport County	4-1	Bergsson,Fradin(og),Pedersen,Ricketts	5821	*	A*							*		*	*					*/			AS	*		BS		*		B*		
4	Feb	5	Tottenham Hotspur	0-4		27093	*	*							*		*	*		BS	*	CS			C*	*			B*		*				A*

Additional players: W.Buchanan 4/AS, D.Norris 3/C*, C.Taylor 3/CS, J.Viander 3/*

League Cup

		Date	Opponent	Result	Scorers	Att	Bank S	Barnes A	Bergsson G	Bobic F	Charlton S	Diawara D	Djorkaeff Y	Espartero M	Farrelly G	Frandsen P	Gardner R	Hansen B	Hendry C	Holdsworth D	Jaaskelainen J	Johnson J	Konstantinidos K	Marshall I	Ngotty G	Nolan K	Pedersen H	Poole K	Ricketts M	Smith J	Southall N	Tofting S	Wallace R	Warhurst P	Whitlow M
2	Sep	11	WALSALL*	4-3	Ricketts,Holdsworth,Nishizawa,Pedersen	5761	*								C*				*	*				*		AS	CS		BS	A*	*				
3	Oct	8	NOTTINGHAM FOREST	1-0	Wallace	6881				*	B*					*	*	AS	*				A*	*	*			CS			*		C*		
4	Nov	27	SOUTHAMPTON * #	2-2	Holdsworth(pen), Ricketts	8404	*				*				*		*	*	C*	*	B*			BS		*		CS			*		AS	*	
5	Dec	11	Tottenham Hotspur	0-6		28430	*								*	C*	BS	*	*	*	*			A*		*				*			CS		AS

* After extra time. # Won 6-5 on penalties.

Additional players: D.Holden 2/*; Nishizawa 2/*, 4/A*, 5/B*; D.Norris 2/B*, 3/BS; L.Richardson 2 & 3/*

Other Games

		Date	Opponent	Result
1	Jul	14	Radcliffe Borough	3-1
2		30	Boston United	4-3
3		31	Halifax Town	1-0
4	Aug	3	Athletic Bilbao	0-1
5		7	Deportivo Alaves	0-1

Football League Opponents Record: 1888-89 to 2001/02

Opponents	Home						Away						Total					
	P	W	D	L	F	A	P	W	D	L	F	A	P	W	D	L	F	A
1 ACCRINGTON	5	3	0	2	20	11	5	2	1	2	9	8	10	5	1	4	29	19
2 ALDERSHOT	2	1	1	0	3	2	2	1	0	1	3	1	4	2	1	1	6	3
3 ARSENAL	49	24	13	12	87	63	49	7	14	28	48	111	98	31	27	40	135	174
4 ASTON VILLA	66	36	13	17	129	69	66	15	15	36	86	142	132	51	28	53	215	211
5 BARNSLEY	16	9	5	2	40	17	16	3	6	7	18	23	32	12	11	9	58	40
6 BIRMINGHAM CITY	51	29	16	6	110	49	51	11	14	26	57	91	102	40	30	32	167	140
7 BLACKBURN ROVERS	63	36	14	13	113	73	63	17	12	34	89	132	126	53	26	47	202	205
8 BLACKPOOL	42	23	8	11	71	42	42	11	15	16	49	57	84	34	23	27	120	99
9 BOURNEMOUTH	9	4	2	3	11	7	9	3	1	5	10	16	18	7	3	8	21	23
10 BRADFORD PA	7	3	0	4	8	8	7	3	1	3	10	12	14	6	1	7	18	20
11 BRADFORD CITY	20	9	7	4	33	18	20	4	6	10	34	45	40	13	13	14	67	63
12 BRENTFORD	16	8	3	5	22	17	16	2	4	10	17	34	32	10	7	15	39	51
13 BRIGHTON & HA	4	0	2	2	2	5	4	1	1	2	5	7	8	1	3	4	7	12
14 BRISTOL CITY	25	11	6	8	30	30	25	3	8	14	26	46	50	14	14	22	56	76
15 BRISTOL ROVERS	13	8	3	2	23	8	13	2	4	7	12	19	26	10	7	9	35	27
16 BURNLEY	55	25	17	13	97	56	55	14	12	29	56	96	110	39	29	42	153	152
17 BURTON UNITED	3	3	0	0	15	1	3	2	0	1	7	4	6	5	0	1	22	5
18 BURY	31	17	4	10	57	46	31	6	10	15	41	50	62	23	14	25	98	96
19 CAMBRIDGE UNITED	6	2	3	1	15	9	6	2	2	2	10	10	12	4	5	3	25	19
20 CARDIFF CITY	32	20	6	6	61	25	32	12	5	15	39	37	64	32	11	21	100	62
21 CARLISLE UNITED	12	6	2	4	22	11	12	2	3	7	9	23	24	8	5	11	31	34
22 CHARLTON ATHLETIC	32	24	4	4	72	27	32	8	6	18	39	54	64	32	10	22	111	81
23 CHELSEA	44	22	13	9	90	59	44	11	10	23	52	77	88	33	23	32	142	136
24 CHESTER CITY	6	3	2	1	8	2	6	2	3	1	5	4	12	5	5	2	13	6
25 CHESTERFIELD	9	8	0	1	25	6	9	2	4	3	9	11	18	10	4	4	34	17
26 COLCHESTER UNITED	1	1	0	0	4	0	1	0	0	1	0	3	2	1	0	1	4	3
27 COVENTRY CITY	7	1	3	3	9	14	7	1	5	1	10	10	14	2	8	4	19	24
28 CREWE ALEXANDRA	6	2	3	1	11	9	6	2	2	2	14	12	12	4	5	3	25	21
29 CRYSTAL PALACE	16	9	7	0	32	12	16	2	7	7	17	23	32	11	14	7	49	35
30 DARLINGTON	4	2	1	1	7	7	4	2	0	2	4	4	8	4	1	3	11	11
31 DARWEN	2	2	0	0	2	0	2	2	0	0	5	2	4	4	0	0	7	2
32 DERBY COUNTY	56	30	6	20	110	76	56	8	11	37	61	131	112	38	17	57	171	207
33 DONCASTER ROVERS	4	3	0	1	7	2	4	1	1	2	5	6	8	4	1	3	12	8
34 EVERTON	59	23	12	24	90	88	59	7	16	36	67	114	118	30	28	60	157	202
35 EXETER CITY	5	4	0	1	8	3	5	1	3	1	9	8	10	5	3	2	17	11
36 FULHAM	28	15	7	6	41	29	28	9	8	11	35	43	56	24	15	17	76	72
37 GAINSBOROUGH	5	5	0	0	20	1	5	1	1	3	7	7	10	6	1	3	27	8
38 GILLINGHAM	6	2	1	3	9	8	6	2	1	3	7	9	12	4	2	6	16	17
39 GLOSSOP	4	3	0	1	10	1	4	3	1	0	9	5	8	6	1	1	19	6
40 GRIMSBY TOWN	27	13	7	7	58	32	27	8	10	9	27	38	54	21	17	16	85	70
41 HALIFAX TOWN	3	2	1	0	6	1	3	1	2	0	2	1	6	3	3	0	8	2
42 HARTLEPOOL UNITED	3	0	1	2	4	6	3	2	1	0	6	0	6	2	2	2	10	6
43 HEREFORD UNITED	2	2	0	0	4	1	2	1	1	0	6	3	4	3	1	0	10	4
44 HUDDERSFIELD TOWN	42	25	10	7	86	42	42	10	8	24	38	59	84	35	18	31	124	101
45 HULL CITY	18	12	5	1	30	11	18	3	8	7	17	24	36	15	13	8	47	35
46 IPSWICH TOWN	15	5	5	5	25	17	15	5	2	8	22	28	30	10	7	13	47	45
47 LEEDS UNITED	24	15	4	5	51	24	24	5	6	13	35	51	48	20	10	18	86	75
48 LEICESTER CITY	29	17	6	6	71	35	29	6	10	13	34	55	58	23	16	19	105	90
49 LINCOLN CITY	8	4	1	3	15	9	8	2	3	3	8	8	16	6	4	6	23	17
50 LIVERPOOL	49	23	11	15	71	61	49	10	16	23	53	89	98	33	27	38	124	150

51	LOUGHBOROUGH	1	1	0	0	7	0	1	1	0	0	3	2	2	2	0	0	10	2
52	LUTON TOWN	15	9	3	3	31	18	15	4	5	6	14	13	30	13	8	9	45	31
53	MANCHESTER CITY	46	25	12	9	94	54	46	10	10	26	54	87	92	35	22	35	148	141
54	MANCHESTER UNITED	49	24	12	13	88	62	49	15	10	24	56	83	98	39	22	37	144	145
55	MANSFIELD TOWN	7	3	3	1	8	4	7	2	3	2	6	9	14	5	6	3	14	13
56	MIDDLESBROUGH	47	30	11	6	104	54	47	14	11	22	58	85	94	44	22	28	162	139
57	MILLWALL	14	10	2	2	32	10	14	1	1	12	7	30	28	11	3	14	39	40
58	NEW BRIGHTON	1	1	0	0	2	1	1	0	0	1	1	3	2	1	0	1	3	4
59	NEWCASTLE UNITED	47	22	12	13	74	71	47	11	4	32	48	102	94	33	16	45	122	173
60	NEWPORT COUNTY	5	3	0	2	15	5	5	3	0	2	8	7	10	6	0	4	23	12
61	NORTHAMPTON TOWN	4	1	1	2	3	6	4	2	0	2	6	8	8	3	1	4	9	14
62	NORWICH CITY	16	9	5	2	25	10	16	3	3	10	14	25	32	12	8	12	39	35
63	NOTTS COUNTY	38	21	8	9	76	40	38	10	13	15	44	50	76	31	21	24	120	90
64	NOTTINGHAM FOREST	35	22	9	4	72	32	35	7	9	19	35	64	70	29	18	23	107	96
65	OLDHAM ATHLETIC	22	17	3	2	51	17	22	4	9	9	29	38	44	21	12	11	80	55
66	ORIENT	20	14	4	2	27	8	20	4	7	9	18	28	40	18	11	11	45	36
67	OXFORD UNITED	10	5	3	2	14	8	10	2	4	4	8	14	20	7	7	6	22	22
68	PETERBOROUGH UTD	3	2	1	0	5	2	3	2	0	1	7	3	6	4	1	1	12	5
69	PLYMOUTH ARGYLE	14	10	1	3	35	14	14	4	1	9	14	25	28	14	2	12	49	39
70	PORTSMOUTH	39	28	5	6	90	33	39	6	13	20	38	63	78	34	18	26	128	96
71	PORT VALE	15	13	2	0	40	7	15	7	7	1	22	13	30	20	9	1	62	20
72	PRESTON NORTH END	59	26	13	20	94	84	59	17	17	25	76	88	118	43	30	45	170	172
73	QPR	12	8	2	2	25	17	12	4	1	7	14	23	24	12	3	9	39	40
74	READING	9	6	2	1	16	7	9	2	1	6	8	14	18	8	3	7	24	21
75	ROCHDALE	3	2	1	0	4	2	3	0	3	0	6	6	6	2	4	0	10	8
76	ROTHERHAM UNITED	15	5	6	4	18	16	15	1	5	9	10	24	30	6	11	13	28	40
77	SCARBOROUGH	1	1	0	0	3	1	1	0	0	1	0	4	2	1	0	1	3	5
78	SCUNTHORPE UNITED	3	0	3	0	0	0	3	0	2	1	2	3	6	0	5	1	2	3
79	SHEFFIELD UNITED	53	33	12	8	116	60	53	11	9	33	66	123	106	44	21	41	182	183
80	SHEFFIELD WEDS	49	26	11	12	79	63	49	8	10	31	44	100	98	34	21	43	123	163
81	SHREWSBURY TOWN	8	4	1	3	8	8	8	4	1	3	11	9	16	8	2	6	19	17
82	SOUTHAMPTON	13	8	2	3	24	8	13	4	4	5	14	18	26	12	6	8	38	26
83	SOUTHEND UNITED	7	4	2	1	10	4	7	2	2	3	8	11	14	6	4	4	18	15
84	STOCKPORT COUNTY	9	3	3	3	12	10	9	3	2	4	11	13	18	6	5	7	23	23
85	STOKE CITY	36	17	11	8	67	43	36	11	6	19	35	73	72	28	17	27	102	116
86	SUNDERLAND	59	33	14	12	109	68	59	9	12	38	61	140	118	42	26	50	170	208
87	SWANSEA CITY	14	7	6	1	16	9	14	3	3	8	13	22	28	10	9	9	29	31
88	SWINDON TOWN	9	5	1	3	18	8	9	3	3	3	18	16	18	8	4	6	36	24
89	TORQUAY UNITED	3	2	0	1	4	2	3	0	1	2	2	5	6	2	1	3	6	7
90	TOTTENHAM HOTSPUR	34	18	5	11	57	44	34	7	6	21	36	66	68	25	11	32	93	110
91	TRANMERE ROVERS	11	8	2	1	18	8	11	2	6	3	10	11	22	10	8	4	28	19
92	WALSALL	9	7	1	1	25	9	9	0	3	6	9	17	18	7	4	7	34	26
93	WATFORD	9	5	1	3	16	10	9	0	3	6	6	16	18	5	4	9	22	26
94	WEST BROMWICH ALB	62	31	16	15	114	64	62	15	21	26	92	118	124	46	37	41	206	182
95	WEST HAM UNITED	21	14	4	3	49	18	21	5	2	14	30	52	42	19	6	17	79	70
96	WIGAN ATHLETIC	9	4	2	3	12	11	9	3	2	4	10	10	18	7	4	7	22	21
97	WIMBLEDON	4	3	1	0	6	2	4	1	1	2	3	7	8	4	2	2	9	9
98	WOLVERHAMPTON W	56	32	10	14	110	70	56	11	10	35	58	132	112	43	20	49	168	202
99	WREXHAM	5	3	1	1	6	3	5	4	0	1	8	4	10	7	1	2	14	7
100	YORK CITY	7	3	2	2	11	7	7	4	1	2	10	7	14	7	3	4	21	14

2078	1142	467	469	3885	2262	2078	486	527	1065	2399	3727	4156	1628	994	1534	6284	5989

NEUTRAL PLAY OFF

4	2	0	2	7	6

TOTAL

4160	1630	994	1536	6291	5995

Seasonal Football League Record: 1888-89 to 2001-02

	Season	P	Home W	D	L	F	A	Away W	D	L	F	A	Pts.	Pos.	Div.
1	1888/89	22	6	0	5	35	30	4	2	5	28	29	22	5	1
2	1889/90	22	6	1	4	37	24	3	0	8	17	41	19	9	1
3	1890/91	22	9	0	2	36	14	3	1	7	11	20	25	5	1
4	1891/92	26	9	2	2	29	14	8	0	5	22	23	36	3	1
5	1892/93	30	12	1	2	43	21	1	5	9	13	34	32	5	1
6	1893/94	30	7	3	5	18	14	3	1	11	20	38	24	13	1
7	1894/95	30	8	3	4	45	23	1	4	10	16	39	25	10	1
8	1895/96	30	12	2	1	34	14	4	3	8	15	23	37	4	1
9	1896/97	30	7	3	5	22	18	5	3	7	18	25	30	8	1
10	1897/98	30	9	2	4	18	13	2	2	11	10	28	26	11	1
11	1898/99	34	6	5	6	24	21	3	2	12	13	30	25	17	1
12	1899/00	34	14	2	1	47	7	8	6	3	32	18	52	2	2
13	1900/01	34	10	5	2	21	12	3	2	12	18	43	33	10	1
14	1901/02	34	10	6	1	38	17	2	2	13	13	39	32	12	1
15	1902/03	34	6	2	9	18	20	2	1	14	19	53	19	18	1
16	1903/04	34	10	3	4	38	11	2	7	8	21	30	34	7	2
17	1904/05	34	15	0	2	53	16	12	2	3	34	16	56	2	2
18	1905/06	38	13	1	5	51	22	4	6	9	30	45	41	6	1
19	1906/07	38	10	4	5	35	18	8	4	7	24	29	44	6	1
20	1907/08	38	10	3	6	35	26	4	2	13	17	32	33	19	1
21	1908/09	38	14	3	2	37	8	10	1	8	22	20	52	1	2
22	1909/10	38	7	2	10	31	34	2	4	13	13	37	24	20	1
23	1910/11	38	17	2	0	53	12	4	7	8	16	28	51	2	2
24	1911/12	38	14	2	3	35	15	6	1	12	19	28	43	4	1
25	1912/13	38	10	6	3	36	20	6	4	9	26	43	42	8	1
26	1913/14	38	13	4	2	41	14	3	6	10	24	38	42	6	1
27	1914/15	38	8	5	6	35	27	3	3	13	33	57	30	17	1
28	1919/20	42	11	3	7	35	29	8	6	7	37	36	47	6	1
29	1920/21	42	15	6	0	53	17	4	8	9	24	36	52	3	1
30	1921/22	42	12	4	5	40	24	8	3	10	28	35	47	6	1
31	1922/23	42	11	8	2	36	17	3	4	14	14	41	40	13	1
32	1923/24	42	13	6	2	45	13	5	8	8	23	21	50	4	1
33	1924/25	42	18	2	1	61	13	4	9	8	15	21	55	3	1
34	1925/26	42	11	6	4	46	31	6	4	11	29	45	44	8	1
35	1926/27	42	15	5	1	54	19	4	5	12	30	43	48	4	1
36	1927/28	42	12	5	4	47	26	4	6	11	34	40	43	7	1
37	1928/29	42	10	6	5	44	25	4	6	11	29	55	40	14	1
38	1929/30	42	11	5	5	46	24	4	4	13	28	50	39	15	1
39	1930/31	42	12	6	3	45	26	3	3	15	23	55	39	14	1
40	1931/32	42	15	1	5	51	25	2	3	16	21	55	38	17	1
41	1932/33	42	10	7	4	49	33	2	2	17	29	59	33	21	1
42	1933/34	42	14	2	5	45	22	7	7	7	34	33	51	3	2
43	1934/35	42	17	1	3	63	15	9	3	9	33	33	56	2	2
44	1935/36	42	11	4	6	41	27	3	9	9	26	49	41	13	1
45	1936/37	42	6	6	9	22	33	4	8	9	21	33	34	20	1
46	1937/38	42	11	6	4	38	22	4	9	8	26	38	45	7	1
47	1938/39	42	10	6	5	39	25	5	9	7	28	33	45	8	1
48	1946/47	42	8	5	8	30	28	5	3	13	27	41	34	18	1
49	1947/48	42	11	2	8	29	25	5	3	13	17	33	37	17	1
50	1948/49	42	10	4	7	43	32	4	6	11	16	36	38	14	1
51	1949/50	42	10	5	6	34	22	0	9	12	11	37	34	16	1
52	1950/51	42	11	2	8	31	20	8	5	8	33	41	45	8	1
53	1951/52	42	11	7	3	35	26	8	3	10	30	35	48	5	1
54	1952/53	42	9	4	8	39	35	6	5	10	22	34	39	14	1
55	1953/54	42	14	6	1	45	20	4	6	11	30	40	48	5	1
56	1954/55	42	11	6	4	45	29	2	7	12	17	40	39	18	1
57	1955/56	42	13	3	5	50	24	5	4	12	21	34	43	8	1
58	1956/57	42	13	6	2	42	23	3	6	12	23	42	44	9	1
59	1957/58	42	9	5	7	38	35	5	5	11	27	52	38	15	1

		P	W	D	L	F	A	W	D	L	F	A			
60	1958/59	42	14	3	4	56	30	6	7	8	23	36	50	4	1
61	1959/60	42	12	5	4	37	27	8	3	10	22	24	48	6	1
62	1960/61	42	9	5	7	38	29	3	6	12	20	44	35	18	1
63	1961/62	42	11	7	3	35	22	5	3	13	27	44	42	11	1
64	1962/63	42	13	3	5	35	18	2	2	17	20	57	35	18	1
65	1963/64	42	6	5	10	30	35	4	3	14	18	45	28	21	1
66	1964/65	42	13	6	2	46	17	7	4	10	34	41	50	3	2
67	1965/66	42	12	2	7	43	25	4	7	10	19	34	41	9	2
68	1966/67	42	10	7	4	36	19	4	7	10	28	39	42	9	2
69	1967/68	42	8	6	7	37	28	5	7	9	23	35	39	12	2
70	1968/69	42	8	7	6	29	26	4	7	10	26	41	38	17	2
71	1969/70	42	9	6	6	31	23	3	6	12	23	38	36	16	2
72	1970/71	42	6	5	10	22	31	1	5	15	13	43	24	22	2
73	1971/72	46	11	8	4	25	13	6	8	9	26	28	50	7	3
74	1972/73	46	18	4	1	44	9	7	7	9	29	30	61	1	3
75	1973/74	42	12	5	4	30	17	3	7	11	14	23	42	11	2
76	1974/75	42	9	7	5	27	16	6	5	10	18	25	42	10	2
77	1975/76	42	12	5	4	36	14	8	7	6	28	24	52	4	2
78	1976/77	42	15	2	4	46	21	5	9	7	29	33	51	4	2
79	1977/78	42	16	4	1	39	14	8	6	7	24	19	58	1	2
80	1978/79	42	10	5	6	36	28	2	6	13	18	47	35	17	1
81	1979/80	42	5	11	5	19	21	0	4	17	19	52	25	22	1
82	1980/81	42	10	5	6	40	27	4	5	12	21	39	38	18	2
83	1981/82	42	10	4	7	28	24	3	3	15	11	37	46	19	2
84	1982/83	42	10	2	9	30	26	1	9	11	12	35	44	22	2
85	1983/84	46	13	4	6	36	17	5	6	12	20	43	64	10	3
86	1984/85	46	12	5	6	38	22	4	1	18	31	53	54	17	3
87	1985/86	46	10	4	9	35	30	5	4	14	19	38	53	18	3
88	1986/87*	48	8	6	10	31	28	2	10	12	17	33	45	21	3
89	1987/88	46	15	6	2	42	12	7	6	10	24	30	78	3	4
90	1988/89	46	12	8	3	42	23	4	8	11	16	31	64	10	3
91	1989/90*	48	12	8	4	33	20	6	8	10	27	31	69	6	3
92	1990/91*	49	15	5	4	34	18	10	7	8	32	34	83	4	3
93	1991/92	46	10	9	4	26	19	4	8	11	31	37	59	13	3
94	1992/93	46	18	2	3	48	14	9	7	7	32	27	90	2	2
95	1993/94	46	10	8	5	40	31	5	6	12	23	33	59	14	1
96	1994/95*	49	17	6	1	45	13	6	8	11	29	37	77	3	1
97	1995/96	38	5	4	10	16	31	3	1	15	23	40	29	20	pl
98	1996/97	46	18	4	1	60	20	10	10	3	40	33	98	1	1
99	1997/98	38	7	8	4	25	22	2	5	12	16	39	40	18	pl
100	1998/99*	49	14	6	4	45	25	7	10	8	37	40	76	6	1
101	1999/2000*	48	14	6	4	45	28	7	8	9	29	29	76	6	1
102	2000/01*	49	11	10	3	43	28	15	6	4	41	19	87	3	1
103	2001/02	38	5	7	7	20	31	4	6	9	24	31	40	16	pl
	Totals	4160	1142	467	469	3885	2262	488	527	1067	2406	3733			

* inc play offs   3 points for a win commenced from 1986-87

1986/87	Aldershot 1 Bolton 0	1994/95	Wolves 2 Bolton 1		1999/00	Bolton 2 Ipswich 2	
	Bolton 2 Aldershot 2 aet		Bolton 2 Wolves 0	aet		Ipswich 5 Bolton 3	aet
1989/90	Bolton 1 Notts Co 1		Bolton 4 Reading 3	aet	2000/01	West Brom 2 Bolton 2	
	Notts Co 2 Bolton 0	1998/99	Bolton 1 Ipswich 0			Bolton 3 West Brom 0	
1990/91	Bury 1 Bolton 1		Ipswich 4 Bolton 3	aet		Bolton 3 Preston 0	
	Bolton 1 Bury 0		Bolton 0 Watford 2				
	Bolton 0 Tranmere 1 aet				Play-offs: P18 W6 D 5 L7 F29 A28		

Major Cups Record

Complete FA Cup Record	P	W	D	L	F	A
Home	165	93	36	36	353	182
Away	159	54	44	61	220	257
Neutral	31	17	2	12	42	34
Total	355	164	82	109	615	473

Complete League Cup Record	P	W	D	L	F	A
Home	76	42	14	20	141	102
Away	72	23	19	30	105	135
Neutral	2	1	0	1	3	3
Total	150	66	33	51	249	240

~ Honours and Records ~

League Highs and Lows

Most Points in a Season	98	1996/97
Most Home Wins in a Season	18	1924/25, 72/73, 92/93, 96/97
Most Home Draws in a Season	11	1979/80
Most Home Losses in a Season	10	1909/10, 63/64, 70/71, 86/87, 95/96
Most Home Goals Scored in a Season	63	1934/35
Most Home Goals Conceded in a Season	35	1952/53, 1957/58, 1963/64
Most Away Wins in a Season	14	2000/01. (15 Inc. Play Off)
Most Away Draws in a Season	10	1986/87, 1996/97, 1998/99
Most Away Losses in a Season	18	1984/85
Most Away Goals Scored in a Season	40	1996/97 (41 2000/01 Inc. Play Offs)
Most Away Goals Conceded in a Season	59	1932/33
Most Wins in a Season	28	1996/97
Most Draws in a Season	17	1991/92
Most Losses in a Season	25	1970/71, 1995/96
Most Goals Scored in a Season	100	1996/97
Most Goals Conceded in a Season	92	1932/33
Least Home Wins in a Season	5	1979/80
Least Home Draws in a Season	0	1888/89, 1890/91, 1904/05
Least Home Losses in a Season	0	1910/11, 1920/21
Least Home Goals Scored in a Season	18	1893/94, 1897/98, 1902/03
Least Home Goals Conceded in a Season	7	1899/1900
Least Away Wins in a Season	0	1949/50, 1979/80
Least Away Draws in a Season	0	1889/90, 1891/92
Least Away Losses in a Season	3	1899/1900, 1904/05, 1996/97
Least Away Goals Scored in a Season	10	1897/98
Least Away Goals Conceded in a Season	16	1904/05
Least Wins in a Season	5	1979/80
Least Draws in a Season	1	1889/90, 1890/91
Least Losses in a Season	4	1899/1900, 1996/97
Least Goals Scored in a Season	28	1897/98
Least Goals Conceded in a Season	25	1899/1900

Most Consecutive :

Wins	11	1904/05
Home Wins	13	1910/11
Away Wins	5	1904/05, 2000/01
Draws	6	1912/13
Losses	11	1901/02-1902/03
Home Losses	4	1902/03
Away Losses	11	1979/80, 1984/85
Games Without Scoring	5	1897/98, 1989/90
Games with Scoring	24	1888/89, 1889/90, 1996/97
Run Without a Defeat	23	1990/91
Run Without a Draw	28	1911/12
Run Without a Win	26	1901/02-1902/03
Home Games Without a Win	10	1902/03, 1979/80
Away Games Without a Win	21	1979/80
Games Without Conceding a Goal	7	1899/1900
Games Conceding a Goal	27	1901/02-1902/03
Unbeaten Home Games	21	1920/21
Unbeaten Away Games	11	1904/05

Record Victories:

League:
Home 8-0 V Barnsley. Division Two. 6.10.1934
Away 7-1 V Aston Villa. Division One. 26.12.1914

FA Cup:
Home 13-0 V Sheffield United. Round Two. 1.2.1890
Away 5-1 V Charlton Athletic. Round Three. 14.1.1933

League Cup:
Home 6-1 V Tottenham H.. Round Four. 27.11.1996
Away 4-0 V Rochdale. Round Two. 10.10.1973

Record Defeats:

League:
Home
0-6 V Manchester U.. Prem. League. 25.02.1996
Away
0-7 V Burnley. Div. One. 1.3.1890
0-7 V Sheffield Weds. Div. One. 1.3.1915
0-7 V Manchester City. Div. One. 21.3.1936

FA Cup:
Home
0-5 V Bristol C.. Round One. 7.02.1903
0-5 V Manchester C.. Round Five. 20.02.1937
Away
1-9 V Preston N.E. Round Two. 10.12.1887

League Cup:
Home
0-6 V Chelsea. Round Four Rep.. 8.11.1971
Away
0-6 V Tottenham H.. Round Five. 11.12.2001

Other Records (Players):

Appearancess:	Eddie Hopkinson	578 (1956-1969) (519 League)
Goalscorer:	Nat Lofthouse	285 (1945-1960) (255 League)
Goals in a Season:	Joe Smith	38 (1920/21) (All League)
Goals in a match:	Billy Struthers	5 (6-1 V Bootle FA Cup 4.11.1882)
	Jim Cassidy	5 (13-0 V Sheffield United FA Cup 1.2.1890).
	Tony Caldwell	5 (8-1 V Walsall Division Three 10.9.1983)
Most Capped :	Mark Fish	(South Africa - 34 appearances)
Record Transfer	Fee Paid	£3.5m. Dean Holdsworth (Wimbledon October 1997)
Record Transfer	Fee Received	£4.5m. Jason McAteer (Liverpool September 1995)
Youngest:	Ray Parry	15 Years 267 Days v Wolves 13.10.1951
Oldest:	Peter Shilton	45 Years 239 Days V Wolves 15.5.1995

Gate Records (Recorded)

Record Attendance:
69,912 v Manchester C.
(FA Cup 5th Round) 18.02. 1933.
Lowest Attendance:
1,507 v Rochdale
(Autoglass Trophy) 10.12. 1991.
Record Receipts:
£335,468 v West Brom. Albion
First Division Play-off. 17.05.2001

Football League and Premiership Record

FA Premiership: 1995/96, 1997/98, 2001/02-
Division One: 1888/89-1898/1899, 1900/01: 1902/03, 1905/06-1907/08, 1909/10, 1911/12-1932/33, 1935/36-1963/64, 1978/79-1979/80
Division One (Formerly Division Two). 1899/1900, 1903/04-1904/05, 1908/09, 1910/11, 1933/34-1934/35, 1964/65-1970/71, 1973/74-1977/78, 1980/81,1982/83, 1993/94-1994/95, 1996/97, 1998/99-00/01.
Division Two (Formerly Division Three): 1971/72-1972/73, 1983/84-1986/87, 1988/89-1992/93.
Division Three (Formerly Division Four): 1987/88
(Old) Division One Best Position: 3rd. 1892. 1921. 1925.
Division One/Two Champions: 1909, 1978, 1997. Runners Up: 1900.1905.1911.1935.
Promoted via Play-offs: 1995. 2001.
Division Two/three Champions: 1973. Runners Up: 1993. Division Three/Four Promotion: 1988.

(Honours and Records Continued)

FA Cup:	Winners: 1923. 1926. 1929. 1958.	Runners Up: 1894. 1904. 1953.
Football League Cup:	Runners Up: 1995	

Sherpa Van Trophy:	Winners: 1989
Freight Rover Trophy:	Runners-up: 1986
FA Charity Shield:	Winners: 1958
Lancashire Cup:	Winners: 1886. 1891. 1912. 1922. 1925. 1927. 1932. 1934. 1948. 1988. 1990.
Central League:	Champions: 1955. 1995.

Football League Record at: Pikes Lane/Burnden Park/Reebok Stadium

		P	W	D	L	F	A	Pts.
Pikes Lane								
Division One		91	57	10	24	243	140	239
Burnden Park								
Division One (Premier League from 92/93)		1082	574	247	261	2029	1280	1285
Division Two (Div. One from 92/93)	Inc. 1 p/off	516	306	104	106	1001	483	778
Division Three (Div. Two from 92/93)	Inc. 3 p/offs	256	139	63	54	392	213	446
Division Four (Div. Three from 92/3)		23	15	6	2	42	12	51
Burnden Park Total		1877	1034	420	423	3464	1988	2560
Reebok Stadium								
Premier League		38	12	15	11	45	53	51
Reebok Stadium First Division	Inc. 3 p/offs	72	39	22	11	133	81	132
Reebok StadiumTotal		110	51	37	22	178	134	183
Overall Total		2078	1142	467	469	3885	2262	2982

Football League Record: Divisional Split

Division		Home							Away							(Additional) Neutral					
	P	W	D	L	F	A	Pts.	P	W	D	L	F	A	Pts.	P	W	D	L	F	A
Division One (Premier from 92/93)	1211	643	272	296	2317	1473	1575	1211	251	272	688	1388	2443	783						
							Total:	2422	894	544	984	3705	3916	2358						
Division Two (Division One from 92/93) Incl. 11 play-offs	588	345	126	117	1134	564	910	588	166	175	247	707	870	558	3	2	0	1	7	5
							Total:	1179	513	301	365	1848	1439	1468						
Division Three (Division Two from 92/93) Incl. 7 play-offs	256	139	63	54	392	213	446	256	62	74	120	280	384	246	1	0	0	1	0	1
							Total:	513	201	137	175	672	598	692						
Division Four (Division Three from 92/3)	23	15	6	2	42	12	51	23	7	6	10	24	30	27						
							Total:	46	22	12	12	66	42	78						
Total	2078	1142	467	469	3885	2262	2982	2078	486	527	1065	2399	3727	1614	4	2	0	2	7	6

Grand Total: | 4160 | 1630 | 994 | 1536 | 6291 | 5995 | 4596 |